COMPLETE

CRIMINAL LAW

TEXT, CASES, AND MATERIALS

COMPLETE

CRIMINAL LAW

TEXT, CASES, AND MATERIALS

SIXTH EDITION

Janet Loveless

Mischa Allen

Caroline Derry

OXFORD

UNIVERSITY PRESS

OXFORD
UNIVERSITY PRESS

Great Clarendon Street, Oxford, OX2 6DP,
United Kingdom

Oxford University Press is a department of the University of Oxford.
It furthers the University's objective of excellence in research, scholarship,
and education by publishing worldwide. Oxford is a registered trade mark of
Oxford University Press in the UK and in certain other countries

Third edition 2012
Fourth edition 2014
Fifth edition 2016

Impression: 1

Public sector information reproduced under Open Government Licence v3.0
(http://www.nationalarchives.gov.uk/doc/open-government-licence/open-government-licence.htm)

Published in the United States of America by Oxford University Press
198 Madison Avenue, New York, NY 10016, United States of America

British Library Cataloguing in Publication Data
Data available

Library of Congress Control Number: 2017961181

ISBN 978–0–19–880327–0

Printed in Great Britain by
Bell & Bain Ltd., Glasgow

To Janet

Preface

This book offers you a fascinating insight into the world of criminal law, a world with which you may already be familiar. Crime thrillers, films or novels, can tell us a good deal about criminal minds and detective work. Television dramas may follow the day-to-day lives of busy barristers and solicitors. Some real-life criminal trials have been televised and investigations have been undertaken into how juries work. Rarely a day passes without a criminal news story, whether international, national or local. Crime is always in the public domain. But the detail of the criminal law itself receives little attention. Strangely, despite our familiarity with the world of criminal justice, the law itself remains a mystery to most people.

In this book you will find the law clearly explained, so that you can get to know what lies behind the news, novels and dramas. You'll be amazed at the diverse ways people find to break the law, and the arguments they use to defend themselves. During your studies, you will discover the principles and structure of criminal law, what you have to do to commit a crime, with what state of mind, and when you might be entitled to a defence. You will also be guided on how to apply the law to typical criminal law questions so as to be ready for that final assessment which comes around all too soon.

The book takes the form of most criminal law courses: fundamental principles such as the conduct and mental element (known as actus reus and mens rea respectively) followed by defences and then the major offences. One diversion occurs in that homicide is placed in the middle of fundamental principles so that at an early stage you can understand this important offence which is the focus of so many of the central principles of criminal liability. The law is explained on a step-by-step basis so that by the end of each chapter you will have fully understood the structure and law of each topic. This gradual progression is achieved through:

- Clear and straightforward narrative
- Explanation of all legal concepts
- Extracts from leading cases and a selection of academic articles
- Point-by-point explanation of judgments in the 'note' section
- Explanation and straightforward questions on academic articles where relevant
- Development of case analysis in the text
- Examples of complex legal points
- Diagrams
- Summaries of the law
- Explanation and regular updating of the law on the accompanying website.

Without further explanation, the book would appear to be a rather remote mass of information interspersed with many curious cases. But criminal law is relevant to all of our lives in many different ways. Therefore, discussion of the context in which the law operates is a special feature of the book. Law does not exist in isolation from you or your social, moral, economic, historical or political environment. Rather, it is a product of them. By relating underlying legal principles to the world in which we live you will acquire a deeper understanding of the reason for law being the way it is.

A significant part of the study of any law is to be able to step back and ask whether it is logical or is fit for its intended purpose. The criminal law is no different. Does this case or that principle make sense? Is it consistent with developments in that or other areas? Consideration of academic opinion and reform proposals published by the Law Commission can be particularly helpful in this respect. Being alive to relevant contradictions and adopting a critical and questioning attitude to your studies will foster greater interest and depth of understanding. If you follow the guidance offered in these pages, there is no reason why criminal law should be as daunting and formidable as it is to those who find themselves caught up in the criminal justice system!

You will find new cases referred to in this edition as well as some new extracts from academic books and journals. As always, several aspects of the book have been thoroughly revised.

One major change for this edition is our addition as joint authors. Janet, a much missed friend and colleague, sadly passed away in 2016. Janet's practical and contextual approach to criminal law was appreciated by both readers of this book and her colleagues and students. We are proud to follow in her footsteps and have tried to preserve her original approach as far as possible.

Our special thanks to our editor, John Carroll, and to the whole OUP production team who have made working on this new edition such a pleasure. Responsibility for all errors and omissions are ours alone.

We hope you enjoy your study of criminal law and bear it in mind for your future careers. As criminal offences continue to grow in number and complexity, as they have done over the last 20 years, never has there been such a need for good criminal lawyers who, incidentally, are never likely to be short of work.

The law is correct as at October 2017. The Supreme Court's decision in *Ivey v Genting Casinos* which will no doubt have lasting implications on the test for dishonesty in criminal law, was included just in time. Chapters 12, 13 and 14 will now need to be read in the light of that decision.

Caroline Derry and Mischa Allen

New to this edition

Among some of the newly included materials in this edition are—

Bowler [2015] EWCA Crim 849 (unlawful act manslaughter)

Brandford [2016] EWCA Crim 1794 (duress)

Chodorek v Poland [2017] ACD 244 (82) (property belonging to another)

Golds [2016] UKSC 61, *Joyce & Kay* [2017] EWCA Crim 647, *Squelch* [2017] EWCA Crim 204, *Wilcocks* [2016] EWCA Crim 2043 (diminished responsibility)

Health and Safety Executive v Sherwood Rise [2015] (corporate liability)

Ivey v Genting Casinos (UK) t/a Crockfords [2017] UKSC 67 (dishonesty)

Jogee [2016] UKSC 8; *Johnson (Lewis)* [2016] EWCA Crim 1613 (secondary participation)

Johnson (Wayne) [2017] EWCA Crim 189 (knowledge, strict liability)

Meanza [2017] EWCA Crim 445 (loss of control)

R (on the application of Conway) v Secretary of State for Justice [2017] EWHC 2447 (assisted dying)

Ray [2017] EWCA Crim 1391 (self-defence)

Law Commission Report on Offences Against the Person (2015)

Law Commission Report on Unfitness to Plead (2016)

Guide to using the book

Complete Criminal Law: Text, Cases, and Materials includes a number of different features that have been carefully designed to enrich your learning and help you along as you develop your understanding of criminal law.

KEY CASES

Robinson [1977] Crim LR 173—robbery: a defence to theft will defeat robbe

Hale [1978] 68 Cr App R 415—force during a continuing act of theft;

B, R v DPP [2007] EWHC 739—an express or implied threat of force will suffi

Corcoran (1980) 71 Cr App R 104—robbery is complete at the time of appro

Key cases Helpful lists of the really key cases at the beginning of each topic highlight those extracts that you should pay special attention to.

12.2.1 Introduction

Robbery is a form of aggravated stealing: theft by the threat or use of
clude the following: muggings, car-jackings, mobile phone and iPod robb
armed robberies of banks and building societies. It comprises serious or

 THINKING POINT 2.2

A child jumps into a swimming pool and gets into difficulty. The follo
serve the child drowning but fail to save her. Who amongst them would
offence if she drowned?

Mother/lifeguard/neighbour/mother's cohabitee/relative by marriage (suc
or uncle)/cousin/baby-sitter/teacher/stranger.
A case relied on in *Dobinson* was the following:

R v Instan [1893] 1 QB 450 COURT FOR CROWN CASES RESE

Thinking points Why was a certain decision reached in a particular case? Is D guilty of murder or manslaughter in the following examples? Regular thinking points throughout the text encourage you to pause and reflect on the key issues. Guidance on answering each one of these questions can be found in the online resources.

! **EXAMPLE** 12.2

If you have £100 in your account and D withdraws £150 from it, he will o
ated the debt owed to you by the bank of £100. The outstanding £50 v
begin with, the bank never owed it to you, you had no right to it and D
appropriate it.

The same would apply to you if you had become overdrawn by tendering ch
for more than the total in your account. This is not theft. It may be an atten
but it cannot be theft because there is no intangible property to appropriat

Examples Short, fictional examples of how the law would be applied in certain situations illustrate the practical application of what you are learning.

 NOTE 2.1

The court said that there could be no conviction unless there was a *duty*
identified such a duty on the basis that Fanny was a blood relative of Mr S
Ds had assumed responsibility for her. The basis of the latter was that she
in Mr Stone's house and Mrs Dobinson had attempted to wash her and ta
what distinguished the situation of the drowning stranger and the passi

The two unfortunate defendants were therefore convicted of one of the mo
the criminal justice system. The judgment was described as 'judicial cruel
'Criminal Omissions—The Conventional View' [1991] 107 *LQR*, at 90. It
problems.

Notes Figuring out exactly what the significance of a long case report or judgment is can be tricky. These short bullet-point sections follow the longer extracts in the book, and pull out the key points that you need to take from your reading of the extract.

SECTION SUMMARY

Self-defence is a complete justificatory defence to all crimes:

■ *Did D honestly believe that it was necessary for him to defend himself?*

■ *If so, and taking the circumstances as the defendant honestly believed them to force reasonable?*

Any mistake must be honest but need not be reasonable.

Excessive force which is unreasonable on the facts as D believed them to be will may be the subject of mitigation.

Murder cannot be mitigated to manslaughter.

Householders can now use disproportionate force provided it is reasonable.

Section summaries Short summaries appear throughout the book at the end of key sections to reinforce your knowledge. You should use these to reflect on what you have just learnt.

SUMMARY

You should now be familiar with the AR/MR definitions, cases, principles and ap ing major offences:

■ Common law assault (intentional/reckless causing another to apprehend ha al/reckless infliction of physical contact/minor harm).

■ ABH contrary to s47 OAPA 1861 (assault/battery causing minor harm).

■ Malicious wounding and malicious infliction of GBH contrary to s20 OAPA 1£ or reckless infliction of serious harm).

■ Intentional wounding and intentional GBH with intent to cause GBH contrar

You should now understand how these traditional offences have also been app STI transmission.

You should now be able to identify and understand the application of the def

Chapter summaries Each chapter ends with a concise summary allowing you to check your understanding and return to any areas that aren't yet completely clear.

PROBLEM SOLVING

Theft, robbery, handling:

During a long motorway journey, D stops off at an off-licence store. She needs party. On seeing a box of expensive bottles, she removes the price label of £100 from a cheaper box of £30. She puts the box in her trolley but notices a bea near the check-out and so replaces it on the shelf. She picks up a few boxes of and conceals three bottles of the expensive champagne in her overcoat pock sparkling wine at the check-out the cashier (Z) gives her £50 too much change rest of the journey home before noticing the overpayment. At her party, she se bottles of champagne to X. X pays a low price and is aware that D has previous sells the bottles to Y for the full price.

D returns to the store one week later and buys some wine. On her way out, Z runs z the return of the £50. Z's wages had been reduced by this amount because of I

Problem solving The questions at the end of each chapter provide the ideal opportunity for you to test your understanding of a topic. They challenge you to apply your knowledge—either by preparing a full answer to a question, or by debating the issues with your fellow students. Again, guidance on how to approach these questions can be found in the online resources.

FURTHER READING

A. Ashworth, 'Robbery Reassessed' [2002] *Crim LR* 851

Argues that the sentencing structure for robbery is in need of review.

S. Gardner, 'Appropriation in Theft: the Last Word?' (1993) 109 *LQR* 194

Gardner discusses the idea of consent in appropriation with reference to the case of *Gomez*.

E. Griew, 'Dishonesty—The Objections to Feely & Ghosh' [1985] *Crim LR* 432

Argues that the *Ghosh* test leads to inconsistent verdicts as it is too difficult for juries to understand.

R. Heaton and A.P. Simester, 'Stealing One's Own Property' (1999) 115 *LQR* 37

A discussion of *Hinks*.

E. Melissaris, 'The Concept of Appropriation and The Offence of Theft' (2007)

Article discussing the inconsistencies in the case law on appropriation by reference to the philosophical no

D. Ormerod, 'R v Vinall: Robbery—Appropriation of Property—Subsequent I

Further reading These suggestions for additional reading have been carefully selected to highlight key areas and to help deepen your knowledge of the subject.

Guide to the online resources

The online resources that accompany this book provide students and lecturers with ready-to-use teaching and learning material. They are free of charge, and are designed to complement the book and maximise the teaching and learning experience.

 www.oup.com/uk/loveless6e/

Regular updates The authors regularly update this section of the site to account for recent cases and developments in criminal law that have occurred since publication of the book. These updates are accompanied by page references to the textbook, so you can easily see how the new developments relate to the existing law.

Web links Links to useful websites enable you to instantly look at reliable sources of online information, and efficiently direct your online study.

Guidance on answering the problem questions and thinking points Here is where you can find guidance on how to correctly answer all the thinking points and problem questions posed throughout the book.

Exam-style questions and guidance Revise for exams and test your knowledge by answering these exam-style questions. Accompanying guidance helps you to assess how you did.

FOR LECTURERS

These resources are password protected to ensure only lecturers can access them; each registration is personally checked to ensure the security of the site. Registering is easy: click on 'registration form', complete a simple registration form which allows you to choose your own username, and access will be granted within three working days subject to verification.

Test bank Containing 150 multiple-choice questions with answers and feedback; this is a fully customisable resource of ready-made revision assessments which you can use to test your students. It can be easily downloaded into your Virtual Learning Environment.

Contents in brief

Detailed Contents

Acknowledgements

Grateful acknowledgement is made to all the authors and publishers of copyright material which appears in this book, and in particular to the following for permission to reprint material from the sources indicated:

Extracts from unreported case reports, Law Commission Reports, consultation papers, and Home Office reports and statistics are Crown copyright material and are reproduced under Class Licence Number C2006010631 with the permission of the Controller of OPSI and the Queen's Printer. Extracts from House of Lords case reports are Parliamentary copyright and are reproduced by permission of the Controller of HMSO on behalf of Parliament.

Cambridge University Press and the author for extracts from A. Norrie: *Crime, Reason and History: A Critical Introduction to Criminal Law* (Cambridge, 1993); and G. Williams: 'The Unresolved Problem of Recklessness', 8 *Legal Studies* 74 (1988).

Incorporated Council of Law Reporting for extracts from the Law Reports: *Appeal Cases* (AC), *Family Division* (FAM), *Queen's Bench Division* (QB), and *Weekly Law Reports* (WLR).

LexisNexis for extract from B. Hogan: 'Omissions and a Duty Myth' in *Criminal Law: Essays in Honour of J.C. Smith* edited by P. Smith (1987).

SAGE Publishing for extract from S. Parsons, 'Joint Enterprise Murder: R v Jogee' [2016] *Journal of Criminal Law* 173.

Sweet & Maxwell Ltd for extracts from the *Criminal Appeal Reports* (Cr App R), *Criminal Law Review* (Crim LR), and *Law Quarterly Review* (LQR).

Web Journal of Current Legal Issues and author for extract from C. Walsh: 'Irrational Presumptions of Rationality and Comprehension', 3 *Web JCLI* (1998).

Wiley-Blackwell Publishing Ltd for extracts from M. Giles: 'R v Brown: Consensual Harm and Public Interest' 57 *Modern Law Review* 101 (1994); and A. Norrie: 'Critique of Criminal Causation' 64 *Modern Law Review* 684 (1991).

Every effort has been made to trace and contact copyright holders prior to publication but this has not been possible in every case. If notified, the publisher will undertake to rectify any errors or omissions at the earliest opportunity.

Table of cases

Where cases are dealt with in detail the relevant page numbers are shown in bold.

Table of legislation

Where sections are reproduced in full or in part the page number is shown in bold.

UK orders and regulations

Other legislation

Introduction and general principles

1

KEY POINTS

WHAT IS CRIME?

This section will help you to identify some common notions of criminal law and to understand the 'harm' principle in criminal law. It also explores some contemporary theories of criminal law, including feminist critique.

PRESUMPTION OF INNOCENCE AND THE BURDEN OF PROOF

This section will help you to understand the key principles which underpin the criminal trial—namely that the accused is to be considered innocent until proven guilty and that this must be proven beyond reasonable doubt. It also explores exceptions to this rule, including the defences of insanity and diminished responsibility along with the idea of 'reverse onus' provisions.

CLASSIFICATION OF CRIMES AND COURTS

This section will help you to understand the classification of criminal offences and the effect of this on procedure. It also explains the hierarchy of the criminal courts.

PROCEDURE AND FAIR TRIAL RIGHTS

This section will help you to understand fair trial rights such as the right to legal representation. It examines the role of the police and the Crown Prosecution Service.

SOURCES OF THE CRIMINAL LAW

The key sources of criminal law are cases and legislation. In addition, this section will help you to understand the impact of the European Convention on Human Rights on criminal law and procedure and the reform work carried out by the Law Commission.

CRIME IN ENGLAND AND WALES TODAY

This section will help you to understand the true extent of criminal offences committed and the ways in which certain groups of people such as ethnic minorities and women are treated by the criminal justice system.

INTRODUCTION

This chapter provides an overview of the criminal justice system, and considers the practical and procedural context in which it operates. It discusses key theoretical views underpinning the criminal law, and challenges to these views. Finally, it assesses approaches to criminality and punishment.

1.1 What is Crime?

1.1.1 Traditional Theory: Harm to Others

1.1.2 Harm to Oneself

1.1.3 Politicisation

1.1.4 Contemporary Theories of Criminal Law

1.1.5 The Need for Minimal Criminalisation—Are There Too Many Crimes?

1.1.6 Punishment

KEY CASES

DPP v Woolmington [1935] AC 462—the burden of proof is on the prosecution.

Any criminal law textbook will explain the principles and structure of criminal law and examine the major offences. This book is no different. We hope, though, that by relating the law to its broader context wherever possible, you will understand how the law 'lives and breathes' and that it is not an abstract concept.

Some of the questions thrown up by the case law in these pages concern matters which might affect any of us. For example, do you commit a crime by failing to rescue a stranger in danger? Should you? Is it a crime to exaggerate your qualifications when seeking employment? Do you commit a crime by lying to obtain your partner's consent to sex? What if you conceal the fact that you have HIV? Can you steal something that has been lawfully given to you? When will medical accidents result in manslaughter? Will you be guilty of murder if you are in a group fight and someone suddenly kills? If you are in a gun-fight (We sincerely hope you never will be), and your opponent kills a passer-by, will you be convicted of murder? Do you commit a crime by consensually branding your partner's bottom with your initials and infection sets in? (This is an actual case, not our imagination!) You may think you would never end up at the wrong end of the criminal law but look at the following cases which have occurred in recent years.

■ A schoolboy aged 14 sent a naked image of himself, taken in his bedroom, to a girl at school by mobile telephone. She saved it on her mobile and sent it on to her friends. The offence of making and distributing a self-generated explicit image sent to other people over the internet was then recorded against him by the police (contrary to s1 Protection of Children Act 1978 and the Criminal Justice Act 1988). It was not well-known that this was an offence. (www.bbc.co.uk/news/uk-34136388, 3 September 2015).

■ Alex Haigh, 21, left his home in Plymouth in July 2012 to find 'opportunities' in London and worked for a time as an apprentice bricklayer. Finding nowhere to live, he squatted in an empty, boarded up house belonging to a housing association. He was convicted and sent to prison for 'squatting in a residential building contrary to Section 144 of the Legal Aid, Sentencing and Punishment of Offenders Act 2012'. This was no offence until 1 September 2012 (*The Guardian*, 27 September 2012: www.theguardian.com).

■ When Doncaster airport was closed due to bad weather, preventing D from meeting his internet girlfriend, he posted a public message on his Twitter account which at the time had 600+ followers. It read: 'Crap! Robin Hood Airport is closed. You've got a week and a bit to get your shit together otherwise I am blowing the airport sky high!!' He was prosecuted for sending by a public electronic communication network a message of a 'menacing character' contrary to s127(1)(a) and (3) Communications Act 2003. The High Court overturned his conviction. There was no evidence that anyone who read the message had found it menacing (*Chambers v DPP* [2012] EWHC 2157 (Admin)).

■ Two defendants were sentenced for four years for posting a message on Facebook in the summer of 2011, during the riots, for a 'Smash down in Northwick Town', encouraging people to meet behind McDonalds at 1.00pm the next day to riot, and commit burglary or criminal damage. They were convicted under s46 Serious Crime Act 2007 for encouraging an offence believing one or more will be committed (*Blackshaw and Sutcliffe* [2011] EWCA Crim 2312).

You might consider these to be excessive in one respect or another. The fact that Mr Chambers' conviction was overturned suggests that his prosecution was over-zealous. The fact that Blackshaw and Sutcliffe were given four years for encouraging an offence which did not happen looks severe. Does the context (the riots of 2011) make a difference? That Mr Haigh should be sent to prison for squatting due to homelessness, no crime until in 2012, appears unjust. The 'sexting' recorded by the police against the schoolboy, with the potential for prosecution and registration as a sex offender, might appear an unwise way to deal with childhood foolishness and experimentation. This is a new way of using an existing offence originally intended for child protection. Politicians, law enforcers, or maybe even some of you, might disagree. But, for students of criminal law, these matters should concern us. They are used here to illustrate different features of what legal scholars identify as being wrong with criminal law and criminal justice today: over-criminalisation, over-charging and over-punishment. These and other matters will be explored in this chapter.

As you read this book, you will be fascinated by the amazingly diverse way some people have found to break the criminal law. Consider, for example, the case of the 'naked rambler', Stephen Gough, who spent ten years walking from John O'Groats to Land's End completely nude. He was charged with various offences including causing alarm and distress or disgust to the public contrary to s5 Public Order Act 1986. He maintained that his numerous convictions breached his freedom of expression under Article 10 of the European Convention on Human Rights (ECHR). Neither the Court of Appeal nor the European Court of Human Rights agreed with him. He has, as a consequence, spent several years in prison. Criminal cases can certainly be amusing and eye-opening. For defendants up against the system, of course, it is quite another matter where loss of reputation, liberty, disruption to employment and family life are all at risk.

First, we will follow conventional textbooks and ask what crime is and how the criminal law is theorised. Then we will turn back to practical reality.

1.1.1 Traditional Theory: Harm to Others

How may we define a 'crime'? Many students when asked this question will say, 'A crime is something which is against the law and if you do it you go to jail or at least end up paying a fine!' But we need to ask why certain conduct is prohibited and why the civil law would not be an alternative way of controlling wrongdoing. Without a common understanding of the basis on which conduct should be criminalised, the criminal law might spiral out of control. Is there a single or unifying definition of crime? Let us note that a crime is an offence against the state, as well as individuals, and a public wrong, which is why prosecutions are not left up to the victim. Most of you will readily identify the major offences which are to be found in every jurisdiction of the world such as homicide, rape, robbery and grievous bodily harm. These are known as crimes of *mala in se* (wrong in themselves). No-one disputes that these offences transgress moral codes as well as universal principles regarding the sanctity of life and freedom from harm. Therefore, one would assume that in order to justify punishment, a crime should necessarily protect us from 'harm'. This concept becomes somewhat overstretched however when you consider that there are over ten thousand offences in the criminal justice system ranging from murder down to selling liqueur chocolates to a child under 16 (s148 Licensing Act 2003)! So, by what criteria are the limits of the criminal law determined?

J.S. Mill provided the traditional rationale for criminalising conduct in his treatise *On Liberty and Other Writings* (1859):

> The only purpose for which power can rightfully be exercised over any member of a civilized community against his will, is to prevent harm to others.

Harm had to be serious and to threaten society. The more serious offences against the person clearly fulfil these two criteria. Laws which protect us from violent aggressors are clearly justified. They also help to preserve social order. They should apply to everyone, including the agencies of the state so that we are protected from both individual and state violence. This is known as the rule of law. Laws prohibiting harm are clearly justified in the interests of individual freedom and the greater good of society.

In the leading modern work on the harm principle, Joel Feinberg, in *The Moral Limits of the Criminal Law: Harm to Others* (1984) considers that crimes should be confined to conduct which is harmful and which displays moral wrongfulness. At pp 33, 34, 215–216 he states:

> A harm in the appropriate sense then will be produced by morally indefensible conduct that not only sets back the victim's interest, but also violates his right . . . Minor or trivial harms are harms despite their minor magnitude and triviality, but below a certain threshold they are not to count as harms for the purposes of the harm principle, for legal interference with trivia is likely to cause more harm than it prevents . . . Where the kind of conduct in question . . . does create a danger to some degree, legislators employing the harm principle must use various rules of thumb as best they can . . .

Not all harmful conduct should be criminalised. There need to be limits. It must be morally indefensible and 'set back' the victim's interests. Feinberg identifies various justifications for criminalising harmful conduct such as gravity, probability and magnitude of risk.

The difficulty is that 'harm' and the 'set back' of interests can be defined so as to justify criminalising a wide range of conduct, regardless of immorality or the degree of harm to others. As we see in the next paragraph, the harm may also affect society and not just individuals, whilst the creation of offences is justified for a range of reasons, explored below, going way beyond mere harm.

Wrongdoing, regulatory offences and welfare

In England and Wales, the criminal law includes many offences not classified as crimes else-where, even though individual fault is frequently unidentifiable. Strict liability, or regulatory, of-fences often carrying severe penalties, are examples. Here the offence consists of conduct which is criminal simply because it has been prohibited, for example: driving or health and safety of-fences. These are known as crimes of *mala prohibita*. Both 'harm' and 'wrongdoing' are used to justify regulatory crimes for the risks they pose to the welfare of society and interference with the liberty of others. Such crimes do not necessarily offend our moral code. It is relevant to ask whether these, or other victimless crimes, over-extend the boundaries of the criminal law. Are there other ways of controlling behaviour which is detrimental to society? Enforcement tends to occur through specific regulatory agencies such as the Health and Safety Executive or the Environment Agency which rely on negotiation or enforcement procedures with prosecution as a last resort. Criminal prosecutions are rare and police prosecutions even more so. Therefore one has to ask whether it is essential that regulatory standards be enforced by the criminal law as opposed to civil law orders, injunctions and awards of compensation. This is particularly so in view of J.S. Mill's requirement that harm needs to be serious before criminal sanctions should be imposed. However, the notion that regulatory offences are not 'real crimes' sometimes involves a value-laden judgement:

 EXAMPLE 1.1

You might assume that an employer who pays her cleaner in cash to avoid paying £50 VAT, a white-collar crime, should be able to get away with it. But few would doubt that the cleaner who steals £50 from her employer should be prosecuted in court. Do you agree? Why?

Moralism

Should the criminal law control individual morality? It is true to say that mainstream moral attitudes are generally upheld by the law. There is a view, however, that the courts should retain a residual power to control moral issues by the criminal law, physical harm or not. Moralism therefore challenges the limitations of the harm principle. Both approaches are apparent in rela-tion to the defence of consent concerning violent offences.

    The moralistic approach is more explicitly applied to the common law offence of outrag-ing public decency. But the courts' role as custodians of public morality was less disguised 30 or so years ago. Conspiracy to corrupt public morals and conspiracy to outrage public decency were judicially created offences in the 1970s to criminalise and censure publica-tions concerning prostitution (*Shaw v DPP* [1962] HL AC 220) and homosexuality (*Knuller v DPP* [1973] AC 435) at a time when neither activity was against the law. Prostitution itself had never been an offence and homosexuality between consenting males in private over the age of 21 had been decriminalised by the Sexual Offences Act 1967. This would now be contrary to Article 7 ECHR on the grounds of retrospectivity. But the moralistic approach continues to be evident, particularly in relation to harm cases involving self-harm. One might put the example of the 14-year-old sexting schoolboy described at the beginning into this category.

→ CROSS-REFERENCE
For a discussion of the defence of consent see Chapter 10, 10.6.

→ CROSS-REFERENCE
Article 7 ECHR on retro-spectivity is discussed in 1.6. See 1.1.2 for harm cases involving self-harm.

The Wolfenden Committee Report on Prostitution and Homosexual Offences 1957

Shaw and *Knuller* followed a major review of prostitution and homosexuality by the Wolfenden Committee which took the view that the criminal law had no role in the enforcement of morality. Its function was to maintain public order and decency, to protect the public from what was offensive or injurious and to protect the vulnerable from exploitation. But given the vagueness of what qualifies as 'decent, offensive, injurious or even exploitation', it is little surprise that this area continues to generate debate.

The liberal views of the Wolfenden Committee were contested by a leading jurist of the time, Lord Devlin, who felt that the law should rightly enforce moral principles and nothing else. The morality of 'right-minded' people was fundamental to the cohesion of society which would disintegrate unless upheld by the law ('The Enforcement of Morals' (1961, 1965)). Endorsement of the liberal views of the Committee came from legal philosopher H.L.A. Hart who argued that the criminalisation of morality led to laws based on ignorance or superstition (H.L.A. Hart: *The Listener*, 30 July 1959). The only justification for the law's intervention into morality was protection of the vulnerable from exploitation.

1.1.2 Harm to Oneself

The liberal view of 'harm' would also permit crimes concerned with 'self-harm', particularly so on the grounds of protecting people from their own risky behaviour. Many types of socially acceptable conduct involve self-harm, such as boxing, tattooing, cosmetic surgery, sex change operations and body piercing. Few people would consider these to be characterised by criminality for there are important social or cultural reasons for permitting them.

But when it comes to minority sexual practices involving consensual self-harm, the law can be severe. We are not allowed to consent to private consensual sexual bodily 'harm' unless there are no injuries. The House of Lords in the famous case of *Brown* [1993] 2 All ER 75 held that one cannot legally consent to even minor injury in the course of a private masochistic homosexual encounter and that any such injury is a crime. Yet, the Court of Appeal decided two years later that more serious harm inflicted in consensual heterosexual activity was no crime (*Wilson* [1996] 3 WLR 125). You might think that if the wider interests of society demand protection from a so-called cult of violence, surely it should apply to everyone in equal measure or it should not apply at all. The objection here is that it is being used to prohibit behaviour regarded by the majority of society as pure 'immorality'.

Under the pretext of protecting us from harm in the area of private morality, the law either prohibits or regulates euthanasia, abortion, the age of consent, consensual sexual harm to oneself and others, drug use, prostitution, homosexuality, incest, female circumcision and pornography to name but a few examples. The boundaries of the criminal law are nowhere more vociferously debated than in this area.

Paternalism

The justification for the law's intrusion into private adult morality is the protection of vulnerable victims from exploitation and abuse. Here the law performs a paternalistic role. One would naturally expect there to be legal safeguards protecting weaker members of society from coercive or degrading exploitation. But paternalism can be used to justify censoring private adult consensual conduct in the absence of exploitation or harm. The criticism is often made that the underlying reason is one of upholding the dominant morality of society at the expense of criminalising minority practices perceived as threatening or deviant. Feminists would argue that paternalism is little more than a disguise for patriarchal attitudes which infuse the law.

The morality/harm debate continues and it raises the question of whether there is any point in a law that cannot be effectively enforced. Abortion was illegal until 1967 but back-street abortions flourished. Possession and the use of recreational drugs such as cannabis and ecstasy are against the law. Despite that, their use has escalated and, meanwhile, the debate continues as to whether the social or personal ills they convey are any worse than those arising from alcohol abuse or smoking. Individuals are allowed by the law to make certain, but not all, moral choices for themselves.

1.1.3 Politicisation

The harm principle is increasingly invoked on the grounds of political expediency when Parliament creates new crimes. Crime and criminal justice have been political issues for the last 20 years when the two major political parties began to compete for votes on the basis of new ways of containing the post-1945 escalation of crime. The legislative response has mostly concerned procedure or sentencing but new crimes are continually being created by Parliament to cater for perceived social problems. Squatting, stalking, raves, hunt-saboteurs, public protests, gun crime, dangerous dogs, beggars, terrorist offences, offences concerned with confiscating the proceeds of crime and breaching the terms of a Criminal Behaviour Order (CBO) or Football Spectator Banning Order, failure to give information in relation to a series of activities such as terrorism—all have been recently criminalised. It is hard to see the criminal wrongdoing in some of these offences. New laws are created not on the basis of principle or enquiry, seemingly, but by successive governments courting popularity with the mass media and pressure groups, all with reference to a vague and undefined notion of 'harm'.

?! THINKING POINT 1.1

Do you think the law should be concerned with what we do with our own bodies or with whom?

Should the law prohibit self-harm?

Should law play a role in the enforcement of morality?

What is the point of an unenforceable law?

Is it morally right to disobey laws which infringe our privacy?

The theories of criminal law discussed in 1.1.4 seek to demonstrate that harm is a socially, morally and politically relative concept.

1.1.4 Contemporary Theories of Criminal Law

Feminist critique

Feminist critique of the criminal law has focused on the fact that the cultural, historical and moral arena in which law operates is male. The law's underlying values and assumptions are therefore male and are not gender-neutral or pluralistic. It is in the realm of violence and defences that we see this most acutely. K. O'Donovan, 'Defences for Battered Women Who Kill', (1991) 18 *Journal of Law & Society* 219:

> Violence and fear have a relationship to gender. When these matters come to court other cultural factors enter in through the law. Definitions of defences are informed by the past history of homicide and its character as primarily a male act. The gender aspects are rarely articulated. Laws are made by judges and legislators who are mainly drawn from one gender and whose experience is limited. When women do kill after experiencing violence they enter an alien culture which lacks an understanding of the context of their act. They encounter legal categories that do not accommodate their behaviour and are 'tried and sentenced by courts that ignore or misunderstand their actions and motivations'.

Until relatively recently, many defences were based on what a 'reasonable man' might do. That language has sometimes yielded to the reasonable 'person' but, as we shall see, there is still some way to go to say that it comprehensively includes the reasonable woman.

You may remember the appointment of Lady Justice Hale, then the only female judge in the Supreme Court, as the first woman President of the Supreme Court in July 2017. She has repeatedly emphasised the need for greater diversity in the judiciary (www.bbc.co.uk):

> I do not think I am alone in thinking that diversity of many kinds on the bench is important for a great many reasons, but most of all because in a democracy which values everyone equally, and not just the privileged and the powerful, it is important that their rights and responsibilities should be decided by a judiciary which is more reflective of the society as a whole, and not just a very small section of it.

Recent improvements now indicate that more than half of all judges under the age of 40 in England and Wales are women; but only 7 per cent are from a black or ethnic minority background (*The Guardian*, 31 July 2015).

Critical legal theory

Many legal scholars today subject the general principles of criminal law to critical analysis. This means they look for inconsistencies and conflicts within the law. A critical and historical analysis of the criminal law is offered by A. Norrie in *Crime, Reason and History*, Weidenfeld and Nicolson, 1993, who argues that the criminal law is the product of historical social class contradictions. Legal principles reflect the interests of the economically powerful middle-class. The law may appear class-neutral but liability is construed from so-called 'voluntary' individual actions, removed, abstractly, from surrounding social and political forces. At p 23 he says:

> In place of real individuals belonging to particular social classes, possessing the infinite differences that constitute genuine individuality, the reformers proposed an ideal individual living in an ideal world. 'Economic man' or 'juridical man' were abstractions from real people emphasising one side of human life – the ability to reason and calculate – at the expense of every social circumstance that actually brings individuals to reason and calculate in particular ways. Crime was a social problem. It arose out of particular social conditions and was brought into being in the midst of struggles between social classes over definitions of right and wrong.

Conclusion: Harm is a relative concept

The harm principle may be vague and permit intrusions by the law into individual autonomy in many contestable ways. But there is no doubt that the concept has facilitated recognition of some serious 'hidden' social harms, and can, therefore be seen as context-dependent in that its scope tends to reflect changing social, moral and political values. It has enabled the law to include the following over recent years: child sex abuse, domestic violence, rape within marriage and workplace deaths, to name but a few. As we have seen, what makes conduct criminal lacks one single comprehensive definition. Serious offences seek to protect our fundamental rights. From time to time, other rights are restricted in the interests of public and moral protection. 'Harm' as such is used in a variety of ways and, as we shall see in 1.1.5, has justified the creation of an ever-increasing number of criminal offences.

?! THINKING POINT 1.2

Do you think people should be deprived of their liberty for causing a nuisance to others or without proof of fault?

Should politics play a role in the creation of criminal offences?

1.1.5 The Need for Minimal Criminalisation— Are There Too Many Crimes?

Over-criminalisation?

The decision to criminalise squatting in 2012 (the second example at the beginning of this chapter) is an example of what may be termed 'over-criminalisation'. This means that crimes will be created and used to deal with a given problem with inadequate justification. There are, for example, effective alternative civil solutions to the problem of squatting. On the other hand, four new offences created since publication of the last edition of this book, 'revenge porn', 'coercive and controlling behaviour' within intimate relationships, 'slavery, servitude and forced or compulsory labour' and 'failure to protect a girl from the risk of female genital mutilation', may be thought to be long overdue. However, the harm principle implies that people should not be punished by the criminal law unnecessarily. The criminal law should be a last resort. We have already seen that regulatory crimes might infringe this principle. But these are not the only examples. Read the following by A. Ashworth, 'Is the Criminal Law a Lost Cause?' [2000] *LQR* 225:

> The number of offences in English criminal law continues to grow year by year.
>
> Politicians, pressure groups, journalists and others often express themselves as if the creation of a new criminal offence is the natural, or the only appropriate, response to a particular event or series of events giving rise to social concern. At the same time, criminal offences are tacked on to diverse statutes by various government departments, and then enacted (or, often, re-enacted) by Parliament without demur. There is little sense that the decision to introduce a new offence should only be made after certain conditions have been satisfied, little sense that making conduct criminal is a step of considerable social significance. It is this unprincipled and chaotic construction of the criminal law that prompts the question whether it is a lost cause. From the point of view of governments it is clearly not a lost cause: it is a multi-purpose tool, often creating the favourable impression that certain misconduct has been taken seriously and dealt with appropriately. But from any principled viewpoint there are important issues—of how the criminal law ought to be shaped, of what its social significance should be, of when it should be used and when not—which are simply not being addressed in the majority of instances.

One reason for the proliferation of offences is the fact that society is becoming far more complex, therefore offences are needed to control new forms of activity. People are finding new ways to commit crimes (particularly internet and cyber-crime) and international treaty obligations compel our government to impose new offences upon us. However, the number continues to increase annually, regardless, it would seem, of which party is in government—see J. Chalmers and F. Leverick, 'Tracking the Creation of Criminal Offences' [2013] *Crim LR* 543:

> In August 2006 it was claimed that the Labour government had created 3,023 offences since elected in May 1997. That figure has been regularly cited as evidence of the overuse of criminal law, and the Liberal Democrats made halting such overuse a commitment in their 2010 election manifesto . . . In November 2010, the Ministry of Justice committed to creating 'a gateway to scrutinise all legislation containing criminal offences' and publishing annual statistics on the number of new offences . . . In December 2011, the Ministry of Justice published statistics on the creation of new criminal offences in England and Wales. According to these, 174 new criminal offences were created in the 12 months ending May 2011, compared to 712 in the 12 months ending May 2010 . . . Our results are rather different . . . our research produced a figure of 634.

The authors go on to say that 'not only do we not know how many criminal offences there are, we are not even sure how many bodies have the power to create them'.

This looks like a system out of control. However, the type of offences now proliferating, like those in the opening examples are low-level, and not the sort that might keep us awake at night. Far more worrying to us as members of society are violent crimes and crimes against our property. Are such concerns justified?

Fear of crime v reality

Despite our fears of becoming a victim of crime, the evidence is that crime is falling and has been since the mid 1990s. Society has never been safer. Yet, fear of crime is pervasive. After all, we are made aware in the media, almost on a daily basis, of the many ways that human beings inflict horrific crimes upon one another. It has been argued by a group of leading scholars with a sociological interest that our fear of crime, which is disproportionate to the evidence, has been manipulated and 'dramatised' by the media and politicians. Fear of crime has increased, due to the economic, social, global and cultural transformations of the last 30 years leading to personal insecurity and a weakening of support for the poor and the welfare state. This has in turn fed the politicisation and increased severity of criminal justice policy. The result is 'over-criminalisation' and 'penal populism': political enactment of popular crime control measures.

Read this by D. Garland in *The Culture of Control*, OUP, 2001, p 10:

> Since the 1970s fear of crime has come to have salience. What was once regarded as a localized, situational anxiety, affecting the worst-off individuals and neighbourhoods, has come to be regarded as a major social problem and a characteristic of contemporary culture. Fear of crime has come to be regarded as a problem in itself, quite distinct from actual crime and victimization and distinctive policies have been developed that aim to reduce fear levels rather than reduce crime . . . . The emergence of fear of crime as a prominent cultural theme is confirmed by public opinion research that finds that there is a settled assumption on the part of a large majority of the public in the US and the UK that crime rates are getting worse, whatever the actual patterns, and that there is little public confidence in the ability of the criminal justice system to do anything about this.

Criminological scholars identify specific features of contemporary crime and criminal justice that would have been unrecognisable 40 years ago: a culture of managerialism in the criminal justice agencies, the return of retributivism in punishment, the political elevation of victims' rights at the expense of those of the defendant, an escalation of fear of crime within society, the reversal of creating alternatives to prison, commercialisation of criminal justice services, payment for probation services by results and a loss of confidence by the public in the system.

1.1.6 Punishment

It might help us to understand the wider need for criminalisation, if we were to ask why we punish. The reasons for punishment are based on the following philosophies, all of which may be described as utilitarian. This means that punishment should only be permitted in order to prevent greater harm to society.

Deterrence—this principle justifies sentences which are harsher than would be deserved simply on the gravity of the offence in order to protect society and reduce crime by deterring others from engaging in similar activity. Sentencing for drug offences would be an example. This, of course, assumes that people always decide to offend as a matter of freedom of choice.

Incapacitation—to remove people from society where they pose a risk of re-offending or danger. This is undoubtedly a current policy choice.

Rehabilitation—to return people back to society in a reformed state of mind. This was the predominant policy until around 25 years ago. It has been replaced by a more punitive attitude to punishment. But any prison will have prison education and training schemes and therapeutic and medical treatment programmes.

Retribution—'Just Desserts', that is: that criminals deserve punishment but that the punishment should be no greater than is proportional to the harm. Therefore, the less serious the gravity of the crime, the lower the punishment. Account should also be taken of mitigating factors.

Sentences

These will range from imprisonment; suspended custody; intermittent custody; community sentences (or community punishment orders); probation (or community rehabilitation orders); combination orders (or community punishment and rehabilitation orders); fines; absolute/conditional discharges; binding over to keep the peace; care/supervision orders; disqualification; compensation; to orders in relation to the mentally ill. Sexual prevention orders and Criminal Behaviour Orders can be attached to other sentences. Penalty Notices for Disorder (on the spot fines) are being increasingly used by the police in respect of low-level offending such as criminal damage, public disorder and theft from shops. Paying the penalty is not an admission of guilt, it will not form part of an individual's criminal record, but it does count as a recordable offence. Whether it is right that the police should be acting as sentencers is a valid question (A. Ashworth, 'Editorial: Penalty Notices for Disorder and Summary Justice' [2013] *Crim LR* 869).

Over-punishment?

Populist views have, since the mid-1990s, dominated criminal justice policy so as to produce greater punitiveness in crime policy. That era marked a high-point in the crime rate and politicians began to express slogans such as 'Prison works', 'Tough on crime and tough on the causes of crime' and 'No more excuses' (originally used by Tony Blair, PM in 1993).

Read this by M. Tonry, *Confronting Crime*, Willan Publishing, 2003, pp 2, 3:

> . . . Parliament enacted tougher sentencing laws, Home Secretaries put those tougher laws into effect, magistrates and judges sent more people to prison and for longer times, the Parole Board became more risk averse and rates of recall and revocation increased, and the probation service shifted away from its traditional supervision and social service ethos to a surveillant and risk-management ethos. In other words, every component of the English criminal justice system became tougher . . . England's record and rising prison population is a remarkable phenomenon because it occurred during a period

of generally declining crime rates . . . we know that crime rates have been falling in every Western country since the mid-1990's, irrespective of whether imprisonment rates have risen . . . or held steady.

Section 142(1) of the Criminal Justice Act 2003 sets out the purposes of sentencing, in no particular order of priority: public protection, punishment, reparation, prevention and crime reduction. Sentencers have to attempt to balance competing justifications for punishment in place of focusing solely on the seriousness of the individual offence. The creation of mandatory sentences (for Class A drug offences, repeat burglary and serious sexual offences) and indeterminate sentences of imprisonment for public protection, the latter depriving anyone convicted of an automatic right to release, have all contributed to a dramatic rise in imprisonment. The result is that England and Wales has had one of the highest rates of imprisonment in Western Europe: 86,220 as of September 2017. In 2008, when the first edition of this book was published, the total was 82,006. It also has the highest number of life sentenced prisoners in Europe, more than Germany, Italy, the Russian Federation and Turkey (Aebi, Tiago & Burkhardt (2017) Council of Europe Annual Penal Statistics (www.coe.int)). The overwhelming majority of people in prison are working class; around 25 per cent have been in care, almost half have no educational qualifications, and more than 70 per cent have at least two mental disorders (www.prisonreformtrust. org.uk). Around 50 per cent of adults and 75 per cent of youths reoffend after release (D. Scott and H. Codd, *Controversial Issues in Prison*, Open University Press, 2010).

Carol Steiker, 'Criminalization and the Criminal Process', in *The Boundaries of the Criminal Law*, OUP, 2010, pp 29 and 23 states that we have reached a situation of 'mass incarceration' which impacts most heavily on the poor and minority communities, but there is little recognition of the family and social problems created by mass imprisonment. The Ministry of Justice itself announced in July 2013 that 'while the number of offenders coming to court is falling, alongside falling crime rates, more people who do commit crime are receiving prison sentences … Statistics published today also show a sharp rise in the use of longer sentences …' (*Reducing Reoffending and Improving Rehabilitation*, 25 July 2013: www.gov.uk/government policies/).

In recent years, some policies have aimed to divert less serious offenders away from prison (eg: Green Paper *Breaking the Cycle: Effective Punishment, Rehabilitation and Sentencing of Offenders* (Ministry of Justice, 2010)). The Legal Aid, Sentencing and Punishment of Offenders Act 2012 imposes a duty upon sentencers to consider compensation and permit sentences to be suspended for up to 24, instead of 12, months (s63 and s68). However, custodial numbers have stabilised at around 85,000 rather than fallen. (Story of the Prison Population: 1993–2016: www. gov.uk/government/collections/prisons-and-probation-statistics).

1.2 Presumption of Innocence and the Burden of Proof

1.2.1 The General Principle

1.2.2 Exceptions to the Prosecution Bearing the Burden of Proof

1.2.1 The General Principle

The following case enshrines a fundamental principle of the common law: that it is for the prosecution to prove the guilt of the accused, not for the accused to prove his innocence. This means that the prosecution have the burden of proving all the facts upon which they rely to establish the guilt of the accused.

Woolmington v DPP [1935] AC 462

D's wife left him after a few months of marriage and went to live with her mother. He wanted her to return. One morning he called at her mother's house and shot her dead. He maintained that it was an accident. His account of the facts was that he had taken an old gun belonging to his employer to show it to his wife to demonstrate his threat to commit suicide if she did not return to him. He sawed off the two barrels of the gun and loaded two cartridges. He attached wire to the gun so as to suspend it from his shoulder under his coat. He asked his wife to return and she said she was going to work. He then threatened to shoot himself and went to show her the gun. As he brought it across his waist it accidentally went off. A note was found in his pocket in which he had written that he wanted to kill both his wife and himself. He claimed to have written it after the shooting. D was convicted and appealed to the Court of Appeal, which dismissed the appeal. He then appealed to the House of Lords which allowed the appeal.

The trial judge, Swift J, had directed the jury as follows:

> Once it is shown to a jury that somebody has died through the act of another, that is presumed to be murder, unless the person who has been guilty of the act which causes the death can satisfy a jury that what happened was something less, something which might be alleviated, something which might be reduced to a charge of manslaughter, or was something which was accidental, or was something which could be justified.
>
> . . .
>
> The Crown has got to satisfy you that this woman, Violet Woolmington, died at the prisoner's hands. They must satisfy you of that beyond any reasonable doubt. If they satisfy you of that, then he has to show that there are circumstances to be found in the evidence which has been given from the witness box in this case which alleviate the crime so that it is only manslaughter, or which excuse the homicide altogether by showing that it was a pure accident.

Lord Sankey LC in the House of Lords:

> If at any period of a trial it was permissible for the judge to rule that the prosecution had established its case and that the onus was shifted on the prisoner to prove that he was not guilty, and that, unless he discharged that onus, the prosecution was entitled to succeed, it would be enabling the judge in such a case to say that the jury must in law find the prisoner guilty and so make the judge decide the case and not the jury, which is not the common law. It would be an entirely different case from those exceptional instances of special verdicts where a judge asks the jury to find certain facts and directs them that on such facts the prosecution is entitled to succeed. Indeed, a consideration of such special verdicts shows that it is not till the end of the evidence that a verdict can properly be found and that at the end of the evidence it is not for the prisoner to establish his innocence, but for the prosecution to establish his guilt. Just as there is evidence on behalf of the prosecution so there may be evidence on behalf of the prisoner which may cause a doubt as to his guilt. In either case, he is entitled to the benefit of the doubt. But while the prosecution must prove the guilt of the prisoner, there is no such burden laid on the prisoner to prove his innocence, and it is sufficient for him to raise a doubt as to his guilt; he is not bound to satisfy the jury of his innocence . . .
>
> *Throughout the web of the English criminal law one golden thread is always to be seen –that it is the duty of the prosecution to prove the prisoner's guilt subject to what I have already said as to the defence of insanity and subject also to any statutory exception. If, at the end of and on the whole of the case, there is a reasonable doubt, created by the evidence given by either the prosecution or the prisoner, as to whether the prisoner killed the deceased with a malicious intention, the prosecution has not made out the case and the prisoner is entitled to an acquittal. No matter what the charge or where the trial, the principle that the prosecution must prove the guilt of the prisoner is part of the common law of England and no attempt to whittle it down can be entertained.* When dealing with a murder case the Crown must prove (a) death as the result of a voluntary act of the accused and (b) malice of the accused. It may prove malice either expressly or by implication. For malice may be implied where death occurs

as the result of a voluntary act of the accused which is (i) intentional and (ii) unprovoked. When evidence of death and malice has been given (this is a question for the jury) the accused is entitled to show by evidence or by examination of the circumstances adduced by the Crown that the act on his part which caused death was either unintentional or provoked. If the jury are either satisfied with his explanation or, upon a review of all the evidence, are left in reasonable doubt whether, even if his explanation be not accepted, the act was unintentional or provoked, the prisoner is entitled to be acquitted. Appeal allowed. [Emphasis added.]

 NOTE 1.1

1. The standard of proof on the prosecution is to prove guilt 'beyond all reasonable doubt'. In other words, the magistrates or jury must be *sure* of the defendant's guilt.
2. The defendant does not have to prove innocence and is entitled to a presumption of innocence until proven guilty. In other words, the defendant has the benefit of the doubt.

Flowing from the presumption of innocence are several other important constitutional protections for the defendant: the right to silence and the privilege against self-incrimination. These are now protected by Article 6(2) ECHR which embodies fundamental fair trial rights.

The right to silence implies that the accused does not need to assist the state to prove its case. It has symbolic significance in confirming the presumption of innocence and placing the legal burden of proof on the prosecution. It defines the balance between the state and the individual and is a vital protection for protecting the innocent, especially suspects who are vulnerable because of age, mental disorder or learning disability. It was qualified by s34 Criminal Justice and Public Order Act 1994. An arrested person is not only told that he has the right to remain silent and that anything he does say may be used in evidence against him. He is advised that if he later relies upon a fact which it would have been reasonable for him to mention, an adverse inference will arise (ie: that he has fabricated a defence not mentioned during detention in the police station). An adverse inference, of course, potentially undermines the right of silence.

The privilege against self-incrimination confers the right not to be compelled to speak in a potentially incriminating way, whether in police detention or in court.

1.2.2 Exceptions to the Prosecution Bearing the Burden of Proof

Insanity and diminished responsibility

There are exceptions to the general rule that the prosecution must bear the burden of proof beyond all reasonable doubt. The defences of insanity and diminished responsibility impose legal burdens of proof on the accused on a balance of probability. They apply where the mental capacity of the accused at the time of the crime was in doubt. What this means is that anyone wishing to rely on either defence must provide sufficient medical evidence to convince a court that it was *more likely than not* that, at the time of the offence, they were acting under a mental disability. As we shall see, insanity can be a defence to any crime whereas diminished responsibility applies only to murder. If successful, it results in a conviction of manslaughter. Various justifications for this reversal of the burden are given by courts from time to time, not the least of which is that an accused who wishes to rely on such a defence is the one best placed to prove it. This is a questionable argument. A legal burden of proof on the accused is more demanding than an evidential burden which must be satisfied where the accused relies on most other defences. An evidential burden means that the accused must have sufficient evidence of his defence, but need not prove it. For example, in a case of self-defence, the defendant must produce some evidence that any assault he committed was in response to an imminent attack. This may be by his own testimony, eye-witnesses, CCTV film footage, or by some other means. A trial for an offence imposing a legal burden of proof upon the accused risks contravening the presumption of innocence and Article 6(2) ECHR. The risk is that he could be convicted where he is unable to prove a defence despite there being a reasonable doubt as to guilt.

Reverse-onus statutory offences

The majority of offences in the criminal justice system are statutory, and many of those are offences of strict liability or negligence as we saw earlier. Contrary to the general rule that an accused does not have to prove his innocence, many of these offences also contain a defence which either expressly, or implicitly, reverses the burden of proof. This means, again, that Parliament expects an accused to prove his innocence on a balance of probabilities.

An example of such an offence is that of producing, supplying or possession of controlled drugs contrary to s4 Misuse of Drugs Act 1971. Section 28(b)(i) provides that the accused shall be acquitted if he proves that he neither believed nor suspected nor had reason to suspect that the substance or product in question was a controlled drug. Another example would be the following offence under s57(1) Terrorism Act 2000:

> A person commits an offence if he possesses an article in circumstances which give rise to reasonable suspicion that his possession is for a purpose connected with the commission, preparation or instigation of an act of terrorism.

Section 57(2) provides a defence if it can be *proved* that possession of the article was not for a purpose connected with terrorism.

Some offences, usually those of strict liability, provide for a 'due diligence' defence which requires the accused to show that he has taken reasonable precautions and exercised due diligence to prevent the offence in question. With other offences, the reversal of the burden of proof will be implied. '*Implied*' statutory exceptions to the general principle that the prosecution bears the burden of proof arise where the offence provides any 'exception, exemption, proviso, excuse or qualification whether or not it accompanies the description of the offence' (s101 Magistrates' Courts Act 1980 and *Hunt* [1987] AC 352). Consequently, the courts have had to deal with the question of whether these reverse-onus provisions are fair and compatible with Article 6(2).

Unfortunately, the House of Lords is unable to state a clear position on reverse-onus defences. It has held that sometimes they do offend the presumption of innocence or Article 6(2) and so impose only an *evidential* burden on the accused on a balance of probabilities not a *legal* burden of proof beyond all reasonable doubt:

KEY CASES

R v Lambert [2001] 3 All ER 577—possession of a controlled drug;

AG's Reference (No 4 of 2002) [2004] UKHL 43—membership of a proscribed organisation under s11 Terrorism Act 2000.

On the other hand, the House of Lords held in *DPP v Sheldrake* [2005] 1 AC 246 that on a drink-driving charge, a reverse-onus defence requiring the accused to prove that he was not likely to drive whilst over the limit, imposes a legal burden of proof which is not incompatible with Article 6(2) provided it is in pursuance of a legitimate aim and it is proportionate. It depends on what mischief the statute is aimed at, how practical it would be to expect the defendant to prove any defence, the seriousness of the punishment and the need to observe basic requirements of fairness. Lord Bingham explained:

> The overriding concern is that a trial should be fair, and the presumption of innocence is a fundamental right directed to that end. The Convention does not outlaw presumptions of fact or law but requires that these should be kept within reasonable limits and should not be arbitrary …
>
> Relevant to any judgment on reasonableness or proportionality will be the opportunity given to the defendant to rebut the presumption, maintenance of the rights of the defendant, flexibility in the application of the presumption, retention by the court of a power to assess the evidence, the importance of what is at stake and the difficulty which a prosecutor may face in the absence of a presumption.

Each case must therefore be considered on all the facts and circumstances. Davis LJ reviewed the law on reverse-onus provisions in *Williams (Orette)* [2012] EWCA Crim 2162. The case concerned possession of a prohibited weapon (imitation gun capable of firing blanks readily convertible into firearm) contrary to s5(1)(a) Firearms Act 1968. Section 1(5) Firearms Act 1982 provides a defence that the accused did not know or had no reason to suspect that it was readily convertible. It was held that this carried a legal burden of proof:

> Firearms offences – any firearms offences – are a very serious problem. Where those firearms stand to be lethal – as in the case of readily convertible imitation firearms – the need for protection of the public is obvious. That is reflected by the (legitimate) creation of a number of strict liability offences in this context … Further, the question of knowledge (or lack of it) involves facts readily available to the accused – he knows the circumstances in which and from whom he obtained the item. Likewise as to the issue of whether he 'had no reason to suspect' that the imitation firearm was so constructed or adapted as to be readily convertible. No great difficulty is placed in the way of a defendant in that regard. On the other hand, it could be very difficult indeed for prosecutors, and would be a real deterrent to prosecution let alone successful prosecution, if the burden were placed on the Crown to obtain the necessary evidence to disprove a case that the accused had neither knowledge nor reason to suspect.

The inroad to the presumption of innocence and Article 6(2) was proportionate given the seriousness of the offence. But this argument is debatable given that offences of violence, which are more serious than offences of firearms possession, do not involve a reversal of the legal burden in any respect.

Most reverse-onus offences are summary, triable only in the magistrates' court. But it has been estimated that 'reverse-onus' offences apply to something over 200 of the 540 or so statutory offences triable in the Crown Court or 40 per cent of all Crown Court offences. (A. Ashworth and M. Blake, 'The Presumption of Innocence in English Criminal Law' [1996] *Crim LR* 306–317.)

➡ CROSS-REFERENCE
For further discussion of this matter and a look at strict liability in detail see Chapter 4.

It is important to note that, in principle, strict liability offences carrying reverse-onus provisions are compatible with the ECHR: *Salibiaku v France* (1988) 13 EHRR 379 provided, again, that they are confined within reasonable limits.

By way of conclusion, we can say that the standard of proof beyond all reasonable, as opposed to all, doubt, represents as fair a balance as possible between the interests of the state, society and the individual. The film 'Twelve Angry Men', 1957, by Sidney Lumet, is one of the clearest illustrations of this important constitutional principle. You should see it if you can.

1.3 Classification of Crimes and Courts

1.3.1 Classification of Crimes

1.3.2 The Courts

1.3.1 Classification of Crimes

Summary offences

These are relatively minor cases, for instance:

- assault;
- battery;
- taking a conveyance without consent.

The magistrates' court has limited sentencing powers (six months for each offence, with a maximum of 12 months for more than one, and fines limited to £5,000). Magistrates' sentencing guidance is contained in the Magistrates' Court Sentencing Guidelines. These cases typically start by either summons or charge.

Either way offences

These may be more or less serious depending on the nature and seriousness of the case, for example:

- assault which is racially or religiously aggravated;
- theft, fraud;
- criminal damage;
- assault occasioning actual bodily harm, wounding/infliction of grievous bodily harm.

If a defendant is charged with an either way offence, the magistrates' court holds a Mode of Trial hearing in which the magistrates decide whether to retain or reject jurisdiction depending on the gravity of the case and the sufficiency of their sentencing powers. If they accept jurisdiction, the defendant has the right to elect Crown Court trial before judge and jury. If the magistrates decline jurisdiction because their sentencing powers are insufficient or the case is complex, the defendant will be sent to the Crown Court for trial and has no right to elect to be tried by the magistrates. Magistrates are able to send a case to the Crown Court after conviction if they feel that their sentencing powers are insufficient (ss2 and 3 Powers of Criminal Courts (Sentencing) Act 2000). Only a very small percentage of defendants elect jury trial.

Indictable offences

These are the most serious offences in the criminal justice system:

- murder, manslaughter;
- rape;
- robbery;
- wounding with intent to cause grievous bodily harm.

They will be tried by judge and jury in the Crown Court. An 'indictment' will be drawn up by the Crown Court, similar to a charge in the magistrates' court, listing the offences for which the defendant will be tried. Sentencing limits will be prescribed by the statutory maximum for each offence, sentencing guidelines from the Court of Appeal or Sentencing Council Guidelines (www.sentencingcouncil.org.uk/). Fines are unlimited.

1.3.2 The Courts

The magistrates' court

The magistrates' court hears all summary cases and offences triable either way where the defendant elects for magistrates' trial. Indictable cases also initially begin here. Well over 90 per cent of all offences will be dealt with in the magistrates' courts from beginning to end. Appeal will be to the Crown Court against conviction/sentence or to the High Court (QBD) by way of 'case stated' on a point of law or excess of jurisdiction. It will also hear applications for judicial review of the magistrates' decision in excess of jurisdiction/breach of natural justice. Appeal can be made to the Supreme Court on a point of law of public importance with leave.

The Crown Court

Crown Court trials will be before a single High Court Judge, Circuit Judge, or part-time Recorder or Assistant Recorder. Juries consist of 12 people selected randomly from the electoral roll. Verdicts must be either unanimous or, if this is not possible, by majority vote of at least 9:3. The role of the judge is to determine questions of law and to direct the jury on the law, evidence and facts. Juries decide questions of fact, guilt or innocence. Appeal will be to the Court of Appeal (Criminal Division) against conviction/sentence. A conviction will be overturned if it is considered to be unsafe (s2 Criminal Appeal Act 1968). The prosecution can appeal to the Court of Appeal against termination or evidential rulings. An example of a termination ruling is where there has been a finding of 'no case to answer'. The Attorney-General can appeal to the Court of Appeal against unduly lenient sentences (s36 Criminal Justice Act 1988).

The Director of Public Prosecutions may apply to the Court of Appeal for a second retrial in serious crimes where there is new and compelling evidence of guilt and it is in the interests of justice (s79 Criminal Justice Act 2003).

See Diagram 1.1 for an overview.

1.4 Procedure and Fair Trial Rights

1.4.1 Procedure

1.4.2 Fair Trial Rights

1.4.1 Procedure

Once an accused has been charged with an offence, the Crown Prosecution Service, on behalf of the state, will institute proceedings if there is sufficient evidence to provide a realistic prospect of conviction and it is in the public interest (Code for Crown Prosecutors: www.cps.gov.uk). In

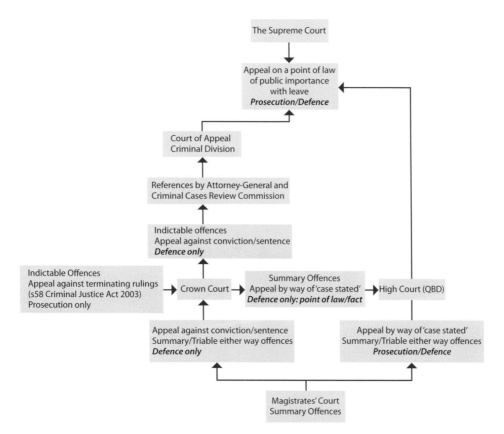

Diagram 1.1

The criminal court system

both the police station and at court, the accused will be represented by a defence lawyer who will be paid for by the Legal Aid Scheme. Pending trial, the accused will either be released on bail or remanded in custody. There will be pre-trial hearings concerning the management of the case. The prosecution is obliged to disclose its evidence, as well as any evidence which would be useful to the defence. The defence is obliged to disclose the nature and basis of any defence (Criminal Procedure and Investigations Act 1996).

All criminal trials will be opened by the prosecution who introduce the evidence upon which they wish to rely, that is: witnesses, the victim, documentary or real evidence such as the murder weapon. They examine their witnesses in chief who are then cross-examined by the defence. The point is to test the evidence and challenge the reliability or credibility of each witness. The defence then presents its case, the prosecution cross-examining. Whereas the prosecution bears *the legal burden* of proof, the onus is on the accused to satisfy *an evidential burden* in respect of a defence so as to cast reasonable doubt on the prosecution case. Each side may re-examine if necessary. Closing speeches follow, the defence always addressing the court last. In the magistrates' court, the verdict is reached by the magistrate who will either sentence immediately or adjourn the case for probation/medical reports. In the Crown Court, the judge gives guidance on the evidence and law, but it is the jury which convicts or acquits. If the jury convicts, the judge passes sentence either immediately or after reports.

See Diagram 1.2 for an overview.

Trial Procedure

1.

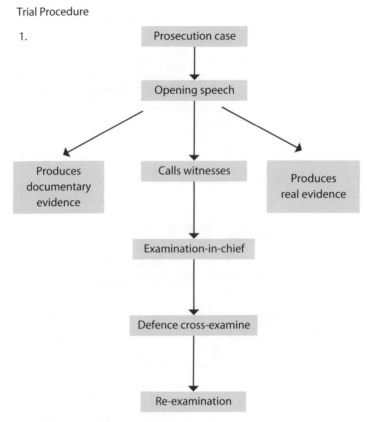

2. Defence case follows same sequence
3. Closing speeches
4. Verdict/Reports/Sentencing

Diagram 1.2
Trial procedure

1.4.2 Fair Trial Rights

In addition to the presumption of innocence, the accused has certain 'fair trial rights'. Besides the right to representation, the accused has the right to be informed of the case against him, to challenge that evidence, to be tried and convicted on evidence lawfully obtained, to be judged by an impartial court, not to be unfairly punished and to appeal against both conviction and sentence.

1.5 Police Powers, Miscarriages of Justice and Victims

1.5.1 Police Powers

1.5.2 Miscarriages of Justice

1.5.3 Victims

1.5.1 Police Powers

Police powers were codified by the Police and Criminal Evidence Act 1984. Codes of Practice issued under the Act, and revised periodically, set out their powers in respect of stop and search, seizure of evidence, arrest, ID parades, detention in the police station and so on. Their powers have increased extensively to deal with our more complex society and have been extended over recent years by a succession of Acts of Parliament. The Criminal Justice Act 2003, for example, increased powers of search and seizure and extended periods of detention in terrorist cases. By virtue of the Serious Organised Crime and Police Act 2005, virtually all offences are now arrestable and the police station detention limit can be extended beyond 24 hours for all offences.

1.5.2 Miscarriages of Justice

Three significant landmarks in criminal justice history were the Philips Royal Commission on Criminal Procedure 1981, the Runciman Royal Commission on Criminal Justice 1993 and the MacPherson Inquiry 1999.

The first two investigated the causes of several serious miscarriages of justice: the conviction of three youths for the murder of Maxwell Confait and the cases of the Guildford 4, the Maguire 7 and the Birmingham 6, all Irish nationals who had been convicted for bombings and murders on mainland Britain of which they were entirely innocent. Some were not released from prison for 13–16 years. Other wrongfully convicted victims were incarcerated for even longer. These miscarriages were the result of systemic failings: inadequate defence representation in police stations, undue pressure to confess, police brutality, withholding of vital forensic evidence, fabricated confessions, the lack of an independent review of the decision to prosecute and a slow and cumbersome appeals procedure. The Royal Commission resulted in the Criminal Cases Review Commission (1995) which investigates and refers unsafe convictions to the Court of Appeal.

The MacPherson Inquiry concerned the failure of the police to prosecute the death of black teenager Stephen Lawrence. It also addressed the violent racism in society and police inability to address it. The outcome was a finding of 'institutional racism' against the police and a standard to which all public institutions must adhere in order to meet ethnic minority demands.

There have been well over 40 new Acts of Parliament on criminal justice since 1997, many of which erode defendant's rights. For example, the Criminal Justice Act 2003 permitted greater admissibility of previous convictions and hearsay evidence in criminal trials, placed new disclosure duties on defendants, and abolished the rule against double jeopardy in serious crimes (ie: you can now be prosecuted more than once for the same offence). All reforms were aimed at convicting the guilty, protecting victims, management and efficiency.

1.5.3 Victims

The Criminal Justice Act 2003 was swiftly followed by several other Acts and proposals all in the spirit of rebalancing the criminal justice system in favour of victims and the public. Victims are now at the heart of criminal justice policy. Yet, tipping the balance of justice too far away from defendants in favour of victims and the fight against crime threatens to undermine defendants' rights and increases the risk of wrongful convictions. Victims' rights, which were always under-valued in practical terms, were given new impetus under the Domestic Violence,

Crime and Victims Act 2004 and the Criminal Justice Act 2003. There is now a Code of Practice for prosecutors to follow in keeping victims informed of proceedings and a Commissioner for Victims.

?!   **THINKING POINT** 1.3

Do you think that criminals have too many rights in the criminal justice system?

What sort of a criminal justice system would you prefer:

A One where the guilty are only convicted by evidence beyond any doubt at all?

B One where the guilty will be convicted by evidence beyond all reasonable doubt?

A rules out the possibility of wrongly convicting the innocent, but it would be virtually impossible to convict anyone. B includes the possibility that the guilty might be wrongfully acquitted. Is that better than wrongfully convicting the innocent?

1.6 Sources of the Criminal Law including the ECHR

1.6.1 Statute and Common Law

1.6.2 The Draft Criminal Code 1989

1.6.3 The European Convention for the Protection of Human Rights and Fundamental Freedoms (ECHR)

1.6.1 Statute and Common Law

Some of our criminal law derives from common law. For example, murder and manslaughter are common law offences for which there are no statutory definitions. These crimes may well be defined in language that is now regarded as historic and imprecise.

As part of an ongoing process of law reform, however, a good deal of criminal law is now defined by statute. Property and sexual offences for example are now mostly codified by the Theft Acts 1968 and 1978, the Fraud Act 2006 and the Sexual Offences Act 2003. Statutory reform tends to be piecemeal and there may be several statutes concerning any particular area of law.

1.6.2 The Draft Criminal Code 1989

This was drawn up by a team of criminal academics. It is not in force but is referred to by the courts for guidance from time to time. There is no comprehensive criminal code in England and Wales. The Law Commission is involved in long-term law reform and periodically produces reports and draft bills to supplement the Draft Criminal Code. We will examine some of them throughout this book. The Law Commission recently announced that it was relinquishing its long-term goal of codification.

1.6.3 The European Convention for the Protection of Human Rights and Fundamental Freedoms (ECHR)

The European Convention for the Protection of Human Rights and Fundamental Freedoms (ECHR) was signed in 1950, ratified by the UK in 1951 and came into force in 1953. It was inspired by the principles declared by the United Nations Universal Declaration of Human Rights in 1948. It is a document of the Council of Europe (not the European Union, which is a separate organisation). It does not include social or economic rights. The rights guaranteed represent minimum human rights which should be protected by the law of each member state which has ratified the ECHR. These rights can be enforced in criminal proceedings in two ways:

(1) They can be the basis of a claim to the European Court of Human Rights at Strasbourg (ECtHR) after all domestic remedies have been exhausted. The ECtHR at Strasbourg has no power to declare UK law to be incompatible with the ECHR. It will find the UK government to be in violation of a protected right wherever there is ambiguity between domestic law and the ECHR.

(2) The Human Rights Act 1998 (HRA) provides that for claims arising after 2 October 2000 most Convention rights can be directly enforced in the domestic courts. This does not prevent anyone from applying directly to Strasbourg after attempting domestic appeals. Section 6 provides that all public authorities, including courts and tribunals, must, if possible, act in a way which is compatible with the Convention. This includes: central and local government, police, immigration officers, and prisons. Section 7 provides that individuals who believe their rights have been infringed by a public authority can assert their rights either as a defence in criminal proceedings; in an appeal or judicial review; or, if no other legal avenue is open, by bringing civil proceedings for damages. No court has the power to strike down incompatible legislation but it can make a Declaration of Incompatibility which means that the task of amending the law is left to Parliament. Section 3 provides that, so far as it is possible to do so, primary and subordinate legislation must be read and given effect in a way which is compatible with Convention rights. This means that the courts must be guided by the rules of statutory interpretation. In addition, they may introduce or remove certain words or meanings so as to achieve compatibility (reading 'in' or 'out'). Alternatively, reading 'down' involves confining the meaning of words in the legislation so as to make it compatible with Convention rights.

The following guaranteed rights and freedoms are set out in section 1 of the Convention and have relevance to the criminal law:

Article 2 The right to life and the prohibition of arbitrary deprivation of life.

Article 3 The prohibition of torture, inhuman and/or degrading treatment or punishment.

Article 4 The prohibition of slavery and forced labour.

Article 5 The right to liberty and security of person including the right of an arrested person to be informed promptly of the reasons for arrest and of any charges against him.

Article 6 The right to a fair trial by an impartial court: the right to be presumed innocent of a criminal charge until proven guilty, the right to be defended by a lawyer and to have free legal assistance when 'the interests of justice so require'.

Article 7 The right to certainty and the prohibition of retrospective application of the criminal law.

Article 8 The right to respect for private and family life.

Article 9 Freedom of thought, conscience and religion.

Article 10 Freedom of expression, including the right to receive and impart information and ideas without interference.

Article 11 Freedom of assembly and association, including the right to form and join trade unions.

Article 12 The right to marry and found a family.

Article 13 The right to an effective remedy in domestic law for arguable violations of the Convention.

Article 14 The right to non-discrimination under any Convention right.

Some rights are qualified. Under Article 5 for example a person's liberty may be denied by lawful arrest. Article 8 may be qualified if necessary in a democratic society in the interests of national security, public safety, the economic well-being of the country, the prevention of crime and disorder, the protection of health or morals or the protection of rights and freedoms of others.

The ECtHR has found the UK to be in breach of the ECHR in relation to the following areas:

- Article 2: the use of lethal force by state security forces and the law of self-defence: *McCann v UK* (1996) 21 EHRR 96 and *Jordan v UK* (2003) 37 EHRR 52.

- Article 3: torture and deprivation of liberty of those interned for long periods without trial in Northern Ireland: *Brogan v UK* (1988) 11 EHRR 117 and *Brannigan v UK* (1993) 17 EHRR 539.

- Article 3: vagueness of the defence of reasonable chastisement by parents against children: *A v UK* (1998) 27 EHRR 611.

- Article 5: the indefinite detention of terrorist suspects based 'solely or to a decisive degree on closed material' amounts to a breach of procedural fairness as guaranteed by the ECHR: *A v UK* (2009) 49 EHRR 29, [2009] All ER (D) 203 (ECHR) [220].

- Article 8: the Northern Irish criminalisation of homosexual conduct between consenting adults in private: *Dudgeon v UK* (1981) 4 EHRR 149. The UK police were held to be in breach of Article 8 by retaining fingerprints, cell samples, DNA and photographs in the absence of criminal conviction: *S v UK* [2009] 48 EHRR 50.

- Article 14: differential age of consent for homosexuals (18) and heterosexuals (16): *Sutherland v UK* [1998] EHRLR 117. Equality in the age of consent was provided for by the Sexual Offences (Amendment) Act 2000.

- Article 3 of Protocol 1: there have been several cases on the blanket ban on prisoners' right to vote.

The ECHR has had by far the greatest impact on procedural rights rather than the substantive law. However, as we progress through this book we shall meet various areas which can be challenged from a human rights perspective. For example, many fundamental criminal concepts of mens rea (MR) such as intention and dishonesty are far from certain. The same applies to many common law offences such as common law conspiracy, offences by omission and gross negligence manslaughter. Throughout this book we will touch upon these issues as we consider the rules and principles underlying the criminal law of England and Wales.

1.7 Crime in England and Wales Today

1.7.1 Women

1.7.2 Black and Ethnic Minorities

Criminal justice statistics are published regularly by the Home Office, the Office for National Statistics (ONS) and the Ministry of Justice. The crime rate in England and Wales has halved since 1995 and is now at its lowest since 1981. The Crime Survey for England and Wales measures crime by asking for people's experiences. It shows that for the year ending March 2017 crime fell by 7 per cent compared to the previous year. However, crime recorded by the police increased by 10 per cent (at least partly accounted for by improved recording and increased offence coverage). Naturally, statistics must be regarded with a certain amount of scepticism. Only a very small proportion of crime is reported to or recorded by the police (23 per cent) of which the clear up rate is only 28.9 per cent. It is estimated that the Crime Survey fails to account for nearly half of violent crime against women, for example (*The Guardian*, 10 June 2015, p 2). The fact remains that only 2–3 per cent of all crime results in conviction (Home Office: Information on the Criminal Justice System in England and Wales (1999)—these are the most up-to-date figures).

See Diagram 1.3 for a breakdown of some of the latest figures.

Contemporary crime is in addition characterised by globalisation, cross-border organisation and the use of the internet, particularly in respect of transnational fraud, drug and human trafficking. This of course creates new problems in detection, investigation and evidence gathering. Other internet crimes which are escalating such as cyber-hate offences, incitement to racist, xenophobic or anti-Semitic hatred or violence, pose new challenges for prosecutors.

The Ministry of Justice publishes biennial statistics on women and BAME ethnic groups in the criminal justice system.

1.7.1 Women

Women are more likely to be victims of intimate violence (ie: domestic violence from a partner or family member) than men and they are far more likely to be murdered by someone they know, rather than by a stranger. As defendants, they commit far less crime than men but those for which they are most commonly sentenced are theft and handling (34 per cent), followed by fraud, violence and drug offences. A significant fact is that a higher proportion of females than men sentenced to custody have no previous convictions. Women are more likely to receive punishments other than custody, such as fines or community sentences, but there is evidence of harsher sentences than for men in drug offending (J. Loveless, 'Women, Sentencing and the Drug Offences Definitive Guideline' [2013] *Crim LR* 594). Currently there are just under 4,000 women in prison in the UK out of a total of approximately 85,000. This represents a fall over previous levels. By contrast, the average population of women in prison increased dramatically by 173 per cent between 1992 and 2002. It is noteworthy that 20 per cent of women in prison were in care as children and around half have experienced violent relationships. Around 13 per cent are foreign nationals. 80 per cent have a diagnosable mental health problem. In 2011, 55 women committed suicide in prison compared to 2 men but that trend is now falling. There is little research on the familial consequences of imprisoning women. (All statistics from Felicity Gerry and Lyndon Harris, *Women in prison: is the justice system fit for purpose?* 2016 (www.halsburyslawexchange.co.uk), Ministry of Justice, *Women in the Criminal Justice System* 2011 (www.gov.uk), Corston Report, *Review of Women with Particular Vulnerabilities in the Criminal Justice System*, 2007.)

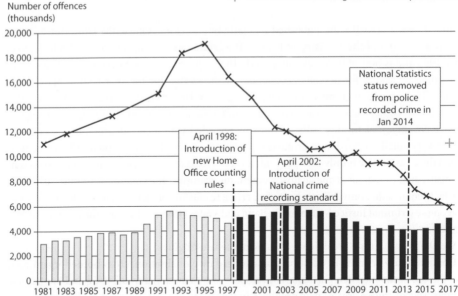

Diagram 1.3

Trends in Crime Survey for England and Wales and police recorded crime, year ending December 1981 to year ending March 2017

Source: ONS Bulletin, year ending March 2017, available at www.ons.gov.uk/peoplepopulationandcommunity/ crimeandjustice/datasets/crimeinenglandandwalesbulletintables

Notes:

1. Police recorded crime data are not designated as National Statistics.

2. CSEW data on this chart refer to different time periods: a) 1981 to 1999 refer to crimes experienced in the calendar year (January to December) b) from year ending March 2002 onwards the estimates relate to crimes experienced in the 12 months before interview, based on interviews carried out in that financial year (April to March).

3. From the year ending March 2012 onwards, police recorded crime data has included offences from additional sources of fraud data.

4. CSEW data relate to adults aged 16 and over or to households.

5. Some forces have revised their data and police recorded crime totals may not agree with those previously published.

6. Data on fraud and computer misuse are published as Experimental Statistics, which are in the testing phase and not yet fully developed. They are published in order to involve users and stakeholders in their development, and as a means to build in quality at an early stage.

7. New victimisation questions on fraud and computer misuse were incorporated into the Crime Survey for England and Wales (CSEW) from October 2015. The questions are currently asked of half the survey sample to test for detrimental effects on the survey as a whole and help ensure that the historical time series is protected

1.7.2 Black and Ethnic Minorities

The risk of being a victim of personal crime is higher for adults from a mixed background than for any other group. The number of stops and searches has increased for everyone, but for black people this occurs 4.5 times more than for white people. Black people are more likely to be arrested than whites by a factor of almost 3. Black persons are more likely to be proceeded against in the magistrates' court than all other ethnic groups. BAME groups are over-represented in the prison system at 25 per cent whilst forming 14 per cent of the general population (*Statistics on Race and the Criminal Justice System 2014*: www.gov.uk).

A study in 1992 could not confirm this was due to racism within the criminal justice system. Read this by M. Tonry, *Confronting Crime*, Willan Publishing, 2003, p 162:

> Black people in England and Wales are, relative to their numbers in the population, six or seven times more likely to be confined in prison than whites, and, when charged with crimes, are more likely to be imprisoned and to receive longer sentences . . . Considerable research effort has been devoted to explaining these differences . . . Findings from Roger Hood's (1992) landmark study of black/white differences in Crown Court sentencing in the Midlands are typical. The overrepresentation of black people in prison is explained in the following way: 70 per cent of the differential resulted from black overrepresentation among persons appearing for sentence . . .; 10 per cent was attributable to offence seriousness and criminal history . . .; 13 per cent was attributable to case processing differences . . .; and 7 per cent was not explained.

A more recent study by *Guardian* journalists of over one million court records found that BAME people were more likely to be imprisoned than whites for offences concerned with drugs, possession of a weapon, driving and public disorder (J. Ball, O. Bowcott, and S. Rogers, *The Guardian*, 26 November 2011).

In 2017, the *Lammy Review*, commissioned in 2016 by Prime Minister David Cameron and led by David Lammy MP, concluded that BAME defendants were disproportionately likely to receive prison sentences for drug offences, even when other factors were taken into account; while youth offending and reoffending overall has decreased in the last decade, the numbers of BAME offenders has increased; and many BAME defendants lacked trust in the court and prison systems (www.gov.uk/government/publications/lammy-review-final-report).

1.8 Conclusion

We have examined the social, moral and political influences on the decision to criminalise, and the reality of crime in England and Wales today. Throughout this book we will touch upon these issues as we consider the rules and principles underlying the criminal law of England and Wales.

SUMMARY

- The reasons for criminalising conduct.
- The standard and burden of proof in criminal proceedings.
- The exceptions to the prosecution bearing the burden of proof.
- The classification of crimes and the criminal court structure.
- The sources of the criminal law.
- The four theories of punishment.
- Crime in England and Wales Today.

How to answer examination questions

At the end of each chapter of this book is an examination-style question for you to attempt before looking at the answer outline on the online resources: www.oup.com/uk/loveless6e/.

PROBLEM QUESTIONS

A useful tool to bear in mind when structuring your answer is the following:

- **I: Identify** relevant issues
- **D: Define** offences/defences
- **E: Explain/evaluate** the law
- **A: Apply** law to facts.

Identify the issues

This means that you will need to work out in general terms what area of criminal law the question is about. Most will concern some particular issue of the actus reus (AR)/MR of an offence or whether the defendant has the benefit of a defence. The facts of problem questions rarely fall squarely within decided cases or legal rules. They generally fall in between and include a range of issues. You will need to highlight these issues for discussion.

Define offences/defences

All questions will expect you to discuss the case for the prosecution and the liability of a defendant. After having identified the issues you therefore need to set out the legal definitions or main elements of all relevant offences/defences. No prosecution lawyer would go into court without first knowing what offence he had to prove nor would a defence lawyer be much good without knowing the elements of his client's defence.

Explain/evaluate the law

Next you are expected to discuss in detail the particular legal issues that arise from the facts. A structured and logical approach to the law is required. Use the sequence of headings in the relevant chapters as a guide. Support your answers with cases (authorities) and statutory definitions. Your work will be improved by references to academic articles.

When referring to cases, do not be too concerned about describing the facts. What matters is the ratio of the case (the point of law decided by the court) and the explanation for it.

You will be expected to examine the law from the point of view of both prosecution and defence. It should be possible for you to construct an argument for both by referring to different cases or to different arguments within some of the judgments.

Apply law to the facts

Once you have fully explained the law relating to each issue, you should then apply the law to the facts of the question. You will need to bear in mind that there is not one single right answer. The questions are not designed to enable you to say, 'Of course, D is guilty because this case says so!' They are never that clear-cut. You will need to examine the law and then argue for or against guilt or innocence in the light of your preceding discussion. A clear and authoritative explanation of the law and a coherent argument/application to the facts is far more important than thinking that there is necessarily one right answer.

Essay questions

All examinations include a mix of essay and problem questions. An essay question will ask you to examine/analyse/compare and contrast a particular area/s of law in depth. Here you would be required to engage in a far more detailed examination of a narrower area of law than with a problem question. Again, you should support your answers with cases and statutory definitions. Greater reference to academic articles would be expected.

FURTHER READING

Crime in England and Wales (for statistics and research): www.ons.gov.uk.

A. Ashworth, 'A Decade of Human Rights in Criminal Justice' [2014] 5 *Crim LR* 325
Considers the impact of the ECHR and Human Rights Act 1988 on criminal law.

F. Gerry and L. Harris, *Women in prison: is the justice system fit for purpose?* **(2016)**
www.halsburyslawexchange.co.uk
Brings together the most recent research and makes recommendations for improvement.

D. Husak, 'The Criminal Law as Last Resort' (2004) 24 *OJLS* **207**
Takes a critical look at increasing criminalisation and asks if it should be a last resort.

G. Lamond, 'What Is a Crime?' (2007) 27 *OJLS* **609**
Considers what distinguishes criminal liability from civil liability and considers crimes as public wrongs.

C.C. Murphy, 'The Principle of Legality in Criminal Law under the European Convention on Human Rights' (2010) 2 *EHRLR* **192**
Discusses case law on Article 7 ECHR (the right to certainty in criminal law and the prohibition of retrospective application).

WEBSITES

www.parliament.uk—bills and Hansard

www.lawcom.gov.uk—Law Commission publications

www.police.uk—news and information on crime and policing

www.gov.uk/police-powers-of-arrest-your-rights—general information regarding police powers

www.ons.gov.uk—criminal justice statistics

www.gov.uk/government/organisations/ministry-of-justice—website of the Ministry of Justice with gateways to legislation, reports, research, statistics and data

www.sentencingcouncil.org.uk—for sentencing guidelines

www.cps.gov.uk—code for crown prosecutors and legal guidance on prosecutions.

2 Actus reus: acts, omissions and causation

Introduction

2.1 Acts

2.2 Omissions: Liability for Failing to Act in Breach of Duty

2.3 Causation

KEY POINTS

ACTUS REUS

This section will help you to understand that:

- a crime consists of conduct (actus reus or AR) and a mental element (mens rea or MR);
- it is a fundamental precondition of criminal liability that the AR must always be proved, that it is voluntary and that it should coincide with MR.

OMISSIONS

This section will help you to understand that:

- the AR can consist of an omission as well as an act but only where there is a pre-existing duty. Duties can arise through statute (failure to act) or in five common law duty situations.

CAUSATION

This section will help you to understand that:

- a defendant's conduct must cause the result prohibited by the offence. There are various tests for legal causation where D's conduct is the main but not the only cause.

INTRODUCTION

A crime consists of two elements: guilty behaviour and a guilty state of mind. Together, they describe the harm prohibited by the offence and the blameworthiness, or fault, of the defendant. Both must occur at the same time. In this chapter we shall explore guilty behaviour, which is typically an act, but which might, in limited circumstances, also consist of a failure to act (an omission). Either way, D's conduct must be the legal cause of the harm. The principles explored in this chapter apply to any crime, whether it is murder, theft, rape or taking and driving away a motor vehicle without consent. In criminal law, guilty conduct committed in prohibited circumstances is labelled 'actus reus' (AR) and the fault element (or guilty state of mind) is called 'mens rea' (MR).

→ **CROSS-REFERENCE**
Mens rea (MR) is explored in Chapter 3.

2.1 Acts

2.1.1 What does Actus Reus Mean?

2.1.2 Coincidence/Correspondence of Actus Reus and Mens Rea

KEY CASES

Bratty v AG for Northern Ireland [1963] AC 386—guidance on voluntariness;

Larsonneur [1933] 24 Cr App R 74—status offences can dispense with voluntariness;

Deller [1952] 23 Cr App R 184—the AR must be proved;

Thabo Meli [1954] 1 All ER 373—the 'continuing act' exception to 'coincidence' in murder;

Fagan [1969] 1 QB 439—the 'continuing act' exception in assault;

Le Brun [1991] 4 All ER 673—the 'continuing act' exception in manslaughter.

2.1.1 What does Actus Reus Mean?

Both AR and MR are required to be proved beyond all reasonable doubt in order to obtain a conviction (see Diagram 2.1). A Latin statement traditionally used to describe these components of an offence is: '*Actus non facit reum nisi mens sit rea*', which means that a man is not liable for his acts alone, but only if he acts with a guilty mind. A number of consequences, set out here, flow from this doctrine and are set out below.

AR and MR are defined by the crime

All crimes will have an AR component. In order to find out what it is, you need to know the definition of the crime in question, which means referring to either the statutory or common law definition. The AR refers to the particular type of *conduct* prohibited by the offence in question, and, where relevant, *the circumstances*. AR refers to all those external elements of an offence which are not concerned with the internal mental element. *Conduct* will usually consist of an act but may also consist of an omission. Sometimes, the AR is defined in general terms:

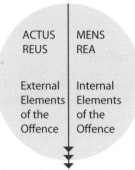

Actus Reus (AR) = guilty conduct   Mens Rea (MR) = fault or mental element

Diagram 2.1

The components of a crime

EXAMPLE 2.1

The AR of homicide, a common law offence, is described as the unlawful killing of a human being under the Queen's peace. If the killing is accompanied by an intention to kill or to cause grievous bodily harm (GBH) the killing becomes murder. The definition does not require death to be caused in any particular way. Therefore, it does not matter if the victim (V) is shot, strangled or starved to death.

On the other hand, some offences will specify the type of conduct required by the AR such as causing death by *dangerous driving* contrary to s1 Road Traffic Act 1988.

Look at the following examples: underline the AR element. What act does it prohibit? Do the offences require a result or simply conduct?

1. *Common Assault:* Any act by which D, intentionally or recklessly, inflicts unlawful personal violence upon V.

2. *Actual bodily harm: s47 Offences Against the Person Act 1861:* Whosoever shall be convicted on indictment of any assault occasioning actual bodily harm shall be liable to imprisonment for not more than 5 years.

3. *Grievous bodily harm: s20 Offences Against the Person Act 1861:* Whosoever shall unlawfully and maliciously wound or inflict any grievous bodily harm upon any other person, either with or without any weapon or instrument, shall be guilty of a misdemeanour, and being convicted thereof shall be liable ... to imprisonment for not more than 5 years.

4. *Murder/Manslaughter:* The unlawful killing of a human who is in being and under the Queen's Peace. For murder, the killing must be intentional.

Which of the above offences are common law crimes?

Circumstances: Many crimes also require the prohibited conduct to have occurred in legally relevant circumstances, for example: criminal damage contrary to s1 Criminal Damage Act 1971, as we shall see, requires D to destroy or damage property belonging to another 'without lawful excuse'. Rape contrary to s1 Sexual Offences Act 2003 requires the penile penetration of the victim to be 'without consent'. Theft requires the property appropriated to 'belong to another'. An act alone will not amount to the AR of a crime, therefore, unless both circumstances and, where relevant, a result can be proved. As you will have gathered, the AR of an offence can consist of more than one element. How many can you identify in the offence of murder in the example box? (The correct answer is four.)

The AR must be voluntary or willed

It is a fundamental precondition of criminal liability that the AR of a crime should require human conduct and be committed voluntarily. Only those who have freely chosen to do wrong should be punished. If voluntariness is lacking, because D has lost physical control through no fault of his own, then it would be unjust to convict and punish. The principle of individual autonomy and free will implies respect for individual freedom, responsibility and protection from harm. The philosophical origins of voluntariness are to be found in the work of John Austin in *Lectures on Jurisprudence* (1869). Guilt should attach to only rational, human agents who have the capacity and conscious ability to make voluntary choices regarding their actions. But the definition of a voluntary act is not as clear as you would think. Consider these examples and decide which actions are involuntary:

> **EXAMPLE** 2.2

a. X is holding a tennis racket in a game of doubles. As he runs to hit the ball he slips, causing his racket to slam into the back of his partner's legs.

b. X is holding an air-rifle. D grips X's hand, points the gun and squeezes X's finger around the trigger. The gun goes off and Z is shot.

c. X is hypnotised by D. D tells X to assault Z. X does so.

d. D falls off his bicycle and receives a knock on the head which causes concussion. He assaults the first person he sees but has no recollection of it later.

e. In a game, X hits D's knee with a small hammer. By a reflex action, D kicks X in the face and breaks his nose.

f. D consumes 12 pints of beer. His friends dare him to set fire to the curtains of the pub in which they are drinking. He does so but later remembers nothing about it.

g. W, an abused woman living with H, a violent man, commits theft because H threatened to break her arm if she did not do so.

h. W steals a loaf of bread from a shop because her child is starving and she has no money.

You might think that an act is only voluntary when accompanied by desire. Or you might think that an act is not voluntary if it is the result of misfortune, coercion or necessity. The law, however, is somewhat different.

Voluntary action is defined at a very basic level: muscular or bodily movement controlled by the will or volition. Read the following by John Austin, *Lectures on Jurisprudence*, 5th edn (xviii–xix) Vol. 1, at p 411:

> Certain movements of our bodies follow invariably and immediately our wishes and desires for those same movements. Provided, that is, that the bodily organ be sane, and the desired movement be not prevented by any outward obstacle … These antecedent wishes and these consequent movements, are human volitions and acts (strictly and properly so-called) … It will be admitted on the mere statement, that the only objects which can be called acts are consequences of volitions. A voluntary movement of my body, or a movement which follows a volition, is an act. The involuntary movements which (for example) are the consequences of certain diseases, are not acts.

Voluntariness enables the law to distinguish between *doing* something and having something *done* to you. By this reasoning, only movements which are undesired, unconscious or physically controlled by another would be involuntary. This would therefore only apply to *a, b, c, d* and *e*. The drunk arsonist in *f*, the abused woman in *g* and the desperate mother in *h* would be considered to have acted voluntarily because their actions were deliberate and conscious at the time.

The condition illustrated in *d* is an example of what the law calls *automatism*. If the link between mind and body is missing through external causes such as concussion, the defence of automatism is available. It is essentially a denial of voluntariness and a plea that there was no AR. Most textbooks deal with automatism in detail as part of the AR. However, we will examine it later where it fits more easily into an explanation of incapacitating defences such as insanity (see Chapter 8). As you can see, the category of involuntary acts is very limited.

Lord Denning in *Bratty v AG for Northern Ireland* [1963] AC 386, a case to which we return in Chapter 8, held that:

> The requirement that it [murder] should be a voluntary act is essential, not only in a murder case, but also in every criminal case. No act is punishable if it is done involuntarily: and an involuntary act in this context … means an act which is done by the muscles without any control by the mind such as a spasm, a reflex or a convulsion; or an act done by a person who is not conscious of what he is doing such as an act done whilst suffering from concussion …

Therefore, an act will not be involuntary simply because the doer does not remember it, or could not control the impulse to do it, or did not intend it.

The requirement of a voluntary act raises a number of problems. For instance, it is artificial to describe actions in terms of muscular contractions. We tend to think in terms of completed actions or results like going to the cinema, driving into town or walking to the shops. Read this by philosopher H.L.A. Hart in (1968) *Punishment and Responsibility*, at p 101:

> [W]hen we shut a door, or when we hit someone, or when we fire a gun at a bird, these things are done without any previous thought of the muscular movements involved and without any desire to contract the muscles … The simple but important truth is that when we deliberate and think about actions, we do so not in terms of muscular movements but in the ordinary terminology of actions.

The reduction of voluntariness to willed muscular action also removes the physical act from its moral or social circumstances, as in *g* and *h* above. We would not say that we voluntarily do something which we are forced to do against our will. As we shall see with the law on intention, however, criminal liability has developed so as to exclude the reason or motive for acting. Confining the criminal act to willed mechanical contraction of the muscles enables the law to avoid the wider social and political context of criminal liability. Read this extract by A. Norrie from *Crime, Reason & History, A Critical Introduction to Criminal Law*, Cambridge University Press, 2014 at p 111:

> The *physical* conception [of voluntariness] operates as a 'technical' criterion for judging conduct involuntary, because it excludes all considerations other than the abstract and general issue of whether or not the act was a conscious one. It therefore parallels the technical conception of intention, which artificially separates out the question of *how* an intention is formed from the question of *why* it is formed. The *moral* conception of involuntariness, on the other hand, opens up questions about the social context in which actions are formed and in which broader judgments, about whether the accused could have helped doing what he did, become relevant. The exclusion of this conception, which is potentially more political in its effect, parallels the exclusion of motive from the law of intent.

Why people commit crime is therefore irrelevant to liability, although it might be relevant to sentencing. Liability is established by reference to proof of the AR and MR of the offence, not motive.

The AR can consist of a state of affairs: status offences—an exception to the voluntariness principle

Exceptionally, the AR will not refer to conduct in an active sense but to 'being found' in a prohibited place in proscribed circumstances, for example: knowingly remaining in the UK without leave or being unfit to drive through drink or drugs. These offences are also labelled 'status' or 'situational' offences because they represent not an act/omission but a state of affairs. They can be committed involuntarily and are an exception to the requirement that the AR should be voluntary. As such, they confer absolute liability upon D. Consider the facts of the following cases:

R v Larsonneur (1933) 24 CR APP R 74 COURT OF APPEAL

A French woman was allowed to enter the UK subject to employment, but not time restrictions. She attempted to go through an arranged marriage ceremony which would have given her indefinite leave to remain. The marriage was halted, she was ordered to leave England that day and her passport was endorsed. Instead of returning to France she left for Eire (the Irish Free State). This was an offence and she was subject to the same immigration limitations as before. An order for her deportation was made from Eire whereupon she was arrested and taken to Holyhead by the Irish police who handed her over to the UK police. She was charged and convicted of being an illegal alien to whom leave to land in the UK had been refused under the Aliens Order 1920. She appealed on the grounds that she had been landed by a superior force over which she had no physical control. The court confirmed the conviction on the grounds that how she got to the UK was immaterial. The offence was committed by simple presence in the UK.

Absolute liability was applied in *Winzar v Chief Constable of Kent* (1983) *The Times*, 28 March, where a drunk was ejected by the police from a hospital and was then charged with being found drunk on the public highway. His being on the highway was entirely due to the police and not the result of his own voluntary act. The Divisional Court upheld his conviction.

Both of these cases were reviewed in *R v Robinson-Pierre* [2013] EWCA Crim 2396. The accused was charged with being the owner of a dog which was dangerously out of control in a public place contrary to s3 Dangerous Dogs Act 1991. Five police officers had been bitten by a pit bull terrier whilst executing a search warrant in D's house. The dog's attack continued when the officers retreated into the street. Pitchford LJ held that s3 was an offence of strict, but not absolute, liability. It was necessary for the owner to have done or omitted to do something which caused the injuries. By contrast, neither Mr Winzar nor Ms Larsonneur needed to have caused their offences, but they were responsible for them:

> While the decision [*Larsonneur*] has been criticised, it is an example of the enforcement of a prohibition upon a state of affairs that the individual did not *cause*, but for which she was deemed to be responsible … we have no doubt that the supremacy of Parliament embraces the power to create 'state of affairs', offences in which no causative link between the prohibited state of affairs and the defendant need be established. The legal issue is not, in our view, whether in principle such offences can be created, but whether in any particular enactment Parliament intended to create one … On analysis of s.3, we do not consider that it was Parliament's intention to create an offence without regard to the ability of the owner (or someone to whom he had entrusted responsibility) to take and keep control of the dog. There must, in our view, be some causal connection between having charge of the dog and the prohibited state of affairs that has arisen.

Since voluntariness in criminal law has a very restricted meaning it is likely that Ms Larsonneur walked whilst under arrest and did not need to be carried. She therefore acted voluntarily in that narrow sense. Whether the same applied to Mr Winzar is another question.

Or one might argue that both were examples of a policy: to exert immigration controls to the UK and to rid public places of drunkenness.

(See further: R.C. Doeggar, in 'Strict Liability in Criminal Law and *Larsonneur* Reassessed' [1998] *Crim LR* 791 and J.C. Smith [1999] *Crim LR* 100.)

Conduct and result crimes

Conduct crimes prohibit certain behaviour. No harm will be required by the offence definition. Result crimes, on the other hand, are more serious and require that conduct occurs in certain legally prohibited circumstances and causes a particular prohibited result (see Diagram 2.2 for a summary). Look at the offences below and decide which is which.

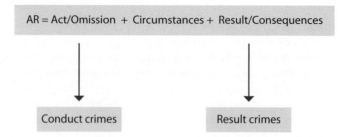

Diagram 2.2
Conduct and result crimes

- *Section 3 Road Traffic Act 1988:* If a person drives a mechanically propelled vehicle on a road or other public place without due care and attention, or without reasonable consideration for other persons using the road or place, he is guilty of an offence.
- *Section 1 Road Traffic Act 1988:* A person who causes the death of another person by driving a mechanically propelled vehicle dangerously on a road or other public place is guilty of an offence.

→ CROSS-REFERENCE
Causation is examined in 2.3.

With a result crime, the proscribed conduct must not only lead to harm, such as death in the second example above, but it must be proved that D's conduct was the cause of that result.

You cannot be convicted of a crime merely for having guilty thoughts

→ CROSS-REFERENCE
Inchoate offences are discussed in Chapter 15.

Given that most crimes, other than those of strict or absolute liability, require both AR and MR, it follows that you cannot be guilty of a crime simply for having a guilty mind. There is no such thing as thought crime. It is only when guilty thoughts are put into practice that the AR of a crime is committed. Even for inchoate crimes, such as attempt or conspiracy, there must be some act, no matter how minimal, even though it is less than would be required for a completed offence.

The AR must be proved

It follows from that which has just been stated that there must always be proof of the AR if one is not to be punished for guilty thoughts alone. One case will illustrate this:

R v Deller (1952) 23 CR APP R 184 COURT OF APPEAL

D induced a man to buy his car by representing that it was free of any outstanding financial loans. This was dishonest because D had previously arranged to mortgage the car to a finance company and had signed a document to that effect. It transpired that the document was void for technical reasons, a fact of which D was unaware. After the sale, D was prosecuted for obtaining by false pretences (it would now be a fraud offence). The document being void, however, the car was actually free of any financial claim. Therefore, although D thought he was being dishonest, the MR of the offence, he had not committed the AR of *obtaining* by false pretences. MR alone was not enough.

Only once there is proof of AR will it be necessary to prove MR.

The AR can include a mental element

The traditional division between the AR, consisting of the external elements of an offence, and MR, consisting of the internal elements, is not always clear-cut. For example, 'possession' of something is categorised as an AR element, but you can only 'possess' something if you are aware of it—a mental state. This overlap of AR and MR has led to the criticism that to describe AR as all the external elements of an offence and MR as the internal elements can be misleading.

The AR can be negated by 'justificatory' defences

A justificatory defence, such as self-defence, consent, or necessity, can be used where an offence has been committed in morally justifiable *circumstances*. The offence will typically be an assault, the definition of which requires *unlawful* violence. Justificatory defences negate the unlawfulness of the AR. Thus it is as though no crime at all was ever committed. The force being lawful, the AR of assault cannot be proved.

→ CROSS-REFERENCE
Chapter 9 explores self-defence.

Conclusion

Some writers agree that the labels AR and MR are not particularly helpful. The criticism is that there is little coherence in designating so many different concepts such as acts, omissions and causation under one umbrella of AR. Read the following by P. Roberts: 'The Actus Reus–Mens Rea Distinction' in *Action and Value* in Clarendon, Shute, Gardner & Horder (eds), *Criminal Law* (1996):

> No doubt the *actus reus—mens rea* distinction is a logical and natural extension of the obvious empirical difference between a person's conduct, which we can directly observe, and his intention, which we cannot. … [W]hat we refer to as *actus reus* requirements or as *mens rea* requirements are in fact a collection of entirely distinct doctrines. Four doctrines typically described as the *actus reus* requirements include what I shall refer to as the act requirement, the rules governing omission liability, the voluntariness requirement, and the objective elements of offence definitions. … Four doctrines typically described as the *mens rea* requirement include what I shall refer to as present-conduct intention, present-circumstance culpability, future-result culpability and future-conduct intention. Whilst these doctrines are grouped together as *actus reus* or as *mens rea*, the doctrines within each group have no common characteristic and no common function. Grouping the doctrines as *actus reus* or as *mens rea* is problematic because it obscures the fact that there are different doctrines at work and it misleadingly suggests that the doctrines share a common characteristic or function.

Despite theoretical criticisms, the AR/MR distinction has practical advantages, and continues to be a useful tool for analysis of criminal liability.

SECTION SUMMARY

A crime consists of AR (conduct) and MR (blameworthiness/fault).
- *AR and MR are always defined by the crime.*
- *The AR must be voluntary or willed.*
- *You cannot be convicted of a crime merely for having guilty thoughts.*
- *In conduct crimes, the AR consists of conduct alone; in result crimes, the AR will include a result.*
- *The AR must be proved.*
- *It can include a mental element.*
- *It can consist of a state of affairs: status offences.*
- *It can be negated by some defences.*

2.1.2 Coincidence/Correspondence of Actus Reus and Mens Rea

Coincidence of AR and MR in time and the continuing act exception

The general principle is that no-one can be criminally liable unless they possess the necessary MR for a crime at the time of committing the AR. The two must coincide together.

> **EXAMPLE** 2.3
>
> If on Monday D decides to shoot X dead the following Saturday, but on Thursday he accidentally shoots X dead whilst out hunting, D has not murdered X because there is no coincidence of AR and MR. D cannot be punished for his criminal thoughts on Monday. Since the AR was committed without MR on Thursday, no murder has occurred.

The need for coincidence has posed a problem in certain cases where there has been a delay between MR and AR. Rather than abandoning the principle, the courts have developed an exception to it: the continuing act exception. Whilst reading these cases, you will find it helpful to refer to the offence definitions at the beginning of this chapter ('AR and MR are defined by the crime').

Thabo Meli v R [1954] 1 ALL ER 373 PRIVY COUNCIL

Two Ds planned to murder V. They took him to a hut, gave him some beer and hit him over the head. Thinking he was dead, they rolled his body over a cliff to make it look like an accident. He was in fact still alive but died from exposure on the cliff during the night due to exceptionally cold weather conditions. The Ds were convicted of murder and appealed.

The problem was that although the first act of hitting V over the head had been performed with an intent to kill, it was not the cause of death. The actual cause was the act of rolling him down the cliff and leaving him but there was no MR to accompany that act. By then, both Ds thought V was already dead.

The Privy Council held that it was impossible to divide up what was really one series of acts or a single transaction and the conviction was confirmed.

Lord Reid:

> It appears to their Lordships impossible to divide up what was really one series of acts in this way. There is no doubt that the accused set out to do all these acts in order to achieve their plan, and as parts of their plan; and it is much too refined a ground of judgment to say that because they were under a misapprehension at one stage and thought that their guilty purpose had been achieved before, in fact, it was achieved, therefore they are to escape the penalties of the law.

R v Fagan [1968] 3 ALL ER 442 QBD DIVISIONAL COURT

D accidentally drove on to a police officer's boot whilst parking his car. On being alerted by the police officer to the situation, D said, 'Fuck you. You can wait'. He switched off the ignition and sat in his car for two or three minutes before moving off. D was convicted of assault and appealed.

In a majority decision, the court held that it was sufficient if there was a continuing act of assault during which D had the relevant MR at some point. His appeal was dismissed.

James J:

Although 'assault' is an independent crime and is to be treated as such, for practical purposes today 'assault' is generally synonymous with the term 'battery', and is a term used to mean the actual intended use of unlawful force to another person without his consent. On the facts of the present case, the 'assault' alleged involved a 'battery'. Where an assault involved a battery, it matters not, in our judgment, whether the battery is inflicted directly by the body of the offender or through the medium of some weapon or instrument controlled by the action of the offender. … we see no difference in principle between the action of stepping on to a person's toe and maintaining that position and the action of driving a car on to a person's foot and sitting in the car while its position on the foot is maintained.

To constitute this offence, some intentional act must have been performed; a mere omission to act cannot amount to an assault. …

On the facts found, the action of the appellant may have been initially unintentional, but the time came when, knowing that the wheel was on the officer's foot, the appellant (i) remained seated in the car so that his body through the medium of the car was in contact with the officer, (ii) switched off the ignition of the car, (iii) maintained the wheel of the car on the foot, and (iv) used words indicating the intention of keeping the wheel in that position. For our part, we cannot regard such conduct as mere omission or inactivity. There was an act constituting a battery which at its inception was not criminal because there was no element of intention, but which became criminal from the moment the intention was formed to produce the apprehension which was flowing from the continuing act ….

Bridge J gave a dissenting judgment:

No mere omission to act can amount to an assault. Both the elements of actus reus and mens rea must be present at the same time, but the one may be superimposed on the other. … I have been unable to find any way of regarding the facts which satisfied me that they amounted to the crime of assault. … after the wheel of the appellant's car had accidentally come to rest on the constable's foot, what was it that the appellant *did* which constituted the act of assault? However the question is approached, the answer which I feel obliged to give is: precisely nothing. The car rested on the foot by its own weight and remained stationary by its own inertia. The appellant's fault was that he omitted to manipulate the controls to set it in motion again. … It is not … a legitimate use of language to speak of the appellant 'holding' or 'maintaining' the car wheel on the constable's foot. The expression which corresponds to the reality is that used by the justices in the Case Stated. They say, quite rightly, that he 'allowed' the wheel to remain.

Bridge J viewed the case as one of omission rather than an act.

→ CROSS-REFERENCE
See *Miller* at 2.2.3.

R v Le Brun [1991] 4 ALL ER 673 COURT OF APPEAL

Whilst walking home at 2.00 am D hit his wife on the jaw, knocking her unconscious. He did not intend really serious harm. Whilst carrying her away, probably to conceal what he had done, he accidentally dropped her. She hit her head, fractured her skull, and died. D was convicted of manslaughter and appealed.

The Court of Appeal held that, applying *Thabo Meli*, there was a continuing act. However, in *Thabo Meli* death was part of a pre-conceived plan to kill. That was not the case here. Given that D did not have the MR for murder at any time, the Court of Appeal decided that he should be guilty of manslaughter by unlawful and dangerous act (ie: the original assault).

Lord Lane CJ:

It seems to us that where the unlawful application of force and the eventual act causing death are parts of the same sequence of events, the same transaction, the fact that there is an appreciable interval of time between the two does not serve to exonerate the defendant from liability. That is certainly so where the appellant's subsequent actions which caused death, after the initial unlawful blow, are designed to conceal his commission of the original unlawful assault. ...

In short, in circumstances such as the present, which is the only concern of this court, the act which causes death and the necessary mental state to constitute manslaughter need not coincide in point of time. ...

The original unlawful, intentional assault (MR) and the subsequent accidental dropping which caused death (AR) were part of the same sequence of events.

An earlier precedent in relation to unlawful and dangerous act manslaughter was relied upon to convict D of manslaughter rather than murder: *R v Church* [1965] 2 All ER 72. Here, D had thrown a woman into a river after knocking her unconscious. He thought he was disposing of a dead body. In fact, she was only unconscious but she subsequently drowned. D was charged with murder but convicted of manslaughter on the basis of lack of intent for murder and the continuing series of acts designed to cause death.

Read this criticism of the judgment and of the coincidence principle by C. Wells in 'Goodbye to Coincidence' (1991) *NLJ* 15 November, at p 1566 in which she argues that coincidence never really had an independent existence and that it is only displayed in order to create another exception to it. Most cases could be dealt with more logically by reference to causation:

In each of these cases (*Thabo Meli* and *Church*), including *Le Brun*, an artificial division of the *actus reus* has been attempted. It is said that the *actus reus* is that which medically is regarded as the cause of death (the skull fracture, the exposure and the drowning) and that the defendant in each case lacked *mens rea* in respect of it. In each case, however, the defendant had done a prior act which was accompanied by *mens rea* for murder or manslaughter. The *actus reus* of homicide is causing the death of another person; in each case the difficulty could be solved by asking 'did the defendant's act which was accompanied by *mens rea* contribute causally to the death'? In dealing with *Thabo Meli* and *Church* on the basis of a 'continuing transaction' analysis, there is an implicit acknowledgement that it is artificial to divide the initial injury from the purported disposal of the 'body'.

This might be thought to raise a certain problem for *Le Brun* since the death was caused not by a purported corpse disposal but by the accidental dropping of what was in fact and what was thought by D to be an unconscious person. ... So why have these cases come to be seen as 'coincidence' cases rather than causation issues? The answer would seem to be partly to do with a rigid devotion to the division between *actus reus* and *mens rea* and partly through a failure to see that causation in homicide is different from causing results such as GBH or criminal damage. Death can be the end result of a protracted process. Some deaths are immediate, but often they are not. Taken together with the fact that most events can be attributed to a multiplicity of causes, this gives homicide cases the potential to place the artificial *actus reus/mens rea* formulation under strain. The *actus reus* becomes confused with 'the act' and when it is argued that *mens rea* must coincide, there is an unfortunate tendency to assume that the *actus reus* of homicide is the act which was the immediate cause of death. If instead the *actus reus* was identified with the 'legal' cause of death then the problem would be presented for what it is: an issue of causation.

Had these two cases been dealt with on the basis of causation, the results would have been just the same. There is, as we shall see, considerable overlap between the principles of coincidence, omissions and causation. This may be because the AR/MR distinction is, as C. Wells states, a very unclear concept.

In the above cases, there was a clearly identifiable medical cause of death. If it is less clear which act in a continuing series was the actual cause of a result, the courts will not resort to the continuing act theory but will decide whether each individual act might have been responsible. In *AG's Reference (No 4 of 1980)* [1981] 2 All ER 617, D killed a woman by causing her to fall down a flight of stairs head first, rendering her unconscious. He then tied a rope around her neck, dragged her upstairs, placed her in the bath, cut her throat to let out her blood and cut up her body to dispose of the pieces. Which act was the cause of death? The Court of Appeal held that it was unnecessary to decide between various acts if it was clear that each act on its own would have established the basis of a homicide offence. The 'continuing act' theory was unnecessary here.

Correspondence of AR and MR

In general, it is said that MR must correspond to every element of the AR. So, for example, if the crime is one of intent, there must be intent in respect of each element of the AR. However, the MR of some crimes consists of recklessness/intention as to a different and less serious AR. They are an exception to the general principle and are known as 'constructive' crimes. For example:

- The AR of murder is the unlawful killing of a human being. MR consists of intention to kill *or* cause grievous bodily harm (GBH).

- The AR of malicious wounding or infliction of GBH contrary to s20 Offences Against the Person Act 1861 is wounding or inflicting really serious harm. MR consists of *malice* (recklessness or intention) but only as to *some* harm and not grievous bodily harm.

- Unlawful and dangerous act manslaughter (also known as constructive manslaughter) requires MR only as to an original unlawful act and not as to death.

SECTION SUMMARY

- *The AR and MR of an offence must coincide in time.*
- *The continuing act theory is an exception to the need for coincidence.*
- *Most cases involving delay between MR and AR will now probably be dealt with under the duty principle.*
- *There must be correspondence of AR and MR in law.*
- *'Constructive' crimes are an exception to this principle.*

?!   THINKING POINT 2.1

D attends a show by a famous hypnotist in the course of which he is conditioned to embrace anyone wearing a uniform. After the show, a police officer (V) approaches D to tell him he is illegally parked. D attempts to embrace the officer but as he stumbles on wet leaves he pulls V to the ground and kicks him. V becomes unconscious. D hides V behind a bush and walks off but 10 minutes later a torrential storm occurs. V drowns in a flash flood. Does D's act satisfy the AR of manslaughter?

2.2 Omissions: Liability for Failing to Act in Breach of Duty

2.2.1 Introduction: Acts and Omissions

2.2.2 Statutory Offences of Failing to Act in Breach of Duty: Conduct Crimes

2.2.3 Common Law Offences: Commission by Omission—Result Crimes and the Five Duty Situations

2.2.4 Criticisms of Omissions Liability

2.2.5 Evaluation

2.2.6 Reform

KEY CASES

Stone & Dobinson [1977] 1 QB 354—duty by assumption of responsibility;

Miller [1983] 2 AC 161, House of Lords—duty by creating a dangerous situation;

Airedale NHS Trust v Bland [1993] 1 All ER 831—an omission by doctors to provide life support in the best interests of a patient is not a breach of duty;

Pittwood [1902] 19 TLR 37—duty arising by virtue of contract.

2.2.1 Introduction: Acts and Omissions

Common law and statutory offences generally prohibit acts not omissions. If, for example, a statute expressly requires an act, no omission will suffice (eg: the Protection from Eviction Act 1977, which contains the words 'does acts' likely to interfere with peace or comfort: *Ahmad* (1986) 84 Cr App R 64). However, the courts will sometimes construe the statutory requirement of an act to cover an omission if it is in the form of passive submission, for example: in *Speck* [1977] 2 All ER 859 an *act* of gross indecency was satisfied by an omission to remove a child's hand from D's penis.

 CROSS-REFERENCE
Breach of statutory duty is discussed in 2.2.2.

Nevertheless, there are numerous statutes which specifically make 'failure to act' an offence. Essentially, these are regulatory crimes and consist of breach of statutory duty.

In addition, it is now well-established that one can commit most serious criminal offences by omission, from criminal damage to manslaughter, even though the offence definition might imply the requirement of a positive act.

This may surprise you. Liability for omitting or failing to act sounds very uncertain and rather wide. Would we, for example, commit a crime by doing nothing in the following examples?

> ⚠ **EXAMPLE** 2.4
>
> 1. An alcoholic wanders into the middle of a busy road, gets knocked down by a car and is killed. A crowd of pedestrians foresee the inevitable accident but fail to rescue him before he is hit. Are they all potentially liable for his death?
> 2. A stranger hammers on your front door one night seeking help because her husband outside in the street is threatening violence against her. You do not open the door or call the police because you do not want to get involved. She is subsequently seriously injured. Are you criminally responsible?

Should the law expect us to intervene, render assistance, rescue people in peril or prevent crimes from occurring on a never-ending basis, regardless of our circumstances, connection to the victim, personal risk or inconvenience? Under the common law, there will only be liability for an omission in five situations where the criminal law imposes a *duty* to act requiring us to act in a reasonable way so as to prevent criminal harm to others.

The scope of these duty situations is not without criticism on the grounds that it is uncertain and is being developed by the courts on an ad hoc basis. It is, therefore, a potential violation of Article 7 ECHR (the need for maximum certainty of the law).

2.2.2 Statutory Offences of Failing to Act in Breach of Duty: Conduct Crimes

Consider the following statutory offences which specifically prohibit 'failure to act':

- *Road Traffic Act 1988*
  - ☐ Failing to provide [without reasonable excuse] a breath test when driving, or being in charge of a motor vehicle, under the influence of alcohol or after commission of a traffic offence (s6(4)).
  - ☐ Failing to produce driving licence to constable or to state date of birth (s164(6)).
- *Education Act 1996*
  - ☐ If a child of compulsory school age who is a registered pupil at a school fails to attend regularly at the school, his parent is guilty of an offence (s444(1)).
- *Terrorism Act 2000*
  - ☐ Where a person believes or suspects that another person has committed an offence [of terrorism or related activity] under any of ss15 to 18, the person commits an offence if he does not disclose to a constable as soon as is reasonably practicable a) his belief or suspicion, and b) the information on which it is based (s19).
- *Domestic Violence, Crime and Victims Act 2004 (as amended)*
  - ☐ Failing to protect a child or vulnerable adult from the risk of death or serious physical harm (s5).

These provisions create statutory duties to act in specific situations. Failure to perform the required act (an omission) will result in liability for breach of statutory duty. They are classified as 'conduct crimes' and tend to be crimes of strict liability or negligence. Most will be dealt with summarily in the magistrates' court, where the maximum penalties are less than those for more serious result crimes.

2.2.3 Common Law Offences: Commission by Omission—Result Crimes and the Five Duty Situations

Under English law there is no general duty to act.

 EXAMPLE 2.5

A sees B drowning and is able to save him by holding out his hand. A abstains from doing so in order that B may be drowned, and B is drowned. A has committed no offence. (This example is from the famous criminal jurist, J.F. Stephen, *History of the Criminal Law of England* (1883).)

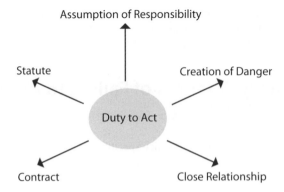

Diagram 2.3
The criminal duty to act

The AR of virtually all result crimes, whether statutory or common law, is capable of being committed by omission and no positive act is required. However, a duty to act is created in five exceptional situations (see Diagram 2.3).

Voluntary assumption of a duty to act

Where responsibility for another person (V) has been voluntarily assumed, the criminal law imposes a duty to act on the basis of expectation or reliance. Therefore, an omission or failure to prevent harm could constitute the AR of an offence.

The offence in the following case was involuntary manslaughter by gross negligence consisting of an omission to ensure the health and safety of a relative for whom it was held that two Ds had assumed responsibility.

R v Stone & Dobinson [1977] 1 QB 354

Mr Stone was 67, a widower, partially deaf, almost totally blind, of low intelligence with no appreciable sense of smell. His mentally subnormal son lived with him. He cohabited with Mrs Dobinson who was 43. She was described by the court as ineffectual and inadequate. Mr Stone's younger sister, Fanny, aged 63, came to live with them in 1972. She suffered from anorexia nervosa and stayed in her room for days at a time. Her room had no ventilation, cooking or washing facilities and only a bucket. It being clear that she was ill, the Ds unsuccessfully attempted to find Fanny's doctor in the spring of 1975. She became confined to bed. In July, D and a neighbour washed her. She was by this time lying in her own excrement and covered in sores. Neither D could use a telephone and the neighbour failed to get another doctor to call. A social worker visited the house periodically to visit the son. She was not informed of Fanny's condition. Fanny died in August 1975 from infected bed sores (toxaemia) arising from prolonged immobilisation. Her condition was one of terrible squalor. Maggots were found in some of her sores. Her mattress was soaked in urine and excrement. The bedding had not been changed for weeks. Medical evidence suggested that Fanny might have survived had she received medical attention after being washed in July. Mr Stone and Mrs Dobinson were charged with manslaughter.

Lane LJ:

There is no dispute, broadly speaking, as to the matters on which the jury must be satisfied before they can convict of manslaughter in circumstances such as the present. They are (1) that the defendant undertook the care of a person who by reason of age or infirmity was unable to care for himself; (2) that the defendant was grossly negligent in regard to his duty of care; (3) that by reason of such negligence the person died. …

At the close of the Crown's case submissions were made to the judge that there was no, or no suffi-cient, evidence that the appellants, or either of them, had chosen to undertake the care of Fanny. …

Is it to be said, asks counsel for the appellants rhetorically, that by the mere fact of becoming infirm and helpless in these circumstances, she casts a duty on her brother and Mrs. Dobinson to take steps to have her looked after or taken to hospital? The suggestion is that, heartless though it may seem, this is one of those situations where the appellants were entitled to do nothing; where no duty was cast on them to help, any more than it is cast on a man to rescue a stranger from drowning, however easy such a rescue might be.

The court rejects that proposition. Whether Fanny was a lodger or not she was a blood relation of the appellant Stone; she was occupying a room in his house; Mrs. Dobinson had undertaken the duty of trying to wash her, of taking such food to her as she required. There was ample evidence that each appellant was aware of the poor condition she was in by mid-July. It was not disputed that no effort was made to summon an ambulance or the social services or the police. … A social worker used to visit [Stone]. No word was spoken to him. All these were matters which the jury were entitled to take into account when considering whether the necessary assumption of a duty to care for Fanny had been proved.

This was not a situation analogous to the drowning stranger. They did make efforts to care. They tried to get a doctor, they tried to discover the previous doctor. Mrs. Dobinson helped with the washing and the provision of food. All these matters were put before the jury in terms which we find it impossible to fault. The jury were entitled to find that the duty had been assumed. They were entitled to conclude that once Fanny became helplessly infirm, as she had by 19 July, the appellants were, in the circumstances, obliged either to summon help or else to care for Fanny themselves …

Appeal dismissed. Stone sentenced to 12 months' suspended imprisonment. Dobinson sen-tenced to 18 months' suspended sentence.

 NOTE 2.1

The court said that there could be no conviction unless there was a *duty of care*. The court identified such a duty on the basis that Fanny was a blood relative of Mr Stone and that the Ds had assumed responsibility for her. The basis of the latter was that she occupied a room in Mr Stone's house and Mrs Dobinson had attempted to wash her and take her food. This is what distinguished the situation of the drowning stranger and the passive observer.

The two unfortunate defendants were therefore convicted of one of the most serious offences in the criminal justice system. The judgment was described as 'judicial cruelty' by G. Williams in 'Criminal Omissions—The Conventional View' [1991] 107 *LQR*, at 90. It created a number of problems.

Read the following extract from 'The Scope of Criminal Liability for Omissions' (1989) 105 *LQR* 424 by A. Ashworth:

The relationship of parent to child is the strongest case for a general duty. How many other relation-ships should be treated in the same way is a matter for debate. A duty towards one's spouse might appear uncontroversial, but a duty towards one's parents begins to reach the boundaries of practicality and desirability for legal obligation. It is one thing to maintain that a person has a legal duty towards a parent who lives in the same house; it is another thing to argue that a person has a legal duty towards a parent who lives alone in the next street, or the next town, or many miles away. Thus with parents, as indeed with husband and wife (who may also be living apart), there should be a proximate requirement of living in the same household before a legal duty is imposed.

The pragmatism of the 'same household' limitation may be accepted, but it remains to decide what family relationships should be covered. If the duty were to extend to any member of the family living in the household, this would go against nineteenth century cases like *R v Smith* (1826) 2 C & P 449 which denied any duty towards a mentally disturbed adult brother and *R v Shepherd* (1862) 9 Cox CC 123 which denied any duty toward a daughter aged 18, but would tend to support the more modern cases such as *R v Chatterway* (1922) 17 Cr App R 7 which imposed a duty towards a daughter aged 25 and *R v Stone & Dobinson* [1977] … which accepted a duty towards an elderly sister. Indeed, one might go further and inquire whether the family relationship should be accorded such significance, rather than simply membership of the same household. Would this mean that the house-owner whose lodger becomes ill has no duty to call for medical assistance? Would it also confirm the acquittal in the famous American case of *People v Beardsley* (1907) 113 NW 1128 (Michigan), where a woman who spent the weekend with D took an overdose of tablets and D, knowing that she was in a serious condition, simply arranged for her to be carried to another apartment, where she subsequently died? These are difficult cases, and they raise the question whether there is any defensible line which can be drawn short of a duty of common humanity owed to any person who is seen or known to be in need of urgent assistance …

The scope of this duty might therefore be considered somewhat uncertain.

Several other questions are posed by the case: if we are to take reasonable steps to assist, how is this to be assessed, and from whose point of view? Given that the duty arose by assumption, might it have been avoided by making no effort whatsoever to assist? Was the defendant's omission the *cause* of death or Fanny's mental illness? The defendants may have neglected Fanny but did they kill her? Why should those least able to assist be pinned with responsibility, when others from the community ought to have intervened?

?!   THINKING POINT 2.2

A child jumps into a swimming pool and gets into difficulty. The following people observe the child drowning but fail to save her. Who amongst them would commit a criminal offence if she drowned?

Mother/lifeguard/neighbour/mother's cohabitee/relative by marriage (such as a step-brother or uncle)/cousin/baby-sitter/teacher/stranger.

A case relied on in *Dobinson* was the following:

R v Instan [1893] 1 QB 450 COURT FOR CROWN CASES RESERVED

A 73-year-old woman died as a result of untreated gangrene in her leg with which she had suddenly become ill. D was her niece who lived with her. D failed to obtain medical help or to nurse or feed her during the last 12 days of her life yet continued to eat her aunt's food. D was charged and convicted of manslaughter.

Lord Coleridge CJ:

It would not be correct to say that every moral obligation involves a legal duty; but every legal duty is founded on a moral obligation. A legal common law duty is nothing else than the enforcing by law of that which is a moral obligation without legal enforcement. There can be no question in this case that it was the clear duty of the prisoner to impart to the deceased so much as was necessary to sustain life of the food which she from time to time took in, and which was paid for by the deceased's own money for the purpose of the maintenance of herself and the prisoner; it was only through the instrumentality of the prisoner that the deceased could get the food. There was, therefore, a common law duty imposed upon the prisoner which she did not discharge. ... The prisoner was under a moral obligation to the deceased from which arose a legal duty towards her; that legal duty the prisoner has wilfully and deliberately left unperformed, with the consequence that there has been an acceleration of the death of the deceased owing to the non-performance of that legal duty.

The basis of the duty here was a moral one: the assumption of a responsibility by the niece for the aunt. But there was also a contractual dimension: the responsibility arose from the contract between them that the aunt would pay for the provision of food for them both.

A duty to act by voluntary assumption of responsibility has been recognised in other cases which support the principle that those engaged in dangerous activities assume a responsibility to one another. The activity may be lawful, such as a dangerous sport, or unlawful, such as drug-taking. In *Khan* [1998] Crim LR 830, an appeal against manslaughter, the Court of Appeal held that a heroin supplier may owe a duty to a user who has overdosed.

Swinton Thomas LJ:

> ... To extend the duty to summon medical assistance to a drug dealer who supplies heroin to a person who subsequently dies on the facts of this case would undoubtedly enlarge the class of persons to whom, on previous authority, such a duty may be owed. It may be correct to hold that such a duty does arise ...

Appeals allowed.

THINKING POINT 2.3

Do you think a duty should exist between drug suppliers and users?

What is the difference, if any, between *Khan* and *Stone & Dobinson*?

A manslaughter conviction was confirmed on this basis in the next case.

R v Ruffel [2003] EWCA CRIM 122 COURT OF APPEAL

V had injected heroin at D's house and had become unwell. D made attempts to revive him that night by splashing water on his face, placing him by a radiator and wrapping him in towels, but early the following morning the victim was still unwell. D put him outside the house and rang V's mother. She asked him to take V back inside the house but D left him there, went back inside and fell asleep. V was later found dead, the cause of death being identified as opiate intoxication and hypothermia, the temperature having dropped to 6 degrees. D was convicted of manslaughter. It was held that the offence had involved either a direct act and/or omission.

His Honour Judge Fawcus:

> The learned judge considered the arguments put before him on that basis and came to the conclusion that the way in which the Crown put the case, namely that the deceased was a guest of the appellant in the appellant's family home and that he was a friend – one thing he did say to the police

when he was first taxed of this matter was that the deceased was a friend of his – and that he had taken upon himself the duty of trying to revive him after what had happened, the learned judge felt that that created a sufficient nexus to give rise, if the jury thought it right to do so, to a duty of care.

What followed, of course, was putting the deceased outside, and that clearly gave rise to the situation in which the jury could consider whether there had been a breach of that duty.

It is unclear why D's efforts to care for a guest should give rise to a duty to act rendering the D liable to such a serious offence. A duty of responsibility towards guests who make up their own minds to engage in dangerous occupations considerably expands the net of potential criminal liability. Perhaps D had a moral duty to call for medical assistance—but should this breach of a moral duty, not a legal one, have rendered him guilty of manslaughter?

Close or special relationship giving rise to a duty to act

Although there is no general duty to assist strangers, there is a duty to assist those with whom we have a close or special relationship. However, there is no definitive list of relationships giving rise to a duty to act. The law has developed on a case-by-case basis. As such, the underlying principles of this type of duty are again somewhat uncertain. The following cases establish that a duty to act exists between:

Parents and children

R v Gibbons & Proctor (1918) 13 CR APP R 134 COURT OF APPEAL

A father (Gibbons) and his female partner (Proctor) were convicted of murdering Gibbons' daughter by starving her to death. Proctor was held to have assumed a duty towards the girl since she had used all Gibbons' regular earnings in order to buy food. Both were held to have intended to cause her grievous bodily harm. There was evidence that Proctor hated the child and hit her. Gibbons knew of this and neglected to do anything to assist the child. Gibbons owed a duty by virtue of his relationship. Proctor owed a duty by virtue of her moral and contractual obligation.

R v Lowe [1973] QB 702 QUEEN'S BENCH DIVISION

A father of low intelligence failed to call a doctor when his 9-week-old daughter fell ill. She died ten days later from dehydration and emaciation. He was convicted of wilful neglect of a child under 16 contrary to s1(1) Children and Young Persons Act 1933 (now amended by s66 Serious Crime Act 2015):

If any person who has attained the age of sixteen years and has responsibility for any child or young person under that age, wilfully assaults, ill-treats, neglects, abandons, or exposes him, or causes or procures him to be assaulted, ill-treated, neglected, abandoned, or exposed, in a manner likely to cause him unnecessary suffering or injury to health … that person shall be guilty of [an offence]. …

You might be able to identify this as a conduct crime creating a statutory duty between parent and child under 16. Mr Lowe was also charged with unlawful and dangerous act manslaughter but the court held that a negligent omission could not fulfil the necessary act. There is no statutory duty on parents to care for their children over the age of 16. The common law will intercede however and impose a duty by virtue of the close nature of the relationship or by assumption of responsibility.

Husband and wife, perhaps also close family members and relatives

R v Hood [2004] 1 CR APP R (S) 73 COURT OF APPEAL

D was the husband of V and her sole carer. She had suffered for several years from diabetes and osteoporosis causing her bones to become brittle. She broke a number of bones in a fall but was reluctant to go to hospital. She laid on the floor three weeks before D called an ambulance and she died in hospital. It was observed that her level of care had been low. D was convicted of gross negligence manslaughter on the basis of an omission to care appropriately for his wife.

A duty will also probably arise in these relationships between:

- Children and guardians or people having the care of children such as other relatives, child-minders or teachers.
- Doctors/hospital authorities and patients. (See 'Withholding medical treatment in the best interests of the patient' later in this chapter.)
- Participants in dangerous sports/activities.

?!   THINKING POINT 2.4

1. F is the father of two children aged 10 and 3. He leaves them in the house for half an hour during the evening bath-time. The 10-year-old fetches a hairdryer and attempts to dry the hair of the 3-year-old whilst he is in the bath. The dryer falls into the water whilst it is switched on and the young child dies from electrocution. Has F committed the AR of any criminal offence/s?

2. M is the mother of a 5-year-old girl, V. They take a friend of V to the countryside for a picnic. Whilst M sets out the food, V and the friend play on a nearby railway line. They are struck by a train and killed. Has M committed the AR of any offence/s?

Creation of a situation of danger

This duty applies where D accidentally does an act which creates a dangerous situation but then deliberately or knowingly fails to counteract that danger so that harm is caused. D will only be convicted of an offence if the relevant MR can also be proved:

R v Miller [1983] 2 AC 161 HOUSE OF LORDS

D was a squatter in a house. He lay on a mattress, lit a cigarette and fell asleep. He awoke to find the mattress on fire. He failed to extinguish it and moved to another room where he continued to sleep. The house caught fire and D had to be rescued; £800 worth of damage was caused. D was charged with arson under ss1(1) and (3) Criminal Damage Act 1971. He did not deny MR (recklessness) but argued that his omission to extinguish a fire which he had accidentally started did not amount to the AR of an offence. This was rejected by the court.

Lord Diplock:

> … In the instant case … it is the use of the expression 'actus reus' that is liable to mislead, since it suggests that some positive act on the part of the accused is needed to make him guilty of a crime and that a failure or omission to act is insufficient to give rise to criminal liability unless some express provision in the statute that creates the offence so provides …

The first question to be answered where a completed crime of arson is charged is: 'Did a physical act of the accused start the fire which spread and damaged property belonging to another (or did his act cause an existing fire which he had not started but which would otherwise have burnt itself out harmlessly, to spread and damage property belonging to another)?' ... The first question is a pure question of causation; it is one of fact to be decided by the jury in a trial upon indictment. It should be answered 'No' if, in relation to the fire during the period starting immediately before its ignition and ending with its extinction, the role of the accused was at no time more than that of a passive bystander. In such a case the subsequent questions to which I shall be turning would not arise. The conduct of the parabolical priest and Levite on the road to Jericho may have been indeed deplorable, but English law has not so far developed to the stage of treating it as criminal; and if it ever were to do so there would be difficulties in defining what should be the limits of the offence.

If on the other hand the question, which I now confine to: 'Did a physical act of the accused start the fire which spread and damaged property belonging to another?' is answered 'Yes' ... the conduct of the accused, throughout the period from immediately before the moment of ignition to the completion of the damage to the property by fire, is relevant; so is his state of mind throughout that period.

Since arson is a result-crime the period may be considerable, and during it the conduct of the accused that is causative of the result may consist not only of his doing physical acts which cause the fire to start or spread but also of his failing to take measures that lie within his power to counteract the danger that he has himself created. And if his conduct, active or passive, varies in the course of the period, so may his state of mind at the time of each piece of conduct. If at the time of any particular piece of conduct by the accused that is causative of the result, the state of mind that actuates his conduct falls within the description of one or other of the states of mind that are made a necessary ingredient of the offence of arson by section 1(1) of the Criminal Damage Act 1971 ... I know of no principle of English criminal law that would prevent his being guilty of the offence created by that subsection. Likewise, I see no rational ground for excluding from conduct capable of giving rise to criminal liability, conduct which consists of failing to take measures that lie within one's power to counteract a danger that one has oneself created, if at the time of such conduct one's state of mind is such as constitutes a necessary ingredient of the offence. I venture to think that the habit of lawyers to talk of '*actus reus*', suggestive as it is of action rather than inaction, is responsible for any erroneous notion that failure to act cannot give rise to criminal liability in English law ...

[The theory of the continuing act] [w]hen applied to cases where a person has unknowingly done an act which sets in train events that, when he becomes aware of them present an obvious risk that property belonging to another will be damaged, both theories [ie: the continuing act and duty theory] lead to an identical result; and since what your Lordships are concerned with is to give guidance to trial judges in their task of summing up to juries, I would for this purpose adopt the duty theory as being the easier to explain to a jury; though I would commend the use of the word 'responsibility', rather than 'duty' which is more appropriate to civil than to criminal law since it suggests an obligation owed to another person, ie: the person to whom the endangered property belongs, whereas a criminal statute defines combinations of conduct and state of mind which render a person liable to punishment by the State itself.

NOTE 2.2

1. The House of Lords held that the creation of a risk of harm or danger gives rise to a duty to take reasonable steps to eliminate the risk provided D is aware of the risk. Failure to do so amounts to a breach of duty and this forms the AR of an offence.

2. The duty arises where the risk of danger has been initiated by a physical act which D personally creates. There is no need for the originating act to be criminal in nature.

   But the question arises as to whether the duty would arise where the sequence of events had been started not by a physical act but by an omission (see *Evans* [2009], later in this section). The distinction between an act and omission is far from clear (see *Bland*, later in this section). What if the events had begun not by D but by the act of someone for whom D was responsible?

4. The House of Lords held that the duty to take reasonable steps will only arise where D is aware of the risk of danger created. The recent case of *Evans* (see later in this section) held that a duty can arise where D knew, or *ought to have known*, of the risk.

5. D's conduct was of a continuing nature, from lighting the cigarette to ignoring the resulting fire. The court preferred the duty principle to that of the continuing act as in *Fagan* [1969] where D inadvertently parked on a police officer's foot and then refused to move for a minute or two after realising the harm. However, the continuing act principle still appears to be relevant to homicide cases (*Le Brun* [1991]).

CROSS-REFERENCE
The facts of *Fagan* are set out in 2.1.2.

It appears that the *Miller* principle, rather than that of the continuing act, was the basis of liability in the next case.

DPP v Santa-Bermudez [2003] EWHC 2908

D was asked to turn out his pockets before being searched by a female police officer. On seeing some syringes without needles, she asked him twice whether that was all and he replied 'Yes.' She pricked her finger on a hypodermic needle in D's jacket pocket. This became the subject of a charge of assault occasioning actual bodily harm contrary to s47 Offences Against the Person Act 1861. Although it was not material to the case, a blood sample from D proved positive for HIV and hepatitis C. Since there had been no act, and *Fagan* had held that there could be no assault by omission, D was acquitted. Allowing an appeal by the DPP, the Divisional Court held, on the authority of *Miller*, that D had exposed the officer to a reasonably foreseeable risk of injury by a combination of acts and words. The court made no reference to either duty or omission. One unresolved question is whether the decision implies that D was under a duty to inform the officer of the danger. A general duty to disclose information is unknown in English law.

The Court of Appeal held in *Gemma Evans* that a failure by one half-sister to summon medical assistance for another to whom she had supplied heroin gives rise to a breach of duty to act by the creation of danger.

→ CROSS-REFERENCE
See Chapter 7 for further discussion of duties of care in criminal law.

Gemma Evans [2009] CRIM LR 631 COURT OF APPEAL

D supplied heroin to her half-sister, V, aged 16. V self-injected and overdosed. She felt and looked unwell. D and her mother had histories of heroin addiction. They recognised the symptoms of an overdose and knew of the danger to V's life. They performed some acts to assist V during the night. Although V appeared better during the evening, by the next morning she was dead. The mother was convicted of manslaughter on the basis of a breach of a duty of care towards her daughter. D was also convicted and appealed.

Lord Judge LCJ:

> The question in this appeal is not whether the appellant may be guilty of manslaughter for having been concerned in the supply of the heroin which caused the deceased's death. It is whether, notwithstanding that their relationship lacked the features of familial duty or responsibility which marked her mother's relationship with the deceased, she was under a duty to take reasonable steps for the safety of the deceased once she appreciated that the heroin she procured for her was having a potentially fatal impact on her health ... The duty necessary to found gross negligence manslaughter is plainly not confined to cases of a familial or professional relationship between the defendant and the deceased. In our judgment, consistently with Adomako and the link between civil and criminal liability for negligence, for the purposes of gross negligence manslaughter, when a person has created or contributed to the creation of a state of affairs which he knows, or ought reasonably to know, has become life threatening, a consequent duty on him to act by taking reasonable steps to save the other's life will normally arise ... Without her involvement in the supply of heroin, the jury was directed that there was no duty on the appellant to act even after she became aware of the serious adverse effect of the drug taking on Carly. If on the other hand she was so involved, that fact, taken with the other undisputed facts would, and on our analysis of the relevant principles did give rise to a duty on the appellant to act. In law the judge's directions about the ingredients of gross negligence manslaughter, as applied to this case, were correct.

 NOTE 2.3

The Court of Appeal held that D was under a duty to take reasonable steps for V's safety having supplied her with drugs. Her failure to obtain help created or *contributed* to a dangerous situation, in accordance with *Miller*. It is not clear from the judgment whether the duty arose from the act of supply or from the later omission as soon as she realised, or ought to have realised, that the heroin she had bought for V was having a potentially fatal effect on V's health.

This was a novel extension of the *Miller* principle: if the duty did not begin until D failed to obtain help, where was the necessary act? If it was the supply, then how did D *cause* V's death? Surely V's autonomous decision to self-inject was the cause of her own death. This problem was side-stepped by the court in holding that D had either caused or *contributed* to the death, a new principle. The case is possibly at odds with *Lewin v CPS* [2002] EWHC 1049 where D was held not to be in breach of duty by leaving his sleeping, intoxicated friend, whom he had driven home from a club on holiday in Spain, in the car where he died in the summer heat. The duty lasted only so long as the car was in motion and ceased upon arriving at their destination. Death was not foreseen and V was an adult, not a child. The distinction from *Evans* appears to be D's lack of knowledge of V's life-threatening position. A. Ashworth, in 'Manslaughter by Omission and the Rule of Law' [2015] *Crim LR* 563, argues that the incremental expansion of the duty principle in *Stone* and *Evans* goes too far and offends the need for certainty of the criminal law under Article 7 ECHR. Neither defendant would have known their omissions were criminal until after the event. *Evans* appears to be a conviction based on morality: D ought reasonably to have done more. But should this result in conviction for manslaughter?

?!   **THINKING POINT** 2.5

D is in the middle of a long telephone conversation when she smells smoke coming from the kitchen. She had forgotten that half an hour ago she put food under the grill. She ignores the smell of smoke and continues talking. A fire breaks out and spreads to an adjoining flat. Z, a passer-by on the street below, watches but does nothing.

1. Have D or Z committed an offence?
2. Would your answer differ if, whilst his mother was speaking on the telephone, the fire had been started by D's young son using a magnifying glass to reflect sunlight on to the tablecloth to see what would happen?

Withholding medical treatment in the best interests of the patient

Act or omission?

Doctors owe patients a duty to preserve their lives by the provision of reasonable medical treatment. Can they be relieved of this duty where it is no longer in the best interests of the patient to be treated? This question was put to the test in the following case:

Airedale National Health Service Trust v Bland [1993] 1 ALL ER 821, [1993] 2 WLR 316 HOUSE OF LORDS

Tony Bland, a young man of 21, had been in a persistent vegetative state (PVS) for three and a half years following a severe crushed chest injury suffered in the 1989 Hillsborough football stadium disaster. Due to severe overcrowding in tunnels and on the terraces, hundreds of people were trampled upon and crushed. 96 were killed. Since the disaster, Tony Bland had been in the care of the health authority. He had suffered brain damage resulting in the destruction of all the higher functions of his brain. The unanimous opinion of all the doctors who examined him was that he had no hope of recovery or improvement of any kind. He was fed artificially and mechanically by a naso-gastric tube. His consultant decided that it would be appropriate to cease further treatment. Other distinguished consultants supported this view. It would mean withdrawing ventilation, artificial nutrition and hydration (ANH) and all further administration of antibiotics in the event of future infection except for medication to enable Tony Bland to end his life with dignity and the least pain and distress. He would die by starvation within 10 to 14 days. With the support of his parents, the health authority applied to the High Court for a declaration that it be permitted to withdraw all life support and medical treatment from the patient. The Official Solicitor representing Tony Bland argued that the health authority would be committing murder by either a positive act of discontinuance or by an omission to continue feeding and treatment which, in the circumstances of a duty of care (*Stone & Dobinson*), was criminal.

The declaration was granted and the Official Solicitor appealed first to the Court of Appeal and then to the House of Lords. All of their lordships, Lords Keith, Goff, Lowry, Browne-Wilkinson and Mustill, dismissed the appeal.

Lord Goff:

In medicine, the cessation of breathing or of heartbeat is no longer death. By the use of a ventilator, lungs which in the unaided course of nature would have stopped breathing can be made to breathe, thereby sustaining the heartbeat. Those, like Anthony Bland, who would previously have died through inability to swallow food can be kept alive by artificial feeding. This has led the medical profession to redefine death in terms of brain stem death, i.e., the death of that part of the brain without which the body cannot function at all without assistance. In some cases it is now apparently possible, with the use of the ventilator, to sustain a beating heart even though the brain stem, and therefore in medical terms the patient, is dead; 'the ventilated corpse'.

I do not refer to these factors because Anthony Bland is already dead, either medically or legally. His brain stem is alive and so is he; provided that he is artificially fed and the waste products evacuated from his body by skilled medical care, his body sustains its own life. I refer to these factors in order to illustrate the scale of the problem which is presented by modern technological developments, of which this case is merely one instance. The physical state known as death has changed. In many cases the time and manner of death is no longer dictated by nature but can be determined by human decision. The life of Anthony Bland, in the purely physical sense, has been and can be extended by skilled medical care for a period of years.

To my mind, these technical developments have raised a wholly new series of ethical and social problems. What is meant now by 'life' in the moral precept which requires respect for the sanctity of human life? If the quality of life of a person such as Anthony Bland is non-existent since he is unaware of anything that happens to him, has he a right to be sustained in that state of living death and are his family and medical attendants under a duty to maintain it? If Anthony Bland has no such right and others no such duty, should society draw a distinction (which some would see as artificial) between adopting a course of action designed to produce certain death, on the one hand through the lack of food, and on the other from a fatal injection, the former being permissible and the latter (euthanasia) prohibited? If the withdrawal of life support is legitimate in the case of Anthony Bland, whose P.V.S. is very severe, what of others in this country also in P.V.S. (whom we were told numbered between 1,000 and 1,500) and others suffering from medical conditions having similar impact, e.g. the Guillain-Barré syndrome? Who is to decide, and according to what criteria, who is to live and who is to die? What rights have the relatives of the patient in taking that decision?

Why is it that the doctor who gives his patient a lethal injection which kills him commits an unlawful act and indeed is guilty of murder, whereas a doctor who, by discontinuing life support, allows his patient to die, may not act unlawfully – and will not do so, if he commits no breach of duty to his patient? Professor Glanville Williams has suggested (see his Textbook of Criminal Law, 2nd ed. (1983), p. 282) that the reason is that what the doctor does when he switches off a life support machine 'is in substance not an act but an omission to struggle,' and that 'the omission is not a breach of duty by the doctor, because he is not obliged to continue in a hopeless case.'

I agree that the doctor's conduct in discontinuing life support can properly be categorised as an omission. It is true that it may be difficult to describe what the doctor actually does as an omission, *for example where he takes some positive step to bring the life support to an end. But discontinuation of life support is, for present purposes, no different from not initiating life support in the first place. In each case, the doctor is simply allowing his patient to die in the sense that he is desisting from taking a step which might, in certain circumstances, prevent his patient from dying as a result of his pre-existing condition; and as a matter of general principle an omission such as this will not be unlawful unless it constitutes a breach of duty to the patient.* [Emphasis added.]

Lord Goff held that the withdrawal of ANH and further medical treatment was an omission and lawful. But to administer a drug to bring about death would be to cross the Rubicon between care of the living and euthanasia. Lord Mustill agreed.

Lord Mustill:

After much expression of negative opinions I turn to an argument which in my judgment is logically defensible and consistent with the existing law. In essence it turns the previous argument on its head by directing the inquiry to the interests of the patient, not in the termination of life but in the continuation of his treatment. It runs as follows. (i) The cessation of nourishment and hydration is an omission not an act. (ii) Accordingly, the cessation will not be a criminal act unless the doctors are under a present duty to continue the regime. (iii) At the time when Anthony Bland came into the care of the doctors decisions had to be made about his care which he was unable to make for himself. In accordance with In Re F [1990] 2 AC 1 these decisions were to be made in his best interests. Since the possibility that he might recover still existed his best interests required that he should be supported in the hope that this would happen. These best interests justified the application of the necessary regime without his consent. (iv) All hope of recovery has now been abandoned. Thus, although the termination of his life is not in the best interests of Anthony Bland, his best interests in being kept alive have also disappeared, taking with them the justification for the non-consensual regime and the correlative duty to keep it in being. (v) Since there is no longer a duty to provide nourishment and hydration a failure to do so cannot be a criminal offence …

[A]lthough in cases near the borderline the categorisation of conduct [as either an act or omission] will be exceedingly hard, I believe that nearer the periphery there will be many instances which fall quite clearly into one category rather than the other. In my opinion the present is such a case, and in company with Compton J. in Barber v. Superior Court of State of California, 195 Cal.Rptr. 484, 490 amongst others I consider that the proposed conduct will fall into the category of omissions.

I therefore consider the argument to be soundly-based. Now that the time has come when Anthony Bland has no further interest in being kept alive, the necessity to do so, created by his inability to make a choice, has gone; and the justification for the invasive care and treatment, together with the duty to provide it have also gone. Absent a duty, the omission to perform what had previously been a duty will no longer be a breach of the criminal law.

 NOTE 2.4

1. The case raised the moral and ethical problem of euthanasia and the distinction between bringing life to an end by positive means, such as lethal injection, and letting die by the withdrawal of life support and medical treatment which the House classified as an omission.

2. A positive act such as a lethal injection would constitute murder but the House held that an omission could not do so unless it constituted a breach of duty.

3. The House acknowledged that doctors owe a duty to do all that they reasonably can to keep their patients alive.

4. A doctor may be absolved of the duty where the patient is in an irrecoverable, unconscious condition and a clinical decision is made that it is in the best interests of the patient to discontinue treatment. It will only be in his best interests if the continuation would be intolerable from the patient's point of view. Artificial nutrition, defined by Lord Goff as medical treatment, may be lawfully discontinued in such circumstances so as to allow a patient in a hopeless case to die with dignity and minimum distress.

5. Lord Mustill rejected the argument that because of incapacity or infirmity one life is intrinsically worth less than another. This would be a dangerous step which could authorise active as well as passive killing. But he held that by looking at the effectiveness of continuing the treatment, Tony Bland had no interest in being kept alive.

6. Reference was made to the ECHR which guarantees the right to life (Article 2), the right to dignity (Article 3) and the right to autonomy (Article 8). The decision in the

case was held to be consistent with those rights. The case pre-dated the incorporation of the ECHR into domestic law by the Human Rights Act 1998. The compatibility of the withdrawal of medical treatment under the HRA 1998 has been endorsed in subsequent cases.

7. Criticisms of the *Bland* judgment:

The act/omission distinction

The case fuelled debate as to whether there was a *moral* distinction between killing by positive act and letting die by omission. The distinction had been recognised in the case of *Doctor Arthur* [1985] Crim LR 705 which concerned the withdrawal of nutrition from a Down's Syndrome baby, the baby having been rejected by its parents. The court held that a doctor has no right to kill a handicapped child, no matter how serious the medical condition. But there was a difference between killing through lethal injection and allowing nature to take its course through not operating or withholding food if the parents did not wish the child to survive (an omission).

But could withdrawal of treatment be equally classified as a positive act, particularly the withdrawal of artificial feeding to which one might be entitled as a basic right?

See this extract from D. Morgan, 'The Greatest Danger' *NLJ*, 27 November 1992, at 1652 in commenting on the High Court decision in *Bland*:

> Shifting conceptual notions of causation, doing violence to common understanding of basic human activities – such as feeding – does not seem a wise or acceptable way to proceed. Withdrawing nutrition and hydration can have only one effect, indeed it is intended to have one effect – to kill the patient. 'Good medical practice' is again allowed to dictate what legally amounts to death, in parallel with the expansion from total circulatory death to encompass brain stem death without a jot of legislative ink or a drop of judicial blood.

→ CROSS-REFERENCE
Re A (Conjoined Twins) is discussed in detail in Chapter 6.

Others argued that it would be kinder to give such patients a lethal injection rather than letting them starve to death. In the case of the separation of the conjoined twins (*Re A (Conjoined Twins)* [2001] 2 WLR 480 Ward LJ in the Court of Appeal held the act/omission distinction to be without foundation. Thus, it would be murder to kill by either method but the act would not be unlawful if a good defence could be established. *Re A*, being a decision of a lower court cannot, of course, overrule *Bland*.

The sanctity of life

Critics of the decision in *Bland* said that the decision was in breach of the 'sanctity of life' principle. This principle, whilst admitting that a doctor does not have to save life at all costs, rejects the argument that a life or death decision can be taken according to the quality of the patient's life. What is required is an evaluation of the 'worthwhileness' of the proposed treatment. Who is to say that the life of a PVS patient has less value than any other? Why should it be in the patient's best interests to be allowed to die, especially through starvation and possible infection?

See this extract from 'Restoring Moral and Intellectual Shape to the Law after *Bland*' by J. Keown (1997) 113 *LQR* 381, commenting on Lord Goff's judgment:

> He observed, first, that it is lawful to kill in self-defence and, secondly, that, in the medical context, there is no absolute rule that a patient's life must be prolonged by treatment or care regardless of the circumstances. Both statements are, as the discussion in Part I made clear, accurate. But they do not show that the principle of the sanctity of life is 'not absolute', unless one thinks, as his Lordship appears to, that the principle prohibits all killings or requires the preservation of life at all costs. Neither proposition is, of course, consistent with the princi-

ple as traditionally formulated and understood. His Lordship observed, thirdly, that the fact that a doctor must respect a patient's refusal of life-prolonging treatment showed that the sanctity of life yielded to the right to self-determination. Again, his Lordship seems to think that the sanctity of life requires the preservation of life, even against the competent patient's contemporaneous wishes. Again, this is not so. Fourthly, he distinguished between a doctor, on the one hand, omitting to provide life-prolonging treatment or care and, on the other, administering a lethal drug. 'So to act', he said 'is to cross the Rubicon which runs between on the one hand the care of the living patient and on the other hand euthanasia – actively causing his death to avoid or to end his suffering'. But, as we saw in Part I, the intentional killing by one person of another person in his care, even if effected by omission, breaches the principle.'

The House of Lords in *Bland* did not attempt to arbitrate these moral questions. They may have employed euphemisms but few could disagree with the decision.

Contractual, official or statutory duty

The type of contract most likely to give rise to a duty to act is a contract of employment by which D, the employee, assumes responsibility for third parties, such as the public. If D fails to act in breach of contract and harm befalls a member of the public, criminal omissions liability may arise.

This contrasts with English contract law where the doctrine of privity of contract prevents anyone who is not a party to the contract from enforcing it, subject to limited exceptions. Further, under tort law, it is D's employer who would owe a duty of care towards an injured member of the public.

Two cases illustrate the position in criminal law but you will note that each D was charged with quite different types of offence. This raises further uncertainty about omissions liability.

R v Pittwood (1902) 19 TLR 37 TAUNTON ASSIZES

A gate keeper on the Somerset and Dorset Railway was under a contractual duty to keep the crossing gates closed whenever a train was passing from 7.00 am to 7.00 pm. He forgot to shut the gates one afternoon and a passing train struck a hay cart. One man was killed and another was seriously injured. D argued that his responsibility was to his employers and not to the public. He was held guilty of manslaughter on the grounds of gross and criminal negligence and an *assumption* of responsibility to the public. His duty was not simply to his employers. *Instan* was applied.

In *Pittwood*, D's contractual duty to protect the public was specifically owed to his employers but this did not prevent conviction. A duty to the public was also inferred from the manager of a cab firm's contractual duty to MOT the tyres of a minibus which was involved in a fatal accident: *Yaqoob* [2005] EWCA Crim 1269.

→ CROSS-REFERENCE
The fact of *Instan* are set out in 2.2.3.

R v Dytham [1979] 3 ALL ER 641 COURT OF APPEAL

A police officer failed to protect a man from being beaten to death by bouncers after he had been ejected from a nightclub at 1.00 am. He did not intervene and drove off. He was convicted of misconduct whilst acting as an officer of justice. His conviction was confirmed on the grounds of his deliberate and wilful neglect of duty.

In both of the above cases, D's actions contributed to death yet only in *Pittwood* did the manslaughter conviction reflect the full consequences of his omission. True, PC Dytham did not beat up the man himself. Others were the more direct and culpable cause of death. But it was his duty to prevent it and he could have done so. Is *Dytham* really that different from *Pittwood*? Ought Pittwood to have been charged with a conduct crime involving breach of some lesser statutory offence?

2.2.4 Criticisms of Omissions Liability

The distinction between acts and omissions

The case of *Bland* left many people unhappy with the interpretation of withdrawal of nutrition and medication as an omission and not as a positive act of unlawful killing.

A. Ashworth argues as follows in 'The Scope of Criminal Liability for Omissions' (1989) 105 *LQR* 424:

> Whether we term certain events 'acts' or 'omissions' may be both flexible in practice and virtually insoluble in theory: for example, does a hospital nurse who decides not to replace an empty bag for a drip feed make an omission, whilst a nurse who switches off a ventilator commits an act? It would seem wrong that criminal liability or non-liability should turn on such fine points, which seem incapable of reflecting any substantial moral distinctions in a context where the preservation of life is generally paramount. ... The proper solution is not to warp the concepts of omission, duty, knowledge and causation, but to provide for such cases to be determined on new principles of justification. This would require the courts to be explicit about the grounds for exonerating doctors or nurses, rather than concealing the reasons behind the act/omission distinction.

Further, a conviction for a straightforward breach of duty conduct offence may be acceptable whereas a conviction for all the *consequences* flowing from the omission (a result crime, eg: manslaughter) leads to injustice.

Moral arguments: individual autonomy v welfare and human rights

Is there a case for extending the law and having a general public duty to rescue strangers in peril? A. Ashworth identifies two contrasting positions on omissions liability: the 'conventional view' and the 'social responsibility view'. The former holds that there is a moral distinction between acts and omissions and liability should only be imposed in clear and serious cases, principally where a duty has been voluntarily assumed.

> The arguments for the conventional view may appear strong and practical, but they depend on a narrow, individualistic conception of human life which should be rejected as a basis for morality and ... as a basis for criminal liability. ... [R]arely is individual autonomy promoted as a supreme value through a moral or legal system. For example, paternalistic considerations are taken to outweigh it when imposing a duty to wear a seat belt in the front seat of a car ... If individual autonomy is truly a supreme value, then it requires social principles rather than this kind of isolationist individualism in order to secure its fulfilment. Individuals tend to place a high value on interpersonal contacts, relationships, mutual support and the fulfilment of obligations, and a society which values collective goals and collective goods may therefore provide a wider range of worthwhile opportunities for individual development.
>
> The social responsibility view of omissions liability grows out of a communitarian social philosophy which stresses the necessary interrelationship between individual behaviour and collective goods. In-

dividuals need others, or the actions of others, for a wide variety of tasks which assist each one of us to maximise the pursuit of our personal goals. A community or society may be regarded as a network of relationships which support one another by direct and indirect means. But the community also consists of individuals, each having certain basic rights (such as the right to life). It is therefore strongly arguable that each individual life should be valued both intrinsically and for its contribution (or potential contribution) to the community. It follows that there is a good case for encouraging co-operation at the minimal level of the duty to assist persons in peril, so long as the assistance does not endanger the person rendering it, and a case may be made for reinforcing this duty by the criminal sanction. ... The argument does not rest on a simple utilitarian calculation of benefits, ensuring a net saving of lives with comparatively little inconvenience to other members of society. Nor does it rest on the prediction that both respect for the law and the level of social co-operation will be improved if the law encourages morally desirable conduct, although those would be beneficial consequences. The foundation of the argument is that a level of social co-operation and social responsibility is both good and necessary for the realisation of individual autonomy ...

The general principle in criminal law should be that omissions liability should be possible if a duty is established, because in those circumstances there is no fundamental moral distinction between failing to perform an act with foreseen bad consequences and performing the act with identical foreseen bad consequences.

The social responsibility view would impose a wider duty on citizens to render assistance in certain situations with no pre-existing duty requirement on the basis that there is no moral distinction between an act and an omission.

Read the opposing views of G. Williams in: 'Criminal Omissions—The Conventional View' (1991) 107 *LQR* 88:

This is a reply, by one who now discovers himself to be a conventionalist, to Professor Ashworth's piece 'The Scope of Criminal Liability for Omissions'. Ashworth stages the debate as a conflict between two contrasting approaches to the subject of criminal omissions: one, the 'conventional view' (which he seems to regard as selfish and callous), and an opposing (virtuous) approach dubbed the 'social responsibility view'. ... The opposing 'conventional view', to which I would subscribe if it were presented with due moderation, is stated by Ashworth in terms of narrow nineteenth-century individualism, so that few people nowadays would wish to support it; but to present the argument in this way is merely shadow-boxing. ...

If there is no fundamental moral distinction between killing and letting die (in breach of duty), it is a fact that has been missed by members of the medical profession, who see a great difference between the two. Whereas killing your patient is absolutely taboo, according to the present law and official medical ethics, letting your patient die is qualifiedly permissible, namely when the patient is dying and there is no point in continuing his agony. ...

The arguments for this [conventional] philosophy may be briefly stated. ... First, society's most urgent task is the repression of active wrongdoing. Bringing the ignorant or lethargic up to scratch is very much a secondary endeavour, for which the criminal process is not necessarily the best suited.

Secondly, our attitudes to wrongful action and wrongful inaction differ. There may be instances where our blood boils at the same temperature on account of both, but these cases are very exceptional. The only likely instance that comes to my mind is that of parents who are charged with killing their baby (i) by smothering it or (ii) by starving it to death. In this instance we are likely to feel more angry and sad about the slow starvation (an omission) than about the comparatively merciful infliction of death with a pillow. But on other occasions we almost always perceive a moral distinction between (for example) killing a person and failing to save his life (the former being the worse); and similarly between other acts and corresponding omissions.

The moral distinction … reflects differences in our psychological approach to our own acts and omissions. We have much stronger inhibitions against active wrongdoing than against wrongfully omitting. … Also, a requirement to do something presupposes the ability to do it (the physical ability, and often the financial and educational ability as well), whereas almost everyone has the ability to refrain from ordinary physical acts.

Thirdly, serious crimes of commission can usually be formulated merely stating the forbidden conduct, but laws creating crimes of omission are rarely directed against the whole world. They are intended to operate only against particular classes of person (and sometimes only for the protection of particular classes), in which case these persons must be singled out in the statement of the crime. To take an example: the courts can, in theory, punish everyone … who knowingly kills, but they cannot punish everyone who fails to save life, without some minimum specification of whose lives are to be saved. I cannot be made criminally responsible when I knowingly fail to save (and do not even try to save) the lives of unfortunate inhabitants of the Ganges delta who are drowned in floods; yet I could do something to help them by selling my house and giving the money to a suitable charity. …

The argument against treating omissions in the same way as positive acts does not go to the extent of saying that omissions running contrary to the public interest should never be punishable. Those who oppose seat belt legislation … do so on the ground that it unjustifiably restricts liberty, not on the ground that it wrongly punishes omissions. The legislation forbids one to drive in a car without belting up, and the forbidden conduct is a hybrid act/omission, which is legally classified as an act, not an omission.

1. What reasons do the authors give for and against having a general duty to act?

2. Whose views do you agree with and why?

In his later work (*Positive Obligations in Criminal Law*, Hart, 2013, ch 2) A. Ashworth argues on human rights grounds in favour of positive duties to act. He would support the creation of specific offences broadly in line with existing common law duties, particularly one related to failing to report abuse against vulnerable victims, such as children. At p 47:

[T]he individual … has duties, and the question is whether it is in any way unreasonable to impose a criminal law duty on the individual to summon emergency services or to report abuse, particularly in view of the principle of urgency, the priority of life and the principles of opportunity and capacity.

He criticises omissions liability as being contrary to the rule of law. At pp 66–67:

First, the list of duty-situations in English law remains open for judicial development, so that individuals often cannot know whether their failure to intervene in a given situation will lead to liability for the serious offence of manslaughter. Surely, if we accept the fundamental principle that the criminal law should not be retroactive, and that fair warning should be given, the judicial recognition of new duty-situations in these serious cases would seem to violate this … The second major problem is that there may be nothing to put the individual on notice of the duty-situations, not least because there may be a widespread belief that there are few legal duties to care for one's fellow human beings … A third and related problem concerns the fault element … the case for liability based on negligence, or even on gross negligence, is precarious. Fourthly, one aspect of the rule of law is that people are entitled to know what is expected of them. Omissions law creates difficulties in this respect insofar as it relies on concepts such as 'reasonable steps' and 'such steps as could reasonably be expected'.

It follows that this creates uncertainty in the law which violates Article 7 ECHR.

Omissions and causation

Should all omissions cases be dealt with under the principles of causation? In criminal law, no-one can be convicted of a result crime unless their act/omission was the legal cause of the prohibited harm.

→ CROSS-REFERENCE
Causation is discussed in 2.3.

How can an omission be said to cause a prohibited result? Read the following extract from B. Hogan, 'Omissions and a Duty Myth' in P. Smith (ed.), *Criminal Law: Essays in Honour of J.C. Smith*, Butterworths, 1987:

> [T]here is no way that you can *cause* an event by doing nothing (or is it, more precisely, by not doing anything?) to prevent it …
>
> But we immediately encounter the problem of what is meant by doing nothing, or, rather, not doing anything. The vexing problem of the distinction between act and omission. … [M]y own view is that the distinction is at best unhelpful and at worst misleading. …
>
> [I]t would be much more conducive to clarity of thought if we spoke of conduct and causation. If any proposition is self-evident (and, arguably, none is) it is that a person cannot be held to have caused an event which he did not cause. …
>
> So in *R v Pittwood* it becomes fruitless to debate whether leaving open the level-crossing gates is to be characterised as omission or commission. The court characterised the conduct as misfeasance and in so doing, though the report is brief, appears to have looked at the totality of the defendant's conduct. And looking at the totality of his conduct it can easily be said that he created a situation of danger which caused harm to the victim.
>
> It is true that in *R v Pittwood* the court also said that a duty might arise out of a contract and the cases on 'omissions' are certainly littered with references to 'duty'. In my view these references to duty are unhelpful. The issue in *R v Pittwood* was simply whether the defendant had caused the deaths of the victims with the relevant mens rea. …
>
> There is perhaps a stronger case for imputing the duty concept in connection with domestic and similar relationships … I am unhappy about the duty concept in the context of 'omission'. It is likely to mislead a jury into thinking of duties in other than legal terms; into a consideration of the immorality of particular conduct; into convicting the defendant merely for his callousness. Better to put the issue as simply one of causation. …
>
> That is not to say that I am against liability for omissions … There are of course numerous in-stances where Parliament (and a handful where the common law) has penalised omissions but what is noteworthy is that the defendant is penalised for the omission but not visited with liability for the consequences of that omission. … I would ask only two conditions of a law punishing omissions. One is that it be clearly articulated and the other is that it seeks to punish the defendant for his dereliction and does not artificially treat him as a cause of the event he has not brought about by his conduct.

The author objects to Pittwood's conviction for manslaughter but would not object to conviction of a lesser breach of duty offence. However, A. Ashworth in 'The Scope of Criminal Liability for Omissions' (1989) 105 *LQR* 424 disagrees:

> Once it is established that there has been a voluntary omission to perform a duty, the next question is whether it can be said to have caused the result. There is considerable uncertainty over the relationship between causation and omissions. … [t]his concept must [of causation] avoid regarding all non-acting as a cause of all events or results which could have been averted by acting – otherwise, I could be said to cause people to sleep rough in London each night (since by selling my share of the house and car and devoting the proceeds to the relief of this problem I could alleviate it), and we would all be responsible for causing myriad misfortunes each day. In this way the argument returns to the duty concept as the

primary criterion, both because it establishes moral (if not strictly causal) responsibility and because it delineates in time and space the number of people who may be said to have omitted – although that may still be a large number on some occasions. In other words, so long as we are satisfied that under certain circumstances an act and an omission are morally equivalent, then under those circumstances no separate causal enquiry is necessary, for a sufficiently close link exists.

For this writer, the duty is pre-eminent and is all that is required. Do you agree that there is a moral equivalence between an act and an omission?

2.2.5 Evaluation

There are strong moral reasons for saying that we should, in every case, render assistance, intervene or do what we reasonably can to aid or rescue strangers. This is particularly compelling in respect of the protection of children and the vulnerable. Indeed, some people, such as doctors, have a specific professional and ethical duty to render assistance to accident victims. But failure to do so is no crime.

On the other hand, there are equally strong arguments for resisting the elevation of a moral duty to a legal one save in exceptional circumstances. Personal freedom and independence would be compromised. If the omission was the result of a conscious decision, it might look as if one could be punished for simply having guilty thoughts for a crime requires an act. One might ask whether the current law offers sufficient certainty, predictability or fairness to defendants as required by Article 7 ECHR. On the other hand, does it offer sufficient protection to individuals in distress?

If a general duty were imposed, would it risk turning us into spies and informers? In many European countries there is a wider obligation on citizens to assist than under English law. For example, an offence of failure to render assistance exists in France. You might recall the prosecution of the French paparazzi who photographed Princess Diana at the scene of the fatal car crash in Paris in 1997. They allegedly delayed calling the emergency services and were charged with an offence under the French Penal Code of failing to rescue (an omission), of which they were, incidentally, later acquitted. However, further than that, under French law there is an obligation to report criminals to the authorities in murder and sexual assault cases. Failure to do so will result in criminal liability. There is also an obligation to prevent other people from committing offences. This has resulted in the conviction of bar owners and dinner hosts for omissions offences where they have failed to stop guests from driving whilst intoxicated and having car crashes (*Times*, 26 October 2004). A wider duty to act might expect us all to become informers. Would society be better or worse for this? There are many moral arguments here. What do you think?

2.2.6 Reform

The Law Commission's Draft Criminal Code Bill (Law Com No 177) preserves omissions liability:

> Cl. 17(1): … a person causes a result … when … (b) he omits to do an act which might prevent its occurrence and which he is under a duty to do according to the law of the offence.

SECTION SUMMARY

Omissions liability concerns the commission of the AR through failing to act. There is no general duty to act. There can only be liability for an omission in the circumstances of a duty imposed by:

■ *Statutory conduct crimes prohibiting 'failure to act';*
■ *Five common law duty situations;*
■ *voluntary assumption of responsibility;*
■ *close/special relationship;*
■ *creation of a dangerous situation;*

■ *withdrawal of medical treatment where there is a continuing obligation to preserve life; and*

■ *contract, statute or official position.*

You should note the criticisms and moral arguments for and against omissions liability.

NB: Omissions liability overlaps with gross negligence manslaughter. A duty to act in the former will amount to a duty of care for the latter.

→ CROSS-REFERENCE
Gross negligence manslaughter is discussed in Chapter 7.

2.3 Causation

2.3.1 Introduction

2.3.2 Factual Causation

2.3.3 Legal Causation

2.3.4 Conclusion

2.3.5 Reform

KEY CASES

Pagett [1983] 76 Cr App R 279—an intervening act must be free, deliberate and informed;

Rafferty [2007] EWCA Crim 1846—assault/robbery: intervening act by drowning will break the chain of causation;

Kennedy [2007] UKHL 38—drugs supply cases: a voluntary act of self-injection will break the chain of causation;

Malcherek & Steel [1981] 1 WLR 690—medical intervention does not break the chain where the original wounds are substantial and operating;

Jordan [1956] 40 Cr App R 152—medical neglect which is independent and palpably wrong will break the chain;

Cheshire [1991] 3 All ER 670—medical neglect does not break the chain where the original wounds are significant.

2.3.1 Introduction

Causation applies to result crimes

A *result* crime requires guilty conduct (act or omission) to be followed by a result or consequence. We saw some examples of result crimes at the beginning of this chapter: homicide, assault, criminal damage. Causation is a set of rules by which the court determines whether D's conduct has caused or contributed significantly to the result as a matter of law. In a result crime, unless causation can be established, the AR will not be proved and D will be acquitted. As with omissions, causation in the criminal law is challenged as being vague and inconsistent, as we shall see. Whether or not D can be found guilty of the offence in question still depends on proof of MR. Proving causation and, thus, the AR of a crime, is only the first stage of criminal liability.

2.3.2 Factual Causation

The 'but for' test

Before the search for *legal* causation can begin, it must first be proved that D's conduct was a *factual* cause of the result. Another way of putting this is to ask whether, *but for* D's conduct, the result would have happened. If it would have happened anyway, D's conduct is not the cause of it. This is sometimes expressed as the *sine qua non* test, where D's conduct is a necessary precondition of the result. For example, consider the two following cases:

R v White [1910] 2 KB 124 COURT OF APPEAL

D put cyanide in his mother's drink with the intention of killing her. She was later found dead next to the cup which was only three-quarters full. Medical evidence revealed that she had died from heart failure not poisoning. Factual causation between D's attempted poisoning and death could not be proved. D could not therefore be convicted of murdering his mother. He was only guilty of attempting to do so.

→ CROSS-REFERENCE
The offence of attempt is explored in Chapter 15.

R v Dalloway (1847) 2 COX 273 CROWN COURT

D was the driver of a horse-drawn cart. Whilst standing in the cart without holding on to the reins as the horse trotted down a hill, a 3-year-old child ran in front of the horse and was killed by one of the wheels of the cart. D did not see the child in the road. He was charged with manslaughter. Although D had been driving negligently the question was whether his negligence was the cause of death. If he could have used the reins to stop the horse before hitting the child, then his negligence would have caused the child's death and he would be guilty of manslaughter. If nothing could have saved the child, he was not the cause of death and therefore not guilty. He was acquitted.

In neither of these cases were D's culpable acts or omissions the factual cause of death. Therefore, the AR of the respective offences could not be proved.

Minimal contributions

→ CROSS-REFERENCE
For example, *Dr. Adams* and *Dr. Cox* are discussed in Chapter 3, 3.1.9.

Minimal causal contributions to a result are disregarded. Thus, a doctor who only *accelerates* death by minutes or hours through the administration to a terminally ill patient of a high dose of a pain-relieving drug for the purpose of palliative care will not cause death.

2.3.3 Legal Causation

Third party interventions: the novus actus interveniens

There may be more than one cause of a result. D may commit an unlawful act or omission which sets in motion a chain of events leading to harm. But suppose a third party intervenes and compounds matters. Will this intervention absolve D of all liability? The basic rule is that D will be responsible for all the natural and probable consequences of his act.

 EXAMPLE 2.6

D assaults V by knocking him unconscious. Ten minutes later Z sees V on the ground and shoots him dead.

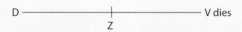

Diagram 2.4
Intervening event/*novus actus interveniens*

The chain of causation between D and V would be broken by Z whose independent act would be regarded as an intervening event (a *novus actus interveniens*). The chain would not be broken if Z was acting in concert with D (see Diagram 2.4).

A *novus actus interveniens* is typically a third person intervention but could theoretically be a natural event such as a hurricane, earthquake, flood, tsunami or bolt of lightning which exacerbates harm originating from D's unlawful act. The Draft Criminal Code includes reference to 'events' as third party interventions as we shall see at the end of this section. We will consider how third party interventions may break the chain of causation in six types of case: homicide, drugs supply, pollution, medical and interventions by the victim. Many of the principles of causation derive from a famous study of the subject by Hart & Honoré, *Causation in the Law*, OUP, 1985. There is an extract from this work at the end of this chapter.

1. Homicide and violent offences: the intervention must be free, deliberate and informed

The following case confirms that before a third party intervention will break a chain of causation it must be voluntary.

R v Pagett (1983) 76 CR APP R 279 COURT OF APPEAL

One evening, Pagett kidnapped his six-months' pregnant girlfriend, Gail Kitchen. Armed with a shotgun, he drove to Gail's home where he assaulted her mother and shot her father in the thigh. Gail was not there and so Pagett took her mother by force in his car to find her. Finding Gail at a friend's house, Pagett forced her and her mother into his car and drove off, hitting both of them before and after they got into the car. Despite being stopped by unarmed police, when the mother escaped, Pagett continued to drive Gail to his flat situated on the first floor of a three-storey block of flats. There were two flats on each floor, opening out on to a central staircase. The two officers inside the block took up position on the first floor landing outside Pagett's flat. There was only one light on in the stairwell at the back of the ground floor. After some time, Pagett's door opened and the shape of a woman was in the doorway. Pagett had his arm around her neck and a gun in his right hand, pointing at the officers. They warned him that they were armed and Pagett moved towards them with Gail in front of him. The officers retreated to the top landing where it was very dark. They could see practically nothing. More warnings were issued by the officers. They could see a figure looming towards them on the upper flight of stairs. The officers shouted another warning. Pagett fired his gun. Six shots were fired by the officers. Pagett fired again. The officers fired three more times instinctively, not taking any particular aim. Three bullets wounded Gail, she shouted out and collapsed on to Pagett. Pagett was disarmed. Thirteen more pellets were found on him. It was clear he had been using Gail as a shield although the officers could not see this. Gail later died. The officers were unhurt. Pagett was acquitted of the murder of Gail but convicted of manslaughter and other firearms and kidnapping offences. He appealed against the manslaughter conviction on the grounds of causation.

Defence counsel argued at the appeal that where the act which immediately resulted in a fatal injury was the act of another, then the ensuing death was too remote. No-one should be convicted of homicide unless he fired the shot which was the immediate cause of death.

Goff LJ:

For the appellant, Lord Gifford criticised the statement of the learned authors [Smith & Hogan] that 'Whether a particular act which is a *sine qua non* of an alleged actus reus is also a cause of it is a question of law.' He submitted that that question had to be answered by the jury as a question of fact. In our view, with all respect, both the passage in Smith and Hogan's *Criminal Law*, and Lord Gifford's criticism of it, are oversimplifications of a complex matter. …

Now the whole subject of causation in the law has been the subject of a well-known and distinguished treatise by Professors Hart and Honoré, Causation in the Law. Passages from this book were cited to the learned judge, and were plainly relied upon by him; we, too, wish to express indebtedness to it. It would be quite wrong for us to consider in this judgment the wider issues discussed in that work. But, for present purposes, the passage which is of most immediate relevance is to be found in Chapter XII, in which the learned authors consider the circumstances in which the intervention of a third person, not acting in concert with the accused, may have the effect of relieving the accused of criminal responsibility. The criterion which they suggest should be applied in such circumstances is whether the intervention is voluntary, ie whether it is 'free, deliberate and informed'. We resist the temptation of expressing the judicial opinion whether we find ourselves in complete agreement with that definition; though we certainly consider it to be broadly correct and supported by authority. Among the examples which the authors give of non-voluntary conduct, which is not effective to relieve the accused of responsibility, are two which are germane to the present case, viz a reasonable act performed for the purpose of self-preservation, and an act done in performance of a legal duty. [Emphasis added.]

There can, we consider, be no doubt that a reasonable act performed for the purpose of self-preservation, being of course itself an act caused by the accused's own act, does not operate as a *novus actus interveniens*. If authority is needed for this almost self-evident proposition, it is to be found in such cases as *Pitts* (1842) Car & M 284 and *Curley* (1909) 2 Cr App R 96. In both these cases, the act performed for the purpose of self-preservation consisted of an act by the victim attempting to escape from the violence of the accused, which in fact resulted in the victim's death. In each case it was held as a matter of law that, if the victim acted in a reasonable attempt to escape the violence of the accused, the death of the victim was caused by the act of the accused. Now one form of self-preservation is self-defence; for present purposes, we can see no distinction in principle between an attempt to escape the consequences of the accused's act, and a response which takes the form of self-defence. Furthermore, in our judgment, if a reasonable act of self-defence against the act of the accused causes the death of a third party, we can see no reason in principle why the act of self-defence, being an involuntary act caused by the act of the accused, should relieve the accused of criminal responsibility for the death of the third party. Of course, it does not necessarily follow that the accused will be guilty of the murder, or even of the manslaughter, of the third party; though in the majority of cases he is likely to be guilty at least of manslaughter. Whether he is guilty of murder or manslaughter will depend upon the question whether all the ingredients of the relevant offence have been proved; in particular, on a charge of murder, it will be necessary that the accused had the necessary intent …

No English authority was cited to us, nor we think to the learned judge, in support of the proposition that an act done in the execution of a legal duty, again of course being an act itself caused by the act of the accused, does not operate as a *novus actus interveniens* … Even so, we agree with the learned judge that the proposition is sound in law, because as a matter of principle such an act cannot be regarded as a voluntary act independent of the wrongful act of the accused. A parallel may be drawn with the so-called 'rescue' cases in the law of negligence, where a wrongdoer may be held liable in negligence to a third party who suffers injury in going to the rescue of a person who has been put in danger by the defendant's negligent act. …

The principles which we have stated are principles of law. … It does not however follow that it is accurate to state broadly that causation is a question of law. On the contrary, generally speaking causation is a question of fact for the jury. … But that does not mean that there are no principles of law relating to causation, so that no directions on law are ever to be given to a jury on the question of causation.

In cases of homicide, it is rarely necessary to give the jury any direction on causation as such. … Even where it is necessary to direct the jury's minds to the question of causation, it is usually enough to direct them simply that in law the accused's act need not be the sole cause, or even the main cause of the victim's death, it being enough that his act contributed significantly to that result. … Occasionally, however, a specific issue of causation may arise. One such case is where, although an act of the accused constitutes a *causa sine qua non* of (or necessary condition for) the death of the victim, nevertheless the intervention of a third person may be regarded as the sole cause of the victim's death, thereby relieving the accused of criminal responsibility. … [T]he Latin term has become a term of art which conveys to lawyers the crucial feature that there has not merely been an intervening act of another person, but that that act was so independent of the act of the accused that it should be regarded in law as the cause of the victim's death, to the exclusion of the act of the accused. …

NOTE 2.5

This case established the following principles in relation to the *novus actus interveniens* or third party intervention:

1. D's act need not be the sole or even the main cause of V's death.
2. D's act need only contribute significantly to that result.
3. In order to constitute a *novus actus interveniens*, a third party intervention had to be voluntary in the sense of being *free, deliberate and informed*.
4. A reasonable act performed in self-preservation or in pursuance of a legal duty is not voluntary.
5. Causation is a question of fact for the jury based on legal principles on which guidance will need to be given to juries from time to time.
6. These rules apply not simply to homicide but to causation in general.

Pagett generated considerable academic criticism. Was it reasonable for the police officers to fire nine shots in virtual darkness in such close proximity to a hostage whose life they were there to protect? If it was unreasonable, could they really be said to be acting in the execution of duty? Gail's mother later received damages as a result of civil proceedings against the police for their negligence in failing to protect her. Ashworth in *Principles of the Criminal Law* has stated that the right to act in self-preservation might be qualified if there is a conflict with the duty to safeguard the life of a hostage. Should the police officers have positioned themselves so that a clearer view was possible if and when Pagett emerged from the block with Gail?

Where D is part of a joint enterprise to commit one type of crime, a different crime committed by a co-defendant will be regarded as a voluntary break in the chain of causation:

R v Rafferty (Andrew Paul) [2007] EWCA CRIM 1846 COURT OF APPEAL

D and two co-defendants attacked V on a beach rendering him unconscious. It appeared that D's role had been to elbow V in the back twice as he lay on the ground to pin him down so that the two others could punch and kick him. They then robbed him. D took V's credit card to a cash machine in order to obtain some money. By the time he returned to the beach, his co-defendants had disappeared. It transpired that in D's absence they had inflicted further serious injuries on V, dragged him 100 metres across the beach, stripped him naked and taken him out some distance into the sea where he drowned. The co-defendants were convicted of murder. D was convicted of manslaughter on the basis that he lacked the intent to seriously injure V. (The MR for murder consists of an intent to kill or seriously injure.) In relation to causation, the judge had directed the jury that drowning was not such a new and intervening act in the chain of events which was so completely different from the injuries for which D was responsible. It did not overwhelm those injuries or destroy any causal connection between them and the death of V. D appealed on this point.

Hooper LJ:

> Mr Spencer [for the Crown] argued that the jury was entitled to find that the post-departure acts of the co-defendants would not break the chain of causation even though Rafferty ceased to be a party to their joint enterprise to inflict violence when he left the scene and even though the immediate cause of death was the drowning. …
>
> Mr Spencer relied upon a passage from the Professor's article Finis for Novus Actus? [1989] Cambridge Law Journal 391, at page 396:
>
> 'If D murderously attacks a victim and leaves him for dead, when in fact he is not dead or even fatally injured, and if X then comes along and, *acting quite independently from D*, dispatches the victim, the killing will be X's act, not D's, and D would be completely innocent of it. It makes no difference that [D's] act reduced the victim to a condition of helplessness so that he could not defend himself against [X]. (D would, however, be guilty of attempted murder). The analysis is not changed if D was aware of the possibility or even probability of X's intervention, *provided that he was not acting in complicity with X …'* (emphasis supplied).
>
> Mr Spencer cited the following passage from Hart and Honore, Causation in the Law (2nd edn., 1985), a passage which was approved by the Court of Appeal in Pagett (1983) 76 Cr.App.R. 279:
>
> 'The free deliberate and informed intervention of a second person, who intends to exploit the situation created by the first, *but is not acting in concert with him*, is normally held to relieve the first actor of criminal responsibility.' (emphasis added) …
>
> If Rafferty had withdrawn from the joint enterprise to assault the deceased, it seems to us there was no 'degree of [relevant] joint enterprise … still running.' …
>
> We have reached the conclusion that no jury could properly conclude that the drowning of Ben Bellamy by Taylor and Thomas was other than a new and intervening act in the chain of events. …'

Appeal allowed. Conviction quashed.

This is one of only three cases where the courts have held that the independent, voluntary intervention of a third party breaks the chain of causation.

2. Drugs supply cases: A voluntary act of self-injection will break the chain of causation between supply and death

Many cases have come before the courts over the years concerning the liability of people who, in the business of supplying a Class A drug such as heroin, prepare syringes for users or help to tie tourniquets to their arms, the user then self-injecting and later dying. An early case of *Dalby & Armstrong* [1982] 1 All ER 916 recognised the principle that in cases of unlawful act manslaughter (involuntary manslaughter) self-injection represented a voluntary act which broke the chain of causation. Supplier D would therefore escape liability for manslaughter. The principle has now been confirmed by the House of Lords in the case of *Kennedy* below.

Kennedy had supplied, prepared and handed V a syringe containing heroin for immediate injection. V injected himself and later died. Kennedy was convicted of manslaughter in 1997. His first appeal in 1998 was rejected but that decision was widely criticised on the grounds that a voluntary act of self-injection breaks the chain and thus his conviction should have been quashed. Kennedy unsuccessfully appealed for a second time in 2004. The Court of Appeal held that Kennedy and V had acted 'in concert' (as co-defendants) and thus the conviction was upheld. The House of Lords considered an appeal in 2007 and finally quashed Kennedy's conviction.

R v Kennedy [2007] UKHL 38 HOUSE OF LORDS

The Judicial Committee of the House consisted of Lord Bingham, Lord Rodger, Baroness Hale, Lord Carswell and Lord Mance. This was the decision of the Committee:

The criminal law generally assumes the existence of free will. The law recognises certain exceptions, in the case of the young, those who for any reason are not fully responsible for their actions, and the vulnerable, and it acknowledges situations of duress and necessity, as also of deception and mistake. But, generally speaking, informed adults of sound mind are treated as autonomous beings able to make their own decisions how they will act, and none of the exceptions is relied on as possibly applicable in this case. Thus D is not to be treated as causing V to act in a certain way if V makes a voluntary and informed decision to act in that way rather than another. There are many classic statements to this effect. In his article *'Finis for Novus Actus?'* (1989) 48(3) CLJ 391, 392, Professor Glanville Williams wrote:

'I may suggest reasons to you for doing something; I may urge you to do it, tell you it will pay you to do it, tell you it is your duty to do it. My efforts may perhaps make it very much more likely that you will do it. But they do not cause you to do it, in the sense in which one causes a kettle of water to boil by putting it on the stove. Your volitional act is regarded (within the doctrine of responsibility) as setting a new "chain of causation" going, irrespective of what has happened before.'

In chapter XII of *Causation in the Law*, 2nd ed (1985), p 326, Hart and Honoré wrote:

'The free, deliberate, and informed intervention of a second person, who intends to exploit the situation created by the first, but is not acting in concert with him, is normally held to relieve the first actor of criminal responsibility ...'

Questions of causation frequently arise in many areas of the law, but causation is not a single, unvarying concept to be mechanically applied without regard to the context in which the question arises. ...

In his article already cited Professor Glanville Williams pointed out (at p 398) that the doctrine of secondary liability was developed precisely because an informed voluntary choice was ordinarily regarded as a *novus actus interveniens* breaking the chain of causation:

'Principals cause, accomplices encourage (or otherwise influence) or help. If the instigator were regarded as causing the result he would be a principal, and the conceptual division between principals (or, as I prefer to call them, perpetrators) and accessories would vanish. Indeed, it was because the instigator was not regarded as causing the crime that the notion of accessories had to be developed. This is the irrefragable argument for recognising the *novus actus* principle as one of the bases of our criminal law. The final act is done by the perpetrator, and his guilt pushes the accessories, conceptually speaking, into the background. Accessorial liability is, in the traditional theory, "derivative" from that of the perpetrator.'

This is a matter of some significance since, contrary to the view of the Court of Appeal when dismissing the appellant's first appeal, the deceased committed no offence when injecting himself with the fatal dose of heroin. It was so held by the Court of Appeal in *R v Dias* [2002] 2 Cr App R 96, paras 21–24, and in *R v Rogers* [2003] EWCA Crim 945, [2003] 1 WLR 1374 and is now accepted. If the conduct of the deceased was not criminal he was not a principal offender, and it of course follows that the appellant cannot be liable as a secondary party. It also follows that there is no meaningful legal sense in which the appellant can be said to have been a principal jointly with the deceased, or to have been acting in concert. The finding that the deceased freely and voluntarily administered the injection to himself, knowing what it was, is fatal to any contention that the appellant caused the heroin to be administered to the deceased or taken by him ...

NOTE 2.6

The House rejected all of the previous arguments which had diverted the Court of Appeal away from the only real issue: that the chain of causation will be broken by a third party intervention which is free, deliberate and informed. Self-injection of a Class A drug, by an informed adult of sound mind, is an autonomous act.

The offence charged was 'unlawful and dangerous act' manslaughter, the unlawful act in question being the supply of drugs. The chain of causation under consideration therefore began with the supply. It was broken by V's self-injection and D was eventually acquitted. How can this be reconciled with *Evans* [2009] EWCA Crim 650 where, on similar facts, the half-sister's conviction was confirmed? The offence in the latter case was gross negligence manslaughter where the court had to find a duty to act. As explained earlier, the judgment is unclear as to whether the duty arose from the supply or from the failure to seek medical help. However, if the danger arose from the supply, then the *Kennedy* argument should have prevailed. If it arose from the omission, where was the original 'act' required by *Miller*?

→ CROSS-REFERENCE
The facts of *Evans* are set out in 2.2.3.

3. The common sense view—strict liability offences

However, despite the general principle that a chain of causation will be broken by a voluntary intervention, this does not appear to apply to pollution cases.

Environment Agency (formerly National Rivers Authority) v Empress Car Co (Abertillery) Ltd [1998] 1 ALL ER 481 HOUSE OF LORDS

The D company brought a tank of oil on to its premises and located it so that if the tap was turned on, oil would flow into a river. There was no proper lock or other precautions against misuse. On one occasion, the tap was turned on by an unknown third party and the entire contents of the tank flowed into the river. D was held to have 'caused' the pollution under s85(1) Water Resources Act 1991 which required proof that the pollution was *caused* by something which D did, rather than merely failed to prevent.

Lord Hoffmann:

The courts have repeatedly said that the notion of 'causing' is one of common sense. So in Alphacell Ltd. v. Woodward [1972] A.C. 824, 847 Lord Salmon said:

'what or who has caused a certain event to occur is essentially a practical question of fact which can best be answered by ordinary common sense rather than by abstract metaphysical theory.'

...

(4) If the defendant did something which produced a situation in which the polluting matter could escape but a necessary condition of the actual escape which happened was also the act of a third party or a natural event, the justices should consider whether that act or event should be regarded as a normal fact of life or something extraordinary. If it was in the general run of things a matter of ordinary occurrence, it will not negative the causal effect of the defendant's acts, even if it was not foreseeable that it would happen to that particular defendant or take that particular form. If it can be regarded as something extraordinary, it will be open to the justices to hold that the defendant did not cause the pollution.

(5) The distinction between ordinary and extraordinary is one of fact and degree to which the justices must apply their common sense and knowledge of what happens in the area.

 NOTE 2.7

1. The court took the common sense view that in the statutory context only something extraordinary will break the chain of causation. But there is one confusing complication where Lord Hoffmann said that even an *unforeseeable* intervention or natural event might not be so extraordinary as to break the chain.
2. *Empress* therefore conflicts with the general causation principle established by *Pagett* which is that the voluntary and deliberate act of a stranger breaks the chain of causation.
3. *Empress* can be seen as a policy approach to causation. The court wished to ensure that the company with overall responsibility for hazardous operations was held accountable for pollution. It has been widely criticised for bringing greater uncertainty to the law (See, eg: JC Smith in [2002] *Crim LR*, 492).

However, the Court of Appeal and House of Lords in *Kennedy* [2007] approved *Empress* in the particular context of industrial pollution and strict liability crimes.

Do children and others acting under a disability break the chain of causation?

 EXAMPLE 2.7

1. D intends to kill V by poisoning. D leaves some poison disguised as a small carton of juice on the table. D's young son X gives the carton to V believing it to be juice. V drinks it and dies.

   D has the MR for murder and commits an act that is more than preparatory for the offence of murder but D is not the one who in fact kills V. It is thought that X's unforeseeable intervention does not break the chain of causation. It could be argued that X's act was not informed, that he acted in ignorance of the facts and that the intervention was not voluntary. The same argument could be applied to *an adult* X. Age is therefore immaterial.
2. D orders X, who might be a child or mentally disordered, to administer some poison to V. Here, X is considered to be an innocent agent whose act will not break the chain between D and V.

To summarise so far, the chain of causation will be broken by the voluntary intervention of a third party. It will not be voluntary where the third party is acting: in the course of duty or self-preservation, in concert with D, or to bring about a strict liability offence, or is an innocent agent.

4. Medical cases

Where V's death is the combined result of D's assault followed by a deterioration in V's pre-existing health condition or medical negligence, the issue of causation will arise. Two main rules apply:

D's act need not be the only or main cause of death

The courts will hold D responsible for death even though injuries inflicted may not be the immediate or medical cause of death.

> ### *R v Dyson* [1908] 2 KB 454 COURT OF APPEAL
>
> D inflicted serious head injuries upon a child on two occasions. By the time of the second assault, the child was suffering from meningitis, the result of earlier head injuries, from which he would certainly have died. The second assault exacerbated the disease with the result that death was accelerated. Although D's conviction for manslaughter was quashed on other grounds it was considered that it was no defence to say that the blows would not have caused death but for the meningitis.

> ### *R v McKechnie* (1992) 94 CR APP R 51 COURT OF APPEAL
>
> D and two others entered the home of an elderly man and caused damage. One man hit V over the head with a chair. D further attacked him causing serious head injuries rendering V unconscious. Because of the risk of death from anaesthesia owing to V's serious head injuries, doctors were unable to operate on V's duodenal ulcer with the result that he died when it burst. It was held that the doctors' decision not to operate was reasonable and the head injuries were the significant cause of V's death. D was rightly convicted of manslaughter.

D's act need not be the sole cause of death but must be a substantial, operating and significant cause

Where D injures V, who then receives negligent medical treatment and dies, the chain of causation between D and V remains unbroken.

> ### *R v Smith* [1959] 2 QB 35 COURTS' MARTIAL APPEAL COURT
>
> This was a case of medical negligence. D, a soldier, twice stabbed V during a barrack-room fight. He was convicted of murder but appealed on the grounds of causation arguing that he was not the sole cause of death. Another soldier had carried V to the medical room but had dropped him twice. In addition, once there, V received harmful and inappropriate treatment: he failed to receive a blood transfusion which would have increased his chances of survival by 75 per cent. V

died after two hours. It was held that if at the time of death the original wound was still an operating and substantial cause, death was the result of the wound albeit that some other cause was also operating.

Lord Parker CJ:

> Only if it can be said that the original wounding is merely the setting in which another cause operates can it be said that the death does not result from the wound. Putting it in another way, only if the second cause is so overwhelming as to make the original wound merely part of the history can it be said that the death does not flow from the wound.

This principle was confirmed in the next two cases.

R v Malcherek, R v Steel [1981] 1 WLR 690 COURT OF APPEAL

M had stabbed his wife causing abdominal injuries. S had attacked a girl causing head injuries. Both Vs were put on life support machines which were switched off after medical confirmation of brain death in each case. Both Ds were convicted of murder and there were joint appeals on grounds that the trial judges in both cases had withdrawn the issue of causation from the jury. The argument was that the doctors did not comply with all necessary criteria to establish death and that, in any event, those tests were not stringent enough.

Lord Lane CJ:

> [T]he fact that the victim has died, despite or because of medical treatment for the initial injury given by careful and skilled medical practitioners, will not exonerate the original assailant from responsibility for the death. …
>
> It is no part of the task of this court to inquire whether the criteria, the royal medical colleges' confirmatory tests, are a satisfactory code of practice. It is no part of the task of this court to decide whether the doctors were, in either of these two cases, justified in omitting one or more of the so called 'confirmatory tests.' The doctors are not on trial: the applicant and the appellant respectively were. …
>
> There is no evidence in the present case that at the time of conventional death, after the life support machinery was disconnected, the original wound or injury was other than a continuing, operating and indeed substantial cause of the death of the victim, although it need hardly be added that it need not be substantial to render the assailant guilty. There may be occasions, although they will be rare, when the original injury has ceased to operate as a cause at all, but in the ordinary case if the treatment is given bona fide by competent and careful medical practitioners, then evidence will not be admissible to show that the treatment would not have been administered in the same way by other medical practitioners. In other words, the fact that the victim has died, despite or because of medical treatment for the initial injury given by careful and skilled medical practitioners, will not exonerate the original assailant from responsibility for the death.

 NOTE 2.8

1. It was held that there was no evidence that at the time of death the original wounds were other than a continuing, operating and substantial cause of death. The doctors had merely ceased artificially to sustain lives which had been ended by the original injuries.

2. It was also acknowledged that the irreversible death of the brain stem, rather than the heart, constituted the medical diagnosis of death.

→ CROSS-REFERENCE
See 2.2.3 for further
details of *Bland*.

These were not PVS cases as in *Bland* where V was unconscious but alive when life support was ended. These patients were already clinically dead when the decision to terminate life support was made. The cause of death was therefore the original injuries.

R v Cheshire [1991] 3 ALL ER 670 COURT OF APPEAL

During an argument in a fish and chip shop in November 1987, D shot V in the thigh and stomach. V developed respiratory problems in hospital and a tracheotomy tube was inserted through his neck and into his trachea. He died in February 1988. Post-mortem tests revealed that V's trachea had become obstructed by scar tissue. D was charged with murder. Medical evidence from the pathologist confirmed that the immediate cause of death was a heart attack produced by respiratory obstruction. D argued that the wounds were no longer a threat to V's life. The cause of death was the doctors' failure to recognise the reason for the respiratory obstruction. A consultant surgeon stated that the doctors had not been grossly negligent or reckless. However, V would not have died had the condition been properly diagnosed and treated.

Beldam LJ:

> Whilst medical treatment unsuccessfully given to prevent the death of a victim with the care and skill of a competent medical practitioner will not amount to an intervening cause, it does not follow that treatment which falls below that standard of care and skill will amount to such a cause. As Professors Hart and Honoré comment, treatment which falls short of the standard expected of the competent medical practitioner is unfortunately only too frequent in human experience for it to be considered abnormal in the sense of extraordinary. Acts or omissions of a doctor treating the victim for injuries he has received at the hands of an accused may conceivably be so extraordinary as to be capable of being regarded as acts independent of the conduct of the accused but it is most unlikely that they will be. … In a case in which the jury have to consider whether negligence in the treatment of injuries inflicted by the accused was the cause of death we think it is sufficient for the judge to tell the jury that they must be satisfied that the Crown have proved that the acts of the accused caused the death of the deceased adding that the accused's acts need not be the sole cause or even the main cause of death it being sufficient that his acts contributed significantly to that result. Even though negligence in the treatment of the victim was the immediate cause of his death, the jury should not regard it as excluding the responsibility of the accused unless the negligent treatment was so independent of his acts, and in itself so potent in causing death, that they regard the contribution made by his acts as insignificant.

Conviction confirmed.

 NOTE 2.8

1. In criminal cases, unlike civil cases, blame cannot be apportioned. The accused is either guilty or innocent.

2. D's acts need not be the sole or main cause of death. It is sufficient that their acts contributed *significantly* to that result.

3. A jury should not regard medical negligence as the cause of death unless the medical treatment was so independent of D's original acts and so potent in causing death that D's contribution can be regarded as *insignificant*.

The following case, being the only decision in a defendant's favour, was distinguished but not overruled by any of the above judgments.

R v Jordan (1956) 40 CR APP R 152 COURT OF APPEAL

D, an American airman, stabbed V, another airman, in Hull. V died eight days later in hospital. D was convicted of murder and appealed on the grounds that the stabbing was not the sole cause of death. V had died from an allergic reaction to an antibiotic, Terramycin, with which he had been treated to prevent infection after the wound had mainly healed. V was intolerant to the drug and although treatment was stopped it was continued the next day by another doctor who administered it in such large quantities that it resulted in pneumonia from which V died.

Hallet J:

> We are disposed to accept it as the law that death resulting from any normal treatment employed to deal with a felonious injury may be regarded as caused by the felonious injury, but we do not think it necessary to examine the cases in detail or to formulate for the assistance of those who have to deal with such matters in the future the correct test which ought to be laid down with regard to what is necessary to be proved in order to establish causal connection between the death and the felonious injury. It is sufficient to point out here that this was not normal treatment. *Not only one feature, but two separate and independent features, of treatment were, in the opinion of the doctors, palpably wrong and these produced the symptoms discovered at the post-mortem examination which were the direct and immediate cause of death, namely, the pneumonia resulting from the condition of oedema which was found.* [Emphasis added.]

The court in *Cheshire* signified that medical negligence was not an extraordinary occurrence these days. It is therefore unlikely that the unique decision in *Jordan* will ever be repeated. There were, of course, significant differences between *Jordan* and the other cases mentioned here. *Jordan* involved the positive administration of a drug not an omission. The wounds were also mainly healed but so they were in *Cheshire*. However, if V would not have died but for the medical omission in question, then surely it was grossly negligent not to have diagnosed the easily preventable cause of his respiratory difficulties? The medical cases raise a potential conflict with the *Pagett* principle that a voluntary and unforeseeable intervention will break the chain of causation. Medical negligence, it appears, is to be expected.

The question arises as to when or why the courts should use one test as opposed to the other. The exceptions to the general rule that a voluntary intervening act will break the chain of causation appear to render the law quite arbitrary and unpredictable. Read the following extract from A. Norrie, *Crime, Reason and History: A Critical Introduction to Criminal Law*, 2nd edn, Cambridge University Press, 1993, at pp 140–149:

> Because of the two-sided nature of actions as both individual and social, what appears from one point of view as a voluntary act can from another point of view appear involuntary, and vice versa. Much depends upon the focus of the enquiry … The more narrowly one analyses the various actions and actors, the more likely it is that they will appear to be discrete, self contained and autonomous phenomena. The more broadly one examines the facts, however, locating what happened within the wider context, the less an act is likely to appear voluntary. …
>
> *Smith's* victim was given 'thoroughly bad' (surely a synonym for 'palpably wrong') treatment and had a 75 per cent chance of recovery. It is hard not to say that the treatment 'made the difference' if the test of abnormality is applied. The counter-argument is that the wound in *Smith* remained an

operating cause, whereas in *Jordan*, it was more or less repaired, no longer operative and therefore only the setting in which maltreatment occurred. This argument only holds on a failure to see the facts in *Jordan* broadly enough, for it was the accused's actions that landed his victim in the hospital, and that led him to be treated in the way that turned out to be palpably wrong. The victim in *Jordan* was only in hospital receiving treatment as a result of the assault by the accused. He was only treated because of the existence of the original wound. Even if the wound had virtually healed, it was still the reason why, and the only reason why, the victim was treated. It therefore remained an operating and substantial cause of the treatment. Thus his actions were a substantial cause of death as in *Smith*, the only difference being that one must look at the former case in a broader focus in order to see it. …

In *Smith*, there is evidence of the poor medical provisions available to soldiers in a peace time medical station in Germany. There were no facilities for example, for blood transfusion, which would have been, in the court's words, 'the best possible treatment' …. In *Smith*, the court evades consideration of the intervening act doctrine entirely, preferring comfortably vague terms like 'substantial cause' in place of a straight confrontation of the argument raised by *Jordan*. Because they do this, they are forced to distinguish the earlier case as a particular one decided on its facts, which is not to distinguish it at all.

The author concludes that the 'operating and substantial' or 'significant cause' test is too vague to do anything but allow courts complete freedom to decide what will or will not break the chain of causation. This they will do on policy grounds.

?! THINKING POINT 2.6

Consider whether D is the cause of V's death in the following circumstances. Is there an intervening event or are D's acts substantial and operating?

1. D knocks V unconscious on a beach: a) V drowns when the tide comes in; b) V dies when a tsunami floods the coast.

2. D assaults V in his flat by breaking his ankles and then leaves. An hour later a fire breaks out. V cannot escape, develops breathing difficulties as a result of the fire and burns to death.

3. In a gun battle between a group of robbers and police, an officer is killed by a police bullet.

---

5. Interventions by V

There are two potentially conflicting rules:

- you must take your victim as you find him; and
- victim escape cases.

Take your victim as you find him

Unforeseeable acts by V following D's unlawful act, even suicide, will not break the chain of causation.

The law of tort has recognised the 'egg shell skull' rule for a considerable time. V's unforeseen physical abnormalities will not prevent D's liability for a tort offence. Thus, if D hits a claimant on the head with a newspaper and fractures his skull, D will be liable for civil trespass to the person under the egg shell skull rule on the basis that you should take your victim as you find him. The next case discussed applied and transferred the civil principle to the criminal law in respect of not simply physical but also psychological abnormalities.

R v Blaue [1975] 1 WLR 1411 COURT OF APPEAL

D stabbed V, a woman, in a street attack, piercing her lung. At hospital, she refused a life-saving blood transfusion for it was contrary to her religious beliefs as a Jehovah's Witness. Consequently, she died and D was convicted of manslaughter on the grounds of diminished responsibility, the court holding that the wounds were the cause of death. D appealed on the grounds that V's decision to refuse the blood transfusion was unreasonable and should break the chain of causation. The court disagreed.

Lawton LJ:

In Reg. v. Holland, 2 Mood. & R. 351, the defendant in the course of a violent assault, had injured one of his victim's fingers. A surgeon had advised amputation because of the danger to life through complications developing. The advice was rejected. A fortnight later the victim died of lockjaw. Maule J. said, at p. 352: 'the real question is, whether in the end the wound inflicted by the prisoner was the cause of death.' That distinguished judge left the jury to decide that question as did the judge in this case. They had to decide it as juries always do, by pooling their experience of life and using their common sense. They would not have been handicapped by a lack of training in dialectic or moral theology.

Maule J.'s direction to the jury reflected the common law's answer to the problem. He who inflicted an injury which resulted in death could not excuse himself by pleading that his victim could have avoided death by taking greater care of himself: see *Hale's Pleas of the Crown* (1800 ed.), pp. 427–428. The common law in Sir Matthew Hale's time probably was in line with contemporary concepts of ethics. A man who did a wrongful act was deemed morally responsible for the natural and probable consequences of that act. Mr. Comyn asked us to remember that since Sir Matthew Hale's day the rigour of the law relating to homicide has been eased in favour of the accused. It has been – but this has come about through the development of the concept of intent, not by reason of a different view of causation …

The physical cause of death in this case was the bleeding into the pleural cavity arising from the penetration of the lung. This had not been brought about by any decision made by the deceased girl but by the stab wound. Counsel for the appellant tried to overcome this line of reasoning by submitting that the jury should have been directed that if they thought the girl's decision not to have a blood transfusion was an unreasonable one, then the chain of causation would have been broken. At once the question arises – reasonable by whose standards? Those of Jehovah's Witnesses? Humanists? Roman Catholics? Protestants of Anglo-Saxon descent? The man on the Clapham omnibus? But he might well be an admirer of Eleazar who suffered death rather than eat the flesh of swine … *It has long been the policy of the law that those who use violence on other people must take their victims as they find them. This in our judgment means the whole man, not just the physical man. It does not lie in the mouth of the assailant to say that his victim's religious beliefs which inhibited him from accepting certain kinds of treatment were unreasonable. The question for decision is what caused her death. The answer is the stab wound. The fact that the victim refused to stop this end coming about did not break the causal connection between the act and death* … (Emphasis added.)

The court might have decided this case on the basis of the 'substantial and operating' test as in *Smith*, for the wounds were the operating cause of death notwithstanding V's unforeseeable decision. The decision may be correct but the 'take your victim as you find him' principle has been criticised. What if, for example, V had refused the treatment through spite? Surely, D was a factual cause but should he have been the legal cause of death? Hart and Honoré suggest that the question is not whether a particular belief is reasonable but whether a person whose life is in danger can reasonably be expected to abandon a firmly held religious belief? (*Causation in the Law*, 2nd edn, 2002, OUP, at 361). V's refusal of the blood transfusion might be seen as bad luck for D. Had it not been for her refusal, she would probably have survived and D might have faced a lesser charge. The next two suicide cases followed *Blaue*.

R v Dear [1996] CRIM LR 595 COURT OF APPEAL

D slashed V repeatedly with a Stanley knife. The attack was prompted by allegations made against V by D's 12-year-old daughter that V had sexually assaulted her. V died two days later from the wounds. D's case was that V had committed suicide by either re-opening the wounds with a blade and bleeding to death or, the wounds having re-opened naturally, by failing to take steps to staunch the blood loss. His appeal against conviction of murder was dismissed, the court holding that the only issue was whether the original injuries were an operating and significant cause of death following *Smith, Malcherek, Cheshire* and *Blaue*. It might have been different if V had acted for a reason unconnected with D's attack, such as shame at his own behaviour.

V's voluntary decision to commit suicide was unforeseeable. It ought to have broken the chain under the *novus actus interveniens* principle. In *Dhaliwal* [2006] EWCA Crim 1139 the Court of Appeal held that suicide following physical violence upon a fragile personality would not break the chain of causation. The context of the case was domestic violence.

These cases conflict with the following group of cases where V's abnormal, unreasonable or 'daft' reaction will break the chain.

→ CROSS-REFERENCE
Unlawful act man-
slaughter is discussed in
Chapter 7, 7.2.4.

Victim escape cases

If D has created a risk of harm or danger to V from which V escapes, provided the escape is reasonably foreseeable it will not break the chain of causation. Only unforeseeable escapes by V will do so. Where, however, V's reaction is unexpected or so 'daft' as to be considered unreasonable, the chain will be broken and D will be acquitted. The question of reasonableness is not determined by D's own foresight but according to that of the reasonable person.

R v Roberts (1971) 56 CR APP R 95 COURT OF APPEAL

V, a young woman, broke her ankle by jumping from a moving car. She alleged that D had made sexual advances to her and had tried to pull off her coat. D was convicted of assault causing actual bodily harm contrary to s47 Offences Against the Person Act 1861. He appealed on the grounds of causation arguing that V's escape was unforeseeable and a break in the chain of causation. It was held that V's escape was the natural result of D's conduct and was reasonably foreseeable.

Stephenson LJ:

> The test is: Was it the natural result of what the alleged assailant said and did, in the sense that it was something that could reasonably have been foreseen as the consequence of what he was saying or

doing? As it was put in one of the old cases, it had got to be shown to be his act, and if of course the victim does something so 'daft,' in the words of the appellant in this case, or so unexpected, not that this particular assailant did not actually foresee it but that no reasonable man could be expected to foresee it, then it is only in a very remote and unreal sense a consequence of his assault, it is really occasioned by a voluntary act on the part of the victim which could not reasonably be foreseen and which breaks the chain of causation between the assault and the harm or injury.

The test of 'reasonable foreseeability' was confirmed in *Mackie* (1973) 57 Cr App R 453 (where a 3-year-old boy died from falling down some stairs while running away from D in fear of ill-treatment) and the next case.

R v Williams and Davis (1992) 95 CR APP R 1 COURT OF APPEAL

V was a hitch-hiker who was picked up in a car driven by W. D was a passenger in the back seat. After travelling about five miles, V jumped from the car whilst it was moving at 30 miles an hour. He sustained head injuries from which he died. The Ds were convicted of manslaughter on the basis that they had planned to rob V and that V died whilst trying to escape. The judge did not give a complete direction on causation and subsequent appeals were allowed.

Stuart-Smith LJ:

> Where the unlawful act was a battery, there was no difficulty with the second ingredient [ie: the second identified in *Dalby*]. However, where the unlawful act was merely a threat unaccompanied and not preceded by actual violence, the position might be more difficult. The nature of the threat was important in considering both the foreseeability of harm to the victim from the threat and the question whether the deceased's conduct was proportionate to the threat, that is to say that it was within the ambit of reasonableness and not so daft as to make it his own voluntary act which broke the chain of causation. The jury should consider two questions: first whether it was reasonably foreseeable that some harm, albeit not serious harm, was likely to result from the threat itself; and second, whether the deceased's reaction in jumping from the moving car was within the range of responses which might be expected from a victim placed in his situation. The jury should bear in mind any particular characteristic of the victim and the fact that in the agony of the moment he might act without thought and deliberation.

Whether an escape is reasonably foreseeable is an objective one according to the standard of a hypothetical onlooker. Therefore, it will be no defence for D to argue that *he* did not foresee V's reaction.

R v Marjoram [2000] CRIM LR 372 COURT OF APPEAL

D was 16. He went with a group of young people to V's hostel room with whom they had a dispute. V's door was locked. There was shouting, banging, threats and the door was broken down. V was on the window ledge at the time. She then either fell or jumped two storeys to the ground, suffering severe injuries. D was charged with being part of a joint enterprise to assault V and that this had caused V to escape through the window and suffer injury. The appeal turned on the question of causation.

Rock LJ:

In a case such as the present the prosecution have to prove, as the judge directed the jury, five elements. First, that the victim had suffered injury of the kind required for the offence charged; in this case really serious physical harm. Second, that the accused's conduct was deliberate. Third, that the accused's conduct was unlawful. Fourth, that the accused's conduct must have caused or materially contributed to the injury suffered by the victim. The accused's conduct will have caused or materially contributed to the injury suffered by the victim if the injury was the natural result of what the accused said and did. The injury will be the natural result of what the accused said and did if a reasonable person could have foreseen the victim's conduct in attempting to escape as a possible outcome of what the accused was saying and doing. The prosecution do not have to prove that the accused himself or herself actually foresaw what occurred as a possibility in order to establish causation.

Appeal dismissed.

The test of causation in relation to victim escapes is based on 'reasonable foreseeability'. It raises yet another contradiction within causation. An intervention will not break the chain of causation in homicide cases unless it is voluntary, deliberate and informed. This includes drug supply cases even though self-injection is foreseeable. An intervention will not be regarded as voluntary in medical cases where the original wound is operating or substantial. In cases where you 'take your victim as you find him', an unforeseeable reaction will not break the chain, but it will do in escape cases.

S. Shute in 'Causation: Foreseeability v Natural Consequences' (1992) 55 *MLR*, at 585, questions what we mean by the terms 'reasonable' and 'foreseeable':

A second source of indeterminacy is the notion of reasonableness. If the natural consequence test is best expressed in terms of reasonableness, we need to know which conception of reasonableness is being referred to. On one view, reasonableness involves thinking and acting in accordance with right reason. Let us call this the 'idealised' conception of reasonableness. An opposing, more 'moderate' conception of reasonableness draws a distinction between the reasonable and the rational, arguing that the reasonable person cannot be expected to possess preternatural powers of judgment or self-control and, in appropriate circumstances, may be capable of thinking and acting irrationally ...

The rival foreseeability test ... is equally problematic. As with the natural consequence test, the character of the foreseeability test remains largely unexplained. What exactly must be foreseeable? At what stage should the test be applied? What difference does the addition of the word 'reasonable' to the test make? Is the test meant to be an explanation of, a substitute for, or an addition to causation?'

■ NB: Where D acts unlawfully and then commits a further accidental act or omission, the chain will not be broken. Therefore, although the ratio of *Le Brun* concerned the 'continuing act', there was no break in the chain of causation when he accidentally dropped his wife after knocking her unconscious.

➜ CROSS-REFERENCE
See 2.1.2 for the facts of *Le Brun*.

■ A finding of causation does not mean that D is guilty of the crime. MR must also be proved. In many of the cases examined, D had the MR for the offence in question but the issue was whether causation was also satisfied. Both must be established before D can be convicted.

SECTION SUMMARY

An intervening act/event will not break the chain where it is performed:

■ *in self-preservation or in the course of duty* (Pagett);
■ *in pollution cases: the common sense approach* (Empress);
■ *in medical cases* (Smith, Malcherek, Cheshire) *where D's act will be regarded as substantial, operating or significant;*

■ by V in pursuance of a physical or psychological abnormality, even where unforeseeable (take your victim as you find him) (Blaue);

■ by V's reasonably foreseeable, but not unreasonable or daft, escape from danger (victim escape cases).

?! **THINKING POINT** 2.7

Is D liable for V's death in the following situations?

1. D shoots V in the stomach. V then slits his own throat and dies within five minutes.

2. D has a violent argument with V who runs away and falls into a gutter. He is struck by a passing car and killed.

3. D injures V's finger. A surgeon advises amputation but V refuses and dies two weeks later from infection.

Causation in dangerous driving cases

The issue of causation was dealt with recently in the case of *Taylor* [2016] UKSC 5. The facts were that a driver was charged with aggravated vehicle taking under s12A Theft Act 1968 (taking a conveyance without authority). He and another man had taken a van which belonged to the other man's employer. His driving was not at fault, but when he collided with a scooter, killing the driver, he was charged with death by dangerous driving. He was found to be over the alcohol limit and also found to be uninsured.

The prosecution contended that these facts alone should lead to the conclusion that the defendant could be convicted of dangerous driving, a much more serious offence. In arguing this, they relied on *R v Hughes* [2013] 1 WLR 2462, a case in which the defendant had also driven without insurance and a licence. In this case, it was accepted that these are separate strict liability offences and that no element of fault need be proven. The defence argued that the element of fault had to be proven, as did the causal connection between the defendant's criminal behaviour and the death of the victim. A certified question was put to the Supreme Court by the Court of Appeal, as follows:

> Was an offence contrary to s12A (1) and (2)(b) of the Theft Act 1968 committed when, following the basic offence and recovery of the vehicle, the defendant drove the vehicle and without fault in his manner of driving the vehicle was involved in an accident which caused injury to a person?

The court held that a causal connection was required between the driving and the injury. This was not present in these circumstances.

The outcome of this case is that the prosecution must prove an element of fault in the defendant's driving in order to secure a conviction. The Supreme Court rejected the prosecution's argument that the necessary fault element was the drink driving. It was necessary to prove a 'causal connection between the driving and the accident'. Here, this fault came from the victim, not the defendant. The appeal was allowed.

2.3.4 Conclusion

It is generally accepted that the rules on causation are based on common sense and policy not science. They are a way of explaining why D's culpable act should be regarded as legally responsible for harm. Hart & Honoré, *Causation in the Law*, 2nd edn, OUP, 1985 at p 29:

The notion that a cause is essentially something which interferes with or intervenes in the course of events which would normally take place, is central to our commonsense concept of cause … [I]n distinguishing between causes and conditions two contrasts are of prime importance. These are the contrasts between what is abnormal and what is normal in relation to any given thing or subject-matter, and between a free deliberate human action and all other conditions … The free, deliberate, and informed intervention of a second person, not acting in concert with the first, and intending to bring about the harm which in fact occurs or recklessly courting it, is normally held to relieve the first actor of criminal responsibility. One must distinguish, however, the situation where the first actor's conduct was sufficient in the existing circumstances to bring about the harm … from that where it was not sufficient without the intervention of the second actor (… here most decisions relieve the first actor of responsibility) …

The criticism is, however, that Hart & Honoré's rules are randomly used and are vague and contradictory. It is not clear when the courts will use any particular test or what the difference is between them, if there is any at all.

A. Norrie, in 'A Critique of Criminal Causation' [1991] 64 *MLR* 658, takes issue with the individualistic notion of criminal causation:

Hart and Honoré argue that where there is a 'free, deliberate and informed act or omission of a human being' intervening in a causal sequence, the initial causal chain is negated … Hart and Honoré's position is most plausible where they draw their examples from situations in which an individual, isolated and alone, acts to bring about some effect in nature, for example, the lighting of a spark which sets a forest on fire. But even here, the picture that is presented is one-sided, for we are told nothing about the conditions in which the act occurs, or how it is perceived … This becomes clear in the crucial distinction they draw between abnormal and normal conditions. An individual is only the moral/legal cause of those events in the world that are accompanied by the normal range of attendant conditions. Where an abnormal condition ensues, it becomes the cause in place of the human intervention, which in turn becomes an antecedent condition to the abnormal element. The problem is that what is normal and what is abnormal, what is cause and what is condition, is a matter of judgment and perspective … Second, there is the question of the law's use of the concept of voluntariness. On the face of it, the idea of a new intervening voluntary act by a third party possesses a measure of solidity that the distinction between the normal and the abnormal does not. However, this is illusory since it all depends on how one defines 'voluntary.' Only a voluntary act will break the causal chain, so the act of a third party may not break the chain if it is adjudged 'involuntary.' … This, they say, 'depends in part on what conduct is regarded from a moral or legal point of view as reasonable in the circumstances,' an issue that 'raises questions of legal policy.' … A second objection stems from the first. What is voluntary may be subject to a more or less individualistic interpretation. If it is a matter of looking at whether an individual was conscious when she acted, this is a narrow focus on the individual and her mental state. If, on the other hand, it is a question of examining social or legal obligations, this locates the individual in a network of social relations and understandings, and presents a broad view of the voluntary/involuntary line. From this latter, more social view, rooting the individual in a context of interpersonal relations, it is questionable whether the voluntariness of human agency should have any particular importance at all … If, on the other hand, it is a question of examining social or legal obligations, this locates the individual in a network of social relations and understandings, and presents a broad view of the voluntary/involuntary line … Hart and Honoré reflect the individualist logic of the law which stipulates that individuals are practical actors who effectively act upon the world, who are producers of causes and consequences by their acts. Their weakness lies in their inability, like the law, to see the other side of individual agency, its inherent rootedness in social and political relations and structures. Because of this, the strength of their concepts, based upon the abstract individualist model, ebbs away when confronted with the broader context within which individuals operate … Hart and Honoré's analysis is a paradigmatic, if late, expression of Enlightenment thought. Rooted in the philosophy of Hume and Mill, it rests upon the analysis of the individual, engaging with other individuals and with nature as a self-contained monad, capable of producing effects in the world as a cause in him/herself. This is the law's approach too, but what is missing from both is any recognition of the way in which individual agency is fundamentally constructed and constituted within pre-existing social relations. It is the gap between the individual and the social that hounds the case law on causation.

2.3.5 Reform

The Law Commission's Draft Criminal Code Bill (Law Com No 177) states:

Cl. 17 *Causation*

(1) Subject to subsections (2) and (3), a person causes a result which is an element of an offence when–

    (a) he does an act which makes a more than negligible contribution to its occurrence; or

    (b) he omits to do an act which might prevent its occurrence and which he is under a duty to do according to the law relating to the offence.

(2) A person does not cause a result where, after he does such an act or makes such an omission, an act or event occurs–

    (a) which is the immediate and sufficient cause of the result;

    (b) which he did not foresee; and

    (c) which could not in the circumstances reasonably have been foreseen.

(3) A person who procures, assists or encourages another to cause a result that is an element of an offence does not himself cause that result so as to be guilty of the offence as a principal except when–

    (a) [he procures the act by an innocent agent]; or

    (b) the offence itself consists in the procuring, assisting or encouraging another to cause the result.

The exception in favour of acts/events which D does not foresee is new and wider than the current law.

SUMMARY

Actus reus

A crime consists of AR (conduct) and MR (mental element).

- AR and MR are defined by the crime.
- There is a distinction between conduct and result crimes.
- You cannot be convicted of a crime merely for having guilty thoughts.
- The AR must be proved.
- It must be voluntary or willed.
- It can include a mental element.
- It can consist of a state of affairs: status offences.
- It can be negated by some defences.

Omissions

Omissions liability concerns the commission of the AR of an offence through failing to act where there is a duty to act. Duties can arise through statute (failure to act) or in five common law duty situations:

- assumption of responsibility;
- close/special relationship;
- creation of a dangerous situation;
- withdrawal of medical treatment where there is a continuing obligation to preserve life;
- contract, statute or official position.

Causation

Causation is the name given to the search for the legal cause of a result where there is more than one potential cause.

- Factual causation: but for D's act the result would not have happened.
- Legal causation: the chain of causation will be broken by a *novus actus interveniens* which must be voluntary: free, deliberate and informed, that is: self-injection with drugs leading to death.
- An intervening act will not break the chain where it is performed:
  - ☐ in self-preservation or in the course of duty;
  - ☐ in pollution cases unless it is extraordinary;
  - ☐ in medical cases where D's act is substantial and operating;
  - ☐ by V in pursuance of even an unforeseeable abnormality—take your victim as you find her;
  - ☐ by V's reasonably foreseeable, but not unreasonable or daft, escape from danger.

PROBLEM SOLVING

1. D is driving his 15-year-old daughter, A, to school. As D approaches the school crossing A, who loves to make her father laugh, suddenly tickles D under his arm. He loses control of the steering wheel and the car rolls on to the foot of the lollipop man. D dislikes the man and leaves the car there for a couple of minutes whilst he scolds A.

2. The following week, D's wife gives birth to a baby. It is severely mentally and physically disabled, requiring 24-hour care. The baby becomes critically ill. After several days the baby's heart stops beating. The doctors do not resuscitate and withdraw artificial nutrition and hydration on the basis that the baby is never going to recover.

3. That night A threatens V, her unusually nervous 9-year-old brother, by breaking into his room and shouting. V jumps out of an upper window and breaks his arm. He is taken to hospital where a junior doctor fails to detect the complexity of the break. The arm is not set properly. It fails to heal and V dies from an infection.

Discuss the criminal liability of D, the doctors and A for the harm in each scenario.

A useful technique for answering questions involving causation (ie: 3) is to draw a chain of causation marked with potential interventions (see Diagram 2.5):

Remember:

- **I: Identify** relevant issues
- **D: Define** offences/defences
- **E: Explain/evaluate** the law
- **A: Apply** law to facts.

It is important to realise that there is no single correct answer. The point of any problem question is to allow you to explore the legal and factual issues. In this way you will develop an ability to formulate

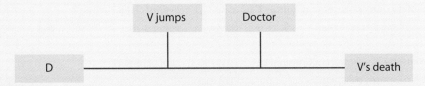

Diagram 2.5
Causation answer diagram

different arguments leading to a particular conclusion. Remember, however, that your conclusion is less important than your explanation, and your application of the law to the facts.

See the online resources for further guidance on solving this problem: www.oup.com/uk/loveless6e/.

FURTHER READING

Actus reus

A. Lynch, 'The Mental Element in the Actus Reus' (1982) 98 *LQR* 127

Discusses whether the conduct element of a crime also contains by implication a mental element.

Omissions

A. Ashworth, 'Manslaughter by Omission and the Rule of Law' [2015] *Crim LR* 563

Considers the extent to which the law should impose criminal liability on people failing to assist a friend or a member of their family where the result is death.

A. Ashworth, 'Positive Duties, Regulation and the Criminal Sanction' (2017) 133 *LQR* 606–630

Considers existing duties to act under the criminal law especially crime prevention.

C. Elliott, 'Liability for Manslaughter by Omission: Don't Let the Baby Drown' (2010) 74(2) *JCL* 163–179

Considers the potential confusion between a duty to act and a duty of care in this area of law and argues that the law should follow the approach in *R v Adomako*.

B. Hogan, 'Omissions and the Duty Myth', in P. Smith (ed.) *Criminal Law: Essays in Honour of J.C. Smith*, Butterworths, 1968

Argues that the act/omissions distinction is unhelpful and that liability for omissions should instead be based on causation.

J. Keown, 'Beyond *Bland*: A Critique of the BMA Guidance on Withholding and Withdrawing Medical Treatment' (2000) 20 *LS* 66

Critiques the BMA guidance which endorses withdrawal of feeding tubes in patients with PVS and other non-terminal illnesses, and argues that this endorsement contradicts its stated anti-euthanasia policy.

Causation

D. Baker, 'Omissions Liability for Homicide Offences' (2010) 74(26) *JCL* 310–320

Discusses these two cases in the context of whether the victim's deliberate self-injection breaks the chain of causation where the victim has self-injected.

H.L.A. Hart and Tony Honoré, *Causation in the Law*, 2nd edn, OUP, 1985

The seminal work on causation.

A. Norrie, 'A Critique of Criminal Causation' (1991) 54 *MLR* 685

Argues that the intricacies of doctrines of causation can only be understood by reference to the social and political constructs within which the criminal law operates.

N. Padfield , 'Clean Water and Muddy Causations' [1995] *Crim LR* **683**

Discusses whether liability for causing a result is clear by comparing decisions in homicide cases with strict liability pollution offences.

A.P. Simester, 'Causation in Criminal Law' (2017) 133(3) *LQR* **416–441**

Examines the interplay of causation and omissions in a practical context.

J.C. Smith, 'Liability for Omissions in the Criminal Law' (1993) 57 *JCL* **88**

Argues that causation should be the determiner of liability for omissions, not duty.

J. Stannard, 'Criminal Causation and the Careless Doctor' (1992) 55 *MLR* **577**

Discusses the decision in *R v Cheshire* on whether negligent medical treatment breaks the chain of causation.

Mens rea: intention, recklessness, negligence and gross negligence

3

KEY POINTS

This chapter will help you to:

- identify the two meanings of intention:
  - direct intent: aim or purpose; and
  - indirect/oblique intent: foresight of a virtually certain result as defined in the *Nedrick/ Woollin* test.
- understand that recklessness has one meaning:
  - recklessness is subjectively defined according to *Cunningham* [1957] as the conscious taking of an unjustified risk;
  - objective *Caldwell* [1982] recklessness, defined as failure to think about a serious and obvious risk, no longer exists.
- distinguish between recklessness, negligence and gross negligence:
  - negligence: unreasonable conduct which creates an obvious risk of harm or damage through genuine inadvertence;
  - gross negligence: an extremely high degree of negligence so as to deserve criminal punishment. It only applies to manslaughter.
- evaluate the relative merits of a subjective/objective approach to MR.

INTRODUCTION

No-one can be convicted of a crime unless their criminal conduct (AR) was accompanied by a criminal mental element known as mens rea (MR). Each offence defines the particular MR which must be proved beyond reasonable doubt in order to secure a conviction. All MR terms reflect varying degrees of blameworthiness or culpability so as to justify punishment. The prosecution will need to prove MR in relation to each element of the AR. Some offences already examined in Chapter 2 such as murder, for example, contain several AR elements, and D must have MR in relation to each one.

We say that MR consists of a guilty 'state of mind', which is usually the case with the more serious crimes requiring intention, recklessness or dishonesty. These terms represent states of mind where D will have decided or chosen to bring about a *result* prohibited by the criminal law or will, at least, have realised to a greater or lesser extent that the result would happen. But in addition, many offences also require mens rea in the form of knowledge or belief in relation to a particular *circumstance*, for example: rape, which requires the absence of reasonable belief in consent.

Gross negligence on the other hand does not represent a definable mental element but an extremely careless and unreasonable standard of conduct. Where grossly negligent conduct leads to harm, it is also regarded as blameworthy. It is nevertheless included here along with the two other major categories of MR.

Other MR terms, such as knowledge or willfulness, will be studied in Chapter 4, 'Strict, Vicarious and Corporate Liability', where they may more logically be placed as belonging to statutory offences.

It is important to note at the outset that, today, the test of MR is subjective. This means that the jury must be sure that D actually did know or foresee the result. No longer should MR be assessed objectively, that is: according to what a reasonable person would have known or foreseen.

3.1 Intention

KEY CASES

Steane [1947] 1 All ER 813—intention confined to motive;

Moloney [1985] 1 All ER 1025—oblique intention: foresight of a moral certainty;

Hancock & Shankland [1986] 1 All ER 641—the greater a consequence is foreseen, the greater the probability it is intended;

Nedrick [1986] 3 All ER 1—the *Nedrick Direction*: foresight of a virtual certainty is oblique intention;

Woollin [1999] 1 AC 82—*Nedrick Direction* confirmed.

3.1.1 Introduction

If we could represent MR and culpability in the form of a diagram, it would look something like the mountain in Diagram 3.1. Intention is the highest, and most culpable, form of MR at the top. Some of the most serious offences can only be proved by reference to intention. Recklessness is not enough. We call these crimes of specific or ulterior intent.

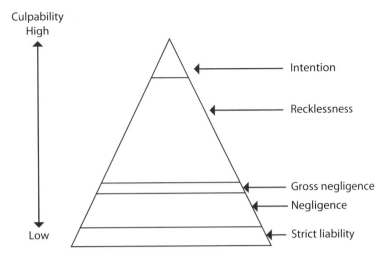

Diagram 3.1
Mens rea and culpability

Crimes of specific and ulterior intent

A crime of specific intent is one where the prosecution must establish intention rather than recklessness in relation to the AR of an offence, for example:

Murder: MR is defined as an intention to kill or cause grievous bodily harm (GBH). The AR is 'the unlawful killing of a human being'.

A crime of ulterior intent is one where MR includes an intention to cause a consequence or result beyond the AR of the crime in question, for example:

Causing grievous bodily harm with intent contrary to s18 Offences Against the Person Act 1861:

Whosoever shall unlawfully and maliciously by any means whatsoever wound or cause any grievous bodily harm to any person . . . with intent . . . to do some grievous bodily harm to any person, shall be guilty . . . [of an offence and liable to imprisonment for life].

Burglary under s9(1)(a) Theft Act 1968:

(1) A person is guilty of burglary if:

(a) he enters any building or part of a building as a trespasser and with intent to commit any such offence as is mentioned in subsection (2) below; or . . .

(2) The offences referred to . . . are stealing anything in the building in question, or inflicting on any person therein any grievous bodily harm and of doing unlawful damage to the building or anything therein.

Crimes of specific or ulterior intent must be distinguished from crimes of basic intent, second in priority in our diagram, where MR can consist of recklessness, such as criminal damage.

The overwhelming majority of offences in the criminal justice system require no fault, being crimes of strict liability or negligence, as you can see, where culpability is low.

3.1.2 Context: Intention and Murder

The discussion regarding intention generally takes place in the context of murder. The MR for murder consists of an intention to kill or cause grievous bodily harm (GBH) (confirmed in *Moloney* [1985] 1 All ER 1025 House of Lords). As the highest form of MR, intention occupies a symbolic place in the criminal law. Given that it applies to the gravest crime in the criminal justice system, you might expect it to have a relatively certain definition. Arguably, this is not the case, as we shall see. Consequently, it is a topic which has attracted much academic debate.

The alternative homicide offence of manslaughter is defined by reference to other forms of MR, the most serious of which is recklessness. The only distinction between the two offences is the mental element. Uncertainty regarding the line between intention and recklessness will therefore result in confusion between murder and manslaughter. This could lead to injustice: a defendant who recklessly kills ought not to be convicted of murder which requires nothing less than an intentional killing. The blurring of the distinction could result in an unsafe murder conviction. As you read through this section, therefore, it might help to bear in mind the question of whether the definition of intention is too wide, too narrow or satisfactory.

The Law Commission report 'Murder, Manslaughter and Infanticide' (Law Com No 304, 2006) concerning homicide reform includes recommendations on intention which we will examine at the end of this section.

3.1.3 Intention: Ordinary Meaning

In ordinary language, we understand the concept of intention to be linked to immediate voluntary actions that we mean, want or desire to do, for example:

> I intend to finish my criminal law coursework tonight.

Usually, desired actions will imply a desired result:

> I intend to work extremely hard on my coursework tonight and get an A grade.

Sometimes, we may act with many intentions in mind. Thus:

> I intend to finish my criminal law coursework tonight and work extremely hard so as to get a good grade. I can then take the weekend off before starting three outstanding courseworks which should have been finished last Friday!

We may also intend a result even though the chances of achieving it are minimal. Doubtless every football team manager says at some point that his team intends to play well so as to win the league title or some other cup. Both immediate action (playing well) and aim/result (winning) are desired and intended even if the chance of success may not be very high!

3.1.4 Legal Meaning: Type 1—Direct Intent

Aim or purpose

There is no statutory definition of intention. Its meaning has evolved through decisions of the higher courts (the common law). Intention in criminal law is defined in two ways: direct and indirect or oblique.

> Direct intent = desire, aim or purpose: *A directly intended result is one which it is the aim or purpose of D to achieve. It will usually be desired. This accords with the ordinary meaning above.*

Direct intent conforms most closely to the ordinary meaning of intention. As we have seen, in ordinary language the meaning of intention coincides with wanting a particular result to occur or having it as one's aim or purpose. See the following homicide scenario.

 EXAMPLE 3.1

I pull the trigger of a gun which I know to be loaded and aimed at the chest of a person three metres away. It is my desire to kill and death is my aim or purpose.
   I have the MR for murder: death or GBH are directly intended.

It would make no difference if the chance of success is less than certain because, for instance, I am a poor shot or the gun is very unreliable. It is still my aim or purpose to kill or seriously injure. To express direct intent in terms of aim or purpose is more certain than desire, perhaps, and connotes control or influence over the result of one's actions. One might want or desire one's national football team to win the World Cup but only the manager or team can have it as their aim or purpose and, thus, directly intend it. You should note that intention need not necessarily imply premeditation. Intention can arise without planning or forethought but it does imply a decision to act in a certain way, or an attitude towards the consequences. Direct intention therefore has a straightforward meaning and this is now a principle of substantive law.

3.1.5 Type 2—Oblique or indirect intent: foresight of a virtual certainty

Indirect or oblique intent is wider than direct intent. Under the criminal law, you can intend a result (eg: a murder) which is not your aim or purpose. This is more problematic in terms of both definition and principle. The test relates to what you think, know or foresee will happen, whether you want it to or not (see Diagrams 3.2 and 3.3). The authorities here are *Nedrick* and *Woollin*, which we shall shortly examine.

Indirect or Oblique intent = The result must be a virtually certain consequence of the achievement of D's primary purpose (objective)

and

D must foresee/appreciate that fact (subjective)

Therefore:

Diagram 3.2
Mens rea by reference to foresight

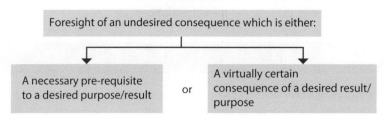

Diagram 3.3
Oblique intent

Indirect/oblique intent will apply to results caused when D acts with some other purpose in mind. An obliquely intended result is therefore a spin-off or side-effect of D's main purpose. This means that you can indirectly intend a result which is either *a pre-requisite* to the achievement of the desired primary purpose or a *virtually certain consequence* of such purpose.

Foresight of a pre-requisite result

 EXAMPLE 3.2

I live 60 miles away and drive to work each day. I wake up late one morning with only 30 minutes to get to work. In order to achieve my desired (primary) purpose of getting to work on time (A) it will be necessary to drive at 120 mph (B: a speeding offence). B is a pre-requisite to the achievement of A and I appreciate this fact.

My only desire or purpose is to arrive on time for work (A). In ordinary language, that is the only result I intend. Under the criminal law, however, I have an indirect or oblique intention to offend (B) because speeding is a necessary pre-requisite to achieving my desired purpose (A). I know this to be so and foresee that it must occur as a means or pre-requisite to the desired end.

The next example is found throughout all criminal law textbooks:

 EXAMPLE 3.3

I wish to shoot V. I see V standing in a house behind a window and I shoot him. I have a direct intent to kill V. According to the law, I also have an indirect or oblique intention to break the pane of glass between us and thus commit criminal damage. Criminal damage is a pre-requisite and necessary means to achieving my desired purpose of killing V. I know this to be so and foresee that it must first occur.

Foresight of a virtually certain result

EXAMPLE 3.4

Suppose I am late in getting up and have just over 50 minutes to drive the 60 miles to work. Breaking the speed limit will not be a pre-requisite in order to achieve my aim of arriving on time but it is a virtual certainty that at some point I will need to do so and thus commit a speeding offence. I know this to be so and foresee the offence as a virtually certain consequence of achieving my desired purpose.

In criminal law, I will be said to have an indirect or oblique intention to commit a speeding offence. Take another example:

EXAMPLE 3.5

If I give a football a hard kick with the purpose of hitting a small target in front of a very large window, it is a virtual certainty that I will break the window. To hit the target is my desired (primary) purpose which I directly intend. Breaking the window is not a pre-requisite to hitting the target but will be a virtually certain consequence. If I know or foresee the damage to be virtually certain then I obliquely intend the offence of criminal damage.

None of these examples concerns murder, but they do illustrate the oblique intent quite clearly. The point is that the offences committed in each case are inevitable. They are so closely connected to D's voluntary act that it would not make sense for D to deny an intention to commit them. This extended meaning of intention was first expressed in *Mohan* [1976] QB 1 where James LJ stated that intention meant:

> a decision to bring about, in so far as it lies within the Accused's power, [the prohibited consequence], no matter whether the accused desired that consequence of his act or not.

There have been many cases on the meaning of oblique intention since then and although the concept is now well-established a good deal of speculation still remains as to whether foresight of a virtual certainty is a separate *definition* of intention or mere *evidence* of it, a point to which we return.

THINKING POINT 3.1

Consider whether A has either a direct or indirect/oblique intention in the following examples:

1. A dislikes B and decides to run him over with his car. He succeeds in doing so with the result that B dies.

2. A, a very short person, has a quarrel with B. B is 6′6″ tall and a fast runner. A wishes to hit B on the nose.

3. A has a toothache and goes to the dentist knowing that the treatment will result in un-wanted pain. Does he intend to suffer pain? (This example is taken from *Norrie/Duff* in the indicative reading.)

4. A puts a bomb on a plane hoping to collect insurance money when it explodes in mid-air. He hopes that the crew and passengers will survive. The explosion kills all on board.

The difference between oblique intention and recklessness

Given that oblique intention extends the ordinary meaning of intention beyond purpose or de-sire, you might wonder how it is different from recklessness? Either direct or oblique intent suffice for murder but reckless killings should result in a conviction of manslaughter. This is an important distinction, not least because of the related sentences. Murder carries a mandatory life sentence whilst, for manslaughter, the sentence is discretionary, ranging from life imprisonment to an absolute discharge.

→ CROSS-REFERENCE
The relevant law
of manslaughter is
explained in 3.1.2.

Both types of MR must be assessed subjectively according to what D actually thought was going to happen at the time of the offence. However, the difference is, in theory, that whilst oblique intention requires D to foresee a *virtually certain* result of death or GBH, such risk being virtually certain to occur, recklessness is concerned with foresight of lower degrees of *risk* rang-ing from *high to low probabilities* but not certainties. Recklessness is often easier to prove than intention for this reason.

At one time, the test of MR for murder seemed to invite an overlap with recklessness. In the case of *Hyam v DPP* [1975] AC 55, for example, the House of Lords held that foresight of a prob-ability, whether high or low, of death or GBH would suffice for murder. Mrs Hyam, a jilted lover, had poured petrol through the letterbox of a house occupied by her rival and ignited it. In the ensuing fire two children were killed. Mrs Hyam claimed that she only wanted to frighten her rival although she foresaw that death or grievous bodily harm was highly probable. The problem here was that a jury might deduce that a low level of foresight was the equivalent of intention. Murder could then effectively be committed recklessly. This was not what the House had meant to convey since the MR for murder, at that stage, did not consist exclusively of intention.

However, this ambiguity was continued by the House of Lords in *R v Moloney* [1985] 1 All ER 1025. Moloney was on leave from the army and had shot his stepfather at close range dur-ing a drunken argument over which of them could load and fire a shotgun in the shortest time. Moloney had been the first to load the gun and in response to his stepfather's statement, 'I didn't think you'd got the guts, but if you have, pull the trigger', Moloney fired the gun and killed his stepfather. He claimed that he had not aimed the gun at his father and denied an intent to kill. Lord Bridge held that a jury should be directed to ask:

First, was death or really serious injury in a murder case (or whatever relevant consequence must be proved to have been intended in any other case) *a natural consequence* of D's voluntary act? Secondly, did D foresee that consequence as being a natural consequence of his act? The jury should then be told that if they answer yes to both questions it is a proper inference for them to draw that he intended that consequence.

Unfortunately, these guidelines diluted the ratio of his judgment, for he had earlier stated that:

. . . [W]here a crime of specific intent was under consideration, including *R. v Hyam* itself, they sug-gest to me that the probability of the consequence taken to have been foreseen must be little short of overwhelming before it will suffice to establish the necessary intent. . . .

The resulting confusion between the very high degree of foresight he meant to attribute to intention and the lower degree set out in his guidelines allowed for potential overlap with recklessness.

The House of Lords similarly failed to resolve the issue in *Hancock and Shankland* [1986] 1 All ER 641. Two striking miners in Wales during the 1984 national miners' strike pushed a concrete block and post over a motorway bridge with the intention of frightening a working miner into joining the strike. The driver of the taxi in which he was travelling was killed. They were convicted of murder on the basis of the *Moloney* guidelines. Lord Scarman held that:

> . . . In my judgment, therefore, the *Moloney* guidelines as they stand are unsafe and misleading. They require a reference to probability. They also require an explanation that the greater the probability of a consequence the more likely it is that the consequence was foreseen and that if that consequence was foreseen the greater the probability is that that consequence was also intended. But juries also require to be reminded that the decision is theirs to be reached upon a consideration of all the evidence.

The ratio of *Moloney* was approved but Lord Bridge's guidelines were held to be defective. The difficulty was that Lord Scarman omitted from his guidelines the need for foresight of a 'moral certainty' as *Moloney* had required. It was not until the case of *Nedrick*, which sought to crystallise the ratios of both *Hancock* and *Moloney*, that greater clarity in respect of the necessary degree of foresight was achieved.

The Nedrick/Woollin *test of oblique intention*

The next two cases are the current authorities on oblique intention.

R v Nedrick [1986] 3 ALL ER 1 COURT OF APPEAL

D poured paraffin through the letterbox of the house of a woman against whom he bore a grudge and set it alight. In the fire a child died. D was charged with murder. He denied the crime and at his trial the judge directed the jury that D was guilty of murder if he knew that it was highly probable that his act would result in serious bodily injury to somebody in the house in accordance with Hancock. On appeal to the Court of Appeal the leading judgment was given by Lord Lane CJ:

> We have endeavoured to crystallise the effect of their Lordships' speeches in R v Moloney and R v Hancock in a way which we hope may be helpful to judges who have to handle this type of case.
>
> It may be advisable first of all to explain to the jury that a man may intend to achieve a certain result whilst at the same time not desiring it to come about. . . .
>
> Where the charge is murder and in the rare cases where the simple direction is not enough, the *jury should be directed that they are not entitled to infer the necessary intention unless they feel* sure that death or serious bodily harm was a virtual certainty (barring some unforeseen intervention) as a result of D's actions and that D appreciated that such was the case.
>
> Where a man realises that it is for all practical purposes inevitable that his actions will result in death or serious harm, the inference may be irresistible that he intended that result, however little he may have desired or wished it to happen. The decision is one for the jury to be reached on a consideration of all the evidence. [Emphasis added.]

 NOTE 3.1

Rather than give a settled definition, the Court of Appeal adopted the model of jury guidelines which were confirmed, subject to one or two words, by the House of Lords in *Woollin* (see next case box) some 12 years later. The case gave rise to what is now known as the *critical* or *Nedrick Direction* (in bold type in the case judgment provided) in murder cases. There are objective and subjective parts.

■ *The objective part of the test requires that death or serious bodily harm be a virtual certainty.*

■ *The subjective part requires D to have foreseen death or serious bodily harm as a virtual certainty.*

This may appear to be clear but many questions arise:

1. What is a virtual certainty and how is it different from a high probability, foresight of which should indicate recklessness and not intention?
   In *Walker and Hayles* (1990) 90 Cr App R 226, D was charged with attempted murder having thrown V from a third floor balcony. Lloyd LJ in the Court of Appeal stated that there was little difference between a very high degree of probability and a virtual certainty and that the dividing line between intention and recklessness had not been blurred. This was somewhat surprising.

2. The test is negatively phrased: if a jury is *not entitled* to infer intention *unless* death or serious bodily harm is foreseen as a virtual certainty then are those requirements sufficient, or is something else required, and, if so, what? The test does not say. Therefore, is a jury free to decide that D did not intend to kill/cause GBH even if he foresaw that result as virtually certain? There seems to be room for flexibility. The test is therefore 'permissive' but not mandatory.

3. Does the *Nedrick* test provide a definition of intention? This depends on whether the necessary degree of foresight represents a definition of intention, or whether it is merely evidence of it. This is important because without a clear definition, it could be possible for a jury to mistake recklessness for intention and arrive at an unjust verdict, a point to which we return.

These arguments were made before the House of Lords in the next case which confirmed the *Nedrick Direction.*

R v Woollin [1999] 1 AC 82

The appellant lost his temper and threw his three-month-old son on to a hard surface as a result of which he sustained a fractured skull and died. Woollin was charged with murder. The Crown did not contend that he wanted to kill his son or to cause serious injury. The issue was nevertheless whether he had the intention to cause serious harm. Woollin denied intent. The judge directed the jury in accordance with the guidance given by Lord Lane CJ in *Nedrick*. However towards the end of his summing up the judge directed the jury further that if they were satisfied that the appellant:

> must have realised and appreciated that when he threw that child that there was *a substantial risk* that he would cause serious injury to it, then it would be open to you to find that he intended to cause injury to the child and you should convict him of murder. [Emphasis added.]

The jury found Woollin had the necessary intention; they rejected a defence of provocation and convicted him of murder. On appeal to the Court of Appeal his main argument was that by directing the jury in terms of substantial risk the judge unacceptably enlarged the mental element of murder and confused intention with recklessness. The Court of Appeal dismissed the appeal on the basis that the *Nedrick Direction* only applied where the only evidence of intention was D's actions and consequences. What that meant was that if there was objectively a virtually certain risk of death/GBH, and no indication as to what D actually foresaw, then the jury should be invited to consider that the result was foreseen as a virtual certainty and thus intended. In other cases, as here, there was other evidence (ie: that the baby was thrown in temper) and it was not necessary to give the *Nedrick Direction*. Before the House of Lords the prosecution argued:

(1) That the conviction was correct because *Nedrick* was wrong or did not apply here. Foresight was only evidence of intention and since the probability of the consequence was only one factor to take into account, it was not necessary to direct a jury in a murder trial in terms of virtual certainty. This would be limiting their discretion, contrary to s8 CJA 1967 and *Hancock*, and substituting a rule of substantive law for a rule of evidence.

(2) 'Substantial risk' was more than 'might' and the trial judge did not blur the distinction between intention and recklessness.

The appellant (Woollin) argued:

(1) *Nedrick* was right and the *Nedrick Direction* should have been given by the trial judge. Foresight in general was evidence of intent and that there was a necessary connection between foresight of a moral or virtual certainty and intention. Therefore, the conviction should be overturned.

(2) The use of the term 'virtual certainty' ensures that a jury will not confuse recklessness and intention.

Lord Steyn gave the leading judgment:

The direct attack on *Nedrick*

It is now possible to consider the Crown's direct challenge to the correctness of *Nedrick*. First, the Crown argued that *Nedrick* prevents the jury from considering all the evidence in the case relevant to intention. The argument is that this is contrary to the provisions of section 8 of the Criminal Justice Act 1967. . . .

The Crown's argument relied on paragraph (b) which is concerned with the function of the jury. It is no more than a legislative instruction that in considering their findings on intention or foresight the jury must take into account all relevant evidence . . . *Nedrick* is undoubtedly concerned with the mental element which is sufficient for murder. So, for that matter, in their different ways were *Smith*, *Hyam*, *Moloney* and *Hancock*. But, as Lord Lane emphasised in the last sentence of *Nedrick*, 'The decision is one for the jury to be reached upon a consideration of all the evidence.' *Nedrick* does not prevent a jury from considering all the evidence: it merely stated what state of mind (in the absence of a purpose to kill or to cause serious harm) is sufficient for murder. I would therefore reject the Crown's first argument.

In the second place the Crown submitted that *Nedrick* is in conflict with the decision of the House in *Hancock*. Counsel argued that in order 'to bring some coherence to the process of determining intention Lord Lane specified a minimum level of foresight, namely virtual certainty'. But that is not in conflict with the decision in *Hancock* which, apart from disapproving Lord Bridge's 'natural consequence' model direction, approved *Moloney* in all other respects. *And in Moloney Lord Bridge said that if a person foresees the probability of a consequence as little short of overwhelming, this 'will suffice to establish the necessary intent.'* Nor did the House in *Hancock* rule out the framing of model directions by the Court of Appeal for the assistance of trial judges. I would therefore reject the argument that the guidance given in *Nedrick* was in conflict with the decision of the House in *Hancock*.

The Crown did not argue that as a matter of policy foresight of a virtual certainty is too narrow a test in murder. Subject to minor qualifications, the decision in *Nedrick*, was widely welcomed by distinguished academic writers: see J.C. Smith (1986) Crim.L.R. 742–744; *Glanville Williams, The Mens Rea for Murder: Leave It Alone*, 105 (1989) L.Q.R. 387; J. R. Spencer, [1986] C.L.J. 366–367; *Andrew Ashworth, Principles of Criminal Law*, 2nd ed. (1995), p. 172. It is also of interest that it is very similar to the threshold of being aware 'that it *will* occur in the ordinary course of events' in the Law Commission's draft Criminal Code: compare also *J.C. Smith, A Note on Intention* (1990) Cr. L.R. 85, at 86. Moreover, over a period of twelve years since *Nedrick* the test of foresight of virtual certainty has apparently caused no practical difficulties. It is simple and clear. It is true that it may exclude a conviction of murder in the often cited terrorist example where a member of the bomb disposal team is killed. In such a case it may realistically be said that the terrorist did not foresee the killing of a member of the bomb disposal team as a virtual certainty. That may be a consequence of not framing the principle in terms of risk taking. Such cases ought to cause no substantial difficulty since immediately below murder there is available a verdict of manslaughter which may attract in the discretion of the court a life sentence. In any event, as Lord Lane eloquently argued in a debate in the House of Lords, to frame a principle for particular difficulties regarding terrorism 'would produce corresponding injustices which would be very hard to eradicate': Hansard (H.L. Debates), 6 November 1989, col. 480. I am satisfied that the *Nedrick* test, which was squarely based on the decision of the House in *Moloney*, is pitched at the right level of foresight.

It follows that the judge should not have departed from the *Nedrick* direction. By using the phrase '*substantial risk*' the judge blurred the line between intention and recklessness, and hence between murder and manslaughter. The misdirection enlarged the scope of the mental element required for murder. It was a material misdirection. At one stage it was argued that the earlier correct direction 'cured' the subsequent incorrect direction. A misdirection cannot by any means always be cured by the fact that the judge at an earlier or later stage gave a correct direction. After all, how is a jury to choose between a correct and an incorrect direction on a point of law?

That is, however, not the end of the matter. For my part, I have given anxious consideration to the observation of the Court of Appeal that, if the judge had used the phrase 'a virtual certainty', the verdict would have been the same. In this case there was no suggestion of any other ill-treatment of the child. It would also be putting matters too high to say that on the evidence before the jury it was an open-and-shut case of murder rather than manslaughter. In my view the conviction of murder is unsafe. The conviction of murder must be quashed.

The status of *Nedrick*

In my view Lord Lane's judgment in *Nedrick* provided valuable assistance to trial judges. The model direction is by now a tried-and-tested formula. Trial judges ought to continue to use it. . . . *But it would always be right for the judge to say, as Lord Lane put it, that the decision is for the jury upon a consideration of all the evidence in the case.* [Emphasis added.]

 NOTE 3.2

1. Use by the judge at Woollin's trial of the term *substantial risk* blurred the line between intention and recklessness and hence the line between murder and manslaughter.

2. The *Nedrick Direction* was approved subject to substituting the words 'to find' for the words 'to infer' which had detracted from the clarity of the model direction. The jury should always be told that the decision is for them on the basis of all the evidence in the case.

The *Nedrick/Woollin* test is very similar to the Law Commission's Draft Criminal Code definition of intention in clause 18(b): 'A person acts intentionally with respect to a result when he acts either in order to bring it about or being aware that it will occur in the ordinary course of events.'

The term 'ordinary course of events' would be easier for a jury to understand that 'virtual certainty'.

?! THINKING POINT 3.2

1. Under the amended *Nedrick/Woollin Direction*, do you think a father who kills his terminally ill son, who can no longer bear being in pain, would necessarily be intentional?

2. D places a bomb on an aeroplane which is timed to explode mid-flight so that he might recover insurance money. His purpose is not to kill or injure those on the plane. Does he nevertheless intend that result?

3. D plants a time bomb in a public building and gives a warning to enable the public to be evacuated. A bomb disposal expert is killed by the explosion whilst attempting to defuse the bomb. Is D guilty of murder?

4. The 'indefinable notion of intent' referred to by Professor Smith below implies flexibility in the meaning of intention. Why should a court want to avoid rigidity?

Does *Woollin* clarify any of the questions raised by *Nedrick*? J.C. Smith commented in [1998] *Crim LR* 890:

> . . . At one point Lord Steyn says of *Nedrick* 'The effect of the critical direction is that a result foreseen as virtually certain is an intended result'. If that is right, the only question for the jury is, did D foresee the result as virtually certain? If he did, he intended it. That, it is submitted is what the law should be; and it now seems that we have at last moved substantially in that direction. The *Nedrick* formula, however, even as modified (entitled to find), involves some ambiguity with the hint of the existence of some ineffable, indefinable, notion of intent, locked in the breasts of jurors.

This brings us onto the next question:

How is a jury to 'find' foresight of a virtual certainty? Section 8 Criminal Justice Act 1967

As you will have gathered from the case law discussed so far in this chapter, in a murder case, D's actual state of mind at the time of the offence must be examined to see whether he intended, either directly or obliquely, to kill or commit GBH. No automatic assumptions can be made. The test is subjective. Therefore, there will be no comparison with what an ordinary or reasonable person would have foreseen, which would be an objective test. The test is not 'what ought D to have foreseen?' It is, instead, 'What did D foresee?' The fact that a reasonable person or onlooker would have foreseen the result, when D claims that he did not, will not establish intention. Therefore, D cannot be held to have intended a result unless it can be proved beyond all reasonable doubt that it was his actual purpose to bring it about (direct intent) or he actually foresaw it occurring as a virtual certainty (oblique intent).

The subjective test was confirmed by s8 Criminal Justice Act 1967 which lays down guidance for juries on *how* to determine D's MR at the time of committing the offence:

A court or jury in determining whether a person has committed an offence–

(a) shall not be bound in law to infer that he intended or foresaw a result of his actions by reason of its being a natural and probable consequence of those actions but

(b) shall decide whether he did intend or foresee that result by reference to all the evidence, drawing such inferences from the evidence as appear proper in the circumstances.

Section 8 explains the *means* by which intention should be inferred or found from the evidence. It does not define intention. If intention is disputed by D, s8 states that the jury will need to take into account all the *evidence* in the case in order to draw an inference of (or to find) intention. Suppose, for example, D denies an intention to kill but has no plausible alternative explanation of his state of mind at the time of committing the crime. The jury will be directed to weigh up the facts and all the evidence tendered on behalf of the parties in order to infer or find D's state of mind at the time of the act. What D thought would happen as a result of his actions and the degree of risk of harm foreseen will be significant. So too the testimony of police officers, other witnesses and experts. The jury will look at forensic and circumstantial evidence such as DNA, motive, fingerprints, weapons, documentary evidence and any earlier admissions, silence or lies by D in the police station. If the evidence is strongly against D, then, despite a denial of intention, and in the absence of any reasonable explanation, the jury will be invited to draw the conclusion, or to find, that the harm was intended. The judge will *direct* the jury, who decide issues of fact, on the legal meaning of intention and on the weight of the evidence, leaving it to the jury to decide whether D's state of mind was intentional or not. Whether a result was actually intended is essentially a question of fact for the jury not the judge.

By abolishing any suggestion that the test for intention was objective, s8 Criminal Justice Act 1967 reversed the House of Lords case of *DPP v Smith* [1960] 3 All ER 161 where an objective test of intention temporarily broadened the MR for murder. D, who had stolen goods in his car, was asked to pull into the kerb by a police officer. Instead of doing so he drove away at high speed, the police officer clinging to the door of the car. D zig-zagged and hit three oncoming vehicles. The police officer was thrown off into the path of a vehicle and was killed. D denied an intent to kill or cause GBH, asserting that his only intention was to escape. Smith was convicted and sentenced to death. The House of Lords confirmed that an objective test was to apply to the question of whether or not death or GBH was intended. In other words, this question should be determined by reference to what a responsible and accountable 'reasonable man' would have foreseen. Smith's conviction for murder but not the sentence was confirmed. The threshold of culpability and MR for murder was therefore very low. That intention should be presumed without an inquiry into D's actual state of mind at the time of the crime was seen as controversial. Parliament subsequently passed s8 Criminal Justice Act 1967 which overruled *Smith*.

3.1.6 Oblique Intent is a Flexible Concept

→ CROSS-REFERENCE
For further discussion of
the *Nedrick/Woollin* test
see 3.1.5.

The uncertainty surrounding the *Nedrick/Woollin* test, (ie: the meaning of 'a virtual certainty' and the negative phrasing of the test) together with s8 Criminal Justice Act 1967 gives rise to an unresolved question: is foresight of a virtually certain risk of death/GBH a *definition* of intent or simply *evidence* of it for the purposes of murder? See Diagram 3.4. If foresight represents a *definition* of intent, then the meaning of intention is reasonably clear. A jury should be instructed

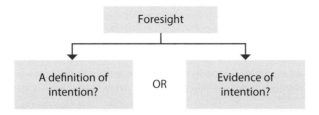

Diagram 3.4
Foresight, intention or evidence

that, if satisfied that D foresaw death/GBH as virtually certain, they must convict. They have no discretion to decide otherwise. Foresight equals intention.

On the other hand, if foresight is regarded as only *evidence* of intent, as indicated by s8 Criminal Justice Act 1967, but is not a definition, then a jury retains discretion to convict of murder or manslaughter.

Confusion has crept in because of an established rule of *evidence.* Look, for example, at Lord Bridge's judgment in *Moloney*:

> I am firmly of the opinion that foresight of consequences, as an element bearing on the issue of intention in murder, or indeed any other crime of specific intent, belongs, not to the substantive law, but to the law of evidence. Here again I am happy to find myself aligned with my noble and learned friend, Lord Hailsham of St Marylebone LC, in [*Hyam v DPP*] [1974] 2 All ER 41, [1975] AC 55, where he said, at p65: 'Knowledge or foresight is at the best material which entitles or compels a jury to draw the necessary inference as to intention.' A rule of evidence which judges for more than a century found of the utmost utility in directing juries was expressed in the maxim: 'A man is presumed to intend the natural and probable consequences of his acts.' . . .
>
> I think we should now no longer speak of presumptions in this context but rather of inferences. . . .

Then look at the two statements in bold type in Lord Steyn's judgment in *Woollin*. Is there any contradiction between them? The first appears to state that the effect of the critical direction in *Nedrick* (or *Nedrick Direction*) is that a result foreseen as virtually certain is an intended result. If so, foresight equals intention by definition. But the second statement appears to say that foresight is only *evidence* of intent because Lord Steyn remarks that *Nedrick* does not prevent a jury from considering all the evidence. It merely stated what state of mind (in the absence of a purpose to kill or cause serious harm) is sufficient for murder.

If the *Nedrick/Woollin Direction* is not a definition, then the meaning of a rather important MR concept is to be left to the jury with the risk that different juries might reach different conclusions on the same facts. This violates the certainty and predictability required by Article 7 ECHR:

> 7 (1) No-one shall be held guilty of any criminal offence on account of any act or omission which did not constitute a criminal offence under national or international law at the time when it was committed nor shall a heavier penalty be imposed than the one that was applicable at the time the criminal offence was committed.

Whether foresight is a separate form of intention or merely evidence by which intention might be established has never been satisfactorily resolved. The Court of Appeal in the following case saw no contradiction in the law:

R v Matthews & Alleyne [2003] EWCA CRIM 192 COURT OF APPEAL

Ds attacked V, an 18-year-old A-level student, on leaving a club one night. They stole his bankcard but could get no money from his account because it was empty. They returned to find him, forced him into their car, drove to a high bridge and threw him into a wide river. V could not swim and drowned. There was evidence that Ds knew V could not swim. The judge directed the jury in terms of an amended *Woollin Direction* that if '. . . drowning was a virtual certainty and Ds appreciated that, and in the absence of any desire or attempt to save him, and if they also realised that the others were not going to save him too they must have had the intent to kill'. Ds were convicted of robbery, kidnapping and murder. They appealed on the basis of a misdirection because the amended *Woollin Direction* was put by the judge as a rule of substantive law rather than evidence. The prosecution argued that *Woollin* moved away from a rule of evidence to a rule of substantive law but the Court of Appeal disagreed. It held that:

1. The law had not yet reached a definition of intent in murder in terms of a virtual certainty and Woollin should not be regarded as laying down a substantive rule of law.

2. The judge had gone further than permitted by directing the jury to find the necessary intent.

3. However, there was very little difference between a rule of evidence and a rule of substantive law where foresight of a virtual certainty, as opposed to foresight of a lesser degree of risk, was concerned. The appeal was dismissed.

Professor Ashworth said in the commentary to the case in [2003] *Crim LR* 553 that the *Woollin* formula remains a rule of evidence:

> The upshot is that a court that is satisfied that D foresaw the prohibited result as a virtual certainty may properly decide not to find that D intended that result. The court cannot find intention if D foresaw the result as less than virtually certain; but foresight of virtual certainty may not be sufficient in some cases.

The consequence of the continuing uncertainty is as follows:

1. D, a terrorist, kills by exploding a bomb in a public place giving a reasonable warning. He thinks death is probable but not certain. The *Nedrick/Woollin* test ought to exclude any D who fails to foresee the undesired consequence as a virtual certainty. But if it is merely a rule of evidence, rather than a definition, the jury has the scope to convict of murder if they think it is deserved.

2. D, a father, kills his child by throwing her from a high window of a burning building into the arms of the crowd below knowing that death/GBH is virtually certain. Again, the *Nedrick* test invokes flexibility, scope or what Professor Ashworth calls 'moral elbow room' to acquit deserving cases.

The Court of Appeal in *R v MD* [2004] EWCA Crim 1391, a case of attempted murder, confirmed that the *Nedrick/Woollin* test need only be given to juries where D does an act causing death without the purpose of killing or causing serious injury and where there is evidence that D would fulfill the criteria of the test. It is not to be given in every case in which there is doubt about D's intention.

It would therefore be wrong for a judge to direct a jury in the terms set out in *R v Royle (Mark)* [2013] EWCA Crim 1461. The case concerned the issue of whether or not, when D used severe force causing head injuries to a 79-year-old woman during a robbery, he intended GBH. If he did, then he had the MR for murder. The judge had said: 'You must be sure that [D] did not just realise that it *could* happen but acted on the basis that it *would* or that he intended that it would.' This was held to be narrower than *Nedrick/Woollin* where the relevant test is one of foresight of a *virtual* not an absolute certainty. The *Direction* may have been beneficial to D but it was not an accurate statement of the test.

Therefore:

Intention includes:

■ Direct intent: desired aim or purpose and

■ Oblique intent as defined in the amended *Nedrick/Woollin Direction:* a result which is not desired but which is either a pre-requisite to D's primary purpose or one which is virtually certain to occur (barring some unforeseen intervention) and which is, in either case, foreseen as such.

■ The jury may but does not have to find intention using this test.

■ Whether *Nedrick/Woollin* provide a definition or evidence of intention is undecided.

Intention distinguished from recklessness:

■ A lower degree of an unreasonable risk of harm foreseen as probable or possible will constitute recklessness.

3.1.7 The Distinction between Motive and Intention

In general, the law draws a distinction between motive and MR. One may have a very good reason or motive for committing an offence but moral justification will not excuse where D intends prohibited harm. Motive is relevant to evidence and punishment and is, in general, no defence. Quite simply, the law is not interested in why you act but in whether you committed the AR of any particular crime with the necessary MR. However, despite that, motive was regarded as intention in the next case which has never been overruled:

Intention confined to motive

R v Steane [1947] 1 ALL ER 813 COURT OF CRIMINAL APPEAL

The appellant had been convicted of an offence under the Defence (General) Regulations, regulation 2A, with doing acts likely to assist the enemy *with intent to assist the enemy*. D had on several occasions in 1940 during the Second World War made propaganda broadcasts from Germany on behalf of the Nazi government. He asserted that he had had no intention of assisting the enemy but that his actions were done for the purpose of saving his wife and children from being sent to a German concentration camp. The question was whether the broadcasts were made with the intention of assisting the enemy.

Lord Goddard CJ gave the leading judgment in which he said the jury would not be entitled to presume intention if the act was done in subjection to the power of the enemy or if it was as equally consistent with *an innocent intent* as with a criminal intent, for example a desire to save his wife and children from a concentration camp. Although likely to assist the enemy, the acts were not intended to do so. The construction of intention here was a narrow one, confined to motive and desire. Steane did not want (or directly intend) to assist the enemy. He wanted to assist his family. The possibility that Steane might use the defence of duress was raised during the trial. This defence arises where a criminal act is performed under threat of violence. The court dismissed this possibility because it was first necessary to find that the conduct was intended. Similar reasoning applied in the case of *Gillick v West Norfolk and Wisbech Area Health Authority* [1985] 1 All ER 553 where the House of Lords held that a doctor giving confidential contraceptive advice to under-age young women would not intend an offence of assisting and encouraging unlawful sexual intercourse if his purpose was to prevent unwanted pregnancy and secure the best interests of the patient. The doctor's motive negated any criminal intent.

Intention corresponding to purpose

In other cases, the courts have ignored motive and concentrated on the ultimate purpose of D's actions.

Chandler v DPP [1964] AC 763 HOUSE OF LORDS

D was charged with conduct revealing *a purpose prejudicial to the safety of the state* under s1 Official Secrets Act 1911 by breaking into a nuclear base and obstructing aircraft from flying. In this offence, as with many others, intention is not specifically identified but it is concealed within the term 'purpose'. D claimed that his purpose was not to prejudice state security but to draw attention to the danger of nuclear weapons by protesting. The House held that purpose should have an objective definition. D's motive may have been political protest but this was irrelevant to whether his purpose, objectively defined as prejudicing state security, was intentional.

Yip Chiu-Cheung v R [1994] 3 WLR 514 PRIVY COUNCIL

D agreed with an American undercover agent to commit an offence of trafficking a dangerous drug (heroin). He was charged with conspiracy. Conspiracy consists of an *agreement* between two or more people to commit a crime, each possessing an intention that the crime should occur. The agent's purpose was to infiltrate and collect evidence on a gang of criminal drug dealers in which D was suspected to be involved. The Council decided that the undercover agent had intentionally committed conspiracy to traffic in heroin. His good motive was irrelevant to his intention. It therefore followed that D the co-conspirator was guilty of conspiracy.

Similar reasoning applied in *Hales* [2005] EWCA Crim 1118. D had stolen a motorcycle and had been pursued by a police car. The police caught up with him and whilst an officer was attempting to handcuff D, he and an accomplice escaped, got into the police car which still had its engine running and deliberately reversed over the police officer, who was seriously injured and who later died. It was argued on appeal that D did not desire death and his motive was to escape arrest. He therefore did not directly intend to kill. This was rejected by the Court of Appeal. If D was prepared to kill in order to escape, that was a case of direct intent. Motive and desire were separate.

3.1.8 Mercy Killings

You might think that the connection in *Steane* between intention and motive should apply to a mercy killing where a person intentionally kills for compassionate reasons. In these cases, however, the motive may be benign but the intention is not regarded as innocent because the law resorts to the conventional distinction between motive and intention. If death is the aim or purpose of acting, or if it is, at least, a known virtual certainty, this constitutes murder in the absence of a relevant defence such as loss of control or diminished responsibility. Death will be either directly or obliquely intended.

3.1.9 Doctors, Palliative Care and Double Effect

Where a doctor administers high doses of palliative/pain-relieving drugs, even if he knows it is virtually certain that death will be accelerated, no question of intent arises unless it is the doctor's purpose or direct intention to kill. The defence of 'double effect' cancels out the effect of the bad consequences by an intention to produce a good effect. We can illustrate this by the case of *Dr Adams* [1957] Crim LR 365 who administered increasing doses of morphine to a terminally ill patient who died. Devlin J explained:

> Murder is an act or series of acts done by the prisoner which were intended to kill and did in fact kill the dead woman. It does not matter for this purpose that her death was inevitable and her days were numbered. If her life was cut short by weeks or months; it is just as much murder as if it were cut short by years . . . But that does not mean that a doctor aiding the sick or dying has to calculate in minutes or hours or perhaps in days or weeks, the effect on a patient's life of the medicines which he administers. If the first purpose of medicine – the restoration of health – can no longer be achieved, there is still much for the doctor to do, and he is entitled to do all that is proper and necessary to relieve pain and suffering even if measures he takes may incidentally shorten life.

This reasoning also applied in the case of *Dr Cox* 12 BMLR 38 (cited in 'The Trial of Dr. David Moor' [2000] *Crim LR* 31) who administered a dose of potassium chloride to a woman who had long suffered from arthritis and other conditions. She died shortly afterwards. Ognall J directed the jury as follows:

> And so, in deciding Dr. Cox's intention, the distinction the law requires you to draw is this. Is it proved that in giving the injection, in that form and in those amounts, Dr. Cox's primary purpose was to bring the life of Lilian Boyes to an end? If it was then he is guilty. If on the other hand, it was, or may have been, his primary purpose in acting as he did to alleviate her pain and suffering, then he is not guilty.

Dr Moor's case concerned a charge of murder against a Newcastle GP for administering a large dose of diamorphine to an 85-year-old cancer patient who was close to death. The charges had been brought following publicity regarding Dr Moor's views on helping patients to die. He was acquitted of murdering the man on the basis of the reasoning in the earlier cases.

The doctrine of double effect received recent attention in the case of *Re A (Children) (Conjoined Twins: Surgical Separation)* [2000] 4 All ER 961 where the parents opposed, on religious grounds, a separation operation. The NHS Trust argued, following *Adams* and *Cox*, that if the surgeon's primary purpose was not to kill then death would not be intended. This was rejected by two of the three Court of Appeal judges. A doctor both intends and causes death but the intention is not culpable and the cause not blameworthy because the law permits such action where it can be justified.

→ CROSS-REFERENCE
For details of the defences see Chapter 10, 10.6.4, 'Capacity to Consent'.

The view that a doctor has the MR of murder when knowingly accelerating death is favoured by the Law Commission in 'A New Homicide Act for England and Wales?' (CP No 177, 2005). However, defences should operate so as to negate liability.

?! **THINKING POINT** 3.3

1. A doctor gives confidential contraceptive advice to a 15-year-old girl whom he knows is virtually certain to commit the offence of unlawful sexual intercourse under s13 Sexual Offences Act 2003. Does the doctor have an intention to encourage the offence?

2. A woman organises and addresses a public meeting on a highway. The meeting blocks the road and she is charged with wilful obstruction of the highway. It was not her purpose to cause an obstruction. Has she intentionally committed the offence?

3.1.10 Evaluation

Here we will concentrate on oblique intent. All of the cases in 3.1.6 were concerned to clarify and crystallise the law on oblique intention. Many questions are left unanswered:

- Why do the courts still maintain such uncertainty?
- Is intention too wide and over-inclusive?
- Is it right to convict someone of murder when death/GBH was not the purpose of D's actions but a virtually certain consequence?
- Does it matter that the distinction between intention and recklessness is still unclear and that there is potential for overlap?
- Would a narrower definition be under-inclusive?

Even though the *Nedrick/Woollin* test of intention will be rarely required, it is not hard to see why such an important concept still generates such uncertainty. Buxton in 'Some Simple Thoughts on Intention' [1988] *Crim LR* 484 is of the view that the current guidelines are workable, but that a state of 'fragile equilibrium' exists which should not be disturbed. Norrie argues that the concept of oblique intention raises questions as to whether consequences foreseen as virtually certain could nevertheless be said to be just as desired as in a case of direct intent where they are *part of the same package*. If foreseen consequences are inescapable, then they too are desired. As to whether foresight is evidence or the same as intention, this remains problematic. Judges tend to say one thing then another within the same judgment: A. Norrie, 'Oblique Intention and Legal Politics' [1989] *Crim LR* 793.

These questions are given force by virtue of the context in which the leading cases arise: murder. The courts have been concerned not only with the meaning of intention but also the dividing line between murder and manslaughter. The distinction is important: following conviction for murder a judge must pass a mandatory life sentence. Following conviction for manslaughter the judge retains discretion as to the most appropriate sentence. The maximum is life but it might, depending on the circumstances, be a short or even a suspended sentence. The difference between these two states of mind is therefore of considerable practical significance. Whether someone should be convicted of one or the other will, in a minority of cases, generate moral or philosophical debate.

The moral context

The moral arguments concern murder and the sanctity of life. If one is prepared to forsake the life of another, not purposely, but as an inevitable consequence of securing a desired aim, then perhaps one deserves the gravest punishment and moral censure that society can impose. A. Norrie identifies within the debate on intention a political tension in the role of the law between liberal ideology and social control. Thus the bomber who kills the bomb disposal officer after a reasonable warning could be convicted of murder despite the lack of foresight of a virtual certainty of death/GBH because society would feel that morally D should be censured. Read this extract at p 806:

Conclusion

The ultimate problem in formulating a law of oblique intent consistent with ordinary or common-sensical usage lies in the contradiction between the form of the law, which through doctrines of mens rea and the various excuses embodies a liberal ideology and logic of individual right and its function as a mechanism of social control wielded by a judicial elite who possess clear perceptions as to what such control requires. Law is formed in this contradictory crucible. Williams has written that 'the law on mens rea illustrates the eternal tension in the position of the judge. He is supposed to be an impartial adjudicator, applying the existing law and protecting the rights and liberties of the subject; but he is also a State instrumentality – in the wider sense, an organ of government. In general it is the second concept of the judge's role that shapes judicial attitudes on the issue of fault in the criminal law.' (Textbook of Criminal Law (1983) pp 143–144.)

In fact the law can go either way – in favour of or against liberal principles – as *Moloney's* correction of *Hyam* shows. But whichever way it goes, we should cease to see the laws as potentially founded on rationality and principle. Rather, it is the site of a struggle between separate and contradictory rationalities and conflicting aims and principles. Contrary to the orthodox view of the standard textbook writers, criminal law is constituted fundamentally as much by lack of liberal principle and logic as by their presence.

A. Ashworth in *Principles of the Criminal Law*, 8th edn, OUP, 2016 argues that a flexible concept of intention leaves a jury a certain amount of 'moral elbow room' to reflect amoral elements. This is why the case of *Steane* has never been overruled. There would be moral objection to convicting a person acting under duress. These remain debatable issues.

Intention as an ordinary concept

Is there anything wrong in leaving the meaning of intention to the good sense of the jury? Are the courts leaving the definition 'up in the air'? N. Lacey in 'A Clear Concept of Intention: Elusive or Illusory?' (1993) 56(5) *MLR* 621 thinks not, because most people have an innate sense of what terms such as intention and dishonesty mean. MR terms are invested with ordinary meaning to reflect society's values and to give the jury, representatives of society, the decision-making power rather than judges. Read this extract at p 636:

For the appeal to 'ordinary' usage has a number of discrete and ideologically significant positive attractions. Although they are related, we need for a moment to distinguish between appeals to 'ordinary' usage at large (some of which are disingenuous) and passing of the determination of a particular question to the jury, the jury to decide on its own, non-technical, 'common sense' understanding of the relevant term. In the case of the former, the appeal to 'ordinary' usage usefully underlines the familiarity and commonality of criminal law: it suggests that criminal law operates on the basis of widely shared meanings and widely endorsed judgments. It hence suppresses the idea that criminal law is hierarchical, an exercise of power, based on meanings which are imposed. So it has a powerful, subtle legitimating effect within legal discourse.

W. Wilson, writing in 'Doctrinal Rationality after *Woollin*' (1999) 62 *MLR*, at 448 agrees because by leaving it to the jury, cases of 'wicked recklessness' such as *Hyam* could be caught, where her conduct was consistent with both intending to kill and intending to frighten. A. Pedain in 'Intention & The Terrorist Example' [2003] *Crim LR* 579 argues that it is possible to include both *Hyam* and the terrorist within the definition of intent on the basis of attitude and endorsement of the outcome. He asks in what sense did Mrs Hyam not want the result to happen? Foresight of a low probability of risk need not signify recklessness if the focus is on prior moral endorsement. References to wicked recklessness are made in the latest proposals for reform to which we now turn.

Of course, the necessity for an expanded definition of intention would evaporate if the mandatory life sentence for murder were to be amended. If judges could dispense sentences to reflect the moral culpability of the crime at hand, there would be no need to tinker with the definition of MR. Justice could also be effectively achieved if defences applied to murder in a more consistent way.

You will need to decide for yourself whether academic criticism of the law is warranted. Does it help to clarify or complicate a difficult concept? In either case, you might conclude that if you have found this topic rather taxing, you are evidently not alone!

3.1.11 Reform

The Law Commission has considered the law on intention in 1989, 1993, 1998, 2005 and 2006, the latter being Law Com Report No 304, 'Murder, Manslaughter and Infanticide' (2006). Here the Law Commission recommends implementation of a proposed definition of intention first advanced in Consultation Paper No 177, Part IV, 'A New Homicide Act for England and Wales?' (2005). It is as follows:

(1) A person is to be regarded as acting intentionally with respect to a result when he or she acts in order to bring it about.

(2) In the rare case where the simple direction in clause (1) is not enough, the jury should be directed that:

they are not entitled to find the necessary intention with regard to a result unless they are sure that the result was a virtual certainty (barring some unforeseen intervention) as a result of D's actions and that the defendant appreciated that such was the case.

(3) In any case where D's chance of success in his or her purpose of causing some other result is relevant, the direction in clause (2) may be expanded by the addition of the following phrase at the end of the clause (2) direction:

or that it would be if he or she were to succeed in his or her purpose of causing some other result, and that D appreciated that such was the case.

Two examples are given where the expanded definition would be required.

V attempts to stop D from stealing a car and leaps on to the bonnet. D drives off, accelerating and V falls off and is killed. D claims he did not intend to kill V or to cause serious injury but simply wanted to escape.

D is jogging along a narrow path that follows a cliff edge. V is walking ahead. D wantonly barges V over the cliff rather than asking that he step aside. V is killed. D was not concerned with whether V lived or died.

In both, D displays homicidal or murderous disregard for human life.

A. Norrie in 'Between Orthodox Subjectivism and Moral Contextualism' [2005] *Crim LR* 497 criticises the definition of intention recommended by the Law Commission. He states that the definition and the consultation document from which it derived adopts a theoretical structure in which the mandatory life sentence for murder is 'totemic' (at 487). What he means is that the proposals work around the existing mandatory life sentence rather than call for its abolition for

→ CROSS-REFERENCE
For a detailed look at the homicide provisions see Chapter 6.

different categories of case or for the creation of more defences for murder such as duress and necessity. It combines both a subjectivist and moral contextual approach. However, he points out that the proposals disclose an inconsistency between the view that the father who throws a child from a burning building would be excluded from intention through use of the proviso yet doctors would be caught and should claim the benefit of a defence, especially when justificatory defences, such as necessity, were excluded from the paper. Further, by continuing to use the word purpose, juries will confuse it with motive. Read the following extract:

Defining intention

The Law Commission develop two positions on intention in Pt 4, one based upon previous Commission attempts to establish a clear definition, the other based upon the existing common law approach established in *Nedrick* and *Woollin*. Most of the work has gone into the former of these two approaches, though the Commission state that it sees competing values in both. While the definitional approach has the attraction of certainty, it has the disadvantage of rigidity. While the common law approach allows for flexibility and 'moral elbow room', it has the countervailing disadvantage of a lack of certainty (para. 4.1). Overall, however, the discussion is coloured by one major issue, the relationship between a cognitivist account of the mental state of intention and the moral work it must do in the law of murder . . .

The common law approach

The second approach is based upon the existing case law, and in particular the failure to provide a common law definition of intention. Instead of providing such, the drift of the cases from *Moloney* onwards has been towards the creation and refinement of a set of guidelines to a jury as to when it may find intention. In its post-*Woollin* form this involves the notion that a jury is not entitled to find intention unless they feel sure that:

> death or serious bodily harm was a virtual certainty (barring some unforeseen intervention) as a result of D's actions, and D appreciated that such was the case (*Nedrick*, as amended, para. 4.64).

The second Law Commission proposal takes this formula up without alteration as a means of finding indirect intent, while direct intent is defined, as in the definitional approach, as acting in order to bring a result about. The argument in support of this approach is that it takes all the strain out of the first proposal. The fact-finder is not required to reach a particular conclusion, but is permitted 'the freedom to find, or not to find, intent, in the way the common law does at present' (para. 4.65), and it therefore avoids 'creating the difficulty which calls for the development of a proviso' (para. 4.66).

In a sense there is nothing new here, and therefore perhaps less to discuss. However, it is worth thinking about the precise status of the 'entitled to find' formula within the law. The Law Commission clearly think that this formula is the means whereby 'moral elbow room' is permitted in the law, but I wonder whether this is really the case. It is true that the cases culminating in *Woollin* and *Matthews and Alleyne* have as their direct ancestor Lord Scarman's observations in favour of a jury's judgment in the earlier *Hancock and Shankland*, but is it the case that this formula makes a genuine moral difference in subsequent cases? . . . in the trial of Dr Moor, a case of injecting drugs which would have the anticipated effect of shortening life, it is reported that the trial judge finessed the issue by instructing the jury in terms of two alternatives, one based on direct intention, the other on recklessness, avoiding consideration of the virtual certainty formula and the possibility of the jury being 'entitled to find' intention. In other cases involving doctors who kill, the formula of 'primary purpose' and the possibility of double effect have been called into service rather than 'entitled to find', though admittedly these cases predate *Woollin* and much of the speculation about how the law works. There is nonetheless an element of speculation in academic writing as to how, or if, 'entitled to find' works, though this is aligned with appreciation of a real problem in the law: that it needs to find a way to deal with cases involving 'good motive'. Academics have put two and two together, but I am unsure that the judges have said that this makes four.

SECTION SUMMARY

- *Intention is the only type of MR required by crimes of specific or ulterior intent. It has two meanings: direct and indirect/oblique.*
- *A directly intended result is the desired aim/purpose of D.*
- *An obliquely intended result is not desired but is one which is:*
  - □ *a pre-requisite or condition to the achievement of D's purpose; or*
  - □ *a virtually certain result of D's primary purpose for acting and which he knows or foresees will occur as a virtual certainty.*
- *The test of intention is subjective by virtue of s8 Criminal Justice Act 1967.*
- *Intention is distinct from motive but recall* Steane.
- *Doctors acting with good motives who kill will either have no intention (Steane) or an innocent intent.*

3.1.12 Transferred Malice

Where D's MR for one crime causes the AR of the same crime but either mistakenly or accidentally causes an unintended consequence, MR can be transferred. For example, A intends to kill B and sets out to do so but mistakenly attacks and kills C instead. The mistaken identity of C makes no difference because the requirements of the offence of murder are satisfied: the intentional killing of a live person. The intention or malice with which the act was performed is transferred to the actual, albeit mistaken, victim of the murder. Therefore, provided MR required by the offence definition exists, it can be transferred.

Malice can only be transferred within the same offence. Suppose that in attacking C, A intended to kill or cause GBH and threw a brick at him which missed C and went straight through a nearby window. The intention to kill or cause GBH to C could not be transferred to criminal damage. There is no equivalence between the MR for murder (intention to kill or cause GBH) and criminal damage (intention or recklessness to damage/destroy property) and thus no transference is possible.

→ CROSS-REFERENCE
The homicide aspect of this case is considered in Chapter 6, 6.1.3.

The case of *Attorney-General's Reference (No 3 of 1994)* concerned the issue of whether intention to seriously injure a pregnant woman could be transferred to her premature child born alive but which then died after a short period of time:

Attorney-General's Reference (No 3 of 1994) [1997] UKHL 31, [1998] AC 245

D, the boyfriend of a young woman who was 22–24 weeks' pregnant, quarrelled with her and stabbed her in the face, back and abdomen with a long-bladed kitchen knife. He intended to cause GBH. The mother survived but gave birth 17 days later. The baby (S) was born alive but grossly premature. S lived for 121 days but then died from bronchial infection as a result of prematurity. D had been sentenced to four years' imprisonment for wounding the mother with intent to cause GBH. Following the baby's death, he was charged with murder and pleaded not guilty. At his trial a submission was advanced that on the evidence no criminal offence relating to the baby was proved. The judge ruled in his favour and the prosecution appealed. The Court of Appeal held that the foetus was as much a part of the mother's body as an arm and a leg. An intent to injure her was, therefore, an intent to injure the foetus. D appealed to the House of Lords:

Lord Mustill:

What explanation is left: for explanation there must be, since the 'transferred malice' concept is agreed on both sides to be sound law today? The sources in more recent centuries are few. Of the two most frequently cited the earlier is *R. v. Pembliton* (1874) L.R. 2 C.C.R. 119. In the course of a fight D threw a stone at others which missed and broke a window. He was indicted for that he 'unlawfully and maliciously did commit damage, injury, and spoil upon a window . . .' The jury found that he did not intend to break the window. On a case stated to the Court for Crown Cases Reserved it was argued for the prosecution that 'directly it is proved that he threw the stone . . . without just cause, the offence is established.' The ancient origins of this argument need no elaboration, and indeed the report of the argument as it developed showed that it was based on a conception of general malice . . . The conviction was quashed. [Blackburn J (at 122) was quoted where he said that if D had been reckless as to damaging the window the conviction might have been sound but he was not.]

This decision was distinguished in *R. v. Latimer* (1886) 17 Q.B.D. 359. Two men quarrelled in a public house. One of them struck at the other with his belt. The glancing blow bounced off and struck the prosecutrix, wounding her severely. The assailant was prosecuted and convicted for having unlawfully and maliciously wounded her, contrary to section 20 of the Offences Against the Person Act 1861. Counsel for D relied on *Pembliton*. In his judgment Lord Coleridge C.J. said, at p. 361,

'It is common knowledge that a man who has an unlawful and malicious intent against another, and, in attempting to carry it out, injures a third person, is guilty of what the law deems malice against the person injured, because the person is doing an unlawful act, and has that which the judges call general malice, and that is enough.'

. . .

My Lords, I find it hard to base a modern law of murder on these two cases. The court in *Latimer* was, I believe, entirely justified in finding a distinction between their statutory backgrounds and one can well accept that the answers given, one for acquittal, the other for conviction, would be the same today. But the harking back to a concept of general malice, which amounts to no more than this, that a wrongful act displays a malevolence which can be attached to any adverse consequence, has long been out of date. And to speak of a particular malice which is 'transferred' simply disguises the problem by idiomatic language. D's malice is directed at one objective, and when after the event the court treats it as directed at another object it is not recognising a 'transfer' but creating a new malice which never existed before. As Dr. Glanville Williams pointed out (*Criminal Law*, the General Part 2nd Ed. (1961), p. 184) the doctrine is 'rather an arbitrary exception to general principles.' Like many of its kind this is useful enough to yield rough justice, in particular cases, and it can sensibly be retained notwithstanding its lack of any sound intellectual basis. But it is another matter to build a new rule upon it . . .

My Lords, the purpose of this enquiry has been to see whether the existing rules are based on principles sound enough to justify their extension to a case where D acts without an intent to injure either the foetus or the child which it will become. In my opinion they are not. To give an affirmative answer requires a double 'transfer' of intent: first from the mother to the foetus and then from the foetus to the child as yet unborn. Then one would have to deploy the fiction (or at least the doctrine) which converts an intention to commit serious harm into the mens rea of murder. For me, this is too much. If one could find any logic in the rules I would follow it from one fiction to another, but whatever grounds there may once have been have long since disappeared. I am willing to follow old laws until they are overturned, but not to make a new law on a basis for which there is no principle.

Moreover, even on a narrower approach the argument breaks down. The effect of transferred malice, as I understand it, is that the intended victim and the actual victim are treated as if they were one, so that what was intended to happen to the first person (but did not happen) is added to what actually did happen to the second person (but was not intended to happen), with the result that what was intended and what happened are married to make a notionally intended and actually consummated crime. The cases are treated as if the actual victim had been the intended victim from the start. To make any sense of this process there must, as it seems to me, be some compatibility between the original intention and the actual occurrence, and this is, indeed, what one finds in the cases. There is no such compatibility here. D intended to commit and did commit an immediate crime of violence to the mother. He committed no relevant violence to the foetus, which was not a person, either at the time or in the future, and intended no harm to the foetus or to the human person which it would become. If fictions are useful, as they can be, they are only damaged by straining them beyond their limits. I would not overstrain the idea of transferred malice by trying to make it fit the present case.... [Emphasis added.]

 NOTE 3.3

1. Lord Mustill went on to dismiss the application of transferred malice to the offence of unlawful act manslaughter for the same reasons he had dismissed it to murder. However, given that unlawful act manslaughter does not require the act to be directed towards V, he thought that problems of transferred malice could be avoided by substituting causation. D had caused the death of the child by the unlawful and dangerous attack on the mother.

2. If this is right, the decision of the trial judge (that there was no offence because the violence must be directed towards another person and the foetus is not a person) was wrong. The Court of Appeal had also been wrong to see the foetus as an integral part of the mother.

There is no concept of 'general malice' which would make D guilty of every type of prohibited harm resulting from his actions. He will only be responsible for accidental harm where the MR of the offence committed is satisfied by the intention accompanying the preceding act so that it can be transferred from one intentional result to another.

?! **THINKING POINT** 3.4

1. Which two cases were cited by Lord Mustill with reference to transferred malice?
2. Which provided authority for the doctrine?
3. Did Lord Mustill approve of the doctrine of transferred malice?
4. Is transferred malice necessary to convict a terrorist who kills by exploding a bomb?
5. Why did Lord Mustill not apply the doctrine of transferred malice in this case?

There are arguments for and against the doctrine of transferred malice. The most contentious issue is what is called 'remoteness'. Consider the example below:

 EXAMPLE 3.6

D strikes a match whilst sitting in a library in order to burn a small piece of paper. The whole box of matches explodes and the vibrations cause a nearby priceless sculpture to fall from its pedestal and shatter.

D's intended offence is criminal damage. However, both damage and means are unintentional. Should there be full liability for criminal damage, or an attempt, or no liability at all on the basis that liability was too remote? There is no real agreement on this.

Reform: The draft Criminal Law Bill, clause 32 confirms that intention or awareness can be transferred within offences, including defences.

3.2 Recklessness

KEY CASES

Cunningham [1957] 2 QB 396—subjective recklessness: the conscious taking of an unreasonable risk;

Parker [1977] 1 WLR 600—subjective recklessness includes closing one's mind to risk;

Caldwell [1982] AC 341—objective recklessness: where D fails to think about a serious and obvious risk of harm;

Elliott v C [1983] 77 Cr App R 103—objective recklessness takes no account of inability to foresee risk;

R v G [2003] UKHL 50—objective recklessness abolished.

3.2.1 Introduction

Recklessness = Unreasonable risk-taking:

◼ **Subjective or Advertent Recklessness:** *Cunningham* **Recklessness**

This is the current test, defined as the conscious (or advertent) taking of an unjustified or unreasonable risk of harm.

Recklessness is concerned with causing harm through taking risks. In the hierarchy of MR, recklessness is second only to intention, but is not as culpable. It appears in offences ranging in gravity from manslaughter at the top end of the scale to criminal damage and a range of statutory offences at the bottom. Here we shall examine recklessness relating to *results*, for example, criminal damage or personal injury, as opposed to the reckless disregard of *circumstances or conduct*. For instance, recklessness can be used in an offence as a description of conduct, such as reckless driving. You can *intend* to drive recklessly but you cannot be both intentional and reckless in relation to *results*. The two mental states are quite different.

Offences involving recklessness are called offences of *basic intent*. We can contrast them with offences requiring proof of intention alone which are called offences of *specific* or *ulterior* intent. Recklessness can be distinguished from intention in that the latter is defined as aim or purpose (direct intent) or requires foresight as to a virtually certain result (oblique intent) whereas recklessness is concerned with foresight of probabilities, that is: lower degrees of risk.

A *basic intent offence* is an offence requiring proof of either recklessness or intention. This means that in reality the prosecution need only prove recklessness which will usually be less onerous than proof of intention, for example:

Criminal Damage Act 1971

'1. **Destroying or damaging property**

 (1) A person who without lawful excuse destroys or damages any property belonging to another intending to destroy or damage any such property or being reckless as to whether any such property would be destroyed or damaged shall be guilty of an offence.

 (2) A person who without lawful excuse destroys or damages any property, whether belonging to himself or another –

 (a) intending to destroy or damage any property or being reckless as to whether any property would be destroyed or damaged; and

 (b) intending by the destruction or damage to endanger the life of another or being reckless as to whether the life of another would be thereby endangered; shall be guilty of an offence.

 (3) An offence committed under this section by destroying or damaging property by fire shall be charged as arson.'

Common Assault

Any act by which D, intentionally or recklessly, causes V to apprehend immediate and unlawful personal violence.

Between 1982 and 2003 recklessness was defined both *subjectively* (*Cunningham* recklessness) and *objectively* (*Caldwell* recklessness), but each applied to different offences. Recklessness now has only one meaning and is *subjectively* assessed. The House of Lords in *R v G* [2003] UKHL 50 abolished objective recklessness.

3.2.2 The Ordinary Meaning of Recklessness

Creating a risk of harm without thinking

Most people would consider a person to be reckless when he acts without thinking, perhaps with a lack of care or indifference to the risk of causing harm to another's safety or property. Such a person may be impulsive, angry or intoxicated and thus not immediately aware of any immediate risk. Provided they were, apart from their behaviour, otherwise normal individuals, we would probably think them reckless if they ought to have known better. We might also apply the terms 'thoughtless', 'stupid', 'callous' to a person who acts with disregard for the interests of other people. In ordinary language therefore recklessness refers both to being aware and being unaware of causing an unreasonable risk of harm to somebody else. The legal definition is, however, narrower and is confined to subjective awareness.

3.2.3 The Current Legal Definition: Subjective Recklessness

The conscious taking of an unjustified risk

Unreasonable risks: Recklessness in the legal sense is concerned with unreasonable risk-taking. Today, it is assessed subjectively, as is intention, and is confined to the conscious taking of an unjustified risk of harm. This means that to be reckless, one needs to be *aware* of an *unreasonable* risk of harmful consequences.

Whether a risk is unreasonable involves a value judgement. Many areas of life require us to take risks. Everyday activities involve a routine risk-assessment exercise of which we are barely aware: crossing a busy road for example. Others in which we engage less often require a more conscious assessment in which we weigh up the risk and compare it to the rewards. Travel, sport, or surgery, for example, may carry a small risk but if we figure that the benefit outweighs the risk, then it is a risk worth taking. The risks we choose to assume and which are incidental to everyday living are justifiable and perfectly reasonable because they have social value, even where the risk of harm is high. It is not until risk-taking loses its social value or utility that we would call it unreasonable. It will always be unreasonable and seldom justifiable to take a risk with another's personal safety or property.

You may have acted recklessly in the current legal sense of the word when, for example, overtaking on the road in risky circumstances, *conscious* that you may be endangering safety or property. If you know that you are taking an unreasonable risk, you are subjectively reckless.

Foresight: Foresight is an essential element of subjective recklessness, just as it is with oblique intention. The risk of harm may be high or low but provided D perceives or foresees some degree of risk then he will be reckless. The type of harm in relation to which recklessness must be proved depends on the offence definition.

Objective *Caldwell* recklessness, which applied to some important offences between 1982 and 2003, concerned the *unconscious/inadvertent* creation of a serious and obvious risk of harm. One could be objectively reckless even though completely unaware of any risk created. This caused injustice and gave rise to a great deal of criticism. It now no longer exists.

?! THINKING POINT 3.5

List the AR/MR elements of criminal damage and assault defined earlier.

Is the interpretation of recklessness clear (ie subjective/objective)?

D slams a shop door so hard on leaving a shop that the plate glass window shatters. Identify his state of mind in the following:

a. he wanted the window to break;

b. he did not want it to break but knew damage was virtually certain;

c. he thought it probable that the window would break;

d. He was unaware of any risk of damage.

You will probably have known that the first three examples were descriptions of a) direct intent, b) oblique intent and c) subjective recklessness. The answer to d) is that today D would not be reckless and would be innocent of criminal damage. Until the House of Lords decision in *R v G* [2003] UKHL 50 however, D would have been considered objectively reckless and guilty. This is the leading case on subjective recklessness:

R v Cunningham [1957] 2 QB 396 COURT OF APPEAL

A building had been divided into two. D's prospective mother in law lived in one part and D and his future wife were to live in the other. He one day entered the cellar of the empty part, wrenched a coin-operated gas meter away from a coal-gas pipe to steal the money inside, and caused the pipe to fracture. Gas escaped and seeped through the cellar wall into the adjoining part of the house where it was inhaled by a sleeping woman who was partially suffocated. D was charged under s23 Offences Against the Person Act 1861 where MR was defined, not as recklessness, but as *maliciously*:

> Whosoever shall unlawfully and maliciously administer to or cause to be administered a noxious thing, so as thereby to endanger the life of such person, or so as thereby to inflict upon such person any grievous bodily harm, shall be guilty of felony . . .

D did not give evidence at his trial but the judge told the jury that he must have known the gas would escape to the neighbouring house. On the meaning of 'maliciously' the judge directed the jury to find D guilty if he had acted in such a way as to be wicked. D was convicted and appealed.

The Court of Appeal adopted a subjective approach to MR and asked two questions:

1. Did D foresee the possibility of the harmful consequences? A person may be held liable if he foresaw any degree of risk however slight.

2. Was it unjustifiable or unreasonable for D to take the risk?

If D did perceive or foresee the possibility of harm then he would be reckless even though he assessed the risk of harm as small. Whether the risk is reasonable or unreasonable will require an objective assessment and the jury will lay down the required standard of care. It will depend on the social utility of the activity. Taking a known risk with another person's body or property is not justifiable.

The court overruled the judge's direction on the interpretation of maliciousness, approving an earlier definition. It stated that in any statutory definition of a crime 'maliciously' should be defined as requiring either:

1. An actual intention to do the particular harm that was done or

2. Recklessness as to whether such harm should occur or not.

Byrne J said: 'In our opinion the word "maliciously" in a statutory crime postulates foresight of the consequences'.

Following *Cunningham*, the courts decided that a D who *deliberately closes his mind* to risk could be considered subjectively reckless:

R v Parker (Daryl) [1977] 1 WLR 600

D, in a fit of temper, broke a telephone by smashing the handset violently down on to a telephone unit. He was convicted under s1(1) Criminal Damage Act 1971. The Court of Appeal held that a man is reckless in the sense required when he carries out a deliberate act knowing or closing his mind to the obvious fact that there is some risk of damage resulting from that act but nevertheless continues in the performance of that act. Lane LJ:

He [Parker] was well aware, of course, of the degree of force which he was using – a degree described by (Defence Counsel) before us as slamming the receiver down and a demonstration by (Defence Counsel), whether wittingly or not, was given of a hand brought down from head height on to whatever the receiving object was.

In those circumstances, it seems to this court that if he did not know, as he said he did not, that there was some risk of damage, he was, in effect, deliberately closing his mind to the obvious – the obvious being that damage in these circumstances was inevitable. In the view of this court, that type of action, that type of deliberate closing of the mind, is the equivalent of knowledge and a man certainly cannot escape the consequences of his action in this particular set of circumstances by saying, 'I never directed my mind to the obvious consequences because I was in a self-induced state of temper.'

The rationale was to draw a distinction between culpable inadvertence and mere negligence or oversight. Reasons for culpable inadvertence would be intoxication, anger, impulsiveness and an attitude of indifference, for example, any of which might suppress an inconvenient, and more conscientious, appreciation of risk. Provided the defendant was otherwise capable of appreciating the risk of his actions, there would be no reason for excusing him from the consequences.

?! THINKING POINT 3.6

1. If Mr Cunningham had failed to think about any risk to others would he have been reckless?
2. After Parker, would Cunningham have been considered subjectively reckless if he had failed to think of any risk because he was impulsive or angry?
3. Would you re-consider your answer if he genuinely did not think there was any risk, for some innocent reason or through carelessness?

Subjectivity takes account of individual characteristics

A subjective approach to MR means that account can be taken of D's individual characteristics. Therefore if D's ability to perceive a risk is less than that of a reasonable person, a subjective approach will be fairer. The next case demonstrates the justice of this approach.

R v Stephenson [1979] 1 QB 695 COURT OF APPEAL

The appellant crawled into a hollow in the side of a large haystack and, feeling cold, lit a small fire which got out of control and damaged the hay at a value of £3,500. He was charged with arson contrary to s1(1) Criminal Damage Act 1971.

D was convicted on the grounds that he had 'closed his mind' to the obvious risk of fire. However, he was a schizophrenic and the judge held that his schizophrenia was the reason why he had closed his mind to the risk. He was therefore reckless. The Court of Appeal allowed his appeal and overturned the conviction. Schizophrenia was, on the evidence, something which might have prevented the idea of danger even entering the appellant's mind at all. Even if he had stopped to think about the risk it is possible that his condition would have prevented him from being aware of it.

Lord Lane:

What then must the prosecution prove in order to bring home the charge of arson in circumstances such as the present? They must prove that (1) D deliberately committed some act which caused the damage to property alleged or part of such damage; (2) D had no excuse for causing the damage; these two requirements will in the ordinary case not be in issue; (3) D either (a) intended to cause the damage to the property, or (b) was reckless as to whether the property was damaged or not. A man is reckless when he carries out the deliberate act appreciating that there is a risk that damage to property may result from his act. It is however not the taking of every risk which could properly be classed as reckless. The risk must be one which it is in all the circumstances unreasonable for him to take.

Proof of the requisite knowledge in the mind of D will in most cases present little difficulty. The fact that the risk of some damage would have been obvious to anyone in his right mind in the position of D is not conclusive proof of D's knowledge, but it may well be and in many cases doubtless will be a matter which will drive the jury to the conclusion that D himself must have appreciated the risk. The fact that he may have been in a temper at the time would not normally deprive him of knowledge or foresight of the risk. If he had the necessary knowledge or foresight and his bad temper merely caused him to disregard it or put it to the back of his mind not caring whether the risk materialised, or if it merely deprived him of the self-control necessary to prevent him from taking the risk of which he was aware, then his bad temper will not avail him. This was the concept which the court in R. v Parker (Daryl) [1977] 1 W.L.R. 600, 604 was trying to express when it used the words 'or closing his mind to the obvious fact that there is some risk of damage resulting from that act . . . ' [Emphasis added.]

The Criminal Damage Act 1971 had replaced the Malicious Damage Act 1861, where MR had been defined as 'maliciously'. Recklessness was not defined in the new Act but the Court of Appeal in *Stephenson* gave it the same subjective interpretation as 'maliciously' under the previous legislation, that is: foresight of a risk of damage.

?! THINKING POINT 3.7

D borrows X's mobile phone to make an urgent call. The phone has run out of credit. D slams down the phone so hard on a table that it breaks.

1. What offence would D be charged with?
2. Would he be considered reckless if the reason for his conduct was:
   a. to see how much force the phone could withstand?
   b. temper or impulse?
   c. momentary distraction?
   d. young age or mental incapacity?

SECTION SUMMARY

- *Recklessness is concerned with unreasonable risk-taking.*
- *It is a definition of MR found in crimes of basic intent.*
- *Subjective recklessness is now the only type of recklessness following R v G.*
- *Liability depends on foresight: the conscious taking of an unjustified risk.*
- *Not all unconscious risk-takers will be acquitted if they have closed their minds to the risk of harm* (Parker).
- *This will ensure the conviction of those who are culpable but not the negligent risk-taker.*

Two years later, *Stephenson* was overturned by the House of Lords in *Caldwell*, which abolished subjective recklessness in criminal damage.

3.2.4 *Caldwell* Recklessness: 1982–2003

This type of recklessness no longer exists and was overruled in 2003 by the House of Lords in *R v G*. It was a controversial area of law and is explained here to assist you to understand why it had to change.

R v Caldwell [1982] AC 341 HOUSE OF LORDS

The respondent had done work in a hotel as a result of which he had quarrelled with the owner, got drunk, and set fire to the building. The fire was extinguished before serious damage occurred or anyone was injured. The respondent had been charged with two counts of arson. The first and more serious count was under s1(2)(b) of the 1971 Act (endangerment of life), the second count under s1(1). He pleaded guilty to the second count but defended the first on the ground of self-induced intoxication: that he was so drunk that the thought there might be people in the hotel had never crossed his mind. His conviction under count 1 was set aside by the Court of Appeal which certified a question for the House of Lords as to whether evidence of self-induced intoxication was relevant to criminal damage.

Held:

1. Intoxication

The House of Lords confirmed that drunkenness was no defence to a crime of basic intent and upheld the conviction. Intoxication is rarely a defence under the criminal law.

Lord Diplock thought that D's unawareness, owing to his drunkenness, of the risk of endangering life was no defence if that risk would have been obvious to him had he been sober. Evidence of self-induced intoxication was relevant to a s1(2) charge based on intention but not recklessness.

2. Recklessness

The significance of this case concerned not only intoxication but primarily recklessness. Lord Diplock gave the leading judgment with which Lord Keith and Lord Roskill agreed. There were two dissenting judgments from Lord Wilberforce and Lord Edmund-Davies.

Lord Diplock stated that it was no less blameworthy for a man whose mind was affected by rage, excitement or drink to fail to give thought to the risk of damaging property and a man whose mind was similarly affected but who had appreciated the risk, but not its seriousness. Recklessness should be given its dictionary meaning of 'careless, regardless, heedless of the consequences'.

He saw no reason to assume that the 1971 Act, which was intended to revise the law of damage to property, meant 'reckless' to be interpreted as 'maliciously' had been. He preferred the ordinary meaning of reckless:

> (which) surely includes not only deciding to ignore the risk of harmful consequences resulting from one's acts that one has recognised as existing, but also failing to give any thought to whether or not there is any such risk in circumstances where, if any thought were given to the matter, it would be obvious that there was.

Therefore the mind of 'the ordinary prudent individual' should be considered.

→ CROSS-REFERENCE
For the law on intoxication see Chapter 8, 8.3.

> Nevertheless, to decide whether someone has been 'reckless' as to whether harmful consequences of a particular kind will result from his act, as distinguished from his actually intending such harmful consequences to follow, does call for some consideration of how the mind of the ordinary prudent individual would have reacted to a similar situation. If there was nothing in the circumstances that ought to have drawn the attention of an ordinary prudent individual to the possibility of that kind of harmful consequence, the accused would not be described as 'reckless' in the natural meaning of that word for failing to address his mind to the possibility; nor, if the risk of the harmful consequences was so slight that the ordinary prudent individual upon due consideration of the risk would not be deterred from treating it as negligible, could the accused be described as reckless in its ordinary sense if, having considered the risk, he decided to ignore it

Lord Diplock proposed what came to be a model direction on objective recklessness, known as the *Caldwell* test:

> . . . a person charged with an offence under s1(1) Criminal Damage Act 1971 is reckless as to whether or not property would be destroyed or damaged if–
>
> (a) he does an act which in fact creates an obvious risk that property will be destroyed or damaged and
> (b) when he does that act he either has not given any thought to the possibility of any such risk or has recognised that there was some risk involved and has nonetheless gone on to do it.

This complicated test combined both *Cunningham* subjective recklessness as well as objective recklessness. What was new was the first limb of the test which stated that D would be reckless where *he fails to give thought to an obvious risk*.

The two states of mind, both subjective and objective, were considered equally blameworthy. In other words, the new test would catch those who deserved to be punished for their harmful actions even though the idea of risk may not have been in the forefront of their minds at the time of acting. No enquiry as to a state of mind was necessary under the new test. Therefore, it would not matter why D had failed to give thought to an obvious risk, whether incapacity or temper. *Stephenson* was overruled.

You may wonder why any change to the law was necessary since *Parker* and *Stephenson* had already decided that the unaware/unconscious risk-taker who had closed his mind to an obvious risk of damage was subjectively reckless.

Caldwell *and* Cunningham *applied to different offences*

Not only were there two different tests of recklessness, but they applied to different offences, which was even more confusing. Wherever a statute used the word '*reckless*' the new objective test applied. Therefore it was not the case that subjective *Cunningham* recklessness was completely replaced. It continued to apply to older statutory offences defined by 'maliciously', principally offences against the person. Objective recklessness was extended to the offences of causing death by reckless driving (*Lawrence* [1982] AC 510) and manslaughter (*Seymour* [1983] 2 AC 493). In 1994 the House of Lords in *Adomako* [1995] 1 AC 171 overturned *Caldwell* in respect of manslaughter, reverting MR to subjective recklessness or gross negligence. It was some years before the courts decided that *Caldwell* did not apply to common law assault. The two tests of recklessness led to some illogical results:

EXAMPLE 3.7

A resident of a caravan park (D) was involved in a dispute with the owner over rent. D went on a rampage with a mechanical digger, destroying the house of the park owner whilst she and her husband were inside and two cars. The owner also suffered damage to her eye from flying debris. D suffered from psychological problems. Criminal damage to the house and cars: *Caldwell* recklessness—guilty. D's state of mind would be irrelevant. Assault/ABH on the woman: *Cunningham* recklessness—this would depend on D's awareness of risk. Lack of mental capacity might have afforded a defence.

Caldwell, *children and the mentally ill*

The effect of an objective approach to MR is that everyone is judged according to the standard of a reasonable adult whether they happen to be a 'reasonable', 'normal', adult or not. Thus, young or mentally disabled people or those who are too ill or exhausted to think carefully would be judged by reasonable standards. Objective liability makes no concessions to disability, age or health. What if D is not ordinary because of an incapacitating condition which might interfere with the ability to perceive a risk? This was the case with the schizophrenic defendant in *Stephenson* but Lord Diplock expressly overruled this case. A rigid interpretation of the *Caldwell* test could lead to injustice, as it did. See the next case.

Elliott v C (A Minor) (1983) 77 CR APP R 103 DIVISIONAL COURT

D was a young girl aged 14 of low intelligence who had spent a night out without sleeping. She wandered into a shed, poured white spirit on the floor and ignited it. The resulting fire destroyed the shed. D was charged with criminal damage under s1(1) Criminal Damage Act 1971. The defence was that she was not reckless because she did not know that white spirit was inflammable. It was found as a fact that she was unaware of the risk of fire and that she would not have appreciated the danger had she stopped to think about it. The justices acquitted her because they interpreted the *Caldwell* test as indicating that the risk had to be obvious to the particular defendant. The prosecution appealed and the appeal was allowed. It was accepted that the risk was one which had to be obvious to a reasonably prudent person and therefore once it was proved that D gave no thought to the possibility of there being such a risk, low intelligence or exhaustion was not a defence. Lord Goff expressed his unhappiness at this decision which the court was obliged to make in deference to *Caldwell*.

You might consider that a test of recklessness which convicted a child with learning difficulties was punitive. Such inflexibility was again illustrated in the further criminal damage convictions of a schizophrenic for use of his car to attack various buildings (*Bell* [1984] 3 All ER 842), and two 15-year-old boys for arson (*Stephen Malcolm R* (1984) 79 Cr App R 334 and *Coles* [1995] 1 Cr App R 157).

Caldwell recklessness was 'over-inclusive' in the sense that it extended the boundaries of MR beyond what most people might consider to be the proper limits of responsibility for inadvertent risk-taking. There were no exceptions for incapacity. The young defendant in *Elliott* had not chosen, in a rational sense, to do wrong. She may have been foolish but to convict on the basis of recklessness was unjust to say the least.

The Caldwell loophole

The test gave rise to a theoretical argument called 'the *Caldwell* loophole', a particular anomaly that might have provided a defence if the courts had ever accepted the argument: *Caldwell* recklessness applied to a defendant who had *failed to give thought* to a serious and obvious risk of harm in certain offences. But if D *had thought* about the risk and had wrongly concluded there was none, he would not be reckless in the *Caldwell* sense. Neither would subjective recklessness apply for D was not taking a known risk, having just dismissed it. D would therefore fall between the two tests and would simply be negligent on the basis of a mistake about a serious and obvious risk.

The *Caldwell* loophole argument never succeeded. For example, in *Chief Constable of Avon & Somerset v Shimmen* (1987) 84 Cr App R 7 a martial art Tae Kwon Do expert kicked and smashed a shop window. He successfully argued that he had eliminated as much risk as possible from his demonstration by aiming to stop two inches short of the glass. The Divisional Court remitted the case back to the magistrates to convict. D had still foreseen some risk and was therefore reckless.

Understandably, there were many other criticisms of *Caldwell* recklessness which was overturned by *R v G*, to which we now turn.

3.2.5 Subjective Recklessness Restored: 2003 Onwards

R v G & Anr [2003] UKHL 50 HOUSE OF LORDS

Two boys aged 11 and 12 went camping one night without their parents' permission. They entered the back yard of the Co-op shop in Newport Pagnell. They found bundles of newspapers which they opened up to read and then lit some of them with a lighter. They threw some of the lit newspaper under a large plastic wheelie-bin and left the yard without putting out the burning papers. The bin caught fire and the fire spread to the bin next to the shop wall. From there it spread to an overhanging eave, then to the guttering, fascia and up into the roof space of the shop until the roof and neighbouring buildings caught fire. The roof collapsed and approximately one million pounds' worth of damage was caused. The appellants stated at trial that they expected the newspapers to extinguish themselves on the concrete floor of the yard. Neither of them thought there was a risk that the fire would spread. They were charged with arson contrary to ss 1(1) and (3) Criminal Damage Act 1971.

On conviction by the Crown Court the boys had received a one-year supervision order, the judge having reluctantly given the jury a direction on the *Caldwell* definition of recklessness to assess the actions of the children by the standard of the ordinary reasonable bystander. The appellants appealed to the Court of Appeal which was unable to depart from *Caldwell*. The matter was referred to the House of Lords and the issue was whether the *Caldwell* objective approach to recklessness in criminal damage was correct.

In this important judgment, you will see why the Lords disagreed with Lord Diplock in *Caldwell* and agreed with the dissenting judgment of Lord Edmund-Davies.

Lord Bingham gave the leading judgment:

> The task confronting the House in this appeal is, first of all, one of statutory construction: what did Parliament mean when it used the word 'reckless' in section 1(1) and (2) of the 1971 Act? In so expressing the question I mean to make it as plain as I can that I am not addressing the meaning of 'reckless' in any other statutory or common law context. In particular, but perhaps needlessly since 'recklessly' has now been banished from the lexicon of driving offences, I would wish to throw no doubt on the decisions of the House in *R v Lawrence* [1982] AC 510 and *R v Reid* [1992] 1 WLR 793.
>
> Since a statute is always speaking, the context or application of a statutory expression may change over time, but the meaning of the expression itself cannot change. So the starting point is to ascertain what Parliament meant by 'reckless' in 1971. As noted above in paragraph 13, section 1 as enacted followed, subject to an immaterial addition, the draft proposed by the Law Commission. It cannot be supposed that by 'reckless' Parliament meant anything different from the Law Commission. The Law Commission's meaning was made plain both in its Report (Law Com No 29) and in Working Paper No 23 which preceded it. These materials (not, it would seem, placed before the House in *R v Caldwell*) reveal a very plain intention to replace the old-fashioned and misleading expression 'maliciously' by the more familiar expression 'reckless' but to give the latter expression the meaning which *R v Cunningham* [1957] 2 QB 396 and Professor Kenny had given to the former. In treating this authority as irrelevant to the construction of 'reckless' the majority fell into understandable but clearly demonstrable error. No relevant change in the mens rea necessary for proof of the offence was intended, and in holding otherwise the majority misconstrued section 1 of the Act.
>
> That conclusion is by no means determinative of this appeal. For the decision in *R v Caldwell* was made more than 20 years ago. Its essential reasoning was unanimously approved by the House in *R v Lawrence* [1982] AC 510. Invitations to reconsider that reasoning have been rejected. The principles laid down have been applied on many occasions, by Crown Court judges and, even more frequently, by justices. In the submission of the Crown, the ruling of the House works well and causes no injustice in practice. If Parliament had wished to give effect to the intention of the Law Commission it has had many opportunities, which it has not taken, to do so. Despite its power under *Practice Statement* (*Judicial Precedent*) [1966] 1 WLR 1234 to depart from its earlier decisions, the House should be very slow to do so, not least in a context such as this.

Lord Bingham gave four reasons to depart from *Caldwell*:

> First, it is a salutary principle that conviction of serious crime should depend on proof not simply that D caused (by act or omission) an injurious result to another but that his state of mind when so acting was culpable. This, after all, is the meaning of the familiar rule *actus non facit reum nisi mens sit rea*. The most obviously culpable state of mind is no doubt an intention to cause the injurious result, but knowing disregard of an appreciated and unacceptable risk of causing an injurious result or a deliberate closing of the mind to such risk would be readily accepted as culpable also. It is clearly blameworthy to take an obvious and significant risk of causing injury to another. But it is not clearly blameworthy to do something involving a risk of injury to another if (for reasons other than self-induced intoxication: *R v Majewski* [1977] AC 443) one genuinely does not perceive the risk. Such a person may fairly be accused of stupidity or lack of imagination, but neither of those failings should expose him to conviction of serious crime or the risk of punishment.
>
> Secondly, the present case shows, more clearly than any other reported case since *R v Caldwell*, that the model direction formulated by Lord Diplock (see paragraph 18 above) is capable of leading to obvious unfairness. As the excerpts quoted in paragraphs 6–7 reveal, the trial judge regretted the direction he (quite rightly) felt compelled to give, and it is evident that this direction offended the jury's sense of fairness. The sense of fairness of 12 representative citizens sit-

ting as a jury (or of a smaller group of lay justices sitting as a bench of magistrates) is the bedrock on which the administration of criminal justice in this country is built. A law which runs counter to that sense must cause concern. Here, the appellants could have been charged under section 1(1) with recklessly damaging one or both of the wheelie-bins, and they would have had little defence. As it was, the jury might have inferred that boys of the appellants' age would have appreciated the risk to the building of what they did, but it seems clear that such was not their conclusion (nor, it would appear, the judge's either). On that basis the jury thought it unfair to convict them. I share their sense of unease. It is neither moral nor just to convict a defendant (least of all a child) on the strength of what someone else would have apprehended if D himself had no such apprehension. Nor, D having been convicted, is the problem cured by imposition of a nominal penalty.

Thirdly, I do not think the criticism of *R v Caldwell* expressed by academics, judges and practitioners should be ignored. A decision is not, of course, to be overruled or departed from simply because it meets with disfavour in the learned journals. But a decision which attracts reasoned and outspoken criticism by the leading scholars of the day, respected as authorities in the field, must command attention. One need only cite (among many other examples) the observations of Professor John Smith ([1981] Crim LR 392, 393–396) and Professor Glanville Williams ('Recklessness Redefined' (1981) 40 CLJ 252). This criticism carries greater weight when voiced also by judges as authoritative as Lord Edmund-Davies and Lord Wilberforce in *R v Caldwell* itself, Robert Goff LJ in *Elliott v C* [1983] 1 WLR 939 and Ackner LJ in *R v Stephen Malcolm R* (1984) 79 Cr App R 334. The reservations expressed by the trial judge in the present case are widely shared. The shopfloor response to *R v Caldwell* may be gauged from the editors' commentary, to be found in the 41st edition of *Archbold* (1982): paragraph 17–25, pages 1009–1010. The editors suggested that remedial legislation was urgently required.

Fourthly, the majority's interpretation of 'recklessly' in section 1 of the 1971 Act was, as already shown, a misinterpretation. If it were a misinterpretation that offended no principle and gave rise to no injustice there would be strong grounds for adhering to the misinterpretation and leaving Parliament to correct it if it chose. But this misinterpretation is offensive to principle and is apt to cause injustice. That being so, the need to correct the misinterpretation is compelling . . .

In the course of argument before the House it was suggested that the rule in *R v Caldwell* might be modified, in cases involving children, by requiring comparison not with normal reasonable adults but with normal reasonable children of the same age. This is a suggestion with some attractions but it is open to four compelling objections. First, even this modification would offend the principle that conviction should depend on proving the state of mind of the individual defendant to be culpable. Second, if the rule were modified in relation to children on grounds of their immaturity it would be anomalous if it were not also modified in relation to the mentally handicapped on grounds of their limited understanding. Third, any modification along these lines would open the door to difficult and contentious argument concerning the qualities and characteristics to be taken into account for purposes of the comparison. Fourth, to adopt this modification would be to substitute one misinterpretation of section 1 for another. There is no warrant in the Act or in the *travaux préparatoires* which preceded it for such an interpretation.

A further refinement, advanced by Professor Glanville Williams in his article 'Recklessness Redefined' (1981) 40 CLJ 252, 270–271, adopted by the justices in *Elliott v C* [1983] 1 WLR 939 and commented upon by Robert Goff LJ in that case is that a defendant should only be regarded as having acted recklessly by virtue of his failure to give any thought to an obvious risk that property would be destroyed or damaged, where such risk would have been obvious to him if he had given any thought to the matter. This refinement also has attractions, although it does not meet the objection of principle and does not represent a correct interpretation of the section. It is, in my opinion, open to the further objection of over-complicating the task of the jury (or bench of justices). It is one thing to decide whether a defendant can be believed when he says that the thought of a given risk never crossed his mind. It is another, and much more speculative, task to decide whether the risk would have been obvious to him if the thought had crossed his mind. The simpler the jury's task, the more likely is its verdict to be reliable. Robert Goff LJ's reason for rejecting this refinement was somewhat similar (*Elliott v C*, page 950). . . .

Lord Bingham agreed with the Law Commission's definition of recklessness in clause 18(b) of the Criminal Code Bill annexed by the Law Commission to 'A Criminal Code for England and Wales Volume 1: Report and Draft Criminal Code Bill' (Law Com No 177, April 1989):

> A person acts–
>
> '(b) 'recklessly' with respect to–
>
> > (i) a circumstance, when he is aware of a risk that it exists or will exist, and
> >
> > (ii) a result when he is aware of a risk that it will occur,
>
> and it is unreasonable, having regard to the circumstances known to him, to take that risk . . . '

 NOTE 3.4

Lord Bingham's four reasons for departing from *Caldwell* can be summarised as follows:

1. *The intention of Parliament and Law Commission recommendations.* The majority's interpretation of 'recklessly' in s1 of the 1971 Act was a misinterpretation causing offence to principle and justice. He asked what Parliament had meant in using the word 'reckless' in s1(1) and (2) of the 1971 Act. Since a statute is always speaking, the context or application of a statutory expression may change over time but its meaning cannot. The Law Commission clearly meant recklessness to mean the same as maliciousness and Parliament cannot have meant anything different from the Law Commission. In treating *Cunningham* as irrelevant, the majority in *Caldwell* fell into 'understandable but demonstrable error'.

2. *In serious crimes, D's state of mind should be culpable.* No-one should be convicted of a serious crime without culpability. But *Cunningham* recklessness was not as under-inclusive as Lord Diplock had thought in *Caldwell.* Not only intention but 'knowing disregard' of a known and unacceptable risk or a deliberate closing of the mind to such risk are culpable. Lord Bingham approved the dissenting judgment of Lord Edmund-Davies in *Caldwell* where he had said that a man cannot close his mind to risk unless he first realises that there is a risk, in which case he is subjectively reckless as had already been decided in *Parker (Daryl)* [1977] 1 WLR 600.

3. *The model direction in Caldwell leads to unfairness*, as in *Elliott* (see 3.2.4) and clearly in this case it offended the jury's sense of fairness. The context of *Caldwell* did not require consideration of the young or mentally handicapped. No modification of *Caldwell* could correct its inherent injustice or error. *Caldwell* had swallowed up large parts of what we would normally call negligence. A lapse of care due to incapacity, absent-mindedness or foolishness would be negligent whereas if it was due to excitability or rage it might be reckless. But none of the Ds in *Elliott*, *Bell*, *Malcolm* or *Coles* had chosen to commit harm in a rational sense.

4. *The academic criticism* of *Caldwell* could not be ignored. Lord Bingham referred to a great deal of academic criticism of *Caldwell*. Here are some examples: J.C. Smith, commentary to *Caldwell* in [1981] *Crim LR* at 392:

> The present decision . . . plainly defeats the intention of the Law Commission which was responsible for the drafting of the [Criminal Damage Act 1971] and whose recommenda-

tions were accepted by Parliament; and it conflicts with the proposals of the Criminal Law Revision Committee in their report on the law of offences against the person. It sets back the law concerning the mental element in criminal damage, in theory to before 1861, and in practice probably to before Kenny formulated the law in the first edition of his *Outlines of Criminal law* in 1902 and certainly to before the decision in *Cunningham* in 1957 . . . What has the majority to offer against this overwhelming evidence as to Parliament's actual intentions? Lord Diplock points out that the purpose of the Criminal Damage Act, as stated in its long title, was 'to *revise* the law' . . . and he could 'see no reason why parliament when it decided to revise the law . . . should go out of its way to perpetuate fine and impracticable distinctions . . . 'With all possible respect, this is a pathetically inadequate reason for ignoring the readily available evidence . . . Beyond any doubt, the intention of the framers was correctly interpreted by *Briggs*, *Stephenson* and Lords Wilberforce and Edmund-Davies and is defeated by the decision of the majority.

And in 'The unresolved problem of recklessness' G. Williams in (1988) 8 *Legal Studies*, at p 74 states:

We seem to be stuck fast over recklessness. The model direction in *Caldwell* is almost universally deplored, particularly in respect of its operation in cases like *Elliott v C* and *R (Stephen Malcolm)*, but the lords show no sign of repenting, even though in both of the cases last cited expressions of disapproval ascended to them from a Divisional Court. . . .

Although the subjective definition requires the jury (or magistrates) to find whether D knew of the risk he was creating, this does not mean that they must rely entirely on his own account of his state of mind. The jury may (and generally should) find that he knew of a risk of which everyone would have known – provided that there is nothing in the facts to indicate that D did not know it.

However, anyone who supposes that subjective recklessness is too narrow a concept to be workable labours under a misconception. At least four rules can be used by a judge to give it reasonable width.

(i) First, on a charge of recklessly causing injury to the person or damage to property, all that the prosecution generally have to show is that D must have realised that he was creating a very small risk of the harm in question . . . This is because it is generally unjustified to create even a small known risk . . . for other people . . . .

(ii) The situation where D seeks to show that he has a low IQ, for the purpose of negativing foresight, is a second area of difficulty . . . The proper rule would be that defendant can always prove his below-average IQ [including mental impairment], with the aid of expert evidence or otherwise, in the hope of gaining an acquittal . . . If an impaired person has accidentally set fire to a house, not realising, because he was stupid, that what he did was dangerous, he can safely be set at large if the accident is not likely to be repeated. The prosecution and conviction of Miss C, the ESN girl who accidentally destroyed a shed, were scandalous . . . .

The argument from preoccupation may be used by way of defence in all kinds of cases if subjective recklessness is in issue, but it may often be countered by inviting the jury to consider D's knowledge not only when he was committing the crime but when he was planning it and even after committing it . . . To that extent, at least, knowledge must be regarded as a continuing state of mind.

A second difficult case for subjective recklessness is that of the man who says that he was acting in a blind rage. One may doubt whether there is in fact any such thing as a blind rage: what rage does is to destroy self-control, not awareness. Anyway, rage, like intoxication, is a common concomitant of aggression, and the law cannot look with sympathy on a defence that 'I was so angry I didn't know what I was doing.'

Furthermore, it was thought that the difficulty perceived by Lord Diplock arose from use of the language of foresight (*knowledge* or *cognition*) to represent recklessness.

Professor D. Birch in 'The Foresight Saga: The Biggest Mistake of All?' [1988] *Crim LR* 4 argued that *attitude* (eg: stupidity, callousness, indifference) would have been a better approach:

> Suppose that D, to impress his friends, vaults over a seaside breakwater without looking before he leaps. The seashore is crowded with holiday makers and their possessions, and it is entirely predictable that he will land on something or someone and cause damage or injury. He lands on a sunbather and causes painful bruising. A jury might well find it plausible that the thought of causing such harm never entered D's head, but in so far as his conduct suggests the indifference to others of one who 'couldn't care less,' and who would have jumped even if he had been fully apprised of the risk, they might well itch to convict him. By what moral principle should they be prevented from doing so?
>
> If the answer is none, then we should have a second means of proving recklessness with an equal claim to recognition along with foresight, and perhaps a superior one, because the attitude of D, if it can be proved, may be a more reliable guide to moral fault than a momentary awareness of risk.

These authors shared the view that failure to think about a risk through anger or indifference would be no defence to recklessness subjectively defined and the law had been changed unnecessarily. On the other hand, failure to think because of preoccupation or lack of ability would amount to a negligent mistake and thus would be a defence.

Lord Steyn in R v G *gave three reasons for allowing the appeal:*

1. The majority in *Caldwell* ignored the fact that before 1971 foresight of consequences was an essential element in recklessness in the context of criminal damage.
2. The purpose of s1 of the Act was to replace the wording of the Malicious Damage Act 1861 but not its meaning.
3. *Caldwell* was potentially unjust and contrary to the UN Convention on the Rights of the Child in force in the UK in September 1999. Article 40.1 provides:

> States Parties recognise the right of every child alleged as, accused of, or recognised as having infringed the penal law to be treated in a manner consistent with the promotion of the child's sense of dignity and worth, which reinforces the child's respect for the human rights and fundamental freedoms of others and which takes into account the child's age and the desirability of promoting the child's reintegration and the child's assuming a constructive role in society.

Subjective standards in MR mean that the special requirements of children and the mentally incapacitated should be respected. *Caldwell* took a wrong turn from the general subjective development of mens rea.

Doubts concerning the majority's view of *Caldwell* were expressed by Lord Rodger but he lent his support to the decision of the House. He was concerned about the subjectivist stance of academics and law reformers. Other views had been legitimately adopted by English judges at different times over the centuries and *Cunningham* may not provide the best solution in all circumstances. *Caldwell* might have been erroneous in so far as the Criminal Damage Act was concerned, but it does not follow that it was bad policy for other offences such as reckless driving.

It now seems that, although the ratio of *R v G* was concerned with criminal damage, *Caldwell* recklessness has been effectively ousted in any offence of recklessness. *AG's Reference (No 3 of 2003)* [2004] EWCA Crim 868 confirms that objective liability no longer applies to statutory offences at all. The case concerned the offence of misconduct in a public office against police officers who had acted in a grossly negligent way in respect of the death of a citizen in police custody. It was held that recklessness must be subjective, that it excludes 'indifference', and the fact that the offence was a conduct not a result crime, in the context of a duty, made no difference. Offences of wilful neglect or misconduct were to be determined subjectively and this was so in so far as awareness of the duty was concerned.

3.2.6 Was the House of Lords in *R v G* right to reverse *Caldwell*?

The court might have modified the *Caldwell* test instead of departing from it but for various reasons declined to do so. Read the following extract from D. Kimel, 'Inadvertent Recklessness in Criminal Law' (2004) 120 *LQR* 548–554:

Lord Bingham's first and most substantial reason for departing from R. v Caldwell is captured in the simple statement that whereas 'it is clearly blameworthy to take an obvious and significant risk of causing injury to another . . . it is not clearly blameworthy to do something involving a risk of injury to another if . . . one genuinely does not perceive the risk. Such a person may fairly be accused of stupidity or lack of imagination, but neither of those failings should expose him to conviction of serious crime or the risk of punishment' (at [32]). This cursory statement is clearly unsatisfactory. The precise nature of the personal flaw revealed through the failure (by a person of sound cognitive faculties) to perceive an obvious risk of injury to another, depends entirely on the risk in question, the actions that brought it about, and the surrounding circumstances. In certain cases the flaw may indeed amount to stupidity or dull imagination, but in others far more serious vices may be at stake: a genuine disregard for the safety of others, a glaring insensitivity to others' legitimate interests or well-being, and the like. Even those who may baulk at the suggestion that the two states of mind in question are always equally blameworthy, should eschew the notion that a failure to advert to an obvious risk is always, or even on most occasions, blameless. Indeed, a failure, even if entirely genuine to advert to the obvious risk that a person does not consent to the sexual advances of another, can hardly ever be dismissed as being owed to no more than stupidity on the part of the latter; and it is precisely that notion which informed the revised offence of rape in the recently enacted Sexual Offences Act 2003.

Lord Bingham's only other substantive reason for departing from R. v Caldwell touches on the 'obvious unfairness' it is capable of generating, and the corresponding sense of unease experienced by juries when asked to apply the model direction formulated in it (at [33]). Both the unfairness and the unease, however, are acute features of those cases where D's capacity to appreciate risks is inherently inferior to that attributable to the ordinary, prudent person. Thus, this reason only begs the question why not modify or limit the scope of application of the Caldwell rule, e.g. along the very lines offered in the certified question before the House, while leaving the rule in place otherwise. One of Lord Bingham's reasons for not doing so was that a modification of the rule so as to prevent it from applying to children would suggest the need to modify it also in relation to other defendants whose relevant cognitive skills may be limited, such as the mentally-handicapped. But rather than serve as a reason against modification, this consideration merely indicates what kind of modification was needed from the outset: namely, that D should only be regarded as having acted recklessly where the risk to which she had failed to give thought would have been obvious to her had she given thought to it. Lord Bingham expressed the concern that such a modification would over-complicate the task of the jury, by rendering it more speculative (at [33]). His point here is sound. It is not clear, however, that such a task would be any more complicated than – or, possibly, as complicated as – various other, somewhat similar tasks juries are routinely invited to perform in criminal cases (e.g. in relation to the defences of provocation and duress, or to 'dishonesty' under the Theft Act 1968, or indeed, in future, with regard to recklessness for the purposes of rape under the Sexual Offences Act 2003).

. . .

Lord Rodger, by contrast, at least hinted at a more balanced approach to the underlying normative issue. Having recognised that the decision in R. v Caldwell involved a 'legitimate choice between two legal policies', that the Caldwell approach 'may be better suited to some offences than to others', and that 'an alternative way to allow the appeal by re-analysing Lord Diplock's speech and overruling Elliott v C . . . might well have been found' (at [70]), he concluded that, in light of the fact that the decision in R. v Caldwell could not be defended as a legitimate interpretation in light of the original intention of Parliament, it should be overruled, leaving it to Parliament to restore inadvertent recklessness under the 1971 Act if it thinks preferable. (Lord Rodger was alone in describing the decision in R. v G as one that overrules R. v Caldwell, whereas Lord Bingham and Lord Steyn both used the phrase 'departing from'. The latter formulation is the more accurate: since the decision in Caldwell concerned evidence of intoxication, which was not at issue in R. v G, departing from its interpretation of 'recklessness' does not, technically speaking, amount to overruling it: the case on its facts would still be decided the same way today.)

By way of conclusion, two ironies need to be pointed out. The first has already surfaced. Within one month of the decision in R. v G, the Sexual Offences Act 2003 received Royal Assent. One of the elements of the new offence of rape, according to s.1(1)(c), is that D does not reasonably believe that V consents. The 'reasonableness' requirement was intended to overrule D.P.P. v Morgan [1976] A.C. 182, incidentally one of the decisions Lord Steyn mentioned in support of his contention that departing from R. v Caldwell and restoring the narrower, 'subjective' interpretation of recklessness for the purposes of the 1971 Act, 'would fit in with the general tendency in modern times of our criminal law' (at [55]). Instead, through the new Sexual Offences Act, inadvertent recklessness has made a swift return into our criminal law, and, at that, in the context of a rather more serious offence than criminal damage to property. . . . '

The author identifies a new objective approach to MR in rape. As we shall see, this is a requirement of reasonableness as to consent, a *circumstance* not a result. Consent might be considered easy to ascertain in the context of sexual conduct. It is submitted that it is therefore not unfair to require D to take reasonable steps to obtain it. Do you agree with the author that the *Caldwell* test might have been more appropriately amended rather than overturned?

3.2.7 How to Distinguish Recklessness from Intention

In a case of murder, remember that the *Nedrick/Woollin* test of oblique intention requires that death or GBH be both objectively virtually certain to occur, excluding any unforeseen interventions, and that D foresees that result as a virtual certainty. In a manslaughter case, recklessness, on the other hand, requires only that D is aware that he is taking an objectively unreasonable risk of harm of death or GBH. With lesser offences, he needs to be aware of a risk of harm.

3.2.8 How to Distinguish Recklessness from Negligence

A negligent person foresees no risk at all and is simply forgetful or careless about an ordinary, minor matter. Negligence is not generally considered to be so culpable as to attract criminal liability. It is a fault element of civil liability involving, for example, road accidents and personal injury claims. Whilst recklessness requires foresight of an unreasonable risk, a person who lacks foresight but whose standard of conduct is unreasonable by ordinary standards may be negligent.

3.2.9 Reform

Subjective recklessness is recommended in clause 18(b) of the Criminal Code Bill annexed by the Law Commission in 'A Criminal Code for England and Wales Volume 1: Report and Draft Criminal Code Bill' (Law Com No 177, April 1989) (see *R v G*, 'Subjective Recklessness Restored', p 146) and the Law Commission's report on offences against the person: 'Legislating the Criminal Code: Offences Against the Person and General Principles' (Law Com No 218, 1993). Clause 1 states that:

> A person is defined as acting 'recklessly' in relation to a result if he is aware of a risk that it will occur, and it is unreasonable, having regard to all the circumstances known to him, to take that risk.

3.2.10 Evaluation and Conclusion

Caldwell raised the issue of how far the criminal law should go in punishing people for their harmful conduct. It drew a critical response from academics and, ultimately, judges: the boundaries of the criminal law were over-extended, catching many people who ought never to have been labelled criminal. A. Ashworth in *Principles of Criminal Law* stated that the *Caldwell* test could be seen as a more accurate representation of a social judgment of blame. You might or might not agree with *Caldwell*. Here are some of the arguments for and against objective liability.

Subjectivist theory

This philosophy rests on the principle that moral guilt and criminal liability should only be imposed on people who have chosen to do wrong. Individuals are autonomous and have the capacity and freedom to decide how to behave. Therefore, a person's state of mind at the time of the offence is significant. MR reflects the principle that liability should be imposed on those who intended or knew of the risks of their behaviour.

Utilitarianism/the welfare principle

The contrasting view is that of utilitarianism which emphasises social needs before those of the individual. Hence, punishment may be necessary to protect society or deter wrong-doing despite the absence of choice on the part of the individual. Subjectivist theory has been subject to criticism over the years on the grounds that it portrays a simplistic view of what constitutes knowledge or awareness of risk. Utilitarianism states that the boundaries between these two states of mind are not clear cut and therefore there may be justification in classifying inadvertence as MR in some offences. One can deservedly be punished for failing to consider the consequences of one's actions where the harm risked is serious and the unawareness is culpable.

Read the following extract from R.A. Duff, 'Recklessness' [1980] *Crim LR* 282:

> [There is a] view that inadvertence, however negligent, cannot constitute *mens rea* since we cannot blame a man for what he does not know. That view has been convincingly demolished: whether I notice some aspect of my action or its context may depend on the attention I pay to what I am doing, and be thus within my control; failures of attention may be as 'voluntary' and culpable as other omissions . . .
>
> . . . to say that I forgot or did not realise something is to admit that I thought it unimportant, and thus to convict myself of a serious lack of concern for it (which is why a bridegroom would hardly mitigate his offence of missing his wedding by the plea that he forgot). If, as I have suggested, an agent is reckless to the extent that his actions manifest a serious kind of 'practical indifference,' a 'willingness' to bring about some harm, then such recklessness, indifference, and willingness can be exhibited as much in his failure to notice obvious and important aspects of his action as in his conscious risk-taking.

R v G favours a subjectivist approach to recklessness but it also recognises that a defendant's state of mind may not be easily described as either advertent or inadvertent. There are some situations where, if one is deliberately blind to an obvious risk of harm, one might still 'know' of the risk and ought to be liable for failing to appreciate it at the time of acting. The decision was also informed by society's more widely held respect for the individual human rights of children and the mentally ill.

Most people would agree that punishment should extend to people who knowingly choose to take a risk of serious harm with others' safety and property. They would also probably agree that, although not necessarily fully aware of the risk of harm at the moment of acting, a person still knows they are creating a risk if they would have been able to realise it given a moment's reflection. *R v G* demonstrates that a subjective test of recklessness should be able to include both of these states of mind.

The fact that it took so long for *Caldwell* to be reversed is surprising but tells us two important things about the law. Parliament can change the law whenever it pleases but the common law evolves slowly on a case-by-case basis because lower courts are bound by precedent. It took many years for the right case to reach the House of Lords, by which time judicial attitudes had evolved to reflect contemporary morality. Secondly, the courts, like the rest of us, are capable of making mistakes but once made, until Parliament intervenes, the timing of an about turn is very much a matter of chance.

SECTION SUMMARY

- *Recklessness is now subjective and is defined according to* Cunningham *[1957] as the conscious taking of an unjustified risk.*
- Caldwell *[1982] objective recklessness applied to criminal damage until it was overturned by* R v G *[2003].*
- Caldwell *also applied to manslaughter until* Adomako *[1995].*
- R v G *overturned* Caldwell *because:*
  - ☐ Caldwell *had wrongly changed the interpretation of recklessness in the Criminal Damage Act 1971;*
  - ☐ Caldwell *led to injustice in respect of children and the mentally ill;*
  - ☐ *no-one should be convicted of a serious crime unless their mind is guilty; and*
  - ☐ *academic criticism of* Caldwell *could not be ignored.*

3.3 Negligence and Gross Negligence

3.3.1 Negligence

3.3.2 Negligent Mistake

3.3.3 The Distinction between Negligence and Recklessness

3.3.4 Should Negligence be a Basis of Fault?

3.3.5 Gross Negligence

3.3.6 Reform

KEY CASES

Bateman (1925) 19 Cr App R 8—test of gross negligence in manslaughter;

Adomako [1995] 1 AC 171—*Bateman* test of gross negligence confirmed in manslaughter.

3.3.1 Negligence

Negligence relates not to a state of mind but to an unreasonable standard of conduct which we might in ordinary language call 'stupid', 'absent-minded', 'inadvertent', an 'error of judgment' or a 'simple mistake'. Here, D's behaviour will fall below an objective standard of conduct.

→ CROSS-REFERENCE
For discussion of negligence as an element of liability, see 3.2.8.

Negligence is not a form of MR and generally falls outside of criminal liability. However, it is relevant to many *conduct* crimes. Some are minor statutory offences such as driving without due care and attention:

Section 3 Road Traffic Act 1988, as substituted by s2 Road Traffic Act 1991:

If a person drives a mechanically propelled vehicle on a road or other public place without due care and attention, or without reasonable consideration for other persons using the road or place, he is guilty of an offence.

Other offences of negligence may be more serious, such as harassment:

Section 1(1)(b) Protection from Harassment Act 1997:

(1) A person must not pursue a course of conduct–

(a) which amounts to harassment of another, and

(b) which he knows or ought to know amounts to harassment of the other.

A defendant *ought* to know . . . if a *reasonable* person in possession of the same information would think the course of conduct amounted to harassment . . .

Recent reforms to sexual offences include elements requiring a *reasonable belief* by D as to consent or age:

Section 1 Sexual Offences Act 2003:

(1) A person (A) commits an offence if–

(a) he intentionally penetrates the vagina, anus or mouth of another person (B) with his penis,

(b) B does not consent to the penetration, and

(c) A does not reasonably believe that B consents.

(2) Whether a belief is reasonable is to be determined having regard to all the circumstances, including any steps A has taken to ascertain whether B consents.

3.3.2 Negligent Mistake

→ **CROSS-REFERENCE**
For further discussion of the defence of mistake see Chapter 9, 9.4. Sexual offences are discussed in Chapter 11.

If D makes a careless mistake resulting in an offence, he may have a defence. An honest mistake can provide a general defence, even if it is unreasonable (*Morgan* [1975] 2 All ER 347). (Note that this no longer applies to sexual offences, which now require any mistaken belief to be reasonable.)

Mistake has also arisen in the context of other statutory crimes such as bigamy which is committed under s57 Offences Against the Person Act 1861 where a person:

being married, shall marry any other person during the life of the former husband or wife. A reasonable belief (or absence of negligence) that the first spouse is dead will be a defence.

In addition, offences of strict liability will occasionally provide a defence based on the absence of negligence. For example:

Section 28 Misuse of Drugs Act 1971:

(2) Subject to subsection (3) below, in any proceedings for an offence to which this section applies it shall be a defence for the accused to prove that he neither knew of nor suspected nor had reason to suspect the existence of some fact alleged by the prosecution which it is necessary for the prosecution to prove if he is to be convicted of the offence charged.

3.3.3 The Distinction between Negligence and Recklessness

Under *Caldwell* recklessness the distinction was blurred. It was possible to be objectively reckless through the negligent, as well as a more culpable indifferent, oversight of a serious and obvious risk. The distinction is now more straightforward:

- *Cunningham*/subjective recklessness involves the conscious taking of an unjustifiable risk of harm or damage. The risk should be serious though need not be obvious to the ordinary person provided it is perceived by D.
- After *R v G*, subjective recklessness includes the person who has deliberately closed his mind to all risk through, for example, temper.
- Negligence involves unreasonable conduct which creates an obvious risk of harm or damage through genuine inadvertence, that is: the unconscious risk-taker who does not appreciate the risk. Risk may never have entered the mind of D at all.

The question arises as to whether the risk needs to be obvious to a reasonable person or to the particular defendant. Opinion seems to favour the more objective position so that even if D lacks the capacity to perceive what might be obvious to an ordinary prudent individual, he will still be negligent. However, in *RSPCA v C* [2006] EWHC 1069, the High Court held that whether a young girl of 15 was negligent in failing to take an injured cat to the vet should be judged according to the standards of a reasonable girl *of her age*.

3.3.4 Should Negligence be a Basis of Fault?

There are arguments both ways. The main argument against making people liable for negligence is that negligence, involving a low or unreasonable standard of conduct, is simply not as culpable as conscious risk-taking or recklessness. Negligence takes the form of a mistake and is unconscious. There is therefore no point in punishing people for their mistakes because no conscious decision was involved that might be deterred next time. On the other hand, it can be said that penalising negligence will force people to be more careful, to stop and think and take precautions next time.

3.3.5 Gross Negligence

➜ CROSS-REFERENCE
For further discussion of gross negligence manslaughter see Chapter 7.

This MR concept is relevant only to involuntary manslaughter by gross negligence. Briefly, as we shall see, involuntary manslaughter consists of unintentional killing. There are now three types: gross negligence, reckless, and constructive/unlawful and dangerous act. Between 1983–1994 gross negligence manslaughter disappeared but re-emerged in a distinct form in 1994 (see Diagram 3.5).

Here we are only concerned with the definition of gross negligence as a form of MR. Historically, where death had occurred as a result of serious neglect, manslaughter could be committed by subjective recklessness or by 'gross' negligence, the term 'gross' indicating that a higher degree of fault was required than that which was sufficient for civil liability for negligence. The definition of gross negligence was given in *R v Bateman* (1925) 19 Cr App R 8, where a doctor had killed a pregnant woman giving birth. It had been necessary for him to insert his hand into the womb in order to physically turn the unborn child which was in the wrong position for birth, a procedure known as 'manual version'. He mistakenly ruptured part of the uterus and ruptured her bladder, as a consequence of which she died. The doctor was convicted of manslaughter but was acquitted on appeal. The case is seen as an important contribution to the definition of gross negligence.

The *Bateman* test of gross negligence was set out by Lord Hewart CJ:

> In explaining to juries the test to be applied, many epithets such as culpable, criminal, gross, wicked, clear and complete have been used . . . In order to establish criminal liability the facts must be such that in the opinion of the jury the negligence of the Accused went beyond a mere matter of compensation between subjects and showed such disregard for the life and safety of others as to amount to a crime against the state and conduct deserving of punishment.

This test makes clear that gross negligence involved not a state of mind but a serious form of negligent conduct. However, it was difficult to be precise about the exact type of negligence required for all occasions and therefore the matter was left to the jury. It led to the criticism that the definition was circular in that the jury could only convict if the negligence was criminal but the designation 'criminal' was up to them. This invited inconsistency. It did,

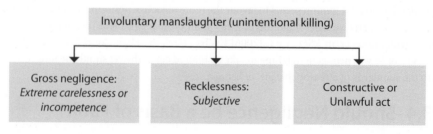

Diagram 3.5
Involuntary manslaughter today

however, have the advantage of flexibility in that all the surrounding circumstances could be taken into account.

Over time, it was not altogether clear if gross negligence was still an independent form of MR or a form of recklessness. Sometimes, it was the term used to describe the very high degree of recklessness applicable to manslaughter. You may recall that in *R v Stone & Dobinson* [1977] the MR for involuntary manslaughter was explained as being either gross negligence or recklessness.

Gross negligence and *Caldwell* recklessness

In 1983, *Caldwell/Lawrence* recklessness was applied to motor manslaughter by the House of Lords in the case of *Seymour* [1983] 2 AC 493 which effectively absorbed gross negligence. Motor manslaughter was the name given to a killing by the driver of a vehicle.

In *Seymour*, Lord Roskill held that for motor manslaughter and for all cases of gross negligence manslaughter *Caldwell* recklessness should henceforth prevail. However, the risk of death created by the manner of D's driving must be very high as opposed to simply serious and obvious as in *Stone*. That objective MR in any form should apply to such a serious offence was seen as unjust. It was not until 1994 that the *Caldwell/Lawrence* test in relation to manslaughter was overturned by the House of Lords in the case of *Adomako*.

R v Adomako [1995] 1 AC 171 HOUSE OF LORDS

This appeal first appeared in the Court of Appeal under the name *R v Sulman, Prentice, Adomako & Holloway* [1994] QB 304.

Four defendants, all professionals, had been convicted of reckless manslaughter in three separate cases. They all appealed and since an identical point of law was raised by each, the appeals were conjoined. Doctors Sulman and Prentice had been convicted of manslaughter following the death of a leukaemia patient to whom they had administered an injection in the wrong part of the body (directly into the spine instead of into a muscle). Both were junior doctors. Neither knew the correct procedure but each thought the other did. There was no supervision at the time of the injection. The box containing the drug had been put on the lumbar puncture trolley instead of the 'cytotoxic trolley'. Mr Holloway was a central heating engineer who had been convicted of manslaughter following the faulty installation of a central heating system. He had left bare wires touching a metal sink which became live when the heating was switched on and which fatally electrocuted a person who used the sink. Dr Adomako was an anaesthetist during the later stages of an eye operation on a patient. During the operation, the tube from the ventilator supplying the patient with oxygen became disconnected. The appellant failed to notice the disconnection for nine minutes as a result of which the patient suffered a cardiac arrest and died. He had had only three and a half hours' sleep before the morning on which the offence was committed. He should have had an assistant during the operation but none was present. Expert evidence at the trial indicated that a competent anaesthetist would have detected the problem in 15 seconds. In the trials of all defendants apart from Dr Adomako, the juries had received directions on objective recklessness following *Caldwell/Lawrence*, not gross negligence. At Dr Adomako's trial, negligence had been admitted but the issue was whether he had been *criminally* negligent. The Court of Appeal considered that gross negligence had survived *Caldwell*. It applied to one type of involuntary manslaughter described as breach of duty manslaughter, which really arose here rather than reckless manslaughter.

It followed that the convictions of the junior doctors and Mr Holloway were wrong. The Crown did not appeal in those cases. Dr Adomako's conviction was confirmed and there was an appeal to the House of Lords:

Lord Mackay LC:

> ... In my opinion the law as stated in these two authorities [*R v Bateman* (1925) and *Andrews v DPP* [1937]] is satisfactory as providing a proper basis for describing the crime of involuntary man-slaughter. Since the decision in *Andrews v DPP* [1937] 2 All ER 552, [1937] AC 576 was a decision of your Lordships' house, it remains the most authoritative statement of the present law which I have been able to find and although its relationship to *R v Seymour* [1983] 2 All ER 1058, [1983] 2 AC 493 is a matter to which I shall have to return, it is a decision which has not been departed from. On this basis in my opinion the ordinary principles of the law of negligence apply to ascertain whether or not D has been in breach of a duty of care towards V who has died. If such breach of duty is established the next question is whether that breach of duty caused the death of V. If so, the jury must go on to consider whether that breach of duty should be characterised as gross negligence and therefore as a crime. This will depend on the seriousness of the breach of duty committed by D in all the circumstances in which D was placed when it occurred. The jury will have to consider whether the extent to which D's conduct departed from the proper standard of care incumbent upon him, involving as it must have done a risk of death to the patient, was such that it should be judged criminal.
>
> It is true that to a certain extent this involves an element of circularity, but in this branch of the law I do not believe that is fatal to its being correct as a test of how far conduct must depart from accepted standards to be characterised as criminal. This is necessarily a question of degree and an attempt to specify that degree more closely is I think likely to achieve only a spurious precision. The essence of the matter, which is supremely a jury question, is whether, having regard to the risk of death involved, the conduct of D was so bad in all the circumstances as to amount in their judgment to a criminal act or omission.

 NOTE 3.5

1. *Bateman* gross negligence was the appropriate test of MR in manslaughter cases involving a breach of duty. Gross negligence is a purely objective test. It was described as:

   ■ A breach of a duty of care. The ordinary principles of the law of negligence apply to ascertain whether or not D has been in breach of a duty of care.

   ■ The breach must involve a risk of death and not just a risk to health or welfare. This is an objective test.

   ■ Did that breach cause death? D's conduct must have fallen below the standard to be expected of a reasonable doctor, driver, whatever the case might be.

   ■ Should that breach be characterised as gross negligence and therefore a crime? The question of whether D's conduct had departed from the proper standard of care involving a risk of death so as to be judged criminal is a jury one.

2. Manslaughter by breach of duty applies to everyone not just professionals. We are all under a duty not to risk someone's life.

3. The case of *Seymour* was effectively overruled. Motor manslaughter was no longer a separate form of manslaughter. *Lawrence* recklessness no longer applied to manslaughter. Recklessness would be subjective. Manslaughter would now become both reckless and by gross negligence.

Gross negligence revived

Caldwell recklessness was too wide and inflexible for manslaughter and caught undeserving people. Therefore, gross negligence requires juries to ask one further question in addition to whether D had failed to think about a serious and obvious risk: was the negligence so bad in all the circumstances as to be deserving of criminal punishment? Gross negligence is therefore more favourable to D than recklessness.

Circularity

The circularity of the *Bateman* test is preserved by *Adomako*. A question of law as to the definition of gross negligence is left to the jury. This could lead to inconsistency of verdicts on similar facts and evidence. However, gross negligence has been held not to violate the certainty or predictability required by Article 7 ECHR.

➔ CROSS-REFERENCE
For further discussion of the compatibility of gross negligence with Article 7 ECHR see Chapter 7, 7.2.3.

Gross negligence and mere negligence

Lord Mackay stated that the ordinary principles of negligence apply to ascertain whether or not D has been in breach of a duty of care towards a victim who has died. This is unclear in a criminal law context for two reasons.

First, a tortious duty of care is undoubtedly wider than any duty existing under the criminal law. There are established but limited duty situations in criminal law relating to liability for omissions, for example:

- relationship between parent and child, doctor and patient, etc;
- an assumption of responsibility;
- a contractual duty to assume the safety of others;
- the creation of a dangerous situation.

Beyond these categories, the law is uncertain. A. Ashworth in *Principles of the Criminal Law* considers that the criminal law imposes general duties of care upon drivers towards road users and upon anyone in possession of a firearm. Smith & Hogan states that where a negligent act is alleged, the existence of a duty is unlikely to cause a problem; we must all be under a duty not to do acts endangering the lives of others in the absence of a defence. However, L.H. Leigh in 'Liability for inadvertence: A Lordly Legacy?' (1995) 58 *MLR* 457 argued that:

> Whatever be the basis of punishment, a body of rules which required us all to be careful in all aspects of our daily lives on pain of punishment would seem totalitarian. It would seem an extreme assertion of the right to punish in order to uphold social values . . . Whether or not one believes that punishment can be justified on educative grounds, it must surely be admitted that at most it can only ever apply in particular situations of obvious and grave danger which are singled out as presenting obvious risks.

Secondly, the ordinary principles of negligence in the context of manslaughter are very uncertain. It has been argued by the Law Commission in 'Legislating the Criminal Code: Involuntary Manslaughter' (Law Com No 237), at 25, that negligence here may mean no more than carelessness. In *Adomako*, the anaesthetist was careless in relation to a positive act towards V. But in cases of manslaughter by omission, the criminal law appears to be wider than the law of negligence (eg: one can remove oneself from a duty to care for another in tort by abandoning all efforts but not in the criminal law: *Stone & Dobinson*). S. Gardner in 'Manslaughter by Gross Negligence' (1995) 111 *LQR* 22 states that:

> The test [that there was a breach of a duty of care] probably originated in lawyers finding it helpful to conceive gross, criminal, negligence by contrasting it with ordinary, tortuous, negligence. But since juries will be equally, if not more, unfamiliar with the latter, they will not be helped, and may even be confused, by being told to consider it.

Degree of risk

It follows that the degree of risk involved in gross negligence is uncertain. Although Lord Mackay stated that it should be a risk of death reference was also made to a possible risk of injury.

Incapacity

If gross negligence is an objective test, does this mean that individual mental incapacity, such as would deprive D of the ability to perceive an obvious risk, is no defence as would be the case with recklessness? The answer appears to be that there would be no defence here, but some writers argue that some parts of Lord Mackay's judgment can be seen as indicating that the risk of death must be obvious to D.

Relationship of gross negligence to recklessness

The test under *Bateman* and *Adomako*, by requiring the jury to ask an additional question of whether the conduct was so bad as to be a crime, although objective, is more favourable than recklessness. But the difficulty is that this question does not indicate that a very serious level of neglect should be required for manslaughter.

3.3.6 Reform

In the section on recklessness we reviewed the criticisms of objective recklessness: that it worked harshly against those who lacked capacity. Can this objection be overcome in relation to manslaughter? Arguably so where the conduct in question poses a very high risk of death and the jury question in *Adomako* exists as a safeguard against penalising people for carelessness. The Law Commission in 'Legislating the Criminal Code: Involuntary Manslaughter', Law Com No 237 suggests that it may be justifiable to impose criminal liability for the unforeseen consequences of a person's acts where the harm risked is great and the actor's failure to advert to this risk is *culpable*. It has recommended that *gross carelessness* should apply to manslaughter where the risk of death or serious injury would have been obvious to a reasonable person in the accused's position: Involuntary Homicide Bill, cl 2(1)(a) annexed to Law Com No 237. In addition, the accused must have been capable of appreciating the risk at the material time.

?!   THINKING POINT 3.8

Consider the examples below (taken from the Law Commission report, No 237, at 36). Would each fall within the Bateman/Adomako test of gross negligence?

In each case you need to identify:

■ A duty of care;

■ Breach of that duty involving an obvious risk of death;

■ That the breach caused death;

■ Whether the breach was accompanied by gross negligence which was so bad as to be regarded as criminal.

1. D is an anaesthetist who causes her patient V's death because she fails to notice that a ventilation tube has become disconnected and that V has turned blue.

2. D, an adult of average intelligence, in the course of a fight hits V over the head with a spanner. In the heat of the moment, D does not realise that death or serious injury may result; but the blow cracks V's skull and causes her death.

3. D, in the course of a fight, slaps V once across the face. V loses her balance and falls to the floor, cracks her skull, and dies.

We will return to gross negligence in Chapter 7.

We have now looked at the three most important mental states in criminal law: intention, recklessness and gross negligence. Here is an illustration which might help you to see the difference between them all. The following scenarios were adapted from an example given by G. Williams in 'Recklessness Redefined' (1981) 40(2) *Cambridge LJ* 252–283, at p 256:

EXAMPLE 3.8

D parks his car on a busy road and opens the driver's door which collides with a cyclist V who was passing D's car at that moment. V is thrown off his bicycle, falls under the wheels of a bus and dies.

Identify the offence and relevant state of mind in the following:

1. D knows V is at that spot and wishes to cause V serious bodily harm.

2. D does not wish to injure V but does wish to win a £100 bet that he has the nerve to knock a cyclist off his bicycle. He knew serious injury to V was a virtual certainty.

3. D does not wish to injure V but D's purpose was to quickly escape from his car which had just burst into flames. He knew serious injury to V was a virtual certainty.

4. D wishes to give V a fright by opening the door, thinking he will probably suffer injury.

5. D did not look in the mirror to see if it was safe to open the car door because he was angry and drunk.

6. D had learning difficulties and did not know it was necessary to check the mirror before opening the car door.

7. D opens the car door and, without looking, flings a large hammer into the road which hits V and throws him off his bicycle and under the bus.

8. D was in a rush and completely forgot to look in the mirror before opening the door.

9. The police discover during the subsequent investigation that the car's rear brake lights were not working.

Answers:

1. Murder: direct intent.

2. Murder: oblique intent.

3. Murder: oblique intent. Under the *Nedrick Direction* the jury may find that D was more culpable in 2 than 3 and may exercise their discretion in 3 to convict of reckless manslaughter.

4. Manslaughter: subjective recklessness *R v G*.

5. Manslaughter: subjective recklessness *R v Parker/R v G*.

6. Negligence. No liability for any serious criminal offence.

7. Manslaughter: gross negligence.

8. Negligence. No liability for any serious criminal offence.

9. Section 2 Road Traffic Act 1991 (Driving without due care and attention)—negligence.

SUMMARY

Intention has two meanings:

■ Direct intent: desired aim or purpose; and

■ Oblique intent as defined in the amended *Nedrick Direction*: a result which is not desired but which is either a pre-requisite to D's primary purpose or one which is virtually certain to occur (barring some unforeseen intervention) and which is, in either case, foreseen as such.

■ The jury may but does not have to find intention using this test.

■ Whether *Nedrick/Woollin* provides a definition or evidence of intention is undecided.

Recklessness has one meaning:

■ Recklessness is now subjective and is defined according to *Cunningham* [1957] as the conscious taking of an unjustified risk.

■ *Caldwell* [1982] objective recklessness applied to manslaughter until *Adomako* [1995] and criminal damage until it was overturned by *R v G* [2003].

■ After *R v G*, subjective recklessness includes the person who has deliberately closed his mind to all risk through, for example, temper.

Negligence is defined as:

■ Unreasonable conduct which creates an obvious risk of harm or damage through genuine inadvertence. Risk may never have entered the mind of D at all.

Gross negligence is defined according to:

■ *Bateman* and *Adomako* as an extremely high degree of negligence so as to deserve criminal punishment. It only applies to manslaughter.

PROBLEM SOLVING

D is an anti-capitalist protestor. He telephones a television company and threatens to release a toxic gas into the underground rail system of a city within 30 minutes unless the government agrees to his demands. Twenty minutes later, D releases poisonous gas at a busy station. V dies within minutes. D later claims that he only wanted to make a political point.

A witnesses V's death. She is 14 years old. In shock, she spends a night out and wanders into a neighbour's shed. To keep warm, she pours paraffin on to old wood and ignites it. The fire burns down the shed. B, the neighbour, suffers burns whilst attempting to put out the fire.

Consider any offences that D and A might have committed, paying particular attention to MR.

Remember:

- **I: Identify** relevant issues
- **D: Define** offences/defences
- **E: Explain/evaluate** the law
- **A: Apply** law to facts.

A note on problem solving

Answering essay questions

Problem questions on recklessness have been simplified because of the decision in *R v G*. Questions now frequently take the form of essays in which the legal development of recklessness requires evaluation. For example:

Analyse whether the House of Lords in *R v G and Another* [2003] was correct to hold that a defendant who lacks the capacity for foresight of a risk of destruction or damage to property is not reckless for the purposes of s1 Criminal Damage Act 1971?

Here, the headings of this section should be used as a guide:

- The difference between a subjective and objective test of recklessness and the development of each illustrated by reference to authorities, particularly *Cunningham* and *Caldwell*.
- Lord Diplock's reasons for changing the law in *Caldwell* and the minority judgment of Lord Edmund-Davies.
- Problems of the objective approach by reference to authorities.
- Discussion of facts and analysis of *R v G*, in particular the judgments of Lord Bingham and Lord Steyn with reference to the criticism of *Caldwell*.
- Analysis of judgment of Lord Rodgers.
- Arguments for and against the decision in *R v G* and reform.

Extra marks would be awarded for including academic criticism of the topic with appropriate references. Exactly the same approach should be adopted when answering essay questions in relation to intention or gross negligence.

Answering problem questions

MR is fundamental to criminal liability and it is always necessary to remember that no matter what problem you are answering, the AR/MR of relevant offences will need to be defined, whatever the offence.

It is not uncommon to hear students make an easy mistake about recklessness: 'D didn't mean to be reckless'. This involves a confusion between recklessness as to a result (eg: criminal damage) and reckless conduct, which can be intentional. To say, 'I intend to drive recklessly tonight', makes sense but here one is not talking about MR in relation to a *result* but to a type of *conduct*. Intention and recklessness as to results are quite separate forms of MR and should not be confused.

Whereas recklessness problem questions before 2003 were aimed at getting the student to identify the appropriate tests of recklessness for different offences, as well as the loophole, now the aim will be to test whether you can recognise various mental states which might, or might not, fall within the subjective test as defined in *R v G*.

For further guidance on solving this problem, see the online resources: www.oup.com/uk/loveless6e/.

FURTHER READING

F. Stark, 'It's Only Words: On Meaning and Mens Rea' (2013) 72(1) *Cambridge LJ* 155
Argues that first, English law defines mens rea terms inconsistently depending on context and second, that they should be used uniformly.

Intention

R. Buxton, 'Some Simple Thoughts on Intention' [1988] *Crim LR* **484**

Considers the current law and argues against further reform.

R. Duff, 'The Politics of Intention: A Response to Norrie' [1990] *Crim LR* **637**

A response to 'Oblique Intention and Legal Politics' (cited later in this section) on the definition and politics of intention.

J. Herring, *Great Debates in Criminal Law***, London: Palgrave Macmillan, 2015 at pp 45–55**

Explores the debate on how intention should be defined and whether it should include oblique intention

J. Horder, 'Two Histories and Four Hidden Principles of Mens Rea' (1997) 113 *LQR* **95**

Argues that there is historical authority for the view that foresight is required to morally justify the imposition of criminal liability.

M. Kaveny, 'Inferring Intention from Foresight' (2004) 120 *LQR* **81, 86**

Discusses the legal relationship between foresight and intention.

I. Kugler, 'Conditional Oblique Intention' [2004] *Crim LR* **284**

Argues that conditional oblique intention should not necessarily suffice for a conviction.

N. Lacey, 'A Clear Concept of Intention: Elusive or Illusory?' (1993) 56(5) *MLR* **621**

Argues that we haven't reached consensus on the definition of intention, and explores the legal use of 'common sense' or 'ordinary' meanings.

A. Norrie, 'Oblique Intention and Legal Politics' [1989] *Crim LR* **793**

Relates the difficulties in defining oblique intention to the contradiction between law's liberal form and its social control function.

A. Norrie, 'Intention—More Loose Talk' [1990] *Crim LR* **642**

Responds to criticisms made by Duff in 'The Politics of Intention' (cited earlier in this section).

A. Norrie, 'After *Woollin***' [1999]** *Crim LR* **532**

Argues that the law on oblique intention remains unclear.

A. Pedain, 'Intention and the Terrorist Example' [2003] *Crim LR* **579**

Uses the terrorist example in *Woollin* to highlight criticisms of the test for intention.

A. Simester & W. Chan, 'Intention Thus Far' [1997] *Crim LR* **704**

Analyses how far the case law has clarified the test for intention, and what scope it allows for moral judgments.

W. Wilson, 'Doctrinal Rationality after Woollin' (1999) 62 *MLR* **448**

Pays particular attention to using the *Woollin Direction* when D was motivated by good intentions.

Recklessness

K. Amirthalingam, '*Caldwell* **Recklessness is Dead, Long Live Mens Rea's Fecklessness' (2004) 63** *MLR* **491**

Argues that *R v G* is too heavily-weighted towards a subjective approach.

A. Ashworth, 'R v G & Anr [2003] UKHL 50 [2004] Crim LR 369 (commentary)'

Summarises and comments on major themes of *R v G*.

J. Herring, *Great Debates in Criminal Law***, London: Palgrave Macmillan, 2015 at pp 55–61**

Suggests that the test for recklessness should not be wholly subjective.

H. Keating, 'Reckless Children' [2007] *Crim LR* **546**

Considers the effect of the Ds' age on the jury in *R v G* and asks whether the age of criminal responsibility should be raised.

Law Commission, 'Legislating the Criminal Code: Involuntary Manslaughter' (Report No 237, 1996)

Reviews the law in this area and makes recommendations for legislation.

Gross negligence

J.C Smith, 'R v Adomako [1994] 3 All ER 79 (HL); [1994] *Crim LR* **757 (commentary)'**

Summarises and highlights key points of the judgment.

S. Shute, 'Causation: Foreseeability v Natural Consequences' (1992) 55(4) *MLR* **585**

Questions what we mean by the terms 'reasonable' and 'foreseeable'.

Strict, vicarious and corporate liability

4

Introduction

4.1 Strict Liability

4.2 Corporate Liability

KEY POINTS

STRICT LIABILITY

This section will help you to:

- understand that strict liability means that no MR needs to be proved in relation to one or more elements of the AR of an offence, typically arising in the areas of social concern or public safety;
- understand that strict liability offences can be defended by general and due diligence defences;
- define statutory MR terms;
- evaluate the arguments concerning strict liability, the presumption of innocence and the ECHR;
- evaluate the arguments for and against strict liability.

VICARIOUS AND CORPORATE LIABILITY

This section will help you to understand:

- the nature of corporate criminal liability, both vicarious and direct;
- the difficulties in prosecuting a company for serious crime;
- the main provisions of the Corporate Manslaughter and Corporate Homicide Act 2007.

INTRODUCTION

We have seen that generally, a person is guilty of a crime if they have both actus reus and mens rea for the offence (and no defence). This chapter considers two situations outside that general rule. First, statutory offences of strict liability can be committed even where D does not have mens rea for all elements of the actus reus. That obviously gives rise to important issues, including fairness and human rights, which are considered here. Many statutory offences which do require mens rea use terms such as knowledge or wilfulness, which will also be considered in this chapter.

Second, while most crimes are committed by natural persons (individual human beings), some can also be committed by legal persons (corporations). Since a corporation is very different to a natural person—it does not have a mind of its own, and cannot be physically placed in prison, for example—there are special rules of corporate liability. Like strict liability, this area of criminal law also raises important and controversial policy issues.

4.1 Strict Liability

KEY CASES

Sweet v Parsley [1970] AC 132—the presumption of MR;

B (A Minor) v DPP [2000] 1 All ER 833—MR can only be displaced expressly or by necessary implication;

R v K [2001] UKHL 41—*B v DPP* confirmed;

R v G [2008] UKHL 37—strict liability offences are not contrary to Article 6(2) ECHR;

Pharmaceutical Society of GB v Storkwain Ltd [1986] 2 All ER 635—strict liability in drug-related offences;

Nasir Zahid v R [2010] EWCA Crim 2158—possession of expanding ammunition.

4.1.1 Introduction

Over half of all offences in English law are offences of strict or no-fault liability. These statutory offences are the result of a massive expansion of state regulation over commercial and public welfare activities since the end of the Second World War. They exist in the areas of health and safety, environmental health, pollution, licensing, motoring, public transport, consumer protection, copyright, financial services, food safety, trade and industry. Most strict liability offences regulate the activities of corporations. The offences are conventionally regarded as quasi-criminal. Although fines and/or imprisonment are possible, they do not usually bear the stigma of a serious conviction.

There are criticisms relating to the fairness and effectiveness of these offences in general which become more accentuated when strict liability is used to penalise individuals as opposed to corporations. Conviction without fault contradicts the accepted approach to criminal liability that only people who have chosen to do wrong should be punished. By holding individuals to account for these crimes which may carry a risk of imprisonment, fundamental principles of proportionality and legitimacy are raised. We will examine the arguments either way in this chapter.

4.1.2 Strict v Absolute Liability

An offence of strict liability is one where no fault needs to be proved to secure a conviction. Sometimes the offence will consist of AR only.

> Section 4 Road Traffic Act 1988:
>
> A person who, when driving or attempting to drive a mechanically propelled vehicle on a road or other public place, is unfit to drive through drink or drugs is guilty of an offence.

Whether a driver is knowingly intoxicated or not is irrelevant. Liability is strict. A new offence of 'Drug Driving' under s5A of the Road Traffic Act 1988 imposes liability for driving or being in charge of a motor vehicle with a concentration of a controlled drug above a specified limit. Unlike s4, there is no need to prove that the driver is unfit to drive. These offences are concerned with public safety and impose tight controls on drink and drug driving.

In other offences, liability can be strict in relation to one element of the AR but require MR as to another:

Section 5 Sexual Offences Act 2003:

(1) A person commits an offence if–

(a) he intentionally penetrates the vagina, anus or mouth of another person with his penis, and

(b) the other person is under 13.

D may intentionally penetrate another but be under a genuine mistake as to the other's age. Nevertheless, although neither intentional, reckless, or knowingly at fault in relation to age, D will still be convicted. Strict liability as to age applies to all sexual offences against children under 13 whereas MR is required in relation to offences against children aged 13–16.

An early strict liability case is *Hobbs v Winchester Corporation* [1910] 2 KB 471 where a butcher was found to have committed the offence of selling unsound meat even though he could not have discovered the defect by any reasonable examination and had not been negligent. The Court of Appeal held that one who engages in business for profit has to take the risk of criminal liability without fault in the interests of public safety.

Many strict liability offences now provide 'no negligence' or 'due diligence' defences by which a blameless defendant may be excused, having taken all reasonable steps to prevent the risk of harm. Other general defences can apply. For example, if D commits an unlawful act under s5 Sexual Offences Act 2003 under threat of death or serious injury, he should be allowed to plead duress. If he acts as an automaton following a blow to the head, the defence of automatism should be available. An offence of absolute liability, on the other hand, is one where involuntariness is no defence. An example would be a status or situational offence (refer back to *Larsonneur* (1933) 149 LT 542: 'being an alien to whom leave to land in the UK has been refused'). Confusingly, some cases adopt the language of absolute as opposed to strict liability in relevant case law.

→ CROSS-REFERENCE
The facts of *Larsonneur* are set out in Chapter 2, 2.1.1.

?! THINKING POINT 4.1

Which of the following are offences of strict liability?

■ Any person who sells to a person under the age of 16 years any tobacco or cigarette papers, whether for his own use or not, shall be liable on summary conviction to a fine not exceeding level 4 ... (s7 Children and Young Persons Act 1933);

■ A person commits an offence if he intentionally touches another person, the touching is sexual and the other person is under 13. (s7 Sexual Offences Act 2003);

■ If a person drives a mechanically propelled vehicle on a road or other public place without due care and attention, or without reasonable consideration for other persons using the road or place, he is guilty of an offence. (s3 Road Traffic Act 1988);

■ Whosoever shall assault any person with intent to resist arrest ... shall be guilty of an offence. (s38 Police Act 1996).

Can you think of any advantages of strict liability?

You might think that strict liability deters people from acting negligently or that it is a more efficient means of prosecuting people or organisations for offences which are not truly criminal, particularly where the risk to public safety or welfare is high. We will now examine the frequently overlapping and uncertain principles used by the courts to decide whether an offence is one of strict liability or not.

4.1.3 The Statutory Context: The Presumption of Mens Rea

The fact that MR is not defined in an offence is not conclusive. The court will need to explore whether the omission of a mental element was deliberate, thereby indicating strict liability, or a matter of poor drafting, indicating that the offence is really one of MR. The guiding principle is that where an offence is silent regarding any mental element, there is a *presumption* of MR. That presumption should only be displaced for very good reason such as social concern, the intention of Parliament or the promotion of law enforcement.

Strict liability has been dealt a heavy blow by the House of Lords in two recent age-related sexual cases (*B* and *K*, see later in this section). These judgments reinforced the presumption of MR. However, the courts continue to apply strict liability to new offences and one may therefore assume that, although less popular than it once was, strict liability is far from redundant. The first case in which the presumption of MR was confirmed was the following:

Sweet v Parsley [1970] AC 132 HOUSE OF LORDS

Miss Sweet, a teacher, let rooms in her farmhouse to students. She was not a resident landlord. She was convicted under s5(b) Dangerous Drugs Act 1965 for being concerned in the management of premises used for the *purposes* of smoking cannabis. The magistrates found that she had no control over her tenants or knowledge that the house was being used for smoking cannabis. Nevertheless, they interpreted the offence as one of strict liability. She appealed by way of case stated to the Divisional Court which dismissed her appeal. She then appealed to the House of Lords.

Lord Reid:

How has it come about that the Divisional Court has felt bound to reach such an obviously unjust result? ... Our first duty is to consider the words of the Act: if they show a clear intention to create an absolute offence that is an end of the matter. But such cases are very rare. Sometimes the words of the section which creates a particular offence make it clear that *mens rea* is required in one form or another. Such cases are quite frequent. But in a very large number of cases there is no clear indication either way. In such cases there has for centuries been a presumption that Parliament did not intend to make criminals of persons who were in no way blameworthy in what they did. That means that whenever a section is silent as to *mens rea* there is a presumption that, in order to give effect to the will of Parliament, we must read in words appropriate to require *mens rea*. ... [I]t is firmly established by a host of authorities that *mens rea* is an essential ingredient of every offence unless some reason can be found for holding that that is not necessary.

It is also firmly established that the fact that other sections of the Act expressly require *mens rea*, for example because they contain the word 'knowingly' is not in itself sufficient to justify a decision that a section which is silent as to *mens rea* creates an absolute offence. In the absence of a clear indication in the Act that an offence is intended to be an absolute offence, it is necessary to go outside the Act and examine all relevant circumstances in order to establish that this must have been the intention of Parliament. I say 'must have been' because it is a universal principle that if a penal provision is reasonably capable of two interpretations, that interpretation which is most favourable to the accused must be adopted.

Lord Reid then doubted whether the public interest demanded the conviction of the innocent for offences of a truly criminal character, particularly in view of the stigma that would attach. The choice for the House was simply between the imposition of MR, which could lead to unjustified acquittals, or strict liability, which could lead to unjustified convictions. He concluded:

> If this section means what the Divisional Court have held that it means, then hundreds of thousands of people who sublet part of the premises or take in lodgers or are concerned in the management of residential premises or institutions are daily incurring a risk of being convicted of a serious offence in circumstances where they are in no way to blame. ... I must now turn to the question what is the true meaning of section 5 of the 1965 Act ... is the 'purpose' the purpose of the smoker or the purpose of the management? ... It is clear that the purpose is the purpose of the management ... So if the purpose is the purpose of the management, the question whether the offence ... is absolute can hardly arise.

Appeal allowed.

This was a landmark case which signalled disapproval of a tendency to define drugs-related offences as imposing strict liability. The modern equivalent of this offence, s5 Misuse of Drugs Act 1971, requires knowledge of the purposes for which the premises are being used.

The presumption of MR was recently confirmed by two House of Lords decisions concerning sexual offences against children. Although the offences in question have now been replaced by others under the Sexual Offences Act 2003, these decisions remain leading cases on strict liability.

B (A Minor) v DPP [2000] 1 ALL ER 833, [2000] CRIM LR 403 HOUSE OF LORDS

The appellant, aged 15, was charged with inciting a girl under 14 to commit an act of gross indecency with him contrary to s1 Indecency with Children Act 1960. He sat next to a girl aged 13 on a bus and asked her several times to perform oral sex with him which she refused to do. The appellant honestly believed the girl to be over 14 but this was held by the magistrates to be no defence. The Divisional Court dismissed his appeal and certified a point of law for appeal to the House of Lords as to whether a defence of honest belief that the child was over 14 applied to the offence. The House held that the offence in question was not one of strict liability. The prosecution must prove that D knew that, or was reckless whether, the child was under 14.

Lord Nicholls:

> The common law presumes that, unless Parliament indicated otherwise, the appropriate mental element is an unexpressed ingredient of every statutory offence. On this I need do no more than refer to Lord Reid's magisterial statement in the leading case of *Sweet v. Parsley* [1970] ...
>
> If a man genuinely believes that the girl with whom he is committing a grossly indecent act is over fourteen, he is not intending to commit such an act with a girl under fourteen. Whether such an intention is an essential ingredient of the offence depends upon a proper construction of section 1 of the 1960 Act. I turn next to that question.
>
> The construction of section 1 of the Indecency with Children Act 1960
>
> In section 1(1) of the Indecency with Children Act 1960 Parliament has not expressly negatived the need for a mental element in respect of the age element of the offence. The question, therefore, is whether, although not expressly negatived, the need for a mental element is

negatived by necessary implication. 'Necessary implication' connotes an implication which is compellingly clear. Such an implication may be found in the language used, the nature of the offence, the mischief sought to be prevented and any other circumstances which may assist in determining what intention is properly to be attributed to Parliament when creating the offence …

The offence so created is a serious offence. The more serious the offence, the greater is the weight to be attached to the presumption, because the more severe is the punishment and the graver the stigma which accompany a conviction. Under section 1 conviction originally attracted a punishment of up to two years' imprisonment. This has since been increased to a maximum of ten years' imprisonment. The notification requirements under Part I of the Sex Offenders Act 1997 now apply, no matter what the age of the offender: see Schedule 1, paragraph 1(1)(*b*). Further, in addition to being a serious offence, the offence is drawn broadly ('an act of gross indecency'). It can embrace conduct ranging from predatory approaches by a much older paedophile to consensual sexual experimentation between precocious teenagers of whom the offender may be the younger of the two. The conduct may be depraved by any acceptable standard, or it may be relatively innocuous behaviour in private between two young people. These factors reinforce, rather than negative, the application of the presumption in this case.

The purpose of the section is, of course, to protect children. An age ingredient was therefore an essential ingredient of the offence. This factor in itself does not assist greatly. Without more, this does not lead to the conclusion that liability was intended to be strict so far as the age element is concerned, so that the offence is committed irrespective of the alleged offender's belief about the age of the 'victim' and irrespective of how the offender came to hold this belief. ….

Accordingly, I cannot find, either in the statutory context or otherwise, any indication of sufficient cogency to displace the application of the common law presumption. In my view the necessary mental element regarding the age ingredient in section 1 of the Act of 1960 is the absence of a genuine belief by the accused that the victim was fourteen years of age or above. The burden of proof of this rests upon the prosecution in the usual way. If Parliament considers that the position should be otherwise regarding this serious social problem, Parliament must itself confront the difficulties and express its will in clear terms. I would allow this appeal.

 NOTE 4.1

The case is significant for two reasons:

1. *Strict Liability*: The House stated that the starting point for offences which are silent on MR was the common law presumption that MR was essential unless Parliament had indicated a contrary intention. Further, it was also held that the presumption of MR applies to all statutory offences unless it is excluded expressly or by *necessary* implication. A reasonable implication is not enough. In other words, courts should now be very slow to find that an offence is one of strict liability.

Lord Steyn stated that the requirement of MR in statutory offences was a constitutional principle:

In successive editions of his classic work Professor Sir Rupert Cross cited as the paradigm of the principle the '"presumption" that mens rea is required in the case of statutory crimes': *Statutory Interpretation* 3 ed. (1995), p. 166. Sir Rupert explained that such presumptions are of general application and are not dependent on finding an ambiguity in the text. He said they 'not only supplement the text, they also operate at a higher level as expressions of fundamental principles governing both civil liberties and the relations between Parliament, the executive and the courts. They operate as constitutional principles which are not easily displaced by a statutory text': ibid. In other words, in the absence of express words or a truly necessary implication, Parliament must be presumed to legislate on the assumption that the principle of legality will supplement the text. This is the theoretical framework against which section 1(1) must be interpreted.

2. *The Defence of Mistaken Belief*: Historically, MR offences required a mistaken belief in relevant facts to be both honest and *reasonable*. Reasonableness indicated an objective approach to MR in the sense that unless the mistaken belief was one which any reasonable person would have held, it would not provide a defence. But over the years, the courts have tended to prefer a subjective approach to MR and mistaken belief in relation to defences. D is now to be judged on the facts as he honestly believed them to be, whether that belief is reasonable or not. The case confirms this subjective approach (see Chapter 9).

?! THINKING POINT 4.2

In order to decide whether the offence required MR, many social issues concerning the sexual exploitation and autonomy of young people arose in the case.

The act in question was accepted as being grossly indecent. Do you think there is a moral difference between an act of gross indecency with a child under 14 and a child under 16— the legal age of consent?

Should it make any difference whether D is around the same age or older than the victim?

The ratio of *B v DPP* was followed in the next case which was also concerned with an age-related sexual offence, this time under the Sexual Offences Act 1956.

R v K [2001] UKHL 41, [2001] 3 ALL ER 897 HOUSE OF LORDS

The 26-year-old appellant was convicted of indecent assault on a 14-year-old girl contrary to s14(1) Sexual Offences Act 1956 (indecent assault on a woman under the age of 16 years). The offence was punishable with a maximum life sentence. His defence was that the activity was consensual and that he believed her to be 16 for that was what she had told him. Section 14(1) did not mention any defence whereas other offences within s14 expressly provided a defence of honest and *reasonable* mistaken belief. The trial judge had ruled that the prosecution had to prove an absence of genuine belief on the part of the defendant that the victim was 16 or over. In other words, MR was required for this offence following *B v DPP*, but a mistaken honest belief as to age would provide a defence. The Court of Appeal allowed the appeal in favour of the prosecution. The House of Lords reversed the Court of Appeal's ruling and found in favour of the appellant.

Lord Bingham stated that the fact that s14(1) did not expressly provide a defence which was available elsewhere was not a conclusive indication that it was an offence of strict liability:

In *B (A Minor) v Director of Public Prosecutions* [2000] 2 AC 428 the House considered section 1(1) of the 1960 Act in the light of the presumption that guilty knowledge is an essential ingredient of a statutory offence unless it is shown to be excluded by express words or necessary implication. It found no express words and no necessary implication having that effect. It was accordingly necessary for the prosecution to prove the absence of a genuine belief on the part of the defendant, whether reasonable or not, that the victim had been 14 or over. The House was invited in that case (see pp 457G, 473A) to treat the Acts of 1956 and 1960 as part of a single code, and that approach seems to me to be plainly correct. It is at once obvious that if an absence of genuine belief as to the age of an under-age victim must be proved against a defendant under section 1 of the 1960 Act but not against a defendant under section 14 of the 1956 Act, another glaring anomaly would be introduced into this legislation. But that conclusion does not relieve the House of the need to carry out, in relation to section 14, the task that it carried out in relation to section 1.

Neither in section 14 nor elsewhere in the 1956 Act is there any express exclusion of the need to prove an absence of genuine belief on the part of a defendant as to the age of an under-age victim. Had it been intended to exclude that element of mens rea it could very conveniently have been so provided in or following subsection (2).

There is nothing in the language of this statute which justifies, as a matter of necessary implication, the conclusion that Parliament must have intended to exclude this ingredient of mens rea in section 14 any more than in section 1. If the effect of the presumption is read into section 14, with reference to the defendant's belief as to the age of the victim, no absurdity results.

NOTE 4.2

As with *B v DPP*, there were two issues:

1. *Strict Liability*: The House decided that, consistently with *B v DPP*, there was nothing in the language of the Act to justify, by necessary implication, the conclusion that Parliament intended to deny a defence of mistaken belief in relation to age in s14(1).

2. *Mistaken Belief*: Any mistaken belief need only be honest and genuine but not reasonable. Reasonableness or unreasonableness is not irrelevant however because the more unreasonable the belief, the less likely it is to be believed as honest. The decision was unanimous but Lord Millett expressed misgivings about providing a defence of honest but unreasonable belief in an offence concerned with the protection of under-age girls.

?! THINKING POINT 4.3

Suppose D is a paedophile who commits a consensual indecent assault upon a 14-year-old victim. He honestly believes that she is 16 because of the adult way she dresses and acts. Would *B and K* provide him with a defence?

Should his own belief provide him with a defence? Alternatively, should there be objective standards against which to measure any belief? Or should this be an offence of strict liability where belief is irrelevant? Under the Sexual Offences Act 2003, sexual offences against children under 13 are now offences of strict liability. Offences against children between 13 and 16 are based on reasonable belief as to age.

You will find it helpful to compare the following commentaries on *B* and *K*.

J.C. Smith, commentary to *B v DPP* [2000] *Crim LR* at p 405:

> It was once asserted in these commentaries that the House of Lords has a dismal record in criminal cases. It still does; but just occasionally, the House hits the jackpot. *Woolmington* (1935), *Morgan* (1976) and now this. …
>
> In his Hamlyn lecture on *Woolmington* ('One Golden Thread?' in *Turning Points of the Common Law* (1997)) … he (Lord Cooke of Thorndon, a NZ judge) writes:
>
> > '… it does seem odd that in the home of Woolmington absolute (or strict) liability is so extensively accepted by the courts, and with some equanimity. It is as if the great case has created a judicial mindset which recoils at a shifting of the onus, yet tolerates a harsher solution …'
>
> There is great force in this criticism. It is certainly odd. English judges, while routinely paying lip-service to a presumption in favour of *mens rea* before finding it ruled out, have jibbed at inferring a requirement of a lower degree of fault … It is in the toleration of the harsher solution where the English courts have gone wrong—though they would doubtless disclaim responsibility, arguing that they were only implementing the intention of Parliament. Sometimes they were; but more often strict liability was their own invention … Of course this is far from being the end of strict liability. *B's* case inevitably creates a degree of uncertainty in the law. Age-related sexual offences provide the most obvious case in point … There are many other offences, other than the sexual offences where the age of the 'victim' is a material—usually the principal—element. … [In relation to *Shah*, Professor Smith continued] … Mitchell J quoted from the well-known authorities, which are cited over and over again when strict liability is in issue, particularly Lord Reid's speech in *Sweet v Parsley* … where he distinguished 'truly criminal acts' and acts which are not truly criminal but which in the public interest are prohibited under a penalty. … But despite the eminence of the judges who have taken this line over so many years, it is questionable. … It is impossible to deny that the regulation in *Shah*, for example, creates a crime. … Unless the sellers are given an absolute discharge, they have a conviction recorded against them. By any test, it *is* a crime. It is entirely different from the imposition of a fine for failure to return a library book. 'Truly' it is a crime and no amount of judicial assertion can change that fact. The assertion that something is so when it is not so cannot be the basis of a sound law – whoever makes the assertion.

→ CROSS-REFERENCE
Shah is discussed in 4.1.4.

J. Horder in 'How Culpability Can, and Cannot, be Denied in Under-age Sex Crimes' [2001] *Crim LR* 15 argues that the law should observe the moral context of the crime and uphold reasonable standards:

> [Speaking of *B v DPP*:] The decision of the House of Lords, a decision that flies in the face of Legislation and case law across much of the rest of the common law world, can be attributed more or less directly to the pervasive influence of a subjectivist understanding of the so-called 'correspondence principle' in criminal law theory. According to subjectivists, this theory requires that defendants should not in general be held criminally liable unless they intended to bring about, or realised that they might bring about, the forbidden consequences in the forbidden circumstances. …
>
> [T]he House of Lords concerned itself exclusively with whether D realised that V might be, as section 1(1) [Indecency with Children Act 1960] demands, aged under 14. That concern is with the wrong issue. Whether V is aged just under or over 14 years is, for the purposes of section 1(1), in itself a matter of *moral* insignificance, in spite of its legal import. There is no moral distinction to be drawn between a case in which a man invites a girl aged just under 14 to commit an act of gross indecency, and a case in which a man does the same to a girl aged just over 14. … It follows that a mistaken belief that V is aged 14 has no moral bearing on whether D is to be blamed for engaging in the *actus reus*, by … inciting an act of gross indecency with a young girl. …

On the face of it, such a holding is capable of producing some unsavoury results. Suppose D, an adult paedophile, invites V, who is in fact 13, to commit an act of gross indecency with him. D believes V is over 14. D's belief is based, however, solely on an inference drawn from the character of previous sexual experiences he has had with V, as compared to his numerous sexual experiences with other children both younger and older than V. The law as it stands after *B (A Minor) v DPP* would acquit D in this example, even though it was nothing more than his experience as a paedophile that led him to believe that V was over 14. … [The author then goes on to argue that a *reasonable* belief that V was *16* would be morally significant.]

Compare this example with one in which D is charged with having sexual intercourse with a girl under 13 … In such a case D's belief that V has just turned 13, whether reasonable or not, cannot be a morally justifiable ground for acting as D does because it has no moral significance …

The basic wrong committed by D … in *B* … was (in broad terms) the sexual propositioning of a child, someone aged under 16. D's basic *mens rea* ought to relate to this. … The '*B* principle' is wholly subjective, and thus focuses on whether D *himself* regarded the conduct as tolerable in society as it is today, even if it was not tolerable in fact … In this regard, as hinted at the outset, what age D believed V to be (if he had any belief about V's age) can have practical normal significance, but of a kind quite different from that emphasised in *B*. … The significance of B's belief about V's age was that he believed her to be *about the same age as him*. Such a belief to some extent furbishes his case for saying that he believed the contact he had with V might be regarded by decent, humane people as tolerable, even if far from admirable.

Which of these authors favours a subjective approach to MR and which an objective?

The offences in *B* and *K* have now been replaced by new child sex offences in the Sexual Offences Act 2003. One example is the offence of rape of a child under 13 which was considered in *R v G* [2008] UKHL 37.

→ CROSS-REFERENCE
See 4.1.5 for the facts
of *R v G*.

The 2003 Act does not affect the significance of *B* and *K* in relation to the principles of strict liability. However, strict liability continues to be applied to current statutes. Therefore we must understand the traditional principles of this area of liability.

4.1.4 The Exceptions to Mens Rea

- Social concern
- Public safety and law enforcement
- Offences which are not 'truly criminal'
- Statutory mens rea terms

Social concern

Two of the earliest cases on strict liability concerned offences which were silent on MR. The social context was the problem of drunkenness. But statutory interpretation and policy were invoked by the courts in each case to produce opposite results.

Drunkenness

Cundy v Le Cocq (1884) 13 QBD 207 QUEEN'S BENCH DIVISION

D, a licensed wines and spirits seller, sold alcohol to a drunk. He did not know the customer was drunk but was still convicted under s13 Licensing Act 1872 of unlawfully selling liquor to a drunken person. On appeal to the Divisional Court it was held that the words of the section imposed an absolute prohibition on the sale of liquor to drunken persons and that a genuine mistake about the customer's condition would not affect liability but would provide mitigation of sentence. The scope of the Act was the repression of drunkenness. Other sections of the Act contained offences where knowledge was plainly required as an element.

Stephen J:

> In old time and as applicable to the common law or to earlier statutes, the maxim [that in every criminal offence there must be a guilty mind] may have been of general application; but a difference has arisen owing to the greater precision of modern statutes. It is impossible now … to apply the maxim generally to all statutes, and the substance of all the reported cases is that it is necessary to look at the object of each Act that is under consideration to see whether and how far knowledge is of the essence of the offence created. Here … the object of this part of the Act is to prevent the sale of intoxicating liquor to drunken persons, and it is perfectly natural to carry that out by throwing on the publican the responsibility of determining whether the person supplied comes within that category.

Conviction affirmed.

Sherras v De Rutzen [1895] 1 QB 918 QUEEN'S BENCH DIVISION

D, a licensed wines and spirits seller, sold alcohol to a police constable on duty without permission from a superior officer contrary to s16(2) Licensing Act 1872. D reasonably believed the constable was off-duty. The word 'knowingly' was used in other offences but not s16(2). The Divisional Court held that the absence of that word merely shifted the burden of proof on to D to prove that he did not know the constable was on duty. The fact that a publican would have no independent means of ascertaining whether a police officer was on duty or not justified interpreting the offence as one of negligence and not strict liability on the principle of fairness.

Can the distinction between these two cases be justified?

 THINKING POINT 4.4

Do you think a publican should be punished for serving alcohol to under-age drinkers where he has done all that is reasonably possible to prevent the offence?

Drug offences

Strict liability defines some drug-related offences.

Pharmaceutical Society of GB v Storkwain Ltd [1986] 2 ALL ER 635 HOUSE OF LORDS

The Pharmaceutical Society prosecuted Storkwain Ltd (a pharmacy) alleging offences under s58(2)(a) and s76(2) Medicines Act 1968 for supplying prescription-only drugs to customers on forged prescriptions. The pharmacist believed himself to be without fault, having acted in good faith and believing on reasonable grounds that the prescriptions were valid. Following conviction by the magistrates, the Divisional Court had dismissed the pharmacy's appeal and it appealed to the House of Lords.

The offence was silent on MR unlike other offences under the Act in question and the House of Lords held that this was very strong evidence of strict liability.

Lord Goff:

> ... For the appellants, counsel submitted [*inter alia*] that there must, in accordance with the well-recognised presumption, be read into section 58(2)(a) words appropriate to require *mens rea* ... [I]n other words, to adopt the language of Lord Diplock in *Sweet v Parsley*, the subsection must be read subject to the implication that a necessary element in the prohibition ... is the absence of belief, held honestly and on reasonable grounds, in the existence of facts which, if true, would make the act innocent. ... [I]t is ... clear from the 1968 Act that Parliament must have intended that the presumption of *mens rea* should be inapplicable to section 58(2)(a). First of all, it appears from the 1968 Act that, where Parliament wished to recognise that *mens rea* should be an ingredient of an offence created by the Act, it has expressly so provided. [His Lordship remarked that mens rea was expressly provided in other sections of the Act.] ... I gratefully adopt as my own the following passage from the judgment of Farquharson J [in the Divisional Court]:
>
> '... it is perfectly obvious that pharmacists are in a position to put illicit drugs and perhaps other medicines on the market. Happily this rarely happens but it does from time to time. It can therefore be readily understood that Parliament would find it necessary to impose a heavier liability on those who are in such a position, and make them more strictly accountable for any breaches of the Act.'

Appeal dismissed.

See this commentary by B.S. Jackson, '*Storkwain*: A Case Study in Strict Liability and Self-Regulation' [1991] *Crim LR* 892 who observes that there was more to the case than the prosecution of a careless pharmacist:

The case of Storkwain, as reported in the Law Reports, appears at first sight to be a paradigm case of strict liability, a harsh – even anomalous – example of preference of public interest over individual responsibility. Indeed, it heads the chapter on strict liability in the current edition of Smith and Hogan, as an example of the imposition of liability despite the absence of 'intention, recklessness or even negligence to one or more elements of the actus reus,' and Professor Smith in his commentary in this journal concluded that Parliament cannot have intended 'such an unjust result as that reached.' Yet further examination of the facts of the case, and of their relationship to the internal regulatory mechanisms of the professional body concerned, reveals a very different, and arguably rather more interesting, story ...

The Divisional Court's sketchy knowledge of the facts is not surprising; the facts had been agreed even before the proceedings in the Magistrates' Court, and in a form such as not to suggest culpability on the part of the pharmacist. The Society wanted to confirm (as it saw it) the principle of strict liability, for reasons which will appear. However, the full facts told a significantly different story, and at the same time illustrate some important practical dimensions of regulatory law-enforcement, and the way in which it is currently affected by changes in the prosecution system.

First, the facts of Storkwain's offence, as understood by the Society. The script was one of a number of private prescriptions containing controlled drugs which were noticed by the Society's Inspector, on his periodic visit. The forgery appeared quite blatant: and indeed the prescription itself was later published on the front cover of The Pharmaceutical Journal. ... However, apart from not spotting what the Inspector took to be an obvious forgery, Storkwain's pharmacist fell short of normal (or at least expected) good practice in another respect.

Since the prescription included 'controlled drugs', as well as 'prescription-only-medicines' (known in the profession as 'POMs'), it was indeed expected that the pharmacist would telephone the doctor for confirmation. Where the doctor is not known to the pharmacist, the Society expects that reliance not be placed upon the telephone number on the prescription. A check should then be made that the doctor's practice does indeed have that telephone number. The reason for this is well illustrated in this case. The name of the doctor was not known to Storkwain's pharmacist; it was not that of a local doctor. The forger had chosen the name and genuine address of a real doctor from out of the locality, but had attached to the 'prescription' a false telephone number (varying only in one digit from the genuine phone number). The pharmacist did indeed telephone the number on the prescription, and asked to speak to the doctor. A male voice replied (the real doctor, as it happens, was female). The voice at the end of the telephone was presumably an accomplice of the forger, who knew that the pharmacist would ring for confirmation, and had arranged with the forger the time at which the prescription would be presented. The pharmacist was completely taken in by the false doctor. On that basis, he issued the drugs. Thus, from the viewpoint of the Society, he was at fault in two respects: first, the prescription on the face of it was suspect; secondly, he contributed to his own deception on the telephone, by not checking initially that he was ringing the real number of the doctor.

The decision in *Storkwain*'s case could be justified on the basis that he was negligent and therefore at fault. Note: he was not dishonest.

By contrast, the offence in the next drugs case, which was concerned with the definition of possession, bore all the hallmarks of being truly criminal, yet it was classified as an offence of strict liability.

?! **THINKING POINT** 4.5

Is the criminal law the best way to enforce higher regulatory standards?

Should *Storkwain* be overturned in the light of *B and K*?

Warner v Metropolitan Police Commissioner [1968] 2 ALL ER 356 HOUSE OF LORDS

The appellant was charged with possession of a prohibited drug contrary to s1 Drugs (Prevention of Misuse) Act 1964. [The relevant offence is now s5 Misuse of Drugs Act 1971.] D was found in possession of two boxes in which were 20,000 tablets containing amphetamine sulphate, a prohibited drug. The appellant's case was that he thought he was in possession of scent not drugs. D was convicted on the basis of strict liability. The House of Lords held that the offence was one of strict liability but that possession required knowledge. In other words, if D could prove he had no knowledge of what he possessed, he would have a defence. This was a 'half-way house' between absolute liability and mens rea.

Lord Reid:

> I understand that this is the first case in which this house has had to consider whether a statutory offence is an absolute offence in the sense that the belief, intention, or state of mind of the accused is immaterial and irrelevant. ... I would think it difficult to convince Parliament that there

was any real need to convict a man who could prove that he had neither knowledge of what was being done nor any grounds for suspecting that there was anything wrong. ... Ignorance of the law is no defence and in fact virtually everyone knows that there are prohibited drugs. So it would be quite sufficient to prove facts from which it could properly be inferred that the accused knew that he had a prohibited drug in his possession. That would not lead to an unreasonable result. In a case like this Parliament, if consulted, might think it right to transfer the onus of proof so that an accused would have to prove that he neither knew nor had any reason to suspect that he had a prohibited drug in his possession; I am unable to find sufficient grounds for imputing to Parliament an intention to deprive the accused of all rights to show that he had no knowledge or reason to suspect that any prohibited drug was on his premises or in a container which was in his possession.

Section 28(3) Misuse of Drugs Act 1971 now confers a statutory defence of mistaken *belief*.

Pollution

In the next case the court decided that the offence was not truly criminal in nature.

Alphacell Ltd v Woodward [1972] AC 824 HOUSE OF LORDS

In the course of their business, the appellants produced a large amount of pollutant which was stored in a tank near a river. The tank possessed pumps so that excess water could be removed to prevent over-flowing. The pumps were fixed with filters so that they would not become blocked. The tank was regularly inspected. Despite this, the pumps became blocked with leaves and other vegetable matter causing the tank to overflow and pollute the river. The appellants were convicted under s2(1) Rivers (Prevention of Pollution) Act 1951 whereby it was an offence for a person to cause or knowingly permit to enter a stream any poisonous, noxious or polluting matter. The case was appealed to the House of Lords on the question of whether the offence was committed if D had no knowledge of the pollution and had not been negligent.

Lord Salmon:

It seems to me that, giving the word 'cause' its ordinary and natural meaning, anyone may cause something to happen ... intentionally or negligently or inadvertently without negligence and without intention. ...

The appellants clearly did not cause the pollution intentionally and we must assume that they did not do so negligently. Nevertheless, the facts so fully and clearly stated by my noble and learned friend Viscount Dilhorne to my mind make it obvious that the appellants in fact caused the pollution. If they did not cause it, what did? There was no intervening act of a third party nor was there any act of God to which it could be attributed. ... It seems plain to me that the appellants caused the pollution by the active operation of their plant. They certainly did not intend to cause pollution but they intended to do the acts which caused it. ...

It is of the utmost public importance that our rivers should not be polluted. The risk of pollution, particularly from the vast and increasing number of riparian industries, is very great. The offences created by the Act of 1951 seem to me to be prototypes of offences which 'are not criminal in any real sense, but are acts which in the public interest are prohibited under a penalty': [His Lordship quoted *Sherras v De Rutzen* and *Sweet v Parsley*.]

If this appeal succeeded and it were held to be the law that no conviction could be obtained under the Act of 1951 unless the prosecution could discharge the often impossible onus of proving that the pollution was caused intentionally or negligently, a great deal of pollution would go unpunished and undeterred to the relief of many riparian factory owners. ...

Alphacell indicated enthusiasm for strict liability at the highest level despite confirmation of the presumption of MR in *Sweet v Parsley*. Not all pollution cases involve offences of strict liability however, for arguments concerning causation and the provision of statutory defences may indicate the reverse (see *Environment Agency (formerly National Rivers Authority) v Empress Car Co (Abertillery) Ltd* [1998] 1 All ER 481 in Chapter 2, 2.3.3).

→ CROSS-REFERENCE
Environment Agency (formerly National Rivers Authority) v Empress Car Co (Abertillery) Ltd is discussed in Chapter 2, 2.3.3.

Public safety and law enforcement

Public safety and social concern were emphasised in the next case but only as an encouragement to law enforcement.

Gammon (Hong Kong) Ltd v AG of Hong Kong [1985] AC 1 PRIVY COUNCIL

During construction work, part of a lateral support system collapsed. The company was charged with a material deviation from an approved plan contrary to s40(2A)(b) Hong Kong Building Ordinance and with carrying out works in a manner likely to cause risk of injury or damage in contravention of (2B)(b) of the Ordinance. The project manager and site agent were also charged. The maximum sentence was a fine and three years' imprisonment.

Lord Scarman:

> In their Lordships' opinion, the law relevant to this appeal may be stated in the following proposition: (1) there is a presumption of law that *mens rea* is required before a person can be held guilty of a criminal offence; (2) the presumption is particularly strong where the offence is 'truly criminal' in character; (3) the presumption applies to statutory offences, and can be displaced only if this is clearly or by necessary implication the effect of the statute; (4) the only situation in which the presumption can be displaced is where the statute is concerned with an issue of social concern; public safety is such an issue; (5) even where a statute is concerned with such an issue, the presumption of *mens rea* stands unless it can also be shown that the creation of strict liability will be effective to promote the objects of the statute by encouraging greater vigilance to prevent the commission of the prohibited act.
>
> The ordinance
> … Its overall purpose is clearly to regulate the planning, design and construction of the building works to which it relates in the interests of safety. It covers a field of activity where there is, especially in Hong Kong, a potential danger to public safety. And the activity which the ordinance is intended to regulate is one in which citizens have a choice whether they participate or not.
> … [T]heir Lordships are satisfied that strict liability would help to promote greater vigilance in the matters covered by the two offences with which this appeal is concerned (the material deviation … and the risk of injury or damage …). [T]he legislature by enacting … (section 40) … clearly took the view that criminal liability and punishment were needed as a deterrent against slipshod or incompetent supervision, control or execution of building works. The imposition of strict liability for some offences clearly would emphasise to those concerned the need for high standards of care in the supervision and execution of work. …
> Put in positive terms, the conclusion of the Board is that it is consistent with the purpose of the ordinance in its regulation of the works to which it applies that at least some of the criminal offences which it creates should be of strict liability. It is a statute the subject matter of which may properly be described as 'the regulation of a particular activity involving potential danger to public health [and] safety … in which citizens have a choice whether they participate or not …'

Appeal dismissed. Case remitted to magistrate.

Possession of firearms

The position here is stricter than with drugs possession. In *Howells* [1977] QB 614 it was held that the offence of possession of a firearm without a certificate, contrary to s1 Firearms Act 1968, carrying a maximum penalty of three years' imprisonment, was an offence of strict liability. There was an exemption under the Act for antique guns. D's gun was a reproduction antique but D's belief that it was genuine was rejected because knowledge or belief was held to be irrelevant. The main reason was silence in the offence on MR and danger to the public of the possession of unlawful lethal firearms. The recent case of *Deyemi* [2007] EWCA Crim 2060 confirmed this approach to possession of an electrical stun gun where the Ds alleged they believed it to be a torch.

In the same vein, the Court of Appeal applied strict liability to possession of a bag containing expanding ammunition, contrary to s5(1A)(f) Firearms Act 1968 in the next case:

Nasir Zahid v R [2010] EWCA CRIM 2158 COURT OF APPEAL

Two bullets were found in D's inside jacket breast pocket. 38 similar bullets inside a taped package of brown paper were found in a wash-bag in his study. D stated at trial that he did not know he possessed the bullets. He thought the packet contained nuts and bolts left by builders and that the two in his pocket must have fallen from the packet. His defence was one of honest mistake following *Warner* [1968]: that although possession of firearms was an offence of strict liability, D should have a defence where he believed the contents of 'the container' to be *innocent*. The Court of Appeal upheld his conviction:

Flaux J:

> … [T]he essence of the defendant's argument is: 'I did not know that the object in my possession was a firearm'. The reasons which this Court has given for concluding that such an argument should not afford a defence are equally applicable whether the defendant's case is that he did not know what was in the bag or that he thought what was in the bag was an innocent object.
>
> The reasons why this Court has reached this conclusion are set out in the judgment of Auld J in *R v Bradish* (1990) 90 Cr App R 271:
>
> > 'The justification for the concession on behalf of the appellant, which we agree has been properly made, that the offence created by section 5 is one of strict liability, at least in the absence of a defence of ignorance, may be summarised as follows:
> >
> > > First, the words of the section themselves, 'A person commits an offence if without … authority … he has in his possession …' any firearm, weapon or ammunition of the type defined, makes plain that this is an offence of strict liability.
> >
> > Secondly, the comparable words and structure of section 1 of the 1968 Act have been held by this Court in *Howells* (supra) and *Hussain* (supra) to create an offence of strict liability.
> >
> > Thirdly, the clear purpose of the firearms legislation is to impose a tight control on the use of highly dangerous weapons … Given that section 1 has been held to create an offence of strict liability, this consideration applies a fortiori to section 5, which is concerned with more serious weapons, such as automatic handguns and machine guns, and imposes a higher maximum penalty.'
> >
> > On the question whether the approach adopted by certain of their Lordships in Warner v. M.P.C. (supra) applies to a 'container' case under section 5, and presumably section 1 too, of the 1968 Act, so as to enable an accused to raise a defence that he did not know what was in the container, we are of the view that it does not. We say that for the following reasons:
> >
> > > First, whilst neither *Howells* (1977) 65 Cr.App.R. 86, [1977] Q.B. 614 nor *Hussain* (1981) 72 Cr.App.R. 143, [1981] 1 W.L.R. 416, was a 'container' case, the Court of Appeal in each case adopted the much stricter line of Lord Morris in Warner than the 'half-way house' approach of Lords Pearce, Reid and Wilberforce …

Fourthly, no provision corresponding to section 28(3) of the Misuse of Drugs Act 1971 has been introduced to the Firearms legislation so as to import the Warner 'half-way house' concept into offences aimed at controlling the possession or use of firearms. In particular, the recent comprehensive extension of that control in the Firearms (Amendment) Act 1988 contains no such provision in relation to offences under section 1 or 5 of the 1968 Act.

Fifthly, the possibilities and consequences of evasion would be too great for effective control, even if the burden of proving lack of guilty knowledge were to be on the accused ... It would be easy for an accused to maintain, lyingly but with conviction, that he did not recognise the object in his possession as part of a firearm or prohibited weapon. To the argument that the innocent possessor or carrier of firearms or prohibited weapons or parts of them is at risk of unfair conviction under these provisions, there has to be balanced the important public policy behind the legislation of protecting the public from the misuse of such dangerous weapons. Just as the Chicago-style gangster might plausibly maintain that he believed his violin case to contain a violin, not a sub-machine gun, so it might be difficult to meet a London lout's assertion that he did not know an unmarked plastic bottle in his possession contained ammonia rather than something to drink.

Accordingly, we are of the view that, whether or not this case is regarded as a 'container' case, and even if the canister had not been clearly marked 'Force 10 Super Magnum C.S.', this was an absolute offence, and it would have been no defence for the appellant to maintain that he did not know or could not reasonably have been expected to know that the canister contained C.S. gas. It follows that, in our view, the assistant recorder was correct in the ruling that he gave, so far as it went, that section 5 creates an offence of strict liability.

 NOTE 4.3

1. The Court of Appeal did not consider this to be a 'container' case but, even if it was, the defence of genuine mistake as to the contents would not apply where D had had an opportunity to examine the contents.

2. The presumption of MR did not apply to s5 Firearms Act 1968 which Parliament had clearly intended to be an offence of strict liability.

The Court of Appeal recently confirmed in relation to the offence of possession of unlawful firearm contrary to s5(1) Firearms Act 1968 that momentary possession of a gun followed by immediate rejection did not constitute possession: *R v Taylor* [2011] EWCA 1646.

 THINKING POINT 4.6

Do you consider that punishment of individuals who have taken all necessary steps to prevent harm will promote greater vigilance and observance of the law?

Can you think of any serious offence that is not concerned with protecting the public from danger?

Does it automatically follow therefore that such an offence should be one of strict liability? Should murder and offences of violence become crimes of strict liability?

Law enforcement

Sometimes the question of whether strict liability would help in obtaining compliance with the law is of paramount importance and if not, then MR should be required. In *Lim Chin Aik v The Queen* [1963] AC 160 PC, D had been convicted of an immigration offence by remaining in Singapore after being prohibited from doing so. The prohibition had not been published or made known to the appellant. It was held that there was no reason to penalise someone who had had no opportunity to change his behaviour:

Lord Evershed (Privy Council):

> Where it can be shown that the imposition of strict liability would result in the prosecution and con-viction of a class of persons whose conduct could not in any way affect the observance of the law, their Lordships consider that, even where the statute is dealing with a grave social evil, strict liability is not likely to be intended. … The subject-matter, the control of immigration, is not one in which the presumption of strict liability has generally been made. … Clearly one of the objects of the Ordinance is the expulsion of prohibited persons from Singapore, but there is nothing that a man can do about it if, before the commission of the offence, there is no practical or sensible way in which he can ascertain whether he is a prohibited person or not.

Offences which are not 'truly criminal'

Gambling

→ CROSS-REFERENCE

B v DPP is discussed in 4.1.3.

Despite the House of Lords' strong statement against strict liability in an age-related sexual offence (*B v DPP* [2000]), Parliament continues to create such offences and the courts continue to dispense with MR, particularly in respect of offences considered to be 'not truly criminal'.

London Borough of Harrow v Shah (D) & Shah (B) [2000] CRIM LR 692 DIVISIONAL COURT

The respondents were newsagents charged with selling a national lottery ticket to a boy aged under 16 contrary to the National Lottery Act 1993 s13(1)(c) and the National Lottery Regulations 1994, reg 3. They had displayed a notice in their shop and had instructed their employees not to sell tickets to under-16s. An employee of the newsagents reasonably but mistakenly believed that the boy was over 16. The respondents were acquitted by the magistrates but the local authority appealed.

The appeal was allowed. Whilst a statutory defence of reasonable diligence was available under other sections of the Act no such defence was available under s13(1)(c). This indicated strict liability. Further, the offence was not truly criminal, the maximum sentence being two years or a fine/both. Finally, the legislation dealt with an issue of social concern, namely, gambling by young people.

?!   THINKING POINT 4.7

If Mr and Mrs Shah had done all they could to prevent the offence, how would strict liability have encouraged greater vigilance?

In view of the penalty for the offence, do you agree that it is not truly criminal in nature?

Was the conviction fair?

Certainly, the offence committed by Mr and Mrs Shah would generally be regarded as far more 'criminal' than something like a parking offence or failure to return a library book which carry no stigma. Is the denial of true criminality justifiable?

R v Muhamad [2003] WLR 1031, [2002] EWCA CRIM 1856 COURT OF APPEAL

The defendant was convicted of materially contributing to the extent of his insolvency by gambling contrary to s362(1)(a) Insolvency Act 1968.

Dyson J:

> It is not clear to us whether an offence under section 362(1)(a) would have been classified by Lord Reid [in *Sweet v Parsley*] as 'quasi-criminal', or 'truly criminal'. A maximum penalty of two years imprisonment is by no means insignificant, although it is towards the lower end of the scale of maximum custodial sentences. On the other hand, it is open to doubt whether, at any rate in 2002, such an offence would be regarded as 'truly criminal'. ... The question whether the presumption of law that mens rea is required applies, and, if so, whether it has been displaced can be approached in two ways. One approach is to ask whether the act is truly criminal, on the basis that, if it is not, then the presumption does not apply at all. The other approach is to recognise that any offence in respect of which a person may be punished in a criminal court is, prima facie, sufficiently 'criminal' for the presumption to apply. But the more serious the offence, the greater the weight to be attached to the presumption, and conversely, the less serious the offence, the less weight to be attached. It is now clear that it is this latter approach which according to our domestic law must be applied.
>
> The starting point, therefore, is to determine how serious an offence is created by section 362(1)(a), and accordingly how much weight, if any, should be attached to the presumption. Some weight must undoubtedly be given to the presumption, but in our judgment it can be readily displaced. As we have said, the maximum sentence indicates that Parliament considered this to be an offence of some significance, but not one of the utmost seriousness. This is not surprising. We do not believe that great stigma attaches to a conviction of this offence. ...
>
> The next point ... is the fact that gambling which harms a gambler's creditors is a matter of social concern. That is obviously right. It follows that this is a case where the fourth and fifth of Lord Scarman's propositions are engaged. So too they were in *Harrow London Borough Council v Shah* [1999]. ...

The denial of 'true criminality' is not altogether convincing and one wonders whether it is a useful classification given that some offences which are undeniably regulatory (such as health and safety) can give rise to loss of life, serious harm and damage on a devastating scale. Think of recent train crashes for instance—all caused by safety failures.

?! THINKING POINT 4.8

Does Dyson J give any clear reason for stating that the offence should not be regarded as truly criminal in 2002?

The offence of bringing a prohibited article into a prison contrary to s40C(1) Prison Act 1952, as amended by the Offender Management Act 2007 and carrying a maximum 10-year penalty, was held to be 'truly criminal' in *R v M and B* [2009] EWCA Crim 2615. The two Ds were solicitor's agents found to have a SIM card and mobile phone battery in their pockets.

Rix LJ:

> The default position is that, despite the absence of any express language, there is a presumption, founded in constitutional principle, that mens rea is an essential ingredient of the offence. Only a compelling case for implying the exclusion of such an ingredient as a matter of necessity will suffice.

The Court of Appeal went on to hold that as the article had to be brought 'knowingly', the offence was not in fact one of strict liability.

These cases indicate that the courts still view strict liability as having continuing validity despite the arguments of the House of Lords in B and K. Does social concern triumph over individual fairness? Or is there really no injustice in convicting someone without fault?

Statutory mens rea terms

The offence may be silent on MR but include adverbs or verbs which imply a mental element.

Knowingly

Many regulatory or conduct crimes will convey a MR requirement by using words which signify knowledge or awareness as to a circumstance or state of affairs, for example: being *knowingly* concerned in the importation of unlawful drugs. A new example would be the offence of squatting in a residential building contrary to s144 Legal Aid, Sentencing & Punishment of Offenders Act 2012:

> a person commits an offence of entry to a residential building as a trespasser if he knows or ought to know that he is a trespasser, and he is living in the building or intends to live there for any period.

The level of knowledge required can be low. The offences of bringing a prohibited article into prison contrary to s40B or s40C Prison Act 1952 must be committed 'knowingly' (*R v M and B*, above). In *R v Johnson (Wayne)* [2017] EWCA Crim 189, D had brought a package containing 'spice' (synthetic cannabis), SIM cards and oxymethalone into a prison. He admitted knowing about the 'spice', but not the SIM cards or oxymethalone. The Court of Appeal held that knowledge that he was conveying prohibited articles sufficed; he did not have to know what the articles were.

Wilful blindness or awareness

The word knowledge implies that one not only knows a fact in reality but that one also knows of an obvious fact to which one has deliberately closed one's mind. The term wilful blindness covers this mental state. *Parker* [1977] 1 WLR 600 and *R v G* [2004] 1 AC 1034 confirm this approach to 'knowing' of the existence of a risk. Parker was aware of the risk of damage to the telephone handset even though he was wilfully blind to the risk at the time of acting.

Mistaken belief

A person who has made an honest mistake is to be judged on the facts as he believed them to be (Chapter 9, 9.4.2, *Morgan* [1975]: and 4.1.3, *B v DPP*). Therefore, he will not have knowledge of the relevant facts. The Sexual Offences Act 2003 is different in requiring the defence of mistaken belief to be both honest and reasonable.

Forgetfulness

Possession requires knowledge. If a person is charged with *possession* of an unlawful item but claims to have genuinely forgotten it was on them or under their control, they will not knowingly be in possession (*R v Russell* (1984) 81 Cr App R 315).

 THINKING POINT 4.9

A man is asked to deliver a box. He believes the box contains stolen goods but asks no questions nor does he open the box to find out. Is he knowingly in possession of the contents?

Where there is more than one AR element, knowledge is required for all

Knowledge is frequently required in licensing offences under the Licensing Act 2003, for example:

- s147: A person ... commits an offence if he knowingly allows the sale of alcohol on relevant premises to an individual aged under 18;

- s141: A person ... commits an offence if, on relevant premises, he knowingly (a) sells or attempts to sell alcohol to a person who is drunk; or (b) allows alcohol to be sold to such a person.

These offences contain more than one AR element. It is clear that knowledge is required for allowing the sale of alcohol but the statute does not make it clear whether actual knowledge is required in respect of the status of the consumer as a child or a drunk.

On the ordinary principles of construction, knowledge should be required for all elements and thus the offence will not be one of strict liability. In *Westminster City Council v Croyalgrange Ltd* [1986] 1 WLR 674 the House of Lords confirmed that in s20(1)(a) of Sch 3 to the Local Government (Miscellaneous Provisions) Act 1982 (knowingly permitting the use of the premises [for the purposes of pornographic films/materials] without a licence) knowledge would be required to all elements of the offence (ie: use and licence).

Knowledge and vicarious liability

You will see in 4.2.2 that knowledge can be imputed to a manager under the delegation principle where all management authority and responsibility has been transferred to another person who committed the offence.

The Draft Criminal Code clause 18(a) states that a person acts:

'knowingly' with respect to a circumstance not only when he is aware that it exists or will exist, but also when he avoids taking steps that might confirm this belief that it exists or will exist.

Wilfully

'Wilfully' is commonly found in statutory offences, for example:

- Wilfully obstructing the public highway under s137(1) Highways Act 1980.

■ Wilfully obstructing a police officer in the exercise of his duty under s89 Police Act 1996.

■ Cruelty to a person under 16 by wilful assault, ill-treatment, neglect, abandonment or exposure in a manner likely to cause unnecessary suffering or injury to health contrary to s1 Children and Young Persons Act 1933.

Sometimes it implies MR and sometimes strict liability.

Wilfulness as strict liability to the result

Wilful obstruction of the highway: *Arrowsmith v Jenkins* [1963] 2 QB 561 held that all that was required was an intention to perform an immediate act (holding a meeting) which in fact obstructed the highway. Knowledge of the fact that the CND public meeting was obstructing the highway was all that was required, not an intention to obstruct.

Wilfulness as intention to the result

Wilful obstruction of a police officer has always required an intention to obstruct or to make it more difficult or to prevent the police from carrying out their duties: *Rice v Connolly* [1966] 2 QB 414 and *Willmott v Atack* [1977] QB 498. In the latter, a police officer was prevented from making an arrest during an altercation. It was held that 'wilful' implied hostility to the police with the intention that the immediate act should obstruct.

Wilful neglect as intention or recklessness

In the offence of wilful neglect of a child under s1 Children and Young Persons Act 1933, wilfulness implies either an intention to cause harm to the child by positive act (ill-treatment or abandonment) or subjective recklessness as to whether harm will be caused in the case of an omission (failure to call a doctor for a sick child). In other words, in the case of positive acts, wilfulness means more than just an intention to commit the act which in fact results in harm. There must be an intention to harm. Where the neglect takes the form of an omission, there

> → CROSS-REFERENCE
> See Chapter 2, 2.2.3 for discussion on *R v Lowe*.

must be foresight of a risk of harm. If there is not, mere negligence is insufficient (*R v Sheppard* [1980] 3 All ER 899). For an illustration of a case under s1 Children and Young Persons Act 1933, refer back to *R v Lowe* [1973] QB 702.

Wilful neglect of a child is therefore an offence of MR, unlike obstruction of the highway. The same interpretation of 'wilful neglect' applies to the offence of wilful neglect of an elderly patient contrary to s44 Mental Capacity Act 2005 (*Turbill (Maxine)* [2013] EWCA Crim 1422, where the staff of a nursing home had left a resident with Alzheimer's disease on the floor overnight; following *Sheppard*, 'wilful' meant deliberate).

?! **THINKING POINT** 4.10

D organises a public protest outside a weapons factory which blocks the road. A police officer attempts to arrest D by putting his arm around D's shoulders but D pulls away and the officer falls over. Has D wilfully committed any offences?

Using, causing or permitting

There is little certainty about the definition of these words. Using a vehicle in contravention of a traffic regulation (defective brakes) is an offence of strict liability but permitting another to use a vehicle in contravention of regulations entails knowledge (*James & Son Ltd v Smee* [1955] 1 QB 78).

Permitting another to drive without insurance is an offence of strict liability (*DPP v Fisher* [1991] Crim LR 787). In other cases, 'permitting' may depend on the context (*Vehicle Inspectorate v Nuttal* [1999] 1 WLR 629, HL).

Suffer, allow and cause

These verbs are frequently found in pollution legislation. The meaning given to each is variable so that sometimes the offence is one of strict liability and sometimes not. See *Alphacell* (discussed earlier in this section).

4.1.5 Strict Liability and the ECHR

The presumption of innocence should be reflected in substantive offences so as to prevent the conviction of morally innocent people. An offence which imposes strict or absolute liability regardless of the lack of MR could contravene Article 6(2) and Article 5.

The ECtHR has held that strict liability offences do not in themselves contravene the right to a fair trial provided they are confined within reasonable limits. This is the leading case:

Salabiaku v France [1988] 13 EHRR 379

The applicant who lived in Paris was found in possession of a trunk containing drugs. He was charged with illegally importing and smuggling narcotics. The appeal concerned the offence of smuggling. Once the prosecution had proved possession of prohibited goods there was no defence unless D could prove a specific event beyond human control which could not be foreseen or averted, something which was clearly likely to be extremely rare. It was argued that the offence provided an *irrebuttable presumption* of liability offering D no chance of a defence:

> In particular, and again in principle, the Contracting States may, under certain conditions, penalise a simple or objective fact as such, irrespective of whether it results from criminal intent or from negligence. Examples of such offences may be found in the laws of Contracting States.

The ECtHR declined to hold that this irrebuttable presumption infringed Article 6(2) provided the presumption was exercised within reasonable limits:

> [I]t requires states to confine them within reasonable limits which take account of the importance of what is at stake and maintain the rights of the defence.

Therefore, the benefit of the doubt could be given to a D with a genuine explanation for being in possession.

The English courts rely on this case to support the view that Article 6 is only concerned with procedural and not substantive fairness. Therefore, strict liability is not automatically incompatible with Article 6(2) under the Convention. This was confirmed in the following case:

R v G [2008] UKHL 37

D, aged 15, was charged with rape of a child under 13 contrary to s5 Sexual Offences Act 2003 (SOA): a person commits an offence if a) he intentionally penetrates the vagina, anus or mouth of another person with his penis, and b) the other person is under 13. A person guilty of an offence under this section is liable, on conviction on indictment, to imprisonment for life.

It was alleged that non-consensual sexual intercourse had taken place in the boy's bedroom. It was admitted that the girl had lied about her age, having told D that she was 15. D's case was that she willingly agreed to sexual intercourse. However, since the offence could be committed irrespective of consent or belief as to age, D pleaded guilty and appealed. He was given a 12-month detention and training order and was notified on the register of sexual offenders. On appeal, it was argued that the prosecution was disproportionate because it was accepted that the girl had lied about her age. Had D been convicted under s13 SOA (sexual activity with another child) he would not have been labelled as a rapist, would have received a lighter sentence and would not have been subject to the notification requirements. Therefore, the conviction infringed his rights under Articles 5, 6 and 8 (right to privacy).

The Court of Appeal had held that Article 6(2) was concerned with procedural fairness not with substantive law. Section 5 was an offence of strict liability and was not therefore incompatible with the requirements of procedural fairness or the presumption of innocence imposed by Article 6. The court further considered that an appropriate sentence would not infringe Article 8. The sentence had been disproportionate and a conditional discharge was substituted. D appealed to the House of Lords, which dismissed his appeal and unanimously agreed with the Court of Appeal on the interpretation of Article 6(2). The substantive law is not engaged by Article 6.

Lord Hoffman:

> Article 6(1) provides that in the determination of his civil rights or any criminal charge, everyone is entitled to a 'fair and public hearing' and article 6(2) provides that everyone charged with a criminal offence 'shall be presumed innocent until proved guilty according to law'. It is settled law that Article 6(1) guarantees fair procedure and the observance of the principle of the separation of powers but not that either the civil or criminal law will have any particular substantive content: see *Matthews v Ministry of Defence [2003] UKHL 4; [2003] 1 AC 1163*. Likewise, article 6(2) requires him to be presumed innocent of the offence but does not say anything about what the mental or other elements of the offence should be. In the case of civil law, this was established (after a moment of aberration) by *Z v United Kingdom (2001) 34 EHRR 97*. There is no reason why the reasoning should not apply equally to the substantive content of the criminal law. In *R v Gemmell [2002] EWCA Crim 1992; [2003] 1 Cr App R 343*, 356, para 33 Dyson LJ said:
>
> > 'The position is quite clear. So far as Article 6 is concerned, the fairness of the provisions of the substantive law of the Contracting States is not a matter for investigation. The content and interpretation of domestic substantive law is not engaged by Article 6.'
>
> The only authority which is said to cast any doubt upon this proposition is the decision of the Strasbourg court in *Salabiaku v France (1988) 13 EHRR 379* and in particular a statement in paragraph 28 (at p.388) that 'presumptions of fact or of law' in criminal proceedings should be confined 'within reasonable limits'. No one has yet discovered what this paragraph means but your Lordships were referred to a wealth of academic learning which tries to solve the riddle.
>
> My Lords, I think that judges and academic writers have picked over the carcass of this unfortunate case so many times in attempts to find some intelligible meat on its bones that the time has come to call a halt. The Strasbourg court, uninhibited by a doctrine of precedent or the need to find a ratio decidendi, seems to have ignored it. It is not mentioned in *Z v United Kingdom (2001) 34 EHRR 97*. I would recommend your Lordships to do likewise. For my part, I would simply endorse the remarks of Dyson LJ in *R v Gemmell [2003] 1 Cr App R 343, 356*.

As to whether D's Article 8 rights had been infringed, Lord Hoffmann, Lord Mance and Baroness Hale held that they had not.

Baroness Hale:

> … there are positive obligations inherent in an effective respect for private and family life. These may require the criminal law to provide effective protection for those who cannot protect themselves from the sexual attentions of others, as well as requiring the state to abstain from arbitrary interference in the sexual lives of individuals …
>
> In effect, therefore, the real complaint is that the appellant has been convicted of an offence bearing the label 'rape'. Parliament has very recently decided that this is the correct label to apply to this activity. In my view this does not engage the article 8 rights of the appellant at all, but if it does, it is entirely justified … The state would have been open to criticism if it did not provide her with adequate protection. This it attempts to do by a clear rule that children under 13 are incapable of giving any sort of consent to sexual activity and treating penile penetration as a most serious form of such activity. This does not in my view amount to a lack of respect for the private life of the penetrating male.

Baroness Hale was primarily concerned with the rights of the victim. 'Rape' was not an inappropriate term for the offence in question, even when it concerned consensual sexual activity between children. The offence was not one of strict liability in relation to the conduct involved: intentional penetration.

Lords Hope and Carswell for the minority expressed a different view which focused on the rights of the 15-year-old defendant. They asked whether the interference with his Article 8 rights could be justified as 'necessary in a democratic society' and whether the prosecution was proportionate given the alternative of a lesser offence under s13 SOA:

Lord Hope:

> … the creation of an unqualified offence of this kind carries with it the risk of stigmatising as rapists children who engage in a single act of mutual sexual activity. A heavy responsibility has been placed on the prosecuting authorities, where both parties are of a similar young age, to discriminate between cases where the proscribed activity was truly mutual on the one hand and those where the complainant was subjected to an element of exploitation or undue pressure on the other. In the former case more harm than good may be done by prosecuting …

Conviction under s5 labels a child as a rapist regardless of consent to sexual intercourse. Can this be right? Consent is a defence in adult rape. Should a lesser offence have been substituted? Should D have even been prosecuted? Parliament clearly intended this offence to carry strict liability. But the courts could have decided that it was unfair by reference to Article 6 and therefore incompatible with the ECHR under s3(1) Human Rights Act 1998. An appeal to the ECtHR was dismissed (*G v UK* [2012] App No 37334/08) on the grounds that it is not the Court's role under Article 6(1) or (2) to dictate the content of domestic law in relation to the inclusion of blameworthy states of mind or defences. The Court agreed that Article 8 was engaged but the legitimate aim of protecting children from premature sexual activity fell within the margin of appreciation. The 'reasonable limits' of strict liability, particularly concerning the criminalisation of a child for a serious offence where a lesser one was available, were not considered.

?! THINKING POINT 4.11

1. Do you think it is right to divide the presumption of innocence into two halves: procedural and substantive?

2. D, the mother of a child, gets a criminal record when she is convicted and fined £75 under s444(1) Education Act 1996: If a child of compulsory school age who is a registered pupil at a school fails to attend regularly at the school, his parent is guilty of an offence. There is no defence. She had done all she could to get her child to attend but he was beyond control.

Do you think the offence offends Article 6(2) ECHR? Is the conviction fair? Look at what was said in *Salabiaku* regarding D's rights and proportionality.

4.1.6 Evaluation: Arguments for and against Strict Liability

For:

1. The argument for strict liability is one of social protection, efficiency and certainty (sexual exploitation, drugs, firearms, pollution, gambling, etc). The argument that society needs protecting from certain types of harm is a utilitarian one: that the greatest happiness of the greatest number should be protected by the law, even at the risk of convicting a few innocent people. It would not in many cases be possible to prove MR if it were required, especially in the case of companies, and so the object of promoting public welfare would be circumvented.

2. Strict liability offences are not real crimes and may in fact be regulated not by police prosecution but by regulatory enforcement processes, such as compliance and warning notices. Only those who are blameworthy will be prosecuted. But this did not appear to assist the Shahs, for instance.

3. A major philosophical exponent of these offences was Baroness Wootton who would have extended strict liability to even more serious crimes on the grounds that the criminal law should not primarily be concerned with punishment but with protection. Read the following in *Crime and the Criminal Law*, 2nd edn, 1981, at p 46:

If, however, the primary function of the courts is conceived as the prevention of forbidden acts, there is little cause to be disturbed by the multiplication of offences of strict liability. If the law says that certain things are not to be done, it is illogical to confine this prohibition to occasions on which they are done from malice aforethought: for at least the material consequences of an action, and the reasons for prohibiting it, are the same whether it is the result of sinister malicious plotting, of negligence or of sheer accident. A man is equally dead and his relatives equally bereaved whether he was stabbed or run over by a drunken motorist or by an incompetent one; and the inconvenience caused by the loss of your bicycle is unaffected by the question whether or not the youth who removed it had the intention of putting it back, if in fact he had not done so at the time of his arrest. ... The conclusion to which this argument leads is, I think, not that the presence or absence of the guilty mind is unimportant, but that *mens rea* has, so to speak – and this is the crux of the matter – *got into the wrong place*. Traditionally, the requirement of the guilty mind is written into the actual definition of a crime. No guilty intention, no crime, is the rule. ... If the object of the criminal law is to prevent the occurrence of socially damaging actions, it would be absurd to turn a blind eye to those which were due to carelessness, negligence or even accident. The question of motivation is *in the first instance* irrelevant.

But only in the first instance. At a later stage, that is to say, after what is now known as conviction, the presence or absence of guilty intention is all-important for its effect on the appropriate measures to be taken to prevent a recurrence of the forbidden act. The prevention of accidental deaths presents different problems from those involved in the prevention of wilful murders. The results of the actions of the careless, the mistaken, the wicked and the merely unfortunate may be indistinguishable from one another, but each case calls for a different treatment.

J.C. Smith, writing in 'Responsibility in Criminal Law' in Bean and Whynes (eds), *Barbara Wootton, Essays in Her Honour* (1986), at p 141 suggested that this would mean that all cases of forbidden harm would need to be prosecuted if the object of the law was to prevent harm rather than punish offenders. The fault test would inevitably creep back into the system for it would be futile to invoke the legal process against the person who had acted reasonably.

A further practical difficulty is that the system would put enormous discretion into the hands of the sentencer. He would apparently have the same power in law over one who caused death accidentally as over a murderer. It is difficult to believe that such a large discretion would be tolerable. It would dilute, if not destroy, the criminal law as a moral force and that at a time when the decline of religious belief has, as Lady Wootton herself says, created a dangerous vacuum. The shift from punishment to prevention may be intended to remove the moral basis of the law; but if, as some believe, one of the major reasons why people do not commit crimes is the sense of guilt which attaches to them, should not the aim be to enhance the sense of guilt rather than otherwise? To remove the element of fault is to empty the law of moral content. If murder were, in law, no different from accidental death, should we be so inhibited from committing murder as most of us are?

The main argument in favour of strict liability is that it can be justified for minor, quasi-criminal offences where little stigma attaches to conviction.

Against:

1. If D has taken all reasonable care to prevent an offence from occurring, imposing strict liability will do nothing to deter offending nor prevent recurrence. If liability is to be imposed, even in the absence of negligence, it will not encourage greater vigilance since liability will be incurred no matter how much effort and expense has been put into preventing accidental harm. Strict liability will therefore achieve nothing that could not be achieved without the requirement of negligence. There is no research proving that strict liability actually achieves higher standards or greater legal compliance. The courts in England and Wales might adopt the principle that all strict liability offences should be interpreted as requiring D to prove that he has not been negligent but they decline to do so.

2. Strict liability leads to individual unfairness, especially when applied to offences which are not minor and which carry a custodial penalty, for example: *Shah*. This is morally unjustifiable. The economic or social protection arguments in favour of strict liability cannot justify punishment for anything other than minor offences, especially where it leads to imprisonment.

3. The presumption of MR is a principle of 'constitutional importance' according to the House of Lords in *B v DPP* and should only be displaced where compellingly clear or by necessary implication. There is every possibility of a fundamental shift in attitude towards strict liability by this case but whether this will prove to be the case remains to be seen. The recent House of Lords decision in *G* and the firearms cases of *Deyemi* and *Zahid* (4.1.4) suggest that change may be slow in coming.

4. The Law Commission in 'Criminal Liability in Regulatory Contexts' (CP No 195, August 2010) recommends that civil law should be used as the primary means of promoting regulatory objectives. The criminal law should be reserved for behaviour which deserves the stigma of criminal conviction because their conduct is seriously reprehensible, risks serious harm or demonstrates moral failing.

■ An offence which is silent on MR carries a presumption of MR.

■ MR may be rebutted by: express terms or by necessary implication, parliamentary intention, social concern, where the offence is not truly criminal or for law enforcement.

■ An offence may indicate a mental element but there is little consistency in interpretation.

■ Many strict liability offences are provided with due diligence defences.

■ You should be familiar with the arguments for and against strict liability.

4.2 Corporate Liability

4.2.1 Introduction: What is a Corporation?

4.2.2 Vicarious Liability

4.2.3 Direct Corporate Liability

4.2.4 Evaluation of the 2007 Act

KEY CASES

Tesco v Nattrass [1972] AC 153—the identification doctrine;

Meridian Global Funds Management Asia Ltd [1995] 3 All ER 918—the attribution principle;

R v St. Regis Paper Company Ltd [2011] EWCA Crim 2527—confirmation of the identification principle;

P&O Ferries [1990] 93 Cr App R 72—the identification doctrine presents a barrier to corporate manslaughter;

Kite v OLL Ltd [unreported]—corporate manslaughter conviction of sole director;

AG's Reference (No 2 of 1999) [2000] 2 Cr App R 207—individual guilt is required before conviction of a company for gross negligence manslaughter.

4.2.1 Introduction: What is a Corporation?

A corporation can be a limited company, a body incorporated by statute or under Royal Charter, an incorporated body formed to run a nationalised industry or a local authority. It is legally distinct from its members. It has legal personality, although no physical existence. It can sue and be sued, enter contracts and hold property. An unincorporated association such as a partnership, trust or government department can incur liability for acts/omissions to the same extent as a person for statutory crimes (Interpretation Act 1898). The term 'corporate liability' will refer to both corporations and unincorporated bodies.

Many of the strict liability cases examined earlier involved the liability of corporations for regulatory offences. There is usually little difficulty in securing a conviction for there is no requirement to prove MR once the AR has been established. It is more difficult to attribute liability to a corporation where the strict liability offence contains an MR element such as knowledge or wilfulness. The usual means of conviction is vicariously, where the employing company will be made liable for the acts of its employees or where knowledge of an employee will be attributed to the employer.

It is extremely difficult, however, to prove that a corporation is directly liable for a serious offence of recklessness, gross negligence or intention. Historically, MR developed in accordance with individual criminal responsibility, meaning that an individual must be found to have committed the AR of an offence with MR before he can be convicted. Such a model is ill-suited to corporate crime unless the company is small and the culpable individuals can be identified. This is difficult in large corporations which are, consequently, able to hide behind their veil of incorporation. After more than ten years of pressure, however, the government enacted the Corporate Manslaughter and Corporate Homicide Act 2007 which now enables organisations to be prosecuted for manslaughter. Corporations will still be able to avoid criminal responsibility for other serious crimes.

4.2.2 Vicarious Liability

▓ Delegation and offences of mens rea/negligence

▓ Attribution: offences of strict liability

▓ Limitations on vicarious liability

Vicarious liability means making one person liable for an offence committed by another. It is the most common way of obtaining a civil judgment against an employer for employee negligence. An employer will be vicariously liable for the unlawful acts and omissions of his employees committed in the performance of an employee's contract of employment. A corporation will be directly criminally liable for crimes which it has actually committed or in which it has participated. Vicarious liability does not generally exist in criminal law subject to two exceptions regarding corporate compliance with public welfare legislation:

▓ *The delegation principle:* vicarious liability will apply in the case of offences of mens rea or negligence.

▓ *The attribution principle:* the act of the employee can be regarded as the act of the employer in law. This applies to statutory offences of strict liability.

Delegation and offences of mens rea/negligence

A corporation will be liable for an offence committed by a junior employee in the course of employment but only where management responsibility has been completely transferred from the senior manager to another person or employee. Most of the cases are concerned with licensing and require knowledge. The principle can be readily understood from the following case:

Allen v Whitehead [1930] 1 KB 211 KINGS BENCH DIVISION

D was the leaseholder of a café and received the profits. He employed a manager and visited the café periodically. He received a written warning from the police concerning prostitutes meeting in his café. He instructed the manager not to allow any prostitutes into the café and put a notice on the door. On eight consecutive days the manager allowed prostitutes to remain on the premises between 8 pm and 4 am. D was charged under s44 Metropolitan Police Act 1839 with 'knowingly permitting or suffering prostitutes or persons of notoriously bad character to meet together and remain in a place where refreshments are sold and consumed'. It was held that D's ignorance was no defence. The offence could only be committed by the person who shall 'have or keep' the house. This could only mean D and not the manager otherwise the purposes of the legislation would be frustrated. The acts of the manager and MR could be imputed to D because management of the house had been delegated.

However, delegation may not always be easy to identify because of the following case:

Vane v Yiannopoullos [1965] AC 486 HOUSE OF LORDS

The licensee of a restaurant was on one floor whilst a waitress was on another. Contrary to instructions, she served two alcoholic drinks to people who did not order a meal. The licensee was charged with 'knowingly selling intoxicating liquor to persons to whom he was not permitted to sell contrary to s22(1)(a) Licensing Act 1961'. His acquittal was confirmed on the basis that delegation required the handing over of all effective management of the premises. The licensee had merely given the waitress authority to sell alcohol and there had been no delegation of authority to manage the business. There had to be a complete delegation of authority to another for management of the premises. Neither was he absent from the premises. The House confirmed that if a requirement of knowledge made the legislation harder to enforce, then the problem lay with Parliament.

Attribution: offences of strict liability

Here, the act of the employee can be regarded as the act of the employer in law. The fact that management may have been transferred is irrelevant. Both *Alphacell* and *Shah* were decided on this principle. Whether a corporation will be vicariously liable depends on the construction of the statute.

Coppen v Moore (No 2) [1898] 2 QB 306 COURT OF APPEAL

D owned six shops in which he sold American hams. He gave strict instructions to his branch managers that they were to be sold as breakfast hams and not according to their place of origin. In the absence and without the knowledge of either D or the branch manager, an assistant of one shop sold some of the ham as 'Scotch' ham. This was an offence under the Merchandise Marks Act 1887: selling goods to which a false trade description is applied.

It was held by the Court of Appeal that if actual knowledge had been required, the legislation could not have been enforced. On the basis of civil law principles of sale of goods D remained the seller, being the owner of the ham, though not the actual salesman. The delegation principle was not employed. D was liable vicariously.

Limitations on vicarious liability

There are two limitations:

1. The employee has to be acting within the scope of his employment or, if an agent, within the scope of authorisation.

2. An employer will not be liable for inchoate offences committed by employees, that is: aiding, abetting or attempting an offence.

4.2.3 Direct Corporate Liability

■ The identification doctrine (or alter ego principle)

■ Corporate manslaughter: The Corporate Manslaughter and Corporate Homicide Act 2007

The identification doctrine (or alter ego principle)

In order to convict an individual of a serious criminal offence, it must be proved that they committed the AR with MR. The same applies to a corporation. A corporation is regarded in law as a legal person but obviously it can only think and act through its board of directors or controlling senior managers. In law, they are identified as the corporation. It is only their acts, as opposed to the acts of subordinate staff, which are identified as being the acts of the corporation. Therefore, if a crime is committed by a senior manager with MR, the corporation can also be made liable. If fault lies lower down the management level, the corporation will escape conviction.

Corporate liability is dependent on liability being established against an individual so that if there is no prosecution against a senior manager or if that person is acquitted, there can be no conviction against the corporation, no matter how negligent or reckless the management may have been. This is known as the 'identification doctrine'. The identification doctrine did not emerge until 1944. It was based on the nineteenth-century model of a corporation: a small company run by a single entrepreneur. Although it permitted the conviction of small corporations, paradoxically it protected larger entities from prosecution for the following reasons. Lord Denning in the House of Lords case of *Bolton (Engineering) Co. Ltd. v T.J. Graham & Sons Ltd* [1957] 1 QB 159 described a company in this way:

> A company may be likened to a human body with a brain, nerve centre which controls what it does and hands which hold the tools. The state of mind of the managers representing the directing mind of the company is treated by the law as the state of mind of the company.

You might imagine that on this basis, only small corporations, with one or two directors, could ever be directly criminally liable. The larger the corporation, the less likely it is to be found guilty. This is indeed the case:

Tesco Supermarkets Ltd v Nattrass [1972] AC 153 HOUSE OF LORDS

Tesco was charged under s24(1) Trade Descriptions Act 1968 for advertising items for sale at the wrong price. The employee responsible was the branch manager. Tesco had over 800 branches at the time. The company raised a defence in s24(1) that the offence was due to the act/default of another (the branch manager) and that it had exercised due diligence. The question was whether the branch manager was independent of the corporation, and therefore another person, or an employee identified with the corporation whose actions were those of the corporation itself. The corporation was convicted and appealed.

It was held that the branch manager was another person and thus the defence ought to have succeeded. The branch manager represented the hands of the corporation not its brain.

Lord Reid:

> [A corporation] must act through living persons, though not always one and the same person. Then the person who acts is not speaking or acting for the company. He is acting as the company and his mind which directs his acts is the mind of the company. There is no question of the company being vicariously liable. He is not acting as a servant, representative, agent or delegate … if it is a guilty mind then that guilt is the guilt of the company.

The identification doctrine fails to take account of the fact that corporations may be complex organisations which conduct their activities according to policies, cultures, rules, habits and customs. An offence may be committed by an employee at any level through failure of the corporation in any of these respects. An employee is acting by virtue of his position within the corporation although not in law as the corporation. An individual senior manager of a large corporation is unlikely to have knowledge of all operational matters or the acts/defaults of employees yet the corporation cannot be made legally responsible in the absence of such knowledge. Tesco might have been held liable under the delegation principle but this was not referred to.

As C. Wells states in 'Corporations: Culture, Risk and Criminal Liability' [1993] *Crim LR*, at p 551:

> Business corporations represent a distinct and powerful force at global, national and regional levels and they wield enormous economic power. The legal structure within which they operate largely serves their interests, corporate personality protects their owners from the full consequences of failure, and the regulation to which they are subject assumes their beneficence ... Problems arise in applying responsibility to corporations for the very reason that they are not human individuals. Contemporary preoccupation with the notion that responsibility derives from and attaches to the autonomous individual renders us bereft of conceptual tools with which to confront corporate accountability. ... If corporations are to be brought within criminal responsibility, the argument should be a normative one not a linguistic one. The relationship between language, concept and culture is not static and I think this helps to explain how there can be at one and the same time a call for more corporate blame and yet an ill-equipped legal vocabulary with which to achieve that.

The identification doctrine prevents the successful prosecution of a company for any offence of knowledge or one with a defence of lack of knowledge or due diligence. It would always be possible for a director to argue that he had no knowledge of the conduct in question at ground level. Over the years however there has been a slow transition in judicial attitudes to the conviction of companies for regulatory crimes. Tesco was successfully prosecuted in 1993:

Tesco Stores Ltd v Brent LBC [1993] 3 ALL ER 138 QUEEN'S BENCH DIVISION

The store was charged with an offence of selling an '18' only video to a child. There was a defence if D had reasonable grounds to believe the purchaser was over 18. Tesco argued that its controlling officers had no means of knowing the age of the purchaser and that the knowledge of the checkout assistant (who knew, in fact, that the purchaser was under-age) was irrelevant. It was held that the argument was absurd since, on that basis, a company would never be guilty of this crime. The case was dealt with under the principles of vicarious liability rather than the identification model.

This approach was continued in the following case:

Meridian Global Funds Management Asia Ltd v The Securities Commission [1995] 3 ALL ER 918 PRIVY COUNCIL

The chief investment officer of Meridian, a Hong Kong investment company, improperly purchased a substantial stake in a publicly listed New Zealand company in order to gain control of it. The transaction was recorded in the accounts but was hidden from the managing director. Meridian was prosecuted under NZ securities legislation for failure to disclose details of the controlling investment. The question was whether the knowledge of the investment officer could be attributed to the company. It was held that the knowledge of the person whom the company had authorised to purchase shares should count as the knowledge of the company even though the investment officer had deliberately hidden the knowledge of the purchase from the managing director.

Lord Hoffmann stated that the identification model of liability was not always appropriate and was one subcategory of a broader rule of attribution. The constitution of the company and company law provided the primary rules for attributing knowledge to a company. The acts of those having the authority to bind the company in its constitution will prima facie bind the company as intended. There is no single rule and each case should be independently considered. Sometimes, actual knowledge will be required by the board of directors. Elsewhere, knowledge by more junior staff will be sufficient. Lord Hoffmann's interpretation of attribution was however rejected by the Court of Appeal in *R v St. Regis Paper Company Ltd* [2011] EWCA 2527 which permitted a company to escape liability for the intentional falsification of records by its technical manager contrary to regulation 32(1)(g) Pollution Prevention and Control (England and Wales) Regulations 2000. The decision would not appear to take into account that the offence was aimed at 'the permit holder', that is: the company, which can only act through its employees. A Supreme Court decision is required to clarify whether companies should be bound by legislation in such circumstances.

Corporate manslaughter

As you will have gathered, the identification doctrine was a legal barrier to prosecuting a company for homicide. This was a serious gap in the law which allowed management, with responsibility for the health and safety of their operations, to escape liability. The Health and Safety Executive (HSE) identified management failure as the cause of 70 per cent of deaths and major injuries in the workplace. Despite this, there were only six convictions of common-law manslaughter against companies, all small scale, between 1927, the year of the first unsuccessful prosecution (*R v Cory Bros Ltd* [1927] 1 KB 810) and 2008. The aim of the Corporate Manslaughter and Corporate Homicide Act 2007 was to overcome the identification doctrine in relation to manslaughter but not other serious offences. So far, there have been 11 convictions under the Act.

Consider these death tolls from the following disasters, and the scale of the problem will become clear:

- 1987: Kings Cross Underground fire: 31
- 1987: Herald of Free Enterprise (capsizing of the P&O cross-channel ferry): 192
- 1984–1994: Channel tunnel construction: 6
- 1988: Sinking of Thames pleasure cruiser (Marchioness): 51
- Rail disasters:
  - 1997: Southall: 7 + 150 injuries
  - 1999: Paddington: 31 + 400 injuries
  - 2000: Hatfield: 4 + 102 injuries
  - 2002: Potters Bar: 7 + 70 injuries
  - 2007: Cumbria: 1 + 5 injuries.
- 2017: Grenfell Tower: 71

If you add to this the number of people killed at work annually, the scale of the problem multiplies:

- 2011/12: 172 + 111,000 injuries
- 2012/13: 150 + 77,310 injuries
- 2013/14: 133 + 76,054 injuries
- 2015/16: 144 + 72,702 injuries
- 2016/17: 137 + 72,702 injuries

[Health & Safety Executive statistics from www.hse.gov.uk/statistics/]

Since 1992, over 1,000 workers in the construction industry alone have lost their lives accounting for 30 per cent of all the deaths at work in 2004. These casualties are overwhelmingly the result of company neglect but they are recorded annually by the HSE as accidents. The figures do not include deaths from work-related illnesses such as mesothelioma (2012: 2,535), occupational cancers and lung diseases: 13,000 each year (www.hse.gov.uk/statistics/index.htm). The HSE estimates that up to 90 per cent of deaths are preventable.

We will briefly consider the background to the Act. Until the following case, it was thought that a company could not be convicted of homicide:

The 'Herald of Free Enterprise' case

This case involved the prosecution of the shipping company, P&O, and seven employees for reckless manslaughter. P&O ran a cross-channel ferry service between Dover and Belgium. One stormy night in 1987, the Herald of Free Enterprise cross-channel ferry set sail from the port of Zeebrugge with the bow doors open. The ship took on water and quickly capsized, with the loss of 192 lives. There was no means by which the captain on the bridge of the ship could know whether the door was open or shut before setting sail. On the night in question, the assistant bosun, whose job it was to shut the doors, had fallen asleep. The chief officer, who had responsibility to ensure the doors were shut, had failed to do so.

Following an inquiry by the Department of Transport, the Sheen Report concluded in 1987 that cardinal fault lay with the board of directors who failed to apply their minds to the question of what orders were required to ensure the safety of the ship. There had been a failure of management which was 'infected with the disease of sloppiness from top to bottom'.

Two directors, a senior manager, the captain, assistant bosun, Master and chief officer and the company were subsequently charged with reckless manslaughter which at the time was defined as *Caldwell* recklessness:

R v P&O Ferries Ltd (1990) 93 CR APP R 72 CENTRAL CRIMINAL COURT

There were three hurdles for the prosecution to overcome in respect of the company:

1. Could a company commit manslaughter?
2. Who were the directing minds of the company?
3. Had the company failed to think about a serious and obvious risk of harm?

Turner J:

> Since the nineteenth century there has been a huge increase in the numbers and activities of corporations whether nationalised, municipal or commercial, which enter the private lives of all or most of 'men and subjects' in a diversity of ways. A clear case can be made for imputing to such corporations social duties including the duty not to offend all relevant parts of the criminal law. By

tracing the history of the cases decided by the English Courts over the period of the last 150 years, it can be seen how first tentatively and, finally, confidently the Courts have been able to ascribe to corporations a 'mind' which is generally one of the essential ingredients of common law and statutory offences. Indeed, it can be seen that in many Acts of Parliament the same concept has been embraced. The parliamentary approach is, perhaps, exemplified by section 18 of the Theft Act 1968 which provides for directors and managers of a limited company to be rendered liable to conviction if an offence under section 15, 16 or 17 of the Act is proved to have been committed – and I quote: 'with the consent, connivance of any director, manager, secretary … purporting to act in such capacity, then such director, manager or secretary shall be guilty of the offence.' Once a state of mind could be effectively attributed to a corporation, all that remained was to determine the means by which that state of mind could be ascertained and imputed to a non-natural person. That done, the obstacle to the acceptance of general criminal liability of a corporation was overcome. … Suffice it that where a corporation, through the controlling mind of one of its agents, does an act which fulfils the prerequisites of the crime of manslaughter, it is properly indictable for the crime of manslaughter. …

The prosecutions were dismissed even before the end of the prosecution case, primarily because of the identification principle (*R v P&O Ferries Ltd* (1990) 93 Cr App R 72).

The company had spent £1 million and had employed 14 counsel in its defence. It had called 138 witnesses, only 66 of whom were heard. The inequality of resources between prosecutor and defendant in this case was obvious. As C. Wells pointed out in 'Law Commission on Involuntary Manslaughter' *Crim LR* [1996], at p 552:

If there is one lesson from the P&O and other corporate killing sagas, it is that corporate defendants are highly motivated and well placed to exploit the metaphysical gap between 'the company' and its members.

Shortly after the failed prosecution, the House of Lords revived the offence of gross negligence manslaughter in the case of *Adomako* [1995] 1 AC 171. For a while it was thought that corporate manslaughter prosecutions might be more successfully achieved by this route but hope was short-lived. There was only one successful case. In *R v Kite & OLL Ltd* (Unreported) 8 December 1994 Winchester Crown Court, the sole director of an educational outdoor adventure company for school-children and the company were convicted of the manslaughter of four teenagers in a canoeing tragedy at Lyme Bay in March 1993. He had ignored storm warnings on the day and also previous warnings regarding low health and safety standards from staff. The teenagers had been inadequately clothed and equipped for capsize and died from hypothermia.

Five disastrous train crashes in England in a decade caused unprecedented loss of life and injury. The identification principle again prevented a single successful prosecution of manslaughter.

AG's Reference (No 2 of 1999) [2000] 2 CR APP R 207 COURT OF APPEAL

In 1997 a high-speed train from Swansea crashed into a freight train at Southall. Seven people were killed and others were injured. The driver had driven through two yellow warning signals and a red stop signal. He was packing his bags at the time. The operator of the train, Great Western Trains, was indicted with seven counts of manslaughter. The alleged gross negligence consisted of allowing the train to operate without either the Automatic Warning System which would have warned the driver that he had driven through a yellow light, or the Automatic Train Protection which would have automatically halted the train. Both systems were installed on the train but neither was operational. No trial took place regarding manslaughter but the company pleaded guilty to Health and Safety at Work Act offences. The prosecution appealed. Although the Court of Appeal held that a company could be convicted of manslaughter by gross negligence in the absence of evidence as to D's state of mind, it could not be convicted in the absence of evidence establishing the guilt of an identified human individual.

Rose LJ:

> In our judgment, unless an identified individual's conduct, characterisable as gross criminal negligence, can be attributed to the company the company is not, in the present state of the common law, liable for manslaughter. ... Indeed, Lord Hoffmann's speech in *Meridian*, in fashioning an additional special rule of attribution geared to the purpose of the statute, proceeded on the basis that the primary 'directing mind and will' rule still applies, although it is not determinative in all cases. In other words, he was not departing from the identification theory but reaffirming its existence. ...

The Court of Appeal rejected Lord Hoffmann's liberal approach to the identification doctrine in *Meridian*.

Given that gross negligence manslaughter is concerned with unreasonable conduct, not states of mind, and there is no reason why cumulative failures of different senior managers should not have been aggregated so as to convict the company, the identification principle need not have been a barrier to conviction.

No manslaughter prosecutions were attempted for either the Paddington train crash in 1999 (31 deaths), the Hatfield train derailment in 2000 (4 deaths), the derailment at Potters Bar in 2002 (7 deaths) or the Cumbria crash (1 death), although health and safety prosecutions resulted in convictions and fines against the rail operator and contractors.

After the Grenfell Tower fire disaster in 2017, it has been suggested that corporate or individual manslaughter charges could follow (*The Guardian*, 19 September 2017). 71 people died in a London tower block when an appliance in a flat caught fire, which spread quickly and fatally. The Royal Borough of Kensington and Chelsea and the management company responsible for the flats, the Kensington and Chelsea Tenant Management Organisation, could, in theory, be charged under the Act. At the time of writing, interviews were taking place.

The Corporate Manslaughter and Corporate Homicide Act 2007

The Act was the result of ten years of political pressure on the government and came into force in April 2008. It substantially replicates Home Office Consultation Document: 'Reforming the law on involuntary manslaughter: the government's proposals' (2000).

Corporate manslaughter in England, and corporate homicide in Scotland, will be committed where death was the result of the way in which an organisation's activities were managed or organised amounting to a gross breach of a relevant duty of care owed to the deceased:

1 The offence

(1) An organisation to which this section applies is guilty of an offence if the way in which its activities are managed or organised—

(a) causes a person's death, and

(b) amounts to a gross breach of a relevant duty of care owed by the organisation to the deceased.

(2)   The organisations to which this section applies are—

    (a)   a corporation;

    (b)   a department or other body listed in Schedule 1;

    (c)   a police force;

    (d)   a partnership, or a trade union or employers' association, that is an employer.

(3)   An organisation is guilty of an offence under this section only if the way in which its activities are managed or organised by its senior management is a substantial element in the breach referred to in subsection (1).

(4)   For the purposes of this Act—

    (a)   'relevant duty of care' has the meaning given by section 2, read with sections 3 to 7;

    (b)   a breach of a duty of care by an organisation is a 'gross' breach if the conduct alleged to amount to a breach of that duty falls far below what can reasonably be expected of the organisation in the circumstances;

    (c)   'senior management', in relation to an organisation, means the persons who play significant roles in—

        i.   the making of decisions about how the whole or a substantial part of its activities are to be managed or organised, or

        ii.   the actual managing or organising of the whole or a substantial part of those activities.

8 Factors for jury

(1)   This section applies where—

    (a)   it is established that an organisation owed a relevant duty of care to a person, and

    (b)   it falls to the jury to decide whether there was a gross breach of that duty.

(2)   The jury must consider whether the evidence shows that the organisation failed to comply with any health and safety legislation that relates to the alleged breach, and if so—

    (a)   how serious that failure was;

    (b)   how much of a risk of death it posed.

(3)   The jury may also—

    (a)   consider the extent to which the evidence shows that there were attitudes, policies, systems or accepted practices within the organisation that were likely to have encouraged any such failure as is mentioned in subsection (2), or to have produced tolerance of it;

    (b)   have regard to any health and safety guidance that relates to the alleged breach.

(4)   This section does not prevent the jury from having regard to any other matters they consider relevant.

 NOTE 4.4

Section 1(1)(a)

1. Section 1(1)(a): *Causation* must be proved between the death and the way in which the corporation's activities are managed or organised. Given that in many cases the immediate cause of death was the gross negligence of an individual employee (eg: *AG's Reference (No 2 of 1999)*) (see earlier in this section), will it be possible for a corporation to argue that the chain of causation was broken? The causal connection may be easier to identify in smaller companies.

→ CROSS-REFERENCE
Gross negligence is
discussed in detail in
Chapter 3, 3.3.

2. Section 1(1)(b): The corporation must owe *a relevant duty of care* to the victim. When would a corporation not owe an implied duty 'not to kill'? Is this not an unnecessary complication? Section 2 defines a duty of care by reference to the law of negligence. This means that corporate manslaughter is a form of gross negligence manslaughter based on the common law model of *Adomako* [1995] 1 AC 171.

   The need for a *'gross breach'* of a duty of care is determined according to the need under s8 for a failure to comply with relevant health and safety legislation and for an assessment of the risk of death. This will enable organisational policy, culture and systems to be taken into account in deciding whether there was a gross breach of a duty of care. But fault must still be related to the role of senior managers. Section 4(b) qualifies the term by requiring the breach to fall 'far below what can reasonably be expected of the organisation in the circumstances'. If standards across an industry are generally low, is it more likely that a breach will be regarded as reasonable in the circumstances? Will the Act encourage negligently low standards rather than insist on standards that the public have a right to expect? What does 'circumstances' add to 'gross breach'?

3. Section 1(2): Section 1(2) applies the Act to a wide range of organisations, both private and public. Concern has so far been directed at company strategy of putting profit before safety. Unincorporated bodies such as police forces, government departments and other public bodies are included. This overcomes human rights criticisms of the preceding bill which excluded them. Crown immunity is therefore removed subject to wide exclusions in ss 3–7 in relation to certain military and policy operations and child protection.

4. Section 1(3): The Act will not apply unless the way in which the organisation's activities are *managed or organised by senior management is a substantial element in the breach of duty of care*. Who are the senior management in complex national, international or global concerns? Section 1(4)(c) restricts the description to those playing *significant* roles in decision-making in relation to at least a *substantial* part of the corporation's activities? How will this be assessed? The Act is aimed at strategic management or organisational failings but this may be too restrictive although there is no insistence on the senior manager belonging to the board of directors or occupying any specific post as required by the identification doctrine. Will relevant junior employees be included? The role of senior managers can be aggregated. But one queries how effective the Act will be if it is necessary to identify knowledge or fault on the part of at least one senior manager before there can be organisational liability, especially where the organisation is incorporated abroad.

5. Section 18 of the Act specifically prohibits the prosecution of any individual as an accomplice to corporate manslaughter. However, an individual will remain personally liable for common law gross negligence manslaughter, and for any offence committed by a corporation attributable to neglect by a senior manager under s37 Health and Safety at Work Act 1974. The possibility of such prosecutions as an ancillary to, or a substitute for, corporate manslaughter might appear to be remote in this context. Directors do not owe a personal duty of care to individual victims and a decision in relation to adoption or implementation of health and safety policies is unlikely to be regarded as grossly negligent. The Act might have had greater impact upon corporate health and safety culture had it allowed prosecution of individual managerial risk-assessors for complicity in corporate manslaughter.

The Police

Since 1 September 2011, the Act has covered deaths in custody. Between 1998 and 2009 there were 333 deaths either in or following police custody, a substantial number of which were linked to physical restraint. In 2017, there were 14 deaths in police custody, the same as in 2016. Very few officers are ever charged, none resulting in conviction. Now, liability is extended to not only the police but also custody providers, both public and private, escorting or transporting detainees to and from prison or immigration detention centres. You may recall the widely reported death of Jimmy Mubenga, an Angolan deportee, who died whilst being restrained on a plane by a G4S guard. A verdict of 'unlawful killing' was returned by the Coroner's Court on 9 July 2013. A decision not to prosecute had already been made by the Independent Police Complaints Commission (IPCC) which has not, as yet, been reversed. (Statistics: K. Grace, *Deaths in or following police custody: Statistics for England & Wales 2010/11* (IPCC, 2011) and K. Grace, *Deaths during or following police contact: Statistics for England and Wales 2016/17* (IPCC and National Office for Statistics, 2017)); M. Hannan et al., *Deaths in or following police custody: An examination of the cases 1998/9–2008/9* (IPCC, 2010)).

Cases under the 2007 Act

Less than 25 prosecutions under the Act so far have resulted in convictions. There is an emerging trend of the prosecution accepting guilty pleas to corporate manslaughter in return for dropping charges of gross negligence manslaughter or breach of health and safety legislation against individual directors. The first conviction concerned the death of a geologist in a pit collapse. The company was small with eight employees and a sole director (*Cotswold Geotechnical Holdings* [2011] EWCA Crim 1137). Pleas of guilty were entered in the second prosecution (*JMW Farms Ltd* [2012] NICC17) and the third (*Lion Steel Equipment Ltd*, Unreported, 2 July 2012, Manchester Crown Court) where an employee was killed after falling through an unsafe roof. Gross negligence manslaughter charges against the directors of both *Geotechnical* and *Lion Steel* were dropped.

Read this by Celia Wells, 'Corporate Criminal Liability: A Ten Year Review' [2014] *Crim LR* 849 at p 861:

> These first prosecutions underline the limitations of the CMCH Act. The number of convictions is low, and as most concerned very small firms, might well have been successfully convicted under the common law had the deaths occurred pre-2008. The plethora of potential charges arising from the same fatality (CHCHA, individual common law manslaughter, HSWA corporate or individual charges) allows plea bargains. On the plus side, the very fact of the corporate manslaughter investigation often serves to put the case in to the headlines. With hefty fines for health and safety offences in some of these cases and with reporting often confusing corporate and director liability, it can be concluded that the Act has achieved some of its purpose, as one mechanism for flagging some of the worst examples of poor workplace safety practices.

The authors conclude that, despite its shortcomings, the Act fulfils a symbolic denunciatory role. Furthermore, its scope would appear to be widening. In 2016, the director of a company owning a care home was convicted under the Act for the death of an elderly patient in its care. (*Health and Safety Executive v Sherwood Rise* [2015] (unreported, February 2016)). Other recent cases include *Health and Safety Executive v Martinisation (London) Ltd* (unreported, 19 May 2017) in which two employees were killed trying to hoist a sofa up from a pavement. They had not had a risk assessment explained to them. Likewise, in *Health and Executive v Linley Developments Ltd* (unreported, 24 September 2015), the defendants were convicted of the corporate manslaughter of a bricklayer who was crushed when a wall collapsed. No risk assessments were carried out. Whether the Act is fit for purpose is of course still open to debate. For example, the Ministry of Defence were not liable in 2016 for the death of new recruits who died during gruelling training exercises; and in *Health and Safety Executive v Maidstone and Tunbridge Wells NHS Trust* (unreported, 27 January 2016), the CPS were not successful in securing a conviction when a woman died following an alleged lack of appropriate care following a caesarian section. As explained earlier, prosecutions are likely to follow in the aftermath of the Grenfell Tower disaster. At the time of writing, the enquiry was ongoing and interviews were being conducted.

4.2.4 Evaluation of the 2007 Act

1. The Act has been criticised for its technicality. Read the following criticism of the Act by D. Ormerod and R. Taylor, 'The Corporate Manslaughter and Corporate Homicide Act 2007' [2008] *Crim LR* 589:

Although relatively short by criminal justice standards … the Act is far from straightforward. Whether liability arises involves working through numerous issues: Is this an organisation that is covered? (s1) Is there a relevant duty? (s2) Is the duty excluded in whole or in part? (ss3–7) Is there a gross breach? (s8) In relation to each of these primary questions, numerous technical secondary issues arise: Is the offence due to the way in which activities are 'managed or organised'? Is the contribution of the 'senior management' a 'substantial element'? Who are the senior management? For the statute to leave so many crucial issues unresolved is disappointing.

Cynical commentators might regard the Act as succeeding primarily in making a symbolic statement about corporate responsibility, which it will struggle to fulfil in practice. Although the Act appears to create a broad reaching offence in terms of bodies to which it will apply and the duties of care which will trigger liability, these are severely curtailed by the technical qualifications integral to the all important duty question and by the numerous and far reaching exclusions designed to protect public bodies. The layers of technicality serve to restrict the scope of liability far more than would at first appear, and may well lead to significant difficulties in practice.

2. The Act has also been criticised for its failure to focus on any form of corporate wrongdoing other than homicide. Read this extract from J. Gobert, 'Corporate Manslaughter & Homicide Act 2007, thirteen years in the making but was it worth the wait?' (2008) 71(3) *MLR* 414:

The problem with the 2007 Act was thus not the lack of an adequate opportunity for reflection and review, but rather that it was too narrowly conceived from the outset. Instead of addressing the generic problem of corporate wrongdoing and how to hold organisations accountable for illegality whatever form it might take, the Act, as well as the Law Commission's recommendations and the Home Office consultation document which preceded it, is restricted to cases of homicide. None of these addressed, for example, corporate liability for causing grievous bodily harm, a statistically far more prevalent problem than corporate manslaughter. Indeed, it can be argued that a crime of corporate grievous bodily harm would be likely to have a far greater impact on risk management decisions than a law of corporate manslaughter. Few, if any, corporate executives or managers deliberately set out to kill or adopt policies that they can foresee will lead to widespread death. The threat of a prosecution of their company for corporate manslaughter is therefore unlikely to enter their thinking. On the other hand, it is axiomatic that these decision-makers will be aware that failing to pay sufficient attention to safety can lead to workplace injuries. Nonetheless, decisions not to install state-of-the-art but costly safety equipment may be rationalised on the basis that legal fines and damages resulting from claims by injured workers will be more than offset by the savings from foregoing installing the expensive equipment.

The last point can be illustrated by the £5.3 million fine against companies owned by BP, Shell and Total for the Buncefield oil depot explosion in 2005 for health, safety and environmental offences. The fine against Total represented 0.003 per cent of its 2011 first three months' profit. The explosion was the worst of its kind since the Second World War. No-one was killed but 43 people were injured, hundreds of homes and businesses were damaged or destroyed and drinking water was polluted.

3. There was no political or social enthusiasm for prosecuting companies for corporate crime until around 25 years ago. That has now changed. Why insist on corporate as opposed to individual senior management accountability? 'Did you ever expect a corporation to have a conscience, when it has no soul to be damned, and no body to be kicked?' asked Baron Thurlow, eighteenth-century Lord Chancellor, quoted in *Real Estate Opportunities Ltd v Aberdeen Asset Managers Jersey Ltd* [2007] 2 All ER 791 at 805.

Read this extract from J. Gobert and M. Punch, *Rethinking Corporate Crime* (Butterworths LexisNexis, 2003), at p 35:

What is needed is a theory of criminal liability that captures the distinctive nature of corporate fault. We start from the insight that a significant proportion of corporate offences are, in fact, crimes of omission rather than commission. Typically, the company's fault will lie in its failure to have put into place protective mechanisms that would have prevented harm from occurring. It is for this failure that the company bears responsibility for the harm. Recognising that corporate crimes are more often crimes of omission than commission reinforces the poverty of derivative theories of corporate liability that attribute the offences of individuals to a company. While it may be feasible to link wrongful acts to particular actors, it is often impossible to determine who should have done something that was not done. The obligation to put into place systems that would avert crime is collective and the failure to do so is a reflection of the way that the company has chosen to conduct its business.

4. There is considerable overlap with regulatory 'breach of duty' offences under the Health and Safety at Work Act 1974, although there is no doubt that the new offence is far more serious and emblematic of corporate criminal neglect. These offences require proof only that the company created a risk to health and safety, not that the risk resulted in death. Individual responsibility, if proven, can result in imprisonment. Where this cannot be achieved the company can be fined and will bear the stigma of conviction. Recent case law appears to confirm that liability for homicide is a complex mix of corporate and individual liability.

5. A serious criticism of the Act is that it does not permit the prosecution of individual directors for assisting manslaughter. A director can be prosecuted under s37 of the 1974 Act for statutory breach of duty if the company's breach was due to neglect. If convicted he can be fined and disqualified. This, though, is a far less significant offence and disqualifications are rare. Common law gross negligence manslaughter prosecutions remain possible provided a relevant duty of care can be identified. Interestingly, the number of such prosecutions against directors appears to be increasing: (S. Antrobus, 'The criminal liability of directors for health and safety breaches and manslaughter' [2013] *Crim LR* 309). The possibility of imprisonment may better reflect public desire for accountability. You cannot put a company behind bars. If the company is fined, surely the shareholders or taxpayer will suffer rather than individual directors? Heavy fines may reduce company resources for safety improvements to prevent similar disasters again, and could be self-defeating. The Sentencing Guidelines for corporate

homicide state that fines must be sufficiently substantial to have a real economic impact (Definitive Guideline on Health & Safety Offences, Corporate Manslaughter and Food Safety and Hygiene Offences (2016)). But can any fine really reflect the harm?

So far, the Act has had little direct impact on corporate responsibility for homicide. This may be due to the many difficulties with the legislation. It might also be because the HSE is a regulatory not an investigative body and its record of investigation and prosecution is poor. However, the Act may incidentally be encouraging more prosecutions of individual directors for gross negligence manslaughter. The identification doctrine does not exist in other common law jurisdictions nor in many European jurisdictions. It is beyond the scope of this book to examine alternative models but you will see comparative information in the Further reading section at the end of this chapter.

SECTION SUMMARY

A company can be liable:

- ■ *vicariously via delegation (offences of mens rea) or attribution (offences of strict liability); or*
- ■ *directly via the identification principle for low-level offences;*
- ■ *but the identification principle prevents a company from being liable for serious crimes, particularly homicide.*

The Corporate Manslaughter and Corporate Homicide Act 2007 enables an organisation to be prosecuted for a death where there has been a gross breach of a relevant duty of care.

SUMMARY

- ■ Offences of strict liability do not require MR to be proved in relation to one or more AR elements.
- ■ Courts should presume MR unless it is excluded expressly or by necessary implication.
- ■ Strict liability offences are mainly regulatory and are the means of enforcing company compliance with regulatory criminal law.
- ■ Strict liability has also been applied to offences which are not minor and which carry a term of imprisonment.
- ■ There are various criticisms relating to fairness, effectiveness and the presumption of innocence.
- ■ Companies can commit regulatory crimes of strict liability or minor MR crimes, but are unlikely to be found guilty of serious offences unless a controlling officer can be identified as having committed the AR with MR.

PROBLEM SOLVING

You are unlikely to meet problem questions on strict liability. The most likely means of assessing your knowledge of this subject will be through essay questions, for example: 'Analyse the arguments in favour or against strict liability'.

You are unlikely to meet problem questions solely on corporate manslaughter although the latter may be included in a question on homicide. Therefore, if you see that D has killed in the course of employment and a company is identified, that is a signal for you to discuss corporate manslaughter, for example: a train driver kills when he crashes his train, through a momentary loss of concentration, or a manager of an adventure centre fails to equip teenagers with life-jackets before sending them out on a sailing trip.

It is more likely that you will be presented with an essay question such as:

To what extent is it possible in England and Wales to prosecute a company for serious harm?

Remember:

- **I: Identify** relevant issues
- **D: Define** offences/defences
- **E: Explain/evaluate** the law
- **A: Apply** law to facts.

See the online resources for further guidance on solving this problem: http://www.oup.com/uk/loveless6e/.

FURTHER READING

Strict liability

A. Ashworth, 'Four Threats to the Presumption of Innocence' (2006) 10 *E & P* 241
Explores why the presumption of innocence is important and ways in which it is circumvented, including strict liability.

C. Manchester, 'Knowledge, Due Diligence and Strict Liability in Regulatory Offences' [2006] *Crim LR* 213
Looking at Licensing Act 2003 offences, it explores 'due diligence' defences to offences of strict liability.

A.P. Simester, *Appraising Strict Liability*, OUP, 2005
A collection of essays providing a wide-ranging exploration of strict liability.

J. Spencer, '"Fare-dodging"—Strict liability for Fraud?' (2014) 3 *Archbold Review* 5
Applies criticisms of strict liability to argue that travelling without a valid train ticket should not be a strict liability offence.

J. Stanton-Ife, 'Strict Liability: Stigma & Regret' (2007) 27(1) *OJLS* 151
A review of Simester (cited earlier in this section) which also offers analysis of the justifications for strict liability.

V. Tadros and S. Tierney, 'The Presumption of Innocence & the Human Rights Act' (2004) 67 *MLR* 402
Examines the ECHR and English courts' approach to the presumption of innocence.

Corporate liability

C.M.V. Clarkson, 'Corporate Manslaughter: Yet More Proposals' [2005] *Crim LR* 677
An article preceding the enactment of the CMCHA 2007, useful for evaluating the changes it made.

S. Field & L. Jones, 'Five Years On: The Impact of the Corporate Manslaughter and Corporate Homicide Act 2007: Plus ça Change?' [2013] 24(6) *ICCLR* 239
Argues that the success of the Act will largely depend on police accountability and the approach of the prosecuting authorities. Much will still rest on the wording of the Act and how the courts interpret the terms within it.

F. Gerry, 'Corporate Manslaughter After Grenfell' (2017) 181(26) *CL & J Weekly* 474
Explores the law on corporate manslaughter in the context of the disaster.

Law Commission: Legislating the Criminal Code: Involuntary Manslaughter (Law Com No 237) 1996
The government's proposals on the changes to involuntary manslaughter overall, including corporate manslaughter.

A. Lodge, 'Gross Negligence Manslaughter on the Cusp: The Unprincipled Privileging of Harm Over Culpability' (2017) 81(2) *JCL* 125–142
Focuses on the basis of liability for gross negligence manslaughter and whether it should focus on the decision to cause harm.

E. Mujih, 'Reform of the Law on Corporate Killing: A Toughening or Softening of the Law' (2008) 29(3) *Company Lawyer* 76
Argues that in disasters such as the Zeebrugge ferry disaster fault was diffused and could not be attributed to any one individual.

S. Ramage, 'Grenfell Tower' (2017) 234 *Criminal Lawyer* 1–2

Comments on whether building contractors could potentially be guilty of corporate manslaughter following the disaster.

Sentencing Guidelines Council: Definitive Guidelines on Corporate Manslaughter and Health & Safety Offences Causing Death (2010) (www.sentencingcouncil.org.uk/wp-content/uploads/web__guideline_on_corporate_manslaughter_accessible.pdf)

The new sentencing guidelines.

F.B. Wright, 'Criminal Liability of Directors and Senior Managers for Deaths at Work' [2007] *Crim LR* 949

Explains how directors and senior managers at fault can be held to account for deaths at work, even though the Corporate Manslaughter and Corporate Homicide Act 2007 imposes liability on organisations but not individuals.

Secondary participation: parties to a crime

5

Introduction

KEY POINTS

This chapter will help you to understand that:

- secondary parties (accessories) can be liable for an offence committed by another and that they will be subject to the same punishment;

- an accessory is someone who assists or encourages another to commit a crime by aiding, abetting, counselling or procuring (AR);

- MR of accessories: intention to assist the principal offender with knowledge or foresight that a particular type of offence might be committed with the MR for that offence;

- following recommendations for reform from the Law Commission and others, *Jogee* made significant changes to accessorial liability in joint ventures;

- an accessory will be liable for another's offence going beyond the joint plan only if they intended to encourage or assist in that offence, albeit conditionally;

- defence: withdrawal.

INTRODUCTION

This chapter concerns the liability of those who assist or encourage another to commit a crime. They are called secondary parties or accessories. An accessory may be convicted of a crime that was committed by another person (the perpetrator or principal offender) and may be subject to the same maximum sentence, even where participation is minor or indirect. The law in this area determines the liability of secondary parties to all crimes, from minor driving offences to murder. There must be a principal offence before a person can be convicted as an accessory.

It has been acknowledged for some time that the law is in an unsatisfactory state and is frequently inconsistent. The Law Commission has published no less than five reports on various aspects of secondary participation since 1993. In the most recent, detailed recommendations for reform were made in relation to secondary participation in homicide. In 2007, the government published a working paper on secondary participation and murder. However, significant change to the law has come not from Parliament but from the Supreme Court decision in *R v Jogee* [2016] UKSC 8.

KEY CASES

Robinson v Queen [2011] UKPC 3—aiding: presence requires a positive act;

Gnango [2011] UKSC 59—accessory to murder of X by participating in attempted murder by P on himself;

NCB v Gamble [1959] 1 QB 11—MR for accessories: intention means knowledge not purpose;

Johnson v Youden [1950] 1 KB 544—knowledge of the essential matters forming the offence;

Maxwell v DPP for NI [1978] 3 All ER 1140—knowledge of a particular type of offence;

Jogee [2016] UKSC 8—abolishes 'joint enterprise' and confirms usual rules for secondary participation apply: A must intend to encourage or assist P to commit the crime with the MR of the offence.

5.1 Definition of Parties

- ■ *Principal (P)*: The person who commits a crime whether by himself, or through an innocent agent (eg: a child) or as a co-defendant. The act of a principal or perpetrator (P) will be the most immediate cause of the crime: the murderer or burglar. If a person contributes to the AR of an offence, he is a principal.

- ■ *Accessory (A)*: All other parties who assist and encourage the crime *before and/or during* commission, also called 'secondary parties', for example: the look-out or supplier of weapons. An accessory will not commit the final offence.

- ■ The *principal offence* must be committed. It includes both completion of and an *attempt* by P to commit a substantive offence.

- ■ *Joint or co-defendant*: A defendant who jointly and intentionally commits the same offence as another defendant, each of whom is equally liable.

When identifying the parties to a crime throughout this book so far we have used the symbol D for defendant. For the purposes of this chapter, a principal will be identified as P and an accessory as A.

5.2 Accessories: Conditions for Liability

5.2.1 Actus Reus

5.2.2 Mens Rea

Liability is governed by s8 Accessories and Abettors Act 1861 (as amended by Criminal Law Act 1977):

> Whosoever shall aid, abet, counsel or procure the commission of any indictable offence, whether the same be an offence at common law or by virtue of any Act passed, shall be tried, indicted and punished as a principal offender.

Section 44 Magistrates' Courts Act 1980 applies similar provisions to summary offences.

5.2.1 Actus Reus

The conduct element for accessories is satisfied by far less than is required by the AR of P's completed offence. The common feature of the first three classifications of accessory is that they all provide *assistance* and *encouragement* to P before or at the time of P's offence (refer to Diagram 5.1 for the three conditions of liability). There is a degree of overlap between these means of participation.

Aiding

The term suggests one who assists P to commit the offence either before or at the time of commission, for example: supplying equipment, keeping a look-out. P need not be aware of A's assistance as in *State v Tally* (1894) 15 So 722 (Supreme Court of Alabama) where, unknown to P, A prevented a warning from being sent to V and was convicted of being a secondary party to murder. Assistance may only amount to very little:

> In an Australian case Brown [1968] S.A.S.R. 467 it was simply a cough. But that cough was a signal, which was intended to tell, and did tell, the killer that the victim was leaving his room. It was intended to assist, and it assisted, the commission of murder. When the killing occurred, the cougher became a murderer.
>
> (J.C. Smith, 'Criminal Liability of Accessories: Law and Law Reform' (1997) 113 *LQR*, at 461)

As with abetting (see next), aiding requires a positive act which encourages P and which is intended to encourage. Aiding and abetting have much in common. Other jointly relevant aspects are covered next.

Abetting

An abettor encourages P to commit the offence. Encouragement must be communicated and P must derive encouragement from it. Again, encouragement may amount to very little, for example: the Court of Appeal in *Giannetto* [1997] 1 Cr App R 1 confirmed that there would be encouragement if a husband, when told of a plan to murder his wife, merely said 'Oh goody!' The husband would thereby become an accessory to murder. The Court of Appeal stated that '[a]ny involvement from mere encouragement upwards would suffice'.

R v Craig & Bentley (1952) *The Times*, 10–13 December, is an illustration of positive encouragement by words. The police were attempting to apprehend both defendants for a crime during a roof-top chase. The words, 'Let him have it', allegedly spoken by Derek Bentley, a 19-year-old epileptic with a mental age of 11, were found to amount to positive encouragement to Daniel Craig, who shot and killed a police officer. Both were convicted of murder. (There is dispute over whether Bentley's words, if spoken, meant 'shoot him' or 'give up, let him have the gun'; his conviction was quashed in 1998, over 45 years after his execution: *R v Bentley (Deceased)* [1998] EWCA Crim 2516.) Assistance or encouragement is a question of fact, as confirmed in the next case.

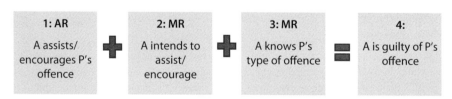

Diagram 5.1
Accessories: Conditions for liability

Stringer [2011] EWCA CRIM 1396

Father (A1), son (A2) and P chased V, who was armed with a baseball bat. A1 and A2 knew P had a knife. Both were guilty of murder for giving encouragement to P to stab V. The original conviction had been based on joint enterprise.

Toulson LJ:

> If D provides assistance or encouragement to P, and P does that which he has been encouraged or assisted to do, there is good policy reason for treating D's conduct as materially contributing to the commission of the offence, and therefore justifying D's punishment as a person responsible for the commission of the offence, whether or not P would have acted in the same way without such encouragement or assistance. Whether D's conduct amounts to assistance or encouragement is a question of fact. Professor Glanville Williams commented in Criminal Law: The General Part (1961) 2nd ed, at page 356, that it is sometimes difficult to know what degree of assistance is to be regarded as aiding. Several centuries of case law have not produced any definitive legal formula for resolving that question. This is unsurprising because the facts of different cases are infinitely variable. It is for the jury, applying their common sense and sense of fairness, to decide whether the prosecution have proved to their satisfaction on the particular facts that P's act was done with D's assistance or encouragement (subject to the qualification that if no fair-minded jury could properly reach that conclusion, the judge should withdraw the case) …

The next case generated much debate because a conviction as accessory to murder was overturned by the Court of Appeal but reinstated by the Supreme Court.

R v Gnango [2011] UKSC 59 SUPREME COURT

Gnango (G) and Bandana Man (BM) engaged in a gunfight in a car park outside a nursing home. A bullet from BM's gun killed a passing care worker, Miss Pniewska. BM was arrested but never charged. G was tried for her murder. The prosecution argued that G was guilty either: (a) as part of a joint enterprise, that is: a *common purpose* to commit an affray (a shoot-out) with foresight that BM might intentionally kill or commit GBH; or (b) as an accessory by way of *encouragement and participation* in the affray with the necessary foresight that BM might intentionally kill or commit GBH. [Ground (a) is referred to in the judgment below as 'parasitic accessory liability'.] G could then be guilty of murder through the doctrine of transferred malice. G was convicted under ground (a) for the judge held that there was no encouragement by G towards BM for the purposes of (b). The Court of Appeal overturned the conviction. There was no *common purpose* to commit an affray given that G and BM had opposing or antagonistic purposes. There were individual acts of affray which were separate and diametrically opposed but there was no common purpose to be shot at. Further, since there had been no *encouragement* of BM by G, G was not guilty of murder on ground (b). The prosecution appealed. The Supreme Court held that G was guilty of murder as an accessory to an offence of violence under the ordinary rules of secondary participation. The respondent in the judgment is party G.

Lord Phillips and Lord Judge:

> Parasitic accessory liability arises where (i) D1 and D2 have a common intention to commit crime A (ii) D1, as an incident of committing crime A, commits crime B, and (iii) D2 had foreseen the possibility that he might do so. Here there was no crime A and crime B. It cannot be said that the two protagonists had a joint intention to commit violence of a type that fell short of the violence committed. Either Bandana Man and the respondent had no common intention, or

there was a common intention to have a shoot out. If they intended to have a shoot out, then each necessarily accepted that the other would shoot at him with the intention to kill or cause serious injury. Neither intended that the other should kill him but each accepted the risk that he might do so.

If the respondent aided, abetted, counselled and procured Bandana Man to shoot at him he was, on my analysis, guilty of aiding and abetting the attempted murder of himself. Had he been killed by Bandana Man, he would have been a party to his own murder. Although he had not intended that Bandana Man should succeed in hitting him, complicity in his attempt to do so would have rendered him a party to the successful achievement of that attempt. As it was, Bandana Man accidentally shot Miss Pniewska. Under the doctrine of transferred malice he was liable for her murder. Under the same doctrine, the respondent, if he had aided, abetted, counselled and procured the attempt, was party to the murder that resulted ... A guilty verdict in this case involves a combination of common law principles in relation to aiding and abetting and the common law doctrine of transferred malice ... We have considered whether to hold the respondent guilty of murder would be so far at odds with what the public would be likely to consider the requirements of justice as to call for a reappraisal of the application of the doctrine in this case. We have concluded to the contrary. On the jury's verdict the respondent and Bandana Man had chosen to indulge in a gunfight in a public place, each intending to kill or cause serious injury to the other, in circumstances where there was a foreseeable risk that this result would be suffered by an innocent bystander. It was a matter of fortuity which of the two fired what proved to be the fatal shot. In other circumstances it might have been impossible to deduce which of the two had done so. In these circumstances it seems to us to accord with the demands of justice rather than to conflict with them that the two gunmen should each be liable for Miss Pniewska's murder.

 NOTE 5.1

1. G was convicted of murder as an accessory on the basis of his *participation* in the offence of *attempted* murder by BM against himself. Since he intended to kill or commit really serious harm to BM as part of that attempt, his intention could be transferred to the victim. The Supreme Court rejected as artificial the judge's finding of a shared common purpose (or joint enterprise) to commit an affray (crime 1) as a result of which A would be guilty of the consequential murder (crime 2). The Court of Appeal's reasoning for overturning that conviction was also rejected as being unduly technical. Joint enterprise was rejected by both Court of Appeal and Supreme Court.

2. Lord Brown and Lord Clarke considered that G was guilty of murder as a joint principal, the difference between an accessory and principal being elusive in the circumstances.

   'The general public would in my opinion be astonished and appalled if in those circumstances the law attached liability for the death only to the gunman who actually fired the fatal shot (which, indeed, it would not always be possible to determine). Is he alone to be regarded as guilty of the victim's murder? Is the other gunman really to be regarded as blameless and exonerated from all criminal liability for that killing? Does the decision of the Court of Appeal here, allowing A's appeal against his conviction for murder, really represent the law of the land? ... it seems to me that A is liable for C's murder as a principal—a direct participant engaged by agreement in unlawful violence (like a duel,

→ CROSS-REFERENCE

Kennedy (No 2) is the drug supplier/manslaughter case discussed in Chapter 2, 2.3.3.

a prize-fight or sado-masochism) specifically designed to cause and in fact causing death or serious injury. But whichever analysis is adopted, A's liability for C's murder seems to me clear and I would regard our criminal law as seriously defective were it otherwise.'

3. Lord Kerr would have dismissed the conviction. There was no agreement to shoot and be shot at and G could not be a joint principal because the voluntary and informed act of BM broke the chain of causation in accordance with *R v Kennedy (No 2)* [2008] 1 AC 269.

This reasoning of the Supreme Court can be criticised for ignoring the basic elements of accessorial liability: (i) A was originally charged with assisting and encouraging murder not attempted murder. Section 8 of the 1861 Act requires A to be indicted and punished for the same crime as P; (ii) aiding and abetting require an intention to encourage P. When G fired at BM, was he intentionally encouraging BM to fire back at him? Read the following by R. Buxton 'Being an Accessory to One's Own Murder' [2012] *Crim LR* 275:

> ... G's participation in the affray was held by the Supreme Court to have amounted to encouragement of BM (to shoot at G): even though that had not been the view of the trial judge who heard the evidence ... It might have been said in *Gnango*, had this issue ever been considered, that G must have appreciated that by participating in the shoot-out he was egging BM on to respond. But the Court of Appeal, when rejecting the argument based on affray, pointed out that the participants did not act in concert, but independently and antagonistically, without a shared purpose to shoot and be shot at. That state of mind does not drive one to think that G had in his mind the encouragement of BM ... It is much less clear that D can be said to *encourage* P to produce consequence x when consequence x is exactly what D does not want to occur ...

It may be the case that the decision is based on policy (Lord Brown and Lord Clarke), but would public opinion demand conviction of the person who did not actually fire the fatal shot? Even if it did, is this a good reason to convict? If BM had been tried and convicted of the murder of Miss Pniewska, would G also have been convicted even though he did not kill her? If, in a fight between two people, injuries are inflicted by D upon V, should V also be convicted as an accessory to the attempt to injure himself? If D injures X, should V be an accessory to those injuries?

Presence at the scene is not necessary—but mere presence alone is insufficient

An accessory (A) may be present, absent or assist or encourage before or at the time of the offence. Mere presence alone is insufficient unless it provides evidence of an intention to encourage the commission of the offence. In *Coney* (1882) 8 QBD 534, D's mere presence at an illegal prize fight was not conclusive evidence of an intention to encourage the fight. Presence was capable of providing such an intention, but was insufficient on its own without further proof of encouragement.

In *Wilcox v Jeffrey* [1951] 1 All ER 464, however, A's presence at an illegal public jazz concert by Coleman Hawkins (P), a famous American saxophonist, was held to have abetted P to contravene immigration controls prohibiting him from taking employment in the UK. A did not applaud P but he did report the performance in his jazz journal and had met P at the airport. There was other evidence, therefore, beyond mere presence, of an intention to encourage.

R v Clarkson [1971] 1 WLR 1402 COURT OF APPEAL

A was charged with aiding and abetting the rape of a woman in an army barracks. The rape was in progress when A and others purposely entered the room to watch. They remained throughout the rape without intervening. It was held on appeal that mere presence was insufficient without an intention to encourage, even if P derived encouragement from their presence.

Megaw LJ:

> In my opinion to constitute an aider and abettor some active steps must be taken by word or action with the intent to instigate the principal or principals. Encouragement does not of necessity amount to aiding and abetting ... He will only aid and abet if he encourages intentionally by expressions, gestures or actions intended to signify approval.

Mere presence and secret approval does not signify an intention to encourage:

Robinson v Queen [2011] UKPC 3 (ON APPEAL FROM THE COURT OF APPEAL, BERMUDA)

P instructed Robinson (R) to drive P and two twin brothers to a house. R and another cleared out some rooms which made space for a murderous attack by P on the brothers with a baseball bat. R continued to remain in the room, guarding the door. He was convicted of aiding P's murders on the basis of his presence. R denied that he had encouraged P to kill. This was rejected.

Sir Anthony Hughes explained that aiding imports a positive act of assistance:

> Of course that positive act of assistance may sometimes be constituted by D2 being present, and communicating to D1 not merely that he concurs in what D1 is doing, but that he is ready and willing to help in any way required. The commission of most criminal offences, and certainly most offences of violence, may be assisted by the forbidding presence of another as back-up and support. If D2's presence can properly be held to amount to communicating to D1 (whether expressly or by implication) that he is there to help in any way he can if the opportunity or need arises, that is perfectly capable of amounting to aiding ... It is, however, important to make clear to juries that mere approval of (ie 'assent' to, or 'concurrence' in) the offence by a bystander who gives no assistance, does not without more amount to aiding. It is potentially misleading to formulate aiding ... without explaining that the communication of willingness to give active assistance is a minimum requirement.

Sir Anthony then went on to approve the direction given by the Chief Justice to the jury:

> i) that mere presence was not enough to constitute aiding; ii) that presence plus secret approval or enjoyment or even secret intention to help if needed does not do so either; and iii) that in order to make a bystander guilty 'he must do something positive, intending to help or to encourage'.

Mere presence, in the absence of an intention to encourage, would convict a person for their thoughts alone if unaccompanied by any physical act. Remember that failing to act, or merely watching another come to harm and failing to intervene, is not in itself a crime unless D is under a duty to act. However, in some circumstances, presence can amount to assistance or encouragement, for example: if it 'provid[es] support by contributing to the force of numbers in a hostile confrontation' (*Jogee*).

➔ CROSS-REFERENCE
For further discussion of *Jogee* and accessorial liability see 5.2.2.

Omissions: Assisting or encouraging by failing to intervene

→ CROSS-REFERENCE
Liability for omissions
is discussed in Chapter 2.

→ CROSS-REFERENCE
For discussion of
duress in the context of
domestic violence see
Chapter 9, 9.1.2 'Mental
characteristics'.

One can commit a criminal offence by failing to intervene in breach of a duty recognised by the criminal law. The five duty situations are relationship, contract, statute, assumption of responsibility and creation of danger. If A is under a duty to intervene and fails to do so he will be liable as an accessory to P's offence.

In *Russell v Russell* [1987] 85 Cr App R 388 the Court of Appeal held that where a duty to act does exist, an omission or failure to intervene may amount to encouragement. Here, one parent ill-treated a child in the presence of another. The other was convicted as accessory to murder. Recall that in such cases issues can arise regarding duress where one carer is too frightened to intervene because of the other's violence.

Evidence of encouragement will be particularly strong if the accessory is expected to exercise some control over P. In *Tuck v Robson* [1970] 1 WLR 741, the Court of Appeal held that a publican (A) who takes no steps to make a customer (P) leave after closing time may be committing the offence of aiding and abetting P's consumption of illegal alcohol. In *Webster* [2006] EWCA Crim 415 it was held that where a car owner allows a drunken driver to drive his car in his presence, and with his consent and approval, he may aid and abet dangerous driving provided he could have intervened and failed to do so. In *Baldessare* (1930) 22 Cr App R 70, two men took a car and drove recklessly, killing V. The passenger was convicted as accessory to manslaughter. Death may have been unforeseen but the common purpose was driving recklessly. It did not matter whose hands were upon the wheel. In a curious reversal of the civil law doctrine of agency (where the principal exercises control over the agent's acts), the driver was held to be the agent of the passenger. You might like to compare the case of *Willett*, where the court held that merely continuing to sit in a passenger seat did not amount to an intention to encourage his brother to run down and murder V. It seems unlikely that Baldessare had any control over the driver's conduct. In the more recent case of *Martin* [2010] EWCA Crim 1450, however, a learner, driving under supervision, lost control of a vehicle and crashed, killing himself and a passenger. The court held that, in the absence of a common venture to drive dangerously, the supervisor would only become an accomplice if he deliberately failed to intervene in the negligent driving, thereby demonstrating an intention to encourage P.

> **?!   THINKING POINT** 5.1
>
> A decides to hold a party at his house. In the course of the evening, A is told that in the upstairs bedroom a guest, P, is about to rape another guest, V, who is the worse for drink. A decides to do nothing. P rapes V. Is A an accessory to rape?

Where A or P cannot be identified

One of the advantages of secondary liability is that where the prosecution cannot prove whether P or A *committed* an offence, but there is evidence of *participation* by both, then each will be fully liable: *Swindall & Osborne* (1846) 2 C & K 230, 175 ER 95 where, in a joint cart-race between an accessory and principal, one cart struck and killed somebody but it was not clear whose. Manslaughter convictions for both were upheld.

In the absence of evidence that either party *participated* in the AR, it will not be clear as to which one is P or A. In such a case, a prosecution will fail for lack of evidence. For example, in *Lane & Lane* (1986) 82 Cr App R 5 each parent had been present for part of a five-hour period during which the death of their child occurred. There was no evidence as to who had been P or A and therefore both were acquitted.

However, where the victim is a child or vulnerable adult in the same household as parents/guardians, s5 Domestic Violence, Crime and Victims Act 2004 now provides that either can be prosecuted for causing or allowing such death. This raises questions concerning the fairness of convicting a parent/guardian (typically a woman) who has failed to protect the child for reasons of violence or fear of violence from the parent killer. *Lane* was relied upon in the following case:

R v Banfield [2013] EWCA CRIM 1394

A wife (W) and daughter appealed against conviction of murdering V. V had disappeared shortly after selling the family home. There was no body, no suggested mechanism of death, no identified day when the murder was said to have occurred, no time and no place and no suggestion of what happened to the body. The proceeds of sale and V's pension were transferred to W. During the proceedings, the daughter admitted that V had been murdered. The appeal turned upon whether there was evidence from which the jury could infer that the two defendants must have killed together and not one in the absence of the other:

Lady Justice Rafferty:

> The test for the jury was whether the Crown had made it sure of joint responsibility. The Crown's difficulty is readily apparent. If at the close of its case the evidence were consistent both with inculpation and exculpation of either defendant then it had not established a prima facie case of murder, against either.
>
> Given its decision to indict murder but not conspiracy to murder. … the Crown's consequential difficulty was its inability to prove that the two women acted in concert to bring about DB's death … As the authors of Smith and Hogan's Criminal Law, 13th Ed, para 8.4.1.5 remark, if all that can be proved is that the principal offence was committed either by the first or the second accused, each must be acquitted: *Richardson* (1785) 1 Leach 387; *R v Abbott* [1955] 2 QB 497. We have reminded ourselves of the example given by Finnemore J and referred to in the judgment of Croom-Johnson LJ in *Lane:* If two sisters were provably in the room when X was murdered, and either both together or one alone were responsible, there is no prima facie case against either since the Crown would be unable to exclude either. We have reminded ourselves too that in that case there had been no suggestion that two had acted in concert, rather that one or the other was responsible. Nevertheless, the logic of the approach is not weaker as a consequence.

Causation is not necessary

A must have contributed to the principal offence but will not have caused it. If he did, by contributing to the AR of P's offence, he would be a joint principal. In many cases the intervention of P, acting independently of A's assistance, will have broken the chain of causation.

THINKING POINT 5.2

1. V has been shot and killed by either P or A but the prosecution cannot prove which of the two pulled the trigger and which one hired the other as hitman. What offence has each committed, if any?

2. Which of the following represents either aiding or abetting by A and for which offence will A be liable?

   a. P tells A that he plans to murder V. A says he thinks it a very good idea. P kills V the following week.

   b. A finds P violently kicking V in the head. A shouts encouragement, smashes a bottle, hands it to P and then leaves the scene. P continues the attack with the bottle. V dies.

Counselling

Broadly speaking, a counsellor is an adviser. The term applies to one who advises, solicits or encourages before the commission of the offence, for example: supplying information, the weapon or equipment. It implies contact between the parties but not causation or presence at the scene of the crime.

R v Calhaem [1985] 1 QB 808 COURT OF APPEAL

A was infatuated with her solicitor and wanted to kill another woman with whom he was having an affair. A hired P to kill the woman. P pleaded guilty to murder but said that he only intended to pretend to attempt the killing. He had gone berserk and killed because the victim had screamed so much. A appealed against conviction for murder on the ground that counselling required a causal connection between the counsellor and the commission of the offence. This was rejected and the appeal dismissed. Counselling required:

1. the offence to be within the authority of the advice of the counsellor, and
2. contact between the parties, and
3. a connection between the counselling and the murder.

Procuring

A procurer causes a crime to be committed. The term covers a range of activities from surreptitiously causing or influencing to threatening or commanding the commission of the offence. Contact is not necessary.

 EXAMPLE 5.1

A compels P to drive whilst disqualified. A procures P to commit a driving offence and is liable for that offence as a secondary party.

→ CROSS-REFERENCE
For further discussion of situations where the secondary party is liable when P is not see 5.4.

Where the conduct element of a principal offence has been committed, A may still be liable as a secondary party even though P is acquitted by virtue of a defence such as duress. P may also be morally innocent and unaware that A is attempting to procure an offence:

AG's Reference (No 1 of 1975) [1975] QB 773 COURT OF APPEAL

A secretly laced P's drink with double measures of spirits, knowing that P would be driving home. A was charged with aiding, abetting, counselling and procuring the offence of driving with excess alcohol under s6(1) Road Traffic Act 1972. On appeal the Court of Appeal had to decide whether there had to be a shared intention to commit the crime or simply encouragement of the offence. The trial judge had concluded that some sort of meeting of minds or mental link between the secondary party and principal was essential but this was rejected on appeal:

Lord Widgery CJ:

So far as aiding, abetting and counselling is concerned, we would go a long way with that conclusion. It may very well be … difficult to think of a case of aiding, abetting or counselling when the parties have not met and have not discussed in some respects the terms of the offence which they have in mind. But we do not see why a similar principle should apply to procuring. We approach section 8 of the Act of 1861 on the basis that the words should be given their ordinary meaning, if possible. …

To procure means to produce by endeavour. You procure a thing by setting out to see that it happens and taking the appropriate steps to produce that happening. We think that there are plenty of instances in which a person may be said to procure the commission of a crime by another even though there is no sort of conspiracy between the two, even though there is no attempt at agreement or discussion as to the form which the offence should take. In our judgment the offence described in this reference is such a case. …

You cannot procure an offence unless there is a causal link between what you do and the commission of the offence, and here we are told that in consequence of the addition of this alcohol the driver, when he drove home, drove with an excess quantity of alcohol in his body.

Giving the words their ordinary meaning in English, and asking oneself whether in those circumstances the offence has been procured, we are in no doubt that the answer is that it has. It has been procured because, unknown to the driver and without his collaboration, he has been put in a position in which in fact he has committed an offence which he never would have committed otherwise.

Appeal dismissed.

NOTE 5.2

1. To procure means to produce by endeavour.
2. Contact or a meeting of minds between A, the procurer, and P is not essential.
3. A must cause the offence.
4. It follows that A needs to procure intentionally and not recklessly.

Point 4 was confirmed by the Court of Appeal in *Blakely and Sutton v Chief Constable of West Mercia* [1991] Crim LR 763, where A1 and A2 laced P's tonic water with vodka so that he would not drive home but stay and spend the night with A1. They intended to tell him but did not do so before P left and drove home whilst drunk. P received an absolute discharge for driving with excess alcohol. A1 and A2 were convicted as secondary parties to procuring P's offence but appealed on the basis that, although they intended to induce drunkenness, they did not intend P to drive and were therefore only reckless as to that fact. Procuring, they argued, should not be reckless. The Court of Appeal agreed and held that procuring, and perhaps also counselling, required an intention that P *might* commit the principal offence.

Procuring and innocent agents

If P is below the age of criminal responsibility (10) or insane, he is an innocent agent and cannot legally commit an offence. An intentional procurer of a child P's offence will therefore be regarded as a principal offender rather than an accessory.

> **EXAMPLE** 5.2
>
> A father gives his 7-year-old son a loaded gun, telling him that it is only a toy and that he should fire it at his mother, whom the father secretly wishes dead. The son does so, killing his mother. The father becomes the principal offender to murder.

The crime needs to have been intentionally procured. So if, instead, the father had forgotten that he had left a loaded gun on the kitchen table and the son had accidentally shot his mother, the father would not be guilty of procuring gross negligence manslaughter. (An example adapted from Law Com No 305, at 4.18.)

The innocent agency doctrine runs into difficulty with certain offences which can only be committed by a certain category of people, for example: only men can commit rape. Therefore, if a woman (A) procures a 9-year-old boy to have sexual penetration with another woman without the latter's consent, A cannot be convicted as principal but only as an accessory.

> **?! THINKING POINT** 5.3
>
> Which of the following represents either counselling or procuring by A and for which offence will A be liable?
>
> 1. A generous host (A) gives too much alcohol to a guest (P):
>   a. hoping, wrongly, that P will be sensible enough to stay the night and not drive home;
>   b. knowing P must drive home.
> In each case P is stopped, charged and convicted of driving with excess alcohol.
> 2. A emails P information about the security system of a shop which P wishes to burgle, on the basis of which P attempts the burglary but is arrested on site.
> 3. A asks P, a 9-year-old boy, to slip through a narrow window of a house and to unlock the front door from the inside so that A can enter in order to steal.

5.2.2 Mens Rea

Intention to assist and knowledge of the circumstances

The MR of an accessory relates to the intentions of another. This is not the case with ordinary criminal liability where MR relates to acts, circumstances and results for which one bears direct responsibility. The MR of an accessory consists of intention to assist and knowledge of the circumstances of P's offence, regardless of whether it is a crime of MR, negligence or strict liability.

Intention to assist or encourage

- A must intend to do the act which assists or encourages.
- A must intend the act to assist or encourage P.
- Intention requires knowledge but not purpose that an offence should be committed.

Does intention mean knowledge or purpose?

NCB v Gamble [1959] 1 QB 11 DIVISIONAL COURT

The National Coal Board (A) operated a weighbridge at a coal colliery. The weighbridge operator, an employee of A, informed a lorry driver (P) that his lorry was overloaded by nearly four tons. It was an offence to drive an overloaded lorry on the road. The driver (P) said he would take the risk. A's employee gave P a weighbridge ticket which passed ownership of the coal to him. A was charged with aiding, abetting, counselling or procuring P's offence of driving an overloaded lorry on the road. It was held that A *intended* to aid the offence by virtue of the employee's voluntary act of giving P an essential item for the commission of the offence (the ticket) with *knowledge of the circumstances* that the lorry was overloaded. A's indifference to the consequences was irrelevant as was the fact that the weighbridge operator was only doing his job.

This case seemed to draw an equation between intention and mere knowledge—a very wide interpretation of intention. Intention in general means purpose (direct intent) or foresight of a virtual certainty (oblique intent). However, according to Devlin J:

> If one man deliberately sells to another a gun to be used for murdering a third, he may be indifferent whether the third man lives or dies and interested only in the cash profit to be made out of the sale, but he can still be an aider and abettor.

A would be liable for P's offence as an accessory not only where he deliberately sold goods to P but also where he gained knowledge of P's unlawful purpose during the ordinary course of business as a shop-keeper, for example: if A ran a hardware store and sold P industrial cutting equipment knowing that P, a convicted burglar, might use the equipment on the next job, A would intentionally encourage burglary. If P committed 20 burglaries with the equipment, A remained an accessory.

R v Jogee [2016] UKSC 8

The Supreme Court in *Jogee* interpreted *Gamble* as stating that *where the principal offence does not require MR*, the secondary party only needs intention to encourage or assist the prohibited act, plus knowledge of any facts necessary for it to be a prohibited act. However, if a crime does require MR, then A must intend to assist P to act *with that MR*. That still encompasses the situation where A does not know (or care) exactly what P will go on to do.

Lord Hughes and Lord Toulson:

> If the crime requires a particular intent, D2 must intend to assist or encourage D1 to act with such intent. D2's intention to assist D1 to commit the offence, and to act with whatever mental element is required of D1, will often be co-extensive on the facts with an intention by D2 that that offence be committed. Where that is so, it will be seen that many of the cases discuss D2's mental element simply in terms of intention to commit the offence. But there can be cases where D2 gives intentional assistance or encouragement to D1 to commit an offence and to act with the mental element required of him, but without D2 having a positive intent that the particular offence will be committed. That may be so, for example, where at the time that encouragement is given it remains uncertain what D1 might do; an arms supplier might be such a case.

The shop-keeper in the earlier example would remain liable as an accessory. By selling cutting equipment to P, he gives intentional assistance to him to commit burglaries with intent to steal, even though he is uncertain what P might actually do.

Knowledge of the circumstances

(a) A must have knowledge of the essential facts constituting the offence.

(b) A need not know the specific offence, only that P will commit a particular type of offence.

(c) A will not be liable for a material or significant variation by P.

In addition to an intention to assist or encourage, A must also have knowledge of the circumstances or essential elements of the offence. Suspicion is not enough. Knowledge includes wilful blindness: where A assists but deliberately refrains from asking too many questions, as in *JF Alford Transport Ltd* [1997] 2 Cr App R at 332 where a company and its directors were convicted of abetting the false making of tachograph records by the company drivers through inactivity.

Remember that the requirement of intention and knowledge also applies to accessories to an offence of strict liability in relation to which P need have no MR at all. A's MR is more stringent than that of P here.

 THINKING POINT 5.4

A sells P a knife which A realises P might use to inflict serious harm. P uses the knife to kill. What offence has A committed?

A must have knowledge of the essential facts constituting the offence—'awareness of risk of an offence'

In *Johnson v Youden* [1950] 1 KB 544, Lord Goddard CJ stated:

> Before a person can be convicted of aiding and abetting the commission of an offence he must at least know the essential matters which constitute that offence. He need not actually know that an offence has been committed, because he may not know that the facts constitute an offence and ignorance of the law is no defence.

The essential facts relate to knowledge of P's *actual* or *future* act. If A is an accessory during the commission of the offence he will 'know' that an offence is being committed. But where A assists P some time beforehand, A may only *foresee or be aware of the possibility or probability of a crime* and may have less than certain knowledge of P's intentions. We would call this recklessness. The fact that knowledge can include subjective recklessness (foresight by A that P might commit an offence) was confirmed in *Blakely and Sutton v Chief Constable of West Mercia* ('Procuring', earlier), and the further cases later.

R v Reardon [1999] CRIM LR 392 COURT OF APPEAL

P shot two victims in a pub and carried them into the garden. He returned to ask A for a knife to kill one, not identifying which, believing that the other was dead. Both died from wounds inflicted by A's knife. A was convicted of two murders as an accessory. Had a particular victim been identified and P had deliberately stabbed the other, A would not have been liable. The conviction was upheld on the basis that A foresaw a *real risk* that there might be two and not one murders with his knife.

R v Bryce [2004] EWCA CRIM 1231, CRIM LR 936 COURT OF APPEAL

A appealed against conviction of murder as an aider and abettor. In a dispute between drug deal-ers he had assisted P to kill by transporting P, and a gun, to a caravan near V's home so that P could wait for an opportunity to kill him. P killed V 12 hours later. On appeal A argued that since P had not formed the intention to kill at the time of A's assistance, A could not have intended to assist the murder. His actions were therefore too remote in time and place to the killing.

The appeal was dismissed. The delay did not negative the intention. It was not necessary for P's intention to exist at the time of A's act. It was necessary to prove an intention to assist P in a way in which A knew would assist towards the commission of an offence. Reference was made to R v Woollin [1999] AC 82 (oblique intention) whereby a person may still intend a result even though he does not desire it. A must have done the act deliberately, realising that it was capable of assist-ing the offence. In the extract below, the court uses 'D' to represent 'A':

Lord Potter:

> We are of the view that … where a defendant, D, is charged as the secondary party to an offence committed by P in reliance on acts which have assisted steps taken by P in the preliminary stages of a crime later committed by P in the absence of D, it is necessary for the Crown to prove intentional assistance by D in the sense of an intention to assist (and not to hinder or obstruct) P in acts which D knows are steps taken by P towards the commission of the offence. … Thus the prosecution must prove:
>
> a. an act done by D which in fact assisted the later commission of the offence;
> b. that D did the act deliberately realising that it was capable of assisting the offence,
> c. that D at the time of doing the act contemplated the commission of the offence by A ie he foresaw it as a 'real or substantial risk' or 'real possibility' and,
> d. that D when doing the act intended to assist A in what he was doing.

 NOTE 5.3

1. The problem here was that A was held to have intended to assist at a time when P might not have himself formed the intention to murder.
2. Liability is based on intention to do an immediate act with realisation of a risk that a final offence might be committed. In other words, A's MR in relation to P's offence is recklessness.

Given such a slender connection between the advice and principal offence, particularly in the case of such a serious offence as murder, it might be thought that a more exacting form of MR should be demanded such as intention/purpose to produce the principal offence. This is exactly the recommendation of the Law Commission, as we shall see.

R v Webster [2006] EWCA CRIM 415 COURT OF APPEAL

This was an appeal against conviction for aiding and abetting causing death by dangerous driving. W had allowed P to drive his car carrying passengers knowing that P had been drinking all day. P drove erratically and crashed, throwing V from the car to his death.

Moses LJ:

In relation to the first way in which the prosecution put the case against this defendant there was no issue but that the prosecution had proved a sufficient *actus reus* for secondary liability. The appellant had permitted Westbrook to drive and had stopped the car and let Westbrook take over the driving. The dispute concerned what knowledge the prosecution had to prove before the appellant could be convicted. It was accepted that the prosecution had to prove knowledge of the 'essential matters' which constituted the offence of dangerous driving (see e.g. *Johnson v Youden* [1951] KB 544 at 546). …

To establish secondary liability against the appellant it is important to appreciate that the real question as to the appellant's state of mind is whether he foresaw the *likelihood* that the driver would drive in a dangerous manner. …

Further, we must emphasise what the prosecution had to prove in relation to the appellant's state of mind. It accepted that it was not sufficient to prove that the appellant ought to have foreseen that Westbrook would drive dangerously. The prosecution had to prove that the appellant did foresee that Westbrook was likely to drive dangerously when he permitted him to get into the driver's seat (see *Blakely, Sutton v DPP* [1991] Crim LR 763).

It is quite apparent from these cases that there is no definitive test of foresight of the essential facts/circumstances of P's case. It might be thought that this is too low a threshold of culpability. Read the following from 'Participating in Crime' (Law Com No 305, 2007), at para 1.16:

The failure to provide a clear and authoritative set of rules manifests itself in a number of ways:

1. There is uncertainty as to what state of mind D must have in relation to P committing the principal offence:

Example 1C: D sells P some petrol believing that P *may* use it to make a petrol bomb with which he *might* commit arson.

Example 1D: D lends his car to P so that P can drive his pregnant wife to the hospital. D believes that P has been drinking alcohol and is *probably* over the prescribed limit.

On this issue, the authorities are in impressive disarray. At common law, there is support for at least four different tests for determining D's liability.

Para: 2.65

… the courts have demonstrated a readiness to dilute the stringent fault requirement of knowledge. With regard to the conduct element of the principal offence, there are authorities that can be cited in support of no less than four different tests, each of which requires something less than a belief that P will commit the conduct element. The tests are:

1. Belief that P might commit the conduct element (*Blakely and Sutton v DPP* [1991] RTR 405)

2. Foresight of the risk of a strong possibility that P will commit it (*Reardon* [1999] Crim LR 392)

3. Contemplation of the risk of a real possibility that P will commit it (*Bryce* [2004] EWCA Crim 1231)

4. Foresight that it is likely that P will commit it (*Webster* [2006] EWCA Crim 415).

An accessory can therefore be convicted of the same principal offence as P on the basis of relatively less conduct and less MR. For example, for murder, P must unlawfully kill intending (either directly or obliquely) to kill or inflict GBH. But A need only intentionally assist or encourage P with foresight that P *will* or *might* intentionally inflict GBH as strong possibility, a real possibility or as a likelihood. The MR for murder does not need to be proved against A. Moreover, A need not want or agree that P should murder. That this is harsh on accessories is widely acknowledged.

A need not know the specific offence, only that P will commit a particular type of offence

The general principle is that the accessory may not know all the details of P's plan but A must know that P plans a particular *type* of offence. Knowledge of the specific offence is not necessary.

R v Bainbridge [1960] 1 QB 129 COURT OF APPEAL

A supplied oxygen-cutting equipment to P who used it to burgle a bank and steal £18,000. A was convicted as an accessory to burglary but appealed on the grounds that it should have been proved that he knew that P intended to burgle a bank. He had only known that something illegal was intended. It was held that knowledge (as opposed to suspicion) of a particular type of offence was required. Knowledge that the equipment was going to be used for an undefined illegal plan would be insufficient.

But what did 'particular type of offence' mean? The following case was approved by the Supreme Court in *R v Jogee*:

Maxwell v DPP for NI [1978] 3 ALL ER 1140 COURT OF CRIMINAL APPEAL FOR NORTHERN IRELAND, AND HOUSE OF LORDS

D drove a car guiding members of a Northern Irish paramilitary army to a public house where he knew a terrorist attack was to be made. He knew that the attack would be either by bombing or shooting. A bomb was thrown into the pub. He was charged as an accessory to the offence of doing an act with intent to cause an explosion likely to endanger life or cause serious injury to property. He appealed against conviction on the basis that he did not know the precise 'type of offence' to be committed. He did not know and it could not be proved that he knew a bomb attack was intended by those whom he was assisting. His conviction was upheld.

Lord Lowry in the Court of Criminal Appeal, Northern Ireland:

> His guilt springs from the fact that he contemplates the commission of one (or more) of a number of crimes by the principal and he intentionally lends his assistance in order that such a crime will be committed. In other words, he knows that the principal is committing or about to commit one of a number of specified illegal acts and with that knowledge he helps him to do so.

This was approved by Lord Scarman in the House of Lords:

> An accessory who leaves it to his principal to choose is liable, provided always the choice is made from the range of offences from which the accessory contemplates the choice will be made.

 NOTE 5.4

1. The test is one of contemplation.
2. It follows that no liability should arise if P commits an offence outside of the accessory's contemplation (eg: murder not rape, assault not theft). Therefore, A will not be liable for every offence that P may commit.

3. Both *Maxwell* and *Bainbridge* introduced an element of reckless knowledge into MR. An accessory will be liable if he knows there is a *possibility* that P will commit a certain *type* of offence.

4. The test is therefore wider than one which would require detailed knowledge but narrower than one requiring knowledge of criminality in general.

5. If A need only know of a risk that P will commit an offence within his contemplation, and not the precise details, then far-sighted or contemplative accessories will be penalised.

?! THINKING POINT 5.5

A lends P his tools for a burglary. P keeps the tools and uses them for 20 other burglaries. Is A an accomplice to all?

A lends P a gun with which to kill V that evening. P uses the gun as expected. The following month he uses it to kill two police officers whilst resisting arrest. Is A an accomplice to all three murders?

If A were to be secondarily liable for all subsequent crimes by P it would represent quite an extension to accomplice liability. It was this prospect that led the Law Commission in 1993 to propose the abolition of secondary liability. However, in practice it does not seem to have been the problem it was feared to be. Read this by J.C. Smith, 'Criminal Liability of Accessories: Law and Law Reform' (1997) 113 *LQR*, at 461:

> What of the Bainbridge problem? Ever since that decision in 1959 academic lawyers and students have been having sleepless nights worrying about the seller of a rather durable jemmy being convicted of endless burglaries, of which he knew nothing, years after the sale. But the issue of multiple convictions did not arise in Bainbridge nor, so far as I know, has it arisen in any reported case in the 38 years which have elapsed since we were alerted to the existence of the problem. We do not know, of course, that it has not caused concern to prosecutors but it can hardly be seen as a pressing practical problem.

A may know the type of offence but will not be liable for a material or significant intentional variation by P

→ CROSS-REFERENCE
For further discussion of transferred malice see Chapter 3, 3.1.12.

Suppose A assists or encourages P to commit murder or grievous bodily harm on V but P intentionally commits the contemplated offence against X. The House of Lords in *Powell* [1999] AC 1 said that A would not be liable unless he foresaw that P might act in this way. The doctrine of transferred malice would only apply to A if P committed the offence against X unintentionally, in a mistaken or accidental attempt to kill/injure V.

The oldest reported case involving deviation from an agreed plan is *Saunders and Archer* (1573) 2 Plowd 473 where S advised A to kill his wife by giving her a poisoned apple so that A could be with another woman. A placed the apple before his wife but did not intervene when she gave the apple to their child who ate it and died. A was convicted of murder but S was held not to have been an accessory on the basis that A's omission to intervene was a deliberate change of plan and represented a break in the chain of causation. The court took two years to decide the verdict. A might today be convicted of conspiracy to murder.

Questions also arise as to how far P's offence must differ in order for the variation to be material or substantial.

?! **THINKING POINT** 5.6

1. A sells P a gun believing that P will use it to kill. P uses it to kill on several subsequent occasions. Is A liable for all murders?

2. A sells P an iron bar believing that P will use it in a burglary or robbery. P uses it to commit murder. Is A liable?

3. A lends P a crowbar for a burglary knowing that there is a risk that P might use it to attack the occupier (V) if he is disturbed. P is disturbed during the burglary and hits V around the head causing serious injury from which V then dies.

The Law Commission recommended that A should only be convicted of the principal offence if his culpability is *comparable* to P's. Therefore, A must intend that P should engage in the conduct element of the principal offence and not be merely reckless as to that fact. One problem is that if P fails to carry out the principal offence, because he is arrested beforehand for example or chooses not to proceed, A will escape all liability despite having given assistance or encouragement at an earlier stage, unless prosecutions for an inchoate offence such as conspiracy or attempt are possible. In Part 2, Serious Crime Act 2007 three new statutory inchoate offences now incriminate A in just this situation. The offences replace incitement and supplement secondary liability.

→ CROSS-REFERENCE
For discussion of the Serious Crime Act 2007 offences see Chapter 15, 15.3.

SECTION SUMMARY

The law has expanded the scope of knowledge for accomplice liability in recent years to include recklessness or awareness of a risk that P might offend in a contemplated way. This is a summary of the current law on the MR of secondary parties:

- ■ *A must intend to do the act which assists or encourages.*
- ■ *A must intend the act to assist or encourage P.*
- ■ *Intention requires knowledge but not purpose that an offence will be committed.*
- ■ *A must know the essential matters forming the offence.*
- ■ *Knowledge means 'awareness of the risk' of P's offence.*
- ■ *A need only contemplate that P might carry out a particular type of offence.*
- ■ *A will not be liable for a material or significant intentional variation by P.*

5.3 Where P Goes Beyond the Joint Plan to Commit Another Offence

5.3.1 Definition

5.3.2 'Joint Enterprise' Before *Jogee*

5.3.3 The Law After *Jogee*

5.3.4 Is the Law After *Jogee* Satisfactory?

5.3.1 Definition

This section is about the situation where several people *participate*, whether by assistance or encouragement, in a common criminal venture or purpose and, typically, one or more persons commit a further offence going beyond that joint venture. The initial venture might be the result of an *agreement* to commit an offence or the result of a sudden or spontaneous shared common *intention*. What is crucial is a unity of purpose, meeting of minds, or understanding of some sort.

Put simply, we are considering the means whereby one person in a group offence (A) may be considered liable for P's offence going beyond the original purpose/venture. Until the Supreme Court decision in *Jogee*, the doctrine of 'joint enterprise' meant that prosecutors did not need to prove that A *intended* to participate in P's further offence. Since *Jogee*, this is no longer the case. We will consider both what the current law is, and why the Supreme Court felt that substantial change was needed. This is a controversial and difficult area of law, as we shall see.

Context

Arguably, when used in order to convict those involved in serious crimes, the law on joint enterprise was not without moral validity. In 2012, Gary Dobson and David Norris were convicted of joint enterprise for the 1993 murder of Stephen Lawrence despite the fact that it was not known which of them actually committed the murder. Joint enterprise was also widely used in the context of gang violence, often for the same reason.

→ CROSS-REFERENCE
For further discussion of *Powell* and *English* see 5.3.2.

The justification for joint liability was that by continuing to participate in the joint venture with *realisation* or *foresight* that P might commit a further offence, A associated himself with that offence and bore some responsibility for it. The underlying policy justification was described by Lord Steyn in *R v Powell & Anr, R v English* [1999] AC 1, the first leading authority:

> The criminal justice system exists to control crime. A prime function of that system must be to deal justly but effectively with those who join with others in criminal enterprises. Experience has shown that joint criminal enterprises only too readily escalate into the commission of greater offences. In order to deal with this important social problem the accessory principle is needed and cannot be abolished or relaxed. …

However, critics argued that joint enterprise law was being used to convict large numbers of young people, including children, for crimes intentionally committed by others for which they, themselves, bore little criminal responsibility (*Joint Enterprise, House of Commons, Justice Committee, Report 1957* (January 2012)). There was concern regarding sentencing, which was harsh. If the joint enterprise resulted in murder, all would be subject to the same mandatory life sentence regardless of their role. From 2005 to 2013, 1,853 people were prosecuted for joint enterprise murder involving four or more defendants and 4,590 involving two or more defendants. 22 per cent of all Court of Appeal rulings related to joint enterprise. It was felt that the law was racially discriminatory: 80 per cent of the 600 prisoners serving long sentences for joint enterprise are black. (Statistics: www.independent.co.uk, 14 July 2015). The objection was that the law was being used to convey a social message against gang violence, based on shaky evidence and at the cost of real injustice (A. Green and C. McGourlay, 'The wolf packs in our midst and other products of criminal joint enterprise prosecutions' (2015) 79(4) *JCL* 280). Recent research (B. Crewe, A. Liebling, N. Padfield, G. Virgo, 'Joint Enterprise: The Implications of an Unfair and Unclear Law' [2015] 4 *Crim LR* 252) on joint enterprise prisoners revealed the following:

> Many of the interviewees felt that joint enterprise was being used as an indiscriminate vacuum cleaner, convicting them with little regard for natural or procedural justice, and sweeping them and their associates into prison with insufficient regard for legal process or humanity.

Two House of Commons Justice Committee reports recommended that the Law Commission review the law (see *Joint Enterprise, House of Commons, Justice Committee, Report 1957* (January 2012) (mentioned earlier) and *Joint Enterprise: Follow Up (2014) HC Paper No 310*). Reflecting public concern with the law, the BBC aired a drama on these issues in 'Common' (July 2014). It was against this background of widespread criticism of joint enterprise that the Supreme Court decided *Jogee* in 2016.

5.3.2 'Joint Enterprise' Before *Jogee*

Although 'joint enterprise' was sometimes used to describe any situations where A and P participated in the same group crime, or where A joined in with P's offence, the most significant use of the term was a narrower one. It described the situation where P went beyond the joint venture and committed a further offence which A knew or foresaw P might intentionally commit and in which he continued to participate, for example:

EXAMPLE 5.3

A and P engage in a burglary in the course of which A foresees that P might commit serious harm to the occupier with a weapon. P pulls out a knife and fatally stabs the occupier. A and P are guilty of burglary and murder by joint enterprise.

Joint enterprise was referred to in some cases as 'parasitic liability', for example: *Gnango*. The old law is summarised in Diagram 5.2.

➜ CROSS-REFERENCE
Gnango is discussed in 5.2.1.

Actus reus: Agreement or common venture/purpose

Once a shared common purpose had been proved, there was no requirement to prove that A *intended* to assist or encourage P's further offence as would be the case under the general principles

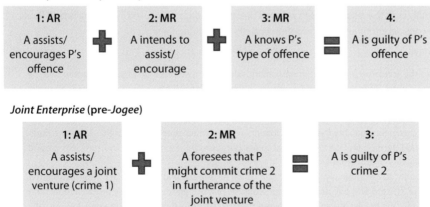

Diagram 5.2
Distinction between secondary participation and joint enterprise

of secondary liability. What mattered was that A participated (or agreed) in the common venture (the first crime, eg: burglary) and *continued* to participate whilst P committed the further offence (the second crime, eg: murder).

However, P's second crime (eg: murder) must have occurred in the course of or furtherance of the common venture. Both the nature of the common enterprise and its scope (ie: its beginning and end) had to be identified.

Mens Rea: Foresight that P might go beyond the joint venture

The basis of A's MR depended on *foresight* or *realisation* that P *might* go further than the joint venture in order to intentionally commit another offence. A's MR therefore depended on *recklessness* as to what another *might* do. Provided A *foresaw* a possibility of P's further offence, he (A) would be guilty of it, even though he had not agreed to it, did not intend that P should commit it, had tried to persuade A not to go through with it, or was not present at the scene of the crime (*Rook* [1993] 2 All ER 955).

The first case on joint enterprise and MR was *Anderson & Morris* [1966] 2 QB 110, in which the basis for liability was revealed as 'tacit agreement'. If one party went further than agreed, the jury should decide whether that act was within or beyond the joint enterprise. In *Chan Wing-Siu v R* [1985] AC 168 (Privy Council) where three accomplices committed a robbery with knives and one of them, it could not be proved which, stabbed the robbery victim to death, the Privy Council held that the doctrine of common purpose depends on *contemplation or authorisation* and foresight. 'Contemplation' as opposed to 'tacit agreement' was regarded as crucial by the House of Lords in the leading case of *Powell* in a conjoined appeal with *English*.

➜ CROSS-REFERENCE

English is discussed later in this section.

R v Powell & Anr, R v English [1999] AC 1 HOUSE OF LORDS

Powell, Daniels and another, X, went to a drug dealer's house. When the dealer came to the door, he was shot dead by either of them or by X. Powell and Daniels were convicted of murder on the basis that if the dealer had been shot by X, then they knew he was armed and must therefore have foreseen that he might use the gun to kill or cause really serious harm.

On appeal, the House of Lords held that the scope of a common purpose was determined by the contemplation of the parties sharing that purpose. A would be liable on the basis of recklessness not simply as to the result but as to whether death/GBH might be caused intentionally by P. Public policy considerations applied to confirm Powell's conviction.

Lord Steyn:

> Under the accessory principle criminal liability is dependent on proof of subjective foresight on the part of a participant in the criminal enterprise that the primary offender might commit a greater offence, that being in these cases foresight that the primary offender might commit murder as defined in law. …
>
> The criminal culpability lies in participating in the criminal enterprise with that foresight. Foresight and intention are not synonymous terms. But foresight is a necessary and sufficient ground of the liability of accessories. …
>
> He ought to be criminally liable for harm which he foresaw and which in fact resulted from the crime he assisted and encouraged. But it would in practice almost invariably be impossible for a jury to say that the secondary party wanted death to be caused or that he regarded it as virtually certain. In the real world proof of an intention sufficient for murder would be well nigh impossible in the vast majority of joint enterprise cases.

NOTE 5.5

1. There was no need for foresight of a real or substantial risk or a virtual certainty of death or GBH.

2. A's liability for murder and the mandatory life sentence were based on relatively little MR: foresight of the possibility that GBH might be caused (the GBH rule). This was a much less culpable state of mind than demanded by primary liability for murder (direct/oblique *intent*, ie: purpose or foresight of a virtual certainty) or that required by the ordinary principles of secondary participation where a further intention to assist/encourage must be proved.

3. Basing liability on foresight of what another person might or might not be intending to do can be quite precarious. In the homicide context, where the only distinction between murder and manslaughter is one of MR, the degree of awareness of P's intentions could make the difference between a mandatory or discretionary life sentence.

If P departed from the joint venture by a fundamentally different act, A would not be liable as accessory to P's offence. The point was captured by Lord Parker in *R v Anderson & Morris* [1966] 2 QB 110:

> Where two persons embark on a joint enterprise, each is liable for the acts done in pursuance of that joint enterprise and that includes liability for unusual consequences if they arise from the execution of the agreed joint enterprise. ... but if one of the adventurers goes beyond what has been tacitly agreed as part of the common enterprise his co-adventurer is not liable for the consequences of that unauthorised act.

The question of whether P was acting in a fundamentally different way so as to take him outside of the joint enterprise was not always easy to answer and generated a significant amount of case law, for example:

- *R v Rafferty* [2007] EWCA CRIM 1846 concerned an appeal against the manslaughter conviction of D who in a joint enterprise with two others, attacked V on a beach and then robbed him. Whilst D took V's credit card to a cash point, two co-defendants inflicted further injuries on V and then took him out to sea where he drowned. The co-defendants were convicted of murder. D successfully appealed against conviction on the grounds of causation, the drowning constituting a break in the chain of causation. However, the court also agreed that a deliberate drowning was a fundamentally different act from the joint enterprise to beat and rob him.

➔ CROSS-REFERENCE
Rafferty is also considered in Chapter 2, 2.3.3.

- *R v Powell; R v English* [1999] AC 1: English and P took part in a joint enterprise to attack and cause injury to a police officer using wooden posts. P used a knife and stabbed the officer to death. English did not know that P had the knife. On appeal to the House of Lords it was held that A must foresee an act of the *type* which P committed, but the use of a knife was *fundamentally different* to the use of a wooden post. P's lethal act went beyond the scope of the joint enterprise. Therefore, English was not guilty of either murder or manslaughter.

- The courts did not agree on what made a weapon 'fundamentally different'. In *Uddin* [1999] 1 Cr App R 319 the court asked whether the contemplated method of death was 'as dangerous' as or 'completely different' from the actual means of committing the offence. In *Greatrex and Bates* [1999] 1 Cr App R 126 the Court of Appeal held that whether kicking and punching was as dangerous as the unexpected use of a spanner or metal bar was a question of fact. In *Yemoh* [2009] EWCA Crim 930, the Court of Appeal held that a Stanley knife was not fundamentally different from a long-bladed knife. In *Mendez and Thompson* [2010] EWCA Crim 516, the Court of Appeal held that the rule concerns not simply a different weapon but the *way in which it is used* and the *degree of injury* likely to be caused.

5.3.3 The Law After *Jogee*

The separate category of joint enterprise liability was abolished by the Supreme Court in *Jogee*. It declared that the law had taken a wrong turn in *Chan Wing-Siu* and *Powell & English*. A's liability should be assessed no differently from any other accomplice under the principles of ordinary secondary liability. Where A sets out to commit Crime A with P, he will only be guilty of crime B if he intended that crime B be committed or if he intended to assist or encourage P in the commission of crime B. Foresight will be evidence of intent, not conclusive of it.

Actus reus: Agreement or common venture/purpose

→ CROSS-REFERENCE
For further discussion of
Gnango see 5.2.1.

1. *Gnango* [2011] UKSC 59 is authority for the proposition that A and P must have a shared 'common purpose' to enter the original venture (eg: burglary), whether spontaneous or planned.

2. *P's further offence must be in the course of or furtherance of the common venture*

   Lord Bridge in *Hui Chi-Ming* [1992] 1 AC 34 said: '[T]he accessory, in order to be guilty, must have foreseen the relevant offence which the principal may commit *as a possible incident of the common unlawful enterprise* and must, with such foresight, still have participated in the enterprise.' If A and P are engaged in a common venture to burgle, for example, A may not foresee P committing rape as a possible incident of the joint venture and will not be liable for this.

3. *P's identity need not be known*

   In *Rahman* [2008] UKHL 45, a joint plan to commit GBH was sufficient to convict an entire group of murder, even if the actual perpetrator (P) could not be known. In *ABCD* [2010] EWCA Crim 1622, a case of murder during a joint venture to assault and beat V, Hughes LJ said this:

   > It is not, of course, necessary for the guilt of D that P be identified. In a multi-handed assault it will often be the case that no-one can say whose hand did the act which proved fatal. But what is necessary is that some (identified or not) be shown to have committed murder.

   In other words, provided a further offence is proved, it does not matter that P is unknown. A's liability derives from P's offence.

4. *P's offence can be separate in time and place*

   It might be thought that if P's second offence occurs after the joint attack has ended, or after V has been chased to an entirely different place, there would be two separate offences and not one continuing joint venture. This is not necessarily so. The fact that V was killed out of sight of the appellants in the next case did not justify finding that there was no joint venture to murder:

5. *The scope, beginning and end of the enterprise must be identified*

Importantly, in *Rajakumar*, Davis LJ issued a reminder that courts need to identify the scope of the enterprise. (This is still the law: although the language of joint enterprise should no longer be used, the need to define the scope of the common venture continues post-*Jogee*.) Unless this is done, it is difficult to know if there has been a second crime going beyond the venture, particularly in spontaneous cases. The trial judge in this case had failed to do so, and therefore his decision that there was no case to answer (an application made after close of the prosecution case) was wrong. It was overturned by the Court of Appeal and the trials were ordered to continue.

To identify the beginning and end of the venture is especially important in fast-moving cases where it is necessary to ensure that all defendants have continued to participate in the final offence. Joint enterprise liability was rejected in the following case for this reason:

Rajakumar [2013] EWCA Crim 1512

Following a planned attack with wooden weapons by one Tamil gang upon another, two men chased the victim round the corner and beat him severely with a wooden pole. The injuries led to his death. All were convicted of murder and appealed. It was held that given the agreed plan and that the killing was committed by a wooden pole (not dissimilar to the weapons brought to the scene), this was one evolving joint venture. Had the violence been spontaneous, or had V been shot or stabbed, there may then have been two incidents (ie: the joint attack and then a separate murder), depending on whether the group knew that things might get out of hand. In such a case, the remaining members of the gang could not have been responsible for the death.

Davis LJ:

> In the present case, of course, the victim was not stabbed by the unforeseen production of a knife. On the contrary he was beaten to death by the use of a wooden implement. He was the subject of an assault which the jury could properly infer was an assault of the kind which had initially been intended, with the necessary intent to cause really serious harm and involving precisely the kind of weapon that some members of the group, to the presumed knowledge of all, had come equipped with, namely a wooden implement or post. That could be inferred to have been all part of the pre-agreed plan and intention from the outset. Putting it another way, there was certainly material here, in our view, on which a jury could conclude that this was to be regarded as a one evolving incident, the culmination of which was the fatal beating of the victim. In such circumstances, in our view, there was no proper basis for the judge concluding that the joint enterprise (the scope of which he himself had never defined) had, so far as these respondents were concerned, necessarily ceased to exist by the time of the final assault in Lewisham High Street.

R v Childs, R v Price [2015] EWCA Crim 265

V was killed in a 15-second spontaneous attack in a car park, the attack taking place by the boot of a car belonging to the two appellants. There had been a previous history of rancour between V (Flitchett) and Childs. The fatal blow caused a 'traumatic tear to an artery at the base of the brain and in turn caused a ... hemorrhage leading to a rapid loss of consciousness and death.' This was very rare. When Price was still in the car, Childs made the first heavy blow to the right of V's head. There was evidence of a further heavy punch to the left which might have been inflicted by either Childs or by Price who had joined the attack within a second. A Home Office pathologist gave uncontested evidence that *either* of these punches could have been responsible for the tear. It was not a question of V dying from the *combination* of blows or from the final kicking and punching V received whilst on the ground, largely carried out by Price. The problem was that there was no evidence regarding which of the two appellants had inflicted the fatal punch. The trial judge asked the jury to focus on the position of each defendant 'from start to finish' of the enterprise and the jury convicted them both of murder against which they appealed.

Davis LJ:

> As we have indicated, the jury could not on the expert evidence exclude the first punch (that is to say, the punch administered by Childs when Price was not present) as the fatal punch. To talk, rather broadly, of 'from start to finish' rather masks this central point. If both the appellants could properly be convicted, the jury would at least have to be sure that before the first blow was administered by Childs there was already in place the necessary joint enterprise with the necessary intent. They would have to be sure of that because they could not be sure to the criminal standard that the fatal blow was not administered at that stage ... We can accept that it may at first sight seem somewhat artificial to break down this altercation in this way. But, as was in substance accepted below, that was essential: precisely because of the unchallenged pathological evidence and the issue of causation that that threw up. Further, as we have said, simply to use the words 'from start to finish' does rather mask, or at least potentially so, the crucial point: which is whether there was sufficient evidence to establish a prior plan *before* the first punch was administered by Childs ... As left to the jury, with all respect, there was no real focus on the evidence, or indeed lack of evidence, as to the forming of a plan of the giving of any encouragement *before* the first blow was administered. In many respects the jury were positively invited simply to look at the incident as a whole.
>
> Furthermore, on one view of the summing-up the case left to the jury was, in effect, joint enterprise homicide or nothing: either both of the appellants were guilty of homicide or neither were. But, we ask, why should that be so? Childs administered, undoubtedly administered, the first punch which may have been the fatal punch. If there was no prior plan or prior encouragement, then Price could not have been guilty. ...
>
> That then leaves the question of Childs' intent. On the face of it, of course, this was a matter of fact for the jury. But if the first blow may have been, as according to the expert evidence it may have been, the fatal blow, one then has to assess Childs' intent at that particular time: which was not a matter on which the jury had really been invited specifically to focus ... the conclusion we feel compelled to reach is that the case against Price of murder on the joint enterprise basis alleged was not one in respect of which a properly directed jury could properly convict, applying the criminal standard of proof, having regard to the pathological evidence and the other evidence. The submission of no case to answer in this regard should have been accepted. The appellant Price therefore has to be acquitted both of murder and of manslaughter.

 NOTE 5.6

1. *Price*—joint venture: The beginning and end of the venture had not been identified. If the fatal blow was the first one, inflicted by Childs, Price did not participate in it, encourage it or agree to it. At that moment, he was still in the car. Consequently, he was not guilty of murder as an accomplice under the ordinary principles of secondary liability (or under the old law of joint enterprise). He therefore had to be acquitted.

2. *Childs* participated in the whole of the short attack during which the fatal blow was inflicted, whenever that was. He must, therefore, have *caused* the death as a principal offender.

3. Because the jury had not been asked to consider whether Childs had intended to kill or cause serious harm at the time of the first blow, which may have been the fatal one, he might not have had the MR for murder. His conviction was unsafe and manslaughter was substituted.

You may see the similarity between Price's situation and the case of *Lane* where a child was killed during a prolonged attack by two parents, but it could not be proved by whose hand the child had died. Both were acquitted of murder, there being no evidence of who had caused the death as principal.

→ CROSS-REFERENCE
Lane is considered in 5.2.1 'Where A or P cannot be identified'.

Mens rea

The law on joint ventures has undergone a virtually complete revision as a result of *Jogee*. The old law of joint enterprise had stated that liability turned on foresight or contemplation by A of what P might do. Thus if A realised that in the course of the joint venture P might kill with intent to cause grievous bodily harm, then A would be guilty of murder even though he had not tacitly agreed to that act. In *Jogee*, the Supreme Court said that this was a wrong turn in the law which needed to be corrected. Courts should apply the ordinary rules of secondary liability which require an *intention to assist or encourage* P to commit grievous bodily harm or murder.

R v Jogee [2016] UKSC 8

Briefly, the facts were that Jogee (J) and a co-defendant, Hirsi (H) were each convicted of the murder of Fyfe (F) at the home of F's girlfriend. The cause of death was a stab wound inflicted by H just inside the front door. At the time of the stabbing, J was outside. Before the stabbing, he had shouted encouragement to H to do something to F and had threatened F with a broken bottle. The Court of Appeal rejected J's argument that whilst he might have encouraged the killing, he did not participate in it. J then appealed to the Supreme Court on the grounds that joint enterprise liability, based as it was on foresight of a possibility of what a co-defendant might do and participation, was wrong. After reviewing extensive case law from 1672 to modern times, Lord Hughes and Lord Toulson gave a joint judgment with which Lord Neuberger, Lady Hale and Lord Thomas concurred. All agreed that the law was wrong.

> From our review of the authorities, there is no doubt that the Privy Council laid down a new principle in *Chan Wing-Siu* when it held that if two people set out to commit an offence (crime A), and in the course of it one of them commits another offence (crime B), the second person is guilty as an accessory to crime B if he foresaw it as a possibility, but did not necessarily intend it. …
>
> The Privy Council judgment … elided foresight with authorisation, when it said that the principle 'turns on contemplation or, putting the same idea in other words, authorisation, which may be express but is more usually implied'. But as Professor Smith observed, contemplation and authorisation are not the same at all.
>
> Nor can authorisation of crime B automatically be inferred from continued participation in crime A with foresight of crime B. As Lord Brown of Eaton-under-Heywood accurately pointed out in *R v Rahman* [2009] AC 129, para 63, the rule in *Chan Wing-Siu* makes guilty those who foresee crime B but never intended it or wanted it to happen. There can be no doubt that if D2 continues to participate in crime A with foresight that D1 may commit crime B, that is evidence, and sometimes powerful evidence, of an intent to assist D1 in crime B. But it is evidence of such intent (or, if one likes, of 'authorisation'), not conclusive of it. …
>
> In *Chan Wing-Siu* [1985] AC 168, 176 Sir Robin Cooke referred to the 'modern emphasis on subjective tests of criminal guilt'. There has indeed been a progressive move away from the historic tendency of the common law to presume as a matter of law that the 'natural and probable consequences' of a man's act were intended, culminating in England and Wales in its statutory removal by section 8 of the Criminal Justice Act 1967. Since then in England and Wales the foreseeability of the consequences has been a matter of evidence from which intention may be, but need not necessarily be, inferred; …

The dangers of escalation of violence where people go out in possession of weapons to commit crime are indisputable, but they were specifically referred to by the court in *R v Reid*, when explaining why it was right that such conduct should result in conviction for manslaughter if death resulted, albeit that the initial intention may have been nothing more than causing fright. There was no consideration in the *Chan Wing-Siu* case, or in *R v Powell ; R v English*, of the fundamental policy question whether and why it was necessary and appropriate to reclassify such conduct as murder rather than manslaughter. Such a discussion would have involved, among other things, questions about fair labelling and fair discrimination in sentencing. …

The rule in *Chan Wing-Siu* is often described as 'joint enterprise liability'. However, the expression 'joint enterprise' is not a legal term of art. As the Court of Appeal observed in *R v A* [2011] QB 841, para 9, it is used in practice in a variety of situations to include both principals and accessories. As applied to the rule in *Chan Wing-Siu*, it unfortunately occasions some public misunderstanding. It is understood (erroneously) by some to be a form of guilt by association or of guilt by simple presence without more. It is important to emphasise that guilt of crime by mere association has no proper part in the common law.

As we have explained, secondary liability does not require the existence of an agreement between D1 and D2. Where, however, it exists, such agreement is by its nature a form of encouragement and in most cases will also involve acts of assistance. The long-established principle that where parties agree to carry out a criminal venture, each is liable for acts to which they have expressly or impliedly given their assent is an example of the intention to assist which is inherent in the making of the agreement. Similarly, where people come together without agreement, often spontaneously, to commit an offence together, the giving of intentional support by words or deeds, including by supportive presence, is sufficient to attract secondary liability on ordinary principles. We repeat that secondary liability includes cases of agreement between principal and secondary party, but it is not limited to them.

It will be apparent from what we have said that we do not consider that the *Chan Wing-Siu* principle can be supported, except on the basis that it has been decided and followed at the highest level. In plain terms, our analysis leads us to the conclusion that the introduction of the principle was based on an incomplete, and in some respects erroneous, reading of the previous case law, coupled with generalised and questionable policy arguments.

… in the common law foresight of what might happen is ordinarily no more than evidence from which a jury can infer the presence of a requisite intention. It may be strong evidence, but its adoption as a test for the mental element for murder in the case of a secondary party is a serious and anomalous departure from the basic rule, which results in over-extension of the law of murder and reduction of the law of manslaughter. Murder already has a relatively low mens rea threshold, because it includes an intention to cause serious injury, without intent to kill or to cause risk to life. The *Chan Wing-Siu* principle extends liability for murder to a secondary party on the basis of a still lesser degree of culpability, namely foresight only of the possibility that the principal may commit murder but without there being any need for intention to assist him to do so. It savours, as Professor Smith suggested, of constructive crime.

 NOTE 5.7

1. The MR for offences which go beyond the joint plan is now in line with that for ordinary secondary liability. A must intend to encourage or assist P to commit the crime, acting with whatever mental element the offence requires of P. Thus, for a conviction of murder, A must *intend* to assist or encourage P to act with intent to cause grievous bodily harm or death. Intending to encourage P to act recklessly, or with intention to cause minor injury, will not suffice.

2. While intention can be inferred from foresight, there is no automatic assumption that simply because A foresaw and participated in a joint enterprise, he intended the crime. In a common venture to commit crime A, it will be necessary for a jury to infer A's intention that P commit crime B from the evidence. Here they will ask whether A shared a common purpose or common intent to commit crime B if things came to it. In other words, was P's act within the scope of the joint venture, or did A expressly or tacitly agree to it?

3. A conditional intention will suffice. For example, if A participates in an armed robbery, hoping that violence will not be used but being prepared to use it if necessary, A will still have intended the crime if guns are fired.

4. Where the necessary intention is lacking, but death occurs, A may be guilty of (unlawful act) manslaughter, not murder. For example, in *Anderson & Morris* [1966] 2 QB 110 a fatal stabbing resulted in conviction of Anderson for murder and Morris for manslaughter. Anderson, acting outside the common design, produced a knife of which Morris had no knowledge. It was held on appeal that Anderson had gone 'beyond what had been tacitly agreed as part of the joint enterprise'. A's liability depends on his own MR.

5. The fundamental difference rule caused difficulties and brought inconsistency to the law as courts attempted to assess whether, for example, one type of weapon was 'fundamentally different' from another. Now, knowledge of a weapon or foresight that P might use it will relate to an assessment of A's MR, which is for the jury to assess as a matter of fact. The fundamental difference escape route therefore loses most of its significance. It will only apply to the rare case where P's deviation from the enterprise was so overwhelming (or unforeseeable by anybody) as to relegate A's acts to history, in which case he will bear no responsibility for the death.

6. The principles established by *Jogee* differ significantly from the Law Commission's proposals for reform. The Law Commission would have retained liability for joint enterprise despite its many difficulties (Law Com No 305 'Participating in Crime'). It also recommended that instead of acquitting A where the principal offence is fundamentally different, he should be held guilty of a new offence of complicity in an unlawful killing ('Murder, Manslaughter and Infanticide', Law Com No 304, November 2006).

7. Following *Jogee*, there were a number of applications for leave to appeal against convictions under the old law. *Jogee* had stated that leave might be granted 'if substantial injustice be demonstrated.' That has proven to be a hard threshold to cross: *R v Johnson (Lewis)* [2016] EWCA Crim 1613 made it clear that 'substantial injustice' is a more stringent requirement than the usual test of whether a conviction is or may be unsafe. It is deliberately so, given the public interest in legal certainty and the interests of the victim (or their family). However, are these being protected at the expense of injustice to some Ds?

5.3.4 Is the Law After *Jogee* Satisfactory?

We have seen that all aspects of the law on joint enterprise attracted considerable criticism, the most important of which was that the required degree of foresight of P's further crime led to a very low threshold of liability and was unjust. Indeed, in 2015, W. Wilson and D. Ormerod in

'Simply Harsh to Fairly Simple: Joint Enterprise Reform' [2015] *Crim LR* 1, 3, at pp 21–25 had called upon the Supreme Court to act:

(i) Accept that legislative reform is not forthcoming

It is important to appreciate that our proposal would require no legislative involvement. The present law of 'joint enterprise' is of relatively recent vintage and exists entirely at common law. … A change in the law can therefore be brought about by the Supreme Court. Admittedly, after *Gnango*, it may take a majority of a nine-member Supreme Court to achieve this. Nevertheless, that may well be a more realistic prospect than legislation given that successive governments have exhibited no interest in adopting Law Commission recommendations and draft Bills. … Our view is that the prospect of legislation in the near future is so minimal that the challenge should be seized by the Supreme Court.

…

(iii) Define 'criminal venture' liability

We submit that a clearer, fairer, practical replacement for 'joint enterprise' liability in homicide cases that meets the problems of practice and principle raised above could be created. Liability for homicides would arise in the following circumstances:

…

3. Where D was party to a criminal venture with P or Ps to commit crime A and in the course of the commission of that crime an unlawful killing was committed by P or Ps with the mens rea for that crime, murder or manslaughter as the case may be, D would be liable:

   a. For murder where, whether or not D had intentionally assisted or encouraged the acts of P which caused V's death, D intended or believed that P would:

      (i) kill, with mens rea for murder, in the execution of the criminal venture in which D was participating; or

      (ii) kill, with mens rea for murder, in the execution of the criminal venture in which D was participating if a particular condition was met, which condition was met; or

      (iii) intentionally cause GBH in the execution of the criminal venture by acts not substantially different from those which resulted in V's death; or

      (iv) intentionally cause GBH in the execution of the criminal venture by acts not substantially different from those which resulted in V's death if a particular condition was met, which condition was met.

   (b) For manslaughter if, in addition to the situations in which D would currently be liable for that crime … he foresaw that P might, in the course of committing crime A, intentionally kill or cause GBH even if D has not intentionally assisted or encouraged P's lethal acts.

…

(vi) Meeting public expectations of justice

One might expect immediate public concerns to be raised that this restricts the scope of liability and hence the pool of those likely to be labelled and punished as murderers. However, bearing in mind the empirical research, this model would reflect public expectations more accurately than the present law. D would, having been involved in a violent group activity leading to a murder, still be charged with manslaughter. D would of course also be liable for any initial crime D has intentionally participated in—affray, ABH, etc. Despite this, we might expect there to be some public concern in relation to cases in which, for lack of evidence, there was no identified murderer and no single member of the group could be convicted as a murderer. We do not regard this as undermining the value of our proposal. Under the proposal it may often be possible for the Crown to establish there was a killing and on the part of some of the participants that they intended at least GBH: that would, provided the jury were sure there was a murder, render all those who held such intent or belief liable as murderers. Where that is not possible, the proposed scheme would result in manslaughter convictions.

Q. Why do the authors argue that the law should be reformed in this way?

Q. How far is *Jogee* consistent with the authors' recommendations?

To the extent that it raises the threshold for accessorial liability, the decision in *Jogee* has been widely welcomed. However, it has been pointed out that the practical consequences of *Jogee* may be more apparent than real (S. Parsons, 'Joint Enterprise Murder: *R v Jogee*' (2016) 80(3) *JCL* 173):

> There were people cheering the judgment outside the Supreme Court. The question is: were they right to do so? The judgment makes it clear that the liberalisation of the law is not retrospective. 'The effect of putting the law right is not to render invalid all convictions which were arrived at over many years by faithfully applying the law as laid down in *Chan Wing-Siu*.' The Court of Appeal can grant leave to appeal out of time and may do so if substantial injustice can be shown, but it will not do so simply because the law has been declared to be wrong. So, many secondary parties convicted under the Chan Wing-Siu principle and residing in prison will be unable to appeal their murder convictions. For them the law remains harsh.
>
> The question to ask is whether there has been a true liberalisation of the law. 'The error identified, of equating foresight with intent to assist rather than treating the first as evidence of the second, is important as a matter of legal principle.' But is it important? Finding intention from foresight implies that the distinction between direct intent and indirect intent has a role to play. In many cases the secondary party will want the principal to murder—a direct intent to assist—but there will also be cases where the secondary party wants only for the original common purpose, such as a burglary, to succeed but not the murder. This is where foresight is evidence from which an indirect intent to assist can be found. There is the old chestnut of what intent means when it is found from foresight. The judgment rules out desire. But, more importantly, there is no real guidance as to the degree of foresight required before an intention to assist can be found. The judgment says 'in the common law foresight of what might happen is ordinarily no more than evidence from which a jury can infer the presence of a requisite intention.' The word 'might' implies that a much wider degree of foresight can be used to find an intention to assist than that for liability for murder as a principal, which requires foresight of the virtual certainty of death or serious injury before the principal's murderous intent can be found from foresight. In addition, when will a jury not find an intention to assist from foresight? For example, when a secondary party foresees the principal might use a weapon, surely the jury will conclude that he realised this not done for a benevolent purpose and find an intention to assist when the principal murders using the weapon. Is the distinction in Jogee more apparent than real?

Q. Does the author think that *Jogee* will correct past injustices?

Q. What degree of foresight does the author argue *Jogee* requires?

F. Stark makes a more fundamental criticism of *Jogee*, offering a different reading of the case law from 1553 onwards to argue that *Chan Wing-Siu* was a development of the existing law rather than a change to it. Read the following from 'The demise of "parasitic accessorial liability": substantive judicial law reform, not common law housekeeping' [2016] *Cambridge LJ* 550 at 578–579:

> The claim that *Chan Wing-Siu* was a 'wrong turn', and departing from it was in large part a matter of precedent (and therefore constitutionally straightforward), is thus unconvincing. The more compelling reading of *Jogee* is that the Supreme Court/Privy Council engaged in substantive law reform. This could have been made explicit, and the decision sold as a continuation of the historical narrowing of PAL. Just as the law had moved from a focus on: (1) furthering the common purpose, to (2) probable collateral offending, to (3) contemplated/foreseen collateral offending, it was now mov-

ing to focus on (4) intentional encouragement/assistance of the collateral crime, thus rendering PAL conceptually identical to ordinary aiding and abetting (and redundant). Many would have viewed such a judicial change as desirable, regarding PAL – a judicial development – as the genesis of much injustice. Being explicit about the change would, however, have meant engaging more directly with the proper process of revisiting previous decisions, and raised more clearly constitutional concerns about judicial activism. Although the Supreme Court/Privy Council is no doubt right that corrections of clear common law 'errors' are largely unproblematic constitutionally, there are clearer concerns raised by more substantive reform of even the common law (as the prosecution maintained in *Jogee*). The reasons the change in *Jogee* is problematic, once the alleged precedential 'error' has been dismissed as a smokescreen, are as follows: (1) the law as stated (defensibly, as shown above) in *Chan Wing-Siu* had been relatively settled for over 30 years; (2) requiring intentional encouragement or assistance for all secondary liability was not a reform the Law Commission had proposed when it had considered accessorial liability; and (3) Parliament had not apparently contemplated reforming the law, despite recent encouragement to do so. Once that shield of precedent and history has been shattered, the question is whether the other reasons provided by the Supreme Court/Privy Council in *Jogee* justified such dramatic law reform being undertaken by the courts, not the legislature. It is unfortunate that this question was so easily avoided in *Jogee*, but this paper opens up the possibility for it to be addressed more straightforwardly in the future. *Jogee* should be seen for what it is: significant judicial law reform, not common law housekeeping.

Q: Why does the author argue that it matters whether *Jogee* was a reform rather than a 'correction' of the previous law?

Whatever view one takes of the decision in *Jogee*, it is unlikely that the law in this area will remain static. D. Ormerod and K. Laird argue that there are still a number of questions which urgently need to be resolved, not least the underlying principle on which the law is based ('*Jogee*: not the end of a legal saga but the start of one?' [2016] *Crim LR* 539 at pp 548–549):

> **The underlying problem of principle—whether there ought to be parity between the accessory and the principal**
>
> As a matter of principle, a major problem remains—what is the definition of mens rea for an accessory to murder and does it differ from the definition that applies when considering the liability of the principal? If so, why? …
>
> Given that the Supreme Court in *Jogee* did not state that it was changing the law on how intent can be inferred from foresight in murder cases, the trial judge must faithfully follow *Woollin*. The jury would still have to be directed that they can only infer that the principal had the requisite intent if death or really serious harm was a virtually certain consequence, barring some unforeseen intervention and the principal appreciated that this was the case.
>
> One of the main criticisms leveled at the law on joint enterprise was the fact a lower threshold of mens rea applied to the accessory as opposed to the principal, which meant that he was convicted despite not necessarily having demonstrated any of the culpability or wrongdoing of the principal. Although the judge would be directing the jury that the same mens rea, i.e. intention, applies to both the principal and the accessory, as a matter of substance a different threshold of foresight would suffice for guilt, depending upon whose liability was being considered. There could be those who argue that this approach means that the accessory would once again be liable to conviction despite the fact he lacks the same level of culpability as the principal.
>
> In *Jogee* the Supreme Court held that it was anomalous to require a lower mental threshold of guilt in the case of the accessory than in the case of the principal. This was catalogued as one of the factors that justified the court departing from *Chan Wing-Siu*. Although not decisive, this strongly suggests that the Supreme Court sought to impose the same mental threshold upon both the accessory and the principal.

Given the outstanding questions to be answered, and the criticisms of *Jogee* which have already emerged, it is likely that there will be further developments in this area of law. Its practical impact will also depend upon prosecutorial decision-making, and the CPS launched a consultation in 2017 upon its Legal Guidance on Secondary Liability (www.cps.gov.uk/consultations). 'Joint enterprise' may be gone, but this area of accessorial liability remains controversial.

SECTION SUMMARY

Summary of A's liability when P goes beyond the joint plan to commit a further offence:

- *This issue arises where P and A have a common design or venture which is the result of agreement or a spontaneous common intention.*
- *Participants will be liable as co-defendants or joint principals where the joint enterprise leads to the intended offence.*
- *Where P goes further than agreed or beyond the intended scope of the enterprise, A will share P's liability for the more serious offence only where he intended to assist or encourage P in committing it with the relevant MR.*
- *That intention may be conditional.*
- *Where P goes beyond the intended scope of the venture in cases of murder, A need only intend to assist or encourage P to intentionally cause grievous bodily harm. If A did not have that intention, he may be guilty of unlawful act manslaughter.*

5.4 Liability of A can be Higher than that of P

5.4.1 Liability of A can be Higher

5.4.2 Accessories and Justificatory Defences

No-one can be guilty as an accessory unless there is a principal offender because the liability of an accessory derives from that of the principal. But in practice, P may be acquitted for a variety of reasons: procedural or evidential, an *excusatory* defence (diminished responsibility, provocation, intoxication, duress), innocent agency or absence of AR. Here, the liability of the accessory A remains and is higher than P's. A's liability is not therefore derivative or dependent on P's.

Initially, the courts were reluctant to convict A of a higher offence than P:

R v Richards [1974] QB 776 COURT OF APPEAL

D, a wife, employed two men to beat up her husband so seriously as to put him in hospital where she believed he would turn to her for love and affection. The two Ps wounded the husband but less seriously than instructed. They were convicted of malicious and unlawful wounding contrary to s20 Offences Against the Person Act 1861 (OAPA) whereas D was originally convicted of a higher offence: wounding with intent contrary to s18 OAPA. She appealed and a lesser offence was substituted on the grounds that the liability of an accessory could not be higher than that of P.

→ CROSS-REFERENCE
For further discussion
of *Howe* see
Chapter 9, 9.1.4.

Lord Mackay in *Howe* [1987] 1 All ER 771 overturned *Richards* on this point. He confirmed the decision of the Court of Appeal in *Howe* which had illustrated the absurdity of the principle in this way:

> Counsel before us posed the situation where A hands a gun to D informing him that it is loaded with blank ammunition only and telling him to go and scare X by discharging it. The ammunition is in fact live, as A knows, and X is killed. D is convicted only of manslaughter, as he might be on those facts. It would seem absurd that A should thereby escape conviction for murder.

5.4.1 Liability of A can be Higher

This may arise in the following circumstances:

1 Where P has an excusatory defence, for example: duress

Several earlier cases had recognised this principle such as *R v Bourne* (1952) 36 Cr App R 125. A threatened his wife and forced her to commit bestiality with a dog. His conviction for aiding and abetting bestiality was upheld despite the fact that his wife would have had a defence of duress if she had been charged.

In *R v Austin* (1981) 72 Cr App R 104 P, a father snatched his child from the custody of his wife and was assisted by A. P was exempt from the offence of 'child-stealing' (now repealed) by virtue of a statutory defence. This did not prevent A's liability as he shared the common intention.

2 Where P commits the AR with no MR

The most significant precedent is:

R v Cogan & Leak [1976] 1 QB 217

L, the accessory, compelled his wife to have sexual intercourse with C, the principal. C put forward the defence of honest belief in consent on the basis of *DPP v Morgan* [1976]. This was not left to the jury and he was convicted. His conviction was overturned on appeal. L, the husband accessory, was also convicted for two reasons. Firstly, he had the intention (MR) that C should rape his wife. C had committed the AR, effectively, as the court held, as an innocent agent. The second reason was that L was the procurer of rape.

The second argument is difficult to sustain. A successful defence of honest belief in consent by C would have resulted in an acquittal for him. How could L have procured an act which might not have been a crime?

The answer to the last question was supplied in effect by:

R v Millward [1994] CRIM LR 527 COURT OF APPEAL

A was convicted of procuring P, his employee driver, to commit death by reckless driving (a crime of intention). A had instructed P to use a tractor to tow a trailer on a main road. A knew that the tractor's hitch was poorly maintained. The trailer became detached, hit a car and killed a passenger. P had committed the AR but was acquitted. A's conviction was upheld on appeal. There was no need for a joint intention to commit the offence.

It is true that there is no need for a joint intention, but there usually needs to be some intention for accessorial liability. This case was different from *Cogan & Leak* in that in *Millward* neither A nor P had any MR for the offence (ie: intention to cause death by reckless driving). This led to speculation that the court had created a new offence of 'procuring the AR' of an offence. Procuring means to cause or bring about the offence.

In 1 and 2 it is a little artificial to regard A as an accessory. The Law Commission recommends that A would be convicted as principal offender in these cases (clause 4 'Participating in Crime' Bill, 2007).

3 But A will not be liable as accessory where P does not commit the AR

Thornton v Mitchel [1940] 1 ALL ER 339 COURT OF APPEAL

A bus conductor (A) negligently directed a bus driver (P) to reverse a bus causing two pedestrians to be knocked down, one of whom was killed. P was found not guilty of careless driving because he was only acting under instructions. He had driven but had not done so carelessly. Thus he had not committed the AR of the offence. A was consequently acquitted of aiding and abetting careless driving. Clearly, he had not driven the bus and therefore the AR of careless driving had not been committed. A might be convicted of gross negligence manslaughter today.

 THINKING POINT 5.7

Which of the above categories, 1–3 applies to the following?

1. A, a man, procures X, aged 9, to commit a burglary.
2. P is threatened with violence by A unless he injures V.

5.4.2 Accessories and Justificatory Defences

Following on from the last point, a successful plea of a *justificatory* defence such as consent, self-defence or necessity in relation to an offence against the person means that an intentional assault, for example, becomes lawful. The AR of assault, which requires force to be unlawful, will not have been committed. There is therefore no crime in respect of which anyone can be convicted, either as P or A. All accomplices will therefore escape liability.

 EXAMPLE 5.4

P, assisted by A, assaults V in self-defence. The AR of an assault is the infliction of unlawful personal violence upon another. Self-defence is a justificatory defence which negates the AR of a crime. It converts the unlawfulness of the assault into one of lawfulness. There being no AR, there can be no liability, either for P or A.

5.5 Defences to Secondary Participation: Withdrawal from a Joint Venture

5.5.1 Planned Enterprises: There must be Timely, Unequivocal Communication of Withdrawal where Practical and Reasonable

5.5.2 Spontaneous Enterprises: Withdrawal without Communication may be Effective

5.5.3 Joint Venture Going beyond the Agreed Plan

5.5.4 Reform of Withdrawal

→ **CROSS-REFERENCE**
For further discussion of *Jogee* see 5.3.3.

If A gives encouragement to P but then experiences a change of heart and withdraws before commission of the offence, he may have a defence. If successful, withdrawal operates so as to provide a defence for the completed crime but liability remains for all criminal offences committed up until that point. While much of the law on this point was developed in relation to joint enterprise, it appears to be left unchanged by *Jogee*.

It will be rare that a party can withdraw once an offence is initiated after having given encouragement. In those rare circumstances, the decision to withdraw must be communicated to P, if it is practicable or reasonable to do so, in order to give him the opportunity to desist rather than complete the crime. It is uncertain whether communication must also be given in situations of spontaneous violence, as we shall see.

Withdrawal is a unique defence applicable only to accessories. Remember that the AR of secondary participation consists of assistance and encouragement to P. Ordinarily, no primary party may argue that, having performed the AR of an offence with MR, they experienced a change of heart and abandoned their plan.

The defence of withdrawal needs to be contrasted with an assertion of lack of AR, which might occur where A 'undoes' or neutralises any complicitous act before commission, or a lack of MR, such as where P goes beyond any agreed venture (eg: *Saunders & Archer* (1576) 2 Plowd 473).

As with other areas of secondary participation, the law on withdrawal is somewhat vague and inconsistent (K.J.M. Smith, 'Withdrawal in Complicity' [2001] *Crim LR* 774):

> Of the potential range of withdrawal measures which the law might expect, the most demanding would be that the accessory should attempt to thwart the commission of the principal offence. At the other extreme, there might be the simple requirement of an attempt to communicate notice of withdrawal to the principal. In fact, the authorities come close to spanning these two extremes, with a steady trickle of case law producing neither clarity nor consistency in establishing the defence's qualifying conditions.

5.5.1 Planned Enterprises: There must be Timely, Unequivocal Communication of Withdrawal where Practical and Reasonable

To escape liability for the completed offence, withdrawal must be effective and communicated, whether verbally or otherwise.

The starting point is the dicta of Sloan JA in *R v Whitehouse* [1941] 1 WWR 172 (Court of Appeal British Columbia):

> After a crime has been committed and before a prior abandonment of the common enterprise may be found there must be in the absence of exceptional circumstances something more than a mere mental

change of intention and physical change of place by those associates who wish to disassociate themselves from the consequences attendant upon their willing assistance up to the moment of the actual commission of the crime. I would not attempt to define too closely what must be done in criminal matters involving participation in a common unlawful purpose to break the chain of causation and responsibility. That must depend on the circumstances of each case, but it seems to me that one essential element ought to be established in a case of this kind. Where practicable and reasonable there must be timely communication of the intention to abandon the common purpose from those who wish to disassociate from the contemplated crime to those who desire to continue with it. What is timely communication must be determined by the facts of each case but where practicable and reasonable it ought to be such communication, verbal or otherwise, that will serve unequivocal notice upon the other party to the common unlawful cause that if he proceeds upon it he does so without the further aid and assistance of those who withdraw.

This was confirmed as a correct statement of the law in:

R v Becerra & Cooper (1975) 62 CR APP R 212 COURT OF APPEAL

B broke into a house with C and another with the intention of stealing. B gave C a knife to use in case they were interrupted. An upstairs tenant came downstairs to investigate the noise. B said, 'There's someone coming. Come on, let's go'. With that, he jumped out of the window. As B ran away, C stabbed and killed the tenant.

Both were convicted of murder. B appealed.

Roskill LJ:

> Can it be said that one who experiences a change of mental intention and who quits the scene of the crime just before a fatal blow is struck is absolved from all consequences performed by the other who strikes in ignorance of his companion's change of heart? There must be more than a mere mental change of intention and physical change of place. There must be timely communication of the intention to abandon the common purpose. …

The words used by B and his act of jumping through the window were inadequate repentance. But there was little indication as to what might have qualified as effective withdrawal. In *R v Grundy* [1977] Crim LR 543, A withdrew from a burglary two weeks before its commission and twice tried to stop P from breaking in. This was deemed to be effective.

Grundy was followed by *R v Rook* [1993] 2 All ER 955 where R tried to dissociate himself from a planned murder by being absent when the other participants came to collect him on their way to the crime. His purpose was to defraud P of money and make off without participating in the offence. It was held by the Court of Appeal that 'absence could not amount to unequivocal communication of withdrawal'. There clearly had to be some attempt to communicate withdrawal whether verbally or physically.

However, the *Whitehouse/Becerra* principle is beset by ambiguity. In *R v Whitefield* (1984) 79 Cr App R 36 it was held that withdrawal from a planned burglary to a neighbouring flat was effective when A told G he would not join in. Although A did nothing when he heard G breaking in via the coal chute it was held that he had effectively withdrawn. He needed to take no steps to prevent it from happening or to notify the police. This appeared to be a very liberal decision, presumably confined to A's provision of advice and encouragement before he gave notice of his intention to withdraw. But it is hard to see how his withdrawal negated the assistance of such information.

5.5.2 Spontaneous Enterprises: Withdrawal without Communication may be Effective

In a spontaneous violent enterprise, it is far easier to see how withdrawal may be effective if A simply walks away even without communication. However, the Court of Appeal decisions are contradictory. In *Mitchell & Anr* [1999] Crim LR 496 (murder by spontaneous joint enterprise) it was held that *Becerra* applies to planned enterprises (timely, unequivocal communication of withdrawal where practical and reasonable) but mere withdrawal from the scene without communication applies to spontaneous enterprises. No guidance was offered as to what type of act would qualify as withdrawal.

This was held to have been too liberal by *Robinson* [2000] 5 Archbold News 2, CA where A initially participated in an attack but then attempted to protect V when it became really violent:

> … the bare minimum requirement is communication to the other members of the joint enterprise of the fact that you are withdrawing, and of course communication can be either by words or by deeds or both. If it is within your power to prevent the commission of the offence after you decide to withdraw then a failure to take steps to prevent it may indicate that you have not in fact withdrawn. It is a question of fact and degree for you to decide. On the other hand again it is a matter of fact and degree for you – efforts to prevent the commission of the offence may provide a basis for suggesting that the person concerned has in fact withdrawn and may perhaps be endeavouring to communicate that fact.

Appeal dismissed.

But *Mitchell* was confirmed by *O'Flaherty & Ors* [2004] EWCA Crim 526, a group attack, where 'two defendants successfully argued withdrawal before V was killed by another wielding a knife on the basis that they had not followed the violent affray into the street where the fatal attack occurred.' This approach, which essentially asks whether A is still in the enterprise at the time of the killing, was confirmed by *Mitchell* [2008] EWCA Crim 2552 where a killing occurred in a car park and A was party to the initial attack but unsuccessfully argued that she was not party to the killing by another stamping on V's head. There was one continuing enterprise which had not been exceeded and from which she had not withdrawn.

5.5.3 Joint Venture Going beyond the Agreed Plan

Withdrawal from a joint venture (as well as lack of MR) may be argued by an accessory or co-defendant where the other goes beyond the scope of the common design. In *R v Baker* [1994] Crim LR 444, A stabbed V three times near the shoulder and throat and then handed back the knife to the co-defendant and said 'I'm not doing it'. The co-defendant continued to stab V who died. A argued on appeal against his conviction for murder that it could not be proven that any of his stabs had killed and that the joint enterprise came to an end when he handed back the knife. It was held that his words and actions were far from unequivocal.

→ CROSS-REFERENCE
For further discussion of *Rajakumar* see 5.3.3.

Following *Powell/English* [1999] 1 AC 1 and *Jogee*, if P's acts go beyond the scope of a joint venture in an unforeseen way, then A may plead lack of MR as well as withdrawal. Withdrawal is only likely to succeed in a spontaneous joint venture according to Davies LJ in *Rajakumar*, approving the direction given in *Mitchell* [2009] 1 Cr App R 30:

> If a group of men, in a spontaneous joint enterprise of violence, are chasing another man armed with weapons, bottles and sticks through the streets of a town, and at a point when the man being chased and the remaining chasers turn a corner out of the sight of the one of the attackers, and that one attacker then stops, puts down his weapon and walks back the way he had come, and does not go round

the corner, he does not participate any further in the attack which culminates two streets later with the death of the man being chased. In such a case, a jury may well conclude that that one man, by stopping and acting as he did, had withdrawn from the joint enterprise of which he was at one stage a willing member. [It] is a question of fact and degree in every case.

The requirement of communication may be harsh in some cases. A may not be able to find P, or may consider that notice of withdrawal would be a futile way of discouraging the crime. A's culpability is no greater, however, than if communication had been successful. On the other hand, it can be argued that no defence should apply unless A demonstrates repentance by notifying the authorities or victim or, indeed, in appropriate cases, physically intervenes to stop an attack.

5.5.4 Reform of Withdrawal

The defence of withdrawal raises many difficult issues. An accessory assists and encourages P to commit a crime. If A withdraws before commission, he may no longer assist but his encouragement cannot be retracted. As Professor Smith said in the *Criminal Law* commentary to *Mitchell* [1999] *Crim LR* 497:

> Once the arrow is in the air, it is no use wishing to have never let it go –'Please God, let it miss!' The archer is guilty of homicide when the arrow gets the victim through the heart. The withdrawer, it is true, does not merely change his mind: he withdraws – but is that relevant if the withdrawal has no more effect on subsequent events than the archer's repentance?

The rationale of the defence is twofold: to induce an accessory to reconsider and to provide evidence of lack of culpability and danger, neither of which is satisfactory. An accessory may withdraw for many reasons, not necessarily laudable ones.

The Law Commission in 'Participating in Crime' (Law Com No 305, 2007) recommends that:

Para. 5.23

… it should be a defence to liability for an offence as a secondary party if D proves that:

    (1) he or she acted for the purpose of:

        (a) preventing the commission of either the offence that he or she was encouraging or assisting or another offence; or

        (b) to prevent or limit the occurrence of harm; and

    (2) it was reasonable to act as D did in the circumstances.

The defence would not apply to a P who uses an innocent agent.

?! THINKING POINT 5.8

Will the defence of withdrawal succeed in the following?

1. A initially participates in the joint ventures below. He then decides that he has had enough and slopes off without attracting P's attention in:

   a. a planned joint violent attack on V;

   b. a spontaneous joint violent attack on V.

2. In a joint violent attack, A offers encouragement by shouting, 'Hit him P'. Five minutes later he tries to protect V who is on the ground.

5.6 Can Victims be Accessories?

The short answer following *Gnango*, is 'yes,' although previous cases decided the issue on far less tortuous reasoning! For instance, in *R v Sockett* (1908) 1 Cr App R 101, by allowing P to perform an unlawful abortion upon her, V was held to have aided and abetted that offence. In *R v Brown* [1993] 2 WLR 556, consenting 'victims' were also co-defendants for injuries deliberately inflicted by homosexuals contrary to s47 and s20 Offences Against the Person Act 1861 in the course of sado-masochistic assaults. In *Gnango* [2011] UKSC 59 the respondent was guilty of murder as an accessory through participation in an attempted murder upon himself.

→ CROSS-REFERENCE
For further discussion of *Brown* see Chapter 10, 10.6.2.

However, the law recognises that certain classes of victim should be protected despite their complicity in an offence to which they have submitted. This primarily concerns sexual offences for the protection of children and the vulnerable. It is known as the *Tyrell Principle*, so-called after the case by that name.

R v Tyrrell [1894] 1 QB 710 COURT FOR CROWN CASES RESERVED

The case concerned an appeal against the conviction of a girl between 13 and 16 for aiding and abetting D to have sexual intercourse with her contrary to s5 Criminal Law Amendment Act 1885. The conviction was quashed.

Lord Coleridge CJ:

> The Criminal Law Amendment Act, 1885, was passed for the purpose of protecting women and girls against themselves. ... With the object of protecting women and girls against themselves the Act of Parliament has made illicit connection with a girl under that age unlawful; if a man wishes to have such illicit connection he must wait until the girl is 16, otherwise he breaks the law; but it is impossible to say that the Act, which is absolutely silent about aiding and abetting or soliciting or inciting, can have intended that the girls for whose protection it was passed should be punishable under it for the offences committed upon themselves. I am of the opinion that this conviction ought to be quashed.

The principle was applied in *Whitehouse* [1977] QB 868 where the conviction of a 15-year-old daughter who had been incited by her father to have incest with him contrary to s11 Sexual Offences Act 1956 was quashed under the same principle.

The Law Commission ('Participating in Crime', Law Com No 305, 2007, para 5.39) recommend that the *Tyrell* principle be confined to offences specifically protecting particular categories of person (eg: children, the elderly and those trafficked for exploitation).

SECTION SUMMARY

■ *The liability of A can be higher than that of P where P has an excusatory defence, or is an innocent agent, or does not commit the AR of an offence.*

■ *Withdrawal is a defence to secondary participation which must be effective and communicated in planned enterprises and possibly just effective in spontaneous enterprises.*

■ *Victims will not be accessories to crimes where the offence is for their protection: the* Tyrrell *principle.*

5.7 Reform

Here we will focus on the recommendations for reform of secondary participation in relation to murder.

Problems and proposals for reform were first identified in 'A New Homicide Act for England and Wales?' (Law Com CP No 177, 2005) Part 5, 'Complicity in First Degree Murder'. The main problems were these:

1. D can be liable for murder and the mandatory life sentence on the basis that he foresaw the *possibility* that non-life-threatening GBH might be caused (the GBH rule). This is a much less culpable state of mind than for primary liability for murder (direct/oblique *intent* to cause GBH or death).

   Note that *Jogee* now goes some way to addressing this by requiring that he *intended* to assist or encourage P to act with intent to cause grievous bodily harm or death; but there are concerns about the level of foresight required to establish that intention, and that conditional intention will suffice.

➡ CROSS-REFERENCE
For further discussion of the criticisms of *Jogee* see 5.3.3.

2. Duress is no defence to murder/attempted murder, either for principal or secondary parties (*Howe* [1987] AC 417, *Gotts* [1992] 2 AC 412). Therefore, an A who acts under duress will receive the mandatory life sentence even where he foresaw that relatively little harm might be caused to V.

➡ CROSS-REFERENCE
Duress and murder/ attempted murder is discussed in Chapter 9, 9.1.4.

The proposal was to restrict secondary liability so that D (ie: the accessory) should only be rendered guilty of P's principal offence in three situations where D's conduct actually encouraged or assisted P. Significantly, the categories represent shared moral culpability between P and D:

Para: 5.43

   1.   it was D's intention that the principal offence should be committed;

   2.   D and P were parties to a joint venture to commit the principal offence or

   3.   D and P were parties to a joint venture to commit an offence other than the principal offence and D foresaw the possible commission of the principal offence in relation to the fulfilment of the venture (which is what happened).

This led to the proposal that in cases other than those of joint ventures, secondary liability should only apply to Ds whose *purpose* was to encourage or assist the commission of the conduct element of first degree murder, and who either *intended* that death should be caused or *foresaw* that, if the conduct element of first degree murder were to be committed, P would act with intent to kill. This largely replicated the common law but would exclude shop-keepers acting in the normal course of business who are aware that their goods will be used with criminal intent.

In relation to joint ventures the proposals were in line with the pre-*Jogee* common law: there needed to be no actual encouragement or assistance for P by D, nor need D act with such a purpose and the element of reckless foresight of P's offence would be maintained. The 'fundamental difference' defence would remain on the basis that the GBH rule in murder continued as it was (ie: inclusive of both life-threatening and non-life-threatening serious harm).

D would remain liable for first degree murder even though P had a defence rendering him liable to second degree murder (diminished responsibility or provocation) and duress should apply to Ps and As in first degree murder.

In addition, two new offences of *complicity in an unlawful killing* were proposed where D did not intend or foresee serious harm or murder but only harm or fear of harm (as in *English, Stewart & Schofield* or *Gilmour*). In the final report, 'Murder, Manslaughter, Infanticide' (Law Com No 304, 2006), the Law Commission recommended that in these circumstances, D's offence was one of manslaughter.

Para 4.47:

We recommend that D should be liable to be convicted of P's offence of first or second degree murder (as the case may be) if:

(1)   D intended to assist or encourage P to commit the relevant offence; or

(2)   D was engaged in a joint criminal venture with P, and realised that P or another party to the joint venture, might commit the relevant offence.

Para 4.48:

We recommend that D should be liable for manslaughter if the following conditions are met:

(1)   D and P were parties to a joint venture to commit an offence;

(2)   P committed the offence of first degree murder or second degree murder in relation to the fulfilment of that venture;

(3)   D intended or foresaw that (non-serious) harm or the fear of harm might be caused by a party to the venture; and

(4)   a reasonable person in D's position, with D's knowledge of the relevant facts, would have foreseen an obvious risk of death or serious injury being caused by a party to the venture.

In the government's Consultation Paper, *Murder, manslaughter and infanticide* (CP 19/08) the Law Commission's recommendations were largely accepted. Two new offences were proposed of intentionally assisting or encouraging murder and manslaughter. Murder in the context of a joint venture would be retained subject to the limitations recommended by the Law Commission. However, the government did not proceed with legislative reform, and the Supreme Court decision in *Jogee* brought changes in relation to joint ventures which differed significantly from the recommendations.

5.8 Evaluation

The question of whether the current law poses suitable limits on the scope of secondary liability needs to be asked. Is it right to base secondary liability on foresight of a risk as opposed to certainty? Is this too harsh? The Law Commission observed that it was the limited scope of inchoate liability which accounted for the common law's over-extension of secondary participation. It was by compensating for the inadequacy of inchoate liability that the ad hoc development of secondary participation occurred. The four new offences of assistance and encouragement under the Serious Crime Act 2007 are designed to address this problem. However, the width of those offences only mirrors and does not reduce the width of secondary liability.

The Supreme Court responded in *Jogee* to the powerful arguments against joint enterprise, particularly in the murder context. However, the resulting changes to the law are limited in scope and by no means address all concerns about unjust convictions for secondary participation. On the other hand, the threat posed by joint ventures with their potential for violence may justify a more policy-driven approach. It seems unlikely that *Jogee* is the final word on how a balance is to be achieved.

SUMMARY

- Under s8 Accessories and Abettors Act 1861, secondary parties (accessories) can be liable for an offence committed by another where they will be subject to the same punishment.

- An accessory is someone who assists or encourages another to commit a crime (AR).

- The MR for accessories depends on intention to assist and encourage plus knowledge of the circumstances.

- Where a member of a joint venture goes beyond the agreed scope of the venture, A will be liable for the more serious offence if he intended to assist or encourage P's intentional act (including when that intention was conditional).

- It is possible for A's liability to be higher than that of P.

- Victims who have participated in an offence will be protected from liability by the *Tyrrell* principle.

- Withdrawal provides a defence.

PROBLEM SOLVING

A1, A2 and P jointly agree to burgle V's house, taking with them a jemmy to break open a window. It is agreed that A2 will act as look out. A1 breaks open the window and hands it to P whilst they climb inside. They hear footsteps on the stairs and see V approaching. P rushes at V wielding the jemmy. A1 jumps back out through the window and runs off. In fact, P drops the jemmy and produces a knife with which he stabs and kills V. The knife had been lent to A by X, an associate who was aware that A had previous convictions for violence and that he might use it for a similar offence.

Discuss the liability of A1, A2, P and X on the basis of the following:

(a) A1 and A2 knew P was violent and that he might kill with the jemmy if disturbed although they sincerely hoped this would not happen.

(b) A1 was P's younger brother who had been threatened by P with violence unless he accompanied him on the burglary.

Remember:

- **I: Identify** relevant issues
- **D: Define** offences/defences
- **E: Explain/evaluate** the law
- **A: Apply** law to facts.

See the online resources for further guidance on solving this problem: www.oup.com/uk/loveless6e/.

FURTHER READING

R. Buxton, 'Joint Enterprise: *Jogee*, Substantial Injustice and the Court of Appeal' [2017] *Crim LR* 123
A brief commentary on *Johnson*, arguing that the test for historic appeals should be that the conviction was unsafe rather than the higher standard of 'substantial injustice'.

D. Ormerod and K. Laird, *Jogee*: Not the End of a Legal Saga but the Start of One?' [2016] *Crim LR* 539
Considers the various legal questions which *Jogee* still leaves unresolved and argues that the Court of Appeal needs to address them swiftly.

C. Sjolin-Knight, 'Killing the Parasite in *R v Jogee*' (2016) 25 *Nottingham Law Journal* 129
A casenote and discussion by junior counsel for *Jogee*.

F. Stark, 'The Demise of "Parasitic Accessorial Liability": Substantive Judicial Law Reform, Not Common Law Housekeeping' (2016) 75(3) *Cambridge LJ* **550**

Reviews and provides an alternative reading of the case law on accessorial liability to argue that *Jogee* reformed the law, rather than simply correcting it.

G.R. Sullivan, 'Inchoate Liability for Assisting and Encouraging Crime—the Law Commission Report' [2006] *Crim LR* **1047**

Discussion of the Law Commission's proposals for reforming secondary liability.

W. Wilson, 'A Rational Scheme of Liability for Participating in Crime' [2008] *Crim LR* **3**

Considers the practical and moral justifications for accessorial liability and discusses the Law Commission's recommendations for reform.

W. Wilson and D. Ormerod, 'Simply Harsh to Fairly Simple: Joint Enterprise Reform' [2015] *Crim LR* **1, 3**

A pre-*Jogee* article which remains valuable for its consideration of the problems with the law as it then was and its foreshadowing of *Jogee* by recommendations for judicial reform.

Homicide 1: murder

6.1 Actus Reus

6.2 Mens Rea

6.3 The Sentence for Murder

6.4 Criticism

6.5 Reform

KEY POINTS

This chapter will help you to:

- identify the AR/MR elements of murder and understand that murder concerns intentional killings whilst manslaughter refers to unintentional killings;

- understand that intention consists of intention to kill or cause really serious harm;

- question whether the mandatory life sentence is appropriate;

- evaluate whether the boundaries of murder are too wide given the extended meaning of 'oblique' intent and the inclusion of intent to cause really serious harm.

INTRODUCTION

The term 'homicide' includes the common law offences of murder and manslaughter which are used to describe many forms of unlawful killing. It also includes statutory offences of killing in specific circumstances such as infanticide and dangerous driving. See Diagram 6.1.

Some facts about homicide that you probably already know

Murder at its worst reflects the heart of violence within society: intentional killing. It is the gravest crime in the legal system justifying the severest punishment of a mandatory life sentence. It includes premeditated assassination, serial or sexual killings, domestic killings and the killing of police officers.

Diagram 6.1
Structure of homicide

Some facts about homicide that you probably do not already know

Homicide also covers killing in a completely different set of circumstances. Murder includes far less culpable killings such as euthanasia which can be carried out with compassion rather than aggression. It includes the abused woman who kills her abuser through fear of further violence. Notwithstanding otherwise blameless lives, the life sentence will be mandatory. Even though a relatively short period of imprisonment may be served, the life sentence carries conditions for the natural life of the offender with the possibility of recall to prison at any time.

Many people would be surprised to learn that you can commit murder without foreseeing death at all where the intention is to do GBH and not to kill. Further, murder includes spontaneous killings that are not premeditated. In reality, therefore, murder is an offence carried out in diverse circumstances with gradations of culpability.

Research by Professor Mitchell on public attitudes to murder submitted to the Law Commission for its report on the 'Partial Defences to Murder' (2004) (Appendix C) confirms that there is profound public ignorance of the breadth of unlawful and lethal conduct falling within the meaning of murder because of public association of murder with the term 'malice afore-thought'. This was the definition of MR for murder until recently.

The dividing line between murder and manslaughter is one of MR: murder requires intention, whereas manslaughter requires recklessness or gross negligence. The uncertainty of oblique intention prohibits a clear distinction between intention and recklessness and, consequently, between murder and manslaughter. Therefore, it is not difficult to see how the difference between the offences can sometimes be a matter of pure chance.

Some offences of reckless killing (manslaughter) might be thought to be as bad as murder, for instance, terrorist killings where death/GBH was foreseen as only probable and not virtually certain. Therefore, putting a bomb in a public place and giving a warning, or pouring paraffin through someone's letterbox and setting light to it, may mean that there was only recklessness regarding death/GBH and not intention. The moral reason for the distinction may be imperceptible. The Law Commission has recommended reforms to the current law by the creation of a ladder of new homicide offences ('Murder, Manslaughter and Infanticide', Law Com No 304, 2006). We shall consider these at the end of the chapter.

Public perceptions of homicide

The general perception of homicide and violent crime is that it is on the increase and that society is less safe today than in the past. However, since peaking in 1995, crime has virtually halved and violent crime has fallen by 43 per cent. The number of recorded homicides has been falling this century and currently stands at 723 for 2017, an increase of 9 per cent from the previous year (571). It is worth noting that the 9 per cent increase excludes 96 cases of recorded homicide as a result of the Hillsborough stadium disaster. Despite these increases, there is still a downward trend in homicide (Office for National Statistics).

Home Office statistics reveal the following: the most likely victim of a homicide is a child. Children under 1 year old were most at risk at 21 per million. Parents were the most likely suspects. The second most common group of victims are males over the age of 16.

British Crime Survey statistics reveal that most murders are committed by men on young men in quarrels and arguments with knives. Women are more likely to be victims of domestic violence. Just over half of female victims are killed by partners. See Diagram 6.2 for more details and a breakdown of offences by apparent method of killing and sex of the victim.

Fear of rising homicidal violence is therefore not to be dismissed but it must be seen in broader context. Almost 4,000 people die each year from falls whilst 1,792 died in 2016/17 in road accidents and 1,201 died in 2016 taking heroin and morphine.

If you were to add the number of fatalities in the workplace and deaths from work-related disease, (see Chapter 4), the risk of death from ordinary activities far outweighs the risk of criminal homicide.

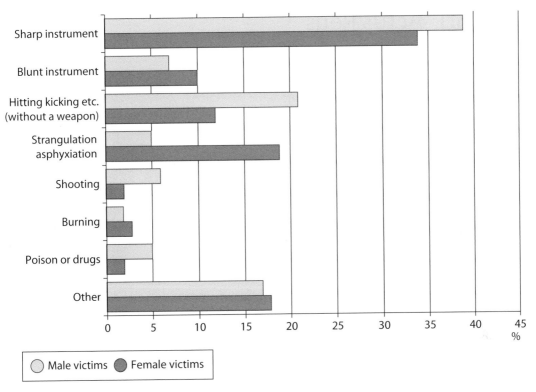

Diagram 6.2

Offences currently recorded as homicide by apparent method of killing and sex of victim, year ending March 2016

Source: Homicide Index: Home Office

Definition of murder:

AR   The unlawful killing of a human being under the Queen's Peace.

MR   Intention to kill or to cause GBH.

KEY CASES

AG's Reference (No 3 of 1994) [1997] UKHL 31, [1998] AC 245—a double transfer of intention (transferred malice) is not possible;

Pretty v DPP [2002] 3 WLR 1598—no right to die by positive act;

Purdy v DPP [2009] UKHL 45—DPP should produce guidelines on prosecutions for assisted suicide;

R (on the application of Nicklinson & Ors) v Ministry of Justice, R (on the application of AM) v DPP [2014] UKSC 38—law on assisted suicide is potentially incompatible with Article 8 ECHR.

Vickers [1957] 2 All ER 741—MR for murder consists of intent to kill or cause GBH;

Cunningham [1981] 2 All ER 863—GBH rule in murder confirmed by HL;

6.1 Actus Reus

6.1.1 Unlawful Killing

6.1.2 Killing and Causation

6.1.3 A Human Being

6.1.4 Under the Queen's Peace

6.1.5 The 'Death Within a Year and a Day' Rule No Longer Applies

Murder carries a mandatory life sentence and is committed when a defendant unlawfully kills another person with an intention to kill, or an intention to do serious harm. The AR of homicide is common to both murder and manslaughter, both of which are common law crimes. The classic description of murder was given by LCJ Coke in 3 Inst 47 as follows:

> Murder is when a man of sound memory, and of the age of discretion, unlawfully killeth within any county of the realm any reasonable creature in rerum natura under the king's peace, with malice aforethought, either expressed by the party or implied by law, [so as the party wounded, or hurt, etc die of the wound or hurt, etc within a year and a day after the same]. [NB: *The year and a day requirement no longer applies.*]

There are four elements to the AR of homicide, each of which must be proved by the prosecution beyond all reasonable doubt.

6.1.1 Unlawful Killing

A person of 'sound mind' and 'of the age of discretion' can commit the AR of murder by unlawfully killing another person. All this means is that D must be legally responsible for his actions: not insane, not under diminished responsibility and be a person not a corporation. The age of criminal responsibility since the Crime and Disorder Act 1998 in England and Wales is ten years.

The killing must be unlawful. This must be distinguished from lawful killings, such as killings in self-defence, killings in time of war and killings of patients close to death by doctors whose purpose is either to relieve pain and suffering or to give the chance of life to another person. You may remember the case of the conjoined twins, Jodie and Mary, only one of whom had any viable prospects of survival following an operation to separate them, the effect of which was to bring about the death of the weaker twin: *Re A (Minors) (Conjoined Twins: Medical Treatment)* [2000] 4 All ER 961. Two out of three judges thought the killing could be murder but necessity or self-defence would provide a defence. You should note that an intentional 'mercy killing' of a sick person for compassionate reasons is murder. Mercy killing is not a separate offence. For example, in *Inglis* [2010] EWCA Crim 2637 a mother killed her paraplegic 18-year-old son who was a physically and mentally healthy teenager until he suffered head injuries after falling from an ambulance on his way to hospital following a fight. Although the Court of Appeal reduced her sentence to reflect the fact that she genuinely believed she was committing a mercy killing, her offence was still murder.

6.1.2 Killing and Causation

The method of killing is unimportant. In reality, a variety of means are revealed by the statistics, stabbing and the use of sharp instruments being the most frequent.

Neither does it matter that V is randomly killed and not known to D. The definition of murder makes no reference to the killing of a specific, identified victim.

What is important is that D caused the death of V and it is in the context of homicide and the more serious result crimes against the person that causation becomes relevant. This may not necessarily be an easy matter to discern where there are multiple causes of death or the involvement of more than one individual. The rules on causation will be examined by the courts to determine whether D was the legal cause of death in the sense of contributing to or accelerating it.

→ **CROSS-REFERENCE**
See Chapter 2, 2.3 for the general rules on causation.

6.1.3 A Human Being

The historic definition of murder referred to the victim as 'a reasonable person in being'. As live human beings we are all capable of being a victim of a homicide. The attribution of 'reasonableness' added nothing to the definition of a person in being but it is clear that V is not 'in being' either before birth or if clinically brain dead. If a foetus is killed before birth, or if death occurs during birth and before the baby is fully expelled, the offence will not be murder but one of several statutory offences concerned with the protection of the unborn child:

- Procuring a miscarriage under s58 Offences Against the Person Act 1861 applies to attempts to procure a miscarriage at any time between conception and birth.
- Child destruction under s1 Infant Life (Preservation) Act 1929 applies to the killing of a child capable of being born alive during child-birth.
- The Abortion Act 1967, as amended by the Human Fertilisation and Embryology Act 1990, legalises abortion by a medical practitioner in prescribed circumstances. The current legal time limit is 24 weeks in most circumstances.

When does life begin?

When does a foetus become a human being? The rule is that the child must have been wholly expelled from the mother and have an independent circulation. It was originally thought that the child must have drawn its first breath, but this is now doubted since there is invariably a delay between birth and the first breath. It is not necessary for the umbilical cord to have been cut. The last case on this topic was in the Victorian era: *Handley* (1874) 13 Cox CC 79 when science was less able to detect whether a premature baby had died from pre-natal injury or complications due to being premature. It is now possible for premature babies born at 22 weeks to survive. Diagnosis of a causal connection between pre-natal injury and death is therefore far more possible. The following case raised related issues:

> ***Attorney-General's Reference (No 3 of 1994)*** [1997] UKHL 31, [1998] AC 245
>
> ....
>
> - Where D intends to cause grievous bodily harm (GBH) on a pregnant woman, is it murder or manslaughter where injury is also caused to the foetus which is then born alive and later dies?
> - Can an intention to cause GBH to the mother be transferred to the unborn child?
>
> You will have read the *transferred malice* aspects of this case in Chapter 3 (3.1.12). A pregnant woman was stabbed by the father of her baby (D). 17 days later she gave birth to a grossly premature baby which died 121 days later from a chest infection due to prematurity. D's conviction for

murder of the baby was overturned by the House of Lords, and manslaughter substituted. Lord Mustill reviewed the rules on murder:

1. It is sufficient to raise a prima facie case of murder (subject to entire or partial excuses such as self-defence or provocation) for it to be proved that D did the act which caused the death intending to kill V or to cause him at least grievous bodily harm. . . . Thus, if M had died as a result of the injuries received B would have been guilty of murdering her, even though in the everyday sense he did not intend her death.

2. If D does an act with the intention of causing a particular kind of harm to X, and unintentionally does that kind of harm to Y, then the intent to harm X may be added to the harm actually done to Y in deciding whether D has committed a crime towards Y. This rule is usually referred to as the doctrine of 'transferred malice', a misleading label but one which is too firmly entrenched to be discarded. . . .

3. Except under statute an embryo or foetus *in utero* cannot be V of a crime of violence. In particular, violence to the foetus which causes its death *in utero* is not a murder. The foundation authority is the definition by Sir Edward Coke of murder by reference to the killing of 'a reasonable creature', '*in rerum natura*'. . . .

4. The existence of an interval of time between the doing of an act by D with the necessary wrongful intent and its impact on V in a manner which leads to death does not in itself prevent the intent, the act and the death from together amounting to murder so long as there is an unbroken causal connection between the act and the death.

5. Violence towards a foetus which results in harm suffered after the baby has been born alive can give rise to criminal responsibility even if the harm would not have been criminal (apart from statute) if it had been suffered *in utero*.'

NOTE 6.1

The House of Lords decided that D's offence was unlawful act manslaughter of the baby (V) on the basis of the violent attack against the mother which did not need to be aimed at V. This would avoid any of the difficulties of transferred malice or coincidence of AR and MR. Death may have been unintentional but D had committed a dangerous intentional unlawful act which caused death.

It is not easy to see why this should not have been a case of murder of the child on the basis of intention to commit GBH on the mother. This would have sufficed as MR for murder had the mother died. A double transfer of intention was rejected for murder but in preferring manslaughter an identical double transfer of intention to injure was implicit. The question arises however whether the decision would have been different had D had an intent to kill rather than an intent to injure. This case provided the precedent for *CP (A Child) v First Tier Tribunal (Criminal Injuries Compensation Authority)* [2014] EWCA Civ 1554, where the Court of Appeal confirmed that an embryo or foetus in the uterus does not have human personality and therefore cannot be the victim of a crime of violence. The Court rejected the claim that an alcoholic mother, who had caused 'foetal alcohol spectrum disorder' to her unborn child, had committed an offence contrary to s23 Offences Against the Person Act 1861 (maliciously administering poison so as to endanger life or cause GBH).

THINKING POINT 6.1

What offence has D committed in the following cases?

- D administers poison to a pregnant woman as a result of which:

  a. her unborn child dies;

  b. she goes into premature labour but the child dies during delivery;

  c. the baby is born prematurely but dies within minutes.

When does life end?

When does a person cease to be regarded as alive? Will a doctor, for example, commit murder by ceasing to treat someone with a very low quality of life such as a seriously handicapped baby, a patient in a long-term persistent vegetative state (PVS) or a terminally ill patient suffering unbearable pain? These questions, which are informed by clinical definitions, raise significant moral issues regarding the sanctity of life. They also need to be scrutinised from a human rights perspective. By virtue of the Human Rights Act 1998, the UK government is required by Article 2 ECHR to protect everyone's right to life.

Switching off life-support machines

We have already seen that doctors rely on a clinical diagnosis of brain stem death in order to determine when life has ended and that they commit no crime by switching off life support to a patient who is already brain-dead, despite the fact that breathing could be artificially sustained.

➜ CROSS-REFERENCE
See the case of
Malcherek [1981] 1 WLR
690 in Chapter 2, 2.3.3.

Letting patients die and the ECHR: omission v positive act

Persistent vegetative state (PVS) patients

But what is the position where patients are not clinically dead but in long-term PVS and are being fed, hydrated and treated artificially?

➜ CROSS-REFERENCE
Bland is discussed in
Chapter 2, 2.2.3

The precedent here is the case of Anthony Bland. This young man had been in a coma for three and a half years before an application was made to the High Court to terminate artificial nutrition and hydration. The House of Lords held on appeal that doctors were not under a duty to continue treating him or to provide nutritional support as there was no hope of his ever recovering. Letting him die, an omission of a previous duty of care, would be no crime despite the fact that he was incapable of giving consent (*Airedale NHS Trust v Bland* [1993] 2 WLR 316).

The High Court subsequently decided in *NHS Trust A v Mrs M and NHS Trust B v Mrs H* [2001] Fam 348, that Article 2 ECHR was not violated by cases such as *Bland*. Mrs M had been a PVS patient for three years following an operation and Mrs H for ten months following collapse whilst on holiday. These cases must be distinguished from a patient with 'minimal consciousness', that is, someone who is alive and sometimes conscious: *W v M* [2011] EWHC 2443. The signing of a 'living will' recording an advanced decision to be allowed to die in such circumstances could have resulted in a different decision.

Severely handicapped babies

The legal position concerning the withdrawal of nutrition and treatment of a severely handicapped baby is that, as a reasonable person in being regardless of the extent of physical or mental impairment, the baby is protected by the law of homicide.

→ CROSS-REFERENCE

Re A (Children) (Conjoined Twins) is discussed further in Chapter 9, 9.2.3.

In *Re A (Children) (Conjoined Twins)* [2000] 4 All ER 961, Brook LJ observed that:

Modern English statute law has mitigated the prospective burden that might otherwise fall on the parents of severely handicapped children and their families if they are willing to avail themselves of its protection at any time up to the time the child (or children) is born . . . Once a seriously handicapped child is born alive, the position changes, and it is as much entitled to the protection of the criminal law as any other human being.

But the quality of life argument will be relevant where the extent of deformity may involve painful invasive treatment so as to render the quality of life intolerable: *Re J* [1990] 3 All ER 930.

Euthanasia

There is no right to die by positive act

Suicide has not been an offence since the Suicide Act 1961 and a failed attempt on oneself will incur no criminal liability. Euthanasia, on the other hand, is unlawful and anyone who commits a positive act to bring about the death of another, even with their consent, will commit murder. If D can prove that he assisted V's suicide, he will be guilty not of murder but of the offence of assisting or encouraging suicide under s2(1) Suicide Act 1961 and will face a maximum sentence of up to 14 years rather than a mandatory life sentence. The DPP must consent to any prosecution (s2(4) 1961 Act).

In several high-profile cases, courts have been asked to confer future immunity from prosecution upon relatives who might provide such assistance:

R (on the application of Pretty) v DPP [2002] 3 WLR 1598

Diane Pretty was terminally ill with motor neurone disease. She wished to take her own life with help from her husband so that she could die with dignity at home. The DPP was asked by letter to confirm that he would not prosecute Mr Pretty if he helped his wife to commit suicide. The DPP refused to do so. The question before the court was what factors would be taken into account by the DPP in deciding whether or not to prosecute. Diane Pretty argued that the uncertainty interfered with her human dignity under Article 2 ECHR, her right to private and family life under Article 8, her freedom of thought, conscience and religion under Article 9 and the right not to be discriminated against under Article 14.

Read the following from Lord Steyn's judgment:

54. The subject of euthanasia and assisted suicide have been deeply controversial long before the adoption of the Universal Declaration of Human Rights in 1948, which was followed two years later by the European Convention on Human Rights and Freedoms (1950). The arguments and counter arguments have ranged widely. There is a conviction that human life is sacred and that the corollary is that euthanasia and assisted suicide are always wrong. This view is supported by the Roman Catholic Church, Islam and other religions. There is also a secular view, shared sometimes by atheists and agnostics, that human life is sacred. On the other side, there are many millions who do not hold these beliefs. For many the personal autonomy of individuals is predominant. They would argue that it is the moral right of individuals to have a say over the time and manner of their death. On the other hand, there are utilitarian arguments to the contrary effect. The terminally ill and those suffering great pain from incurable illnesses are often vulnerable. And not all families, whose interests are at stake, are wholly unselfish and loving. There is a risk that assisted suicide may be abused in the sense that such people may be persuaded that they want to die or that they ought to want to die. Another strand is that, when one knows the genuine wish of a terminally ill patient to die, they should not be forced against their will to endure a life they no longer wish to endure.

Such views are countered by those who say it is a slippery slope or the thin end of the wedge. It is also argued that euthanasia and assisted suicide, under medical supervision, will undermine the trust between doctors and patients. It is said that protective safeguards are unworkable. The countervailing contentions of moral philosophers, medical experts and ordinary people are endless. . . . It is not for us, in this case, to express a view on these arguments. But it is of great importance to note that these are ancient questions on which millions in the past have taken diametrically opposite views and still do.

The Relevance of Existing English Law

55. Given the fact that Mrs Pretty's arguments are founded on the European Convention, the existing position under English law, even if in large measure very similar to that under other European legal systems, cannot be decisive. But it demonstrates how controversial the subject of the legalisation of euthanasia and assisted suicide is in Europe. In outline the position in England is as follows. By virtue of legislation suicide is no longer an offence and a suicide pact may result in a verdict of manslaughter. Mercy killing in the form of euthanasia is murder and assisted suicide is a statutory offence punishable by 14 years' imprisonment. A competent patient cannot be compelled to undergo life saving treatment: *St George's Health Care Trust v S* [1999] Fam 26. Under the double effect principle medical treatment may be administered to a terminally ill person to alleviate pain although it may hasten death: *Airedale NHS Trust v Bland* [1993] AC 789, 867D, per Lord Goff of Chieveley. This principle entails a distinction between foreseeing an outcome and intending it: see also Anthony Arlidge, *The Trial of Dr David Moor*, [2000] Crim LR 31. The case of *Bland* involved a further step: the House of Lords held that under judicial control it was permissible to cease to take active steps to keep a person in a permanent vegetative state alive. It involved the notion of a distinction between doctors killing a patient and letting him die: see also *NHS Trust A v H* [2001] 2 FLR 501. These are at present the only inroads on the sanctity of life principle in English law.

The application was refused on the ground that s2(1) Suicide Act 1961 did not contravene the ECHR and this decision was confirmed by the ECtHR (*Pretty v UK* [2002] 3 WLR 1598). Unlike the House of Lords, however, the Court found that s2(1) of the 1961 Act did represent an interference with the right to private and family life under Article 8(1), but it was justified by Article 8(2) which prohibits any interference by a public authority with this right unless it is for certain reasons, one of which is the 'protection of the rights and freedoms of others'. Thus, the right of the sufferer to die was outweighed by the need to protect other vulnerable, incapacitated people from pressure to die.

THINKING POINT 6.2

1. Did the House of Lords take a moral stand on euthanasia?
2. Was Diane Pretty mentally competent to make the decision to die?
3. If she had wanted to die through starvation would the decision have been different?

R (on the application of Purdy) (Appellant) v DPP (Respondent) [2009] UKHL 45 HOUSE OF LORDS

The House of Lords was sympathetic to the dilemma of the applicant, an MS sufferer who, like Diane Pretty, wanted information from the DPP as to whether her husband was likely to face prosecution should he assist her in her decision to end her life abroad. The House held that the DPP should immediately draw up a policy to clarify when a prosecution would be instituted.

The Guidelines were duly published on 25 February 2010 (Policy for Prosecutors in Respect of Cases of Assisting or Encouraging Suicide: www.cps.gov.uk/publications/prosecution/assisted_ suicide_policy.html). Factors were listed which will be taken into account in determining whether it is in the public interest that a prosecution for assisted suicide should take place. Those motivated by compassion to help a relative or close friend with a 'clear, settled and informed' wish to die are unlikely to be prosecuted. On the other hand, healthcare professionals assisting a terminally ill person to die are more at risk of prosecution. The guidelines were at the heart of the next important appeal.

R (on the application of Nicklinson & Ors) v Ministry of Justice, R (on the application of AM) v DPP [2014] UKSC 38

Tony Nicklinson (represented in the appeal by his widow), Paul Lamb and AM (Martin) appealed to the Supreme Court for a declaration that the law relating to assisted suicide and the DPP's Policy for Prosecutors were incompatible with Article 8. All three had suffered permanent and catastrophic physical disabilities leaving them paralysed and unable to speak without the aid of technology. Each was living such a distressing and undignified life that he had made a settled wish to end it. Like Diane Pretty, none could do so without assistance other than by self-starvation, a painful, protracted and distressing process. The Divisional Court had refused Tony Martin a declaration that it would be lawful for a doctor to assist him to die, or that the current law was incompatible with the ECHR. He then embarked on self-starvation and died six days after that judgment. Martin's application for a declaration in respect of the DPP's policy had also failed. He had sought clarification of the prosecution guidelines relating to family members or carers who wished to assist a person to die by arranging for their travel to the Dignitas Clinic in Switzerland, where assisted suicide was lawful. Subsequent appeals to the Court of Appeal were unsuccessful on the ground that any change to the law on assisted suicide was a matter for parliament, not the courts. M's appeal succeeded, however, to the extent that the DPP's guidelines were considered to offer insufficient clarity with respect to healthcare professionals. The parties appealed to the Supreme Court which effectively adjudicated three issues:

1. *Whether the unqualified ban on voluntary euthanasia under s2(1) Suicide Act 1961 was compatible with Article 8 and whether the Court had jurisdiction to determine that issue.* Seven of the nine justices declined to give an opinion on this question in this case and considered that it was for Parliament to decide the width of the law.

   Lord Neuberger:

   > [The appellants] say that the harmful effect that liberalising the law on assisting suicide may have on vulnerable and weak people is no more than speculative, because no evidence has been adduced to suggest otherwise, and because in jurisdictions where assisted suicide is permitted, there do not seem to have been any undesirable consequences for the weak and vulnerable. ... It is true that the Falconer Report, supported by the reports of the two Canadian panels, states that in the Netherlands, Oregon and Switzerland there is no evidence of abuse of the law, which permits assisting a suicide in prescribed circumstances and subject to conditions. However, negative evidence is often hard to obtain, there is only a limited scope for information given the few jurisdictions where assisted suicide is lawful and the short time for which it has been lawful there, and different countries may have different potential problems.

In other words, the evidence on that point plainly falls some way short of establishing that there is no risk. The most that can be said is that the Falconer commission and the Canadian panels could find no evidence of abuse. As Lord Sumption points out in paras 224–225 below, however, while the factual evidence in this connection is sparse, anecdotal, and inconclusive, the expert experienced and professional opinion evidence does provide support for the existence of the risk. In all the circumstances, this concern cannot, in my opinion, possibly be rejected as fanciful or unrealistic.

Lady Hale and Lord Kerr, held, by contrast, that current law is incompatible with Article 8 and would have granted a declaration now:

Lady Hale:

> Why then is the present law incompatible? Not because it contains a general prohibition on assisting or encouraging suicide, but because it fails to admit of any exceptions. … The most important [distinction in our law] is between the positive and the negative, between killing and letting die, between taking active steps to end a patient's life, even though this is what the patient herself earnestly desires, and withholding or withdrawing life-sustaining medical treatment or intervention to which a patient refuses her consent (whether at the time or in advance). While this distinction may make sense to us, it must often make little sense, especially to those who suffer the cruel fate of paralysis: those who can breathe without artificial help are denied a choice which those who cannot do so may make, should they wish to do so. For some of the people looking after them, it will be a mystery why they must switch off the machine or withdraw artificial nutrition and hydration if this is what the patient wants, but they may not painlessly administer a lethal dose of medication which the patient wants just as much.

However, it was held by a five to four majority that the Supreme Court did have jurisdiction to make a future declaration of incompatibility in the absence of a parliamentary review of the law.

Lord Neuberger:

> … the arguments raised by the Secretary of State do not justify this Court ruling out the possibility that it could make a declaration of incompatibility in relation to section 2. The interference with Applicants' article 8 rights is grave, the arguments in favour of the current law are by no means overwhelming, the present official attitude to assisted suicide seems in practice to come close to tolerating it in certain situations, the appeal raises issues similar to those which the courts have determined under the common law, the rational connection between the aim and effect of section 2 is fairly weak, and no compelling reason has been made out for the court simply ceding any jurisdiction to Parliament.

2. *Whether the DPP's guidelines, by recommending flexibility in prosecutorial policy, should be taken into account in determining whether s2(1) was lawful.* Various views were expressed by the justices here. It was noted that 215 people had travelled from England to Switzerland to commit suicide and no prosecutions had taken place. The majority held, however, that if s2(1) is disproportionate to the need to protect the vulnerable, it cannot be rendered compatible by a discretionary, practical policy.

3. *Whether the guidelines required clarification in respect of healthcare professionals.*

Lord Sumption:

> The most that the Director can reasonably be expected to do in the face of such a complex process of evaluative judgment is to identify the main factors that will be relevant. It is neither possible nor proper for him to attempt a precise statement in advance of the facts about when a professional will or will not be prosecuted. Either such a statement will have to be so general and qualified as to be of limited value for predictive purposes, or else it is liable to tie the Director's hands in a way that would in practice amount to a dispensation from the law.

The Supreme Court unanimously reversed the Court of Appeal's decision to order the DPP to amend the guidelines concerning healthcare professionals. The purpose of the policy was not to inform prospective offenders how to escape prosecution. However, clarification of the guidelines on healthcare workers was made by amendment in October 2014. A prosecution is now more likely to be required if the victim 'is in the care' of a medical professional. The question of whether the unqualified ban on euthanasia is lawful now awaits a further Supreme Court decision.

There is a right to die by omission.

→ CROSS-REFERENCE
See Chapter 9, 9.2.3 for further discussion on *Re A (Children) (Conjoined Twins)*.

A crucial distinction was noted by Lady Hale in *Nicklinson* between the prohibition on assisting a paralysed individual to die by positive act and allowing such a person to die by withdrawing medical treatment. She saw no logic in the distinction. Contrast the cases of Diane Pretty and Tony Nicklinson with *Re B (Consent to Treatment: Capacity)* [2002] 2 All ER 449 where the Family Division of the High Court held that a 43-year-old quadriplegic woman who had been paralysed from the neck down by a burst blood vessel in her neck was mentally competent to decide that she wished to die. She had the same right to personal autonomy as any other person with mental capacity. Non-consensual treatment would constitute an assault and would be an infringement of Article 8.

The legal distinction between these cases is one of acts and omissions, a distinction recognised in *Bland* [1993]. But is there any moral distinction? Why was Diane Pretty's application refused yet Ms. B's allowed? The act/omission distinction was regarded as having no foundation in the case of the conjoined twins (*Re A* [2001]).

Lord Neuberger in *Nicklinson* also doubted the validity of the distinction and considered the issue was one of 'personal autonomy'. You should note that under s25 Mental Capacity Act 2005 an advance decision may be made to refuse life-sustaining treatment by a patient and a doctor will commit no crime by allowing the patient to die naturally.

A recent challenge to the Suicide Act 1961 was brought to the High Court in October 2017 in the case of *Conway v Secretary of State for Justice* [2017] EWHC 2447. Noel Conway argued that the Act, which sets out the relevant law on assisted dying, is incompatible with Article 8 ECHR, which guarantees the right to respect for private and family life. The High Court followed the decision of *Nicklinson*, regarding it as 'institutionally inappropriate' to depart from it. In other words, any decision on a change in the law is for Parliament to make. No declaration of incompatibility would be made. In January 2018, the Court of Appeal gave permission to appeal this ruling.

6.1.4 Under the Queen's Peace

The Queen's Peace extends to anyone in the UK who is thus protected by the law. The protection will not apply to enemy aliens in war time. In addition, English courts have jurisdiction over:

- any homicide committed by a British citizen anywhere in the world under s9 Offences Against the Person Act 1861 and s3 British Nationality Act 1948;

- homicides committed on British ships and aircraft by anyone; and

- homicides by British subjects on foreign ships.

6.1.5 The 'Death Within a Year and a Day' Rule No Longer Applies

This requirement no longer applies to deaths occurring after 17 June 1996 having been abolished by the Law Reform (Year and a Day Rule) Act 1996. There is no time limit on prosecutions for murder except that the permission of the Attorney-General is required for prosecutions for murder, manslaughter, infanticide or assisting suicide after three years of death. The Year and a Day rule was abolished because advances in technology allow people with brain damage to be kept alive for prolonged periods of time.

SECTION SUMMARY

- Homicide consists of murder and manslaughter.
- The AR of both is the same: the unlawful killing of a human being under the Queen's Peace.
- The AR raises questions concerning the sanctity of life: when does life begin or end?
- A person is not in being until born with an independent circulation.
- A person who has been clinically diagnosed as having no quality of life may be allowed to die by a medical practitioner through discontinuance of life-support treatment. This is an omission and not a breach of a duty of care.
- Positive acts of assisted death are currently unlawful.

6.2 Mens Rea

6.2.1 Background: Malice Aforethought

6.2.2 Criticisms of Intention

6.2.3 Intention to Commit GBH/Serious Harm

6.2.1 Background: Malice Aforethought

If you look at the historic common law definition of murder by LCJ Coke at 6.1, you will see that MR is described as 'malice aforethought'. This term distinguished murder from involuntary manslaughter. But in no sense was the term ever an accurate definition of the MR for murder which, over the years, was narrowed by the courts to mean not malice but intention. Malice was said to be 'a mere arbitrary symbol … for the "malice" may have in it nothing really malicious; and need never be really "aforethought"' (C.S Kenny, *Outlines of the Criminal Law*, Cambridge University Press, at p 158).

Lord Mustill in *AG's Reference (No 3 of 1994)* said the following of the definition of murder:

Murder is widely thought to be the gravest of crimes. One could expect a developed system to embody a law of murder clear enough to yield an unequivocal result on a given set of facts, a result which conforms with apparent justice and has a sound intellectual base. This is not so in England, where the law of homicide is permeated by anomaly, fiction, misnomer and obsolete reasoning. One conspicuous anomaly is the rule which identifies the 'malice aforethought' (a doubly misleading expression) required for the crime of murder not only with a conscious intention to kill but also with an intention to cause grievous bodily harm.

Until 1957, malice aforethought for murder was defined as either express, implied or constructive:

→ CROSS-REFERENCE
Mens rea (MR) is
explored in detail in
Chapter 3.

- An intention to kill (express malice).

- An intention to commit GBH (implied malice).

- Knowledge that death or GBH would probably be caused: in other words, recklessness (implied malice).

- Killing in the course of a felony (constructive malice). This was abolished by s1 Homicide Act 1957.

- An intention to oppose by force any officer of justice in the execution of his duty.

Malice aforethought was a vague and potentially wide definition of the MR for murder. It was strongly disapproved of by the House of Lords in *Moloney* [1985] AC 905 which held that MR was defined as *intention* to kill or cause GBH, whether direct (purpose) or oblique (foresight of a moral/virtual certainty). (Remember the *Nedrick/Woollin* test for oblique intent is now one of foresight of a virtual certainty of death/GBH.) See Diagram 6.3 for a summary.

6.2.2 Criticisms of Intention

Despite such high-level attention, the MR for murder is subject to the criticisms we previously encountered in Chapter 3:

- The *Nedrick/Woollin* test is not a rule of law because the jury *may* find intention but does not have to do so.

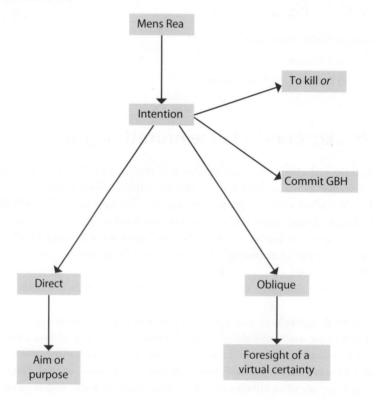

Diagram 6.3
Murder: mens rea

■ The *Nedrick/Woollin* test is over-inclusive because it extends the scope of intention beyond its ordinary meaning of 'purpose'.

■ On the other hand, it is under-inclusive because the exclusion of recklessness would acquit the terrorist who kills following an unsuccessful warning and who did not foresee death/GBH as a virtual certainty.

6.2.3 Intention to Commit GBH/Serious Harm

This aspect of the MR for murder is also controversial. The criticism is that it makes murder a constructive crime—one where MR of a lesser crime (GBH) constitutes liability for a more serious one (murder). The 'GBH rule' was confirmed as a form of malice aforethought in the next case:

R v Vickers [1957] 2 ALL ER 741 COURT OF APPEAL

D broke into a shop in order to steal knowing that a 72-year-old woman was living over the shop. He thought he would not be disturbed because she was deaf. She came downstairs and approached D who was hiding. He struck her many times and kicked her in the face. She died from her injuries. Medical evidence indicated that a moderate degree of violence had been used. D was convicted of murder.

Lord Goddard LCJ held that malice aforethought consisted of either an intention to kill or an intention to cause GBH, even in the absence of knowledge or belief that life would be endangered. This was, in fact, different from what he had said to the Royal Commission on Capital Punishment in 1953 which was that a person must *know* that life is being endangered. It also went beyond the intention of Parliament when passing the Homicide Act 1957: that D must realise his conduct might cause death.

The rule was nevertheless confirmed by the next case:

R v Cunningham [1981] 2 ALL ER 863 HOUSE OF LORDS

The appellant attacked V in a pub with a chair. He was motivated by jealousy and killed V by breaking his skull. The judge directed the jury to find the appellant guilty of murder if he intended to cause really serious harm. The Court of Appeal dismissed the appeal and the appellant appealed to the House of Lords.

It was held that the GBH rule constituted an historic form of malice aforethought. The rule was not a form of constructive malice and it was therefore not abolished in 1957.

The meaning of GBH

The House of Lords in *Smith* said that the term GBH is to be given its natural meaning: 'bodily harm' needs no explanation and 'grievous' means really serious. Since the House of Lords decisions in *Ireland/Burstow* [1997] UKHL 34 'bodily' harm has been extended to psychiatric injury. But the harm need not be so serious as to be life-threatening. Thus, one can be convicted of murder even though one has not even foreseen or contemplated death. Lord Mustill in *AG's Reference (No 3 of 1994)* observed:

It is, therefore, possible to commit a murder not only without wishing the death of V but without the least thought that this might be the result of the assault. Many would doubt the justice of this rule, which is not the popular conception of murder and (as I shall suggest) no longer rests on any intellectual foundation. The law of Scotland does very well without it, and England could perhaps do the same.

> **?!   THINKING POINT 6.3**
>
> Look at the following and decide whether A is guilty of murder:
>
> 1. A punches B intending to break his arm. B falls against a barbed wire fence and incurs a superficial flesh wound to the upper arm. In hospital, B's wound becomes infected. He is resistant to antibiotics and dies some weeks later.
> 2. A jabs a broken glass in B's face intending to do serious harm. B refuses a potentially life-saving blood transfusion and dies.
> 3. A shoots B intending to do serious harm. B receives negligent treatment in hospital and dies two months later.
> 4. A slaps B around the head intending to do slight harm and causing B to become unconscious. In attempting to conceal his crime, A drags B behind a bush, dropping her. B dies from a fractured skull.

Criticisms of the GBH rule

1. GBH is an ambiguous term. In England and Wales it has an unclear meaning and includes harm which is not life-threatening.

2. More fundamentally, the GBH rule contradicts what J. Horder in *Ashworth's Principles of Criminal Law*, OUP, 2016 calls the 'correspondence' and 'subjectivity' principles. Under the correspondence principle, MR should relate to the harm done whilst under the subjectivity principle, MR should be concerned with D's state of mind at the time of the act.

3. On the other hand, it can be argued that whoever chooses to take the risk of endangering life must accept the consequences. D is just as blameworthy as one who intends to kill. Further, there must be at least oblique intention to cause GBH, not recklessness.

Read the following extract from Robert Goff, 'The Mental Element in the Crime of Murder' (1988) 104 *LQR* 30:

'. . . I turn from intention to kill to intention to cause grievous bodily harm . . . The most fundamental objection is that the crime of murder is concerned with unlawful killing of a particularly serious kind; and it seems very strange that a man should be called a murderer even though not only did he not intend to kill V, but he may even have intended that he should not die. There are cases known to occur where D does indeed intend not to kill but only to cause serious injury – as, for example, in the case of terrorists who punish traitors from their ranks by 'knee-capping' them – shooting them in the knee with a gun. This they do with a positive intent not to kill but to leave V maimed, *pour encourager les autres*. If a man so injured were to die in consequence, perhaps because he contracted an infection from his wound, the man who 'knee-capped' him would, in English law, be held to have murdered him, even though he positively intended not to kill him . . .'

Consideration was then given to the Criminal Law Revision Committee's proposal in its 14th Report (1980) to include the GBH rule only where there is a known risk of causing death.

... So what of the case where he only intends to cause a slight injury or indeed no injury at all, but knows that his action involves a risk of causing death? Why should that be any different? For example, a nick in the skin of a haemophiliac could be as dangerous to life as a more serious wound to a normal man . . . .

[In Scots Law] 'when death results from the perpetration of any serious or dangerous crime, murder may have been committed, although the specific intent to kill be absent. This is so where the crime perpetrated involves either wilful intent to do grave personal injury, or the wilful use of dangerous means implying wicked disregard of consequences to life.'

If this approach is right, then both English and Scots law should abandon intention to cause grievous bodily harm or grave personal injury as constituting of itself a sufficient mental element for the crime of murder, if indeed this be Scots law.

?! THINKING POINT 6.4

Where there is no intent to kill but D is charged with murder, would 'wicked disregard' instead of intent to cause GBH be a more satisfactory MR for murder? Can you think of any difficulties with this concept?

6.3 The Sentence for Murder

The mandatory death penalty for murder was abolished by s1(1) Murder (Abolition of Death Penalty) Act 1965. It was abolished for treason and piracy by s36 Crime and Disorder Act 1998 in order to comply with Protocol 6 of the European Convention. The penalty for murder for an offender over the age of 21 is now the mandatory life sentence. Section 269 and Sch 21 Criminal Justice Act 2003 provide a statutory scheme for minimum terms in murder cases. This is divided into three:

- The minimum term imposed by the trial judge, reflecting gravity, which will be served in full.
- A portion reflecting the need for public protection, until the Parole Board considers he is safe for release.
- After release, the offender remains on licence for life and is subject to recall should he re-offend.

The power of the Home Secretary to decide on minimum terms and release dates was removed by the ECtHR decision in *Stafford v UK* (2002) 35 EHRR 1121 and the House of Lords decision in *R (on the application of Anderson) v Secretary of State for the Home Department* [2003] 1 AC 837 on the grounds of lack of impartiality. This followed a decision which went against the Home Secretary for increasing the tariff (now called the minimum sentence) to 15 years for the young 10-year-old killers of the toddler Jamie Bulger on the grounds of unfairness: *R v Secretary of State for the Home Department, ex p Venables* [1998] AC 407.

Read the following extract from D.A. Thomas, 'Form and Function in Criminal Law' in Glazebrook (ed), *Reshaping the Criminal Law*, at pp 21–25 regarding the mandatory life sentence for murder:

The results of maintaining a separation between the development of the substantive criminal law on the one hand and procedure and penal policy on the other is a system of dealing with homicide and grave personal violence which makes no sense at all in functional terms. A man strikes another with a broken glass in a public-house fight in circumstances which would normally lead to a sentence of three or four years' imprisonment for causing grievous bodily harm with intent; fortuitously V dies from his injuries, and unless either the prosecution or jury will relax the law the assailant is convicted of murder and subject to a mandatory sentence of life imprisonment. In another case D makes a determined attempt to kill his victim, using carefully contrived means based on thoughtful preparations; despite his best endeavours his plans miscarry and he is convicted of attempted murder; his sentence is absolutely within the discretion of the sentencing judge . . .

Other examples abound. The present definition of murder (whatever its precise terms may be) is clearly not a satisfactory basis for selecting offenders for a unique variety of sentencing procedure. In so far as the mandatory life sentence is justified by the special problems of estimating the chances of future violence by those who have killed once, the existence of special defences such as diminished responsibility and provocation, introduced in earlier times for different purposes, undermines the logic of the sentence by excepting from its scope just those offenders who are most likely to prove dangerous for the future. If the justification for the mandatory life sentence is the unique gravity of the offence and the need to emphasise the particular abhorrence of society for the murderer, that justification is at least diluted by the extension of the definition of murder by the felony-murder rule and the recognition of an intention to inflict grievous bodily harm as a sufficient mental state for conviction may have made some sense in the days when the offence was capital, as directing the supposedly unique deterrent effect of the death sentence at the potential offender who was prepared to risk the use of grave violence to achieve his objects. Now that justification has gone, the effect of the extension of the definition of murder beyond intentional killing weakens whatever morally educative force the mandatory life sentence possesses.

> ## ?! THINKING POINT 6.5
>
> Can you think of other arguments for and against retention of the mandatory life sentence?

6.4 Criticism

Murder is the most serious offence in the criminal justice system but is the definition too wide and the sentence too inflexible? The justification for the mandatory life sentence is a moral and social one underscored by the sanctity of life and the finality of death. The life sentence imposes moral and social censure for the gravest of offences. However, the following questions need to be asked:

- Is the murder/manslaughter division in the right place?
- Is the definition of murder too wide in respect of the GBH/serious harm rule? Does it therefore label as murderers those whose crimes do not deserve the strongest form of condemnation?
- On the other hand, is it too narrow so as to exclude some heinous forms of reckless killing, such as those committed by terrorists, which might be thought to be the moral equivalent of murder?
- Should it be possible to commit murder by anything less than direct intention? Is the oblique intention/recklessness boundary too uncertain?
- Is the mandatory life sentence for murder correct? Should not judges be able to pass lower sentences on deserving cases, such as mercy killings and women who kill their abusive partners? The partial defences of diminished responsibility and loss of control exist to mitigate the mandatory life sentence for some of these cases, but these defences are complicated, technical and do not comprehensively cover all deserving cases as we shall see.

→ CROSS-REFERENCE
See Chapter 7 for further discussion on partial defences to murder.

As you will appreciate, the arguments regarding the reform of murder are inextricably inter-twined with criticisms of intention and the partial defences to murder. This has led the Law Commission (Law Commission Consultation Document No 177 (2005) 'A New Homicide Act for England and Wales?' para 1.4) to recently observe that:

> The law governing homicide in England and Wales is a rickety structure set upon shaky foundations. Some of its rules have been unaltered since the seventeenth century, even though it has long been acknowledged that they are in dire need of reform. Other rules are of uncertain content or have been constantly changed, so that the law cannot be stated with certainty or clarity.

On the other hand, it has been argued that murder should be abolished not reformed. Sir Louis Blom-Cooper and Professor Terence Morris in *With Malice Aforethought: A Study of the Crime and Punishment for Homicide* (2004) argue that there should be a single offence of criminal homicide. Excuse or justification for the killing providing loss of control, diminished respon-sibility and other mitigating factors should be reflected in sentencing not through a series of complicated defences, partial and otherwise.

6.5 Reform

Reform of murder and the mandatory sentence has been considered many times. Here are the most recent:

(1) Law Commission, Draft Criminal Code, clause 54(1): 'A person is guilty of murder if he causes the death of another (a) intending to cause death, or (b) intending to cause serious personal harm and being aware that he may cause death.'

(2) Law Commission report on the Partial Defences to Murder (2004), Consultation Docu-ment LCCP No 177 'A New Homicide Act for England and Wales?' (2005) and final report No 304 on 'Murder, Manslaughter and Infanticide' (2006). In the latter, the Law Commission recommend that there should be a new Homicide Act for England and Wales. A ladder of offences was proposed:

- *First degree murder:* intentional killings and killings with the intent to do serious in-jury where the killer was aware that his or her conduct involved a serious risk of caus-ing death. Mandatory life sentence. This is a crime of specific intent.

- *Second degree murder:* 1) killings intended to cause *serious* injury (even without an awareness of a serious risk of causing death); or 2) killings intended to cause injury or fear or risk of injury where the killer was aware that his or her conduct involved a serious risk of causing death; or 3) killings intended to kill or to cause serious injury where the killer was aware that his or her conduct involved a serious risk of causing death but successfully pleads loss of control, diminished responsibility or that he or she killed pursuant to a suicide pact. Maximum life sentence. This is a crime of specific intent.

- Killing through simple recklessness remains manslaughter.

Read the following extracts from 'The Structure of Criminal Homicide' by William Wilson [2006] *Crim LR* 471 for a critique of earlier Law Commission proposals preceding the final report:

First degree murder

The Law Commission takes the uncomplicated view that the moral basis of the crime of murder—the sanctity of life ideal—renders intentional killing specially heinous, worthy of being accorded a separate offence label and the symbolic mandatory sentence. There are reasons for limiting first degree murder to intentional killings, other than the evident desire to sidestep the mandatory sentence. Limiting first degree murder to cases of intentional killing will better align the law of murder with that of attempted murder, whose fault element is an intention to kill. It will also enable sentencing discretion for accomplices to murder, who are presently sentenced as if they were the killers themselves.

I am not convinced, however, that, mandatory sentence aside, this would or should form any part of the reform package and I am not sure the Law Commission is either. For a start, it is dependent upon the existence of a fully worked-out system of defences to ensure that no partly or fully-justified or excusable killings remain subject to the penalty. The consultation paper understandably does not seek to deliver such a system, but its absence destabilises the proposed grading structure. More generally, as is well understood, there is nothing in the concept of an intentional killing which makes it morally worse than a reckless killing. An intentional killing is simply a different wrong from a reckless killing … Some reckless killings attract far more revulsion and indignation than some intentional killings …

Second degree murder

… The key task, for purposes of consistent (if not necessarily fair) labelling is to cut up the murder/manslaughter cake in a way which renders the two wrongs meaningfully distinct and makes it clear exactly how citizens must behave to avoid the relevant prohibition. I take the uncomplicated view, as the Criminal Law Commissioner has elsewhere argued, that those who intentionally attack others are morally responsible for and so fully legally accountable for the consequences of so doing whether or not such consequences were foreseen so long as these consequences are not out of proportion to the nature of the attack launched.

What is clearly crucial, however, is that serious injury is defined with sufficient precision for this purpose. The Commission's current working definition—that harm is not to be regarded as serious unless it is 'of such a nature as to endanger life, or to cause or to be likely to cause, permanent or long term damage to a significant aspect of physical integrity or mental functioning' is, in this respect, not yet adequate for the task. In its own terms, it would render jury directions particularly difficult to follow. …'

The Law Commission's recommendations on degrees of murder were not implemented; however its recommendations on the partial defences to murder were largely incorporated into the Coroners and Justice Act 2009.

SUMMARY

Homicide consists of murder and manslaughter:

- AR of homicide: the unlawful killing of a reasonable person in being under the Queen's Peace.
- MR of murder: intention to kill or cause GBH. MR of manslaughter: recklessness, gross negligence or an intended unlawful act.
- Intention can be direct or oblique.
- GBH means very serious bodily (or possibly psychiatric) harm.
- Note the criticisms of the 'GBH Rule' and the width of murder.
- Murder is a constructive crime: the MR of a lesser crime (GBH) satisfies liability for a more serious one (murder).
- The sentence for murder is the mandatory life sentence whilst for manslaughter sentence is discretionary.

PROBLEM SOLVING

D punches his girlfriend V in the stomach very hard intending to injure her. She is 24 weeks pregnant. V falls and is knocked unconscious when her head hits a marble fireplace. D takes her to hospital. V undergoes a Caesarian section. Her child (B) is born alive but grossly premature. V is paralysed from the neck down. After three months, B dies from a chest infection. V no longer wishes to live and asks her doctor (M) to let her die. M agrees and terminates life support, V dies one month later.

Have D or M committed any criminal offences?

Remember:

- **I: Identify** relevant issues
- **D: Define** offences/defences
- **E: Explain/evaluate** the law
- **A: Apply** law to facts.

See the online resources for further guidance on solving this problem: www.oup.com/uk/loveless5e/.

FURTHER READING

A. Ashworth, 'Principles, Pragmatism and the Law Commission's Recommendations on Homicide Law Reform' [2007] *Crim LR* **333**

A commentary on the Law Commission's 1996 recommendations, including those for degrees of murder classification.

A. Clough, 'Mercy Killing: Three's a Crowd' (2015) 79(5) *JCL* **358**

Discusses whether mercy killing should be included in the defences of loss of control or diminished responsibility.

J. Goss, 'A Postscript to the Trial of Dr. David Moor' [2000] *Crim LR* **568**

Discusses the problems arising from the prosecution of a doctor for murder following the injection of drugs to relieve pain.

M. Hirst, 'Assisted Suicide after Purdy: The Unresolved Issue' [2009] *Crim LR* **87**

Discusses whether the aiding and abetting of a suicide to take place abroad would be a criminal offence.

H. Keating and J. Bridgeman, 'Compassionate Killings: The Case for a Partial Defence' (2012) 75(5) *MLR* **69**

An article proposing a defence of compassionate killing. It asks why there are defences of fear and anger and not one for compassionate killing.

S. Ost, 'Euthanasia & the Defence of Necessity: Advocating a More Appropriate Legal Response' [2006] *Crim LR* **355**

Analyses the doctrine of double effect, diminsihed responsibility and necessity in the context of euthanasia.

N. Papadopoulou, 'From Pretty to Nicklinson: Changing Judicial Attitudes to Assisted Dying' (2017) 3 EHRLR 298–307

Discusses whether judicial attitudes on this area of law are taking account of how, and whether, the law ought to change.

7 Homicide 2: voluntary and involuntary manslaughter

Introduction

7.1 Voluntary Manslaughter

7.2 Involuntary Manslaughter: Unintentional Killings

7.3 Homicide-related Offences

KEY POINTS

This chapter will help you to identify the AR/MR elements of:

- *Voluntary manslaughter:* intentional killings which would otherwise be murder may be reduced to voluntary manslaughter where D succeeds in establishing any of the following partial defences:
  - diminished responsibility; or
  - loss of control; or
  - suicide pact;
- *Involuntary manslaughter* by recklessness, gross negligence, or by unlawful and dangerous act.

INTRODUCTION

The dividing line between murder and manslaughter is the boundary between a mandatory life sentence and a discretionary sentence up to and including life imprisonment. The vast range of discretionary sentencing possible in manslaughter reflects the many types of manslaughter which exist, and the endlessly varied circumstances in which they may be committed.

Manslaughter takes two broad forms: voluntary and involuntary. For voluntary manslaughter, D must have the AR and MR of murder but also a partial defence. These defences are now all statutory, and their definitions are partly the outcome of vigorous debates around who should or should not benefit from a partial excuse for killing. Most recently, the partial defences were reformed by the Coroners & Justice Act 2009, but those changes have themselves led to further debate.

Involuntary manslaughter requires the same AR as murder/voluntary manslaughter, but some lesser form of MR. We have already encountered two forms of MR for manslaughter—recklessness and gross negligence. In addition, D may commit unlawful act manslaughter when he kills V in the course of committing some other crime. Thus D can be guilty of one of the most serious offences, manslaughter, despite having a lower level of MR than that required for many less serious crimes.

7.1 Voluntary Manslaughter

7.1.1 Introduction to Voluntary Manslaughter

Intentional killings which would otherwise be murder can be reduced to voluntary manslaughter where D succeeds with any of the three partial defences to murder: diminished responsibility, loss of control or suicide pact (see Diagram 7.1 for a summary). These partial defences are unique to murder. As we have seen, a life sentence is mandatory following a murder conviction and cannot be reduced to reflect even overwhelming mitigation due to the circumstances or D's mental capacity. The partial defences, by substituting a voluntary manslaughter conviction in place of murder, enable the judge to exercise discretion to achieve a sentencing outcome which reflects the crime and does justice to the individual. The sentencing options range from a discretionary life sentence in the most culpable cases to shorter periods of imprisonment, community sentences, or an absolute discharge. In cases of diminished responsibility, less culpable killings can also be dealt with by restriction and hospital orders.

The Coroners and Justice Act 2009 (C&JA 2009) reformed diminished responsibility and introduced a new partial defence of loss of control, replacing the former defence of provocation. The 2009 Act was the culmination of three Law Commission reports and much dissatisfaction with the partial defences to murder. The reforms represent a narrowing of the previous defences and are likely to result in more defendants being convicted of murder rather than voluntary manslaughter. We will examine the extent to which the new law represents an improvement on the old in the relevant sections which follow. An outline of suicide pact is included for information only.

➔ **CROSS-REFERENCE**
For further discussion of the Law Commission reports see 7.1.2 'Conclusion'.

7.1.2 Diminished Responsibility

KEY CASES

Byrne [1960] 2 QB 396—Diminished responsibility includes defects of *will*;

Ahluwahlia [1992] 4 All ER 889—Diminished responsibility includes the psychological effect of domestic violence;

Dietschmann [2003] UKHL 10—sets the test for both an abnormality and intoxication;

Stewart (James) [2009] EWCA Crim 593—alcoholism short of brain damage if not voluntary may amount to an abnormality;

Dowds [2012] EWCA Crim 281—voluntary acute intoxication alone is not sufficient;

Foye [2013] EWCA Crim 475—diminished responsibility includes psychopathic personality disorder;

Golds [2016] UKSC 61—'substantial' impairment must be significant;

Brennan [2014] EWCA Crim 2387—uncontested expert evidence should be followed.

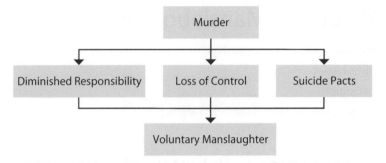

Diagram 7.1
Voluntary manslaughter

Introduction: Why do we need this partial defence?

Diminished responsibility is a relatively new statutory defence, unlike loss of control/provocation, the origins of which could be traced back to the twelfth century. It came about as a result of public opposition in the 1950s to the use of capital punishment for murder and also as a result of increasing awareness of the problems of mental illness. Capital punishment was used relatively rarely and most convicted murderers were sentenced to life imprisonment. However, one hanging in the 1950s was particularly controversial. In 1953, Derek Bentley (*R v Craig & Bentley* (1952) *The Times*, 10–13 December) took part in the murder of a police officer, PC Sidney Miles. Bentley was aged 19, suffered from epilepsy, and had a mental age of 11. The trial and his hanging were conducted speedily. But the evidence of his MR continued to be questioned and in 1998 his conviction was quashed and he received a full posthumous pardon. This case undoubtedly fuelled public concern regarding capital punishment.

The Royal Commission on Capital Punishment was established in 1949–53. It reported that the greatest defect with the law of murder, given that it can be committed in such widely different circumstances, was the single punishment. To mitigate such severity, diminished responsibility was proposed, which might cover mental deficiency falling short of insanity where the accused was still fit to plead but not wholly responsible at the time of the offence. However, public concerns regarding capital punishment were not addressed until introduction of the partial defences to murder by the Homicide Act 1957. Diminished responsibility originally consisted of a two-part test: there had to be proof of an abnormality of mind and substantial impairment of mental responsibility for the killing. As you will see, this has now become a four-part test. We will examine each component in turn.

Definition of diminished responsibility

Section 2 Homicide Act 1957 (HA 1957) (as amended by s52 Coroners and Justice Act 1999 (C&JA 2009)):

(1) A person ('D') who kills or is a party to the killing of another is not to be convicted of murder if D was suffering from an abnormality of mental functioning which –

    (a) arose from a recognised medical condition,

    (b) substantially impaired D's ability to do one or more of the things mentioned in subsection (1A), and

    (c) provides an explanation for D's acts and omissions in doing or being a party to the killing.

(1A)   Those things are –

    (a)   to understand the nature of D's conduct;

    (b)   to form a rational judgment;

    (c)   to exercise self-control.

(1B)   For the purposes of subsection (1)(c), an abnormality of mental functioning provides an explanation for D's conduct if it causes, or is a significant contributory factor in causing, D to carry out that conduct.

    (1)   On a charge of murder, it shall be for the defence to prove that the person charged is by virtue of this section not liable to be convicted of murder.

    (2)   A person who but for this section would be liable, whether as principal or as accessory, to be convicted of murder shall be liable instead to be convicted of manslaughter.

There are therefore four requirements which the defendant must prove (see Diagram 7.2):

◼ an abnormality of mental functioning;

◼ which arose from a recognised medical condition;

◼ which substantially impaired D's ability to understand his/her conduct, form a rational judgment or exercise self-control;

◼ which provides an explanation for D's killing in the sense of being a cause or contributory factor.

1. Abnormality of mental functioning: s2(1)

The previous law referred to an 'abnormality of mind'. This term was vague and problematic. Psychiatrists had to testify to the presence of a mental state the formulation of which was not linked to a medical definition of mental illness. It was not a psychiatric term and this had been

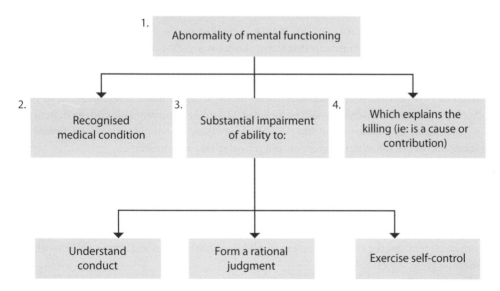

Diagram 7.2
Diminished responsibility

a profound cause of criticism of the defence. In addition, the abnormality of mind had to arise from four specified causes: arrested or retarded development, any inherent cause, disease or injury. These categories were interpreted very widely in practice, from the unendurable anguish of a relative committing a mercy killing to the most serious mental disorders suffered by defendants committing horrific murders. But in theory, they imposed limits upon the sort of abnormality of mind that would satisfy the defence.

The rationale of the C&JA 2009 reform was to confine the defence within narrower limits more closely related to medical conditions and to clarify the requirement of 'substantial impairment' of mental ability. Two recent cases, *Golds* and *Brennan* (see '3. Which substantially impaired D's ability to: understand his/her conduct; form a rational judgment; or exercise self-control', later in this section), confirm that all four parts of the test are now dependent on medical evidence and that a serious degree of mental impairment will be required to satisfy the defence. Therefore, some defendants previously able to use the defence may now be excluded, for example: mercy killers suffering temporary mental disturbance or children under 18 suffering 'developmental immaturity'. The latter concept was left out of the new reform. The term 'abnormality of mental functioning' is not intended to represent a change of substance to the previous requirement of an 'abnormality of mind' but it implies an emphasis on the mental processes spelt out in s2(1). However, it must arise from a recognised medical condition, to which we now turn.

2. Recognised medical condition (s2(1)(a))

D will need to produce psychiatric evidence of an abnormality of mental functioning arising from a recognised medical condition, but the court does not necessarily have to accept it if there is other evidence of substance which conflicts with and outweighs it. There is no requirement that any recognised medical condition should be confined to mental disorder. The term will include recognised physical, psychiatric and psychological conditions. Some of these require explanation.

Medically classified mental disorders

Current classificatory systems consist of those compiled by the World Health Organization (ICD-10 (2007)) and the American Psychiatric Association (DSM-5 (2013)). Therefore, schizophrenia, psychosis, psychopathy, organic brain disorder, endogenous depression, serious neurotic conditions and emotional disorders, for example, will clearly be covered. A recent example would be *Foye* [2013] EWCA Crim 475 where the CA accepted that a severe dissocial or psychopathic personality disorder would be included. D, who had murdered his girlfriend, went on to murder another prisoner in a deliberate and planned way. The disorder was characterised by callous unconcern for others, aggression and refusal to take responsibility.

Reactive conditions (ie: those brought on by circumstances) such as depression and anxiety were already recognised under the previous concept of 'abnormality of mind' and are likely to be included in the new test. In *Seers* (1984) 79 Cr App R 261, for example, a chronic reactive depression suffered by a man who had killed his wife, was included. Other recognised medical conditions include Autistic Spectrum Disorders (*Conroy* [2017] EWCA Crim 81). It was, however, and it remains, the case that the sort of mild emotional stresses and strains of life to which we are all prone are excluded.

The case of *Byrne* considerably extended the scope of the previous defence by including defects of will. Such conditions may continue to be relevant under the new law provided they can be medically classified.

Defect of will

R v Byrne [1960] 2 QB 396 COURT OF CRIMINAL APPEAL

The appellant had been sentenced to life imprisonment for strangling a young woman in a YMCA hostel whom he had then horrifically mutilated. The conclusion of three doctors called by the defence was that D was a sexual psychopath suffering from an abnormality of mind which arose from a condition of arrested or retarded development of mind or inherent causes. Further, he found it difficult or impossible to control his perverted sexual desires. The doctors found that he was not legally insane but his sexual psychopathy could be described as partial insanity. In the Court of Appeal, Lord Parker put forward a definition of the term 'abnormality of mind' which served as a precedent under the previous law:

'Abnormality of mind', which has to be contrasted with the time honoured expression in the M'Naghten Rules, 'defect of reason', means a state of mind so different from that of ordinary human beings that the reasonable man would term it abnormal. It appears to us to be wide enough to cover the mind's activities in all its aspects, not only the perception of physical acts and matters and the ability to form a rational judgment whether an act is right or wrong, but also the ability to exercise will-power to control physical acts in accordance with that rational judgement.

 NOTE 7.1

1. The question of whether or not the defence succeeded was to be determined by the jury on the basis of all the evidence. This remains the case. The continuing validity of *Byrne* was preserved by *Bunch* [2013] EWCA Crim 2498 which held that medical evidence was a 'practical necessity' given that the onus in proving the defence was on D.

   Brennan (see '3. Which substantially impaired D's ability to: understand his/her conduct; form a rational judgment; or exercise self-control' later in this section) acknowledges that the psychiatric expert may express an opinion, not simply on matters within their medical expertise, but also as to whether or not the defence should succeed. The jury, however, must weigh up all relevant evidence such as the facts, medical reports, statements and demeanour of the accused. They are not bound to accept the medical evidence.

2. The difference between 'he did not resist the impulse to kill' and 'he could not resist it' was incapable of scientific proof and should be decided by the jury on the basis of common sense. This will remain the case.

Psychological injury

This was one of the specified causes of diminished responsibility under the previous law. Decided cases may continue to be relevant. An abnormality of mind was held to include psychiatric or psychological conditions which were the result of organic or physical injury. But the Northern Irish case of *McQuade* [2005] NICA 2 said that injury included the psychological, as opposed to physical, injury arising from sexual abuse because what was crucial was the degree of abnormality and the effect on the individual's mental capacity rather than the type or cause of injury. Exceptionally, pre-menstrual tension has been included (*Reynolds* (1988) 23 April) where after hearing psychiatric evidence of pre-menstrual tension and postnatal depression, the Crown

Court acquitted Anne Reynolds of killing her mother and substituted a verdict of manslaughter. (See S. Edwards, 'Mad, bad or pre-menstrual?' *NLJ*, 1 July 1988.) Battered woman syndrome (BWS) was also included, which might be thought to be a reactive 'dissociative' condition, but which was recognised in the next case as a disease.

Battered Woman Syndrome (BWS)

R v Ahluwalia [1992] 4 ALL ER 889 COURT OF APPEAL

D had been married for ten years to a man who was frequently violent towards her. On the night in question she threw petrol in his bedroom and set it alight. He died from severe burns six days later. No medical evidence was presented at her trial. At her appeal following a murder conviction the court was invited to consider the defence of provocation. However, the Court of Appeal considered that she might have had the defence of diminished responsibility because fresh medical evidence suggested that she was suffering from 'a major depressive disorder at the material time'. A retrial was therefore ordered and her conviction for murder was reduced to manslaughter on the grounds of diminished responsibility.

The case of *Hobson* [1997] EWCA Crim 1317 confirmed that BWS, having been included in the American DSM 4th edn in 1994, was a form of diminished responsibility. However, DR was not unambiguously helpful to abused women: if you look at the pre-reform victim statistics on cases of diminished responsibility (see 'Context' later) you will see that most were female. This generated the criticism that the law was being exploited by men who killed out of jealousy or anger rather than any abnormality, and who were therefore punishing a partner or former partner. This was one of the reasons for the reform.

➜ CROSS-REFERENCE
The part of the judgment dealing with provocation is considered in 7.1.3.

➜ CROSS-REFERENCE
The plight of battered women who kill is further considered in 7.1.3.

Intoxication

a. Alcoholism (alcohol dependency syndrome)

As we shall see, intoxication is not a defence to most crimes but may be a partial defence to crimes of intention, such as murder, provided D lacks MR (see Chapter 8). These are known as crimes of specific/ulterior intent. To what extent might intoxication also provide the defence of diminished responsibility?

Intoxication alone will not be regarded as a recognised medical condition unless it has resulted in alcohol dependency syndrome (alcoholism) or brain damage and is involuntary. The case of *Tandy* [1988] 87 Cr App R 45 was the first to hold that where the drinking is involuntary or the craving is irresistible the defence might apply: Mrs Tandy had killed her 11-year-old daughter shortly after the daughter's revelation that she was being sexually abused. She had suspected the abuser to be her husband, the child's step-father. She was alcoholic and on the day in question consumed almost one bottle of vodka. Her appeal against conviction failed because the intoxication would need to be involuntary so that she could not resist the impulse to drink. The first drink of the day would need to be irresistible.

The question of mixed voluntary and involuntary intoxication was then considered in two cases. It was held in *Wood* [2008] EWCA Crim 1305 that alcoholism (alcohol dependency syndrome) short of brain damage could give rise to the defence depending on the extent and nature of the illness, although *voluntary* intoxication could never do so. Sir Igor Judge P explained:

> Dealing with the point very broadly, the consumption of alcohol before a defendant acts with murderous intent and kills cannot, without more, bring his actions within the concept of diminished responsibility.

On its own, voluntary intoxication falls outside the ambit of the defence . . . [T]he jury should focus exclusively on the effect of alcohol consumed by the defendant as a direct result of his illness or disease and ignore the effect of any alcohol consumed voluntarily.

Tandy and *Wood* were regarded as being too rigid by the next case, *Stewart*, because the distinction between voluntary and involuntary intoxication was not always clear:

R v Stewart (James) [2009] EWCA CRIM 593

The appellant, who suffered from alcohol dependency syndrome, and the deceased, were sleeping rough in the area of Marble Arch in London. Both men and others had been drinking heavily, and were all severely intoxicated. Minor trouble developed in the early evening during which the deceased struck the appellant, causing a laceration across his nose and bleeding under his eye. Much later that night the appellant attacked the deceased with extreme violence causing fatal injuries. There were numerous blunt force impacts as well as injuries to the deceased's head and neck caused by a sharp jagged object, probably glass. His body was found slumped in some flower beds in the early hours. The cause of death was brain damage and blood loss. The appellant had been drinking for about 10 days continuously and had drunk particularly heavily on the day of the attack which was his birthday.

Lord Judge LCJ:

> Whether or not brain damage is discernible, alcohol dependency syndrome is a disease (ICD10) or disorder of the mind (DSM-IV-TR). It is not excluded from the operation of section 2 of the Homicide Act 1957. If the defence of diminished responsibility is to operate according to its statutory structure, the law must take account of advances in medical knowledge. Nevertheless, when the issue arises, it must be addressed in the context of a further principle, that the voluntary consumption of alcohol, and the defendant's voluntary intoxication, does not provide a defence to murder, although it may, in an extreme case, bear on the question of the defendant's intent (*R v Sheehan and Moore* [1974] 60 CAR 208]. These principles have to be reconciled . . . .
>
> With these considerations in mind we have re-examined paragraph 41 of the judgment in *Wood*, and in particular the sentence which reads ' . . . the jury should focus exclusively on the effect of alcohol consumed by the defendant as a direct result of his illness or disease and ignore the effect of any alcohol consumed voluntarily'. Taken with the references to 'voluntary' drinking later in this paragraph, we accept that the clause, ' . . . and ignore the effect of any alcohol consumed voluntarily' may appear to require the jury to 'separate out' (to use Mr Richardson's words) each and every drink consumed by the defendant and decide whether it was taken voluntary or involuntarily. As he argues, that would be unrealistic, when, at some levels of severity what may appear to be 'voluntary' drinking may be inseparable from the defendant's underlying syndrome . . . . '

The Court of Appeal set out new guidelines for diminished responsibility and alcohol dependency syndrome which might also include some episodes of voluntary intoxication:

(1) Was D suffering from an abnormality of mind? (Remember: the relevant term now is 'abnormality of mental functioning'.) The nature and extent of the syndrome would need to be considered as well as whether the drinking before the killing was the involuntary result of an irresistible craving.

(2) Was the abnormality caused by disease or illness?

(3) Was D's mental responsibility substantially impaired? (Remember: the relevant requirement is now for substantial impairment of ability to do any of the three things in s2(1A) 1957 Act.) This would involve consideration of the distinction between a failure to resist the impulse to drink and inability to do so.

The decision will be one for the jury on the basis of all the evidence, especially the drinking on the days leading up to the killing and on the day of the killing itself, taking into account whether D was able to make sensible and rational decisions on everyday matters at the relevant time. However, in the absence of such a condition, mere drunkenness alone, even if extreme, will be excluded from the defence, as the first appeal under the amended Act confirmed:

R v Dowds [2012] EWCA Crim 281

D, a 49-year-old college lecturer, and his girlfriend were habitual heavy binge drinkers. The relationship was violent. On the night of her death they had bought and consumed a 1 litre bottle of vodka at 5 pm and another at 10 pm. Shortly afterwards, he stabbed her to death 60 times. He had no recollection of the killing but did not dispute responsibility. He pleaded diminished responsibility on the grounds that voluntary acute intoxication was a 'recognised medical condition' under s2(1)(a) Homicide Act 1957 as amended. He was not an alcoholic or dependent on alcohol.

Hughes LJ:

It was established in 1975 in R v Fenton (1975) 61 Cr App R 261 that the effect on the mind of voluntary intoxication could not give rise to diminished responsibility . . . The law as explained in Fenton was never significantly questioned. It was in due course endorsed by the House of Lords in R v Dietschmann [2003] UKHL 10; [2003] 1 AC 1209 . . . This court's judgment in Wood [2008] EWCA Crim 1305 usefully explains what is very clearly the case. The axiomatic rule that simple voluntary drunkenness, without more, cannot found diminished responsibility is not a rule special to the partial defence. It is but one example of the general approach of English criminal law to voluntary drunkenness . . . The World Health Organization ('WHO') has for many years sponsored the publication of an International Statistical Classification of Diseases and Related Health Problems ('ICD') of which the current edition is ICD-10. As its full title suggests, it is a general classification of the whole range of medical conditions and health problems; it is in no sense limited to diseases or conditions of the mind . . . The American Medical Association has for many years sponsored a similar classification under the title 'Diagnostic and Statistical Manual' ('DSM'). That part of it which relates to conditions of the mind is now known as DSM-IV, published under the auspices of the American Psychiatric Association. It is a very substantial volume. Like ICD-10, and as its title makes clear, it is a tool for clinical diagnosis and for statistical analysis. Its introduction begins with a statement of its priority aim 'to provide a helpful guide to clinical practice,' and refers also to the goal of improving communications between clinicians and researchers and to its usefulness in the collection of clinical information . . . . It is enough to say that it is quite clear that the re-formulation of the statutory conditions for diminished responsibility was not intended to reverse the well established rule that voluntary acute intoxication is not capable of being relied upon to found diminished responsibility. That remains the law. The presence of a 'recognised medical condition' is a necessary, but not always a sufficient, condition to raise the issue of diminished responsibility.

 NOTE 7.2

Inclusion of a medical condition in ICD-10 is a tool for medical analysis. It is not a guide as to whether any such condition should provide a criminal defence. Voluntary, acute intoxication is not, and never has been, a form of diminished responsibility.

b. Intoxication as one of the factors for killing

Where D is not alcoholic but is suffering from diminished responsibility for other reasons and kills whilst intoxicated, the former position was that the jury would be directed to ask whether D would have killed as he did if he had not been intoxicated: *Atkinson* [1985] Crim LR 314 and *Egan* [1993] Crim LR 131. The test was modified in the following case:

R v Dietschmann [2003] UKHL 10 HOUSE OF LORDS

D had had a relationship with his aunt, a drug addict, who had died leaving him her watch. After her death he began to drink heavily and because of depression was prescribed anti-depressants and sleeping tablets. He got into a drunken dispute one night with a friend whom he accused of breaking the watch. He began to punch and stamp on his head whilst the friend was on the floor. By the time police arrived, the friend was dead. D admitted kicking him but denied an intention to kill and pleaded diminished responsibility. At his trial two psychiatric experts had given evidence that the abnormality was 'an adjustment disorder' which was described as an unusually severe grief reaction to the death of the aunt. The judge gave the *Atkinson* direction. D was convicted and appealed to the House of Lords on the following certified question:

(1) Does a defendant seeking to prove a defence of diminished responsibility ... in a case where he had taken drink prior to killing V, have to show that if he had not taken drink

   (a) he would have killed as he in fact did; and

   (b) he would have been under diminished responsibility when he did so?

(2) If not, what direction ought to be given to a jury as to the approach to be taken to self-induced intoxication which was present at the material time in conjunction with an abnormality of mind which falls within s2(1) of the 1957 Act?

Lord Hutton:

The policy of the criminal law in respect of persons suffering from mental abnormality is to be found in the words of section 2 ... [A] brain-damaged person who is intoxicated and who commits a killing is not in the same position as a person who is intoxicated, but not brain-damaged, and who commits a killing ... I consider that the jury should be directed along the following lines:

'Assuming that the defence has established that D was suffering from mental abnormality as described in section 2, the important question is: did that abnormality substantially impair his mental responsibility for his acts in doing the killing? [Author's comment: Note that the previous concepts of abnormality of mind and substantial impairment of responsibility referred to here no longer apply.] You know that before he carried out the killing D had had a lot to drink. Drink cannot be taken into account as something which contributed to his mental abnormality and to any impairment of mental responsibility arising from that abnormality. But you may take the view that both D's mental abnormality and drink played a part in impairing his mental responsibility of the killing and that he might not have killed if he had not taken drink. If you take that view, then the question for you to decide is this: has D satisfied you that, despite the drink, his mental abnormality substantially impaired his mental responsibility for his fatal acts, or has he failed to satisfy you of that? If he has satisfied you of that, you will find him not guilty of murder but you may find him guilty of manslaughter.'

The test put forward by this case presented the jury with a task barely less difficult than previous law. Whereas *Atkinson* required the jury to consider whether D's underlying difficulties other than alcohol (or drugs) amounted to an *abnormality of mind*, *Dietschmann* required them to consider whether D's *mental responsibility* was impaired by the abnormality ignoring the drink (or drugs). This might be just as difficult for a jury, or indeed, anyone to answer as the previous test. However, it was clear that the focus was to be on the underlying medical condition and that intoxication may have played a contributory part in that. Note that the test has now become one of 'substantial impairment of ability' to do any of the three things set out in s2(1A) HA 1957.

The approach in *Dietschmann* and *Stewart* is unchanged under the amended test. Where D has a mental abnormality, but it would not have substantially impaired his responsibility but for voluntary intoxication, then DR will not be available:

R v Joyce and Kay [2017] EWCA Crim 647 COURT OF APPEAL

D had paranoid schizophrenia and knew that unlawful drug use could exacerbate his condition, triggering psychotic episodes. He nonetheless took large quantities of alcohol and unlawful drugs over three days, resulting in a psychotic eopisode during which he brutally stabbed V to death in a frenzied attack. Hallett LJ:

> The appellant in this case, therefore, had to establish either that his intoxication was involuntary and together with the schizophrenia substantially impaired his responsibility (as the defence experts argued) or that the schizophrenia standing alone substantially impaired his responsibility.
>
> The difficulty facing the appellant was that . . . there was no medical evidence available to him that his underlying illness was of such a degree that, independent of drug or alcohol abuse, it impaired his responsibility substantially. On the contrary this appellant's condition was stable. There was therefore no medical evidence to support a partial defence based on schizophrenia alone. Once the jury rejected the defence assertion that he was suffering from dependency syndrome, he no longer had a defence.

Physical conditions

Physical conditions such as epilepsy (*Campbell* [1997] Crim LR 495), sleepwalking and diabetes, all of which have the capacity to affect mental ability, are recognised medical conditions for the purposes of diminished responsibility.

You might consider that the term 'recognised medical condition' actually appears to be quite wide in view of the examples discussed so far. It is thought, however, that it will exclude certain types of mental conditions previously included within the defence, particularly developmental and emotional immaturity and low intelligence (R.D. Mackay 'The New Diminished Responsibility Plea' [2010] *Crim LR* 290). However, an autistic spectrum condition (a developmental disability) was accepted as a 'recognised medical condition' in *Conroy* [2017] EWCA Crim 81.

3. Which substantially impaired D's ability to: understand his/her conduct; form a rational judgment; or exercise self-control

Substantial impairment (s2(1)(b))

The abnormality of mental functioning must substantially impair D's mental abilities in any of three specific ways. They are much clearer but also narrower than the previous law which required a 'substantial impairment of mental responsibility'. This was a vague term implying somewhat less than full moral responsibility for the killing. For example, it allowed flexibility in relation to mercy killers suffering unendurable distress who killed on compassionate grounds.

The law is now quite specific as to which mental abilities must be 'substantially impaired'. As Davis LJ stated in *Brennan*:

> The original provisions of the 1957 Act are broadly phrased and rather more obviously couched in terms of a value judgment, by the references to *substantial* impairment of mental *responsibility*. But the provisions as substituted by the 2009 Act are altogether more tightly structured: for example by removing the (undefined) reference to mental responsibility, even while retaining the concept of substantial impairment. As stated by Lord Judge LCJ in *Brown* [2012] 2 CAR(S) 27 (at paragraph 23 of the judgment) it appears that one purpose of the amendments was to ensure 'a greater equilibrium between the law and medical science'. The new wording gives significantly more scope to the importance of expert psychiatric evidence.

Substantial: The meaning of this word has given rise to several appeals. Until recently, it was held to mean 'more than trivial' as under the previous law (*Lloyd* [1967] 1 QB 175, *Brown (Robert)* [2011] EWCA Crim 2796). However, in *Golds* [2016] UKSC 61, the Supreme Court held that 'substantial' required something more than this. Lord Hughes:

> . . . as a matter simply of dictionary definition, 'substantial' is capable of meaning either (1) 'present rather than illusory or fanciful, thus having some substance' or (2) 'important or weighty', as in 'a substantial meal' or 'a substantial salary'. The first meaning could fairly be paraphrased as 'having any effect more than the merely trivial', whereas the second meaning cannot. . . .
>
> The existence of the two senses of the word 'substantially' identified above means that the law should, in relation to diminished responsibility, be clear which sense is being employed. If it is not, there is, first, a risk of trials being distracted into semantic arguments between the two. Secondly, there is a risk that different juries may apply different senses. Thirdly, medical evidence (nearly always forensic psychiatric evidence) has always been a practical necessity where the issue is diminished responsibility. If anything, the 2009 changes to the law have emphasised this necessity by tying the partial defence more clearly to a recognised medical condition, although in practice this was always required. Although it is for the jury, and not for the doctors, to determine whether the partial defence is made out, and this important difference of function is well recognised by responsible forensic psychiatrists, it is inevitable that they may express an opinion as to whether the impairment was or was not substantial, and if they do not do so in their reports, as commonly many do, they may be asked about it in oral evidence. It is therefore important that if they use the expression, they do so in the sense in which it is used by the courts. If there is doubt about the sense in which they have used it, their reports may be misunderstood and decisions made upon them falsified, and much time at trials is likely to be taken up unnecessarily by cross examination on the semantic question. . . .
>
> The sense in which 'substantially impaired' is used in relation to diminished responsibility is, for the reasons set out above, the second of the two senses. It is not synonymous with 'anything more than merely trivial impairment'.

However, no more specific definition was given by the Supreme Court. This approach was followed in *Squelch* [2017] EWCA Crim 204, where the Court of Appeal emphasised that it was best to direct the jury using the words of s2 'without undue elaboration'. As M. Gibson points out ('Diminished responsibility in *Gold* and beyond: insights and implications' [2017] *Crim LR* 543 at p 545), leaving the definition to the jury 'presents one obvious challenge: inconsistency'.

Impairment: There must be psychiatric evidence of how D's abilities were impaired, that is: how he failed to understand what he was doing. He might be suffering from a recognised medical condition and kill, but that does not automatically mean that the defence should succeed. He may, despite his condition, bear a high degree of responsibility for his actions. This is ultimately an issue for the jury. Sometimes juries have rejected unchallenged expert evidence and convicted. An example would be *Khan (Dawood)* [2009] EWCA Crim 2015, decided before the C&JA 2009, where, despite uncontested medical evidence of a mental illness, D was convicted of murder on the grounds that there was no substantial impairment of mental responsibility. D was schizophrenic and had bludgeoned V to death. In confirming the conviction, the Court of Appeal held that the jury must determine the degree to which the accused comprehended the physical acts he was doing, and the degree to which he had, at that time, any power to exercise control over his actions. Each case was fact-specific. However, is there a risk that a jury might substitute their own inexperienced opinion for that of the expert, particularly in a more shocking case? In *Khan*, D disputed that he had killed at all and simultaneously pleaded diminished responsibility, so there were serious issues of fact and credibility for the jury to consider. The new law, however, is more closely tied to the medical evidence and the Court of Appeal has recently held that, in the absence of a good reason, juries must accept uncontested expert evidence:

Brennan v R [2014] EWCA Crim 2387

D, a male escort with a history of mental health problems, had been convicted of a savage and brutal murder of a man. The victim had been stabbed 22 times with a variety of knives and bludgeoned with a hammer. Scratchings had been made on the victim's back 'to release his spirit into the after-life'. After the murder, D had cleaned, changed his clothes, and gone to the police station. There was uncontested psychiatric evidence that he was suffering from Schizotypal Disorder and Emotionally Unstable Personality Disorder which had substantially impaired his ability to form a rational judgment or to exercise self-control. The jury rejected the evidence and convicted of murder. The question on appeal was whether, in view of the expert's evaluation, the defence should have been left to the jury at all. Davis LJ said this:

> The problem that a case of this kind throws up derives from the fact that there are two relevant but potentially conflicting principles that are brought into play. The first principle is the general principle that in criminal trials cases are decided by juries, not by experts. Indeed experts are permitted by reason of their expertise to express *opinions* by way of evidence: but cases ultimately fall to be decided by juries, and they decide on the *entirety* of the evidence. The second principle, however, is that juries must base their conclusions on the *evidence*. That fundamental principle finds reflection, for example, in directions conventionally given to juries not to speculate and not to allow their views to be swayed by feelings of distaste or emotion. There can, as we see it, be no room for departure from so fundamental a principle as the second principle. It reflects the very essence of the jury system and of a just and fair trial. But the first principle, whilst most important and undoubtedly descriptive of the general position, is also capable, as it seems to us, of admitting of degree of qualification in a suitably exceptional case. Clearly no difficulty arises (normally) where there is a dispute as to the expert evidence. The jury decides. But suppose, for example, a matter arises falling exclusively within the domain of scientific expertise; suppose, too, that all the well qualified experts instructed on that particular matter are agreed as to the correct conclusion and no challenge is made to such conclusion. Can it really be said that the jury nevertheless can properly depart from the experts as to that conclusion on that particular matter: simply on the basis that it is to be said, by way of mantra, that the ultimate conclusion is always for the jury? We would suggest not. Where there simply is no rational or proper basis for departing from uncontradicted and unchallenged expert evidence then juries may not do so. . . . As we see it, most, if not all, of the aspects of the new provisions relate entirely to psychiatric matters. In our view it is both legitimate and helpful, given the structure of the new provisions, for an expert psychiatrist to include in his or her evidence a view on all four stages, including a view as to whether there was substantial impairment.

NOTE 7.3

Juries are no longer making a value judgment on D's moral responsibility for the killing. They must now base their decision on the *expert evidence* of whether or not a recognised medical condition substantially impairs D's ability in one of the three specified ways. This can only be rejected for a good reason. All of the elements of the defence now relate to psychiatric matters.

The three abilities in (s2(1A)) are as follows:

a. Understand his/her conduct (s2(1A)(a))

This test of substantially impaired ability is similar to the test for insanity where D needs to prove that he suffers from a disease of the mind and did not know the *nature and quality* of the act he was doing or did not know that it was *wrong* (*M'Naghten Rules* 1843). The specified causes of an abnormality of mind as previously required were always inclusive of and wider than insanity, particularly in respect of defects of will, and this will continue to be the case.

→ CROSS-REFERENCE
For discussion of insanity see Chapter 8, 8.1.

b. Form a rational judgment (s2(1A)(b))

Unless this concept is widely interpreted, it risks excluding those whose perception of reality is distorted by their mental disorder but whose ability to exercise self-control or to form a rational judgment are not substantially impaired. People with some personality disorders may therefore fall outside of the defence.

c. Exercise self-control (s2(1A)(c))

As we will see later, a person who kills through fear or anger, having been seriously provoked, may be able to use an alternative partial defence of 'loss of control', formerly called 'provocation'. The difference between the defence of loss of control and diminished responsibility is that the latter requires proof of a recognised medical condition as we have seen. Some defendants under the previous law, notably women suffering from BWS, would rely on both defences at their murder trials. Thus, weaknesses in one defence or the other would not necessarily be so crucial. It is thought that, elsewhere, the possibility of running both defences together is now reduced given the more limited definition of diminished responsibility.

4. Which provides an explanation for D's acts and omissions in doing or being a party to the killing (s2(1)(c))

The abnormality of mental functioning will provide an explanation for the killing if it causes, or is a significant contributory factor in causing D's conduct (s2(1B) HA 1957). There was no such requirement under the previous law. Responsibility was likely to be regarded as impaired simply on the basis of a medical diagnosis alone.

The government's intention behind this new provision was to rule out cases of 'random coincidence', that is: where there is no connection between the abnormality and the killing. However, if D can prove that his abnormality of mental functioning was due to a recognised medical condition which did substantially impair his ability to do one of the three specified things in s2(1A) then it might be thought that any further enquiry into causation would be unnecessary. Insanity does not require a specific causal connection between D's disease of the mind and his conduct. This extra requirement may therefore impose another limitation upon the defence.

?!   THINKING POINT 7.1

Consider whether the following fall within the definition of s2:

1. A has been physically and mentally abused for several months by her husband B. She has become extremely depressed. One night she stabs and kills B.

2. A hears voices which tell him to kill his neighbours. A does so.

3. A becomes depressed when his girlfriend, B, leaves him for another man. After one week, A kills B.

4. A suffers from a depressive condition causing him to become aggressive. He gets into an argument with B over some tools which he accuses B of having stolen. The argument becomes heated and A stabs and kills B.

5. A's terminally ill wife has suffered great pain and discomfort for a prolonged period. A has become depressed and kills his wife by suffocation.

Burden of proof and the ECHR

One significant feature of this defence is that there is a legal burden of proof on D to prove the defence on a balance of probabilities. The only other defence where this occurs is insanity. With diminished responsibility, psychiatric reports must be presented to the court on behalf of D testifying to a relevant abnormality of mental functioning. The justification for this is twofold. First, that the reverse-burden of proof relates not to an element of the offence of murder but to a statutory exception, that is: that once P has proved murder, D may prove that he should be excepted from the mandatory life sentence and convicted of voluntary manslaughter (*McQuade* [2005] NICA 2 and *Lambert, Ali & Jordan* [2001] 2 WLR 211). Therefore, Article 6(2) ECHR, which guarantees the presumption of innocence and the imposition of a burden of proof upon the prosecution, is not contravened. Second, on practical grounds, the medical matters relied upon by D relating to his state of mind are solely within his knowledge and can only be investigated with his cooperation. The Court of Appeal concluded in *Foye* [2013] EWCA Crim 475, considering the unamended law, that the converse could involve him being forced to undergo medical examination on behalf of P in order to disprove the defence, which would be unacceptable. *Wilcocks* [2016] EWCA Crim 2043 confirmed that the legal burden remains on D, and that this is compatible with Article 6(2), under the amended definition.

This is an anomaly however for no other defence, apart from insanity, needs to be proved. The same observation regarding the facts being within D's own knowledge could likewise be made of them. Ordinarily, D merely has to produce some evidence of a defence which the prosecution must disprove beyond all reasonable doubt.

How is diminished responsibility different from insanity?

Section 2 does not include the term 'diminished responsibility'. Instead it refers to 'abnormality of mental functioning', 'recognised medical condition' and 'substantially impaired ability'. There is therefore the possibility of overlap with insanity which, as we shall see, is based on a disease of the mind and a *defect of reason*.

Insanity, defined in the *M'Naghten Rules* 1843, will only apply to mental disorder which is serious enough to deprive D of either:

- knowledge of the nature and quality of his actions; or
- knowledge that what he had done was wrong.

It is distinguished from diminished responsibility in that the insanity defence is concerned with the intellectual or cognitive faculties of memory, reason and understanding. If D is able to appreciate the physical act and/or knows that it is wrong, the fact that he is unable to control the impulse to do it is irrelevant.

Diminished responsibility is not concerned with knowledge or cognition but with all types of mental disorder. D may know that he is killing a person but be unable to control the impulse to do it or suffer from some other volitional disorder.

Insanity is a general defence applying to any crime. Diminished responsibility, on the other hand, only applies to murder.

Where D has raised diminished responsibility, the prosecution may put forward available evidence of insanity under s6 Criminal Procedure (Insanity) Act 1964. If the prosecution wish to assert that D is insane they must prove it beyond all reasonable doubt. Where D pleads insanity, the prosecution may also assert that he is suffering from diminished responsibility and again will need to prove this to the higher standard. If no argument relating to diminished responsibility is raised by the defence and the judge considers it appropriate to do so, he may raise the issue with defence counsel.

The defence in context

There has been a decline in the use of the diminished responsibility plea from 109 in 1979 to 16 in 2013/14 (ONS Statistical Bulletin, *Crime Statistics, Focus on Violent Crime and Sexual Offences, 2012/13* (Feb 2015), Table 2.14).

Research in 2017 revealed the following facts:

- most defendants were male (almost 85 per cent);
- approximately half of victims were female, a significant proportion of whom were killed by a current or former lover/partner (confirming national and international data that women are most at risk from being killed by a partner);
- the most frequent mental disorders were: depression, schizophrenia, personality disorder, psychosis, with a range of less serious conditions appearing less frequently;
- while the former defence rarely needed to be proved in court, because in approximately 77 per cent of cases the prosecution would accept a plea of guilty to manslaughter on the basis of diminished responsibility, this is no longer true. Under the amended defence, almost half (43.3 per cent) of cases did go to trial. (R. Mackay and B. Mitchell, 'The new diminished responsibility plea in operation: some initial findings' [2017] *Crim LR* 18)

Certain criticisms of the former defence in relation to the role that a jury must perform remain valid for the new: in order to assess whether D is suffering from an abnormality of mental functioning, it is they who must evaluate the expert evidence on abnormality. Where there is a conflict between experts on each side, the jury must choose between them. How is a jury to know which expert testimony is more authoritative? On what basis will a jury then decide? Juries do not give reasons for their verdicts and it is not possible to know why they might decide one way or the other. Evidence suggests that contested trials are more likely to result in a murder conviction. Ultimately, the question the jury will ask themselves is whether it is right in all the circumstances to convict such a person of murder. But greater sympathy may be extended to one with milder mental conditions, whose crime is viewed with compassion, than to one who is seriously ill. The case of Peter Sutcliffe, the Yorkshire Ripper, is an example. He was charged with the murder of 13 prostitutes in the North of England in the 1980s. There was medical evidence that he suffered from diminished responsibility which the prosecution was initially prepared to accept in the form of a plea of guilty to manslaughter. However, this was refused by the judge who ordered the trial to proceed. The defence was then successfully contested by the prosecution with the result that Peter Sutcliffe was convicted of the 13 murders.

Conclusion

The current law is the result of two Law Commission Reports: 'Partial Defences to Murder' (Law Com No 290, 2004) and 'Murder, Manslaughter and Infanticide' (Law Com No 304, 2006).

The 2004 Law Commission Report acknowledged that the partial defences to murder owe their existence solely to the mandatory life sentence for murder. Consideration was given to merging diminished responsibility and provocation but was rejected. The current reforms reflect the 2006 Law Commission report except that the Law Commission specifically included in the definition of abnormality of mental functioning 'developmental immaturity in a defendant under the age of 18' alongside the need for a recognised medical condition. There was no requirement that D's mental condition be a cause of the killing. The amended defence of diminished responsibility is therefore undoubtedly narrower than it was, but the vagueness surrounding its former requirements has been improved. The requirements of a medical condition and substantial impairment of ability are more capable of scientific assessment. Fears surrounding its new limitations have perhaps been borne out by the Supreme Court's approach in *Golds*, where Lord Hughes stated that 'it is appropriate, as it always has been, for the reduction to the lesser offence to be occasioned where there is a weighty reason for it and not merely a reason which just passes the trivial.' If use of the defence continues to fall, and this is likely given its narrower scope which could make it more difficult to prove, more defendants will be convicted of murder.

SECTION SUMMARY

Diminished responsibility:

- ◼ *is a partial defence to murder;*
- ◼ *where successful, reduces the conviction to voluntary manslaughter (s2(3) HA 1957).*

Under s2 Homicide Act 1957 diminished responsibility consists of:

- ◼ *an abnormality of mental functioning;*
- ◼ *a recognised medical condition;*
- ◼ *substantial impairment of D's ability to do any of the three things specified in s2(1)(b):*
  - ☐ *understand the nature of D's conduct;*
  - ☐ *form a rational judgment;*
  - ☐ *exercise self-control;*
- ◼ *an explanation that the abnormality of mental functioning caused, or was a significant contributory factor in causing, D's conduct.*

7.1.3 Loss of Control

KEY CASES

Duffy [1949] 1 All ER 932—subjective test: sudden and temporary loss of self-control;

Camplin [1978] 2 All ER 168—objective 'reasonable man' test: age, sex and 'other' characteristics relevant to the gravity of the provocation are relevant;

Holley [2005] UKPC 23—only mental characteristics relevant to the gravity of provocation will be relevant;

Clinton, Parker, Evans [2012] EWCA Crim 2—sexual infidelity is excluded as a qualifying trigger, but the effects may be regarded as 'circumstances' in relation to the objective test;

Dawes, Hatter & Bowyer [2013] EWCA 332—*Clinton* confirmed. Considered desire for revenge considered;

Asmelash [2013] EWCA Crim 157—intoxication is excluded from the objective test;

Jewell [2014] EWCA Crim 414—definition of 'loss of control';

Gurpinar [2015] EWCA Crim 178—sufficient evidence of all three parts of the test for the defence required.

Introduction

This defence, along with diminished responsibility, is a partial defence to murder and is unique to that offence. As with a successful plea of diminished responsibility, loss of control will reduce the murder conviction to one of voluntary manslaughter. If a defendant wishes to allege that any crime other than murder was committed under provocation, that fact may form the basis of a plea in mitigation of sentence but cannot provide a defence. We saw with diminished responsibility that the onus of proving it was on D on a balance of probabilities. This is not so with loss of control. D must produce sufficient evidence to raise the defence but need satisfy no legal burden of proof in that respect. It will then be up to the prosecution to disprove it beyond all reasonable doubt.

As with the former defence of provocation, this defence remains a concession to human frailty and a partial defence to 'heat of the moment' intentional killings committed through moral outrage and, now, fear. The rationale of provocation, explained by A. Ashworth in 'The Doctrine of Provocation' [1976] *CLJ* 292, remains true of the new defence:

> Provocation mitigates moral culpability to the extent that a person acted in a less-than-fully-controlled manner in circumstances in which there was reasonable justification for him to feel aggrieved at the conduct of another.

Historically, the defence developed in the typical scenario of a husband murdering upon finding his wife in the act of adultery, or his son being sexually abused. It was thought that the husband's self-control would have been pushed beyond reasonable limits, thus partially justifying the murder, since V was thought to bear some responsibility for her own death. A far wider range of circumstances will now fall within the defence. In recognition of modern social values, however, sexual infidelity is no longer regarded as a justification for murder.

Context

Approximately two women per week are killed by violent partners, the most common cause of death being strangulation and asphyxiation. In 2015/16, 50 per cent of female victims were killed

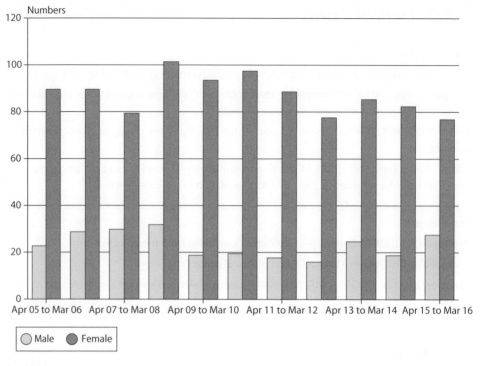

Diagram 7.3

Number of homicide victims aged 16 and over killed by partner/ex-partner, by sex of victim, 2005/06 to 2015/16

Source: ONS, 'Focus on violent crime and sexual offences, England and Wales: year ending Mar 2016 - Compendium: Homicide' www.ons.gov.uk/peoplepopulationandcommunity/crimeandjustice/compendium/focusonviolentcrime-andsexualoffences/yearendingmarch2016/homicide#how-are-victims-and-suspects-related.

by a current or former sexual partner, compared to 7 per cent of male victims. See Diagram 7.3 for further information.

What was wrong with provocation?

This defence was defined by s3 Homicide Act 1957 and the common law. The first problem was that, over time, the defence was invoked to excuse, rather than justify, a killing on rather trivial grounds, for example: *Doughty* [1986] 83 Cr App R 319 where a father killed his persistently crying small baby having snapped under great stress. This was hard to justify on moral grounds. Domestic homicide by violent men against women for the merest provocation also fell into this category, for example: *Weller* [2003] EWCA Crim 815, where the victim was killed on packing her bags to leave or *Bisla* (1992) *The Telegraph*, 30 January, where a wife was killed for nagging her husband.

Second, women who killed men were largely excluded by the first, subjective test of the defence. This required that the killing be committed under *a sudden and temporary* loss of self-control. In other words, there had to be a 'heat of the moment' killing involving a spontaneous reaction. The fundamental flaw was that it excluded people who killed through fear or desperation, those who experienced a delayed reaction to provocation, or killings involving the use of a weapon. This became clear from certain notorious cases involving women who killed violent partners. A famous case was that of Ruth Ellis who, in 1955, was convicted of the murder of her lover, David Blakely.

This case had involved infidelity, jealousy and violence by him against her which culminated in a fatal shooting some two weeks after the last act of violence. On the morning of her hanging 1,000 people stood silently outside Holloway Prison in protest. Despite continuing allegations of a miscarriage of justice, on the grounds that she had been provoked into the killing, she has never been pardoned, and the Court of Appeal confirmed that her conviction was in accordance with the law as it was in 1955 (*Ellis* [2003] EWCA Crim 3556). Over the years, much research established that women do not typically respond to violence with an immediate angry, physical retaliation. They lack not only the strength but also the psychological make-up and are, consequently, more likely to delay their reaction or to use a weapon. One example was the case of Sara Thornton which you will read about later, where a delay of one or two minutes was fatal to her defence (*Thornton [No 1]* [1992] 1 All ER 306). However, this did not stop courts from allowing the defence to men when pre-armed, for example: *Wells* [1966] 66 Cr App R 271 where a husband shot his wife twice at close range with a gun purchased that morning following her alleged confession of adultery. The criticism that the law was not gender-neutral eventually filtered through, but it took many years of academic, political and campaigning opposition to achieve the necessary change.

Third, the objective test required a jury to consider whether a reasonable person with reasonable self-control would have killed. This became immensely complicated. What if D was not 'reasonable' but mentally incapacitated with reduced powers of self-control? The problem was that the defence only existed for 'ordinary' people who might snap when seriously provoked. It was not supposed to excuse killings by people who were more aggressive or hot-tempered than a person without such incapacity.

Underlying the case law was a doctrinal difference as to the scope of the defence: should the so-called 'reasonable man' resemble the defendant with all his mental characteristics, even those reducing his self-control, such as depression or drug addiction? Or should these be excluded so that the reactions of the defendant be compared to that of a normal person with reasonable self-control? Most of the cases followed the latter test, which made the defence harder to use, but there were certain exceptions related to the provocation being aimed at a particular characteristic which, therefore, increased its gravity. One of the difficulties of this compromise was that it left abused women, in particular, in a difficult position. An abused woman with a relevant characteristic such as '*battered woman syndrome*' (BWS) would have found it hard to deny that her condition reduced her powers of self-control or to show that the violence she had received was aimed at the BWS. Worse still, she would have found it even harder to establish the objective test without reference to any such characteristic. The problem of mental characteristics was, therefore, essentially unresolved in several respects.

In short, the law had become so complex and technical that it was virtually unintelligible to a jury and lacking in moral validity. The Law Commission's final report on 'Murder, Manslaughter and Infanticide' (2006) contained recommendations for reform of provocation. The defence was abolished by ss 54 and 55 C&JA 2009. Many of the previous shortcomings of provocation are addressed by the new law. Whether the defence has achieved any greater moral validity than the old will be examined at the end of this chapter.

Definition of the defence

■ Definition

■ What amounts to loss of control?

■ The qualifying trigger

■ The objective test.

See Diagram 7.4 for an overview.

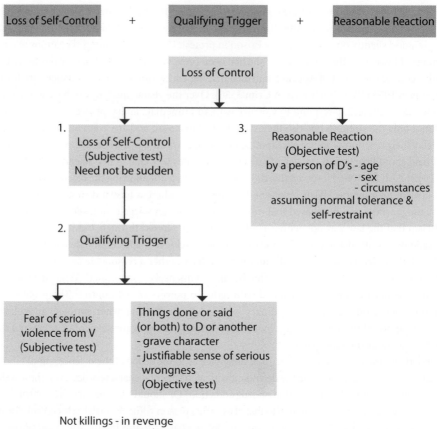

Diagram 7.4
The test for loss of control

Section 54 C&JA 2009: Partial defence to murder: loss of control

(1) Where a person ('D') kills or is a party to the killing of another ('V'), D is not to be convicted of murder if—

(a) D's acts and omissions in doing or being a party to the killing resulted from D's *loss of self-control,*

(b) the loss of self-control had *a qualifying trigger* and,

(c) a person of D's sex and age, with a *normal degree of tolerance and self-restraint and in the circumstances of D,* might have reacted in the same or in a similar way to D.

(2) For the purposes of subsection (1)(a), *it does not matter whether or not the loss of control was sudden.*

(3) In subsection (1)(c) the reference to 'the circumstances of D' is a reference to all of D's circumstances other than those whose only relevance to D's conduct is that they bear on D's general capacity for tolerance or self-restraint.

(4) Subsection (1) does not apply if, in doing or being a party to the killing, D acted in a considered desire for *revenge*.

(5) On a charge of murder, if sufficient evidence is adduced to raise an issue with respect to the defence under subsection (1), the jury must assume that the defence is satisfied unless the prosecution proves beyond reasonable doubt that it is not.

(6) For the purposes of subsection (5), sufficient evidence is adduced to raise an issue with respect to the defence if evidence is adduced on which, in the opinion of the trial judge, a jury, properly directed, could reasonably conclude that the defence might apply. [Emphasis added.]

Section 55 Meaning of 'Qualifying Trigger'

...

(3) This subsection applies if D's loss of control was attributable to D's *fear of serious violence* from V against D or another identified person.

(4) This subsection applies if D's loss of control was attributable to a *thing or things done or said (or both)* which—

(a) constituted circumstances of an *extremely grave character*, and

(b) caused D to have a *justifiable* sense of being *seriously wronged*.

(5) This subsection applies if D's loss of self-control was attributable to a combination of the matters mentioned in subsections (3) and (4).

(6) In determining whether a loss of self-control had a qualifying trigger—

(a) D's fear of serious violence is to be disregarded to the extent that it was caused by a thing which D *incited* to be done or said for the purpose of providing an excuse to use violence;

(b) a sense of being seriously wronged by a thing done or said is not justifiable if D *incited* the thing to be done or said for the purpose of providing an excuse to use violence;

(c) *the fact that a thing done or said constituted sexual infidelity is to be disregarded.* [Emphasis added.]

Section 56(1) The common law defence of provocation is abolished and replaced by sections 54 and 55.

There are therefore three limbs to the test for Loss of Control:

■ There must first be evidence of a *loss of self-control* (a subjective test);

■ This must be due to a 'qualifying trigger' (a semi-subjective/objective test):

☐ fear of *serious violence* from V towards D or another; and/or

☐ a thing done or said of an extremely grave character causing a justifiable sense of being seriously wronged (ie: anger);

■ D must finally demonstrate that *a person of his age and sex with normal capacity for tolerance and self-restraint* would have killed in such circumstances (an objective test).

There are three general points to make about the new defence at the outset. First, the Court of Appeal in *Clinton* [2012] EWCA Crim 2 held that the new defence is self-contained and that its common law heritage is irrelevant. Rarely will it be necessary to refer to previous provocation case law. Any such references here are purely to enable you to make comparisons. Second, in *Dawes, Hatter & Bowyer* [2013] EWCA 332 the Court of Appeal held that the defence should not be left to the jury unless there is sufficient evidence of *all the elements* of the defence. The old law simply required some evidence of loss of self-control. Third, the new defence requires the judge to give a more thorough evaluation of the evidence to a jury than before. Lord Thomas CJ in *Gurpinar* [2015] EWCA Crim 178 said:

> We therefore accept the submission of the appellants that a judge needs to proceed on the premise that the jury may take a different view of the evidence to that which the judge may have found . . . However as the Act refers to 'sufficient evidence,' it is clearly the judge's task to analyse the evidence closely and be satisfied that there is, taking into account the whole of the evidence, sufficient evidence in respect of each of the three components of the defence. The judge is bound to consider the weight and quality of the evidence in coming to a conclusion . . .

In other words, the defence is now more legally defined and much narrower than it used to be. The three requirements of the defence will be examined in turn.

1. Loss of self-control: s54(1)

This entails a subjective test which broadens the previous law. Loss of self-control was concerned with having been caused by anger, but the term will now cover fear, so as to include domestic abuse victims who kill.

The defendant's emotional state, whether despair, terror, hysteria, exhaustion or isolation, will need to satisfy the requirement of loss of control.

We must now exclude earlier cases which attempted to interpret this concept such as *R v Duffy* [1949] 1 All ER 932: D must be *no longer be 'master of his mind'*; *R v Richens* (1994) 98 Cr App R 43: defendant *went berserk*; *R v Brown* [1972]: defendant *snapped, exploded, blacked out*.

However, mere anger or fear, even if serious, is unlikely to suffice (Lord Judge CJ in *Dawes, Hatter, Bowyer* [2013] EWCA 332 ('Sexual infidelity') later):

> 'For the individual with normal capacity of self-restraint and tolerance, unless the circumstances are extremely grave, normal irritation, and even serious anger do not often cross the threshold into loss of control . . . '

Beyond that, it has to be said that loss of self-control remains a rather elusive concept. Neither defendant in the following cases succeeded for that reason: Each had relied on loss of control due to fear of serious violence.

Jewell [2014] EWCA Crim 414

Jewell, an otherwise normal, well-balanced man, shot a work colleague twice when picking him up for work one morning. He explained to the police that over the preceding two weeks he had thought the victim had been intimidating him and had actually threatened him the night before by saying that he had 'two days left'. On the morning of the shooting, Jewell said that something snapped and that he had shot the victim as in a dream. Over the previous night, however, Jewell had borrowed guns from his father and carefully planned the murder, an escape and his own suicide.

Lady Justice Rafferty:

> His explanation that he was in fear of serious violence from Mr Prickett, who the night before had made a threat to kill him, must be seen in context. That context includes that the applicant went home and during the next 12 hours failed . . . to seek help from the police or from his family or from his friends, save his father who was persuaded to loan him a shotgun.. . . . We remind ourselves of the words of the Lord Chief Justice in *Clinton*: 'In reality, the greater the level of deliberation, the less likely it will be that the killing followed a true loss of self-control.'

In the course of the judgment, loss of control was defined as follows:

'... loss of self-control' in the Act could be best understood as 'founded on whether the D has lost his ability to maintain his actions in accordance with considered judgment or whether he had lost normal powers of reasoning.'

Whether this will be regarded as a standard interpretation remains to be seen. It could indicate that a mere loss of temper is sufficient, without defining whether the loss of control needs to be complete or partial.

Gurpinar [2015] EWCA Crim 178

Gurpinar, aged 14, stabbed and killed another 14-year-old, larger, aggressive boy who was threatening to attack him. Gurpinar claimed to have found the knife near the scene of the killing. He stated that he had acted without thinking in the heat of the moment under pressure of a sudden violent attack. The event had been filmed on a mobile phone. The Court of Appeal held that the evidence was 'indicative of an instinctive reaction to hit out at the deceased both in panic to stop the attack and in order to defend himself.' Gurpinar had a background of making violent threats on Facebook and this was also taken into account. At no point had he claimed to have lost control.

The fact that this crucial first component of the defence has been left undefined is extremely unsatisfactory. If D is acting purposively, or instinctively, does he always retain self-control? If the killing is a rational response to domestic abuse, does it entail a loss of control? Whether the courts will require the killing to have been committed in anything less than 'a frenzied attack' remains to be seen. Undoubtedly, the use of a weapon, unless spontaneous, will be seen as evidence of deliberation, and deliberation is excluded. This makes the defence hard to use, especially for abused women who, because of their weaker physical strength, more typically kill abusers with a weapon.

Remember that D will have formed an intention to kill or commit GBH despite the loss of self-control. The point is that this defence is not a denial of MR for murder. It can only be pleaded where D would otherwise be guilty of murder.

The loss of control need not be sudden: s54(2)

One of the most important changes introduced by the new law is that the loss of self-control need no longer be sudden and spontaneous. This represents a relaxation of the previous law and will theoretically extend the defence to those who kill after the heat of the moment has passed. The reason for the change was the injustice caused, primarily to women, by the subjective test in provocation (see 'What was wrong with Provocation' earlier). This 'immediacy principle' was the result of *Duffy* [1949] 1 All ER 932 in which, following an assault and threat of violence one evening, Mrs Duffy killed her violent husband with a hammer and an axe whilst he was asleep.

Fatal to her defence was the delay between the last assault upon her and the murder. At her trial, Devlin J gave a famous direction, approved by the Court of Criminal Appeal, which restricted the defence until it was abolished by the C&JA 2009:

'... circumstances which induce a desire for revenge are inconsistent with provocation, since the conscious formulation of a desire for revenge means that a person has had time to think, to reflect, and that would negative a sudden and temporary loss of self-control, which is of the essence of provocation.'

Note that the delay here was presumed by the court to represent a cooling down and time for conscious formulation of a plan for revenge rather than a 'slow burn' and chronic 'boiling over'.

Duffy was followed in the famous case of *Thornton [No 1]* [1992] 1 All ER 306. Sara Thornton stabbed and killed her violent husband with a carving knife which she had gone to the kitchen to sharpen. He was lying on the couch and had threatened to kill her when she was asleep. A delay of seconds between threat and reaction was, again, fatal to the defence for the Court of Appeal held that the distinction between a person who has had time to think and one who acts whilst out of control is more important in a case of domestic dispute. The court did, however, confirm that domestic violence might be regarded as 'cumulative provocation' but unless it led to a loss of control, the defence would fail. The lack of gender-neutrality of the defence was unacknowledged by the courts until *Ahluwalia* [1992] 4 ALL ER 889, previously considered under diminished responsibility.

Karanjit Ahluwalia killed her husband after prolonged serious domestic violence and degradation. On the night in question he held a hot iron to her face threatening to burn her. That night, she poured petrol over him whilst he was in bed asleep and ignited it. He died six days later. On appeal against conviction of murder, LCJ Taylor stated that:

> We accept that the subjective element in the defence of provocation would not as a matter of law be negatived simply because of the delayed reaction in such cases, provided that there was at the time of the killing 'a sudden and temporary loss of self-control' caused by the alleged provocation. However, the longer the delay and the stronger the evidence of deliberation on the part of D, the more likely it will be that the prosecution will negative provocation. [Emphasis added]

The prosecution accepted a plea of guilt to manslaughter on the basis of diminished responsibility. The running of both defences together would then become viable in future cases. The long-term psychological effects of domestic violence were subsequently recognised at Sara Thornton's second appeal where the possibility that she might have been suffering from BWS was decisive to the Court of Appeal's decision to order a retrial. Arguably, s54(2) encapsulates Lord Taylor's stance regarding the timing of a loss of self-control in *Ahluwalia*.

Under s54(2) the length of any delay will continue to have a bearing on the question of whether the killing was premeditated or in revenge. Such killings are specifically excluded from the defence by s55(4) which restates the common law position. We do not yet know how s55(4) will work in practice but it may threaten any potential extension of the subjective test in reality.

2. The two qualifying triggers

These provisions are also new and represent a simplification of the old law. In addition to providing evidence of loss of control, D must next provide evidence of one or both of the new 'qualifying triggers': fear of *serious violence* or justifiable offence taken in response to *a thing said or done of a grave nature* or both. In either case, the 'qualifying trigger' must be directed from V towards D (or a third party). The law is extended by the first qualifying trigger but it is narrowed by the second.

Fear of serious violence from V against D or another identified person (s55(3))

This provision allows the defence to be used where the killing is the result of loss of self-control attributable to fear of serious violence. It is new and represents an extension of the old law. The old law would have required the killing to have been an immediate response to a threat of, or actual, violence constituting the provocation. Whether D killed through fear will be subjectively assessed although the violence feared must be objectively serious. This provision will now include abused women who kill their violent partners through fear of serious violence, despite the fact that they have delayed or over-reacted and used excessive force in response to a future, rather than an immediate, threat. It will also include the person who kills through fear using disproportionate, pre-emptive force, that is: a householder killing an intruder. Such defendants may, in fact, use either this or the alternative qualifying trigger of 'a thing done or said' where they were motivated to kill by anger instead of fear.

However, there is still a requirement for a loss of self-control although it need not be sudden (s54(2), see earlier). The heat of the moment might have passed but the fear of future violence still needs to be such as to cause a loss of control. Domestic violence, for example, is unpredictable and the cumulative psychological impact of this upon an abused victim is likely to constitute fear and desperation. In an extreme case, a serious traumatic condition such as BWS might develop. The new law attempts to take this into account.

There is no express limitation regarding the time at which the feared violence is to be expected. It might in practice be within the next minute, the next morning or, indeed, at an unknown time within the foreseeable future provided there is, at the time of the killing, a loss of self-control. Clearly, one can envisage difficulties in establishing such a degree of fear as to amount to a loss of self-control in cases where the harm is not anticipated for some time. Whether loss of control is a normal sequel to fear is also debatable. Will women who kill violent partners through fear risk exclusion from the defence for lack of evidence of this vital requirement? The counter-argument is that the killing might have been motivated by a considered desire for revenge, expressly excluded by s54(4). Note that abused women suffering BWS might also plead diminished responsibility.

Violence against third parties

Section 55(3) permits the defence to be used where the violence is directed by V towards another identified person. This might be D's child, sibling or someone to whom D is close. An example would be *Pearson* [1992] Crim LR 193 where an elder brother killed his father on the basis of the latter's violence towards his younger brother.

Revenge or incitement

Section 54(4) states that the defence will not be available to those acting in a 'considered' desire for revenge. In *Evans* [2012] EWCA Crim 2 ('Sexual infidelity' discussed later) it was held that this would be inconsistent with a loss of self-control.

Section 55(6)(a) states that D's fear of serious violence is to be disregarded to the extent that it was caused by a thing which D incited *for the purpose* of providing an excuse to use violence. D may still use the defence if behaving badly in a general way and looking for violence but not if he provoked a reaction. Lord Judge CJ in *Dawes, Hatter & Bowyer* [2013] EWCA 332 explained:

> One may wonder (and the judge would have to consider) how often a defendant who is out to incite violence could be said to 'fear' serious violence; often he may be welcoming it. Similarly, one may wonder how such a defendant may have a justifiable sense of being seriously wronged if he successfully incites someone else to use violence towards him. Those are legitimate issues for consideration, but as a matter of statutory construction, the mere fact that in some general way the defendant was behaving badly and looking for and provoking trouble does not of itself lead to the disapplication of the qualifying triggers based on s.55(3)(4) and (5) unless his actions were intended to provide him with the excuse or opportunity to use violence.

The overlap of loss of control and self-defence

The inclusion of fear as a qualifying trigger effectively grants a partial defence to those denied self-defence because the killing is not a reasonable response to an immediate threat. A successful plea of self-defence results in complete acquittal. Where the fearful killing is an excessive over-reaction to a threat of violence, self-defence will fail but loss of control may still be relied upon. This represents an extension of the law. There may be occasions where both defences might be used, but these will be rare as Lord Judge CJ explained in *Dawes, Hatter & Bowyer*:

> Self-defence may still apply where the facts create an overlap, but this will be in very limited circumstances. Loss of control requires fear of serious violence, not necessarily imminent, whilst any threat might justify self-defence provided it is imminent. If self-defence is rejected, a court should still consider loss of control. The circumstances in which the defendant, who has lost control of himself, will nevertheless be able to argue that he used reasonable force in response to the violence he feared, or to which he was subjected, are likely to be limited. But even if the defendant may have lost his self-control, provided his violent response in self-defence was not unreasonable in the circumstances, he would be entitled to rely on self defence as a complete defence.

A thing or things done or said (or both) which constituted circumstances of an extremely grave character, and caused D to have a justifiable sense of being seriously wronged (s55(4))

This provision allows the defence to be used where the killing was the result of loss of control attributable to anger. Under the old law, provocation could be either verbal (such as a threat or abuse) or physical (such as violence) and be directed against a third party, such as a sibling or child. Section 55(4) is not, in this respect, entirely new. However, as we saw earlier in this section, the nature of the provocative conduct could be quite minor, for example: *Doughty* where D killed his persistently crying small baby. It is unlikely that such conduct would fall within the new law. Now, anything done or said must be of a 'grave character' and must give rise to a 'justifiable' sense of being 'seriously wronged'. It appears that, apart from D's sense of being wronged (a subjective matter), all other aspects of the provision should be measured against objective standards: *Clinton, Parker, Evans* [2012] EWCA Crim 2 (discussed later). The sense of being wronged must itself be objectively justifiable: thus in *Meanza* [2017] EWCA Crim 445 it was accepted that D felt seriously wronged by conditions imposed on him by hospital and restriction orders. However, '[t]he emphasis must be on the adjective "justifiable". The appellant could have no justifiable grievance in relation to hospital and restriction orders that were lawfully imposed.'

Section 55(4) represents a narrowing of the old law. Lord Judge CJ confirmed in *Clinton* that the qualifying triggers in s54 have 'raised the bar' by contrast with the former law of provocation. It is, therefore, unlikely that some previous cases would now succeed. For example, in *Morhall* [1995] 3 All ER 659, D killed on being taunted about his addiction to glue-sniffing. He was allowed the defence of provocation on the grounds that the taunting was directed at his particular habit and was therefore serious to him. Whether his sense of being seriously wronged would now be considered objectively justifiable is questionable. One can also predict juries struggling to fit many cases of domestic violence within this requirement, particularly where, following cumulative violence, the last act is relatively less serious.

Sexual infidelity

Section 55(6)(c) states for the first time that sexual infidelity is to be disregarded as a thing done or said. This is in recognition of the fact that many men successfully used the former defence where they had killed their partners through extreme jealousy and possessiveness, for example: *Weller* [2003] EWCA Crim 815 (see 'Introduction' in this section). But sexual infidelity is not defined. Could it be said, therefore, that things done or said which are peripheral to or associated with sexual infidelity are not excluded? The first case to be decided under the new law held that context, taunting and humiliation arising from sexual infidelity were still relevant.

R v Clinton, Parker, Evans [2012] EWCA CRIM 2

Three conjoined appeals were heard by the Court of Appeal against murder convictions by husbands on the grounds that loss of control should take account of sexual infidelity despite its exclusion from the C&JA 2009 by s55(6)(c). We will concentrate on *Clinton*, the focus of the judgment.

D and his wife (W) had lived together for 16 years. D was obsessional and suspicious. W went to live with her mother two weeks before her death, leaving their two children with D. On the day before her death in November 2010, W confessed to an affair. D also found evidence of sexual infidelity on W's Facebook site and believed her to have had affairs with five men. W returned home next day at 2.00 pm. That morning, D had consumed drink and drugs and had had suicidal thoughts. By 2.50 pm W had been beaten with a wooden bat around the head and strangled to death with a belt. At the time of arrest, he was in the loft with a rope around his neck and said he was hearing voices. He alleged W had taunted him about committing suicide. D pleaded guilty to manslaughter on the grounds of diminished responsibility and loss of control. The former was dismissed by the jury. The trial judge refused to allow loss of control to go to the jury on the grounds that sexual infidelity was excluded by the C&JA 2009 and there was no other evidence capable of being regarded as grave or justifiably wrong. D was convicted of murder and appealed.

Lord Judge CJ:

> To begin with, there is no definition of 'sexual infidelity'. Who and what is embraced in this concept? Is sexual infidelity to be construed narrowly so as to refer only to conduct which is related directly and exclusively to sexual activity? Only the words and acts constituting sexual activity are to be disregarded: on one construction, therefore, the effects are not. What acts relating to infidelity, but distinguishable from it on the basis that they are not 'sexual,' may be taken into account? Is the provision directly concerned with sexual infidelity, or with envy and jealousy and possessiveness, the sort of obsession that leads to violence against the victim on the basis expressed in the sadly familiar language, 'if I cannot have him/her, then no one else will/can?' The notion of infidelity appears to involve a relationship between the two people to which one party may be unfaithful. Is a one-night-stand sufficient for this purpose? . . .
>
> It would be illogical for a defendant to be able to rely on an untrue statement about the victim's sexual infidelity as a qualifying trigger in support of the defence, but not on a truthful one. Equally, it would be quite unrealistic to limit its ambit to words spoken to his or her lover by the unfaithful spouse or partner during sexual activity. In our judgment things 'said' includes admissions of sexual infidelity (even if untrue) as well as reports (by others) of sexual infidelity. Such admissions or reports will rarely if ever be uttered without a context, and almost certainly a painful one. In short, the words will almost invariably be spoken as part of a highly charged discussion in which many disturbing comments will be uttered, often on both sides . . .
>
> It may not be unduly burdensome to compartmentalise sexual infidelity where it is the only element relied on in support of a qualifying trigger, and, having compartmentalised it in this way, to disregard it. Whether this is so or not, the legislation imposes that exclusionary obligation on the court. However, to seek to compartmentalise sexual infidelity and exclude it when it is integral to the facts as a whole is not only much more difficult, but is unrealistic and carries with it the potential for injustice. In the examples we have given earlier in this judgment, we do not see how any sensible evaluation of the gravity of the circumstances or their *impact on the defendant* could be made if the jury, having, in accordance with the legislation, heard the evidence, were then to be directed to excise from their evaluation of the qualifying trigger the matters said to constitute sexual infidelity, and to put them into distinct compartments to be disregarded. In our judgment, where sexual infidelity is integral to and forms an essential part of the context in which to make a just evaluation whether a qualifying trigger properly falls within the ambit of subsections 55(3) and (4), the prohibition in section 55(6)(c) does not operate to exclude it.

> For present purposes the most significant feature of the third component is that the impact on the defendant of sexual infidelity is not excluded. The exclusion in section 55(6)(c) is limited to the assessment of the qualifying trigger. In relation to the third component, that is the way in which the defendant has reacted and lost control, 'the circumstances' are not constrained or limited. Indeed, section 54(3) expressly provides that reference to the defendant's circumstances extends to 'all' of the circumstances except those bearing on his general capacity for tolerance and self-restraint. When the third component of the defence is examined it emerges that, notwithstanding section 55(6)(c), account may, and in an appropriate case, should be taken of sexual infidelity. [Emphasis added]

Conviction in *Clinton* was overturned and a retrial ordered.

 NOTE 7.4

1. The exclusion of sexual infidelity as a qualifying trigger is extremely problematic, particularly in relation to things 'said'. Confessions of betrayal may or may not be true and may or may not disclose actual sexual infidelity. The relevant words may take the form of reports from third parties or things said in a highly charged, emotional discussion, which, again, may or may not be true. Nevertheless, sexual infidelity as a thing 'done or said' is to be disregarded as a qualifying trigger.

2. However, *taunting or humiliation*, if sufficiently serious, could provide the necessary qualifying trigger, just as much as betrayal or humiliation of sufficient gravity in respect of other matters.

3. The *impact* of sexual infidelity is not excluded from the objective test in s54(1)(c), in considering the circumstances in which D has reacted and lost control. Section 54(3) extends to 'all' of the circumstances except those bearing on D's general capacity for tolerance and self-restraint. That does not mean that the *context* of infidelity should be excluded altogether in respect of such *effects* as taunting or humiliation, but they would need to be sufficiently serious objectively.

This judgment has not been universally welcomed because it appears to permit the very thing that Parliament wished to exclude from the defence: the killing of women by violent, angry men. Sexual infidelity plus humiliation might now provide the necessary qualifying trigger: 'infidelity *plus*'.

One might query whether the real trigger in such cases is humiliation as opposed to infidelity. The taunting in *Clinton* concerned suicide. It was presumably regarded by the court as insignificant since the judgment was concerned more or less entirely with sexual infidelity. The reasoning here does appear to undermine parliamentary intention: if sexual infidelity, whether done or said, is to be excluded as a qualifying trigger, as Lord Judge CJ confirms, then the defence should be withdrawn from the jury. If there is no qualifying trigger, the defence does not arise. On what basis, therefore, is a jury to take account of the impact of sexual infidelity? Read this critique by D. J. Baker and LX. Zhao, 'Contributory qualifying and non-qualifying triggers in the loss of control defence: a wrong turn on sexual infidelity' [2012] *JCL* 254:

> Sexual infidelity cannot be considered as a circumstance merely to try to show that even though the potential qualifying conduct is too mild to qualify as a trigger under s. 55(4), that it might if it is considered in light of the fact that the defendant felt aggrieved by his partner's sexual infidelity. Clearly,

allowing such evidence to be considered under the third prong of the defence undercuts Parliament's aim to exclude sexual infidelity from being used as a qualifying trigger. It is clear that Parliament did not intend sexual infidelity to be used in this way. It is a form of provocation that is expressly excluded from counting as a qualifying trigger, and the legal effect of this is that it is also excluded from the inquiry that is conducted under s. 54(1)(c). How could the jury consider whether sexual infidelity prevented the defendant from exercising *self-restraint* under the third prong of the defence without compromising its inquiry under the qualifying trigger provision? . . . If sexual infidelity were considered as a circumstance under the third prong, it would effectively allow D to use a non-qualifying trigger to establish the defence . . .

The decision seems to ignore that a core aim of reforming the law in this area was to give women greater protection. The aim was to deny angry and jealous men a concession for killing in revenge or out of jealousy. The government took a bold and commendable step in expressly excluding sexual infidelity as a qualifying trigger. The law was not changed on the basis that a person never loses control when he or she is provoked by sexual infidelity; it was changed because society no longer views a loss of control resulting from this as reasonable. Society expects a person to maintain control in such cases even though the provocation may in fact be immense for him or her. Some people will in fact lose control in such circumstances, but Parliament is no longer willing to recognise this type of loss of control as an excuse for killing.

Clinton has, predictably, generated further appeals on the issue of sexual infidelity. There is little to be said about the next case except that it held that the concepts of cumulative provocation and slow burn, previously recognised under the previous defence, should continue under the new. These concepts were, of course, of great assistance to abused women who had killed violent men after a delay or after a last incident of relatively trivial provocation. The context here, ironically, concerned the killing of women by men for sexual infidelity. Presumably, after *Clinton*, the arguments could be described as 'infidelity plus'. None of the appeals succeeded, but for a different reason:

Dawes, Hatter & Bowyer [2013] EWCA CRIM 332

Three conjoined appeals concerned sexual infidelity. Dawes killed a man, with a kitchen knife, whom he found lying on the sofa with his estranged wife. The appeal against conviction concerned the fact that, since *Clinton* had not prohibited the emotional effect of infidelity, loss of control should have been considered on the *cumulative effect* of various incidents of suspected infidelity. Hatter was convicted for stabbing his estranged girlfriend, who had begun to see another man, after breaking into her home. On appeal, it was argued that there was evidence that D might have lost his self-control due to emotional 'slow burn', a sense of abandonment and anxiety. Bowyer killed V, with whom he shared a prostitute, whilst burgling V's house. He pleaded loss of control on the basis of his fear of V and hurtful comments made by V against the prostitute. All three appeals were dismissed on the basis of insufficient evidence of loss of control. Lord Judge CJ explained:

Dawes: In our judgment, however, the decision that the loss of control should not be left to the jury was fully justified. There was no sufficient evidence that the appellant ever lost his self-control. His own evidence was that he had not killed Mr Pethard in a rage. He was shocked rather than angry. He simply wanted him out of the flat.

Hatter: The defence was accident. Once again, for entirely understandable reasons, the jury rejected the defence. It did not follow from the rejection of the defence that the loss of control defence might then arise. Dealing with it generally, we agree that the fact of the break up of a relationship, of itself, will not normally constitute circumstances of an extremely grave character and entitle the aggrieved party to feel a justifiable sense of being seriously wronged. However we also appreciate that circumstances vary, and just as issues relating to sexual infidelity have to be examined in their overall circumstances, so the events surrounding the circumstances in the breakdown of a relationship will often but not always fall to be disqualified by s.55(6). In the present case, however, we agree with Judge Goldsack that . . . there was no particular feature of the evidence to suggest any justifiable sense in the appellant of being seriously wronged. If the jury was sure about the main thrust of the Crown's case, this was premeditated murder. If the jury concluded that the defendant's account of events may have been correct, but nevertheless rejected accident, there was no evidence that the fatal injuries were inflicted by him in consequence of loss of control.

Bowyer: The deceased was entitled to say and do anything reasonable, including the use of force, to eject the burglar from his home. Even taking the appellant's evidence at face value (and we bear in mind that the jury must have rejected it) it is absurd to suggest that the entirely understandable response of the deceased to finding a burglar in his home provided the appellant with the remotest beginnings of a basis for suggesting that he had any justifiable sense of being wronged, let alone seriously wronged. On that basis alone, one essential ingredient of this defence was entirely absent. Furthermore, we can detect no evidence of loss of control. The tragic events which occurred in the home of the deceased bore all the hallmarks of appalling violence administered in cold blood.

 NOTE 7.5

1. The approach to sexual infidelity as set out in *Clinton* was confirmed, namely that it is to be excluded as a qualifying trigger. In *Dawes*, there was nothing in the circumstances leading up to the relationship breakdown that might admit the defence and Hatter's appeal was dismissed on the grounds that the killing was a direct response to the relationship breakdown.

2. A considered desire for revenge will defeat the defence. It remains an open question as to whether the defence will apply where a mix of anger/fear and a desire for revenge arise. Bowyer's killing was considered to be due to cold-blooded violence during a burglary. There was no evidence of loss of control. As such, the defence should never have been left to the jury at all.

Given that none of the appellants were found to have lost self-control, perhaps the more fundamental issue raised here is the meaning of that concept. Look back at '1. Loss of self-control: s54(1)' in this section for some observations.

Provocation was in the past accepted in relation to 'honour killings' in order to 'wipe away the shame' of cultural moral transgressions. Honour killings are unlikely to fall within s55(4) for lack of objective justification, save for exceptional cases, particularly given the prohibition on sexual infidelity as a qualifying trigger (see A. Clough, 'Honour killings, partial defences and the exclusionary conduct model' (2016) 80(3) *JCL* 177).

Revenge or incitement

Again, s54(4) applies so that the defence will not be available to those acting in a considered desire for revenge. Section 55(6)(b) states that D's sense of being seriously wronged is not justifiable where the thing done or said is incited by D as an excuse for violence.

SECTION SUMMARY

- *The defence of loss of control is a concession to human frailty where a defendant kills through fear or anger;*
- *D will have intentionally killed but will be able to plead the defence, reducing the conviction to one of voluntary manslaughter, where under ss 54 and 55 C&JA 2009 there is:*
  - ☐ *s54(1)(a): a loss of self-control which can arise after a delay; AND*
  - ☐ *s54(1)(b): which is due to either or both of the following qualifying triggers:*
  - ☐ *s 55(3): fear of serious violence;*
  - ☐ *s55(4): a thing done or said (or both) of an extremely grave character causing D to have a justifiable sense of being seriously wronged; AND*
  - ☐ *s54(1)(c): D must also satisfy the objective test*

?! THINKING POINT 7.2

1. Ahmed suspected that his wife, Sophia, was conducting an affair with his best friend, Brian. One day, he found them together and Sophia confessed to Ahmed that the child of their marriage was Brian's. Ahmed immediately strangled Brian to death.

   Would the defence of loss of control apply? Give reasons for your answer.

2. Anne and Bill lived together for eight months. Bill frequently punched and threatened her. One day, she told him she was going out. He said that she could only go out with him and that if she tried to leave on her own she would get what was coming to her. The next evening, Anne stabbed Bill repeatedly with a knife as he lay sleeping in a drunken stupor on the settee. He died in hospital the next day.

   a. What offence/s might Anne have committed?

   b. Did Anne have the mens rea for the offence?

   c. Does Anne have a defence?

   d. What difficulties will Anne face in arguing any defence and how might she overcome them?

3. The objective test: A person of D's sex and age, with a normal degree of tolerance and self-restraint and in the circumstances of D, might have reacted in the same or in a similar way to D: s54(1)(c)

The fact that there has been a loss of self-control due to a qualifying trigger is insufficient. The jury must be satisfied that a person of similar age and sex, with normal powers of tolerance and self-restraint and in similar circumstances, would have killed in a similar way. This is an objective test. It reflects, but is wider than, the objective 'reasonable man' test under provocation because it permits D's circumstances to be taken into account. The point of this test is to remind the jury that there must be some objective expectations of behaviour in the face of provocative conduct. People are expected to exert reasonable 'self-restraint' over their responses. This test will therefore exclude those who are naturally hot-tempered, possessive, jealous, intoxicated or otherwise likely to fly off the handle at the slightest provocation. However, tolerable variations can be accepted depending on age, sex and circumstances.

The core features of the corresponding part of the old defence, which are essentially preserved, were stated by A. Ashworth in 'The Doctrine of Provocation' [1976] CLJ 292, as follows:

> The objective condition looks to the element of partial justification and, inevitably, to the conduct of the provoking party. It requires of the jury an assessment of the seriousness of the provocation, and a judgment as to whether the provocation was grave enough to warrant a reduction of the crime from murder to manslaughter. This question of sufficiency is one of degree, and the legal rules, although they can take the court so far, cannot determine this ultimate question. Of course there will be clear cases—as, for example, where a teenage son loses control and attacks his bullying father—and there will be doubtful cases . . . . Each case is for the decision of the jury, properly directed as to the law.

In principle, the test is one of objective reasonableness, but s54(1)(c) envisages three ways in which D's specific attributes marking him out from the ordinary may be relevant:

- age, sex (general physical attributes);
- tolerance, self-restraint (mental attributes); and
- circumstances.

Age, sex and general physical attributes

Section 54(1)(c) states that the jury should compare D's reaction to that of a person of D's age and sex. These two characteristics may have a bearing on a person's capacity for self-restraint. The fact that they have been specifically mentioned derives from the following important precedent on provocation:

R v Camplin [1978] 2 ALL ER 168 HOUSE OF LORDS

Camplin was a 15-year-old youth who killed a man by whom he had been forcibly sexually assaulted and then taunted. Camplin had hit V over the head with a chapatti pan. The question for the court was whether to assess the provocation against the standard of a reasonable adult or whether Camplin be judged against the standard of a reasonable 15-year-old youth.

It was held that youth was not a personal idiosyncrasy or infirmity and was relevant for the jury to take into account. Lord Diplock said in a model direction:

> The reasonable man is a person having the power of self-control to be expected of an ordinary person of the sex and age of the Accused but in other respects sharing such of the Accused's characteristics as they think would affect the gravity of the provocation to him.
> . . . the reasonable man is an ordinary person of either sex, not exceptionally excitable or pugnacious, but possessed of such powers of self-control as everyone is entitled to expect that his fellow citizens will exercise in society as it is today.

 NOTE 7.6

The case was concerned with physical as opposed to mental characteristics. Historically, D's fatal reaction was judged against the standard of a reasonable man who was of sound mind and able-bodied. No account could be taken of any unique attributes or characteristics. Therefore, the reasonable man was not allowed to be: excitable or unusually unstable

(*Lesbini* [1914] 3 KB 116—where D killed a girl in an amusement arcade firing range after she had taunted him); pregnant (*Smith* (1915) 11 Cr App R 81) or impotent (*Bedder* [1954] 2 All ER 801—where an impotent young man killed a prostitute who had jeered at him). The rule was relaxed after s3 Homicide Act 1957 extended the defence of provocation to include both physical and verbal provocation. This opened the possibility that verbal insults could be directed at D's unusual characteristics. The so-called reasonable man might therefore bear greater similarity to the D on trial with the qualification that sobriety and reasonable self-control were standards to be expected from everyone.

Section 54(1)(c) reflects this case. Sex was doubtless included due to the physical inequality of women compared to men, which may lead to a lower degree of self-restraint. Women get pregnant and abused which may also reduce their tolerance and self-restraint. Whether this view is right or wrong can be debated, but it is possible that gender may be relevant to the killing of a violent assailant by a vulnerable defendant. It is not clear why race, ethnicity or religion are not also expressly included since, as S. Edwards argues, a jury applying an objective test may need reminding of the impact of such taunting ('Anger and Fear as Justifiable Preludes for Loss of Self-Control' (2010) 74(3) *JCL* 223).

The reference to age may be considered problematic given that, in the case of children and teenagers, age is not always the best indication of maturity or capacity for self-restraint. Some 14-year-olds have greater maturity than some 18-year-olds. The stipulation of age may exclude mentally immature children and adults. Recall that developmental immaturity is excluded from the new diminished responsibility defence. Such defendants may now be left without a defence to murder. Sex and age are not the only physical characteristics which will be relevant to the objective test. Unique physical attributes such as those mentioned earlier, for example, impotency, as in *Bedder*, and pregnancy, as in *Smith* will continue to be relevant to s54(1)(c).

Tolerance, self-restraint and mental attributes

This aspect of s54(1)(c) requires a comparison between the actual defendant on trial and a person with a normal degree of tolerance and self-restraint (replacing the previous test of reasonable self-control). This apparently straightforward test belies some of the most complex historical case law to be found in criminal law, as indicated in the introduction.

Tolerance and self-restraint may not be normal because of a mental problem. Under the old law of provocation, there were two irreconcilable approaches to such a 'characteristic': The first was flexible and semi-subjective. It asked, 'what would it be reasonable to expect from a person with all of his mental characteristics under the circumstances'? This approach could have included *any* mental characteristic, even one reducing D's self-control, for example: BWS as in *Thornton*, *Ahluwalia* discussed earlier, or serious clinical depression as in (*Morgan*) *Smith* [2000] 3 All ER 289. In the latter, the majority of the House of Lords held that the crucial question was what degree of self-control was it fair and just to expect from a person with the accused's characteristics?) The second, and dominant, approach excluded all mental characteristics except for those which were related to the gravity of the provocation, that is: if V was insulted about a particular mental characteristic, the gravity of the insult would be more serious than had it been a more abstract provocation. So, the House of Lords in *Morhall* [1995] 3 All ER 659, held that an addiction to glue-sniffing was an admissible characteristic because it was the target of provocative taunting and, as such, had affected the gravity of the provocation to D. This was logical but surprising, since the reasonable person was always assumed to be sober. The Privy Council in *Luc Thiet Thuan* [1996] 2 All ER 1033 confirmed that brain damage rendering D less able to control his impulses would be relevant if it was the subject of taunts by the deceased. The Privy Council in *Holley* (discussed next) confirmed this strict, objective approach, that only those attributes which had a bearing on the gravity of the provocation would be relevant, and disapproved of *Smith*. This then became the precedent for s54(1)(c), although the term 'character- istics' was avoided. In other words, the particular characteristic, whether a serious mental disorder or a disability such as dyslexia, compulsive behaviour or an addiction, must be the target of pro- vocative insults, taunts or jokes so as to render the provocation more serious to the defendant. If D's mental characteristic is sufficiently severe, diminished responsibility should be used instead.

AG for Jersey v Holley [2005] UKPC 23 PRIVY COUNCIL

D, an alcoholic, killed his girlfriend while under the influence of drink following her confession that she had had sex with another man. He pleaded not guilty to murder on the grounds of provo- cation and was convicted. The Court of Appeal of Jersey, applying *Smith*, allowed his appeal on the ground that the disease of alcoholism from which he suffered could be taken into account in considering whether the provocation was enough to make a reasonable man act as he had done. A manslaughter conviction was substituted. The Crown appealed to the Privy Council.

Lord Nicholls:

> The law of homicide is a highly sensitive and highly controversial area of the criminal law. In 1957 Parliament altered the common law relating to provocation and declared what the law on this subject should thenceforth be. In these circumstances it is not open to judges now to change ('develop') the common law and thereby depart from the law as declared by Parliament. However much the contrary is asserted, the majority view [in *Morgan Smith*] does represent a departure from the law as declared in section 3 of the Homicide Act 1957. It involves a significant relaxation of the uniform, objective standard adopted by Parliament. Under the statute the sufficiency of the provocation ('whether the provocation was enough to make a reasonable man do as [D] did') is to be judged by one standard, not a standard which varies from defendant to defendant. Whether the provocative act or words and D's response met the 'ordinary person' standard prescribed by the statute is the question the jury must consider, not the altogether looser question of whether, hav- ing regard to all the circumstances, the jury consider the loss of self-control was sufficiently excus- able. The statute does not leave each jury free to set whatever standard they consider appropriate in the circumstances by which to judge whether D's conduct is 'excusable'.
>
> [T]heir Lordships, respectfully but firmly, consider the majority view expressed in the Morgan Smith case is erroneous.
>
> Points arising
>
> The first is relevant to the facts in the present case. It concerns application of the principles dis- cussed above in circumstances where D acted under the influence of alcohol or drugs and, there- fore, at a time when his level of self-control may have been reduced. If D was taunted on account of his intoxication, that may be a relevant matter for the jury to take into account when assessing the gravity of the taunt to D. But D's intoxicated state is not a matter to be taken into account by the jury when considering whether D exercised ordinary self-control. The position is the same, so far as provocation is concerned, if D's addiction to alcohol has reached the stage that he is suffering from the disease of alcoholism.

Nevertheless, the majority did not disturb the decision of the Court of Appeal to overturn D's conviction.

NOTE 7.7

The appeal specifically concerned the relevance of D's alcoholism to the defence. Had D been taunted about this instead of infidelity, it might have been relevant to the gravity of the provocation. The defence should then have been left to the jury. It was rightly excluded because his alcoholism was irrelevant to the actual provocation.

The new objective test in s54(1)(c) reflects the reasoning of this case. The problem here is that there may well be no moral basis for confining the test to only those attributes which relate to the gravity of the provocation. Read the following by A. Norrie, 'The Coroners and Justice Act 2009—Partial Defences to Murder' [2010] *Crim LR* 281–282:

> Thus after *Holley*, being addicted to glue-sniffing still provided the basis for an excusable provocation, provided the taunt was directed at the addiction, but not if it was not. At the same time, otherwise sympathetic psychological conditions such as the stress and pressure of caring for a new-born baby (*Doughty*), or suffering from emotional immaturity (*Humphreys*), or being of low intelligence (*Acott*) would not. Yet, these were cases that were, or could in principle have been, admitted under the compassionate excuse approach of the old law. For these defendants to have a defence to murder after *Holley*, they would need to find refuge in diminished responsibility. In all three cases this might have been possible under the existing law, though it would have involved very sympathetic psychiatric testimony, especially in *Doughty* . . . . Thus post-*Holley*, under the old law, the law's irrationality is seen in that morally unworthy characteristics are still admissible provided that they are directly related to the provocation, while morally sympathetic characteristics are not, unless there is the direct link. The old law was based upon a concession to human frailty, recognising that people could not always reach the standard of the reasonable person, yet be worthy of compassion in their personal situation. That law developed in a way that lost sight of the need to judge which characteristics were worthy of compassion, and hit upon the need for a direct connection between provocation and loss of self-control to narrow its application, but without ever recognising the underlying problem. . . .
>
> Under the new ethical approach [of the new law], this sympathy for human frailty is rejected in favour of a recognition of imperfectly justified anger. Anger is partially rightful in the new understanding, while loss of self-control fails to qualify one for the defence. The person who loses self-control falls short of a standard to which he or she has to conform. . . . [In relation to *Doughty*:] That case in particular requires us to have compassion for the weakness of one who in sad or tragic circumstances did what was wrong without justifiable sense of being seriously wronged. No jury, properly directed or otherwise, could find that the defendant had such a sense. Under the old law, his loss of self-control was condemnable, but having lost it in the context of a sympathetic or tragic plight could lead the jury to grant him a partial concession based on human frailty. Under the old provocation law, someone like Doughty may be shown compassion and become a manslaughterer; under the new law, he will not get the defence. One might wonder if moral progress has been made here.

Do you agree with the author's views? Would someone like Doughty be able to use the defence of diminished responsibility? Would someone like Morhall still be able to use the defence of loss of control?

Circumstances

Section 54(3) states that 'the circumstances of D' is a reference to all of D's circumstances other than those whose only relevance to D's conduct is that they bear on D's general capacity for tolerance and self-restraint.

D's external circumstances can be taken into account here, that is: the fact that D is a householder using force to defend himself or his family, an abused woman who kills against a background of violence or, controversially, anyone who kills against a background of sexual infidelity, so it would seem (see *Clinton* earlier). On this reading, there is no reason why it should not also include D's 'internal' circumstances such as a particular mental state but s54(3) specifically excludes those which might reduce D's general capacity for tolerance and self-restraint. Diminished responsibility might be used in the alternative. The Court of Appeal has held that a firm line will be taken to exclude alcoholism or intoxication from the new defence.

R v Asmelash [2013] EWCA CRIM 157

D angrily stabbed a man in the chest following several hours of argument, insults and aggression towards him by V. Both had been drinking all day. D claimed to have lost his self-control and to have swung the knife at V in order to protect himself. He was convicted and appealed on the ground that voluntary intoxication should be a relevant circumstance for the purposes of s54(1)(c) because it did not solely relate to the issue of self-restraint.

Lord Judge CJ:

> In essence, therefore, Mr Davey's submission proceeds on the basis that in the absence of any express statutory provision, in the context of 'loss of control', a new approach to the issue of voluntary drunkenness is required. We disagree. We can find nothing in the 'loss of control' defence to suggest that Parliament intended, somehow, that the normal rules which apply to voluntary intoxication should not apply. If that had been the intention of Parliament, it would have been spelled out in unequivocal language. Moreover, faced with the compelling reasoning of this court in *Dowds* in the context of diminished responsibility, it is inconceivable that different criteria should govern the approach to the issue of voluntary drunkenness, depending on whether the partial defence under consideration is diminished responsibility or loss of control. Indeed, given that in a fair proportion of cases, both defences are canvassed before the jury, the potential for uncertainty and confusion which would follow the necessarily very different directions on the issue of intoxication depending on which partial defence was under consideration, does not bear contemplation. . . . Our conclusion does not bear the dire consequences suggested by Mr Davey. It does not mean that the defendant who has been drinking is deprived of any possible loss of control defence: it simply means, as the judge explained, that the loss of control defence must be approached without reference to the defendant's voluntary intoxication. If a sober individual in the defendant's circumstances, with normal levels of tolerance and self-restraint might have behaved in the same way as the defendant confronted by the relevant qualifying trigger, he would not be deprived of the loss of control defence just because he was not sober. And different considerations would arise if a defendant with a severe problem with alcohol or drugs was mercilessly taunted about the condition, to the extent that it constituted a qualifying trigger, the alcohol or drug problem would then form part of the circumstances for consideration.

Therefore, the reaction of the hypothetical other person with a normal degree of tolerance and self-restraint had to be judged as if he were sober, as established in *Camplin* and *Holley* (see earlier).

The inclusion of 'circumstances' could mean that it will be less crucial for abused women to prove BWS in relation to loss of control. A background of abuse, whether resulting in BWS or not, may thus be relevant to the gravity of the injustice done to her. Otherwise, her history and experience of violence will form part of her background circumstances.

?! **THINKING POINT** 7.3

Consider whether the following characteristics are relevant to either D's capacity for tolerance/self-restraint or the gravity of V's words or conduct. Comment on their relevance in relation to the objective test under s54(1)(c) C&JA 2009.

1. Dan has a hot-tempered and jealous disposition. When his girlfriend, Eileen, attempts to leave him one day, he strangles her.

2. Yolanda is 16 and kills an older man with whom she has a relationship because he wishes to force her into prostitution.

3. Nigel, an alcoholic, thinks all Asians are terrorists. Mohammed calls him a racist pig. Nigel then throws a petrol bomb through Mohammed's window and Mohammed is killed in the fire.

4. Zohra has an attention-seeking personality and self-harms. She kills her boyfriend when he threatens her with a gang rape.

5. Delia is dyslexic and cannot read very well. Her boyfriend taunts her about it frequently. One night in desperation, Delia stabs him with a pair of scissors.

6. Look at the question on Anne and Bill at the end of the last section on the tests for loss of self-control and qualifying triggers. Suppose that as a consequence of Bill's violence, Anne became anxiety ridden, nervous, depressed and suffered from insomnia. What other defence might Anne plead?

Conclusion

The new defence of loss of control introduced by ss 54 and 55 C&JA 2009 in October 2010 was the culmination of three Law Commission reports: 'Partial Defences to Murder' (Law Com No 290, Cm. 630, 2004), 'A New Homicide Act for England and Wales' (CP No 177, 2005) and 'Murder, Manslaughter and Infanticide' (Law Com No 304, 2006). Consideration was given to merging the two partial defences of diminished responsibility and provocation but this was rejected because each served a different purpose and the potential for overlap was limited. It was possible but less likely that mental characteristics would be regarded as relevant to provocation. The question is whether the new defence of loss of control has greater clarity than provocation? Will it be any easier for juries to understand? Several new concepts were not defined, such as sexual infidelity and a 'considered' desire for revenge. This task has, therefore, been left to the courts, a process which has now begun. *Clinton* and *Dawes* confirm that the defence is narrower than before, although many previous features of the defence, such as cumulative 'impact' and 'slow burn' remain. Objective standards have an ever-more important part to play, as intended. The question of 'what does society expect of a person in such circumstances?' remains central to the defence. However, the defence remains technical and not easy for a jury to understand. The relationship of the objective test to the qualifying triggers is obscure and the meaning of self-control is opaque. To be 'not the master of one's mind' is capable of both scientific and emotional analysis. Either way, it involves an objective evaluation. Is it an unnecessary complication? One thing of which we can be sure, in view of the lingering uncertainties, is that the new defence is likely to generate as many colourful cases as the old!

SECTION SUMMARY

The partial defence of loss of control rests upon a three-limbed test:

■ *s54(1)(a): there must first be evidence of a loss of self-control (a subjective test);*

■ *s54(1)(b): this must be due to a 'qualifying trigger' (a semi-subjective/objective test):*

   ☐ *s55(3): fear of serious violence from V towards D or another; and/or s55(4): a thing done or said of an extremely grave character causing a justifiable sense of being seriously wronged;*

■ *s54(1)(c): D must finally demonstrate that a person of his age and sex with normal capacity for tolerance and self-restraint would have killed in such circumstances (an objective test).*

7.1.4 Suicide Pacts: The Third Partial Defence to Murder

Section 4 Homicide Act 1957 substitutes manslaughter for murder in these circumstances:

(1) It shall be manslaughter, and shall not be murder, for a person acting in pursuance of a suicide pact between him and another to kill the other or be a party to the other . . . being killed by a third person.

(2) Where it is shown that a person charged with the murder of another killed the other or was a party to his . . . being killed, it shall be for the defence to prove that the person charged was acting in pursuance of a suicide pact between him and the other.

(3) . . . 'suicide pact' means a common agreement between two or more persons having for its object the death of all of them, whether or not each is to take his own life, but nothing done by a person who enters into a suicide pact shall be treated as done by him in pursuance of the pact unless it is done while he has the settled intention of dying in pursuance of the pact.

In addition:

■ **Section 1 Suicide Act 1961** abolishes the offence of suicide.

■ **Section 2 Suicide Act 1961** as amended by s59 Coroners and Justice Act 2009, creates an offence of intentionally encouraging or assisting suicide.

7.2 Involuntary Manslaughter: Unintentional Killings

7.2.1 Introduction

7.2.2 Reckless Manslaughter

7.2.3 Manslaughter by Gross Negligence

7.2.4 Unlawful and Dangerous Act (Constructive) Manslaughter

KEY CASES

Gross Negligence Manslaughter

Adomako [1995] 1 AC 171—gross negligence manslaughter defined;

Misra & Srivastava [2004] EWCA Crim 2375—gross negligence manslaughter was not contrary to Article 7 ECHR;

Gemma Evans [2009] EWCA Crim 650—the existence of a duty is a matter of law.

7.2.1 Introduction

We have seen that the offence of murder consists of intentional killings and that voluntary manslaughter consists of intentional killings in the circumstances of a partial defence to murder such as loss of control, diminished responsibility or suicide pact. Involuntary manslaughter consists of three categories of unintentional killing, by recklessness, gross negligence and unlawful and dangerous act, where D is convicted of causing death even though he did not intend or foresee the possibility of death or serious harm. The offence applies to a wide range of conduct leading to death, from intentional unlawful activity, such as a robbery or arson, to lawful activity carried out with a high degree of incompetence, such as surgery or driving.

Unlawful and dangerous act manslaughter appears to be the most frequently committed of the three offences comprising involuntary manslaughter (B. Mitchell & R.D. Mackay 'Investigating Involuntary Manslaughter: An Empirical Study of 127 Cases' (2011) 31(1) *OJLS* 165). This study revealed a broad range of contexts and circumstances in which killings occurred, from young parents who found it difficult to cope with crying babies to revenge killings, killings during robberies or burglaries, and street fights. As such, the range of moral blame in this offence is vast and unique in English law.

Involuntary manslaughter is therefore a very wide offence covering a huge range of conduct with varying degrees of culpability (see Diagram 7.5). This has given rise to criticism and calls for reform.

7.2.2 Reckless Manslaughter

This category of manslaughter lacks a secure definition. When the House of Lords revived gross negligence manslaughter in *Adomako* [1995] 1AC 171, no attention was paid to whether or not reckless manslaughter would continue or as to the definition. Clearly, any recklessness would be subjective rather than objective according to *Caldwell*. Beyond that nothing was certain. Previous authority in the case of *Stone & Dobinson* [1977] 1 QB 354 had set a very low threshold of liability (recklessness as to an obvious risk of injury to health). It is now considered that if, when acting, D is aware of a high risk of death or serious injury and he nevertheless goes on unreasonably to take that risk, reckless manslaughter will have been committed provided the acts were the cause of death. This might occur in the context of either lawful or unlawful activity. The offence of reckless manslaughter overlaps with both gross negligence and unlawful act manslaughter.

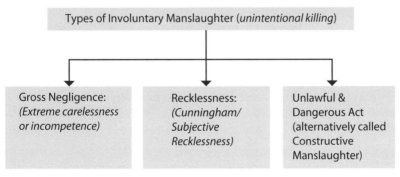

NB: The AR of manslaughter is the same as for murder.

Diagram 7.5
Types of involuntary manslaughter

The main difficulty here is to distinguish recklessness from oblique intention. If you think back to *Hyam* for instance, in pouring paraffin through a letter box and igniting it, D foresaw a highly probable risk of death/GBH but no certainty. The court considered that such foresight was sufficient MR for murder. *Hyam* was implicitly overruled by *Moloney* however when the MR for murder was confined to direct and oblique intention, the latter consisting of foresight of death/GBH as a 'moral certainty'. Mrs Hyam would now be considered subjectively reckless and guilty of either reckless or unlawful and dangerous act manslaughter but not murder. The following case confirms the elements of this offence:

R v Lidar (Narinder Singh) [2000] (UNREPORTED) 4 ARCHBOLD NEWS 3 COURT OF APPEAL

D was the driver of a moving car on to which V (Kully) was clinging whilst fighting with D. V fell and was killed when the car ran him over. The appeal against conviction was dismissed.

Evans LJ:

Nothing here suggests that for the future 'recklessness' could no longer be a basis for proving the offence of manslaughter; rather, the opposite. *Smith & Hogan* records that 'For many years the courts have used the terms "recklessness" and "gross negligence" to describe the fault required for involuntary manslaughter .... without any clear definition of either term. It was not clear whether these terms were merely two ways of describing the same thing, or whether they represented two distinct conditions of fault' (page 375). After referring to *Adomako*, the learned author continues:

'*Reckless manslaughter*. Gross negligence is a sufficient, but not necessarily the only fault for manslaughter. To some extent manslaughter by overt recklessness, conscious risk-taking still survives' (p.377) . . .

Recklessness

The direction given by the judge might be said to be open to criticism for failing to specify, first, that there had to be a high probability of physical harm to Kully, and secondly, that the risk was of serious injury rather than, as the judge put it, 'injury to health' and 'some physical harm, however slight'. This criticism was not advanced as a ground of appeal, but we should nevertheless consider what force there might be in it. In our judgment, there is none, because in the circumstances of this case both requirements undoubtedly were satisfied. The risk of harm to Kully, of which the jury has found that the appellant was aware, was clearly and unarguably a high degree of risk of serious injury to him. In the circumstances, therefore, we are satisfied that the verdict could not be considered unsafe if there was a mis-direction in this respect.

?! THINKING POINT 7.4

1. Can you think of a manslaughter case by omission in which recklessness was described as foresight of an obvious risk of injury to health?

2. How does *Lidar* establish a more limited mens rea for reckless manslaughter?

SECTION SUMMARY

Reckless manslaughter consists of:

■ *Causing death by a lawful or unlawful act and*

■ *With foresight of a high degree of risk of serious injury.*

7.2.3 Manslaughter by Gross Negligence

The offence consists of four elements:

1. A duty owed by D towards V to take care;

2. D's conduct must breach that duty in such a way as to give rise to a risk of death;

3. Causation;

4. Gross negligence showing such disregard for the life and safety of others as to amount to a crime.

The concept of gross negligence applies only to manslaughter and to no other offence. It means extreme carelessness or incompetence and arises where a very serious mistake causes death. The conduct may take the form of a seriously negligent act or omission. Sometimes there will be an overlap between unlawful and dangerous act manslaughter and gross negligence manslaughter.

One of the growth areas of this offence concerns the prosecution of doctors for causing death by neglect and mistreatment. Between 1867–1989 there were only seven reported prosecutions whereas, between 1995 and 2005, there were 38 (H. Quirk, 'The Need for Guidance in Medical Manslaughter Cases' [2013] *Crim LR* 871).

The two points concerning gross negligence manslaughter that you need to bear in mind as you read through this section are:

- The definition of gross negligence has been criticised as being so vague that it is capable of including lower degrees of ordinary negligence (carelessness).

- A duty of care is determined according to civil law principles. These are sometimes unclear. But a duty *to act*, as required by omissions liability, is determined by the criminal law. Are the two consistent? Is this a satisfactory basis of criminal liability for manslaughter? Recall the case of *Stone & Dobinson* [1977] 1 QB 354 and the criticism that liability for an assumption of a duty of care represented a wide extension of criminal liability for manslaughter.

➡ CROSS-REFERENCE
For further discussion of *Stone & Dobinson* see Chapter 2, 2.2.3.

We already know that negligence is found throughout both civil and criminal law. Ordinary negligence will not usually attract criminal liability but may be the basis of minor criminal conduct crime such as careless driving. There ought to be a clear distinction between the very high degree of negligence required for manslaughter and ordinary negligence. We will assess whether this is the case.

Background to the current law

We have seen that gross negligence manslaughter emerged at the beginning of the twentieth century (*Bateman* (1925) 19 Cr App R 8 and *Andrews v DPP* [1937] AC 576). However, it fell into obscurity after 1983 when *Caldwell* recklessness was applied to manslaughter. Gross negligence was not revived as an identifiable independent fault element until the leading case of *Adomako* [1995] 1 AC 171 (HL). It is distinguishable from subjective recklessness which involves the conscious or advertent running of an unreasonable risk of harm. The main criticism of this concept is that the *Adomako/Bateman* test does not indicate exactly how bad the negligence must be before it should amount to manslaughter as opposed to a lesser crime. It therefore follows that gross negligence manslaughter may offend the principle of legal certainty as required by Article 7 ECHR.

➡ CROSS-REFERENCE
The development of gross negligence manslaughter was considered in Chapter 3, 3.3.

1. Duty of care

The ordinary principles of negligence will be used in order to determine whether a duty of care exists between D and V. This might arise from either an omission or an act, both of which will now be considered.

Duty arising by omission

→ **CROSS-REFERENCE**
Liability for omissions was discussed in Chapter 2.

Gross negligence manslaughter is a result crime which can be committed by omission. We have already seen that omissions liability involves a breach of a duty to act, the duty arising in rare situations. For example, there is no duty upon any of us to rescue a drowning stranger and therefore no criminal liability will arise even though we might have easily performed a rescue. The limited categories of duty to act concern: doctor–patient; voluntary assumption; contract/statute; relationship; creation of danger.

Whether a duty exists is a matter of law

→ **CROSS-REFERENCE**
For further discussion of *Evans* see Chapter 2, 2.2.3.

It was held in the following case that the judge had been wrong to leave this matter of law to the jury. The facts concerned the failure by one half-sister to summon medical assistance for another to whom she had supplied heroin.

R v Gemma Evans [2009] EWCA CRIM 650 COURT OF APPEAL

Lord Judge LCJ:

The starting point is to reflect on first principles. Subject to any statutory exceptions, in the criminal trial decisions of fact are the exclusive responsibility of the jury and questions of law are for the judge. In principle therefore the existence, or otherwise, of a duty of care or, we would add, a duty to act, is a stark question of law: the question whether the facts establish the existence of the duty is for the jury …

In some cases, such as those arising from a doctor/patient relationship where the existence of the duty is not in dispute, the judge may well direct the jury that a duty of care exists. Such a direction would be proper. But if, for example, the doctor were on holiday at the material time, and the deceased asked a casual question over a drink, it may very well be that the question whether a doctor/patient relationship existed, and accordingly whether a duty of care arose, would be in dispute. In any cases where the issue is in dispute, and therefore in more complex cases, and assuming that the judge has found that it would be open to the jury to find that there was a duty of care, or a duty to act, the jury should be directed that if facts a + b and/or c or d are established, then in law a duty will arise, but if facts x or y or z were present, the duty would be negatived. In this sense, of course, the jury is deciding whether the duty situation has been established. In our judgment this is the way in which *Willoughby* should be understood and, understood in this way, no potential problems arising from article 6 and article 7 of the ECHR are engaged.

▤ NOTE 7.8

1. The case has now clarified that it is for the judge to define the duty by instructing the jury that if they find the facts of the case to be X, a duty will be established. The jury must then decide whether they find that the facts occurred.

2. This was not a case of *unlawful act* manslaughter where the culpable act concerned the supply of drugs as in *Kennedy (No 2)* [2007] UKHL 38. Had it been so, V's free decision to

self-inject would have broken the chain of causation between supply and death. Here, D's guilt arose from a grossly negligent omission in breach of a duty to act by creating a dangerous situation, that is: the failure to call for medical assistance in full awareness of the risks. Other duty situations have also given rise to gross negligence manslaughter prosecutions, that is: 'Voluntary assumption of a duty to act': *Khan* [1998] Crim LR 830.

→ CROSS-REFERENCE
For further discussion of *Kennedy (No 2)* and *Khan* see Chapter 2, 2.2.3.

It is, however, doubtful whether the issue of causation was convincingly dealt with in *Evans* and would seem to contradict *Kennedy*. D created or *contributed* to the dangerous situation by failing to protect the safety of V *once she became aware that her condition was life-threatening*, whereas *Kennedy* confirmed that self-injection breaks the chain of causation. This decision will undoubtedly enlarge the group of potential defendants in manslaughter cases. For example, it was followed in *Bowler* [2015] EWCA Crim 849, where D wrapped V in cellophane and PVC for their mutual sexual satisfaction (a lawful but dangerous activity). He then left V alone; when he later found him lifeless, D panicked and delayed calling emergency services. V died of heart failure caused by overheating and dehydration. D was convicted of gross negligence manslaughter since he had created a dangerous situation and then failed to monitor V or get timely help for him.

The next case confirms that contributory negligence by V will not exonerate D from a duty of care.

R v Winter & Winter [2010] EWCA CRIM 1474 COURT OF APPEAL

A director of a fireworks company and his son stored dangerous display-type fireworks of a kind they were not licensed to make or store in contravention of the Explosives Regulations 2003. A fire broke out on the farm they owned and spread to a container in which the fireworks were stored. It exploded killing a fire officer and a fire-service civilian media awareness officer (V) who was filming the fire for training purposes. He had ignored instructions from fire officers to keep back. The issue on appeal against convictions of gross negligence manslaughter concerned whether a duty was owed to the media awareness officer whose presence was not foreseeable. Alternatively, had the duty ceased when he disobeyed instructions? Hooper LJ:

> In our view it is reasonably foreseeable that civilian employees of the fire service in the position of Mr Wembridge may come on to and close to the site of a fire in order to film or photograph it. . . . Does that duty cease to be owed because Mr Wembridge may have disobeyed instructions? Counsel for the applicants conceded that they could show us no authority to suggest that a failure to comply with instructions resulted in there being no duty owed. Such a failure may be relevant on the issue of causation and, in civil cases, to the issue of causation, *volenti* and contributory negligence. It is not arguable, in our view, that any failure to comply with instructions in this case had the consequence that no duty of care was owed to Mr Wembridge. . . . To whom such a duty extends must depend upon all of the facts of the individual case. Suffice it to say that we are satisfied that it is not arguable that a duty was not owed to Mr Wembridge.

 NOTE 7.9

The existence of a duty of care must be distinguished from causation, to which a failure to follow instructions may be relevant. Remember: the breach of duty must cause death. The civil doctrine of *volenti non fit injuria*, referred to in the judgment, is a defence to an action in negligence. It means that V has voluntarily assumed the risk of injury.

Duty arising by positive act

Here, the courts will examine ordinary principles of the law of negligence in order to determine whether a duty was owed by D to V in circumstances which may arise outside of the 'omissions' categories. For the purposes of negligence, where the loss is purely physical, a duty of care will arise where the injury would have been in the contemplation of the reasonable man. The test is one of reasonable foreseeability. This is a wider test than for omissions. The civil position, however, is not entirely conclusive. For example, the criminal courts have found the existence of a duty between participants in a criminal enterprise even though this would not give rise to a duty in tort.

R v Wacker [2002] EWCA CRIM 1944, [2003] 4 ALL ER 295 COURT OF APPEAL

The bodies of 58 illegal Chinese immigrants were discovered in the back of a container lorry at Dover by Customs and Excise officers, having been carried from Rotterdam. They had died from suffocation. The container had been ventilated by a small vent which was open at the beginning of the journey but which had been closed from the outside during a stop shortly before boarding the ship. The lorry driver's fingerprints were discovered on the vent. The driver was convicted of conspiracy to facilitate the entry into the UK of illegal immigrants. He appealed.

Did the driver owe a duty of care to the deceased victims of the enterprise? His chief argument was that Adomako states that the ordinary principles of the law of negligence apply to ascertain whether or not D is in breach of a duty of care towards V who has died. One of the ordinary principles of negligence law is *ex turpi causa non oritur actio* (the law of negligence does not recognise a duty of care between participants in a criminal enterprise). It followed that he therefore owed no duty of care towards the illegal immigrants because they were participants in the illegal importation. The Court of Appeal rejected the appellant's argument on the grounds of public policy and dismissed the appeal. Kay LJ:

> Thus looked at as a matter of pure public policy, we can see no justification for concluding that the criminal law should decline to hold a person as criminally responsible for the death of another simply because the two were engaged in some joint unlawful activity at the time or, indeed, because there may have been an element of acceptance of a degree of risk by V in order to further the joint unlawful enterprise. Public policy, in our judgment, manifestly points in totally the opposite direction.
>
> The next question that we are bound to ask ourselves is whether in any way we are required by authority to take a different view. The foundation for the contention that *ex turpi causa* is as much a part of the law of manslaughter as it is a part of the law of negligence is the passage from the speech of Lord Mackay in *Adomako*. . . . In particular it is Lord Mackay's reference to 'the ordinary principles of negligence.'
>
> *Adomako* was a case where an anaesthetist had negligently brought about the death of a patient. It, therefore, involved no element of unlawful activity on the part of either the anaesthetist or the victim. We have no doubt that issues raised in the case we are considering would never have crossed the minds of those deciding that case in the House of Lords. Insofar as Lord Mackay referred to 'ordinary principles of the laws of negligence' we do not accept for one moment that he was intending to decide that the rules relating to *ex turpi causa* were part of those ordinary principles. He was doing no more than holding that in an 'ordinary' case of negligence, the question whether there was a duty of care was to be judged by the same legal criteria as governed whether there was a duty of care in the law of negligence. . . . The next question which is posed is whether it is right to say in this case that no duty of care can arise because it is impossible or inappropriate to determine the extent of that duty. We do not accept this proposition. If at the moment when the vent was shut, one of the Chinese had said 'you will make sure that we have enough air to survive,'

the appellant would have had no difficulty understanding the proposition and clearly by continu-ing with the unlawful enterprise in the way that he did, he would have been shouldering the duty to take care for their safety in this regard.... One further issue merits consideration, namely is it any answer to a charge of manslaughter for a defendant to say 'we were jointly engaged in a criminal enterprise and weighing the risk of injury or death against our joint desire to achieve our unlawful objective, we collectively thought that it was a risk worth taking'. In our judgment it is not. The duty to take care cannot, as a matter of public policy, be permitted to be affected the by countervailing demands of the criminal enterprise.

 NOTE 7.10

1. Participants to a criminal enterprise could owe a duty to one another, even though they are not covered by the civil law of negligence (*ex turpi causa*).

2. The rules relating to *ex turpi causa* were never intended by Lord Mackay in *Adomako* to be considered part of the ordinary principles of negligence when applying to *lawful* negligent activity. But that did not mean that a duty should be excluded from negligent *unlawful* activity.

No mention was made by the Court of Appeal in *Wacker* of *Khan* in which the Court of Appeal had already decided that a duty of care might arise in the joint criminal enterprise between a heroin dealer and his customer on suitable facts.

➜ CROSS-REFERENCE
For further discussion of *Khan* see 2.2.3.

Some confusion remains between the tortious 'duty of care' which is essential to manslaughter by gross negligence and the 'duty to act' which forms the basis of omissions liability in the crimi-nal law. *Wacker* confirms that there is not a complete overlap. See this comment from 'The Duty of Care in Gross Negligence Manslaughter' [2007] *Crim LR* 24 by J. Herring and E. Palser:

> Whilst there may be some areas in which policy considerations and objectives differ between tort and criminal law, only rarely will these justify a significant deviation from the well-established principles governing the tortious duty of care, upon which *Adomako* clearly appears to have been predicated. In this light, though there may be calls for the criminal law to develop its own understanding of the duty of care, distinct from that in tort, we would suggest that use is made of the development of the concept of a duty of care in the law of tort as the normal meaning of 'duty of care' in gross negligence manslaughter but recognising that there may be rare cases where the judge can direct that the tortious duty will not be relied upon. These will be in cases where the blameworthiness of the victim leads to there being no duty of care in tort when it may still be appropriate to impose a criminal liability (eg: the *ex turpi causa* doctrine) and cases involving omissions, where the court will need to find not only a duty of care, but also a duty to act. Such an approach is the best way to achieve clarity and consistency in the law.

2. Breach of the duty

As will be obvious from the cases discussed earlier, the duty, once established, may be breached in a wide variety of ways, both lawful and unlawful. But it is clear that gross negli-gence manslaughter is to be kept within strict and narrow limits. Thus, *Adomako* held that D's conduct must give rise to a serious and obvious risk of *death* as opposed to a risk of *serious harm* as laid down in *Stone & Dobinson*.

→ CROSS-REFERENCE
Stone & Dobinson was discussed in Chapter 2, 2.2.3.

The *Bateman/Adomako* definition establishes that the test is objective. Therefore, the jury will need to consider the extent to which D's conduct departed from a proper standard of care and ask whether the risk of death was obvious to a reasonable person in the same position as D, that is: a reasonable doctor, engineer, driver, carer and so on. Lord MacKay in *Adomako* [1995] 1 AC 171 defined the risk as follows:

> The essence of the matter, which is supremely a jury question, is whether, having regard to *the risk of death* involved, the *conduct* of D was so bad in all the circumstances as to amount in their judgment to a criminal act or omission. . . . [Emphasis added.]

Often, particularly in medical negligence cases, the breach itself may prevent D realising that there is a serious risk of death. D will not then be liable, for reasons set out in *Rose v R* [2017] EWCA Crim 1168:

> The question of whether there is a serious and obvious risk of death must exist at, and is to be assessed with respect to, knowledge at the time of the breach of duty.
>   A recognisable risk of something serious is not the same as a recognisable risk of death.
>   A mere possibility that an assessment might reveal something life-threatening is not the same as an obvious risk of death: an obvious risk is a present risk which is clear and unambiguous, not one which might become apparent on further investigation.

Gross negligence manslaughter is therefore more limited than reckless manslaughter, which only requires foresight of risk of serious injury.

3. Causation

→ CROSS-REFERENCE
For further discussion of the rules on causation see Chapter 2.

The breach must cause death and so the rules on causation must be satisfied.

4. Gross negligence

Lord MacKay in *Adomako*:

> In cases of manslaughter by criminal negligence involving a breach of duty, it is a sufficient direction to the jury to adopt the gross negligence test set out by the Court of Appeal in the present case following *R v Bateman* and *Andrews v DPP* and it is not necessary to refer to the definition of recklessness in *R v Lawrence*, although it is perfectly open to the trial judge to use the word 'reckless' in its ordinary meaning as part of his exposition of the law if he deems it appropriate in the circumstances of the particular case.

The *Bateman* test was as follows:

> In explaining to juries the test to be applied, many epithets such as culpable, criminal, gross, wicked, clear and complete have been used . . . In order to establish criminal liability the facts must be such that in the opinion of the jury the negligence of the Accused went beyond a mere matter of compensation between subjects and showed such disregard for the life and safety of others as to amount to a crime against the state and conduct deserving of punishment.

Two issues arise: the distinction between ordinary and gross negligence and the relevance of recklessness.

The unclear distinction between civil negligence and gross negligence

Are the boundaries of gross negligence certain enough so as to exclude ordinary negligence? In determining whether the negligence was bad enough to amount to a crime, is the jury answering a question of law? The test is criticised as being circular. This means that a jury can decide whether a crime has been committed because they think it ought to be a crime. The point arose in this case where the question was whether the captain of a ship owes a duty of care to his crew.

R v Lichfield [1998] CRIM LR 508 COURT OF APPEAL

The appellant was the owner and master of a square-rigged schooner which became ship-wrecked on rocks off the Cornish coast and broke up. Three of the 14 crew died.

The appellant was accused of gross negligence manslaughter for 1) steering an unsafe course too close to a dangerous coast and 2) for setting sail knowing that he might have to rely on the ship's engines which he knew contained contaminated fuel and which might therefore fail. He had therefore knowingly assumed a serious and obvious risk of death but had carried on regardless. The appellant argued that the existence of a statutory crime of (mere) negligence in s27(2) Merchant Shipping Act 1970, providing an offence of breach of duty where a ship's master negligently causes damage to his ship or death or injury to any person, precluded a finding of gross negligence. The appellant was convicted and appealed.

The appellant's argument that there was no room for a shipping manslaughter case was described as impossible because it would make nonsense of *Adomako* and would advantage those who were subject to statutory liability under the 1970 Act.

NOTE 7.11

J.C. Smith in the *Criminal Law Review* commentary has stated that it is one thing to decide that the negligence was 'more than a matter of mere compensation between the parties' but quite another to decide whether it was bad enough to amount to manslaughter. Negligence may be criminal in regulatory offences but not necessarily so bad as to amount to manslaughter. The test for gross negligence fails to make this clear. At p 509 he states:

> It would, at least, make sense in circumstances like the present to ask a jury whether they are sure that the case is so bad that it is not adequately dealt with by a conviction under the 1970 Act. It makes no sense to ask them whether they are sure it is not adequately dealt with by damages at civil law . . .

The relevance of recklessness

The *Adomako* definition of the offence refers to the need for D's conduct to breach a duty of care in a grossly negligent way. Where it is clear that D consciously took a risk and was subjectively reckless, how is D's *state of mind* relevant to the question of whether his *conduct* was so bad as to amount to the crime of manslaughter? Three approaches are apparent:

    a. *Subjective recklessness is not a prerequisite to a finding of gross negligence. The test for gross negligence is objective*

DPP, ex parte Jones [2000] CRIM LR 858, [2000] IRLR 373 DIVISIONAL COURT

This was an application for judicial review by the brother of a young male student who had been killed on his first day of a holiday job in Portsmouth unloading cargo from the hold of a ship. The bags of cargo were lifted by a dockside crane using a grab bucket and the jaws of the bucket had closed on the deceased whilst he was on deck and decapitated him. The crane had been adapted by the managing director of the employing company to facilitate the lifting of open bags. The DPP had decided that there was insufficient evidence of gross negligence for the purposes of manslaughter because of the absence of subjective recklessness. The application was allowed. At paragraph 23, Buxton LJ stated:

> The law is, therefore, quite clear. If the accused is subjectively reckless, then that may be taken into account by the jury as a strong factor demonstrating that his negligence was criminal, but negligence will still be criminal in the absence of any recklessness if on an objective basis D demonstrated what, for instance, Lord Mackay quoted the Court of Appeal in *Adomako* as describing as:
>
> > 'failure to advert to a serious risk going beyond mere inadvertence in respect of an obvious and important matter which D's duty demanded that he should address.'
>
> That is a test in objective terms.

The only issue should have been whether the unsafe system of work represented such a high degree of negligence that it should be judged criminal. In other words, was there an obvious risk of death such that the employer should be convicted of manslaughter?

b. *Evidence of a state of mind is generally irrelevant but could have a bearing on grossness or criminality*

→ CROSS-REFERENCE
For discussion of *AG's Reference (No 2 of 1999)* in relation to corporate manslaughter see Chapter 4, 4.2.3.

AG's Reference (No 2 of 1999) [2000] QB 796, [2000] CRIM LR 475 COURT OF APPEAL

This was the failed prosecution of South West Trains for the Southall Rail crash in which seven people died. The case is primarily relevant to the issue of whether it is possible to prosecute a corporation for homicide. However, the Court of Appeal confirmed that the *state of mind of D* is not relevant to a successful conviction for gross negligence manslaughter. Rose LJ said at p 809:

> Although there may be cases where D's state of mind is relevant to the jury's consideration when assessing the grossness and criminality of his conduct, evidence of his state of mind is not a prerequisite to a conviction for manslaughter by gross negligence. The *Adomako* test is objective but a defendant who is reckless as defined in *R v Stone* may be the more readily found to be grossly negligent to a criminal degree.

Recall that recklessness had been defined in *Stone & Dobinson* [1977] 2 All ER 341 as follows:

> A reckless disregard of danger to the health and welfare of the infirm person. Mere inadvertence is not enough. D must be proved to have been indifferent to an obvious risk of injury to health, or actually to have foreseen the risk but to have determined nevertheless to run it. (Lane LJ at p 363)

?! THINKING POINT 7.5

1. In what ways are subjective recklessness and gross negligence different?
2. In what way could it be useful to a jury to be told that a defendant who was reckless is more likely to be grossly negligent?

c. *Evidence of a subjective state of mind is relevant to gross negligence manslaughter because it is part of all the circumstances of the case that fall to be determined by a jury*

?! THINKING POINT 7.6

Are *Jones* and *Rowley* compatible?

R (on the application of Rowley) v DPP [2003] EWHC 693 (ADMIN) QBD, DIVISIONAL COURT

This was an application for judicial review of the DPP's decision not to prosecute the managers of a care home for the death of the applicant's disabled son who drowned when he was left unattended in a bath by a carer. The DPP had considered that a lack of awareness of risk on the part of the carer was a factor weighing against the existence of an obvious risk of death posed by the neglect.

It was held in this case that D's state of mind was relevant as forming part of the overall circumstances of the case which the jury had to take into consideration when assessing whether D's conduct was grossly negligent. Evidence of subjective recklessness was not only relevant in helping to establish a prosecution case but was also relevant if tendered in favour of D. It was further relevant to the grossness and criminality of D's conduct, as confirmed by *AG's Reference (No 2 of 1999)*. The application was dismissed. This would appear to be more favourable to D than the two previous tests and indicates that some prosecutors may only be charging gross negligence manslaughter when there has been, in fact, recklessness. This surely demonstrates a concern regarding the vagueness of gross negligence.

?! THINKING POINT 7.7

1. Looking at the Bateman test, what is the standard of negligence against which the jury are asked to compare D's negligence?
2. Do you think this would help a jury to identify gross negligence?
3. The jury are asked if the negligence is so bad as to amount to a crime. Why could this be confusing?
4. How do you think the test could be improved?

Does gross negligence manslaughter offend Article 7 ECHR?

Despite its difficulties, the concept of gross negligence was held not to be so uncertain as to offend the principle of uncertainty under Article 7 in the following case:

R v Misra & Srivastava [2004] EWCA CRIM 2375, [2005] CRIM LR 234 COURT OF APPEAL

This was a medical case of negligent omission in which doctors had failed to notice that following knee surgery a patient had developed toxic shock syndrome from which he died. The negligence relied upon by the prosecution was a failure to diagnose serious illness, a failure to obtain the results of blood tests and a failure to consult senior colleagues. The appellants' arguments (doctors) on appeal were as follows:

(1) That gross negligence manslaughter was uncertain and unclear.

(2) It suffered from the defect of 'circularity' in that it was left to the jury to decide whether the acts in question should amount to a crime. This was, indeed, an additional specific ingredient of the offence.

(3) After *R v G* [2003] UKHL 50 gross negligence manslaughter should be abandoned in favour of subjective reckless manslaughter because no serious offence could be committed without MR.

Article 7 ECHR provides:

(1) No-one shall be held guilty of any criminal offence on account of any act or omission which did not constitute a criminal offence under national or international law at the time when it was committed nor shall a heavier penalty be imposed than the one that was applicable at the time the criminal offence was committed.

Judge LJ:

Looking at the authorities since *Bateman*, the purpose of referring to the differences between civil and criminal liability . . . is to highlight that the burden on the prosecution goes beyond proof of negligence for which compensation would be payable. Negligence of that degree could not lead to a conviction for manslaughter. The negligence must be so bad, 'gross,' that if all the other ingredients of the offence are proved, then it amounts to a crime and is punishable as such . . .

Accordingly, the value of references to the criminal law in this context is that they avoid the danger that the jury may equate what we may describe as 'simple' negligence, which in relation to manslaughter would not be a crime at all, with negligence which involves a criminal offence. In short, by bringing home to the jury the extent of the burden on the prosecution, they ensure that D whose negligence does not fall within the ambit of the criminal law is not convicted of a crime. They do not alter the essential ingredients of this offence. A conviction cannot be returned if the negligent conduct is or may be less than gross. If however D is found by the jury to have been grossly negligent, then, if the jury is to act in accordance with its duty, he must be convicted. This is precisely what Lord Mackay indicated when, in the passage already cited, he said, ' . . . The jury must go on to consider whether that breach of duty should be characterised as gross negligence and *therefore* as a crime' (our emphasis). The decision whether the conduct was criminal is described not as 'the' test, but as 'a' test as to how far the conduct in question must depart from accepted standards to be 'characterised as criminal'. On proper analysis, therefore, the jury is not deciding whether the particular defendant ought to be convicted on some unprincipled basis. The question for the jury is not whether D's negligence was gross, and whether, *additionally*, it was a crime, but whether his behaviour was grossly negligent and *consequently* criminal. This is not a question of law, but one of fact, for decision in the individual case. Appeals dismissed.

NOTE 7.12

1. The court in this case examined the concept of gross negligence against the requirements of Article 7 ECHR. The offence is not unclear or uncertain. If negligent conduct is less than gross it will not count as criminal. The jury must decide whether a breach of

duty should be characterised as gross negligence and consequentially therefore as a crime. This is a question of fact. The jury is not deciding a matter of law.

2. Any inherent circularity in the definition of gross negligence does not offend Article 7.

3. *R v G* was confined to the offence of criminal damage and had no bearing on gross negligence manslaughter.

It is doubtful whether this decision satisfies the arguments of the appellants. It does little to clarify the definition of gross negligence so as to avoid the risk of confusing ordinary negligence with the high degree of negligence which ought to be required for this offence. Expert evidence will clearly assist in some cases where the conduct of D can be compared to that of the reasonable doctor or engineer for example. But is there not a risk of confusing mere carelessness and gross negligence in ordinary activities such as driving, child-minding, repair and maintenance of installations in rented accommodation, etc? Recall too that the Court of Appeal in *Gemma Evans* held that provided the duty of care is seen as a question of law, neither Article 6 (right to a fair trial) nor Article 7 is engaged.

?! THINKING POINT 7.8

Is there a parallel between asking a jury to decide whether D's negligence is gross and therefore a crime and asking a jury to decide whether a defendant was dishonest, intentional or reckless?

Reform

The appellants' arguments in *Misra & Sivastrava* were based on the Law Commission's criticisms of gross negligence in its report 'Involuntary Manslaughter' (Law Com No 273, 1996). The Law Commission would abolish involuntary manslaughter and replace it by two separate offences of reckless killing and killing by gross carelessness. The problems identified by the Law Commission in respect of gross negligence were listed at the beginning of this section.

Consequently, a new offence of 'killing by gross carelessness' was proposed in clause 2(1) of the draft Involuntary Homicide Bill:

A person who by his conduct causes the death of another is guilty of killing by gross carelessness if—

(a) a risk that his conduct will cause death or serious injury would be obvious to a reasonable person in his position;

(b) he is capable of appreciating that risk at the material time; and

(c) either—

(i) his conduct falls far below what can reasonably be expected of him in the circumstances; or

(ii) he intends by his conduct to cause some injury or is aware of, and unreasonably takes, the risk that it may do so.

In its Consultation Paper, 'A New Homicide Act for England and Wales?' (Law Com No 177, 2005) the Law Commission proposes that gross negligence and recklessness should be the fault elements for two new manslaughter offences. The relevant risk required to be intended/foreseen by D should be one of *death* and not *some* injury.

This would ensure compliance with the *subjectivity* and *correspondence* principles as well as with the current law as stated in *Adomako*. We already understand the meaning of *subjectivity*: that no-one should be convicted of an offence unless they have the capacity to appreciate the relevant risk of harm at the time of the offence. The *correspondence* principle means that the fault element of an offence should correspond to the harm done. Therefore, liability should not be incurred for harm greater than that which was foreseen.

→ CROSS-REFERENCE

The correspondence principle is examined in greater detail in 7.2.4.

SECTION SUMMARY

Manslaughter by gross negligence consists of four elements:
- *A duty of care arising by omission or positive act;*
- *Breach of that duty in such a way as to give rise to a risk of death;*
- *A causal link between the breach and death;*
- *Gross negligence defined by* Adomako *which is so bad as to amount to a crime.*

7.2.4 Unlawful and Dangerous Act (Constructive) Manslaughter

KEY CASES

Church [1965] 2 All ER 72—the 'unlawful act' in manslaughter must be objectively dangerous;

DPP v Newbury & Jones [1976] 2 ALL ER 365—lack of foresight of danger is irrelevant;

JF and NE [2015] EWCA Crim 351—*Church* and *Newbury* confirmed in relation to 14-year-old with mental functioning of a 6-year-old;

Bristow [2013] EWCA Crim 1540—a burglary may be dangerous because of circumstances and foresight;

R v JM; R v SM [2012] EWCA Crim 2293—danger may take the form of a risk of physical shock;

Kennedy [2007] UKHL 38—drug supply cases: self-injection is not an unlawful act and will break the chain of causation.

Introduction

Unlike either reckless or gross negligence manslaughter, unlawful and dangerous act manslaughter ('unlawful act' manslaughter for short) can only be committed in the course of a crime (see Diagram 7.6). This category of involuntary manslaughter is controversial. It imposes liability for death despite the fact that D is engaged in criminal activity that carries no intrinsic risk of injury to the person. Moreover, D can be convicted despite a lack of foresight of a risk of even minor harm. The death may have been a matter of pure bad luck: perhaps V suffered from a rare health condition causing an adverse reaction to the shock of a minor

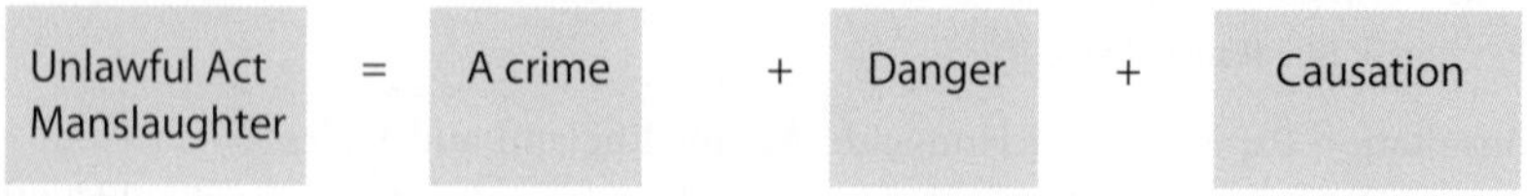

| Unlawful Act Manslaughter | = | A crime | + | Danger | + | Causation |

Diagram 7.6
Unlawful and Dangerous Act (Constructive) Manslaughter

assault or burglary; perhaps, having been mildly injured, V then receives negligent hospital treatment and dies. It might be considered harsh to attribute blame to D for the unforeseen and unintended consequence of death where, subsequent to the unlawful act, events unfold beyond his control. On the other hand, it can be argued that he has taken a risk of serious harm simply by engaging in criminal activity and therefore has to accept all the consequences. Unlawful act manslaughter can be criticised for amounting to a 'constructive' crime, where blame is attributed for a result going beyond D's MR. It offends the 'correspondence principle' of criminal law as we noted earlier. Whether this criticism is valid will be examined at the end of this section. It can also be criticised for lacking certainty. The boundaries of the offence appear to expand or contract on a case by case basis. Newer cases, as we shall see, would seem to confirm this point.

Definition

There are five components of this offence:

- D's unlawful act must be a crime which must be identified and proved.
- The unlawful act must be dangerous.
- The test of danger is objective.
- The unlawful act must be a crime by virtue of a positive act as opposed to an omission.
- The unlawful act need not be directed at V but must be the cause of death.

The unlawful act must be a crime which must be identified and proved

There appears to be no limit as to what sort of crime can constitute an unlawful act.

One might imagine that it would, at least, need to be an offence against the person because such crimes carry the highest risk of personal injury. Cases reveal, however, that it can be an assault, affray, criminal damage or burglary. It is also now clear that the unlawful act must amount to a crime requiring MR and must be more than an act of civil negligence or an omission. This was not always so, however, for historically, the unlawful act might be no more serious than a civil wrong or tort. Recall that until 1957 murder could be committed by killing in the course of an intentional felony (unlawful act), where there need not have been any intention or foresight of death or GBH. A parallel offence existed in relation to manslaughter when the killing occurred as a result of an intentional criminal or civil unlawful act. Constructive murder has been abolished but constructive manslaughter remains. Two early cases demonstrate that the unlawful act could once be defined as a civil wrong.

> ### R v Fenton (1830) 1 LEW CC 179
> ....
> D threw stones down a mine and broke some scaffolding. A coal bucket fell and hit and killed a victim. It was held by Tindall CJ that killing in the course of a wrongful act, such as trespass to the person, was manslaughter and D was convicted.

R v Franklin (1883) 15 COX CC 163

D took a box from another man's stall on Brighton pier and threw it into the sea. The box hit and killed a swimmer. The prosecutor argued that negligence was irrelevant and that it was manslaughter where death ensued in the course of any unlawful act (trespass). D was convicted of manslaughter on the broad ground of negligence, Field J commenting that a civil wrong ought not to be used as a step in a criminal case.

Franklin left open the question of what an unlawful act had to be. It is now clear that it must be a crime of commission (a positive as opposed to a negative act). It should follow therefore that in establishing the elements of manslaughter the criminal unlawful act should be defined and proved by the court. Sometimes however this technicality is overlooked and proof of no more than a voluntary act is taken to satisfy the requirements of the unlawful act.

R v Lamb [1967] 2 QB 981 COURT OF APPEAL

Lamb and his best friend were playing a game of Russian Roulette, a game of chance, with a loaded revolver containing five chambers. Three were empty and two contained bullets. Lamb did not realise that when he pulled the trigger the chamber would rotate and that therefore there was an extremely high risk of causing death or serious injury if one of the two bullets was fired. One bullet was fired at his friend who was shot and killed. The judge directed the jury that merely pointing a gun and pulling a trigger was an unlawful act even though there was no intention to frighten or injure his friend. It was not necessary for the jury to consider whether an assault had been committed. Lamb's defence was one of 'accident' which was not put to the jury.

Sachs LJ:

> Counsel for the Crown, however, had at all times put forward the correct view that for the act to be unlawful it must constitute at least what he then termed 'a technical assault'. In this court, moreover, he rightly conceded that there was no evidence to go to the jury of any assault of any kind.... Another way of putting it is that mens rea being now an essential ingredient in manslaughter ... this could not in the present case be established in relation to the first ground except by proving that element of intent without which there can be no assault. It is perhaps as well to mention that when using the phrase 'unlawful in the criminal sense of that word' the court has in mind that it is long settled that it is not in point to consider whether an act is unlawful merely from the angle of civil liabilities.... The general effect of the summing-up was thus to withdraw from the jury the defence put forward on behalf of the appellant.... In the present case it would, of course, have been fully open to a jury, if properly directed, to find the accused guilty because they considered his view as to there being no danger was formed in a criminally negligent way.

Appeal allowed.

 NOTE 7.13

Not only was there no MR but D had committed no assault and, therefore, no guilty act. An assault requires the intentional or reckless causing of another to apprehend immediate and unlawful personal violence. V was participating in a joke and did not think it was likely to be harmful.

?! **THINKING POINT** 7.9

1. If there was no unlawful act for the purposes of unlawful act manslaughter, what other offence might Lamb have committed?

2. Could Lamb have been guilty of that offence even though he thought there was no risk of harming his friend?

The House of Lords similarly failed to identify the criminal unlawful act in *DPP v Newbury & Jones* [1976] 2 All ER 365 where two boys killed a train guard when they threw stones over a railway bridge. (See later in this section: 'Dangerousness is assessed objectively'.)

Recent cases take a more stringent approach towards the unlawful act, so as to confine the offence within strict limits, but there is no consistency of such an approach. The absence of an unlawful criminal act secured acquittals in the next three cases.

R v Simon Slingsby [1995] CRIM LR 570 CROWN COURT

D consensually penetrated V's vagina and rectum with his hand, whilst wearing a signet ring which caused V internal cuts. She did not appreciate that the cuts were potentially very serious and she later died of septicaemia (blood poisoning). The prosecution alleged that the unlawful act was a battery (the intentional or reckless infliction of unlawful violence). D was acquitted, Judge J holding that the consensual sexual activity here did not involve the *deliberate* infliction of injury, it was the accidental consequence of consensual vigorous sexual activity. Because no injury had been foreseen or intended, there was no battery and therefore no unlawful act.

In *R v Dhaliwal* [2006] EWCA Crim 1139 the Court of Appeal declined to hold that psychological harm caused by a husband's domestic violence against his wife resulting in her suicide amounted to the unlawful act of GBH under s20 Offences Against the Person Act 1861 for the purposes of manslaughter. On the night of death, the husband had inflicted a minor head wound upon his wife but this was not so significant to be a cause of death. It could not, therefore, supply the necessary unlawful act for manslaughter. In order to amount to this offence, the psychological harm had to be so serious as to amount to a recognised psychiatric disorder. There was no evidence of this because she had not been examined before her death. It could be different where there was unlawful physical violence on an individual with a fragile and vulnerable personality which was proved to be a material cause of death, even if by suicide.

In *R v Carey* [2006] EWCA Crim 17 an affray was held to be insufficient to amount to an unlawful act. (NB: An affray is defined, contrary to s3 Public Order Act 1986, as the use or threat of unlawful violence against another such as would cause a person of reasonable firmness present at the scene to fear for his personal safety.) V, a young girl, had run 109 metres to escape from a threatening group which had inflicted minor injuries against her friends. V had also suffered a minor assault. She collapsed and died later that evening from ventricular fibrillation (a heart attack). The judge had said that it was enough to establish manslaughter that all sober and reasonable persons would have realised that the actual infliction of violence on V would subject her to some physical harm and that it was not necessary to prove causation. The Court of Appeal held this to be wrong. The only dangerous act perpetrated on V, a punch, was not the cause of her death.

On the other hand, a more tolerant approach to the unlawful act was demonstrated in the next case. This, along with two further cases, *Bristow* and *JM*, (see 'The unlawful act must be dangerous' later) appears to indicate that the boundaries of the offence are expanding once more:

R v Meeking [2013] EWCA CRIM 641

D, the passenger in a car being driven at 60 mph by her husband, pulled on the handbrake during an argument. The car spun across the road, collided with an oncoming car, and the husband was killed. She was convicted of manslaughter. The unlawful act was identified as endangering road users contrary to s22(A)(1)(b) Road Traffic Act 1988: 'A person is guilty of an offence if he intentionally and without lawful authority or reasonable cause—. . . (b) interferes with a motor vehicle, trailer or cycle . . . in such circumstances that it would be obvious to a reasonable person that to do so would be dangerous.' On appeal, D argued that to commit such an offence, she had to do something which changed the vehicle in some way, not simply interfere with the driving. The appeal was dismissed. There were no such limitations in s22(A)(1). The braking system was part of the car with which she had interfered whilst it was being driven.

Toulson LJ:

> There is no discernible policy reason why Parliament should have wanted to criminalise interference with a car creating a danger before it is driven, but not interference creating a danger while it is in the process of being driven. We are therefore unable to accept the appellant's first submission. Nor are we persuaded by the argument that the conduct has to be in some way external to the vehicle itself, such as dropping objects onto it. If a bomber carried a bomb on a bus intending it to go off and it did so, we have no doubt that the bomber would be guilty of an offence under the section, whether the bomber was a suicide bomber or succeeded in getting off the bus before the bomb went off. . . .

> There remains Miss Bradberry's [defence counsel] final argument that it is necessary to distinguish between something which interferes with the vehicle in the sense that the vehicle itself is damaged or otherwise altered, for example by dropping a brick on it, and something which is essentially an interference with its driving by the motorist. We can see that if the act is simply one of distraction of the motorist, that would not be an interference with the vehicle. But the braking system is a mechanical part of the car and we reject the argument that pulling the brake on while the car is being driven does not amount to or cannot be regarded by a jury as amounting to interfering with the motor vehicle. In the ordinary and natural sense of the words it is an interference with the vehicle. It is an interference with the vehicle by interfering with a mechanical part of it.

The court did note, however, that the case might have been charged as gross negligence manslaughter given the obvious risk of death concerned. Mere negligence would, of course, not suffice in respect of either offence. But this case represents a more tolerant approach to unlawful act manslaughter. It is clear that it is potentially a very wide offence unless all elements are scrupulously observed.

The unlawful act has to be positive and not by omission

Since this offence requires an unlawful act which must be dangerous, the act itself will typically be an intentional positive act. Therefore, a negligent omission is insufficient.

Recall the case of *Lowe* [1973] 1 All ER 805. A father had failed to summon medical help for his 9-week-old child who subsequently died. He was convicted of child cruelty under s1 Children and Young Persons Act 1933. The Court of Appeal held that mere neglect was insufficient for manslaughter. Whether an omission can ever supply the unlawful act for unlawful and dangerous act manslaughter is unclear. It might be justified where the omission is deliberate. There may be no moral distinction between an act or omission in such a case. See A. Ashworth [1976] *Crim LR* 529:

> In the absence of strong and clear arguments in favour of treating homicide by neglect as less serious than other forms of homicide, the distinction set out in *Lowe* can only be based on superstition.

→ CROSS-REFERENCE
For further discussion of *Lowe* see Chapter 2, 2.2.3.

The unlawful act must be dangerous

Dangerousness is assessed objectively

The unlawful act must also be dangerous in that it carries an obvious risk of some harm. An assault will be inherently dangerous because it poses a risk of personal injury. A burglary or robbery are not inherently dangerous because they do not necessarily pose such a risk. The element of danger therefore requires assessment over and above proof of the unlawful act. The risk of obvious harm is defined at quite a low level and requires an objective assessment. You may find it surprising that the foreseeable harm need not be serious. Remember that murder requires an intention to kill or cause GBH; yet unlawful act manslaughter does not require any awareness of harm by D provided it would have been obvious to a reasonable man.

R v Church [1965] 2 ALL ER 72 COURT OF APPEAL

Church had sex with a woman in the back of his van. She reproached him for his inadequacy and slapped his face. They fought and he hit her, rendering her unconscious. He dragged her out of the van and dumped her in a river where she subsequently drowned. Church said at his trial that he thought she was already dead when he put her in the river. The judge directed the jury that it did not matter whether she was dead or alive when he put her there. In other words, knowledge or mens rea was unimportant. He was convicted of manslaughter and appealed.

Edmund-Davies J stated, in relation to the judge's direction:

> . . . in the judgment of this court it was misdirection. It amounted to telling the jury that, whenever any unlawful act is committed in relation to a human being which resulted in death there must be, at least, a conviction for manslaughter. This might at one time have been regarded as good law: see, for example, *Fenton* [1830] 1 Lew CC 179. It appears to this court, however, that the passage of years has achieved a transformation in this branch of the law and, even in relation to manslaughter, a degree of mens rea has become recognised as essential. To define it is a difficult task, and in *Andrews v DPP* [1937] AC 576 at 582 . . . Lord Atkin spoke of the element of '"unlawfulness" which is the elusive factor'. Stressing that we are here leaving entirely out of account those ingredients of homicide which might justify a verdict of manslaughter on the grounds of (a) criminal negligence, or (b) provocation or (c) diminished responsibility, the conclusion of this court is that an unlawful act causing the death of another cannot, simply because it is an unlawful act, render a manslaughter verdict inevitable.

There then followed what has become a classic definition of the element of danger:

> For such a verdict inexorably to follow, the unlawful act must be such as all sober and reasonable people would inevitably recognise must subject the other person to, at least, the risk of some harm resulting therefrom albeit not serious harm . . .

The direction to the jury should have been put like this:

> . . . they were entitled . . . to regard the conduct of the appellant in relation to Mrs Nott [the deceased] as constituting throughout a series of acts which culminated in her death, and that, if that was how they regarded the accused's behaviour, it mattered not whether he believed her to be alive or dead when he threw her in the river.

Appeal dismissed on the grounds that the judge had properly directed the jury on criminal as opposed to mere negligence and D's conduct was a series of acts culminating in death.

NOTE 7.14

1. The basis of the conviction appears to have been gross negligence manslaughter but the case is significant for its contribution to unlawful and dangerous act manslaughter.

2. The case confirmed the continuing act theory of *Thabo Meli* [1954]. However, there was no plan to kill V here as in *Thabo Meli* and so whether there was a continuing act designed to cause death or GBH was really questionable.

→ **CROSS-REFERENCE**
For further discussion of *Thabo Meli* see Chapter 2, 2.1.2.

3. When D threw V into the river he thought he was disposing of a corpse. G. Williams stated in *Criminal Law: The General Part* (1961) that if a killing by the first act would have been manslaughter, a later destruction of the corpse should also be manslaughter. The court accepted this proposition.

Dangerousness need not be foreseen by D

The next case applied the objective *Church* test.

DPP v Newbury & Jones [1976] 2 ALL ER 365 HOUSE OF LORDS

Two 15-year-old boys pushed part of a paving stone over a railway bridge wall. The stone struck an oncoming train, went through the driver's cab window and killed the guard who was sitting next to the driver. Their appeal was dismissed by the Court of Appeal which certified a point of law for the House of Lords:

Can a defendant be properly convicted of manslaughter, when his mind is not affected by drink or drugs, if he did not foresee that his act might cause harm to another?

Lord Salmon:

The direction which he [the judge] gave is completely in accordance with established law, which, possibly with one exception to which I shall presently refer, has never been challenged. In *Larkin* [[1943] 1 All ER 217 at 219] Humphries J said:

'Where the act which a person is engaged in performing is unlawful, then if at the same time it is a dangerous act, that is, an act which is likely to injure another person, and quite inadvertently he causes the death of that other person by that act, then he is guilty of manslaughter.'

...The test is still the objective test. In judging whether the act was dangerous, the test is not did the accused recognise that it was dangerous but would all sober and reasonable people recognise its danger...

NOTE 7.15

1. Where D performs an unlawful act which is dangerous and which is likely to injure and quite inadvertently the act causes death, D is guilty of manslaughter.

2. What must be proved is an intention to commit an unlawful and dangerous act and that that act inadvertently caused death. It is not necessary to prove that D knew it was unlawful or dangerous. The test is objective.

?! **THINKING POINT** 7.10

The House of Lords failed to identify any relevant unlawful act in this case. What do you think it was? Do you agree that the boys should have been convicted of this serious offence?

The House of Lords abolished objective recklessness in *R v G* [2004] 1 AC 1034 and ruled that age and mental capacity were relevant to an assessment of D's awareness for the purposes of subjective recklessness. You might reflect that this case ought to have a bearing on the liability of children who commit manslaughter, but you would be wrong.

→ **CROSS-REFERENCE**
For discussion of *R v G* see Chapter 3, 3.2.

R v JF & NE [2015] EWCA CRIM 351

JF, aged 14 with the mental functioning of a 6-year-old, and NE, aged 16, set fire to a discarded duvet in the basement of a derelict building in Croydon. The fire spread to some tyres and the acrid smoke killed a homeless man sleeping in the basement. Neither defendant knew anyone was there at the time, although they did know that people slept there. Although they were both acquitted of aggravated arson (arson intending or being reckless as to whether life was endangered) they were convicted of simple arson and manslaughter. This was confirmed on appeal.

Lord Thomas CJ:

> In the present appeal, the jury were directed to consider whether the appellants had subjectively appreciated both the risk of damage to the building by fire and the risk that some person would be in the building. It is clear from the jury's verdict on manslaughter that the jury must have found they appreciated both risks, but from the verdict on arson have concluded that the appellants did not appreciate the risk of endangering the life of any such person by the smoke and carbon monoxide that could kill a person in no more than 5 minutes in that basement. It would appear from the facts of the case that the appellants must therefore have appreciated the risk of some harm to a person from the setting of the fire, but not harm to the extent of endangering life. It is therefore not clear on this case that the verdict would have been different if the requirement in respect of dangerous act were modified so that the subjective realisation of the appellants of some harm was required.
>
> In any event, neither Parliament nor the Executive have sought to carry forward the recommendations in respect of unlawful act manslaughter. As is evident from the Law Commission Reports to which we have referred the issue as to the scope of the offence of manslaughter is one on which there has been significant debate. In commenting on the decision of this court in *R v JM* [2013] 1 WLR 1083 where a different issue was involved, Professor Andrew Ashworth wrote at [2013] Crim LR 335:
>
>> 'In the longer term, common law manslaughter ought to be revisited by the Law Commission, since its most recent review of homicide law was focused on other matters and consequently treated this form of manslaughter rather cursorily: *Law Com. No.304, Murder, Manslaughter and Infanticide (2006)*, pp. 61-64. It is unlikely that the conflict of principle referred to [earlier in the comment] will be resolved to the satisfaction of all, but it is more appropriate that there be wide consultation on detailed questions about the ambit of any such offence than that these issues be resolved piecemeal by the courts, without clear parameters to guide them.'
>
> We agree. As we have explained, the law is clear and well established. It must be for Parliament to determine whether the long established law needs changing in the light of the Law Commission's various recommendations or whether a further examination is needed by the Law Commission.

NOTE 7.16

1. The reference by Lord Thomas CJ to the article by Professor Ashworth concerned the conflict at the heart of this offence: where death is inadvertent, should those who kill by a relatively minor crime be penalised for what might be termed a matter of bad luck, or do they deserve to be convicted for the consequences of their wrongful act?

2. The court considered here that, even if the objective test of danger had been modified, it would have made no difference. Although the defendants did not realise there was a risk of endangering life, they were aware of the risk of some harm.

Note that the objective test may be modified in the defendant's favour. The reasonable person is not expected to have extra knowledge of hidden facts which might affect the victim's reaction: Following *Newbury*, the objective test was modified by:

R v Dawson [1985] CR APP R 150 COURT OF APPEAL

It was held that the sober and reasonable man is credited with the same knowledge as the accused at the time of the offence. Therefore any peculiarities of V that would not be obvious should be ignored in the assessment of danger. Dawson and others had committed armed robbery on a petrol station wearing masks and armed with a pickaxe handle and replica gun. The garage attendant died of a heart attack shortly afterwards. Two Ds were convicted of manslaughter but their convictions were overturned on appeal. The attendant had been suffering from heart disease and that condition would not have been obvious to a reasonable man with the same knowledge as the men attempting to rob. It was not obvious therefore that the robbery posed an additional risk of danger.

?! **THINKING POINT** 7.11

In the course of an argument in a shop D punches V slightly. V hits her head against a metal object. She is knocked unconscious and later dies from internal bleeding to the brain. Has D committed unlawful act manslaughter?

This principle was confirmed in *Watson* [1989] 2 All ER 865 where on this occasion V was an 87-year-old man who died one and a half hours after being verbally abused during a burglary on his home. It would have been obvious to a reasonable and sober bystander that such unlawful conduct carried a risk of some harm to a frail and elderly V and was therefore dangerous. D's conviction of manslaughter was quashed, however, because it was not proved that the burglary caused death.

This implies that death might be inadvertent—neither foreseen nor intended by D. In *Watson* it was not obvious that the robbery/burglary was dangerous until the elderly V was assaulted. This was what might have transformed the burglary into manslaughter. In other cases the danger will be obvious from the outset, particularly if it is D's intention to cause harm to V, come what may:

Bristow [2013] EWCA CRIM 1540

One night, six burglars raided farm workshops located next to a farmhouse using two cars. They stole quad bikes, tyres and a Land Rover. They left via the only escape route at speed. It is likely that the owner intervened whilst the burglary was taking place. His body was found the following morning on the forecourt outside the workshops. The pathologist's conclusion was that death had been caused by the deceased being struck and/or run over by one or more of the motor vehicles at the scene. All defendants were convicted, the judge agreeing with the prosecution that the burglary was obviously dangerous from the start because the escape would necessarily have involved a risk of injury to anyone who tried to intervene. In dismissing an appeal, Treacy LJ held:

> This is not a case like *Dawson* or *Watson* where the circumstances demonstrating the risk of harm to the occupier of property did not arise until a point during the burglary or at all. Whilst burglary of itself is not a dangerous crime, a particular burglary may be dangerous because of the circumstances surrounding its commission. We consider that the features identified by the Crown, as set out earlier in this judgment, were capable of making this burglary dangerous when coupled with foresight of the risk of intervention to prevent escape.
>
> In those circumstances we consider that the features of this crime were sufficient for the burglary to be capable of being an unlawful act which a reasonable bystander would inevitably realise must subject any person intervening to the risk of some harm resulting.

Any offence, even a property offence, may be dangerous from the outset if committed in such a way as to give rise to a foreseeable risk of some harm. The defendants were charged with manslaughter by joint enterprise, but the drivers and occupiers of the vehicles during the escape could not be precisely identified. This might have prevented conviction of anyone had the danger arisen only during the escape. It was no problem if the burglary was dangerous from the beginning.

Danger means some physical, psychological or psychiatric harm

In the vast majority of cases, the unlawful act will be dangerous because it gives rise to an immediate risk of some *physical* harm, such as a wound or broken bone. Since *psychiatric/psychological* harm is now recognised as actual or grievous bodily harm for the purposes of offences against the person, this may also be relevant. But the offence is widened considerably by the fact that physical harm also includes shock, a condition induced by extreme fear which can cause lethal consequences, such as a heart attack. It is to be distinguished from mere emotional shock, which is not a physical condition.

→ CROSS-REFERENCE
For discussion of psychiatric/psychological harm as ABH or GBH see Chapter 10, 10.4.2.

Shock

Dawson (see earlier) indicated that shock emanating from fright was an injury to the person. But it would need to be *obvious to the reasonable man* and the *cause* of *physical* harm leading to death. In *Carey* (see earlier: 'The unlawful act must be a crime which must be identified and proved') the Court of Appeal declined to convict D where he punched a 15-year-old V during an affray and she later died from a heart attack. It was held that the assessment of danger might include V's characteristics. If V had died from *physical shock* then manslaughter could have been left to the jury. But there was no objective danger of shock from the affray as would have been recognised by a sober and reasonable bystander. V had been an apparently healthy 15-year-old. The question of both shock and affray was again reviewed in the next case.

R v JM; R v SM [2012] EWCA Crim 2293

V, a nightclub doorman, collapsed and died following an altercation with the defendants on a fire-escape outside the club. It is possible that he was not physically struck. Unbeknown to any-one, however, he suffered from a renal artery aneurysm (excessive enlargement of the artery) and died from blood loss following a rupture of the aneurysm within minutes of the fight. The two defendants were charged with manslaughter, the unlawful act being an affray. The prosecution contended that V had died as a result of shock. The defendants were acquitted, the trial judge ruling that the *physical harm* to V, rupture of the aneurysm, was not reasonably foreseeable. This was held to be wrong on appeal by the prosecution. It would create a fourth requirement and a restriction of the offence. The *Church* test referred only to 'some harm;' the particular type need not be specific. Lord Judge CJ explained:

> [The trial judge] believed that in order to sustain a conviction for manslaughter in this case at any rate there was a fourth requirement [the others being the unlawful act, the need for danger and causation]—'*namely that the victim died as a result of the sort of physical harm that any reasonable and sober person would inevitably realise the lawful act in question risked causing.*' He concluded his judgment:
>
> 'The jury could not reasonably conclude that they were sure that any sober and reasonable person, having the knowledge that the defendants had during the incident, would inevitably realise that there was a risk that Peter Jopling—an apparently fit, 40 year old experienced door-man—would suffer an increase in blood pressure leading to a fracture of an aneurism as a result of anything that occurred on that night . . . This is a completely different form of physical harm than that harm of which there was a recognisable danger such as the danger of his being hit or suffering injuries from a fall in attempting to deal with the defendants.'
>
> Unless it is appreciated that the level of danger required for the offence is not high, the reference to 'dangerous' as part of the definition of involuntary manslaughter is liable to mislead. The risk of harm to be recognised is not dangerous in the sense that it must be potentially lethal or even serious harm: it is dangerous for this purpose because of the risk of 'some harm'. The principle, now long established, is explained in *Church* [1966] 1 QB 59 . . . Mr Robert Smith QC (who did not appear in the court below) accepted that the judge misdirected himself when he required the Crown to establish the fourth ingredient, that is, that the reasonable and sober person envisaged in *Church* must realise that that was a risk that the unlawful act would cause the sort of physical harm as a re-sult of which the victim died. *We agree that such a requirement provided a gloss on the ingredients of this offence which is not justified by the authorities and does not follow from the reasoning in Dawson and Carey. Indeed, the observations at the end of the judgment appear to elevate the requisite risk from an appreciation that some harm will inevitably occur into foresight of the type of harm which actually ensued and indeed the mechanism by which death occurred.* Of course, unless the Crown can prove that death resulted from the defendant's unlawful and dangerous act, the case of manslaughter would fail on causation grounds. However a requirement that the bystander must appreciate the 'sort' of injury which might occur undermines the 'some' harm principle explained in *Church*, and on close analysis, is not supported or suggested by *Dawson* or *Carey*. [Emphasis added.]

Appeal allowed.

 NOTE 7.17

1. An affray can supply the unlawful act in manslaughter, even, it seems, if V is not physi-cally struck. But V must be involved in the affray. This much was accepted in obiter by the Court of Appeal in *Carey*.

2. There is no fourth requirement in manslaughter that the reasonable bystander must recognise *the type* of harm risked by the defendant's unlawful act.

3. Causation would need to be proved. This, of course, would be extremely difficult in a case where an apparently healthy individual later dies from shock-induced heart attack

The reasonable bystander is not expected to know of any of V's characteristics which are not obvious, such as an underlying health risk. Following *JM*, it will not be necessary to identify the risk of shock or any other type of harm, but simply that the risk of some form of harm exists. This would seem to threaten the modified objective approach to danger created by *Dawson*. The risk of widening the law beyond the most obvious type of dangerous conduct is that manslaughter becomes an uncertain and unpredictable offence. Recent cases on shock would seem to warrant greater analysis of this proposition.

Causation: the unlawful act must cause death

As with any homicide offence, it must be proved that there was an unbroken chain of causation between D's act and death. Normally this will not present a problem where D's act was the sole or main cause of death. But where, for example, V commits suicide and it is difficult to gauge the extent to which D's prior physical or psychological violence was a contributory factor, causation is problematic. (See *Dhaliwal* [2006] EWCA Crim 1139 at the beginning of this section where the Court of Appeal held that suicide following physical violence upon a fragile personality would not break the chain of causation.) In suicide causation cases, a serious wound has always been found to be substantial and operating at the time of death, notwithstanding a decision to commit suicide (eg: *Blaue, Dear*). Whether a lesser wound would suffice is unclear. If so, the offence would be wider than it is currently considered to be. (For a discussion of the issues of this case see J. Horder and L. McGowan, 'Manslaughter by Causing Another's Suicide' [2006] *Crim LR* 1035.)

However, for many years, causation presented a problem to the courts in a series of cases concerning the liability of Class A drug suppliers whose victims self-injected the drug and then died. We first looked at some of these cases in Chapter 2 where you will recall that the House of Lords, in a welcome and long-overdue decision, recently clarified the law in this area: *R v Kennedy* [2007] UKHL 38 (see next section). The current legal position is as follows:

Where D injects V with an unlawful drug

The law here remains generally clear although certain obiter comments in the case discussed remain a little dubious.

R v Cato [1976] 1 ALL ER 260 COURT OF APPEAL

The appellant supplied heroin and injected V with a mix of heroin and water which V had prepared. V had also injected the appellant with heroin which the appellant had prepared. The appellant was convicted of unlawful and dangerous act manslaughter and of an offence under s23 Offences Against the Person Act 1861: 'Whosoever shall unlawfully and maliciously administer to or cause to be administered to or taken by any other person any poison or other destructive or noxious thing, so as thereby to endanger the life of such person, or so as thereby to inflict upon any such person any grievous bodily harm, shall be guilty of an offence, and being convicted thereof shall be liable . . . to imprisonment for any term not exceeding ten years . . .'

It was held that:

1. The unlawful act was the offence of administration under s23.
2. Even if the unlawful act had not been the s23 offence, there would have been an alternative unlawful act of *possession* by the appellant.

Lord Widgery CJ:

> . . . had it not been possible to rely on the charge under s23 of the 1861 Act, we think there would have been an unlawful act here, and we think the unlawful act would be described as injecting the deceased Farmer with a mixture of heroin and water which at the time of the injection Cato had unlawfully taken into his possession.

Appeal dismissed. This decision was problematic. Under s23, the administration needs to be unlawful and malicious and 'so as to endanger life'. There was no evidence that the appellant knew or foresaw any risk of harm to V's life, particularly since V had himself prepared the mix of drug and water in the syringe. Further, the thing administered must be noxious. Whether heroin is inherently noxious or dangerous is debatable. The ordinary view would probably be that taking heroin is dangerous because it is an addictive drug with adverse effects on health and risks to life from overdoses and disease transmission from the shared use of needles, such as HIV and hepatitis. The pharmacological view of heroin itself is that, taken in tolerable doses, it is safe and predictable.

The obiter comments in the case identifying possession as the unlawful act were generally considered to be flawed from the point of view of causation: neither the supply nor indeed possession could have been the cause of death.

D supplies the drug—V self-injects

R v Kennedy [2007] UKHL 38 HOUSE OF LORDS

Kennedy had supplied, prepared and handed the deceased a syringe containing heroin for immediate injection. The deceased injected himself and later died. Kennedy was convicted of manslaughter. The first appeal was dismissed on the grounds that where D supplies drugs and prepares a syringe for self-injection by another, D becomes an accomplice to a s23 offence by *assisting and encouraging* self-injection and is thus guilty of manslaughter. The problem was that the court did not clarify why the self-injection was unlawful since it is no offence under any statute or at common law. The appeal was generally considered to have been wrongly decided because if self-injection is no crime, there would be no principal offender for D to assist. The second appeal was dismissed on the grounds that D and V were acting in concert.

This was reversed on appeal to the House of Lords, the Judicial Committee consisting of Lord Bingham, Lord Rodger, Baroness Hale, Lord Carswell and Lord Mance. This was the decision of the Committee:

> There is now, as already noted, no doubt but that the appellant committed an unlawful (and criminal) act by supplying the heroin to the deceased. But the act of supplying, without more, could not harm the deceased in any physical way, let alone cause his death. As the Court of Appeal observed in *R v Dalby* [1982] 1 WLR 425, 429, 'the supply of drugs would itself have caused no harm unless the deceased had subsequently used the drugs in a form and quantity which was dangerous'. So,

as the parties agree, the charge of unlawful act manslaughter cannot be founded on the act of supplying the heroin alone. . . .

The parties are further agreed that an unlawful act of the appellant on the present facts must be found, if at all, in a breach of section 23 of the Offences against the Person Act 1861. Although the death of the deceased was the tragic outcome of the injection on 10 September 1996 the death is legally irrelevant to the criminality of the appellant's conduct under the section: he either was or was not guilty of an offence under section 23 irrespective of the death. . . .

The sole argument open to the crown was, . . . that the appellant administered the injection to the deceased. It was argued that the term 'administer' should not be narrowly interpreted. Reliance was placed on the steps taken by the appellant to facilitate the injection and on the trial judge's direction to the jury that they had to be satisfied that the appellant handed the syringe to the deceased 'for immediate injection'. But section 23 draws a very clear contrast between a noxious thing administered to another person and a noxious thing taken by another person. It cannot ordinarily be both. In this case the heroin is described as 'freely and voluntarily self-administered' by the deceased. This, on the facts, is an inevitable finding. The appellant supplied the heroin and prepared the syringe. But the deceased had a choice whether to inject himself or not. He chose to do so, knowing what he was doing. It was his act . . .

At the trial of the present appellant there was no consideration of section 23 and the trial judge effectively stopped defence counsel submitting to the jury that the appellant had not caused the death of the deceased. In dismissing his first appeal the Court of Appeal said:

'We can see no reason why, on the facts alleged by the Crown, the appellant in the instant case might not have been guilty of an offence under section 23 of the Offences Against the Person Act 1861. Perhaps more relevantly, the injection of the heroin into himself by Bosque was itself an unlawful act, and if the appellant assisted in and wilfully encouraged that unlawful conduct, he would himself be acting unlawfully.'

But the court gave no detailed consideration to the terms of section 23, and it is now accepted that the deceased's injection of himself was not an unlawful act.

In *R v Dias* [2002] 2 Cr App R 96 the defendant had been convicted of manslaughter. He had prepared a syringe charged with heroin which he had handed to the deceased, who had injected himself. The court recognised that the chain of causation had probably been broken by the free and informed decision of the deceased, and noted the error in the decision on the appellant's first appeal as to the unlawfulness of the deceased's injection of himself.

In rejecting the appellant's second appeal in the decision now challenged, the Court of Appeal reviewed the history of the case and the authorities in some detail. The court expressed its conclusion in these paragraphs:

51 In view of the conclusions that we have come to as a result of our examination of the authorities, it appears to us that it was open to the jury to convict the appellant of manslaughter. To convict, the jury had to be satisfied that, when the heroin was handed to the deceased 'for immediate injection,' he and the deceased were both engaged in the one activity of administering the heroin. These were not necessarily to be regarded as two separate activities; and the question that remains is whether the jury were satisfied that this was the situation. If the jury were satisfied of this then the appellant was responsible for taking the action in concert with the deceased to enable the deceased to inject himself with the syringe of heroin which had been made ready for his immediate use. . . .

53 The point in this case is that the appellant and the deceased were carrying out a 'combined operation' for which they were jointly responsible. Their actions were similar to what happens frequently when carrying out lawful injections: one nurse may carry out certain preparatory actions (including preparing the syringe) and hand it to a colleague who inserts the needle and administers the injection, after which the other nurse may apply a plaster. In such a situation, both nurses can be regarded as administering the drug. They are working as a team. Both their actions are necessary. They are interlinked but separate parts in the overall process of administering the drug. In these circumstances, as Waller LJ stated on the first appeal, they 'can be said to be jointly responsible for the carrying out of that act' . . .

The court went on in the next paragraph to refer to the deceased and the appellant acting in concert in administering the heroin. Thus the essential ratio of the decision is that the administration of the injection was a joint activity of the appellant and the deceased acting together. It is possible to imagine factual scenarios in which two people could properly be regarded as acting together to administer an injection. But nothing of the kind was the case here. As in *R v Dalby* and *R v Dias* the appellant supplied the drug to the deceased, who then had a choice, knowing the facts, whether to inject himself or not. The heroin was, as the certified question correctly recognises, self-administered, not jointly administered. The appellant did not administer the drug. Nor, for reasons already given, did the appellant cause the drug to be administered to or taken by the deceased.

The answer to the certified question is: 'In the case of a fully-informed and responsible adult, never'. The appeal must be allowed and the appellant's conviction for manslaughter quashed. The appellant must have his costs, here and below, out of central funds. . . .'

NOTE 7.18

1. This is the current position on drug deaths and is a welcome simplification of the law. The boundaries of this offence for drug suppliers are considerably narrowed by this decision (although this is not necessarily true of gross negligence manslaughter). The House approved *Dalby* [1982] 1 All ER 916 in which Walker LJ had said this:

   'The difficulty in the present case is that the act of supplying a controlled drug was not an act which caused direct harm. It was an act which made it possible, or even likely, that harm would occur subsequently, particularly if the drug was supplied to somebody who was on drugs. In all the reported cases, the physical act has been one which inevitably would subject the other person to the risk of some harm from the act itself.'

2. The House overturned previous cases which had given rise to creative arguments for convicting drug suppliers, for example: participation in the administration (*Rogers* [2003] Crim LR 555), no extraordinary intervention (*Finlay* [2003] EWCA Crim 3868), accomplice liability (*Kennedy* [2005] EWCA Crim 685).

3. There remains the possibility of convicting a supplier where he and the deceased were acting in concert.

?! THINKING POINT 7.12

Given that D does not commit unlawful act manslaughter where he supplies Class A drugs and prepares a syringe for immediate injection by V, who then self-injects and dies, can you think of an alternative homicide offence?

What are the elements of the offence? Can you think of any relevant cases? Would causation continue to be a problem?

The unlawful act does not need to be directed at V

One case may illustrate this principle—but remember that there still needs to be an unbroken chain of causation. In *Goodfellow* (1986) 83 Cr App R 23, D killed three people, two of whom were his wife and child, by setting fire to his council flat in order to obtain alternative accommodation. His conviction was upheld on the basis that it was not necessary for the unlawful act to be directed at Vs provided it was a direct cause of death, there was no intervening act, and it was objectively dangerous. This may indeed have been an extremely reckless and dangerous act but whether the conviction of manslaughter was justifiable is questionable.

> **?!**   **THINKING POINT** 7.13
>
> D is standing in a post office queue and gets into an altercation with the person standing behind him (A). He pushes A, who falls on top of an elderly woman (V). V sustains fractured bones and later dies from her injuries. Is D guilty of unlawful act manslaughter in respect of V's death?

The unlawful act and defences

The act causing death must be unlawful. It follows that if D has a particular defence which negates the unlawfulness of his actions, such as consent, self-defence or necessity, there can be no conviction for unlawful act manslaughter. These defences are justificatory.

→ CROSS-REFERENCE
Justificatory defences are discussed in Chapter 9.

But if the defence is one which does not negate unlawfulness, such as intoxication (or other excusatory defence), D may still have committed an unlawful act and therefore manslaughter. Intoxication is no defence to a crime of basic intent. This will be so despite the fact that D was so intoxicated as to lack MR or even consciousness of the AR. If the unlawful act is also dangerous and leads to death, D will be guilty of manslaughter despite knowledge of what he was doing. Understandably, this is controversial.

→ CROSS-REFERENCE
Intoxication as a defence is discussed in Chapter 8.

R v Lipman [1970] 1 QB 152, [1969] 3 ALL ER 410 COURT OF APPEAL

D killed his girlfriend by cramming nine inches of sheet into her mouth and hitting her whilst he was on an LSD trip. He believed he was descending to the centre of the Earth and was being attacked by snakes. His defence was intoxication producing automatism—a denial of MR and AR. The Court of Appeal confirmed his conviction of manslaughter on the grounds that he had committed an unlawful act of battery for which intoxication was no defence. Because the act was dangerous, he was guilty.

Conclusion

Clearly, unlawful act manslaughter is a very wide offence and has been criticised as being fundamentally wrong in principle. Here is the main argument:

Breadth of conduct falling within the offence: the Correspondence Principle

The fact that manslaughter can be committed by a minor offence causing death, in which death was neither foreseen nor intended nor even foreseeable by an ordinary person, is wrong in principle. The Law Commission in 'Legislating the Criminal Code, Involuntary Manslaughter' (Law Com No 237, 1996) states:

3.6 For reasons we explain in more detail below, we consider that it is wrong in principle for the law to hold a person responsible for causing a result that he did not intend or foresee, and which would not even have been *foreseeable* by a reasonable person observing his conduct. Unlawful act manslaughter is therefore, we believe, unprincipled because it requires only that a foreseeable risk of causing *some* harm should have been inherent in the accused's conduct, whereas he is convicted of actually causing death, and also to some extent punished for doing so.

The Law Commission bases all law reform on the guiding principle of subjectivity. It means that criminal liability should only be imposed on those who have chosen to do wrong. That is why criminal liability in serious crimes requires MR (intention or foresight) as to the consequences. Furthermore, the fault element of a crime should correspond to the conduct element.

> 4.5 . . . according to the 'principle of correspondence', subjectivists insist that the fault element of a crime *correspond* to the conduct element; for example, if the conduct element is 'causing serious injury', the fault element ought to be 'intention or recklessness as to causing serious injury'. This ensures that D is punished only for causing a harm which she *chose* to risk or to bring about.

How can the law deter future offending where the consequence occurs by chance? On this basis, involuntary manslaughter is unprincipled and in need of reform.

However, there are powerful contrary arguments against the correspondence principle which allege that it is based on a simplistic view of knowledge or awareness of risk. Read the following from R.A. Duff, *Intention, Agency and Criminal Liability* (1990), at p 160 quoted in the Law Commission Report at para 4.12:

> . . . while we do indeed sometimes make our knowledge of what we are doing explicit to ourselves in . . . silent mental reports, it is absurd to suggest that such knowledge can be actual only if it is made thus explicit. When I drive my car, my driving is guided by my (actual) knowledge of my car and of the context in which I am driving; but my driving is not accompanied by a constant silent monologue in which I tell myself what to do next, what the road conditions are, whether I am driving safely or not, and all the other facts of which I am certainly aware while I am driving . . .

It is also argued that a person should be legally and morally at fault for *failing* to consider the consequences of their criminal conduct. See this example from J. Horder, 'A Critique of the Correspondence Principle in Criminal Law' [1995] *Crim LR*, at p 764:

> I suggest that the existence of an intention to do wrong may make it legitimate to hold someone criminally responsible for any adverse consequences of which there was a risk in committing the intended wrong, whether it could be said that the risk would reasonably foreseeably turn into reality or not. Suppose I am unlawfully cleaning my gun in the garden, and it goes off. My neighbour, V, given a severe shock by the noise, consequently dies of a heart attack. Despite my unlawful act, this is probably not manslaughter, as the risk of some harm to V was not obvious. This conclusion might be the same even if the unsuspecting V dies of shock after I deliberately discharged the gun close to him, in order to frighten him. Paying scant regard to the nature of the unlawful act, the law makes a conviction hang principally on whether the risk of resulting harm was obvious. This gets things the wrong way around. In the second case, the fact that I *deliberately* wrong V arguably changes my normative position *vis a vis* the risk of adverse consequences of that wrongdoing to V, whether or not foreseen or reasonably foreseeable. Subject to any questions about causation, I should be criminally responsible in the second case, but not in the first. In the first case, my unlawful conduct is not directed at V, so (if my liability is not to depend crudely on causation and the unlawfulness of my actions) its relevance should be merely evidential: can it be inferred that I foresaw harm, or should obviously have foreseen it? Yet if, as in the second case, my unlawful act is meant to wrong V, its relevance is normative, and not merely evidential. Its deliberateness changes my relationship with the risk of adverse consequences stemming there from, for which I may now be blamed and held criminally responsible, irrespective of their reasonable foreseeability.

The underlying philosophical argument here is one of 'moral luck' which would hold a person morally and legally responsible for the consequences of their actions even though they were unforeseen and unintended. In the interests of justice, a defendant should not be allowed to escape liability for manslaughter where he ought to have foreseen the risk of serious harm and was capable of doing so. On the other hand, it is morally unfair to penalise a person under the criminal law for consequences which occur as a result of chance or bad luck. Therefore, striking a balance, if there is to be liability for unintended consequences, it should only be for actions which can be regarded as morally culpable. Too low a threshold is harsh and gives rise to the criticisms of the current offence. Too high, on the other hand, would be over lenient to defendants and give rise to injustice to victims and their families.

Clearly, this is a very wide offence which raises substantial problems. We shall now turn to proposals for reform.

Reform

In its report 'Legislating the Criminal Code: Involuntary Manslaughter' (Law Com No 237, 1996) the Law Commission was persuaded that it was acceptable to retain an offence of manslaughter based upon inadvertent killings where the harm risked was very serious and the risk of such harm was obvious. This would provide the necessary degree of moral culpability which ought to attract liability.

> 4.19 As a matter of strict principle, the accused ought only to be held liable for causing death if the risk to which she culpably failed to advert was a risk of *death*. In practice, however, there is a very thin line between behaviour that risks serious injury and behaviour that risks death, because it is frequently a matter of chance, depending on such factors as the availability of medical treatment, whether serious injury leads to death. Admittedly it is possible for conduct to involve a risk of serious injury (such as a broken limb) though not a risk of death; but intention to cause serious injury constitutes the mens rea of murder although the actus reus is the causing of death, and we see no compelling reason to distinguish between murder and manslaughter in this respect. We consider, therefore, that it would not be wrong in principle if a person were to be held responsible for causing death through failing to advert to a clear risk of causing death *or* serious injury—subject of course to a second criterion, to which we now turn.
>
> 4.20 The second criterion of culpability which we consider to be essential is that the accused herself would have been *capable* of perceiving the risk in question, had she directed her mind to it. Since the fault of the accused lies in her failure to consider a risk, she cannot be punished for this failure if the risk in question would never have been apparent to her, no matter how hard she thought about the potential consequences of her conduct. If this criterion is not insisted upon, the accused will, in essence, be punished for being less intelligent, mature or capable than the average person.

It would follow that death resulting from a relatively minor offence would not necessarily become manslaughter, which would only be committed where there was an *obvious* risk of causing death or serious injury.

On this basis they recommended the abolition of involuntary manslaughter and its replacement by two separate offences of *reckless killing* and *killing by gross carelessness*:

> (1) A person who by his conduct causes the death of another is guilty of reckless killing if–
>
> (a) he is aware of a risk that his conduct will cause death or serious injury and
>
> (b) it is unreasonable for him to take that risk having regard to the circumstances as he knows or believes them to be.

(2)   A person guilty of reckless killing is liable on conviction on indictment to imprisonment for life.

2(1)   A person who by his conduct causes the death of another is guilty of killing by gross carelessness if–

   (a)   a risk that his conduct will cause death or serious injury would be obvious to a reasonable person in his position;

   (b)   he is capable of appreciating that risk at the material time; and

   (c)   either–

      (i)   his conduct falls far below what can reasonably be expected of him in the circumstances; or

      (ii)   he intends by his conduct to cause some injury or is aware of, and unreasonably takes, the risk that it may do so.

The government subsequently proposed an amended manslaughter offence which would narrow the current offence by requiring D to intend or be reckless as to injury (Home Office, 'Reforming the Law on Involuntary Manslaughter: The Government's Proposals', 2000). This has never been implemented.

In Law Commission Report, 'Murder, Manslaughter and Infanticide' (Law Com No 304, 2006) second degree murder would include some reckless killings where D realised there was a serious risk of death only if, in addition, D intended to cause injury, fear or risk of injury. Other reckless killings will be subsumed within either gross negligence or criminal act manslaughter.

Therefore, inadvertent killings without foresight of the risk of harm by D would no longer exist.

SECTION SUMMARY

Unlawful and dangerous act manslaughter consists of the following elements:
- *D's unlawful act must be a crime which must be identified and proved;*
- *The unlawful act must be dangerous;*
- *The test of danger is objective;*
- *The unlawful act must be a crime by virtue of a positive act as opposed to an omission;*
- *The unlawful act need not be directed at V but must be the cause of death.*

7.3 Homicide-related Offences

7.3.1 Causing Death by Dangerous Driving

7.3.2 Causing Death by Careless or Inconsiderate Driving

7.3.3 Causing Death by Driving While Unlicensed, Disqualified or Uninsured

7.3.4 Infanticide

7.3.5 Infant and Child Killing

The following homicide-related offences are set out briefly so that you can identify the definition of each.

7.3.1 Causing Death by Dangerous Driving

Along with liability for omissions, this is a special case of gross negligence manslaughter. There are two alternative offences where death is caused by dangerous driving:

1. Gross negligence manslaughter where the manner of driving fell so far below reasonable standards as to create a risk of *death* following *Adomako*.

2. A statutory offence of causing death by dangerous driving under s1 Road Traffic Act 1988:

(1) A person who causes the death of another person by driving a mechanically propelled vehicle dangerously on a road or other public place is guilty of an offence. . . .

(2A) for the purposes of sections 1 and 2 above a person is to be regarded as driving dangerously if (and, subject to subsection (2) below, only if)–

(a) the way he drives falls far below what would be expected of a competent and careful driver, and

(b) it would be obvious to a competent and careful driver that driving in that way would be dangerous.

(2) A person is also to be regarded as driving dangerously for the purposes of sections 1 and 2 above if it would be obvious to a competent and careful driver that driving the vehicle in its current state would be dangerous.

(3) In subsections (1) and (2) above 'dangerous' refers to danger either of injury to any person or of serious damage to property; and in determining for the purposes of those subsections what would be expected of, or obvious to, a competent and careful driver in a particular case, regard shall be had not only to the circumstances of which he could be expected to be aware but also to any circumstances shown to have been within the knowledge of the accused.

7.3.2 Causing Death by Careless or Inconsiderate Driving

Section 2B Road Traffic Act 1988:

A person who causes the death of another person by driving a mechanically propelled vehicle on a road or other public place without due care and attention, or without reasonable consideration for other persons using the road or place, is guilty of an offence.

Section 3A Road Traffic Act 1988 added an aggravated offence of causing death by careless driving when under the influence of drink or drugs. It has a maximum penalty of 14 years' imprisonment, while that for the s2B offence is five years' imprisonment.

7.3.3 Causing Death by Driving While Unlicensed, Disqualified or Uninsured

Section 3ZB Road Traffic Act 1988:

A person is guilty of an offence under this section if he causes the death of another person by driving a motor vehicle on a road and, at the time when he is driving, the circumstances are such that he is committing an offence [of driving while unlicensed, disqualified, or uninsured] ...

This offence carries a maximum sentence of two years' imprisonment. It has been criticised for the lack of any necessary connection between unlicensed or uninsured driving which, while unlawful, are not obviously dangerous, and causing death. The Supreme Court ruled in *Hughes* [2013] UKSC 56 that there does have to be 'some act or omission in the control of the car, which involves some element of fault . . . which contributes in some more than minimal way to the death of an individual.'

7.3.4 Infanticide

Section 1(1) Infanticide Act 1938:

> Where a woman by any wilful act or omission causes the death of her child being a child under the age of twelve months, but at the time of the act or omission the balance of her mind was disturbed by reason of her not having fully recovered from the effect of giving birth to the child or by reason of the effect of lactation consequent upon the birth of the child, then, if the circumstances were such that but for this Act the offence would have amounted to murder or manslaughter, she shall be guilty of [an offence], to wit of infanticide, and may for such offence be dealt with and punished as if she had been guilty of the offence of manslaughter of the child.

Infanticide is both an offence and a partial defence to murder for women accused of killing their young baby.

7.3.5 Infant and Child Killing

Section 5 Domestic Violence, Crime and Victims Act 2004:

(1) A person ('D') is guilty of an offence if–

    (a) a child or vulnerable adult ('V') dies as a result of the unlawful act of a person who–

        (i) was a member of the same household as V, and

        (ii) had frequent contact with him,

    (b) D was such a person at the time of that act,

    (c) at that time there was a significant risk of serious physical harm being caused to V by the unlawful act of such a person, and

    (d) either D was the person whose act caused V's death or–

        (i) D was, or ought to have been, aware of the risk mentioned in paragraph (c),

        (ii) D failed to take such steps as he could reasonably have been expected to take to protect V from the risk, and

        (iii) the act occurred in circumstances of the kind that D foresaw or ought to have foreseen.

(2) The prosecution does not have to prove whether it is the first alternative in subsection (1) (d) or the second (sub-paragraphs (i) to (iii)) that applies.

This offence provides that where a child or vulnerable adult dies at the hands of either of two responsible adults in the same household, typically the parents, but it cannot be proved which of them actually killed, either can be prosecuted for this offence. Even if it is clear who performed the killing, a partner can be convicted for failing to protect the child. Formerly, in the absence of proof of evidence against either parent, they would both have had to be acquitted.

SUMMARY

Homicide consists of:

- Murder.
- AR: the unlawful killing of a reasonable person in being; MR: intention to kill or cause GBH.
- Voluntary manslaughter—murder can be defended by the partial defences of:

  (1) Diminished responsibility (s2 Homicide Act 1957): an abnormality of mental functioning arising from a recognised medical condition which substantially impairs D's ability to: understand the nature of his actions, form a rational judgment or exercise self-control and which causes or is a significant cause of D's conduct.

- *or*

  (2) Loss of control: a loss of self-control due to a qualifying trigger (either fear of serious violence or justifiable offence in response to a thing done or said of a grave nature) which would cause a person of D's age and sex, of normal tolerance and self-restraint, to react in the same or a similar way.

- *or*

  (3) Suicide pacts.

- Involuntary manslaughter—reckless, gross negligence or unlawful and dangerous act.

PROBLEM SOLVING

Amelia has an aggressive disposition. She has a stormy relationship with Bill, who physically and mentally abuses her. He threatens to run her over unless she stops seeing all her friends. She becomes depressed and begins hearing voices which tell her to kill Bill. On the night in question, she drinks four vodkas and stabs him with a kitchen knife. She knows that it is wrong but cannot stop the impulse to kill him. Bill dies four days later. Amelia then purchases some heroin for herself and her friend, Cynthia. She loads up a syringe and gives it to Cynthia who says she will take it later. After several hours, Cynthia self-injects herself with the heroin and dies. Discuss whether Amelia has committed the murder of Bill and Cynthia.

Remember:

- **I: Identify** relevant issues
- **D: Define** offences/defences
- **E: Explain/evaluate** the law
- **A: Apply** law to facts.

See Table 7.1 for a suggested approach to this question.

A helpful problem-solving technique is to construct a chart setting out the main issues. This will assist you to structure your answer. See the online resources for a fuller answer: www.oup.com/uk/loveless6e/.

Table 7.1

Defences	Murder of Bill	Voluntary Manslaughter of Bill	Involuntary Manslaughter of C by Unlawful act
	AR/MR. Death appears to have been intended. Murder can be mitigated to voluntary manslaughter by either of the partial defences.		Unlawful act? (s23 OAPA 1861?). Danger? Causation? (All of these could be discussed in the context of: *Kennedy*).
Diminished Responsibility		S2 Homicide Act 1957: 1. Abnormality of mental functioning due to; 2. A recognised medical condition; 3. Which substantially impaired D's ability to: understand the nature of his conduct, form a rational judgment or exercise self-control; 4. And which caused or was a significant cause of his conduct. A question of fact.	
Loss of Control		S54 & S55 C&JA 2009 1. Subjective test: A loss of self-control? 2. Subjective/objective test: A qualifying trigger (either fear of serious violence or justifiable offence in response to a thing done or said of a grave nature)? 3. The objective test? 4. Characteristics–aggression/intoxication?	

FURTHER READING

Diminished responsibility

M. Gibson, 'Diminished Responsibility in *Golds* and Beyond: Insights and Implications' [2017] *Crim LR* 543

Explores the impact of the Supreme Court's decision, drawing on three subsequent cases to argue that it narrows the scope of DR and reflects a changing attitude to partial defences generally.

R. Mackay and B. Mitchell, 'The New Diminished Responsibility Plea in Operation: Some Initial Findings' [2017] *Crim LR* 18

Reviews the impact of the updated definition of DR upon homicide prosecutions.

Loss of control

D. J. Baker and L.X. Zhao 'Contributory Qualifying and Non-qualifying Triggers in the Loss of Control Defence: A Wrong Turn on Sexual Infidelity' (2012) 76(3) *JCL* 254

Criticises *Clinton* for failing to understand the workings of the loss of control defence and overlooking policy issues.

A. Clough, 'Honour Killings, Partial Defences and the Exclusionary Conduct Model' (2016) 80(3) *JCL* 177

Considers whether honour killings might come under the defence, and concludes that while this is unlikely, more explicit exclusion in the wording of the Act would have been welcome.

S.M. Edwards, 'Mr Justice Devlin's Legacy: Duffy—A Battered Woman "Caught" in Time' [2009] *Crim LR* 851

Explores the facts and judgment in *Duffy* in detail, considering whether it was a miscarriage of justice.

S.M. Edwards, 'The Strangulation of Female Partners' [2015] 12 *Crim LR* 949

Argues that English law should treat strangulation, a common and gender-specific method of killing women, as more rather than less heinous than other forms of killing.

R.D. Mackay and B.J. Mitchell, 'But is this Provocation? Some Thoughts on the Law Commission's Report on Partial Defences to Murder' [2005] *Crim LR* 44

Critically examines the Law Commission proposals which formed the basis of the loss of control defence.

C. Morgan, 'Loss of Self-Control: Back to the Good Old Days' (2013) 77(2) *JCL* 119

Argues that the underlying principle of loss of control is to account for human emotion and behaviour, and that this could be done using a more objective test.

A. Norrie, 'The Coroners and Justice Act 2009—Partial Defences to Murder: (1) Loss of Control' [2010] *Crim LR* 275

Focuses on the Law Commission proposals on provocation and their relationship to the defence of loss of control.

C. Withey, 'Loss of Control: Loss of Opportunity?' [2011] *Crim LR* 263

Examines the statutory provisions on loss of control, their theoretical underpinnings and potential problems.

Involuntary manslaughter

J. Herring, 'Familial Homicide, Failure to Protect & Domestic Violence' [2007] *Crim LR* 923

Expresses concern about the use of s5 Domestic Violence, Crime and Victims Act 2004 to prosecute victims of domestic violence for 'failure to protect'.

J. Herring and E. Palser, 'The Duty of Care in Gross Negligence Manslaughter' [2007] *Crim LR* 24

Examines the duty of care in gross negligence, its correspondence to tort law and suggestions for reform.

G. Leigh, 'Deconstructing Unlawful Act Manslaughter' (2017) 81(2) *JCL* 112

Suggests that unlawful act manslaughter could usefully be considered as having two forms: manslaughter by act of intended bodily harm, and manslaughter by unlawful and dangerous act.

B. Mitchell, 'More Thoughts about Unlawful and Dangerous Act Manslaughter and the One Punch Killer' [2009] *Crim LR* 502

Explores unforeseen consequences of risk-taking and the levels of culpability in unlawful act manslaughter, raising possible arguments for creation of a lesser offence.

B. Mitchell and R.D. Mackay, 'Investigating Involuntary Manslaughter: An Empirical Study of 127 Cases' (2011) 31(1) *Oxford JLS* 165

Analyses over 100 involuntary manslaughter cases, considering the nature and categorisation of the offences and the offenders' culpability.

F. Stark, 'Reckless Manslaughter' [2017] *Crim LR* 763

Considers whether reckless manslaughter exists separately from gross negligence/unlawful act manslaughter, and whether it should.

G. Williams, 'Gross Negligence Manslaughter—Duty of Care in Drugs Cases: R v Evans' [2009] *Crim LR* 631

Critically examines omissions liability in 'drug homicide' cases.

8 Defences of incapacity and mental conditions

KEY POINTS

INSANITY

This section will help you to:

- [ ] understand the general principles of the defence of insanity so as to be able to distinguish it from automatism and diminished responsibility;
- [ ] critically think about:
  - whether the legal distinction between insanity and automatism is logical;
  - whether insanity is out of date and unrelated to contemporary classifications of mental illness;
  - the social role of the defence.

AUTOMATISM

This section will help you to:

- [ ] understand the general principles of the defence of automatism so as to distinguish it from insanity and diminished responsibility;
- [ ] critically think about:
  - whether the legal distinction between insanity and automatism is logical;
  - the criticisms of the defence and the arguments for reform.

INTOXICATION

This section will help you to:

- [ ] understand:
  - that intoxication is not a defence but that it may negate MR so as to provide a partial defence to crimes of specific intent;
  - that neither voluntary nor involuntary intoxication provide any defence where D acts with mens rea;

- distinguish the effect of a drunken mistake on statutory and common law defences and between drunken mistake, intoxication and mistaken self-defence;
- evaluate the policy basis of the rules.

INFANCY

This section will help you to understand and critically reflect upon the arguments for and against the age of criminal responsibility in the UK.

INTRODUCTION

In this chapter we consider four defences concerning the mental and age-related capacity of D. These defences are available to all crimes but if successfully argued, they do not all result in complete acquittals. A finding of 'not guilty by reason of insanity' can result in detention, while intoxication is rarely a complete defence.

Burden of Proof

As we saw earlier in this volume, in a criminal trial, the burden of proof is on the prosecution to adduce evidence beyond all reasonable doubt that D committed the AR of the offence with MR.

Provided there is sufficient evidence to establish a prima facie case, D will have the opportunity to introduce a defence which the prosecution must then disprove beyond all reasonable doubt. If they cannot do so and D manages to cast a reasonable doubt on the prosecution case, the defence will succeed and D will be entitled to an acquittal. Note that the prosecution have a legal burden of proving all elements of the AR and MR of the crime. D does not have to prove a defence. He is entitled to the presumption of innocence and is not guilty of any charge until it has been proved beyond all reasonable doubt. There are only two defences which impose a legal burden of proof on D: insanity and diminished responsibility.

Recall also that in the case of some statutory defences, the onus of proof can reverse so as to cast upon D an evidential as opposed to a legal burden of proof in respect of a defence.

In either case, if there is insufficient evidence of a defence it will fail but the court may consider that certain factors of the case or D's personal circumstances warrant a more lenient sentence. Those factors will be used to mitigate or reduce the sentence.

→ CROSS-REFERENCE
The burden of proof in a criminal trial is discussed in Chapter 1, 1.2.

Classification

Defences fall into two categories: excusatory and justificatory. Theories of 'excuse' and 'justification' primarily help to explain the legal development of defences, most falling into the former category. A relevant excuse will arise where D intended to commit an offence but only did so because of coercion (duress) or an incapacitating condition such as automatism or insanity. Such a defence excuses D from liability, notwithstanding that he might have intended a crime. Justificatory defences on the other hand amount to a denial of intention to commit an unlawful act. This means that no crime was committed. D's actions will be considered justified or morally right in the circumstances and thus no offence, such as where D inflicts harm in the course of using self-defence to prevent an attack. In general terms, actors are excused, but actions are justified. Both types of defence, if successful, result in acquittal.

The only practical consequence of the distinction is that an accessory to an offence whose principal benefits from a justificatory defence commits no crime. So, if D is an accessory to an assault inflicted by P in self-defence, both will have the benefit of a justificatory defence and neither will be convicted.

Theories of excuse and justification are not generally adhered to by the courts and there is no general agreement on how to classify certain defences such as loss of control or duress of circumstances. For this reason, defences have been divided between two chapters (see also Chapter 9) bearing in mind the more practical distinction of incapacity and compulsion.

In addition to a specific defence, it is always open to D to admit that he committed the crime but did so accidentally or without MR. The latter will typically be an indication of a mistake. Either of these assertions amount to a denial of MR rather than a defence.

8.1 Insanity

KEY CASES

M'Naghten [1843] 10 Cl & R 200—definition of insanity: defect of reason due to an internal disease of the mind;

Bratty v AG for Northern Ireland [1963] AC 386—any mental disorder which has manifested itself in violence and is prone to recur is a disease of the mind;

Sullivan [1984] AC 156—epilepsy as insanity: 'mind' means reason, memory and understanding;

Hennessy [1989] 89 Cr App R 10—diabetes as insanity;

Windle [1952] 2QB 826—knowledge of legal wrongness.

8.1.1 Introduction

Insanity provides a general defence to those suffering from a narrow range of mental disorders who are so ill as to not know what they are doing at the time of the offence or who do not know that it is wrong. The defence offers protection to those suffering primarily from psychotic (ie: delusional) or serious dissociative conditions (where D does not understand the consequences of his actions). Neurotic, emotional or volitional disorders are excluded (eg: depression/anxiety/compulsive disorders). However, the defence is also somewhat surprising because although it excludes all but the most seriously mentally ill, it does, strangely, include defendants with common physical illnesses such as diabetes, sleepwalking and epilepsy.

The rationale of the defence is to protect mentally ill defendants from being unjustly punished. It is, however, unclear as to whether this should be because such defendants lack legal responsibility, or whether they lack mens rea. Before the abolition of capital punishment by the Murder (Abolition of Death Penalty) Act 1965, insanity was primarily used as a means of avoiding the death penalty following conviction for murder. A successful plea of insanity led to a special verdict of 'not guilty by reason of insanity' (NGRI), as it still does, but it was accompanied by automatic and indefinite hospitalisation in a secure mental institution under the Criminal Procedure (Insanity) Act 1964, whether the offence was petty theft or murder. Consequently, insanity was rarely used for anything other than the most serious crimes. There are only about 30 successful insanity pleas in Crown Courts each year. The Criminal Procedure (Insanity and Unfitness to Plead) Act 1991 abolished mandatory and indefinite detention for all crimes apart from murder and introduced a range of disposal options. This brought about an increase in use of the defence: between 1997 and 2001 insanity was successfully used in 72 cases. Further disposal options were introduced by the Domestic Violence, Crime and Victims Act 2004 resulting in 122 successful cases between 2007 and 2011: R. Mackay, B. Mitchell and L. Howe, 'Yet More Facts about the Insanity Defence' [2007] *Crim LR* 399,

R. Mackay 'Ten More Years of the Insanity Defence' [2012] *Crim LR* 946. However, given the prevalence of mental disorders amongst the prison population use of the defence is surprisingly low.

Insanity is relevant at three stages of the criminal process:

→ CROSS-REFERENCE
For further discussion on mental disorders among prisoners see 8.1.6.

- *Mental condition rendering trial impractical:* If D is in custody and too ill to stand trial because of mental illness or impairment, he may be detained in a hospital following reports from two medical practitioners provided the Home Secretary is satisfied that this is necessary in the public interest (ss47, 48 Mental Health Act 1983).

- *Fitness to plead:* D may be unfit to plead guilt or innocence or to participate in the trial. The current test focuses on D's ability to understand the proceedings, instruct a lawyer, plead to the indictment and understand the evidence: *Pritchard* (1836) 7 C & P 303. The emphasis is on intellectual ability but not decision-making capacity or ability to rationalise. One may be unfit to plead even if one is not mentally disordered and, conversely, fit to plead despite mental disorder. Any doubt about fitness to understand the proceedings will result in a *trial of the facts*. If the court finds that D is under a disability, a jury will be empanelled to hear evidence as to whether D did the act or made the omission charged (ie: the AR of the offence). If the jury are not satisfied, they will acquit. If they are satisfied, they do not convict but a disposal will be made by the court from a range of options, such as hospital orders with or without restriction, supervision/treatment orders or an absolute discharge (s5 Criminal Procedure (Insanity) Act 1964 as amended by the Domestic Violence, Crime and Victims Act 2004). This issue will not be considered in any more detail here save to note two criticisms: (1) The emphasis on whether or not D did the act or made the omission assumes that there is a clear distinction between the AR and MR of a crime. This is not always the case (see 2.1.1 and Sir Leveson P in *R v Wells & Others* [2015] EWCA Crim 2). (2) The current test is thought to set the level of unfitness at too high a level. In Law Com CP No 197 (2010) the Law Commission proposed a new, fairer test of unfitness based on decision-making capacity. In 2016, the Law Commission produced a report on unfitness to plead (Law Com CP No 364 (2016)) in which it considered that unfitness to plead should be a last resort, the full trial process ensuring that a defendant in this situation is treated fairly. In determining this, diversion from the criminal trial process and the seriousness of the offence should be considered. The current law was not always consistently applied. Consequently, the Commission recommended that judicial discretion should be introduced, along with a robust fact finding procedure. Disposals (sentences) should be limited to hospital orders, supervision orders or absolute discharges. This paper was followed in early 2016 by a draft Bill—the Criminal Procedure (Lack of Capacity) Bill which would allow a court to determine capacity in clearly defined circumstances.

- *At trial:* D may be fit to plead but can raise insanity as a defence if he was insane at the time of the crime.

The defence is based on the much criticised M'Naghten Rules which have not changed since 1843. The absence of reform is a source of repeated criticism.

→ CROSS-REFERENCE
Law Commission proposals for abolition of the defences of 'insanity' and 'automatism' are considered in 8.1.6.

8.1.2 The Relationship between Insanity, Automatism and Diminished Responsibility

Automatism

Before examining the case law on insanity, it is helpful to note that the defence is closely related to automatism. Both arise where D is in a mental state of automatism, meaning loss of complete voluntary control over one's actions. Insanity is sometimes referred to as insane automatism and automatism as non-insane automatism. The more straightforward labels of insanity and automatism will be used in this book.

A successful plea of automatism negates voluntariness. Recall that this is a fundamental precondition of any criminal act. Insanity, on the other hand, undermines either AR or MR. The distinction between the defences in terms of presentation is that insanity is due to an internal cause whilst the cause of automatism is external. The consequences of such a distinction can be radically different. A burden of proof is imposed on D under insanity whereas it remains on the prosecution in the case of automatism. Automatism is a complete defence whereas the technical verdict following a successful plea of insanity is NGRI but this can be followed by one of a range of hospitalisation or supervision orders.

Diminished responsibility

A plea of diminished responsibility relates to a lack of moral responsibility for a murder that D *intended* to commit whilst suffering from an *abnormality of mental functioning*. D will therefore have acted with MR. This partial defence will, if successfully proved by D, result in a conviction of manslaughter. The definition of diminished responsibility (s2 Homicide Act 1957 as amended in Coroners and Justice Act 2009) is wide enough to encompass insanity and other mental disorders.

See Diagram 8.1 for a summary of the relationship between insanity, automatism and diminished responsibility.

8.1.3 The Test for Insanity: The M'Naghten Rules

M'Naghten's Case (1843) 10 CL & R 200; 8 ER 718

Daniel M'Naghten shot and killed the secretary to the Prime Minister, Sir Robert Peel, under a morbid delusion that he was being persecuted by the police on the instructions of the Tory Party. He was acquitted by reason of insanity. The ensuing public outrage led to the referral of a number of questions to the judges of the House of Lords whose answers have provided the legal test of insanity ever since.

In answer to the second question (what directions should be given to a jury regarding an insanity plea?) and the third question (as to D's state of mind at the time of the act) Tindal CJ said this:

> … we have to submit our opinion to be, that the jurors ought to be told in all cases that every man is to be presumed to be sane, and to possess a sufficient degree of reason to be responsible for his crimes, until the contrary be proved to their satisfaction; and that to establish a defence on the ground of insanity, *it must be clearly proved that, at the time of the committing of the act, the party accused was labouring under such a defect of reason, from disease of the mind, as not to know the nature and quality of the act he was doing; or, if he did know it, that he did not know he was doing what was wrong …* (Emphasis added.)

In answer to the fourth question (regarding the verdict) Tindal CJ continued:

> … we think he must be considered in the same situation as to responsibility as if the facts with respect to which the delusion exists were real. For example, if under the influence of his delusion he supposes another man to be in the act of attempting to take away his life, and he kills that man,

as he supposes, in self-defence, he would be exempt from punishment. If this delusion was that the deceased had inflicted a serious injury to his character and fortune, and he killed him in revenge for such supposed injury, he would be liable to punishment.

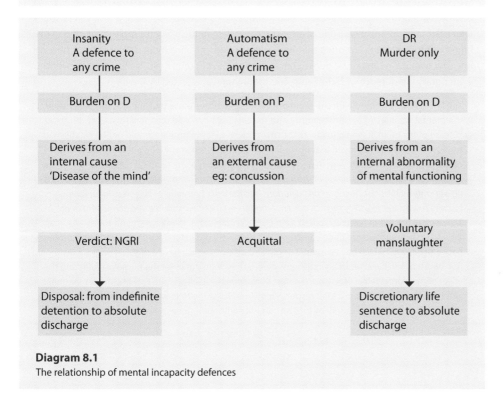

Diagram 8.1
The relationship of mental incapacity defences

The M'Naghten Rules therefore consist of three elements each of which needs to be proved by D on a balance of probabilities:

- Disease of the mind.
- Defect of reason.
- The two cognitive tests: D must not know the nature and quality of his actions or, if he does, he must not know that it is wrong.

Disease of the mind

The insanity defence is symbolic of the court's role in protecting society from violence. To that end it has been decided that a *disease of the mind* need not necessarily arise from mental disorder. The disease must affect the *mind* not the brain. Two implications follow: (1) the faculties comprising 'the mind' are narrowly defined as the intellectual/cognitive faculties of 'reason, memory and understanding'; (2) this is far narrower than the four categories of mental disorder defined in the Mental Health Act 1983: mental illness, severe mental impairment, mental impairment and psychopathic disorder; or by the Mental Health Act 2007: any disorder or disability of the mind. All are inclusive of emotional/developmental and volitional impulses.

The following cases have classified as a disease of the mind these non-psychiatric illnesses: arteriosclerosis, epilepsy, diabetes, sleepwalking.

Arteriosclerosis

R v Kemp [1957] 1 QB 399 BRISTOL ASSIZES

D was charged with causing grievous bodily harm to his wife having made a motiveless attack with a hammer during an episode of arteriosclerosis (where the oxygen supply is cut off due to a blood clot to the brain). D argued that he was not suffering from a mental disease but a physical one which might in time cause degeneration of the brain but until it did, it should be regarded as a temporary interference with the brain. This argument was rejected by Devlin J:

> The law is not concerned with the brain but with the mind, in sense that 'mind' is ordinarily used, the mental faculties of reason, memory and understanding. If one read for 'disease of the mind' 'disease of the brain', it would follow that in many cases pleas of insanity would not be established because it could not be proved that the brain had been affected in any way, either by degeneration of the cells or in any other way. *In my judgment the condition of the brain is irrelevant and so is the question of whether the condition of the mind is curable or incurable, transitory or permanent. There is no warranty for introducing those considerations into the definition in the M'Naghten Rules. Temporary insanity is sufficient to satisfy them. It does not matter whether it is incurable and permanent or not ... The primary thing that has to be looked for is the defect of reason.* In my judgment, the words 'from disease of the mind' are not to be construed as if they were put in for the purpose of distinguishing between diseases which have a mental origin and diseases which have a physical origin, a distinction which in 1843 was probably little considered. They were put in for the purpose of limiting the effect of the words 'defect of reason'. A defect of reason is by itself enough to make the act irrational and therefore normally to exclude responsibility in law. But the Rule was not intended to apply to defects of reason caused simply by brutish stupidity without rational power. [Emphasis added.]

Verdict: Guilty but insane.

Epilepsy

Bratty v AG for Northern Ireland [1963] AC 386 HOUSE OF LORDS

D killed a girl whom he was driving in a car by taking off her stocking and strangling her with it. In his statement to the police he said that he had had 'a terrible feeling' and 'a sort of blackness' had come over him. Medical evidence at his trial for murder supported the view that he might have been suffering from psychomotor epilepsy. He pleaded automatism, lack of intent for murder and insanity. The judge refused to leave the first two to the jury and D was convicted, the jury having rejected insanity. Most of the leading judgment of Lord Denning is concerned with automatism but, on insanity, he said the following:

> The major mental diseases, which the doctors call psychoses, such as schizophrenia, are clearly diseases of the mind ... **It seems to me that any mental disorder which has manifested itself in violence and is prone to recur is a disease of the mind. At any rate it is the sort of disease for which a person should be detained in hospital rather than be given an unqualified acquittal ...**
>
> I am clearly of the opinion that, if the act of George Bratty was an involuntary act, as the defence suggested, the evidence attributed it solely to a disease of the mind and the only defence open was the defence of insanity. There was no evidence of automatism apart from insanity. There was, therefore, no need for the judge to put it to the jury. And when the jury rejected the defence of insanity, they rejected the only defence disclosed by the evidence. (Emphasis added.)

Appeal dismissed.

The statement in bold type should be treated with some caution for insanity has been found to apply to a range of offences other than those of violence, although the latter are, by far, the most frequent. Nevertheless, the requirement of violence, although not recurrence, was confirmed by the Court of Appeal in *Burgess* [1991] (see 'Sleepwalking').

The evidence in *Bratty* that D was suffering from epilepsy was very weak and the jury had rejected it. In the next case, the evidence of epilepsy was more persuasive.

R v Sullivan [1984] AC 156 HOUSE OF LORDS

D, aged 51 and a life-long sufferer of epilepsy, kicked an 80-year-old friend during one of his fits, and was charged with inflicting grievous bodily harm with intent under ss20 and 18 Offences Against the Person Act 1861. Having no recollection of the attack, D pleaded automatism but the trial judge ruled that the defence was one of insanity due to a disease of the mind. D then pleaded guilty to assault occasioning actual bodily harm to avoid mandatory indefinite detention in a mental hospital which would automatically follow a verdict of NGRI. He was convicted and appealed to the House of Lords where Lord Diplock gave the leading judgment in which the *Kemp* definition of disease of the mind was approved:

> *I agree with what was said by Devlin J in R v Kemp, that 'mind' in the M'Naghten Rules is used in the ordinary sense of the mental faculties of reason, memory and understanding. If the effect of a disease is to impair these faculties so severely as to have either of the consequences referred to in the latter part of the rules, it matters not whether the aetiology of the impairment is organic, as in epilepsy, or functional, or whether the impairment itself is permanent or is transient and intermittent, provided that it subsisted at the time of commission of the act. The purpose of the legislation relating to the defence of insanity, ever since its origin in 1800, has been to protect society against recurrence of the dangerous conduct …*
>
> *My Lords, it is natural to feel reluctant to attach the label of insanity to a sufferer from psychomotor epilepsy of the kind to which Mr. Sullivan was subject, even though the expression in the context of a special verdict of 'not guilty by reason of insanity' is a technical one which includes a purely temporary and intermittent suspension of the mental faculties of reason, memory and understanding resulting from the occurrence of an epileptic fit. But the label is contained in the current statute, it has appeared in the statute's predecessors ever since 1800. It does not lie within the power of the courts to alter it. Only Parliament can do that. It has done so twice; it could do so once again.* [Emphasis added.]

Appeal dismissed.

 NOTE 8.1

1. The court confirmed that the crucial distinction between the related defences of automatism and insanity was the internal/external divide. Since epilepsy was due to an internal cause, it was a disease of the mind.

2. The court viewed insanity as a social defence: one which protected the public from violence. But since Mr Sullivan had pleaded guilty to a lesser crime and was subsequently sentenced to far less than indefinite detention, the protection the court could offer to society in reality was somewhat illusory.

Diabetes

R v Hennessy (1989) 89 CR APP R 10 COURT OF APPEAL

D, a diabetic, was charged with taking a conveyance and driving away while disqualified. He pleaded automatism for he had acted involuntarily, having forgotten to take his insulin due to stress, anxiety and depression following a failed relationship. Consequently, he was hyperglycaemic (an excess of blood sugar and too little insulin). The trial judge ruled that his condition was the result of diabetes, an internal cause of involuntary action, and that his defence was insanity. To avoid being despatched for life to a mental institution in respect of such a minor transgression, Mr Hennessy pleaded guilty and appealed on the grounds that his depression and relationship troubles were external factors overriding the effect of a lack of insulin.

Lord Lane CJ:

> In our judgment, stress, anxiety and depression can no doubt be the result of the operation of external factors, but they are not, it seems to us, in themselves separately or together external factors of the kind capable in law of causing or contributing to a state of automatism. They constitute a state of mind which is prone to recur. They lack the feature of novelty or accident which is the basis of the distinction drawn by Lord Diplock in *R v Sullivan* …

Appeal dismissed.

 THINKING POINT 8.1

Was Hennessy's driving offence violent or likely to recur as required by *Bratty*?

Sleepwalking

R v Burgess [1991] 2 ALL ER 769 COURT OF APPEAL

Burgess and his neighbour spent an evening at her flat watching video tapes. She fell asleep but awoke when Burgess hit her over the head with the video recorder and a bottle and grasped her around the throat. As soon as she shouted he appeared to come to his senses and showed distress. He was charged with malicious wounding with intent contrary to s18 Offences Against the Person Act 1861. He claimed to have been sleepwalking and pleaded automatism for which there was previous authority. Lord Denning in Bratty had classified sleepwalking as a case of automatism:

> An involuntary act … means an act done by the muscles, without any control by the mind, such as a spasm, a reflex action or a convulsion, or an act done by a person who is not conscious of what he is doing, such as an act done whilst suffering from concussion or whilst sleepwalking.

Further, in *Boshears* (1961) The Times, 8 February, D was cleared of killing his wife during a 'night terror' on the basis of automatism and in the unreported case of *Lillienfield* (1985) The Times, 17 October, a Crown Court had classified sleepwalking as automatism. D was acquitted of murder, despite the fact that he had stabbed his victim 20 times.

The prosecution in *Burgess* argued that D either knew what he was doing, and had therefore been intentional, or if he did not, he was insane. Faced with the prospect of indefinite detention, Burgess changed his plea to guilty and appealed.

Lord Lane CJ:

> The appellant plainly suffered from a defect of reason from some sort of failure (for lack of a better term) of the mind causing him to act as he did without conscious motivation …
>
> One can perhaps narrow the field of inquiry further by eliminating what are sometimes called the 'external factors' such as concussion caused by a blow on the head. There were no such factors here. Whatever the cause may have been, it was an 'internal' cause …

Lord Lane then approved of Lord Denning's definition of disease of the mind with this qualification:

> It seems to us that if there is a danger of recurrence that may be an added reason for categorising the condition as a disease of the mind. On the other hand, the absence of the danger of recurrence is not a reason for saying that it cannot be a disease of the mind …
>
> There have been several occasions when during the course of judgments … sleepwalking has been used as a self-evident illustration of non-insane automatism. [Reference was made to *Bratty* and a Canadian case of *R v Parks* (1990) 56 CCC (3d) 449 where D successfully claimed automatism after having driven 23 km to the house of his wife's parents and stabbed them whilst sleepwalking. He was acquitted of murder and attempted murder, this being confirmed by the Canadian Supreme Court. Lord Lane then reviewed the expert medical evidence in the case which was to the effect that Burgess suffered either from an internal sleep disorder or from an hysterical dissociative state, both of which were likely to recur.]
>
> *It seems to us that on this evidence the judge was right to conclude that this was an abnormality or disorder, albeit transitory, due to an internal factor, whether functional or organic, which had manifested itself in violence. It was a disorder or abnormality which might recur, though the possibility of it recurring in the form of serious violence was unlikely …* [Emphasis added.]

Appeal dismissed.

?! THINKING POINT 8.2

If Burgess did not represent a continuing danger, why was it necessary to label him insane? Was this decision made on 'legal principle' or for reasons of 'public protection'?

If D murders his father (V) whilst sleepwalking, having been provoked by V during the evening and having drunk an excessive amount of alcohol, should the cause of involuntary action be regarded as internal or external?

Contrary to English law, the Canadian Supreme Court has defined sleepwalking as automatism. In *Parks* (1992) DLR (4th) 27 it was held that before sleepwalking could be defined as insanity there would have to be evidence of a link with D's state of mind rather than with the normal condition of sleep. It was said that the dichotomy between internal and external causes was blurred and unhelpful in this context. Other Canadian cases have called for a more 'holistic approach' to disease of the mind. Read this extract by W. Wilson, Dr I. Ebrahim, Dr P. Fenwick and R. Marks from 'Violence, Sleepwalking and the Criminal Law: (2) The Legal Aspects' [2005] *Crim LR* 615:

> … sleepwalking is a common enough activity and sleepwalkers are known to be able to perform any number of activities while 'unconscious'. The apparent consequence of *Burgess* is that activities which would, in a conscious person, result in criminal liability, will convert an otherwise normal person who

performs them while sleepwalking into a person who is legally insane. This is difficult to support on any ground, medical, legal or practical. It would mean that a sleepwalker who dropped a cup while making a cup of fantasy midnight tea, or who urinated in a hotel cupboard would be insane for the purpose of the law of criminal damage, a serious departure from the notion that the verdict of criminal courts communicates desert.

Further, more recent English Crown Court cases have held that sleepwalking defendants are entitled to acquittals, presumably on the basis of automatism: *Bilton* (2005) *The Guardian*, 20 December, a rape case, and *Davies* (2006) *The Times*, 11 February, a sexual assault case. Perhaps this reflects a concern to adhere to Article 5 ECHR where deprivation of liberty for persons of 'unsound mind' can only be justified on medical grounds in respect of the mentally ill. However, the precedent of *Burgess* remains.

Stress and dissociative states

In Canadian law, a dissociative state of mind deriving from a psychological blow has been held to constitute a disease of the mind (*Rabey* [1980] SCR 513, 54 CCC (2d) 1). Rabey was an infatuated student who assaulted a girl by whom he had been rejected. The court held that the source of the disassociation was D's internal psychology and emotional make-up which had caused him to over-react. Therefore, the *ordinary* stresses and strains of life are not external but internal causes of involuntary action. This accords with the principles of English law.

But what of *extraordinary* stresses and strains? The Court of Appeal in *Re T* [1990] Crim LR 256 stated that stress, anxiety and depression arising from an external cause may provide the basis of automatism. The young woman defendant had been raped the week before she committed a robbery whilst suffering from post-traumatic stress disorder.

Mental disorder and intoxication

An important case, involving three conjoined appeals, reviewed the inter-relationship between insanity, automatism and intoxication. Two of the appellants suffered from both a mental condition and intoxication at the time of the offence.

Coley, McGhee, Harris [2013] EWCA CRIM 223

Coley concerned an appeal against conviction of attempted murder. D, a 17-year-old youth, addicted to cannabis, stabbed a neighbour after watching violent video games. He entered the neighbour's house with a key and, whilst wearing dark clothes and a balaclava, conducted the attack with a hunting (or 'Rambo') knife. He claimed to have 'blacked out' and had no recollection of the events. He had smoked cannabis during the evening. There was expert evidence that he had suffered a brief psychotic episode arising from voluntary intoxication and may have been delusional, 'acting out' a role from a video game. On appeal, defence counsel argued that insanity and automatism should have been put before the jury:

Hughes LJ:

> We do not doubt that the possible state of mind in which this defendant stabbed the man next door can properly be called a mental abnormality (or, in the nineteenth century language of *M'Naghten*, a defect of reason) which is recognised medically by psychiatrists ... Well understood

ones certainly include schizophrenia and bi-polar disorder, which are no doubt mental disorders or illnesses. Another well known possible cause of psychotic *symptoms* is drug abuse, which is not a mental disorder. But with that caveat, we agree that to speak of a psychotic episode is no doubt to speak of a temporary abnormality of the brain or mind and thus of a defect of reason for the purposes of the *M'Naghten* rules.

However, the key thing to understand is that whether there is or is not a 'disease of the mind' for the purpose of the *M'Naghten* rules is, and has to be, a question of law and not of medical usage ... *[T]he law has to cope with the synthesising of the law of insanity with the law of voluntary intoxication. The first calls for a special verdict of acquittal and very particular means of disposal. The latter is generally no defence at all, but may be relevant to whether the defendant formed a specific intention, if the offence in question is one which requires such: DPP v Majewski [1977] AC 443 ... For all the reasons explained in Majewski, the law refuses as a matter of policy to afford a general defence to an offender on the basis of his own voluntary intoxication. The pressing social reasons for maintaining this general policy of the law are certainly no less present in modern conditions of substance abuse than they were in the past.*

The precise line between the law of voluntary intoxication and the law of insanity may, we do not doubt, be difficult to identify in some borderline cases. But the present case falls comfortably on the side of the line covered by voluntary intoxication ... In order to engage the law of insanity, it is not enough that there is an effect on the mind, or, in the language of the M'Naghten rules, a 'defect of reason'. There must also be what the law classifies as a disease of the mind. Direct acute effects on the mind of intoxicants, voluntarily taken, are not so classified. [Emphasis added.]

Conviction confirmed.

NOTE 8.2

1. Whilst the appellant may have been suffering from a *defect of reason*, the direct, acute effects of voluntary intoxication could never amount to a *disease of the mind*. The defence of insanity was therefore rejected on policy grounds.

2. A distinction has existed in English law since *Beard* (1920) 14 Cr App R 160 at 194 between intoxication and a disease of the mind produced by the intoxicant. If the appellant had been suffering from a more serious long-term psychiatric condition, rather than a temporary one, insanity might have succeeded.

→ CROSS-REFERENCE
Other aspects of this are case are discussed in 8.3.3 and 8.3.4.

Most cases of insanity do not include common physical illness which, at most, account for only around 10 per cent of cases. Research shows that the most common diagnostic group is schizophrenia (around 50 per cent), the rest comprising acute or transient psychosis (approximately 6.9 per cent), hypomania (4.2 per cent), depressive/anxiety disorders (11.1 per cent), with drug induced psychosis, post-traumatic stress disorder, brain damage and other cases (collectively around 20 per cent) (Statistics from R.D. Mackay, B.J. Mitchell and L. Howe, 'Yet More Facts about the Insanity Defence' [2006] *Crim LR* 399). Therefore, for the most part, the defence is used appropriately to secure psychiatric treatment for those with mental disorders. Nevertheless, it would surprise most people to learn that sleepwalkers, diabetics and epileptics risk being regarded by the law as insane. It was held by the Divisional Court in *DPP v H* [1997] 1 WLR 1406 that insanity does not apply to strict liability offences.

?! THINKING POINT 8.3

D commits a sexual assault on V whilst sleepwalking. He later claims to remember nothing about it. He suffers from anxiety due to a job loss as well as relationship breakdown. Does he have a defence?

Defect of reason

The M'Naghten Rules require a defect of *reason* due to a disease of the mind. The defect must affect the cognitive or intellectual faculties of memory, reason and understanding (*Bratty*). It is here that the law's concern with the superficial aspects of mental disorder parts company with the far more complex classifications of contemporary psychiatry. The rules do not include defects of the emotions or will (unlike diminished responsibility).

As a concept, defect of reason is vague and could apply to many people who are simply forgetful or confused, but when put together with *disease of the mind* it clearly indicates something rather more serious:

A temporary period of absent-mindedness during diabetic depression is not a defect of reason

> #### *R v Clarke* [1972] 1 ALL ER 219 COURT OF APPEAL
>
> D was diabetic and suffered various domestic problems. She was charged with theft for stealing three items from a supermarket, having removed them from the basket and placed them in her shopping bag without paying for them at the check-out. Her defence was one of lack of intent to steal and that she had acted during a moment of absent-mindedness. There was medical evidence that she was suffering from diabetic depression. To avoid the verdict of 'not guilty' and mandatory, indefinite hospitalisation, she had pleaded guilty and appealed:
>
> Ackner J:
>
> > It may be that on the evidence in this case the assistant recorder was entitled to the view that the appellant suffered from a disease of the mind but we express no concluded view on that. However, in our judgment the evidence fell very far short either of showing that she suffered from a defect of reason or that the consequences of that defect in reason, if any, were that she was unable to know the nature and quality of the act she was doing. The *M'Naghten* rules relate to accused persons who by reason of a disease of the mind are deprived of the power of reasoning. They do not apply and never have applied to those who retain the power of reasoning but who in moments of confusion or absent-mindedness fail to use their powers to the full.

Knowledge of nature and quality—the two cognitive tests

The scope of the defence is considerably narrowed by the following tests. The M'Naghten Rules require D to be suffering from a defect of reason from a disease of the mind as *not to know the nature and quality of what they are doing* or, if they do, as *not to know that it is wrong*. These elements, being entirely dependent on *knowledge*, are referred to as the 'two cognitive tests'.

Nature and quality of the act

D must not know the nature and quality of his act, or, in other words, must not know what he is doing in a physical sense. The courts do not look to the underlying cause of mental illness but to an absence of cognition/understanding.

EXAMPLE 8.1

D is under the delusion that he is killing a snake whereas the victim is, in fact, D's partner. The test is satisfied and D has a defence to murder.

On the other hand, if D is delusional and thinks he is killing a partner but the victim is, in fact, the postman, D would fail the test because he would know that he was physically killing *a person*. However, should it be right that a major delusional disorder should fail to excuse D's responsibility for the act? The test has the effect of distinguishing between delusions. Partial delusions are not included.

THINKING POINT 8.4

Would D succeed under the nature/quality limb of the insanity test?

1. D is under the delusion that God has told him to kill all prostitutes because they are evil. He kills six such young women.

2. D kills his daughter under the delusion that he is acting under divine authority which is superior to the law of the land.

3. D pulls out her daughter's teeth believing them to be possessed by the devil.

4. D is paranoid and believes that all shop-keepers are spying on him. He kills a butcher (V) believing that his life is under threat when he sees V chopping meat.

5. D believes he is cutting down a tree whereas he is chopping a neighbour to pieces.

Knowledge that what they are doing is wrong

If D knows what he is doing, the insanity defence may still be proved by reference to the second test: that he did not know it was wrong. In England, 'wrong' means *legally* as opposed to *morally* wrong. Therefore, if D, under a disease of the mind, commits a mercy killing, knowing that murder is a crime, he would fail the test even in the presence of a belief that the killing was morally excusable. On the other hand, if the test was one of *moral wrongness*, D would pass. By adhering to legal wrongness, far more people are excluded from the insanity defence. You would need to be extremely disturbed to not know that murder or another major offence was against the law.

R v Windle [1952] 2 QB 826 COURT OF APPEAL

D was convicted of murdering his wife by giving her a fatal dose of 100 aspirin tablets. She was probably certifiably insane and was obsessed with committing suicide. D was thought to be suffering from a form of communicated insanity known as folie à deux. It can arise when one is constantly caring for an insane person. It was D's pre-occupation with his wife's condition that led him to commit the murder. On his arrest he told the police that he supposed he would hang for it. His plea of insanity at the trial was rejected and he appealed.

Lord Goddard CJ:

> The argument in this appeal really has been concerned with what is meant by the word 'wrong'. The evidence that was given on the issue of insanity was that of the doctor called by the appellant and that of the prison doctor who was called by the prosecution. Both doctors expressed without hesitation the view that when the appellant was administering this poison to his wife he knew he was doing an act which the law forbade. I need not put it higher than that. It may well be that in the misery in which he had been living with this nagging and tiresome wife who constantly expressed the desire to commit suicide, he thought she was better out of the world than in it. … The question … in all these cases is one of responsibility. A man may be suffering from a defect of reason, but, if he knows that what he is doing is wrong—and by 'wrong' is meant contrary to law—he is responsible.

Appeal dismissed.

The narrow test was recently confirmed in *Johnson* [2007] EWCA Crim 1978. Other common law jurisdictions have not followed the English example and apply a more flexible test of moral wrongness. The two cognitive tests exclude from the insanity defence people who are conscious of what they are doing at the time of the offence but who cannot control the impulse to do it due to an emotional or volitional disorder.

The Butler Report commented that (para. 18.8):

> Knowledge of the law is hardly an appropriate test on which to base ascription of responsibility to the mentally disordered. It is a very narrow ground of exemption since even persons who are grossly disturbed generally know that murder and arson are crimes.

➔ **CROSS-REFERENCE**
For details of the Butler Report see 8.1.7.

?!   **THINKING POINT** 8.5

If the test had been one of moral wrongness, or ordinary standards of wrongness, do you think Windle's appeal would have been allowed?

If Windle were to be charged with murder on the same facts today, what defence would you advise him to use?

Research indicates that in practice the 'wrongness limb' is used more regularly in psychiatric reports than the 'nature and quality' limb. However, the narrow interpretation of 'wrong according to law' is not always followed in practice: R.D. Mackay, 'More Fact(s) about the Insanity Defence' [1999] *Crim LR* 715:

> Perhaps the most interesting finding is in the way that the 'wrongness' limb of M'Naghten continues to be interpreted by psychiatrists. In previous research it was remarked that 'the general impression gained from reading the documentation in these cases was that the wrongness issue was being treated in a liberal fashion by all concerned, rather than in the strict manner regularly depicted by legal commentators'. Within the current research sample (44 cases) it was found that in 25 reports (18 cases) the psychiatrists specifically used the term that the defendant did not know that his act was 'wrong'. However, it is safe to say the vast majority of these reports made no reference to knowledge of legal wrongness. Rather in most of the case reports the 'wrongness' limb was interpreted widely to cover whether the defendant thought his/her actions were morally justified, and/or whether the actions were

in perceived self-defence of themselves or others, in the sense of protecting their physical or spiritual well-being … In short, the overwhelming impression is that the question the majority of psychiatrists are addressing is: if the delusion that the defendant was experiencing at the time of the offence was in fact reality, then would the defendant's actions be morally justified?—rather than the narrow cognitive test of legal wrongness required by the M'Naghten Rules.

?! **THINKING POINT** 8.6

Look at the examples in Thinking point 8.4. Which of those might succeed under the alternative wrongness test?

For example, do they know whether:

■ They are committing a legal wrong (as strictly required by the law)? *or*

■ Their actions would be justified by the delusion (as seems to be the test in practice)?

8.1.4 Burden of Proof

In all criminal trials, the prosecution bear the legal burden of proving all elements of an offence (AR and MR) and disproving any defence beyond all reasonable doubt.

This is in accordance with the fundamental presumption of innocence. If MR cannot be proved, D is entitled to an acquittal.

However, the insanity defence transfers the burden of proof to D on a balance of probabilities. This is because the M'Naghten Rules presume that everyone is sane. Therefore, that presumption must be disproved by D. Of course, this does not stop the prosecution from attempting to prove that D was not insane and knew perfectly well what he was doing.

As with unfitness, D is required to produce written or oral evidence of insanity from two medical practitioners, one of whom is duly approved. If D succeeds, he will not be set free but will be subject to one of a range of orders (see 8.1.5). If D fails to prove insanity, he will be convicted provided there is proof beyond reasonable doubt of the act/omission. Under the *nature/ quality* test, the prosecution need only prove that D did the act or made the omission in question and do not have to prove MR (s2 Trial of Lunatics Act 1883 and *AG's Reference (No 3 of 1998)* [1999] 3 WLR 1994).

This is of course exceptional. D's burden is more onerous than the burden on the prosecution and is subject to the criticism that if the prosecution have failed to prove MR, it should not also be necessary for D to also prove its absence, especially when success results not in freedom but a potential prolonged or even indefinite period of detention in hospital. There is a risk of injustice if D can lose his freedom without proof of all elements of the offence in the usual way.

Either the judge or the prosecution may raise insanity where D puts his mental capacity in issue by introducing evidence of automatism or diminished responsibility. Here the burden of proof will be borne by the prosecution beyond all reasonable doubt (s6 Criminal Procedure (Insanity) Act 1964). It is now clear, however, that it will only be in exceptional cases that a judge can leave insanity to the jury against D's wishes such as in murder cases: *R v Thomas (Sharon)* [1994] Crim LR 314.

The justification for reversing the burden of proof is that defendants who wish to raise insanity are best placed to prove it. Prosecutors would find proving or disproving the defence too difficult. This remains a contentious issue however since the same argument might also apply to self-defence, automatism or intoxication. It is thought that the reversal of the burden is an historical anomaly, stemming from a time when the distinction between legal and evidential burdens of proof was less certain and when most defences had to be proved by defendants. It is doubtful whether any special rules were ever intended to be established for insanity, yet they have endured since the Victorian era.

8.1.5 The Verdict and Disposal Provisions

Verdict

By virtue of s2 Trial of Lunatics Act 1883, a successful plea of insanity will amount to the special verdict that at the date of the act or omission charged, D was 'not guilty by reason of insanity' (NGRI).

Disposal provisions

Before 1991, under the Criminal Procedure (Insanity) Act 1964, indefinite detention was mandatory following all special verdicts regardless of the crime and it was commonly perceived as the equivalent of a life sentence. It was a little known fact, however, that some acquittees were sent to local hospitals and released after a few months. Even some who had been sent to special units were only detained for a few years (R.D. MacKay, 'Fact and Fiction About the Insanity Defence' [1990] *Crim LR* 247). The Criminal Procedure (Insanity and Unfitness to Plead) Act 1991 abolished mandatory detention for all crimes other than murder.

Now, s24 Domestic Violence, Crime and Victims Act 2004 has amended the 1964 Act to provide that indefinite detention following murder will only be mandatory where D's mental health is such that the court can make a hospital order within the terms of s27 of the Mental Health Act 1983, as for unfitness. Otherwise, the courts have greater flexibility for all cases (Home Office Circular, 24/2005, para 12).

The following powers exist to deal with persons not guilty by reason of insanity or unfit to plead:

- a hospital order with or without a restriction order;
- a supervision and treatment order; or
- an order for an absolute discharge.

These options now give sentencers the power to order a much wider and more appropriate range of hospital and community-based disposals.

8.1.6 Criticisms of Insanity

Many of the criticisms of the M'Naghten Rules have already been noted. They can be summarised as follows:

a. In 1953, the Royal Commission on Capital Punishment described the M'Naghten Rules as obsolete and misleading and the superficiality of 'disease of the mind' as outdated and inaccurate. Certainly, the label 'insanity' is outdated and a potential disincentive to those who might otherwise plead the defence. The definition of *disease of the mind* is so wide as to include epileptics, sleepwalkers and diabetics. 600,000 people in the UK have epilepsy; 2.7 million have diabetes (Law Commission Discussion Paper, *Criminal Liability: Automatism and Insanity* (July 2013), p 8).

b. However, the test of defect of reason under the two cognitive tests is, by contrast, too narrow and excludes those who know what they do but who cannot help themselves. A lack of reason is only one cause of mental illness. Emotional or volitional disorders are excluded. The result is that a person suffering non-legally insane mental disorder is more likely to be convicted of a crime, sent to prison and fail to receive necessary psychiatric treatment. The rules therefore fail to offer a safety net to some of the most disturbed offenders and they remain at greater risk of mental deterioration, self-harm and suicide, particularly children. Approximately 36 per cent of prisoners are considered to have a disability, 10 per cent are estimated to be seriously mentally ill and 25 per cent could have actual or borderline learning disability (Law Commission Discussion Paper, *Criminal Liability: Automatism and Insanity* (July 2013), para 1.75). This of course raises concerns regarding compliance with Article 3 ECHR, the UN Convention on the Rights of Persons with Disabilities, the UN Convention on the Rights of the Child and the UK's other international obligations.

c. The distinction between insanity and automatism is a very fine, yet rather blunt, determination of whether the cause of involuntary action is internal (a disease of the mind) or external (automatism). Diabetics can be classified as one or the other depending on the presence of an external factor such as medication. One justification for the distinction is the policy that those suffering from an internal condition are more likely to be dangerous and more likely to re-offend (*Bratty*). This is arbitrary. An insane defendant, especially one not suffering from mental disorder, is no more likely to re-offend that one classified as an automaton.

d. Psychiatric medicine no longer defines mental disorder in terms of insanity. Psychiatrists tend to excuse people for not being completely 'normal' whereas the courts hold people to account because they are not completely 'mad'. The M'Naghten Rules, based upon a legal rather than a medical definition of insanity, prevail. This reinforces the rationale of insanity as a social defence.

e. As with diminished responsibility, conflicting expert evidence can be submitted to the court on behalf of either prosecution or defence. The question of whether or not a defendant is legally insane is then determined by medically unqualified jurors who are left to choose between the experts.

f. A finding of insanity can be avoided by a defendant changing his plea to guilty, thus circumventing both justice and social protection.

g. In terms of the width of disease of the mind and the reversal of the burden of proof, the rules potentially conflict with the ECHR.

Article 5 ECHR states that everyone has the right to liberty and security and that no-one shall be deprived of his liberty save in prescribed cases and in accordance with a procedure prescribed by law. One of the prescribed cases in Article 5(1)(e) refers to detention of persons of *unsound mind*. *Winterwerp v Netherlands* (1979) 2 EHRR 387 stated that whether someone was of *unsound mind* was a matter of objective medical expertise and that detention is unlawful unless the mental disorder warrants compulsory hospitalisation. Therefore, the detention of people with physical diseases is contrary to this provision.

> The presumption of innocence is guaranteed by Article 6 ECHR. which is contravened by the defence to the extent that the burden of proof is reversed whereas, under normal circumstances, D would only need to raise a reasonable doubt about his guilt.

Since the prosecution are not required to prove MR in insanity cases the criticism arises that if D fails to prove insanity, yet the prosecution prove the act/omission, D can be convicted despite the presence of reasonable doubt concerning MR.

The criticisms can be answered to some extent by pointing to the role of insanity as a social defence so that it affords protection to society not only to those who need help (even sleepwalkers can be referred to sleep-clinics) but from violent and dangerous individuals who need treatment or supervision.

8.1.7 Reform

The rules have not been reformed since they were formulated in 1843. This is despite strong criticism by the Royal Commission on Capital Punishment 1949–1953 (Cmd 8932), the Butler Committee 1975 and by a welter of academic literature.

The Law Commission in its discussion paper *Criminal Liability: Insanity and Automatism* (July 2013) provisionally propose to abolish the common law rules on both defences and realign them:

> 4.158 Proposal 1: We provisionally propose that the common law rules on the defence of insanity be abolished.
>
> 4.159 Proposal 2: We provisionally propose the creation of a new statutory defence of *not criminally responsible by reason of recognised medical condition*.
>
> 4.160 Proposal 3: The party seeking to raise the new defence must adduce expert evidence that at the time of the alleged offence the defendant wholly lacked the capacity:
>
>   (i)   rationally to form a judgment about the relevant conduct or circumstances;
>
>   (ii)   to understand the wrongfulness of what he or she is charged with having done; or
>
>   (iii)   to control his or her physical acts in relation to the relevant conduct or circumstances
>
> as a result of a qualifying recognised medical condition.
>
> 4.161 Proposal 4: We provisionally propose that certain conditions would not qualify. These include acute intoxication or any condition which is manifested solely or principally by abnormally aggressive or seriously irresponsible behaviour.

The qualifying recognised medical condition would include physical conditions such as diabetes, epilepsy, sleepwalking and PTSD. It would therefore include some conditions currently classified as automatism but with a verdict of not criminally responsible.

D will bear an 'elevated burden of proof' from two experts which P will have to disprove.

As seen earlier, reform to the unfitness to plead procedure has taken precedence over reform to the insanity defence. The Law Commission has acknowledged the need for reform, citing unfairness and the facts that the law 'lags behind' psychiatric understanding.

8.2 Automatism

8.2.1 Introduction

8.2.2 Definition

8.2.3 Burden of Proof

8.2.4 External Causes of Involuntary Action

8.2.5 Self-induced Automatism is No Defence

8.2.6 Automatism Requires Total Destruction of Voluntary Control/Consciousness in Driving Cases

8.2.7 Criticisms of the Defence

8.2.8 Reform

KEY CASES

Quick [1973] 3 All ER 347—automatism derives from an external source; self-induced automatism no defence to crimes of basic intent;

Bailey [1983] 2 All ER 503—self-induced automatism may be a defence to a crime of specific intent;

Coley, McGhee, Harris [2013] EWCA Crim 223—automatism requires complete destruction of voluntary control.

8.2.1 Introduction

There is a very fine line between insanity and automatism and many of the insanity cases already examined have involved a search for the distinction. Both insanity (insane automatism) and automatism (non-insane automatism) amount to a plea of lack of voluntary action. However, whereas a successful plea of insanity leads to a conditional acquittal of NGRI followed by an order for hospitalisation or supervision, automatism leads to an unconditional acquittal. Both can be pleaded in relation to any crime.

8.2.2 Definition

Automatism is a claim that D's actions at the time of the offence were involuntary in the sense of not being controlled by the brain. The link between mind and behaviour was absent. Lord Denning in *Bratty* [1963] AC 386 described automatism as:

> An involuntary act … means an act done by the muscles, without any control by the mind, such as a spasm, a reflex action or a convulsion, or an act done by a person who is not conscious of what he is doing, such as an act done whilst suffering from concussion or whilst sleepwalking.

Implicit in this statement is the idea that D becomes an automaton if his actions are either *uncontrollable and spontaneous* or more purposeful but *lacking in* consciousness. This reinforces the fundamental principle of criminal liability that conviction and punishment are only justified where D voluntarily chooses to do wrong. Otherwise, the AR of a crime is not satisfied.

It is now clear that the source of involuntary action must be external whereas insanity is based upon an internal disease resulting in violent or otherwise unpredictable behaviour. The internal/external divide is fundamental. Recall that the reference by Lord Denning to sleepwalking must now be ignored for the House of Lords held in *Burgess* [1991] that this would be a case of insanity arising from an internal disease of the mind. Therefore, if D kills during a 'night terror', the correct defence is one of insanity.

8.2.3 Burden of Proof

Besides the verdict, there is one other consequence of the distinction: where D pleads automatism, the legal burden of proof remains with the prosecution. But D has an evidential burden to discharge and must adduce medical evidence that his actions were involuntary so as to cast reasonable doubt on the prosecution case that D acted voluntarily. The evidence will need to show that D acted as an automaton, independently of his will, without the assistance of the mind. It is insufficient for D to plead that he simply 'blacked out' without further medical evidence. A blackout will be seen as 'one of the first refuges of a guilty conscience and a popular excuse' (Stable J in *Cooper v McKenna, ex p Cooper* [1960] Qd R 406, at 419).

By contrast, the legal burden of proving insanity lies with D on a balance of probabilities.

8.2.4 External Causes of Involuntary Action

The internal/external distinction assists a court to identify mental abnormalities which are part of a person's identity and which therefore are more likely to lead to recurrence (insanity) as opposed to abnormalities which happen by chance (automatism). Here are some examples of automatism where D is conscious yet cannot physically control his actions:

- sneezing, spasm, reflex action. An example was given in *Hill v Baxter* [1958] 1 All ER 193 of the dangerous driver attacked by a swarm of bees thus prohibiting any directional control over the car whilst the movements of his arms and legs are controlled by the bees.

Examples where D lacks consciousness and is unaware of his actions:

> **CROSS-REFERENCE**
> *Re T* [1990] *Crim LR* 256 is discussed further in 8.1.3.

- concussion from a blow to the head, head injuries, hypnosis or anaesthetic drugs, medication, post-traumatic stress disorder/dissociative condition following an extraordinary event such as rape (*Re T* [1990] Crim LR 256).

This is the leading precedent on automatism which we encountered in 8.1.3 (in relation to insanity):

Bratty v AG for Northern Ireland [1963] 3 ALL ER 523 HOUSE OF LORDS

(D had killed a female passenger in his car by taking off her stocking and strangling her with it. He claimed to have had an epileptic fit and pleaded automatism and insanity.)

Lord Denning stated that the category of involuntary acts will be very rare. Although a voluntary act is essential to liability, not every act that might ordinarily be described as involuntary would be regarded as legally involuntary:

> [So also] it seems to me that a man's act is presumed to be a voluntary act unless there is evidence from which it can reasonably be inferred that it was involuntary ... The necessity of laying this proper foundation is on the defence: and if it is not so laid, the defence of automatism need not be left to the jury, any more than the defence of drunkenness ... or self-defence ... need be.
>
> What, then, is a proper foundation? The presumption of mental capacity of which I have spoken is a provisional presumption only. It does not put the legal burden on the defence in the same way as the presumption of sanity does. It leaves the legal burden on the prosecution, but nevertheless, until it is displaced, it enables the prosecution to discharge the ultimate burden of proving that the act was voluntary. Not because the presumption is evidence itself, but because it takes the place of evidence.
>
> *In order to displace the presumption of mental capacity, the defence must give sufficient evidence from which it may reasonably be inferred that the act was involuntary. The evidence of the man himself will rarely be sufficient unless it is supported by medical evidence which points to the cause of the mental incapacity. It is not sufficient for a man to say 'I had a black-out': for 'black out' ... is one of the first refuges of a guilty conscience, and a popular excuse ... Once a proper foundation is thus laid for automatism, the matter becomes at large and must be left to the jury ...* There was [in the present case] no evidence of automatism apart from insanity. There was therefore no need for the judge to put it to the jury.' [Emphasis added.]

> **CROSS-REFERENCE**
> *Kemp* is discussed under 'Arteriosclerosis' in 8.1.3).

Appeal dismissed.

In his judgment, Lord Denning cited one case of automatism: *Charlson* [1955] 1 All ER 859 where D, a devoted father suffering from a cerebral tumour, hit his 10-year-old son on the head with a hammer and threw him in the river, injuring him. Automatism was accepted since D would have had no control over his actions at all. If this case were to come before the courts today, it would be regarded as one of insanity for it is irreconcilable with *Kemp*.

The internal/external divide is regarded with scepticism by the medical profession. Read this extract from 'Violence, Sleepwalking and the Criminal Law: (1) The Medical Aspects' by Dr I. Ebrahim, W. Wilson, R. Marks, K. Peacock and Dr P. Fenwick [2005] *Crim LR* 601:

> Problems arise with the legal insistence on dividing automatisms into two categories, sane ... and insane ... These categories are 'lawyer speak' and make little medical sense.
>
> At the limit it should be easy, medically, to distinguish these two categories. And at the limit it is. For example, an attack by a swarm of bees resulting in a reflex turning of the steering wheel of a car is easy to see as a sane automatism. An epileptic fit arising from a damaged brain and leading to a violent killing is clearly an insane automatism. But between these two extremes the medical and legal grounds do not coalesce happily.
>
> From a medical point of view any abnormality of brain function, which has led to a disorder of behaviour, will usually contain components of both sane and insane automatism. For example, the blow to the head (external) only produces the automatism because it disrupts the functioning of the neurones in the brain (internal) ... Neither does the categorisation take into account the severity of the offence. A severe and prolonged attack in a confusional state following a head injury is a sane automatism; walking naked through a crowded hotel bar in a sleepwalking episode is insanity.

8.2.5 Self-induced Automatism is No Defence

Given that the outcome of a successful plea of automatism is a complete acquittal, the courts are naturally concerned to confine it within strict limits so as to avoid releasing on to the streets potentially violent people. Therefore, if D has been at fault in inducing a state of automatism, the defence will fail. He will not lack complete legal or moral responsibility for his actions.

The clearest example of this principle is the case of *Kay v Butterworth* (1945) 173 LT 191 where D fell asleep at the wheel of his car after working a night-shift and knocked down a file of marching soldiers. He was convicted of careless and dangerous driving, his defence of automatism having failed on the basis that, although lacking in control of his actions, he ought not to have been driving in that condition.

This principle was affirmed by the Court of Appeal in the next case, which is a leading authority on the internal/external divide.

R v Quick & Paddison [1973] 3 WLR 26 Court of Appeal

P and Q, both mental health nurses, had been convicted of assault occasioning actual bodily harm upon a paraplegic mentally ill patient at a hospital. Q had been diabetic since childhood and had taken his insulin on the day in question. He had had a small breakfast but no lunch. Before the assault he had drunk some whiskey and a quarter of a bottle of rum. He had no recollection of the assault and pleaded not guilty on the basis of automatism and hypoglycaemia (ie: a confusional state due to low blood sugar). The trial judge ruled that Q's condition was due to the disease of diabetes, an internal disease of the mind and thus insanity. Q changed his plea to guilty and appealed. P was found guilty of abetting Q. The Court of Appeal held that the cause of Q's involuntary action was not his underlying diabetes but the insulin, an external factor, of which there was an excess in his body at the time of the offence.

Lawton LJ:

> Our task has been to decide what the law means now by the words 'disease of the mind'. In our judgment the fundamental concept is of a malfunctioning of the mind caused by disease. A malfunctioning of the mind of transitory effect caused by the application to the body of some external

factor such as violence, drugs, including anaesthetics, alcohol and hypnotic influences cannot fairly be said to be due to disease. Such malfunctioning, unlike that caused by a defect of reason from disease of the mind, will not always relieve an accused from criminal responsibility. *A self-induced incapacity will not excuse nor will one which could have been reasonably foreseen as a result of either doing, or omitting to do something, as for example, taking alcohol against medical advice after using certain prescribed drugs, or failing to have regular meals whilst taking insulin.* From time to time difficult borderline cases are likely to arise. When they do, the test suggested by the New Zealand Court of Appeal in Cottle is likely to give the correct result, viz can this mental condition be fairly regarded as amounting to or producing a defect of reason from disease of the mind?

In this case Quick's alleged mental condition, if it ever existed, was not caused by his diabetes but by his use of the insulin prescribed by his doctor. Such malfunctioning of his mind as there was, was caused by an external factor and not by a bodily disorder in the nature of a disease which disturbed the working of his mind. It follows in our judgment that Quick was entitled to have his defence of automatism left to the jury and that Bridge J's ruling as to the effect of the medical evidence called by him was wrong. Had the defence of automatism been left to the jury, a number of questions of fact would have had to be answered.

If he was in a confused mental condition, was it due to a hypoglycaemic episode or to too much alcohol? If the former, to what extent had he brought about his condition by not following his doctor's instructions about taking regular meals? Did he know that he was getting into a hypoglycaemic episode? If Yes, why did he not use the antidote of eating a lump of sugar as he had been advised to do? On the evidence which was before the jury Quick might have had difficulty in answering these questions in a manner which would have relieved him of responsibility for his acts. We cannot say, however, with the requisite degree of confidence, that the jury would have convicted him. It follows that his conviction must be quashed on the ground that the verdict was unsatisfactory. [Emphasis added.]

Appeals allowed.

NOTE 8.3

1. An external factor, such as medication, causing a transitory malfunctioning of the mind will lead to automatism rather than insanity.

2. Self-induced incapacity will not excuse. Equally, a state which could have been reasonably foreseen by D. This would be recklessness, the MR for the offence here.

3. Therefore, the question of whether Q knew of the risk of hypoglycaemia was crucial. This was not pursued at his trial because the judge had not allowed automatism to go to the jury. The defect rendered the conviction unsafe even though a jury might well have decided that Q was reckless in not eating properly contrary to medical advice. If so, he would have been rightly convicted.

?! THINKING POINT 8.7

On Monday, Diane, a diabetic, takes her insulin injection but is so busy at work that she has no time to eat properly. She becomes confused and throws her telephone at a work colleague when he asks her the time, injuring him.

On Tuesday, Diane is late for work and forgets to take her insulin. During the day, she becomes confused and throws her telephone at another work colleague when he asks her the time, injuring him. What defence/s does Diane have?

Self-induced automatism was considered again in *Bailey*. Here, the offence was more serious and can be distinguished from *Quick* by reference to MR.

R v Bailey [1983] 2 ALL ER 503 COURT OF APPEAL

D was charged with wounding with intent (s18 OAPA 1861) and unlawful wounding (s20 OAPA 1861) for assaulting a rival with an iron bar, the rival having stolen his girlfriend. D was diabetic and had failed to eat sufficient food after taking insulin although he had taken some sugar and water. He pleaded automatism because he lacked the specific intent required by s18 and the basic intent required by s20. He claimed to be hypoglycaemic at the time of the offence. The judge ruled that self-induced automatism was no defence, following Quick D was convicted of the s18 offence and appealed.

Griffiths LJ:

> Automatism resulting from intoxication as a result of a voluntary ingestion of alcohol or dangerous drugs does not negative the mens rea necessary for crimes of basic intent, because the conduct of the accused is reckless and recklessness is enough to constitute the necessary mens rea in assault cases where no specific intent forms part of the charge: see *R v Majewski* …
>
> *It is common knowledge that those who take alcohol to excess or certain sorts of drugs may become aggressive or do dangerous or unpredictable things, they may be able to foresee the risks of causing harm to others but nevertheless persist in their conduct. But the same cannot be said without more of a man who fails to take food after an insulin injection. If he does appreciate the risk that such a failure may lead to aggressive, unpredictable and uncontrollable conduct and he nevertheless deliberately runs the risk or otherwise disregards it, this will amount to recklessness. But we certainly do not think that it is common knowledge, even among diabetics, that such is a consequence of a failure to take food and there is no evidence that it was known to this appellant.* Doubtless he knew that if he failed to take his insulin or proper food after it, he might lose consciousness, but as such he would only be a danger to himself unless he put himself in charge of some machine such as a motor car, which required his continued conscious control.
>
> In our judgment, self-induced automatism other than that due to intoxication from alcohol or drugs, may provide a defence to crimes of basic intent. The question in each case will be whether the prosecution have proved the necessary element of recklessness … [Emphasis added.]

Griffiths LJ then concluded that although there had been a misdirection by the trial judge, there had been no miscarriage of justice because it was clear that D had armed himself with the iron bar and had sought out his rival in order to attack him.

 NOTE 8.4

1. The court confirmed that if D's actions were involuntary, the cause was external, namely the insulin. The defence was therefore automatism.

2. Self-induced automatism is in general no defence, especially to crimes of recklessness. These are labelled crimes of *basic intent* (eg: assault occasioning actual bodily harm contrary to s 47 OAPA 1861) where MR consists of subjective recklessness. Automatism is no defence if D is aware that he is inducing such a condition. The reckless assumption of the risk of aggression will supply the recklessness for the crime (*Quick*).

3. However, self-induced automatism will provide a defence to crimes of basic intent if D is not aware of the risk because, for example: he does not know that taking the drug would lead to aggression. In this case, he will not be reckless and will lack MR.

4. It can even be a defence to crimes of specific intent (eg: s18 OAPA 1861) where D lacks the necessary intention.

5. This leads to the distinction between intoxicants known to be dangerous on the one hand (such as alcohol and drugs, the consumption of which will always be reckless and will never provide the basis of automatism), and drugs not known to be dangerous, on the other, such as medication taken pursuant to medical advice (eg: insulin, the consumption of which might provide the basis of the defence if D did not know it was likely to lead to aggression).

6. The court considered that it was not well known that failure to eat after taking insulin could result in aggression but there was little evidence of hypoglycaemia in this case and so the appeal was dismissed. Whether the nutritional requirements of diabetics are better known today remains to be legally clarified.

The result of *Quick* and *Bailey* is that D is more likely to be granted a complete, unconditional acquittal to a more serious offence than to a less serious assault.

There is, therefore, a strong incentive to limit the scope of automatism. This is achieved by either construing cases involving 'prior fault' as insanity or intoxication, or by finding that D acted with MR. *Coley, McGhee, Harris* [2013] EWCA Crim 223 is an example. Recall that *Coley* had stabbed a neighbour after smoking cannabis. Hughes LJ rejected insanity. He also rejected automatism:

→ CROSS-REFERENCE
For a discussion of the rejection of the mental defences see 8.1.3.

The essence of [automatism] is that the movements or actions of the defendant at the material time were wholly involuntary. The better expression is complete destruction of voluntary control: Watmore v Jenkins [1962] 2 QB 572 and Attorney-General's Reference (No 2 of 1992) [1994] QB 91. Examples which have been given in the past include the driver attacked by a swarm of bees or the man under hypnosis. 'Involuntary' is not the same as 'irrational'; indeed it needs sharply to be distinguished from it. In the present case the doctors were asked several times whether the defendant was acting 'consciously' when he did what he did. We understand the difficulties of selecting appropriate adverbs, but this one carries some risk of difficulty. He was plainly not unconscious, in the sense of comatose. But automatism does not require that, and if it did it would be even more exceptional than it undoubtedly is. On the other hand, his mind may well, if the doctors were right, have been affected by delusions or hallucinations and in that sense his detachment from reality might be described by some as an absence of conscious action. Such condition, however, clearly falls short of involuntary, as distinct from irrational, action ... The doctor said 'He is conscious in a way but it is conscious in the belief that he is a character. He does not have an awareness of what he is doing.' That is a description of irrational behaviour, with a deluded or disordered mind, but it is not a description of wholly involuntary action ...

Quite apart from the fact that the evidence was of voluntary, if irrational action, the defence of automatism is not available to a defendant who has induced an acute state of involuntary behaviour by his own fault. This court so held in Quick, and approved the decision in Bailey and Hennessy ... [t]he voluntary consumption of intoxicants leading to an acute condition is the prime example of self-induced behaviour ... We are satisfied that automatism simply did not run in this case for the reasons already explained: (a) the defendant was clearly not acting wholly involuntarily and (b) he had induced his condition by voluntary intoxication.' [Emphasis added.]

NOTE 8.5

1. Automatism requires a complete loss of voluntary control. Previous references to *un-consciousness* were unhelpful. D's behaviour was delusional and irrational rather than involuntary.

2. D had formed an intent to kill. Therefore, self-induced automatism was no defence.

3. Neither should D have the defence of intoxication, given that he had acted intentionally.

The first point is new. As we shall see, complete lack of voluntariness has, until now, only been required in driving cases.

➔ CROSS-REFERENCE
Driving cases are discussed in 8.2.6.

It had always been assumed that automatism permitted some degree of consciousness or otherwise the D would be comatose and on the floor. Hughes LJ considered, rightly, that reference to 'consciousness,' as in Denning LJ's famous quotation in 8.2.2, was unhelpful. The degree of involuntariness required to fulfil the defence, though, remains debateable, but it does not apply to someone who is delusional. This is a narrowing of the defence.

The facts of *McGee* were as follows: *McGee* had taken Tamezepam, an anti-anxiety tablet, allegedly for the treatment of severe tinnitus (an ear problem). He then drank alcohol despite warnings on the bottle of medication. He attacked two men in a 24-hour off-licence shop, pressing his fingers into the eye of one and stabbing another in the arm with a kitchen knife. He had no later recollection of this. He appealed a conviction of grievous bodily harm with intent contrary to s18 OAPA 1861 on the grounds that he had acted whilst in a state of automatism and lacked MR. One expert gave evidence that D had been aware of his actions, even if his judgment had been impaired. The other considered that the drug, when accompanied by alcohol, can reduce self-restraint and lead to disinhibition, aggression and over-reaction to trivial provocation. Hughes LJ:

> Thus the evidence made it clear that what Professor Birch was speaking about were the paradoxically disinhibiting effects of temazepam plus alcohol and the manner in which that can lead to a person behaving in an aggressive fashion from which he would normally be restrained in the absence of the substances taken. *Disinhibition is exactly not automatism.* [Emphasis added.]

Given that the context of *Coley* and *McGee* was one of self-induced intoxication, or prior fault, is the court imposing a moral judgment here when exploring the fine distinction between voluntariness and involuntariness? More importantly, what is involuntariness? If it does not require total unconsciousness, what extent of consciousness is permitted? Will the defence ever apply where D's act is purposeful? Would descriptions such as 'deliberative control,' 'impaired consciousness' or 'a lack of control' be any clearer? (*Criminal Liability: Automatism and Insanity* (July 2013), para 5.2). Automatism is clearly an extremely rare defence but it could, on the basis of this judgment, be limited to only cases where there was no prior fault and total loss of control. Hughes LJ referred to the ongoing review of mental defences by the Law Commission and future debate as to whether the inter-relationship between them is currently correct.

?!   THINKING POINT 8.8

D, a diabetic, fails to eat after taking insulin. Whilst disorientated, he commits a serious assault upon V1 as a result of which V1 is permanently disabled. He then punches V2 in the face, bruising him mildly. Does D have a defence?

8.2.6 Automatism Requires Total Destruction of Voluntary Control/Consciousness in Driving Cases

In relation to most offences, there has never been a requirement of a total lack of control (*Quick* and *Bailey*). That may have changed as a result of *Coley*. However, in driving cases, the courts have always demanded complete unconsciousness before conceding the defence.

In *Watmore v Jenkins* [1962] 2 All ER 868, a case of dangerous driving/driving without due care and attention, D, who was diabetic and hypoglycaemic, drove for a five-mile stretch of road in a dazed state, veering from one side to the other, passing through traffic lights, narrowly missing various vehicles and finally crashing into the rear of a stationary car at a place well past his home. It was held by the Divisional Court that D must have been able to exercise some control over his car and could not have been in a state of automatism throughout the whole distance. In *Broome v Perkins* [1987] Crim LR 271 D was guilty of driving without due care and attention, even though hypoglycaemic, because although he had exercised sufficient control over his vehicle to drive home, he had crashed the car en route. Partial or impaired control was insufficient. (Recall that hypoglycaemia is a state of food/sugar deficiency.)

This was also confirmed in *AG's Reference (No 2 of 1992)* [1993] 4 All ER 683 where the Court of Appeal held that a trance-like state of 'driving without awareness' caused by repetitive visual stimuli experienced on long journeys on straight, flat, featureless motorways was rejected because what was required was total destruction of voluntary control. And in *C* [2007] EWCA Crim 1862 a hypoglycaemic driver who had committed a road traffic offence needed to show he was totally unable to control the car due to an unforeseen onset of his condition and had had no warning symptoms.

8.2.7 Criticisms of the Defence

Both automatism and insanity refer to lack of voluntary action. Both are social defences but it is evident that the law lacks a satisfactory means of determining which defendants fall into one or other category. New doubts have been raised about the definition of 'voluntariness' and the basis of the defence since *Coley*. Might automatism succeed where D lacks moral responsibility but acts with MR? Presumably not in cases of prior fault. But the basis of automatism needs to be clarified.

The major problem is the internal/external distinction between automatism and insanity which focuses on the source of incapacity rather than on its effect. Defendants who have acted involuntarily in a similar way can be categorised differently. The distinction is not linked to medical classifications and is therefore arbitrary. Diabetes can be classified as insanity or automatism depending on whether D has taken insulin or not. An epileptic who commits an offence involuntarily during a fit is insane yet a diabetic who does likewise during a hypoglycaemic coma is an automaton. Is the former any more dangerous than the latter? What if hypoglycaemia is caused by the internal pancreatic over-production of insulin? This condition should be classified as insanity yet it is not permanent or integral to D's character and could be remedied by simply eating sugar.

→ CROSS-REFERENCE

Re T is discussed in 8.1.3.

Other common law jurisdictions seem to have abandoned the internal/external divide.

The nature of the external cause must be novel, accidental or extraordinary. This included the rape in *Re T* but not the ordinary stresses and strains of life in *Hennessy*.

Underlying this selective element, however, is the need for the courts to exercise control over potentially violent defendants. Where evidence is submitted in support of either automatism or insanity, the shift in the burden of proof is difficult for the jury to understand. The prosecution must prove that D's acts were voluntary to disprove automatism, in respect of which D has an evidential burden. If insanity is raised, D has a legal burden of proof.

SECTION SUMMARY

Automatism and insanity can be represented by Diagram 8.2.

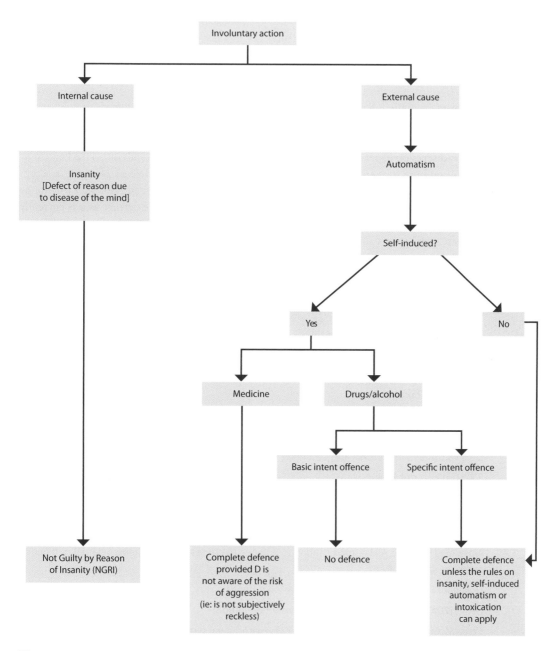

Diagram 8.2
Flow chart: insanity and automatism

8.2.8 Reform

Clause 33 Law Commission Draft Criminal Code Bill:

Automatism and physical incapacity

(1) A person is not guilty of an offence if–

    (a) he acts in a state of automatism, that is, his act–

        (i) is a reflex, spasm or convulsion; or

        (ii) occurs while he is in a condition (whether of sleep, unconsciousness, impaired consciousness or otherwise) depriving him of effective control of the act; and

    (b) the act or condition is the result neither of anything done or omitted with the fault required for the offence nor of voluntary intoxication.

Commentary to the Bill provides that the main purpose of this clause is to provide a defence of automatism to a strict liability crime. For other crimes of MR, D will continue to assert lack of AR/MR as at present.

In its discussion paper *Criminal Liability: Insanity and Automatism* (July 2013) the Law Commission propose to merge automatism and insanity within a new defence requiring a recognised medical condition (RMC). It will require a total loss of control and prior fault will not be recognised. This would be a clarification, but also a narrowing of the defence as it is currently understood. A defence of automatism will remain for those who do not suffer from a RMC, that is: where total loss of control followed a chance event.

→ CROSS-REFERENCE
The defence is explained in 8.1.7.

8.3 Intoxication

KEY CASES

Majewski [1977] AC 443—intoxication: no defence to crimes of basic intent, a partial defence to crimes of specific intent;

Gallagher [1963] AC 349—Dutch courage: no defence;

Heard [2007] EWCA Crim 125—specific intent definition;

Coley, McGhee, Harris [2013] EWCA Crim 223—withdrawal symptoms producing mental illness are the opposite of intoxication;

Kingston [1994] 3 WLR 519 House of Lords—involuntary intoxication: no defence if MR is present.

8.3.1 Introduction

Alcohol is a factor in a high proportion of criminal cases. In the year ending March 2015, of all violent offences occurring in the evening, 25% happened in a pub or club. The rule on intoxication can be quite simply stated: intoxication is never a defence but may be the reason why D lacked the intention required by the more serious crimes. To this extent only, if intoxication negates intention, it may result in conviction of a lesser offence. For example, D could be convicted of manslaughter instead of murder, as shown in Diagram 8.3. But intoxication is no defence to the vast majority of crimes which can be committed recklessly. The underlying policy is that people should not be entitled to an acquittal simply because they were drunk when they committed the crime. Intoxication is no excuse. This is known as the *Majewski* rule.

The *Majewski* rule works in different ways according to whether the intoxication is voluntary or involuntary and whether the crime is one of 'specific' or 'basic' intent. The crucial question is whether, *despite intoxication*, D has MR for the offence. The *Majewski* rule represents an objective approach to criminal liability and is not without criticism as we shall see.

8.3.2 Crimes of Basic and Specific Intent

In *Majewski*, Lord Elwyn-Jones drew a distinction between crimes of specific and basic intent, the former requiring an ulterior intent (one going beyond the immediate act), the latter being characterised by recklessness. But there was no general agreement. Lord Simon considered that specific intent referred to a crime requiring 'proof of a purposive' element. Burglary (entry with intent to commit, eg: theft) or grievous bodily harm with intent under s18 Offences Against the Person Act 1861 would be examples but murder would not, for the MR of murder does not contain a purposive element. Lord Salmon thought that any distinction at all was strictly illogical but justifiable on the basis of common sense.

In *Caldwell* [1982] AC 341 (where D set fire to a hotel whilst drunk), Lord Diplock confirmed that a crime of basic intent was one in which recklessness was an element of MR. Consequently, for many years, the courts operated on the basis of the list in Diagram 8.3.

➔ CROSS-REFERENCE
Caldwell is discussed in Chapter 3.

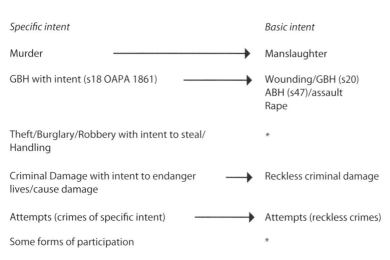

Specific intent	Basic intent
Murder ——————————➔	Manslaughter
GBH with intent (s18 OAPA 1861) ———➔	Wounding/GBH (s20) ABH (s47)/assault Rape
Theft/Burglary/Robbery with intent to steal/ Handling	*
Criminal Damage with intent to endanger lives/cause damage ——➔	Reckless criminal damage
Attempts (crimes of specific intent) ——➔	Attempts (reckless crimes)
Some forms of participation	*

Diagram 8.3
Basic and specific intent offences

If intoxication negates specific intent, D will be convicted of the lesser crime of basic intent. Therefore, a charge of murder will result in a conviction of manslaughter; a charge under s18 OAPA 1861 will result in a conviction under s20 and so on. There is no lesser offence for some offences marked * in the Diagram.

Rape is classified as a basic intent offence despite MR under s1 Sexual Offences Act 2003 consisting of two elements: intentional penetration + lack of reasonable belief in consent. However, uncertainty has been cast upon this rule by the next case which equated specific intent with ulterior intent.

R v Heard [2007] EWCA CRIM 125, [2007] CRIM LR 654 COURT OF APPEAL

D was heavily intoxicated by alcohol. He exposed his penis and rubbed it against the thigh of a police officer. He was charged and convicted of sexual assault contrary to s3(1)(a) Sexual Offences Act 2003, which concerns intentional sexual touching of another. On appeal it was argued on his behalf that the offence was one of specific intent since recklessness was insufficient MR. It followed that voluntary intoxication might afford a partial defence in the absence of intention. The argument was rejected.

Hughes LJ:

> It is necessary to go back to Majewski in order to see the basis for the distinction there upheld between crimes of basic and of specific intent. It is to be found most clearly in the speech of Lord Simon … It was that crimes of specific intent are those where the offence requires proof of purpose or consequence, which are not confined to, but amongst which are included, those where the purpose goes beyond the actus reus (sometimes referred to as cases of 'ulterior intent'). Lord Simon put it in this way at 478H:
>
> > 'The best description of "specific intent" in this sense that I know is contained in the judgment of Fauteux J in Reg v George (1960) 128 Can CC 289, 301–
> >
> > > "In considering the question of mens rea, a distinction is to be made between (i) intention as applied to acts considered in relation to their purposes and (ii) intention as applied to acts apart from their purposes. A general intent attending the commission of an act is, in some cases, the only intent required to constitute the crime while, in others, there must be, in addition to that general intent, a specific intent attending the purpose for the commission of the act."'
>
> That explanation of the difference is consistent with the view of Lord Edmund-Davies that an offence contrary to s 1(2)(b) Criminal Damage Act is one of specific intent in this sense, even though it involves no more than recklessness as to the endangering of life; the offence requires proof of a state of mind addressing something beyond the prohibited act itself, namely its consequences. We regard this as the best explanation of the sometimes elusive distinction between specific and basic intent in the sense used in Majewski, and it seems to us that this is the distinction which the Judge in the present case was applying when he referred to the concept of a 'bolted-on' intent.

Ulterior intent requires an intention to do something beyond the immediate act. It is possible the Court of Appeal meant to confine this new definition to sexual offences alone, many of which contain divisible MR (intent and recklessness). Read the following from the Criminal Law Review commentary at [2007] 654 by D. Ormerod:

Reinterpreting Majewski more widely? Will the court's obiter rejection of the orthodox interpretation of *Majewski* be applied throughout the criminal law? There are several reasons why it is respectfully submitted that this would be undesirable. First, it is more difficult to apply: looking for the element of additional *mens rea* in a crime in order to categorise it appropriately is less straightforward than asking simply whether it was one for which recklessness suffices. Secondly, looking for this ulterior *mens rea* creates no fewer anomalies than the established interpretation of *Majewski*: murder should be a specific intent offence but where is the 'bolt-on' intent beyond that to kill? … Thirdly, the complexity will be exacerbated by the fact that an offence can be one of specific intent even if it contains no element of intent at all—provided there is an ulterior *mens rea* … Fourthly, the court even hints at rejecting the twofold classification by suggesting that it is not to be assumed that every offence is one of basic or specific intent. But what is this other category that now exists? And what offences might fall into it?

?! THINKING POINT 8.9

Will intoxication provide a defence?

Look at the scenarios in the following list. What offence has D committed? Is it a crime of basic or specific intent? Will intoxication provide a defence?

After drinking eight double vodkas and six pints of beer, D does the following whilst blind drunk. Assume there is reasonable doubt as to MR:

- In throwing beer over V, she accidentally lets go of the glass which hits V in the face and causes him to lose an eye;
- She picks up a chair and deliberately hits the barman over the head with it, causing his skull to fracture from which he later dies;
- She helps herself to £50 from the cash-till;
- She sets fire to the pub intending to injure the occupants.

8.3.3 Intoxication is not a 'Defence' but a Denial of MR

In a criminal trial, if D wishes to introduce evidence of intoxication, its only relevance is to show that he lacked the mental element for the crime. If charged with a crime of specific intent, D will therefore have to establish a reasonable doubt that he acted intentionally. This could be done by showing that he was not aware or did not foresee a particular circumstance or result (remember that intention and recklessness depend on foresight or awareness). However, if, despite intoxication, D formed the necessary intention, he will be guilty: a drunken intent is still an intent (*Doherty* (1887) 16 Cox CC 306, 308; *R v Sheehan and Moore* (1975) 60 Cr App R 308 at 312, a case of murder by arson). Intoxication is therefore not a defence in the usual sense.

Note that we are not concerned here with *crimes* consisting of drunken actions, such as being drunk in a public place, or driving when under the influence of drink or drugs, both crimes of strict liability where being drunk forms the AR of the offence. We are concerned with the extent to which intoxication forms a defence to general offences.

You may wonder how it is physically possible to commit a serious crime of specific intent, such as murder or burglary, whilst so drunk as to lack an intention to do it. There are in fact very few cases where a plea of intoxication has actually succeeded. Here are five general points:

- It was once thought that D needed to be so extremely intoxicated as to be *incapable* of forming the necessary intention for a crime of specific intent: *DPP v Beard* [1920] AC 479, a case of rape and murder by suffocation. This is no longer necessary for the courts have considered that it would be wrong to impose a burden on D to prove incapacity.

■ The question is straightforwardly one of intent, determined on the basis of all the evidence, including evidence of intoxication: *Sheehan and Moore*, confirmed by *R v Pordage* [1975] Crim LR 575 (a case of wounding with intent contrary to s18 Offences Against the Person Act 1861).

■ If D is so intoxicated as to be *incapable* of forming the necessary intent the jury will take that incapacity into account. More usually the evidence will show impaired control, understanding, perception, awareness or knowledge as to conduct, circumstances or consequences. Thus, D's state of mind would more accurately be described as reckless, inadvertent or negligent. At the extreme end of the spectrum it could be that the act is done during a 'blackout' or whilst D is so 'blind drunk' as to not know what he is doing. He may be hallucinating or in a state of near automatism or insanity.

■ However, evidence of intoxication, no matter how slight, can negate MR provided it prevented D from foreseeing or knowing what he would have foreseen/known had he been sober.

■ Loss of inhibition, poor judgement or inability to recollect events are not the same as lack of MR. The crucial question in all cases is, taking the intoxication into account, 'did D act with MR?' Once intoxication has been raised by D, the burden is on the prosecution to prove intention despite the intoxication.

?! **THINKING POINT** 8.10

1. Do you agree that intoxication should be no excuse for criminal behaviour?

2. If D's actions were involuntary and he pleaded automatism, the fundamental principle that one should not be convicted in the absence of MR would apply. Should an intoxicated D whose actions were involuntary be treated differently?

3. In your opinion, should it make any difference whether the offence is committed under the influence of 20 pints of beer or a cocktail of barbiturates, LSD and amphetamines?

8.3.4 Voluntary Intoxication: The *Majewski* Rule

A partial defence to crimes of specific intent

D will be voluntarily intoxicated where he knowingly consumes alcohol or drugs, even if mistaken as to the strength, quantity or effect (*Allen* [1988] Crim LR 698—wine with an unknown high alcohol content). The crucial question is whether, despite the intoxication, he has MR.

DPP v Majewski [1977] AC 443, [1976] 2 ALL ER 142 HOUSE OF LORDS

D had been convicted of assault occasioning actual bodily harm and assault on a police constable in the execution of his duty. His defence had been that he was too intoxicated to form MR, having taken, over the previous two days, large amounts of amphetamines and barbiturates, and having spent an evening drinking in the pub where the offences were committed. He claimed to have 'blacked out'. Medical evidence at trial established that it was more likely that D knew what he was doing at the time but could not remember later. The certified question for the House concerned whether a D should be convicted notwithstanding that he lacked intention due to voluntary intoxication.

Lord Elwyn-Jones LC:

If a man consciously and deliberately takes alcohol and drugs not on medical prescription, but in order to escape from reality, to go 'on a trip,' to become hallucinated, whatever the description may be, and thereby disables himself from taking the care he might otherwise take and as a result by his subsequent actions causes injury to another—does our criminal law enable him to say that because he did not know what he was doing he lacked both intention and recklessness and accordingly is entitled to an acquittal? …

There are, however, decisions of eminent judges in a number of Commonwealth cases in Australia and New Zealand, (but generally not in Canada nor in the United States) as well as impressive academic comment in this country, to which we have been referred, supporting the view that it is illogical and inconsistent with legal principle to treat a person who of his own choice and volition has taken drugs and drink, even though he thereby creates a state in which he is not conscious of what he is doing, any differently from a person suffering from the various medical conditions like epilepsy or diabetic coma and who is regarded by the law as free from fault. However our courts have for a very long time regarded in quite another light the state of self-induced intoxication. The authority which for the last half century has been relied upon in this context has been the speech of Lord Birkenhead L.C. in *Director of Public Prosecutions v Beard* [1920] A.C. 479: who stated (at page 494):'Under the law of England as it prevailed until early in the 19th century voluntary drunkenness was never an excuse for criminal misconduct; and indeed the classic authorities broadly assert that voluntary drunkenness must be considered rather an aggravation than a defence. This view was in terms based upon the principle that a man who by his own voluntary act debauches and destroys his will power shall be no better situated in regard to criminal acts than a sober man.' …

It has to be said that it is on the latter footing that the judges have applied the law before and since *Beard's* case and have taken the view that self-induced intoxication, however gross and even if it has produced a condition akin to automatism, cannot excuse crimes of basic intent such as the charges of assault which have given rise to the present appeal.

If a man of his own volition takes a substance which causes him to cast off the restraints of reason and conscience, no wrong is done to him by holding him answerable criminally for any injury he may do while in that condition. His course of conduct in reducing himself by drugs and drink to that condition in my view supplies the evidence of mens rea, of guilty mind certainly sufficient for crimes of basic intent. It is a reckless course of conduct and recklessness is enough to constitute the necessary mens rea in assault cases; see R v. Venna [1975] 3 W.L.R. 737 per James L.J. at page 743. The drunkenness is itself an intrinsic, an integral part of the crime, the other part being the evidence of the unlawful use of force against the victim. Together they add up to criminal recklessness. [Emphasis added.]

The Majewski rule is therefore as follows:

■ Voluntary intoxication may provide a partial defence to a D lacking the intention of a specific intent crime but is no defence to a crime of basic intent whether D has MR or not.

■ In crimes of basic intent, the prosecution may, but need not, prove intention, foresight or any other state of mind. It must simply prove that D would have had MR if he had not been intoxicated.

Without this rule, defendants lacking intention/recklessness for basic intent crimes due to intoxication would be entitled to an acquittal. Lord Elwyn-Jones held that the recklessness in becoming intoxicated supplied the recklessness for a crime of basic intent. It should be noted, however, that intoxication should not automatically lead to conviction. For the purposes of subjective recklessness, the risk of harm arising from D's act needs to be objectively obvious. Intoxication is not, as yet, an exception to this principle.

The Majewski rule is contrary to three fundamental principles of criminal liability:

1. It assumes that recklessness in the ordinary sense of the word (generally related to unreasonable *conduct*) is a sufficient substitute for recklessness in the legal sense of the word (ie: *a state of mind*, such as awareness or foresight (*Cunningham*)). The latter requires awareness of the

risk of committing the AR of an offence whereas the former is a colloquial description of non-criminal conduct.

2. It ignores the principle that AR and MR should coincide. The recklessness in becoming intoxicated would typically occur prior to the commission of a crime.

3. It is contrary to the general principle that MR must be proved by the prosecution. It is also contrary to s8 Criminal Justice Act 1967 which does not apply to cases of intoxication. Section 8 states:

A court or jury in determining whether a person has committed an offence–

a. shall not be bound in law to infer that he intended or foresaw a result of his actions by reason of its being a natural and probable consequence of those actions but

b. shall decide whether he did intend or foresee that result by reference to all the evidence, drawing such inference from the evidence as appears proper in the circumstances.

This is a rule directing juries that for offences requiring proof of MR (intention or foresight) they must consider D's subjective state of mind. Clearly, if D is so intoxicated as to not know what he is doing or fails to foresee something that they ordinarily would not miss, D will have no 'state of mind' that could be described as one of MR. The *Majewski* rule is contrary to the usual subjective approach to MR which has become a striking feature of criminal law in recent years, particularly after the abolition of *Caldwell* objective recklessness by *R v G* [2003] UKHL 50.

 THINKING POINT 8.11

Acquittal or conviction can therefore depend on as little as two pints of lager! Compare the following:

1. D has just been made redundant. On her way home from work, she assaults V in response to being jostled. She claims she lacked MR and over-reacted inadvertently because she was tired, worried, depressed and did not think properly.

   ■ Is assault a crime of basic or specific intent?

   ■ What MR would the prosecution need to prove for an assault?

   ■ Would they succeed in proving MR here?

2. On the same facts, suppose D gave evidence that in addition to her emotional state she had also just had a couple of pints of lager before committing the assault.

   ■ Under *Majewski*, would the prosecution need to prove MR?

   ■ Will D be convicted or acquitted?

Where D suffers from an alcohol-related condition, but is not drunk at the time of the offence, the *Majewski* rule does not apply. Therefore, D's MR will need to be assessed in the usual way.

Coley, McGhee, Harris [2013] EWCA CRIM 223

Harris suffered clinical depression with a history of heavy drinking. He stopped drinking several days before setting fire to his home but began hearing voices. Expert evidence suggested delirium tremens (acute impact of the withdrawal of alcohol). The fire was controlled before it spread to neighbouring properties but he was convicted of aggravated arson contrary to s1(2)

Criminal Damage Act 1971 for recklessly endangering the lives of his neighbours in the next door semi-detached house. He appealed on the grounds that his mental condition prevented him from foreseeing possible risks to his neighbours from setting his own home on fire. The judge had regarded the appellant's mental condition as one induced by voluntary intoxication. He was convicted under the *Majewski* rule. D appealed.

Hughes LJ:

> The argument for the Crown in this case is that the mental illness from which the defendant was suffering was brought on by his past voluntary drinking. Therefore, it is contended, it should be treated in the same way as if he were still drunk. We agree that there is scope for the argument that an illness caused by his own fault ought as a matter of policy to be treated in the same way as is drunkenness at the time of the offence. This would, however, represent a significant extension of *DPP v Majewski* and of the similar principle expounded in *Quick*, which likewise concerned a case where what was asserted was an acute condition (there of automatism) induced arguably by the defendant's fault … But in the present state of the law, *Majewski* applies to offences committed by persons who are then voluntarily intoxicated but not to those who are suffering mental illness. This defendant was, it is clear, suffering from a condition of mental illness when he set fire to his own house. That it was not long-lasting does not mean that it was not a true illness. In our view he was entitled to have tried the question of whether, in the condition in which he was, he was actually aware of the risk which he created for his neighbours.

Conviction overturned.

 NOTE 8.6

Harris was not intoxicated. Quite the opposite. He was suffering from the effects of the withdrawal of alcohol. The Court decided that neither was he legally insane. His MR therefore needed to be proved for the *Majewski* rule did not apply. But if the cause of his actions was internal, was he not insane? Specifically, if he had failed to appreciate the risk of the fire spreading, could this have been interpreted as a failure to appreciate the 'nature and quality of his actions'?

8.3.5 Dutch Courage

If D has planned a crime and consumes alcohol in order to get Dutch courage to commit it, he cannot deny intention because of intoxication, even where the intoxication was so extreme as to negate the necessary intent (although it would be extremely unlikely that intention would ever be completely negated in the circumstances of premeditation).

Attorney-General for Northern Ireland v Gallagher [1963] AC 349, [1961] 3 ALL ER 299 HOUSE OF LORDS

D, a psychopath, decided to kill his wife and bought a knife and a bottle of whiskey. He drank the whiskey to give himself the courage to commit the crime and killed his wife. He was charged with murder. His defence was that he was so intoxicated as to be either insane or incapable of forming MR and, accordingly, should be convicted of manslaughter. The judge had said that the M'Naghten Rules should apply to the time when the alcohol was taken and not to the time of the murder. Lord Denning observed that although insanity caused by intoxication is an exception to the general rule that intoxication is no defence, D was not legally insane so as to not know what he was doing or that it was wrong. He knew full well what he was doing and remembered it afterwards.

> If a man by drinking brings on a distinct disease of the mind such as delirium tremens, so that he is temporarily insane within the M'Naghten Rules, that is to say, he does not at the time know what he is doing or that it is wrong, then he has a defence on the ground of insanity … [h]e was not suffering from a disease of the mind brought on by drink. He was suffering from a different disease altogether …
>
> My Lords, I think the law on this point should take a clear stand. If a man, whilst sane and sober, forms an intention to kill and makes preparation for it, knowing it is a wrong thing to do, and then gets himself drunk so as to give himself Dutch courage to do the killing, and whilst drunk carries out his intention, he cannot rely on this self-induced drunkenness as a defence to a charge of murder, nor even as reducing it to manslaughter. He cannot say that he got himself into such a stupid state that he was incapable of an intent to kill. So also when he is a psychopath, he cannot by drinking rely on his self-induced defect of reason as a defence of insanity …

?! THINKING POINT 8.12

1. Would Gallagher have had any other defence to murder?
2. D plans to kill a rival (V) at the end of the week but V goes away for a month. D, whilst in a drunken state, unexpectedly meets V on his return. He kills V with a single stab to the heart. He later claims that he was so drunk as to lack MR. Will D have a defence?

8.3.6 Involuntary Intoxication

Involuntary intoxication is rare but it can occur where D is unaware of the intoxicant because it is secretly concealed in a soft drink, administered without consent (eg: under duress or trick), the result of automatism (one who drinks wine instead of water whilst concussed) or the *unforeseen* effect of medication. Here, the court is not concerned with moral fault, only with culpability.

The crucial question remains one of MR, whether intoxication is voluntary or involuntary. Involuntary intoxication provides a complete defence to all crimes provided D lacks MR. But it is no defence at all to one who acts with MR.

R v Kingston [1994] 3 WLR 519 HOUSE OF LORDS

D was a man with paedophiliac homosexual tendencies which he had kept under control. He was in a business dispute with third parties who wished to blackmail him. The third parties hired a man named Penn to obtain damaging information against D. Penn lured a 15-year-old boy to his flat and surreptitiously drugged him. D was then invited to the flat. He sexually abused the boy along with Penn who photographed and taped the incident. Both were charged with indecent assault. D's defence was that he could remember nothing after having consumed coffee in the flat. He alleged that Penn had surreptitiously laced his coffee with a drug which caused him to commit the offence. Both were convicted of indecent assault. Penn was also convicted of causing the youth to take a stupefying drug with intent.

The judge directed the jury that if D had no intent for the crime, he should be acquitted. On the other hand, if he did have MR, he was guilty because a drugged intent was still an intent. The Court of Appeal quashed the conviction on the grounds that if D had formed the intent to assault, but that he would not have done so but for the surreptitious administration of drugs which had caused him to lose self-control, the involuntary intoxication negatived MR. In other words, if blame was absent, so too was MR. Lord Taylor CJ in the Court of Appeal had said this:

> Having paedophiliac inclinations and desires is not proscribed; putting them into practice is. If the sole reason why the threshold between the two has been crossed is or may have been that the inhibition which the law requires has been removed by the clandestine act of a third party, the purposes of the criminal law are not served by nevertheless holding that the person performing the act is guilty of an offence. A man is not responsible for a condition produced 'by stratagem, or the fraud of another.' If therefore drink or a drug, surreptitiously administered, causes a person to lose his self-control and for that reason to form an intent which he would not otherwise have formed, it is consistent with the principle that the law should exculpate him because the operative fault is not his … the law recognises that, exceptionally, an accused person may be entitled to be acquitted if there is a possibility that although his act was intentional, the intent itself arose out of circumstances for which he bears no blame.

This was rejected by the House of Lords. Lord Mustill gave the leading judgment:

> In ordinary circumstances the respondent's paedophiliac tendencies would have been kept under control, even in the presence of the sleeping or unconscious boy on the bed. The ingestion of the drug (whatever it was) brought about a temporary change in the mentality or personality of the respondent which lowered his ability to resist temptation so far that his desires overrode his ability to control them. Thus we are concerned here with a case of disinhibition. The drug is not alleged to have created the desire to which the respondent gave way, but rather to have enabled it to be released …
>
> Each offence consists of a prohibited act or omission coupled with whatever state of mind is called for by the statute or rule of the common law which creates the offence. In those offences which are not absolute the state of mind which the prosecution must prove to have underlain the act or omission—the 'mental element'—will in the majority of cases be such as to attract disapproval. The mental element will then be the mark of what may properly be called a 'guilty mind' … [t]o assume that contemporary moral judgments affect the criminality of the act as distinct from the punishment appropriate to the crime once proved, is to be misled by the expression 'mens rea,' the ambiguity of which has been the subject of complaint for more than a century. Certainly, the 'mens' of the defendant must usually be involved in the offence: but the epithet 'rea' refers to the criminality of the act in which the mind is engaged, not to its moral character …

Appeal allowed.

 NOTE 8.7

1. Lord Mustill refused to recognise a new defence of involuntary intoxication on the grounds that, unlike other excusatory defences, it would be a general and complete defence, unlike, for example, loss of control or diminished responsibility. Moreover, it was unclear as to whether it would only apply where a third party had caused the intoxication or whether D's own mistake might have done so. Lord Mustill was concerned that the more susceptible the D to temptation, the easier it would be to establish.

2. Following *Kingston*, it is irrelevant whether intoxication is voluntary or involuntary or, if the latter, whether D lacks moral fault. The crucial question in all cases is whether MR can be proved or not.

Voluntary intoxication:

Assuming proof of AR:

■ Did D have MR for the offence, whether specific or basic intent?

■ If yes, D is guilty.

■ If no, D may have a partial defence to a crime of specific intent but will have no defence to a basic intent crime.

Involuntary intoxication:

Assuming proof of AR:

■ Did D have MR for the offence, whether specific or basic intent?

■ If yes, D is guilty.

■ If no, D may have a complete defence (subject to the rules on medication).

?!   **THINKING POINT** 8.13

D suffers a migraine attack and experiences visual disturbances. She accidentally takes some of her husband's tranquillisers instead of pain killers and feels worse. She abuses and kicks a child who rings the doorbell to ask if she can retrieve her football from D's garden. D is frequently troubled by this child whose football games D regards as anti-social behaviour. Does D have a defence to assault and battery?

Kingston raised interesting arguments about moral fault and criminal liability. Read the following by G.R. Sullivan, 'Involuntary Intoxication and Beyond' [1994] *Crim LR* 272 following the decision of the Court of Appeal:

The Court of Appeal's decision does not fit certain accounts of criminal liability. An intent in the conventional sense seemed clearly present; D conceived what it was he wanted and obtained it by goal-directed conduct. Although in a state of disinhibition, his conduct was in no sense compelled. From the perspective of 'fair opportunity and capacity to conform conduct to law' he arguably retained sufficient cognitive and volitional resources to comply with the law. If the Court of Appeal's decision is confirmed as it stands, then, as regards any offence with which D is charged involving proof of mens rea, should he adduce evidence of involuntary intoxication, it will be for the prosecution to prove that it was voluntary. Failing that, it must prove the hypothetical proposition that D would have offended in the same way had he been sober. Compared, say, to a defendant raising duress, the Court of Appeal's decision appears indulgent and could well be overturned.

Yet if we ask some very basic questions about the nature and point of criminal liability for stigmatic offences, a case can be made for sustaining the Court of Appeal's decision, provided certain qualifications are made … The drugs did not necessarily produce an alien character, they brought to the surface proclivities he might otherwise have suppressed. The intent that D formed was his own intent and no one else's. Yet Lord Taylor's intuition that D may have lacked sufficient culpability for a conviction is, with respect, convincing if we can make the assumption that D was not a practising paedophile. Taking the assumption to be correct, it is not a fair test of character to remove surreptitiously a person's inhibitions and confront him with that temptation he ordinarily seeks to avoid. Character, in this context, is a matter of attained status, public record, not of private dispositions or proclivities. In Kingston, D was afflicted with a sexuality which if he expressed would lead inevitably to criminal conduct. To the extent that he was able to restrain this tendency, he was entitled to that respect and non-intervention on the part of the State which is the due of law-abiding subjects. The Court of Appeal effectively concluded that D's conduct in all the circumstances of the particular occasion did not merit loss of this status.

Do you agree with the views of this author and the Court of Appeal or with those of the House of Lords?

See Diagram 8.4 for an overview of the intoxication rules.

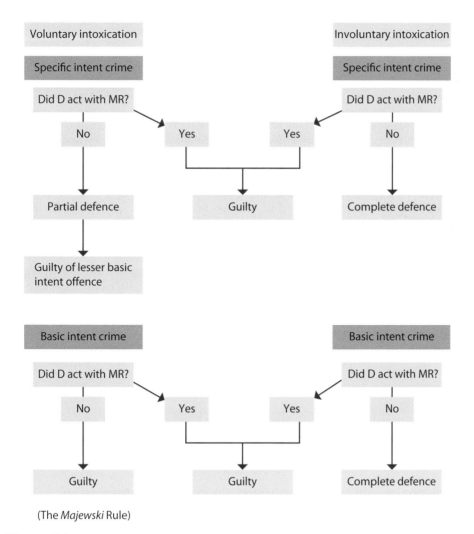

(The *Majewski* Rule)

Diagram 8.4
Flow chart: The intoxication rules

8.3.7 Dangerous Drugs

Drugs known to be dangerous—voluntary intoxication

Basic intent crimes: Where D consumes a drug which is known to be dangerous in the sense that it can cause unpredictable and aggressive behaviour, he will be regarded as voluntarily intoxicated and will have no defence to a crime of basic intent. This will be so even where D has acted involuntarily and was acting as an automaton.

> ### R v Lipman [1970] 1 QB 152 COURT OF APPEAL
>
> D and his girlfriend were tripping on LSD, an hallucinogenic drug. D crammed eight inches of sheet into the girl's mouth, asphyxiating her, in the belief that he was descending to the centre of the earth and was being attacked by snakes. On the charge of manslaughter by recklessness or gross negligence, the jury was directed that the prosecution need only prove that D would have known his actions in voluntarily taking the drugs to have been dangerous. D was convicted and appealed on the ground that the jury should also have been directed on the need for proof of intention or foresight that his actions were likely to result in harm.
>
> Widgery LJ:
>
> > For the purposes of criminal responsibility we see no reason to distinguish between the effect of drugs voluntarily taken and drunkenness voluntarily induced. As to the latter there is a great deal of authority. [The cases of *Beard*, *Bratty* and *Gallagher* were cited.] These authorities show quite clearly, in our opinion, that it was well established that no specific intent was necessary to support a conviction for manslaughter based on killing in the course of an unlawful act and that, accordingly, self-induced drunkenness was no defence to such a charge …
>
> Widgery LJ held that D was responsible for the act of killing whilst drugged (a different point from the responsibility for taking the drugs). Further, such unlawful and obviously dangerous actions were all that was required for unlawful act manslaughter (as opposed to gross negligence manslaughter as charged).

Lipman has been strongly criticised. D would have been correctly convicted of reckless/gross negligence manslaughter as directed by the trial judge, having voluntarily taken dangerous drugs with the requisite MR. However, the Court of Appeal convicted him of unlawful and dangerous act manslaughter and held that no MR was required for his act of killing. Under the usual rules MR must be proved for the unlawful act.

→ CROSS-REFERENCE
The case is discussed in this context in 8.2.5.

Specific intent crimes: As a result of *Coley, McGhee, Harris* [2013] EWCA Crim 223 (prior fault and automatism), it seems that voluntary intoxication is unlikely to ever be regarded as resulting in the total loss of voluntary control. D will either have MR or the rules on voluntary intoxication will apply.

There is no certainty as to which drugs the court will regard as dangerous and thus the rule is somewhat vague. Drugs legislation may provide some guidance but not all classified drugs produce dangerous aggression (Misuse of Drugs Act 1971 as amended by the Drugs Act 2005).

Drugs not known to be dangerous—involuntary intoxication

If D commits an offence under the influence of a medicinal drug taken in accordance with medical advice which is not known to be dangerous and the drug has an unforeseen side-effect causing D to become aggressive or unpredictable, involuntary intoxication will provide a defence to all crimes provided there was a lack of MR. But awareness of the risk of aggression/unpredictability will defeat the defence because D will be (subjectively) reckless.

R v Hardie [1985] 1 WLR 64 COURT OF APPEAL

To calm his nerves, D took several Valium tablets belonging to his former partner following the break-up of their relationship. He did not know what effect they would have. Whilst she and her daughter were in an adjoining room, D started a fire in a wardrobe. He was charged with damaging property with intent to endanger life or being reckless whether life would be endangered contrary to s1(2) Criminal Damage Act 1971. He argued in his defence that the Valium had prevented him from having MR. The judge rejected this defence because D had voluntarily taken the drug. D was convicted and appealed.

Parker LJ:

It is true that Valium is a drug and it is true that it was taken deliberately and not taken on medical prescription, but the drug is, in our view, wholly different in kind from drugs which are liable to cause unpredictability or aggressiveness. It may well be that the taking of a sedative or soporific drug will, in certain circumstances, be no answer, for example in a case of reckless driving, but *if the effect of a drug is merely soporific or sedative the taking of it, even in some excessive quantity, cannot in the ordinary way raise a conclusive presumption against the admission of proof of intoxication for the purpose of disproving mens rea in ordinary crimes, such as would be the case with alcoholic intoxication or incapacity or automatism resulting from the self-administration of dangerous drugs …*

In the present case the jury should not, in our judgment, have been directed to disregard any incapacity which resulted or might have resulted from the taking of Valium. They should have been directed that if they came to the conclusion that, as a result of the Valium, the appellant was, at the time, unable to appreciate the risks to property and persons from his actions they should then consider whether the taking of the Valium was itself reckless … [Emphasis added.]

Appeal allowed.

 NOTE 8.8

The outcome of a prosecution therefore depends on (a) whether a drug voluntarily taken is known to be dangerous or not. This is entirely dependent on the availability of publicised research, medical advice concerning unusual side-effects and public knowledge. (b) Even if the drug is generally thought to be safe, D may still be reckless in taking it for he may be actually aware of a risk of unpredictability/aggression as, for instance, where a medicinal drug is taken for non-medicinal purposes (to get high).

?! **THINKING POINT** 8.14

Would intoxication from the following be classified as voluntary or involuntary?

a. Insulin and alcohol, D being diabetic and having taken no food

b. Magic mushrooms

c. Valium

d. Crack

e. Cannabis.

8.3.8 Voluntary Intoxication and Defences: Drunken Mistake

There appears to be a strange anomaly between a straight plea of intoxication and a plea of drunken mistake in relation to a defence. Whilst intoxication under the *Majewski* rule may result in a partial defence for crimes of specific intent, a plea of drunken mistake will result in conviction. A drunken mistake is irrelevant and no defence at all. This is contrary to general principles of MR and the *Majewski* rule. Statutory defences of reasonable belief or lawful excuse are, however, unaffected by this rule.

Statutory defences and drunken mistake

If D commits a statutory crime and the statute provides a defence of reasonable belief or lawful excuse, a drunken mistake of fact giving rise to an erroneous belief on D's part will provide a complete defence, even to crimes of basic intent.

Jaggard v Dickinson [1980] 3 ALL ER 716 QUEEN'S BENCH DIVISION

D's friend had invited her to treat his home as her own. She attempted to enter the wrong house one night by a drunken mistake. Finding it locked, she broke a window and damaged some curtains. When charged with criminal damage (a crime of basic intent) she relied on the defence in s5(2) Criminal Damage Act 1971 of lawful excuse based on a belief that the person entitled to consent to the damage (ie: her friend) would have consented had he known her circumstances. Under s5(2) it is immaterial whether a belief is justified or not provided it is honest.

She was acquitted. The prosecution had argued that since drunkenness in a crime of basic intent did not negate recklessness under *Majewski*, it could not be relied upon as a defence.

Mustill J:

> In the first place, the argument transfers the distinctions between offences of specific and of basic intent to a context in which it has no place. The distinction is material where the defendant relies on his own drunkenness as a ground for denying that he had the degree of intention or recklessness required in order to constitute the offence. Here, by contrast, the appellant does not rely on her drunkenness to displace an inference of intent or recklessness; indeed she does not rely on it at all.
> Her defence is founded on the state of belief called for by s5(2). True, the fact of the appellant's intoxication was relevant to the defence under s5(2) for it helped to explain what would otherwise have been inexplicable, and hence lent colour to her evidence about the state of her belief. This is not the same as using drunkenness to rebut an inference of intention or recklessness. Belief, like intention or recklessness, is a state of mind; but they are not the same states of mind.

 NOTE 8.9

In 1980, criminal damage was an offence of *Caldwell* recklessness (where D was reckless for having failed to think about an obvious risk of harm). Evidence of intoxication would normally have supported a finding of *Caldwell* recklessness regardless of the *Majewski* rule. However, the court decided that D's actual belief was the real issue which took priority over *Caldwell* and *Majewski*.

Read this extract by G. Williams, 'Two Nocturnal Blunders' *NLJ*, 9 November 1990:

> The defendant Jaggard had spent the evening in the local boozer, and the prosecution brought out this
> fact in evidence … Note that the Diplock rule does not shut the defendant out from any defence. [The
> Diplock rule comes from *Caldwell*: D's unawareness, owing to intoxication, of a risk is reckless if the
> risk would have been obvious to him had he been sober.] It is a common misapprehension that vol-
> untary intoxication in the case of a crime of basic intent precludes any defence of lack of *mens rea*. In
> truth there is no rule that evidence of intoxication at the time of a criminal act turns the crime into one
> of strict liability and must inevitably lead to a conviction. Under the Diplock rule the defendant will
> still get off if the court thinks that a sober person might have made the same mistake … Many people,
> irrespective of intoxication, must have mistaken a house in a street … We do not know whether the
> magistrates considered the Diplock question, but anyway the Divisional Court held … that it was not
> the right question, because the matter was regulated by s5(2)(a), which is wholly a subjective provi-
> sion. The issue under the Act is what the defendant believed: it says nothing about intoxication. Al-
> though the Diplock rule applies to charges of recklessness in general, the Act supersedes it for charges
> of criminal damage, asking not what the defendant would have believed but for intoxication, but what
> he did in fact believe, taking account of his intoxication.

Common law defences and drunken mistake

Mistaken self-defence

→ CROSS-REFERENCE
See Chapter 9, 9.3.2 for
the facts of the case and
further discussion on the
subjective test.

Imagine that D mistakenly believes that it is necessary to use force to defend himself from attack
when, in reality, there is no threat at all. Under the usual rules of self-defence, an honest belief
will result in acquittal. The test is subjective (*Gladstone Williams*).

You might expect an honest belief based on a drunken mistake to follow the same rule. It did
in *Jaggard*. Or perhaps the test should follow *Majewski*, so that a drunken mistake would provide
a partial defence to crimes of specific intent but no defence to crimes of basic intent? Three cases
have confirmed, however, that a drunken mistake is no defence to any crime, whether specific or
basic, regardless of the absence of MR and D will be convicted.

R v O'Grady [1987] 3 ALL ER 420 COURT OF APPEAL

D and his friend fell asleep in D's flat, both of them extremely drunk. D alleged that he awoke to
find his friend assaulting him with a piece of glass in his hand. D retaliated with another piece of
glass. The friend died from his injuries. D was convicted of manslaughter following the judge's
direction to the jury on mistaken belief in self-defence, which would constitute a defence if the
mistake was honest, but that the amount of force used was excessive or unreasonable.

Lord Lane CJ:

> We have come to the conclusion that, where the jury are satisfied that the defendant was mistaken
> in his belief that any force or the force which he in fact used was necessary to defend himself and
> are further satisfied that the mistake was caused by voluntarily induced intoxication, the defence
> must fail. We do not consider that any distinction should be drawn on this aspect of the matter
> between offences involving what is called specific intent, such as murder, and offences of so called
> basic intent, such as manslaughter. Quite apart from the problem of directing a jury in a case such
> as the present where manslaughter is an alternative verdict to murder, the question of mistake can
> and ought to be considered separately from the question of intent. A sober man who mistakenly
> believes he is in danger of immediate death at the hands of an attacker is entitled to be acquitted of
> both murder and manslaughter if his reaction in killing his supposed assailant was a reasonable one.
> What his intent may have been seems to us to be irrelevant to the problem of self-defence or no.

NOTE 8.10

The question of mistake was (inexplicably) 'separate' from that of MR. The decision meant that one could be convicted of murder in the absence of intention to kill or cause grievous bodily harm. This was extremely contentious.

O'Grady gives rise to the following consequences: a drunken mistake might produce different outcomes at trial for a crime of specific intent depending on how it is presented:

- as a plea of intoxication—a partial defence;
- as mistaken self-defence—a complete defence;
- as a drunken mistake in self-defence—no defence at all.

The Law Commission criticised *O'Grady* in 'Criminal Law, A Criminal Code' (Law Com No 177, 1989), para 8.42, as follows:

… it would, we believe, be unthinkable to convict of murder a person who thought, for whatever reason, that he was acting to save his life and who would have been acting reasonably if he had been right.

Reversal of the case was recommended in 'Intoxication and Criminal Liability' (Law Com No 229, 1995) para 7.12.

Despite its ambiguity, the *O'Grady* rule signifies a policy to protect victims and society from the excesses of intoxication producing violence. The Court of Appeal in *O'Connor* [1991] Crim LR 135, confirmed that *O'Grady* was binding in relation to murder. *O'Connor* concerned a head-butting causing death in a public house in drunken self-defence. Both cases were approved in *R v Hatton (Jonathan)* [2005] EWCA Crim 2951 where, after consuming over 20 pints of beer, D battered V to death with a sledgehammer. Under V's body was a five-foot-long stick belonging to D which D had fashioned to resemble a samurai sword. D was charged with murder and pleaded self-defence induced by drunken mistake.

The appeal was dismissed. *O'Grady* was confirmed by the Court of Appeal as having decided a general point of law that where mistaken force in self-defence was caused by voluntary intoxication, the defence must fail.

Mistaken belief in consent

Consent can be a defence to assault and sexual offences. A mistaken belief in consent will arise where D mistakenly believes that V is consenting because, due to intoxication, he fails to notice what would have been an obvious refusal had he been sober. The same rule applies here. *O'Grady* was confirmed by the Court of Appeal in *R v Fotheringham* (1988) 88 Cr App R 206 (a rape case involving drunken belief that a babysitter was D's wife). Strangely, this approach was not applied by the Court of Appeal in *R v Richardson & Irwin* [1999] 1 Cr App R 392, [1999] Crim LR 494 where two university students pleaded drunken belief in consent when, for a prank, they dropped a friend over a balcony and were charged with unlawfully and maliciously inflicting grievous bodily harm contrary to s20 OAPA 1861 for the ensuing broken bones. The court focused on MR. If Ds lacked awareness due to a mistaken belief in consent, albeit a drunken and unreasonable one, they were not reckless and were wrongly convicted.

This decision is generally regarded as flawed. Even under *Majewski*, intoxication is no defence to a crime of basic intent.

?!   THINKING POINT 8.15

D, who has drunk six vodkas, commits the following mistakes. Will she have a defence? In each case:

■ Identify the offence.

■ Is there a statutory defence?—mistaken belief is relevant.

■ Is there a common law defence?—mistaken belief is irrelevant.

1. D kills V thinking that V is pointing a gun at her whereas it is in fact a stick.

2. D breaks into a neighbour's house (V) to turn off a persistently ringing burglar alarm, believing that V would not mind. The alarm is ringing from a different house.

3. D jokingly trips V up, causing V to break his wrist.

Intoxication, insanity and automatism

Where excessive drinking has produced insanity (as a result of either alcohol dependency syndrome or delirium tremens) so that D does not know what he is doing or that it is wrong, the M'Naghten Rules will apply (*Beard, Gallagher*).

Where D suffers from a pre-existing disease of the mind and also drinks excessively, it is unclear whether the defence should be insanity (*Beard*) or intoxication (*Gallagher*). *Coley*, where a delusional D stabbed a neighbour, now confirms that the 'direct acute effects' of intoxicants do not produce a disease of the mind.

If D is so intoxicated by alcohol or dangerous drug as to be acting as an automaton, the rules on intoxication will apply (*Lipman*—where D took LSD and killed his girlfriend believing she was a snake). Further, it is unlikely, following *Coley, McGee, Harris* that intoxication producing disinhibition will be regarded as having negated MR or created total loss of voluntariness. Policy requires the courts to invoke the rules for the purposes of social defence. Where the automatism is the result of non-dangerous drugs, automatism will apply provided D was not aware of the risk. The Law Commission, in its ongoing project on mental defences, is considering the relationship between these defences.

→ CROSS-REFERENCE
For details of *Coley* and discussion on disease of the mind
see 8.1.3.

→ CROSS-REFERENCE
See 8.2.8 and 8.3.10 in relation to reform proposals.

8.3.9 Criticisms of *Majewski*

The *Majewski* rule has been subject to a good deal of criticism. Read the following by G. Virgo, 'The Law Commission Consultation Paper on Intoxication and Criminal Liability: Reconciling Principle and Policy' [1993] *Crim LR* 415:

> *Majewski* secures a rough form of criminal justice, since it means that for many offences it is possible to convict a defendant for causing harm, even though intoxication prevented the formation of a mental element. This is so even in respect of some specific intent offences where the defendant can be convicted of a lesser, basic intent offence. In *Majewski* the House of Lords acknowledged principle by allowing intoxication to be adduced to show that the mental element for specific intent offences did not exist, but were swayed by policy objectives in convicting of basic intent offences despite intoxication. This compromise is defensible on policy grounds, but it fails to accord with accepted principles of the criminal law …
>
> The very distinction between specific intent and basic intent offences is open to criticism, for it is difficult to discern any logical rationale for drawing such a distinction between offences. The lack of

an accepted rationale for the distinction makes it difficult to characterise new crimes as being either specific or basic intent offences. It is also uncertain whether it is the offence itself that is characterised as one of specific or basic intent, or whether each mental element of the offence should be so characterised ...

The policy objectives of the *Majewski* distinction, in seeking to secure convictions for crimes committed whilst intoxicated, are only partially fulfilled, in that there are a number of specific intent offences which cannot be reduced to lesser, basic intent offences, most notably a number of offences involving dishonesty, such as theft. If the defendant is charged with such offences and he was intoxicated at the time of committing them, then he will not be liable for anything. Also, by convicting intoxicated offenders of basic intent crimes rather than for a specific offence of causing harm whilst intoxicated, the existing law fails to identify the offender's real culpability and punish this accordingly.

This survey shows that, because the law on the relevance of intoxication does not accord with the accepted principles for establishing criminal liability, because the law is uncertain, illogical and unnecessarily complex and because the desired policy, of securing convictions for those causing harm whilst intoxicated, is not accurately achieved, the case for Parliamentary reform of this area of law is compelling.

On the other hand, the *Majewski* rule has its supporters. S. Gardner in 'The Importance of Majewski' (1994) 14 *Oxford JLS* 280 argued against the accusation of illogicality:

... [t]here is clearly no difficulty about the idea that a crime may have more than one style of *mens rea*, one of which is advertence. This is the situation, for example, with crimes which can be committed either intentionally or recklessly, and also with crimes of strict liability or negligence, which can normally be committed intentionally or recklessly too. The fact that a crime has advertence as a basis for liability thus provides no ground for the supposition that advertence *must* be its exclusive basis for liability, leaving no room for intoxication.

That seems to be as far as 'logic' takes us. There is no technical reason for thinking that *Majewski* must be out of place in the law ... The argument needs now to be recast along the lines that advertence alone should be regarded as adequate to inculpate [ie: convict] for offences of recklessness. If this proposition can be found embedded in the law or salient in the relevant philosophy, *Majewski* might still be denounced as 'contrary to principle'. But it is questionable whether that is the case.

The proposition is, of course supported by the well-known subjectivist platform. But it is clear that that platform is itself far from universally accepted. At the lowest, there seems to be a popular notion that when a person has done some misdeed, to say 'I didn't realize' is not necessarily a satisfactory answer to an accusation of culpability for it: the retort, 'Well, you should have done,' is felt supportable. A specific manifestation of this seems to be the further popular idea that one who fails to realize what he is doing because he is voluntarily intoxicated is not to be exonerated; if anything, the intoxication gives especially sharp focus and added power to the retort.

Q. Of the two views in these extracts, whose do you find more persuasive?
As we shall see at 8.3.10 the Law Commission currently favours retention of the *Majewski* rule despite its shortcomings.

The *Majewski* principle, resulting in conviction for crimes of basic intent despite the absence of MR, is not followed throughout the common law world.

- New Zealand: a lack of MR due to intoxication results in complete acquittal and there is no distinction between intentional and reckless crimes.

- Australia: under a federal legal system, some states provide that drunkenness might be a defence wherever it negated MR but reforms in others have moved towards a *Majewski* rule.

- Canada: *Majewski* has not been followed since 1995 (*Daviault* (1995) 118 DLR (4th) 469). The case concerned a sexual assault upon a woman wheel-chair user by a chronic alcoholic who had consumed almost a whole bottle of brandy and who might not have known what he was doing.

- Scotland: MR is treated rather more objectively than in England. Intoxication is no defence in general.

SECTION SUMMARY

Intoxication is a denial of MR.

Voluntary intoxication by alcohol or dangerous drugs:
- *Did D have MR for the offence, whether specific or basic intent?*
- *If yes, D is guilty.*
- *If no, D may have a partial defence to a crime of specific intent but will have no defence to a basic intent crime.*
- *Intoxication in the form of Dutch courage is no defence.*

Involuntary intoxication:
- *Did D have MR for the offence, whether specific or basic intent?*
- *If yes, D is guilty.*
- *If no, D may have a complete defence.*
- *This includes medication (ie drugs not generally known to be dangerous) unless D is reckless.*

Intoxication and defences:
- *A drunken mistake in relation to common law defences is no defence at all but might be where a statutory defence is based on reasonable belief or lawful excuse.*

8.3.10 Reform

In 1993, the Law Commission recommended the abolition of the *Majewski* rule and the introduction of a crime of criminal intoxication (Law Com CP No 127 (1993)). This was rejected by the government.

In 1995, it recommended general codification of *Majewski* subject to amendment ('Legislating the Criminal Code: Intoxication and Criminal Liability', Law Com No 229 (1995)). A Home Office draft bill was attached to a Consultation Paper on 'Violence: Reforming the Offences Against the Person Act 1861' (1998) as follows:

Clause 19(1):

For the purposes of this act a person who was voluntarily intoxicated at any material time must be treated–

(a) as having been aware of any risk of which he would have been aware had he not been intoxicated, and

(b) as having known or believed in any circumstances which he would have known or believed in had he not been intoxicated.

In 2009, the Law Commission proposed that voluntary intoxication should support a defence based on the absence of fault: 'Intoxication and Criminal Liability' (Law Com No 314).

In discussion paper 'Criminal Liability: Insanity and Automatism' (July 2013), the Law Commission propose amending involuntary intoxication so that those who have an adverse reaction to prescription medicine and commit an offence without MR would no longer benefit from an acquittal on the grounds of involuntary intoxication but would fall within the proposed 'recognised medical condition' defence (insanity as amended) to receive a verdict of 'not criminally responsible'. This would prevent disparity between, for example: diabetic defendants who fail to take insulin and those who do but then fail to eat.

8.4 Infancy

8.4.1 The Age of Criminal Responsibility: *Doli Incapax*

8.4.2 Criticism: Was it Right to Abolish the Presumption?

8.4.3 Innocent Agents

8.4.1 The Age of Criminal Responsibility: *Doli Incapax*

The age of criminal responsibility is 10. Children under the age of 10 are irrebuttably presumed incapable of committing a criminal offence (s50 Children and Young Persons Act 1933). This presumption is known as *doli incapax*. Children above 10 are capable of committing an offence. Between 10 and 21 there is age differentiation in relation to procedure and sentencing but not legal responsibility.

Criminal Justice Classifications:

- 10–14 years (children)
- 14–17 years (young persons)
- 17–21 years (young offenders).

Until 1998, the age of criminal responsibility was 14. Between the ages of 10 and 14 the presumption that a child was incapable of crime (*doli incapax*) was rebuttable. This protection for children had existed for 700 years. It could be rebutted by prosecution evidence that the child knew his act was seriously wrong or had mischievous discretion. There was pressure to abolish this presumption in the early 1990s but the House of Lords refused to do so in *C (A Minor) v DPP* [1995] 3 WLR 888 on the grounds that only Parliament could change the law. In this case, D, a 12-year-old boy charged with attempted taking and driving away contrary to s12 Theft Act 1968, held the handlebars of a motorbike while another boy tried to force the padlock and chain securing it. The House held that there needed to be clear evidence that D knew his act to be seriously wrong in addition to proving the AR and MR of the offence.

Much of the 1993 trial of the 10-year-old defendants, Thompson and Venables, for the murder of two-year-old Jamie Bulger concerned whether they knew what they had done was seriously wrong. The ECtHR ruled in 1999 that the age of criminal responsibility in England was not contrary to the Convention but the Crown Court trial process was a violation of their right to a fair trial (*T v UK, V v UK* [2000] Crim 187).

Doli incapax was completely removed by s34 Crime and Disorder Act 1998, ironically as part of the Labour government's criminal justice programme on youth justice. That the presumption had been removed was confirmed in *R v T* [2009] UKHL 20. The removal of such an historic protection for children under the guise of welfare so as to cast upon them greater punishment was politically popular but repressive. Had *doli incapax* survived, the two boys in *R v G* [2004] 1 AC 1034 (reckless criminal damage) would probably never have been convicted, or even brought to trial.

Compare the age of criminal responsibility in the following European countries:

- Ireland 7
- Scotland 8
- France/Holland 13
- Germany/Austria/Italy 14
- Scandinavia 15
- Portugal, Poland, Andorra 16
- Luxembourg/Belgium/Spain 18

Article 3 of the UN Charter on the Rights of the Child (the 'Beijing Rules') 1989 states that in all actions concerning children, the rights of the child shall be a primary consideration. The United Nations Committee on the Rights of the Child has issued three reports (1995, 2002 and 2008) criticising the UK and Scotland for their lack of a child-centred and rights approach to criminal justice, particularly in relation to the low age of criminal responsibility in England, Wales and Scotland. The UK imprisons more children than almost any other European country—approximately 3,000 at any one time (*The Guardian*, 20 November 2007).

?! THINKING POINT 8.16

Do you consider that a child of 10–14 automatically has the same understanding, knowledge, ability to reason or knowledge of wrongfulness as an adult?

At what age do you consider a child/young person should be exposed to the full consequences of criminal activity?

Are criminal sanctions the answer to youth offending?

8.4.2 Criticism: Was it Right to Abolish the Presumption?

The government abolished the presumption because it was archaic, illogical and unfair. Read this extract by C. Walsh, 'Irrational Presumptions of Rationality and Comprehension' [1998] 3 *Web JCLI*:

> The crux of their (the government's) overall approach is summed up in their slogan 'No More Excuses'. Evidently, the assumption that a ten year old does not have the same capacity to reason as an adult is a prime example of the sort of excuse which Labour has vowed to remove from the system ….
>
> i. The contention that the presumption of *doli incapax* is archaic:
>
> While it is true that a child's understanding, knowledge and ability to reason are still developing, the notion that the average 10–14 year old does not know right from wrong seems contrary to

common sense in an age of compulsory education from the age of five, when children seem to develop faster both mentally and physically. (Consultation Paper 1997, p6).

The above argument can be criticised on a number of counts. In answering a similar contention arising from the judgement of the Divisional Court in *C (A Minor) v DPP* [1995] 2 Cr App R 166, Lord Lowry responded with the following:

> It is true that there is (and has been for a considerable time) compulsory education and, ... perhaps children now grow up more quickly. But better formal education and earlier sophistication do not guarantee that the child will more readily distinguish right from wrong (p396).

... Paul Cavadino (Cavadino 1997) adds further criticism of the 'universal education' argument by making the valid point that,

> [I]n view of the association between truancy and offending and the recent sharp rise in school exclusions, ... many of the children concerned have in practice failed to benefit from universal compulsory education. (p167) ....

> [F]ar from being an outmoded survival from an earlier era, the *doli incapax* rule is fully consistent with our increasing knowledge of child development and learning, which tells us that children mature and learn over differing time spans. (p168) ...

> [I]t is submitted that a system which allocates a flexible four year period during which moral culpability can be assessed is preferable to a system which assumes that by the age of ten all children have reached the same level of moral culpability as an adult.

> At the time the doctrine developed the need for protection was undoubted—the death penalty was available for children, for crimes less serious than murder. But the criminal law is very different and for most young offenders, the court's emphasis is as much on preventing re-offending as on punishment for the crime (Consultation Paper 1997, p6).

> [T]his welfare argument overlooks the fact that very substantial penalties are available for ten to thirteen year olds found guilty of criminal offences. The Criminal Justice and Public Order Act 1994 extended the range of offences for which children aged ten to thirteen inclusive can be sentenced to long term detention under s53 Children and Young Persons Act 1933. It also provided for a new secure training order, which is a custodial sentence for twelve to fourteen year old offenders with a minimum length of six months and a maximum of two years. (Penal Affairs Consortium 1995) ...

> [T]he Labour Government's approach to youth justice is distinctly victim-orientated: even if rehabilitation were to result from whatever penalty is imposed on young offenders in this age group in the future, their own good is not at the forefront of New Labour's agenda.

> ... [M]any experts in this area support the view that children should be kept out of the criminal justice system wherever possible ... Most children commit criminal offences and most children grow out of committing crime ... However, one way of interfering with this natural progression is to give these children a criminal label.

The author goes on to observe that the presumption provided a 'benevolent safeguard' and was not illogical.

8.4.3 Innocent Agents

➔ CROSS-REFERENCE
Secondary parties to crime are covered in Chapter 5.

The consequence of the limited *doli incapax* presumption is that although a child under the age of 10 is incapable of committing a crime, a person above that age who procures or assists a child to commit a crime is criminally liable not as a secondary party but as a principal offender through an innocent agent (child).

SUMMARY

- A defence of mental incapacity may excuse D's liability for an offence by negating MR.

- This applies to insanity where special arguments regarding lack of moral responsibility apply. These arguments do not apply to intoxication, which is never a defence but may be the reason why D lacked MR.

- Automatism, where D lacks voluntariness, negates the AR of the crime.

- Infancy, applying to children under 10 years old, prevents the offence from being regarded as criminal at all.

PROBLEM SOLVING

D is a soldier just returned from war where he was on active service. His unit was involved in a serious armed confrontation three months ago in which D sustained head injuries. Since then, he has had nightmares, depression and frequent fits for which he takes medication. D's relationship with V has just ended because V could no longer tolerate D's mood swings. One night after drinking alcohol and taking a double dose of Valium, D gets out of bed whilst in a dream and drives to V's flat where he lets himself in with a key. D sees V in bed. Thinking she is about to attack him, he smothers her with a pillow, killing her. On his way out, D comes to his senses but as he is about to leave, he sneezes violently and knocks a valuable vase on to the carpet, breaking it. He then drives to the nearest police station, giving himself up. At his trial he informs his barrister that aliens from space inserted a micro-chip into his ear last year so that God could give him orders as to when to kill V.

Does D have any defence/s to the crimes in this scenario?

Remember:

- **I: Identify** relevant issues
- **D: Define** offences/defences
- **E: Explain/evaluate** the law
- **A: Apply** law to facts.

   A useful problem-solving technique is to construct a chart representing the headings of an outline answer, as shown in Table 8.1.

   Always conclude as to which defence/s it would be in D's interests to plead and which are most likely to succeed.

   See Table 8.1 for a sample approach.

   See the online resources for further guidance on solving this problem: www.oup.com/uk/loveless6e/.

FURTHER READING

Insanity
J. Child and G.R. Sullivan, 'When Does the Insanity Defence Apply? Some Recent Cases' [2014] 11 *Crim LR* 788
Examines the interplay between the defence of insanity and other important defences.

H. Howard, 'Lack of Capacity: Reforming the Law on Unfitness to Plead' (2016) 80(6) JCL 428–435
Considers the proposals put forward by the Law Commission and the pros and cons of including a diagnostic threshold.

T. Jones, 'Insanity, Automatism and the Burden of Proof on the Accused' (1995) 111 *LQR* 475–516
Examines the way in which the insanity defence is dealt with in criminal trials from an evidential perspective.

Table 8.1

Problem-solving chart

Defence	Murder MR? *Basic/specific intent?*	Criminal Damage *MR?* *Basic/specific intent?*
Unfitness to plead	Sufficient understanding of the proceedings?	As for murder.
Insanity	Are there internal causes of involuntary action? What is the test/burden of proof? Outcome of a successful plea?	As for murder.
Automatism	Are there external causes of involuntary action? Self-induced? Test/burden/likely outcome? Which provides a better result for D: insanity or automatism?	As for murder.
Intoxication	Explain the *Majewski* rule. How does the *Majewski* rule apply to this crime? Was intoxication voluntary or involuntary? Possible to argue either way? Likely outcome?	How does the *Majewski* rule apply to this crime? What difference does involuntary intoxication make?
Diminished Responsibility	Test: s2 Homicide Act 1957. Does D qualify?	Does this defence apply?

Law Commission, 'Criminal Liability: Insanity and Automatism—A Discussion Paper' (July 2013) (www.lawcom.gov.uk)

Law Commission, 'Unfitness to Plead: Consultation Responses & Analysis of Responses' (2013) (www.lawcom.gov.uk)

Law Commission, 'Unfitness to Plead Volumes 1 and 2' (Unfitness to Plead and Draft Legislation) (Law Com No 364, 2016)

Law Commission reports proposing reforms to the insanity defence and to unfitness to plead.

R.D. Mackay, 'Yet More Fact(s) about the Insanity Defence' [2006] *Crim LR* 399

On the relationship between the insanity defence and unfitness to plead. Includes an analysis of the way in which the M'Naghten Rules were used and the final outcomes for the defendant.

R.D. MacKay, 'Righting the Wrong?—Some Observations on the Second Limb of the N'Naghten Rules' [2009] *Crim LR* 80

Examines the second limb of the M'Naghten Rules—that although the defendant understands the nature and quality of his act, he does not know that it is wrong. Includes empirical studies of the insanity defence.

Automatism

Dr I. Ebrahim, W. Wilson, R. Marks, K. Peacock and Dr P. Fenwick, 'Violence, Sleepwalking and the Criminal Law: (1 and 2) The Medical Aspects' [2005] *Crim LR* 601–623

Articles discuss the medical and legal aspects of sleepwalking to automatism and insanity.

J. Rumbold and M. Wasik, 'Diabetic Drivers, Hypoglycaemic Unawareness, and Automatism' [2011] *Crim LR* 863

A commentary on the decision in *R v Clarke* on suffering a hypoglycaemic episode whilst driving and whether this should lead to criminal liability.

A. Samuels, 'The Diabetic Driver' (2017) 181(33) *CL & J Weekly* 354

Discusses the difficulties in proving non-insane automatism and insanity when a driver blames his diabetes for a collision

Intoxication

J. Child, 'Drink, Drugs and Law Reform: A Review of Law Commission Report No 314' [2009] *Crim LR* 488

Discusses the interplay of mens rea and voluntary intoxication and the Law Commission's proposals, including for inchoate offences and secondary participation.

S. Gardner, 'The Importance of Majewski' (1994) 14 *Oxford JLS* 280

Discusses the scope of the *Majewski* rule and the emphasis on crimes of specific intent.

Law Commission, 'Intoxication and Criminal Liability' (Law Com No 314, 2008)

An evaluation of the Law Commission's proposals.

J. Tolmie, 'Alcoholism and Criminal Liability', (2001) 64(5) *MLR* 688

Article questions whether alcoholism should be considered to be a 'disease' or a behaviour of choice, and if the latter, how other defences such as insanity and loss of control should deal with it.

R. Williams, 'Voluntary Intoxication: A Lost Cause?' (2013) 129 *LQR* 264–289

Assesses the limits of *DPP v Majewski* in intoxication cases and proposes a new element to an offence.

Age of criminal responsibility

F. Bennion, 'Mens Rea and Defendants Below the Age of Discretion' [2009] *Crim LR* 757

Argues that the doctrine of *doli incapax* has and should not have been abolished by the House of Lords.

L. Hoyano, 'Coroners and Justice Act 2009: Special Measures Direction Take Two,' [2010] *Crim LR* 345

Discusses the effectiveness of special measures directions for child witnesses and other vulnerable defendants.

9

Defences of compulsion

Introduction

9.1 Duress and Duress of Circumstances

9.2 Necessity

9.3 Public and Private Defence

9.4 Mistake

KEY POINTS

DURESS/DURESS OF CIRCUMSTANCES

This section will help you to:

- understand:
  - the general principles of these two excusatory defences so as to distinguish them from the justificatory defences of necessity and self-defence;
  - how recent case law has set strict, objective limits to the defences;
- critically think about:
  - the underlying policy issues and whether the defence is based on principles of fairness;
  - whether the exclusion of these defences from murder should be reformed.

NECESSITY

This section will help you to:

- understand:
  - the general principles of this justificatory defence so as to distinguish it from duress/duress of circumstances;
  - that necessity has only been acknowledged in relation to medical but not self-help cases and that, in relation to the former, it could apply to murder;
  - that necessity has been recently merged with duress of circumstances to form a new defence of 'necessity of circumstances';
- evaluate whether the general limitations in respect of murder and self-help cases are justifiable.

SELF-DEFENCE/DEFENCE OF OTHERS/PROPERTY/PREVENTION OF CRIME

This section will help you to:

- understand the general principles of the justificatory defence of self-defence (etc) so as to be able to distinguish it from necessity and duress;

- evaluate whether the defence is clear and certain;
- think critically about whether the imminence rule conflicts with the underlying principle of necessity in the defence;
- consider whether excessive force in self-defence should provide mitigation in murder cases and whether the defence contravenes Article 2 ECHR.

MISTAKE

This section will help you to understand:

- that mistaken belief is a complete defence to all crimes;
- that in excusatory defences it negates and excuses MR so that D will not be guilty of an offence;
- that in justificatory defences it negates and justifies AR so that there is no offence.

INTRODUCTION

The defences in this section will all result in complete acquittals if successfully established. They provide a defence to all crimes with one major exception: duress/duress of circumstances cannot be used as a defence to murder, treason or attempted murder. D bears no legal burden of proof in any of these defences but he must satisfy an evidential burden, that is: produce sufficient evidence so as to cast reasonable doubt on the prosecution case.

You will see that the tests for most of these defences consist of subjective and objective elements. Duress/duress of circumstances/necessity tend to be more objective whereas self-defence and mistake are predominantly subjective. They are divided between justifications and excuses, as with defences of incapacity in Chapter 8.

9.1 Duress and Duress of Circumstances

9.1.1 Introduction

9.1.2 The Test for Duress

9.1.3 Limitations on the Defence: Voluntary Association with Criminals: *R v Hasan*

9.1.4 Limitations on the Defence: Murder, Attempted Murder and Treason

9.1.5 Duress of Circumstances

9.1.6 Reform

KEY CASES

R v van Dao (Vinh) [2012] EWCA Crim 1717—a threat of false imprisonment in the absence of serious injury is insufficient;

Hasan [2005] UKHL 22—duress is excluded in voluntary association cases and unless the threat is of immediate harm;

R v Howe & Bannister [1987] 2 WLR 568 House of Lords—duress is excluded from murder, attempted murder and treason;

R v GAC [2013] EWCA 1472—duress and BWS;

Pommell [1995] 2 Cr App R 607—duress of circumstances applies to all crimes except for the *Howe* limitations.

9.1.1 Introduction

Duress is a complete defence to all crimes apart from murder, attempted murder and some forms of treason, to which it is no defence at all. The defence is not a plea that the AR was involuntary or lawful. It is a plea that, despite having committed the offence, D's wrongdoing or fault (MR) should be *excused* because his will was overborne by threats of death or physical violence. Lord Wilberforce in *DPP for NI v Lynch* [1975] AC 653 described the essence of the defence as follows:

> Duress is something which is superimposed on the other elements of the offence so as to prevent the law from treating what s/he has done a crime.

The defence is a concession to human frailty. It acknowledges that under serious threats, D will face a moral dilemma: to commit the crime or suffer death or serious violence. The harm need not be directed at D personally and may be threatened against his family or others to whom responsibility is owed. The burden of disproving the defence is on the prosecution. The focus will be on D's state of mind, unlike justificatory defences where the emphasis is on the circumstances of the offence. It is the only area of criminal law where motive is allowed to excuse D from liability. The Law Commission has recently considered duress/duress of circumstances in the context of homicide reform and has recommended that the murder/attempted murder limitation be removed.

→ CROSS-REFERENCE
For further discussion of the Law Commission proposals see 9.1.6.

The defence takes two forms: duress by threats and duress of circumstances. They derive from the same tests and common principles. The distinction can be seen from the examples below:

Duress by threats ('Commit this offence or else!')

D is threatened as follows:

- 'If you do not rob that post office, I will blow your brains out.'
- 'If you do not burgle that house, I will shoot your husband/wife/children.'
- 'Unless you give me the keys to the school safe, I will kill your pupils one by one.'

The above threats are clear-cut. D effectively has no choice. It would be *reasonable* that he should be excused from liability in choosing to protect innocent life. Less clear is the example of a threat that unless D shoots V in the knee-caps, both of D's ears will be blown off. Would it be reasonable for D to commit the offence?

Duress of circumstances

- D sees an aggressive group charging towards him. In order to escape, he drives away dangerously and knocks down a pedestrian, injuring her.
- D is pursued by a ferocious pit bull terrier which his rival, X, has set upon him. D breaks down a locked gate (criminal damage) to escape into a nearby garden.

The threat arises from a perception of immediate danger arising from the circumstances, not from a verbal threat.

Necessity

Necessity is a related defence. It derives from the same theoretical root of 'overpowerment' or 'compulsion' to commit crime but the threat need not be criminal in nature. Theoretically, it provides a wider defence than duress or duress of circumstances but, as we shall see, its ambit has been restricted to medical cases. Necessity is viewed as a justification rather than an excuse.

9.1.2 The Test for Duress

■ Was D forced to act as he did because of a reasonable fear of death or personal injury?

■ Would a sober person of reasonable firmness, sharing D's characteristics, have responded to D's belief in the same way?

➔ CROSS-REFERENCE
For further discussion of
Howe & Bannister
see 9.1.4.

The test derives from two cases: *Graham* (next) and *R v Howe & Bannister* [1987] 2 WLR 568 House of Lords.

R v Graham [1982] 1 WLR 294 COURT OF APPEAL

Graham, a homosexual, lived with his wife, W, and another homosexual, King. King was violent and had attacked W but Graham had intervened. Whilst W was out, King suggested to Graham that they kill W. Graham telephoned W and asked her to return. King then put a flex around her neck and told Graham to pull the other end which he did. W was killed. Graham claimed to have acted only because he was afraid of King. Graham was convicted of murder and appealed on the grounds of duress.

Lord Lane CJ:

As a matter of public policy, it seems to us essential to limit the defence of duress by means of an objective criterion formulated in terms of reasonableness. Consistency of approach in defences to criminal liability is obviously desirable. Provocation and duress are analogous. In provocation the words or actions of one person break the self-control of another. In duress the words or actions of one person break the will of another. The law requires a defendant to have the self-control reasonably to be expected of the ordinary citizen in his situation. It should likewise require him to have the steadfastness reasonably to be expected of the ordinary citizen in his situation. So too with self-defence, in which the law permits the use of no more force than is reasonable in the circumstances. And, in general, if a mistake is to excuse what would otherwise be criminal, the mistake must be a reasonable one. . . .

[T]he correct approach on the facts of this case would have been as follows. (1) Was the defendant, or may he have been, impelled to act as he did because, as a result of what he reasonably believed King had said or done, he had good cause to fear that if he did not so act King would kill him or (if this is to be added) cause him serious physical injury? (2) If so, have the prosecution made the jury sure that a sober person of reasonable firmness, sharing the characteristics of the defendant, would not have responded to whatever he reasonably believed King said or did by taking part in the killing?. . . . We doubt whether the Crown were right to concede that the question of duress ever arose on the facts of the case. The words and deeds of King relied on by the defence were far short of those needed to raise a threat of the requisite gravity. [Emphasis added.]

The subjective and objective elements were comprehensively reviewed by the House of Lords in *R v Hasan* [2005] UKHL 22, [2005] 2 WLR 709, the most important authority on duress for many years. The House asserted a strict, objective approach which makes duress more difficult to use than before. Although *Hasan* was directly concerned with the limitations of the defence, we will take account of its impact upon the defence as we proceed.

➔ CROSS-REFERENCE
For further discussion of
Hasan see 9.1.3.

The subjective question

The question is subjective in that it must be established that D acted through fear. However the fear must also be reasonable, an objective element. We need to consider six aspects to this question.

1. The threats must be of death or serious personal physical violence to D, D's family or others for whom D is responsible

The threats will come from a person in the case of duress and threatening circumstances, such as a gang, in the case of duress of circumstances. The fear must be of death or serious physical injury. Fear of damage to property, blackmail, imprisonment or psychological injury are insufficient.

R v Baker & Wilkins [1997] CRIM LR 497 COURT OF APPEAL

A mother (D) was charged with threatening behaviour and criminal damage. In an attempt to rescue her child, whom she believed had been kidnapped by the child's father and his new wife, she broke through a front door of premises where the child was being held. It was submitted that duress of circumstances should be available where D believed the act was immediately necessary to avoid serious psychological injury (ie: her nervous breakdown). The appeal was dismissed. Duress or duress of circumstances exist to accommodate human frailty when D's mind is so overpowered by some threat of death or serious physical injury that he cannot reasonably be expected to act otherwise. The court called for codification of the defence.

J.C. Smith called the case 'muddling' and 'inconsistent' ([1997] *Crim LR Report*, 499) because the courts have now accepted that psychological harm can amount to actual bodily harm or grievous bodily harm (Burstow [1997] UKHL 34).

→ **CROSS-REFERENCE**
For further discussion of psychological harm and ABH/GBH, see Chapter 10, 10.3.2 'Psychiatric Harm'.

A threat of false imprisonment in the absence of serious injury is also insufficient:

R v Van Dao (Vinh) [2012] EWCA CRIM 1717

Three workers at a cannabis factory were convicted of cultivating cannabis and possession of criminal property. Two appealed against conviction on the grounds that they had been duped into believing that they were to have been cleaners, not cultivators and that when they tried to leave they were threatened with violence so that their will had been overcome. They were locked in with no means of escape and their work had been under duress. Extending duress to a threat of false imprisonment would comply with Article 26 of the Council of Europe Convention on Action against Trafficking in Human Beings: non-punishment of victims of trafficking for involvement in unlawful activities under compulsion.

The Court of Appeal dismissed the appeal on the grounds that duress, on the facts, was fanciful. The defendants were found with mobile phones and keys to the building. But the view was expressed that a threat of imprisonment without an accompanying threat of serious harm would be insufficient, given the narrowness of the defence following *Hasan*.

Gross LJ:

> *Policy:* In our judgment, even if only provisionally, policy considerations point strongly towards confining the defence of duress to threats of death or serious injury and against extending the defence to treat threats of false imprisonment as sufficing. Our reasons follow. First, there are the difficulties of proof alluded to by Lord Bingham in *Z (supra)*, at [20] [*Z* was the sub-nom of *Hasan*]. These should not

be underestimated. If once the evidence is sufficient to permit the defence to be raised, the burden is on the prosecution to disprove it to the criminal standard. In practical terms, the defence may consist of little more than assertions, only expanded upon at trial. It would be all too easy to assert a threat of false imprisonment, especially if it is unnecessary for any such assertion to be underpinned by a threat of death or serious injury . . . Fourthly, confining the defence within its present relatively narrow limits does not preclude doing justice when sentencing, to reflect a defendant's true culpability even if, on the facts, falling short of the requirements for reliance on duress.

2. The threats must cause the crime but need not be the sole reason for acting

R v Valderrama-Vega [1985] CRIM LR 220 COURT OF APPEAL

D was charged with offences concerning the illegal importation of dangerous drugs. He pleaded duress on three grounds: that he had only committed the offence under threat of death from a Mafia-type organisation; that there had also been a threat to disclose his homosexual orientation and that he needed the money.

He was convicted and appealed. The Court of Appeal held that it was wrong to direct a jury that the death threats must be the only cause of the crime. Although the second and third reasons would have been insufficient alone, the defence was available if D acted because of the cumulative effects of all the threats. The appeal was allowed.

?! THINKING POINT 9.1

Which of the following threats do you think amounts to serious injury?

a. a broken arm/leg

a dislocated finger

one slap around the head

a hundred slaps around the head

an electric shock?

b. Economic ruin, damage to reputation, the destruction of a home or object with monetary or sentimental value?

3. The threat must be of immediate harm so that D could not reasonably be expected to take evasive action

Consider the following:

 EXAMPLE 9.1

a. D is told to commit a crime whilst a gun is pointing at his head or whilst his child or spouse are being held under threat of death.

b. X threatens D, 'I will shoot you unless you steal £500 from X by the end of the week.'

With a threat of imminent or future harm (as in b), D might be expected to go to the police. If it would be reasonable to do so, but D nevertheless commits theft through fear, the defence will be unavailable. Clearly, no such opportunity is possible in the case of the immediate threat in a.

The requirement of immediacy, excluding delay, has been recently reaffirmed by *R v Hasan* [2005] UKHL 22.

Previous authorities were divided on the meaning of 'immediacy'. Some, such as the two following cases, held that an uncertain delay following a threat can be just as compelling as an immediate one. If the rationale of the defence is to accommodate those whose will has been overborne, a short delay should not matter provided the reason for acting was D's fear of violence at some time in the future. *Hudson & Taylor* [1971] 2 QB 202 concerned two teenage girls who committed perjury (lying under oath in court) whilst giving evidence in a criminal trial against a violent gang, one of whom had threatened to 'cut them up'. Some members of the gang were in the public gallery at the time. Their appeal against conviction for perjury was allowed.

Lord Widgery CJ:

> It is essential to the defence of duress that the threat shall be effective at the moment when the crime is committed. The threat must be a 'present' threat in the sense that it is effective to neutralise the will of the accused at that time. . . . When, however, there is no opportunity for delaying tactics, and the person threatened must make up his mind whether he is to commit the criminal act or not, the existence at that moment of threats sufficient to destroy his will ought to provide him with a defence even though the threatened injury may not follow instantly, but after an interval. . . .
>
> The threats . . . were likely to be no less compelling because their execution could not be effected in the court room, if they could be carried out in the streets of Salford the same night.

Lord Widgery refused to confine the defence to situations where D was unable to go to the police. The guiding principle was the *reasonableness of D's actions in the circumstances*. This would include such factors as D's age, circumstances and the inherent risks.

Hudson had been followed by *Abdul Hussain & Others* [1999] Crim LR 570 (unreported) Court of Appeal where six Shiite Muslims, who had fled to Sudan from Southern Iraq, hijacked a plane to London. They had fled Iraq to Sudan through fear of government persecution and feared deportation back to Iraq. On appeal against convictions of hijacking on the grounds of duress of circumstances, the Court of Appeal held that although the feared violence was imminent rather than immediate, the significant factor was whether the threat had operated on their minds at the time of the offence so as to overbear their will. A period of delay was relevant but not conclusive as to whether D's will had been overborne. In the course of his judgment Rose LJ wisely remarked:

> [I]f Anne Frank had stolen a car to escape from Amsterdam and been charged with theft, the tenets of English law would not, in our judgment, have denied her a defence of duress of circumstances, on the ground that she should have waited for the Gestapo's knock on the door.

Both of these cases have been effectively overruled by *Hasan*, which has now decided that any delay at all between the threat and harm will be detrimental to the defence:

➔ CROSS-REFERENCE
The facts of *Hasan* are explained in 9.1.3.

R v Hasan [2005] UKHL 22 HOUSE OF LORDS

Lord Bingham:

The commonsense starting point of the common law is that adults of sound mind are ordinarily to be held responsible for the crimes which they commit. To this general principle there has, since the 14th century, been a recognised but limited exception in favour of those who commit crimes because they are forced or compelled to do so against their will by the threats of another. Such persons are said, in the language of the criminal law, to act as they do because they are subject to duress.

Where duress is established, it does not ordinarily operate to negative any legal ingredient of the crime which the defendant has committed. Nor is it now regarded as justifying the conduct of the defendant, as has in the past been suggested. . . . Duress is now properly to be regarded as a defence which, if established, excuses what would otherwise be criminal conduct: . . .

Duress affords a defence which, if raised and not disproved, exonerates the defendant altogether. It does not, like the defence of provocation to a charge of murder, serve merely to reduce the seriousness of the crime which the defendant has committed. And the victim of a crime committed under duress is not, like a person against whom a defendant uses force to defend himself, a person who has threatened the defendant or been perceived by the defendant as doing so. The victim of a crime committed under duress may be assumed to be morally innocent, having shown no hostility or aggression towards the defendant. The only criminal defences which have any close affinity with duress are necessity, where the force or compulsion is exerted not by human threats but by extraneous circumstances, and, perhaps, marital coercion under section 47 of the Criminal Justice Act 1925. . . .

I must acknowledge that the features of duress to which I have referred . . . incline me, where policy choices are to be made, towards tightening rather than relaxing the conditions to be met before duress may be successfully relied on. In doing so, I bear in mind in particular two observations of Lord Simon of Glaisdale in R v Lynch above (dissenting on the main ruling, which was reversed in R v Howe, above):

'. . . your Lordships should hesitate long lest you may be inscribing a charter for terrorists, gang-leaders and kidnappers.' (p 688).

'A sane system of criminal justice does not permit a subject to set up a countervailing system of sanctions or by terrorism to confer criminal immunity on his gang.' (p 696)

In *Perka v The Queen* [1984] 2 SCR 232, 250, Dickson J held that

'If the defence of necessity is to form a valid and consistent part of our criminal law it must, as has been universally recognised, be strictly controlled and scrupulously limited to situations that correspond to its underlying rationale.'

The recent English authorities have tended to lay stress on the requirement that a defendant should not have been able, without reasonably fearing execution of the threat, to avoid compliance. Thus Lord Morris of Borth-y-Gest in *R v Lynch*, above, at p 670, emphasised that duress

'must never be allowed to be the easy answer of those who can devise no other explanation of their conduct nor of those who readily could have avoided the dominance of threats nor of those who allow themselves to be at the disposal and under the sway of some gangster-tyrant.'

In the view of Lord Edmund-Davies (p 708) there had been

'for some years an unquestionable tendency towards progressive latitude in relation to the plea of duress.'

It should . . . be made clear to juries that if the retribution threatened against the defendant or his family or a person for whom he reasonably feels responsible is not such as he reasonably expects to follow immediately or almost immediately on his failure to comply with the threat, there may be little if any room for doubt that he could have taken evasive action, whether by going to the police or in some other way, to avoid committing the crime with which he is charged. [Emphasis added.]

By requiring immediacy, is there a risk that *Hasan* could lead to injustice? If duress now only applies to threats which are immediate or almost immediate, the opportunity for going to the police will hardly arise at all. But this denies two facts: that a person's will can be overborne no less by threats of future than immediate harm and that one can have good reason for not going to the police. Look at these examples:

EXAMPLE 9.2

1. D is a battered woman who is threatened with violence by her husband unless she par-ticipates in drug dealing the next day. She genuinely believes that she will be killed if she refuses to participate or goes to the police.

2. A forces Class A drugs on D and tells him to sell them. A threatens D that if he throws them away or goes to the police he and his family will be attacked. D intends to return the drugs to A but is arrested before he can do so (*Rahman* [2010] EWCA Crim 235).

3. D has experienced racism at the hands of the police in the past. He is threatened with serious harm unless he commits an offence the next day. In the belief that the police will not wish to help, he commits the crime.

In each case, taking D's circumstances into account, failure to go to the police might be consid-ered reasonable. *Hudson & Taylor* inclined towards this view. *Hasan* states that the issue, to the extent that it is relevant at all, must be reasonable according to the reasonable person. Thus, Rose LJ's wise statement in *Abdul Hussain* regarding Anne Frank may be no longer relevant. It would be unfortunate if objectively reasonable grounds for D's belief were regarded as inconsistent with the defence. It follows that a failure to seek police assistance over two and a half years of violent threats, causing D to commit VAT fraud offences, will be impermissible (*R v Batchelor* [2013] EWCA Crim 2638). This was, probably, always the case.

4. The threatener must nominate the crime

There must be a connection or *nexus* between the threat and the crime.

→ CROSS-REFERENCE
For discussion of voluntary association see 9.1.3.

R v Cole [1994] CRIM LR 582 COURT OF APPEAL

D robbed two building societies because he owed debts to money lenders who had threatened him, his girlfriend and child with violence. They had hit him with a baseball bat. He was convicted of robbery and appealed on the grounds of duress.

The Court of Appeal held that the necessary precondition of an imminent peril was lacking. More-over, duress by threats only applied when the threatener nominated the crime. The money lend-ers had not stipulated that D commit robbery to meet their demands.

However, as J.C. Smith in the Criminal Law Review commentary indicated, there is no difference between, 'Get the money from X building society or else', and 'How you get the money is up to you, but get it somehow or else'. If the rationale of the defence is overpowerment of will, D's will might be equally overpowered in either case.

5. The threat need not exist in fact so long as D reasonably fears that it does

This point raises two interconnected issues: whether the threat must exist in fact and the type of belief D needs to have in relation to it.

What matters is D's perception not actual reality.

R v Cairns [1999] CRIM LR 827 COURT OF APPEAL

D, believing that he was being followed by a threatening group, drove off, injuring V who had climbed on to the bonnet of his car. V fell off and D drove over him. V was seriously injured and D was charged with dangerous driving and grievous bodily harm contrary to s20 Offences Against the Person Act 1861. The group of friends were actually trying to prevent V from behaving as he did. D pleaded duress of circumstances. On appeal against conviction it was held that what mattered was D's reasonable belief in the threat not whether the threat actually existed in fact. This point was confirmed in *Safi* and *Hasan*.

R v Safi [2003] CRIM LR 721 COURT OF APPEAL

This was an appeal against convictions on a retrial for hijacking and weapons offences. Safi and eight others had hijacked an aircraft from Afghanistan to Stansted. Their appeal was based on duress: that they feared death and serious injury because other members of their organisation had been tortured by the Taliban. There were two issues:

1.   Did there need to be an actual threat/circumstances of duress in fact or merely a reasonable belief in one?

2.   If the latter, to whom did the belief need to be reasonable—a reasonable person or D?

The Court of Appeal held that the threat need not exist in reality. It noted the ease with which the defence might become a 'mask for anarchy', as with the wider defence of necessity. As we have seen, this was one of the reasons for tightening up the defence in *Hasan*. But the court in *Safi* considered that if public policy demanded the existence of an actual threat, it was for Parliament to change the law. The convictions were overturned because D's beliefs had been disregarded.

The risk of mistake as to whether a threat actually exists may be highest when it is indirect. Nonetheless, *Brandford* [2016] EWCA Crim 1794 held that a threat need not be delivered directly. In this case, it was conveyed to D by her boyfriend, who told her his life was threatened if the couple did not transport drugs. The Court of Appeal held that such 'hearsay' threats can support a defence of duress. However, D's appeal was dismissed as the threat was not sufficiently immediate and she had opportunity to escape; she had also voluntarily associated with known criminals.

6. A genuine belief in an immediate threat is sufficient

It follows from the preceding paragraphs that if D is genuinely mistaken about the existence of a non-existent threat, he should not be denied the defence. Or suppose that D, in hearing a threat uttered by X, mistakenly perceives it to be more threatening than it really is, and, on the strength of that mistake, proceeds to commit a crime. Or suppose that D thinks he is being pursued by a gang that he mistakenly perceives to be more threatening than it really is, as in *Cairns*. The following case confirms that any mistake need only be honest and need not be reasonable:

R v Martin (David Paul) [2000] CR APP R 42 COURT OF APPEAL

D, a paranoid schizophrenic, appealed against convictions of two robberies on the grounds of duress from two men. Psychiatric evidence was given at his trial that his condition would render him more likely to believe that he had been threatened and that the threats would be executed. The judge had directed the jury to assess D's belief according to what a mentally healthy reasonable man would have believed. This was held to be wrong. There was no requirement of reasonable grounds for D's mistake. He was to be judged on the facts as he believed them to be, whether his perception was reasonable or not.

> It is to be observed that Lord Simon [in *Graham*] left open the question whether or not the fear had to be well grounded and whether the words 'reasonable belief' should be tested subjectively or objectively. The passage cited from *Graham* might suggest the latter. However, Lord Lane considered that duress and self-defence were analogous. It is now accepted that 'the test to be applied for self-defence is that a person may use such force as is reasonable in the circumstances as he honestly believes them to be in the defence of himself or another' (see *Beckford v R* (1987) 85 Cr App Rep 378 . . .). The same subjective approach has been approved by this Court in case of duress of circumstances or duress of necessity (see *Cairns* (1999) 2 Cr App Rep 137 . . .) We cannot see that any distinction should be made in a case of straightforward duress by threats. It follows that in our view the learned judge was in error in directing the jury as he did with regard to the appellant's understanding or perception of the words alleged to have been used.

The House of Lords in *Hasan* did not overrule this case, but did consider that any belief must be both genuine and objectively reasonable. Lord Bingham:

> I am conscious that application of an objective reasonableness test to other ingredients of duress has attracted criticism . . . But since there is a choice to be made, policy in my view points towards an objective test of what the defendant, placed as he was and knowing what he did, ought reasonably to have foreseen. . . .
>
> . . . the words used in *R v Graham* and approved in *R v Howe* were 'he reasonably believed'. It is of course essential that the defendant should genuinely, ie. actually, believe in the efficacy of the threat by which he claims to have been compelled. But there is no warrant for relaxing the requirement that the belief must be reasonable as well as genuine. There can of course be no complaint of this departure from authority, which was favourable to the defendant.

If this is right, the status of *Martin* and *Safi* are in doubt. Hasan represents a return to a traditional and strictly objective approach to duress. In the interests of fairness, one hopes that the objective approach will not ignore that people can make mistakes in the heat of the moment.

It is worth noting here that the Law Commission in 'Murder, Manslaughter and Infanticide 2006 Part 6: Duress' (Law Com No 304, 2006) confirmed a view that Martin was correctly decided and, moreover, that Hasan cast no doubt upon it. The report stated that the particular circumstances of D should be taken into account in determining whether or not his or her belief was reasonably held. Thus, age, vulnerability and recognised psychiatric conditions should all be allowed on the question of D's belief.

The objective question

Would a sober person of reasonable firmness, sharing D's characteristics, have responded to D's belief in the same way?

D must satisfy the court not only that he reasonably believed in a violent threat, but that any reasonably brave person would have committed the crime with which he is charged. This part of the test is designed to exclude frivolous and false claims of duress. It mirrors the objective test in loss of control where a reasonable person of D's sex and age, with a normal degree of tolerance and self-restraint and in similar circumstances, might have reacted in the same or a similar way (s54(1)(c) Coroners and Justice Act 2009). The test in duress has always been interpreted strictly and few characteristics are permitted.

Physical characteristics: age and sex

The case of *Graham* held that the threat must be one which would overcome the will of an ordinary person of the *sex* and *age* of D, sharing such of D's characteristics as would affect the gravity of the threat to him. The case of *Bowen* below adds pregnancy and serious physical disability.

➜ **CROSS-REFERENCE**
For discussion of *Graham* see 9.1.2.

Mental characteristics

Timidity: The defence is not granted to the D who succumbs to a threat because he is naturally timid. The faint-hearted lack reasonable fortitude by definition.

Psychiatric conditions: The law admits only those conditions which are verifiable by medical classification to render D *less able to resist threats*, thereby excluding the naturally timid.

R v Bowen [1996] 2 CR APP R 157, [1996] CRIM LR 576 COURT OF APPEAL

D, a man with low IQ, was convicted of obtaining services by deception. He claimed that two men had threatened to petrol bomb his house unless he obtained the goods. Evidence was called at trial to show that he was abnormally vulnerable and suggestible. The judge refused to allow these characteristics to be put before the jury. D was convicted and appealed. The appeal was allowed on the following grounds:

1. Mere personality traits are to be excluded. Psychological evidence tending to show that D is more timid, pliable, vulnerable or susceptible to threats than a normal person will be excluded for it has no bearing on the question of characteristics. This confirms an earlier case of *Horne* [1994] *Crim LR* 584 in which it was decided that it was a contradiction in terms to ask whether a D of reasonable firmness who was also 'pliant or vulnerable' could have resisted the threat.

2. Characteristics due to self-induced abuse, such as alcohol, drugs or glue sniffing, are never relevant.

3. Any characteristic to be attributed to the reasonable person must be such as makes him less able to resist the threats than persons without that characteristic:

Stuart Smith LJ:

> The defendant may be in a category of persons who the jury may think less able to resist pressure than people not within that category. Obvious examples are age, where a young person may well not be so robust as a mature one; possibly sex, though many women would doubtless consider they had as much moral courage to resist pressure as men; pregnancy, where there is added fear for the unborn child; serious physical disability, which may inhibit self protection, recognised mental illness or psychiatric condition, such as post traumatic stress disorder leading to learned helplessness. . . .
>
> Psychiatric evidence may be admissible to show that the accused is suffering from some mental illness, mental impairment or recognised psychiatric condition provided persons generally suffering from such condition may be more susceptible to pressure and threats and thus to assist the jury in deciding whether a reasonable person suffering from such a condition might have been impelled to act as the defendant did. It is not admissible simply to show that in the doctor's opinion an accused, who is not suffering from such illness or condition, is especially timid, suggestible or vulnerable to pressure and threats.

NOTE 9.1

No mental illness or psychiatric condition will be allowed to modify the objective test unless it leads to 'learned helplessness'. This condition derives from the definition of Battered Woman Syndrome (BWS) which can be experienced by women who have suffered domestic abuse. There have been no successful reported appeals involving duress and BWS. The next case illustrates why.

R v GAC [2013] EWCA CRIM 1472

This was an appeal against importation of drugs by a 24-year-old mother of two on grounds of duress from her partner and BWS:

Lady Justice Hallett:

> Learned helplessness would be of particular relevance to a possible defence of duress. The term is used to describe the reaction of a victim to chronic and repeated abuse, whereby they feel that whatever they do nothing will change. They have no way of physically or emotionally breaking free from their abuser and the abuse. They cannot extricate themselves from the violent situation no matter how many cries for help they may make. They become increasingly passive. Traumatic bonding is the attachment that a victim has to their abusers which may make them supportive of the abuser and loyal to them. It may mean a victim will stay with their abuser through a variety of emotions but particularly through fear . . . It is essential to analyse, with some care, the extent and timing of the domestic violence, the impact upon the person concerned and their presentation at the relevant time . . .

Appeal dismissed.

This explanation may provide assistance in future cases. However, the appeal failed for lack of learned helplessness, which would appear to be far harder to establish than the conventional objective test in duress. Learned helplessness seems to be regarded as a preliminary obstacle which must be overcome if duress is to succeed (see also *Emery* (1992) 14 Cr App R 391). This makes the defence more complicated for abused women than for other defendants. Read this critique of the judgment in *GAC* by J. Loveless in '*R v GAC*: Battered Woman "Syndromization"' [2014] 9 *Crim LR* 655:

> The premise in the article is that BWS possesses insufficient scientific integrity for it to be relevant to criminal defences, a premise which may run counter to the prevailing body of scientific opinion on BWS. This is especially true of 'learned helplessness,' which is crucial not only to BWS, but also to the objective test of reasonable fortitude in duress when reliance is placed on a recognized mental illness or psychiatric condition such as post-traumatic stress disorder (PTSD) . . . the 'learned helplessness' theory was described, soon after BWS was launched into the world, as logically inconsistent, empirically vacuous, poorly substantiated and methodologically flawed . . . The focus on learned helplessness and passivity suggested an illness or clinical disorder, irrationality, emotional disturbance and that abused women are all the same. But it has been recognized for many years that there is no one model of how abused women respond to violence . . . Rigorous research over the last 30 years has now been conducted on many aspects of abused women's lives . . . such research shows that women who experience abuse are typically highly motivated to terminate the violence and vigorously engaged in seeking help. Consequently, the discourse of BWS and learned helplessness has now yielded to more contemporary understandings of the complex effects of, and responses to, abuse and many books have been written on this subject.

The article concludes by suggesting that, instead of looking for learned helplessness, a court should ask whether the woman's reactions were reasonable given her circumstances. Note that where duress has been accepted as a factor for women, it tends to operate so as to mitigate sentence rather than to acquit (eg: conditional discharge as in *Hudson & Taylor*). This, of course, reflects structural gender bias in duress, similar to self-defence and loss of control, both of which rely on 'reasonable' responses. Read the following by J. Loveless, 'Domestic Violence, Coercion and Duress' [2010] *Crim LR* 93:

> . . . [o]ver half of the 4000+ women in prison are the victims of domestic violence and one in three has suffered sexual abuse . . . 42% of a sample of 200 women prisoners reported recent histories of abuse . . . evidence from the US tells us that half of all US female inmates commit offences to avoid further battering . . . If this estimate is in any sense a reflection of what is happening in England and Wales then coercion of women by domestic violence is potentially an unrecognized problem . . . one interesting observation is that women rarely feature in reported cases on this defence and this leads to speculation that the defence may not be working for them . . . One reason may be that domestic violence can be all too easily perceived as 'falling short of duress' thus putting the defence out of their reach. It will be suggested that this is because the defence is based on the way in which men may more typically experience coercion through clearly identifiable specific threats of serious harm rather than by the incremental destruction of self-esteem characteristic of prolonged domestic violence. A court or jury will more readily identify with the reasonableness of a male response to a specific threat rather than with the reaction of a woman who has 'chosen' to remain with her abusive partner. She is far more likely to be perceived as weak and undeserving of legal protection . . . '

Marital coercion was an alternative defence available to married women between 1925 and 2014. Coercion implied psychological pressure rather than a threat of physical harm. It was, however, abolished by s177 Anti-social Behaviour, Crime and Policing Act 2014.

The narrow range of admissible characteristics in duress is considered to be unsatisfactory. Is it morally fair to exclude the timid and fearful from the defence? This could put the defence out of range of a good many ordinary people. Read the following from K.J.M. Smith, 'Duress & Steadfastness: In Pursuit of the Unintelligible' [1999] *Crim LR* 366:

> Why should someone of such a disposition be denied a defence granted to one with a 'recognised impairment' for example, evidence that a defendant was more susceptible to intimidation because of the long-term emotional damage caused by parental or spouse abuse would be deemed irrelevant to the issue of reasonable firmness. To be relevant not only must the defendant's condition be 'recognized' but it must also make the defendant 'more susceptible to pressure'. Thus in Emery (1992) 14 Cr App R 391, where the defendant claimed that long-term abuse had resulted in post-traumatic stress disorder, the court was concerned to find that the level of abuse was sufficient to have produced a 'condition of dependent helplessness'. More generally, are a person's age and sex relevant because of expectations as to their physical ability or moral courage? The specifically identified relevance of 'serious physical disability which may inhibit self-protection' appears to suggest the former. If this is true, an unqualified gender distinction makes no sense.

Further, it has been pointed out that medical classifications may be of limited use in determining which psychiatric conditions are capable of influencing susceptibility to threats. Read the following by A. Buchanan and G. Virgo, 'Duress & Mental Abnormality' [1999] *Crim LR* 528:

> Many psychiatric conditions are capable of influencing susceptibility to threats . . . The difficulty is that the value of a diagnostic label, in terms of distinguishing those abnormally susceptible to threats from the rest of the population, is limited. Classification in science serves many purposes. One cause of the confusion regarding the implications of psychiatric diagnosis is that classificatory systems de-

signed for one purpose are being used for another. Diagnostic categories designed to enable doctors to communicate with each other have been co-opted to enable the law to distinguish a group of people for whom a defence may be considered. . . . the absence of a mental disorder does not mean that someone's mental state at the time they acted was normal. Some victims of psychological trauma have no symptoms until they are placed in a situation which leads them to recall the traumatic event. . . . It follows that the test propounded by the Court of Appeal in *Bowen*, namely that the defendant's mental disorder will only be a relevant characteristic where it can be characterised as a recognised psychiatric condition, is unworkable and needs to be reformulated.

→ **CROSS-REFERENCE**
For discussion of the Law Commission recommendations see 9.1.6.

The Law Commission recommend retention of the *Bowen* characteristics except in respect of murder, to which they would extend duress.

?!   THINKING POINT 9.2

Which of the following characteristics would be admissible in relation to the standard of reasonable firmness to be expected of a reasonable person after *Bowen*:

- being 18;
- schizophrenia;
- mild depression/anxiety;
- weakness and timidity;
- weakness/timidity of grandmothers aged 57 or 75;
- low IQ;
- Battered Woman Syndrome;
- blindness;
- suicidal tendencies?

9.1.3 Limitations on the Defence: Voluntary Association with Criminals: *R v Hasan*

The defence will fail where D associates with others whom he knew or ought to have known might subject him to any compulsion through threats of violence.

It was always the case that the defence would fail where D freely associated with others whom he knew might coerce him, by violent threat, to commit a crime. This well-established principle first arose in *R v Fitzpatrick* [1977] NI 20, an IRA case in which D claimed to have been forced to participate in a robbery. The Northern Irish Court of Criminal Appeal held that voluntary exposure to *illegal compulsion* precluded the defence. This was extended to association with a gang of robbers (*R v Sharp* [1987] QB 853) and to a shoplifting gang (*R v Shepherd* (1987) 86 Cr App R 47). In each case, D knew of the potential for violence. However, there was disagreement as to whether the defence was available where D *ought* to have known but did not.

Further uncertainty concerned whether D had to know which type of crime he might be forced to commit. If he thought it was likely he would come under pressure to commit shoplifting, but was forced to commit an assault, would the defence succeed? *Baker & Ward* [1999] 2 Cr App R 335 held that it would. A heroin dealer was forced to commit robbery by his supplier. The Court of Appeal, taking a subjective approach, held that the defence would continue to be available to D where he was unaware of the risk of being forced to commit anything other than drug-related crimes. The Law Commission's Draft Criminal Code Bill 1989 and J.C. Smith ([2000] *Crim LR* 109) supported this approach:

> It is one thing . . . to be aware that you are likely to be beaten up if you do not pay your debts, it is another to be aware that you may be required under threat of violence to commit other, though unspecified, crimes if you do not . . . [I]t is presumably only the latter kind of foresight which rules out the defence.

All other authorities, however, had said the opposite.

Baker & Ward has now been firmly rejected by *Hasan* which has reasserted a strict objective approach. The defence will now fail where D knows or ought to have known that he would be subjected to *any compulsion* by threats of violence. The compulsion need not be to commit criminal activity.

R v Hasan [2005] UKHL 22 HOUSE OF LORDS

D worked for T who was involved in prostitution. Her boyfriend, S, was involved in the supply of drugs and had a reputation for violence. D alleged that S had boasted to him that he had committed three murders and had offered to show D a body in the boot of his car. D further alleged that he had been ambushed by S and an unknown man armed with a gun and made to carry out a burglary. He had been threatened by S with deadly consequences to himself and his family unless he did so. They drove D to a house, gave him a knife and forced him to commit a burglary. D broke into the house but ran off when he saw the occupier. D alleged that he had had no chance to go to the police. No harm had subsequently come to D's family. At D's trial for aggravated burglary he raised the defence of duress. He was convicted but this was overturned by the Court of Appeal on the authority of *Baker & Ward*. The defence should not fail where D does not foresee pressure to commit a crime of the kind with which he was charged.

The House of Lords unanimously and decisively dismissed this interpretation of the law. Lord Bingham gave the leading judgment:

> In its Working Paper No 55 of 1974, the Law Commission in para 26 favoured 'a limitation upon the defence [of duress] which would exclude its availability where the defendant had joined an association or conspiracy which was of such a character that he was aware that he might be *compelled to participate in offences of the type with which he is charged.*'. . .
>
> But there was no warrant for this gloss in any reported British authority until the Court of Appeal . . . gave judgment in *R v Baker and Ward* [1999] 2 Cr App R 335 [where] the appellants claimed that they had been specifically instructed to rob the particular store which they were convicted of robbing. . . .
>
> The principal issue between the Crown on one side and the appellant and the Court of Appeal on the other is whether *R v Baker and Ward* correctly stated the law. . . . The defendant is seeking to be wholly exonerated from the consequences of a crime deliberately committed. . . . The defendant is, *ex hypothesi*, a person who has voluntarily surrendered his will to the domination of another. Nothing should turn on foresight of the manner in which, in the event, the dominant party chooses to exploit the defendant's subservience. There need not be foresight of coercion to commit crimes, although it is not easy to envisage circumstances in which a party might be coerced to act lawfully. In holding that there must be foresight of coercion to commit crimes of the kind with which the defendant is charged, *R v Baker and Ward* mis-stated the law.
>
> There remains the question, which the Court of Appeal left open in . . . their judgment, whether the defendant's foresight must be judged by a subjective or an objective test. . . . *since there is a choice to be made, policy in my view points towards an objective test of what the defendant, placed as he was and knowing what he did, ought reasonably to have foreseen. I am not persuaded otherwise by*

analogies based on self-defence or provocation for reasons I have already given. The policy of the law must be to discourage association with known criminals, and it should be slow to excuse the criminal conduct of those who do so. If a person voluntarily becomes or remains associated with others engaged in criminal activity in a situation where he knows or ought reasonably to know that he may be the subject of compulsion by them or their associates, he cannot rely on the defence of duress to excuse any act which he is thereafter compelled to do by them. . . .

I would answer this certified question by saying that the defence of duress is excluded when as a result of the accused's voluntary association with others engaged in criminal activity he foresaw or ought reasonably to have foreseen the risk of being subjected to any compulsion by threats of violence. [Emphasis added.]

 NOTE 9.2

1. It is not necessary that D foresaw, or ought to have foreseen, compulsion to commit a crime, only the risk of compulsion to do anything by threats of violence. It is the *risk* that must be foreseen rather than the nature of the activity. This was a policy decision taken in light of the increasing frequency with which the defence was being used, particularly in drugs cases.

2. The test of foresight is objective. It will not matter that D did not foresee the risk of compulsion provided a reasonable person would have been aware of it.

   There are probably very few situations where involvement with criminals would not give rise to the suspicion of violence or compulsion but consider the following:

   D regularly smokes cannabis for medicinal purposes, supplied by X for altruistic reasons. X unwisely fritters away D's payments and gets into debt with his supplier. Under pressure and not knowing what to do, X threatens D with violence unless D steals some money from the local post office to satisfy X's debt. D does so through fear. It might be reasonable to assume that D did not know that he was associating with a violent criminal until that point.

3. Baroness Hale was in broad agreement with Lord Bingham, subject to some important qualifications:

   I accept that even the person with a knife at her back has a choice whether or not to do as the knifeman says. The question is whether she should have resisted the threat. But, perhaps because I am a reasonable but comparatively weak and fearful grandmother, I do not understand why the defendant's beliefs and personal characteristics are not morally relevant to whether she could reasonably have been expected to resist. . . .

   There are, however, two other questions.

   The first is that the cases tend to talk about exposing oneself to the risk of 'unlawful violence'. That, it seems to me, is not enough. The foreseeable risk should be one of duress: that is, of threats of such severity, plausibility and immediacy that one might be compelled to do that which one would otherwise have chosen not to do. The battered wife knows that she is exposing herself to a risk of unlawful violence if she stays, but she may have no reason to believe that her husband will eventually use her broken will to force her to commit crimes. For the same reason, I would say that it must be foreseeable that duress will be used to compel the person to commit crimes of some sort. I have no difficulty envisaging circumstances in which a person may be coerced to act lawfully. The battered wife knows very well that she may be compelled to cook the dinner, wash the dishes, iron the shirts and submit to sexual intercourse. That should not deprive her of the defence of duress if she is obliged by the same threats to herself or her children to commit perjury or shoplift for food.

But this brings me to a concern which I have had throughout this case. It is one thing to deny the defence to people who choose to become members of illegal organisations, join criminal gangs, or engage with others in drug-related criminality. It is another thing to deny it to someone who has a quite different reason for becoming associated with the duressor and then finds it difficult to escape. I do not believe that this limitation on the defence is aimed at battered wives at all, or at others in close personal or family relationships with their duressors and their associates, such as their mothers, brothers or children. The Law Commission's Bills all refer to a person who exposes himself to the risk 'without reasonable excuse'. The words were there to cater for the police infiltrator (see Law Com No 83, para 2.37) but they are also applicable to the sort of association I have in mind.

4. Baroness Hale would have preferred a subjective approach to voluntary association assessed by reference to the circumstances as D believed them to be. She drew attention to the risk of excluding from an objectively determined duress the victims of domestic violence. They associate with a duressor for reasons other than criminal activity but are then victimised and find it difficult to escape.

5. Baroness Hale would only deny duress to those who knew they might be compelled to commit crimes. Simple exposure to the risk of violence was insufficient. She would therefore have preferred a wider defence.

A subjective approach to this issue would permit individual standards of fortitude to be taken into account. It has been said that this is fairer to the individual and more just, bringing the law within the reach of the ordinary person. Read this from 'Necessity, Duress and Self-Defence' by D.W. Elliott [1989] *Crim LR* 610:

If D is to be excused in respect of his reaction to pressure, that reaction must have been reasonable by objective standards. But the statement of the policy in *Graham* requires that D's appreciation of the factual situation he is in must also be reasonable, and that does not follow from the policy. A person who yields to a strong but imaginary fear may be stupid in imagining it, but he is no more blameworthy than one whose fear is based on reasonable grounds . . . The requirement that mistake must be reasonable is also inconsistent with the rule as to self-defence and prevention of crime . . . [where] the judges have since laboriously laid down the wholly different rule, that D is to be judged on the facts as he reasonably or unreasonably saw them; *Williams, Beckford*.

9.1.4 Limitations on the Defence: Murder, Attempted Murder and Treason

Duress is not currently a defence to murder, attempted murder or treason. There was previously judicial disagreement as to whether it should apply or not.

In *Lynch v DPP for NI* [1975] 1 All ER 913 D was threatened with violence unless he drove an IRA gunman to a place where a policeman was to be shot. Lynch did so and then drove the gunman away. He claimed that he believed he would be shot if he had disobeyed the order. In establishing the general principles of the defence, the House of Lords held that duress was available to a secondary party to murder.

In *Abbot v R* [1976] 3 All ER 140, the Privy Council held that duress was not available to principals to murder. D had been threatened with his own and his mother's death unless he participated in a murder. He dug a hole and held V as she was stabbed by another. She was left dying in the hole which D helped to fill in whilst V was still alive. She died from the stab wounds and inhalation of dirt. D's argument that he was only a secondary party was rejected. He was considered to have been a principal in the first degree to which duress should be no defence.

Graham [1982] followed but since there was insufficient evidence of duress, it was not necessary for the court to do any more than set down general principles. The leading authority on duress and murder remains the following:

R v Howe & Bannister [1987] 2 WLR 568 HOUSE OF LORDS

Howe and Bannister had participated with two others, Murray and Bailey, in the torture, sexual assault and killing of two 17- and 19-year-old boys. They had participated in the assault of the first victim but did not kill him. They jointly strangled the second victim. They were both charged with murder and conspiracy to murder and pleaded duress on the grounds that they feared for their lives as a result of threats from one of the others. They were convicted and appealed.

The House confirmed the test for duress as set out in *Graham* but denied that it should be available for murder. In the course of the leading judgment, Lord Hailsham had to reconcile the earlier cases of *Lynch* and *Abbot*.

Lord Hailsham LC:

> I begin by affirming that, while there can never be a direct correspondence between law and morality, an attempt to divorce the two entirely is and has always proved to be doomed to failure, and, in the present case, the overriding objects of the criminal law must be to protect innocent lives and to set a standard of conduct which ordinary men and women are expected to observe if they are to avoid criminal responsibility . . .
>
> In general, I must say that I do not at all accept in relation to the defence of murder it is either good morals, good policy or good law to suggest, as did the majority in *Lynch* and the minority in *Abbott* that the ordinary man of reasonable fortitude is not supposed to be capable of heroism if he is asked to take an innocent life rather than sacrifice his own . . . . I have known in my own lifetime of too many acts of heroism by ordinary human beings of no more than ordinary fortitude to regard a law as either 'just or humane' which withdraws the protection of the criminal law from the innocent victim and casts the cloak of its protection upon the coward and the poltroon in the name of a 'concession to human frailty'. . . . But surely I am entitled to believe that some degree of proportionality between the threat and the offence must, at least to some extent, be a prerequisite of the defence under existing law. Few would resist threats to the life of a loved one if the alternative were driving across the red lights or in excess of 70 mph on the motorway. But . . . it would take rather more than the threat of a slap on the wrist or even moderate pain or injury to discharge the evidential burden even in the case of a fairly serious assault. In such a case the 'concession to human frailty' is no more than to say that in such circumstances a reasonable man of average courage is entitled to embrace as a matter of choice the alternative which a reasonable man would regard as the lesser of two evils. *Other considerations necessarily arise where the choice is between the threat of death or a fortiori of serious injury and deliberately taking an innocent life. In such a case a reasonable man might reflect that one innocent human life is at least as valuable as his own or that of his loved one. In such a case a man cannot claim that he is choosing the lesser of two evils. Instead he is embracing the cognate but morally disreputable principle that the end justifies the means.* [Emphasis added.]

Lord Griffiths agreed with Lord Hailsham that duress should be denied both to principal offenders (ie: actual killers) and to accomplices, for the latter can be morally less deserving than principals, for example: the contract killer or the intelligent man who manipulates a weak-minded individual to kill.

Lord Griffiths:

> We face a rising tide of violence and terrorism against which the law must stand firm recognising that its highest duty is to protect the freedom and lives of those that live under it. The sanctity of human life lies at the root of the ideal and I would do nothing to undermine it, be it ever so slight . . .

NOTE 9.3

1. Following *Howe*, duress is never a defence to murder, whatever the circumstances. *Howe* rejected an alternative view, proposed in the Court of Appeal by Lord Lane CJ, that duress might be mitigated to manslaughter.

2. Morality and proportionality were the most significant reasons for denying the defence to murder. It is here that one sees justificatory or utilitarian arguments pervading the issues (ie: rational balancing of harms to protect the safety of society).

3. Excluding murder from duress poses an inconsistency with other serious offences, particularly grievous bodily harm with intent contrary to s18 Offences Against the Person Act 1861. If D, under threat, seriously *injures* V intending GBH, duress is available. If V *dies* from his injuries and D is charged with murder on the basis of an intent to commit GBH, duress is unavailable. This is illogical.

4. Lord Hailsham did not consider the plight of someone whose entire family will be shot unless he kills a single victim. In this respect, he considered that sympathetic cases would be dealt with by administrative procedures (ie: they would never be prosecuted or lenient sentences would be preferred). Such measures would of course be discretionary.

?! THINKING POINT 9.3

1. Do you think that ordinary people are heroes?
2. What moral principle is reflected in *Howe's* stance on duress?
3. Is there a 'social good' or utilitarian principle to the judgment?
4. If you were threatened that your two children would be shot unless you shot a stranger, what would you do? Would duress provide a defence?

The decision to exclude murder from duress was partly based on the old precedent of *Dudley & Stephens*, a case of necessity which is an analogous defence in the sense that D faces a choice between competing harms. Because of its importance in relation to duress and murder we will examine it here.

R v Dudley & Stephens (1884) 14 QBD 273 QUEEN'S BENCH DIVISION

Three men and a 17-year-old cabin boy were shipwrecked in the South Atlantic more than a thousand miles from land. They were drifting in an open life-raft and what little food they had, two tins of turnips, was quickly eaten. After 18 days one mariner proposed to another that they should draw lots to see who should be killed and eaten so that the other three should live. They had had no food for seven days and no water for five. On the twentieth day, the mariners killed the boy, who was close to death, and fed on his body. Four days later they were rescued. Two mariners were put on trial for murder upon their return to England. Their defence was that at the time of the cabin-boy's death there was no reasonable prospect of rescue and that they were all likely to die of starvation. The jury returned a special verdict: that the two men would probably have died before rescue if they had not eaten the boy, who would have likely died sooner, but there was no greater necessity to kill him than any of the others. They were sentenced to death.

The court rejected their appeal but the death sentence was commuted to six months' imprisonment with no hard labour. However, the judgment left considerable doubt about the defence of necessity and murder.

Coleridge LJ:

> . . . it appears sufficiently that the prisoners were subject to terrible temptation, to sufferings which might break down the bodily power of the strongest man, and try the conscience of the best . . . . But nevertheless this is clear, that the prisoners put to death a weak and unoffending boy upon the chance of preserving their own lives by feeding upon his flesh and blood after he was killed, and with the certainty of depriving him of any possible chance of survival . . . . They might possibly have been picked up next day by a passing ship; they might possibly not have been picked up at all; in either case it is obvious that the killing of the boy would have been an unnecessary and profitless act . . . .
>
> Now it is admitted that the deliberate killing of this unoffending and unresisting boy was clearly murder, unless the killing can be justified by some well-recognized excuse admitted by the law. It is further admitted that there was in this case no such excuse, unless the killing was justified by what has been called 'necessity'. But the temptation to the act which existed here was not what the law has ever called necessity. Nor is this to be regretted. Though law and morality are not the same, and many things may be immoral which are not necessarily illegal, yet the absolute divorce of law from morality would be of fatal consequence; and divorce would follow if the temptation to murder in this case were to be held by law an absolute defence of it. It is not so. To preserve one's life is generally speaking a duty, but it may be the plainest and the highest duty to sacrifice it. War is full of instances in which it is a man's duty not to live, but to die . . . . It is not correct, therefore, to say that there is any absolute or unqualified necessity to preserve one's life . . . . *Who is to be the judge of this sort of necessity? By what measure is the comparative value of lives to be measured: Is it to be strength, or intellect, or what? . . . In this case the youngest, the most unresisting, was chosen. Was it more necessary to kill him than one of the grown men? The answer must be 'No' . . . .*
>
> *We are often compelled to set up standards we cannot reach ourselves, and to lay down rules which we could not ourselves satisfy. But a man has no right to declare temptation to be an excuse, though he might have yielded to it, nor allow compassion for the criminal to change or weaken in any manner the legal definition of the crime . . .* [Emphasis added.]

 NOTE 9.4

There are two possible interpretations of Coleridge LJ's judgment:

That the men's suffering would have provided an excuse for killing, but there was no more necessity to kill the cabin boy than any of the others and that, in the absence of an obvious victim, necessity would afford no defence to murder. It followed that necessity might justify murder if it was clear from the threat which innocent victim had to die.

That necessity could never justify murder, regardless of the circumstances. Society needed to be protected from survival cannibalism and other atrocious crimes—a utilitarian argument (ie: the greater good).

It is hard to reconcile Coleridge LJ's conflicting sentiments of sympathy and morality.

A. Norrie on this case from *Crime, Reason and History: A Critical Introduction to Criminal Law*, 2nd edn, Cambridge University Press, at p 159:

In general, the reasoning in the case conflates questions of justification and excuse . . . . These observations all relate to the terrible position of the accused, not the justifiability of their acts. Having recognised the plight of the men, Lord Coleridge's tone shifts significantly . . . . Lord Coleridge expresses compassion for the accused in terms of a morality that recognises normal human standards of conduct, but he nonetheless condemns them in terms of an Old Testament morality for their lack, not of normal human standards, but of heroism. These are the main arguments, but behind these shifts in moral gear there is a narrower but without doubt significant utilitarian consideration . . . . Dudley and Stephens must be condemned both for their lack of heroism and to secure the greater social good . . . . Thus arguments of moral principle and utility both cancel out moral compassion and the excuse of necessity.

There is however paradox in this grandiloquence . . . . Dudley and Stephens must be condemned but at the same time he recommends 'to the Sovereign to exercise that prerogative of mercy which the Constitution has entrusted to the hands fittest to dispense it.' Who could this judgment satisfy? . . . Simpson (1986) in fact tells us that the impact of the case upon the seafaring communities was to confirm that survival cannibalism was acceptable . . . .

What did the judges of the Queen's Bench Division really know of the plight of shipwrecked and starving people, or of the judgment of the seafaring communities on such situations? In the nineteenth-century world of the sailing ships, survival cannibalism was a not uncommon phenomenon sanctioned by the custom and morality of the sea. Public attitudes to the particular plight of Dudley and Stephens were 'all one way' in favour of the accused . . . By contrast it was only among the literate upper classes that there was support for the prosecution, with the Home Secretary agreeing to it to negate 'the popular idea that Dudley was a hero'. Even the dead boy's family bore no ill will to the two accused . . . '

Upon this shaky precedent, the House of Lords in *Howe* decided that duress should be no defence to murder. This harsh rule cannot be lifted even for children. In *R v W* [2007] EWCA Crim 1251 the Court of Appeal held that a 13-year-old boy had no defence to murder even though he had complied with his father's instruction through fear. It follows that duress should also not apply to attempted murder:

R v Gotts [1992] 1 ALL ER 832 HOUSE OF LORDS

D, aged 16, was threatened with death by his father unless he killed his mother who had fled to a refuge for battered women with her two other children to escape her husband's violence. D stabbed his mother and he was charged with attempted murder. The trial judge ruled that duress was not a defence to attempted murder. D pleaded guilty and appealed. The trial judge's ruling was upheld by both the Court of Appeal and the House of Lords.

This was a majority House of Lords judgment 3:2. The leading judgment was given by Lord Jauncey who observed that there was no precedent on the question of whether duress should apply to attempted murder. Therefore the decision was really one of policy:

> As Lord Griffiths pointed out in [*Howe*, at p.303] an intent to kill must be proved in the case of attempted murder but not necessarily in the case of murder. Is there logic in affording the defence to one who intends to kill but fails and denying it to one who mistakenly kills intending only to injure? . . .
>
> It is of course true that withholding the defence in any circumstances will create some anomalies but I would agree with Lord Griffiths . . . that nothing should be done to undermine in any way the highest duty of the law to protect the freedom and lives of those that live under it.

The question of whether D's response to the death threat from his father was reasonable given his age was not considered. There was to be a blanket exclusion of the defence from attempted murder regardless of D's excusing factors.

All judges were in agreement that Parliament should review the defence and consider whether it should be extended to all crimes.

The minority judgment of Lord Lowry highlighted the illogicality of the exclusion from calculated, attempted murder. It would provide no deterrent since one who sets out intending to murder and succeeds will be denied duress under Howe:

> To withhold in respect of *every* crime the defence of duress, leaving it to the court . . . . to take mitigating circumstances into account, seems logical. But to withhold that defence only from a selected list of serious crimes . . . . is questionable from a sentencing point of view, as indeed the sentence in the present case shows. The defence is withheld on the ground that the crime is so odious that it must not be palliated; and yet, if circumstances are allowed to mitigate the punishment, the principle on which the defence of duress is withheld has been defeated.

However, duress remains a defence to conspiracy to murder, thus highlighting the illogicality of denying it to murder and attempted murder.

EXAMPLE 9.3

A agrees with B, under threat of serious injury, to shoot V dead. A is arrested as he aims a gun at V. A will be denied the defence of duress to attempted murder but will be allowed it in relation to conspiracy to murder (subject, of course, to the limitation regarding voluntary association).

?!   THINKING POINT 9.4

Are all murders morally the same? Do you think that any of the following murders are morally justifiable? Should duress be allowed?

■ A mother kills X when her child, who is being held hostage, is threatened with death.

■ A young child is threatened with death by his psychotic father if he does not assist in killing his mother.

■ A pregnant woman kills X rather than submit to being killed, in order to save the life of her unborn child.

■ A woman subject to domestic violence from her husband assists in killing his adversary.

Should duress be a defence to these murders?

Reform of duress and murder

The Law Commission in 'Legislating the Criminal Code; Offences Against the Person and General Principles' (Law Com No 218, 1993) paras 31.1–31.8 thought that duress should be available to both murder and attempted murder. Lord Bingham in *Hasan* was of a similar view, stating that '[t]he logic of this argument is irresistible'.

In the Law Commission's 'A New Homicide Act for England and Wales?' (CP No 177, 2005) the extension of duress/duress of circumstances as partial defences to first degree murder and attempted murder was proposed. Recall that this document proposed restructuring homicide so as to form a ladder of offences.

In, 'Murder, Manslaughter and Infanticide' (Law Com No 304, 2006) Part 6: Duress, the Law Commission recommended:

> We recommend that for duress to be a full defence to first degree murder, second degree murder and at-tempted murder, the threat must be one of death or life threatening harm . . . .
>
> We recommend that on a charge of first degree murder, second degree murder and attempted murder the defendant should bear the legal burden of proving the qualifying conditions of the defence of duress on a balance of probabilities. [para. 9.23]
>
> The argument that duress should be a full defence to first degree murder has a moral basis. It is that the law should not stigmatise a person who, on the basis of a genuine and reasonably held belief, intentionally killed in fear of death or life-threatening injury in circumstances where a jury is satis-fied that an ordinary person of reasonable fortitude might have acted in the same way. If a reasonable person might have acted as D did, then the argument for withholding a complete defence is under-mined. In the words of Professor Ormerod, 'if the jury find that the defendant has, within the terms of the defence, acted reasonably, it seems unfair to treat him as a second degree murderer or even a manslaughterer'. [paras 6.41 and 6.43] [Emphasis added.]

➜ CROSS-REFERENCE
For further discussion of the Law Commission proposals see Chapter 3, 3.3.6 and Chapter 6, 6.5.

Duress and the partial defences

In recommending that duress/duress of circumstances should be complete (not partial) defences to all types of homicide for both principals and accomplices, the Report goes further than the recommendation in respect of provocation (now loss of control) and diminished responsibility which will continue to provide partial defences to first degree murder resulting in liability for second degree murder and not manslaughter as under the current law.

One justification is that under the partial defences, D has not killed in order to save innocent life. More importantly, some cases of duress are closer to a justification rather than an excuse, for example: the mountaineer who cuts the rope to prevent both the dangling companion and himself from being pulled over the precipice. Duress also involves 'a more calculated choice', rather than the more instantaneous killing under provocation (para 6.78).

Reversing the burden of proof under the ECHR

The reversal of the burden of proof was justified on the grounds that the defence presents difficulties for the prosecution in disproving it beyond all reasonable doubt.

Read the following criticisms by A. Ashworth, 'Principles, Pragmatism and the Law Commission' [2007] *Crim LR* 333:

> If duress is to be a complete defence, it is understandable that it should be tightly defined, as the House of Lords has insisted. This leads the Commission to insist that the threat must be believed to be life-threatening, and that D's belief that the threat has been made must be based on reasonable grounds. The latter stipulation applies the anomalous and under-reasoned decision in *Graham*. The Commission supports this on the ground that, compared with provocation and self-defence (which have no such reasonableness requirement), there is a less immediate temporal or physical nexus between the threat and the killing in duress cases. This also becomes the primary argument in favour of transferring the burden of proving duress to the defendant in homicide cases – that the separation of the making of the threat from the killing creates extra difficulties for the prosecution. Is this right? Whereas on provocation and diminished responsibility there has been research, on duress we merely have the unsupported assertion that this occurs 'in many cases'. Moreover, the House of Lords held that the carrying out of the threat must be immediately in prospect (so the temporal separation cannot be great), and the Commission fails to give sufficient recognition to the great emotional turmoil brought about by threats of this magnitude, not least when directed at family members. Thus the Commission's argument that the reasonableness requirement is right because the duressee usually has 'time to reflect' does not convince; and its claims about the relative difficulties of proving the qualifying conditions of duress are inadequately grounded.

On the reversed burden of proof, the author continues:

> The Commission claims that proof is particularly difficult in the few cases relating to acts done outside the jurisdiction; if substantiated, it is not clear that this is good reason for reversing the burden of proof in the majority of cases, not to mention cases where young or vulnerable duressees are involved . . . When the most serious of criminal offences is the focus, no one should be liable to conviction for failing to establish their innocence.

9.1.5 Duress of Circumstances

The test for duress of circumstances is identical to duress:

■ Was D forced to act as he did because of a reasonable fear of death or personal injury?

■ Would a sober person of reasonable firmness, sharing D's characteristics, have responded to D's belief in the same way?

Purpose: To provide a complete defence to those whose will is overborne through fear of death or serious violence arising from a *circumstantial* threat.

This defence may be seen as an outgrowth of duress except that the feared violence or death arises not from a direct personal threat but from circumstances perceived to be threatening. Given that the two defences are essentially concerned with the impact of coercion upon D's will, the distinction is in reality only in name. The plea will only succeed if the offence is:

- a proportionate response to the feared violence. No more must be done than is absolutely necessary to avoid the threat;
- not murder, attempted murder or treason, which are excluded.

The rationale of the defence is that it would be wrong to allow a defence to one whose will was overborne where the threat was personal and to deny it where the threat was circumstantial. The defence is excusatory.

Duress of circumstances is sometimes difficult to distinguish from necessity. Necessity is recognised where D is free to choose between an offence, as the lesser of two competing harms, or risk greater harm. The choice is between competing values and may be seen as morally justifiable. The threat need not be criminal in nature and D's will need not be overborne by emergency.

The earliest cases in which it was recognised that one might commit a crime under circumstantial as opposed to personal threat were all concerned with driving. By 1994 the defence was declared to be of general application to all offences except as mentioned above.

R v Willer (1986) 83 CR APP R 225 COURT OF APPEAL

D was driving his car around Hemel Hempstead. With him were two school friends. They came across a gang of 20 or 30 aggressive youths in a narrow alleyway. D heard one shout threats to kill both himself and one of his passengers. D stopped and tried to turn the car around. The youths set upon the passenger in the rear of the car. D then drove to the local police station through a shopping precinct, the fighting in the back of the car still going on. He was charged with reckless driving. At his trial, D claimed his actions had been necessary to escape harm to person and property.

Watkins LJ:

> Thus the defence of duress, it seems to us, arose but was not pursued. What ought to have happened here, therefore, was that the assistant recorder on those facts should have directed that he would leave to the jury the question whether or not on the outward or the return journey, or both, the appellant was wholly driven by force of circumstances into doing what he did and did not drive the car otherwise than under that form of compulsion.

Appeal allowed.

No precedents were mentioned in the judgment. There followed more cases in which the defence of duress of circumstances was recognised as a defence to reckless driving. For instance, in *Conway* [1989] QB 290 the *Graham* test was followed by Woolf LJ. D's passenger had been shot at previously and on the day of the offence two men ran towards D's car in which the passenger was sitting. D drove off at speed and was apprehended for reckless driving. The two men were plainclothed police officers who wished to question the passenger. The defence succeeded.

These cases appeared to cast doubt on the state of the law as observed by Lord Denning in an earlier case: *Buckoke v GLC* [1971] 2 All ER 254 in which he had said that a fireman who drove through a red light in order to rescue a man from a burning building 200 yards down the road, rather than risk the man's life by waiting for the lights to change, would commit a traffic regulation offence and necessity would be no defence. Necessity was not recognised as a defence at that time on the grounds that it might be seen as encouragement to self-help with consequent anarchic results. Duress of circumstances was a narrower aspect of necessity.

Following *Conway*, general principles of duress of circumstances were set down in the following case:

R v Martin [1989] 1 ALL ER 652 COURT OF APPEAL

D had pleaded guilty to driving whilst disqualified. D's stepson was late for work and risked losing his job. D's wife, who had suicidal tendencies, threatened to commit suicide if D did not drive the son to work. D believed her threat and drove even though he was disqualified. He was stopped by the police within about a quarter of a mile from the house. The Court of Appeal held that D might have had a defence which ought to have been left to the jury.

Simon Brown LJ:

> The authorities are now clear. Their effect is perhaps most conveniently to be found in the judgment of this court in *R v Conway* [1988] 3 All ER 1025. The decision reviews earlier relevant authorities . . . . first, English law does, in extreme circumstances, recognize a defence of necessity. Most commonly this defence arises as duress, that is pressure on the accused's will from the wrongful threats or violence of another. Equally however it can arise from other objective dangers threatening the accused or others. Arising thus it is conveniently called 'duress of circumstances.'
>
> Second, the defence is available only if, from an objective standpoint, the accused can be said to be acting reasonably and proportionately in order to avoid a threat of death or serious injury.
>
> Third, assuming the defence to be open to the accused on his account of the facts, the issue should be left to the jury, who should be directed to determine these two questions: first, was the accused, or may he have been, impelled to act as he did because as a result of what he reasonably believed to be the situation he had good cause to fear that otherwise death or serious physical injury would result; second, if so, would a sober person of reasonable firmness, sharing the characteristics of the accused, have responded to that situation by acting as the accused did? If the answer to both those questions was Yes, then the jury would acquit; the defence of necessity would have been established.

The general principles of the defence were parallel with those of duress by threats. Duress of circumstances was held to be of general application to all criminal offences, except murder, attempted murder and treason, in the following case:

R v Pommell [1995] 2 CR APP R 607 COURT OF APPEAL

D was charged with being in possession of a sub-machine gun, contrary to s5(1)(a) Firearms Act 1968, and 55 rounds of ammunition without a firearm certificate contrary to s1(1)(b) of the Act. His explanation was that he had taken the gun off a friend, Erroll, who had visited him the previous night. Erroll was going to shoot some people whom he thought had killed a friend. He was going to give the gun to his brother in the morning so that he could hand it to the police. Necessity was argued at trial but it was rejected. D appealed.

Kennedy LJ:

> '. . . There is an obvious attraction in the argument that if A finds B in possession of a gun which he is about to use to commit a crime, and if A is then able to persuade B to hand over the gun so that A may hand it to the police, A should not immediately upon taking possession of the gun become guilty of a criminal offence . . .
>
> The strength of the argument that a person ought to be permitted to breach the letter of the criminal law in order to prevent a greater evil befalling himself or others has long been recognised (see, for example, *Stephen's Digest of Criminal Law*), but it has, in English law, not given rise to a recognised general defence of necessity . . . '

His Lordship then reviewed the previous road traffic authorities of *Willer* [1986], *Conway* [1989], *Martin* [1989] and *Bell* [1992].

> Commenting on the case of *Bell*, Professor Sir John Smith has written:
>> All the cases so far have concerned road traffic offences but there are no grounds for supposing that the defence is limited to that kind of case. On the contrary, the defence, being closely related to the defence of duress by threats, appears to be general, applying to all crimes except murder, attempted murder and some forms of treason, . . . see [1992] Crim LR 176.
>> We agree . . . . That leads to the conclusion that in the present case the defence was open to the appellant in respect of his acquisition of the gun. The jury would have to be directed to determine the two questions identified in the passage which we have cited from the judgment in *Martin*. That leaves the question as to his continued possession of the gun thereafter. In our judgment, the test laid down in *Martin* may not be satisfied: there would then be no immediate fear of death or serious injury. In our judgment, a person who has taken possession of a gun in circumstances where he has the defence of duress by circumstances must 'desist from committing the crime as soon as he reasonably can.

However, the court concluded that the delay and reloading of the gun ought not to have denied D the defence which should have been put to the jury. The appeal was allowed.

?! THINKING POINT 9.5

Consider whether duress of circumstances applies to the following:

- D was approached in his car by a plain-clothed police officer. He thought he was going to be attacked and drove away at high speed. He was charged with reckless driving.
- D, who had been assaulted by her husband and threatened with death, drove 72 miles to her home town whilst intoxicated in order to escape. Would it make any difference if she had only driven to the nearest place of safety?
- D was forced to drive whilst drunk in order to escape from a threatened arson attack on her home.

SECTION SUMMARY

- *Duress/duress of circumstances are two excusatory defences to crimes committed under threat where D's will has been overborne.*
- *In duress, the threat is from a person whereas in duress of circumstances the threat is from the circumstances.*
- *They are complete defences to all crimes apart from murder, attempted murder and treason.*
- *The test for each consists of two questions: (1) did D reasonably believe in a threat of death or serious injury; and (2) would a sober person of reasonable firmness, sharing such of D's characteristics as are relevant, have responded to the threats in the same way?*

General principles of duress:

- *The threatened harm must be immediate or almost immediate.*
- *They need not be the sole reason for acting.*
- *There must be a connection between the threat and the offence.*
- *The threat need not exist in fact so long as D believes that it does.*
- *D's belief must be honest and reasonable.*

- *Age, sex and medical conditions are admissible relevant characteristics in the second question* (Bowen).
- *The defences will not apply in the case of voluntary association with criminals* (Hasan) *or murder, attempted murder or treason* (Howe).

General principles of duress of circumstances:

- *A defence where D acts in order to avoid a threat from circumstances.*
- *D must have done no more than was necessary to avoid the threat.*
- *The test and principles of duress apply. A complete defence to all offences except murder, attempted murder and treason.*

9.1.6 Reform

Duress

The following text is proposed in the Draft Criminal Law Bill (Law Com No 218):

(25)(1) No act of a person constitutes an offence if the act is done under duress by threats.

(2) A person does an act under duress by threats if he does it because he knows or believes–

(a) that a threat has been made to cause death or serious injury to himself or another if the act is not done, and

(b) that the threat will be carried out immediately if he does not do the act or, if not immediately, before he or that other can obtain effective official protection, and

(c) that there is no other way of preventing the threat being carried out, and the threat is one which in all the circumstances (including any of his personal characteristics that affect its gravity) he cannot reasonably be expected to resist.

It is for the defendant to show that the reason for his act was such knowledge or belief as is mentioned in paragraphs (a) to (c).

(3) this section applies in relation to omissions as it applies in relation to acts.

(4) This section does not apply to a person who knowingly and without reasonable excuse exposed himself to the risk of the threat made or believed to have been made.

If the question arises whether a person knowingly and without reasonable excuse exposed himself to such a risk, it is for him to show that he did not.

Duress of circumstances

The following text is proposed in the Draft Criminal Law Bill (Law Com No 218):

(26)(1) No act of a person constitutes an offence if the act is done under duress of circumstances.

(2) A person does an act under duress of circumstances if–

(a) he does it because he knows or believes that it is immediately necessary to avoid death or serious injury to himself or another, and

(b) the danger that he knows or believes to exist is such that in all the circumstances (including any of his personal characteristics that affect its gravity) he cannot reasonably be expected to act otherwise.

If is for the defendant to show that the reason for his act was such knowledge or belief as is mentioned in paragraph (a).

(3) This section applies in relation to omissions as it applies in relation to acts.

(4) This section does not apply to a person who knowingly and without reasonable excuse exposed himself to the danger known or believed to exist.

If the question arises whether a person knowingly and without reasonable excuse exposed himself to that danger, it is for him to show that he did not.

9.2 Necessity

9.2.1 Introduction

9.2.2 The Test for Necessity

9.2.3 Medical Cases

9.2.4 Non-medical Cases: Self-help and Direct Action

9.2.5 Reform

KEY CASES

Re A (Conjoined Twins) [2001] 4 All ER 961—necessity justifies murder where V is otherwise designated for death.

9.2.1 Introduction

Necessity does not exist as a general defence. It is thought it might apply to medical cases and the courts have developed some general principles in this context. But it is elsewhere uncertain and unresolved. To the extent that it exists, necessity is thought to encompass a general 'balancing of harms' defence where D believes that it is necessary to commit a crime to avoid greater harm, the offence being the lesser of two evils. The threat of harm need be neither criminal nor urgent. It might arise from a natural source, such as a flood or fire, or other circumstantial danger.

9.2.2 The Test for Necessity

General principles:

- Necessity is a defence to crimes committed to avoid a greater harm.
- No more should be done than is reasonably necessary to avoid such harm.
- The offence should not be disproportionate to the harm avoided.
- Necessity is a justification.

Necessity is similar to duress of circumstances but the focus is on the reasonableness of D's choice. His will need not be overborne, his choice need not be urgent but it must be rational and more morally justifiable.

Necessity is not a defence that the courts wish to encourage. If it were allowed to justify offences preventing such harm as social deprivation, starvation, hunger and homelessness, for instance, people would be encouraged to take the law into their own hands. As Lord Denning put it in the civil homelessness case of *Southwark London Borough v Williams* [1971] 2 All ER 175:

> If homelessness were admitted as a defence to trespass, no one's house could be safe. Necessity would open a door which no man could shut.

Quite simply, self-help could become a 'mask for anarchy' (per Edmund-Davies LJ in that case).

Further, if serious crimes such as murder were justified by necessity, the connection between morality and law could be undermined. You should recall Coleridge LJ's judgment in *Dudley and Stephens* (1884) (where two mariners were guilty of murder for killing a boy in order to save their own lives).

But of course, the law would be too rigid if it refused to acknowledge that law-breaking can sometimes be justified. Recall that Lord Denning said in *Buckoke v GLC* [1971] 2 All ER 254 that a fireman driving through a red light in order to rescue a man from a burning building 200 yards down the road, rather than risk the man's life by waiting for the lights to change, would commit a traffic regulation offence and necessity would be no defence, even though he might be congratulated for doing so. There is consequently a good deal of tension surrounding this defence.

We will now examine relevant case law which can be divided into:

- medical cases; and
- non-medical cases: direct action.

9.2.3 Medical Cases

The threat need not be of death or serious injury (NB: compare duress of circumstances)

In all of the following cases, D's choice was dictated by the circumstances. Should he commit an offence or should he permit harm to come to another person, which need not be serious violence or death as required by duress/duress of circumstances?

Pipe v DPP [2012] EWHC 1821

D drove at above 70mph in order to get his partner's son, who had broken his leg, to hospital. The accident had occurred at a football match and the ambulance had been delayed. D was convicted of speeding and appealed by way of case stated. The magistrates dismissed his defence of necessity because the circumstances were not life-threatening. The Divisional Court upheld the appeal. The harm D seeks to avoid on the grounds of necessity need not be confined to a threat to life, provided D's offence is proportionate. For duress of circumstances to apply, the threatened harm would need to amount to death or grievous bodily harm.

Threat of patient becoming 'a physical or mental wreck'

R v Bourne [1938] 3 ALL ER 615 CENTRAL CRIMINAL COURT

An obstetric surgeon was charged with procuring an unlawful miscarriage on a 14-year-old rape victim contrary to s58 Offences Against the Person Act 1861.

The jury acquitted on being directed that D had not acted unlawfully if he had acted in good faith to save the girl's life. MacNaghten J's interpretation of preserving the life of the mother was to include preserving her from becoming 'a physical or mental wreck'. Although it was not mentioned, it was implicit that the surgeon's choice was determined by necessity. The terms of the defence were borrowed from a defence provision of the Infant Life (Preservation) Act 1929 in relation to child destruction.

Today, abortion is regulated by the Abortion Act 1967 which permits abortion of a foetus on the grounds of risk to the physical or mental health or life of the mother or physical or mental abnormality of the foetus (s1). This is a statutory defence of necessity.

Threat to 'physical, mental and emotional health'

Gillick v West Norfolk and Wisbech Area Health Authority [1985] 1 ALL ER 553 HOUSE OF LORDS

The case concerned a civil application by the mother of five girls challenging the lawfulness of Department of Health advice to area health authorities enabling doctors to give confidential contraceptive advice to young women below the age of 16. It was argued that the medical advice, given without parental consent, might lead to the young woman participating in an offence of unlawful sexual intercourse, aided and abetted by the doctor. The House considered that the doctor faced a choice: giving confidential advice, which was likely to lead to an offence on the one hand, and the risk of an unwanted pregnancy with psychological suffering for the young woman (note, not death or serious violence). It held by a majority that provided the doctor's advice was guided by the best interests of the young woman, who had to be competent to receive it, no criminal intent arose and thus no offence would be committed. Necessity was not explicitly recognised, but it was clearly implicit in the judgments.

Lord Scarman:

He may prescribe only if she has the capacity to consent or if exceptional circumstances exist which justify him in exercising his clinical judgment without parental consent.

The adjective 'clinical' emphasises that it must be a medical judgment based on what he honestly believes to be necessary for the physical, mental and emotional health of his patient. The bona fide exercise by a doctor of his clinical judgment must be a complete negation of the guilty mind which is an essential ingredient of the criminal offence of aiding and abetting the commission of unlawful sexual intercourse.

Threat of 'disastrous psychiatric consequences'

F v West Berkshire Authority [1989] 2 ALL ER 545, [1990] 2 AC 1 HOUSE OF LORDS

This case concerned a forced sterilisation upon F, aged 36, who was a voluntary in-patient in a mental hospital. She had the mental capacity of a 5-year-old and had formed a sexual relationship with a male patient. Medical evidence indicated that it would be disastrous for her psychologically if she became pregnant. Ordinary methods of contraception were unsuitable. She was incapable of consenting to the sterilisation. A declaration in favour of the operation was confirmed by the House of Lords.

Lord Brandon:

> In my opinion, the principle is that, when persons lack the capacity, for whatever reason, to take decisions about the performance of operations on them, or the giving of other medical treatment to them, it is necessary that some other person or persons, with the appropriate qualifications, should take such decisions for them. Otherwise they would be deprived of medical care which they need and to which they are entitled. In many cases, however, it will not only be lawful for doctors, on the ground of necessity, to operate on or give other medical treatment to adult patients disabled from giving their consent; it will also be their common law duty to do so.

Appeal dismissed.

 NOTE 9.5

The medical test of necessity: 'best interests':

1. The case is authority for the proposition that necessity will provide a doctor with a defence to assault, battery or the civil offence of trespass to the person in non-consensual operations where the offence is the only means of avoiding 'disastrous' mental and psychological consequences to the patient (note: not death or serious violence as with duress). The offence is the lesser of two evils. The justification is one of best interests and public interest.

2. The consequences to the patient in this case had to be balanced against the fact that an irreversible sterilisation would deprive any woman of the right to bear children, with significant physical and psychological consequences—a potential violation of Articles 8 and 14 ECHR (the right to privacy and the prohibition against discrimination). There was also the risk that granting the defence and sanctioning the operation would open the door to applications for sterilisations upon non-consenting women for all sorts of non-medical social or welfare reasons.

Threat to life of an unborn child

Re Mrs S [1992] 4 ALL ER 671 FAMILY DIVISION

This was an emergency application by Bloomsbury & Islington Health Authority for a declaration to authorise a non-consensual caesarean operation upon Mrs S. She had been in the final stages of labour for two days and was likely to die without the operation, as would her unborn child. She was a 'Born Again' Christian and the operation was against her religious beliefs. The court granted the application on the grounds that the operation was in the best interests of Mrs S and that it was necessary to protect the life of the unborn child. In fact Mrs S's baby died and Mrs S survived.

 NOTE 9.6

1. Mrs S was forced to submit to a caesarean operation against her will. In the absence of necessity, such invasive action would have constituted not only an assault but also a violation of Mrs S's personal autonomy and her right to refuse potentially life-saving surgery, a right held to be inviolable by Lord Goff in *Re F*. The court appeared to recognise that Mrs S was competent to make decisions and that she was sincere in her religious beliefs.

2. The decision was seen as a dangerous precedent which would legitimise coercive treatment of pregnant women throughout the common law world. It was followed by two similar cases in which caesarean operations were authorised against the mothers' competent refusal of consent. Ian Kennedy, professor of medical law and ethics at Kings College wrote in *The Times*, 15 October 1992:

> It has massive implications for the status of women in regarding them as chattels and ambulatory wombs. It is so potentially intrusive as to reduce women back to the status of slaves.
>
> It implied that pregnant women in labour were not autonomous or entitled to the normal protections of the adversarial process. (See B. Hewson, 'Women's rights and legal wrongs' *NLJ*, 27 September 1996.)

Mrs S's case, in fact, contravened the English precedent of *Re F (In Utero)* [1980] 3 EHRR 408, which had rejected forced caesareans, and *Paton v UK* (1980) 19 DR 244 which said that an unborn child has no right to life under Article 2 ECHR and, therefore, no greater right to life than the mother. Forced caesareans can now only take place where the woman lacks capacity to make a decision and the principles and procedure set out in the Mental Capacity Act 2005 are followed, including that the treatment must be in her best interests.

?! **THINKING POINT** 9.6

Answer the following. In each case, think of whether the harm outweighs the offence and the best interests criterion.

1. A 15-year-old anorexic girl is refusing to eat. Can a hospital force-feed her against her wishes? (*Re F and Re W (A Minor) (Refusal of Medical Treatment)*, CA, 10 July 1992.)

2. A 20-year-old woman refuses a blood transfusion under the influence of her mother who is a Jehovah's witness. Can the hospital force it upon her? (*Re T*, CA, 14 October 1992.)

3. A 12-year-old pregnant girl wishes to have an abortion but her mother will not give consent because she does not agree with it. Can the hospital perform the operation? (*Re B (A Minor)*, Family Division, 20 May 1991.)

The current leading authority on medical necessity is that of the Maltese conjoined twins, Jodie and Mary, who were separated at Manchester Royal Infirmary in August 2000.

Threat to life of conjoined twin: 'calculated murder' can be justified by necessity

Re A (Children) (Conjoined Twins: Surgical Separation) [2001] FAM 147, [2000] 4 ALL ER 961 COURT OF APPEAL

This was an appeal by the parents of two conjoined twins against judgment of the Family Division in which a declaration had been granted that it was lawful for doctors to carry out a separation even though it would lead to the death of Mary, the weaker twin. The twins were joined at the lower abdomen. Mary only lived because a common artery enabled the stronger twin (Jodie) to circulate life-sustaining oxygenated blood for her. Mary's own heart and lungs were too deficient to pump blood through her body. Medical evidence had been submitted that both would die unless separation occurred within six months because Jodie's heart would fail. The effect of the separation would be the almost immediate death of Mary.

The parents were devout Roman Catholics and could not consent to the killing of one child even to save the other. The court had allowed various interested parties to intervene, such as the Catholic Church, in the interests of canvassing as wide a range of views as possible. The case raised the issue of whether the doctors would be committing murder and, if so, whether they would have a defence.

It was held that the operation would be lawful because it was in Jodie's best interests to live although it was clearly not in Mary's interests to die. The court was facing the 'sharp horns of a dilemma' in trying to reconcile such irreconcilable moral and ethical interests. It was held that 'calculated murder' can be justified where:

■ one twin is designated for death; and

■ the operation is in the best interests of the stronger twin.

The issues can be summarised as follows:

The parents refused their consent to the operation on religious grounds. Ward LJ, on reviewing Re F and Bland held that necessity can justify medical intervention. Parental right to refuse treatment is secondary to the best interests of the child.

The welfare of the children—it was not in Mary's best interests to die. Could the sanctity of life, which held that Mary's right to life was inviolable, be outweighed by the opportunity of saving Jodie's life? It was in Jodie's best interests to live but it was clearly not in Mary's best interests to die. Ward LJ stated that Mary's life, desperate as it was, still had ineliminable value and dignity. Given that each life had equal value, one had then to consider the 'worthwhileness' or merits of the operation. Medically, Mary had always been 'designated for death'. Only the doctors could save Jodie whereas Mary was beyond help. The least detrimental alternative was to permit the separation. Only Walker LJ thought that it was in Mary's best interests to die.

Act or omission?

→ CROSS-REFERENCE
Bland was discussed in Chapter 2, 2.2.3.

Recall that in *Bland* the House of Lords had held that the withdrawal of medical treatment from an irrecoverable and unconscious patient was not in breach of duty where discontinuance of medical treatment was in the best interests of the patient. The distinction between killing by positive act and letting die by omission was crucial, the former constituting murder by euthanasia, the latter being lawful. The proposed separation in *Re A* would be a positive act and would thus satisfy the AR of murder. However, Ward LJ held that the act/omission distinction was irrelevant:

> The first important feature is that the doctors cannot be denied a right of choice if they are under a duty to choose. They are under a duty to Mary not to operate because it will kill Mary, but they are under a duty to Jodie to operate because not to do so will kill her. It is important to stress that it makes no difference whether the killing is by act or by omission. That is a distinction without a difference: see Lord Lowry in *Bland* at p. 877. There are similar opinions in the other speeches . . .'

Intent to kill?

The court had to decide whether a doctor who acts in accordance with his clinical judgement but whose act causes the death of a patient has a guilty mind for the purposes of murder. Ward LJ and Brooke LJ agreed that a doctor would have an oblique intention to kill although death may not be the desired result or, indeed, the purpose of acting. Walker LJ thought, on the basis of Gillick, that the exercise of clinical judgement would negate a guilty mind but by failing to operate and thus save Jodie, the doctors would be in breach of duty and thus guilty of murder.

The court concluded that operating would prima facie amount to murder unless a reason could be found for declaring it to be lawful.

Defence (1): self-defence

In this respect, Ward LJ stated that Mary was killing Jodie and that Jodie was entitled to defend herself. Walker LJ was slightly more equivocal.

Ward LJ:

> The reality here – harsh as it is to state it, and unnatural as it is that it should be happening – is that Mary is killing Jodie. That is the effect of the incontrovertible medical evidence and it is common ground in the case. Mary uses Jodie's heart and lungs to receive and use Jodie's oxygenated blood. This will cause Jodie's heart to fail and cause Jodie's death as surely as a slow drip of poison . . . . I have no difficulty in agreeing that this unique happening cannot be said to be unlawful. But it does not have to be unlawful. The six-year-old boy indiscriminately shooting all and sundry in the school playground is not acting unlawfully for he is too young for his acts to be so classified. But is he 'innocent' within the moral meaning of that word? . . . . I am not qualified to answer that moral question . . . If I had to hazard a guess, I would venture the tentative view that the child is not morally innocent. What I am, however, competent to say is that in law killing that six-year-old boy in self-defence of others would be fully justified and the killing would not be unlawful . . . . '

Defence (2): necessity

Recall that the cases of *Howe* and *Dudley & Stephens* had excluded duress and necessity from murder. Brooke LJ stated that neither *Dudley & Stephens* nor *Howe* prevented necessity from ever being a defence to murder for neither was comparable to the unique facts of this case. There were cogent arguments in favour of doing whatever would save the greatest number of lives—a utilitarian principle. Where the identity of the victim was obvious and there was no choice, killing may be justified (as in the case of a person frozen with fear on an escape ladder in a sinking ship who is blocking the escape route for other people). But there was a moral dilemma where a decision had to be made as to who to sacrifice from amongst a group of people. Everyone's life is equal.

Brooke LJ:

> The usual view is that necessity is no defence to a charge of murder. This, if accepted, is a non-utilitarian doctrine; but in the case of a serious emergency is it wholly acceptable? If you are roped to a climber who has fallen, and neither of you can rectify the situation, it may not be very glorious on your part to cut the rope, but is it wrong? Is it not socially desirable that one life, at least, should be saved? Again, if you are flying an aircraft and the engine dies on you, it would not be wrong, but would be praiseworthy, to choose to come down in a street (where you can see you will kill or injure a few pedestrians), rather than in a crowded sports stadium.
>
> But in the case of cutting the rope you are only freeing yourself from someone who is, however involuntarily, dragging you to your death. And in the case of the aircraft you do not want to kill anyone; you simply minimise the slaughter that you are bound to do one way or the other. *The question is whether you could deliberately kill someone for calculating reasons.* [Emphasis added.] . . .
>
> I have considered very carefully the policy reasons for the decision in *R v Dudley and Stephens*, supported as it was by the House of Lords in *R v Howe*. These are, in short, that there were two insuperable objections to the proposition that necessity might be available as a defence for the Mignonette sailors. The first objection was evident in the court's questions: Who is to be the judge of this sort of necessity? By what measure is the comparative value of lives to be measured? The second objection was that to permit such a defence would mark an absolute divorce of law from morality.
>
> In my judgment, neither of these objections are dispositive of the present case. Mary is, sadly, self-designated for a very early death. Nobody can extend her life beyond a very short span. Because her heart, brain and lungs are for all practical purposes useless, nobody would have even tried to extend her life artificially if she had not, fortuitously, been deriving oxygenated blood from her sister's bloodstream.
>
> It is true that there are those who believe most sincerely – and the Archbishop of Westminster is among them – that it would be an immoral act to save Jodie, if by saving Jodie one must end Mary's life before its brief allotted span is complete . . . . The court is not equipped to choose between

these competing philosophies. All that a court can say is that it is not at all obvious that this is the sort of clear-cut case, marking an absolute divorce from law and morality, which was of such concern to Lord Coleridge and his fellow judges.

There are sound reasons for holding that the existence of an emergency in the normal sense of the word is not an essential prerequisite for the application of the doctrine of necessity. The principle is one of necessity, not emergency: see Lord Goff (in *In re F* at p 75D) . . . '

The court emphasised that this was a unique case and the judgment should not become a precedent.

Ward LJ:

Lest it be thought that this decision could become authority for wider propositions, such as that a doctor, once he has determined that a patient cannot survive, can kill the patient, it is important to restate the unique circumstances for which this case is authority. They are that it must be impossible to preserve the life of X without bringing about the death of Y, that Y by his or her very continued existence will inevitably bring about the death of X within a short period of time, and that X is capable of living an independent life but Y is incapable under any circumstances (including all forms of medical intervention) of viable independent existence.

The operation proceeded and Mary died. Jodie survived to become a healthy child.

 NOTE 9.7

1. Necessity would justify the murder of Mary because she was 'designated for death' and it was better that one twin should survive rather than that both should die. Look at these analogous situations quoted by Brooke LJ:

    1. A captain on a sinking ship denies room in a life raft to anyone other than children and pregnant women knowing that all the crew and male passengers will perish in icy waters. He shoots dead a man who is about to jump into the over-full raft.

    2. Two men jump from a burning aeroplane. The parachute of the second man does not open and as he falls past the first man he grabs his legs. The first man kicks the second away.

    3. A gang demand that a particular individual amongst a group be turned over for execution; the rest to go free. The group surrender the individual to save everyone else.

2. However, given that it was accepted by Ward LJ and Brooke LJ that the operation was not in Mary's best interests, the decision represents a utilitarian view of necessity which is at variance with the 'best interests' interpretation in other medical cases.

3. The court held that a failure to save Jodie would have been homicide. This conflicts with *Doctor Arthur* [1985] Crim LR 705 who had allowed a Down's syndrome baby to die on the wishes of the parents. In *A*, the act/omission distinction was held to be irrelevant.

4. Some commentators thought that Article 2 ECHR was cursorily examined. Article 2 protects everyone's right to life from intentional killings. An intentional killing means an act done with the *purpose* of killing. Although there is an exception so that lethal force can be used where absolutely necessary in self-defence, the court decided that where an intentional killing is not performed with the *purpose* of killing, Article 2 does not apply.

5. Other criticisms can be made, for instance, why was Mary and not both twins 'designated to die?' Read the following by J. Rodgers, 'Necessity, Private Defence and the Killing of Mary' [2001] *Crim LR* 515:

→ CROSS-REFERENCE
For further discussion of *Doctor Arthur* see Chapter 2, 2.2.3.

The Court assumed, quite without argument, that if the welfare principle required the sacrifice of Mary, then it would follow that the proportionality test . . . would be decided in the same way. But in applying the welfare principle, the paramount consideration is the benefits and detriments for the children. There is no reason why the proportionality test in necessity should not take into account the benefits and the detriments to other persons closely involved *as well*. One might have thought that the effect of the decision upon the girls' parents should have been weighed in the process of balancing evils. There can be little doubt that, on account of their beliefs, they suffered greatly as a result of the operation . . . It would also mean that it would be easier to use the defence of necessity to justify the sacrifice of one conjoined twin if the parents have given their agreement (because less harm in total would then be caused by the operation) . . . .

Indeed, the result in *Re A (Children)* conflicts with a fundamental principle which Parliament can be taken to have accepted when it passed the Abortion Act 1967, namely that a foetus does not have equal rights to a human being. For the paradoxical result of the present case is that although Mary could not be killed whilst in the womb (and no court would have ordered the mother, a competent but non-consenting person, to undergo a selective abortion) yet she *could* be killed when she had been born alive (because she was no longer protected, in effect, by her mother's absolute right to bodily integrity). One might also imagine that the more serious the harm to be inflicted (in this case, death) the more cautious a court should be to infer that Parliament overlooked a defence which it would otherwise have enacted. It is most unfortunate that none of their Lordships discussed any of these issues.

> **?! THINKING POINT** 9.7
>
> Following *Re A*, would necessity provide a defence in the following murder cases?
>
> 1. A mountaineer (D) whose companion (V) falls over a precipice is in danger of being pulled over the edge. D cuts the connecting rope and V falls to a certain death.
>
> 2. D climbs a ladder whilst leading a group to safety in an upturned and sinking ship. He pulls from the ladder a man who has frozen with fear so that the others may escape. The man is swept away to certain death.
>
> 3. State security forces shoot down an airliner full of passengers which has been taken over by terrorists and is about to crash into a crowded skyscraper. It is the only way to save more lives.

Necessity could, of course, be invoked by *the state* in order to justify torture or death: where police officers torture a suspect to obtain information regarding an anticipated attack on the public, or shoot a suspected terrorist whom they believe to be about to detonate a bomb.

Can torture/death ever be justified on the 'best interests' or utilitarian argument (eg: sacrificing a few lives to save more)? Or should there be limits to 'state necessity'? You decide.

9.2.4 Non-medical Cases: Self-help and Direct Action

In non-medical contexts there is great reluctance to grant necessity (justificatory) an existence independent from the narrower duress of circumstances (excusatory).

Necessity was rejected as a separate defence in the following cases, some of which had political overtones. Here, the courts confirmed a substantial merger of necessity and duress of circumstances to produce a new defence: *necessity of circumstances*.

MI5 whistle-blowing and state security

R v Shayler [2001] CRIM LR 987, [2001] EWCA CRIM 1977 HOUSE OF LORDS

D, a former MI5 officer, was charged under ss1 and 4 Official Secrets Act 1989 for having disclosed to the Mail on Sunday newspaper classified and top secret information regarding the shortcomings of MI5. His motive was to avoid loss of life and protect state security. Both the Court of Appeal and the House of Lords held that his defence should have been duress of circumstances but this was unavailable on the facts. The threat perceived was insufficiently imminent, there was no threat of death or serious injury, and an uncertain definition of the public was likely to be affected.

Innocent deaths in the Iraq War

R v Jones & Milling [2004] EWCA CRIM 1981, [2005] CRIM LR 122, [2006] UKHL 16 COURT OF APPEAL; HOUSE OF LORDS

A group of protestors entered an airbase at RAF Fairford in order to commit unlawful damage so that UK/USA planes would be prevented from taking off, bombing Iraq and causing innocent civilian deaths. The Court of Appeal held that necessity would be unavailable for the reasons in *Shayler*.

Alleviation of pain by medicinal cannabis: 'necessity of circumstances'

R v Quayle; AG's Reference (No 2 of 2004), Re Ditchfield [2005] EWCA CRIM 1415, [2006] CRIM LR 148 COURT OF APPEAL

Conjoined appeals were brought regarding the application of medical necessity to cannabis offences where D genuinely and reasonably believed it was necessary to smoke the drug to avoid pain from a pre-existing medical condition. D had had both legs amputated below the knee and had been using cannabis grown in his loft to treat serious pain. Medical evidence from his GP and a pharmacology expert verified that cannabis offered effective relief from pain and insomnia. The Court of Appeal held that the defence should fail. Necessity was indistinct from duress of circumstances.

Mance LJ:

> *Extraneous circumstances*. Lord Bingham spoke in *Hasan* of the need for 'a just and well-founded fear', while accepting that threats of death or serious injury will suffice. He noted that the relevant requirements had been defined objectively, and went on (with the majority of the House) to apply the same approach when he decided that the defence was not available if the defendant ought reasonably to have foreseen the risk of coercion. It is by 'the standards of honest and reasonable men' therefore that the existence or otherwise of such a fear or such threats falls to be decided . . . .
>
> There is therefore considerable authority pointing towards a need for extraneous circumstances capable of objective scrutiny by judge and jury and as such, it may be added, more likely to be capable of being checked and, where appropriate, met by other evidence . . . .

> *Pain.* There is, on any view, a large element of subjectivity in the assessment of pain not directly associated with some current physical injury. The legal defences of duress by threats and necessity by circumstances should in our view be confined to cases where there is an imminent danger of physical injury . . . .
>
> *Imminence and immediacy.* We consider that these requirements represent another reason why, even at the detailed level, it is difficult to accept that there could be any successful defence of necessity in the cases of *Quayle, Wales* and *Kenny.* Their defences amount to saying that it is open to defendants on a continuous basis to plan for and justify breaches of the law . . .

Appeals dismissed.

Pain is not 'injury': The court did not think pain, being internal and subjective, was the equivalent of injury. However, it is apparent that necessity in its traditional form has been allowed to go to the jury in other cases concerning the medicinal use of cannabis (*Lockwood* [2002] EWCA Crim 60, *Brown* [2003] EWCA Crim 2637).

The requirement of an external threat is based on the following: W. Wilson, 'The Structure of Criminal Defences' [2005] *Crim LR*, at p 111:

> The external prompt performs two key functions. First, it provides criminal excuses with their moral and political validation. It is only in response to crisis that it is plausible to claim that our actions are not authentically ours or, if authentically ours, nevertheless not indicative of censurable indifference to the interest of others . . . Additionally it ensures the actor was not simply 'taking the law into his own hands'. . . More broadly, the external prompt provides practical focus to the claim present, in one form or other, in all core excuses, namely that the infringement is rooted in the characteristics of human beings generally rather (than) the specific, perhaps anti-social or dangerous, characteristics of the actor.

The case represents a fairly clear denunciation of necessity in cases of continuous, deliberate and unlawful 'self-help'. See this general comment from A. Norrie, *Crime, Reason and History: A Critical Introduction to Criminal Law*, 2nd edn, Cambridge University Press, ch 8, at p 162:

> The law may either recognise the social consequences for individuals of a world of rich and poor and incorporate such recognition through a socially centred exculpation such as necessity . . . or it may insist that individuals are responsible in order to protect the status quo. It cannot do both, and the significance of the necessity defence is that it permits an opening for the former approach, one which the law has historically turned its back on . . . . It is for this reason that the defence of 'duress of circumstances' is likely to experience severe restriction on its growth . . . .

?! THINKING POINT 9.8

Is necessity/necessity of circumstances available in the following?

[Remember: it involves a balancing of harms. The offence must be proportionate, the action must be taken to avoid a greater harm, the threat must be extraneous, possibly criminal, and must not involve self-help/direct action.]

a. A prisoner escapes from a burning gaol in order to save his life.

b. D smuggles through customs a parcel of cannabis for medicinal supply to others.

c. D, whose wife is suicidal because of enduring pain from multiple sclerosis, drives her to hospital despite being disqualified from driving.

d. D, who is suicidal because of enduring pain from multiple sclerosis, drives himself to hospital despite being disqualified from driving.

9.2.5 Reform

→ CROSS-REFERENCE
Suggested reforms to
duress of circumstances
are set out in 9.1.

There are no proposals for reform of necessity other than those related to duress of circumstances.

SECTION SUMMARY

■ *Necessity is a complete defence to offences taken to avoid greater harm provided:*
   ☐ *no more should be done than is necessary;*
   ☐ *the offence should not be disproportionate to the harm.*
■ *The threatened harm need not be of death or serious injury.*
■ *Necessity is a justification.*
■ *It does not apply to murder, attempted murder or treason but the limitation in respect of murder for medical and possibly other reasons of necessity has been relaxed by Re A.*
■ *Medical cases: it is a defence recognised as justifying assault/battery in non-consensual operations.*
■ *In Re A necessity was held to justify murder where the weaker twin was designated for death and the operation was in the best interests of the stronger twin.*
■ *Direct action/self-help: where the defence exists at all it will be merged with duress of circumstances to form 'necessity of circumstances' which will be narrower than necessity in medical cases.*
■ *The threat must be extraneous and possibly criminal in nature.*
■ *Recent self-help cases conflict with the wider view of the defence put forward in Re A.*

9.3 Public and Private Defence

9.3.1 Introduction

9.3.2 The Necessity for Force: A Subjective Test

9.3.3 The Degree of Force Must be Reasonable: An Objective Test: s76(7)

9.3.4 Lethal Force and the ECHR

9.3.5 Reform

KEY CASES

Williams (Gladstone) [1984] 78 Cr App R 276—self-defence: mistaken belief need only be honest not reasonable;

Martin [2002] 1 Cr App R 323—D's characteristics are not relevant to self-defence;

Oye (Seun) [2013] EWCA Crim 1725—mistaken belief due to insanity still is relevant to the subjective test but the force used must be reasonable;

Keane [2010] EWCA Crim 2514—self-defence may be pleaded by one who initiates violence;

Burns [2010] EWHC 1604—defence of property: self-help must be necessary.

9.3.1 Introduction

This section concerns the use of reasonable force in self-defence, defence of another, prevention of crime and defence of property. These justificatory defences are complete defences to all crimes. They will most frequently be used against offences of violence or criminal damage.

Much debate has been generated by certain high profile trials involving the use of lethal force in self-defence. We shall read, for example, about the conviction of the farmer, Tony Martin, who in 2002 shot and killed a young burglar whilst defending his isolated farmhouse. It received a great deal of media attention, as did the conviction of two Luton businessmen for GBH with intent for attacking a violent, knife-wielding, masked burglar whom they seriously injured with a cricket bat after chasing him away from the house (*Hussain & Anr* [2010] EWCA Crim 94). Many people questioned whether burglars were given more protection by the law than house-holders. In response to this concern, rightly or wrongly, the government changed the law in 2013 to allow householders to use disproportionate force in defence of themselves and their property. Public concern has also been expressed in relation to the use of lethal force by the police and armed forces in defence of state security. The mistaken fatal shooting of Jean Charles De Menezes in July 2005 by an armed police officer, following the London Underground terrorist bombings, is a case in point. Drone killings in Syria are another. Can such killings be defended under the law of self-defence? If so, is English law compatible with the ECHR?

General principles:

- Force in self-defence, etc., will be lawful if used to repel, resist or ward off an attack or immediate threat.
- To be lawful, it must be necessary and reasonable.
- The test for necessity is subjective: D is judged on the facts as he honestly believed them to be.
- The amount of force must be objectively reasonable according to D's subjective belief about the facts.
- Householders can use disproportionate force in self-defence and defence of property.

Statutory provisions govern the following:

- s3(1) Criminal Law Act 1967—Prevention of crime:

A person may use such force as is reasonable in the circumstances in the prevention of crime, or in effecting or assisting in the lawful arrest of offenders or suspected offenders or of persons unlawfully at large.

- s5 Criminal Damage Act 1971—Defence of property where the charge is one of simple criminal damage.

→ **CROSS-REFERENCE**
For discussion of criminal damage see Chapter 14, 14.3.

The defences overlap so that force used in self-defence will also generally be used in the prevention of a crime. They also overlap with duress/necessity, where force may be either excused or justified if it is the unavoidable result of an immediate threat of death or serious violence.

The common law on self-defence has been restated by s76 Criminal Justice and Immigration Act 2008. It largely replicates the common law. The changes in respect of householders are new:

Section 76

(1) This section applies where in proceedings for an offence—

    (a) an issue arises as to whether a person charged with the offence ('D') is entitled to rely on a defence within subsection (2), and

    (b) the question arises whether the degree of force used by D against a person ('V') was reasonable in the circumstances.

(2)　The defences are—

(a)　the common law defence of self-defence; and

(aa)　the common law defence of defence of property; and . . .

(3)　The question whether the degree of force used by D was reasonable in the circumstances is to be decided by reference to the circumstances as D believed them to be, and subsections (4) to (8) also apply in connection with deciding that question.

(4)　If D claims to have held a particular belief as regards the existence of any circumstances—

(a)　the reasonableness or otherwise of that belief is relevant to the question whether D genuinely held it; but

(b)　if it is determined that D did genuinely hold it, D is entitled to rely on it for the purposes of subsection (3), whether or not—

(i)　it was mistaken, or

(ii)　(if it was mistaken) the mistake was a reasonable one to have made.

(5)　But subsection (4)(b) does not enable D to rely on any mistaken belief attributable to intoxication that was voluntarily induced.

(5A)　In a householder case, the degree of force used by D is not to be regarded as having been reasonable in the circumstances as D believed them to be if it was grossly disproportionate in those circumstances.

(6)　The degree of force used by D is not to be regarded as having been reasonable in the circumstances as D believed them to be if it was disproportionate in those circumstances.

(6A)　In deciding the question mentioned in subsection (3), a possibility that D could have retreated is to be considered (so far as relevant) as a factor to be taken into account, rather than as giving rise to a duty to retreat.

(7)　In deciding the question mentioned in subsection (3) the following considerations are to be taken into account (so far as relevant in the circumstances of the case)—

(a)　that a person acting for a legitimate purpose may not be able to weigh to a nicety the exact measure of any necessary action; and

(b)　that evidence of a person's having only done what the person honestly and instinctively thought was necessary for a legitimate purpose constitutes strong evidence that only reasonable action was taken by that person for that purpose.

(8)　Subsections (6A) and (7) are not to be read as preventing other matters from being taken into account where they are relevant to deciding the question mentioned in subsection (3).

(9)　. . .

(10)　In this section—

(a)　'legitimate purpose' means—

(i)　the purpose of self-defence under the common law, or

(ia)　the purpose of defence of property under the common law, or . . .

Sections 2(aa), 5A, 6A and 10(ia) were added by the Legal Aid, Sentencing and Punishment of Offenders Act 2012 and the Crime and Courts Act 2013. Section 76 aims to clarify the law so that people will know how far they can go in repelling burglars and assailants. In so far as it merely replicates some common law principles and omits others (such as pre-emptive action, force against police officers and unknown circumstances of justification) it has been deemed 'a pointless exercise' (I. Dennis, 'Editorial' [2008] *Crim LR* 507). The new extensions now give wider rights to householders. Whether they add clarity, or, indeed, permit unreasonably extreme force, will be considered. Hughes LJ in *Keane* [2010] EWCA Crim 2514 neatly summed up the approach of the courts:

> For the avoidance of doubt, it is perhaps helpful to say of section 76 three things: (a) it does not alter the law as it has been for many years; (b) it does not exhaustively state the law of self-defence but it does state the basic principles; (c) it does not require any summing-up to rehearse the whole of its contents just because they are now contained in statute.

It is thought that self-defence, etc, is *justificatory* because a balancing of interests is involved: that of the defender and that of the aggressor. The balance is in favour of the defender provided no more than reasonable force is employed, in which case harm inflicted upon an aggressor will be lawful. It follows that the AR of any assault will not have been intentionally committed. D is entitled to an acquittal, as is anyone charged as an accomplice. The defence will be referred to as simply 'self-defence' throughout.

?! THINKING POINT 9.9

1. Why do you think the law is based on 'reasonable' force in self-defence?
2. Is this an objective test (one which is measured against the standard of a reasonable person) or a subjective test (one which is measured against D's own standards)?
3. Do you think reasonable force has been used in the following?
   - D shoots a burglar in the arm with an air rifle as he is making off with D's television;
   - D finds an intruder in her bedroom at 3.00 am. Fearing she will be raped, she stabs him fatally in the neck with some scissors;
   - D stabs and injures a burglar whilst he is still outside D's house on the pavement;
   - D knocks unconscious a youth who is about to break a priceless vase;
   - D breaks the arm of a youth whom he sees mugging a man.

9.3.2 The Necessity for Force: A Subjective Test

The general requirement is that defensive force will only be lawful if it is *necessary*. It will only be necessary if it is used to resist, repel or ward off an unjust imminent threat: an act of self-defence is not retaliatory or revengeful. The need for force is assessed according to D's honest belief of the circumstances (a subjective test). But the amount of force D may use must be reasonable (an objective test). This does not mean equal or proportionate force. The law takes account of the urgency of the moment.

Palmer v The Queen [1971] AC 814 PRIVY COUNCIL

Lord Morris:

> If there has been an attack so that defence is reasonably necessary it will be recognized that a person defending himself cannot weigh to a nicety the exact measure of his necessary defensive action. If a jury thought that in a moment of unexpected anguish a person attacked had only done what he honestly and instinctively thought was necessary that would be most potent evidence that only reasonable defensive action had been taken.

→ CROSS-REFERENCE
The position of house-holders is discussed at 9.3.3.

Section 76(7) confirms this common law principle. But otherwise, what is reasonable in the circumstances involves balancing the interests of the parties: the nature of the threat, the physical capacities of the parties, age, sex, the urgency or opportunity for reflection, and the state of mind of the defendant. We must now, it seems, add that householders may use unreasonable or disproportionate force provided it is not grossly disproportionate.

Section 76(3)–(4): D may make an honest but unreasonable mistake about the necessity for self-defence (a subjective test)

The defence will not fail if D inflicts harm under a mistaken belief that he is under attack. The mistake must be genuine and honest but need not be reasonable. In other words, D will be judged on the facts and circumstances as he believed them to be. This subjective approach to mistake derives from the following:

R v Williams (Gladstone) (1984) 78 CR APP R 276 COURT OF APPEAL

D had been charged and convicted of assault. His victim was a man, Mason, who had seen a youth grab a woman's handbag. Mason caught the youth and held him with a view to taking him to a nearby police station. The youth broke free and Mason caught him again, knocked him to the ground and twisted one of his arms behind his back. The youth struggled and called for help. D intervened, having seen only the later stages of the incident. Mason maintained that he told D why he was holding the youth and (untruthfully) that he was a police officer. D asked to see his warrant card which naturally could not be produced. A struggle occurred. Mason sustained injuries to his face, loosened teeth and bleeding gums. D stated that he had seen Mason dragging the youth and striking him repeatedly. He was so concerned that he got off his bus and asked Mason what he thought he was doing. He punched Mason because he thought if he did so he would save the youth from further beating and torture.

Lord Lane CJ:

One starts off with the meaning of the word 'assault'. 'Assault' in the context of this case, that is to say using the word as a convenient abbreviation for assault and battery, is an act by which the defendant, intentionally or recklessly, applies unlawful force to the complainant. There are circumstances in which force may be applied to another lawfully. Taking a few examples: first, where the victim consents, as in lawful sports, the application of force to another will, generally speaking, not be unlawful. Secondly, where the defendant is acting in self-defence: the exercise of any necessary and reasonable force to protect himself from unlawful violence is not unlawful. Thirdly, by virtue of section 3 of the Criminal Law Act 1967, a person may use such force as is reasonable in the circumstances in the prevention of crime or in effecting or assisting in the lawful arrest of an offender or suspected offender or persons unlawfully at large. In each of those cases the defendant will be guilty if the jury are sure that first of all he applied force to the person of another, and secondly that he had the necessary mental element to constitute guilt . . . .

What then is the situation if the defendant is labouring under a mistake of fact as to the circumstances: What if he believes, but believes mistakenly, that the victim is consenting, or that it is necessary to defend himself, or that a crime is being committed which he intends to prevent? He must then be judged against the mistaken facts as he believes them to be. If judged against those facts or circumstances the prosecution fail to establish his guilt, then he is entitled to be acquitted.

The next question is, does it make any difference if the mistake of the defendant was one which, viewed objectively by a reasonable onlooker, was an unreasonable mistake . . .

The reasonableness or unreasonableness of the defendant's belief is material to the question of whether the belief was held by the defendant at all. If the belief was in fact held, its unreasonableness, so far as guilt or innocence is concerned, is neither here nor there. It is irrelevant. Were it otherwise, the defendant would be convicted because he was negligent in failing to recognise that the victim was not consenting or that a crime was not being committed and so on. In other words the jury should be directed first of all that the prosecution have the burden or duty of proving the unlawfulness of the defendant's action; secondly, if the defendant may have been labouring under a mistake as to the facts, he must be judged according to his mistaken view of the facts; thirdly, that is so whether the mistake was, on an objective view, a reasonable mistake or not.

In a case of self-defence, where self-defence or the prevention of crime is concerned, if the jury came to the conclusion that the defendant believed, or may have believed, that he was being attacked or that a crime was being committed, and that force was necessary to protect himself or to prevent the crime, then the prosecution have not proved their case.

If however, the defendant's alleged belief was mistaken and if the mistake was an unreasonable one, that may be a powerful reason for coming to the conclusion that the belief was not honestly held and should be rejected.

Even if the jury come to the conclusion that the mistake was an unreasonable one, if the defendant may genuinely have been labouring under it, he is entitled to rely upon it. [Emphasis added.]

Appeal allowed. Conviction quashed.

 NOTE 9.8

1. An honest mistake negates the intention to act unlawfully. The mistake does not need to be reasonable, that is: one that anyone would make. The only relevance of reasonableness is that the more unreasonable the belief, the less likely it is to be honest.

2. An honest mistake regarding the necessity for self-defence justifies the force which then becomes lawful. Since the prosecution are unable to prove an essential element of the AR (unlawfulness) neither D nor anyone charged with D is guilty. There is, in effect, no crime.

3. Williams followed the earlier authority of *Morgan* [1976] AC 182 which held that, in relation to rape, a mistaken belief in consent need only be honest, not reasonable. [NB: *Morgan* no longer applies to sexual offences.]

4. The *amount* of force must still be reasonable on the facts as D believed them to be. The test is therefore not completely subjective or completely objective. A purely subjective test would acquit those who use *excessive* force on the basis of a mistaken belief that they are under attack. This might cater to racist or other prejudiced beliefs that certain people are threatening when, in fact, they are not. The requirement of *reasonable* force on the facts as D believed them to be therefore denies the defence to extremists/vigilantes.

➜ CROSS-REFERENCE
Morgan is discussed in relation to mistaken belief at 9.4.2 and in relation to sexual offences in Chapter 11.

?! THINKING POINT 9.10

Look at the facts of the American case of *People v Goetz* 497 NE 2d 41 (NY 1986) where D was twice acquitted of murder at a trial and retrial:

D, a racist, was approached by four black youths on the underground who asked him for money. D took out a gun and shot them dead. When charged with murder, D asserted that he honestly believed the youths were going to rob and assault him and that he acted in self-defence. Would his defence succeed in England?

A subjective/objective approach to mistake of fact applies not only to self-defence, but has also been held to apply to the subjective test in duress *(Martin (David Paul)* [2000] 2 Cr App R 42—the schizophrenic who committed two robberies under duress). *Williams* was relied upon by the Privy Council in *Beckford v Queen* [1987] 3 All ER 425 to overturn the conviction of an armed police officer who had shot and killed a fleeing criminal in the back under the mistaken impression that he was armed.

There are not infrequent appeals regarding the nature of D's belief in self-defence. The trial judge's direction on this point was successfully challenged in both of the next two cases.

R v Yaman [2012] EWCA Crim 1075

D was charged with wounding with intent to do grievous bodily harm and of having an offensive weapon after hitting a man on the head, allegedly with a hammer, causing a gash. The incident had occurred in D's kebab shop, which was, at the time, closed, in which D had found three plain-clothed men. D asserted that he had struck out in self-defence at someone he believed to be a burglar. The men were, in fact, a gas engineer, a warrant officer and a locksmith who, pursuant to a distress warrant, had entered the premises to disconnect the gas for non-payment. The judge directed the jury to consider whether D's mistaken belief that the men were burglars was reasonable.

Hooper LJ:

> Section 76 makes it clear that the trigger for using force is assessed subjectively and the defendant's response is to be assessed objectively. Thus if a person uses force in the belief that he is being attacked, then his response must be assessed objectively in the light of that subjective belief . . . No reference was made by the judge to section 76(7)(b). If the jury reached the conclusion that the appellant was only doing what he honestly and instinctively thought was necessary faced by three burglars (as he believed them to be) for public or private defence, then that constitutes strong evidence that only reasonable action was taken . . . The judge did not say – given that there was no dispute that the appellant believed that the three men were burglars – that the jury must approach the case from the point of view of the appellant, namely that the three men were burglars and, for example that he was 18 years old and outnumbered. Indeed, as we shall show later, he left open for the jury to decide whether the appellant believed that the men were burglars . . .'

R v Morris [2013] EWCA Crim 436

The Court of Appeal ruled that the trial judge had made an error of law by refusing D's defence of honest belief in the need for reasonable force in the prevention of a crime (pursuant to s3 Criminal Law Act 1967). D was a taxi driver, three of whose passengers ran from his car, having failed to pay their fare. D had not noticed a fourth passenger still in the back of the taxi, who did intend to pay. D drove onto the pavement and knocked down one of the escapees, breaking his ankle, believing that he was preventing an offence of 'making off without payment' contrary to s3 Theft Act 1978. The judge's error had been to hold that D's belief needed to have been not simply honest, but also reasonable.

Section 76(5) Criminal Justice and Immigration Act 2008 confirms the common law position that an intoxicated mistake concerning self-defence cannot be relied upon and provides no defence.

➡ **CROSS-REFERENCE**
For further discussion of intoxicated mistake see Chapter 8, 8.3.8.

?!   **THINKING POINT** 9.11

D is sitting in a café. He is approached by a plain-clothed county court bailiff (V) who enquires about an unpaid judgment debt. D does not know who V is. A fracas ensues and D hits V in the face. D is charged with assault. Does he have a defence?

D's perception of danger is relevant to his mistaken belief

The Court of Appeal held in the famous case of *Martin* (see next case) that if D is more sensitive to danger than a normal person, and over-reacts to a threat with excessive force, or perceives a threat where a normal person would not, expert evidence regarding any such characteristic will be inadmissible in relation to self-defence. Since that case, however, the law has been refined, but let us first consider *Martin*. Recall that for the purposes of the subjective test in duress, such characteristics are admissible (*Martin (David Paul)* [2000] 2 Cr App R 42).

This case generated much public debate:

R v Martin (Anthony) [2002] 1 CR APP R 323 COURT OF APPEAL

Tony Martin (D) was a Norfolk farmer living in an isolated farmhouse called 'Bleak House'. He shot at two teenage burglars who had entered his house one night with a pump action shot gun. One named Fearon was injured in both legs and the other, Fred Barras aged 16, was killed by a bullet in the back. D fired the gun without warning. Barras crawled into undergrowth to die. Fearon staggered half a mile to summon help. D was tried for murder and wounding with intent. He claimed to have acted in self-defence. He was convicted and appealed. Fresh evidence was submitted to the Court of Appeal from two psychiatrists who had concluded that D was suffering from a long-standing personality disorder amounting to diminished responsibility. The break-in to his house would be perceived by him as being a greater danger than to a normal person.

D's argument on appeal concerned one point: that in assessing the reasonableness of force used to repel an attack, D should be judged not only on the facts and circumstances as he believed them to be but also on his *perception of danger* which may be exaggerated in the case of persons suffering from psychiatric conditions.

Lord Woolf:

'... Provocation only applies to murder, but self-defence applies to all assaults. In addition, provocation does not provide a complete defence; it only reduces the offence from murder to manslaughter. There is also the undoubted fact that self-defence is raised in a great many cases resulting from minor assaults and it would be wholly disproportionate to encourage medical disputes in cases of that sort ...

We accept that the jury are entitled to take into account in relation to self-defence the physical characteristics of the defendant. However, we would not agree that it is appropriate, except in exceptional circumstances which would make the evidence especially probative, in deciding whether excessive force has been used to take into account whether the defendant is suffering from some psychiatric condition ....'

After considering the psychiatric evidence in relation to diminished responsibility, the murder conviction was quashed and one of manslaughter by reason of diminished responsibility was substituted.

NOTE 9.9

The decision was based on procedural and policy reasons. Self-defence is frequently invoked against minor assaults for which the gravity and penalty do not merit trials complicated by expert evidence. Provocation (now loss of control), on the other hand, permits expert evidence on the objective test because the defence mitigates the mandatory life sentence for murder only. There is no analogy between the two.

This argument was not, however, entirely convincing. Although the court was concerned that self-defence should not be determined by purely subjective standards, the 'exceptional circumstances' that might warrant consideration of D's mental characteristics in relation to self-defence were not explained. If murder is not an 'exceptional case' it would be hard to find one that is.

However, the Privy Council subsequently held in *Shaw v R* [2002] 1 Cr App R 77, an appeal against murder conviction from Belize concerning a dispute over cocaine, that it was necessary for a judge to pose two questions to the jury: (1) Did D honestly believe that it was necessary for him to defend himself? (2) If so, and taking the circumstances *and danger* as the defendant honestly believed them to be, was the amount of force reasonable?

Here it is clear that perception of danger is part of the subjective question of belief. This avoids the complexity of characteristics. This ruling was reflected in s76(4) and confirmed by the next case:

R v Oye (Seun) [2013] EWCA CRIM 1725

Did an insanely held delusion on the part of the appellant that he was being attacked or threatened, causing him violently to respond, entitle him to an acquittal on the basis of reasonable self-defence or a qualified verdict of Not Guilty by Reason of Insanity (NGRI)?

Whilst in custody for affray, D assaulted two police officers under a psychotic delusion that they were evil and trying to exterminate him. At his trial for s20 GBH, two psychiatrists agreed that he was suffering from psychotic disorder. On appeal against conviction it was held that the delusions were relevant to D's belief. But, following *Martin*, 'an insane person cannot set the standards of reasonableness as to the degree of force used by reference to his own insanity . . . It could mean that such an individual who for his own benefit and protection may require hospital treatment or supervision gets none . . . . As s.76(6) makes clear, the position still requires objective assessment by reference to those circumstances' per Davis LJ. A verdict of NGRI was substituted.

 NOTE 9.10

The decision here makes it clear that a delusional belief that one is being attacked, although relevant to D's belief, is not relevant to whether the degree of force used in response is unreasonable. Insanity is likely to be considered the more relevant defence.

Press & Thompson [2013] EWCA Crim 1849 similarly confirmed that hypersensitivity due to post-traumatic stress disorder, involving a tendency to over-react and catastrophise, was relevant to D's subjective belief that he was being threatened. It was not relevant to whether the amount of force was proportionate, and therefore, reasonable, in the circumstances as D believed them to be. This is an objective question for the jury.

?! THINKING POINT 9.12

D stabbed her husband (V) fatally with a kitchen knife whilst he grabbed her throat in a struggle. She believed her life was in danger. D suffered from Battered Woman Syndrome and was extremely sensitive to danger. The facts did not disclose a life-threatening struggle. Does D have a defence to murder?

The law is clearly struggling to balance the interests between defendant and victim given that the subjective test permits the use of an honest but unreasonable mistake.

Pre-emptive strikes

It is clear that it is not necessary for an attack to have begun. D may use pre-emptive force where an imminent attack is apprehended.

Beckford v Queen [1987] 3 ALL ER 425, [1988] AC 130 PRIVY COUNCIL

A police officer (D) had been charged with murder. He had shot and killed a fleeing man in the back whilst investigating a report that an armed man was terrorising his family. He believed the fleeing man to have been armed and to have shot at other officers. At his appeal against conviction of murder, Lord Griffiths stated:

> The common law recognises that there are many circumstances in which one person may inflict violence on another without committing a crime, as for instance in sporting contests, surgical operations or, in the most extreme example, judicial execution. The common law has always recognised as one of these circumstances the right of a person to protect himself from attack and to act in the defence of others and if necessary to inflict violence on another in so doing. If no more force is used than is reasonable to repel the attack such force is not unlawful and no crime is committed. Furthermore, a man about to be attacked does not have to wait for his assailant to strike the first blow or fire the first shot: circumstances may justify a pre-emptive strike.
>
> It is because it is an essential element of all crimes of violence that the violence or the threat of violence should be unlawful that self-defence, if raised as an issue in a criminal trial, must be disproved by the prosecution. If the prosecution fail to do so the accused is entitled to be acquitted because the prosecution will have failed to prove an essential element of the crime, namely that the violence used by the accused was unlawful.

'Imminent' means 'immediate'

The threat which D believes to exist must be imminent. This excludes an attack at some future point. Imminent really means 'fairly immediate' so that although an attack need not have begun, a confrontation does need to be immediately apprehended.

Devlin v Armstrong [1971] NILR 13 COURT OF APPEAL

D was Bernadette Devlin, Britain's youngest female MP at 21, who had been elected to Parliament in 1969. The appeal was against her conviction of four offences of riotous behaviour and incitement to riotous behaviour in Londonderry, Northern Ireland, for which she was sentenced to six months' imprisonment. She had exhorted a crowd who had stoned the police to build a barricade to prevent the police from entering an area of the city, and to use petrol bombs. She had thrown a stone at the police. Her defence was one of justification in that she honestly and reasonably believed her actions to be necessary to protect the Catholic minority in the Bogside from the apprehended violence of the police.

It was held by the Court of Appeal that the danger which D was alleged to have anticipated was not sufficiently specific or imminent to justify her actions. Lord MacDermott LCJ:

> . . . However reasonable and convinced the appellant's apprehensions may have been, I find it impossible to hold that the danger she anticipated was sufficiently specific or imminent to justify the actions she took as measures of self-defence. The police were then in the throes of containing a riot in the course of their duty, and her interventions at that juncture were far too aggressive and premature to rank as justifiable effort to prevent the prospective danger of the police getting out of hand and acting unlawfully which, as I have assumed, she anticipated . . . . '

NOTE 9.11

1. The case is authority for the point that a pre-emptive attack in the face of a future, as opposed to an immediate, threat will not be justified. As with duress, where 'imminent' has now been ruled to mean 'immediate' (*Hasan* [2005] UKHL 22), the rule exists to prevent people from taking the law into their own hands when they have the opportunity to call on the police for assistance. The imminence requirement therefore discourages vigilantism or revenge attacks. The roots of self-defence are in 'necessity' rather than 'retribution'.

2. The imminence requirement is mandatory in English law. Therefore, if D honestly believes the police are unlikely to help and so kills or injures in fearful anticipation of future violence, D will be unable to rely on self-defence. Thus, the victim of domestic violence who believes it is necessary to kill or injure her partner in order to escape from an inevitable but not imminent death is excluded from the defence. She must wait until she is attacked again. Read this extract by K. O'Donovan, 'Defences for Battered Women Who Kill' 18(2) *Journal of Law & Society* 1991 who describes the law as culturally specific to male standards:

> '. . . The appeal is to a concept of equality under the law. But does it propose that women fall under the male standards? . . . there is a distinction between a double standard, a male-centred standard, and an all-encompassing standard . . . . Many articles on the subject of battered wives who kill argue that, given women's lesser violence, it is likely that the law of self-defence evolved in the context of male patterns of behaviour . . . . The problem here for women is that, being on average of a smaller size than men, being less likely to have training in controlled aggression, the requirement of reasonable force in countering the attack may be inappropriate . . . With regard to the attack, the question is whether 'imminent danger' is confined to an immediate act of violence, or whether well-founded fear of a future attack, based on previous experience, suffices. Several cases concern the killing of an assailant who has gone to bed. Hitherto the courts have insisted that 'imminent danger' means that a violent attack has occurred to which there has been an immediate response in fear of personal safety. This is the rock on which many cases have foundered . . . .'

The imminence rule might be thought to defeat the more fundamental justificatory basis of the defence, that of *necessity*. Perhaps the right to self-defence should apply where force is believed to be necessary and not simply in response to an imminent threat? See the following by J. Horder from 'Redrawing the Boundaries of Self-Defence', (1995) 58 *MLR* 431, at p 442:

> . . . If 'imminent' means 'live' or 'being put into effect', the insistence on an imminent threat or attack seems more restrictive than the insistence that the use of force be necessary in meeting the threat. After all, pre-emptive strikes can be necessary and proportionate, even though the very pre-emptiveness of the strike implies that the threat being averted was not 'live'. Suppose A (a notoriously violent criminal) is holding B hostage. A tells B that A may well kill B as a ransom demand has not been met. Knowing of A's reputation, B kills A two days later, when A falls asleep on guard duty, and escapes. If we assume that it was necessary (as well as proportionate) for B to kill A in order to escape, is anything added by the requirement that the threat posed by A be 'imminent'? I doubt it. The imminence of a threat is simply one of those factors taken into account in deciding whether the use of force was necessary.

In other jurisdictions, for example Australia, the imminence requirement is only one of many relevant factors to take into account in assessing whether self-defence was necessary.

The Law Commission would dispense with the requirement (Clause 27(1) of the Draft Criminal Law Bill (Law Com No 218)). Furthermore, the Law Commission Report on 'Murder, Manslaughter and Infanticide' (Law Com No 304, 2006) recommends that killing through the use of excessive force in self-defence should result in a conviction of second degree murder to which a discretionary sentence will apply. Note that now, s54 Coroners and Justice Act 2009 permits a partial defence of loss of self-control to murders committed through fear of serious violence. Immediacy is not required.

➜ CROSS-REFERENCE
For further discussion of the Law Commission recommendations see 9.3.5.

Preparing for an attack with weapons

Statute law, but not common law, sometimes permits preparation (ie: arming oneself) for a specific, imminent attack. However, strangely, the common law does allow use of weapons in self-defence during confrontation. The next case illustrates the distinction between *preparing* for an attack and *acting* in self-defence. As you will see, under the common law, arming oneself by being in possession of a weapon may be unlawful until the point at which it needs to be used:

Attorney-General's Reference (No 2 of 1983) [1984] QB 456 COURT OF APPEAL
....

D was a shop-keeper in Toxteth, Liverpool. His shop had been attacked during a spate of riots which had also broken out amongst other deprived areas of English cities, such as Brixton, London and Bristol. Fearing further attack, D made petrol bombs which he intended to use as a last resort in self-defence. He was acquitted of an offence under s4 Explosive Substances Act 1883: 'making an explosive substance in such circumstances as to give rise to a reasonable suspicion that he had not made it for a lawful object'. The Attorney-General referred the acquittal to the Court of Appeal:

> . . . The fact that in manufacturing and storing the petrol bombs the respondent committed offences under the [Explosives] Act of 1875 . . . did not necessarily involve that when he made them his object in doing so was not lawful. The means by which he sought to fulfil that object were unlawful, but the fact that he could never without committing offences reach the point where he used them in self-defence did not render his object in making them for that purpose unlawful. The object or purpose or end for which the petrol bombs were made was not itself rendered unlawful by the fact that it could not be fulfilled except by unlawful means . . . .

NOTE 9.12

1. The point of the case was quite narrow: the *object* for which D had made the petrol bombs (ie: self-defence) was held to be lawful under the 1883 Act. Therefore, D had not committed the offence charged. But he had committed another offence under the Explosive Substances Act of 1875 of *manufacturing and storing* explosives without a licence. The implication was that possession was unlawful until the moment the explosives were required for use in self-defence of an imminent attack. This is slightly confusing since the court also confirmed that self-defence did not only apply to acts done spontaneously.

2. Read widely however, the decision signified that the carrying or possession of offensive weapons was illegal even though carried for a lawful object, for example: self-defence. This was hard to reconcile with weapons possession offences, for example: s1(1) Prevention of Crime Act 1953 provides a defence of reasonable excuse:

   . . . any person who without lawful authority or reasonable excuse . . . has with him in any public place any offensive weapon shall be guilty of an offence.

   Evans v Hughes [1972] 3 All ER 412 explained that D could have a 'reasonable excuse' for possessing an offensive weapon on a public highway (a metal bar) if there was 'an imminent particular *threat* affecting the particular circumstances in which the weapon was carried', that is: self-defence. When it comes to the legality of carrying around, for example, pepper sprays, knuckle dusters, truncheons for use in case of attack, therefore, none would be lawful in the absence of a specific threat of imminent attack.

   Section 139(1) Criminal Justice Act 1988 prohibits the possession in a public place of a bladed article, but s139(4) provides a defence of good reason or lawful authority. The defence must be proved and is objectively assessed but court opinion seems to differ as to the relative significance of D's belief, whether it should be as to the reasonableness of carrying a weapon in the circumstances (*Clancy (Louise)* [2012] EWCA Crim 8 or as to the reasonableness of the belief (*N* [2011] EWHC 1807)). (Both of the Acts above are now amended by s139AA 1988 Act and s1A Prevention of Crime Act 1953 which provide new either-way offences of having an offensive weapon or an article with a blade or point in a public place or school.)

J.C. Smith in the *Criminal Law Review* commentary to *AG's Reference (No 2)* questioned why self-defence should not be available to preliminary 'possession' offences in the same way as assault offences:

> . . . If I am being shot at by a dangerous criminal and I pick up the revolver which has been dropped by a wounded policeman and fire it in self-defence, am I really guilty of an offence under the Firearms Act 1968, s.1, of being in possession of firearms without holding a firearm certificate? It seems strange that the circumstances might justify me in killing my assailant with the revolver and yet not justify me in being in possession of it. If self-defence is justifiable, it surely ought to be a defence to all crimes. If it is not justifiable, it is a defence to none.

The distinction between lawful and unlawful possession can therefore be so small as to be imperceptible. A defendant in circumstances similar to those in *AG's Reference (No 2 of 1983)* may have a defence of duress of circumstances if his actions are the unavoidable means of escaping death or serious injury.

Provoked attacks

If D provokes an attack, and V's retaliation is such as to justify D in using reasonable force to defend himself, the defence remains available. The only proviso is that D must not have deliberately provoked V as an excuse for violence.

Three cases confirm this point: *Rashford* [2006] Crim LR 547 (revenge murder); *Harvey* [2009] EWCA Crim 469 (ABH: where D bit the nose of her opponent in self-defence during a fight on being pinned to the ground); and *Keane*:

R v Daniel Keane [2010] EWCA CRIM 2514 COURT OF APPEAL

D, a passenger in a car, inflicted GBH (a fractured skull) on driver V in response to V's assault upon him which was in retaliation for D's original violence against a female passenger in the car. This took place in a petrol garage. D pleaded self-defence. The Court of Appeal confirmed that the defence is not automatically denied to one who initiates violence.

Hughes LJ:

> . . . self-defence may arise in the case of an original aggressor but only where the violence offered by the victim was so out of proportion to what the original aggressor did that in effect the roles were reversed . . . . In *Harvey* [2009] EWCA Crim 469 the court considered a direction given by the judge inviting the jury to consider whether 'the tables had been turned'. It seems to us that that kind of homely expression, like 'the roles being reversed', can quite well encapsulate the question which may arise if an original aggressor claims the ability to rely on self-defence. We would commend it as suitable for a great many cases, subject only to this reminder. Lord Hope's formulation of the rule makes it clear that it is not enough to bring self-defence into issue that a defendant who started the fight is at some point during the fight for the time being getting the worst of it, merely because the victim is defending himself reasonably. In that event there has been no disproportionate act by the victim of the kind that Lord Hope is contemplating. The victim has not been turned into the aggressor. The tables have not been turned in that particular sense. The roles have not been reversed . . . . We need to say as clearly as we may that it is not the law that if a defendant sets out to provoke another to punch him and succeeds, the defendant is then entitled to punch the other person. What that would do would be to legalise the common coin of the bully who confronts his victim with taunts which are deliberately designed to provide an excuse to hit him. The reason why it is not the law is that underlying the law of self-defence is the commonsense morality that what is not unlawful is force which is reasonably necessary.

In order to assess whether 'the tables have turned', a jury will need to be satisfied that D was not deliberately seeking an excuse for violence but that D's use of force was in response to unreasonable violence by V, despite D having provoked the V's violence to begin with.

The court will rarely be concerned with whether the initial aggressor was D or V. It is more important to decide whether the aggressive act was done in self-defence. If it was a pre-emptive strike, then it needs to be proportionate to the anticipated retaliation:

Marsh v DPP [2015] EWHC 1022 (Admin)

D made a pre-emptive strike on V by head-butting him because V approached him with his arms wide, a puffed-out chest and an aggressive manner. D said he used his head as he suffered osteoporosis, and he could not use his arm as it might shatter. V sustained injuries and D was charged with assault by beating. The court could not identify who the aggressor was, but held that the prosecution had discharged its burden beyond a reasonable doubt that the appellant went over the top and used force out of all proportion to the anticipated attack. Sir Stephen Silber:

> The issue of self defence arises when there is a focus, as there had to be in this case, on the aggressive act which was the subject matter of the charge which is headbutting.

?! THINKING POINT 9.13

D armed himself with a rice-flail: two pieces of wood joined by a chain sometimes used in martial arts. He and others went to confront someone known to be violent. He carried the weapon because of fear of imminent attack. Has D committed an offence and what is his defence?

Unknown circumstances justifying force in self-defence

What is the position where D uses force for the purposes of an arrest or in the prevention of crime unaware of circumstances justifying such force? In other words, where the use of force is actually justified, does D have to know that it is or can he rely upon a mistake? A nineteenth-century case, *R v Dadson* (1850) decided that it was necessary for D to actually be aware of the circumstances justifying the use of force. In the absence of knowledge, such force would be unlawful. The modern application of the *Dadson* principle would be in respect of police arrests under s24 Police and Criminal Evidence Act 1984 which are unlawful for lack of reasonable suspicion of a relevant statutory ground justifying arrest, even where such a ground actually exists.

R v Dadson (1850) 4 COX CC 358 COURT FOR CROWN CASES RESERVED

D, a police officer, was on duty watching a forest from which wood had been stolen. V emerged carrying stolen wood. D called out and V ran off whereupon D shot him in the leg so that he could arrest him. D was convicted of unlawfully and maliciously shooting at V with intent to do grievous bodily harm under s12 Offences Against the Person Act 1828. D's defence had been one of justification because he was shooting to arrest an escaping felon which it was apparently lawful to do. However, V's offence of stealing wood was only a felony if he held two such previous convictions, otherwise it was only a non-arrestable misdemeanour. V in fact held many convictions of which D was unaware and V was therefore committing a felony, but D did not know this to be so. The court held that D was not justified in shooting V and confirmed his conviction. Knowledge was an essential element of the offence. It can be argued that this decision was illogical given that self-defence is a justificatory defence and that D's actions were objectively justified.

Section 76(6A): There is no duty to retreat

There were once technical rules regarding a duty to retreat as far as possible from a threatening situation before using force in self-defence. It no longer exists. Such a duty would be impossible for some to comply with, such as abused women living with their violent abusers. It would also be incompatible with justifiable pre-emptive force and provoked attacks. A person has the right to 'stand their ground' but the opportunity of retreating will be considered as part of the question of whether the force used was necessary and reasonable. Section 76(6A) confirms this principle.

R v Field [1972] CRIM LR 435 COURT OF APPEAL

D appealed against a conviction of manslaughter for having fatally stabbed a victim whom he knew was part of a group intent on attacking him. He decided to remain outdoors. It was held that it was not the law that a man could be driven off the streets and compelled not to go to a place where he might lawfully be because he had reason to believe he would be met by people intending to attack him. D's conduct was relevant to the question of whether it was reasonable for him to use force. The appeal was allowed.

Neither is there a requirement that D must demonstrate an unwillingness or reluctance to fight before the use of force is regarded as lawful (*Bird* [1985] 1 WLR 816).

The threat of force need not be unlawful

In some situations the feared attack may not be criminal yet self-defence will be justifiable:

- Where the aggressor is under 10 years old, the age of criminal responsibility. Recall the case of the conjoined twins (*Re A* [2000] 4 All ER 961) where Ward LJ held that Jodie was entitled to defend herself from Mary's innocent 'attack' on her life.
- Where the aggressor is legally insane or suffering from automatism.

➜ CROSS-REFERENCE
See the discussion of necessity at 9.2.3, and of infancy in Chapter 8, 8.4.

Prevention of crime: The threat must be criminal

Prevention of crime

Recall the case of *Jones & Milling* [2004] EWCA Crim 1981 where the Ds sought to invoke necessity and prevention of crime to charges of criminal damage at an RAF/US airbase. The defences were also rejected on the basis that the harm to be avoided needed to arise from a criminal act under domestic law. The 'crime of aggression', although existing in international law, had not been incorporated into English jurisdiction.

➜ CROSS-REFERENCE
For further discussion of *Jones & Milling* see 9.2.4.

In rare circumstances, prevention of crime may be used to defend an assault on an innocent person to prevent another from committing an imminent crime. An example would be where a police officer pushes a person out of the way to get at a man about to shoot a gun or detonate a bomb. Another would be where car keys are snatched from someone's hand to prevent him from giving them to a driver who was drunk (*Hitchens* [2011] EWCA Crim 1626).

Defence of property: s76(2)(aa)

Since the seventeenth century, it has been possible to eject a trespasser from your land by using 'self-help' or 'lawful force'. It was once thought that it would be reasonable to kill to prevent dispossession of one's home (*Hussey* (1924) 18 Cr App R 160, CCA). Now that civil remedies are available to householders against unlawful occupiers, a killing in such circumstances would be excessive, or *grossly disproportionate*, using the language of s76(2)(aa) and (5A). But, provided the threat is criminal, force can be used to defend property from damage. It is only in exceptional cases that such a threat will not be criminal since unlawful entry onto another's property by an intruder, for example, will constitute both civil and criminal offences (ie: trespass or criminal damage). However, look at the following two unusual cases.

The Divisional Court held in *DPP v Bayer* [2003] EWHC Admin 2567 that defence of property was unavailable to protestors who had disrupted the lawful planting of GM seeds on farmland by attaching themselves to tractors. GM seed-planting was not against the law and convictions of aggravated trespass were therefore confirmed.

In *Burns* [2010] EWHC 1604 D appealed to the High Court against conviction of assault occasioning actual bodily harm on a prostitute (V) who had agreed to sex for £50. D had invited V into his car but had then changed his mind. She refused to leave whereupon D ejected her causing scratches and grazing. The High Court held that he had not acted in self-defence of himself or his property. She was not a trespasser and force was unnecessary.

Lord Judge, LCJ:

> The question in this appeal is whether the violence to which the complainant was subjected was unlawful. The appellant did not act in self-defence nor in defence of anyone else, nor to prevent a crime, nor in defence of his property from the threat or risk of damage, nor indeed for any of the purposes envisaged either by the Criminal Law Act 1967 or the Criminal Damage Act 1971 or well-established common law defences to allegations of violence which would otherwise be criminal, such as participation in sports like rugby which involve an element of violence. Even as a matter of legal theory we doubt the validity of the analogy between the appellant seeking to remove the complainant from his car and the rights of the house or landowner to remove a trespasser from his property. If anything, the appellant's activities could be said to amount to self-help, that is action to recover exclusive possession and occupation of his car, a concept sometimes described as recaption of property. . . . '

?! THINKING POINT 9.14

D wished to protect the habitat of Great Crested Newts, occupying a site for which planning permission had been granted. V was legitimately using a mechanical digger on the site. D struck the digger with a stake. V chased D who struck V on the arm with the stake. D was charged with assault. Can D plead prevention of crime or defence of property?

→ **CROSS-REFERENCE**
The implications of this change in the law are discussed in 9.3.3.

Householders: s76(2)(aa) and s76(5A)

Taking s76(2)(aa) and s76(5A) together, householders are permitted to use disproportionate force to defend their property, provided it is not grossly disproportionate.

9.3.3 The Degree of Force Must be Reasonable: An Objective Test: s76(7)

There is no separate test in relation to the degree of force. Reasonableness is determined by asking whether force was reasonably necessary in all the circumstances (objective) as D believed them to be (subjective). A reasonable degree of force in self-defence will be commensurate with the degree of danger posed by the threat. 'Reasonable' force is not exact but is intended to prevent gross violations of another's safety for the sake of protecting some minor harm. It is a matter for the jury. The law does not expressly require 'proportionate' force but the degree of force must be capable of being seen as only so much as is necessary to repel an attack.

There can be a fine line between reasonable and excessive force. The law does not demand precision (*Palmer* [1971] AC 814). As a rule, 'reasonableness' implies that killing in self-defence will only be justified where life is being threatened and that it will only be justifiable to seriously injure where serious injuries are threatened. Section 76(6) provides that disproportionate force is not 'reasonable'. Section 76(7) otherwise confirms *Palmer*.

➔ CROSS-REFERENCE
For further discussion of *Palmer* see 9.3.2.

Householders and disproportionate force: s76(5A)

This 2013 amendment to s76 was a government response to a perceived need to clarify the concept of 'reasonable' force for householders seeking to defend themselves from burglars or intruders. The provision is phrased in the negative: while s76(6) provides that force is not regarded as reasonable if it was disproportionate, 76(5A) states that for householders 'the degree of force used by D is not to be regarded as having been reasonable . . . if it was *grossly* disproportionate' (emphasis added). Does that mean householders can now use disproportionate force in self-defence, so long as it is not 'grossly' disproportionate? While that seems to have been Parliament's intention, the courts are taking a different view.

The High Court considered the provision in *R (on the application of Collins) v Secretary of State for Justice* [2016] EWHC 33 (Admin) ('*Denby Collins*'). Leveson P stated that 's. 76(5A) of the 2008 Act does not extend the ambit in law of the second limb of self-defence'. The force used must still be reasonable in all the circumstances; in householder cases, disproportionate force may but will not automatically be unreasonable. The Court of Appeal then considered s76(5A) in the following case:

R v Ray [2017] EWCA Crim 1391 COURT OF APPEAL

D was at home with his partner KA and her children when V, KA's violent ex-partner, came to the house. D tried to get V to leave, but the two men then fought and D fatally stabbed V. D claimed that he believed V had a weapon and was about to grab a kitchen knife which was next to his hand; D did not mean to stab V but did so because he was scared.

Lord Thomas of Cwmgiedd:

. . . In our view the interpretation placed in *Denby Collins* on the householder's defence under s.76 of the 2008 Act as amended by the 2013 Act was correct.

Once the jury have determined the circumstances as the defendant believed them to be, the issue, under s.76(3), for the jury is (as it always has been at common law) whether, in those circumstances, the degree of force used was reasonable.

In determining the question of whether the degree of force used is reasonable, in a householder case, the effect of s. 76 (5A) is that the jury must first determine whether it was grossly disproportionate. If it was, the degree of force was not reasonable and the defence of self defence is not made out.

If the degree of force was not grossly disproportionate, then the effect of s.76(5A) is that the jury must consider whether that degree of force was reasonable taking into account all the circumstances of the case as the defendant believed them to be. The use of disproportionate force which is short of grossly disproportionate is not, on the wording of the section, of itself necessarily the use of reasonable force. The jury are in such a case, where the defendant is a householder, entitled to form the view, taking into account all the other circumstances (as the defendant believed them to be), that the degree of force used was either reasonable or not reasonable.

The terms of the 2013 Act have therefore, in a householder case, slightly refined the common law in that a degree of force used that is disproportionate may nevertheless be reasonable.

As subsection (6) makes clear, in a non-householder case the position is different; in such a case the degree of force used is not to be regarded as reasonable if it was disproportionate.

Thus in our judgment the amendments to s.76 put the householder relying on self defence in a position different from all others relying on the defence. This is clear on the language of the Act. But it is narrow and not of the wide-ranging effect for which the appellant contended. We accordingly reject the contention that provided the degree of force used by a householder is not grossly disproportionate then it is necessarily reasonable.

NOTE 9.13

1. The court recognised that trying to explain distinctions between 'disproportionate' and 'unreasonable' to juries would be unhelpful. Suggestions for jury directions were made: once the jury have decided that the force was not grossly disproportionate, the sole issue on which they should focus is whether it was unreasonable. The difference between what is unreasonable when confronting an aggressive individual in a club and in one's own home could be pointed out. Relevant circumstances to consider might include the shock, the time of day, the desire to protect one's home and its occupants, picking up an object lawfully to hand, and the intruder's conduct.

2. The law was always flexible; strictly proportionate force has never been required. Juries are relied upon to determine the boundary between reasonable and unreasonable force. Presumably, from time to time, householders will use a tolerable amount of disproportionate force and the new provision reflects that. In doing so, it largely mirrors existing law: the change in householders' legal position is indeed 'narrow'.

→ **CROSS-REFERENCE**
For further discussion of the compatibility of self-defence law with Article 2 ECHR see 9.3.4.

3. Disproportionate force is, by definition, excessive and potentially contravenes Articles 2 (right to life), 3 (torture) and 8 (private life) ECHR. *Denby Collins* considered Article 2 and held that s76 is not incompatible with the right to life. However, that is open to argument.

4. This amendment, if only intended to clarify existing law, is unnecessary and a futile means of achieving greater clarity. If it is impossible to define or set out all the circumstances in which force might be considered 'reasonable', the distinction between 'disproportionate' and 'grossly disproportionate' is even more elusive.

5. If intended to permit householders to use greater violence against intruders than the previous law allowed, s5(A) creates a potentially dangerous message: householders can do whatever *they* consider necessary to an intruder, that is: a subjective approach to the degree of force. *Ray* resisted such an interpretation, and that is to be welcomed. To have decided otherwise would have diluted the established principle that it will rarely be reasonable to kill or seriously injure in defence of property, with potentially unhappy consequences. 'Stand your ground' laws in US states appear to have failed to deter violent burglaries, but have produced an 8 per cent increase in homicides (C. Cheng and M. Hoekstra, 'Does Strengthening Self-Defense Law Deter Crime or Escalate Violence? Evidence from Expansions to Castle Doctrine' (2013) 48(3) *Journal of Human Resources* 821, 823). These are not encouraging statistics.

6. A finding of 'excessive' force in self-defence may entitle a trespasser/burglar to successfully claim damages for his injuries against an occupier. *Revill v Newberry* [1996] QB 567 held that occupiers owe a duty towards trespassers. Brendon Fearon began civil proceedings against Tony Martin for damages in respect of his injuries, to which Tony Martin counter-claimed in respect of damages for the break-in. The case settled in 2003 without going to court. Might s76(5A) curtail this type of civil action?

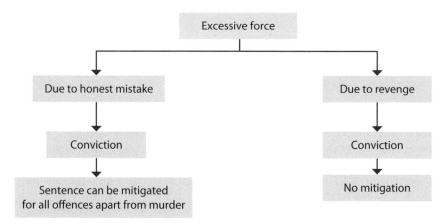

Diagram 9.1
Excessive force in self-defence

Excessive force which is the result of an honest mistake can be used in mitigation of sentence for all crimes apart from murder

Self-defence is all or nothing. It will either succeed, in which case an acquittal will follow, or it fails, and D will be convicted. If it fails, it is not possible to substitute a lesser offence. D will be convicted and sentenced for the offence charged. Excessive force will usually be evidence that the killing was retaliatory and not in self-defence.

But where excessive force is the result of an honest mistake, the circumstances can be used to mitigate the severity of the sentence for all offences other than those for which there is a mandatory penalty. An example would be the case of *Hussain & Anr* [2010] EWCA Crim 94 mentioned in the introduction to this chapter. See Diagram 9.1 for a summary.

Murder and lethal force in self-defence: an 'all or nothing' defence

It is not possible, however, to mitigate the mandatory life sentence where excessive force results in murder, however deserving the circumstances. Murder cannot be reduced to manslaughter. There is no specific defence of 'excessive force' in English law as there was, for example, in Australia between 1957 and 1987. This was argued before the House of Lords in two murder cases in Northern Ireland but was rejected:

AG for Northern Ireland's Reference (No 1 of 1975) [1976] 2 ALL ER 937 HOUSE OF LORDS

A British soldier (D) serving in Northern Ireland had been charged with the murder of a young man (V). During a foot-patrol V had been ordered to halt but he had run off. D, mistakenly believing V to be a member of the IRA, shot and killed him. D was acquitted of the crime but the Attorney-General for Northern Ireland referred the case to the Court of Criminal Appeal for Northern Ireland. The Court of Criminal Appeal gave an opinion and referred the matter to the House of Lords.

Lord Diplock:

> If a plea of self-defence is put forward in answer to a charge of murder and fails because excessive force was used though some force was justifiable, as the law now stands the accused cannot be convicted of manslaughter. It may be that a strong case can be made for an alteration of the law to enable a verdict of manslaughter to be returned where the use of some force was justifiable but that is a matter for legislation not for judicial decision.

Subsequent Law Commission reports recommended that a person who, in public or private defence, uses force which is excessive in the circumstances as he believed them to be should be guilty not of murder but of manslaughter provided his belief was honest. This was confirmed by the Report of the Select Committee of the House of Lords on Murder and Life Imprisonment (HL Paper 78–1, session 1988–89, para 83).

The arguments were rejected by the House of Lords in the next case.

R v Clegg [1995] 1 AC 482 HOUSE OF LORDS

Private Clegg (D) was on road patrol at night with other members of his unit in Northern Ireland in 1990. Another member of the patrol stopped a stolen car at a checkpoint some distance down the road. The car then accelerated away with its headlights full on in the centre of the road towards D and three other members of the patrol. D and his colleagues opened fire. D fired four shots, three as it approached and a fourth after the car had passed. The driver and a rear passenger were killed. The passenger was found to have been killed from the back. Scientific evidence showed that the fourth shot was fired when the car was already over 50 feet along the road, by which time the perceived danger had passed.

D was convicted of murder. His appeal reached the House of Lords.

Lord Lloyd did not consider soldiers or police officers to be in a different category from ordinary members of the public:

> The special position of a soldier in Northern Ireland is reflected in Lord Diplock's speech in the same case [*AG for Northern Ireland's Reference (No. 1 of 1975)* [1976] 2 All ER 937] . . . In most cases of a person acting in self-defence, or a police officer arresting an offender, there is a choice as to the degree of force to be used, even if it is a choice which is to be exercised on the spur of the moment, without time for measured reflection. But in the case of a soldier in Northern Ireland, in the circumstances in which Pte Clegg found himself, there is no scope for graduated force. The only choice lay between firing a high-velocity rifle which, if aimed accurately, was almost certain to kill or injure, and doing nothing at all.
>
> It should be noticed that the point at issue here is not whether Pte Clegg was entitled to be acquitted altogether, on the ground that he was acting in obedience to superior orders. There is no such general defence known to English law, nor was any such defence raised at the trial . . . The point is rather whether the offence in such a case should, because of the strong mitigating circumstances, be regarded as manslaughter rather than murder. But so to hold would . . . be to make entirely new law. I regret that under existing law, on the facts found by the trial judge, he had no alternative but to convict of murder . . .
>
> *Should the law be changed?*
> I am not averse to judges developing law, or indeed making new law, when they can see their way clearly, even where questions of social policy are involved . . . But in the present case I am in no doubt that your Lordships should abstain from law-making. The reduction of what would

otherwise be murder to manslaughter in a particular class of case seems to me essentially a matter for decision by the legislature, and not by the House in its judicial capacity. For the point in issue is, in truth, part of the wider issue whether the mandatory life sentence for murder should still be maintained. That wider issue can only be decided by Parliament. I would say the same for the point at issue in this case. Accordingly I would answer the certified question of law as follows. On the facts stated, and assuming no other defence is available, the soldier or police officer will be guilty of murder, and not manslaughter. It follows that the appeal must be dismissed.

The House rejected the argument that there was a distinction between the use of excessive force in self-defence and excessive force in the prevention of crime or arrest. The defences frequently overlap and one is not less culpable than the other. Furthermore, police officers and soldiers are subject to the same law as ordinary people.

But is there an argument for saying that there should be greater restrictions on the use of force by armed officers than ordinary citizens given that specialist use of a firearm is more likely to result in at least serious injury and probably death? It was clear from evidence at the trial in *Clegg* that the fatal shot against the passenger could not have been fired in self-defence, even on the basis of a mistake.

Private Clegg was freed on licence after serving four years of a life sentence on 3 July 1995. There had been a public and political outcry against the sentence and an immediate campaign began to secure his release. The Home Secretary, Michael Howard, announced a review of the law the following week but, a year later, no change was recommended in the absence of a more fundamental review of the life sentence for murder.

→ CROSS-REFERENCE
ECtHR case law on armed officers' use of force is considered in 9.3.4.

The Law Commission's Draft Criminal Code supported a defence of 'excessive force'. However, the more recent report on 'Murder, Manslaughter and Infanticide' (Law Com No 304, 2006) retracts the Code's proposal and recommends that killing through the use of excessive force in self-defence should result in a conviction of second degree murder to which a discretionary sentence will apply. The change is in reality only one of labelling, but murder signifies greater moral censure than manslaughter. You should recall that force used in fear of serious violence resulting in murder will now give rise to the partial defence of loss of control under s55(3) Coroners and Justice Act 2009 even though the fatal force was excessive and not immediate. The resulting conviction of voluntary manslaughter will allow discretion in sentencing.

?! **THINKING POINT** 9.15

V entered a public house, the worse for drink, and demanded to be served. D, the publican, told him to leave. V refused. D bundled V out of the bar by pinning his arms to his side from behind and pushing him violently towards the door. V fell backwards down a flight of five steps, struck his head and received injuries from which he later died. D was charged with manslaughter and raised self-defence. Which of the following statements correctly represent the law?

a. The use of force in self-defence is subjectively assessed.

b. D can make an unreasonable but honest mistake that he is under attack.

c. D can use an unreasonable amount of force on the facts as he honestly believes them to be.

d. The use of force is assessed in an objective sense as to whether or not force is reasonably necessary in the circumstances as D honestly believed them to be.

9.3.4 Lethal Force and the ECHR

If D intentionally kills an innocent victim, mistaking the victim for a terrorist posing a threat of deadly force, D will be innocent of murder provided the mistake was honest and the lethal force was reasonable in the circumstances as D believed them to be. If D is a police officer or a member of the armed forces, it is unlikely that he would be prosecuted unless the force was clearly excessive. Based on a semi-subjective interpretation of reasonableness, domestic law potentially conflicts with the higher standards of Article 2 ECHR which states:

1. Everyone's right to life shall be protected by law. No one shall be deprived of his life intentionally save in the execution of a sentence of a court following his conviction of a crime for which this penalty is provided by law.

However, there are exceptions to the right to life:

2. Deprivation of life shall not be regarded as inflicted in contravention of this Article when it results from the use of force which is *no more than absolutely necessary*:

   (a) in the defence of any person from unlawful violence;

   (b) in order to effect a lawful arrest or to prevent the escape of a person lawfully detained;

   (c) in action lawfully taken for the purpose of quelling a riot or insurrection.

[Emphasis added.]

The requirement in Article 2 of no more force than is absolutely necessary sets a stricter and higher standard than the reasonable force or honest mistake permitted by *Gladstone Williams* and domestic law. Section 76 does not address this conflict. The problem arises not only when lethal force is used by the state against citizens to prevent crime, effect arrest or in self-defence, but also when lethal force is used in private killings by one individual in mistaken self-defence against another. Now that householders may perhaps use disproportionate force to defend themselves or their property, the conflict with Article 2 becomes even more acute.

Honest belief v good reason

The UK was held to be in breach of Article 2 in the following case:

McCann et al v United Kingdom (1996) 21 EHRR 97 EUROPEAN COURT OF HUMAN RIGHTS

Three members of the IRA were shot and killed in Gibraltar by SAS soldiers in the mistaken belief that they had planted a car bomb and were going to detonate it by remote control from a device concealed on their person. The intelligence information of a planned terrorist attack by an IRA active service unit, on the basis of which the SAS had been sent to assist the authorities in Gibraltar, had been mistaken. An inquest in Gibraltar returned a verdict of lawful killing and no prosecution was brought. An application was made to the ECtHR by the families of the deceased.

The government submitted that the deprivations of life were justified under Article 2(2)(a) as resulting from the use of force which was no more than absolutely necessary in defence of unlawful violence. The applicants submitted that the planning and execution of the operation was not in accordance with Article 2 and therefore the deaths were not absolutely necessary.

Held:

> . . . All four soldiers admitted that they shot to kill. They considered that it was necessary to continue to fire at the suspects until they were rendered physically incapable of detonating a device. According to the pathologists' evidence Ms Farrell was hit by eight bullets, Mr McCann by five and Mr Savage by sixteen . . . .
>
> *It [the Court] considers that the use of force by agents of the State in pursuit of one of the aims delineated in paragraph 2 of Article 2 of the Convention may be justified under this provision where it is based on an honest belief which is perceived, for good reasons, to be valid at the time but which subsequently turns out to be mistaken. To hold otherwise would be to impose an unrealistic burden on the State and its law enforcement personnel in the execution of their duty, perhaps to the detriment of their lives and those of others.*
>
> *It follows that, having regard to the dilemma confronting the authorities in the circumstances of the case, the actions of the soldiers do not, in themselves give rise to a violation of this provision . . . .* [Emphasis added.]

However, the Court stated that in protecting life under Article 2, the state must plan any law enforcement operation so as to minimise recourse to lethal force.

> *In sum, having regard to the decision not to prevent the suspects from travelling into Gibraltar, to the failure of the authorities to make sufficient allowances for the possibility that their intelligence assessments might, in some respects at least, be erroneous and to the automatic recourse to lethal force when the soldiers opened fire, the Court is not persuaded that the killing of the three terrorists constituted the use of force which was no more than absolutely necessary in defence of persons from unlawful violence within the meaning of Article 2(2)(a) of the Convention. Accordingly, it finds that there has been a breach of Article 2 of the Convention.* [Emphasis added.]

 NOTE 9.14

The UK government was in violation of Article 2 because the immediate reaction of the soldiers in shooting the suspects dead lacked the necessary degree of caution to be reasonably expected. The decision was by majority: 10 votes to 9.

Fiona Leverick in 'English Self-defence Law and Article 2' [2002] *Crim LR* 357 claims that these decisions render English law incompatible:

> . . . in allowing the unreasonably mistaken defendant to escape punishment. . . . English law fails to respect the right to life of the person who, through no fault of their own, is mistaken for an attacker. An examination of relevant case law leads to the conclusion that the substance of English law does indeed contravene Article 2 . . .

J.C. Smith in 'The Use of Force in Public or Private Defence and Article 2' [2002] *Crim LR* 958, disagreed. Article 2 proscribes only intentional killings done with the purpose of killing. For example, the doctors in *Re A (Children) (Conjoined Twins)* [2000] 4 All ER 961 may have killed intentionally but not with the purpose of killing. They acted to save Jodie's life and there was, therefore, no conflict with Article 2. The same would apply to a soldier who killed in self-defence. The ECtHR confirmed this view in *Bubbins v UK* [2005] All ER (D) 290.

➜ **CROSS-REFERENCE**
Re A (Children) (Conjoined Twins) was discussed at 9.2.3.

Nevertheless, the *potential* incompatibility between self-defence and Article 2 is not an abstract point given that there have been more than 50 fatal shootings of civilians by armed police in England and Wales since 1985; six people were killed in police shootings in the year 2016–17.

Prosecutions for homicide are rare and convictions rarer. The Commissioner for the Metropolitan Police was found guilty of breaches of health and safety legislation in respect of the shooting of Jean Charles De Menezes at Stockwell underground station, London on 22 July 2005 but there were no prosecutions of individual officers. The civil division of the Court of Appeal held in *R (on the application of Bennett) v HM Coroner for Inner South London* [2007] EWCA Civ 617 that if any officer reasonably decides to use lethal force, it will inevitably be because it is absolutely necessary to do so. The case concerned the killing of Harry Stanley, shot six times by a police officer. He had been told by a witness that the deceased was Irish and carrying a gun. Harry Stanley was Scottish and carrying a table leg.

SECTION SUMMARY

Self-defence is a complete justificatory defence to all crimes:

- *Did D honestly believe that it was necessary for him to defend himself?*
- *If so, and taking the circumstances as the defendant honestly believed them to be, was the amount of force reasonable?*

Any mistake must be honest but need not be reasonable.

Excessive force which is unreasonable on the facts as D believed them to be will defeat the defence but may be the subject of mitigation.

Murder cannot be mitigated to manslaughter.

Householders can now use disproportionate force provided it is reasonable.

9.3.5 Reform

Murder and excessive force

In the Law Commission's final report, 'Murder, Manslaughter and Infanticide' (Law Com No 304, 2006), the previous proposals were largely confirmed. Where excessive force is used, provocation would provide a defence to first degree murder reducing a conviction to second degree murder. As the reason for the defence is the mandatory life sentence, this would permit a discretionary life sentence. The recommended reform is as follows:

(1) Unlawful homicide that would otherwise be first degree murder would instead be second degree murder if:

    (a) D acted in response to:

        (i) gross provocation (meaning words or conduct or a combination of words and conduct) which caused D to have a justifiable sense of being seriously wronged; or

        (ii) fear of serious violence towards D or another; or

        (iii) a combination of both (i) and (ii); and

    (b) a person of D's age and of ordinary temperament, ie., ordinary tolerance and self-restraint, in the circumstances of D might have reacted in the same or in a similar way.

(2) In deciding whether a person of D's age and of ordinary temperament, ie., ordinary tolerance and self-restraint, in the circumstances of D, might have reacted in the same or in a similar way, the court should take into account D's age and all the circumstances of D other than matters whose only relevance to D's conduct is that they bear simply on his or her general capacity for self-control.

The defence should not apply where the victim was incited by D so as to provide an excuse for violence or where D acts in revenge. If the reaction is based on fear and anger, that is not to be considered revenge. If D acts, or over-reacts, in fear or panic of serious violence rather than anger, the defence should apply. This represents an extension of the defence to cover excessive force in self-defence.

9.4 Mistake

9.4.1 Introduction

9.4.2 Relevant Mistakes

9.4.3 Mistake and Strict Liability

9.4.4 Mistake and Offences of Negligence

9.4.5 Irrelevant Mistakes

This section is more appropriate to Chapter 8 but is included here because it is easier to understand once you have read through general defences. It contains very little new material and effectively consolidates previously discussed principles.

KEY CASES

Morgan [1975] 2 All ER 347—mistaken belief of fact need only be honest not reasonable.

9.4.1 Introduction

Mistake is not a defence in the usual sense. It is a simple plea that D lacks MR because he acted under a mistake of fact. There are many types of mistake that are relevant to this plea but it is not in every case that a mistake will negate fault. Look at the examples below and work out whether the mistakes are relevant or irrelevant to fault:

1. D intends to steal a bottle of champagne from a shop but steals a cheap bottle of fizzy wine by mistake.

2. D intends to donate his old jacket to a charity shop but mistakenly gives away the best jacket of his best friend.

3. D intends to shoot a pheasant in a bush and pulls the trigger. It is, in fact, a small child playing hide and seek.

4. D mistakenly thinks that he is under attack and so hits a man in self-defence.

5. D mistakenly believes that he is being threatened with death unless he commits robbery. He commits the crime.

6. D drunkenly believes the woman with whom he has sexual intercourse is consenting when she is not.

In 1 the mistake is irrelevant. D intended to steal at the outset. Both AR and MR of theft would be satisfied. By contrast, the mistake in 2 is relevant for, although D has committed the AR of theft by 'appropriating property belonging to another', he thought he was giving away his own jacket and therefore did not intend to dishonestly appropriate property belonging to another. His mistake explains why D lacked the MR of theft. The mistake in 3 can be explained in the

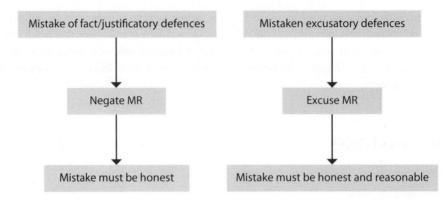

Diagram 9.2
Mistake: the tests

same way. D lacked the MR to unlawfully kill a person. The mistakes in 4 and 5 are also relevant because they explain why D committed the crime in question and, in each case, deny MR (self-defence (4)) or excuse fault (duress (5)). The mistake in 6 is irrelevant. Remember from 'Intoxication' that a drunken mistake is no defence.

→ CROSS-REFERENCE
Intoxication is discussed
in Chapter 8.

The law is only concerned with relevant mistakes. However, the test to be satisfied depends on the type of relevant mistake: does it *justify* D's act and thus deny MR or does it *excuse* D's actions?

9.4.2 Relevant Mistakes

See Diagram 9.2 for a summary.

Mistakes of fact

→ CROSS-REFERENCE
Morgan is considered
in greater detail in
Chapter 11.

If an offence is one of MR (intention or recklessness) and D makes a genuine mistake of fact as to the result (eg: death of a *person* as opposed to a pheasant) or a circumstance (eg: appropriating property belonging to another when he thinks it is his own) he will lack MR. For many years, it was thought that the mistake had to be a reasonable one but this is no longer the case. An honest mistake will excuse D from liability. The main authority is *Morgan*:

> ### *DPP v Morgan* [1975] 2 ALL ER 347 HOUSE OF LORDS
>
> Morgan invited three friends to have sexual intercourse with his wife informing them that she was likely to struggle to increase her sexual arousal. She was dragged by her husband from the bedroom which she shared with her small son and was held down whilst all three men and her husband had sexual intercourse with her. She repeatedly called out to her husband to tell the men to stop. At the trial all three men maintained that they believed she consented. The judge directed the jury that unless their belief was based on reasonable grounds there was no defence to rape. This reflected established law. They were convicted of rape whilst Morgan was convicted of aiding and abetting rape. The case was appealed to the House of Lords which reversed the objective nature of the defence yet upheld the convictions.

Lord Hailsham stated that mistake is not a defence but a matter of MR:

> Once one has accepted, what seems to me abundantly clear, that the prohibited act in rape is
> non-consensual sexual intercourse, and that the guilty state of mind is an intention to commit it,
> it seems to me to follow as a matter of inexorable logic that there is no room either for a 'defence'
> of honest belief or mistake, or of a defence of honest and reasonable belief and mistake. Either the
> prosecution proves that the accused had the requisite intent, or it does not. In the former case it
> succeeds, and in the latter it fails.

This principle has been recently confirmed by the House of Lords in *B (A Minor) v DPP* [2000] 1 All ER
833, [2000] Crim LR 403 where Lord Nicholls confirmed in the context of a strict liability offence that:

> When mens rea is ousted by a mistaken belief, it is as well ousted by an unreasonable belief as by
> a reasonable belief.

These two cases expressly disapproved of an earlier precedent which had established the 'honest
and reasonable' mistake test: *Tolson* (1889) 23 QB 168 CCR, concerning bigamy. *Tolson* was not
overturned and it may be, therefore, that in relation to bigamy the traditional test remains.

NB: *Morgan* has been reversed by the Sexual Offences Act 2003 in relation to rape and other
sexual offences which now require D to have a belief in consent that is both honest and reasonable. *Morgan* remains relevant to all other offences.

➜ CROSS-REFERENCE
For further discussion
of *B (A Minor) v DPP*
see Chapter 4.

Mistake in relation to justification defences

In the case of self-defence, for example, which is a justificatory defence, a mistake as to the necessity for force need only be honest but does not have to be reasonable: *R v Williams (Gladstone)*
(1984) 78 Cr App R 276. Force used in self-defence is justified and lawful. An honest mistake
negates the MR to inflict *unlawful* force.

Mistake in relation to excusatory defences

An example of an excusatory defence would be duress where D intentionally commits an offence
under coercion. A mistake here does not *negate* MR but *excuses* fault or liability. It was always
considered that a mistaken belief in threats had to be both honest and reasonable (*Graham* [1982]
1 All ER 801—murder by tying flex around V's neck). But *Martin (David Paul)* [2000] 2 Cr App R
42 (robberies by schizophrenic) held, consistently with self-defence, that in relation to the subjective test, it need only be honest. Doubt was cast on that by Lord Bingham in *Hasan* where he said:

> It is of course essential that the defendant should genuinely, ie. actually, believe in the efficacy of the
> threat by which he claims to have been compelled. But there is no warrant for relaxing the requirement
> that the belief must be reasonable as well as genuine.

There must therefore be doubt about *Martin* and it is probably the case that any mistake must
be both honest and reasonable. Mistake in relation to the objective test would however need to
be reasonable.

9.4.3 Mistake and Strict Liability

Liability for such an offence is strict, regardless of the lack of MR. The existence of a mistake
would therefore be irrelevant except that many such crimes are only strict in respect of one
element. MR may be required in respect of others. If the mistake of fact is one which negates
MR, this will be a relevant mistake.

9.4.4 Mistake and Offences of Negligence

These are offences which depend upon unreasonable conduct. If D makes a reasonable mistake of fact, the offence will not be committed. If the mistake is unreasonable, he will be liable. For the purposes of gross negligence manslaughter, a reasonable mistake might provide a defence. A grossly unreasonable one would not.

9.4.5 Irrelevant Mistakes

Fact: Some mistakes of fact are irrelevant as in illustration (1) at 9.4.1. The mistake did not negate D's MR for theft for it was unrelated to any AR element of the offence.

Law: Ignorance of the criminal law is no excuse. Most people will know that it is morally wrong to commit the major crimes but ignorance of any crime, whether it be one of the 4,000 plus crimes of strict liability in the English system, or any other more serious crime, will not avail. Knowledge that the act is against the law would be an unusual requirement.

→ CROSS-REFERENCE
For discussion of transferred malice see Chapter 3, 3.1.12.

Mistake of civil law may afford a defence. For example, taking something that you believe legally belongs to you when you may have no entitlement to it would amount to a defence of lack of dishonesty under s2(1) Theft Act 1968.

Transferred malice: If harm is caused to a mistaken or accidental victim or object of an intentional crime, the intention is simply transferred from the intended to the actual victim/object.

SUMMARY

- Duress and duress of circumstances are in reality two forms of a single defence. Overpowerment of D's will by threats of death or serious injury is allowed to excuse where reasonable. *Howe* imposed limits on duress in relation to murder and *Hasan* reinforces the need to control the defence within narrow objective limits lest it become a charter for gangs and terrorists. Therefore, voluntary association will be excluded.

- Self-defence and necessity justify D's actions so as to negate liability. Self-defence requires the use of reasonable force in the circumstances as D believes them to be.

- Necessity requires a balancing of interests entitling D to commit an offence in order to avoid greater harm.

- Mistake, if relevant, will either negate MR (mistakes of fact/justificatory claims) or excuse liability (excusatory defences).

PROBLEM SOLVING

D, a timid 19-year-old woman, moves in with her boyfriend, X. The relationship degenerates into violence against her. X is facing trial for unrelated GBH offences and demands that D gives false evidence on his behalf. D is too frightened to refuse and does so as a result of which X is acquitted. The following week, X takes D on a holiday to the Welsh mountains but his violence continues. Near the summit of Snowdon he puts his hands around her neck. Fearing for her life, D pushes him over a precipice. As they are roped together, X's weight soon threatens to pull D over the ledge. He manages to shout that all he wanted to do was to adorn her neck with a diamond necklace, a surprise present concealed in his hands. D catches a glimpse of it as it falls from his grip. Unable to stop her inevitable fall in any other way, D cuts the rope and X falls to his death. Does D have any defence/s to the offences in this question? (You are not expected to discuss perjury but are required to identify and explain relevant defences to this and any other crimes.)

Remember:

- **I: Identify** relevant issues
- **D: Define** offences/defences
- **E: Explain/evaluate** the law
- **A: Apply** law to facts.

As with the problem question at the end of the last chapter, a good problem-solving technique is to draw a chart for the main headings of an answer (see Table 9.1):

Always conclude as to which defence/s it would be in D's interests to plead and which are most likely to succeed.

See the online resources for further guidance on solving this problem: www.oup.com/uk/loveless6e/.

Table 9.1
Problem-solving chart

Defences	Murder - *Was death intentional?*	Perjury
Duress	Not applicable on the facts	Subjective/objective tests following *Hasan*? Will duress be defeated by delay? Relevant characteristics? Voluntary association?
Self-defence/ mistaken belief	Test: was force reasonable on the facts as D believed them to be taking account of her mistake? Test for mistaken belief in necessity for force? Was her mistake honest? Was the force excessive?	
Necessity	Was it necessary for D to cut the rope? Balance of harms—loss of one life instead of two? Can this apply to murder? (*Re A*).	
Diminished Responsibility	Is D suffering from Battered Woman Syndrome—an abnormality of mind?	

FURTHER READING

Duress

J. Loveless, 'R v Hasan' (2005) 39(3) *The Law Teacher* 375

Explores the factual and legal background to the leading duress case.

N. Padfield, 'Duress, Necessity and the Law Commission' [1992] *Crim LR* 778

Evaluates and discusses the Law Commission's proposals for reforming duress, and argues it should recommend codification of necessity as well.

Necessity

S. Gardner, 'Direct Action and the Defence of Necessity' [2005] *Crim LR* 371

Considers the principles underpinning necessity and the defence's application in political direct action cases.

R. Huxtable, 'Separation of Conjoined Twins: Where Next for English Law?' [2002] *Crim LR* 459

Analyses the conflicts between criminal, family and human rights law in conjoined twin cases and the need for legislation in this area.

J. Rodgers, 'Necessity, Private Defence and the Killing of Mary' [2001] *Crim LR* 515

Argues that *Re A* used a utilitarian theory of necessity which is dangerous, and extending private defence would have been preferable.

F. Stark, 'Necessity & Nicklinson' [2013] 12 *Crim LR* 949

Analyses the argument in this 'right to die' case that a doctor killing a willing patient may have a defence of necessity.

W. Wilson, 'The Structure of Criminal Defences' [2005] *Crim LR* 111

Analyses the framework of defences, their common elements, and the ways in which they do and should converge.

Self-defence

L. Bleasdale-Hill, "'Our home is our haven and refuge—a place where we have every right to feel safe": Justifying the Use of Up to "Grossly Disproportionate Force" in a Place of Residence' [2015] 6 *Crim LR* 407

Considers the householder provision and whether the use of disproportionate force can be justified.

J. Collins and A. Ashworth, 'Householders, Self Defence and the Right to Life' (2016) *LQR* 377

Analyses the compatibility of the householder provision as interpreted in *Collins* with Article 2 ECHR.

S. Gardner, 'The Domestic Criminal Legality of the RAF Drone Strike in Syria in August 2015' [2016] 1 *Crim LR* 35

Discusses whether a fatal drone strike carried out by UK forces in Syria was lawful under English criminal law.

J. Horder, 'Redrawing the Boundaries of Self-Defence' (1995) 58 *MLR* 431

Considers how a theoretical analysis of self-defence may help in the formulation of just and coherent law.

S. Miller, "'Grossly Disproportionate": Home Owners' Legal Licence to Kill' (2013) 77(4) *JCL* 299

Questions the rationale and impact of the householder provision and its compatibility with human rights law.

M.P. Thomas, 'Defenceless Castles: The Use of Grossly Disproportionate Force by Householders in Light of R (Collins) v Secretary of State for Justice' (2016) 80(6) *JCL* 407

Explores the decision in *Collins* and considers how far it accords with Parliament's intention.

Non-fatal offences against the person

10

KEY POINTS

This chapter will help you to identify the AR/MR elements of and the distinction between the major offences against the person:

- assault and battery;
- actual bodily harm;
- GBH and malicious wounding;
- GBH and wounding with intent.

You will understand how these traditional offences are also applied to modern social problems such as stalking, harassment and sexually-transmitted infection (STI) transmission.

You will be able to identify and understand the application of the following defences which are specific to offences against the person:

- consent;
- lawful chastisement.

INTRODUCTION

Unwanted violence from another is an infringement of our individual autonomy. We all have the right to personal integrity and autonomy, free from unlawful interference or harm from others. To protect us from violence there is a structure of offences against the person, primarily the creation of the Offences Against the Person Act 1861 (OAPA 1861). These offences range from assault and battery, which can be committed in the absence of physical harm, to wounding and grievous bodily harm (GBH) which represent serious and potentially life-threatening violence.

These offences, having worked well for many years, are now widely considered to be in need of overhaul. The Victorian OAPA 1861 has been criticised as being (J.C. Smith in his commentary on *Parmenter* [1991] Crim LR 43):

> a rag-bag of offences brought together from a wide variety of sources with no attempt, as the draftsman frankly acknowledged, to introduce consistency as to substance or as to form.

The Act consolidated numerous offences more specifically related to injuries of particular parts of the body. Offence definitions are now regarded as imprecise and out of date, and the offence structure is illogical and incoherent. For example, s20 and s18 GBH include wounding which need only amount to minor harm. The MR for s20 GBH need only amount to foresight of 'some' bodily harm, not necessarily GBH. The offence of causing actual bodily harm (ABH) under s47 may be caused without realisation of any harm. Furthermore, in response to new forms of recognised injury, such as psychiatric harm and sexually-transmitted infections (STIs), the courts have applied the offences to conduct going beyond that which was originally envisaged in 1861, a task for which they are often ill-suited. These offences may, therefore, be criticised for failing to clearly define the exact nature of the harm they seek to prohibit. As such, they risk contravening Article 7 ECHR. The sentencing structure is also illogical. For example, both s47 ABH and s20 GBH carry the same maximum sentence of five years which is illogical. Consequently, the Law Commission has published recommendations for reform of the ladder of offences against the person (see 10.10). In this chapter, we begin with the least serious and most common offences of assault and battery followed by others as they ascend in gravity. In the final sections we look at two specific defences to assault: consent and lawful chastisement. Finally, three recent statutory offences will be examined: racial/religiously aggravated assaults, harassment and stalking. All section numbers refer to the OAPA 1861 unless otherwise stated.

Context

Violent crime accounts for approximately 19 per cent of all crime, a 66 per cent reduction since 1995, with levels remaining stable over the past year. These statistics now include female genital mutilation and modern slavery offences. However, around 55 per cent of violent crime consists of assault without injury. Young men aged 16–24 are most at risk of injury. Levels of firearms offences are 65% lower than in March 2004, despite small annual rises between 2014 and 2016. Similarly, offences involving knives or sharp instruments declined between 2009 (when records began) and 2014, but increased in the following two years. See Diagrams 10.1 and 10.2 for more details.

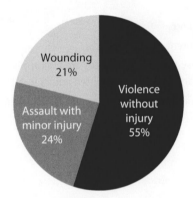

Diagram 10.1

Types of violent crime, year ending March 2016, CSEW

Source: *Crime Survey for England and Wales* (ONS) as appears in Overview of violent crime and sexual offences, 2015/16 Release (ONS) www.ons.gov.uk/peoplepopulationandcommunity/crimeandjustice/compendium/focuson-violentcrimeandsexualoffences/yearendingmarch2016/overviewofviolentcrimeandsexualoffences

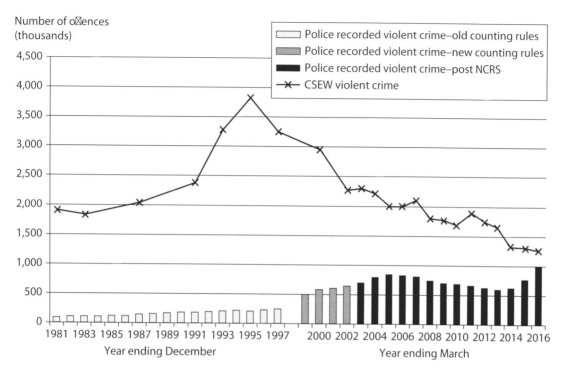

Number of offences
(thousands)

Legend:
- Police recorded violent crime–old counting rules
- Police recorded violent crime–new counting rules
- Police recorded violent crime–post NCRS
- CSEW violent crime

Diagram 10.2

Trends in police recorded and Crime Survey for England and Wales violent crime, year ending December 1981 to year ending March 2016

Notes:

1. Police recorded crime data are not designated as National Statistics.

2. The Home Office Counting Rules for police recorded crime were expanded in April 1998 to include certain additional summary offences. Figures before and after that date are not directly comparable.

3. The National Crime Recording Standard (NCRS) was introduced in April 2002, although some forces adopted NCRS practices before the standard was formally introduced. Figures before and after that date are not directly comparable.

Source: ONS, Police recorded crime, Home Office and Crime Survey for England and Wales, Office for National Statistics, www.ons.gov.uk/peoplepopulationandcommunity/crimeandjustice/compendium/focusonviolentcrimeandsexualoffences/yearendingmarch2016/overviewofviolentcrimeandsexualoffences

Domestic violence

Not surprisingly, there are gender differences in violent crime. In 2011, for example, domestic violence accounted for one third of all violent crime in London. Roughly 80 per cent of victims of domestic violence were women while 77 per cent of victims of stranger violence were men. The most common perpetrators of female intimate violence are males aged 16–24. To get an idea of the scale of the problem, see these statistics:

A Call to End Violence against Women and Girls, Progress Report 2010–15, p 12

Domestic violence and abuse

From the 2013/14 Crime Survey for England and Wales it is estimated that 1.4 million women were victims of domestic abuse in the last year:

■ 85 women were killed by a partner or ex-partner in 2013/14. This is slightly lower than in 2011/12 (89) but higher than the 77 victims in 2012/13.

- The number of referrals for domestic abuse and violence from the police for prosecution is higher than ever before (over 100,000).
- The number of cases of domestic abuse reaching court has also risen. In 2013/14, there were just over 78,000 prosecutions nationally. Current projections expect that figure to increase to nearly 90,000 by the end of 2014/15.
- The conviction rate for domestic violence and abuse is also at its highest ever level at almost 75 per cent in 2013/14—up from 72 per cent in 2009/10.

Source: www.gov.uk/government/uploads/system/uploads/attachment_data/file/409510/VAWG_Progress_Report_2010-2015.pdf

These figures are, of course, shocking. Domestic violence is a serious problem and pervasive within society. Due to feminist campaigns over the last 30 years, it is no longer regarded as purely 'domestic' or private, but a matter of national concern, and government policies are now being implemented to combat it.

Domestic violence is now defined by Sch1, Legal Aid, Sentencing and Punishment of Offenders Act 2012 as 'any incident of, or pattern of incidents, of controlling, coercive or threatening behaviour, violence or abuse (whether psychological, physical, sexual, financial or emotional) between those aged 16 or over who are, or have been, intimate partners or family members regardless of gender or sexuality'.

There is no specific offence of domestic violence except in Wales (Violence Against Women, Domestic Abuse and Sexual Violence (Wales) Act 2015). But a new offence of 'coercive and controlling behaviour' was created by s76 Serious Crime Act 2015. Otherwise, domestic violence will be dealt with by a range of criminal offences, from stalking to murder, as well as by various civil orders against the abuser, such as non-molestation injunctions and restraining orders. Statistics suggest that prosecutions have fallen (by 13 per cent since 2010) despite reports to the police continuing to rise. Reliance on the legal process is inevitably inadequate. Welcome though intervention now is, the problem will not of course be properly addressed without a transformation in social and cultural attitudes towards women.

10.1 Assault

10.1.1 Definition

10.1.2 Actus Reus

10.1.3 Mens Rea

KEY CASES

Ireland & Burstow [1997] UKHL 34—assault by silence; ABH/GBH can consist of psychological harm;

Smith [2006] EWHC 94 (Admin)—cutting off a substantial amount of hair is capable of amounting to ABH;

Brown [1994] 1 AC 212, [1993] 2 WLR 556—deliberate infliction of pain for sado-masochistic reasons is unlawful and contrary to the public interest;

Dica [2004] EWCA Crim 1103—reckless GBH, fraud and consent for the transmission of HIV;

Konzani [2005] EWCA Crim 706—consent to intercourse with an HIV-positive partner must be informed;

Golding [2014] EWCA Crim 889—conviction of GBH for transmission of genital herpes simplex.

10.1.1 Definition

> Assault: Any act by which the defendant intentionally or recklessly causes the victim to apprehend immediate unlawful personal violence.
>
> **Actus reus**
>
> ■ Causing the apprehension of
> ■ Immediate
> ■ Unlawful personal violence.
>
> **Mens rea**
>
> ■ Intention or
> ■ Subjective *Cunningham* recklessness.

Technically, no harm whatsoever need be inflicted for an assault. Prosecutions, however, may be instituted in cases of minor harm such as minor bruising, grazing, cuts and scratches.

Assault and battery are separate common law offences for which the penalty is prescribed by s39 Criminal Justice Act 1988:

> Common assault and battery shall be summary offences and a person guilty of either of them shall be liable to a fine not exceeding level 5 [£5,000] on the standard scale, to imprisonment for a term not exceeding six months, or to both.

Assault and battery are typically charged together as common assault for there will rarely be a battery without an assault but they are technically distinct offences. The term assault is often referred to as being inclusive of battery. However, in this section we consider the two offences separately.

10.1.2 Actus Reus

Apprehension

Technically, no physical contact at all is required for an assault. Typically, D will do something to cause the victim to anticipate or apprehend an immediate battery—that he is going to be struck. This will occur where, for example, D raises a fist, aims a gun, points a knife or some other weapon, or gestures in a threatening way against the victim (V). The assault consists of causing V to apprehend immediate violence. If V does not apprehend immediate violence, because, for example, he thinks D is only joking, there is no assault. V's perceptions are important here. Recall in this respect the case of *Lamb* [1967] 2 QB 981 where D, who had pointed a gun at V in a game of Russian roulette and then proceeded to shoot him by mistake, probably did not commit an assault because he did not cause V to apprehend immediate violence, V being aware that it was only a prank.

→ CROSS-REFERENCE
For further discussion of *Lamb* see Chapter 7, 7.2.4.

Assault being triable only summarily, it is not possible to be liable for an attempted assault. Once violence has been inflicted, it becomes a battery.

Apprehension need not mean 'fear' of immediate violence. In most cases it will probably do so but the requirement is apprehension (ie: anticipation or expectation) not fear. Therefore threatening gestures towards a blind man, aiming a weapon at a sleeping person, or stealthily creeping up behind someone in order to strike them would technically present no assault.

Immediate

This requirement is viewed flexibly so that immediate need only mean *imminent*: the harm need only be apprehended in the immediate future, not the next minute. For example, an assault was committed in the following cases:

- *Lewis* [1970] Crim LR 647 where the defendant uttered threats from another room;
- *Logdon v DPP* [1976] Crim LR 121 where the defendant showed the victim, a tax inspector, a gun in a drawer. The victim feared imminent harm and the defendant intended to cause such fear but he could not have inflicted it because it was an imitation firearm;
- *Smith v Chief Superintendent of Woking Police Station* (1983) 76 Cr App R 234 where D, standing in an enclosed garden of a block of flats, looked through a bed-sitting room window at the victim in her night-clothes, intending to cause her fear. In order to commit battery he would have had to break in.

On the other hand, if it is obvious that the threat cannot be immediately carried out then there will be no assault. This may be the case where for example D is threatening violence from a moving car travelling in the opposite direction, or where violence is threatened to occur after a period of time, for example, 'I will beat you up next Thursday'.

Unlawful personal violence

This requirement is common to both assault and battery. It need not mean violence as we commonly understand it. Violence will be committed as much by unwanted touching (eg: a hand on your shoulder) as by a punch on the nose. It need not be hostile in the colloquial sense or aggressive.

Unlawfulness

Not all unwanted physical contact will constitute assault or battery. Consent is a defence to battery rendering lawful some forms of violence which would otherwise be unlawful. We implicitly consent to reasonable degrees of physical contact in everyday activities, whether on public transport, busy streets, football matches or rock concerts. Other defences, however, will also negate the unlawfulness of an assault or battery: the use of a reasonable degree of force in the punishment of children (parental chastisement), self-defence, the prevention of crime, and necessity. Reasonable physical force to effect an arrest will also be lawful.

Collins v Wilcock [1984] 3 ALL ER 374 QUEEN'S BENCH DIVISION

Wilcock, a police officer, grabbed hold of Collins' arm in order to detain her for questioning in relation to a suspected offence of soliciting as a common prostitute. Collins, in turn, scratched the police officer's forearm with her fingernails and was arrested for assaulting a police officer in the execution of her duty. The issue was whether Wilcock had exceeded her duty by grabbing hold of Collins' arm.

It was held that a distinction can be drawn between touching another to gain attention, which is generally lawful, and physical restraint, which is not. A police officer may, in order to question, lay a hand on a person's sleeve or tap another's shoulder and may do so more than once. But police officers have no greater rights than ordinary persons and must behave according to acceptable standards.

Lord Goff:

> But if, taking into account the nature of his duty, his use of physical contact in the face of non-co-operation persists beyond generally acceptable standards of conduct, his action will become unlawful; and if a police officer restrains a man, for example by gripping his arm or his shoulder, then his action will also be unlawful, unless he is lawfully exercising his power of arrest. A police officer has no power to require a man to answer him, though he has the advantage of authority, enhanced as it is by the uniform which the state provides and requires him to wear, in seeking a response to his inquiry. What is not permitted, however, is the unlawful use of force or the unlawful threat (actual or implicit) to use force; and, excepting the lawful exercise of his power of arrest, the lawfulness of a police officer's conduct is judged by the same criteria as are applied to the conduct of any ordinary citizen of this country.

Collins & Wilcock was applied where a police community support officer (PCSO) had attempted to detain a suspect until the arrival of a police officer:

D v DPP [2010] EWHC 3400

Was a PCSO acting in the execution of her duty by putting out her hand to stop D from leaving the scene of an altercation? She intended that he should await the arrival of a police officer who would conduct a search for prohibited drugs. A PCSO has no power to detain. Ousley J held that an intention to unlawfully detain after a short while did not render a lawful request to stop unlawful:

> At the moment when the appellant pushed the CSO, there had been no detention, and the CSO was continuing to act, and would have continued so to act, in the execution of her duty up until the point at which there was an unlawful detention. That point had not yet arisen on the findings of fact by the magistrates, even though it might do so imminently …
>
> I note what Robert Goff LJ said [in *Collins v Wilcock*] about the purpose of the officer in that case, namely that a laudable intention of carrying out a cautioning procedure could not make the grabbing of the defendant's arm lawful. Conversely, I conclude, a request to stop, which involved no detention and no threat of force, cannot be rendered unlawful by the fact that the CSO intended to detain him in a mistaken belief as to the extent of her powers and in a relatively short while, might have detained the appellant unlawfully …
>
> I have come to the clear conclusion that the question of the point at which an officer acting in the execution of a duty ceases to do so is the point at which she actually acts unlawfully and not the point at which she does something which is not unlawful, but which is intended to lead to an act which is unlawful …

The same point was reiterated in *Tester v DPP* [2015] EWHC 1353 (Admin), where a police officer gave chase in a police car to a drunk and disorderly defendant, got out of the car, and asked the defendant to stop, at which point the defendant pushed him. The officer intended to detain, but not to arrest.

Sir Stephen Silber:

What is relevant is what the officer was doing immediately before he was pushed and all he was doing was approaching the appellant to speak about his behavior. Thus he was not acting outside the scope of his duty ... the intention of the officer does not matter. What was important was what was said and done.

Therefore, D's conviction of assaulting a police officer in the execution of his duty was upheld.

 THINKING POINT 10.1

Has D committed the AR of assault in the following cases?

1. D waits until V has passed him and then jumps on V from behind a bush.
2. D angrily shakes his fist at V but V thinks it is funny.
3. D shakes his fist at V who is standing on the other side of a four-laned road.
4. D thrusts a weapon towards V who is sitting inside a locked car.
5. D is on a train and leans out of the window as it is leaving the station to shake his fist at V who he sees standing on the platform.

You can assault by words alone or even by silence

→ CROSS-REFERENCE
The Protection from Harassment Act 1997 offences are examined at 10.9.

The question of whether or not it is possible to commit an assault verbally is relevant in stalking cases where stalkers cause fear and anxiety through telephone calls, emails, social media or letters. There are now separate offences under the Protection from Harassment Act 1997 specifically aimed at stalking. But before that Act there was no immediately identifiable relevant offence apart from assault.

It had always been thought that it was not possible to assault by mere words: 'no words or singing are equivalent to an assault' (Holroyd J in *Meade's and Belt's Case* (1823) 1 Lew CC 184 at 185).

However, if words could not constitute an assault, they might at least be capable of *negating* an assault. Thus in *Tuberville v Savage* (1669) 1 Mod Rep 3, D said, in laying his hand upon his sword, 'If it were not assize time I would not take such language'. His words counteracted his gestures.

Despite the traditional view, it was thought that a verbal assault would probably occur where there was clear evidence of intention to cause fear.

EXAMPLE 10.1

'Your money or your life!' spoken by a man at the victim's back or 'Be quiet, or I will blow your brains out!' where the threat is conditional on the victim behaving in a certain way.

The House of Lords has now established that words and even silent telephone calls can amount to an assault. Furthermore, 'harm' as defined by s47 (actual bodily harm) and s20 (grievous bodily harm) can mean psychiatric as well as physical harm.

R v Ireland; R v Burstow [1997] UKHL 34

Ireland had been convicted contrary to s47 OAPA 1861 of assault occasioning actual bodily harm. He had made repeated silent telephone calls to three women who suffered psychiatric illness as a result. The Court of Appeal held that he had committed assault by causing the victims to apprehend immediate and unlawful violence, the ABH being psychiatric harm.

Burstow had been convicted contrary to s20 OAPA 1861 of unlawfully and maliciously inflicting GBH. He had applied no physical violence directly or indirectly to the body of the victim but had conducted an eight-month campaign of harassment against her, including silent and abusive telephone calls. As a result, she had become severely depressed and was afraid of personal violence from him. The Court of Appeal had upheld the conviction.

There were three issues in the joint appeals to the House of Lords relevant to assault:

1. whether words can constitute an assault for the purposes of common assault and s47;

2. whether immediate fear of the possibility of harm arising from a telephone call can satisfy the requirement of immediate unlawful personal violence in the definition of an assault; and

3. whether *psychiatric* harm can amount to unlawful personal violence for the purposes of assault, bodily harm for the purposes of s47 and GBH for the purposes of s20.

Lord Steyn (Lord Goff and Lord Slynn agreeing):

> My Lords, it is easy to understand the terrifying effect of a campaign of telephone calls at night by a silent caller to a woman living on her own. It would be natural for the victim to regard the calls as menacing. What may heighten her fear is that she will not know what the caller may do next. The spectre of the caller arriving at her doorstep bent on inflicting personal violence on her may come to dominate her thinking. After all, as a matter of common sense, what else would she be terrified about? The victim may suffer psychiatric illness such as anxiety neurosis or acute depression. Harassment of women by repeated silent telephone calls, accompanied on occasions by heavy breathing, is apparently a significant social problem. That the criminal law should be able to deal with this problem, and so far as is practicable, afford effective protection to victims is self evident.
>
> From the point of view, however, of the general policy of our law towards the imposition of criminal responsibility, three specific features of the problem must be faced squarely. First, the medium used by the caller is the telephone: arguably it differs qualitatively from a face-to-face offer of violence to a sufficient extent to make a difference. Secondly, ex hypothesi the caller remains silent: arguably a caller may avoid the reach of the criminal law by remaining silent however menacing the context may be. Thirdly, it is arguable that the criminal law does not take into account 'mere' psychiatric illnesses.
>
> At first glance it may seem that the legislature has satisfactorily dealt with such objections by section 43(1) of the Telecommunications Act 1984 which makes it an offence persistently to make use of a public telecommunications system for the purpose of causing annoyance, inconvenience or needless anxiety to another. The maximum custodial penalty is six months imprisonment. This penalty may be inadequate to reflect a culpability of a persistent offender who causes serious psychiatric illness to another. For the future there will be for consideration the provisions of sections 1 and 2 of the Protection from Harassment Act 1997, not yet in force, which creates the offence of pursuing a course of conduct which amounts to harassment of another and which he knows or ought to know amounts to harassment of the other. The maximum custodial penalty is six months imprisonment. This penalty may also be inadequate to deal with persistent offenders who cause serious psychiatric injury to victims. Section 4(1) of the Act of 1997 which creates the offence of putting people in fear of violence seems more appropriate. It provides for maximum custodial penalty upon conviction on indictment of five years imprisonment. On the other hand, section 4 only applies when as a result of a course of conduct the victim has cause to fear, on at least two occasions, that violence will be used against her. It may be difficult to secure a conviction in respect of a silent caller: the victim in such cases may have cause to fear that violence may be used against her but no more. In my view, therefore, the provisions of these two statutes are not ideally suited to deal with the significant problem which I have described. One must therefore look elsewhere ...

In relation to the case of Ireland, Lord Steyn continued:

> Before the Court of Appeal there were two principal issues. The first was whether psychiatric illness may amount to bodily harm within the meaning of section 47 of the Act of 1861. Relying on a decision of the Court of Appeal in Reg. v. Chan-Fook [1994] 1 W.L.R. 689 the Court of Appeal in Ireland's case concluded that psychiatric injury may amount to bodily harm under section 47 of the Act of 1861. The second issue was whether Ireland's conduct was capable of amounting to an assault. In giving the judgment of the court in Ireland's case Swinton Thomas L.J. said (at p. 119):
>
> > 'It has been recognised for many centuries that putting a person in fear may amount to an assault. The early cases predate the invention of the telephone. We must apply the law to conditions as they are in the 20th century.'
>
> The court concluded that repeated telephone calls of a menacing nature may cause victims to apprehend immediate and unlawful violence. Given these conclusions of law, and Ireland's guilty plea, the Court of Appeal dismissed the appeal. The Court of Appeal certified the following question as being of general public importance, namely 'As to whether the making of a series of silent telephone calls can amount in law to an assault.' But it will also be necessary to consider the question whether psychiatric illness may in law amount to bodily harm under section 47 of the Act of 1861. Those are the issues of law before the House in the appeal of Ireland.

In relation to Burstow:

> Two questions of law were canvassed before the Court of Appeal. First, there was the question whether psychiatric injury may amount to bodily harm under section 20. The Court of Appeal regarded itself as bound by the affirmative decision in Reg. v. Chan-Fook [1994] 1 W.L.R. 689. The second issue was whether in the absence of physical violence applied directly or indirectly to the body of the victim an offence under section 20 may be committed. The Court of Appeal concluded that this question must be answered in the affirmative ....
>
> It is now necessary to consider whether the making of silent telephone calls causing psychiatric injury is capable of constituting an assault under section 47. The Court of Appeal, as constituted in Ireland's case, answered that question in the affirmative. There has been substantial academic criticism of the conclusion and reasoning in Ireland. ... Counsel's arguments, broadly speaking, challenged the decision in Ireland on very similar lines. Having carefully considered the literature and counsel's arguments, I have come to the conclusion that the appeal ought to be dismissed.
>
> The starting point must be that an assault is an ingredient of the offence under section 47. It is necessary to consider the two forms which an assault may take. The first is battery, which involves the unlawful application of force by the defendant upon the victim. Usually, section 47 is used to prosecute in cases of this kind. The second form of assault is an act causing the victim to apprehend an imminent application of force upon her: see Fagan v. Metropolitan Police Commissioner [1969] 1 Q.B. 439, 444D-E.
>
> One point can be disposed of, quite briefly. The Court of Appeal was not asked to consider whether silent telephone calls resulting in psychiatric injury is capable of constituting a battery. But encouraged by some academic comment it was raised before your Lordships' House. Counsel for Ireland was most economical in his argument on the point. I will try to match his economy of words. In my view it is not feasible to enlarge the generally accepted legal meaning of what is a battery to include the circumstances of a silent caller who causes psychiatric injury.
>
> It is to assault in the form of an act causing the victim to fear an immediate application of force to her that I must turn. Counsel argued that as a matter of law an assault can never be committed by words alone and therefore it cannot be committed by silence. The premise depends on the slenderest authority, namely, an observation by Holroyd J. to a jury that 'no words or singing are equivalent to an assault': Meade's and Belt's case 1 (1823) 1 Lew. C.C. 184. The proposition that a gesture may amount to an assault, but that words can never suffice, is unrealistic and indefensible. A thing said is also a thing done. There is no reason why something said should be incapable of causing an apprehension of immediate personal violence, e.g. a man accosting a woman in a dark alley saying 'come with me or I will stab you.' I would, therefore, reject the proposition that an assault can never be committed by words.

That brings me to the critical question whether a silent caller may be guilty of an assault. The answer to this question seems to me to be 'yes, depending on the facts.' It involves questions of fact within the province of the jury. After all, there is no reason why a telephone caller who says to a woman in a menacing way 'I will be at your door in a minute or two' may not be guilty of an assault if he causes his victim to apprehend immediate personal violence. Take now the case of the silent caller. He intends by his silence to cause fear and he is so understood. The victim is assailed by uncertainty about his intentions. Fear may dominate her emotions, and it may be the fear that the caller's arrival at her door may be imminent. She may fear the possibility of immediate personal violence. As a matter of law the caller may be guilty of an assault: whether he is or not will depend on the circumstances and in particular on the impact of the caller's potentially menacing call or calls on the victim. Such a prosecution case under section 47 may be fit to leave to the jury. And a trial judge may, depending on the circumstances, put a common sense consideration before the jury, namely what, if not the possibility of imminent personal violence, was the victim terrified about? I conclude that an assault may be committed in the particular factual circumstances which I have envisaged. For this reason I reject the submission that as a matter of law a silent telephone caller cannot ever be guilty of an offence under section 47. In these circumstances no useful purpose would be served by answering the vague certified question in *Ireland*.

Having concluded that the legal arguments advanced on behalf of Ireland on section 47 must fail, I nevertheless accept that the concept of an assault involving immediate personal violence as an ingredient of the section 47 offence is a considerable complicating factor in bringing prosecutions under it in respect of silent telephone callers and stalkers. That the least serious of the ladder of offences is difficult to apply in such cases is unfortunate.

 NOTE 10.1

1. Verbal assault: Conscious of the need to protect the victims of stalking by criminal sanction, the Protection from Harassment Act 1997 being not then in force, the House confirmed the traditional definition of assault (causing apprehension of violence to another) and extended it to words as well as deeds: 'a thing said is also a thing done'.

2. Silent telephone calls: Lord Steyn stated that an assault may be committed where V fears the *possibility* of immediate personal violence. Here, he may have extended the traditional definition to cover fear of violence that is not immediate. He goes on to say, however, that it would depend on the facts.

3. Psychiatric harm: The judgment clarified that inflicting psychiatric harm can never amount to the physical violence required by the offence of battery but if serious it can amount to harm for the purposes of ABH or GBH.

4. Immediacy: The judgment does not make clear how long a delay is permissible in assault between the telephone call generating fear and the violence. How long is too long?

 EXAMPLE 10.2

Suppose that D in Edinburgh emails V in London and says that unless she agrees to him visiting he will run her over and break both her legs. Has D assaulted V? V would apprehend violence but not immediately and *Ireland* really has no answer beyond leaving the matter to the jury. Whether the uncertain lapse of time between the threat and the intended infliction would prevent the threat from counting as an assault is an open question.

The requirement in the traditional definition of apprehension of 'immediate' violence has made the offence ill-suited to this social problem. Read the following extract by J. Horder 'Reconsidering Psychic Assault' [1998] *Crim LR* 392:

The meaning of 'imminence' in the common law of assault

Glanville Williams tells us that it has been settled law since the middle ages that the *actus reus* of assault had a technical meaning, different from battery, and focused on the apprehension that unlawful force was about to be applied to the victim .... '[I]t is immaterial that the actor is not at that moment within striking distance, but he must, it seems, be sufficiently near to apply the force then and there ... [The author then referred to the decision in *Ireland* [1997].] One implication of this dictum appears to be that Williams' understanding of the imminence requirement, cited above, cannot stand as an interpretation of the modern law. Ireland could not conceivably have been regarded as 'sufficiently near to apply the force then and there'. That leaves us with the puzzle of what imminence does mean, in the law of psychic assault, and that puzzle inevitably raises the question of what the rationale for the requirement of imminence really is ....

With reference to Lord Steyn's comment regarding the caller who threatens to arrive at a victim's door in a minute or two:

Whether true or not, this example raises the awkward question, not addressed in *Ireland*, of when a threat of future violence could not be regarded as an assault because of the length of delay between the threat itself and the infliction of the violence. What if Lord Steyn's hypothetical caller had said, 'I will be at your door within the hour?', or 'I will be at your door later tonight?' It is not a sufficient answer to say that the question of whether such threats amount to a threat of *imminent* violence, and are thus an assault, can be left to the jury. For what is lacking in such an answer is an account of the qualitative—as opposed to the quantitative—difference between (say) a threat of violence 'in a minute or two,' and a threat of violence 'later tonight,' that warrants marking out the former alone as an assault ....

On considering several cases, including *Smith v Superintendent of Woking Police Station* and *Logdon* the author continued:

In all of these cases the nature of the conditions holding threat in suspense is different; but it is the fact that there is such a threat, inducing a fear of violence, that matters. And in this regard, the amount of time during which the threat's implementation is suspended, the degree of imminence, should be regarded as of little moral significance. Taken together, all these cases are good illustrations of the weakness of the case for an imminence requirement in the law governing the *actus reus* of psychic assault.

Q. Does the author favour the requirement of any time limit at all for an assault?
Give reasons for your answer.

➔ CROSS-REFERENCE
The stalking offences are discussed at 10.9.

You can see that traditional offences are a very imperfect medium for controlling the problem of persistent stalking. No assault offence will have been committed until V has suffered harm and so early legal intervention to prevent stalking from becoming persistent is not possible. Amendments to the Protection from Harassment Act 1997 in 2013 now target stalking more specifically.

?! **THINKING POINT** 10.2

D is a former acquaintance of V now living 50 miles away. He sends her frequent emails, letters and flowers which V finds annoying and to which she does not respond. After several months, the emails become threatening and D says that he will burn down her house. D then begins to make late night silent telephone calls to her. V becomes distraught. Has D committed the AR of assault?

You can assault by omission

You may recall two assault cases from Chapter 2: *Fagan* [1969] 1 QB 439 and *DPP v Santa-Bermudez* [2003] EWHC Div Ct, [2004] Crim LR 417. In the former, D accidentally parked his car on a police officer's foot and deliberately delayed moving off after becoming aware of his actions. It was held that he had committed an assault and battery through a series of events or a continuing act, though some doubt was expressed as to whether his failure or omission to remove the car would be capable of constituting the assault. However, in *Santa-Bermudez* the drug-user's omission or failure to disclose to the police officer that he had a sharp object in his pocket (a syringe needle) was regarded as the AR of assault under the *Miller* duty principle. The duty principle is now preferred to that of the 'continuing act'.

→ CROSS-REFERENCE
Fagan is considered in Chapter 2, 2.1.2. *Santa-Bermudez* is discussed in Chapter 2, 2.2.3 'Creation of a Situation of Danger'.

10.1.3 Mens Rea

This will be dealt with as part of battery below since assault and battery share a common MR.

10.2 Battery

10.2.1 Definition

10.2.2 Actus Reus

10.2.3 Mens Rea of Assault and Battery

10.2.1 Definition

Battery: Any act by which the defendant intentionally or recklessly inflicts or applies unlawful personal violence or force upon the victim.

Actus Reus

- Application/Infliction of
- Unlawful and personal violence.

Mens Rea of Assault and Battery

- Intention or
- Subjective *Cunningham* recklessness.

10.2.2 Actus Reus

Application/infliction

There is no need for the victim to *apprehend* violence. A battery occurs when physical force is *inflicted* upon the victim. As with assault, it need be neither aggressive nor hostile and need only consist of unwanted physical contact, not harm. We implicitly consent to reasonable force in social situations such as jostling on the underground or high street, for example, and this is not an offence of battery.

Battery by omission

Infliction will typically be a positive act but *Santa-Bermudez* [2003] confirms that violence may also be inflicted by omission.

Violence need not be directly inflicted

Unlawful personal violence or force need not be directly inflicted upon the victim.

An intermediate medium for the application, such as a weapon, will suffice. In *Fagan* for example, the intermediate means of applying force to the police officer's foot was the defendant's car. There are three cases in point:

Haystead v Chief Constable of Derbyshire [2000] 3 ALL ER 890 QUEEN'S BENCH DIVISION

The defendant twice punched a woman who was holding her baby, causing the baby to fall and sustain injury. He was convicted of battery. The QBD rejected his argument that the application of force was insufficiently direct.

> Here the movement of Miss Wright whereby she lost hold of the child was entirely and immediately the result of the appellant's action in punching her. There is no difference in logic or good sense between the facts of this case and one where the defendant might have used a weapon to fell the child to the floor, save only that this is a case of reckless and not intentional battery.

→ CROSS-REFERENCE
For further discussion of transferred malice see Chapter 3, 3.1.12.

It was unnecessary to invoke 'transferred malice' because D had been reckless whether he injured the baby. Even if he had not been reckless, he had caused the child's injuries, for which the test is objective.

R v Martin (1881) 8 QBD 54 DIVISIONAL COURT

D put out the gas lights on a stairway of a crowded theatre shortly before the end of a play and also placed an iron bar across the doorway of an exit. Panic took hold of the audience who rushed down the stairs forcing people against the barred exit. Many were thrown to the floor or severely injured. The defendant was convicted of GBH contrary to s20. The Divisional Court confirmed the conviction apparently on the basis of a battery not an assault.

DPP v K (A Minor) [1990] 1 WLR 1067 DIVISIONAL COURT

This was a case of s47 Offences Against the Person Act 1861: assault causing actual bodily harm. A schoolboy had taken hydrochloric acid from a school laboratory into a cloakroom. He panicked when he heard someone approaching and poured the acid into a drying machine. He then abandoned the room. The acid blew into the face of a young victim who next used the machine.

Violence/force

There must be some force applied to the body of the victim. *Ireland* says that the infliction of psychiatric harm alone is not a battery.

→ CROSS-REFERENCE

Ireland is discussed at 10.1.2.

 THINKING POINT 10.3

Has D committed the AR of battery in the following situations?

1. D digs a pit outside V's front door. V falls into it when emerging from his house one night.
2. D sets his dog on V in order to attack V.
3. D throws a firework into a crowd of people who barge into each other to escape.
4. D slaps V hard on the back in greeting him at a party.
5. A store security guard suspects V of shoplifting and in order to detain her for questioning he grabs hold of her sleeve.

10.2.3 Mens Rea of Assault and Battery

The following case confirms the MR for these offences as intention or recklessness.

R v Venna [1975] 3 ALL ER 788 COURT OF APPEAL

A police officer was struck on the hand by D's foot during an attempted arrest in a street disturbance. A bone was fractured. D was convicted of assault occasioning ABH and appealed. The Court of Appeal held:

> We see no reason in logic or in law why a person who recklessly applies physical force to the person of another should be outside the criminal law of assault. In many cases the dividing line between intention and recklessness is barely distinguishable. This is such a case. In our judgment the direction was right in law; this ground of appeal fails ….

Appeal dismissed.

It is now clear that the type of recklessness required is *Cunningham* subjective recklessness:

R v Spratt [1990] 1 WLR 1073 COURT OF APPEAL

A subjective test of recklessness in common assault was approved to acquit D, who had fired an air pistol from a flat into a square below, of assault occasioning actual bodily harm contrary to s47 Offences Against the Person Act 1861. Two pellets had hit a child playing there. He had stated that he was aiming at a sign and would not have fired if he had known the child was there.

The House of Lords in *R v Savage, DPP v Parmenter* [1991] 3 WLR 914, confirmed that recklessness in assault/battery must be subjective. *R v G* [2003] AC 1034 (the two boys who set fire to a wheelie-bin) has now abolished *Caldwell* recklessness in any event.

→ CROSS-REFERENCE
For further discussion of *R v Savage, DPP v Parmenter* see 10.4.3.

?! **THINKING POINT** 10.4

On a street, D pushes V out of the way, causing V to bump into a lamp-post and hurt herself. Does D have the MR for battery on V if:

a. D disliked V and wanted to cause harm?

b. D knew she pushed V harder than was reasonable?

c. D was in a hurry and did not even think about the possibility of harm?

SECTION SUMMARY

Definition of assault:

- *AR: causing another to apprehend unlawful, personal violence;*
- *MR: either intentionally or by subjective recklessness.*

It can be committed by:

- *words or silence (Ireland/Burstow); or*
- *omission (Santana-Bermudez).*

Definition of battery:

- *AR: the infliction of unlawful, personal violence;*
- *MR: which must be intentionally or (subjective) recklessly inflicted.*

It can be committed by:

- *omission; or*
- *the indirect use of force (Haystead, Martin, DPP v K).*

10.3 Aggravated Assaults: Actual Bodily Harm, s47 OAPA 1861

10.3.1 Definition

10.3.2 Actus Reus

10.3.3 Mens Rea

10.3.1 Definition

Section 47 OAPA 1861:

'Whosoever shall be convicted on indictment of any assault occasioning actual bodily harm shall be liable to imprisonment for not more than five years.' The offence is triable either way (in either the magistrates' or Crown Court).

Actus reus

■ Assault or battery

■ Either must cause actual bodily harm.

Mens rea

■ MR of assault/battery.

See Diagram 10.3 for a summary.

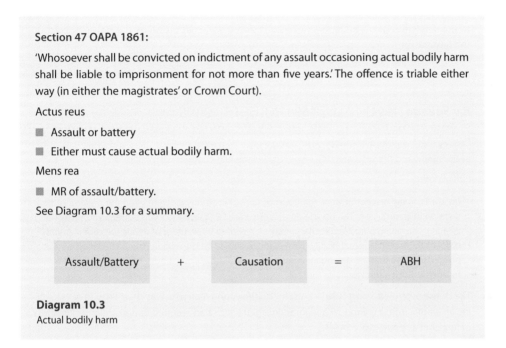

Diagram 10.3
Actual bodily harm

This offence is an example of an aggravated assault, attracting higher penalties. In other offences, an assault will be aggravated because it involves an intent to resist arrest (s38 OAPA 1861), an assault on a constable (s51 Police Act 1964) or a sexual assault (s3 Sexual Offences Act 2003). ABH would be the charge for relatively minor injuries such as bruising, a broken nose or teeth, a fractured wrist or ankle and minor cuts. It also includes psychiatric harm which can of course be considerably more serious than the former categories. It does not include emotional harm. There is therefore some vagueness about the definition of ABH and the distinction from battery.

10.3.2 Actus Reus

Assault/battery

There must first be proof of a technical assault or battery (common assault). This means that the AR/MR of either must be proved. The common assault must, in turn, occasion or *cause* ABH.

Occasioning/causation

There must be an unbroken causal connection between the assault/battery and harm. Recall that an unforeseen intervention, a *novus actus interveniens*, will break the chain of causation:

Roberts (1971) 56 CR APP R 95

The Court of Appeal held that a victim of an assault/battery who jumped from a moving car and suffered a broken ankle, did not break the chain of causation. The defendant driver had asked her to remove her clothes and begun to pull off her coat. She jumped fearing a sexual assault. He argued that he lacked the MR for ABH. It was held that the voluntary decision to jump was the natural and foreseeable result of what D said and did and that there was no need to prove MR in relation to the harm. This decision received approval by the House of Lords in the next case:

R v Savage [1991] 4 ALL ER 698 HOUSE OF LORDS

One woman assaulted another by throwing a glass of beer at her. The glass was broken, possibly accidentally, and the woman's wrist was cut. Savage was charged with ABH.

Lord Ackner:

> My Lords, in my respectful view, the Court of Appeal in *Parmenter* were wrong in preferring the decision in *Spratt's* case. The decision in *Roberts'* case 56 Cr.App.R. 95 was correct. The verdict of assault occasioning actual bodily harm may be returned upon proof of an assault together with proof of the fact that actual bodily harm was occasioned by the assault. The prosecution are not obliged to prove that the defendant intended to cause some actual bodily harm or was reckless as to whether such harm would be caused

The House overruled *Spratt* [1991] 2 All ER 210 (the young man who was charged with ABH for firing an air rifle from his window and injuring a girl) which had required *Cunningham* recklessness or foresight as to the risk of ABH.

 NOTE 10.2

There were criticisms of this judgment. Did it mean that an assault can be committed accidentally for the purposes of ABH? Was Ms Savage punished simply for the consequences of her act? Where was the consideration of her MR? If she had intended only an assault by throwing beer, to convict her of greater harm (ABH) would offend the correspondence principle that MR should correspond to the AR of an offence and not to lesser harm.

→ CROSS-REFERENCE
The correspondence principle is discussed in Chapter 3, 3.1.7.

Actual bodily harm

ABH was defined in *Miller* [1954] 2 QB 282 to mean any hurt or injury calculated to interfere with the health or comfort of the victim. It need not be serious or permanent but must be more than trifling or transient. *Miller* was a case of rape within marriage where the husband was convicted of ABH.

Psychiatric harm

In *R v Chan-Fook* [1994] 1 WLR 689 the Court of Appeal held that psychiatric injury may amount to ABH. D had aggressively questioned and locked in a suspected thief. There was a dispute as to whether D had physically assaulted the victim. But the prosecution alleged that even if the victim had suffered no physical injury, he had been put into a mental state which amounted to ABH. No psychiatric evidence was given. The judge directed the jury that an assault which caused an hysterical and nervous condition was sufficient. On appeal against conviction Hob-house LJ said (at pp 695–696):

> The body of the victim includes all parts of his body, including his organs, his nervous system and his brain. Bodily injury therefore may include injury to any of those parts of his body responsible for his mental and other faculties …. it does not include mere emotions such as fear or distress nor panic nor does it include, as such, states of mind that are not themselves evidence of some identifiable clinical condition.

He observed that whether or not an assault occasioned psychiatric injury should be left to the jury on hearing psychiatric evidence. The appeal was dismissed.

Chan-Fook was a step on the path to the classification of psychological harm as ABH by the House of Lords in the next case:

→ CROSS-REFERENCE

The facts of *Burstow* are set out in 10.1.2.

Burstow: R v Ireland; R v Burstow [1997] UKHL 34

Lord Steyn:

> It will now be convenient to consider the question which is common to the two appeals, namely, whether psychiatric illness is capable of amounting to bodily harm in terms of sections 18, 20 and 47 of the Act of 1861. The answer must be the same for the three sections ….
>
> The case was that they [the victims] developed mental disturbances of a lesser order, namely neurotic disorders. For present purposes the relevant forms of neurosis are anxiety disorders and depressive disorders. Neuroses must be distinguished from simple states of fear, or problems in coping with everyday life. Where the line is to be drawn must be a matter of psychiatric judgment. But for present purposes it is important to note that modern psychiatry treats neuroses as recognisable psychiatric illnesses: see Liability for Psychiatric Injury, Law Commission Consultation paper No. 137 (1995) Part III (The Medical Background); Mullany and Hanford, Tort Liability for Psychiatric Damages, (1993), discussion on 'The Medical Perspective,' at pp. 24–42, and in particular at 30, footnote 88. Moreover, it is essential to bear in mind that neurotic illnesses affect the central nervous system of the body, because emotions such as fear and anxiety are brain functions ….

Having approved *R v Chan-Fook* [1994] Lord Steyn continued:

> The proposition that the Victorian legislator when enacting sections 18, 20 and 47 of the Act 1861, would not have had in mind psychiatric illness is no doubt correct. Psychiatry was in its infancy in 1861. But the subjective intention of the draftsman is immaterial. The only relevant enquiry is as to the sense of the words in the context in which they are used. Moreover the Act of 1861 is a statute of the 'always speaking' type: the statute must be interpreted in the light of the best current scientific appreciation of the link between the body and psychiatric injury.
>
> For these reasons I would, therefore, reject the challenge to the correctness of Chan-Fook [1994] 2 All ER 552, [1994] 1 WLR 689. In my view the ruling in that case was based on principled and cogent reasoning and it marked a sound and essential clarification of the law. I would hold that 'bodily harm' in sections 18, 20 and 47 must be interpreted so as to include recognisable psychiatric illness.

Minor harm

Further cases have confirmed that a relatively low threshold of harm can amount to ABH. The Court of Appeal in *R (on the application of T) v DPP* [2003] EWHC 266 held that a momentary loss of consciousness was sufficient. It constituted harm and an injurious impairment to the victim's sensory functions which was more than transient and trifling. V had been kicked in the eye by a member of a group and was subsequently kicked by D as he lay on the ground causing the momentary loss of consciousness. The whole attack had caused facial injuries to V but the only injury directly attributable to D was the momentary loss of consciousness.

The Divisional Court in *DPP v Smith* [2006] EWHC 94 (Admin), [2006] Crim LR 528 held that cutting off a *substantial* amount of a person's hair, or putting paint or other substances in it, even though it is dead tissue, is *capable* of constituting ABH. Ordinarily, this might constitute battery but in extreme cases could amount to ABH. There is no need for either pain or for the skin to be cut or bruised or for the harm to be permanent. D had cut off his ex-girlfriend's pony tail and some of the hair on the top of her head.

Judge LJ:

15 As there are no decisions directly in point, we must address the problem on first principles, noting that, according to Viscount Kilmuir LC in *Director of Public Prosecutions v Smith* [1961] AC 290, 'bodily harm' needs no explanation, and that the phrase 'actual bodily harm' consists of 'three words of the English language which require no elaboration and in the ordinary course should not receive any [*R v Chan-Fook*]'. So actual bodily harm means what it says.

16 It is necessary to look at definitions because there is nothing to assist us in the decided cases. In ordinary language, 'harm' is not limited to 'injury', and according to the Concise Oxford Dictionary extends to 'hurt' or 'damage'. According to the same dictionary, "bodily," whether used as an adjective or an adverb, is 'concerned with the body'. 'Actual', as defined in the authorities, means that the bodily harm should not be so trivial or trifling as to be effectively without significance.

17 Recent authority shows that evidence of external bodily injury, or a break in or bruise to the surface of the skin, is not required. *Chan-Fook* established that actual bodily harm was not limited to 'harm to the skin, flesh and bones of the victim'. It applies to all parts of the body, 'including the victim's organs, his nervous system and his brain'. The significant words in that sentence are 'all' and 'includes'. By identifying specific parts of the body, the observations in this judgment were not excluding any others. An assault occasioning actual bodily harm may be committed by words or gestures alone, without the need for any physical contact between the assailant and the body of the victim (*R v Ireland and Burstow* [1998] AC 147). It follows that physical pain consequent on an assault is not a necessary ingredient of this offence (see also *R(T) v DPP* [2003] Crim LR 622).

18 In my judgment, whether it is alive beneath the surface of the skin or dead tissue above the surface of the skin, the hair is an attribute and part of the human body. It is intrinsic to each individual and to the identity of each individual. Although it is not essential to my decision, I note that an individual's hair is relevant to his or her autonomy. Some regard it as their crowning glory. Admirers may so regard it in the object of their affections. Even if, medically and scientifically speaking, the hair above the surface of the scalp is no more than dead tissue, it remains part of the body and is attached to it. While it is so attached, in my judgment it falls within the meaning of 'bodily' in the phrase 'actual bodily harm'. It is concerned with the body of the individual victim.

19 In my judgment, the respondent's actions in cutting off a substantial part of the victim's hair in the course of an assault on her—like putting paint on it or some unpleasant substance which marked or damaged it without causing injury elsewhere—is capable of amounting to an assault which occasions actual bodily harm. The justices were wrong in law.'

Appeal allowed.

ABH by omission

Recall the case of *Santa-Bermudez* in relation to assault by omission discussed earlier in this chapter. It was held that D was under a duty to inform the police officer of the needles in his pocket, and his failure to do so constituted an omission rendering him liable for assault occasioning ABH.

10.3.3 Mens Rea

The case of *Savage* confirmed that *Cunningham* recklessness or intention to *assault* is all that is required. D does not need to realise that ABH might occur. Therefore, it is no defence to argue, as in *Savage*, that the cut to V's wrist was accidental. The actual harm does not need to be foreseen by D. He will be convicted if he foresaw a risk of apprehension or harm (ie: the MR for assault or battery).

→ CROSS-REFERENCE
For discussion of *Savage* see 10.3.2.

> **?! THINKING POINT 10.5**
>
> In a neighbour dispute, D threatens to set his dog on V. V is scared of the dog. He jumps over a fence and falls, breaking his wrist. Has D committed ABH under s47?
>
> You will first need to consider whether:
>
> ■ the harm amounts to ABH
>
> ■ D committed the AR/MR elements of an assault
>
> ■ there is a causal link to the harm.

SECTION SUMMARY

ABH under s47 is defined as:

■ *assault occasioning actual bodily harm;*

■ *the assault must occasion or cause ABH;*

■ *ABH consists of interference with health and comfort. It can also include psychological harm; and*

■ *there is no need for MR in respect of the ABH but there must be MR (intention or recklessness) for the assault.*

10.4 Malicious Wounding and Grievous Bodily Harm: s20 OAPA 1861

10.4.1 Definition

10.4.2 Actus Reus

10.4.3 Mens Rea

10.4.1 Definition

> Section 20: Whosoever shall unlawfully and maliciously wound or inflict any grievous bodily harm upon any other person, either with or without any weapon or instrument shall be guilty of [an offence triable either way] and being convicted thereof shall be liable to imprisonment for five years.
>
> Section 20 creates two offences:
>
> ■ Malicious wounding (which need not be really serious); or
>
> ■ Malicious infliction of GBH.

Actus reus

■ Wounding; or

■ Infliction of GBH.

Mens rea

■ Maliciously (intention or *Cunningham* recklessness as to some harm).

See Diagram 10.4 for a summary.

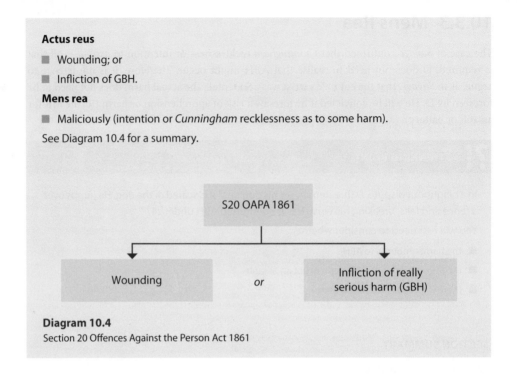

Diagram 10.4
Section 20 Offences Against the Person Act 1861

10.4.2 Actus Reus

Wounding

Case law has established the following technical rules:

■ The continuity of the whole skin must be broken: *Moriarty v Brookes* (1834) 6 C&P 684.

■ A scratch which does not break the inner skin is not a wound: *R v McLoughlin* (1838) 8 C&P 635.

■ Neither is an internal rupture of a blood vessel such as in the eye: *C (a minor) v Eisenhower* [1984] QB 331.

■ There is no wound if bone is broken but skin remains intact, for example: a collar-bone: *R v Wood* (1830) 1 Mood CC 278.

■ Rupture of the inner skin of the cheek or urethra resulting in bleeding is a wound: *R v Waltham* (1849) 3 Cox CC 442.

Therefore, although a wound must be more than a superficial scratch, it need not amount to GBH.

Grievous bodily harm

→ CROSS-REFERENCE
For further discussion of
DPP v Smith see
Chapter 6, 6.2.3.

GBH was defined as 'really serious harm' in *DPP v Smith* [1961] AC 290. It is an imprecise description which has not really been clarified by any later cases. The injury does not need to be permanent or life-threatening and clearly what might be serious to one person, for instance a child or a person with a particular disability, need not be to another.

Physical harm

Section 20 would be charged where there is permanent disability or disfigurement, broken or displaced bones, a fractured skull, or injuries causing substantial loss of blood or lengthy incapacity, as well as serious psychiatric injury.

Psychiatric harm

Burstow and *Ireland* provide that serious psychological/psychiatric injury, even if caused by telephone calls, may constitute both ABH and GBH. Injury need not be the result of physical force. It could be difficult to prove mens rea here for the requirement is for recklessness or intention in respect of *some* harm. Therefore, there would need to be proof of foresight of at least some form of psychological harm.

➜ CROSS-REFERENCE
For further discussion of *Burstow* and *Ireland* see 10.3.2. Mens rea for s20 GBH is discussed at 10.4.3.

Sexually transmitted infections

It was but a short step from the admission of psychiatric harm to the inclusion of HIV as a form of GBH. *Dica* (discussed here) transmitted HIV to two women through consensual sex, having concealed from them his state of health. The trial judge ruled that Dica had recklessly inflicted GBH. This was the first time that STI transmission had ever been held to constitute an assault. Dica appealed.

R v Dica [2004] EWCA CRIM 1103

Judge LJ:

Since R v Chan-Fook [1994] 99 CAR 147, as approved in the House of Lords in R v Ireland; R v Burstow [1998] 1 CAR 177, it has been recognised that for the purposes of both s.20 and s 47 'bodily harm' includes psychiatric injury, and its effects. Although the impact of Chan-Fook is reflected in that now well-established principle, it is perhaps worth noticing that:

'... an injury can be caused to someone by injuring their health; an assault may have the consequence of infecting the victim with a disease or causing the victim to become ill. The injury may be internal and may not be accompanied by any external injury ...' (per Hobhouse LJ at p. 151)

... if the remaining ingredients of s.20 are established, the charge is not answered simply because the grievous bodily harm suffered by the victim did not result from direct or indirect physical violence. Whether the consequences suffered by the victim are physical injuries or psychiatric injuries, or a combination of the two, the ingredients of the offence prescribed by s.20 are identical. If psychiatric injury can be inflicted without direct or indirect violence, or an assault, for the purposes of s.20 physical injury may be similarly inflicted ...

➜ CROSS-REFERENCE
Dica is considered in more detail at 10.6.3.

Subsequent convictions have occurred in respect of the transmission of gonorrhea through the use of a shared towel (*Maranguanda* [2009] EWCA Crim 60), of genital herpes (*Golding* [2014] EWCA Crim 889) and Hepatitis B (unreported, listed by the Terrence Higgins Trust, www.tht.org.uk). As to whether a transmissible sexual, or possibly non-sexual, infection is accurately classified as 'grievous bodily harm', the jury must apply 'contemporary social standards', according to *Golding*. The condition need not require treatment nor be long lasting. This might be thought to be somewhat vague.

Infliction

'Infliction' does not require either an assault or the direct application of force.

It was once thought that *infliction* of a wound or GBH was a technical term requiring proof of a prior assault (ie: non-consensual contact or violence). The authority on this was *Clarence* (1888) 22 QBD 23 where a husband transmitted a serious STI (gonorrhoea) to his wife through consensual sexual intercourse, concealing from her his true state of health. He successfully appealed against convictions of GBH under s20 and ABH under s47. One of the reasons for overturning his conviction was that the majority of the nine judges considered it essential to identify a prior assault for both offences. Consensual sexual intercourse was not an unlawful act of violence and was thus no assault. This was considered further in *Dica*, to which we return later.

The House of Lords held in *Wilson* [1984] AC 242, however, that infliction was not based on an assault but that force must be *directly* applied to the victim's body. This was ambiguous. Would force be directly applied where, for example, the defendant infected the victim with an STI through consensual sexual intercourse? Would force be directly applied where he placed an iron bar across an emergency exit in a crowded theatre, having turned off the lights and shouted fire (*Martin* (1881))? Apparently not, yet the case was approved in *Wilson*. The House of Lords in *Burstow* dispensed with the requirement of both an assault/battery and the direct application of

→ CROSS-REFERENCE
For further discussion of *Martin* see 10.2.2.

force for the purposes of s20. This stalking case established, along with *Ireland* as we have seen, that one can assault by silent telephone call and that serious psychiatric harm could amount to s20 GBH. No physical violence need be directly or indirectly applied to the body of the victim.

R v Ireland; R v Burstow [1997] UKHL 34

Lord Steyn:

Reg. v. Burstow: the meaning of 'inflict' in section 20

The decision in Chan-Fook opened up the possibility of applying sections 18, 20 and 47 in new circumstances. The appeal of Burstow lies in respect of his conviction under section 20. It was conceded that in principle the wording of section 18, and in particular the words 'cause any grievous bodily harm to any person;' do not preclude a prosecution in cases where the actus reus is the causing of psychiatric injury. But counsel laid stress on the difference between 'causing' grievous bodily harm in section 18 and 'inflicting' grievous bodily harm in section 20. Counsel argued that the difference in wording reveals a difference in legislative intent: inflict is a narrower concept than cause. This argument loses sight of the genesis of sections 18 and 20 ..... .

Instead I turn to the words of the section. Counsel's argument can only prevail if one may supplement the section by reading it as providing 'inflict by assault any grievous bodily harm.' Such an implication is, however, not necessary. On the contrary, section 20, like section 18, works perfectly satisfactorily without such an implication. I would reject this part of counsel's argument ....

But counsel had a stronger argument when he submitted that it is inherent in the word 'inflict' that there must be a direct or indirect application of force to the body. Counsel cited the speech of Lord Roskill in Reg. v. Wilson (Clarence) [1984] A.C. 242, 259E-260H, in which Lord Roskill quoted with approval from the judgment of the full court of the Supreme Court of Victoria in Reg. v. Salisbury [1976] V.R. 452. There are passages that give assistance to counsel's argument. But Lord Roskill expressly stated (at p. 260H) that he was 'content to accept, as did the [court in Salisbury] that there can be the infliction of grievous bodily harm contrary to section 20 without an assault being committed.' In the result the effect of the decisions in Wilson and Salisbury is neutral in respect of the issue as to the meaning of 'inflict.' Moreover, in Burstow [1997] 1 Cr.App.R. 144, 149, the Lord Chief Justice pointed out that in Reg. v. Mandair [1995] 1 A.C. 208, 215, Lord Mackay of Clashfern L.C. observed with the agreement of the majority of the House of Lords: 'In my opinion ... the word "cause" is wider or at least not narrower than the word "inflict"'. Like the Lord Chief Justice I regard this observation as making clear that in the context of the Act of 1861 there is no radical divergence between the meaning of the two words.

That leaves the troublesome authority of the decision of the Court for Crown Cases Reserved in Reg. v. Clarence (1888) 22 Q.B.D. 23. At a time when the defendant knew that he was suffering from a venereal disease, and his wife was ignorant of his condition, he had sexual intercourse with her. He communicated the disease to her. The defendant was charged and convicted of inflicting grievous bodily harm under section 20. There was an appeal. By a majority of nine to four the court quashed the conviction. The case was complicated by an issue of consent. But it must be accepted that in a case where there was direct physical contact the majority ruled that the requirement of infliction was not satisfied. This decision has never been overruled. It assists counsel's argument. But it seems to me that what detracts from the weight to be given to the dicta in Clarence is that none of the judges in that case had before them the possibility of the inflicting, or causing, of psychiatric injury. The criminal law has moved on in the light of a developing understanding of the link between the body and psychiatric injury. In my judgment Clarence no longer assists.

This appeal therefore established that psychiatric harm can amount to an offence under either ss 47, 20 or 18. It also established that there was no need for a prior assault in relation to s20, overruling *Clarence*. Consequently, there was no real distinction between s20 infliction and s18 causing GBH. The case of *Dica* explained further that this was so in relation to physical as well as psychiatric GBH.

10.4.3 Mens Rea

'Malicious' means 'foresight'

The two s20 offences of wounding or GBH must be inflicted maliciously. We have already seen that, following *Cunningham*, this means 'with foresight' and implies either intention or subjective recklessness. Recklessness in this context means that D foresaw that he might cause some harm, not necessarily GBH, and that he unreasonably took that risk.

➜ CROSS-REFERENCE
The meaning of 'maliciously' is explored in Chapter 3, 3.2.

Only foresight of the risk of some harm

It was confirmed by the Court of Appeal in *R v Mowatt* [1968] 1 QB 421, a violent assault and theft of £5, that only *some* physical harm needs to be foreseen by D and not harm of the gravity described in s20, that is: wounding or GBH. This was confirmed by the House of Lords in *Parmenter*, an appeal conjoined with *Savage* (discussed earlier).

R v Parmenter [1992] 1 AC 699 HOUSE OF LORDS

A father broke the leg of his 3-month-old son by handling him roughly and was convicted under s20. He had not realised that he was handling him in an inappropriate way. He was convicted following a direction by the judge to the jury that D should have foreseen some physical harm might result. The conviction was overturned by the Court of Appeal on the basis that D ought only to have been convicted if he had actually foreseen some harm. As it was not clear from the jury's decision whether D had foreseen harm or not, no lesser conviction of s47 was substituted. The House of Lords confirmed that for s20 D actually needed to foresee harm but only some harm. However, lack of foresight of harm was no barrier to conviction of s47 which could be committed without foresight of harm provided the initial assault/battery caused the harm. D was accordingly convicted of that offence.

Lord Ackner:

[Mr. Sedley—Counsel for D] contends that, properly construed, the section requires foresight of a wounding or grievous bodily harm. He drew your Lordships' attention to criticisms of R v Mowatt made by Professor Glanville Williams and by Professor JC Smith in their text books and in articles or commentaries. They argue that a person should not be criminally liable for consequences of his conduct unless he foresaw a consequence falling into the same legal category as that set out in the indictment.

Such a general principle runs contrary to the decision in R v Roberts (1971) … , which I have already stated to be, in my opinion, correct. The contention is apparently based on the proposition that, as the actus reus of a s20 offence is the wounding or the infliction of grievous bodily harm, the mens rea must consist of foreseeing such wounding or grievous bodily harm. But there is no such hard and fast principle. To take but two examples, the actus reus of murder is the killing of the victim, but foresight of grievous bodily harm is sufficient and, indeed, such bodily harm need not be such as to be dangerous to life. Again, in the case of manslaughter death is frequently the unforeseen consequence of the violence used ….

My Lords, I am satisfied that the decision in R v Mowatt was correct and that it is quite unnecessary that the accused should either have intended or have foreseen that his unlawful act might cause physical harm of the gravity described in s20, ie a wound or serious physical injury. It is enough that he should have foreseen that some physical harm to some person, albeit of a minor character, might result.

NOTE 10.3

1. Despite the fact that the Law Commission had recommended the reversal of *Mowatt*, this was not referred to in the judgment. Consequently, both s47 and s20 can be committed without any foresight in respect of the harm described by the offences. Again, this represents an infringement of the correspondence principle: that MR should correspond to the AR of any offence.

2. The judgment was criticised because it appeared that Mr Parmenter did not foresee any harm at all. He thought he was handling his baby appropriately. Therefore, lacking the foresight of even an assault, he should have been acquitted.

It follows that provided D does an act that he knows might cause some harm to someone, and he goes on to unreasonably take that risk, D has the MR for s20. Therefore, when D drunkenly perched on a night-club balcony and lost his balance, falling onto the dance-floor below and severely injuring a woman, he would have the MR for s20 if he realised there was a risk of some harm from the whole of his actions (perching and falling) and he unreasonably took that risk. The question is not whether falling was 'accidental' or intentional. Accidents can be reckless where people *knowingly* take risks (*Brady* [2006] EWCA Crim 2413).

?! THINKING POINT 10.6

A police officer, V, attempts to arrest D for breach of the peace and grabs D roughly by the arm. D is wearing a large metal studded arm-band. Has D committed an offence under s20 in any of the following situations (ignore the offences of assaulting or obstructing a police officer in the execution of duty)?

You will need to consider whether:

- The harm amounts to wounding or GBH;
- D has committed the AR of s20 (infliction);
- D has MR (intention or recklessness).
    a. D pulls away from V but in so doing his arm-band causes a 2 centimetre cut to V's face.
    b. D runs off leading V round the corner where D sticks out his leg, hoping V will fall over it and into a shallow hole left unprotected by workmen. V falls in and breaks his arm.

SECTION SUMMARY

Section 20 consists of two offences: malicious wounding or malicious infliction of GBH.
- *AR: Wounding need not amount to serious harm but must penetrate all layers of the skin.*
- *GBH is really serious harm.*
- *Infliction means no more than 'cause'.*
- *MR: GBH must be recklessly or intentionally inflicted but there need only be foresight of some harm.*

10.5 Causing Grievous Bodily Harm with Intent: s18 OAPA 1861

10.5.1 Definition

10.5.2 Actus Reus

10.5.3 Mens Rea

10.5.1 Definition

Section 18: Whosoever shall unlawfully and maliciously by any means whatsoever wound or cause any grievous bodily harm to any person with intent to do some grievous bodily harm to any person or with intent to resist or prevent the lawful apprehension or detainer of any person shall be guilty of an offence and liable to imprisonment for life.

Section 18 creates two separate offences:

Actus reus

- wounding; or
- causing of GBH.

Mens rea

- Maliciousness + Intention to cause GBH/resist arrest.

See Diagram 10.5 for a summary.

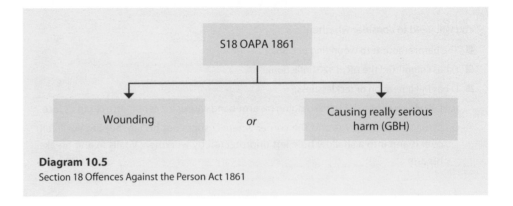

Diagram 10.5
Section 18 Offences Against the Person Act 1861

This is the more serious offence of GBH and is a crime of specific/ulterior intent (which means that it includes an intention to cause a result going beyond the AR of the crime). CPS Charging Standards indicate that the gravity of the injuries does not determine whether D should be charged with s20 or s18. More crucial is evidence of intent. Therefore, a serious injury may be charged as s20 if there is only evidence of recklessness and s18 where there is evidence of intent.

10.5.2 Actus Reus

Wounding bears the same meaning as for s20 and need not amount to GBH. *GBH* means the same as for s20. After *Burstow*, there is no practical difference between s20 inflicting and s18 causing GBH.

10.5.3 Mens Rea

The difference between s18 and s20 is that s18 wounding or GBH requires proof of an *ulterior* intention to commit GBH or resist/prevent the lawful arrest of any person. An intent merely to wound is insufficient. There must be an intent to cause really serious bodily injury: *Taylor* [2009] EWCA Crim 544. Therefore, if D is charged with wounding with intent under s18, but asserts the wound was accidentally caused during a struggle, the jury should consider the alternative offence of malicious wounding under s20. In *R v Brown* [2014] EWCA Crim 2176, a woman (D) slashed her partner's face with a knife. The prosecution alleged this was accompanied by a threat to kill. D alleged the injury was accidental and that she had picked up the knife in self-defence during a physical and verbal altercation. Both parties submitted that D was either guilty of s18 or nothing. In substituting a conviction of s20 for that under s18, the Court of Appeal held that the jury should have had the opportunity of deciding which version of events they believed and of convicting of the lesser offence if appropriate.

Given that the definition also requires the offences to be committed *maliciously* we need to ask what relevance that can have. Recall that 'maliciously' means with foresight.

A conviction of GBH where GBH has actually been caused, based on an intention to do it, is understandable. In such a case, the word maliciously really has no independent significance. Either one has the intention or not.

However, a conviction of GBH on the basis of an intention to resist lawful arrest is illogical. It might imply that one could be convicted for simply causing GBH in the course of arrest without MR. This would be unsatisfactory and it is here that there would need to be proof of 'maliciously' causing GBH, that is: at least foresight of GBH.

EXAMPLE 10.3

During an arrest, D pushes V so that V falls over a nearby obstruction, rolls into a road and is hit by a car. D has caused GBH. Whether or not he should be guilty of an offence under s18 will depend on (a) intention to resist lawful arrest and (b) whether or not he foresaw (maliciously) GBH.

The same would apply to causing a minor wound where there is an intention to commit GBH by breaking a bone, for instance. One would expect there to be a requirement of at least foresight in respect of the wound.

Intention is defined as in the law of murder: (a) *Direct intent*: purpose to cause GBH; or (b) *Oblique intent*: foresight of GBH as a virtually certain consequence of the defendant's act (*R v Woollin* [1998] 4 All ER 103).

→ CROSS-REFERENCE

For discussion of *Woollin* see Chapter 3, 3.1.6.

THINKING POINT 10.7

Is D guilty of s20 or s18 GBH in the following situations?

1. D pushes a broken bottle into V's face causing serious wounding. It was his intention to cause really serious harm.
2. D forcefully throws beer at V aware of the risk that the glass might slip out of her hand at the same time. She causes wounds to V's face.

SECTION SUMMARY

Section 18 consists of two offences: malicious wounding and malicious GBH.

■ *Both must be accompanied by intention to cause GBH or resist arrest;*
■ *The wounding need not be serious but there must be proof of the requisite intention;*
■ *Intention means either direct or oblique intent.*

10.6 Defences to Assault: Consent

10.6.1 The Public Interest

10.6.2 'Public Interest Exceptions': Consent Provides a Defence

10.6.3 Consent Induced by Fraud is No Defence

10.6.4 Capacity to Consent

10.6.5 D's Mistaken Belief in Consent

Any of the defences discussed in Chapters 8 and 9 may be relevant to violent offences. Self-defence is the most typical. But there is one defence which is specific to sexual and violent offences against the person: consent. Consent arises in a wide range of contexts. It may be *implied* in the sort of everyday activities giving rise to minor batteries such as jostling in public places or playing sports. If the activity is more unusual, D may assert that consent was *expressly* given by the 'victim'.

Non-consensual force is unlawful. Unlawful force is an AR element of the definition of all violent offences. A successful plea of consent will negate unlawfulness. Without proof of unlawfulness, the AR will be incomplete and no offence will have been committed. Consent therefore goes directly to the element of unlawfulness. It is regarded as a *justificatory* defence. The defence of consent raises two related issues:

■ **The public interest:** this determines the violent activities to which consent will provide a defence;

■ **Fraud/incapacity:** consent will be no defence if induced by a narrow range of frauds or where D lacks legal capacity.

10.6.1 The Public Interest

'The public interest' is a concept used by the courts in order to distinguish lawful from unlawful violent activities. If lawful, they can be consented to and therefore any harm arising, even if serious, will be within the public interest, for example: an accidental injury in a football match. If unlawful, consent is legally impossible even where V consents in fact.

It is not lawful to consent to being killed, for example, because it is not considered to be in the public interest to allow euthanasia, or in other words, murder. Consent on the part of the victim would be irrelevant. The public interest allows us to consent to surgery for both medical and non-medical reasons, for example: cosmetic surgery, male circumcision, body piercing and tattooing. Our own autonomy is thus protected as well as that of the doctor. The public interest, however, dictates that other forms of non-medical surgery, such as female circumcision contrary to the Female Genital Mutilation Act 2003, can never be consented to because there is no justification for it.

The public interest is a variable and unpredictable measure of what is regarded as lawful. It is a concept in which the following factors are weighed:

■ personal autonomy: we should be allowed a private sphere of integrity, free from state interference and unwanted interference from others without good reason;

■ protection of society from violence;

■ paternalism: protecting us from ourselves;

■ moralism: protecting us from immoral harm.

The current position regarding the public interest is that the courts place the dividing line between assault and battery on the one hand, which can always be consented to, and ABH/GBH which can only be consented to where the activity is lawful by virtue of a good reason. If there is a good reason, the conduct will be in the public interest and lawful.

The activities to which consent provides a defence are known as 'the public interest exceptions'.

10.6.2 'Public Interest Exceptions': Consent Provides a Defence

The following case established that consensual harm is prima facie unlawful unless it falls within a recognised public interest exception:

AG's Reference (No 6 of 1980) [1981] 2 ALL ER 1057 COURT OF APPEAL

Two men decided to settle an argument by fighting and one sustained a bleeding nose and bruises. It was held that his consent to the fight and, therefore, injury, was not in the public interest. The assailant was convicted of ABH. The court commented that minor injuries inflicted during an assault or battery may be consented to but it was not in the public interest that people should cause ABH without good reason, whether the act is public or private. However, Lord Lane stated:

> Nothing which we have said is intended to cast doubt on the accepted legality of properly conducted games and sports, lawful chastisement or correction, reasonable surgical interference, dangerous exhibitions, etc.

These activities are lawful by virtue of being in the public interest even though the physical contact they involve carries the risk of physical harm. For instance, before treating a patient, a doctor usually requires express consent. A competent patient is entitled to withhold consent to treatment even if this leads to death. Doctors imposing physical contact or harm upon a patient without consent will accordingly be guilty of assault. Surgery may well amount to ABH or GBH. Consent can be implied in emergencies and dispensed with in cases of necessity.

Rough horseplay

The public interest categories have been extended to include 'manly diversions' and 'rough horseplay' where consent has been allowed as a defence to serious injuries.

R v Jones (1986) 83 CR APP R 375 COURT OF APPEAL

A group of school boys tossed two others nine or ten feet into the air to prevent them from running away. One suffered a ruptured spleen and the other a broken arm. On appeal against conviction of GBH, the Court of Appeal held that boys have always indulged in rough and undisciplined horseplay and the Ds ought to have been able to rely on the defence of consent.

This represents quite a degree of legal tolerance of male violent activities in circumstances where V is given no real right of refusal. The court stressed that the criminal law is not concerned with physical contact provided it does not go too far. Playground pranks amongst consenting friends or the exercise of strength and skill are one thing, however, but here the boys were running away and had no choice.

The same point was confirmed in:

R v Aitken [1992] 1 WLR 1006 (COURTS' MARTIAL APPEAL COURT)

RAF officers got drunk, poured white spirit over one member of their group wearing a fire-resistant suit, and set fire to it. He was seriously burned. It was held that although intoxication is no defence to s20 (this being a basic intent offence, ie: one where recklessness is sufficient MR) a genuine mistaken belief in consent to rough, undisciplined horseplay can be. The implication was that actual consent would again have been a defence.

Also recall the case of *Richardson & Irwin* [1999] 1 Cr App R 392 where a group of university students threw V over a balcony causing serious harm. Their drunken mistake in consent, sufficient to negate the recklessness of s20, was also allowed to excuse their violence (wrongly in the view of many commentators).

These cases have been rightly questioned on the grounds that it surely ought not to be in the public interest to condone violence, especially drunken violence, where serious injuries have been inflicted. In addition, a defence based on gender creates inequality. The approach of the courts was in effect to assume the legality of the activity and the absence of a public interest reason for criminalising it. Contrast the opposite assumptions generally made in the following section.

→ CROSS-REFERENCE
For further discussion of *Richardson & Irwin* see Chapter 8, 8.3.8.

Intentional injury inflicted during private consensual sexual activity

Two cases established that it was not in the public interest to cause intentional harm during private consensual sexual activity: *Donovan* [1934] 2 KB 498 (ABH: spanking with a cane) and *Boyea* (1992) Crim LR 574 (indecent assault: insertion of fist into the vagina and anus, although consent in this case was doubted in *Dica*). In the next case the House of Lords had to consider whether the public interest exception should be extended to cover intentional bodily harm inflicted during consensual homosexual sado-masochism for the purposes of sexual gratification.

The task of the House was to decide whether there was a line below which harm could be consented to and above which it would never be possible to consent. In this case, the Law Lords sometimes discuss assault and not s47 or s20. This is because assault is a necessary element of s47 (*assault* occasioning ABH). Until recently, it was also thought to be an element of s20.

R v Brown [1994] 1 AC 212, [1993] 2 WLR 556
. . . .

The appellants willingly and enthusiastically participated in the commission of acts of violence against each other during the course of private consensual homosexual sado-masochistic encounters for the sexual pleasure it engendered in the giving and receiving of pain. The victim was usually manacled. There was branding and torture to genitals, thighs, buttocks, anus, penis, testicles and nipples. The victims were degraded and humiliated, sometimes beaten, sometimes wounded with instruments. There was blood-letting and the smearing of blood. Some activities involved excrement. The events were videoed and the prosecutions occurred after the films fell into the hands of the police. The appellants pleaded guilty to offences under s47 and s20 after the trial judge ruled that the prosecution did not need to prove lack of consent on the part of the victim. De facto consent was therefore irrelevant. The convictions were confirmed by both the Court of Appeal and House of Lords.

Lord Templeman:

> In some circumstances violence is not punishable under the criminal law. When no actual bodily harm is caused, the consent of the person affected precludes him from complaining. There can be no conviction for the summary offence of common assault if the victim has consented to the assault. Even when violence is intentionally inflicted and results in actual bodily harm, wounding or serious bodily harm the accused is entitled to be acquitted if the injury was a foreseeable incident of a lawful activity in which the person injured was participating. Surgery involves intentional violence resulting in actual or sometimes serious bodily harm but surgery is a lawful activity. Other activities carried on with consent by or on behalf of the injured person have been accepted as lawful notwithstanding that they involve actual bodily harm or may cause serious bodily harm. Ritual circumcision, tattooing, ear-piercing and violent sports including boxing are lawful activities ....

My Lords, the authorities dealing with the intentional infliction of bodily harm do not establish that consent is a defence to a charge under the 1861 Act. They establish that the courts have accepted that consent is a defence to the infliction of bodily harm in the course of some lawful activities. The question is whether the defence should be extended to the infliction of bodily harm in the course of sado-masochistic encounters. The Wolfenden Committee did not make any recommendations about sado-masochism and Parliament did not deal with violence in 1967. The 1967 Act is of no assistance for present purposes because the present problem was not under consideration.

The question whether the defence of consent should be extended to the consequences of sado-masochistic encounters can only be decided by consideration of policy and public interest. Parliament can call on the advice of doctors, psychiatrists, criminologists, sociologists and other experts and can also sound and take into account public opinion. But the question must at this stage be decided by this House in its judicial capacity in order to determine whether the convictions of the appellants should be upheld or quashed.

Counsel for some of the appellants argued that the defence of consent should be extended to the offence of occasioning actual bodily harm under s 47 of the 1861 Act but should not be available to charges of serious wounding and the infliction of serious bodily harm under s 20. I do not consider that this solution is practicable. Sado-masochistic participants have no way of foretelling the degree of bodily harm which will result from their encounters. The differences between actual bodily harm and serious bodily harm cannot be satisfactorily applied by a jury in order to determine acquittal or conviction.

Counsel for the appellants argued that consent should provide a defence to charges under both ss 20 and 47 because, it was said, every person has a right to deal with his body as he pleases. I do not consider that this slogan provides a sufficient guide to the policy decision which must now be made. It is an offence for a person to abuse his own body and mind by taking drugs. Although the law is often broken, the criminal law restrains a practice which is regarded as dangerous and injurious to individuals and which if allowed and extended is harmful to society generally. In any event the appellants in this case did not mutilate their own bodies. They inflicted bodily harm on willing victims. Suicide is no longer an offence but a person who assists another to commit suicide is guilty of murder or manslaughter.

The assertion was made on behalf of the appellants that the sexual appetites of sadists and masochists can only be satisfied by the infliction of bodily harm and that the law should not punish the consensual achievement of sexual satisfaction. There was no evidence to support the assertion that sado-masochist activities are essential to the happiness of the appellants or any other participants but the argument would be acceptable if sado-masochism were only concerned with sex as the appellants contend. In my opinion sado-masochism is not only concerned with sex. Sado-masochism is also concerned with violence. The evidence discloses that the practices of the appellants were unpredictably dangerous and degrading to body and mind and were developed with increasing barbarity and taught to persons whose consents were dubious or worthless.

A sadist draws pleasure from inflicting or watching cruelty. A masochist derives pleasure from his own pain or humiliation. The appellants are middle-aged men. The victims were youths some of whom were introduced to sado-masochism before they attained the age of 21….

The evidence disclosed that drink and drugs were employed to obtain consent and increase enthusiasm. The victim was usually manacled so that the sadist could enjoy the thrill of power and the victim could enjoy the thrill of helplessness. The victim had no control over the harm which the sadist, also stimulated by drink and drugs, might inflict …. Two members of the group had died from AIDS and one other had contracted an HIV infection although not necessarily from the practices of the group …. It is fortunate that there were no permanent injuries to a victim though no one knows the extent of harm inflicted in other cases. It is not surprising that a victim does not complain to the police when the complaint would involve him in giving details of acts in which he participated. Doctors of course are subject to a code of confidentiality.

In principle there is a difference between violence which is incidental and violence which is inflicted for the indulgence of cruelty. The violence of sado-masochistic encounters involves the indulgence of cruelty by sadists and the degradation of victims. Such violence is injurious to the participants and unpredictably dangerous. I am not prepared to invent a defence of consent for sado-masochistic encounters which breed and glorify cruelty and result in offences under ss 47 and 20 of the 1861 Act ….

Society is entitled and bound to protect itself against a cult of violence. Pleasure derived from the infliction of pain is an evil thing. Cruelty is uncivilised. I would answer the certified question in the negative and dismiss the appeals of the appellants against conviction.

Lord Lowry would also have dismissed the appeal.

 NOTE 10.4

The House of Lords decided, by a majority of 3:2, that:

- The paramount question was whether the injuries were lawful or not and the need for public protection. Consent and individual rights were secondary issues. The deliberate infliction of pain and violence in sado-masochistic activity is prima facie *unlawful* and there was no good reason for declaring it to be lawful in the public interest. The satisfying of a sado-masochistic libido does not come within the category of good reason. Society is entitled and bound to protect itself against a cult of violence.

- ABH, wounding, or GBH intentionally inflicted and foreseeable in a *lawful* activity can be consented to. But the public interest does not permit a new defence of consent to otherwise *unlawful* ABH or GBH. Injuries inflicted during unlawful activities, such as sado-masochism, can never be consented to. A subsidiary question concerned the evidential burden of proof: whether lack of consent is an element of ABH and GBH which must be proved.

- Consent can always operate as a *defence* to common assault, battery and indecent assault. Consent was not an *element* of assault, therefore the prosecution did not need to prove lack of consent.

The defendants had argued that the activity was lawful private, consensual sexual activity, not violence. Alternatively, consent should be allowed as a defence. The public interest prohibits only serious harm. It is not in the public interest to classify such conduct as criminal. Further, the OAPA 1861 was being wrongly used to selectively prosecute a sexual minority for their morality. As such, it offended Articles 7 (right to legal certainty) on the grounds of retrospectivity and 8 (right to privacy) on the ground that privacy includes sexual personality. The House rejected these arguments, but not so the dissenting Lords:

R v Brown [1994] 1 AC 212, [1993] 2 WLR 556

Lord Mustill (dissenting for the minority):

My Lords, this is a case about the criminal law of violence. In my opinion it should be a case about the criminal law of private sexual relations, if about anything at all …. I must confess that this distribution of the charges against the appellants at once sounds a note of warning. It suggests that the involvement of the 1861 Act was adventitious. This impression is reinforced when one considers the title of the statute under which the appellants are charged, 'Offences against the Person'. Conduct infringing ss 18, 20 and 47 of the 1861 Act comes before the Crown Court every day. Typically it involves brutality, aggression and violence, of a kind far removed from the appellants' behaviour which, however worthy of censure, involved no animosity, no aggression, no personal rancour on the part of the person inflicting the hurt towards the recipient and no protest by the recipient. In fact, quite the reverse. Of course we must give effect to the statute if its words capture what the appellants have done, but in deciding whether this is really so it is in my opinion legitimate to assume that the choice of the 1861 Act as the basis for the relevant counts in the indictment was made only because no other statute was found which could conceivably be brought to bear upon them ….

My Lords, I have stated the issue in these terms to stress two considerations of cardinal importance. Lawyers will need no reminding of the first, but since this prosecution has been widely noticed it must be emphasised that the issue before the House is not whether the appellants' conduct is morally right, but whether it is properly charged under the 1861 Act. When proposing that the conduct is not rightly so charged I do not invite your Lordships' House to indorse it as morally acceptable. Nor do I pronounce in favour of a libertarian doctrine specifically related to sexual matters. Nor in the least do I suggest that ethical pronouncements are meaningless, that there is no difference between right and wrong, that sadism is praiseworthy, or that new opinions on sexual morality are necessarily superior to the old, or anything else of the same kind. What I do say is that these are questions of private morality; that the standards by which they fall to be judged are not those of the criminal law; and that if these standards are to be upheld the individual must enforce them upon himself according to his own moral standards, or have them enforced against him by moral pressures exerted by whatever religious or other community to whose ethical ideals he responds. The point from which I invite your Lordships to depart is simply this, that the state should interfere with the rights of an individual to live his or her life as he or she may choose no more than is necessary to ensure a proper balance between the special interests of the individual and the general interests of the individuals who together comprise the populace at large. Thus, whilst acknowledging that very many people, if asked whether the appellants' conduct was wrong, would reply 'Yes, repulsively wrong', I would at the same time assert that this does not in itself mean that the prosecution of the appellants under ss 20 and 47 of the Offences against the Person Act 1861 is well founded ….

Let it be assumed however that we should embark upon this question. I ask myself, not whether as a result of the decision in this appeal, activities such as those of the appellants should cease to be criminal, but rather whether the 1861 Act (a statute which I venture to repeat once again was clearly intended to penalise conduct of a quite different nature) should in this new situation be interpreted so as to make it criminal. Why should this step be taken? Leaving aside repugnance and moral objection, both of which are entirely natural but neither of which are in my opinion grounds upon which the court could properly create a new crime, I can visualise only the following reasons.

(1) Some of the practices obviously created a risk of genito-urinary infection, and others of septicaemia. These might indeed have been grave in former times, but the risk of serious harm must surely have been greatly reduced by modern medical science.

(2) The possibility that matters might get out of hand, with grave results. It has been acknowledged throughout the present proceedings that the appellants' activities were performed as a prearranged ritual, which at the same time enhanced their excitement and minimised the risk that the infliction of injury would go too far. Of course things might go wrong and really serious injury or death might ensue. If this happened, those responsible would be punished according to the ordinary law, in the same way as those who kill or injure in the course of more ordinary sexual activities are regularly punished. But to penalise the appellants' conduct even if the extreme consequences do not ensue, just because they might have done so, would require an assessment of the degree of risk, and the balancing of this risk against the interests of individual freedom. Such a balancing is in my opinion for Parliament, not the courts; and even if your Lordships' House were to embark upon it the attempt must in my opinion fail at the outset for there is no evidence at all of the seriousness of the hazards to which sado-masochistic conduct of this kind gives rise ….

(3) I would give the same answer to the suggestion that these activities involved a risk of accelerating the spread of auto-immune deficiency syndrome (AIDS), and that they should be brought within the 1861 Act in the interests of public health. The consequence would be strange, since what is currently the principal cause for the transmission of this scourge, namely consenting buggery between males, is now legal. Nevertheless, I would have been compelled to give this proposition the most anxious consideration if there

had been any evidence to support it. But there is none, since the case for the Crown was advanced on an entirely different ground.

(4) There remains an argument to which I have given much greater weight. As the evidence in the present case has shown, there is a risk that strangers (and especially young strangers) may be drawn into these activities at an early age and will then become established in them for life. This is indeed a disturbing prospect but I have come to the conclusion that it is not a sufficient ground for declaring these activities to be criminal under the 1861 Act. The element of the corruption of youth is already catered for by the existing legislation; and if there is a gap in it which needs to be filled the remedy surely lies in the hands of Parliament, not in the application of a statute which is aimed at other forms of wrongdoing ... The only question is whether these consensual private acts are offences against the existing law of violence. To this question I return a negative response ....

Lord Mustill would have allowed the appeals, as would Lord Slynn. The minority would have declared the activity *lawful* on the basis that a conviction under the OAPA 1861 would be an unwarranted interference with private sexual morality. This was not the sort of violent behaviour the legislation was aimed at prohibiting. For the minority, the presence of full and free consent, the fact that no harm had been or was likely to be caused to anyone else, and individual autonomy were highly significant factors. The minority were more concerned with the offence whilst the majority focused on the public interest exceptions of the defence.

You should bear in mind that the presence of actual consent can be decisive in the determination of *sexual* offences although, after *Brown*, it is irrelevant in violent offences. P. Murphy, 'Flogging Live Complainants and Dead Horses' [2011] *Crim LR* 758:

Time and public mores have moved on since 1994 ... Indeed, even at the time of *Brown*, a different view was canvassed [a reference to the view of Lord Mustill] ... This alternative view is now widely accepted. The Law Commission proposed a limited reform, ie: that consent should be a defence except in cases of 'serious' injury ... But academic opinion goes much farther, accepting that the law regarding consensual sado-masochism should now be dealt with as an issue of consensual sexual activity, and should not become an issue of violence ... If a defendant is charged today ... with assault occasioning ABH and sexual assault arising from the same facts, the changes in the law of sexual offences places the trial judge in a truly invidious position. The jury must be directed to consider consent in relation to sexual assault, but under *Brown*, must be directed to disregard it in relation to ABH.... It is absurd and unworkable ... If the Supreme Court were now to be faced with this dilemma, I submit it is highly likely that they would depart from the strict holding in *Brown*.

The academic literature overwhelmingly casts *Brown* as a moralistic, anti-civil libertarian decision which served to discriminate against a sexual minority. Read the following extract from M. Giles, '*R v Brown*: Consensual Harm and the Public Interest' (1994) 57 *MLR* 101. In discussing first the judgment of Lord Lane CJ in *AG's Reference (No 6 of 1980)* she states:

In trying to evolve a more modern approach to public interest, he rejects dicta in older cases and finds that it is not in the public interest for people to harm each other for no good reason. This is the stage at which, without relying on any authority and disregarding *obiter dicta* comments which might have taken him in other directions, Lord Lane adds a further layer to the test of what is or is not unlawful. This approach is adopted by the majority in *Brown*.... By adding to the concept of 'public interest' that of 'good reason' he requires a court to in effect ask the same question twice, and at the same time he complicates the burden of proof issue and reverses the basic assumption from that of lawfulness to unlawfulness. In addition, his explanation of 'good reason' is vague in the extreme, consisting as it does only of examples of areas already established which he fails to evaluate or enlarge upon .... As a result of this case, therefore, we have moved from a starting point in line with earlier authority that lack of consent is an element of assault unless the case falls within a category of recognised exceptions, (*ie: consent is relevant to liability, unless the conduct is unlawful in which case consent would be impossible eg: prize-fighting*) to a situation where consensual assault causing harm is *prima facie* unlawful unless the behaviour falls within one of the categories legalising conduct. This case is, therefore, a crucial turning point in the approach to this issue. It is the basis on which Lord Lane again gives judgment in the Court of Appeal in *Brown*, and the confusion it causes is compounded by the majority judgments in the House of Lords.

The Main Issue

The basic issue which presents itself to the House of Lords, therefore, is the question of whether one looks to the public interest in order to legalize *prima facie* illegal behaviour (the paternalistic approach) or whether one uses public interest to criminalise potentially lawful behaviour (the civil libertarian approach). An added complication is that the choice of approach itself is inextricably a policy issue, and a preference for one approach over the other is likely also to influence and be influenced by what one considers is in the public good or the public interest. This is exactly what happens in *Brown*.... In those cases where there IS full and free consent to harm, it is clear that under English law there can be liability, and the question for any court is where and, just as importantly, how to draw the line .... Although their Lordships emphasise the role of parliament rather than the judiciary in policy making, and in effect justify their approach partly on that basis, it is clear that public policy has a major effect on their Lordships' reasoning and influences them either towards a paternalistic or a civil libertarian approach .... The minority approach emphasises consent as an element which legitimises the harm-doing. The majority marginalise consent; it becomes one possible relevant element within policy reasons for creating exceptions to the rule that causing actual bodily harm is unlawful. The practicality of paternalism triumphs over the theory of individual freedom. [Emphasis added.]

But there is a feminist view which would support *Brown* on the grounds that there is no clear divide between sex (the minority view) and violence (the majority view). Sado-masochism is a form of sexual violence which carries the potential to cause harm to anyone, whether homosexual or not. Consent is a nebulous term and difficult to distinguish from submission. The law should protect the weak and vulnerable from harm, not protect those with a libido for violence. The activities were rightly regarded as unlawful. Which view do you agree with?

A further appeal to the ECtHR under Article 8 failed on the grounds that the activity in question was rightly punishable on public health and moral grounds. The state was entitled to have regard not only to the actual *seriousness* of the harm caused, which was considered to be significant, but also to the *potential* for harm (*Laskey, Jaggard & Brown v UK* (1997) 24 EHRR 39).

But was the harm in *Brown* significant? No-one required medical treatment. Regarding the potential for harm, should people be punished for harm actually inflicted or for harm that might have happened? Surely it is the former.

Accidental injury in private consensual activity

Compare the case of *Brown* to the next case:

R v Wilson [1996] 3 WLR 125

The appellant branded his initials on to his wife's buttocks with a hot knife at her instigation. Her skin became infected. The husband was charged and convicted under s47 (ABH). He appealed to the Court of Appeal. The court put forward five reasons for overturning his conviction: consent on the part of Mrs Wilson; the branding was a personal adornment, the equivalent of a tattoo; lack of aggressive intent on the part of D; that although Brown established that consent was no defence to ABH, that case was confined to sado-masochistic encounters. The court held that consent may provide a defence in other circumstances. Finally, it was held that it was not in the public interest that the activities in question should amount to a criminal offence. Consensual activity between husband and wife, in the privacy of the matrimonial home, should not be subject to the criminal law.

In commenting on this case at [1996] *Crim LR* 573, J.C. Smith said that the only real distinction between *Wilson* and *Brown* was that Mr Wilson derived no sexual pleasure from the branding. Otherwise, the judgment was really in accordance with the minority view in *Brown* that there was no public interest reason for criminalising the activity, the focus being on the scope of the offence rather than the scope of the defence. He mused on whether bottom-branding is now a public interest exception to the general rule that ABH can never be consented to! This decision supported the view that *Brown* had been a moralistic judgment.

The assumption that the activity in question was prima facie lawful was followed in *Slingsby* [1995] *Crim LR* 570 where the Court of Appeal held that unintentional, accidental fatal injury in the course of consensual sexual activity (the insertion of D's fist into V's rectum, D wearing a signet ring) was not criminal, even though death had ensued. This approach was endorsed in *Meachen* [2006] EWCA Crim 2414 where D's conviction of indecent assault and s20 for causing unforeseeable injury to V's rectum through the insertion of three fingers was quashed on a similar basis.

→ CROSS-REFERENCE
For further discussion of *Slingsby* see Chapter 7, 7.2.4 'Constructive Manslaughter'.

However, the majority approach in *Brown* was followed in *R v Emmett* (1999) Unreported, *The Independent*, 19 July, where as part of consensual heterosexual activity, a woman agreed to having a plastic bag tied over her head causing unconsciousness, and on another occasion, to lighter fuel being poured over her breasts and set alight causing burns which became infected. Her partner was convicted of s47 and appealed. The Court of Appeal held that consent was no defence on the basis that the masochistic activity, in which injury was intentional, went beyond that which was evident in *Wilson*. In other words, the activity was prima facie unlawful and contrary to the public interest.

It follows that a court will view consensual sexual conduct in which injuries are intentional or foreseeable as prima facie violent and unlawful. Where accidental minor injuries are caused, the activity will be viewed as prima facie lawful. However, the attitude to rough and undisciplined horseplay is inconsistent and surely lacks moral justification.

Properly conducted sport and games

Most sports carry the risk of physical injury, especially contact sports. Boxing is unique in this respect as it is within the rules to assault or commit GBH on an opponent and knock them out. Participants in sport implicitly consent to the risk of reasonable accidental injuries or physical hazards of the game. However, the boundaries of implied consent can be difficult to discern. Harm caused by spontaneous, reflex reactions is one thing, but the defence should not be a licence for violence and thuggery. An increasing number of prosecutions for violence on the sports field culminated in the *Barnes* case. Observance of the rules of any game is not necessarily the end of the matter. Although injuries 'off the ball' in rugby or football are unlikely to be viewed as accidental, it is a question of fact in every case.

R v Barnes [2005] 1 WLR 910 COURT OF APPEAL

In an amateur football match the defendant seriously injured the right leg of an opponent by a crushing, late, unnecessary, reckless and high tackle. He was charged with GBH under s20 and argued at trial that the tackle was fair and the injury accidental. He was convicted following a ruling that he would be guilty if what he had done was not by way of legitimate sport. He was acquitted on appeal.

Woolf LCJ:

The issue which this appeal raises, is an important one. It goes to the heart of the question of when it is appropriate for criminal proceedings to be instituted after an injury is caused to one player by another player in the course of a sporting event, such as a football match. It is surprising that there is so little authoritative guidance from appellate courts as to the legal position in this situation. The explanation for this may be the fact that, until recently, prosecutions in these circumstances were very rare. However, there is now a steady but, fortunately, still modest flow of cases of this type coming before the courts, and thus the need for guidance.

In determining what the approach of the courts should be, the starting point is the fact that most organised sports have their own disciplinary procedures for enforcing their particular rules and standards of conduct. As a result, in the majority of situations there is not only no need for criminal proceedings, it is undesirable that there should be any criminal proceedings. Further, in addition to a criminal prosecution, there is the possibility of an injured player obtaining damages in a civil action from another player, if that other player caused him injuries through negligence or an assault. The circumstances in which criminal and civil remedies are available can and do overlap. However, a criminal prosecution should be reserved for those situations where the conduct is sufficiently grave to be properly categorised as criminal ….

The fact that the participants in, for example, a football match, implicitly consent to take part in a game, assists in identifying the limits of the defence. If what occurs goes beyond what a player can reasonably be regarded as having accepted by taking part in the sport, this indicates that the conduct will not be covered by the defence. What is implicitly accepted in one sport will not necessarily be covered by the defence in another sport. In R v Cey (1989) 48 C.C.C. (3d) 480, the Saskatchewan Court of Appeal was concerned with ice hockey which is a very physical game. Despite the nature of ice hockey, in giving the majority judgment, Gerwing JA (Cameron JA concurring), made it clear that even in ice hockey:

'some forms of bodily contact carry with them such a high risk of injury and such a distinct probability of serious harm as to be beyond what, in fact, the players commonly consent to, or what, in law, they are capable of consenting to.' (At page 490)

The general position as to contact sports was helpfully considered by the Law Commission in 'Consent and offences against the person: Law Commission Consultation Paper No. 134.' The Commission indicated its approval of the approach adopted by the Criminal Injuries Compensation Board which we would also approve. This is that 'in a sport in which bodily contact is a commonplace part of the game, the players consent to such contact even if, through unfortunate accident, injury, perhaps of a serious nature, may result. However, such players do not consent to being deliberately punched or kicked and such actions constitute an assault for which the Board would award compensation.' (10.12)

14. Subject to what we have to say hereafter we would in general accept the view of the Commission that:

'the present broad rules for sports and games appear to be:

(i)   the intentional infliction of injury enjoys no immunity;

(ii) a decision as to whether the reckless infliction of injury is criminal is likely to be strongly influenced by whether the injury occurred during actual play, or in a moment of temper or over-excitement when play has ceased, or "off the ball";

(iii) although there is little authority on the point, principle demands that even during play injury that results from risk-taking by a player that is unreasonable, in the light of the conduct necessary to play the game properly, should also be criminal.' (10.18)

On the other hand, the fact that the play is within the rules and practice of the game and does not go beyond it, will be a firm indication that what has happened is not criminal. In making a judgment as to whether conduct is criminal or not, it has to be borne in mind that, in highly competitive sports, conduct outside the rules can be expected to occur in the heat of the moment, and even if the conduct justifies not only being penalised but also a warning or even a sending off, it still may not reach the threshold level required for it to be criminal. That level is an objective one and does not depend upon the views of individual players. The type of the sport, the level at which it is played, the nature of the act, the degree of force used, the extent of the risk of injury, the state of mind of the defendant are all likely to be relevant in determining whether the defendant's actions go beyond the threshold.

Whether conduct reaches the required threshold to be criminal will therefore depend on all the circumstances. However, there will be cases that fall within a 'grey area,' and then the tribunal of fact will have to make its own determination as to which side of the line the case falls. In a situation such as we have on this appeal, to determine this type of question the jury would need to ask themselves among other questions whether the contact was so obviously late and/or violent that it could not be regarded as an instinctive reaction, error or misjudgement in the heat of the game.

 NOTE 10.5

1. The jury needed to know what was legitimate in the relevant sport and to be told where the ball was during the tackle.
2. Accidental injuries can be lawful even if outside of the rules, but intentional injuries are not.
3. Reckless injuries may also be lawful depending on whether or not D had shown reckless disregard for the safety of an opponent. Objective criteria were to be employed to determine the criminality of D's conduct.

A topical question concerns the legality of popular television programmes which present men intentionally inflicting pain/injury upon each other for entertainment purposes. These would, presumably, be regarded in the same way as sport.

?! **THINKING POINT** 10.8

1. If D intentionally injures V's genitals, in which of the following would D have committed an offence against the person: Female circumcision? Sex reassignment surgery? A street-fight? Whilst committing a youthful prank? In a television entertainment programme?

Example outline answer

You need first to consider the relevant offence with which D might be charged and then whether there is a relevant defence.

Offence: ABH/GBH contrary to either s47, s20 or s18 plus an offence under the prohibition of Female Circumcision Act 1985. You would need to explain the AR/MR of each. Defence: The only relevant potential defence under the common law could have been consent. [There could also have been arguments regarding respect for cultural customs which might fall within Article 9 ECHR (religious freedom).] Consent depends on the activity being in the public interest unless falling within a relevant exception. The exceptions concern sport, reasonable surgical interference and rough horseplay. Therefore, the operation and prank might be considered to be within the public interest. In a longer answer you would refer to all relevant cases, explaining the ratio and reasoning of each.

2. D, a man, canes V by consent, causing minor bruises and cuts. D's motive was sexual. Has D committed a criminal offence in any of the following situations: V is a female prostitute? V is an 18-year-old boy? V is D's long-term homosexual partner? V is a long-term heterosexual partner?

This question invites you to consider the majority and minority judgments in *Brown*.

3. In a game of rugby, player D head-butts player V as they are standing at the back of a scrum. V suffers a broken nose.

This question invites you to consider and apply *Barnes*.

10.6.3 Consent Induced by Fraud is No Defence

The following frauds will negate consent under the common law:

- nature or identity;
- quality;
- HIV and STI transmission.

If consent is given to physical conduct which is not harmful in itself, such as sexual intercourse, there is no crime; such activity is unquestionably lawful. But if V contracts an unexpected infection because D has fraudulently concealed his state of health from her, he may be charged with an offence under s20. Consent to the physical act of intercourse will provide no defence.

The law on fraud in relation to non-fatal offences is determined by the common law. Fraud is currently used to denote: deception, misrepresentation, concealment, or silence in the face of mistake by a victim. Despite the violation and exploitation inflicted, few deceptions turn otherwise lawful conduct into a crime. The legal categories are very narrow. Until recently, apparent consent would only be undermined when induced by fraud as to the *nature* of the act or the *identity* of the actor. Recent case law has added further categories: deception as to the *quality* of the act and concealment of HIV. But the overall scope of the law excludes nearly all other circumstantial deceptions and D will be able to rely on consent as a defence, even where he knows that V only consented because of the deception. The law is not based on the perceptions, or indeed the interests, of the victim of fraud but focuses instead on the type of deception made by D.

Fraud as to nature and identity

The narrow common law categories of fraud as to nature and identity were originally established by the infamous case of *Clarence*.

R v Clarence (1888) 22 QBD 23 COURT OF CROWN CASES RESERVED

A husband transmitted a serious STI (gonorrhoea) to his wife through consensual sexual inter-course, concealing from her his true state of health. He was convicted of the reckless infliction of GBH under s20 and ABH under s47. These were overturned on appeal. The court held that s47 and s20 required an assault. Consensual sexual intercourse was not an unlawful act of violence and was thus no assault. Further, the uncertain and delayed process of infection could not constitute the type of immediate violence envisaged by s20. More to the point, it was held that not every deception vitiates (or negates) consent. Only deceptions as to the nature of the act or the identity of the assailant were regarded as sufficiently fundamental to do so in assault cases. Clarence's deception was as to neither of these and thus his wife's consent remained valid.

→ CROSS-REFERENCE
For discussion of the assault requirement in *Clarence* see 10.4.2.

Much of the majority judges' reasoning was obscure and moralistic and the case is now discredited. But, the legacy for the common law of consent is that very few frauds result in criminal liability. If the victim consents to what is being done and who is doing it, consent, by and large, provides a defence regardless of any other deception, even if serious to the victim. Until 2003, the common law applied not only to violent offences, but also to sexual offences. *Clarence* remained the law for 100 years.

Fraud as to quality

It was not until the sexual assault case below that the *Clarence* orthodoxy began to disintegrate:

R v Tabassum [2000] 2 CR APP R 328 COURT OF APPEAL

The appellant was convicted of indecent assault for persuading women to allow him to measure their breasts for the stated reason that he was preparing a medical dossier for sale to doctors in connection with breast cancer. The women had all consented because they thought he was medically qualified when he was not. No sexual motive was apparent. At his appeal it was argued on his behalf that he had reasonably believed in the consent of the victims. The Court of Appeal agreed with the trial judge that there had been consent as to the nature of the act but not its quality.

Rose LJ:

> On the evidence, if the jury accepted it, consent was given because they mistakenly believed that the defendant was medically qualified or, in the case of the third complainant, trained at Christie's and that, in consequence, the touching was for a medical purpose. As this was not so, there was no true consent. They were consenting to touching for medical purposes not to indecent behaviour, that is, there was consent to the nature of the act but not its quality.

D's motive was irrelevant. The appeal was dismissed and the conviction confirmed.

 NOTE 10.6

→ CROSS-REFERENCE
Section 76(2)(a) Sexual Offences Act 2003 is discussed in Chapter 11, 11.2.2.

This was an important case:

1. It was enshrined in s76(2)(a) Sexual Offences Act 2003, relating to sexual offences, where it will be conclusively presumed that V does not consent if D's fraud relates to the nature of the act or D's *purpose*;

2. It also prepared the ground for *extensions* to the common law of consent in respect of violent offences. Although the deception in *Tabassum* was referred to as a 'quality' of the *act*, the case was essentially no different from *Richardson* [1998] 3 WLR 1292 in which a similar deception was viewed as one of 'attributes', or *identity* of the defendant. A dishonest dentist had failed to disclose her suspension from practice to six patients whom she continued to treat. Here, the court concluded that there had been no deception as to identity (ie: who—not what—she was).

Fraud and sexually-transmitted infection: 'biological GBH'

Tabassum was preferred over *Richardson* in the next case. The fraud here was identified by reference to neither act nor identity. Instead, the court concentrated on *consent to the risk of infection*. The case was concerned with HIV transmission. *Dica* effectively overturned *Clarence*, the facts being identical except for the nature of the infection and the unmarried status of the parties.

R v Dica [2004] EWCA CRIM 1103 COURT OF APPEAL

D was charged on two counts of s20 GBH having knowingly and recklessly transmitted HIV to two unsuspecting women through consensual, unprotected sexual intercourse, having concealed from them his HIV status. He did not intentionally transmit the infection. The prosecution alleged that the women would not have agreed to sexual intercourse had they known the truth. There were two questions for the court:

▨ Can reckless infection constitute an offence under s20 OAPA 1861?

and

▨ Can V's consent to unprotected sexual intercourse be relied upon as a defence?

We have already seen why the court reasoned that infection should constitute GBH. The second question concerned the fact that the trial judge had withdrawn the issue of consent from the jury because, following *Brown*, consent was no defence to GBH deliberately inflicted. Judge LJ:

> In our judgment, the reasoning which led the majority in Clarence to decide that the conviction under s.20 should be quashed has no continuing application. If that case were decided today, the conviction under s.20 would be upheld. Clarence knew, but his wife did not know, and he knew that she did not know that he was suffering from gonorrhoea. Nevertheless he had sexual intercourse with her, not intending deliberately to infect her, but reckless whether she might become infected, and thus suffer grievous bodily harm. Accordingly we agree with Judge Philpot's first ruling, that notwithstanding the decision in Clarence, it was open to the jury to convict the appellant of the offences alleged in the indictment.
>
> Concealment of the truth by the appellant
>
> … The judgments of the majority in Clarence included considerable discussion about the issue of fraud (in the sense of concealment), and the consequences if consent were vitiated. Again, however, the observations have to be put into the context of the perceived requirement that in the absence of an assault Clarence could not be guilty of the s.20 offence, and the deemed consent of the wife to have sexual intercourse with her husband ….
>
> The present case is concerned with and confined to s.20 offences alone, without the burdensome fiction of deemed consent to sexual intercourse. The question for decision is whether the victims' consent to sexual intercourse, which as a result of his alleged concealment was given in ignorance of the facts of the appellant's condition, necessarily amounted to consent to the risk of

→ CROSS-REFERENCE
For discussion of STIs as GBH see 10.4.2.

being infected by him. If that question must be answered 'Yes,' the concept of consent in relation to s.20 is devoid of real meaning ….

In our view, on the assumed fact now being considered, the answer is entirely straightforward. These victims consented to sexual intercourse. Accordingly, the appellant was not guilty of rape. Given the long-term nature of the relationships, if the appellant concealed the truth about his condition from them, and therefore kept them in ignorance of it, there was no reason for them to think that they were running any risk of infection, and they were not consenting to it. On this basis, there would be no consent sufficient in law to provide the appellant with a defence to the charge under s.20.…

In our judgement the impact of the authorities dealing with sexual gratification can too readily be misunderstood. It does not follow from them, and they do not suggest, that consensual acts of sexual intercourse are unlawful merely because there may be a known risk to the health of one or other participant. These participants are not intent on spreading or becoming infected with disease through sexual intercourse. They are not indulging in serious violence for the purposes of sexual gratification. They are simply prepared, knowingly, to run the risk—not the certainty—of infection, as well as all the other risks inherent in and possible consequences of sexual intercourse, such as, and despite the most careful precautions, an unintended pregnancy. At one extreme there is casual sex between complete strangers, sometimes protected, sometimes not, when the attendant risks are known to be higher, and at the other, there is sexual intercourse between couples in a long-term and loving, and trusting relationship, which may from time to time also carry risks.

The court decided that the issue of consent should not have been withdrawn from the jury and allowed the appeal. Dica was retried and sentenced to four and a half months' imprisonment.

NOTE 10.7

➜ CROSS-REFERENCE
Transmission of STIs is considered at 10.4.2.

1. **Biological GBH**: This case confirmed that the reckless transmission of HIV by consensual sexual intercourse amounted to an offence of GBH under s20. Although the ratio is concerned with HIV, the prevalence of other sexually transmitted infections such as Chlamydia was noted in the judgment. As we have already seen, the offence has now been extended to the transmission of other types of STI.

2. **Consent and fraud**: The court held that although consent is no defence to *intentionally* inflicted GBH on public policy grounds (*Brown*), it may be a defence where an STI is *recklessly* inflicted and the risk of infection is known and agreed to. Judge LJ gave two examples: (1) consensual unprotected sex between a Catholic couple one of whom is HIV positive; and (2) consensual unprotected sex between a young couple wishing to have a baby where there is a risk to the life of the woman if she becomes pregnant.

   Whether or not the victim actually consents in any particular case is a question of fact.

3. **Unknown risks**: *Dica* was concerned not with a known risk of infection but an unknown one. To say that because there had been consent to sexual intercourse there had also been consent to the risk of infection would render the word 'consent' devoid of all meaning. It followed that *Clarence* had no continuing relevance either as to whether transmission of an STI constituted GBH or as to whether consent to sexual intercourse implied consent to the risk of transmission.

4. **Rape:** Judge LJ nevertheless stated (obiter) that consent to sexual intercourse remained valid for the purposes of rape. Thus, an HIV positive defendant who conceals his infection from a consenting partner will commit s20 GBH but not rape.

By concentrating on consent, rather than fraud, therefore, we seem to have arrived at a situation whereby fraud regarding health status, leading to serious harm, is regarded as criminal in the context of non-sexual offences against the person but lawful in the context of sexual offences. This cannot be satisfactory.

Consequences of Dica

The Canadian case of *Cuerrier* [1998] 127 CCC (3d) 1, a case of HIV transmission and aggravated assault, of persuasive authority in *Dica*, abolished the *nature/identity* categories of fraud altogether. It held that *any* fraud inducing consent to an act which leads to significant harm should negate consent for the purposes of all personal offences whether of a sexual nature or otherwise.

Whether STI transmission should become an offence had been widely discussed since the early nineties. As a legal response to sexually transmitted infections, many jurisdictions have introduced both public health education policies and specific public health, nuisance, or endangerment offences to deal with the problem, but until the decision in *Dica*, there was no relevant offence in this country. There had been reluctance to criminalise either intentional or reckless infection on the grounds of social/public policy that such an offence would run counter to individuals assuming responsibility for their own health, that it could deter people from seeking HIV testing, and would be discriminatory against those who are HIV positive, have AIDS or carry viral hepatitis. The Law Commission, in 'Reform of Offences against the Person' (Law Com No 361, 2015), recommended that no new offences in relation to STI transmission should be created, but that it should remain within the definition of injury under the general offences. The report did not reach a firm view on decriminalising reckless transmission, instead recommending a wider review.

There have been convictions in Scotland, Cyprus, Canada and Australia for assault and HIV infection. Twenty-seven people in England and Wales have been prosecuted for the reckless transmission of STIs, mainly HIV, as at September 2015 (Terence Higgins Trust, www.tht.org.uk). European convictions for transmitting or exposing another person to HIV infection have led to imprisonment, fines and deportation raising concerns regarding defendants' human rights and discrimination which might impact negatively upon control of the infection. Here are some views on this new legal development:

A.T.H. Smith, 'Criminal Law: The Future' [2004] *Crim LR* 971, at p 977:

> Who knows, when the law is thus unleashed, whither it will subsequently wander? To the infliction of diseases other than those caused through unprotected sexual intercourse? How far are persons now entitled to take the risk of contracting disease when the activity in question is informed and wholly consensual? How critical is it to the reasoning of the Court of Appeal that the risk of infection could have been significantly reduced had the defendant used a condom?

J. Loveless & C. Derry, 'R v Dica' (2004) 38(3) *The Law Teacher* 287:

> [T]he issue of consent is not immune from … uncertainty. How will a court view a complainant who did not wish to become infected but who had unprotected intercourse on a few occasions genuinely thinking infection was not possible? Or the complainant who was aware of the defendant's condition but who through inadvertence or intoxication did not address her mind to the risk at the time? The issues of both risk awareness and consent may assume more public knowledge of the attendant risks of disease transmission than is actually the case … [T]here is little assistance in the judgment as to what factors are relevant to the contours or requirements of consent and this is particularly crucial in the area of private sexual relationships. To leave such an important issue as consent to the jury as a question of fact may well produce injustices parallel to those long apparent in the rape trial process, such as prejudicial jury and judicial attitudes towards certain complainants, particularly those with a sexual history …

M. Weait, '*Dica*: Knowledge, consent and the transmission of HIV' (2004) *NLJ*, 28 May 2004:

> Professor Spencer suggests that the judgment in *Dica* applies not only to those who know their in-fected status, but also to those who know that they *may* be infected. With all due respect, this goes far further than the decision in *Dica*, which concerned a person who knew their HIV-positive status .... [T]here are other ways of conceptualizing both facts and knowledge, and risk in respect of these. For example, a woman to whom HIV is transmitted may know that there was a *risk* that her partner was HIV-positive. She may know for a fact that one of his previous sexual partners is HIV-positive, or that he was sexually active with a number of people and did not practice safer sex, or that he belongs to a high-risk group for HIV infection. Or she may recognize that, in the absence of conclusive proof to the contrary, there is always a *risk* that a partner may be HIV-positive (or be infected with an STI). Ac-cording to *Dica*, the answer depends not on knowledge, but on consent to intercourse that carries the risk of infection. It is submitted that where a person consents to sexual intercourse with knowledge of these facts, and becomes infected, the defence should be available because in each of these cases she is (knowingly) consenting to intercourse that carries the risk of transmission.

Consent must be informed

The Court of Appeal has now gone one step further in defining fraudulently induced consent to STI transmission: consent must be informed.

R v Konzani [2005] EWCA CRIM 706 COURT OF APPEAL

After having been informed that he was HIV positive, D transmitted the infection to three part-ners through consensual sexual intercourse concealing from them his state of health. He was convicted of inflicting GBH contrary to s20 and appealed against the judge's ruling on consent. It was argued on his behalf that by consenting to unprotected sexual intercourse, each partner had implicitly consented to all the risks associated with sexual intercourse.

Judge LJ:

> There is a critical distinction between taking a risk of the various, potentially adverse and possibly problematic consequences of sexual intercourse, and giving an informed consent to the risk of infection with a fatal disease. For the complainant's consent to the risks of contracting the HIV virus to provide a defence, it is at least implicit from the reasoning in R v Dica, and the observa-tions of Lord Woolf CJ in R v Barnes confirm, that her consent must be an informed consent. If that proposition is in doubt, we take this opportunity to emphasise it. We must therefore examine its implications for this appeal.
>
> The recognition in R v Dica of informed consent as a defence was based on but limited by po-tentially conflicting public policy considerations. In the public interest, so far as possible, the spread of catastrophic illness must be avoided or prevented. On the other hand, the public interest also requires that the principle of personal autonomy in the context of adult non-violent sexual relation-ships should be maintained. If an individual who knows that he is suffering from the HIV virus con-ceals this stark fact from his sexual partner, the principle of her personal autonomy is not enhanced if he is exculpated when he recklessly transmits the HIV virus to her through consensual sexual inter-course. On any view, the concealment of this fact from her almost inevitably means that she is de-ceived. Her consent is not properly informed, and she cannot give an informed consent to something of which she is ignorant. Equally, her personal autonomy is not normally protected by allowing a de-fendant who knows that he is suffering from the HIV virus which he deliberately conceals, to assert an honest belief in his partner's informed consent to the risk of the transmission of the HIV virus. Silence in these circumstances is incongruous with honesty, or with a genuine belief that there is an informed consent. Accordingly, in such circumstances the issue either of informed consent, or honest belief in it will only rarely arise: in reality, in most cases, the contention would be wholly artificial.

The appeal was dismissed. But if concealment of information is now unlawful, how much information has to be revealed in order to be able to say that the victim's consent was informed? In English law, there is no general duty of disclosure. Does this case impose a duty to disclose HIV status? Recall that *Santa-Bermudez* (2003) established that D was in breach of duty by failing to inform the police officer of needles in his pockets. Do these cases signify an emerging duty to inform?

→ **CROSS-REFERENCE**
For further discussion of *Santa-Bermudez* see Chapter 2, 2.2.3 'Creation of a Situation of Danger'.

S. Ryan, 'Reckless Transmission of HIV: Knowledge and Culpability' [2006] *Crim LR* 981, at p 990:

> While the defendant in *Matias* [*The Guardian*, 30 April 2005] had received a positive HIV diagnosis, Judge Michael Stokes Q.C., during sentencing observed that Matias might be in need of further information about issues relating to HIV and hoped that he would be provided with such information while in prison. It seems that despite medical diagnosis and treatment, Matias's knowledge regarding risks of transmission was in real doubt. The case of *Adaye* [*The Times*, 10 January 2004] is even more problematic. Although there was evidence that the defendant had been informed by a doctor treating him in Africa that he was at high risk of HIV infection, there was no evidence that he had received any counselling regarding the risks associated with HIV.... Elliott argues that in order to be held criminally liable, the HIV positive person must both understand that HIV is a communicable disease and know how it may be transmitted. Basic principles of fairness would suggest that this is the correct position to adopt. It is simply unfair to punish someone who has no knowledge that their activity risks harming another .... If it is accepted that knowledge regarding the risks of transmission is required, how is such knowledge to be proven?.... [T]here has been a tendency in both the case law and academic commentary to date, to make assumptions as to knowledge regarding means of transmissions .... A Mori poll conducted in November 2005 ... revealed a 12 per cent drop in the number of people who knew that HIV could be passed from a man to a woman during unprotected sexual intercourse.

SECTION SUMMARY

- Consent is a defence to assault and battery.
- Consent is a defence to ABH or GBH where the activity is in the public interest (Brown).
- It will be in the public interest if it is regarded as lawful, for example: sports, surgery, horseplay (AG's Reference (No 6 of 1980) and Brown).
- The deliberate infliction of sexual harm is not in the public interest (Donovan, Boyea, Emmett, Brown, Laskey).
- Consent will be negated by frauds as to the nature of the act or the identity of the actor, some frauds as to a quality of the act, and as to HIV status (Tabassum, Dica, Konzani).
- Consent must be informed. This means that the sexual transmission of HIV will not be consented to where the condition is concealed from the victim but can be consented to where the victim is informed of it (Dica, Konzani).

?! **THINKING POINT** 10.9

In which of the following situations will D have committed s20 GBH?

D has an STI and conceals it from V to whom he transmits the infection through:

a. unprotected consensual sexual intercourse;

b. oral sex; or

c. kissing.

You need to consider the AR/MR elements of any relevant offence followed by any relevant defence.

Example: Offence—s20. What are the AR/MR elements and which authorities are relevant? Look at *Burstow/Ireland* and *Dica*.

Defence:

- Can you consent to STI transmission?
- Will apparent consent be negatived by fraud?
- Look at *Tabassum*, *Dica* and *Konzani*.

10.6.4 Capacity to Consent

Whether or not a person has the capacity to consent to harm is in general terms a question of competence, intelligence and understanding. This may be lacking because they are too young, mentally disabled or lack the ability to communicate.

Age

The only test of competence is not a question of age but of 'maturity, understanding and intelligence': *Gillick v Wisbech & West Norfolk AHA* [1986] AC 112, where a mother of a teenage girl under 16 challenged government advice that GPs could give confidential advice to teenagers under 16 regarding contraception. The House of Lords held that a combination of maturity, understanding and intelligence was more important than age.

An earlier case of *Burrell v Harmer* [1967] had held that two boys aged 12 and 13 were unable to consent to tattooing because they had no understanding of the nature of the act. Their skin had become inflamed and the tattooist was convicted of ABH.

Mental incapacity

The test of capacity in relation to non-sexual offences is determined by the same considerations as in relation to children. This means that, in medical cases, a competent patient who wishes to refuse treatment has the right to do so, even if it may lead to death. A doctor who continues to administer treatment to a competent patient against their wishes will be committing an assault. The common law principles of competence are reinforced by the Mental Capacity Act 2005 which sets out a test of capacity for the purposes of a person's ability to make decisions regarding their care and welfare. A person will lack capacity if at the material time his understanding, or ability to retain, evaluate or communicate information prevents him from making a decision because of an impairment of, or a disturbance in the functioning of, the mind or brain, whether temporary or permanent (ss2 and 3).

10.6.5 D's Mistaken Belief in Consent

→ CROSS-REFERENCE
For further discussion of *Morgan* see Chapter 11, 11.2.3.

D may assert that he mistakenly believed V consented to an act, when there was, in fact, no consent. Provided the act falls within one of the public interest exceptions, D may assert a defence of honest belief, entitling him to be judged on his mistaken view of the facts. The test derives from the case of *Morgan* [1975] 2All ER 347. There is no need for D's belief to be reasonable.

10.7 Defences to Assault: Lawful Chastisement

10.7.1 Parents

10.7.2 Teachers

10.7.1 Parents

Parents and people in parental positions may use reasonable force to discipline their children. If charged with assault, the defence of lawful chastisement may be used provided the force used was moderate.

A v UK (1999) 27 EHRR 611, ECtHR, held the UK to be in violation of Article 3 for allowing a defence of chastisement that failed to provide an adequate or effective deterrent against inhuman or degrading treatment. In this case, a stepfather had hit his child with a garden cane causing multiple bruising on his thighs, back and bottom and was acquitted of a s47 offence. In *R v H* [2002] 1 Cr App R 59, an appeal against conviction of ABH where a father had hit his child with a leather belt, guidelines were set out as to how to evaluate 'reasonableness'. It was a question of the context, nature, duration and reason for the defendant's behaviour as well as the age, characteristics of, and consequences for the child.

Section 58 of the Children Act 2004 has now confined the defence to common assault or battery. The fact that there is no clear distinction between battery and ABH and that reasonableness still needs to be evaluated by a jury means that this defence remains problematic.

10.7.2 Teachers

Under the Education Act 1996, members of staff of a school cannot use corporal punishment on a pupil but can use reasonable force to restrain violent or disruptive children or where there is an immediate danger of personal injury or damage to property.

10.8 Racially and Religiously Aggravated Assaults

10.8.1 Racial and Religious Aggravated Offences

10.8.2 Section 28 Crime and Disorder Act 1998

10.8.3 Section 28(1)(a): Demonstration of Racial/Religious Hostility

10.8.4 Section 28(1)(b): Racial/Religious Motivation

10.8.5 Section 28(4): 'Racial Group'

10.8.1 Racial and Religious Aggravated Offences

In order to confront the problem of racially motivated *violent* crime, as opposed to racist incidents and *public order* offences of racial hatred, s28 Crime and Disorder Act 1998 provides enhanced sentences for nine existing crimes on the basis of racial aggravation. For example, the maximum sentence for common assault rises from six months to two years; for ABH, five years' imprisonment rises to seven. D must be found guilty of a basic offence before the court determines whether a separate offence of racial or religious aggravation has been committed which would justify an enhanced sentence. Despite concerns regarding free speech, s28 was amended by s39 Anti-Terrorism, Crime and Security Act 2001 to include 'religious hostility' which does not require reference to race or ethnicity. Under ss 145 and 146 Criminal Justice Act 2003, the sentencing for any offence may be increased if related to any of five 'protected characteristics': race, religion, sexual orientation, disability and transgender identity. There were 30,234 police recorded offences of racially and religiously aggravated crime in 2012/13. It has fallen by around 21 per cent in the last five years (Ministry of Justice, Statistics on Race and the Criminal Justice System 2012: www.gov.uk). The Public Order Act has now been amended by the Racial and Religious Hatred Act 2006 so as to include incitement to religious hatred. The right to free speech, guaranteed by Article 10 ECHR, is qualified by these offences which seek to promote social cohesion and tolerance.

10.8.2 Section 28 Crime and Disorder Act 1998

Section 28(1) 1998 Act defines 'racial or religious aggravation' as present if:

(a) at the time of committing the offence, or immediately before or after doing so, the offender *demonstrates* towards the victim of the offence *hostility* based on the victim's membership (or presumed membership) of a racial or religious group; or

(b) the offence is *motivated* (wholly or partly) by *hostility* towards members of a racial or religious group based on their membership of that group. [Emphasis added.]

Section 28(4) defines 'racial group' by reference to race, colour, nationality (including citizenship) or ethnic or national origins. Section 28(5) defines 'religious group' as a group of persons defined by reference to religious belief or lack of religious belief, thus covering atheists.

Section 28(1)(a) is concerned with the outward manifestation of racial or religious hostility. Section 28(1)(b) is concerned with the inner motivation of the defendant. It is important to note that the two are distinct. Acquittals under s28(1)(a) should not occur because the hostility was not racially motivated as required by s28(1)(b). In *R (Jones) v Bedfordshire Magistrates' Court* [2010] EWHC 523 the High Court confirmed that the test for hostility required by s28(1)(a) is objective. No subjective intent need be proved. This would only be relevant to s28(1)(b).

10.8.3 Section 28(1)(a): Demonstration of Racial/Religious Hostility

Racism/religious hostility need not be racially motivated or the only reason for hostility

Under s28(1)(a), hostility must be *demonstrated* at the time of the offence and be based on racial or religious grounds.

The need for 'demonstration' was considered in *R v SH* [2010] EWCA Crim 1931, where the Court of Appeal upheld an appeal against D's acquittal of racially aggravated fear or provocation of violence: Leveson LJ:

… [W]hether the repeated references to OA as a 'monkey' or 'black monkey' constituted a demonstration of hostility based on race (whether or not that hostility was also based, to any extent, on any other factor) or mere vulgar abuse unconnected with hostility based on race, was eminently a matter of fact for the jury to consider on all the evidence.

Under s28(3) hostility may be based on factors other than V's presumed race. For example, hostility based partly on V's presumed membership of a racial group is sufficient even if it is also based partly on V's duties as a parking attendant: *Johnson v DPP* [2008] EWCH 509. It does not require proof of motivation, which is relevant only to s28(1)(b). Therefore, 'you black bastard' uttered during an assault on a door supervisor who had refused D entry to a club was held to fall within s28(1)(a): *DPP v Woods* [2002] EWHC Admin 85. Kay LJ:

… if the Justices had had regard to that provision [s28(3)], it is inevitable that a conviction would have followed. Section 28(1)(a) was not intended to apply only to those cases in which the offender is motivated solely, or even mainly, by racial malevolence. It is designed to extend to cases which may have a racially neutral gravamen but in the course of which there is demonstrated towards the victim hostility based on the victim's membership of a racial group. Any contrary constriction would emasculate section 28(1)(a).

Case law confirms that the circumstances must go beyond 'vulgar abuse' into an outward manifestation of racial hostility.

At the time of/immediately before or after

A 20-minute delay between the assault and the racist insult was too long: *Parry v DPP* [2004] EWHC 3112 (Admin).

10.8.4 Section 28(1)(b): Racial/Religious Motivation

One motivation for the crime must be racial or religious hostility, but not necessarily towards the actual victim. Motivation is clearly a difficult concept to prove beyond all reasonable doubt. One may act with several different motives. For example, if D, a white man, discovers V, an Indian man, in the act of adultery with D's wife and D calls V 'a black bastard' whilst assaulting him, the offence may be perceived as motivated by jealousy. However, D may not escape the provisions of the Act since by virtue of s28(1)(a) racial hostility would have been displayed at the time of the basic offence, thus justifying a two-year instead of six-month sentence for common assault.

10.8.5 Section 28(4): 'Racial Group'

People who are not of British origin constitute a racial group

The statute intends a broad, non-technical approach to the definition of racial group, the aim of which is to attack racism and xenophobia. Racial hostility towards V under s28(1)(a) may therefore be general and need not necessarily reflect hostility towards V's actual race. D might be unaware of the specifics of V's racial origins yet insult V by words or actions related to a racial grouping to which V does not belong.

R v Rogers [2007] UKHL 8, [2007] 2 AC 62 HOUSE OF LORDS

Three young Spanish women were called 'bloody foreigners' and told to 'go back to your own country.' D was convicted of a racially aggravated public order offence. He appealed on the grounds that the insult under s28 needed to relate to V's racial group, that is: Spaniards, not simply to foreigners or non-British. The House adopted a broad view of 'racial group'.

Baroness Hale of Richmond:

The point at issue is the meaning of 'racial group'. This is defined in section 28(4):

'In this section, "racial group" means a group of persons defined by reference to race, colour, nationality (including citizenship), or ethnic or national origins'. . .

It is accepted on [D's] behalf that had he called them 'bloody Spaniards' or any other pejorative word associated with natives of the Iberian peninsular, he would have been guilty. But it is argued that the hostility must be shown towards a particular group, rather than to foreigners as a whole. Mere xenophobia, it is said, does not fall within the ordinary person's perception of hostility to a racial group.

This may be true, but the definition of a racial group clearly goes beyond groups defined by their colour, race or ethnic origin. It encompasses both nationality (including citizenship) and national origins. This was quite deliberate. In Ealing London Borough Council v Race Relations Board [1972] AC 342, a majority of this House declined to interpret 'national origins' in the list of prohibited grounds of discrimination under the Race Relations Act 1968 so as to include 'nationality': discriminating against the non-British was allowed. Following this decision, the list of prohibited grounds was deliberately expanded in the Race Relations Act 1976 so as to include nationality. The list of grounds contained in the 1976 Act was adopted for the purposes of defining racial groups in the 1998 Act. An obvious advantage is that it helps to reduce argument about whether particular terms of abuse which are generally considered racist are or are not covered: does 'Paki,' for example, demonstrate hostility towards everyone who might hail from the Indian subcontinent or only towards citizens of Pakistan? …

There are, as Mr David Perry QC for the respondent has pointed out, other indications that the statute intended a broad non-technical approach, rather than a construction which invited nice distinctions. Hostility may be demonstrated at the time, or immediately before or after, the offence is committed (section 28(1)(a)). The victim may be presumed by the offender to be a member of the hated group even if she is not (section 28(1)(a)). Membership of a group includes association with members of that group (section 28(2)). And the fact that the offender's hostility is based on other factors as well as racism or xenophobia is immaterial (section 28(3)).

This flexible, non-technical approach makes sense, not only as a matter of language, but also in policy terms. The mischiefs attacked by the aggravated versions of these offences are racism and xenophobia. Their essence is the denial of equal respect and dignity to people who are seen as 'other'. This is more deeply hurtful, damaging and disrespectful to the victims than the simple versions of these offences. It is also more damaging to the community as a whole, by denying acceptance to members of certain groups not for their own sake but for the sake of something they can do nothing about. This is just as true if the group is defined exclusively as it is if it is defined inclusively.

It therefore comes as no surprise that the Divisional Court and Court of Appeal have generally taken the same view, as did the Court of Appeal in this case. In Director of Public Prosecutions v M [2004] EWHC 1453 (Admin), [2004] 1 WLR 2758 the Divisional Court held that 'bloody foreigners' could, depending on the context, demonstrate hostility to a racial group. In Attorney General's Reference No 4 of 2004 [2005] EWCA Crim 889, [2005] 1 WLR 2810 the Court of Appeal held that 'someone who is an immigrant to this country and therefore non-British' could be a member of a racial group for this purpose. In R v White (Anthony) [2001] EWCA Crim 216; [2001] 1 WLR 1352, it was held that 'African' could demonstrate hostility to a racial group, because it would generally be taken to mean black African. However, it was doubted whether the same would apply to 'South American'. It is not easy to imagine a scene in which hostility to South Americans as such is demonstrated, but as with 'African,' it is quite easy to imagine a scene in which hostility is demonstrated to racial, national or ethnic groups within that continent. The context will illuminate what the conduct shows.

A case which might be thought to go the other way is Director of Public Prosecutions v Pal [2000] Crim LR 756. There the Divisional Court dismissed the prosecution's appeal when magistrates acquitted the defendant, of Asian origin, who had assaulted the victim, also of Asian origin, and called him a 'white man's arse-licker' and a 'brown Englishman'. It was held that this did not demonstrate hostility towards Asians. But it is difficult to understand why it did not demonstrate hostility based on the victim's presumed association with whites (within the meaning of section 28(2)). That would undoubtedly cover, for example, a white woman who is targeted because she is married to a black man. It may well be that this way of looking at the matter did not feature in the case presented to the Divisional Court ....'

Appeal dismissed.

Evaluation

Views are divided on either the necessity or effectiveness of these provisions. The criticisms are that race and religion have been singled out for separate offences over and above other forms of discrimination. Racial and religious hostility were always capable of being regarded as aggravating features in the sentencing process in any event. Other forms of aggravation, such as homophobia for example, are dealt with in this way. The provisions studied here require victims to be identified as part of a racial or religious grouping. They may, instead, prefer to be seen as individuals and the crime as an affront to their individual liberty.

However, before the racial and religious aggravation provisions were introduced, there was greater risk that these more prevalent features of violent crime would be minimised or dismissed by the legal system altogether. These provisions should assist in providing an objective basis of assessment of racist and religiously aggravated crime.

THINKING POINT 10.10

Suppose that an assault is accompanied by the following insults, some of which are racially stereotypic. Consider whether they are racially aggravated under s28(1)(a) or (b) Crime and Disorder Act 1998.

1. A Scot is called 'a skirt-wearing sheep-shagger'. (This was held to amount to racial hostility in an unreported case cited by E. Burney in 'Using the Law on Racially Aggravated Offences' [2003] *Crim LR* at 33.)

2. An Asian doctor is called 'an immigrant doctor'.

3. A Turkish chef of a takeaway shop is called a 'bloody foreigner'.

SECTION SUMMARY

Section 28(1) creates two offences of racial or religious aggravation by which the sentences for nine base offences, including assault, ABH and malicious wounding may be extended:

■ *demonstration of hostility based on racial or religious grouping;*

■ *motivation of racial or religious hostility.*

10.9 The Protection from Harassment Act 1997

10.9.1 Introduction

10.9.2 Actus Reus: Harassment

10.9.3 Mens Rea

10.9.4 Stalking

10.9.1 Introduction

We will consider the offences created by this Act in outline only. The Act was introduced, primarily, to prohibit stalking, an example of harassment. Stalking is one of Britain's fastest growing crimes, committed primarily through digital media, that is: email, Facebook and Twitter. There has been a sharp rise in the number of prosecutions for improper use of electronic messages and the sending of offensive and threatening messages contrary to s127 Communications Act 2003 and the Malicious Communications Act 1988. In response to one unpleasant aspect of this problem, a specific offence of 'revenge porn' came into effect on 13 April 2015 ('Disclosing private sexual photographs and films with intent to cause distress': s33 Criminal Justice and Courts Act 2015). It is one of the most frequent types of intimate violence, affecting twice as many women each year as men. The rationale of the 1997 Act, as amended, is to 'nip stalking in the bud' before it becomes a serious problem and causes psychological or physical harm. If that should occur, assault offences will be resorted to.

→ **CROSS-REFERENCE**
Assault offences in stalking cases, for example *Ireland* and *Burstow*, are discussed at 10.1.2.

For this reason, stalking has now been specifically criminalised by s2A and s4A, in force since 25 November 2012, the result of s111 Protection of Freedoms Act 2012. The CPS also published guidelines in June 2013 on prosecuting various offences, including stalking and harassment, involving offensive communications sent via social media.

Under the Act, as amended, harassment may be committed in three ways and the new s2A and s4A create three stalking offences:

Section 1 Prohibition of harassment

(1) A person must not pursue a course of conduct (a) which amounts to harassment of another, and (b) which he knows or ought to know amounts to harassment of the other.

(1A) A person must not pursue a course of conduct –

    (a) which involves harassment of two or more persons, and

    (b) which he knows or ought to know involved harassment of those persons, and

    (c) by which he intends to persuade any person (whether or not one of those persons mentioned above)

        (i) not to do something that he is entitled or required to do, or

        (ii) to do something that he is not under any obligation to do.

(2) For the purposes of this section, the person whose course of conduct is in question ought to know that it amounts to or involves harassment of another if a reasonable person in possession of the same information would think the course of conduct amounted to or involved harassment of the other.

Section 2 Offence of harassment

(1) A person who pursues a course of conduct in breach of section 1(1) or (1A) is guilty of an offence.

(2) A person guilty of an offence under this section is liable on summary conviction to imprisonment for a term not exceeding six months, or a fine not exceeding level 5 on the standard scale or both ....

Section 2A Offence of stalking

(1) A person is guilty of an offence if –

 (a) the person pursues a course of conduct in breach of section 1(1), and

 (b) the course of conduct amounts to stalking.

(2) For the purposes of subsection (1)(b) and section 4A(1)(a) a person's course of conduct amounts to stalking of another person if –

 (a) it amounts to harassment of that person

 (b) the acts/omissions are associated with stalking, and

 (c) the person whose course of conduct knows or ought to know that the course of conduct amounts to harassment of the other person.

(3) [Various examples of acts/omissions associated with stalking are given, for example: Following, contacting, publishing material, electronic monitoring, loitering, interference with property, watching or spying.]

(4) [Summary offence: max. 51 weeks imprisonment or fine on level 5.]

Section 4 Putting people in fear of violence

(1) A person whose course of conduct causes another to fear, on at least two occasions, that violence will be used against him is guilty of an offence if he knows or ought to know that his course of conduct will cause the other so to fear on each of those occasions.

(2) For the purposes of this section, the person whose course of conduct is in question ought to know that it will cause another to fear that violence will be used against him on any occasion if a reasonable person in possession of the same information would think the course of conduct would cause the other so to fear on that occasion .... This offence is triable either way with a maximum 5 year sentence, or a fine, or both.

S4A Stalking involving fear of violence or serious alarm or distress

(1) A person ('A') whose course of conduct—

 (a) amounts to stalking, and

 (b) either—

  (i) causes another ('B') to fear, on at least two occasions, that violence will be used against B, or

  (ii) causes B serious alarm or distress which has a substantial adverse effect on B's usual day-to-day activities,

 is guilty of an offence if A knows or ought to know that A's course of conduct will cause B so to fear on each of those occasions or (as the case may be) will cause such alarm or distress.

(3) For the purposes of this section A ought to know that A's course of conduct will cause B serious alarm or distress which has a substantial adverse effect on B's usual day-to-day activities if a reasonable person in possession of the same information would think the course of conduct would cause B such alarm or distress.

(5) [Penalty on indictment: maximum five years imprisonment, or fine, or both.]

The Act also creates an offence of breach of a civil injunction. Since September 2009, restraining orders may be imposed on a person acquitted of an offence of harassment (Domestic Violence, Crime and Victims Act 2004). This is possible to protect an individual or corporation from future harassment (*Buxton* [2011] 4 Crim LR 332).

10.9.2 Actus Reus: Harassment

The first element which is common to all offences is that the conduct must be targeted at an individual. The same victim must be harassed by the course of conduct although V need not be actually present. In *Dunn* [2001] Crim LR 130, V was held by the Court of Appeal to have been harassed by D, despite her absence, when he intentionally frightened all members of her home. The second requirement is that D pursues 'a course of conduct' and many of the cases under the Act have concerned the definition of this concept. Section 7(1) states that a course of conduct must involve conduct on at least two occasions. What is important is the *connection* between the acts, not necessarily the time factor. Therefore, a delay between two actions of four months in *Lau v DPP* [2000] Crim LR 580 was not objectionable, nor three months in *Pratt v DPP* [2001] EWHC Admin 483 between a husband (1) throwing water over his wife and (2) chasing her through the matrimonial home. Abuse in four telephone conversations within a 36-hour period by a social services client to the acting manager was within s7(1) (*James v DPP* [2009] EWHC 2925). On the other hand, six incidents of domestic violence by D against his partner over nine months, interspersed with periods of affection, did not automatically amount to a course of conduct amounting to harassment (*Curtis (James Daniel)* [2010] Cr App R 31). Each case will depend on its own facts.

Section 7(2) states that harassment includes causing fear and distress to the victim, but there is no other definition of the term. Whereas the offence under s2 expressly requires the course of conduct to amount to harassment of another, s4 does not. However, the Court of Appeal in *Curtis* held that harassment is also fundamental to this more serious offence of causing fear of violence on at least two occasions. 'Harassment' was held to require proof that 'the conduct must be unacceptable to a degree which would sustain criminal liability and also must be oppressive'. In *Haque* [2011] EWCA Crim 1871 the Court of Appeal also considered that D's conduct must be oppressive and unreasonable.

Section 1A was added by the Serious Organised Crime and Police Act 2005. It criminalises harassment 'by persuasion'. This provision was aimed at protestors.

10.9.3 Mens Rea

MR is entirely objective, amounting to negligence, so that mental illness or other incapacitating factors will be no defence: *Colohan* [2001] EWCA Crim 1251, a case involving a schizophrenic.

10.9.4 Stalking

There are now three new stalking offences. It is only s4A(1)(b)(ii) which effectively adds greater protection to the victims of stalking over and above the existing law.

The new s2A(1) offence of stalking requires that D must first be proved to have committed harassment as explained earlier. Secondly, to prove stalking, the court must decide that 'the acts or omissions involved are ones associated with stalking.' Stalking is not defined, but examples are given in s2A(3).

The new s4A(1)(b)(i) offence of stalking involving fear of violence is identical to the existing s4 offence with the added new requirement of stalking.

The new s4A(1)(b)(ii) offence of stalking involving serious alarm or distress is completely new and fills a gap between s2 harassment and s4 causing fear of violence from harassment. It is the cumulative effect of all relevant conduct which needs to produce alarm or distress so as to have a substantial adverse effect on B's usual day-to-day activities, and not any particular incident.

It has been argued that, given the need for impact upon the victim, some forms of cyber-stalking fall outside the ambit of the new provisions, principally where V may be being electronically monitored, or her identity used, without her knowledge. Whilst this may pose difficulty in terms of both impact and MR, provided that when V does become aware of the offence, she is afraid, distressed or alarmed, and this is something D either is or ought to be aware of, the offence should be satisfied. (See the articles by A. Gillespie and N. MacEwan listed in the Further Reading section at the end of this chapter.)

Evaluation

Until now, most prosecutions have been for harassment following relationship break-down and neighbour disputes involving money, property or jealousy. The injunction provisions of the Act have also been successfully used against animal rights and anti-war protestors (eg: *Huntingdon Life Sciences Ltd v Curtin* (1997) QBD 28 November 1997).

Under s32 Crime and Disorder Act 1998, as amended by the Anti-Terrorism, Crime and Security Act 2001, offences of harassment and putting people in fear of violence may be racially and religiously aggravated.

SECTION SUMMARY

The Protection from Harassment Act 1997 provides that stalking and other forms of harassment may now be prosecuted under any of the provisions below:

▪ *s2 (offence of harassment)*
▪ *s2A (stalking)*
▪ *s4 (putting people in fear of violence).*

10.10 Reform

10.10.1 Offences Against the Person

10.10.2 Consent

10.10.1 Offences Against the Person

As we have seen, offences against the person are somewhat illogical both structurally and in terms of sentencing. The Home Office Consultation Paper 'Violence: Reforming the Offences Against the Person Act 1861' (1998) contains a draft bill for reform of offences against the person. It is still awaiting parliamentary approval yet, in the meantime, legislation in respect of harassment and racial/religious aggravation has been passed. It might be thought that piecemeal reform does nothing to eradicate the more fundamental problems. The Home Office Consultation Paper provides for the following reforms:

1. Intentional serious injury

(1)   A person is guilty of an offence if he intentionally causes serious injury to another.

(2)   A person is guilty of an offence if he omits to do an act which he has a duty to do at common law, the omission results in serious injury to another, and he intends the omission to have that result.

(3)   An offence under this section is committed notwithstanding that the injury occurs outside England and Wales if the act causing injury is done in England and Wales or the omission resulting in injury is made there.

(4)   A person guilty of an offence under this section is liable on conviction on indictment to imprisonment for life.

2. Reckless serious injury

(1)   A person is guilty of an offence if he recklessly causes serious injury to another.

(2)   An offence under this section is committed notwithstanding that the injury occurs outside England and Wales if the act causing injury is done in England and Wales.

(3)   A person guilty of an offence under this section is liable–

(a)   [on conviction on indictment … to a term not exceeding seven years]

(b)   [… on summary conviction to 6 months or a fine or both.]

3. Intentional or reckless injury

(1)   A person is guilty of an offence if he intentionally or recklessly causes injury to another. [five years/six months imprisonment and/or fine.]

4. Assault

(1)   A person is guilty of an offence if–

(a)   he intentionally or recklessly applies force to or causes an impact on the body of another, or

(b)   he intentionally or recklessly causes the other to believe that any such force or impact is imminent.

(2)   No such offence is committed if the force or impact, not being intended or likely to cause injury, is in the circumstances such as is generally acceptable in the ordinary conduct of daily life and the defendant does not know or believe that it is in fact unacceptable to the other person. [Summary only: six months imprisonment/fine.]

In 'Reform of Offences against the Person' (Law Com No 361, 2015) the Law Commission proposes adopting the first three offences just outlined. It also suggests that assault and battery should become two completely separate offences, physical assault and threatened assault, and that a new offence of aggravated assault should be added, committed where physical or threatened assault causes minor injuries.

10.10.2 Consent

The Law Commission, in its paper 'Consent in the Criminal Law' (Law Com CP No 139), called for a uniform definition of consent across the criminal law. It proposed that seriously disabling injury, whether intentional or reckless, should continue to be criminal even if consented to. However, the intentional or reckless causing of other injuries should not be criminal where the person consented to injury of the type caused at the time.

SUMMARY

You should now be familiar with the AR/MR definitions, cases, principles and application of the following major offences:

- Common law assault (intentional/reckless causing another to apprehend harm); battery (intentional/reckless infliction of physical contact/minor harm).
- ABH contrary to s47 OAPA 1861 (assault/battery causing minor harm).
- Malicious wounding and malicious infliction of GBH contrary to s20 OAPA 1861 (reckless wounding or reckless infliction of serious harm).
- Intentional wounding and intentional GBH with intent to cause GBH contrary to s18 OAPA 1861.

You should now understand how these traditional offences have also been applied to harassment and STI transmission.

You should now be able to identify and understand the application of the defence of consent which is specific to assault/battery and more serious offences against the person where the activity concerns public interest exceptions.

You should also understand that lawful chastisement is a defence to assault/battery only.

You should be able to identify the main elements of the following recent statutory offences:

- Racial and religious hostility/motivation contrary to s28 Crime and Disorder Act 1998.
- Stalking and harassment contrary to the Protection from Harassment Act 1997.

PROBLEM SOLVING

Al and Beryl had a sexual relationship which Beryl decided to end after several months owing to Al's possessiveness. Al made many silent telephone calls and sent her several threatening letters causing Beryl some distress. Beryl began to go out with Clem with whom she liked to engage in aggressive spanking. On one occasion this caused Beryl minor grazes which became infected. She was successfully treated by Dr Dave who concealed the fact that he had been struck off the medical register six months earlier.

Al followed Beryl and Clem around a supermarket one day. Clem warned him that if he did not go away he would punch Al on the nose. They started to fight during which Al shoved a trolley towards Clem. It hit a stack of tins which fell on top of him. One hit Clem in the eye causing his sight to be permanently damaged. Al then head-butted PC Ed who had arrived on the scene. PC Ed hit his head on a check-out desk, causing his skull to fracture with a profuse loss of blood. After several months, Beryl discovered that she was HIV positive. She had not had sex with anyone but Al.

Discuss the criminal liability of Al, Clem and Dr Dave.

Remember:

- **I: Identify** relevant issues
- **D: Define** offences/defences
- **E: Explain/evaluate** the law
- **A: Apply** law to facts.

See the online resources for further guidance on solving this problem: www.oup.com/uk/loveless6e/.

FURTHER READING

J. Anderson, 'No Licence for Thuggery: Violence, Sport and the Criminal Law' [2008] *Crim LR* 751
Considers consent to injuries during sport, and draws comparisons with Canadian case law.

J. Anderson, 'The Right to a Fair Fight: Sporting Lessons on Consensual Harm' (2014) 17 *New Criminal Law Review* 55

Reviews the history and justifications of the legality of boxing, and whether they can tell us anything about the wider law on consent to harm.

C. Clarkson, 'Violence and the Law Commission' [1994] *Crim LR* 324

Analyses the Law Commission's draft Bill; its criticism of the failure to reform consent has not been addressed by the 2015 report.

S. Cooper and M. James, 'Entertainment—The Painful Process of Rethinking Consent' [2012] *Crim LR* 188

Explores criminal liability and consent in 'painful entertainment' such as *Jackass* and *Dirty Sanchez*.

S. Edwards, 'No Defence for a Sado-masochistic Libido' (1993) NLJ 406

Discusses the issues raised by *Brown* and argues that the sexual element should not obscure the violence involved.

S. Gardiner, 'The Law and the Sports Field' [1994] *Crim LR 513* and M. James and S. Gardiner, 'Touchlines and Guidelines' [1997] *Crim LR* 41

These articles consider consent to injury in sport and the dangers of increasing criminal regulation of organised sports; the second article focuses on the Scottish approach.

M. Gibson, 'Getting Their "Act" Together? Implementing Statutory Reform of Offences Against the Person' [2016] *Crim LR* 597

A critique of the Law Commission's proposals which finds that on balance, they are welcome.

A. Gillespie, 'Cyberstalking and the Law: A Response to Neil MacEwan' [2013] *Crim LR* 1

Considers how the criminal law can address online stalking behaviour, taking a more optimistic view than MacEwan (cited later in this section).

D. Gurnham, 'Legal Authority and Savagery in Judicial Rhetoric: Sexual Violence and the Criminal Courts' (2011) *International Journal of Law in Context* 117

Analyses the narrative devices used in legal judgments on consensual violence.

J. Harris, 'An Evaluation of the Use and Effectiveness of the Protection from Harassment Act 1997' (Home Office, Research Study 203, London: HMSO, 2000), 4

Results of a study following a number of harassment cases through the criminal justice system.

Law Commission, *Hate Crime: Should the Current Offences be Extended?* (Law Com No 348, 2014)

Detailed overview of hate crimes, the current law and recommendations for reform.

J. Loveless, 'Criminalising Failure to Disclose HIV to Sexual Partners: A Short Note on Recent Lessons from the Canadian Supreme Court' [2013] *Crim LR* 215

Contrasts Canadian and English approaches to criminalising HIV transmission, with particular attention to issues of mens rea.

N. MacEwan, 'The New Stalking Offences in English Law: Will They Provide Effective Protection from Cyberstalking?' [2012] *Crim LR* 10

Evaluates new offences included in the Protection of Freedoms Act 2012 to address online stalking. Also see Gillespie's response (see earlier in this section).

S. Ryan, 'Reckless Transmission of HIV: Knowledge and Culpability' [2006] *Crim LR* 981

Considers what knowledge of HIV status and transmission risks is required for criminal liability.

J.R. Spencer, 'Liability for Reckless Infection: Part 2' (2004) 154 *NLJ* 448

Looking at the specific arguments around criminalisation of STI transmission.

J. Tolmie, 'Consent to Harmful Assaults: The case for moving away from category based decision making' [2012] *Crim LR* 656

Advocates a move away from basing the law on consent around specific categories of behaviour.

S. Walklate, 'What is to be Done About Violence Against Women?' (2008) 48(1) *British Journal of Criminology* 39

Takes a critical approach to the use of criminal law to respond to violence against women.

M. Weait, 'Criminal Law and the Sexual Transmission of HIV: *R v Dica*' (2005) 68 *MLR* 121

Considers *Dica* and the law and policy around criminalising HIV transmission.

Sexual offences

11

KEY POINTS

This chapter will enable you to:

- understand the policy and background to the Sexual Offences Act 2003;
- identify and apply the key elements of the following sexual offences:
  - s1: rape—non-consensual penile penetration where D lacks a reasonable belief in consent;
  - s2: assault by penetration—non-consensual penetration by part of body or other objects;
  - s3: sexual assault—non-consensual sexual touching;
  - s4: causing sexual activity without consent—causing non-consensual sexual activity;
- examine the social context of rape and the reasons for recent low conviction rates.

INTRODUCTION

The idea of sexual equality has produced a profound change in society's attitudes towards sex over the last 50 years. Alongside the era of 'sexual liberation' or 'sexual autonomy' for women in the 1960s, there emerged a growing dissatisfaction with the law. Feminists focused on the relative freedom allowed by the law to pornography, for example, whilst sexual offences against women were largely unacknowledged and under-enforced, much like domestic violence. The legal definition of rape was thought to be particularly problematic. Until the 1970s, many judges refused to hold that a woman had been raped unless the act was accompanied by violence. The law failed to protect those who simply did not wish to participate in sex. Energy was devoted in the 1980s and 1990s to challenging the legal definition of rape and the use of the woman's previous sexual history in court. The Sexual Offences Act 2003 has now changed the definition of rape. But conviction rates have fallen dramatically over the last 30 years. This is a European phenomenon and is occurring despite the fact that rape in England and Wales is now gender neutral, that rape within marriage has been a crime since 1991, that the definition now includes different types of penetration, and that police and court procedures have improved.

It is now widely accepted that sexual offending is prevalent within society, much of it hidden. High profile celebrity offences against children and the scandal of offending in children's homes have recently revealed an ugly depth and tolerance of sexual crimes against those who require special protection in a civilised society. New concerns include the risks of HIV infection and unwanted pregnancies. The debate about what the law needs to do to protect the right of the victim to refuse unwanted sex, and how this is to be achieved, will be explored in this chapter.

Context

Sexual violence has been a growing problem. In 2015/16, for example, reports of sexual offences rose by 20 per cent over the previous year. There has been an increase in the number of recorded historic offences as a result of Operation Yewtree connected to the Jimmy Savile inquiry. Detection rates for sexual offences are notoriously low at 29 per cent. These statistics are undoubtedly an underestimate because it is well-known that much sexual crime is under-reported. An NUS survey in 2010 found that one in seven female students had suffered a serious sexual assault over the previous year but few had reported the attack (www.bbc.co.uk/news). In 2013/14, over 60 per cent of serious sexual assaults against women were committed by a partner/ex-partner or family member (*Focus on Violent Crime & Sexual Offences 2013/14*: www.ons.gov.uk, see Diagram 11.1 for further details). Most controversial is Britain's falling conviction rate for rape: 6 per cent in 2009/10 (*Stern Review*: www.gov.uk/government/organisations/home-office).

All sexual offences are now contained in the Sexual Offences Act 2003 (SOA). In this chapter we will look at four of the most important: rape, assault by penetration, sexual assault and causing sexual activity without consent, all of which prohibit different types of serious non-consensual sexual violence. Rape is a sex-specific offence since its commission requires a penis. The victims may be women, other men or children. Around 90 per cent of rapes are by people known to the victim. Over 90 per cent of all rapes are against women. For these reasons, in this chapter the victim or complainant of rape and other sexual offences will be referred to here as female. This is not to underestimate the prevalence or trauma of sexual offences against males.

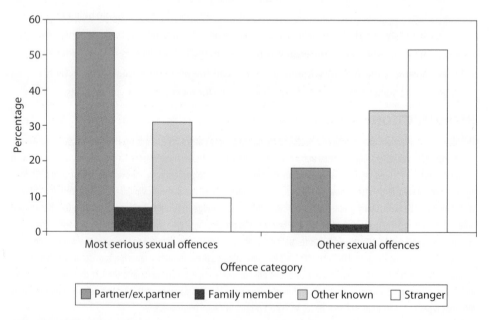

Diagram 11.1

Victim–offender relationship for serious sexual offences and less serious sexual offences experienced by females in the last year, 2009/10, 2010/11 and 2011/12 CSEW combined

Source: Police recorded crime (Home Office) as appears in Crime in England and Wales, Year Ending December 2014 (ONS) 23 April 2015—www.ons.gov.uk/ons/dcp171778_401896.pdf

KEY CASES

Rape and consent: s74

Olugboja [1981] 3 All ER 443—rape: consent is not the same as submission;

Malone [1998] 2 Cr App R 447—submission through intoxication is not consent;

Bree [2007] EWCA Crim 256—capacity to consent: a question of understanding and knowledge;

Assange v Swedish Judicial Authority [2011] EWHC 2849—deception regarding use of condom;

R (F) v DPP [2013] EWHC 945—deception regarding ejaculation;

R v McNally [2013] EWCA Crim 1051—deception regarding D's gender;

R v B [2006] EWCA Crim 2945—ignorance of risk of HIV infection does not negate consent to sexual intercourse for rape;

Linekar [1995] 2 WLR 237—consent and fraud as to circumstances;

Mens rea

R v B [2013] EWCA Crim 3—irrational belief in consent is not reasonable;

Definition of 'sexual': s78

R v H [2005] EWCA Crim 732—sexual assault: 'sexual' is defined according to nature and circumstances.

11.1 The Sexual Offences Act 2003

The Act was a response to greater acknowledgement of sexual abuse and exploitation in society, particularly against children and the vulnerable, and reflected a concern that the victims of abuse were inadequately protected by the law. It set out to modernise sexual offences in such a way as to promote protection, non-discrimination, and justice to victims and defendants alike. In recognising the traumatic nature of a sexual offence, the Act defines consent for the first time and makes sexual autonomy a guiding principle.

Background: The former law was considered by the government to be incoherent. It was spread throughout a network of statutory and common law offences. For example, the definition of rape was confined to sexual intercourse, meaning penile penetration of the vagina or anus (the latter was only included after 1994 bringing male victims within the ambit of rape for the first time). It attracted a maximum discretionary life sentence. However, penetration by other objects, equally if not more damaging and traumatic, was excluded. This offence was charged as indecent assault and only attracted a maximum penalty of ten years' imprisonment. If both types of penetration had occurred in one incident, charges of rape and indecent assault for the separate parts of the attack were necessary. Where force had been used to obtain a woman for sexual purposes, there was a separate offence of procurement of a woman by threats or false pretences. If she had been overpowered by drugs or alcohol prior to the abuse, yet another offence of administration of drugs to obtain or facilitate intercourse was possible. Separate charges therefore had to be matched to different aspects of the same incident.

The former law was also considered to be archaic and discriminatory. It failed to reflect 'changes in society and social attitudes' (Home Office, 'Protecting the Public' (Cm 5668, 2002)). The discriminatory nature of some of the previous offences was to be seen, for example, in the offence of intercourse with a 'defective' under s7 Sexual Offences Act 1956 (meaning a person with mental incapacity) or offences of buggery and gross indecency between consenting males, since homosexuality between consenting males had been only partially decriminalised by the Sexual Offences Act 1967.

On the other hand, the lack of clarity surrounding the fundamental concept of consent in sexual offences allowed all sorts of prejudicial jury attitudes towards women to play a decisive role in determining whether a female victim had, despite evidence of protest, consented to sexual conduct or not. In short, therefore, the former law failed in many respects either to acknowledge sexual privacy on the one hand or to offer adequate protection from harm on the other.

The Act: One of the guiding principles of the SOA 2003 was that the law should not intrude into consensual sexual behaviour between those over the age of consent without good reason. The rationale for any such intrusion was protection from harm, reflecting the principles of the Wolfenden Committee Report that there was a line in private sexual matters beyond which the law should not interfere.

→ CROSS-REFERENCE
The Wolfenden Report principles are discussed in Chapter 1.

For background information to the Act, see Home Office Consultation Document 'Setting the Boundaries' (2000), and Home Office White Paper, 'Protecting the Public' (Cm 5668, 2002).

The underlying principles of the Act are:

- to set out clearly what is unacceptable behaviour;
- to reflect the seriousness of a crime by appropriate penalties;
- to clarify the law on consent;
- to make offences gender-neutral so far as possible.

All section numbers refer to the Sexual Offences Act 2003 unless otherwise stated.

11.2 Rape

11.2.1 Definition of Rape

11.2.2 Actus Reus

11.2.3 Mens Rea

11.2.4 Marital Rape

11.2.5 The Rationale of Rape

11.2.6 Why is Rape so Controversial? The Justice Gap

11.2.1 Definition of Rape

Section 1 Sexual Offences Act 2003 (SOA 2003):

(1) A person (A) commits an offence if–

   (a) he intentionally penetrates the vagina, anus or mouth of another person (B) with his penis,

   (b) B does not consent to the penetration, and

   (c) A does not reasonably believe B consents.

(2) Whether a belief is reasonable is to be determined having regard to all the circumstances, including any steps A has taken to ascertain whether B consents.

(3) Sections 75 and 76 apply to an offence under this section.

(4) A person guilty of an offence under this section is liable, on conviction on indictment, to imprisonment for life.

Section 1 has been adapted by s5 to provide a new strict liability offence of rape of a child under 13.

> Basic intent: The Court of Appeal has clarified in *R v Heard* [2007] EWCA Crim 125, [2007] Crim LR 654 that specific intent means ulterior intent. Therefore rape and other sexual offences, although containing an element of intention, are regarded as crimes of basic intent.

Actus reus

The structure of the offence of rape is illustrated in Diagram 11.2.
    From the extract we can see that the AR consists of:

- Penile penetration,
- Of the vagina, anus or mouth,
- Without consent.

Mens rea

- Penetration must be intentional,
- A must not reasonably believe B consents,
- Whether a belief is reasonable is to be determined having regard to all the circumstances, including any steps A has taken to ascertain whether B consents.

These provisions replaced the previous definition of rape which was intentional non-consensual *sexual intercourse* with a man or a woman, the defendant either *knowing* of lack of consent or

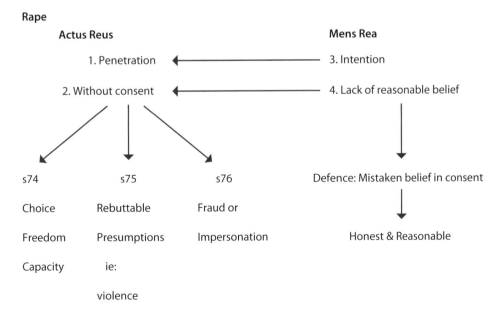

Rape

Diagram 11.2
Structure of the offence

being *reckless* as to that fact (s1(1) Sexual Offences Act 1956 as substituted by the Sexual Offences (Amendment) Act 1976 and s142 Criminal Justice and Public Order Act 1994). Reckless rape has now disappeared.

11.2.2 Actus Reus

Section 1(1)(a): Penile penetration

The new definition of rape is restricted to penetration by the penis of the vagina, anus or mouth of the victim. This makes it clear that the offence, as before, can only be committed by a man (or certain transgender women) although a woman is capable of being an accomplice.

Penile penetration is a clarification of the former requirement of *sexual intercourse* because it was at one time unclear as to whether sexual intercourse could occur before completion. The cases of *R v Kaitamaki* [1985] AC 147 and *Cooper v Schaub* [1994] Crim LR 531 confirmed however that sexual intercourse was a continuing act, meaning that should consent be withdrawn at any time before completion, the conduct element of the offence had been committed. The new law confirms that principle. Section 79(2) states that penetration is a continuing act from entry to withdrawal. Therefore, the AR will be satisfied by the slightest penetration of the external genitalia, vagina or anus, whether sexual intercourse has been completed or not.

The former law excluded penetration of anything but the vagina or anus. The new definition of rape includes penile penetration of the mouth. This extension is a welcome recognition that many rapes are accompanied by forced oral sex.

The rape definition excludes penetration by objects. The Sexual Offences Review (SOR) team which produced Home Office Consultation Document 'Setting the Boundaries' (2000) on which the new reforms were based, gave the following reasons for confining rape to penile penetration:

- Rape was clearly understood by the public as an offence committed by men against women and men;
- Penile penetration was of a personal kind, carrying risks of pregnancy and disease transmission;
- Penetration of the body orifices by objects would become a new offence of assault by penetration in place of the former offence of indecent assault.

Arguments had also been put to the SOR that there should be gradations or degrees of rape to signify that stranger rape was more serious than date rape. This was rejected. Evidence established that a betrayal of trust, whether or not accompanied by violence, can be even harder to overcome than the appalling consequences of stranger rape.

Transsexuals with surgically constructed sexual organs, whether penile or vaginal, are included within the offence (s79(3)—the general interpretation provision).

The offence can be committed by boys over the age of 10. The presumption that boys under the age of 14 were incapable of sexual intercourse was abolished by s1 Sexual Offences Act 1993.

Of the vagina, anus or mouth

The SOR recognised that forced oral sex is 'as horrible, as demeaning and as traumatising as other forms of forced penile penetration, and we saw no reason why rape should not be defined as penile penetration of the anus, vagina or mouth without consent' (para 2.8.5).

Oral sex represents an extension of the former law of rape which was confined to penile penetration of the vagina and, since 1994, the anus. Section 79(5) defines vagina as including the vulva.

Section 1(1)(b): Without consent

The victim must not consent to the penetration: s1(1)(b). Sections 74–76 provide new definitions of consent. For the sake of continuity, they will be considered in this section on rape. However, they also apply to all other offences in the Act including assault by penetration, sexual assault and causing sexual activity without consent.

Consent is the central element of the AR of rape and most other sexual offences. In rape, the onus is on the prosecution to prove that the victim did not consent to penile penetration by the defendant. Consent is also crucial to MR: it must be proved beyond all reasonable doubt that D did not reasonably believe in consent.

The new consent definitions aim to make the meaning of consent as clear as possible. The SOR stated in 'Setting the Boundaries' at para 2.10, that verbal and non-verbal messages can be mistaken and assumptions about appropriate behaviour can lead to significant misunderstanding and, in extreme cases, to forced and unwelcome sex. The SOA therefore sets out new guidance on consent:

- s74 defines consent;
- s75 provides a set of circumstances in which consent will be deemed to be absent. Absence of consent can be rebutted by the defendant;
- s76 sets out two circumstances concerned with fraudulently obtained consent where consent will be conclusively presumed to be absent. Absence of consent cannot be rebutted by the defendant.

Section 74: the definition of consent

Section 74: 'Consent'

For the purposes of this Part, a person consents if she agrees by choice, and has the freedom and capacity to make that choice.

This definition makes it clear that one will not be consenting unless there is:

- *agreement* by choice and
- the agreement was freely entered into
- by a person with capacity.

Until the SOA 2003 there was no definition of consent. Under the previous common law, whether the victim had consented or not to sexual intercourse was to be decided by the jury as a matter of fact. This was unsatisfactory as it had the potential for uncertainty and inconsistency. Moreover, it allowed for the intrusion into the trial process of prejudices and value judgements about the character of the victim. Section 74 emphasises that consent is a matter of agreement by choice. The following three points are implied:

Free agreement v submission

The s74 emphasis on agreement by choice implies freedom from pressure or coercion to submit. The distinction between submission and consent was considered in the next case. This was the only common law guidance on consent before the SOA was enacted:

R v Olugboja [1981] 3 ALL ER 443 COURT OF APPEAL

A girl submitted to intercourse with D through fear. She and a friend had been raped by his companion and she could hear her friend in the next room being beaten up by the companion for resisting a further assault. D claimed that she had consented because consent could only be negated by a threat of death or serious harm.

Dunn LJ:

> The issue of consent should be left to the jury on being directed that consent is to be given its ordinary meaning and by way of example – that there is a difference between consent and submission. Every consent involves a submission but it by no means follows that a mere submission involves consent.

The judgment made it clear that consent was to be regarded as an ordinary word and that a jury should be capable of appreciating the difference between consent and non-consensual submission or reluctant acquiescence. But the problem was that consent was not defined. Different types of pressure might yield either mere submission or consent but Olugboja failed to explain how the difference might be discerned. Look at these examples which all illustrate pressure or coercion in unequal relationships:

?! THINKING POINT 11.1

If sexual intercourse takes place after the following words are spoken to a reluctant 'victim', would it be merely submissive or consensual?

1. A police officer says to a young woman, 'If you do not have sex with me, I will arrest you.'

2. A boss says to a secretary, 'If you sleep with me, I will not make you redundant.'

3. A journalist says to a person, 'Sleep with me or I will publicise some embarrassing fact about your past.'

4. A husband says to his wife, 'Sleep with me or I will give you no housekeeping money for the family this week.'

5. A cab driver says to a passenger with low IQ, 'Have sex with me or I will drive you miles from where you want to go.'

Acquiescence induced by coercion may perhaps indicate consent, depending on the nature of the pressure, but it may also indicate no more than mere submission. *Olugboja* said there was a difference between the two in respect of violent threats but the point at which apparent consent became merely submissive in other contexts was not dealt with. S. Gardner stated in 'Appreciating Olugboja' (1996) 16 LS 275, at 287:

> . . . a threat which had a devastating effect on one victim might appear trivial to another, and if both had intercourse the latter might be held to have consented when the former did not.

The Court of Appeal recently confirmed (Pitchford LJ in *Doyle* [2010] EWCA Crim 119) that submission means the absence of free agreement. The only circumstances in which a judge should give a direction on this is when drawing a comparison between:

> . . . reluctant but free exercise of choice on the one hand, especially in the context of a long term and loving relationship, and unwilling submission to demand in fear of more adverse consequences from refusal on the other.

D had attacked his former girlfriend at her flat, held her head under water in a cold bath, tied her up with a scarf and then raped her by removing her underclothes and forcing her legs apart. V protested until after penetration when she gave in. On appeal against conviction, the Court of Appeal held that this was not a case where the distinction between reluctant consent and submission required guidance. On the facts, V had not consented, having resisted both physically and verbally until penetration.

The Court of Appeal in *Robinson* [2011] EWCA Crim 916 held that submission might arise through *unwilling acquiescence* perhaps through embarrassment or some other reason. Whether this helps to clarify matters is debatable. There will, inevitably, be difficulties here. What of acquiescence out of a sense of duty or to avoid unpleasant consequences? Section 74 leaves the ultimate decision to the jury.

> **?! THINKING POINT** 11.2
>
> Do you think s74 helps you to distinguish consent from submission in relation to the illustrations in Thinking point 11.1? Remember that consent under s74 is defined as agreement by choice, with freedom and capacity to make that choice.
>
> If you are unsure, you are not necessarily wrong.

Consent means informed choice

Inherent in the concept of agreement is the principle of informed choice. This, in turn, means that the context in which consent was given will now be important. Context should include the parties' relationship, knowledge and circumstances. For example, *R v C* [2012] EWCA Crim 2034 decided that if a child-victim, under 16, had been subjected to long-term grooming by a domineering defendant, her later consent to sex as an adult was deprived of real substance.

Three new cases have arisen under s74 where *deception* was held to have negated consent on the basis of a denial of choice. It is necessary to understand at this stage that deception regarding the 'nature or purpose' of the act is covered by s76(2)(a), where D will be conclusively presumed guilty if the deception is intentional. Section 76(2)(a) is being narrowly construed, however, whilst more circumstantial deceptions tend to be dealt with under s74.

Assange v Swedish Judicial Authority [2011] EWHC 2849

D, facing extradition to Sweden on rape charges, was alleged to have removed, or torn, a condom before ejaculation. V had given consent to sexual intercourse on condition that D wear a condom. The High Court held that the facts were capable of invalidating consent within s74.

Sir John Thomas, President of the Queen's Bench Division, explained:

The question of consent in the present case is to be determined by reference to s.74. The allegation is clear and covers the alternative; it is not an allegation that the condom came off accidentally or was damaged accidentally. *It would plainly be open to a jury to hold that, if (the complainant) had made clear that she would only consent to sexual intercourse if Mr Assange used a condom, then there would be no consent if, without her consent, he did not use a condom, or removed or tore the condom without her consent. His conduct in having sexual intercourse without a condom in circumstances where she had made clear she would only have sexual intercourse if he used a condom would therefore amount to an offence under the Sexual Offences Act 2003, whatever the position may have been prior to that Act.* [Emphasis added.]

It had been argued on D's behalf that if the deception was not covered by s76, then it could not be covered by s74. To that, Sir John Thomas said:

> It appears to have been contended by Mr Assange, that if, in accordance with the conclusion we have reached, the deception was not a deception within s.76 (a deception as to the nature or quality of the act or a case of impersonation), then the deception could not be taken into account for the purposes of s.74. It would, in our view, have been extraordinary if Parliament had legislated in terms that, if conduct that was not deceptive could be taken into account for the purposes of s.74, conduct that was deceptive could not be.

NOTE 11.1

1. The court held that a positive lie or deception regarding the condition on which V agreed to sexual penetration (use of a condom) would undermine her choice of whether or not to consent to unprotected sex. It was not a question of deception as to the 'nature' of the act as required by s76. Whether or not sex is protected is irrelevant to the definition or nature (AR/MR) of rape, the AR of which is concerned with non-consensual *penetration*. As such the issue was one of agreement by choice under s74.

2. No *accidental* tearing or removal of a condom will ever amount to rape.

However, not all lies inducing apparent consent will be regarded as sufficiently important as to negate choice under s74. The High Court pointed out that a distinction exists between the type of deception practised by the defendant in *Assange* and 'common or garden' lies used in order to seduce, an issue to which we return when considering s76.

Assange was confirmed in the next case:

R (F) v DPP [2013] EWHC 945

This case concerned an application for judicial review of the DPP's refusal to prosecute following an allegation of rape. The context concerned a relationship demonstrating a pattern of sexual force, dominance and control to which there was at least a degree of reluctant acceptance on V's part. The method of contraception used was withdrawal. V was not using the contraceptive pill for medical reasons. The incident in question concerned D intentionally ejaculating inside V shortly after penetration. He knew that she did not consent because she did not wish to have another child. V subsequently became pregnant. The Divisional Court confirmed that this incident involved a lack of choice under s74, for the reasons set out in *Assange*.

Judge LCJ:

> Consensual penetration occurred. The claimant consented on the clear understanding that the intervener would not ejaculate within her vagina. She believed that he intended and agreed to withdraw before ejaculation. The intervener knew and understood that this was the only basis on which she was prepared to have sexual intercourse with him . . . In short, there is evidence that he deliberately ignored the basis of her consent to penetration as a manifestation of his control over her.
>
> In law, the question which arises is whether this factual structure can give rise to a conviction for rape. Did the claimant consent to this penetration? She did so, provided, in the language of s.74 of the 2003 Act, she agreed by choice, when she had the freedom and capacity to make the choice.

What Assange underlines is that 'choice' is crucial to the issue of 'consent', and indeed we underline that the statutory definition of consent provided in s.74 applies equally to s.1(1)(c) as it does to s.1(1)(b). The evidence relating to 'choice' and the 'freedom' to make any particular choice must be approached in a broad commonsense way. If before penetration began the intervener had made up his mind that he would penetrate and ejaculate within the claimant's vagina, or even, because 'penetration is a continuing act from entry to withdrawal' (see s.79(2) of the 2003 Act) he decided that he would not withdraw at all, just because he deemed the claimant subservient to his control, she was deprived of choice relating to the crucial feature on which her original consent to sexual intercourse was based. Accordingly her consent was negated. Contrary to her wishes, and knowing that she would not have consented, and did not consent to penetration or the continuation of penetration if she had any inkling of his intention, he deliberately ejaculated within her vagina. In law, this combination of circumstances falls within the statutory definition of rape. [Emphasis added.]

 NOTE 11.2

1. The positive deception here related to a 'crucial feature' of the circumstances on which V's consent was based. A 'common sense' approach should prevail. Her choice as to whether or not D should ejaculate during penetration had been denied.

2. The background of sexual dominance here was essential, as, indeed it was in *R v C* mentioned earlier (where V had been groomed as a child).

3. Again, if there had been a deception as to the 'nature' or a feature of the act, s76 might have applied. That was not the case. Deception as to ejaculation is not an element of the offence of rape, the AR of which is concerned with non-consensual penetration. Accidental ejaculation will never amount to rape.

Read the next case where s74, rather than s76, was also applied.

McNally v R [2013] EWCA Crim 1051

This concerned an appeal against conviction for assault by penetration contrary to s2 Sexual Offences Act 2003, rather than rape. The parties had conducted a relationship over three and a half years via MSN. They agreed to marry, and to have a family, without ever meeting. V, aged 13, understood that she was communicating with a 15-year-old male named 'Scott' whereas, in fact, 'Scott' was female. Four meetings took place in which D, who disguised herself as a male, performed oral sex on V, and penetrated her digitally and with a dildo. D was convicted and sentenced to three years in a young offender institution. She appealed against conviction and sentence.

Leveson LJ:

The case for the Crown was that M's [the victim's] consent was obtained by fraudulent deception that the appellant was a male and that had she known the truth, she would not have consented to acts of vaginal penetration. Mr Wainwright [for the defence] argues that deception as to gender cannot vitiate consent; in the same way deception as to age, marital status, wealth or, following EB, HIV status being deceptions as to qualities or attributes cannot vitiate consent. Thus, he submits that Assange and R(F) can be distinguished as the deceptions in those cases were not deceptions as to qualities or attributes but as to the features of the act itself . . . In reality, some deceptions (such as, for example, in relation to wealth) will obviously not be sufficient to vitiate consent. We reject this analysis. First and foremost, EB was not saying that HIV status could not vitiate consent if, for example, the complainant had been positively assured that the defendant was not HIV positive: it left the issue open . . . In our judgment, Lord Judge's observation that 'the evidence relating to "choice" and the "freedom" to make any particular choice must be approached in a broad commonsense way' identifies the route through the dilemma. As Mr McGuinness for the Crown contends, *the argument that in Assange and R(F) the deceptions were as to the features of the act is not sustainable: the wearing of a condom and ejaculation are irrelevant to the definition of rape and are not 'features' of the offence and no such rationale is suggested* . . .

Thus while, in a physical sense, the acts of assault by penetration of the vagina are the same whether perpetrated by a male or a female, the sexual nature of the acts is, on any common sense view, different where the complainant is deliberately deceived by a defendant into believing that the latter is a male. Assuming the facts to be proved as alleged, M chose to have sexual encounters with a boy and her preference (her freedom to choose whether or not to have a sexual encounter with a girl) was removed by the appellant's deception. It follows from the foregoing analysis that we conclude that, depending on the circumstances, deception as to gender can vitiate consent . . . [Emphasis added.]

Given D's clearly troubled emotional state, the Court of Appeal substituted a sentence of nine months, suspended for two years.

NOTE 11.3

1. It was accepted that the conclusive presumptions against consent under s76(2)(b)—impersonation of a person known personally to V—did not apply.

2. It was 'common sense' that V had been deceived as to the physical, *sexual nature* of the act. Gender was far more important than a mere *quality* or *attribute* of the act. V's freedom of choice under s74 as to whether or not to have sex with a girl had been removed by D's deliberate, active deception.

3. It is not clear why, given the last point, s76(2)(a) did not apply. *Assange* and *R(F)* concerned deceptions regarding circumstances of the act in question whereas *McNally* concerned the *nature* of the act.

Did this case criminalise what might be termed a 'moral' as opposed to a 'criminal' deception and unnecessarily stigmatise a troubled, transgender young person? These cases all beg the same issue: the distinction between moral and criminal wrongs. Fundamental to this is what we understand consent, and the nature of the wrong in rape, to be. The law does not go so far as to say that all deceptions should be punished by the criminal law. The deceptions in *Assange* and *R(F)* created serious potential risks for the victims (unwanted pregnancy or disease transmission). The deception in *McNally* related to a 'crucial' matter of gender. Just how far the guiding principle of 'common sense' will take these developments remains to be seen.

One matter raised in *Assange* and *R(F)* concerned deception as to HIV status. A positive lie in respect of such a serious health condition would presumably not be regarded as merely 'common or garden' (*Assange*). Common sense would dictate that such a deception would be of crucial importance to a victim. It is therefore open to a future court to find that an HIV positive defendant, having lied about his health status in order to induce consent, commits rape. V's freedom to choose whether or not to have sex with an infected partner will have been denied. *R(F)* envisages this possibility. Mere concealment of HIV status, as opposed to a positive lie, would be insufficient (*R v EB* [2006] EWCA Crim 2945, discussed later). HIV, where actually transmitted, would remain a s20 OAPA 1861 offence.

→ **CROSS-REFERENCE**
The nature of the wrong in rape is considered at 11.2.5.

Capacity to consent

This is not defined in the Act but the observations on a victim's capacity to consent in relation to non-sexual offences would all equally apply here:

Mental incapacity where it affects V's ability to understand the nature of the sexual act would be determined by *Gillick*. Therefore if V suffers from immaturity, a learning disability or age-related vulnerability, she may lack capacity to consent. The House of Lords held in *R v C* [2009] UKHL 42 that a woman diagnosed with schizo-affective disorder and an emotionally unstable personality disorder, who feared death if she refused sexual activity, lacked the ability to choose under s30. This provides a separate offence of sexual activity with a person with a mental disorder impeding choice. In order to have the capacity to make a decision, the House of Lords held that one must be able to *understand* relevant information and to *weigh* that information so as to arrive at a *choice*. Therefore, it is not enough that one understands the nature of the act in general. One must also be able to appreciate the *circumstances and risks* associated with it so as to make a choice. V might therefore lack either the mental or physical capacity to make a decision. This was confirmed in *R v A (G)* [2014] EWCA Crim 299, a case concerning a sexual encounter between two 21-year-old friends of low intelligence at a special school.

→ CROSS-REFERENCE
Gillick is explained in Chapter 10, 10.6.4.

Incapacity through intoxication: All three cases discussed next raise the question of exactly how drunk a victim must be in order to lack the capacity to consent in cases falling short of outright unconsciousness. Unconsciousness would be a matter for s75:

R v Malone [1998] 2 CR APP R 447 COURT OF APPEAL

D was alleged to have had intercourse with a 16-year-old who was so drunk she could not walk. He was convicted of rape and appealed to the Court of Appeal on the grounds that he had used no force, deceit or threats and there was no dissent by the complainant offering resistance by speech or physical conduct.

It was held that the absence of consent did not have to be demonstrated or communicated. It was not the law that the victim had to say no or put up physical resistance, or had to be incapable of saying no. The evidence of lack of consent might consist of the complainant's simple assertion that she did not consent:

> Submitting to an act of sexual intercourse, because through drink she was unable physically to resist though she wished to, is not consent. If she submits to intercourse because of the drink she cannot physically resist, that, of course, is not consent. No right thinking person would say that in those circumstances she was genuinely consenting to what occurred. What occurred . . . not wishing to have intercourse but being physically unable to do anything about it . . . would plainly, as a matter of common sense be against her will. It would be without her consent.

R v Dougal [2005] (*THE OBSERVER*, 25 JUNE 2006, *THE GUARDIAN*, 24 NOVEMBER 2005) SWANSEA CROWN COURT (UNREPORTED)

A female student at Aberystwyth University made an allegation of rape against a fellow student and part-time security guard who had been asked by university staff to escort her to her room. She had been at a party and was extremely drunk. She had no recollection of the events but did remember lying in the corridor and that someone was attempting to have sex with her. Under cross-examination she said that she could not remember whether she had given consent to sex or not because she had been so drunk. She knew that she would not have consented to sex in a corridor. The judge informed the jury that 'drunken consent is still consent' and directed the jury to find the defendant not guilty 'even if you don't agree'.

What was not considered at the trial was the victim's capacity to consent given her level of intoxication. A jury might well have thought that she was unable to give valid consent to sex whilst so intoxicated. This was the significance of the ratio in *Malone*.

In 2006, in response to *Dougal*, the government proposed an amendment to the Act in the form of a statutory definition of capacity: that a victim will lack the capacity to agree by choice where their understanding or knowledge is so limited that they are not in a position to decide whether or not to agree. The SOR team had originally proposed that s75 should include the situation where the complainant was 'too affected by alcohol or drugs to give free agreement' (para 2.10.9) but this was rejected. See this extract by Professors Tempkin and Ashworth in 'The Sexual Offences Act 2003 (1) Rape, Sexual Assaults and the Problems of Consent' [2004] *Crim LR*, at p 339:

> Whilst contributory negligence has no place in the criminal law, it is apparent that such ideas had an influence on the government's thinking. Those who take alcohol or drugs voluntarily are placed in a different moral category from those who have had alcohol or drugs 'administered' to them by the defendant. Thus, the list of presumptions, which the government has invested with great moral symbolism, is there to protect those who can be constructed as the 'innocent' victims of sexual assault. The many women who get raped when they are drunk and whose inebriation is more or less voluntary will have to take their chances in the legal process without the benefit of evidential presumptions.

The government's proposals were not referred to but were implicitly approved in the following precedent on intoxication and consent:

R v Bree [2007] EWCA CRIM 256 COURT OF APPEAL

V, a 19-year-old student at Bournemouth University, alleged she had been raped by the 25-year-old brother of her male flat-mate (D) after an evening of heavy drinking. D and V walked back to V's flat in the early hours where, once inside, she was alternately sick and unconscious. At some point whilst on her bed, she curled into a ball and turned to the wall. She felt D penetrate her. Her evidence was that she felt 'like it wasn't happening. I knew I didn't want this but I didn't know how to go about stopping it'. D then left. D's case was that although V may have become less inhibited because she was intoxicated, she was lucid enough to consent to sexual intercourse, that she did so, and that he reasonably believed that she was consenting. The prosecution originally presented the case on the basis of unconsciousness and incapacity. However, they amended the case to one of simple lack of consent on the basis that V had capacity but did not consent.

Judge LJ, President of the Family Division:

> In cases which are said to arise after voluntary consumption of alcohol the question is not whether the alcohol made either or both less inhibited than they would have been if sober, nor whether either or both might afterwards have regretted what had happened, and indeed wished that it had not. If the complainant consents, her consent cannot be revoked. Moreover it is not a question whether either or both may have had very poor recollection of precisely what had happened. That may be relevant to the reliability of their evidence . . . .
>
> We should however highlight R v Lang [1976] 62 CAR 50 which summarised the relevant principle . . . . The court observed
>
> > '. . . there is no special rule applicable to drink and rape. If the issue be, as here, did the woman consent? the critical question is not how she came to take the drink, but whether she understood

her situation and was capable of making up her mind. In Howard [1965] 50 CAR 56 the Court of Criminal Appeal had to consider the case of a girl under 16. Lord Parker CJ . . . . said: . . . 'in the case of a girl under 16 the prosecution . . . must prove either that she physically resisted, or, if she did not, that her understanding and knowledge was such that she was not in a position to decide whether to consent or resist'. In our view these words are of general application when ever there is present some factor, be it permanent or transient, suggesting the absence of such understanding or knowledge . . . .'

In the context of the statutory provision in section 74, it is noteworthy that Lang decided thirty years or so ago, directly focused on the 'capacity' of the complainant to decide whether to consent to intercourse or not. These are the concepts with which the 2003 Act itself is concerned . . . .

In our judgment, the proper construction of section 74 of the 2003 Act, as applied to the problem now under discussion, leads to clear conclusions. If, through drink (or for any other reason) the complainant has temporarily lost her capacity to choose whether to have intercourse on the relevant occasion, she is not consenting, and subject to questions about the defendant's state of mind, if intercourse takes place, this would be rape. However, where the complainant has voluntarily consumed even substantial quantities of alcohol, but nevertheless remains capable of choosing whether or not to have intercourse, and in drink agrees to do so, this would not be rape. We should perhaps underline that, as a matter of practical reality, capacity to consent may evaporate well before a complainant becomes unconscious. Whether this is so or not, however, is fact specific, or more accurately, depends on the actual state of mind of the individuals involved on the particular occasion.

Considerations like these underline the fact that it would be unrealistic to endeavour to create some kind of grid system which would enable the answer to these questions to be related to some prescribed level of alcohol consumption. Experience shows that different individuals have a greater or lesser capacity to cope with alcohol than others, and indeed the ability of a single individual to do so may vary from day to day. The practical reality is that there are some areas of human behaviour which are inapt for detailed legislative structures. In this context, provisions intended to protect women from sexual assaults might very well be conflated into a system which would provide patronising interference with the right of autonomous adults to make personal decisions for themselves. [Emphasis added.]

Conviction quashed.

NOTE 11.4

1. The Court of Appeal quashed the conviction for two main reasons. Firstly, *Olugboja* correctly identified that a jury should not be left to determine consent without further direction. The trial judge had not given the jury any assistance with the meaning of 'capacity' to consent. Essentially confirming *Malone*, the *Bree* direction holds on this point that capacity to consent may evaporate before V lapses into unconsciousness but it was not possible to give a definition of capacity because individuals vary in their tolerance to alcohol and a rigid definition may infringe individual autonomy. The question of capacity to consent is therefore fact-specific in every case.

2. Secondly, the judge's summing up to the jury inadequately reflected the changed basis of the prosecution (from one of unconsciousness and incapacity to one of lack of consent). The judge had not explained to the jury that when drunk one might behave in a way which, if sober, one would not and that, therefore, she might have consented or D's belief in consent might have been reasonable.

The case demonstrates the difficulties in determining the distinction between disinhibition and lack of capacity. The court did not consider whether instead of the possibility of consent, there may have been a mere submission which, as *Malone* indicates, is not the same thing.

Section 74 is not without criticism. Professors Temkin and Ashworth argue in 'The Sexual Offences Act 2003 (1) Rape, Sexual Assaults and the Problems of Consent' [2004] *Crim LR* 339 that the term consent 'positively sprouts uncertainties':

> It might be thought that 'freedom' and 'choice' are ideas which raise philosophical issues of such complexity as to be ill-suited to the needs of criminal justice – clearly those words do not refer to total freedom or choice, so all the questions about how much liberty of action satisfies the 'definition' remain at large. What the philosopher J.L. Austin said of the term 'freedom' applies equally to 'choice':
>
>> 'While it has been the tradition to present this as the "positive" term requiring elucidation, there is little doubt that to say we acted "freely". . . is to say only that we acted *not* unfreely, in one or another of the heterogeneous ways of so acting (under duress, or what not). Like 'real', 'free' is only used to rule out the suggestion of some or all of its recognized antitheses.'

As a definition of consent, it might be thought to be somewhat vague and insufficiently robust to offer protection to all victims of sexual crimes. With that aside, however, recent case law does demonstrate a more critical attempt to engage with the principles of agreement, freedom and choice so as to lend greater substance to this vital concept. This is a welcome improvement on the previous status quo.

Section 75: circumstances giving rise to a rebuttable presumption of lack of consent

Section 74 applies where there is evidence that is capable of establishing consent, including any evidence from D. On the other hand, where there is no evidence at all that is capable of amounting to consent, s75 will apply. This section does two things: 1) it lists the circumstances in which consent will be presumed absent; and 2) it gives rise to a presumption that D did not reasonably believe in consent. However, if there is insufficient evidence on one or either of these issues, s75 will not apply and the jury will be directed on s74.

Section 75 sets out the circumstances in which consent will be *evidentially* presumed absent. The presumption can be rebutted by D.

75 Evidential presumptions about consent

(1) If in proceedings for an offence to which this section applies it is proved–

    (a) that the defendant did the relevant act,

    (b) that any of the circumstances specified in subsection (2) existed, and

    (c) that the defendant knew that those circumstances existed, the complainant is to be taken not to have consented to the relevant act unless sufficient evidence is adduced to raise an issue as to whether he consented, and the defendant is to be taken not to have reasonably believed that the complainant consented unless sufficient evidence is adduced to raise an issue as to whether he reasonably believed it.

(2) The circumstances are that–

    (a) any person was, at the time of the relevant act or immediately before it began, using violence against the complainant or causing the complainant to fear that immediate violence would be used against him;

(b) any person was, at the time of the relevant act or immediately before it began, causing the complainant to fear that violence was being used, or that immediate violence would be used, against another person;

(c) the complainant was, and the defendant was not, unlawfully detained at the time of the relevant act;

(d) the complainant was asleep or otherwise unconscious at the time of the relevant act;

(e) because of the complainant's physical disability, the complainant would not have been able at the time of the relevant act to communicate to the defendant whether the complainant consented;

(f) any person had administered to or caused to be taken by the complainant, without the complainant's consent, a substance which, having regard to when it was administered or taken, was capable of causing or enabling the complainant to be stupefied or overpowered at the time of the relevant act.

(3) In subsection (2)(a) and (b), the reference to the time immediately before the relevant act began is, in the case of an act which is one of a continuous series of sexual activities, a reference to the time immediately before the first sexual activity began.

Section 75 sets up a presumption of an absence of consent. The prosecution must present sufficient evidence to the court that one of the circumstances applies to the case, for example, that the victim was asleep at the time of the act. An evidential burden of proof then passes to D for him to raise evidence casting doubt on the presumption that the victim did not consent. He might do this, for example, by putting forward evidence that she did consent and was not asleep at the time or, if she was asleep, that she had previously indicated that she would consent to sex whilst asleep. There must be material evidence to rebut s75. A mere belief is not enough: *Cicerelli* [2011] EWCA Crim 2665. Once consent has become an issue (which means that there is evidence either way) the prosecution must prove beyond all reasonable doubt that the victim did not consent in the normal way. If D fails to dislodge the presumption of lack of consent by evidence, the judge will direct the jury to find him guilty. The presumption of consent under s75 will only arise in a rape case where the prosecution prove:

- penile penetration of the victim by the defendant;
- the specified circumstance under s75;
- that D was aware of the circumstance, as required by s75(1)(b).

Some of the listed circumstances are based on common law precedents which will be referred to later. There are points to be made about each of the s75 circumstances.

Section 75(2)(a): threats of immediate violence against the complainant

The threat does not need to come from D. The provision does not seem to include threats of future or imminent rather than immediate violence. What of threats of *detrimental harm* rather than violence? The examples given in 'Setting the Boundaries' were losing a job or killing the family pet. The point was made that the seriousness of the harm or detriment should relate to the circumstances and perception of the victim. However, neither imminent harm nor detriment made it into the Act. Therefore, the presumption will not apply to such cases which will be dealt with by reference to s74 and the general law on consent.

Section 75(2)(d): asleep/unconscious

a. Asleep

The law seems to have been turned backwards here regarding the sleeping victim. Under the common law, there was a *conclusive* presumption that a victim who was asleep or unconscious during intercourse did not consent (*Mayers* (1872) 12 Cox CC 311 and *Turner* (1872) 12 Cox CC 313). This was a point of law which ought to have precluded any dispute regarding consent. However, *Olugboja* held that consent in general was a question of fact in every case. Therefore, the rape of a 14-year-old sleeping girl in *Larter and Castleton* [1995] Crim LR 75 was regarded as non-consensual not as a matter of law but as a question of fact. The Court of Appeal actually confirmed D's conviction because, on its ordinary meaning, there was a difference between consent and submission. The prosecution had to prove neither physical resistance nor incapacity. However, had the issue been regarded straightforwardly as one of law there would have been no possibility of an appeal. Now, penetration with a sleeping victim raises only a *rebuttable* presumption of lack of consent.

b. Unconscious

An unconscious victim clearly lacks the capacity to consent. The victim might be unconscious because of injury, illness or *self-induced* intoxication due to drugs or alcohol. Unconsciousness is one thing but inebriation short of unconsciousness falls outside of this provision remaining a matter of simple consent under s74.

Section 75(2)(e): physical disability and inability to communicate

The implication is that mental capacity need not be lacking, simply the physical ability to communicate. It is not clear why there should be a s75 presumption for physical but not mental inability.

Section 75(2)(f): administration/cause to be taken a substance capable of causing stupefaction or overpowerment

This provision was aimed at drug assisted date-rape where a drug, the most common being Rohypnol and GHB (gamma hydroxyl butyrate acid), is surreptitiously given to the victim so as to stupefy or overpower in order to obtain sexual intercourse. The provision is not limited to specific substances however and could therefore include any drug or the secret administration of alcohol by spiking the victim's soft drinks. A crucial distinction here is whether the administration is in order to obtain *sexual intercourse* by causing incapacity or to obtain *consent* by altering mood and lowering resistance. The latter would seem to fall outside of s75. As we have seen, the Act does not currently provide a definition of capacity. Therefore, if D knows that the victim will not consent to sex but intoxicates her by spiking her drinks until she does consent, the presumption of lack of consent will not apply but consent may still be regarded as absent under s74.

You should note that there is a reason for the inclusion of both *administration* and *causing to be taken*: administration refers to the surreptitious spiking of a drink whereas causing could occur where the victim takes the drug herself under duress or deception, for example, where V is deceived into thinking that the drug will cure her headache.

The administration/causing to be taken must be without consent. Difficulties arise here in relation to cases where the victim is pressurised into drinking more alcohol than she wishes or where her alcoholic drink is spiked with stronger alcohol which she consumes herself. It is likely that such cases will fall outside of the presumption.

The substance must be capable of causing or enabling stupefaction or overpowering the victim. Stupefaction is not defined. Does it mean unconsciousness? If so, the provision will fail to render protection to those who are conscious but senseless and in a variety of degrees of inebriation. Not even Rohypnol renders the victim unconscious but instils confusion, disinhibition and euphoria with later sedative and memory loss effects. The previous law was clear: the issue was not how the victim came to take a drink, but whether she understood her situation and was capable of making up her mind (*R v Lang* (1976) 62 Cr App R 50).

The question must be asked whether the Act goes far enough to protect vulnerable victims. Why should it not be *conclusively* as opposed to *evidentially* presumed that consent was absent in a case of drug-assisted rape? There appears to be no logic in the distinction. It has been observed that the evidential presumptions do not tell us what consent is, only what it is not. Rather confusingly, they treat as 'evidential' what ought to constitute the definition of rape (V. Tadros, 'Rape without Consent' (2006) 26(3) *OJLS* 515).

EXAMPLE 11.1

D and V go for a drink on a first date. D pours a triple vodka into V's wine glass whilst she is in the bathroom. She drinks it on her return. D suggests they go back to his flat to spend the night together. Feeling rather drunk, V refuses. D insists she drinks three more glasses of wine and V eventually agrees to accompany D although she is hardly aware of what is going on. In D's flat she lays down in a semi-conscious condition. D has sexual intercourse with her. Does s75 apply?

The issue in this question is whether V had the capacity to consent given her intoxicated condition which was partly the result of self-intoxication and partly the result of D lacing her drink with vodka. There are three routes to proving lack of consent—s74, s75 and s76.

Section 75 presumption of lack of consent: The prosecution must prove:

- Penile penetration
- The s75 circumstance/s
- That D was aware of the circumstances.

The two relevant provisions are:

1. Section 75(2)(d): that V is asleep or unconscious

V is semi-conscious at the time of sexual intercourse and therefore s75(2)(d) would appear not to be directly relevant although the facts raise the issue of V's capacity to consent. The cases on capacity concern intoxicated consent: *Malone, Dougal* and *Bree*. Discussion is required of the problems of intoxicated consent with reference to the government's proposals regarding capacity and whether there is a level of intoxication beyond which one lacks the capacity to consent which as *Bree* confirms, is a matter of understanding and knowledge.

2. Section 75(2)(f): Administration or causing to be taken a substance capable of causing stupefaction or overpowerment

It would appear that she was both stupefied and that her will was eventually overpowered by the intoxicating vodka because she was hardly aware of what was being said and she later becomes semi-conscious. It is thought that causing a victim to drink more heavily will not fall within the provision. But where stronger alcohol or drugs have been administered the provision should apply.

If D cannot rebut the presumption of the absence of consent, the prosecution will have succeeded in proving this AR element beyond all reasonable doubt.

Section 74: Agreement by choice

If D can produce evidence which casts doubt on the presumption of lack of consent under s75, the burden of proof is then transferred back to the prosecution to prove the absence of consent under s74.

Did V consent to sexual intercourse in the sense of agreeing by choice with the freedom and capacity to make that choice? The prosecution will need to prove this beyond all reasonable doubt. Even if she had the capacity, which is doubtful, did she merely submit rather than consent? Some jurors may be against V because of her initial drinking, willingness to accompany D back to his flat, etc.

The outcome here may well depend on societal attitudes to autonomy and consent and thus offer little improvement over the previous situation.

?!   **THINKING POINT** 11.3

D and V were former partners. V was a transgender woman who had wanted a loving relationship with D but he was only ever interested in sex. In a chance encounter in a bar, V suggested to D that they get back together. D said that he would think about it.

D went to buy some drinks and slipped a drug into V's sherry to make sure V would not resist his advances. Later in V's flat, V allowed D to have sexual intercourse but she fell asleep halfway through. The next morning she could not remember what had happened but realised that D must have had sex with her. Does s75 apply?

Fraud and consent: s76—circumstances giving rise to a conclusive presumption of lack of consent

76 Conclusive presumptions about consent

(1) If in proceedings for an offence to which this section applies it is proved that the defendant did the relevant act and that any of the circumstances specified in subsection (2) existed, it is to be conclusively presumed –

    (a) that the complainant did not consent to the relevant act, and

    (b) that the defendant did not believe that the complainant consented to the relevant act.

(2) The circumstances are that –

    (a) the defendant intentionally deceived the complainant as to the nature or purpose of the relevant act;

    (b) the defendant intentionally induced the complainant to consent to the relevant act by impersonating a person known personally to the complainant.

Where D is found to have intentionally deceived V about a matter relating to the nature or purpose of the act, or where he impersonates someone that she knows, it will be conclusively presumed that she did not consent and he knew it. In other words, he will be prevented from alleging that V consented and he is likely to be considered guilty. Consent in relation to violent offences will be negated by fraud as to nature, identity, quality or sexual disease status. Remember that originally, under the common law, only frauds or deception as to the *nature* of the act or the *identity* of the perpetrator would negate consent. *Clarence* (1888) 22 QBD 23, who transmitted a sexual disease to his wife through consensual sexual intercourse, having concealed from her his state of health, was cleared of assault charges because his deception was as to neither nature nor identity. The *Clarence* categories were rejected by *Dica* [2004] QB 1257 as being too narrow and were extended in relation to assault offences to include fraud as to HIV transmission. Therefore, Clarence would now be guilty of s20 GBH. Section 76 amends the common law position on fraudulently induced consent but it continues a restrictive approach. Neither Clarence nor Dica would be guilty of rape.

→ CROSS-REFERENCE
Fraudulently induced consent in relation to violent offences is considered in Chapter 10, 10.6.3.

Section 76(2)(a): fraud as to nature or purpose

Nature:

Section 76(2)(a) preserves the previous common law in relation to frauds as to the nature of the act. There have only been two successful prosecutions for rape on this basis which are very old:

R v Flattery [1877] 2 QBD 410

D induced a woman to submit to intercourse by deceiving her that he was performing a surgical operation. He was convicted of rape since his deception had been as to the nature of the act.

R v Williams [1923] 1 KB 340

A singing master was convicted of rape where he claimed that sexual intercourse would improve a female pupil's breathing by creating an air passage. Again, this was held to be a deception as to the nature of the act.

It was clear that there had to be a deception as to the sexual nature of the act. It is unlikely that, in today's climate of sexual awareness, the nature of the sexual act would be misunderstood by a person competent to consent. These provisions apply, however, across all sexual offences, not just rape, and may well have greater relevance elsewhere, particularly in relation to child sexual offences. However, the deception in the next case was not as to the sexual nature of the act but as to payment for it:

R v Linekar [1995] 2 WLR 237 COURT OF APPEAL

Agreement to sexual intercourse by a prostitute was induced by a fraudulent promise of payment of £25. Linekar was originally convicted but it was held on appeal that consent had not been negated because the deception was as to neither nature nor identity, both previous common law categories. It is interesting to see how the court arrived at its conclusion and to bear in mind whether the case might now be decided differently in accordance with either s74 or s76.

Morland J:

The importance of Clarence, in our judgment, is that it exposes the fallacy of the submission that there can be rape by fraud or false pretences. Wills J says (22 QBD 23 at 27):

'That consent obtained by fraud is no consent at all is not true as a general proposition either in fact or in law. If a man meets a woman in the street and knowingly gives her bad money in order to procure her consent to intercourse with him, he obtains her consent by fraud, but it would be childish to say that she did not consent. In respect of a contract, fraud does not destroy the consent. It only makes it revocable.' . . .

Moving to more recent times, there is the highly persuasive authority of Papadimitropoulos v R (1957) 98 CLR 249, a decision of the High Court of Australia . . . . The facts of that case were that the complainant believed that she had gone through a marriage with the appellant.

In its judgment the court said (at 260–261):

'It must be noted that in considering whether an apparent consent is unreal it is the mistake or misapprehension that makes it so. It is not the fraud producing the mistake which is material so much as the mistake itself . . . The identity of the man and the character of the physical act that is done or proposed seem now clearly to be regarded as forming part of the nature and character of the act to which the woman's consent is directed. That accords with the principles governing mistake vitiating apparent manifestations of will in other chapters of the law . . . . To say that in the present case the facts which the jury must be taken to have found amount to wicked and heartless conduct on the part of the applicant is not enough to establish that he committed rape. To say that in having intercourse with him she supposed that she was concerned in a perfectly moral act is not to say that the intercourse was without her consent.'

Respectfully applying those dicta to the facts of the present case, the prostitute here consented to sexual intercourse with the appellant. The reality of that consent is not destroyed by being induced by the appellant's false pretence that his intention was to pay the agreed price of £25 for her services. Therefore, he was not guilty of rape.

NOTE 11.5

The court in *Linekar* was influenced by the contractual arguments regarding fraud and revocation put forward by Wills J in *Clarence*. Provided there was agreement on the physical character of the act, the deception regarding payment was irrelevant. Do you agree that the question of whether or not a person had been raped should be determined by notions of contract? Is the nature of commercial sex different from other types of sex from a victim's point of view?

The Court of Appeal recently confirmed in *Jheeta* (see later in this section) that s76 should be narrowly defined so as to exclude cases like *Linekar*. Presumably, the case would have had no greater chance of success on the basis of deception as to *purpose* (not paying for sexual intercourse) for, as we shall see, this is a difficult concept. However, would the victim in *Papadimitropoulos v R* (1957) 98 CLR 249, cited in *Linekar*, have consented to sexual intercourse had she known the truth behind D's deception? If she had said to D 'I agree to sex only on the condition that we are married', would she now have greater protection given the developments seen in relation to s74 just discussed? *Papadimitropoulos* has now been overturned in Australia by the New South Wales Crimes Act 1900 s61R(2)(a)(ii), the facts now constituting rape.

Note that fraudulent *concealment* of HIV to a consenting partner will not amount to rape because V will have agreed to the physical sexual nature of the act:

R v EB [2006] EWCA CRIM 2945

Sex took place between D, who was HIV positive, and V one night just off the street. Whether it was non-consensual was inconclusive. However, it was clear that V did not ask, and D did not lie, about his HIV positive status. He was convicted of rape and appealed.

Latham LJ:

> As has been indicated in an article by Professor Tempkin and Professor Ashworth, in the 2004 Criminal Law Review, page 328, the Sexual Offences Act 2003 does not expressly concern itself with the full range of deceptions other than those identified in section 76 of the Act, let alone implied deceptions. It notes that this leaves, as a matter of some uncertainty, the question of, for example, as it is put: 'What if D deceives C into thinking that he is not HIV positive when he is?' There is no suggestion in that article that whatever may be the answer to that question, an implied deception can be spelt out of the mere fact that a person does not disclose his HIV status, or his or her infection by some other sexually transmissible disease, that such a deception should vitiate consent . . . But the extent to which such activity should result in charges such as rape, as opposed to tailormade charges of deception in relation to the particular sexual activity, seems to us to be a matter which is a matter properly for public debate. All we need to say is that, as a matter of law, the fact that the appellant may not have disclosed his HIV status is not a matter which could in any way be relevant to the issue of consent under section 74 in relation to the sexual activity in this case.

 NOTE 11.6

1. Non-disclosure of HIV status will not give rise to liability for rape under either s74 or s76. But *Assange* and *R(F)* potentially envisage the possibility of a rape conviction where D makes a positive *lie* regarding his health status.
2. The court identified that a more appropriate offence for concealment would have been s3 Sexual Offences Act 1956 (procuring sexual activity by false pretences), but this was repealed in 2003.

➜ **CROSS-REFERENCE**
For further discussion of *Assange* and *R(F)* see 11.2.2, 'Section 74, the definition of consent'.

Purpose:

Whilst intentional deception as to nature is very narrow, the meaning of *purpose* appears to be elusive. In *Jheeta* [2007] EWCA Crim 1699, D had perpetuated an unusual and unpleasant fraud on his girlfriend over two or three years to prevent her from ending their relationship. He had sent her many threatening emails and text messages, some anonymously and others as a police officer. She unwillingly continued their relationship and some occasions of sex were non-consensual. On appeal against conviction for rape, the court held that s76(2)(a) did not apply because V had not been deceived as to either the nature and purpose of the sexual act. Neither had she been deceived as to D's identity under s76(2)(b). The court observed that deception as to purpose might apply to cases such as *Tabassum* (the breast-examiner) or *Green* [2002] EWCA Crim 1501 where bogus medical examinations for impotence were conducted by a qualified doctor on young men who were wired up whilst they masturbated. In both, the deceptions as to D's purpose (sexual gratification) were clear. Section 76 was applied in *Devonald* [2008] EWCA Crim 527, where D, a father of a jilted daughter, pretended to be a young woman on the internet and persuaded his daughter's former 16-year-old boyfriend to masturbate in front of a webcam. The purpose was identified as humiliation rather than, as V believed, sexual gratification. This decision was criticised in the next case:

➜ **CROSS-REFERENCE**
Tabassum is discussed in Chapter 10, 10.6.3.

R v Bingham [2013] EWCA 813

It was doubted whether *Devonald* was right, and *Jheeta* was preferred. In *Bingham*, D assumed two false identities and persuaded V, his girlfriend, to perform penetrative acts over a webcam. He intended to blackmail her. His conviction was overturned because V had never been asked what she thought the purpose of the relevant sexual acts was. In the absence of such evidence, the more appropriate route to conviction was s74. It follows that s76 is obviously not going to be useful to the vast majority of deception cases, particularly where D's purpose is obscure. Although the Act professes to have a *subjective* approach to consent, therefore, very little may have changed in terms of consent and fraud.

?! THINKING POINT 11.4

Do you think there should be a conclusive presumption against consent under s76(2)(a) if the following fraudulent statements are made?

1. These words, spoken by a man to his partner:
   - 'I love you.'
   - 'I am not married.'
   - 'If you have sex with me I promise to buy you a fur coat.'
   - 'I am a famous TV producer and can get you a role in my next programme.'
2. These words, spoken by a man to a prostitute: 'I will pay you £100 for sex.'
3. To a woman with low IQ who allows full sexual intercourse after being told: 'This is the medical treatment for your problem.'
4. A man arranges for a friend to secretly watch him having sex with a woman from whom the arrangement has been concealed.
5. A victim has sexual intercourse with a man under the mistaken impression that he is wealthy when he is not and he, knowing of the mistake, does not correct it.
6. A man has sexual intercourse with a woman, concealing from her the fact that he is infected with HIV, chlamydia or genital herpes (sexual diseases).

The problem with a wide interpretation of nature or purpose is that it might include *any* or *all* deceptions, even minor ones. To criminalise all deceptions during sexual encounters would be clearly wrong and rather futile, for morality cannot be taught by the criminal law alone. Deceptions always have been and presumably always will be part of the 'seduction process'. Those deceptions occupying the doubtful ground between immorality and crime might be unacceptable but not necessarily criminal. However, sexual morality has evolved since *Clarence* and it might be said that the Act was a missed opportunity for re-evaluating the law on mistaken consent more widely, especially where the deception is particularly serious to the victim.

It has been argued that the real question concerns what we understand consent to mean. See the following extract by J. Herring, 'Mistaken Sex' [2005] *Crim LR*, at p 511–518 in which the author examines the '*caveat emptor*' (or 'buyer beware') traditional common law approach to mistaken consent to sexual relations:

If, therefore, we are to regard the right to sexual autonomy or integrity seriously then we need to be strict about what is meant by consent. We should require 'genuine, morally significant consent' not spurious or morally trivial consent . . . . If we are to move to a position which starts with a norm of people engaging in mutual sexual relationships based on trust and respect for each other; if we are to regard the question of consent not as a 'yes or no' issue but one that gives due respect to the parties' understandings of what the act means; and if we are to understand consent in a rich sense, then we will develop a different approach to understanding 'mistaken consent' in the sexual context. We could formulate a legal rule that would look something like this:

If at the time of the sexual activity a person:

(i)   is mistaken as to a fact; and

(ii) had s/he known the truth about that fact would not have consented to it then s/he did not consent to the sexual activity. If the defendant knows (or ought to know) that s/he did not consent (in the sense just described) then s/he is guilty of an offence . . . .

The proposal has no difficulty in supporting the conviction of a defendant like *Tabassum* . . . . More controversially, it would support the conviction of people who do not disclose the fact that they are carrying a sexually-transmitted disease, where had they informed their partners of the truth they would not have consented.

The author proposes that in order to give meaning to sexual autonomy, the underlying principle of the SOA 2003, a more thorough evaluation of mistaken consent is required even in the case of lesser deceptions. But would the boundaries of rape then become too wide? Read the following extract from H. Gross 'Rape, Moralism and Human Rights' [2007] *Crim LR* 220:

My doubts about Herring's proposal go well beyond the law of rape to the foundations of criminal jurisprudence where nagging questions remain about how the criminal law ought to be used and what its proper limits are. His proposal is one among a number of recent suggestions that the criminal law be used to bring about moral improvement in the way men and women relate to each other sexually. I have serious misgivings about such a project, which seems to me to be a serious abuse of public power. It is not personal morality but public morality where the important issues arise. Principles of political morality that place limits on the exercise of the powers of government to prescribe crimes and put people in prison for committing them are at issue. It is basic human rights that provide the strongest argument I know against making conduct criminal simply because it is morally wrong.

The liberal tradition in opposition to the enforcement of morals stresses preserving freedom of choice when the conduct in question is not palpably harmful or dangerous, or when the enforcement of a legitimate policy of government does not genuinely require a particular kind of conduct to be made unlawful. But however obnoxious may be illicit interference with what free people choose to do, it is a far greater wrong to deprive people of their freedom *tout court* as we do when we inflict punishment for serious crime. It is in fact a prima facie violation of basic human rights. What I am suggesting is that human rights do not allow the creation of criminal liability for the sort of deception that we have been discussing, nor for any other conduct that comes recommended for criminalisation by nothing more compelling than the fact that it is morally wrong. This is not because there is any bar to such legislation in human rights law. Quite the contrary, human rights law leaves open the possibility of punishing people for crimes that amount to nothing more than moral turpitude so long as prohibiting such conduct is not in contravention of some *legally*-recognised human right. What concerns me are human rights in the raw, that is, those basic human rights that exist independent of any legal recognition that is given to them, rights that are therefore pre-legal and enduring no matter what any political authority or any legal institutions may choose to say about them. These basic human rights do in fact receive the strongest legal recognition, but even if legal recognition were withdrawn or had never come about in the first place, so that legal enforcement of these rights would be impossible, the rights themselves would exist no less than they do now.

In giving legal recognition to these rights, and in the political evolutions (and revolutions) that provide a foundation for such recognition, punishment for crime is granted a special status because a condition of universal impunity would be an intolerable state of affairs. But serious criminal punishment, even in its most enlightened and least damaging embodiments, is a paradigm of basic human rights violation.

Which author do you agree with?

Section 76(2)(b): fraud as to identity

This provision confines the conclusive presumption regarding lack of consent to intentional impersonation of persons *known personally* to the complainant. But what 'knowing' means or how long you have to know someone before they become 'known' is an open question. Would you know someone if you had never met them but had only ever communicated by correspondence or email?

 EXAMPLE 11.2

V contacts a former boyfriend, X, through an internet website. She has not seen him for many years. They agree to meet. D, an acquaintance of X, turns up in place of X, impersonating him. V does not realise because she has not seen D for ten years and assumes that he has changed through age. She agrees to have sex with D.

X was personally known to V at some point and so s76(2)(b) should apply. It could be different if D was impersonating someone V had never actually met before.

Section 76(2)(b) was intended to deal with the situation that arose in the case of *R v Elbekkay* [1995] Crim LR 163 where a man impersonating the victim's boyfriend climbed into her bed and had sexual intercourse with her.

 THINKING POINT 11.5

D introduces himself to V as HRH Prince Ralph, a distant cousin to the monarch. V agrees to have sex with him. He later pretends to be the brother of a famous footballer who plays for an English Premiership team. V2 agrees to have sex with him. Has D committed rape?

Deception as to *attributes*, for example, professional qualifications or authority, is not included despite the recommendations of the Law Commission's Consultation Paper, 'Consent in the Criminal Law' (Law Com CP No 139, 1995).

The distinction between s75 and s76

The advantage of the s75 list is that in the specified circumstances the question of consent is no longer a matter for the jury but a question of law. It is right and necessary that consent should be legally defined. Juries will now have no discretion to acquit if D fails to rebut the presumption of lack of consent provided the prosecution continue to prove the case to the required standard.

However, this short list really does no more than state the obvious regarding the specified situations. It is obvious, in the absence of evidence to the contrary, that an unconscious or sleeping woman, for example, would not ordinarily consent to sexual intercourse. Most juries would also readily comprehend a lack of consent in the face of violent threats. It might be thought that these categories were the least problematic under the previous law and that they will contribute little to public understanding of consent. Originally, they were only intended by the SOR team to be a starting point, not an exhaustive list and were wider but were cut down during the parliamentary process. Unfortunately, there is no provision for extending the list by future case law. Amendment requires parliamentary reform, as with the example of capacity.

It is doubtful whether the conclusive presumptions in s76 represent either the worst cases of deception or non-consent. Why should being raped while asleep give rise to only a rebuttable presumption against consent whilst being raped under a deception a conclusive presumption? Is it more serious to be raped under a deception than whilst asleep? Why does violent rape only give rise to a rebuttable presumption against consent and not a conclusive one? Is it worse that consent is obtained by deception rather than by violence? There appears to be little logic in the underlying rationale for the distinction between s75 and s76. Where the facts fall outside of s75 or s76, the general consent provisions of s74 can be relied upon. Recent case law suggests that s74 is more useful to prosecutors than either s75 or s76.

SECTION SUMMARY

Rape (AR):

- *penile penetration;*
- *of the vagina, anus or mouth;*
- *without consent.*
- *Consent is defined by:*
  - ☐ *s74 as agreement by choice;*
  - ☐ *s75 lists circumstances giving rise to a rebuttable presumption of lack of consent;*
  - ☐ *s76 applies to consent obtained by fraud.*

Sections 74, 75 and 76 are alternative routes to proving lack of consent by the prosecution.

11.2.3 Mens Rea

[NB: The mens rea provisions on reasonable belief in consent for rape are identical to the MR provisions on reasonable belief in consent for assault by penetration, sexual assault and causing sexual activity without consent.]

- Section 1(1)(a) Penetration must be intentional.
- Section 1(1)(c) A does not reasonably believe B consents.
- Section 1(2) Whether a belief is reasonable is to be determined having regard to all the circumstances, including any steps A has taken to ascertain whether B consents.

Intentional penetration: s1(1)(a)

Very little needs to be said about this as unintentional penetration is extremely unlikely. Penetration might be unintentional where there was mistaken penetration of an orifice in respect of which there was no consent. For instance, there might have been an intention to penetrate the vagina but not the anus. This MR element is unlikely to give rise to challenge.

Unreasonable belief in consent: s1(1)(c)

If D knows that the victim does not consent, or does not care one way or another, or fails to ask in circumstances where it would be reasonable to do so, or believes that she is consenting because no-one could ever refuse him, then his belief in consent will not be reasonable and he will be guilty of rape. The Court of Appeal has confirmed that such belief must be reasonable according to the standards of the reasonable man: *R v M* [2011] EWCA Crim 1291. This is fairer to victims and not unfair to defendants because it is not a wholly objective test. The belief must still be reasonable in *all the circumstances*—a semi-objective test.

Reasonable belief takes account of circumstances: s1(2)

'All the circumstances' may include the mental capacity of D. Would a defendant who lacked the ability to appreciate an obvious lack of consent have this fact taken into account? A recent example would be the next case:

R v B [2013] EWCA CRIM 3

D was a paranoid schizophrenic with a number of delusional beliefs, including that he was a healer with special powers and that he was being poisoned. He appealed against a conviction of rape on the grounds that his delusional state could have led him to reasonably believe that his partner consented when she did not. The CA held that D's delusional beliefs or mental illness generally should not be taken into account in determining whether a belief is reasonable. Expert evidence suggested that D's delusions concerned his belief that he was entitled to have sex with V without her consent, not that he believed her to be consenting when she was not. Continuing with this, the Hughes LJ said:

> If, however, we are wrong about that, and the defendant's delusional beliefs could have led him to believe that his partner consented when she did not, we take the clear view that such delusional beliefs cannot in law render reasonable a belief that his partner was consenting when in fact she was not . . . the Act asks . . . whether the belief in consent was a reasonable one. A delusional belief in consent, if entertained, would be by definition irrational and thus unreasonable, not reasonable. If such delusional beliefs were capable of being described as reasonable, then the more irrational the belief of the defendant the better would be its prospects of being held reasonable. . . .
>
> *We conclude that unless and until the state of mind amounts to insanity in law, then under the rule enacted in the Sexual Offences Act beliefs in consent arising from conditions such as delusional psychotic illness or personality disorders must be judged by objective standards of reasonableness and not by taking into account a mental disorder which induced a belief which could not reasonably arise without it. The defendant's mental condition, and its impact on his behaviour, is of course extremely relevant to sentence* . . . [Emphasis added.]

    NOTE 11.7

The court was drawing a distinction here between irrational and reasonable beliefs. If a belief in consent was objectively irrational in the circumstances, most likely because of mental illness, it would be unreasonable. But a rational, although ill-judged belief arising as a result of low IQ or another inability, might conceivably be reasonable. It goes without saying that a drunken belief in consent would not be reasonable (*Whitta* [2007] 1 Cr App R (S) 122, where D, whilst drunk, mistakenly digitally penetrated not a girl, but her mother).

During the legislative process, the government stated that it was for the jury to decide which circumstances were relevant. It might be D's attributes such as youth or capacity, or other matters entirely. However, will the reference to circumstances dilute the requirement of reasonableness? The government stated that the level of responsibility exercised by both partners could be relevant. It was up to the judge and jury in each particular case. Read the following extract by Tempkin and Ashworth from the *Criminal Law Review* article cited earlier, at p 341:

> In *Protecting the Public* the Government expressed its concern that the *Morgan* test 'leads many victims who feel that the system will not give them justice, not to report incidents or press for them to be brought to trial.' Accordingly, it decided to alter the test 'to include one of reasonableness under the law.' But the present formulation is unlikely to provide the incentive to report or pursue the case that the Government is seeking. The broad reference to 'all the circumstances' is an invitation to the jury to scrutinise the complainant's behaviour to determine whether there was anything about it which could have induced a reasonable belief in consent. In this respect the Act contains no real challenge to society's norms and stereotypes about either the relationship between men and women or other sexual situations, and leaves open the possibility that those stereotypes will determine assessments of reasonableness . . . . Further, it is true that s.1(2) requires consideration of 'any steps A has taken to ascertain whether B consents,' however, if A enquires about consent, B says no, but A concludes that B's 'no' is tantamount 'yes,' is his culturally engendered belief to be regarded as reasonable or not? In deciding what it is 'relevant' to consider, what is to prevent the influence of stereotypes about B's dress, B's frequenting of a particular place, an invitation to have a drink, and so forth?

There is therefore a risk that the issue of whether the victim did consent will be obscured by prejudicial views of the circumstances.

The defence of mistaken belief in consent

A mistaken belief must be reasonable

Section 1(2) encompasses not only the MR in rape but also the *defence* of mistaken belief in consent. D may assert that he mistakenly believed the victim to be consenting to penetration. The law in this area has undergone fundamental change. Any belief in consent that D possesses, whether mistaken or not, must be *reasonable*. An *honest* belief is no longer sufficient.

Before the SOA 2003, an honest belief, which might have been unreasonable, would have sufficed. This was known as the '*Morgan*' defence after the case of that name: *DPP v Morgan* [1975] 2 All ER 347 HL. Clearly the more unreasonable the belief, the less likely it was to be honest. This case concerned the defendant who invited three friends home from a public house to have sexual intercourse with his wife, informing them that she was likely to struggle to increase her sexual arousal. She was held down whilst all three men and her husband had sexual intercourse with her. At the trial all three men maintained that they believed she consented. They were convicted of rape whilst Morgan was convicted of aiding and abetting rape. The case was appealed to the House of Lords which reversed the previous objective nature of the defence (as established by *Tolson* (1889) 23 QBD 168 CCR) yet upheld the convictions. It established that there can be no conviction for rape where a man honestly believes in consent and that belief does not have to be reasonable.

➡ CROSS-REFERENCE
For further discussion of *Morgan* and unreasonable belief see Chapter 9, 9.4.2.

A subjective approach to MR is generally considered to be a good thing. It judges a defendant on the facts as he believed them to be, not on the facts as he ought to have believed them to be. But in rape, we are not talking about facts which are hard to establish. If D is in any doubt about whether or not his partner consents to sexual intercourse, it would be reasonable to expect him to ask. By allowing an unreasonable belief in consent, the House of Lords disregarded the context and seriousness of rape. It was far too lenient a defence.

The Sexual Offences (Amendment) Act 1976 which followed the widescale disapproval of this case stated for the first time that rape was non-consensual sexual intercourse, thus abolishing any requirement of force or resistance. But the *Morgan* principle of honest but unreasonable belief in consent remained until it was abolished in relation to sexual offences by s1(1)(b) SOA. However, it remains elsewhere in the criminal law.

EXAMPLE 11.3

D and V work together and stay late in the office one night to prepare for an important deadline. D offers V a lift home. She accepts and invites him in for a glass of wine. D asks if he can stay the night. V agrees but says that she does not have casual sex. On that basis, she allows him to embrace her. Whilst doing so, D goes too far and has non-consensual sexual intercourse with V. Does D have the MR for rape?

Here, should D assert a defence of mistaken belief in consent, the issue must be determined not simply by V's evidence on consent, but also by reference to all the circumstances and steps taken by D to ascertain consent (s1(2)). We can see how this might cloud the jury's perception of what happened. V's style of dress, for example, her conduct and background may well be viewed prejudicially by a jury and obscure the facts. Section 1(2) also states that the jury must have regard to the steps taken by D to ascertain consent. D does not seem to have taken any steps in that direction. He is not required by the Act to do so, but failure in these circumstances may be considered unreasonable. There is a possibility, though, that the circumstances here will overshadow this requirement.

?! THINKING POINT 11.6

D is charged with rape in each of the scenarios below. At each trial D asserts that he reasonably believed V had consented to sexual intercourse. Will the defence succeed?

(In each case, the test is whether a reasonable person would believe that V is consenting. The jury's decision as to whether D's belief was reasonable must be based on the circumstances and any steps taken by D to ascertain consent.)

1. D, a stranger, follows V after she gets off a bus late one night. She turns into an unlit alleyway where D pulls her into the bushes after putting his hand over her mouth. He then has sexual intercourse with her.

2. D is a former boyfriend of V. He has a very low IQ. She invites him to her flat one day to discuss their relationship. She makes him a meal and becomes flirtatious. When they later sit on the settee together D climbs on top of V. She protests but D still manages to have sexual intercourse with her.

3. D and V go out on a date. V wears revealing clothes. D knows that V has had several sexual partners. V invites D back to her flat for coffee where he forces her into the bedroom. Ignoring her protests and overcoming her physical resistance, he has sexual intercourse with her.

Would it make any difference if, in each case, V had signs of physical injury, such as bruising, as a result of her resistance?

11.2.4 Marital Rape

Historically, a man was immune from prosecution for raping his wife. Immunity no longer applies.

Until 1994, the definition of rape referred to 'unlawful' sexual intercourse. It was not clear what this meant but the House of Lords in the case of *R v R* [1991] 2 All ER 257 decided that it could only be a reference to the historical rule that rape within marriage was lawful and that all other rapes were unlawful. The rule that a man could not be guilty of raping his wife derived from an eighteenth-century statement of LCJ Hale in Pleas of the Crown Vol. 1 1736:

> By their mutual matrimonial consent and contract the wife hath given herself in this kind unto her Husband which she cannot retract.

The marriage contract therefore implied matrimonial consent to sexual intercourse regardless of violence, indignity, consent or the wife's state of health. Over the years, the marital rape exception was criticised, even by the judges in *Clarence*. In order to mitigate its severity, exceptions were developed: a husband could be guilty of raping his wife where the marriage was the subject of court order or where they were no longer cohabiting. It remained law, however, until the case of *R v R* in which the House of Lords held that the exception was a legal fiction, that marriage in modern times was a relationship of equals, and that a wife may revoke her consent in any circumstances. The word 'unlawful' in the statutory definition was surplus to requirements. It was unlawful to have sexual intercourse with any woman without her consent.

The word 'unlawful' was not however removed from the definition of rape until 1994 by s142 Criminal Justice and Public Order Act 1994. The husband convicted of rape in *R v R* unsuccessfully appealed to the ECHR under Article 7, which prohibits retrospective criminal laws: *CR v United Kingdom* [1996] 1 FLR 434. A conviction against a husband in 2002 for a rape upon his wife in 1970 was also upheld by the Court of Appeal in *R v C* [2005] Crim LR 238 despite the Article 7 argument.

SECTION SUMMARY

Rape (MR):
- *Penetration must be intentional.*
- *Lack of reasonable belief in consent.*
- *Whether a belief is reasonable is to be determined having regard to all the circumstances, including any steps taken to ascertain consent.*

11.2.5 The Rationale of Rape

Rape derives from the Latin word meaning 'to seize or carry off'. In ancient times, raiding tribes would seize and carry off not only goods, cattle and other spoils of war but also women. The rationale of the offence was the protection of a man's proprietorial right to control access to his wife or daughter. It was narrowly identified as theft of virginity until the thirteenth century. From theft of virginity it evolved to an offence against the will of the victim and this required evidence of force or resistance, as it still does in most American states. In the mid-twentieth century, rape became 'the protection of woman's discretion by proscribing coitus contrary to her wishes' or, in other words, non-consensual sexual intercourse ('Forcible and Statutory Rape' [1952] 62 *Yale Law Journal* 62 at p 71). There was, however, considerable leeway in the interpretation of consent, for the law reflected a tacit concession to the man's freedom to 'seduce' by all manner of means: forcible, coercive, fraudulent and dishonest.

Feminist theory from the 1960s onwards focused on gender power relationships. Rape law reflected unequal power relationships in society between men and women and a masculine image of sexuality in which consent was constructed for women according to male perceptions. This was replicated in the trial process. Rape law sustained male dominance by interpreting sexual violence as sex. Female sexual autonomy was denied by the law (C. Mackinnon, *Towards a Feminist Theory of the State*, Harvard University Press, 1989).

This seemed particularly apt for, despite the emphasis in the law on consent, evidence of resistance was still required by judges in rape trials until comparatively recently. The House of Lords in *DPP v Morgan* [1976] AC 182, for example, held that rape consisted of unlawful sexual intercourse with a woman without her consent and by force. This mis-perception was corrected by the Sexual Offences (Amendment) Act 1976 which placed the emphasis on 'lack of consent.' Notwithstanding, prejudicial attitudes towards victims within the judicial process continued until recent years, as witnessed by graphic judicial pronouncements that girls who hitchhike at night are 'in the true sense asking for it' (Sir Melford Stevenson, 25 March 1982) or that 'when a woman says no she doesn't always mean it' (Judge Raymond Dean, 11 April 1990).

Current academic literature reveals a search for the real 'wrong' in rape and other sexual offences. Sexual autonomy is now recognised as the guiding principle. It was described by the SOR team as the freedom and responsibility to make decisions about one's own sexual conduct and to respect the rights of others. But what does this mean? An American legal philosopher, S. Schulhofer, considers that the current approach to consent favours stronger parties who are able to exploit power imbalances to secure consent to sex. Their autonomy is relatively unchecked, whereas the autonomy of the weaker party to refuse is unprotected (*Unwanted Sex: The Culture of Intimidation and the Failure of the Law*, Harvard University Press, 1998). J. Gardner and S. Shute in 'The Wrongness of Rape' in J. Horder (ed), *Oxford Essays in Jurisprudence*, OUP, 2000 consider that consent is not the issue. Rape is the 'sheer use' of a person and when accompanied by humiliation it is a denial of their personhood and is literally dehumanising. For M. Childs, it is a question of psychic and emotional, as well as physical, integrity. It is more than just the violation of proprietary interest in bodily autonomy ('Sexual Autonomy and Law' (2001) 64 *MLR* 309). Other feminist academics also identify the violation of 'oneself' or 'personhood', something not transgressed in non-consensual property crimes (eg: J. Nedelsky 'Reconceiving Autonomy' (1989) 1 *Yale Journal of Law & Feminism* 7).

11.2.6 Why is Rape so Controversial? The Justice Gap

The number of rapes *reported* to the police have soared in the UK over the last 20 years. Yet, conviction rates have plummeted. Whilst in 1977 one in three reported rapes resulted in conviction (32 per cent), the national conviction rate hovered at around 5.6 per cent from 2000 onwards and only rose to 7 per cent in 2013, one of the lowest in Europe (Home Office & Ministry of Justice (2013) *An Overview of Sexual Offending in England and Wales, Sexual offending overview tables*). This is despite legal changes and policy initiatives to tackle the problem. So what is going wrong?

The decision to report

The increase in reported rape is due to many factors such as wider official acknowledgement of its prevalence, less social tolerance of the offence, improvements in police response to complaints through sexual assault referral centres, and the emergence of organisations such as Rape Crisis Centres and Victim Support. In addition, since 1994, the statistics have been increased by the inclusion of male rapes. The most significant factor is the recognition and reporting of acquaintance rape.

But it remains a fact that an extremely high number of all rapes remain unreported. Until about 30 years ago, rape was not regarded as real unless committed upon an unsuspecting victim by a stranger. This undoubtedly meant that rapes falling outside this narrow definition were not reported or, indeed, not regarded as rape even by the victims. It has been known for many years that most rapes are in fact committed by people known to the victim whether it be an acquaintance, current or previous partner, or family member.

Many studies have found that women do not report rape for different reasons, such as fear of disbelief, unsympathetic police treatment, the shame of disclosure to family and friends, self-blame, fear of further attack, divided loyalty where the assailant was known, the wish to avoid court appearances or publicity, and cultural or language reasons. The Court of Appeal recently instructed judges to advise juries that delay by a victim in complaining to the police should not be seen as prejudicial. It may be because of shame and guilt: *R v D* [2008] EWCA Crim 2557. Male rape is under-reported because of the myths and stigma associated with being the victim of a sexual offence.

The police decision to record an offence

It is widely acknowledged that rape is not only under-reported but also under-recorded by the police. An Independent Police Complaints Commission report in 2013 concluded that a policy had been followed across several London boroughs of persuading women to drop their cases so as to boost police performance figures (www.ipcc.gov.uk). Recent empirical research of rape allegations reported to the Metropolitan Police reveals the following (K. Hohl and E.A. Stanko, 'Complaints of rape and the criminal justice system: fresh evidence on the attrition problem in England and Wales' (2015) 12(3) *European Journal of Criminology* 324–41):

> We find that a central factor in attrition is what police and prosecutors perceive as evidence against the victim's allegation: the police record noting a previous false allegation by the victim, inconsistencies in the victim's recollection of the rape, and evidence or police opinion casting doubt on the allegation. In the sample none of the allegations with any of these features were prosecuted. Furthermore, we found that a white suspect with no prior police record is likely to avoid a full police investigation, whilst the police and CPS appear more inclined to believe and pursue an allegation that involves a non-white suspect or a suspect with a prior police record.

Police investigation

Home Office research has found that there is an over-estimation of the scale of false allegations by both police officers and prosecutors, leading to scepticism, poor communication, and loss of confidence of complainants. A Joint Inspectorate Report in 2007, 'Without Consent', confirmed that nearly one in three cases recorded as 'no crime' should have been properly investigated. This was confirmed by a report by the office of the DPP in 2013 negating the misplaced belief that false allegations of rape are rife (*Charging Perverting the Course of Justice and Wasting Police Time in Cases Involving Allegedly False Rape and Domestic Violence Allegations*, CPS March 2013). It has been known for the police to prosecute women who are considered to have made false allegations or false retractions for wasting police time or perverting the course of justice, for example: *R v A* [2012] EWCA Crim 434. Recent DPP legal guidance on such prosecutions

(2013) may affect such practice but 'Rape Crisis' evidence suggests that this is not the case. At the root of police scepticism is an attitude that only rapes committed by strangers or those accompanied by the use of violence are serious or worth pursuing.

The trial process

Going to court as a victim can be traumatic. Studies have shown that victims have expected to be treated with kindness and consideration and to be kept informed but the reality is frequently otherwise. Pre-trial, the victim may not have had clear information about the police investigation or case progress. At court, she may not have met prosecuting counsel until the first morning of the hearing and may not even have been formally introduced. As both witness and victim, she is not entitled to independent representation. She may feel that prosecuting counsel does not adequately represent her interests. In three European countries, Norway, Denmark and Sweden, the victim of rape is separately represented in both the police station and court. The representative's role is limited to supporting the victim through the criminal justice system and is not to prosecute or influence the case. The schemes, introduced in the 1980s, are seen as successful. It is unlikely that this will ever occur in England and Wales however. The Criminal Law Revision Committee, Fifteenth Report, *Sexual Offences* (1984) objected to the idea on principle because it would be anomalous in our adversarial system.

Gradual procedural improvements are being introduced and the introduction of specialised prosecuting counsel in particular could secure improvement in the conviction rates. (See the online resources at **www.oup.com/uk/loveless6e/** for further details.)

The trial: cross-examination and previous sexual history

Cross-examination: Most of the criticisms which follow apply to both male and female rape trials. The task of the prosecutor is to prove that intentional non-consensual penile penetration was committed by D upon the victim. D is unlikely to contest that the act occurred or that it was intentional. The most likely defence will be either consent or mistaken belief in consent. The trial stands or falls on the issue of consent. It thus becomes a strongly contested issue.

The victim is not a party to the trial nor is she represented. She is the chief prosecution witness in the case. Most of the time, she will be the only witness, for there will rarely have been any other eye witnesses to the event, especially where D is known to the victim, such as a husband, partner, former partner, member of the family or acquaintance. The onus will therefore be on her alone to prove that the act of sexual intercourse was non-consensual. The task of defence counsel will be to undermine her evidence through cross-examination. She will be cross-examined on each and every detail of the rape. Research has shown that in the course of this process, many offensive and degrading questions may be put in order to suggest that she is lying or fabricating the allegation. Suggestions will be made which invite the jury to cast her in as discreditable a light as possible.

Prejudices and stereotypes regarding sexual women will be invoked. Therefore, despite her protests, 'no' will be interpreted as 'yes' because she was, for example, flirtatious, wore short skirts, provocative clothing, too much make-up, contributed to the crime by accepting a late night lift from a stranger or invited D back for coffee. The trial process has been slow to combat two myths in particular: that a late complaint is necessarily false, and that victims are always upset and emotional when giving evidence. Much research relates the myths and stereotypes surrounding the concept of consent. Read this extract from M.W. Steward, S.A. Dobbin and S.I. Gatowki, 'Definitions of Rape: Victims, Police and Prosecutors' (1996) 4 *Feminist Legal Studies* 159, at p 160:

Common cultural myths and stereotypes about rape include the belief that rape is a sex act rather than an assault, that raped women are somehow less respectable, that women lie about being raped, and the belief that women are responsible for their own victimization. For example, cultural myths tell us that: 'Only bad girls get raped'; 'Women provoke rape by the physical appearance'; 'All women want to be raped'; and 'Women ask for it'. They also tell us that 'Any healthy woman can resist a rapist if she really wants to' and that 'Women "cry rape" only when they've been jilted'.

(For further research on this aspect of the trial see, for instance, S. Lees, *Ruling Passions: Sexual Violence, Reputation and the Law*, Buckingham: Open University Press, 1997.)

Previous sexual history: There is also every possibility that an application will be granted by the judge under s41 Youth Justice and Criminal Evidence Act 1999 to admit evidence of her sexual history. She will be cross-examined on this, the purpose of which will be to suggest that because she has had sex with D or other men in the past, she is more likely to have consented on the occasion in question. Such allegations of promiscuity will, of course, reinforce her denigration in the eyes of the jury.

It has been found that the rules under s41, which were designed to prevent routine degrading and prejudicial cross-examination by defence barristers on irrelevant previous sexual history are being 'evaded, circumvented and resisted' by barristers and judges alike (L. Kelly, J. Tempkin, and S. Griffiths *Section 41: An evaluation of new legislation limiting sexual history evidence in rape trials*, HO Online Report 20/06, 20 June 2006).

Previous bad conduct or D's convictions are withheld from the jury (although applications to admit them are more likely now under the Criminal Justice Act 2003). The victim's sexual past is, by contrast, open to cross-examination and revealed to the court. It increases the risk that the victim will be judged not on the evidence but on her background, status and morality.

Corroboration: Until 1994, juries had to be given what was known as a mandatory corroboration warning in rape trials where the only evidence came from the victim: that it was unsafe to convict solely on the basis of the evidence of the victim. The jury would be told that women might fabricate allegations of a sexual nature through jealousy, spite, revenge, lies or fantasy. The warning was based on the supposed sexual proclivities and weaknesses of women who might easily make an allegation which could be very difficult to defend. Section 32 of the Criminal Justice and Public Order Act 1994 abolished the mandatory corroboration warning and made it discretionary. Had women given uncorroborated evidence of any other offence such as a theft or murder, a warning regarding female weakness and proclivities would have been grounds for appeal.

Societal attitudes: Research by Amnesty International in November 2005 (www.amnesty.org. uk) found that a third of people in the UK believe that a woman is either totally or partially responsible for being raped if she has behaved in a flirtatious manner. Similar attitudes were expressed in relation to clothing, drink, perceived promiscuity or where she has clearly failed to say 'no'. Amnesty termed the low conviction rates on rape in the UK a gross human rights violation.

The court trial for a rape victim is an extremely traumatic experience. Many rape victims describe the trial as a second rape for the indignity and humiliation inflicted upon them. Some rape victims say they feel they are on trial in place of the defendant. None of this augurs well for successful prosecutions.

There is undoubted government motivation for improvement. How this will translate into practice is yet to be seen. There is clearly still a long way to go to convince many men and women that going to court is worth the trouble. C. McGlynn in 'Feminism, Rape & The Search for Justice' (2011) 31 *OJLS* 4 suggests that restorative justice should be used as an alternative form of punishment:

> I will suggest that feminist strategy and activism must rethink its approach to what constitutes justice for rape victims. It must move beyond a predominant focus on punitive state outcomes, with its emphasis on

convictions and high prison sentences, to encompass broader notions of justice, including an expansive approach to restorative justice. . . . It has been presumed that punishing offenders is necessarily beneficial for victims. But this is not necessarily so, particularly in the case of sexual offences where a much wider challenge to the culture and attitudes which condone sexual violence is required if victims' rights and sense of justice are to be genuinely improved. The end result is a culture where the 'recognition of harm' is equated with the 'length of a prison term' and 'criminal justice responses which are not punitive are seen to be unresponsive to victim's/women's harms'.

The following offences can be committed by either a man or a woman.

11.3 Assault by Penetration

Section 2 SOA 2003:

(1) A person (A) commits an offence if–

    (a) he intentionally penetrates the vagina or anus of another person (B) with a part of his body or anything else,

    (b) the penetration is sexual,

    (c) B does not consent to the penetration, and

    (d) A does not reasonably believe that B consents.

(2) Whether a belief is reasonable is to be determined having regard to all the circumstances, including any steps A has taken to ascertain whether B consents.

(3) Sections 75 and 76 apply to an offence under this section.

(4) A person guilty of an offence under this section is liable, on conviction on indictment, to imprisonment for life.

Section 78

Penetration, touching or any other activity is sexual if a reasonable person would consider that–

    (a) whatever its circumstances or any person's purpose in relation to it, it is because of its nature sexual, or

    (b) because of its nature it may be sexual and because of its circumstances or the purpose of any person in relation to it (or both) it is sexual.

Therefore, the AR consists of:

- sexual penetration of the vagina or anus;
- with a part of the defendant's body other than his penis or any other object;
- without consent.

The MR consists of:

- intentional penetration;
- A does not reasonably believe B consents;
- whether a belief is reasonable is to be determined having regard to all the circumstances, including any steps A has taken to ascertain whether B consents.

→ CROSS-REFERENCE

Sections 75 and 76 are discussed in 11.2.

The consent and MR provisions are identical to those for the offence of rape. You will need to refer back to ss 75 and 76 for this.

This is a new offence and covers all sexual penetrations by any part of the body other than a penis, and all other objects, such as bottles and knives. Oral sex would be included as would penetration by an unknown object where, for example, V is asleep or drunk (*Lyddaman* [2006] EWCA Crim 383). The offence is regarded as being as serious as rape and therefore carries a maximum life sentence. It does not appear that a specific mental element is required in respect of the AR element of 'sexual'.

→ CROSS-REFERENCE

For the meaning of 'sexual' see 11.4.1.

11.4 Sexual Assault

Section 3 SOA 2003:

(1) A person (A) commits an offence if–

   (a) he intentionally touches another person (B),

   (b) the touching is sexual,

   (c) B does not consent to the touching, and

   (d) A does not reasonably believe that B consents.

(2) Whether a belief is reasonable is to be determined having regard to all the circumstances, including any steps A has taken to ascertain whether B consents.

(3) Sections 75 and 76 apply to an offence under this section.

(4) A person guilty of an offence under this section is liable–

   (a) on summary conviction, to imprisonment for a term not exceeding 6 months or a fine not exceeding the statutory maximum or both;

   (b) on conviction on indictment, to imprisonment for a term not exceeding 10 years.

'Sexual' is defined as in s78 [see 11.4.1].

'Touching' is defined in s79(8):

Touching includes touching–

(a) with any part of the body,

(b) with anything else,

(c) through anything,

(d) and in particular includes touching amounting to penetration.

The AR consists of:

◼ touching of another person;

◼ the touching must be sexual;

◼ and without consent.

MR consists of:

◼ intentional touching;

◼ lack of reasonable belief in consent;

◼ whether a belief is reasonable is to be determined having regard to all the circumstances, including any steps A has taken to ascertain whether B consents.

This offence replaces the former offence of indecent assault which was unsatisfactory because of its width: it covered not only serious assaults, such as penile penetration or penetration by other objects, but also sexual touching. The new offence is designed to cover a range of unacceptable touching which is less serious than rape or assault by penetration but which can be distressing to the victim because of its sexual intention, such as rubbing up against someone else in a sexual manner perhaps on public transport, fondling, groping and more serious assaults. An example would be *Heard* [2007] EWCA Crim 125 where D rubbed his penis against the thigh of a police officer. It is not clear whether 'touching' must be by positive act or includes an omission, as, for example, in the case of *Speck* [1977] 2 All ER 859 (passive submission to child voluntarily placing hand on D's genitals which then became erect). It can be committed by either a man or a woman, is triable in either the magistrates or Crown Court, and has a maximum sentence of ten years.

→ **CROSS-REFERENCE**
For further discussion of *Heard* see Chapter 8, 8.3.2.

11.4.1 Section 78: 'Sexual'

This is an objective test: is the touching (a) obviously sexual or (b) sexual by virtue of circumstances or purpose?

Section 78 does not provide a definition but an approach to determining the question of whether the penetration (as in s2 Assault by penetration) or touching (as in s3 sexual assault) is sexual. There is unlikely to be any difficulty about this in respect of assault by penetration. Under s78(a) the question is to determine whether the touching is obviously sexual regardless of the circumstances. If it is, then there is no need to consider s78(b) which is only for cases of doubt. Under s78(b) where the touching *may* be sexual, the circumstances or purpose of the defendant are examined.

Under the previous law of indecent assault, conduct which was not apparently sexual could not be defined as such by reference only to purpose or circumstances. For example, if a man removed a girl's shoe from her foot because it gave him sexual gratification, his purpose was not relevant and the conduct would not be criminal. These were the facts of *R v George* [1956] Crim LR 52. If you read the report of *R v H* which follows, Lord Woolf appeared to think that the decision would not be quite so clear cut under s78.

Although the word assault appears in the title, there is no element of the offence which refers to the requirements of an assault. Therefore, where there is no touching but only a verbal insinuation, the offence is not committed.

There has been one case so far on the definition of 'sexual' under s78:

> ### *R v H* [2005] EWCA CRIM 732 COURT OF APPEAL
>
> The defendant approached the victim one evening as she walked across a field and said to her 'Do you fancy a shag?' She ignored him. He then grabbed her tracksuit bottoms by pulling at a side pocket and attempted to pull her towards him whilst attempting to put his hand over her mouth. The victim escaped. The defendant was convicted under s3 Sexual Offences Act 2003 and appealed. There were two issues:
>
> 1. Whether the touching of the tracksuit fabric alone amounted to touching for the purposes of s79(8).
> 2. Whether a reasonable person might regard the conduct as sexual within s78.

Lord Woolf CJ:

8. In this case we are concerned with section 78(b). Miss Egerton who appears on behalf of the Crown accepts that (a) has no application. The nature of the touching with which we are concerned was not inevitably sexual. It is important to note that there are two requirements in section 78(b). First, there is the requirement that the touching because of its nature may be sexual; and secondly, there is the requirement that the touching because of its circumstances or the purpose of any person in relation to it (or both) is sexual.

9. Miss Egerton agreed with the view of the court expressed in argument that if there were not two requirements in (b), the opening words 'because of its nature it may be sexual' would be sur-plus. If it was not intended by the legislature that effect should be given to those opening words, it would be sufficient to create an offence by looking at the touching and deciding whether because of its circumstances it was sexual. In other words, there is not one comprehensive test. It is neces-sary for both halves of section 78(b) to be complied with.

10. It is no doubt because of this aspect of section 78(b) and the article in the Criminal Law Re-view that Mr. West who appeared on behalf of the appellant referred to R v Court. That case dealt with an alleged indecent assault. An assistant in a shop struck a 12 year old girl visitor twelve times, for no apparent reason, outside her shorts on her buttocks. The assistant was convicted. Both this court and the House of Lords dismissed the assistant's appeal . . . .

In referring to the case of George (just discussed), Lord Woolf continued:

11. We would express reservations as to whether or not it would be possible for the removal of shoes in that way, because of the nature of the act that took place, to be sexual as sexual is defined now in section 78. That in our judgment may well be a question that it would be necessary for a jury to determine.

12. The fact that there are two different questions which we have sought to identify complicates the task of the judge and that of the jury . . . . He [the judge] will answer that question by determin-ing whether it would be appropriate for a reasonable person to consider that the touching because of its nature may be sexual. Equally, the judge will have to consider whether it would be possible for a reasonable person to conclude, because of the circumstances of the touching or the purpose of any person in relation to the touching (or both), that it is sexual. If he comes to the conclusion that a reasonable person could possibly answer those questions adversely to the defendant, then the matter would have to be left to the jury.

13. We would suggest that in that situation the judge would regard it as desirable to identify two distinct questions for the jury. First, would they, as twelve reasonable people (as the section requires), consider that because of its nature the touching that took place in the particular case before them could be sexual? If the answer to that question was 'No', the jury would find the de-fendant not guilty. If 'Yes', they would have to go on to ask themselves (again as twelve reason-able people) whether in view of the circumstances and/or the purpose of any person in relation to the touching (or both), the touching was in fact sexual. If they were satisfied that it was, then they would find the defendant guilty. If they were not satisfied, they would find the defendant not guilty.

14. In that suggested approach the reference to the nature of the touching in the first half refers to the actual touching that took place in that case. In answering the first question, the jury would not be concerned with the circumstances before or after the touching took place, or any evidence as to the purpose of any person in relation to the touching . . . .

24 . . . Where a person is wearing clothing we consider that touching of the clothing constitutes touching for the purpose of the section 3 offence.

26 . . . We have no doubt that it was not Parliament's intention by the use of that language to make it impossible to regard as a sexual assault touching which took place by touching what the victim was wearing at the time.

Appeal dismissed.

?!   THINKING POINT 11.7

Decide whether the following fall within the definition of 'sexual' under s78 or 'touching' under s 79:

1. A man strips another man against his will in public.

2. A man touches the bottom of V's skirt. His motive is sexual.

3. A hospital radiographer carries out an unnecessary gynaecological scan upon a woman by inserting a probe into her vagina.

11.5 Causing Sexual Activity without Consent

Section 4

(1) A person (A) commits an offence if–

    (a) he intentionally causes another person (B) to engage in an activity,

    (b) the activity is sexual,

    (c) B does not consent to engaging in the activity,

    (d) A does not reasonably believe that B consents.

(2) Whether a belief is reasonable is to be determined having regard to all the circumstances, including any steps A has taken to ascertain whether B consents.

The s75 and s76 consent provisions apply. Punishment: six months/10 years maximum.

No touching is required for this offence. Therefore, if D causes the victim to commit a sexual act without physical force the offence will be committed. This might take the form of a threat or deception. It could include the following:

- indecent text messaging;
- women who obtain penetration from non-consenting males;
- forced prostitution;
- forced masturbation (*R v Sargeant* [1997] Crim LR 50).

Sexual activity must be 'caused' by D (usual principles will apply) and it must be intended.
There is no requirement that D be present when sexual activity is engaged in.

SUMMARY

You should now be familiar with the policy of the SOA 2003, the background on sexual violence and with the definitions, cases, principles and application of the following offences:

- Section 1: Rape—law and social context;
- Section 2: Assault by penetration;
- Section 3: Sexual assault;
- Section 4: Causing sexual activity without consent.

You should know that under the SOA 2003 there are common provisions on the following issues which apply to all sexual offences:

- Sections 74–76: Consent;
- Reasonable belief in consent.

PROBLEM SOLVING

Dan approached a prostitute, Vera, outside a tube station one night. He offered her £50 if she would give him a massage. Vera refused because she knew of Dan's reputation for violence. Dan happened to know that Vera was studying law at university and needed the money to support her children. He began to fondle her breasts and said, 'If you don't do what I ask, I will tell the Law Society that you have convictions for being a common prostitute'. Vera pushed him off and became worried. At that point, Dan was joined by his friend, Ali, who said that she should do as Dan asked or something nasty might happen to her children next week. Ali then said that she should come to their flat. Vera reluctantly agreed. At the flat, they entered a bedroom and Dan locked the door. Ali threatened her with a knife before tying her to the bed where they both had sexual intercourse with her. D then penetrated her anus with his fist. No money was paid to Vera. Dan and Ali were later arrested. They gave statements to the police in which they said they believed Vera had consented. Discuss whether Dan and Ali have committed any sexual offences.

Remember:

- **I: Identify** relevant issues
- **D: Define** offences/defences
- **E: Explain/evaluate** the law
- **A: Apply** law to facts.

See the online resources for further guidance on solving this problem: www.oup.com/uk/loveless6e/.

FURTHER READING

M. Dempsey and J. Herring, 'Why Sexual Penetration Requires Justification' [2007] 27(3) *OJLS* 467
Argues that while the law assumes a man's sexual penetration is prima facie lawful unless proven non-consensual, it should be seen as prima facie wrong and requiring justification.

L. Ellison and V. Munro 'Reacting to Rape: Exploring Mock Jurors' Assessments of Complainant Credibility' (2009) 49(2) *British Journal of Criminology* 202
Discusses findings from a study which explored the impact of V's behaviour on jurors by using simulated rape trials.

Home Office & Ministry of Justice, 'An Overview of Sexual Offending in England and Wales' (January 2013) (www.gov.uk/government/statistics/an-overview-of-sexual-offending-in-england-and-wales)
Provides an overview and discussion of the statistics on sexual offences.

L. Kelly, J. Lovett and L. Regan, *A Gap or a Chasm? Attrition in Reported Rape Cases, Home Office Research Study 293, London: HMSO, 2005*
Explores the reasons behind the very low conviction rate for rape.

K. Laird, 'Rapist or Rogue? Deception, Consent and the Sexual Offences Act 2003' [2014] *Crim LR* 491
Considers the relationship between s74 and s76, and the principles and policy issues underlying the law on consent gained by deception.

S. Lees, *Ruling Passions: Sexual Violence, Reputation and the Law*, Open University Press, 1997
Explores the ways in which women's sexual reputations are constructed and used in sexual offences trials.

C. McGlynn, 'Feminism, Rape and the Search for Justice' (2011) 31(4) *OJLS* **825**

Considers whether restorative justice approaches may be appropriate for sexual offences, and if so, what would be required.

N. Padfield, Editorial 'The Growing Number of Convicted Sex Offenders' [2015] *Crim LR* **12, 927**

Notes that a growing number of sexual offences convictions, combined with longer sentences, means more offenders in prison or on the sex offenders' register, and asks what the implications of this are.

S. Schulhofer, *Unwanted Sex: The Culture of Intimidation and the Failure of Law***, Harvard University Press, 1998**

This book argues that the law on sexual offences needs to be refocused upon safeguarding sexual autonomy.

A. Sharpe, 'Criminalising Sexual Intimacy: Transgender Defendants and the Legal Construction of Non-Consent' [2014] 3 *Crim LR* **207**

Analyses the position of transgender defendants prosecuted on the basis of fraudulent consent, and questions the public policy and law leading to their conviction.

J.R. Spencer, 'Three New Cases on Consent' (2007) 66(3) *Cambridge LJ* **493**

Analyses the decisions in *Bree*, *B*, and *Jheeta*.

V. Tadros, 'Rape Without Consent' (2006) 26(3) *OJLS* **515**

Suggests substantial reformulation of the law on sexual offences, which removes 'consent' as the central element.

J. Temkin, *Rape and the Legal Process***, Sweet & Maxwell, 2000**

Examines how the legal system deals with rape and how it might be reformed.

J. Temkin and B. Krahe, *Sexual Assault & The Justice Gap: A Question of Attitude***, Hart, 2008**

Investigates the attrition rate for sexual offences, using interviews with judges, lawyers and the public, and suggests steps for improvement.

Property offences 1

12

Introduction

KEY POINTS

THEFT

This section will help you to understand:

- the s1 Theft Act 1968 definition of theft:
  - actus reus: appropriation, property, belonging to another;
  - mens rea: dishonesty, intention permanently to deprive;
- that each AR/MR element is further defined in the Theft Act 1968;
- the distinction between theft and fraud and that it is possible for them to overlap;
- and to critically examine the contours of the offence.

ROBBERY

This section will help you to:

- understand the s8 Theft Act 1968 definition of robbery:
  - actus reus: theft accompanied by the use or fear of force;
  - mens rea: the MR for theft, intentional use of force; and
- evaluate whether robbery is too wide an offence in that it includes theft with serious violence as well as theft with minor harm.

HANDLING

This section will help you to understand:

- the s22 Theft Act 1968 definition of handling:
  - actus reus: stolen goods and their proceeds, handling, otherwise than in the course of stealing;
  - mens rea: knowledge or belief/dishonesty;
- that handling must be preceded by a prior property offence and that this can include a previous offence of handling.

INTRODUCTION

There is a wide range of property offences. Most are concerned with dishonesty and all are the creation of statute, principally the Theft Acts 1968 and 1978 and the Fraud Act 2006. Property offences cover a wide spectrum of crimes. At the more serious end are robbery (theft accompanied by force) and aggravated burglary (burglary accompanied by a weapon), both carrying maximum life sentences. At the lower end is pickpocketing or minor criminal damage. In between are a number of offences which can be more or less serious depending on the circumstances and the value of the property involved.

For the year ending December 2014, property offences collectively accounted for 70 per cent of all recorded crime, that is: robbery, burglary, offences against vehicles, thefts from the person, other thefts, shoplifting, fraud and forgery, and have fallen by 46 per cent since 2002/3. Theft of mobile phones account for almost half of all thefts from the person, with theft of metal having become a recent trend. (ONS Statistical Bulletin: Crime in England and Wales, Year Ending December 2014: www.ons.gov.uk/ons/rel/crime-stats/crime-statistics/year-ending-december-2014/crime-in-england-and-wales-year-ending-december-2014.html#tab-Theft-offences). Diagram 12.1 provides further details on recent trends. In this and Chapters 13 and 14 we will look at ten of the most important, and most common, property offences. All sections in relation to theft refer to the Theft Act 1968 unless otherwise stated.

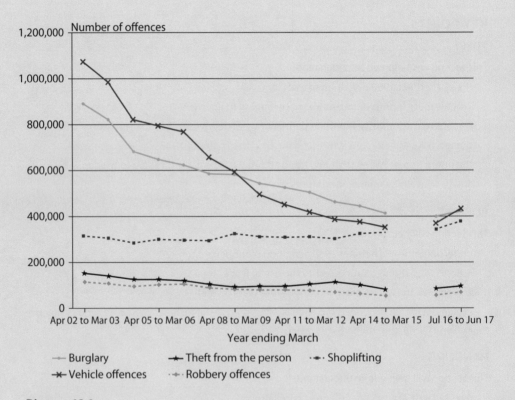

Diagram 12.1

Trends in police recorded theft offences in England and Wales, March 20/03 to year ending June 2017

Notes: 1. Police recorded crime data are not designated as National Statistics

Source: (ONS) www.ons.gov.uk/peoplepopulationandcommunity/crimeandjustice/bulletins/crimeinenglandandwales/june2017#what-is-happening-to-theft

12.1 Theft

KEY CASES

Lawrence [1972] AC 626—theft: consent is irrelevant to appropriation;

Morris [1984] AC 320—appropriation must be non-consensual;

Gomez [1993] AC 442—*Lawrence* approved as correct;

Hinks [2000] 3 WLR 1590—a valid gift can be appropriated;

Ghosh [1982] QB 1053—dishonesty according to ordinary standards and D's belief;

Ivey v Genting Casinos (UK) t/a Crockfords [2017] UKSC 67—*Ghosh* test rejected;

Vinall [2011] EWCA Crim 6252—abandonment and s6(1) intention.

12.1.1 Introduction

Definition of Theft (see Diagram 12.2):

Section 1(1) Theft Act 1968:

A person is guilty of theft if he dishonestly appropriates property belonging to another with the intention of permanently depriving the other of it; and 'thief' and 'steal' shall be construed accordingly.

The penalty is a maximum of seven years' imprisonment.

There are three elements to the actus reus and two mens rea elements:

Actus reus

- Appropriation
- Property
- Belonging to another

Mens rea

- Dishonestly
- Intention permanently to deprive

| Appropriation | + | Property | + | Belonging to another | + | Dishonestly | + | Intention to permanently deprive |

Diagram 12.2
Definition of theft

12.1.2 Actus Reus

Appropriation

Definition

> **Section 3(1):**
>
> Any assumption by a person of the rights of an owner amounts to an appropriation and this includes where he has come by the property (innocently or not) without stealing it, any later assumption of a right to it by keeping or dealing with it as owner.

Note: The word 'consent' does not appear in this definition and s3(1) makes no reference to whether an assumption of ownership rights can occur with the consent of the owner.

Several questions arise from the definition of appropriation in s3(1): What are the rights of an owner? Can there be an appropriation where the owner consents? At what point does an appropriation occur where there is a later assumption, keeping or dealing with property of which one may be already in possession?

Rights of ownership

Under the civil law, you can do anything with your own property: use it, abuse it, destroy it, give it away, lend it, use it as financial security or sell it. Ownership represents a bundle of rights.

Although you might think that you do not appropriate until you assume all the rights of an owner to property (ie: literally take it away from the owner completely), it has been held that an assumption of a single right will do (ie: possession or control). Therefore, acts which might otherwise be simply preparatory or an attempt are included. This has naturally widened the scope of theft.

Appropriation and consent

On a literal interpretation of s3(1), an appropriation or assumption of ownership does not need to be *without the consent of the owner* because those words are not included. Historically, no crime would have been committed if the owner had consented to a taking (Larceny Act 1916). The House of Lords has considered the question as to whether there can be an appropriation where the owner consents to the removal of his property. The answer is 'yes'. This is only ever likely to occur where an owner has been induced to part with property by fraud or trick (or in other words, by deception or false representation). You might wonder why this issue is important. The answer is that the scheme of the Theft Act 1968 was to keep a clear distinction between deception and fraud offences on the one hand and theft on the other. Fraud offences existed to deal with fraudsters who induced another to part with *ownership* by consent whereas theft existed to deal with thieves who took *possession* of property non-consensually. The former acquire ownership but the latter do not. Despite the intention of Parliament when enacting the Theft Act 1968, the courts have now abolished this distinction. Deception offences have now been replaced by a single fraud offence in the Fraud Act 2006 but the possibility of overlap between fraud and theft still remains.

Until 1993, there were two conflicting House of Lords authorities on this point, *Lawrence* and *Morris*:

Lawrence v Metropolitan Police Commissioner [1972] AC 626 HOUSE OF LORDS

D, a taxi driver, was convicted of theft contrary to s1(1) Theft Act 1968 for dishonestly appropriating £6 from an Italian student, a Mr Occhi. Having arrived at Victoria Station on his first visit to this country, and speaking little English, Mr Occhi requested a ride to Ladbroke Grove and was told by D that the fare was £7 when it was in fact only 10s 6d (52p). Mr Occhi gave D £1 and then simply held out his wallet to him from which D took a further £6. In other words, the money having been voluntarily offered, D had obtained it by a clear and unambiguous deception or misrepresentation.

The Court of Appeal upheld D's conviction and in granting leave to appeal to the House of Lords certified the following questions as involving a point of law of general public importance:

> (1) Whether section 1(1) of the Theft Act 1968 is to be construed as though it contained the words 'without the consent of the owner' or words to that effect and (2) Whether the provisions of section 15(1) [obtaining by deception] and of section 1(1) of the Theft Act 1968 are mutually exclusive in the sense that if the facts proved would justify a conviction under section 15(1) there cannot lawfully be a conviction under section 1(1) on those facts.

Viscount Dilhorne:

> Prior to the passage of the Theft Act 1968, which made radical changes in and greatly simplified the law relating to theft and some other offences, it was necessary to prove that the property alleged to have been stolen was taken 'without the consent of the owner' (Larceny Act 1916, section 1(1)).
>
> These words are not included in section 1(1) of the Theft Act, but the appellant contended that the subsection should be construed as if they were, as if they appeared after the words 'appropriates.' Section 1(1) reads as follows:
>
> A person is guilty of theft if he dishonestly appropriates property belonging to another with the intention of permanently depriving the other of it; and 'thief and 'steal' shall be construed accordingly.
>
> I see no ground for concluding that the omission of the words 'without the consent of the owner' was inadvertent and not deliberate, and to read the subsection as if they were included is, in my opinion, wholly unwarranted. Parliament by the omission of these words has relieved the prosecution of the burden of establishing that the taking was without the owner's consent. That is no longer an ingredient of the offence.

Appeal dismissed.

It was further held that belief in consent is relevant, not to consent, but to MR: dishonesty and s2(1)(b) (see later).

 NOTE 12.1

1. The effect of this judgment was that one could appropriate and therefore steal property with or without the consent of the owner. Therefore, in theory, most cases of deception could also be prosecuted as theft. This raises an important principle. If the route to conviction is less important than the type of conviction the rule of law is undermined. This would signify uncertainty and unpredictability in the criminal law—a potential violation of Article 7 ECHR (this article guarantees the right to certainty in the law).

2. The decision was contrary to the scheme of the Theft Act 1968 which had been preceded by the Criminal Law Revision Committee's Eighth Report on 'Theft and Related Offences'. Critical to its recommendations was the need for a clear distinction between theft and deception and the use of simplified language that ordinary members of a jury might easily comprehend. The word 'appropriation' was hardly that! In 1984, and without overruling it, the House of Lords in *Morris* decided that *Lawrence* was wrong.

R v Morris, Anderton and Burnside [1984] AC 320 HOUSE OF LORDS

The appeal involved two cases of price label switching in a supermarket. This was not by consent, of course. But observations in the HL concerned consensual undertakings. In the first case D had removed the price label from a joint of meat and replaced it with a label showing a lesser price which he had removed from another joint. He was detected at the check-out before he had paid for the joint and later convicted of theft contrary to s1(1) Theft Act. In the second case D had in similar manner switched price labels on goods in a supermarket but was not arrested until after he had passed the check-out and paid the lesser prices for the goods. He was also convicted of theft. Appeals against conviction by both Ds were dismissed by the Court of Appeal and by the House of Lords.

Lord Roskill:

> *In the context of section 3(1), the concept of appropriation in my view involves not an act expressly or impliedly authorised by the owner but an act by way of adverse interference with or usurpation of those rights.* When the honest shopper acts . . . . he or she is acting with the implied authority of the owner of the supermarket to take the goods from the shelf, put them in the trolley, take them to the checkpoint and there pay the correct price, at which moment the property in the goods will pass to the shopper for the first time. It is with the consent of the owners of the supermarket, be that consent express or implied, that the shopper does these acts and thus obtains at least control if not actual possession of the goods preparatory, at a later stage, to obtaining the property in them upon payment of the proper amount at the checkpoint. [Emphasis added.]

It was further held that in establishing appropriation, it is enough for the prosecution to prove the assumption by D of any of the rights of an owner, not necessarily all of the rights.

 NOTE 12.2

1. The case held that if V consented to the taking, there was no appropriation and, therefore, no theft. An appropriation would need to be something that V would not ordinarily consent to because it interfered with, or usurped, V's rights of ownership. A consensual acquisition of property would never become theft.

2. *Morris* was regarded as binding in preference to *Lawrence* in most subsequent appeals even though Lord Roskill's comments on authorised appropriations were obiter and not ratio. This was because the facts of *Morris* concerned *unauthorised* appropriations.

Unfortunately, clarity on this issue was short-lived. Eight years later, the House of Lords disapproved of *Morris* in *Gomez*. The same legal issue arose here because Gomez was charged with theft instead of obtaining property by deception. Note that this offence has now been replaced by the Fraud Act 2006.

R v Gomez [1993] AC 442 HOUSE OF LORDS

Gomez was employed as assistant manager in a retail electrical goods shop. He and an acquaintance, Ballay, agreed to take goods from the shop by presenting two stolen building society cheques, one for £7,950 and the other for £9,250, which were undated and bore no payee's name. On the first occasion, the manager instructed Gomez to confirm with the bank that the cheque was acceptable. Gomez later told him that he had done so and that the cheque was 'as good as cash'. The manager agreed to the transaction, Gomez paid the cheque into the bank, and a few days later Ballay took possession of the goods. Shortly afterwards, a further consignment of goods (to the value of £9,250) was ordered and supplied in similar fashion against the second stolen building society cheque. The manager agreed to this transaction without further enquiry. Later the two cheques were returned by the bank marked 'Orders not to pay. Stolen cheque'. Convictions of theft followed. The Court of Appeal quashed the convictions, Lord Lane CJ stating the following:

> What in fact happened was that the owner was induced by deceit to agree to the goods being transferred to Ballay. If that is the case, and if in these circumstances the appellant is guilty of theft, it must follow that anyone who obtains goods in return for a cheque which he knows will be dishonoured on presentation, or indeed by way of any other similar pretence, would be guilty of theft. That does not seem to be the law.

The matter was referred to the House of Lords which decided against *Morris* and in favour of *Lawrence* by 3:2. Lord Keith gave judgment for the majority:

> Prior to the passage of the Theft Act 1968, which made radical changes in and greatly simplified the law relating to theft and some other offences, it was necessary to prove that the property alleged to have been stolen was taken 'without the consent of the owner' (Larceny Act 1916, s1(1)). These words are not included in s1(1) of the Theft Act, but the appellant contended that the subsection should be construed as if they were, as if they appeared after the word 'appropriates' . . . . I see no ground for concluding that the omission of the words 'without the consent of the owner' was inadvertent and not deliberate, and to read the subsection as if they were included is, in my opinion, wholly unwarranted. *Parliament by the omission of these words has relieved the prosecution of the burden of establishing that the taking was without the owner's consent. That is no longer an ingredient of the offence . . . . Belief or the absence of belief that the owner had with such knowledge [of the circumstances of whether V had agreed or not to the assumption] is relevant to the issue of dishonesty, not to the question whether or not there has been an appropriation.* [Emphasis added.]

In relation to the conflict between *Morris* and *Lawrence*, Lord Keith said this:

> On the facts of the two cases it was unnecessary to decide whether . . . the mere taking of the article from the shelf and putting it in a trolley or other receptacle amounted to the assumption of one of the rights of the owner, and hence an appropriation. There was much to be said in favour of the view that it did, in respect that doing so gave the shopper control of the article and the capacity to exclude any other shopper from taking it. However, Lord Roskill expressed the opinion that it did not, on the ground that the concept of appropriation in the context of section 3(1) 'involves not an act expressly or impliedly authorised by the owner but an act by way of adverse interference with or usurpation of those rights.' While it is correct to say that appropriation for purposes of section 3(1) includes the latter sort of act, it does not necessarily follow that no other act can amount to an appropriation and in particular that no act expressly or impliedly authorised by the owner can in any circumstances do so. Indeed, *Lawrence v. Commissioner of Metropolitan Police* is a clear decision to the contrary since it laid down unequivocally that an act may be an appropriation notwithstanding that it is done with the consent of the owner. It does not appear to me that any sensible distinction can be made in this context between consent and authorisation.

In agreement, Lord Browne-Wilkinson observed:

> *The description of appropriation in Morris was tantamount to a 'misappropriation', introducing into the word the mental state of both owner and accused . . . . I regard the word 'appropriation' in isolation as*

being an objective description of the act done irrespective of the mental state of either the owner or the accused. It is impossible to reconcile the decision in *Lawrence* (that the question of consent is irrelevant in considering whether there has been an appropriation) with the views expressed in *Morris*, which latter views in my judgment were incorrect. [Emphasis added.]

In giving judgment for the minority, Lord Lowry noted the observation of the Court of Appeal that anyone who obtained goods in return for a cheque which was known would be dishonoured would be guilty of theft, and not simply a potential breach of contract:

'Fraudulent conversion' is accepted as the starting point for the new and comprehensive definition of theft and 'dishonest appropriation' is chosen as a synonym. Both expressions embody the notion of an adverse unilateral act done to the prejudice of the owner and without his authority; indeed, fraudulent conversion can have no other meaning.

The extension will also have the effect that the offences of theft and criminal deception (ie: s 15 Theft Act 1968) will overlap . . . My Lords, as I would submit, the [Eighth Report of the CLRC] contains a great deal which confirms and nothing which contradicts the interpretation of the word 'appropriates' which I have preferred, and a comparison of the Act with the draft Bill gives no support to the contrary view . . . . The Crown say that section 15 merely describes a particular type of theft and that all stealing by means of deception can be prosecuted under section 1 just as well as under section 15. I would point out that section 15 covers what were formerly two offences, obtaining by false pretences (where the ownership of the property is transferred by the deceived victim) and theft (or larceny) by a trick (where the possession of the property passes, but not the ownership). In the former case, according to the interpretation which I prefer, the offender does not appropriate the property, because the ownership (in colloquial terms, the property) is transferred with the owner's consent, albeit obtained by deception. In the latter case the offender does appropriate the property because, although the owner has handed over possession by consent (which was obtained by deception), he has not transferred the property (that is, the ownership) and the offender, intending to deprive the owner permanently of his property, appropriates it, not by taking possession, but by the unilateral act, adverse to the owner, of treating as his own and taking to himself property of which he was merely given possession. Thus, the kind of obtaining by deception which amounts to larceny by a trick and involves appropriation could be successfully prosecuted under section 1, but the old false pretences type of obtaining by deception could not . . . .

As I have already said, in my view mere removal from the shelves without more is not an appropriation. Further, if a shopper with some perverted sense of humour, intending only to create confusion and nothing more both for the supermarket and for other shoppers, switches labels, I do not think that that act of label switching alone is without more an appropriation, though it is not difficult to envisage some cases of dishonest label switching which could be. In cases such as the present, it is in truth a combination of these actions, the removal from the shelf and the switching of the labels, which evidences adverse interference with or usurpation of the right of the owner. Those acts, therefore, amount to an appropriation and if they are accompanied by proof of the other three elements to which I have referred, the offence of theft is established. Further, if they are accompanied by other acts such as putting the goods so removed and relabelled into a receptacle, whether a trolley or the shopper's own bag or basket, proof of appropriation within section 3(1) becomes overwhelming. [Emphasis added.]

 NOTE 12.3

1. *Assumption of any of the rights of ownership*: By a majority, the House confirmed that Lord Roskill in *Morris* had been right to hold that the assumption of any one of the rights of ownership, as opposed to all, was an appropriation.

2. *Appropriation and consent*: On the issue of consent, however, the majority held that *Lawrence* and *Morris* were irreconcilable. *Lawrence* should prevail for the issue was ratio whereas in *Morris* it was obiter.

3. *The minority judgments*: Whereas the majority of the law lords held that an appropriation occurs as soon as the customer assumes a right of ownership over property (ie: possession or control), Lord Lowry for the minority considered that an appropriation would not occur until the assumption is accompanied by MR. If the arguments are fairly evenly balanced then that interpretation which involves the least alteration to the existing law should be chosen. He was unwilling to adopt a neutral meaning of the word appropriation which dissolved the distinction between theft and deception. Unfortunately, his view did not prevail and so appropriation now occurs at a very early stage. Of course, this makes no difference in practice. You are unlikely to be arrested for theft until you are seen to be doing something suspicious. In terms of theory, however, once you assume possession or control over somebody else's property, even with their consent, dishonestly intending to deprive them of it in the future, you have stolen it. Nothing adverse to the owner need have happened. A later change of heart makes no difference. This would previously have been an attempt. Now, however, theft has become a virtually instantaneous event.

Gomez was of immense importance and had the following far-reaching implications for the offence of theft:

■ *Appropriation by consent is not limited to situations where consent has been induced by deception*

The majority decision was not confined to appropriation induced by deception because deception was not referred to in the majority judgments, and by overruling certain other cases, namely, *Skipp* and *Fritschy* (discussed in the next few paragraphs), a more general interpretation of appropriation was confirmed.

The case of *Skipp* [1975] Crim LR 114 had concerned the collection of three consignments of oranges/onions from London by D who posed as a haulage contractor. He was to deliver them to Leicester. He intended to make off with the consignments from the beginning and did so after loading all three. It was held, in accordance with *Morris*, that appropriation did not occur until he diverted from the authorised destination for only this was inconsistent with the true owner's rights. This case was overruled by *Gomez* for the House held that, consent being irrelevant, D appropriated the goods as soon as he took possession of each load.

It followed from this that if D had collected property in England for transfer outside the jurisdiction, he would have appropriated immediately upon taking possession and if MR existed at that point, theft would have occurred here and not abroad. This was contrary to *Fritschy* [1985] Crim LR 745, again overruled by *Gomez*, where the Court of Appeal had held that D did not commit theft of a number of Krugerrands (South African currency) until he dishonestly disposed of them in Switzerland having bought them in London.

Consequently, appropriation is not a continuing act and can only occur once. Therefore, when Ds imported hired cars into England from Germany and Belgium with the intention of selling them, appropriation occurred outside the jurisdiction of England and Wales: *Ataakpu* [1994] QB 69. Somewhat confusingly, *Ashcroft* [2003] EWCA Crim 2365, holds the opposite. A haulier was held not to have appropriated items from sealed containers he was carrying from Scotland to England until he removed them in England. This decision was contrary to *Gomez* and in line with *Skipp*! Despite its shortcomings, *Gomez* ought to have prevailed.

■ Appropriation by sole company directors

The majority in *Gomez* confirmed an earlier case of *Philippou* [1989] Crim LR 585 concerning theft from a bank account by two sole directors and shareholders of a company. They withdrew money from the company bank account in order to purchase a block of flats in Spain for themselves. On appeal they had argued that, as the company's sole representatives, the company had consented to the taking. Therefore, they had done nothing adverse to the company's interests. The Court of Appeal disagreed. *Lawrence* had held that consent was irrelevant to appropriation. Therefore, by transferring money from the company account to buy a block of flats, the profit from the sale of which would go straight into their pockets, there was evidence of appropriation, dishonesty and an intention to permanently deprive.

■ The conflict with civil law

Gomez represented a dislocation between the civil and criminal law. Removing goods from a supermarket shelf with a dishonest future intention of walking out without paying is not a civil offence until the thought is put into action. After *Gomez*, removal plus a future intention is theft. Could this lead to punishment for one's thoughts alone? Does it make sense to say that you can steal property of which you had become the owner?

■ Later keeping or dealing

At what point does an appropriation occur where there is a later assumption, keeping or dealing with property of which one may be already in possession? Look back at the definition of appropriation in s3(1) which contains reference to a later assumption, etc. At the time, it was clearly meant to convey that one did not appropriate property belonging to another merely by taking possession. It was not until one assumed a right to treat the property as an owner that this would occur. Consequently, borrowing a library book with the consent of the library and taking it home, for instance, would not amount to an appropriation. Failing to return it would. If accompanied by dishonesty and intention to permanently deprive, the appropriation would become theft. *Gomez* holds that consent of the owner is irrelevant to appropriation. Therefore, appropriation occurs immediately the borrower does anything whatsoever with the book, whether by consent or not. The latter part of s3(1) becomes redundant. If a dishonest intent exists at the moment of appropriation, notwithstanding the consent of the owner, theft is immediate.

?!   THINKING POINT 12.1

Consider whether or when an appropriation occurs in these supermarket scenarios:

1. If consent is irrelevant, when does the customer appropriate: when they remove an item from a shelf, when they place it in their basket or when they leave without paying?
2. Does the shop assistant or shelf-filler appropriate?
3. D carelessly knocks an article off the shelf and then replaces it.
4. D removes an item intending not to pay for it but changes her mind and replaces it.
5. D lifts an item off the shelf to read the label and puts it back.

The academic world was split as to whether it was right or wrong. Consider these views from J.C. Smith, commentary to *Gomez* [1993] Crim LR 304:

> *A case of wilful blindness.* The crux of this case was the decision of the majority not to refer to the Eighth Report of the CLRC. 'In my opinion,' said Lord Keith, 'it serves no useful purpose at the present time to seek to construe the relevant provisions of the Theft Act by reference to [the Eighth Report].' No useful purpose! Except of course that it demonstrated conclusively that the decision of the majority flatly contradicted the intention of Parliament – intention which was readily apparent from the fact that Parliament, having received the CLRC's clear exposition of the effect of their draft bill, enacted legislation identical in all material respects with it. Of course, the majority were in fact aware of all this . . . . As for the dissent, one can only echo the editorial comment in *Archbold News* . . .: 'It is a mystery how the majority of their Lordships failed to be persuaded by the elaborate and scholarly dissenting speech delivered by Lord Lowry which they do not answer.' . . .
>
> *The ratio decidendi*: The certified question was limited to the case where the consent of the owner has been obtained by a false representation and the House might have confined its decision to that point. It did not. The fact that, in the instant case, consent was obtained by a false representation is nowhere treated as material. Cases where the defendant makes no representation, like the taker of goods in a supermarket, are regarded as the same in principle as the deception cases. The decision is that the consent of the owner to the act done, or the fact that he authorised that act, is irrelevant.
>
> *Theft and obtaining: sections 1 and 15.* The effect is that all cases of obtaining by deception contrary to section 15 are also theft with the negligible exception of obtaining land . . .
>
> *The effect on the law of theft.* The full effect on the law of theft can be appreciated only when account is taken of the approval given to the ruling in *Morris* that the assumption of any of the rights of an owner amounts to an appropriation; and that it may amount to theft even though *that* act will not deprive the owner permanently, or at all, of his property; it is sufficient that the defendant has a present intention to deprive by some future act. Merely switching the labels in a supermarket, dishonestly intending to buy the article for the lower price, amounts to the complete offence of theft, even though the enterprise is immediately interrupted or abandoned. We now have to couple this extraordinary ruling with the proposition that consent and authority are irrelevant and we reach this conclusion:
>
> ANYONE DOING ANYTHING WHATEVER TO PROPERTY BELONGING TO ANOTHER, WITH OR WITHOUT THE AUTHORITY OR CONSENT OF THE OWNER, APPROPRIATES IT: AND, IF HE DOES SO DISHONESTLY AND WITH INTENT, BY THAT ACT OR ANY SUBSEQUENT ACT, PERMANENTLY TO DEPRIVE, HE COMMITS THEFT.
>
> Of course the object of the Theft Act was to get away from the troublesome concepts of taking and carrying away but this reduced the actus reus of theft almost to vanishing point. Acts which common sense would regard as attempts or merely preparatory acts are the full offence of theft . . . . Millions of employees are 'appropriating' their employers' property, millions of customers are 'appropriating' the property of shopkeepers, husbands are 'appropriating' the property of their wives and vice versa every hour of the day. Fortunately, no legal consequences follow unless they have an intention dishonestly and permanently to deprive.

Others, however, consider that the decision in *Gomez* was justified: see this from S. Gardner, 'Appropriation in Theft—The Last Word' (1993) 109 *LQR* 194:

> Lord Keith now points out that since Lawrence is a clear authority on the issue and has never been displaced, it is right to follow it.
>
> In its own terms, this summary resolution is unimpeachable. The only question is whether the answer is desirable from first principles. It is suggested that it is. Most fundamentally, it is submitted that the quality of dishonest conduct is not necessarily altered by the victim's consent. Consider,

above all, cases where the victim consents to the taking, but does so in a state of low-level, non-specific confusion. For example, elderly people are often exploited by rogues who dishonestly overcharge them for work, or underpay them for their treasures. The victim in such a case has consented to the taking, and her consent is not obviously vitiated, but it is very possible to sense that the rogue's conduct should be criminal. However, in such circumstances it is not easy to convict for anything except ordinary theft. There can be no conviction for obtaining by deception under section 15 of the Theft Act, for want of a clear deception (cf. R. v. Silverman (1988) 86 Cr.App.R. 213); nor for the special form of theft established under section 5(4), for want of a true mistake; nor for blackmail or robbery, for want of any pressure. If theft were negatived by the victim's consent, then, such cases would constitute no offence. By their Lordships' decision in Gomez, however, theft does lie here. That result is to be applauded.

Another argument in favour of Gomez is that, even were we attracted to a requirement of non-consent, we should reject it as making theft difficult of administration by the criminal courts, with their lay judges of fact. Consent is a problematic concept. Even if it simply meant 'saying yes', difficulties would remain. As the facts in Lawrence show, the practical boundaries of 'saying yes' are not altogether clear. And making a victim say 'yes' at the point of a gun would apparently negate theft, and so too robbery. That would be absurd. The answer would have to be that consent means 'true consent' – that is, an owner's 'yes' would be subject to vitiation by such factors as mistake or pressure. This approach is familiar from other branches of the law, above all contract. To adopt it in theft, however, would require magistrates' benches and Crown Courts to handle notions which have been found elusive even in the higher courts on the civil side. Directions on the law would consequently be prone to error, and so to appeal; and even if a direction was sound (or even, perhaps, the more sound it was), the task of applying it might well baffle the lay judges of fact (cf. Whittaker v. Campbell [1984] Q.B. 318). Neither meaning of 'consent', therefore, would leave the law of theft in a happy condition, if non-consent were a constituent of the offence.

One other consideration in favour of the decision in Gomez is to be found in the opinion of Lord Browne-Wilkinson. It is a narrower point, but still important. His Lordship wishes theft to lie against a person who occupies a controlling position in a company and who purloins that company's assets. Theft might lie to such a case even if the law required the owner's non-consent (cf. Attorney-General's Reference (No. 2 of 1982) [1984] Q.B. 624), but there are problems, if only of a jury's comprehension of the concepts involved. With the new ruling that there is no such requirement, however, the aptness of theft to such a case has become simple and incontrovertible . . . .

The real point is this. What is true after Gomez is that all the activities which are covered by section 15 are also, give or take mushrooms and the like, contained within theft. But that is also true of robbery and burglary (in its theft variant). These nevertheless exist as separate offences because the harm suffered by the victim is both a loss of property and a further form of injury as well. In robbery this further injury is the feeling of physical powerlessness. In burglary it is the feeling of lost territorial security. Reflecting this combination of loss of property and additional injury, robbery and burglary have always been aggravated forms of theft, each carrying a maximum sentence higher than that for simple theft. It should be noted that in neither case does the simple offence of theft discontinue where the aggravated offence begins. This seems wise, for otherwise an accused could defeat a prosecution for simple theft by showing that, having used force or intrusion, he was in fact guilty of an aggravated offence instead: which would be unedifying. Even though they overlap with theft, therefore, it is impossible to say that the offences of robbery and burglary are otiose. Obtaining by deception fits the same pattern. It too responds to the victim's suffering both a loss of property and an additional injury: in this case a feeling of intellectual vulnerability. It too now carries a higher maximum sentence than simple theft. It thus seems entirely supportable that, after Gomez, it should operate in the same way as robbery and burglary, as an aggravated form of theft, with simple theft allowed to overlap it.

Q. Which type of victim does the author consider will be given greater protection by Gomez?

Q. How many reasons can you identify in the extract which support *Gomez*?

?! THINKING POINT 12.2

1. V lends D his bicycle for two weeks. D fails to return it. When does D appropriate?

2. Right now, you are presumably sitting on some sort of a chair whether at home/in the university or on the bus/tube. According to whose view in *Gomez* are you appropriating it and why?

3. V advertises his Rolex watch for sale. D, a rogue, agrees to buy it and one week later gives V a forged building society cheque for the price. V hands the watch to D. The cheque bounces. Has D stolen the watch?

4. A nurse responsible for mentally handicapped patients is authorised to deposit cheques into trust accounts in their name from which she can draw for their needs. She receives a cheque for £4,250 on behalf of one and opens a trust account in a building society in his name. She opens a further two accounts in his name when further cheques are received, one at a different and one at the existing building society. She intends to use the money for herself. When does appropriation occur?

The next time appropriation was considered by the House of Lords, it proceeded to take *Gomez* one stage further and applied the same reasoning not just to property obtained by deception, but to valid gifts:

Appropriation and gifts: theft by a lawful act?

In the 1990s, four conflicting Court of Appeal cases disagreed as to whether the receiver of a *valid gift* could appropriate that gift, even in the absence of any deception. *Lawrence*, *Morris* and *Gomez* had all been concerned with deceptions in a commercial transaction. Gifts were a different matter entirely. The circumstances of the cases were broadly similar in that they all involved gifts of large sums of money or valuable property by elderly or vulnerable donors to people in a position of trust: nurses (*Gallasso* [1992] 98 Cr App R 284), maids (*Mazo* [1996] Crim LR 435), carers or residential home managers (*Hopkins, Kendrick* [1972] 2 Cr App R 524). In the first two, the validity of the gift according to civil law prevented an appropriation, and theft, from occurring. This was contradicted by the last two, where the civil law position was regarded as irrelevant. The House of Lords in *Hinks* resolved the conflict by holding that the only issue was one of dishonesty and that one can, consequently, appropriate a valid gift.

R v Hinks [2000] 3 WLR 1590, [2001] CRIM LR 162 HOUSE OF LORDS

V, a 53-year-old naïve and gullible man of limited intelligence, transferred £60,000 and a television set to D, a young female friend. He understood what it meant to make a gift of his property. There was evidence of undue influence but no deception. The Court of Appeal held that the *validity* of the gifts was irrelevant to the question of appropriation. A question was certified for an appeal to the House of Lords:

> Whether the acquisition of an indefeasible title to property is capable of amounting to an appropriation of property belonging to another for the purposes of s1(1) Theft Act 1968?

The word 'indefeasible' meant that V retained no proprietary interest or any right to resume or recover any proprietary interest in the property.

In the House of Lords, the majority answered the question affirmatively (Lords Steyn, Lord Jauncey, Lord Slynn). Guilt hinged on the question of dishonesty as decided by *Gomez*.

Lord Steyn for the majority:

> In other words it is immaterial whether the act was done with the owner's consent or authority. It is true of course that the certified question in *Gomez* referred to the situation where consent had been obtained by fraud. But the majority judgments do not differentiate between cases of consent induced by fraud and consent given in any other circumstances. The ratio involves a proposition of general application. *Gomez* therefore gives effect to section 3(1) of the Act by treating 'appropriation' as a neutral word comprehending 'any assumption by a person of the rights of an owner.' If the law is as held in *Gomez*, it destroys the argument advanced on the present appeal, namely that an indefeasible gift of property cannot amount to an appropriation.
>
> Counsel for the appellant submitted in the first place that the law as expounded in *Gomez* and *Lawrence* must be qualified to say that there can be no appropriation unless the other party (the owner) retains some proprietary interest, or the right to resume or recover some proprietary interest, in the property. Alternatively, counsel argued that 'appropriates' should be interpreted as if the word 'unlawfully' preceded it. Counsel said that the effect of the decisions in *Lawrence* and *Gomez* is to reduce the actus reus of theft to 'vanishing point' (see *Smith and Hogan, Criminal Law*, 9th ed., (1999) p. 505). He argued that the result is to bring the criminal law 'into conflict' with the civil law. Moreover, he argued that the decisions in *Lawrence* and *Gomez* may produce absurd and grotesque results. He argued that the mental requirements of dishonesty and intention of permanently depriving the owner of property are insufficient to filter out some cases of conduct which should not sensibly be regarded as theft. He did not suggest that the appellant's dishonest and repellent conduct came within such a category . . . .
>
> If the law is restated by adopting a narrower definition of appropriation, the outcome is likely to place beyond the reach of the criminal law dishonest persons who should be found guilty of theft. The suggested revisions would unwarrantably restrict the scope of the law of theft and complicate the fair and effective prosecution of theft. In my view the law as settled in *Lawrence* and *Gomez* does not demand the suggested revision. Those decisions can be applied by judges and juries in a way which, absent human error, does not result in injustice.
>
> Counsel for the appellant further pointed out that the law as stated in *Lawrence* and *Gomez* creates a tension between the civil and the criminal law. In other words, conduct which is not wrongful in a civil law sense may constitute the crime of theft. Undoubtedly, this is so. The question whether the civil claim to title by a convicted thief, who committed no civil wrong, may be defeated by the principle that nobody may benefit from his own civil or criminal wrong does not arise for decision. Nevertheless there is a more general point, namely that the interaction between criminal law and civil law can cause problems . . . . The purposes of the civil law and the criminal law are somewhat different. In theory the two systems should be in perfect harmony. In a practical world there will sometimes be some disharmony between the two systems. In any event, it would be wrong to assume on a priori grounds that the criminal law rather than the civil law is defective. Given the jury's conclusions, one is entitled to observe that the appellant's conduct *should* constitute theft, the only available charge. The tension between the civil and the criminal law is therefore not in my view a factor which justifies a departure from the law as stated in *Lawrence* and *Gomez*. Moreover, these decisions of the House have a marked beneficial consequence. While in some contexts of the law of theft a judge cannot avoid explaining civil law concepts to a jury (e.g. in respect of section 2(1)(a)), the decisions of the House of Lords eliminate

the need for such explanations in respect of appropriation. That is a great advantage in an overly complex corner of the law.

As with *Gomez*, the minority judgments in *Hinks*, adhering to the traditional view of appropriation, were persuasive but unsuccessful.

Lord Hobhouse for the minority (with Lord Hutton):

The reason of the Court of Appeal . . . depends upon the disturbing acceptance that a criminal conviction and the imposition of custodial sanctions may be based upon conduct which involves no inherent illegality and may only be capable of being criticised on grounds of lack of morality. This approach itself raises fundamental questions. An essential function of the criminal law is to define the boundary between what conduct is criminal and what is merely immoral. Both are the subject of the disapprobation of ordinary right-thinking citizens and the distinction is liable to be arbitrary or at least strongly influenced by considerations subjective to the individual members of the tribunal. To treat otherwise lawful conduct as criminal merely because it is open to such disapprobation would be contrary to principle and open to the objection that it fails to achieve the objective and transparent certainty required of the criminal law by the principles basic to human rights . . . .

The truth is that a crime which relates to civil property and, inevitably, property concepts from the civil law have to be used and questions answered by reference to that law. Lord Roskill . . . was no doubt right in *R v Morris* [1984] AC 320 at 334 to warn in general terms against introducing into the criminal law questions whether particular contracts were void or voidable on the ground of mistake or fraud or whether any mistake was sufficiently fundamental to vitiate a contract. But the act at times expressly requires civil law concepts to be applied. [Lord Hobhouse then considered three significant theft cases concerned with 'belonging to another' which had all been determined by reference to the civil law.] . . .

If . . . the transferee [D] has already had validly transferred to him the legal title to and possession of the chattel without any obligation to make restoration, a later retention of or dealing with the chattel by the transferee, whether or not 'dishonest' and whether or not it would otherwise amount to an appropriation, cannot amount to theft. However much the jury may consider that his conduct in not returning the chattel falls below the standards of ordinary and decent people, he has not committed the crime of theft. The property did not belong to another.

The making of a gift is the act of the donor [V]. It involves the donor in forming the intention to give and then acting on that intention by doing whatever it is necessary for him to do to transfer the relevant property to the donee [D] . . . . Unless the gift was conditional, in which case the condition must be satisfied before the gift can take effect, the making of the gift is complete once the donor has carried out this step. The gift has become the property of the donee . . . . Once the donor has done his part in transferring the property to the defendant, the property, subject to the special situations identified in the subsections of s5, ceases to be 'property belonging to another'. However wide a meaning one were to give to 'appropriates', there cannot be a theft.

The harm principle was explored further by A.L. Bogg and J. Stanton-Ife in 'Protecting the Vulnerable: legality, harm and theft' (2003) 23 *Legal Studies* 402:

The harm principle sets institutional constraints on the legitimate scope of the criminal law. Like the rule of law, it 'reflects the importance of making the law compatible with people's need to be, to a substantial degree, the author of their own lives'; it should act as a bulwark against Lord Hobhouse's worry that conduct be treated as criminal *merely* because it is open to moral disapprobation . . . It permits the criminalisation of wrongfully inflicted harm. Additionally, it permits the criminalisation of harmless wrongs if that reduces their occurrence, and their wider occurrence would tend to cause harm, by threatening people's prospects . . . . . Was the supposed victim in *Hinks* actually harmed? Was he wronged? And what is the significance of his consent or otherwise in the matter?

It seems clear that there had been harm to Mr Dolphin in the sense that his interests had been set back: he had been deprived of his property rights . . . . What of the second question we distinguished, whether this harm was wrongful? The most obvious response is that it was, since Mr

Dolphin was exploited . . . . The victim . . . was a vulnerable individual of limited intelligence, said to be trusting, generous and exceptionally naïve. The defendant had taken unfair advantage of the victim's vulnerability, and abused his trust, in order to procure the transfer of his property . . . . the defendant had exploited the victim. Exploitation is a wrong, though the degree of wrongfulness will depend on a number of features . . .

The authors go on to question whether V's consent should have rendered Hinks's conduct criminal rather than simply immoral. They concluded that her coercion and manipulation had violated his autonomy and that his consent was not 'independent'.

NOTE 12.4

1. *Dishonesty*: *Hinks* says that everything depends on dishonesty. If D dishonestly acquires ownership of property belonging to another by way of a valid gift, he will have appropriated and stolen it. *Hinks* is the logical extension of *Gomez* which held that the acquisition of ownership of another's property acquired by deception or trick amounts to an appropriation and theft.

2. *Fraud*: There is no longer any distinction between theft and fraud (previously deception) offences. The latter was always considered applicable where D had acquired ownership by deception/fraud. The former applied where possession but not ownership had been acquired.

3. *Attempt*: Pre-*Gomez*, if D was in possession of V's property by consent but with a view to a later non-consensual appropriation, this would have been an act preparatory to theft which might have constituted an attempt. Since *Gomez/Hinks* has made consent irrelevant, there is no longer such a thing as an act preparatory to appropriation or attempt. Appropriation is coincident with an assumption of any right of ownership.

4. *Conflict with the civil law*: After *Hinks*, appropriation includes conduct which under the civil law is not unlawful. If as a result of undue influence, a mentally competent V makes a gift of property to D, the transaction is valid under the general rules of contract. D will acquire a voidable title to the property in question. In other words, it belongs to D until or unless the gift is avoided by V. It is only a fundamental mistake going to the root of the contract which renders a contract void. This will prevent ownership from passing, giving rise to a potential fraud offence. But until *Hinks*, it was no crime to acquire a gift through dishonest means.

Gomez had begun to dismantle that conventional view and in *Hinks* the House of Lords completed the process. The result of *Hinks* is that despite acquiring a voidable title, D has appropriated and stolen the property. The Privy Council in 2006 confirmed the wider *Gomez/Hinks* interpretation of appropriation and held that gain or loss were irrelevant to appropriation. The case arose from the British Virgin Islands which has the same law on theft as England and Wales.

Wheatley & Anr v Commissioner of Police of the British Virgin Islands
[2006] UKPC 24, [2006] 1 WLR 1683 PRIVY COUNCIL

This was a case of corruption by a government employee (D1) who authorised a building contract to D2 in return for payment. Lord Bingham:

> It is certainly true that in most cases of theft there will be an original owner of money or goods who will be poorer because of the defendant's conduct. But in one of the two cases in *R v Morris* the defendant was arrested before paying the reduced price for the goods, so that the supermarket suffered no loss . . . In providing that an appropriation may be dishonest even where there is a willingness to pay, section 204(2) shows that the prospect of loss is not determinative of dishonesty.

The result of *Gomez* is that appropriation as defined by s3(1) has more or less vanished from sight. The only real question left for determination is one of dishonesty, by no means an easy issue as you will read below. Read the following by J.C. Smith writing in the *Criminal Law Review* commentary on *Hinks* [2001] 144:

> The decision, with all respect, is contrary to common sense. It is absurd that a person should be guilty of stealing property which is his and in which no-one else has any legal interest whatsoever. There is theft, but there are no stolen goods because the donor, *ex hypothesi*, never has any right to restitution . . . . '[The 1968 Act] is expressed in simple language as used and understood by ordinary literate men and women'; per Lord Diplock, *Treacy v DPP* [1971] AC 537 at 565. Whoever heard of ordinary literate people describing the receipt of a gift as an appropriation? 'Appropriate your present from Santa Claus, dear.

For an alternative view, read the following by S. Shute, 'Appropriation and the Law of Theft' [2002] *Crim LR* 445:

> Following *Hinks* it is now safe to conclude that there is nothing in the concept of appropriation that requires a jury to consider whether a gift has been validly made. It is thus perfectly possible for the prosecution to bring a charge of theft where someone receives property from a donor in the knowledge that the donor only agreed to the transfer because she assumed, wrongly, that the donee had done something to deserve it . . . .
>
> For many this enlargement of the scope of the criminal law to include cases where title passes as a result of an unimpeachable transaction is unjustified. One argument against such an expansion is that it rides roughshod over the intentions of the framers of the Theft Act 1968 . . . . A second objection to the decision in *Hinks* is that it opens the door to inappropriate prosecutions . . . . A third objection to *Hinks* is that it pares down excessively the *actus reus* of theft; indeed, some have argued that the combined effect of *Hinks* and *Gomez* is to reduce the *actus reus* of theft to 'vanishing point'. Of course, as the *actus reus* of the crime shrinks, so the role played by the *mens rea* concept of dishonesty will necessarily increase: it will have to take much more of the strain of filtering out cases that ought not to be regarded as theft from those that are clearly theftuous. This, in turn, generates two interconnecting objections to the *Gomez/Hinks* position: one based on the rule of law; the other on the harm principle.
>
> It is a foundational (although not an unqualified) principle of our criminal law that citizens ought to be able to predict in advance whether or not their actions or omissions will fall foul of criminal prohibitions. Honouring this principle enhances a number of significant rule of law values: it imposes constraints on the use of arbitrary power; it goes some way towards ensuring that state authorities show proper respect for human dignity and autonomy; it assists citizens who wish to plan for the future; and it increases human freedom by allowing citizens to choose effectively between various life options. Relying on dishonesty to take most of the definitional strain in the crime of theft is said to work against these values because it is far from easy to predict in advance whether one's actions will or will not be adjudged dishonest . . . .
>
> A connected argument against *Hinks* derives from the role of the liberal 'harm principle'. This states that in a liberal society criminalization is justified only if it serves to prevent harm. The prin-

ciple operates as a principle of exclusion: it identifies activities that ought not to be criminalized because their criminalization cannot be shown to serve the goal of preventing harm. The objection to *Hinks* is that it breaches the harm principle because it expands the scope of the offence of theft to include cases where no civil wrong has been committed . . . .

Two points can be made in response to this argument; both are controversial. The first is that there are good grounds for thinking that the conditions of the harm principle are met not only where an activity is itself harmful but also where it is a member of a class of acts that *tend* to cause harm . . . . The second point is that, in any case, the harm principle does not say that only harmful wrongs may be criminalized. Rather, it states that even harmless wrongs may be criminalized if criminalization diminishes their occurrence and if their wider occurrence would detract from other people's prospects – for example, by diminishing some public good . . . . Once the harm principle is understood in this way it becomes possible to see why, even if the main reason for criminalizing theft is to protect property rights, it may nonetheless be justifiable to extend the crime of theft to cases where no property right has been infringed. This is because a State's failure to criminalize wrongs that do not infringe property rights may itself undermine those rights or indeed some other public good.

Q. Which two principles does the author concede may be challenged by the decision in *Hinks*?

Q. On what basis does he support this judgment?

Q. Do you agree with the views of this or the previous author?

?! THINKING POINT 12.3

There is an old adage that what the civil law protects is no crime. But look at these questions:

1. D befriends an elderly, wealthy man (V). V makes all sorts of valuable gifts to D in the genuine wish to give her tokens of his friendship. The gifts are not the result of any deception, pressure, undue influence or coercion on V's part. She does, however, take knowing advantage of V's loneliness in the hope that he will give her some of his wealth. Has she appropriated V's gifts?

2. Have you sold a car/house knowing there were defects which the purchaser did not discover? The contract would be valid under the civil law. Would this now be theft?

3. V buys a painting from D under the impression that it is an old master when it is not. D knows of V's mistake but says nothing. Is this theft? Does it make any difference whether the contract is valid or not?

Bona fide purchasers

There is an exception from liability for theft in s3(2) Theft Act 1968 for innocent purchasers who pay a reasonable price for stolen property:

> Where property or a right or interest in property is or purports to be transferred for value to a person acting in good faith, no later assumption by him of rights which he believed himself to be acquiring shall, by reason of any defect in the transferor's title, amount to theft of the property.

Even if the purchaser later discovers the defect in title, he does not commit theft by keeping or dealing with the property. However, the protection does not extend to handling nor does it mean that the purchaser has acquired good title or ownership.

→ CROSS-REFERENCE
Handling is discussed in 12.3.

Therefore, if, after discovering the defect, he sells the property to X falsely representing that he is the owner, this is a fraud offence.

Property

There is a very wide and comprehensive definition of property in s4(1). The only exceptions from that definition are land, things growing wild on land and wild creatures in s4(2)–(4).

Section 4:

'Property' includes money and all other property, real or personal, including things in action and other intangible property.

This subsection makes it clear that virtually all tangible items are within the definition of property and can, therefore, be stolen. *Things in action* and *intangible* property are interests which one can own but not possess because they lack a physical existence. They can only be asserted by legal action: debt, shares, trade marks, copyright.

There are six types of property that need specific examination:

a. Intellectual property

b. Bank accounts

c. Tickets

d. Electricity

e. Bodies

f. Land.

Intellectual property

Intellectual property, information or services are excluded. Therefore, the acquisition of trade secrets is not theft.

Oxford v Moss (1978) 68 CR APP R 183 QUEEN'S BENCH DIVISION

D, an engineering student of Liverpool University, obtained a copy of an examination paper for Civil Engineering due to be held the following month. He did not intend to steal the actual piece of paper on which the examination was written, merely the information. He was convicted of theft of intangible property, namely, the confidential examination information. On appeal it was held that there was no property in the information and therefore he had not stolen it. Conviction quashed.

The exclusion of trade secrets once gave rise to the comment in Parliament that, 'it is not too much to say that we live in a country where . . . the theft of the boardroom table is punished far more severely than the theft of the boardroom secrets' (Rt Hon Sir Edward Boyle MP, *Hansard*, HC 13.12.68, vol 75 col 806—*Blackstone's Guide to the Fraud Act 2006*, at p 18).

The Law Commission has recommended a new offence of misuse of trade secrets ('Legislating the Criminal Code: Misuse of Trade Secrets' (Law Com CP No 150, 1997)).

Bank accounts

A credit balance in an account and a right to overdraw up to an agreed amount is *a thing in action* in the form of a debt owed by the bank to the customer. The relationship is therefore one of debtor-creditor.

 EXAMPLE 12.1

If you have £100 in your bank account, the bank owes you a debt of that amount. You do not have a right to possess any particular notes or coins. Consequently, as a creditor, you have a right to draw on your account up to that limit including the right to draw on a contractually agreed overdraft. If the bank refuses to recognise the debt it owes to you, you can enforce it through legal action.

a. Unauthorised cheques

If D, a third party, makes an unauthorised withdrawal from your account, and causes your credit balance or agreed overdraft to be reduced, D assumes a right of ownership over the debt your bank owes to you. He *appropriates* a thing in action at that point, before any money is actually received by him (see *Williams* later); but if more is withdrawn than was in your account in the first place, no debt or thing in action can be appropriated for it does not exist.

 EXAMPLE 12.2

If you have £100 in your account and D withdraws £150 from it, he will only have appropriated the debt owed to you by the bank of £100. The outstanding £50 was never yours to begin with, the bank never owed it to you, you had no right to it and D cannot therefore appropriate it.

The same would apply to you if you had become overdrawn by tendering cheques to third parties for more than the total in your account. This is not theft. It may be an attempt or a fraud offence but it cannot be theft because there is no intangible property to appropriate.

R v Kohn (1979) 69 CR APP R 395 COURT OF APPEAL

A director was authorised to draw cheques on a company bank account. He drew some cheques for *unauthorised* amounts. It was held that an unauthorised cheque for an amount which reduces or eliminates the credit balance amounts to theft of a debt owed by the bank to the account holder. The company's right of action against its bank is thereby stolen. The cheques were not a nullity since he had authority to draw them. However, there was no theft where the account was in excess of an agreed overdraft, as was in fact the case. The bank had no legal obligation to meet such cheques. There was no chose of action against the bank and therefore nothing for D to steal. His convictions of theft were quashed. Indeed, *R v Navvabi* [1986] 3 All ER 102 held that there is no theft where a cheque is presented backed with a cheque card on an overdrawn account. This is more likely to be a fraud offence. The principle in *Kohn* was applied in *Hilton* [1997] 2 Cr App R 445 where D instructed a charity's bank, over whose account he had control, to pay money to him. This was theft of a debt belonging to the charity.

b. Account holder writes a cheque in favour of D: appropriation of credit balance

If an account holder (V) writes a cheque in D's favour and gives it to him, D becomes the owner of that cheque and of the right to sue V for that amount. V is known as the drawer and D the payee. This is so even if D caused V to hand over the cheque by dishonest means. D commits no theft so far. However, once D presents the cheque to V's bank for payment, he commits an act which triggers the reduction of V's credit balance and this is an appropriation.

 EXAMPLE 12.3

You pay a rogue decorator to paint your house and pay him in advance by cheque. He does some work but leaves the job half done. He then pays the cheque into his bank account. The cheque is transferred to your account for payment. Your credit balance is reduced. The decorator appropriates your credit balance.

Williams (Roy) [2001] 1 CR APP R 23

D was a builder and targeted elderly householders. He charged reasonable prices for initial work in order to gain the trust of his victims but then charged exorbitant amounts for subsequent work. The Court of Appeal held, in accordance with *Kohn*, that theft of a chose in action may be committed when it is destroyed by D's act of appropriation—the act being the physical presentation of the cheque. D appropriates the thing in action consisting in V's credit balance in the bank *when he presents the cheque and it is honoured, thus destroying that thing or part of it.* The same would apply where funds are transferred electronically or by automated transfer provided the process is personally initiated by D.

Williams might also have committed fraud if he had made either an express or implied representation. Note that a fraud offence no longer requires an active physical 'obtaining' (as was the case with the previous offence under s15 Theft Act 1968 of 'Obtaining by deception'). It can now be passive. Consider the next example:

D applies to several building societies for loans to be secured by mortgages, fraudulently concealing the fact that he has made several applications. He obtains more than £100,000 by a combination of cheque, telegraphic transfer and an electronic automated payment system into his account. He intends to commit fraud and run off with all the money.

D will undoubtedly commit a fraud offence under s2 Fraud Act 2006. But has he also appropriated the credit balance of the respective building societies? In the absence of a triggering act by D, as in *Williams*, the answer is probably 'no'. However, D will also commit the offence discussed in the following paragraph.

→ CROSS-REFERENCE
Section 2 Fraud Act 2006 is cited in Chapter 13, 13.1.2.

> ### Section 24A Theft (Amendment) Act 1996: Retaining a wrongful credit
>
> This is a type of handling offence where money has been wrongfully credited to a bank account. A credit is 'wrongful' if it derives from: theft, blackmail, stolen goods or fraud (contrary to s1 Fraud Act 2006). D must know/believe the credit was wrongful and dishonestly fail to take reasonable steps to secure that the credit is cancelled.

The example reflects the sort of mortgage fraud which occurred in *Preddy & Slade & Dhillon* [1996] 3 WLR 1996. The offence charged was 'obtaining by deception' contrary to s15 Theft Act 1968, now abolished. The House of Lords held that the defendants had obtained no property belonging to the victims and therefore were not guilty. The debiting of V's credit balance and the consequent crediting of D's account as a result of a dishonest misrepresentation did not represent the *obtaining* of property belonging to another. V's chose in action (ie: the credit balance in V's bank account) had been extinguished and a new chose in action (ie: the credit balance in D's bank account) was created by the transfer of funds, even though it had come into existence through deception. The new chose in action represented a debt in an equivalent sum owed by a different bank to D. Since mortgage fraud was apparently, therefore, no offence, s24A Theft (Amendment) Act 1996 was hurriedly created. Section 2 Fraud Act 2006 specifically prohibits fraud by misrepresentation.

→ CROSS-REFERENCE
Fraud is discussed in detail in Chapter 13.

However, it follows that, if D withdraws money from a bank cash dispenser in excess of the amount in his bank account or agreed overdraft, he will commit theft, not of a credit balance, but of money. That money will not have come out of his own bank account. It might be recorded as a debit on his account later but, at the time of appropriation, the money belongs to the bank: *Poland v Ulatowski* [2010] EWCA Crim 2673 (Admin).

c. Forged cheques are void

It was held in *Chan Man-Sin v AG for Hong Kong* [1988] 1 All ER 1 that if a forged cheque is presented for payment or money is otherwise transferred from one bank account to another, although the intended victim of the theft is the account holder, a forged cheque is a nullity. Therefore, it is the bank which suffers the loss if it debits a customer's account. The account holder, the owner of the debt, is reimbursed and will suffer no loss.

Tickets/Cheques

A ticket, such as a rail or bus ticket, or a cheque, is a piece of paper and that piece of paper can be stolen. But all have greater value: they also represent a thing in action. A ticket, for example, has intrinsic economic or practical value—a contractual right to travel. A purchaser whose ticket is stolen will be permanently deprived of both the physical ticket and that right to travel. A customer whose cheque is stolen will lose the thing itself and the value it represents. But does D have the necessary intention permanently to deprive if he knows that either ticket or cheque are likely to be returned to the rail company at the journey's end or to the drawer's bank on completion of the transaction? The answer is that, although the piece of paper may not be lost, the value may have been reduced or extinguished so that it is in such a changed form as to be a completely different thing.

J.C. Smith argues in 'Stealing Tickets' [1998] *Crim LR* 723 that here D commits theft because he has a conditional intent: to only return the ticket in return for a free ride. If the condition is fulfilled, then D has the necessary intention to permanently deprive. The same would apply to gambling chips and all sorts of tokens which, if taken from the owner, are returned only on condition that something of value is provided in exchange.

If you purchase a rail ticket, you own it. If you give it away, you retain no proprietary right in it. You might imagine, then, that, having given it away, it cannot be stolen. But in *Marshall* [1998] 2 Cr App R 282, D collected part-used underground tickets from passengers and resold them to other potential users. He was held to have stolen the tickets from London Underground Ltd which had been deprived of revenue. The tickets bore a clause to the effect that they continued to belong to the company. Whether a company will continue to have a proprietary right in a ticket depends not only on such a contractual term, but also on whether that term has been brought to the attention of the customer—a matter of contract law.

Electricity

A separate offence of 'Abstracting Electricity' exists under s13 Theft Act 1968 and this is not theft. In *Low v Blease* [1975] Crim LR 513 it was held that as electricity could not be appropriated, D could not be convicted of burglary (entry of premises with intent to steal) when he entered premises and made a telephone call. Neither can heat be appropriated (*Clinton v Cahill* [1998] NI 200) where D diverted V's hot water pipes to warm his property. This was not theft.

Bodies

At common law, there is no property in a corpse, meaning that strictly speaking, a corpse belongs to no-one and thus, if taken away, cannot be legally stolen. It was once a felony to steal a corpse for the purposes of witchcraft until that offence was repealed under the Witchcraft Act 1735. It is an offence to disinter a corpse without lawful authority. An interim right to *possession* of a corpse vests in those charged with burial such as executors, administrators or undertakers who may take a civil action in *conversion* against a person who deprives them of possession, but it cannot be stolen from them.

However, a limited right to possession extends to body parts if used as medical specimens or exhibits where the item has acquired different attributes by undergoing the lawful application of skill. Therefore, under s4, limbs, organs, liquids, corpses and dead body parts can be defined as property. Less certain is the position of human embryos/body parts for transplant.

R v Kelly [1998] 3 ALL ER 741 COURT OF APPEAL

Body parts preserved as anatomical specimens were taken by K, an artist, from the Royal College of Surgeons. K had permission to enter the college to draw the specimens. He asked a junior technician to remove 35 to 40 body parts of which he made casts. He then buried most of the parts in a field, kept a leg in his attic and stored the others in a friend's flat. K and the technician were convicted of theft and appealed.

Rose LJ:

We accept that, however questionable the historical origins of the principle, it has now been the common law for 150 years at least that neither a corpse, nor parts of a corpse, are in themselves and without more capable of being property protected by rights . . . . If that principle is now to be changed, in our view, it must be by Parliament, because it has been express or implicit in all the subsequent authorities and writings to which we have been referred that a corpse or part of it cannot be stolen.

To address the point as it was addressed before the trial judge and to which his certificate relates, in our judgment, parts of a corpse are capable of being property within s4 of the Theft Act, if they have acquired different attributes by virtue of the application of skill, such as dissection or preservation techniques, for exhibition or teaching purposes: see . . . *Dobson v North Tyneside Health Authority* [1996] 4 All ER 474 . . .

Furthermore, the common law does not stand still. It may be that if, on some future occasion, the question arises, the courts will hold that human body parts are capable of being property for the purposes of s4, even without the acquisition of different attributes, if they have a use or significance beyond their mere existence. This may be so if, for example, they are intended for use in an organ transplant operation, for the extraction of DNA or, for that matter, as an exhibit in a trial.

So far as the question of possession by the Royal College of Surgeons is concerned, in our judgment the learned judge was correct to rule that the college had possession, sufficiently for the purposes of and within s5(1) of the Theft Act 1968.

Conviction confirmed.

a. Property of corpses

If the property of a dead person is stolen, the question of whether it still belongs to another (required by definition to be alive) will be decided according to the civil law.

R v Sullivan & Ballion [2002] CRIM LR 758 CROWN Court

Two Ds appropriated £50,000, the illegal proceeds of drug dealing, from the body of their friend who had died the previous night. The trial judge ruled that the property did not belong to another and the charges were dismissed. Had the Ds been charged with theft of property of a 'person unknown' the outcome might have been different. The Court of Appeal held that if the £50,000 no longer belonged to the deceased, it must have belonged to someone (his beneficiaries or the Crown if he was intestate?). His 'clients' or purchasers, having given the money to him, no longer retained any proprietary right to it. But should it really make any difference to whom it belonged provided the Ds knew it did not belong to them?

Land

Section 4(2):

A person cannot steal land, or things forming part of land and severed from it by him or by his directions, except in the following cases, that is to say–

(a)   when he is a trustee or personal representative, or is authorised by power of attorney, or as liquidator of a company, or otherwise, to sell or dispose of land belonging to another, and he appropriates the land or anything forming part of it by dealing with it in breach of the confidence reposed in him; or

(b)   when he is not in possession of the land and appropriates anything forming part of the land by severing it or causing it to be severed, or after it has been severed; or

(c)   when, being in possession of the land under a tenancy, he appropriates the whole or part of any fixture or structure let to be used with the land . . . .

a. Land cannot generally be stolen

Land is in general excluded from the s4(1) definition of property and thus it cannot be stolen. There are civil remedies for the unlawful interference with land by third parties.

EXAMPLE 12.4

If your neighbour moves your boundary fence during the night so as to take for herself three metres of your garden, she does not steal it and you will need to resort to a civil action in trespass to enforce your right of ownership over the land.

Section 4(2) prohibits the interference with land belonging to another person from being regarded as theft subject to the exceptions in s4(2)–(4).

b. The exceptions

1. *Trustees/Personal Representatives:* s4(2)(a) provides that land can be stolen by trustees or personal representatives appointed by a will, etc. This would be where they dispose of the land, structure or fixtures other than in a way authorised by the relevant trust deed or will in breach of confidence.

2. *Severing/Fixtures:* s4(2)(b) applies to people not in possession (ie: non-occupiers). Although land cannot be stolen, things on land can be stolen by people not in possession but only by severing or if already severed. It applies to:

   - fixtures (ie: things fixed to the land such as bricks, roof slates, woodwork, cupboards, basins, glass, greenhouses, sheds, conservatories, fireplaces, plumbing, boilers, radiators, etc);

   - growing things (plants, trees) and even the substance of the land itself (eg: turf, topsoil, gravel, clay, etc).

Therefore D, who may be a neighbour, passer-by or someone on the look-out, may steal something provided he severs it or it is already severed.

EXAMPLE 12.5

D sees a pile of lead pipes which have been stripped from a house in the front yard and takes them. He also cuts two dozen roses from the garden.

3. *Fixtures/Structures:* s4(2)(c) applies to tenants in possession (ie: occupiers). There is no need for severing here. A tenant in possession can steal fixtures/fittings or structure within s4(2)(c) but cannot steal the land/dwelling of which he is in possession. Therefore, T can steal the doors/carpets/garden plants of her rented flat, but not the top soil etc from the garden. There is no reason to suppose that the topsoil etc could not be stolen by T's partner or family member if they have no tenancy relationship to the landlord (eg: joint tenants). Further, if a tenant steals something which is not fixed to the structure, eg: a painting, washing machine or television, then that will be theft under the general s4 provisions. Presumably fixtures can be stolen even though T does nothing to dismantle or remove them, eg: contracting to sell a conservatory fixed to the house of which he is a tenant.

EXAMPLE 12.6

A tenant moves out of her flat before the expiry of her tenancy taking with her the land-lord's television (theft under s4(1)) and Victorian fireplace which she has to remove from the wall and dismantle (theft under s4(2)(c)).

Section 4(2)(c) does not include licensees (ie: guests) who, under the general s4(1) provisions, will be unable to steal land.

Intangible rights, such as rights of way, right to light, rights to profit and rent (otherwise known in land law terms as easements or incorporeal hereditaments) are also covered by s4(2).

c. Wild fruit and flowers

Section 4(3):

A person who picks mushrooms growing wild on any land, or who picks flowers, fruit or foliage from a plant growing wild on any land, does not (although not in possession of the land), steal what he picks, unless he does it for reward or for sale or other commercial purpose. For the purposes of this subsection 'mushroom' includes any fungus, and 'plant' includes any shrub or tree.

There is a long tradition in England and Wales of picking wild fruit/foliage from the hedgerows and fields in the summer/autumn, for example: mushrooms, berries such as blackberries and blackcurrants, foliage and flowers for drying, etc. This is preserved by s4(3) provided they are not to be commercially sold after picking. It will be theft where a plant is uprooted or obtained but not by picking, that is: if it is hacked, chopped or sawn.

d. Wild creatures

Section 4(4):

Wild creatures, tamed or untamed, shall be regarded as property; but a person cannot steal a wild creature not tamed nor ordinarily kept in captivity, or the carcase of any such creature, unless either it has been reduced into possession by or on behalf of another person and possession of it has not since been lost or abandoned, or another person is in course of reducing it into possession.

The only animals which can be stolen are:

- those tamed or ordinarily kept in captivity (ie: in zoos or in cages/hives/ponds at home);
- those reduced into and remaining in possession of another person or in the course of being put into possession.

Wild animals which are free and not in anyone's possession, if taken, will not be stolen. The owner of property with rivers full of fish or land full of rabbits/pheasants, all wild, has no pro-prietary right in them but does have a right to take them. Once taken, they belong to him. If taken by another, the offence is not theft, owing to the protection of s4(4), but poaching. Once a poacher has them in his own possession, they can be stolen by a third party.

Consequently, badgers enticed into traps set by a government agency were not property since they were not in the possession of the landowner: *Cresswell v DPP* [2006] EWHC 3379 (Admin).

Belonging to another

This AR element rarely gives rise to difficulty, for most of the time it is clear that D has appropriated something belonging to somebody else to which he has absolutely no legal right at all. However, the Theft Act protects not just ownership or possession but virtually all lesser legal and equitable rights.

Section 5(1):

Property shall be regarded as belonging to any person having possession or control of it, or having in it any proprietary right or interest, whether it be a right of ownership, possession or equitable right (except any equitable interest arising only from an agreement to transfer or grant an interest).

Therefore, although you can only steal what belongs to another, they do not need to own it outright provided they have a legally recognised interest in the property such as those discussed in the following paragraphs.

Possession or control

You can steal something from anyone who has mere possession or control of it provided all other elements of theft can be proved. 'Possession' means physical control and an intention to possess. 'Control' means simply physical control. This means that if V has possession or control of your property (because you have lent it to them or allowed them to take it for repairs) you can steal it from them.

R v Turner (No 2) [1971] 1 WLR 901 COURT OF APPEAL

D took his car to a garage for repairs. He found it parked outside the garage in the road, the repairs almost completed. D told the garage proprietor that he would return the next day and settle his bill. Using a spare key, he drove the car away without paying. It was held that he had stolen his car. In the course of the case, there were arguments on D's behalf that the garage exercised inferior civil law rights to the car by virtue of a lien (limited right to possession for a particular purpose) since the car was in fact the subject of a hire purchase agreement and although legal ownership resided in the HP company, D's right to possession by virtue of that agreement was greater than that of the garage.

Lord Parker CJ:

This court is quite satisfied that there is no ground whatever for qualifying the words 'possession or control' in any way. It is sufficient if it is found that the person from whom the property is taken, or to use the words of the Act, appropriated, was at the time in fact in possession or control. At the trial there was a long argument as to whether that possession or control must be lawful, it being said that by reason of the fact that this car was subject to a hire-purchase agreement, Mr Brown (the garage proprietor) could never even as against the defendant obtain lawful possession or control. As I have said, this court is quite satisfied that the judge was quite correct in telling the jury they need not bother about lien, and that they need not bother about hire purchase agreements. The only question was whether Mr Brown was in fact in possession or control.

The garage proprietor had a proprietary right or interest over the car in his possession until the bill was paid but the court was only concerned with his *intention to possess*. This interest was superior to that of the owner.

One needs to contrast *Turner* with a later Crown Court case of *Meredith* [1973] Crim LR 253 where it was held that a car owner who removed his vehicle which had been impounded during a football match from a police station yard without paying the fine committed no theft in doing so. The statutory charge regulations gave the police no power to prevent the vehicle from being repossessed by its owner.

→ CROSS-REFERENCE
The AR of Robbery is discussed in 12.2.2.

Note that unlawful drugs may be stolen. It is no defence to argue that Class A drugs are not property and that possession/control is unlawful. Illegality is not an exception to sections 4 or 5: *Smith, Plummer, Haines* [2011] EWCA Crim 66.

Abandonment

The general position is that abandoned items do not belong to anyone and they cannot, therefore, be stolen. The only qualification concerns whether the owner intended to abandon. If the owner demonstrates an intention to exclude others from the items in question, they are not abandoned.

R v Woodman [1974] QB 754 COURT OF APPEAL

D removed some scrap metal from a disused factory belonging to English China Clays. They had sold all the scrap metal to a company which had left some inaccessible items on the premises. The factory had then been surrounded by a barbed wire fence to exclude trespassers. D was convicted of theft and appealed on the ground that he had not removed the metal from anyone's possession or control. It was held that D had committed theft.

Lord Widgery CJ:

> We have formed the view without difficulty that the recorder was perfectly entitled to do what he did, that there was ample evidence that English China Clays were in control of the site and had taken considerable steps to exclude trespassers as demonstrating the fact that they were in control of the site, and we think that in ordinary and straightforward cases if it is once established that a particular person is in control of a site such as this, then prima facie he is in control of the articles which are on that site . . . . The fact that it could not be shown that they were conscious of the existence of this or any particular scrap iron does not destroy the general principle that control of a site by excluding others from it is prima facie control of articles on the site as well.

 NOTE 12.5

One ought to ask the obvious question of whether 'unconscious' possession is consistent with possession as defined in *Warner v Metropolitan Police Commissioner* [1968] 2 All ER 356.

Following *Woodman*, in *Hibbert v McKiernan* [1948] 2 KB 142 a trespasser on a golf course was guilty of stealing lost golf balls from the secretary and club members. This was confirmed in *Rostron and Collinson* [2003] 3 All ER (D) 269 where Ds retrieved lost golf balls for the purposes of resale, a lucrative business, from a lake and water features on a course. The issue was whether there was evidence that the balls were property belonging to another.

Consequently, placing items for collection by the local authority in a dustbin is not an abandonment. Neither is depositing items outside a charity shop. In *Ricketts* both points were argued:

R (Ricketts) v Basildon Magistrates Court [2010] EWHC 2358 (ADMIN)
HIGH COURT

D took bags of clothes from outside a charity shop and clothes from a wheelie bin at the back of another charity shop. He admitted he was going to sell them. He appealed to the High Court from the magistrates' court decision that there was evidence of theft on which to commit him to the Crown Court. His argument was that the property in the bags and the bin had been abandoned.

Wyn Williams J:

> In my judgment it cannot be said that the British Heart Foundation acquired possession of the items or assumed control of them or even acquired a proprietary interest in them simply by virtue of the fact that they were left in close proximity to the shop. However it is clearly the case, in my judgment, that it was open to the court to infer that the items had not been abandoned. The obvious inference on the bare facts before the magistrates was that persons unknown had intended the goods to be a gift to the British Heart Foundation. Those persons had an intention to give; they had also attempted to effect delivery. Delivery would be complete however only when the British Heart Foundation took possession of the items. Until that time, although the unknown would-be donor had divested himself of possession of the items, he had not given up his ownership of the items. I accept that it would have been more appropriate to lay a charge of stealing property belonging to persons unknown, though as I have said it is not material to the resolution of this case that the claimant was charged with appropriating items belonging to the British Heart Foundation . . . .
>
> I turn to the charge alleging theft from Oxfam since it is somewhat different on the facts. The claimant admits that the items taken from Oxfam were items which had been placed in bins in close proximity to the rear of the shop. In my judgment, it would be open to a court to infer either that would-be donors had placed the items in the bin for receipt by Oxfam or that employees of Oxfam had placed the items in the bin for onward disposal by the local authority. This analysis assumes of course that the bins belonged to or were controlled by Oxfam, which is not presently disputed. Upon that assumption it would be open to a court to infer that Oxfam had taken delivery of the items once placed within the bin. Alternatively, it could infer that Oxfam had taken possession of the items and had then placed them in the bin for disposal. Either way, Oxfam were in possession of the items at the time of the appropriation by the claimant . . . .

Therefore, provided all other elements of theft could be established, D committed theft.

Leaving things on premises and forgetting about them is not abandonment, neither is losing things and forgetting about them. Treasure trove and antiquities which are 200 or 300 years old are not abandoned and once discovered vest in the Crown. If found on private or public property, the owner or possessor of the land is entitled to possession as against third parties provided there is evidence of an intention to possess or control the land and anything on it. Therefore, using a metal detector and digging for antique jewellery in a public park is trespass and theft (*Waverley Borough Council v Fletcher* [1995] 4 All ER 756).

?!   THINKING POINT 12.4

Does D steal the following items?

1. X takes his bicycle to a shop for repair. The repairer, R, does the work but X fails to collect it as arranged. After three weeks, R puts the bicycle outside the shop because he needs the space. It remains there for a further week when D, a passer-by, sees the bike and takes it.

2. D, a workman dredging a pool on local authority open space, finds two antique gold rings. He decides to keep them.

Proprietary right or interest

Whether a victim retains a proprietary right or interest in property can only be determined by reference to civil law principles which define ownership, possession or equitable rights. Some older theft cases were decided in accordance with the principles of contract or equity in order to determine whether D had become the owner or mere possessor of appropriated property. For instance in the next case the Court of Appeal had to decide whether D had become the owner of three gallons of petrol and two pints of oil which a garage attendant had poured into D's car before he drove off without paying.

Edwards v Ddin [1976] 1 WLR 942 COURT OF APPEAL

Croom-Johnson J:

> The whole question therefore was: whose petrol and oil was it when the defendant drove away? Property passes under a contract of sale when it is intended to pass. In such transactions as the sale of petrol at a garage forecourt ordinary common sense would say that the garage and the motorist intended the property in the petrol to pass when it is poured into the tank and irretrievably mixed with the other petrol that is in it, and I think that is what the justices decided . . . .
>
> By pouring the petrol into the tank the goods have been appropriated to the contract with the assent of both parties. If that is done unconditionally, then the property in the petrol passes to the motorist . . . The garage owner does not reserve the right to dispose of the petrol once it is in the tank, nor is it possible to see how effect could be given to any such condition wherever petrol has been put in and is all mixed up with what other petrol is already there.
>
> Section 5, which deals with but is not definitive of the expression 'belonging to another', is concerned with all manner of interests in property. It was urged upon us that the motorist is under an implied obligation to retain his car with the petrol in its tank on the garage premises and not to take it away until such time as he has paid for it, and that until that has been done the garage owner retains some proprietary interest in the petrol in the tank . . . . That section in my view is not apt to cover a case such as the present where there has been an outright sale of the goods and the property in the goods has passed and the seller is only waiting to be paid. Therefore the provisions of s5 do not affect the conclusion in the present case.

 NOTE 12.6

1. Under contract law, it is a matter of intention as to when ownership will pass from seller to purchaser. Usually, it is upon payment. Section 18 Sale of Goods Act 1979 provides various rules for determining *the intention* of the parties so that it is possible for ownership to be transferred before payment. *Edwards v Ddin* decides that in garages, ownership passes as soon as D pumps the petrol into his tank, even before payment. There is an unconditional intention between the parties that ownership should be transferred at that point. Therefore, in driving off without paying for it, D committed no theft. The petrol already belonged to him and did not therefore belong to another.

2. The same applies if you leave a restaurant without paying for a meal which you have consumed. Once the food is in your stomach, it belongs to you and you cannot steal anything unless it belongs to another. That is not to say that you have not committed other offences (see later).

3. Would a different outcome have been reached if the issue in *Edwards v Ddin* had been whether D had *appropriated* property belonging to another instead of to whom the property belonged? Probably and for these reasons:

Under *Gomez/Hinks*, appropriation occurs at a much earlier point in time: as soon as D assumes one of the rights of ownership, consent being irrelevant. If, when filling the tank, D's mind is dishonest because he intends not to pay, he will appropriate property belonging to another dishonestly and with intent. At that point when the petrol is being put into his tank it still belongs to another. Therefore, he steals the petrol even before driving away without paying.

On the other hand, if D intends to pay whilst filling the tank, but has a change of mind afterwards, the appropriation does not become dishonest until the change of mind. At that later point, the petrol already being in his tank, it belongs to him. D does not therefore steal property belonging to another.

In practice, D is more likely to be charged with 'making off without payment' under s3 Theft Act 1978 which does not depend on whether ownership is transferred, merely on whether D's failure to pay for goods or services as expected is dishonest.

?! THINKING POINT 12.5

D goes into a restaurant and orders a meal. He eats the meal and leaves without paying. Has D committed theft?

Proprietary right and mistake

When property has been acquired under a mistake, the courts will sometimes decide whether or not D has stolen property belonging to another according to the transfer of proprietary rights under the civil law. Here, as we saw earlier, a seller's intention to transfer ownership of goods may be completely negated where the mistake is fundamental (ie: a mistake of identity or nature of the property). This renders the contract void, meaning that no title passes at all and D therefore steals property belonging to another.

If the mistake is not fundamental (ie: a mistake of quality), the contract will become voidable meaning that ownership can pass to the buyer until the seller rescinds the contract (takes steps to end it). In the meantime, D becomes the owner and therefore the property belongs to him. It should not be possible to steal what already belongs to you.

The court held in the next case that D did not commit theft because the contract was made under a mistake of quality:

Kaur v Chief Constable of Hampshire [1981] 2 ALL ER 430 COURT OF APPEAL

D, a customer in a shop, saw some shoes, some pairs of which were priced at £6.99 and others at £4.99. She came across a more expensive pair one of which was marked at the lower price. Without concealing either label, she took the shoes to the cashier hoping to be charged the lower price as indeed she was. She left the shop but was apprehended, charged and convicted of theft. Her conviction was quashed on appeal. The only question for the court was whether the contract was void or voidable. It was held that the mistake as to price was little different from one as to quality (ie: non-fundamental). Therefore, the contract was voidable and D became the owner of the shoes upon payment. Neither appropriation nor theft were possible.

?!   THINKING POINT 12.6

If the facts of *Kaur* occurred today, would Ms Kaur have appropriated and stolen the shoes? (Consider how *Gomez* might have affected the outcome.)

Trust property—equitable rights

The inclusion of equitable rights within s5(1) has allowed theft to expand into the area of the trust. A trust is an equitable concept whereby property is placed under the control of a trustee(s) subject to certain conditions for the benefit of a beneficiar(y/ies). Trustees have a legal interest and beneficiaries have an equitable interest in trust property. Theft by a trustee of trust property held for the benefit of a beneficiary is now covered by s5(1) and this might include property held under a constructive trust.

a. Constructive trusts

A constructive trust is one which operates in the interests of conscience and justice irrespective of the express or presumed intentions of the parties. It may arise in many different situations, for example, where an employee accepts a bribe in the course of his employment. A court might decide that the employee who retains that bribe becomes trustee of it under a constructive trust for the benefit of his employer. If so, he would commit theft of trust property. However, in the absence of a trust, the only remedy is a debt action under the civil law because there would be no trust property belonging to another and, therefore, no theft. Despite the Privy Council case *AG for Hong Kong v Reid* [1994] 1 All ER 1 PC, which said that bribes are held under constructive trust (and are, therefore, potentially, theft), most decisions take the opposite view. The courts are reluctant to extend s5(1) too far.

In *Powell v MacRae* [1977] Crim LR 571, for example, the Court of Appeal held that a turnstile operator at Wembley Stadium who had taken a bribe to admit someone without a ticket did not hold the bribe on trust for his employers and had not therefore stolen it.

This argument was also accepted by the Court of Appeal in *Attorney-General's Reference (No 1 of 1985)* where a manager of a public house, an employee of a brewery, sold beer purchased privately from a wholesaler in breach of contract so as to increase his profits. The court did not consider these circumstances would give rise to a trust. A dishonest employee who kept some profit was far removed from ordinary notions of stealing.

A more recent civil case has held, however, that bribes or wrongful profit should be regarded as trust assets (*FHR European Ventures v Cedar Capital Partners* [2014] UKSC 45). Theoretically, therefore, theft in such circumstances is more of a possibility.

Further provisions of s5 provide that in three specified situations, D can steal property belonging to another even though he becomes the owner of it under the civil law:

b. Trust property

Section 5(2):

Where property is subject to a trust, the persons to whom it belongs shall be regarded as including any person having *a right to enforce the trust*, and an intention to defeat the trust shall be regarded accordingly as an intention to deprive of the property any person having that right.

It is thought that charitable trusts or discretionary trusts for a very large class of beneficiary might fall under this subsection. Since these trusts are unenforceable until beneficiaries have been selected, charitable trusts, for example, are enforceable by the Attorney General. Trustees who wrongfully retain or divert trust property, therefore, steal it.

c. Property received on account

Section 5(3):

Where a person receives property from or on account of another, and is under an obligation to the other to retain and deal with that property or its proceeds in a particular way, the property or proceeds shall be regarded (as against him) as belonging to the other.

This section applies to those holding money for another under an obligation to deal with it in a particular way, for example: estate agents, solicitors, stockbrokers, pension fund holders.

EXAMPLE 12.7

Under the civil law, if you pay £500 to an estate agent or solicitor (D) by way of deposit or on account of work, he becomes the owner of that money subject to your instructions but you retain an equitable interest in it. If D dishonestly appropriates the money, he steals it from you and s5(1) applies. But, the prosecutor may rely on s5(3) without the need to investigate any underlying equitable interest that you may retain under s5(1).

There must be a legal as opposed to a moral obligation to retain or deal with the property.

Section 5(3) applies not only to those in financial relationships holding client money, but to anyone in receipt of money for a specific purpose, such as £500 paid in advance to your decorator to purchase paint/paper to decorate your lounge next week.

But it can be difficult to distinguish money received *on account* from an ordinary contractual debtor-creditor situation where the only remedy would be to sue for return of the money in a civil debt action. The difference appears to lie in a combination of whether the money goes into a separate client or a general account and whether there is a specific instruction to 'retain and deal' with the money in a particular way. One case has held that a dishonest travel agent had no obligations under s5(3):

R v Hall [1973] 1 QB 126 COURT OF APPEAL

D, a travel agent, received client deposits and money for air tickets to America. He paid the money into his firm's general account. The tickets were never supplied and the money was never refunded. He was convicted of theft and appealed on the ground that he had not received the money under an obligation to retain or deal with it in a particular way.

Edmund-Davies LJ:

> . . . when a client goes to a firm carrying on the business of travel agents and pays them money, he expects that in return he will, in due course, receive the tickets and other documents necessary for him to accomplish the trip for which he is paying, and the firm are 'under an obligation' to perform their part to fulfil his expectation and are liable to pay him damages if they do not. But, in our judgment, what was not here established was that these clients expected them 'to retain and deal with that property or its proceeds in a particular way', and that an 'obligation' to do so was undertaken by the appellant. We must make clear, however, that each case turns on its own facts. Cases could, we suppose, conceivably arise where by some special arrangement (preferably evidenced by documents), the client could impose on the travel agent an 'obligation' falling within s5(3). But no such special arrangement was made in any of the seven cases here being considered . . . . It follows from this that, despite what on any view must be condemned as scandalous conduct by the appellant, in our judgment on this ground alone this appeal must be allowed and the convictions quashed.

The money was regarded as business income to be used as D saw fit. Had the agent stated that the money would be held in a separate trust account to be repaid if the arrangements failed, the decision might have been different. As it was, the relationship was purely one of debtor–creditor entitling the clients to sue in the county court. Section 5(3) did not apply and therefore no theft had been committed. A conviction was overturned in the next case for broadly similar reasons:

Foster [2011] EWCA Crim 1192

D ran an unauthorised pyramid investment scheme for work colleagues, collecting money from over 8,500 investors, to be used in large bets on football and other sports. He invested the money for his own use. The question was whether he had an obligation to retain and deal with that money in a particular way, or, as he alleged, whether he had made it clear that he would use the money at his discretion.

Elias LJ:

> . . . the funds which come from the investors will be mixed. If some of those funds are . . . restricted funds, not to be used for other purposes than gambling and networking, but some of those funds can be used more generally, but the two funds are mixed and are not divided in some way – and in practice they will not be – then it is not possible to say whether the funds which were drawn upon to pay for the personal benefits was derived from the tainted section of the funds or the untainted section. If the situation is that some of those funds were given without restriction and they are used for personal benefits, that of course is dishonest but it is not an appropriation of another's property within the meaning of the Theft Act, because in those circumstances, the property does not belong to the investors. . . .
>
> It will have been transferred, effectively to the appellant, and he could not then steal his own money.

The principle of mixed funds here is very similar to the principle we met in *Edwards v Ddin* above: when a motorist puts petrol into his tank and drives off without paying, he leaves with his own property for the new cannot be distinguished from his own petrol already in the tank.

However, each case turns on its own facts. The opposite decision had been reached in *Klineberg & Marsden* [1999] 1 Cr App R 427 where purchasers paid £500,000 to a timeshare company for the purchase of apartments on the understanding that the money would be held by an independent trust company until completion. Only £233 was ever deposited with the company. The Court of Appeal held that there was an obligation to deal with the purchasers' money in a particular way and therefore the company had committed theft. Section 5(3) could even apply to theft of charitable funds. An example would be the unreported case of *Wain* (1995) 2 Cr App R 660, where D diverted donations obtained for 'The Telethon Trust' into his own bank account and spent it. It was held that he was under an obligation to retain if not the actual notes and coins, at least their proceeds.

> ## ?! THINKING POINT 12.7
>
> V gives D £1,800 to buy a particular type of car on V's behalf. D spends the money on himself. Has D committed theft?

d. Property obtained under another's mistake

Section 5(4):

> Where a person gets property by another's mistake, and is under an obligation to make restoration (in whole or in part) of the property or its proceeds or of the value thereof, then to the extent of that obligation the property or proceeds shall be regarded (as against him) as belonging to the person entitled to restoration, and an intention not to make restoration shall be regarded accordingly as an intention to deprive that person of the property or proceeds.

In *Moynes v Cooper* [1956] 1 QB 439 a labourer was paid an advance of £6 19s 6d by a site agent. At the end of the week, the wages clerk also paid him his full weekly wage of £7 3s 4d which the labourer dishonestly kept. It was held that he became the owner of the full amount and had not committed theft.

This case is now overturned by s5(4) which imposes on the recipient a legal obligation to restore the overpayment to the mistaken payer. Therefore, in *AG's Reference (No 1 of 1983)* [1985] QB 182, it was held to apply to mistaken overpayments of salary by direct debit from the account of an employer to an employee police woman, even though she had not withdrawn it. Of course, once the money was in her account, it became, in law, a debt owed by her bank to her. Had she spent all her money before realising the mistake, she would have been under no obligation to restore because there would have been no debt, or chose in action, in existence. The question of 'obligation' is one of civil law. There is some debate as to whether s5(4) is really necessary because the employer probably retains an equitable interest in the overpayment and the case could probably be dealt with under s5(1).

Section 5(4) also applies to mistakes which have been fraudulently induced. In *Gresham* [2003] EWCA Crim 2070 D continued to collect his deceased mother's pension for ten years after her death from the Department of Education and did not inform them of her death. The Court of Appeal regarded this as an unforced mistake caused by D's fraudulent conduct. The pension credited to her account still belonged to the Department.

It can be said by way of conclusion that the provisions of s5 represent a rather unclear divide between ordinary debt situations and theft. For the most part, debts are enforced through the civil courts. Section 5 states that in a few legally technical situations failing to repay a debt will also be a crime.

Note that when a person uses a debit card to withdraw cash from a cash machine when he knows he has no funds in his account and there is no overdraft agreement in place, this may amount to theft of the amount withdrawn. This is because at the time of the appropriation the cash would be 'property belonging to another' (as long as all the other elements of theft were present: *Chodorek v Poland* [2017] ACD 244 (82)).

12.1.3 Mens Rea

The appropriation of property belonging to another must be proved to be dishonest and accompanied by an intention permanently to deprive. There must be proof of both elements of MR in relation to all three aspects of the AR.

Dishonesty

Dishonesty is not defined in the Theft Act other than a partial definition in s2(1) relating to certain beliefs and a willingness to pay in s2(2). The statute gives examples of behaviour and intent which will not be regarded as dishonest, rather than giving a definition of what is. Ordinarily, the issue will be left to the jury as a question of fact and in the majority of cases, requires no legal explanation at all. The jury will be free to apply their common sense to the issue. In certain cases the issue will require legal guidance but the final decision rests with the jury.

Section 2(1) beliefs

Section 2(1) contains a partial definition of dishonesty. Conduct will not be dishonest if D has any of three specified *beliefs*. These beliefs will operate as a defence to an allegation of theft. D may assert that he was not dishonest according to s2(1). On the other hand, s2(2) states that D may be dishonest notwithstanding an intention to pay.

a. Section 2(1)(a): belief in right

> A person's appropriation of property belonging to another is not to be regarded as dishonest (a) if he appropriates the property in the *belief* that he has *in law the right to deprive* the other of it, on behalf of himself or of a third person.

This is known as the 'claim of right' defence. The belief must be honest but need be neither correct nor reasonable. If D is ignorant of the civil law and honestly believes that he is legally entitled to property, s/he does not have the MR for theft.

In *R v Small* (1988) 86 Cr App R 170 the Court of Appeal held that in considering whether or not a belief is honest, reasonableness is a factor to take into account. The more unreasonable, the less likely it is that the belief will be honest. It is necessary to distinguish a belief in a *legal* as opposed to a *moral* right.

 EXAMPLE 12.8

D's aunt promised her that when she died she would leave D her diamond ring.
    After the aunt's death D discovers that by her will the ring is left to D's cousin. D takes the ring from her aunt's house in the belief that it ought to belong to her.

Here, D could not honestly assert a belief in a legal right. The defence would not apply. See also the next case:

R v Forrester [1992] CRIM LR 793 COURT OF APPEAL

D's landlord refused to repay him a £200 deposit at the end of his tenancy. D entered the landlord's flat by force, locked him in a room and took £200 worth of belongings. On appeal against conviction for robbery (theft by the use/threat of force) the Court of Appeal held that D may believe himself to be entitled to act unlawfully but there was little substance in his argument that he was honest.

However, it may not be hard to envisage situations where unlawful actions may be accompanied by an honest belief. See the following problem.

THINKING POINT 12.8

V owes D £50 and has been avoiding D for several weeks. D badly needs the money. D bumps into V one day who has a bundle of notes in his pocket. As V takes his mobile phone from his pocket a £50 note falls out and D takes it in the belief that it is his.
    Does D commit theft?

b. Section 2(1) (b): belief in consent

A person's appropriation of property is not to be regarded as dishonest:

> if he appropriates the property in the *belief* that he would have the other's *consent* if the other knew of the appropriation and the circumstances of it.

As earlier, the belief must be honest and genuine but need not be reasonable.

EXAMPLE 12.9

D needs some money quickly but is overdrawn at the bank. He happens to know his flat-mate's debit bank card PIN number and takes her card whilst she is out to withdraw £100 from a cash machine. D intends to repay her later and therefore believes that she will not mind.

Whether he will have a defence that his actions were not dishonest depends on the genuineness of his belief in consent. The circumstances of their relationship and conduct towards each other may or may not provide a basis for a genuine belief.
    One problem might be s2(2) which states that:

> A person's appropriation may be dishonest notwithstanding that he is willing to pay for the property.

It will be a question of fact for the jury as to whether D's belief is genuine.

c. Section 2(1)(c): belief that the property is lost

A person's appropriation of property is not to be regarded as dishonest:

> if he appropriates the property in the *belief* that the person to whom the property belongs cannot be discovered by taking reasonable steps.

In general, lost property still belongs to the owner. A charge of theft can lay against D in respect of appropriation of property from 'persons unknown'. Therefore, if D steals from a lost property office or is discovered to have found a valuable object to which he believes he has no legal right, it can still be regarded as stolen. Section 2(1)(c) states that this will not be theft however if D asserts a genuine belief that the owner cannot be found by reasonable means.

Clearly, greater effort would be considered reasonable for more valuable items. Distinguish the situation where you find a £5 note on the pavement in Oxford Street, London (where ownership would be virtually impossible to trace) from that where you discover a Renaissance painting leaning against the railings of the National Gallery, Trafalgar Square (where ownership could be easily ascertained).

Reasonable steps do not mean absolutely exhaustive steps—just what a reasonable person would do. Remember that this is part of MR—there is no requirement that the defendant should actually take reasonable steps to recover the property.

> **?! THINKING POINT** 12.9
>
> Are the following Ds dishonest under s2(1)(c)?
>
> 1. V is a legal trainee working on a large conveyancing case. On her way to a completion meeting, she absent-mindedly leaves a file of documents containing a bankers' draft for £1 million on the seat of her train. D finds the draft and keeps it, taking no steps to trace the firm on whose account it has been drawn.
>
> 2. D finds a copy of the latest best-selling detective novel on the seat of a bus. There are only one or two people sitting at the back of the bus and they do not appear interested in it. She decides to keep the book.

Dishonesty will be a question of fact in every case and must be left to the jury to decide. This is so whether or not D asserts a belief under s2(1).

Dishonesty

The way in which juries are asked to assess dishonesty will be substantially affected by the recent civil case of *Ivey v Genting Casinos (UK) Limited (Crockfords)* [2017] UKSC 67. Prior to this decision, where D raised a defence that he did not believe that what he had done was dishonest, and that most people would agree, the jury were directed on the *Ghosh* test. It applied where D's conduct appeared dishonest but D had a belief that, despite appearances, he was not actually dishonest.

The *Ghosh* test ran as follows:

1. Was what was done dishonest according to the ordinary standards of reasonable and honest people?
2. Must D have realised that what he was doing was dishonest according to those standards?

Under the test, if the answer was 'yes' to both questions, then D had to be considered dishonest. If the answer was 'no' to the first or second question then D would not be regarded as dishonest.

The test was not straightforward and was somewhat circular. At one time, the test for dishonesty had been purely objective, but the second *Ghosh* question introduced a subjective element. It seems that now, the test is once again of an objective nature.

The starting point is that in most cases, no explanation of 'dishonest' should be given to the jury:

R v Feely [1973] QB 530 COURT OF APPEAL

D was employed by a firm of book-keepers as manager of a branch. His employers sent round a circular to all managers saying that the practice of borrowing from tills was to stop. Knowing this, D borrowed £30. He was owed more than twice this amount in unpaid wages. When the loss was discovered but before being attributed to him he placed a note in the till recording the taking. The trial judge directed the jury that D's intention to repay the money was no defence. A belief that his employers would not have consented to the taking meant that he was dishonest. This was held by the Court of Appeal to be wrong.

Lawton LJ:

> In s1(1) of the Act of 1968, the word 'dishonestly' can only relate to the state of mind of the person who does the act which amounts to appropriation. Whether an accused person has a particular state of mind is a question of fact which has to be decided by the jury when there is a trial on indictment, and by the magistrates when there are summary proceedings .... We do not agree that judges should define what 'dishonestly' means. This word is in common use whereas the word 'fraudulently' which was used in s1(1) of the Larceny Act 1916, had acquired as a result of case law a special meaning. Jurors, when deciding whether an appropriation was dishonest can be reasonably expected to, and should, apply the current standards of ordinary decent people. In their own lives they have to decide what is and what is not dishonest. We can see no reason why, when in a jury box, they should require the help of a judge to tell them what amounts to dishonesty .... it is clear in our judgment that the jury should have been left to decide whether the defendant's alleged taking of the money had been dishonest ....

Appeal allowed. On the face of it, this test appears to be sensible enough. Most people would agree on most cases of dishonesty. But one criticism was that it could be confused with an entirely objective approach so that conduct which appeared dishonest according to reasonable standards would be regarded as such irrespective of D's genuine belief that he was not dishonest. In order to circumscribe the severity of such a harsh test, the next case attempted to clarify that what was really required was a subjective/objective approach. The unfortunate consequence, however, was a good deal more confusion.

R v Ghosh [1982] QB 1053 COURT OF APPEAL

D, a locum consultant surgeon, falsely claimed anaesthetist's fees in respect of an NHS operation. The same amount of money was owed to him and had been outstanding for a period of time. He was charged with obtaining property by deception under s15 Theft Act 1968. The judge directed the jury to apply their own standards of dishonesty. D was convicted and appealed to the Court of Appeal.

Lord Lane CJ:

> ... *R v Feeley* ... is often treated as having laid down an objective test of dishonesty for the purpose of s1 of the Theft Act 1968. But what it actually decided was (i) that it is for the jury to determine whether the defendant acted dishonestly and not for the judge, (ii) that the word 'dishonestly' can only relate to the defendant's own state of mind, and (iii) that it is unnecessary and undesirable for judges to define what is meant by 'dishonestly'. ... Is 'dishonestly' in s1 of the Theft Act 1968 intended to characterise a course of conduct? Or is it intended to describe a state of mind? If the former, then we can well understand that it could be established independently of the knowledge or belief of the accused. But if, as we think, it is the latter, then the knowledge and belief of the accused are at the root of the problem.

Take for example a man who comes from a country where public transport is free. On his first day here he travels on a bus. He gets off without paying. He never had any intention of paying. His mind is clearly honest; but his conduct, judged objectively by what he has done, is dishonest. It seems to us that in using the word 'dishonestly' in the Theft Act 1968, Parliament cannot have intended to catch dishonest conduct in that sense, that is to say conduct to which no moral obloquy could possibly attach. This is sufficiently established by the partial definition in s2 of the Theft Act itself. All the matters covered by s2(1) relate to the belief of the accused. Section 2(2) relates to his willingness to pay. A man's belief and his willingness to pay are things which can only be established subjectively. It is difficult to see how a partially subjective definition can be made to work in harness with the test which in all other respects is wholly objective.

If we are right that dishonesty is something in the mind of the accused . . ., then if the mind of the accused is honest, it cannot be deemed dishonest merely because members of the jury would have regarded it as dishonest to embark on that course of conduct.

So we would reject the simple uncomplicated approach that the test is purely objective, however attractive from the practical point of view that solution may be.

There remains the objection that to adopt a subjective test is to abandon all standards but that of the accused himself, and to bring about a state of affairs in which 'Robin Hood would be no robber': *R v Greenstein*. This objection misunderstands the nature of the subjective test. It is no defence for a man to say 'I knew what I was doing is generally regarded as dishonest; but I do not regard it as dishonest myself. Therefore I am not guilty.' What he is however entitled to say is 'I did not know that anybody would regard what I was doing as dishonest.' He may not be believed . . . . But if he *is* believed, or raises a real doubt about the matter, the jury cannot be sure that he was dishonest.

In determining whether the prosecution has proved that the defendant was acting dishonestly, a jury must first of all decide whether according to the ordinary standards of reasonable and honest people what was done was dishonest. If it was not dishonest by those standards, that is the end of the matter and the prosecution fails.

If it was dishonest by those standards, then the jury must consider whether the defendant himself must have realised that what he was doing was by those standards dishonest. In most cases, where the actions are obviously dishonest by ordinary standards, there will be no doubt about it. It will be obvious that the defendant himself knew that he was acting dishonestly. It is dishonest for a defendant to act in a way which he knows ordinary people consider to be dishonest, even if he asserts or genuinely believes that he is morally justified in acting as he did. For example, Robin Hood or those ardent anti-vivisectionists who remove animals from vivisection laboratories are acting dishonestly, even though they may consider themselves to be morally justified in doing what they do, because they know that ordinary people would consider these actions to be dishonest. [Emphasis added.]

Appeal dismissed.

The italicised type above became known as the *Ghosh* test and consisted of the two questions posed above which can be summarised as follows:

a. Was D's act dishonest according to ordinary standards of reasonable and honest behaviour? *and*

b. Did D believe himself to be dishonest according to those ordinary standards?

?!   THINKING POINT 12.10

Question (a) derives from *Feely* and (b) derives from *Ghosh*. Identify the objective and subjective parts of the test.

NOTE 12.7

1. Lord Lane held that dishonesty characterises not a course of conduct but a state of mind. The correct test should therefore be a balance between an objective test (conduct: *Feely*) and a subjective test (D's belief: *Ghosh*). The latter was introduced to allow justice to be done in genuine cases.

2. To abandon all standards but those of D (a subjective test) could lead to a state of affairs whereby Robin Hood would be no robber. This had to be balanced against ordinary common standards to say that D should not know that he was dishonest according to reasonable standards.

3. There was a distinction to be drawn here between beliefs and values. One may hold certain values or principles on the basis that they are morally right. If one appropriated property belonging to another in accordance with those values (eg: Robin Hood) it did not necessarily mean that one could claim the defence because one may still believe that most people would regard such actions as dishonest.

4. However, it was here that the test became technically complex because if D was genuinely ignorant of ordinary common standards, then the *Ghosh* test, applied literally, should lead to acquittal regardless of how unreasonable his actions. This was clearly not what Lord Lane intended.

The test was criticised as it left the meaning of the word up to the jury whereas it ought to be defined according to legal principle offering clear guidance. Read this extract by E. Griew, 'Dishonesty: The Objections to *Feely* and *Ghosh*' [1985] *Crim LR* 341 in discussing each part of the *Ghosh* test in turn:

A. Objections to the *Feely* question

A1. *More, longer and more difficult trials*

. . .

(a) The question tends to increase the number of trials. Whereas a different approach to the dishonesty issue might make clear that given conduct was dishonest as a matter of law and therefore constituted an offence, the *Feely* question leaves the issue open. It may be worth a defendant's while to take his chance with the jury. One defendant will claim that he intended to repay the substantial sum of money that he borrowed from the fund entrusted to him and argue that his unjustified optimism about being able to do so bespeaks a temperamental flaw but not a moral one. Another will assert his intention and expectation that the use of invested money for a purpose different from that to which he had represented that it would be applied would in good time have realised a handsome profit to the deceived investor, and he will invite the jury to say that he was not dishonest because he intended the substantial advantage of his deceived victim. Defences such as these provide ground for a contest where, before *Feely*, the defendants might have felt constrained to plead guilty . . . .

A2. *Inconsistent decisions*

The *Feely* question carries an unacceptable risk of inconsistency of decision . . . . It is only in a minority of cases that the matter will truly admit of argument. But within this crucial marginal group different juries, as the presumptive embodiment of ordinary decent standards, may take different views of essentially indistinguishable cases. The law of the relevant offence will then vary as between different defendants. This must be unacceptable.

A3. *Fiction of community norms*

The *Feely* question implies the existence of a relevant community norm. In doing so it glosses over differences of age, class and cultural background which combine to give the character of fiction to the idea of a generally shared sense of the boundary between honesty and dishonesty. This is the more obvious in a society with the range of cultural groups that ours now has; and it is the more relevant since jury service was extended to the generality of electors between 18 and 65. It is simply naïve to suppose – surely no one does suppose – that there is, in respect of the dishonesty question, any such single thing as 'the standards of ordinary decent people.'

A4. *'Dishonestly' as an 'ordinary word'*

The premise [of the *Feely* reasoning] is a semantic one; whether the defendant acted 'dishonestly' depends upon what 'dishonestly' means. The conclusion is that the issue requires the application of ordinary 'standards'. Between the premise and the conclusion lies the proposition that the meaning of the word 'dishonestly' will be found by a reference to standards . . . . What must be expressed here is a doubt about the 'ordinary word.' It simply does not follow from the truth that a word such as 'dishonestly' is an ordinary word that all speakers of the language share the same sense of its application or non-application in particular contests. Once again, it is to the marginal case, where the issue is live and crucial, that this common sense objection particularly applies. Even judges, a relatively homogeneous group of uniformly high linguistic competence, have been known to differ on the application of the epithet 'dishonest' in a marginal case. It is not acceptable that the meaning of 'dishonestly' should be 'whatever in a particular case it conveys to the mind or minds of the tribunal of fact without any instruction as to the meaning . . .'

A7. *'Anarchic' verdicts*

The *Feely* question, offered without qualification to the jury, is a question of moral estimation without guidelines and permits 'anarchic' verdicts which are not technically perverse. . . . A consequence of this . . . is that members of unpopular groups may receive inadequate protection from the law.

B. Objections to the *Ghosh* question . . .

B3. Inept correction of error

Once a relevant state of mind has been found, the only question remaining to be answered is whether . . . the jury's sense of ordinary decent standards makes the defendant's conduct with that state of mind dishonest. This is a question, not as to what state of mind the defendant had, but as to how that state of mind is to be characterised.

The confusion on this point in the *Ghosh* judgment is clear to see in the treatment of the hypothetical of a visitor from a foreign country where public transport is free. He travels on a bus without paying. Does he do so dishonestly? The court says that 'his conduct, judged objectively by what he has done, is dishonest.' The error enters the argument at this point. It cannot be right, as the structure of the court's argument plainly implies, that the visitor's conduct would be regarded as dishonest by ordinary standards. If the jury knew that he believed public transport to be free, they would say that, according to ordinary standards, he had not behaved dishonestly. There is no need to go further; his 'state of mind' has already been taken into account. But the court, having declared him dishonest when 'judged objectively', has to introduce a further 'subjective' element to rescue him. That leads to the question: 'did he know it was dishonest?' – an entirely unnecessary question . . . .

B5. The 'Robin Hood defence'

A person may defend his attack on another's property by reference to a moral or political conviction so passionately held that he believed (so he claims) that 'ordinary decent' members of society would regard his conduct as proper, even laudable. If the asserted belief is treated as a claim to have been ignorant that the conduct was 'dishonest' by ordinary standards (and it has been assumed that it might be so treated), and if the jury think (as exceptionally as they might) that the belief may have been held, *Ghosh* produces an acquittal. The result is remarkable. Robin Hood must be a thief even if he thinks the whole of the right-thinking world is on his side.

?! THINKING POINT 12.11

1. Do you consider D to be dishonest in the following situations:

   a. D spends half an hour at work each day using the firm's computer for her personal emails?

   b. D takes home from work pens, staplers and paper for her personal use?

   c. D buys a cheap CD player from a friend knowing that it has 'come off the back of a lorry' (ie: that it is stolen)?

   d. D inflates her expenses claims at work so as to receive more than she has spent?

   e. D takes three bags of chips, which have passed the 'sale-by' date, from a skip at the rear of a supermarket?

2. D has been accused of theft and puts forward the *Ghosh* defence. The jury consists of grey-haired, professional men. What are the risks of leaving the definition of dishonesty to the jury if D is alternately a single mother, mentally disabled, inarticulate or a scruffy and ill-educated young man?

3. D is a fanatical member of an animal liberation movement. She sees a kitten in a cage by the front door of a research establishment. The kitten is clearly destined for experimentation. D takes it away with the conviction that she is honestly appropriating property belonging to another. Is she dishonest under the *Ghosh* test? Or the *Feely* test?

In several subsequent cases it was asserted that the full *Ghosh* direction to the jury would only be required in those situations where D asserted a belief that what he had done was generally regarded as honest. For example, in *Jouman* [2012] EWCA Crim 1850, Mackay J, in dismissing an appeal by an autistic defendant, stated that the full *Ghosh* direction need only be given 'if the state of the evidence is such that [D] might have believed that what he or she is alleged to have done was in accordance with the ordinary person's view of honesty.' The direction was not required when D appeared dishonest but stated that he was merely forgetful or where the sole question was whether D's assertion of a lack of dishonesty was genuine. See, for example, the next three cases.

R v O'Connell [1991] CRIM LR 781 COURT OF APPEAL

D obtained building society mortgages fraudulently, concealing the fact that he already had several mortgages on different properties. He intended to let and then re-sell them so as to take advantage of increased values. At his trial for obtaining by deception contrary to s15 Theft Act 1968 (it would now be fraud) he submitted that he was not dishonest because he intended to repay the mortgages and thus he did not intend to deprive the building societies of their money. In upholding D's conviction, the Court of Appeal held that a defendant who says that, although he lied to obtain money, he was not dishonest is entitled to have his case considered by the jury.

R v Clarke (Victor) [1996] CRIM LR 824 COURT OF APPEAL

D, a private investigator, falsely told a group of potential clients that he was a former fraud squad officer and court bailiff when he was not. D performed the job satisfactorily. He was convicted of deception contrary to s16 Theft Act 1968 (now a potential fraud offence). His appeal was allowed. It was not necessarily dishonest to tell lies to obtain employment. D's belief and intention could amount to evidence of honesty.

In neither case did the Court of Appeal confirm that what each D had done was necessarily honest. But each was entitled to have the jury consider the issue before reaching a verdict.

We looked at the following case earlier under s5 (see 'Abandonment'). It concerned the collection of golf balls from ponds on a course.

R v Rostron and Collinson [2003] EWCA CRIM 2206, [2003] 3 ALL ER (D) 269 COURT OF APPEAL

Mantell LJ:

The second ground of appeal is that the learned judge failed to give what is sometimes termed a *Ghosh* . . . direction. *A* Ghosh *direction is such as may be necessary where it is said on behalf of a defendant accused of theft, or indeed of any other form of dishonesty, that he believed he was entitled to do what he did. Then the question may arise whether or not he truly held that belief and whether he would have considered that other reasonable persons in the same position might have been of the same mind.*

Here the learned judge chose to give a simple, straightforward, clear and fair direction . . . He told the jury in terms that the prosecution had to prove that the defendant whose case was being considered knew that he was not entitled to go on to the golf course and remove golf balls. If that was established, then the necessary element of dishonesty had been proved, and, of course, if that were the case it would matter not what other people might think, because he could not in such circumstances have had an honest belief that he was entitled to do what he did. [Emphasis added.]

The Law Commission in 'Legislating the Criminal Code: Fraud and Deception Law' (Law Com CP No 155, 1999) is critical of the *Ghosh* test:

5.11 The *Ghosh* approach requires fact-finders to set a moral standard of honesty and determine whether the defendant's conduct falls short of that standard . . . . But it is also a *moral* enquiry, and requires the making of a *moral* judgment. To say that something is dishonest is to characterise the existing facts, not add another fact. This, we believe, is an unusual kind of requirement in English criminal law. Traditionally, offences consist of objectively defined conduct (or circumstances, or events) and mental states (or other fault elements, such as negligence), subject to objectively defined circumstances of justification or excuse (such as self-defence or duress). In general the fact-finders' task is to determine whether the defendant's conduct falls within the legal definition of the offence, not whether they think it sufficiently blameworthy to be an offence. A requirement that the conduct in question fall short of an undefined moral standard is out of keeping with this approach . . . .

5.13 A closer analogy to *Ghosh* dishonesty, perhaps, is gross negligence manslaughter. The law requires the jury to determine whether the defendant's conduct was careless enough to be criminal, but does not tell them how careless it needs to be. It therefore requires the jury not just to *apply* a standard, but also to *set* it. Arguably this is no different in principle from the kind of enquiry required by *Ghosh*. But in one sense it is more objective, because the riskiness of a person's conduct is more quantifiable than its dishonesty. Given enough facts, risk can be mathematically assessed . . . . In the case of dishonesty, however, even this degree of objectivity does not exist. Dishonesty is not quantifiable, even in theory . . . . The fact-finders are required not merely to place the defendant's conduct at an appropriate point on the scale, but to construct their own scale. . . .

5.17 The test in *Ghosh* provides a way for fact-finders to apply the 'ordinary standards of reasonable and honest people', presumably by applying their common understanding of the word. But this amounts to an appeal to a unified conception of honesty which we do not think is workable in modern society. We live in a heterodox and plural society which juries (and to a lesser extent magistrates) presumably replicate. To assume that there is a single community norm or standard of dishonesty, discernible by twelve (or even ten) randomly selected people of any age between 18 and 65, and of widely varied class, cultural, educational, racial and religious backgrounds, is unrealistic. How juries cope with these problems we cannot tell, given the prohibition on research into jury discussion. It seems inconceivable, however, that different juries do not come to different decisions on essentially similar facts . . . .

The dishonesty test redefined: *Ivey v Genting Casinos [2017]—Ghosh* overruled?

This is a recent case concerning a civil suit taken by a professional gambler against a Mayfair casino. Mr Ivey sought to recover his winnings (£7.7 million) from the casino after playing a game called Punto Banco Baccarat. He used a technique called edge-sorting which involved looking at the edges of cards and spotting very small differences, which he did by persuading the croupier to rotate the cards so that he could see them clearly. He told her that he always did this as he was superstitious. The technique improved his chances of winning. The casino refused to pay out his winnings, alleging that he had cheated and was therefore in breach of his contract with them. He argued that he could not have cheated, as he was not dishonest—instead, what he had done was simply an example of good gamesmanship. The definition of dishonesty under the *Ghosh* test required that that defendant knew that was he was doing was dishonest according to the standards of reasonable people. It was this limb, he argued, which was not satisfied: he did not consider himself to be dishonest according to the standards of reasonable people.

The concept of 'cheating' is defined under s42 Gambling Act 2005. It had been found to include dishonesty (*R v Scott* [1975] AC 819). However, that was not a gambling case, but a case of conspiracy to defraud. Nonetheless, *Ivey* contended that as a matter of ordinary English the idea of cheating includes the idea of dishonesty. The Supreme Court rejected this contention, stating that cheating need not involve dishonesty. Lord Hughes (delivering a judgment with which Lord Neuberger, Lady Hale, Lord Kerr and Lord Thomas agreed) then went on to discuss the concept of dishonesty in greater detail.

Lord Hughes:

49 . . . where it applies as an element of a criminal charge, dishonesty is by no means a defined concept. On the contrary, like the elephant, it is characterised more by recognition when encountered than by definition. Dishonesty is not a matter of law, but a jury question of fact and standards. Except to the limited extent that section 2 of the Theft Act 1968 requires otherwise, judges do not, and must not, attempt to define it: R v Feely [1973] QB 530 . . . accordingly. dishonesty cannot be regarded as a concept which would bring to the assessment of behaviour a clarity or a certainty which would be lacking if the jury were left to say whether the behaviour under examination amounted to cheating or did not . . . .

53 This reflects the view of the Criminal Law Revision Committee that dishonesty is a matter left to the jury: it said at para 39 that 'dishonesty is something which laymen can easily recognise when they see it'. That is not to suggest that there is not room for debate at the fringes of whether particular conduct is dishonest or not, but the perils of advance definition would no doubt have been greater than those associated with leaving the matter to the jury. Over the succeeding half century whilst there have undoubtedly and inevitably been examples of uncertainty or debate in identifying whether some conduct is dishonest or not, juries appear to have coped well with applying an uncomplicated lay objective standard of honesty . . .

He went on to say that the *Ghosh* test has had problems:

> 56 The occasion for the analysis of dishonesty in Ghosh was a tangle of what was perceived to be incon-
> sistent decisions, some of which were said to apply a subjective test, and others of which were said to
> apply an objective one. Those terms were not always as plain to jurors as they have become to lawyers . . .
>
> 57 . . . however, it can be seen that there are a number of serious problems about the second leg of
> the rule adopted in *Ghosh*.
>
> (1)   It has the unintended effect that the more warped the defendant's standards of dishonesty are,
>   the less likely it is that he will be convicted of dishonest behaviour.
>
> (2)   it was based on the premise that it was necessary in order to give proper effect to the principle
>   that dishonesty and especially criminal responsibility for it, must depend on the actual state of
>   mind of the defendant, whereas the rule is not necessary to preserve this principle.
>
> (3)   It sets a test which jurors and others often find puzzling and difficult to apply.
>
> (4)   It has led to an unprincipled divergence between the test for dishonesty in *criminal* proceed-
>   ings and the test of the same concept when it comes to a civil action.
>
> (5)   It represented a significant departure from the pre Theft Act 1968 law, when there is no indica-
>   tion that such a change had been intended.
>
> (6)   Moreover, it was not compelled by authority. Although the *pre-Ghosh* cases were in a state of some
>   entanglement, the better view is that the preponderance of authority favoured the simpler rule that
>   once the defendant's state of knowledge and belief has been established, whether that state of mind
>   is dishonest or not is to be determined by the application of the standards of the ordinary honest
>   person, represented in a criminal case by the collective judgment of jurors or magistrates.

In *Ghosh*, the second leg of the test is formulated according to the defendant's perception of society's expectations. If his behaviour does not conform to a general standard he would not be guilty. It is not based on the entirely subjective view of the defendant alone. The *Ghosh* test attempts to avoid the pure subjectivity of this view. Nonetheless. this subjective test still has substantial problems. Firstly, the defendant's view of society's standards may not be correct:

> . . . it is not in the least unusual for the accused not to share the standards which ordinary honest people
> set as standards as a whole . . . the acquisitive offender may, it is true, be this cheerful character who
> frankly acknowledges he is a crook, but very often he is not, but justifies his behaviour to himself. Just
> as convincing himself is frequently the stock in trade of the confidence trickster, so the capacity of all of
> us to persuade ourselves that what we do is excusable knows no bounds . . . there is no reason why the
> law should excuse those who make a mistake about what contemporary standards of honesty are . . . .

In short, the two limbed test in *Ghosh* was rejected by this case:

> there can be no logical or principled basis for the meaning of dishonesty . . . to differ according to
> whether it arises in a civil action or a criminal prosecution. Dishonesty is a simple, if occasionally
> imprecise, English word. It would be an affront to the law if its meaning differed according to the kind
> of proceedings in which it arose.
>
>   these several considerations provide convincing grounds for holding that the second leg of the test
> propounded in *Ghosh* does not correctly represent the law and that directions based on it ought no
> longer to be given . . . when dishonesty is in question the fact finding tribunal must first ascertain
> (subjectively) the actual state of the individual's knowledge or belief as to the facts. The reasonableness
> or otherwise of his belief is a matter of evidence going to whether he held the belief, but it is not an
> additional requirement that his belief must be reasonable; the question is whether it is genuinely held.
> When once his actual state of mind as to knowledge or belief as to facts is established, the question
> whether his conduct was honest or dishonest is to be determined by the fact finder by applying the ob-

jective standard of ordinary decent people. There is no requirement that the defendant must appreciate that what he has done is, by those standards, dishonest.

Appeal dismissed.

Note that the discussion of dishonesty is strictly obiter since the Supreme Court held that dishonesty did not have to be proved in this case. However, given the terms in which it was set out and the fact that it was agreed unanimously by five Supreme Court judges, it is unlikely that future courts will not follow it.

This decision will have far-reaching consequences for the law on property offences, including fraud, as it seems to suggest that the test for dishonesty will be an objective one. It means that the prosecution will no longer need to prove that the defendant is aware that his actions are dishonest according to the standards of reasonable and honest people. A court can therefore conclude that a defendant is dishonest on the basis of his actions and thoughts at the time of committing an offence. It will be up to the jury to decide whether these thoughts and actions are dishonest according to the standards of ordinary people.

Do you think that this test represents a better approach than that in *R v Ghosh*?

Intention permanently to deprive another of property

This is the second element of MR which must be proved against D in accordance with s1 Theft Act 1968. D must be dishonest in the appropriation of property belonging to another and must also intend permanently, not temporarily, to deprive at the time of appropriation. The term 'intention permanently to deprive' is not defined in the Theft Act. In most cases, it will be self-evident. Let us suppose that D surreptitiously takes your mobile telephone out of your bag and sells it or takes £10 from your wallet and spends it. D's intention to permanently deprive you of your property at the time of appropriation is clear and may be inferred from the facts. D might be apprehended before he either sells or spends. You may recover your property. That does not matter. The focus is on D's state of mind at the time.

Intention is given its ordinary meaning (purpose) or is defined in accordance with *Nedrick/ Woollin*, that is: foresight of a virtual certainty of deprivation. Therefore, foresight of a possibility or probability is not enough.

Temporary deprivations

a. Abandonment

Suppose D appropriates property and then abandons it? Abandonment of property is not inconsistent with an intention to permanently deprive:

 EXAMPLE 12.10

a. I appropriate your briefcase and, finding nothing in it, throw it away. My intention/ knowledge that you are virtually certain never to recover your briefcase may be inferred.

b. However, suppose I drive away your car and abandon it after 50 miles. The chances of you recovering your car are far higher than recovering your briefcase because the registration of car ownership is well known to be centrally controlled and traceable. In this case, there can be no inference of intention for I will know that you will eventually recover the car, even if it is a wreck.

Taking and driving away a vehicle and then abandoning it after appropriation is therefore not theft but a separate offence under s12(1) Theft Act 1968:

Section 12(1) Taking an unauthorised conveyance:

. . . a person shall be guilty of an offence if, without having the consent of the owner or other lawful authority, he takes any conveyance for his own or another's use or, knowing that any conveyance has been taken without such authority, drives it or allows himself to be carried in or on it.

Moreover, under s1(2) Theft Act 1968, 'it is immaterial whether the appropriation is made with a view to gain or for the thief's own benefit'.

b. Temporary deprivations under s6(1)

Treating something as your own to dispose of contrary to the owner's rights
Section 6(1) gives a partial definition of intention to permanently deprive. It states in a rather complicated way that 'treating somebody else's property as your own and disposing of it' will amount to such an intention as can a borrowing. In other words, under s6(1) an intention to permanently deprive is *deemed* to arise in certain situations of *temporary* deprivation.

Section 6(1):

A person appropriating property belonging to another without meaning the other permanently to lose the thing itself is nevertheless to be regarded as having the intention of permanently depriving the other of it if his intention is *to treat the thing as his own to dispose of regardless of the other's rights*; and a borrowing or lending of it may amount to so treating it if, but only if, the borrowing or lending is for a period and in circumstances *making it equivalent to an outright taking or 'disposal'*.

Note that s6(1) is in two parts: 'to treat the thing as his own to dispose of . . .' and 'a borrowing or lending . . .'

(i) 'to treat the thing as his own to dispose of ...'

The first part applies to the following two situations where it is intended that the property taken should find its way back to the owner:

■ The 'buy-back' principle

 EXAMPLE 12.11

This principle was clearly illustrated in the following case. The offence was conspiracy to rob but the issue on appeal concerned intention to permanently deprive:

Raphael [2008] EWCA Crim 1014, [2008] Crim LR 995

V was robbed of his car by two Ds who then offered it back to him for £500. The car was abandoned when the police became involved. Both Ds were charged and convicted of conspiracy to rob. One issue on appeal was whether there was an *intention to permanently deprive* at the time of appropriation. It was held by the Court of Appeal that this was exactly the sort of case envisaged by s6(1) whereby something was taken and then offered back for V to buy if he wished. An intention permanently to deprive was deemed to arise in such circumstances.

■ The 'ransom' principle

 EXAMPLE 12.12

If I take your watch with the intention of returning it only after you have fulfilled a condition such as agreeing to pay me £30, the first part of s6(1) may again apply.

In the only case to come before the Court of Appeal on this point however, it was held that the taking must be 'for so long as to amount to an outright taking' which, according to s6(1) strictly appears to apply only to the second part and borrowing.

R v Coffey [1987] CRIM LR 498 COURT OF APPEAL

D obtained machinery from another with whom he had a business dispute. He decided to retain the machinery as ransom until the other complied with his demands. He was convicted of theft and appealed. The Court of Appeal allowed the appeal. The jury should not have convicted unless satisfied that the intended period of detention was so long as to amount to an outright taking.

 NOTE 12.8

The court did not wish to confuse a conditional taking with an intention to permanently deprive. In any event, the words 'to dispose of' appear to be crucial to s6(1) in the dictionary sense: to deal with definitely, to get rid of, to get done with, to finish (*Cahill* [1993] Crim LR 141) and are essential to any direction to the jury.

Obvious examples of s6(1) would be leaving V's property at the pawn-brokers or re-selling a part-used train ticket (*Marshall* [1998] 2 Cr App R 282, 'Property'). It applied in *DPP v J* [2002] EWHC 291 where two 14-year-olds snatched V's headphones, broke them in half and gave them back. There had been 'a disposal' by breaking. By rendering the property useless, an intention permanently to deprive could be inferred. But unless 'disposal' is given a narrow interpretation, s6(1) could be used in order to circumvent the narrowness of theft so as to apply to any type of temporary taking. It was always clear, for example, that abandoning a vehicle would not amount to a disposal (earlier in this section). Therefore, using a car as a getaway and then abandoning it does not give rise to s6(1) (*Mitchell* [2008] EWCA Crim 850). However, a wider view has sometimes been taken, eg: *Vinall* [2011] EWCA Crim 6252 where D abandoned V's bicycle, after a forcible taking, at a nearby bus shelter on a busy street in full public view. Pitchford LJ explained that:

> If the prosecution is unable to establish an intent permanently to deprive at the moment of taking it may nevertheless establish that the defendant exercised such a dominion over the property that it can be inferred that at the time of the taking he intended to treat the property as his own to dispose of regardless of the owner's rights . . .

This would be an unusual view of 'disposal' which has usually been considered to involve some sort of commercial dealing.

(ii) Borrowing or lending

The second part of s6(1) refers to borrowing or lending where it is equivalent to an outright taking or disposal. *Borrowing* something signifies an intention to return it. The usual position is illustrated by the following example:

EXAMPLE 12.13

If I legitimately borrow your bicycle and then *forget* to return it to you, there would be no intention to permanently deprive at the time of appropriation (ie: at the time of taking it), nor, indeed, later in keeping it. This will not be theft.

On the other hand, if I borrow £20 from your drawer, intending to return an equivalent amount later, the law says that I have permanently deprived you of the notes or coins appropriated unless I return exactly the same ones: *Velumyl* [1989] Crim LR 299.

However, it would be pedantic to say that an intention to restore property of equal value represents an intention permanently to deprive.

Borrowing and the essential value principle

Section 6(1) could theoretically apply to the situation where I take your Oyster card (London Underground pass) which you have credited with £15 and I use up £13 on journeys before returning it to you. You will not lose the card but will lose most of its value. However, s6(1) has been interpreted as establishing that unless all the essential quality of the property is lost, an intention to permanently deprive will not arise.

R v Lloyd [1985] QB 829 COURT OF APPEAL

Films were removed from a cinema for a few hours and private copies were made as pirate copies for resale. The original films were replaced. D was convicted of conspiracy to steal and appealed.

Lord Lane CJ held that, since there was only an intention to temporarily deprive the owners of the film, this was the opposite of an intention to permanently deprive. A mere borrowing is never enough to constitute a guilty mind unless the intention is to return the thing in such a changed state that all the goodness or virtue has gone. In this case, the goodness, virtue or practical value of the films to the owners had not disappeared.

[s6(1)] . . . has been described by JR Spencer . . . as a section which 'sprouts obscurities at every phrase' and we are inclined to agree with him. It is abstruse. But it must mean, if nothing else, that there are circumstances in which a defendant may be deemed to have the intention permanently to deprive, even though he may intend the owner eventually get back the object which has been taken . . .

In general we take the same view as Professor Griew in *The Theft Act 1968 and 1978* . . . ., namely, that s6 should be referred to in exceptional cases only. In the vast majority of cases it need not be referred to or considered at all . . .

. . . the first part of s6(1) seems to us to be aimed at the sort of case where a defendant takes things and then offers them back to the owner for the owner to buy if he wishes. If the taker intends to return them to the owner only upon such payment, then, on the wording of s6(1), that is deemed to amount to the necessary intention permanently to deprive.

It seems to us that in this case we are concerned with the second part of s6(1) . . . . This half of the subsection, we believe, is intended to make it clear that a mere borrowing is never enough to constitute the necessary guilty mind unless the intention is to return the 'thing' in such a changed state that it can truly be said that all its goodness or virtue has gone: for example *R v Beecham* (1851) 5 Cox CC 181, where the defendant stole railway tickets intending that they should be returned to the railway company in the usual way only after the journeys had been completed. He was convicted of larceny. The judge in the present case gave another example, namely, the taking of a torch battery with the intention of returning it only when its power is exhausted.

That being the case, we turn to inquire whether the feature films in this case can fall within that category. Our view is that they cannot. *The goodness, the virtue, the practical value of the films to the owners has not gone out of the article.* The film could still be projected to paying audiences, and, had everything gone according to the conspirators' plans, would have been projected in the ordinary way to audiences at the Odeon Cinema, Barking, who would have paid for their seats. Our view is that those particular films which were the subject of this alleged conspiracy had not themselves diminished in value at all. What had happened was that the borrowed film had been used or was going to be used to perpetrate a copyright swindle on the owners . . . . *That borrowing, it seems to us, was not for a period, or in such circumstances, as made it equivalent to an outright taking or disposal. There was still virtue in the film.* [Emphasis added.]

We can conclude from *Lloyd* that very few borrowings will amount to theft. There would be no problem if the Theft Act prohibited temporary borrowings. Indeed, one might say that the value of many articles of temporary duration (a football season ticket for example) is so high that even temporary deprivation should be regarded as a protected loss.

The reference in the second part of s6(1) to 'if, but only if, the borrowing or lending is for a period and in circumstances making it equivalent to an outright taking or disposal' needs to be remembered. If D forcibly takes V's car and then abandons it, there is only an intention to temporarily deprive (ie: not theft) unless the circumstances indicate an intention to retain the car so as to make it equivalent to an outright taking or disposal: *Zerei* [2012] EWCA Crim 114.

c. Disposal of property held under a condition

Section 6(2):

Without prejudice to the generality of subsection (1) above, where a person, having possession or control (lawfully or not) of property belonging to another, parts with the property under a condition as to its return which he may not be able to perform, this (if done for purposes of his own and without the other's authority) amounts to treating the property as his own to dispose of regardless of the other's rights.

Section 6(2) refers to a very specific example falling within s6(1), where D, having possession or control of V's property, parts with it under a condition as to its return which he may not be able to fulfil. This amounts to treating the property as his own to dispose of regardless of V's rights.

 EXAMPLE 12.14

I borrow your expensive camera. I am in debt and take the camera to a pawn broker/money lender and leave it as security for a loan. I intend to repay the loan in three weeks but am unable to do so. The broker keeps the camera and cannot return it to you. Section 6(2) deems there to be an intention to permanently deprive in these circumstances.

?!   THINKING POINT 12.12

Does D have an intention to permanently deprive in the following situations?

1. D uses V's mobile phone without permission intending to replace it. He makes so many calls that the batteries run flat. He then returns the phone.

2. D takes V's Arsenal season ticket without permission intending to return it later. He uses it for nine months before returning it to V.

3. D takes a booklet of supermarket loyalty coupons from an empty check-out. When she does the next week's shopping she hands vouchers to the cashier and receives a substantial discount on the bill.

Conditional intent

→ CROSS-REFERENCE

The offence of attempt is discussed in detail in Chapter 15, 15.1.

Where D explores an item of property in order to see whether it is worth stealing but decides not to do anything further, D is said to have a conditional intent to steal. This is insufficient for theft. If worthwhile property does not actually exist, there can be no appropriation of it although D might be guilty of an attempt under s1(2) and (3) Attempts Act 1981 if the facts had been as D believed them to be.

One case will illustrate this:

R v Easom [1971] 2 QB 315 COURT OF APPEAL

D picked up and rummaged through a handbag belonging to another at a cinema. Finding nothing in it worth stealing he replaced it. The bag had been attached to a woman police officer's wrist by a thread. His conviction for theft was overturned on appeal. D did not have an intention to permanently deprive of any of the contents in which he was not interested. Consequently, he also lacked the necessary MR for an attempt.

The real problem here is less concerned with the substantive offence of theft than with an attempt. At the time, there was no offence of 'attempting the impossible'. That is no longer the case. But so far as actual theft is concerned, a conditional intent is insufficient. The Court of Appeal did make a proposal in *AG's Reference (Nos 1 and 2 of 1979)* that the problem might be overcome if the indictment were worded in a general way (eg: theft of the handbag rather than of specific items such as contents). But D did not intend to steal the bag, only the contents had they been of interest to him.

SECTION SUMMARY

Theft consists of five elements each of which has its own definition and each has to be proved:

Actus reus

■ *appropriation—s3(1)*

■ *property—s4*

■ *belonging to another—s5*

The most difficult issue is that of appropriation where the owner consents.

Gomez *says that consent is irrelevant and that appropriation is a neutral concept.*

Hinks *says that the dishonest receiver of a valid gift appropriates it.*

Therefore D appropriates either with or without such consent.

Whether D has committed theft now depends on dishonesty.

Note the overlap with fraud where property has been appropriated by false representation.

Mens rea

- ▨ *dishonesty—s2(1) and the* Ghosh *test*
- ▨ *intention permanently to deprive—s6*

The s2(1) beliefs provide a partial definition of dishonesty: D will not be dishonest, and will therefore have a defence to theft, if he acts with one of those beliefs (legal right, consent, owner cannot be found).

The Ghosh *test provides a defence to theft if D believes that his conduct was not dishonest according to ordinary reasonable standards.*

Theft is defined by an intention to permanently deprive. Section 6 deems that such an intention will arise even where D intends to temporarily deprive

12.2 Robbery

12.2.1 Introduction

12.2.2 Actus Reus

12.2.3 Mens Rea

KEY CASES

Robinson [1977] Crim LR 173—robbery: a defence to theft will defeat robbery;

Hale [1978] 68 Cr App R 415—force during a continuing act of theft;

B, R v DPP [2007] EWHC 739—an express or implied threat of force will suffice;

Corcoran (1980) 71 Cr App R 104—robbery is complete at the time of appropriation.

12.2.1 Introduction

Robbery is a form of aggravated stealing: theft by the threat or use of force. Robberies include the following: muggings, car-jackings, mobile phone and iPod robberies, bag-snatching, armed robberies of banks and building societies. It comprises serious organised violent crime involving large hauls of money as well as the mugging of pocket money from a child. Robbery offences peaked in 2001/2 but now account for only 2 per cent of all police recorded crime and they continue to fall (13 per cent over the previous year). Robberies at knife point have also fallen by 14 per cent for the year ending December 2014. As you will read, in general the force required to convert a theft into a robbery need only be slight and thus the distinction between these offences is unclear. All the elements of theft must be proved before there can be a conviction.

Definition of robbery (see Diagram 12.3):

Section 8(1) Theft Act 1968:

A person is guilty of robbery if he steals, and immediately before or at the time of doing so, and in order to do so, he uses force on any person or puts or seeks to put any person in fear of being then and there subjected to force.

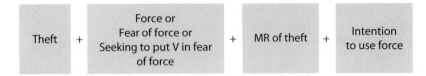

Diagram 12.3
Definition of robbery

Section 8(2):

A person guilty of robbery, or assault with intent to rob, shall on conviction on indictment be liable to imprisonment for life.

The AR consists of five main elements:

1. Theft must be proved (AR + MR).
2. Force must be used immediately before or at the time of stealing and in order to do so *or* someone must be put in *fear* of force *or* D must *seek* to put someone in fear.
3. Force must be used against a person not property.
4. Any amount of force will do.
5. Robbery is complete at the time of appropriation.

The MR has two elements:

1. MR of theft (dishonesty + intention to permanently deprive).
2. Intention to use force in order to steal.

There are many grey areas in the law of robbery in relation to which the jury must exercise common sense. We will examine each element in turn.

12.2.2 Actus Reus

Theft

Theft must be proved but note that any defence to theft will also be a defence to robbery. Therefore, if D establishes that although he appropriated property belonging to another with intention permanently to deprive, he lacked dishonesty because of a belief under s2(1) such as a belief in his right to the property, both theft and robbery will be defeated.

> ### *R v Robinson* [1977] CLR 173 COURT OF APPEAL
> ....
>
> D ran a clothing club to which V's wife owed £7. D and others met V and threatened him. In the fight, £5 fell from V's pocket. D took it and claimed that he was still owed £2. His conviction for robbery was quashed because of his honest belief in entitlement to the money. It was not necessary for him to establish an honest belief that he was entitled to take the money in the way that he did.
>
> It follows that any other defence to theft will work so as to negate robbery. Therefore, D may argue that there was no intention *permanently* to deprive. So where D forces V out of her car and,

using it as a getaway, drives it a short distance before abandoning it, there will be no theft and, in consequence, no robbery: *Mitchell* [2008] EWCA Crim 850.

The same will apply where a bicycle is taken by force with an intention to abandon it, unless it is possible to say that, when the bicycle is first taken, an intention to permanently deprive arose by virtue of s6(1). If, on the other hand, an intention to permanently deprive, whether by virtue of s6(1) or not, only arises upon abandonment, that is when theft occurs. In such a case, there will be no robbery because the force will not have been used at the time of or in order to steal: *Vinall* [2011] EWCA Crim 6252 (see 'Intention permanently to deprive another of property'). Remember that theft only protects permanent not temporary deprivation unless the temporary deprivation falls within s6 (the 'buy-back' principle, the 'ransom' principle, borrowing and lending).

Similarly, where, for example, Class A drugs are stolen from V by force, it will be no defence to argue that V's possession of the drugs was unlawful and that, consequently, no property had been stolen. The Court of Appeal held in *Smith, Plummer, Haines* [2011] EWCA Crim 66 that s4 (the property definition) is clear in providing specific and detailed exceptions and that unlawful possession is not one of them. Otherwise, the drug-misusing community would be free to steal and rob from each other with impunity.

Force must be used immediately before or at the time of stealing and in order to do so *or* someone must be put in *fear of force or* D must *seek* to put someone in fear.

There are three ways in which robbery can be committed: using force, putting someone in fear of force or seeking to do so.

Historically, the law required violence. Section 8, however, refers to force, which connotes the use of exertion, pressure or contact but not injury. Force must be used immediately before or at the time of stealing and in order to do so. Therefore there needs to be a causal connection between the use or threat of force and the theft. It follows that if the force was independent of a subsequent theft, or if the theft following the use of force was spontaneous, the causal link will not be established and robbery will be defeated.

EXAMPLE 12.15

If D strikes V to the ground with an intention to inflict violence but then notices V's iPod on the ground nearby and takes it, there will be theft (and an assault) but no robbery.

Less clear, however, is the situation where force is used during what might be seen as 'a continuing act of theft':

R v Hale (1978) 68 CR APP R 415 COURT OF APPEAL

Two men entered V's house in order to steal. D stayed downstairs and tied up the owner whilst the other went upstairs to steal a jewellery box. D's argument on appeal against conviction was that the other might have appropriated the jewellery box upstairs before he used force against the owner and that therefore the force would not have been immediately before or at the time of stealing and in order to do so. The Court of Appeal held that as appropriation is a continuous act, it was a matter of fact for the jury to decide whether or not the appropriation upstairs had finished by the time force was used. Since the intention to deprive the owner permanently was a continuing one, as a matter of common sense, D was in the course of stealing and the force used was in order to steal.

R v Lockley [1995] CLR 656 COURT OF APPEAL

D took cans of beer from an off-licence and when approached by the shop-keeper used violence. He appealed against a conviction of robbery and submitted that the theft had been completed before he used force. It was held that *Gomez* did not preclude the conclusion that appropriation was a continuing act and that therefore the force was used in order to steal. These two cases arguably extended the concept of robbery beyond the clearly defined incident of theft.

Force must be used against a person not property

Force must be used against a person not property. If force is used on any person in order to steal, the offence will be robbery and not theft. A pickpocket, applying no force to the person, would be guilty of theft. An armed bank-robber would be guilty of robbery. Between these two extremes, however, force assumes many shades of grey (see the section which follows 'Any amount of force will do—no matter how slight').

Force need not necessarily be used against the person in possession. In *Smith v Desmond* [1965] 1 All ER 976 the House of Lords confirmed the convictions of two men who had robbed a night-watchman and a maintenance engineer in a bakery where force was used on them in order to steal from an office under their care but some distance away.

If force does not need to be used against the person in possession of the property, D. Ormerod in *Smith & Hogan's Criminal Law*, 9th edn, OUP, 2009 surmises that robbery could be committed where D tells his wife that he is going out to steal a new suit and locks her in a cupboard when she threatens to telephone the police.

Any amount of force will do—no matter how slight

In *Dawson v James* (1976) 64 Cr App R 64 the Court of Appeal held that a push or a nudge causing V to lose balance would be sufficient. Force was an ordinary word that could be left to the jury. A sailor on shore leave at Liverpool Pier Head waiting for a ferry was surrounded by two men, one standing on either side of him, who nudged him on the shoulder, causing him to lose his balance. While trying to keep his balance, a third man got his hand into the sailor's pocket and took his wallet. This was followed in *R v Clouden* [1987] Crim LR 56 where D wrenched a shopping bag from V's hands and ran off. The Court of Appeal held that s8 required any amount of force to be used against a person in order to steal and not only that which was sufficient to overpower or prevent resistance from the victim as under the former law. In the next case, it was held that where D snatches a cigarette from V's hand with no physical contact between them, the absence of physical force against the victim precludes a finding of robbery:

DPP v RP [2012] EWHC 1657 (ADMIN)

Mitting J:

There was, on the facts found by the court, no physical contact between the hand of RP and the hand of Mrs Gill. The court was invited to consider the case on the basis that the mere snatching of a cigarette from between the fingers of Mrs Gill was sufficient to amount to the use of force on her person. I remind myself that borderline questions, such as a question of what amounts to the use of force on a person when the force used is minimal, are questions for the court at first instance and that it is not for an appellate court to put a gloss on the words in Section 8 of the Theft Act.

However, in the stated case, the court did not find as a fact that RP used force on Mrs Gill. What the court found clearly was that a cigarette was snatched, on the prosecution case, without there being contact with Mrs Gill, that that amounted to the use of force by RP and that the force was used in order to steal the cigarette. Those findings were clearly all open to the court but they do not amount to a finding that force was used on the person of Mrs Gill, unless the mere removal of a cigarette from between her fingers itself is capable of amounting to the use of force upon her person.

A mere threat of force is sufficient

The threat does not need to result in actual fear or the actual infliction of force. Section 8 requires that D puts or *seeks* to put any person *in fear of being then and there* subject to force. Therefore, a futile threat against a deaf, blind or sleeping person will suffice.

B, R v DPP [2007] EWHC 739 (ADMIN) QUEEN'S BENCH DIVISION

A 16-year-old schoolboy (W) was surrounded on the street by a group of teenage males aged around 14 or 15 demanding he hand over his mobile phone and wallet. W refused to do so. A number of the males, including the appellant (B), went into his pockets and took his wallet from his inside pocket, his watch from an outside pocket and his travel card. A £5 note was removed from the wallet; the wallet was then thrown to the ground. The victim did not feel 'particularly threatened' or 'scared' and he was not physically assaulted. He was 'a bit shocked'. Two of the group were convicted of robbery and appealed.

It was argued on behalf of another appellant R that he had been involved in a theft but not robbery. On behalf of B it was argued that, in the absence of actual force, the victim not being frightened, there was no robbery.

Smith LJ:

As a matter of common sense, on the facts of the case, W was subjected to some force and the threat of force by an intimidating group of boys. The intent was to steal his possessions or some of them. He did not stand there, allowing his pockets to be searched with his arms held, simply as an act of generosity. There was furthermore ample evidence from the police officers who observed the incident to justify these conclusions. The precise semantic description of the incident by W does not require any contrary conclusion. In any event it is worth underlining that W himself, if one is to take his evidence literally, said on the findings in the case that he had been threatened, albeit not particularly threatened, and he was a bit shocked. . . . The fact that the victim did not feel threatened or put in fear in no way requires the conclusion that the assailant did not seek to put him in fear. Were it otherwise, the bravery of the victim would determine the guilt of the assailant. That cannot be right. The fact that in *Grant v CPS*, unreported, decision of 10th February 2000, the victim was in fear does not mean that a conviction cannot stand if the fortitude of the victim in any particular case was such that he was not. . . . *Applying the wording of the statute and in cases where property is in fact stolen, it is the intention of the perpetrator rather than the fortitude of the victim which is the touchstone of whether the offence is robbery or theft. The answer to question (1)(a) and (b) is 'yes'.*

A threat of force can be express, that is stated in so many words, or implied, that is implied from other words or conduct or both. Here, on the facts set out in the case, there was every reason to conclude that there was an implied threat of force. The answer to question (2) is 'no'. [Emphasis added.]

Appeals dismissed. A threat of future force is probably not sufficient unless it can be said that D will still be on the job of stealing at that point.

Robbery is complete at the time of appropriation

In *Corcoran v Anderton* (1980) 71 Cr App R 104 two Ds tried to take V's handbag by force and snatched it from her grasp. It was then dropped and they ran off without it. The Court of Appeal held that theft was complete when it was snatched from V's grasp. Ds' argument that this was only an attempt was rejected. The snatching constituted the appropriation and provided all other elements of theft existed at that point, this was theft accompanied by the use of force and hence a robbery.

Intention to deprive is not to be confused with appropriation

In *R v Vinall (George Alfred)* [2011] EWCA 2652 a youth and his friend had been cycling when they met the appellants. One of the appellants punched D and said 'I have a knife'. They then followed D and took his bicycle. They then walked off with it and abandoned it by a bus shelter. The Court of Appeal allowed their appeals against conviction. The trial judge had been wrong to direct the jury it could be robbery if theft had been committed at the moment of abandonment: the force would not then have been used in order to steal. However, the jury could have used the abandonment (that is: treating the bicycle as their own to dispose of) to infer that they had intention to permanently deprive at the time of taking the bicycle.

12.2.3 Mens Rea

As you can see from the preceding section the MR for theft must be proved. Dishonesty will be determined according to the *Ivey* test. In addition, accidental, negligent or reckless force is insufficient. Use of force must be intentional.

It is easy to see how the crime figures for robbery are on the rise given that the element of force is so easily satisfied. Read the following by A. Ashworth, 'Robbery Re-assessed' [2002] *Crim LR* 851:

. . . the dividing line between robbery and theft is anything but robust. This is not necessarily a criticism of the legal definition, since many offences inevitably have fuzzy edges. But the term 'uses force' has been interpreted so as to include relatively slight force, such as barging into someone or tugging at a handbag in such a way that the owner's hand is pulled downwards. The effect is to label such offences as robbery rather than theft, and to put them in a category which has life imprisonment as the maximum penalty.

. . . robbery is a single offence: 'robbery with violence' and armed robbery are not legal terms of art, however often they may appear in crime novels. The single offence is also extraordinarily broad. The maximum penalty for theft is seven years' imprisonment; but, where force or the threat of force is used in order to steal, the category of robbery covers everything from a push or a raised hand in order to snatch a bag, to the most violent robbery of a security vehicle with guns fired and so forth. The single maximum penalty, life imprisonment, covers the whole range. The contrast with other offences involving violence is stark. Although English law remains in a rather antiquated state, the Offences Against the Person Act 1861 provides a ladder of non-fatal crimes . . . . However, no one has been heard to suggest that we should have a single offence of violence, such as 'using force on another person', to replace everything from common assault to wounding with intent . . . . If we (rightly) reject a single offence of violence, should we not also object to such a broad and undifferentiated offence as robbery, based on using or threatening force of any degree? I would argue that the offence of robbery is objectionable because it fails to mark in a public way the distinction between a mere push and serious violence, and because the label 'robbery' is therefore too vague and too liable to stereotypical interpretations – some may assume that serious violence, or a weapon, was involved when this was not necessarily the case.

?! THINKING POINT 12.13

Has D committed robbery?

1. D enters a museum just before closing time with the intention of stealing ancient antiquities from the third floor. As he descends the stairs with the property he is confronted by a museum attendant. D hits him over the head and knocks him unconscious.

2. D approaches a blind person (V) from behind and shouts 'Give me your bag or you'll get this'. He waves a knife at V's back. Unknown to D, V is also deaf and does not hear. D grabs V's bag from her hand.

SECTION SUMMARY

Robbery is defined in s8(1) Theft Act 1968 as theft accompanied by the use or threat of force:

Actus reus

The AR consists of five main elements:

- *Theft must be proved (AR + MR). Failure to prove theft will defeat robbery.*
- *Force must be used immediately before or at the time of stealing and in order to do so OR someone must be put in fear of force OR D must seek to put someone in fear. Robbery is a serious offence. If the theft is not accompanied by one of the above as part of the incident of theft, the offence is theft not robbery.*
- *Force must be used against a person not property.*
- *Any amount of force will do. A common sense approach is taken to this.*
- *Robbery is complete at the time of appropriation. Appropriation can be continuing.*

Mens rea

- *MR of theft (dishonesty + intention to permanently deprive).*
- *Intention to use force in order to steal.*

12.3 Handling

12.3.1 Introduction

12.3.2 Actus Reus

12.3.3 Mens Rea

KEY CASES

AG's Reference (No 1 of 1974)—goods cannot be handled if under police control;

Pitham & Hehl [1976] 65 Cr App R 45—handling must be 'otherwise than in the course of stealing'.

12.3.1 Introduction

The crime of handling stolen goods concerns acts of assistance following theft, including receiving, transporting, keeping, hiding, negotiating for the sale of stolen property and selling it. The maximum sentence is higher than for theft on the basis that handling, by facilitating disposal of the proceeds of theft, contributes to its prevalence.

Definition of handling

Section 22 Theft Act 1968:

(1) A person handles stolen goods if (otherwise than in the course of the stealing) knowing or believing them to be stolen goods he dishonestly receives the goods, or dishonestly undertakes or assists in their retention, removal, disposal or realisation by or for the benefit of another person, or if he arranges to do so.

(2) A person guilty of handling stolen goods shall on conviction on indictment be liable to imprisonment for a term not exceeding 14 years.

This definition is illustrated in Diagram 12.4. The actus reus consists of four elements:

Actus reus

1. The goods must be 'stolen'.

2. Goods includes proceeds of sale.

3. Handling means *receiving, undertaking, assisting or arranging*.

4. Handling must be otherwise than in the course of stealing.

The MR has two elements:

Mens rea

1. Knowledge or belief.

2. Dishonesty.

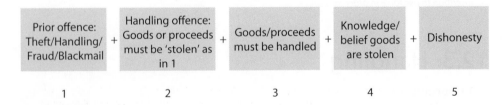

Diagram 12.4
Definition of handling stolen goods

12.3.2 Actus Reus

The goods must be stolen

Goods obtained by theft, handling, blackmail or fraud are regarded as 'stolen.' Therefore, the goods in question must be the ill-gotten gains of one of these crimes. It follows that the original crime must already have been completed and all elements of that crime must be proved. Therefore, if the original thief/blackmailer/handler or fraudster successfully pleads a specific property defence, such as lack of dishonesty, this will defeat his offence and the goods will not be 'stolen' or previously 'handled' and so on. In that case, no-one can subsequently be convicted of handling.

On the other hand, a successful plea of an excusatory defence such as duress or insanity by the original 'thief', will not prevent a later handling conviction. Such a defence will be personal to him but that does not mean that the original crime did not occur or that the goods cannot later be handled.

→ CROSS-REFERENCE
Defences of compulsion are discussed in detail in Chapter 9.

The goods must be 'stolen' at the time of handling. This may not be the case if they have been restored to the owner. Section 24(3) provides the following:

> But no goods shall be regarded as having continued to be stolen goods after they have been restored *to the person from whom they were stolen or to other lawful possession or custody*, or after that person and any other person claiming through him have otherwise ceased as regards those goods to have any right to restitution in respect of the theft. [Emphasis added.]

The question of whether goods have been restored before being handled by D can be quite technical. If they have been restored to the person from whom they were stolen there is no difficulty. But the Act says that they can be restored to 'other lawful possession or custody'.

> **▼ EXAMPLE** 12.16
>
> A police officer enters a flat at which stolen property is being stored and keeps watch from a cupboard to see who will come to collect it with a view to trapping the handler. Has the property been restored by being under his/her supervision? It all seems to depend on the intention of the police officer concerned: were his actions intended to exercise control over the property or was it simply a case of wait and see?
>
> In the first case, restoration will have occurred and there can be no handling. In the second case, they will not have been restored and handling will still be possible.

AG's Reference (No 1 of 1974) [1974] QB 744 COURT OF APPEAL
· ·

A police officer found an unlocked, unattended car containing packages of new clothing which he suspected to be and which proved to be stolen. He immobilised the car and kept watch. After ten minutes, D appeared and attempted to start the engine. He was questioned and arrested. Had the goods ceased to be stolen?

Lord Widgery CJ:

> After hearing argument, the judge accepted the submission of the respondent and directed the jury that they should acquit on the receiving count . . . . it will be observed that from the earliest times it has been recognised that if the owner of stolen goods resumed possession of them, re-

duced them into his possession again, that they thereupon ceased to be stolen goods for present purposes and could certainly not be the subject of a later charge of receiving based on events after they had been reduced into possession . . . .

When the police officer discovered these goods and acted as he did, was the situation that he had taken possession of the goods, in which event, of course, they ceased to be stolen goods? Or was it merely that he was watching the goods with a view to the possibility of catching the receiver at a later stage? . . .

In our judgment it depended primarily on the intentions of the police officer. If the police officer seeing these goods in the back of the car had made up his mind that he would take them into custody, that he would reduce them into his possession or control, take charge of them so that they could not be removed and so that he would have the disposal of them, then it would be a perfectly proper conclusion to say that he had taken possession of the goods. On the other hand, if the truth of the matter is that he was of an entirely open mind at that stage as to whether the goods were to be seized or not and was of an entirely open mind as to whether he should take possession of them or not, but merely stood by so that when the driver of the car appeared he could ask certain questions of that driver as to the nature of the goods and why they were there, then there is no reason whatever to suggest that he had taken the goods into his possession or control. [Emphasis added.]

If the original owner loses the right to have the goods restored under the civil law (the right to restitution) then the goods cease to be stolen. For example, if goods are acquired by D fraudulently but the owner discovers the fraud and nevertheless affirms the transaction, his right to restitution will be lost.

Further, if D believes the goods to be stolen when they are not, there can be no handling offence although there may be an attempt: *Haughton v Smith* [1975] AC 476 (HL).

→ **CROSS-REFERENCE**
See Chapter 15 for detailed discussion on the offence of attempt.

?!   **THINKING POINT** 12.14

D1 meets D2 in a pub—a well-known spot for the exchange of stolen Rolex watches. A police officer observes D1 handing several watches to D2. He calls for further police assistance and five minutes later he and other officers arrest D1 and D2. Has D2 handled stolen property?

Goods and their proceeds

There is a definition of goods in s34(2)(b) which equates to the definition of property for the purposes of theft in s4:

'goods', except in so far as the context otherwise requires, includes money and every other description of property except land, and includes things severed from the land by stealing.

Further, under s24(2), 'goods' includes the proceeds of sale and parts of the original goods:

For the purposes of those provisions references to stolen goods shall include, in addition to the goods originally stolen and parts of them (whether in their original state or not)–

(a) any other goods which directly or indirectly represent or have at any time represented the stolen goods in the hands of the thief as being the proceeds of any disposal or realisation of the whole or part of the goods stolen or of goods so representing the stolen goods; and

(b) any other goods which directly or indirectly represent or have at any time represented the stolen goods in the hands of a handler of the stolen goods or any part of them as being the proceeds of any disposal or realisation of the whole or part of the stolen goods handled by him or of goods so representing them.

Therefore, it is possible to handle either the original item, the proceeds of sale if it has been sold or any constituent part provided the handler knows he is acquiring stolen goods.

EXAMPLE 12.17

A thief steals computers, mobile telephones and car radios for resale either whole or in parts. D will be guilty of handling where, knowing the goods to be stolen, he:

- receives, transports, stores, keeps and finds buyers for the stolen goods;
- receives the stolen goods and sells them to X;
- receives the proceeds of sale from X;
- uses the proceeds to buy other goods ('goods so representing the stolen goods');
- receives parts of goods and either transports, stores, keeps or finds buyers for them, sells them or receives the proceeds of any sale.

If X also knows the goods are stolen, he also handles them. If X then sells the goods on to Y and Y sells them on to Z, they will all be guilty of handling (both goods and proceeds) provided they knew the goods were stolen.

In the hands of a handler

If the goods, proceeds, parts or representative goods have never been in the hands of the 'handler' then there can be no offence of handling. So, where the proceeds of sale of stolen goods are paid into the thief's bank account and an equivalent amount is transferred to X's bank account, under the common law X does not handle the money credited to that account. The case of *Preddy* confirmed that the transfer, no matter how it is made, does not involve property belonging to another. The Theft Amendment Act 1996 created two new offences to deal with this problem: one was a deception offence and is now included within s1 Fraud Act 2006. The other was dishonestly retaining a wrongful credit (s24A) and dishonest withdrawals from accounts which have been wrongfully credited.

Section 24A Retaining a wrongful credit:

(1) A person is guilty of an offence if–

 (a) a wrongful credit has been made to an account kept by him or in respect of which he has any right or interest;

 (b) he knows or believes that the credit is wrongful; and

 (c) he dishonestly fails to take such steps as are reasonable in the circumstances to secure that the credit is cancelled.

(2) References to credit are to a credit of an amount of money.

A credit is 'wrongful' if it derives from: theft, blackmail, stolen goods or fraud (contrary to s1 Fraud Act 2006). The account holder (X) must know/believe the credit was wrongful and dishonestly fail to take reasonable steps to secure that the credit is cancelled.

If the account holder (X) dishonestly withdraws money which has been wrongfully retained, he commits *handling* under s24A(8):

> References to stolen goods include money which is dishonestly withdrawn from an account to which a wrongful credit has been made, but only to the extent that the money derives from the credit.

Therefore, it matters little whether the thief/fraudster/blackmailer, having wrongfully obtained a money transfer into his account as a result of deception etc, obtains *cash* and gives it to another or makes a *credit transfer* to another's bank account. The money will have been handled in either case provided the handler knew of its origins.

 EXAMPLE 12.18

D steals £5,000 from his business partner. He pays it into his wife's bank account. She withdraws it in order to buy two plane tickets to Spain. D's wife knows the money is stolen. By failing to cancel the credit to her account and by dishonestly withdrawing the money she commits two offences: retention of a wrongful credit and handling.

Handling

Section 22 states that the handling must be (otherwise than in the course of stealing) receiving or undertaking, assisting or arranging in the retention, removal, disposal or realisation by or for the benefit of another person, or any arrangement to do so.

Handling is a comprehensive term for the various ways in which the offence may be committed.

- The goods must be *stolen* at the time of handling.
- *Receiving* need not be for anyone else's benefit. Receiving means that D must take possession or control of the stolen goods, either individually, jointly, temporarily or permanently. Unloading a lorry of stolen goods with a thief does not amount to taking possession or control (*Hobson v Impett* (1957) 41 Cr App R 138).
- *Undertaking or assisting* (or arranging to do so) must be for the benefit of another *and* the handler must assist another person to do the act. Something may only be undertaken for another person if that person could have done it for themselves.

The House of Lords in *R v Bloxham* [1982] 1 All ER 582 said that merely selling a stolen car to another person did not amount to undertaking the sale for their benefit. This would only apply where D sold on X's behalf as agent. Neither was it something that the purchaser could do for themselves for they were not in possession of the car.

Undertaking or assisting (or arranging to do so) must be in respect of retention, removal, disposal or realisation, each of which has a specific meaning:

- *Retention*: To keep possession of or not lose, that is: storing, hiding or doing anything so as to retain possession. It includes where D retains goods innocently but later discovers they are stolen and continues to keep them. D does not retain goods by failing to answer police enquiries regarding their whereabouts. Intent to retain must be proved.
- *Removal*: Transporting or carrying.
- *Disposal*: Destroying, dumping, giving away or transforming.
- *Realisation*: Selling or exchanging for something of value.

Otherwise than in the course of stealing

This qualification in s22 prevents the original thief from also being liable for handling simply on the basis of conduct constituting the original theft. It excludes liability for handling where there is continuing conduct.

> **EXAMPLE 12.19**
>
> D steals cars in one part of the country and drives them to another part where he intends to sell them. D will be guilty of theft for the dishonest appropriation of the cars with an intention to permanently deprive when the cars are taken. He will not be guilty of handling at the point of sale.

It can be difficult to determine whether a course of stealing has ended:

> ### *R v Pitham & Hehl* (1976) 65 CR APP R 45 COURT OF APPEAL
>
> Millman invited P and H into V's house and offered to sell them V's furniture which he had no right to do. They paid for it and took it away. Millman was convicted of burglary and P and H of handling. They appealed on the basis that the handling was not 'otherwise than in the course of stealing'.
>
> Lawton LJ:
>
>> What had Millman done? He had assumed the right of the owner. He had done that when he took the two appellants to 20 Party Road, showed them the property and invited them to buy what they wanted. He was then acting as the owner. He was then, in the words of the statute, 'assuming the rights of the owner.' The moment he did that he appropriated McGregor's goods to himself. The appropriation was complete. After this appropriation had been completed there was no question of these two appellants taking part, in the words of section 22 in dealing with the goods 'in the course of stealing'.
>
> Appeals dismissed.

As you can see, there may be an overlap here between handling and burglary, that is: entry as a trespasser with intent to steal.

12.3.3 Mens Rea

Knowledge or belief

D must know or believe the goods to be stolen at the time of the handling. D's participation may initially be innocent but he will be guilty of handling if he later knows or believes the goods to be stolen. Remember that under s3(2), a bona fide purchaser of stolen goods who later learns they are stolen will be protected from theft but there is no exclusion of liability for handling. If D then undertakes or assists (or arranges) in their retention, removal, disposal or realisation he will commit an offence.

The test for knowledge or belief is subjective as with all other MR elements of Theft Act offences. Therefore, D must actually know or believe the goods to be stolen but it does not matter that he does not know the precise nature of the goods (eg: where they are inside a container).

Belief must be distinguished from suspicion which is insufficient. Shutting one's eyes to the obvious (wilful blindness) does not necessarily count as knowledge or belief. It may only indicate suspicion but it is a question of fact in each case.

The doctrine of recent possession

Knowledge that goods are stolen may be inferred from the fact that D is found in possession of stolen goods and can offer no reasonable explanation for having them. Possession provides circumstantial evidence of knowledge or belief.

In addition, s27(3) states that where there is evidence of handling, evidence of an earlier handling (which need not be a conviction) before the last year can be tendered so as to dispense with MR. A conviction of handling within the previous five years can also be tendered.

All of these presumptions dispense with the usual requirement of proof of MR both in relation to the current offence and the previous incidents. It may be thought that this is less than a satisfactory way of obtaining a criminal conviction.

➜ CROSS-REFERENCE
The mens rea of theft is discussed in 12.1.

Dishonesty

The *Ghosh* test and the s2(1) Theft Act 1968 beliefs apply.

> **?!** **THINKING POINT** 12.15
>
> D would like to buy a new washing machine but cannot afford one. She meets X one day who offers her a brand new, top of the range Italian-made machine for £150 provided she buys it that day. D knows the retail price is over £500. D jumps at the chance and hands over £150 in cash to X upon delivery. The next day, D's friend, Z, admires the machine and says she would like one just like it. D tells her she can have it for £250 cash. Z, who knows the retail price, agrees and pays on delivery. D buys another identical machine from X with the money and pays the surplus £100 into her bank account. She later uses the money to buy shoes and clothes for her children. X was working for W who had stolen a consignment of Italian machines. Have D, Z or X handled stolen goods?

SECTION SUMMARY

Handling is defined by s22 Theft Act 1968:

■ *A person handles stolen goods if (otherwise than in the course of the stealing) knowing or believing them to be stolen goods he dishonestly receives the goods, or dishonestly undertakes or assists in their retention, removal, disposal or realisation by or for the benefit of another person, or if he arranges to do so.*

Actus reus

The actus reus consists of four elements:

■ *The goods must be 'stolen'.*

■ *Goods includes proceeds of sale.*

■ *Handling means receiving, undertaking, assisting or arranging.*

■ *Handling must be otherwise than in the course of stealing.*

Mens rea

■ *Knowledge or belief.*

■ *Dishonesty.*

PROBLEM SOLVING

Theft, robbery, handling:

During a long motorway journey, D stops off at an off-licence store. She needs some champagne for a party. On seeing a box of expensive bottles, she removes the price label of £100 and substitutes a label from a cheaper box of £30. She puts the box in her trolley but notices a beady-eyed security guard near the check-out and so replaces it on the shelf. She picks up a few boxes of sparkling wine instead and conceals three bottles of the expensive champagne in her overcoat pockets. On paying for the sparkling wine at the check-out the cashier (Z) gives her £50 too much change by mistake. D drives the rest of the journey home before noticing the overpayment. At her party, she sells the three expensive bottles of champagne to X. X pays a low price and is aware that D has previous convictions for theft. X sells the bottles to Y for the full price.

D returns to the store one week later and buys some wine. On her way out, Z runs after her and demands the return of the £50. Z's wages had been reduced by this amount because of her mistake. D refuses whereupon Z threatens her with a black eye and grabs D's bag. She takes £50 from D's purse, drops both bag and purse, and runs off.

Discuss the liability of D, X, Y and Z for theft, handling or robbery.

Remember:

■ **I: Identify** relevant issues

■ **D: Define** offences/defences

■ **E: Explain/evaluate** the law

■ **A: Apply** law to facts.

In dealing with property offences, you need to make sure that all elements (AR/MR) of each offence are examined. It is best to take each item in turn and address each element in relation to it. A useful technique is to think in terms of charts so as to be comprehensive. Examples are included in Tables 12.1–12.3. They illustrate a technique and not a full answer. You would be expected to write a fully argued answer, supported by clearly explained definitions, authorities and principles which you then apply to the facts.

See the online resources for further guidance on solving this problem: www.oup.com/uk/loveless6e/.

Table 12.1
D's liability: Theft Define theft (s1 Theft Act 1968): AR/MR

	Appropriation S3	Property S4	Belonging to another S5	Dishonesty S2(1) beliefs + *Ivey*	Intention permanently to deprive S6
Box of champagne/ label switching	Yes—on switching the labels: *Gomez**.	Yes	Yes	Yes	Yes
3 bottles of champagne	Yes—on picking them up and certainly by concealing them: *Gomez*.	Yes	Yes	Yes	Yes
£50 change	Yes—on taking possession. However, s3(1) also refers to a later keeping or dealing.	Yes	S5(4) applies: property obtained by another's mistake. D is under an obligation to restore.	*Ivey* may apply.* This is a question of fact for the jury.	Yes

Table 12.2

X's liability: Handling Define handling (s22 Theft Act 1968): AR/MR.

	Stolen	Goods	Handling	Otherwise than in the course of stealing	Knowledge/belief	Dishonesty
Bottles of champagne	Yes—on taking possession: *Gomez*.	Yes	Yes	Yes—D stole them.	X knows of D's previous convictions and pays a low price. She might therefore know but this would need to be proven.	Unless she can assert a belief under the *Ghosh* test, she will be regarded as dishonest.

Table 12.3

Z's liability: Robbery Define robbery (s8(1) Theft Act 1968): AR/MR

	Theft	Force/fear	Force against a person	Any amount of force	Robbery is complete at the time of appropriation	MR of theft	Intention to use force
£50	Appropriation: *Gomez*. All other AR elements are satisfied.	Yes—(a) threat of black eye: *Lockley*.	Yes by grabbing D's bag: *Clouden*.	Force used in grabbing the bag will suffice.	It does not matter that she drops the bag and purse: *Corcoran v Anderton*.	Intention is satisfied but she may have a belief of right under s2(1)(a): *Robinson*.*	Yes

* See online resources for explanation.

FURTHER READING

A. Ashworth, 'Robbery Reassessed' [2002] *Crim LR* **851**

Argues that the sentencing structure for robbery is in need of review.

S. Gardner, 'Appropriation in Theft: the Last Word?' (1993) 109 *LQR* **194**

Gardner discusses the idea of consent in appropriation with reference to the case of *Gomez*.

E. Griew, 'Dishonesty—The Objections to Feely & Ghosh' [1985] *Crim LR* **432**

Argues that the *Ghosh* test leads to inconsistent verdicts as it is too difficult for juries to understand.

R. Heaton and A.P. Simester, 'Stealing One's Own Property' (1999) 115 *LQR* **372**

A discussion of *Hinks*.

E. Melissaris, 'The Concept of Appropriation and The Offence of Theft' (2007) 70(4) *MLR* **581–597**

Article discussing the inconsistencies in the case law on appropriation by reference to the philosophical notion of actions and intentions.

D. Ormerod, 'R v Vinall: Robbery—Appropriation of Property—Subsequent Disposal' [2012] 5 *Crim LR* **387–390**

Discusses this case in which it was held that the trial judge had conflated the concepts of appropriation and intentional deprivation.

S. Shute, 'Appropriation and The Law of Theft' [2002] *Crim LR* **712**

An assessment of disagreements that *R v Hinks* is the wrong decision in cases where the owner has consented to the appropriation.

S. Thomas, 'Do Freegans Commit Theft' (2010) 30(1) *Legal Studies* **98–125**

Considers whether 'freegans' (who forage for unused food in supermarket bins) commit theft or whether they can rely on the principle that such property has been abandoned.

Property offences 2

13

Introduction

13.1 Fraud

13.2 Making off Without Payment

KEY POINTS

FRAUD

This section will help you to:

- understand the new, single offence of fraud under s1 Fraud Act 2006, which can be committed in one of three ways:
  - s2 (fraud by false representation);
  - s3 (fraud by failing to disclose information); and
  - s4 (fraud by abuse of position).
- distinguish fraud from the previous offences of deception;
- understand the new offence of dishonestly obtaining services under s11(1) Fraud Act 2006 and to distinguish it from previous offences of obtaining services by deception.

MAKING OFF WITHOUT PAYMENT

This section will help you to:

- understand that this offence under s3(1) Theft Act 1978 involves no deception but that D must dishonestly make off from the spot where payment for goods or services is required with intent never to pay.

INTRODUCTION

Fraud offences are economic crimes. They have been reformed and extended by the Fraud Act 2006 which came into force in January 2007. The old law consisted of a range of deception offences and these still apply to conduct prior to this date. The aim of the reforms was to simplify the law by introducing a single, comprehensive definition of criminal fraud. However, conspiracy to defraud was left untouched and so the aim only partially succeeded. There are many other fraud offences not covered by the Act but as these are outside the undergraduate criminal law syllabus, they will not be covered in this book: false accounting, money laundering, forgery and counterfeiting, miscellaneous offences under the Companies Acts, copyright offences, computer misuse, social security fraud, trade marks, VAT and financial services fraud.

There were two main incentives for reform:

1. Since 1968, the nature and scale of fraud dramatically changed. Internet fraud, identity fraud, fraud from individuals, charities, the public and private sector have all escalated. Fraud is estimated by the National Fraud Agency to cost the UK economy £193 billion, the largest component of which is cheque, plastic card and online banking fraud. This accounts for 75 per cent of all fraud offences. It has increased by 58 per cent since 2007/8 and has increased steadily year by year (a 4 per cent increase between 2016 and 2017). Individual victims naturally suffer emotional trauma whilst businesses can suffer damage to their reputation. Private sector business suffer the highest level of costs. With links to organised crime, terrorism and other forms of serious crime, it is a particularly difficult challenge (For more information see ONS, Statistical Bulletin, Crime in England & Wales, Year Ending September 2017: www.ons.gov.uk/peoplepopulationandcommunity/crimeandjustice/bulletins/crimeinenglandandwales/june2017#what-is-happening-to-trends-in-fraud).

2. This volume of fraud imposed considerable strain on the old deception offences for a machine, such as a computer or bank cash dispenser could not be deceived. Deception offences were result crimes and the definition of deception required someone to actually believe in a false representation and to act in reliance on that belief. Therefore, only people and not machines could be conned or deceived. Now, rather than concentrating on the impact of deception on the mind of the victim, the new offence of fraud focuses on the intentions of the defendant.

It is in this area of law that traditional notions of serious or real crime are confronted particularly when considering white-collar economic fraud offences. No individual offence of dishonesty, irrespective of its impact on the victim, can be regarded as minor. Yet society tends to perceive the mugging of mobile phones, classified as robbery, more seriously than white-collar fraud which has the potential to inflict serious economic harm upon many individuals. On a large scale, economic fraud can cause irreparable damage to the interests of companies, investors and employees. For instance, thousands of investors and account-holders in the UK lost savings when the middle-eastern Bank of Credit and Commercial International (BCCI) collapsed in 1991 with undeclared debts of £7 billion, the world's largest banking fraud. The deception extended to false accounts, fictitious transactions and theft of money from individual depositors' accounts. More than £400 million was stolen from the Mirror Group Newspapers employees' pension fund in 1991 by Robert Maxwell (the proprietor) which left 30,000 pensioners with an uncertain financial future. The sort of fraud brought to our attention by the media usually concerns long, complex and costly trials prosecuted by the Serious Fraud Office. Regardless of how small or large the case, however, the law is the same.

More recently, the Serious Fraud Office has brought a prosecution against the former chief executive of Barclays along with three of his colleagues alleging conspiracy to commit fraud by false representation relating to the receipt of funds from Qatar to save the bank from being bailed out by the government during the banking and financial crisis in the early part of the decade.

→ CROSS-REFERENCE

Ivey v Genting Casinos Ltd (t/a Crockfords Club) is discussed in detail in Chapter 12.

The way in which fraud offences are proven will be affected by changes to the way that juries will be directed to find whether a defendant is dishonest, as a result of the decision in *Ivey v Genting Casinos Ltd (t/a Crockfords Club)* [2017] UKSC 67.

The offence of making off without payment contrary to s3 Theft Act 1978 is conventionally dealt with in a separate chapter in most criminal law textbooks. But it is included here because it arises in situations that might appear to closely resemble fraud. There are, however, significant differences that need to be understood.

13.1 Fraud

13.1.1 The Fraud Act 2006

13.1.2 Section 2: Fraud by False Representation

13.1.3 Section 3: Fraud by Failing to Disclose Information

13.1.4 Section 4: Fraud by Abuse of Position

13.1.5 Section 11: Obtaining Services Dishonestly

13.1.1 The Fraud Act 2006

All sorts of euphemisms are used to describe fraud: scam, con, swindle, bamboozle and cheat. The offence is, essentially, one of dishonest representation.

The Fraud Act has introduced a new fraud offence with a maximum ten-year sentence. Fraud is not defined and is more straightforwardly based on dishonesty. It is a 'conduct' offence and does not therefore depend on V being induced to believe in the fraud. Key concepts such as dishonesty and property continue to be defined in accordance with s4 Theft Act 1968 and the *Ghosh* test (now changed by *Ivey*). The new reforms are not without criticism as we shall see.

KEY CASES

Ray [1974] AC 370—deception by silence or conduct;

Silverman [1988] 86 Cr App R 213—deception by silence in a situation of trust;

Charles [1977] AC 177—implied representation by use of cheque card;

Lambie [1982] AC 449—implied representation by use of credit card;

Gilbert & Ors [2012] EWCA Crim 2392—the intent to gain/risk/cause loss must arise from the specific false representation alleged;

Valujevs (Juris) [2015] 3 WLR 109—meaning of position of trust.

Definition

Section 1 Fraud:

(1) A person is guilty of fraud if he is in breach of any of the sections listed in subsection (2) (which provide for different ways of committing the offence).

(2) The sections are–

    (a) section 2 (fraud by false representation),

    (b) section 3 (fraud by failing to disclose information), and

    (c) section 4 (fraud by abuse of position).

(3) A person who is guilty of fraud is liable–

    (a) on summary conviction, to imprisonment for a term not exceeding 12 months or to a fine not exceeding the statutory maximum (or to both);

    (b) on conviction on indictment, to imprisonment for a term not exceeding 10 years or to a fine (or to both).

The Fraud Act 2006 abolished eight previous offences, the most prevalent of which were obtaining property (including money) by deception (s15 Theft Act 1968), obtaining a pecuniary advantage by deception (such as an overdraft: s16 Theft Act 1968) and obtaining services by deception (s1 Theft Act 1978). They have been replaced by a single fraud offence under s1 above which can be committed in one of three ways in ss2–4.

13.1.2 Section 2: Fraud by False Representation

(1) A person is in breach of this section if he–

    (a) dishonestly makes a false representation, and

    (b) intends, by making the representation–

        (i)   to make a gain for himself or another, or

        (ii) to cause loss to another or to expose another to a risk of loss.

(2) A representation is false if–

    (a) it is untrue or misleading, and

    (b) the person making it knows that it is, or might be, untrue or misleading.

(3) 'Representation' means any representation as to fact or law, including a representation as to the state of mind of–

    (a) the person making the representation, or

    (b) any other person.

(4) A representation may be express or implied.

(5) For the purposes of this section a representation may be regarded as made if it (or anything implying it) is submitted in any form to any system or device designed to receive, convey or respond to communications (with or without human intervention).

Section 2 fraud by false representation consists of the following elements:

- ■ AR: D must make a false representation;
- ■ MR: D must *know* that the representation was false or that it might be false and that he acted *dishonestly* with *intent* to gain or cause loss.

Section 2 covers the obtaining of property including cheques or other financial advantage by fraud and an attempt to do so. It covers fraud in any commercial context from false mortgage or life insurance applications, the fraudulent use of credit and cheque guarantee cards, to filling up the car with petrol, making a false representation about later payment and driving off. Electronic/internet fraud would be included. The offence covers all that was covered by the repealed deception offences. It is therefore a wide offence.

There is a degree of overlap with s3 Fraud Act (fraud by failing to disclose information) where the contract applied for is one where there is a legal duty of utmost good faith, such as insurance contracts. This implies a duty to disclose all material facts before entering the contract. There is also an overlap with theft. Remember that following *Gomez*, appropriation has a neutral definition and can apply where property has been appropriated either with or without consent. If property has actually been obtained therefore, whether by consent or not, it will be both stolen and acquired by false representation.

Actus reus

The false representation must be made by D: s2(1)(b).

A representation is a statement or an assertion of fact, law, intention, or opinion which is important in the transaction at hand. A false representation is simply a false statement, trick, con or lie. It can be made orally, in writing, by silence, by omission or by conduct. It may be made face to face but may also be made to a machine, such as a computer, an automated cash-dispenser or a chip and PIN machine (s2(5)). Whatever form it takes, it must be made by D.

Two examples of false representation by conduct would be: *Stonehouse* [1977] AC 55 where D left his clothes on a beach and disappeared, representing to the world and his wife that he was dead, and *Darwin* [2008] 2 Cr App (S) 115 where a husband's disappearance during a canoeing trip to the coast impliedly represented that he had drowned whereas he and his wife had planned the events so as to make a false insurance claim and disappear to South America.

Written or oral representations are frequently used in commercial transactions as an inducement to enter a contract. Situations will be as diverse as mortgage/loan applications, shop/internet/private purchases or bank fraud. An example would be *Cleps* [2009] EWCA Crim 894 where a 74-year-old man opened a building society account with a stolen passport and obtained £184,000 from the true account holder's account. An example of a non-commercial fraud would be *Hamilton* [2008] EWCA Crim 2518, where two defendants misrepresented themselves to an elderly woman as being authorised to remove, for £60, new fence panels she had left outside her house for collection since they were the wrong size. Further examples of representations by silence appear below.

The false representation: s2(1)(a)

Under s2(2) falsity is defined as being misleading or untrue. This is not defined in the Act but the government expressed the view that misleading meant 'less than wholly true and capable of an interpretation to the detriment of the victim' (*Fraud Law Reform*, Government response to consultation, at para 19; *Blackstone's Guide to the Fraud Act 2006*, at p 7). Many aspects of buying and selling might involve potentially misleading practices such as advertising. In contract law, there is a distinction between the acceptable mere puff (ie: obvious exaggeration) and the misleading inducement involving misrepresentation. There might be a fine line here between 'sharp practice' and an offence under s2.

> **EXAMPLE** 13.1
>
> D, a second-hand car dealer, turns back the mileage reading on all cars for sale and displays a notice to customers stating that the mileage may not be correct.
>
> The implied representation here is that D has no actual reason to believe the mileage readings to be incorrect whereas he knows very well that they are wrong. This would be held to be a false representation and an offence within s2.

Section 2(2)(b) requires that D knew the representation was false. The test is subjective. This was confirmed in *Augunas* [2013] EWCA Crim 2046 where D's conviction was overturned after he denied knowing that the bank card he used to purchase a laptop computer at Harrods was counterfeit.

By making the representation: s2(1)(b)

Although V no longer needs to rely on the false representation (see later in this section, 'V need not rely on the false representation'), there needs to be a causal link between the false representation and D's intention to make a gain or risk cause loss. The Act requires that 'by making the representation' D intends to gain, for example. This could present problems. Take the example of the car seller who falsely advertises that it has only had 'one previous lady owner' as an inducement to purchasers or some other false statement regarding the car's condition, that is: 'Engine in tip-top condition'. If this is merely one of several representations it may be possible for D to assert that he did not intend to gain by making the representation. If so, his intention will need to be considered within the MR requirements (see later in this section, Mens rea).

D may also assert that by his false representation he intended to secure a contract, such as a contract of employment, or official documents, and not to make a gain. The case against D would need to focus on his intent to make a gain by virtue of the contract secured by misrepresentation: *Dziruni* [2008] EWCA Crim 3348 (false identity documents), *Haboub* [2007] EWCA Crim 3327 (false driving licence), *Idress* [2011] EWHC 624 (driving test sat by X representing himself as D).

If gain/loss are intended due to any means other than the representation, the necessary causal link will not be satisfied:

Gilbert & Ors [2012] EWCA CRIM 2392

D and her husband gave false details to a bank to open an account for a new property company. At a meeting with the bank, her husband represented that the new company would be financed by, amongst other things, 'savings and other assets' and that the estimated turnover would be £700,000 to £800,000. D signed the application form containing this information. She and others then used post-dated company cheques to buy £130,000 worth of computers from a supplier, but stopped the cheques before they had cleared. At the time, there was only £40 in the company account. She was charged with fraud contrary to s2 Fraud Act 2006. The prosecution case against her was that the representations on the application form were false. The obtaining of the bank account was the first dishonest step towards using the company to make financial gains. Lord Judge CJ:

> The substantive ground of appeal arises out of the way the Recorder dealt with the issue of intended gain or loss and it is on this that the single judge, Hamblen J, focused when granting leave. Mrs Devas submits that at no point did the prosecution, or indeed the judge, identify a particular gain or loss. The Recorder allowed the case to go to the jury at the close of the prosecution case on the basis of the possibility of a gain arising from future legitimate property development, rather than a gain arising directly from any representation made at the meeting at the bank, or directly from the opening of the bank account. This, and the direction to the jury that it was open to them to find that a gain could be inferred if they concluded that the opening of the bank account was simply to enable development or the sale of the company, left the case on too vague a basis. The link, it is submitted, between any representation and such a possible future gain, is too tenuous. . . .
>
> An intention to make a gain (or to cause loss to another or expose another to risk of loss) is not of itself enough to meet the requirements of the section. In order to commit fraud by representation, a defendant must (a) make a false representation as defined in s.2(2)–(5) of the Act, (b) do so dishonestly and (c) intend, by making the representation, to make a gain (or to cause loss to another or expose another to a risk of loss). The jury must, therefore, be sure that the defendant intended to make a gain or cause loss or exposure to loss by making the false representation and it is a matter for the jury on the facts of each case whether the causative link between the intention and the making of the false representation, required by the section, is established. [Emphasis added.]

Appeal allowed.

The need for causation might also present a problem with credit card fraud: D may say that it was not *by* his representation that the gain was made. Instead, the gain was the result of the pre-existing agreement between stores and banks/credit companies to guarantee payment.

Neither V nor the recipient of the false representation need suffer loss

There is no need for actual harm or risk to V's property, only for D to *intend* to expose V to, or cause, loss. Therefore, the full offence can be committed in the absence of any actual threat to V's economic interests. Thus, what might previously have been an attempt now becomes a complete offence. As such, fraud offences are not result crimes. This has led D. Ormerod in 'Criminalising

Lying' [2007] *Crim LR* 193 to suggest that s2 creates an inchoate (incomplete) offence which appears to criminalise lying.

A false representation will be made even though it is not made to the ultimate victim who suffers actual loss. For example, in the triangular credit card transaction (involving fraudster, retailer and credit card company), D may use a stolen credit to purchase goods from a store. The false representation (that he has authority to use the card (see *Lambie* later)) is made to the store. But this recipient of the misrepresentation suffers no loss or risk of loss because the store will get paid by the credit company, payment being guaranteed in such cases. The loss is suffered by the credit company not by the store.

V need not rely on the false representation

The Fraud Act 2006 does not require either the deception of, or reliance by, a victim on any false representation, both characteristics of the former law. This was one of the reasons why previous deception offences were unsatisfactory. In the absence of deception or reliance, V was not deceived. The definition of deception derived from a statement of Buckley LJ in *Re London & Globe Finance Co.* [1903] 1 Ch 738:

> To deceive is, I apprehend, to induce a man to believe that a thing is true which is false . . . . to deceive is by falsehood to induce a state of mind.

Laverty [1970] 3 All ER 432 will illustrate this point. D sold to V a reconstructed second-hand car which V bought in good faith. The number plates had been changed. D was charged with obtaining property by deception under s15, the indictment identifying the false representation that the car bore its original number plates. V gave evidence at trial that he was not concerned with the number plates, only with whether D had title to sell the car. D's conviction was quashed on appeal since he had not relied on the false representation.

It followed that under the previous law, the false representation needed to precede the obtaining otherwise it would not be possible to say that D had *obtained by deception*. One case will illustrate this point. In *Collis-Smith* [1971] Crim LR 716 D went to a garage for petrol and after he had pumped it into his tank he falsely stated that he was using the car for business purposes and that his firm would pay. His conviction for obtaining property by deception was quashed by the Court of Appeal since the deception occurred after the obtaining.

The need for causation or for an 'operative' deception became a particular difficulty in relation to cheque and credit card fraud. It was virtually impossible to prove that a seller of goods had *relied* on any misrepresentation regarding either the state of the card holder's account or the validity of a card when the seller was guaranteed payment in any event by the issuing bank or company. To overcome this problem, the House of Lords in *Charles* and *Lambie* (see later in this section, 'Express or implied representation (s2(4))—cheque cards and credit cards') interpreted deception as implying a fiction: that the seller would not have completed the sale had he known that any particular card was stolen or unauthorised. The fact that the retailer had not even considered the possibility of fraud was irrelevant. The implication of a fiction was the only way to secure convictions for card fraud. The need for causation is not entirely overcome by the new law in view of the need for a link between the false representation and D's intent to make a gain or cause loss (discussed earlier).

Representations as to fact, law and states of mind (s2(3))

An example of a false representation of fact is the statement '*this ring is made of gold*', when it is known to be, in fact, made from brass or tin. The most common false statements of fact will concern the ownership of goods sold at very cheap prices, in markets, for example. It can some-times be difficult to distinguish fact from opinion: 'in my opinion, this ring is as good as gold' is clearly opinion. But 'this ring is as good as gold' could be either a statement of fact or opinion. What of 'the price of the ring is very reasonable': fact or opinion? An example of a false statement of law would be a deliberate misinterpretation or misconstruction of a legal document or notice. A false representation of a state of mind would concern the present intentions of D to use goods or money in a particular way in future, for example: 'Pay me £100 now and I will buy paint and materials to decorate your house'.

Express or implied representation (s2(4))—cheque cards and credit cards

Express representations should not be difficult to identify. Implied representations are less obvi-ous, for example: as in the previous example box. Representations are implied, for example, in the use of cheques, cheque guarantee cards and credit cards. Here, D may be in excess of any agreed overdraft or credit level or may not be the authorised card holder.

Cheque guarantee cards: Here, the representation is that the cheque will be honoured, not that there is enough money in the account at the date of the cheque.

MPC v Charles [1977] AC 177 HOUSE OF LORDS

D, who was overdrawn at the bank, was told by his bank manager he could draw one cheque a day for up to £30. He went to a casino and cashed 25 cheques for £30 each backed by a cheque guarantee card. He was clearly not a good gambler because he lost his money, the cheques being met by his bank in due course. D was convicted under s16(2)(b) of obtaining a pecuniary advan-tage (an unauthorised overdraft) and appealed.

The use of a cheque card implies a representation that when presented to the paying bank, the cheque will be honoured. Therefore, on the face of it, D's representation that his bank would honour all of his cheques was correct and not false. However, his use of the card was obviously dishonest and unauthorised because he was overdrawn. It was held that the use of a cheque card implied a further representation that one had authority to use it so as to create a contractual re-lationship between the bank and the payee. If the cheque was one that would not be met but for the use of the cheque card, D lacked authority and that was a misrepresentation.

Credit cards: Here, the representation is that the user has the bank's or credit company's authority to use the card and that payment will be made. No representation is made regarding the state of D's account or creditworthiness.

R v Lambie [1982] AC 449 HOUSE OF LORDS

D had a Barclays bank credit card with a limit of £200. She ran up a debit balance of over £900. The bank sought to recover the card and D agreed to surrender it but failed to do so. She continued to use it and spent £10.35 on one transaction in Mothercare. The transaction went through but she was traced, arrested and convicted under the repealed s16(1) Theft Act 1968 for having used the card without authority. The store manager had given evidence at trial that she had made no assumption about D's credit standing with the bank. The House of Lords held that the reasoning of Charles applied equally to credit cards.

Lord Roskill:

> Following the decision of this House in *Charles*, it is in my view clear that the representation arising from the presentation of a credit card has nothing to do with the appellant's credit standing at the bank but is a representation of actual authority to make the contract with, in this case, Mothercare on the bank's behalf that the bank will honour the voucher upon presentation. Upon that view, the existence and terms of the agreement between the bank and Mothercare are irrelevant, as is the fact that Mothercare, because of that agreement, would look to the bank for payment.

False representation by silence

The representation must be made expressly or by implication. Whether an implied representation would include silence is unclear. Here are four examples of such cases under the previous law which might be relied upon in future cases:

R v Ray [1974] AC 370 HOUSE OF LORDS

D and some friends entered a restaurant and ordered a meal with the intention of paying. Some time after consuming the food, D changed his mind and decided not to pay. When the waiter was out of the room D ran out of the restaurant. He was charged with a deception offence (s16(2)(a) Theft Act 1968—evasion of an obligation to pay—it was later repealed because of its complexity).

Lord MacDermott:

> In my opinion the transaction must for this purpose be regarded in its entirety, beginning with the respondent entering the restaurant and ordering his meal and ending with his running out without paying. The different stages of the transaction are all linked and it would be quite unrealistic to treat them in isolation.
>
> Starting then, at the beginning one finds in the conduct of the respondent in entering and ordering his meal evidence that he impliedly represented that he had the means and the intention of paying for it before he left. . . . If this representation had then been false and matters had proceeded thereafter as they did (but without any change of intention) a conviction for the offence charged would . . . have had ample material to support it. But as the representation when originally made in this case was not false there was therefore no deception at that point. Then the meal is served and eaten and the intention to evade the debt replaces the intention to pay. Did this change of mind produce a deception?
>
> My Lords, in my opinion it did . . . . it did falsify the representation which had already been made because that initial representation must, in my view, be regarded not as something then as spent and past but as a continuing representation which remained alive and operative and had already resulted in the respondent and his defaulting companions being taken on trust and treated as ordinary, honest customers. It covered the whole transaction up to and including payment and must therefore, in my opinion, be considered as continuing and still active at the time of the change of mind . . . . Was the respondent's evasion of the debt obtained by that deception?
>
> I think the material before the justices was enough to show that it was. The obvious effect of the deception was that the respondent and his associates were treated as they had been previously, that is to say as ordinary, honest customers whose conduct did not excite suspicion or call for precautions. In consequence the waiter was off his guard and vanished into the kitchen. That gave the respondent the opportunity of running out without hindrance and he took it.

In order to implement the law, the House of Lords had to devise a fictional representation implied by D's silence or conduct: that the deception consisted of either the initial representation made on entering and ordering the meal which continued, remained alive and operative and then became false, or that by remaining at the table after forming his dishonest intention, he continued to make from moment to moment a false representation that he intended to pay.

These representations were fictional because the victim (waiter) in leaving the room, relied on neither. True, D was dishonest and the waiter would not have left the room had he known the truth, but he did not. Reliance, as we saw earlier, is now no longer necessary.

R v Frith [1990] 91 CR APP R 217 COURT OF APPEAL

A consultant obstetrician referred private clients to an NHS hospital for treatment, omitting to declare that they were private. He was convicted under s2(1)(a) Theft Act 1978 (exemption from liability to make a payment). His silence was an implied representation relied upon by the hospital and he was in breach of a duty to declare the truth.

R v Rai [2000] 1 CR APP R 242 COURT OF APPEAL

D's mother obtained a local authority grant for the installation of adaptations and a bathroom in her house. She died before the works began but D did not inform the authority until after the works were complete. He was charged under s1 Theft Act 1978 with dishonestly obtaining building services from the authority by deception. On appeal against conviction the Court of Appeal held that D's conduct amounted to a continuing representation that his mother was alive. He had practised a straightforward deception.

Judge David Clarke QC:

> The central issue before us was whether, on the facts of the present case, there was conduct capable of constituting that deception and in particular the circumstances in which an omission to act or silence can amount to such conduct . . .
>
> The learned judge gave a reasoned judgment, deciding this issue in favour of the Crown and ruling that his silence in those circumstances did amount to conduct sufficient to constitute a deception on the local authority. It seems to us that, in effect, he found it was capable of amounting to such conduct. Whether it did would have been, no doubt, an issue for the jury.
>
> The underlying facts which underpinned that finding were, not only that the appellant did not tell the council, but that—as was undisputed—this was his house and at all material times he lived there. When, after the learned judge's ruling, the appellant pleaded guilty, he did so on the specific factual basis that his only relevant conduct was his failure to inform the council of the death of his mother. He did not acknowledge any other conduct on his part by which the council might have been deceived . . . .
>
> The basis in the present case of the learned judge's ruling was that this appellant's conduct was equivalent to that conduct on the part of the students (in DPP v Ray [1974] AC 370), and the question for this Court is whether that was correct . . . .
>
> The learned judge held . . . in his ruling, that by simply sitting there doing nothing and allowing the work to be done, the appellant was committing a straightforward deception, because, as he was aware, the local authority were still of the mind that the mother would occupy the premises. He was living there at all material times. In the judgment of this Court, that, against the background of it being his home and he having made the application, was conduct sufficient to amount to conduct within the terms of s15(4) of the 1968 Act . . . . But, on a common-sense and purposive construction of the word 'conduct', it does, in our judgment, cover positive acquiescence in knowingly letting this work proceed as the appellant did in the present case.

The next case illustrated how easily a criminal deception might be committed by silence in a commercial setting—a controversial case:

R v Silverman [1988] 86 CR APP R 213 COURT OF APPEAL

D charged two elderly sisters excessive prices for electrical work to their central heating and wiring. He was known and trusted by them. He had applied no pressure to have his high quote accepted. The work was done satisfactorily. He was convicted of obtaining property by deception under s15 and appealed, the question of law being whether an excessively high price for work amounted to a false representation. It was conceded that he had been dishonest but he had made no positive representations that the price was reasonable. He had merely made a quote which the sisters were free to accept or reject.

It was held by the Court of Appeal that his silence on the matter amounted to a false representation. The sisters were gullible and reliant. D had taken dishonest advantage of a situation of mutual trust built up over a long period of time.

Watkins LJ:

> His silence on any matter other than the sums to be charged was as eloquent as if he had said that he was going to make no more than a modest profit.

This case demonstrated the fine line between economic exploitation, the pursuit of profit and fraud. Not all sharp practice is necessarily dishonest. Not all dishonest practice is necessarily fraudulent. The case turned on the specific facts of the case.

In contract law, silence does not amount to misrepresentation except in four situations: statements of half-truth, positive concealment, change of circumstances and contracts of utmost good faith. The rule caveat emptor (buyer beware) applies. So when you buy a house or a car, it is up to you to make the necessary inspections and surveys. It remains to be seen to what extent the civil law will influence the development of s2. In any event, s3 (failure to disclose) might be a preferable route to conviction.

Mens rea

- *Dishonesty:* The beliefs under s2(1) Theft Act 1968 do not apply (belief in right, consent and that the owner cannot be found). They did not expressly apply to old deception offences. The jury were, until recently, therefore left with the *Ghosh* test which will most certainly include reference to any relevant belief on D's part, including such beliefs to be found in s2(1). After *Ivey*, the test will be an objective one.

- *Knowing that the representation is or might be false:* This is more demanding than belief, suspicion or, indeed, recklessness which was required under the previous law. It is intended to cover knowledge of future facts. Remember that 'closing one's mind to the obvious' can amount to knowledge. It is likely it will blur into dishonesty.

- *With intent to gain or cause loss to another or to expose another to a risk of loss* by the false representation: This is the only causal link in the offence: D's false representation must be made with the intention of gaining or causing V to lose or exposing V to such risk. Gain and loss are defined in s5 very broadly (in money or other property) and include temporary deprivation, unlike theft and the old deception offences.

EXAMPLE 13.2

D sells tickets to V for a local charity event promising several attractions. D knows that the event will almost certainly be cancelled because the local authority are not satisfied with the health and safety conditions of the venue and have threatened to close it down. D is exposing V to the risk of loss.

?! **THINKING POINT** 13.1

Has D committed fraud by false representation under s2 Fraud Act 2006?

An auction house sells a painting by Picasso, believing it to be genuine. It turns out to be a forgery. Do they have MR for s2?

13.1.3 Section 3: Fraud by Failing to Disclose Information

A person is in breach of this section if he–

    (a)   dishonestly fails to disclose to another person information which he is under a legal duty to disclose, and

    (b)   intends, by failing to disclose the information–

        (i)   to make a gain for himself or another, or

        (ii) to cause loss to another or to expose another to a risk of loss.

This is a narrower offence than s2 but to some extent overlaps with it in relation to silence. The circumstances in which one is under a legal duty to disclose information derive from contract law principles. The following are included: insurance contracts (contracts of utmost good faith), statutory obligations in respect of company prospectuses and reports, the express and implied terms of a contract, custom and practice and wherever there is a fiduciary relationship between the parties. A fiduciary relationship is one of trust and confidence, for example solicitor/client or trustee/beneficiary. There will be an overlap with s4. If there is no legal duty to disclose, then the conduct will not be caught by this section. The section does not cover moral duties to disclose or moral/financial exploitation, for example:

➜ CROSS-REFERENCE

Section 4 Fraud Act 2006 is cited in 13.1.4.

- where it would be reasonable to expect disclosure in any type of commercial transaction such as house selling (*caveat emptor*);
- where an expert takes knowing advantage of someone less skilled, for example in buying antiques, art, vintage cars, etc.

The Court of Appeal in *Razoq* [2012] EWCA Crim 674 considered that a doctor who failed to disclose his suspension from practice when applying for locum positions, and who also falsified his qualification, had committed offences under s2 and s3. The latter arose because his contracts of employment expressly required disclosure.

D applies for foreign travel insurance for a forthcoming holiday and deliberately fails to disclose a recent operation involving major surgery. Whilst on holiday, her condition deteriorates and she requires expensive medical treatment. She submits a claim for this under the insurance policy.

Has she committed fraud under s3?

13.1.4 Section 4: Fraud by Abuse of Position

(1) A person iexts in breach of this section if he –

    (a) occupies a position in which he is expected to safeguard, or not to act against, the financial interests of another person,

    (b) dishonestly abuses that position and

    (c) intends, by means of the abuse of that position–

        (i) to make a gain for himself or another, or

        (ii) to cause loss to another or to expose another to a risk of loss.

(2) A person may be regarded as having abused his position even though his conduct consisted of an omission rather than an act.

'Position' is not defined. A person in a position of trust would be clearly included, for example professional and client, trustee and beneficiary, director and company, partner or councillor. A person in a position of trust may be able to abuse their position and damage the interests of a dependent person quite readily. Other examples would be employer/employee, agent/principal, within a family, voluntary work or any context where the parties are not at arm's length. This section is not restricted to fiduciary relationships although may overlap with it.

Valujevs (Juris) [2015] 3 WLR 109

Unlicensed gang-masters in Cambridgeshire allegedly abused their position by making unwarranted deductions from Latvian vegetable pickers' legitimate earnings, charging excessive rental payments for poor quality accommodation and imposing unwarranted fines, sometimes for swearing. Some workers received less than £1pw.

It was held by Fulford LJ:

    . . . to establish an abuse of position for the purposes of section 4 of the 2006 Act it is necessary for the prosecution to demonstrate a breach of a fiduciary duty, or a breach of an obligation that is akin to a fiduciary duty. This can conveniently be described, for instance, as a breach of trust or a breach of a privileged position in relation to the financial interests of another person. Section 4 does not apply to those who simply supply accommodation, goods, services or labour, whether on favourable or unfavourable terms and whether or not they have a stronger bargaining position. . . . We therefore concur with the conclusion of the judge that section 4 should not apply in 'the general commercial area where individuals and businesses compete in markets of one kind or another, including labour markets, and are entitled to and expected to look after their own interests'. We repeat, the critical factor in this case is that there is evidence that the defendants arguably assumed control of, and responsibility for, collecting the wages of the workers, or they controlled the wages at the moment that they were paid over, and the fact that they were acting as gangmasters merely provided the vital context relied on by the prosecution in which that role was assumed.

NOTE 13.1

1. To establish an abuse of position, for the purposes of s4(1)(b), s4 is not confined to situations of fiduciary duty.

2. Section 4 does not apply to the simple supply of accommodation, goods, services, nor to the overcharging for them.

3. The case fell within s4 because of the context: the gang-masters assumed control and responsibility for the workers' wages and thus each *occupied a position in which he would be expected to safeguard, or not to act against, the financial interests of that worker,* within s4(1)(a). The test for expectation here was objective according to the reasonable person.

In other words, s4 does not apply to commercial contracts in general. *Blackstone's Guide to the Fraud Act 2006* states that the section was intended to cover employees who make use of their employer's premises and equipment for their own purposes. An example would be *Gale* [2008] EWCA Crim 1344, where an office manager for DHL at Heathrow airport was convicted contrary to s4 Fraud Act 2006 after accepting a bribe in order to place a crate on a plane bound for the USA with false documentation stating that the contents were 'known' when they were not. In fact the contents consisted of 500 kilos of khat, a drug which is illegal in the USA. The court declared that D's job carried a high degree of probity and trust and that such a position was vulnerable to serious criminals aiming to smuggle contraband through customs. A further case was *Woods* [2011] EWCA Crim 1305 where the deputy manager of a betting shop changed a customer's bet from £1 to £100, enabling her to collect £990 from her employer whilst the customer correctly received £10. D. Ormerod points out that the range of possible defendants is extremely wide, from the dishonest waiter profiting from the sale of his own wine, to the company director making a personal fortune by unauthorised share transactions, to the trustee of a will/charity fraudulently dealing with legacies.

'Abuse' is not defined in s4. Omission is specifically included, unlike false representation under s2. There is therefore no need for a positive act.

Consequently, this is a very wide provision and risks contravening the ECHR requirement of legal certainty under Article 7. There will now be overlap with s3 (failure to disclose) and offences under the relatively new Bribery Act 2010. This Act creates offences of bribing or being bribed (the offer or taking of a 'financial advantage' to induce another to act improperly or to reward the improper performance).

Jennifer Collins argues that the legislation does not make it clear whose expectation is relevant here and therefore that this section is not clear. She asks whether the case 'sheds new light on the principled operation of the offence' and argues that there are dangers in using the section to cover this type of situation. There is no clear guidance from Parliament on this point. In this case, the offence was put to the jury not because the workers' rights should be safeguarded, but because the defendants had assumed responsibility and control over the workers' money, so deducting wages was problematic, and secondly, because the defendants ought to have held a licence. Collins questions the court's reasoning in deciding that a licensed gang-master is expected to safeguard the financial interests of workers:

> arguments for criminalization should not be used as trump cards in the state's response to exploitation of persons. . . . criminal lawyers must resist assuming that existing criminal offences cover exploitative conduct either intrinsically or through judicial interpretation without supporting argument.

In a further article, J. Collins in 'Fraud by Abuse of Position: Theorising Section 4 of the Fraud Act 2006' [2011] *Crim LR* 513 argues that the vagueness of s4 is due to an uncertain theoretical foundation. At its heart are the concepts of exploitation and disloyalty:

Disloyalty . . . is criminalized because it has a corrosive effect on an important basic value held by society: the importance of trust relationships where an individual is entrusted with the oversight of financial affairs of another. The risk of harm to these trust relationships (in themselves a public good) passes the threshold for criminalization. It is desirable that as citizens we can trust those who are entrusted with our financial affairs if the relevant expectation has arisen.

?!   THINKING POINT 13.3

Has D committed fraud under s4?

1. D, a Citizen's Advice Bureau adviser, professing to offer free advice and assistance, obtains compensation of £5,000 on behalf of an elderly client for whom she had taken legal proceedings. The adviser retains £1,000 for her efforts without disclosing the fact to the client.

2. D, the manager of a building society, is in dispute with her employer. She refuses to carry out her contractual duties and spends every day dealing with her own investments whilst at work. One day, she fails to notice a robbery taking place at the counter. The society loses a substantial amount of money.

Section 5: 'gain' and 'loss'

(1)   The references to gain and loss in sections 2 to 4 are to be read in accordance with this section.

(2)   'Gain' and 'loss'–

   (a)   extend only to gain or loss in money or other property;

   (b)   include any such gain or loss whether temporary or permanent;

   and 'property' means any property whether real or personal (including things in action and other intangible property).

(3)   'Gain' includes a gain by keeping what one has, as well as a gain by getting what one does not have.

(4)   'Loss' includes a loss by not getting what one might get, as well as a loss by parting with what one has.

This section follows the s4 Theft Act 1968 definition of property. Therefore, the same limitations in respect of land and intangible property, such as trade secrets, apply. The explanation for the exclusion of trade secrets is that a person committing fraud is not necessarily interested in the information for its own sake but in the financial advantage that it might secure. Other offences such as the Computer Misuse Act 1990 cover the obtaining of unauthorised data. Conspiracy to defraud would apply to agreements to obtain trade secrets.

13.1.5 Section 11: Obtaining Services Dishonestly

(1)   A person is guilty of an offence under this section if he obtains services for himself or another–

   (a)   by a dishonest act, and

   (b)   in breach of subsection (2).

(2)   A person obtains services in breach of this subsection if–

   (a)   they are made available on the basis that payment has been, is being or will be made for or in respect of them,

(b) he obtains them without any payment having been made for or in respect of them or without payment having been made in full, and

(c) when he obtains them, he knows–

    (i) that they are being made available on the basis described in paragraph (a), or

    (ii) that they might be,

but intends that payment will not be made, or will not be made in full.

(3) A person guilty of an offence under this section is liable–

    (a) on summary conviction, to imprisonment for a term not exceeding 12 months or to a fine not exceeding the statutory maximum (or to both);

    (b) on conviction on indictment, to imprisonment.

Actus reus

- Obtaining (act not omission),
- Services that require payment,
- Failure to pay in full.

Mens rea

- Knowledge that services require payment,
- Dishonesty,
- Intent to avoid full or part payment at the time of obtaining.

D must obtain a service requiring payment. Therefore, this is a result offence. D's dishonest *act* must cause the obtaining. An omission is insufficient. D must intend to fail to pay in whole or part at the time of the obtaining and do so.

Actus reus

Section 11 replaces the offence of obtaining services by deception under s1 Theft Act 1978. The old offence included the obtaining of all services for which payment was due as well as the obtaining of loans and mortgages. Service is not defined in s11 and so all services would seem to be included except that they must be the sort for which payment is expected, for example: all professional, financial and commercial services. The requirement of payment is probably satisfied even though it is not expressly stated in any agreement.

'Services' will include: banking/building society/credit card services which are paid for by interest and other charges. This was confirmed by *R v Sofroniou* [2004] QB 1218 in relation to an amendment to the previous law (s1(3) Theft (Amendment) Act 1996). Given that s11 overlaps with s2 of the 2006 Act however, the latter may be a preferable option.

Under the previous law, the service could be obtained for another and this still probably applies. There is nothing to suggest that the service need be lawful, as before. Therefore, obtaining prostitution services and failing to pay would be included.

The main difference between s11 and the previous law is that no operative deception is required. Again, this reflects the fact that in many cases, a false representation does not necessarily operate on the mind of a victim. Therefore, electronic fraud is now also covered. The emphasis is on dishonesty and the offence is thus considerably wider than previously.

There must be an intention never to pay for the services *at the time of the obtaining*. Therefore, D who enters a restaurant with the intention of paying for a meal but who subsequently changes his mind would not commit a s11 offence. The relevant provision would be 'making off without payment' under s3 Theft Act 1978.

All services obtained over the internet or telephone touchpad such as travel/theatre tickets will be included. Further services include the setting up of a company, downloading software or music downloading.

→ CROSS-REFERENCE
For further discussion on 'making off without payment' see 13.2.

Mens rea

- ■ Dishonesty—the *Ivey* test applies.
- ■ D must know the services are to be paid for or know they might have to be paid for, *plus*
- ■ D must intend to avoid payment in whole or part at the time of the obtaining.

?! THINKING POINT 13.4

Has D obtained services contrary to s11 Fraud Act 2006?

1. D enters a football ground through a hole in a fence to watch a game without buying a ticket.
2. D books two tickets to a music concert over the internet using his mother's credit card without her consent.
3. D buys the cheapest underground ticket that covers only part of his journey. At his destination, he leaves the station by jumping over the barrier.

Further offences under the Act, such as possession/supply of articles for use in frauds (s6) and fraudulent trading (s9) are not included here.

Criticisms of the Fraud Act 2006

Read the following by D. Ormerod, 'The Fraud Act 2006—Criminalising Lying?' [2007] *Crim LR* 193:

> General fraud offences offer many *practical* advantages including the clearer expression of large scale criminality in one charge; the ability to render complex schemes more readily understood by jurors; the avoidance of fragmenting factual chronologies to meet technical requirements of specific counts on the indictment; the removal of the risk of duplicity or of overloading the indictment; and the ease of cross-admissibility of evidence. These practical advantages must not, however, be allowed to produce a general offence that is overbroad, based too heavily on the ill-defined concept of dishonesty, too vague to meet the obligation under Art. 7 of the ECHR, and otherwise deficient in principle. It is certainly questionable whether the Act has secured these practical advantages at the cost of undermining important principles. The offences are so wide that they provoke the kind of astonishment that Professor Green expresses when considering the lowest common denominator of the moral content of fraud:
>
> > 'if fraud really were to encompass not just stealing by deceit, but also deceptive and non-deceptive breaches of trust, conflicts of interest, non disclosure of material facts, exploitation, taking unfair advantage, non-performance of contractual obligations, and misuse of corporate assets, it would be virtually impossible to distinguish between different offences in terms of their nature

and seriousness, and even to know whether and when one had committed a crime.' (SP Green, *Lying, Cheating and Stealing*)

In addition to creating broad offences which remove the technicality of the old law, the government's other stated objective included improving the efficiency of the process from investigation to trial. It is submitted that the changes to the substantive offences will have only a limited impact in this regard. In particular, they will do little to assist in the types of case in which length and cost have hit the headlines in recent years. Greater impact in larger frauds is likely to be felt as a result of the procedural changes being introduced including the Lord Chief Justice's *Complex Trial Management Protocol* (2005) and the proposals from the ongoing Fraud Review. As the Attorney-General accepted, it is the complexity of fact and not law which prolongs fraud trials.

The Protocol mentioned concerns the introduction of case management guidelines regarding the conduct and length of trials. Further provision was made in s43 Criminal Justice Act 2003 for judge-only trials in complex cases, a somewhat controversial innovation to criminal justice in this jurisdiction. The proposals have now been abandoned.

SECTION SUMMARY

The main fraud offences of which you should be aware are as follows:

1. *Under s1 Fraud Act 2006, a person commits a fraud offence if he is in breach of any of the sections listed in subsection (2) (which provide for different ways of committing the offence):*
    a. *s2 (fraud by false representation);*
    b. *s3 (fraud by failing to disclose information); and*
    c. *s4 (fraud by abuse of position).*
    ■ *Fraud has replaced 'deception' and is a very wide offence.*
    ■ *There is no need for V to believe in the truth of the s2 false representation or to rely on it.*
2. *Under s11(1) a person is guilty of an offence if he obtains services that must be paid for, whether for himself or another:*
    ■ *by a dishonest act;*
    ■ *D knows that payment is expected;*
    ■ *intending to avoid payment either in full or in part at the time of the obtaining.*

13.2 Making off Without Payment

13.2.1 Actus Reus

13.2.2 Mens Rea

This offence under s3(1) Theft Act 1978 still remains:

(1) Subject to subsection (3) below, a person who, knowing that payment on the spot for any goods supplied or service done is required or expected from him, dishonestly makes off without having paid as required or expected and with intent to avoid payment of the amount due shall be guilty of an offence.

(2) For the purposes of this section 'payment on the spot' includes payment at the time of collecting goods on which work has been done or in respect of which service has been provided.

This section was designed to deal with the person who makes off from a restaurant or petrol garage without paying and against whom a dishonest intention to permanently deprive (theft) or a false representation (fraud/deception) cannot be proved at the time of the obtaining. It was designed to fill a gap in the law.

Recall the case of *Edwards v Ddin* (1976) 63 Cr App R 218.

→ CROSS-REFERENCE
Edwards v Ddin is discussed in detail in Chapter 12.

When the petrol was put into his tank, D became the owner of it. He therefore could not steal what was already his and thus committed no theft by driving off without paying.

Further, under the previous law on obtaining property by deception (s15 Theft Act 1968), the deception had to precede the obtaining, not the other way round. Therefore, if D obtained the petrol (and ownership) before making a false representation, he would not have *obtained property by deception*. The deception would have followed the obtaining and thus there would have been no liability for that offence either. *Making off without payment* filled that gap. The same argument applies to the dishonest restaurant customer in *Ray* earlier.

→ CROSS-REFERENCE
The facts of *Ray* are set out in 13.1.2, 'False representation by silence'.

Here, D had not stolen the food because at the time of dishonestly deciding not to pay, he had already eaten it and ownership had passed to him (ie: it could not belong to the restaurant because it was in his stomach). Neither had he obtained the food by deception because, again, the decision not to pay, and therefore any false representation that he would pay before leaving, arose after the food was obtained.

(Note: There may now be an overlap between s3 and theft following *Gomez* in the sense that D appropriates petrol/food in a restaurant as soon as he does anything with them. If D is dishonest at that moment and intends not to pay, theft is instantaneous.)

Under the Fraud Act 2006, the dishonest motorist who makes a false representation regarding petrol intending to make a gain or to cause another to lose will be caught by s2. But the offence of *making off without payment* will still be required to catch the motorist who makes no such representation or who is not dishonest at the time of appropriation for theft purposes as in *Edwards v Ddin*. Nor is there any requirement that the goods belong to another.

13.2.1 Actus Reus

Makes off

The offence consists of the dishonest departure from the spot at which immediate payment is expected. What counts as the relevant 'spot'? This will clearly be an issue of fact in every case:

- In *Brooks and Brooks* (1982) 76 Cr App R 66 it was held that in restaurants, the 'spot' is the cash point not the restaurant. Therefore, a customer who heads for the door without paying, subject to MR, has made off within s3.

- A D attempting to leave an underground station through the exit barrier without paying for a journey is also on the spot.

- The 'spot' may be 'in motion' as in *R v Aziz* [1993] Crim LR 708 where D and another ordered a taxi to take them to a club 13 miles away. On arrival, they refused to pay the £15 fare. The driver said he would take them back to the hotel but decided to go to a police station en route. One of the defendants damaged the car. The driver stopped at a garage and asked the attendant to call the police. Both Ds ran off, one was caught and convicted under s3. On appeal it was argued that the requirement for payment had ceased once the driver announced his intention to return to the hotel. The Court of Appeal held that the Act did not require payment to be made at any particular spot. The words 'dishonestly makes off without payment' were not qualified in any way and involved a departure without paying from the place where payment might normally be made. In the case of taxis, this might be whilst sitting in the taxi or standing by the window.

'Making off', since it is not qualified in the Act, may be in any manner whether it be running or driving away, done in a more sedate fashion, or simply disappearing without leaving a trace. Therefore, leaving a worthless cheque on a hotel counter or restaurant table would be included.

Goods supplied or service done

Any service or supply of goods where immediate payment is expected will be covered. Therefore, petrol garages, restaurants, hotels, self-service stores, emergency call-out services (eg: plumbers/electricians), taxis, but not the supply of rented accommodation. The element of 'supply' is important. Ordinary non-self-service shops are not regarded as 'supplying' goods whereas self-service stores are.

The offence will not be committed until the service or goods are actually supplied and payment is expected. The service/goods must be those which D is permitted to use. If the obtaining is unauthorised (eg: D stealthily helps himself to a block of cheese from the delicatessen counter at a supermarket), the appropriate offence is theft.

The service must be lawful. Therefore, the supply of drugs, alcohol to under-age drinkers, sex or gambling (agreements which are unenforceable under contract law) are excluded.

'Without having paid as required or expected'

The payment must be lawfully due. Therefore, if the supplier commits a breach of contract and does not render the service or supply the goods agreed upon, there is no liability to pay.

In *Troughton v Metropolitan Police* [1987] Crim LR 138 a taxi driver broke off from his route to take a drunken D to a police station for assistance. He then demanded the full fare. D left without paying. It was held on appeal against conviction that this unilateral change of service supplied entitled D not to pay.

13.2.2 Mens Rea

Dishonesty

D must be dishonest when he makes off. He may have been dishonest from the outset or simply when making off. Either way, the offence is committed although, in the former case, D might also have committed either theft or fraud. A genuine mistaken belief that payment was not required on the spot will negate dishonesty.

'Knowing that payment on the spot . . . is required or expected from him'

This would be a question of fact in every case. Again, a genuine mistaken belief would negate such knowledge.

With intent to avoid payment

An intent to delay or defer payment is insufficient. There must be an intention never to pay.

In *R v Allen* [1985] AC 1029 the Court of Appeal quashed D's conviction for having left a hotel without paying a bill of over £1,000 on the grounds that the section requires an intention never to pay. Therefore, an intention to pay at some future point will defeat the offence.

However, if there is no expectation that the goods/service will be paid for on the spot D will not be guilty. Suppose that D leaves a hotel without paying because he has obtained an agreement from the hotel manager that payment will be made later. The court will not enquire into whether the agreement was obtained by dishonest deception. The mere fact of an agreement will preclude conviction. Section 3(1) was intended to create a simple and straightforward offence and the section does not permit or require analysis of any deception. It is not a debt-collecting provision.

This principle was applied in *R v Vincent* [2001] Crim LR 488 by the Court of Appeal where D, who had stayed at two hotels in Windsor, left without paying the bills after first obtaining agreements to pay later when he could. He denied dishonesty and his conviction was quashed.

?!   **THINKING POINT** 13.5

Does D commit the offence of 'making off without payment' under s3(1) Theft Act 1978?

D goes to a self-service petrol station five times and serves himself telling the attendant to charge the account of a former employer which he is no longer entitled to do.

SUMMARY

In this chapter we have looked at the following:

- The new, single offence of fraud under s1 Fraud Act 2006, which can be committed in one of three ways:

    a. s2 (fraud by false representation),

    b. s3 (fraud by failing to disclose information), and

    c. s4 (fraud by abuse of position).

    We have distinguished the new offence from previous deception offences.

    Fraud consists of a dishonest statement and requires no reliance by V.

- The new offence of dishonestly obtaining services under s11(1) Fraud Act 2006. We have distinguished it from previous offences of obtaining services by deception.

- Making off without payment under s3 Theft Act 1978.

    AR: A person who makes off without paying for any goods supplied or service done. D must make off from the spot where payment is expected.

    MR: D must know that payment on the spot is required or expected and must dishonestly make off without having paid and with intent to avoid payment and never to pay. Dishonesty is likely to be assessed using the *Ivey v Genting Casinos* test.

→ **CROSS-REFERENCE**
See Chapter 12 for details of the amendment to *R v Ghosh* in *Ivey v Genting Casinos* test.

PROBLEM SOLVING

D applies for a lucrative post of chief accountant with a large firm stating, falsely, that she possesses a considerable array of high-level professional qualifications. She is, in fact, newly qualified with only basic certificates. The firm are impressed by her enthusiasm and energy and she is appointed to the post with immediate effect. She spends most of the first week browsing the internet looking for designer shoes and buys several pairs using a cancelled credit card. She also applies for several other credit cards, falsifying her credit history. During one lunch-hour, D goes to a café for a coffee, drinks it and leaves without paying. One of the firm's clients suffers serious financial losses as a result of D's inattention to her work. D maintains that, although she is easily distracted, she is perfectly capable of doing her job and therefore she is not dishonest. Discuss D's criminal liability.

Remember:

- **I: Identify** relevant issues
- **D: Define** offences/defences
- **E: Explain/evaluate** the law
- **A: Apply** law to facts.

See the online resources for further guidance on solving this problem: www.oup.com/uk/loveless6e/.

FURTHER READING

J. Collins, 'Fraud by Abuse of Position: Theorising Section 4 of the Fraud Act 2006' [2011] *Crim LR* 513

Examines the theoretical basis for this section and discusses the concept of fiduciary duty as it relates to the section.

J. Collins, 'Exploitation of Persons and the Limitations of the Criminal Law' [2017] *Crim LR* 169

Argues that the use of fraud legislation to cover the exploitation of persons is complex and can be inappropriate.

Law Commission, 'Legislating the Criminal Code: Fraud and Deception' (Consultation Paper No 155, 1999: www.lawcom.gov.uk/wp-content/uploads/2015/03/Cp155_Legislating_the_Criminal_Code_Fraud_and_Deception_Consultation_Summary.pdf)

A summary of the Law Commission's recommendations which led to the Fraud Act 2006.

C. Monaghan, 'To Prosecute or Not to Prosecute? A Reconsideration of the Over Zealous Prosecution of Parents under the Fraud Act 2006' (2010) *JCL* 75(3) 259

An article commenting on whether it is appropriate to prosecute under the Fraud Act 2006 when a mother lied on her son's school application form.

D. Ormerod, 'Criminalising Lying' [2007] *Crim LR* 193

Provides an assessment of the Fraud Act 2006 and argues that its key concepts are drafted too widely.

A. Reed, 'Making Off Without Payment' (2001) 114 *JCL* 1–2

Examines whether agreement to defer payment was a defence to the offence of making off without payment.

C. Withey, 'Comment: The Fraud Act 2006—Some Early Observations and Comparisons with the Former Law' (2007) 70(4) *JCL* 581–597

Discusses whether the provisions of the Act are an improvement on the previous law of deception.

Property offences 3

KEY POINTS

BURGLARY/AGGRAVATED BURGLARY

This section will help you to understand:

- that, under s9(1) Theft Act 1968, burglary consists of two offences related to the entry of a building/part as a trespasser:
  - s9(1)(a): where D has an intent to commit one of several ulterior offences: stealing, grievous bodily harm or criminal damage (here burglary is a crime of specific intent); OR
  - s9(1)(b): having entered as a trespasser, D goes on to steal or commit grievous bodily harm or attempts to do so;
- that the civil concept of trespass applies to burglary with the addition of MR;
- that any defence to the offences committed or attempted in s9(1)(b) will act as a defence to burglary.

BLACKMAIL

This section will help you to understand that under s21 Theft Act 1968 blackmail consists of an unwarranted demand with menaces with a view to gain or causing loss to another.

CRIMINAL DAMAGE

This section will help you to understand that under s1 Criminal Damage Act 1971 there are three significant offences:

- criminal damage (s1(1));
- criminal damage by endangering life (s1(2));
- arson (s1(3)).

INTRODUCTION

The offences in this chapter are the three outstanding major property offences. They are grouped together here for no better reason than convenience, for each might easily occupy a chapter on its own. There is no pretension of any inherent link between these topics other than that burglary and criminal damage are amongst the most frequently committed property offences, often occurring together. Blackmail is a less commonly committed but equally serious offence. Links have been drawn between them for problem-solving purposes at the end of the chapter.

14.1 Burglary

KEY CASES

Collins [1972] 2 All ER 1562—entry must be a trespass;

Hudson v Crown Prosecution Service [2017] Crim LR 703—whether the property entered was a 'dwelling' for the purposes of s9;

Jones & Smith [1976] 3 All ER 54—entry in excess of authorisation;

Flack (Perry) [2013] EWCA Crim 115—a question of fact as to whether an empty house undergoing renovation was a building;

R v Coleman [2013] EWCA Crim 544—a houseboat can be a dwelling.

14.1.1 Introduction

Burglary is a property offence consisting of unauthorised entry of premises and either an intention to commit or actual commission of certain specified offences. Burglary has decreased over time. Between 2005 and 2011 there was little change, with a sharp decrease in 2011. The year ending March 2017 showed the lowest number to date. In this year, 2 in 100 households had been burgled, compared with 9 in 100 in 1995. Households are four times less likely to be burgled than they were in 1995. This is likely to be due to improvements in household security (see Diagram 14.1).

You are more likely to be a victim of burglary if you live in an urban area, social or privately rented accommodation or have few home security protections.

Source : John Flatley, Office for National Statistics, 'Overview of Burglary and Other Household Theft', 2017—www.ons.gov.uk/peoplepopulationandcommunity/crimeandjustice/articles/overviewofburglaryandotherhouseholdtheft/englandandwales#introduction.

Sentences for domestic burglaries are higher than for non-domestic burglaries. This reflects the fact that entry into a home can cause fear and psychological distress to the occupier. It is akin to an offence against the person.

Section 9 Theft Act 1968 provides two separate offences of burglary (see Diagram 14.2).

Section 9(1)(a) requires proof of entry as a trespasser and of an ulterior intent to commit one of three offences (see Diagram 14.3):

(1) A person is guilty of burglary if–

    (a) He enters any building or part of a building as a trespasser and *with intent* to commit any such offence as is mentioned in subsection (2) below; . . .

    (b) Having entered as a trespasser he steals or attempts to steal anything in the building or that part of it or inflicts or attempts to inflict on any person therein any grievous bodily harm.

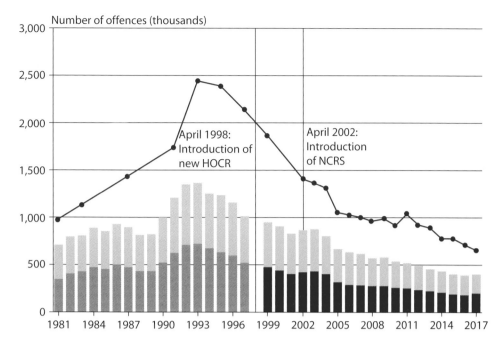

Number of offences (thousands)

- Crime Survey for England and Wales-domestic burglary
- Police recorded crime-non-domestic burglary year ending December
- Police recorded crime-non-domestic burglary year ending March
- Police recorded crime-domestic burglary year ending December

Diagram 14.1

Trends in Crime Survey of England and Wales and police recorded burglary, year ending December 1981 to year ending March 2017

Notes:

1. The data on this chart refer to different time periods: a) 1981 to 1999 refer to crimes experienced in the calendar year (January to December) b) from 2001/02 onwards the estimates relate to crimes experienced in the 12 months before interview, based on interviews carried out in that financial year (April to March) c) the last two data points relate to interviews carried out in the rolling 12 month periods for the latest available two years (January to December).

2. The numbers of incidents are derived by multiplying incidence rates by the population estimates for England and Wales Crime Survey for England and Wales (ONS) as appears in Crime in England and Wales, Year Ending March 2017— www.ons.gov.uk/peoplepopulationandcommunity/crimeandjustice/bulletins/crimeinenglandandwales/june2017#what-is-happening-to-theft

(2) The offences referred to . . . are stealing anything in the building in question, or inflicting on any person therein any grievous bodily harm and of doing unlawful damage to the building or anything therein.

(3) A person guilty of burglary shall on conviction on indictment be liable to imprisonment for a term not exceeding–

    (a) where the offence was committed in respect of a building or part of a building which is a dwelling, fourteen years;

    (b) in any other case, ten years.

(4) References in subsections (1) and (2) above to a building which is also a dwelling, shall apply also to an inhabited vehicle or vessel, and shall apply to any such vehicle or vessel at the times when a person having a habitation in it is not there as well as at times when he is.

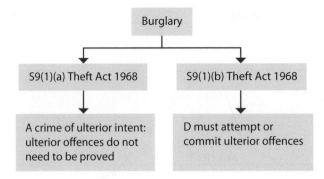

Diagram 14.2
Definition of burglary

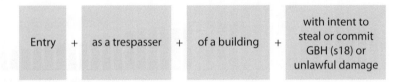

Diagram 14.3
Definition of s9(1)(a) burglary

→ CROSS-REFERENCE
Intention is discussed
fully in Chapter 3.

This is a crime of specific or ulterior intent. It may be charged where D is apprehended at the point of entry to a building as a trespasser provided there is evidence of an intention to commit an ulterior offence. Actual commission of the ulterior offences is not necessary. Remember that intoxication can be a partial defence to a crime of specific intent.

Rape was a fourth ulterior offence until it was removed by the Sexual Offences Act 2003. An alternative offence exists in s63(1) SOA 2003 of trespassing on any premises with intent to commit a relevant sexual offence.

A person commits an offence if–

    (a)   he is a trespasser on any premises,

    (b)   he intends to commit a relevant sexual offence on the premises, and

    (c)   he knows that, or is reckless as to whether, he is a trespasser.

NB: This offence applies to all sexual offences under Part 1 SOA 2003 and not just rape as was the case under the previous law of burglary.

Section 9(1)(b) requires proof of entry as a trespasser and of the actual or attempted commission of either of two offences (see also Diagram 14.4):

Having entered as a trespasser he steals or attempts to steal anything in the building or that part of it or inflicts or attempts to inflict on any person therein any grievous bodily harm.

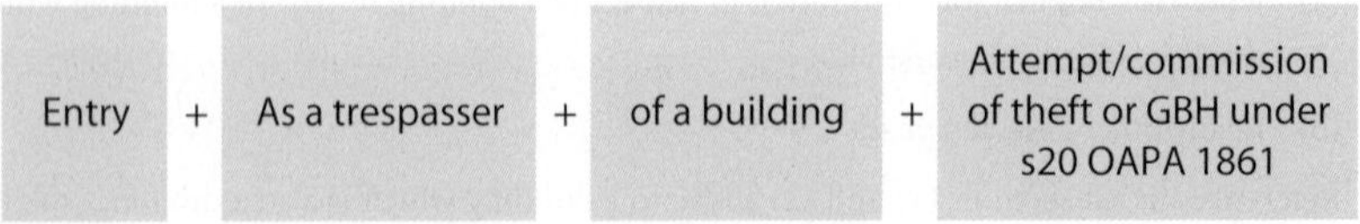

| Entry | + | As a trespasser | + | of a building | + | Attempt/commission of theft or GBH under s20 OAPA 1861 |

Diagram 14.4
Definition of s9(1)(b) burglary

Again, D must have entered a building as a trespasser, whether a dwelling or not, but this is not a crime of ulterior intent for he need not intend to commit a crime at the point of entry. Such intention will not arise until after entry. The specified offences must be committed or attempted. Therefore, this invites the possibility of defences such as lack of dishonesty in theft or self-defence in GBH in which case, if successful, burglary will be defeated. In either case, a conditional intent will suffice, for example: D enters a building intending to steal anything of value but finds nothing.

14.1.2 Actus Reus of Both Offences

The three AR elements are common to both offences:

- ◼ Entry
- ◼ As a trespasser
- ◼ Any building or part thereof.

Entry

The term 'entry' is not defined and so a jury will need to exercise common sense when deciding whether D has actually entered premises. Ultimately, this is a question of fact. A number of issues concerning the AR of burglary, including entry, were considered in the following case. At the time, rape was a specified ulterior offence under s9(1)(a). Since 2003 it no longer is.

➔ CROSS-REFERENCE
See the definition in 14.1.1.

R v Collins [1972] 2 ALL ER 1562 COURT OF APPEAL

At 2.00 am an 18-year-old woman went to bed at her mother's home after spending the evening with her boyfriend during which they had been drinking. Her bed was near the window which she always kept wide open. Some one or two hours later she awoke to find a vague form crouching at the open window. She could not remember whether the form was on the outside or the inside of the window sill. This was a significant omission. She realised that it was a naked man with an erect penis. His hair was blond and she therefore concluded that it was her boyfriend. She beckoned him in. He joined her in bed. It was not until after full sexual intercourse had taken place that she realised she had made a mistake. The defendant was someone who had done some work in the house and knew the victim. He was passing when he saw her open bedroom window. Intent on having sex that night he found a step-ladder, climbed up and looked through her bedroom window to find that she was naked and asleep. He descended the ladder, removed all his clothes apart from his socks and went back up to the window sill. He claimed that he was pulling himself into the room when she awoke. He was convicted of burglary and appealed.

The vital question of 'entry as a trespasser' had not been considered by a court before. Essentially, in order to trespass, entry has to be without consent. However, on the basis of the evidence, the victim's account was unclear.

It appeared that she had invited him into her room. But it was uncertain where he was when she made the invitation—whether on the outside of the window sill or on the inside. If still outside, then his entry was by her consent and he had not trespassed. If on the inside, then he would already have entered before she had said or done anything to indicate her consent and this was a trespass. The jury at D's trial had never been invited to consider this vital question.

Edmund-Davies LJ:

> There was no doubt that his entry into the bedroom was 'intentional'. But what the appellant had said was, 'She knelt on the bed, she put her arms around me and then I went in'. If the jury thought he might be truthful in that assertion, they would need to consider whether or not, although entirely surprised by such a reception being accorded to him, this young man might not have been entitled reasonably to regard her action as amounting to an invitation to him to enter . . . . Unless the jury were entirely satisfied that the appellant made an effective and substantial entry into the bedroom without the complainant doing or saying anything to cause him to believe that she was consenting to his entering it, he ought not to be convicted of the offence charged. The point is a narrow one, as narrow maybe as the window sill which is crucial to this case. But this is a criminal charge of gravity and, even though one may suspect that his intention was to commit the offence charged, unless the facts show with clarity that he in fact committed it he ought not to remain convicted.

Appeal allowed.

We return to this case in relation to the element of 'trespass' later in this section. A number of other issues arise in the context of 'entry':

Entry must be effective

The Court of Appeal in *Collins* considered that any entry for the purposes of burglary had to be *effective and substantial*. These were not prescriptive terms and were, again, a question of fact in each case. The court in *Collins* rejected the pre-Theft Act law that entry could be committed by any part of the body.

In *R v Brown* [1985] Crim LR 611, however, the test was reduced to just 'effective' by the Court of Appeal. Thus, D had entered a building even though he was standing on the pavement with the top half of his body through a broken window rummaging for goods inside. And in *R v Ryan* [1996] Crim LR 320, D was held by the Court of Appeal to have entered a building when he was found with his head and right arm through a small window, the top half of the window having fallen on his neck trapping him there. This was so even though he was incapable of stealing anything. He had to be extricated by the police and fire-brigade—not his lucky day!

Whether the criterion of 'effective' is unambiguous is debatable. Is entry effective if D is standing on the pavement and the object of an intended theft is on the other side of the room, out of reach?

Use of tools to gain entry

Before the Theft Act, if a tool was used to gain access to carry out the ulterior offence before D physically entered a building, it constituted entry. If the tool was used simply to gain entry it constituted an attempt. Thus, if D used a jemmy simply to force open a locked door, this was attempted burglary. If D also wanted to use the jemmy to reach and obtain articles out of reach, this was entry. Whether or not entry is committed now is a question of fact for the jury. Entry was committed in *Horncastle* [2006] EWCA Crim 1736 (use of bamboo canes with hooks to hook V's keys from a hallway) and *Richardson and Brown* [1998] 2 Cr App R (S) 87 (use of a mechanical digger to steal a cash dispenser by ripping it from the wall of a bank).

The same question arises if D uses an innocent agent, such as a child, to enter through a small window in order to steal. The child will be regarded in the same way as a tool.

?! **THINKING POINT** 14.1

Has D entered a building as a trespasser?

1. D inserts a long hook on the end of a pole through the window of a warehouse to drag out some expensive oriental carpets.

2. D points a gun through a window to shoot someone inside.

3. D puts a child through the window of a building so that she may unlock a door and admit D into the building.

As a trespasser

There must be entry 'as a trespasser'. Trespass is a civil law concept denoting voluntary entry which can be committed with any mental state such as intention, recklessness or negligence. Liability is strict and the civil offence is committed simply by the act. There are two problems when applying this civil concept to burglary: What are the boundaries of trespass and does it require its own MR in addition to the statutory requirement of MR for burglary?

The boundaries of trespass under the civil law

Trespass under the civil law is an interference with possession. Only the person in possession of premises can give permission to another to enter. If you have permission to enter you do not trespass. But it can be difficult under the civil law to determine precisely who is in possession and therefore who has the legal right to authorise entry:

a. Tenants

A clear-cut case would be that of a tenant in possession of premises who has the right to invite or exclude anyone, even, in the latter case, the landlord who may only enter for agreed purposes.

b. Guests

A guest, on the other hand, is a licensee and is not regarded as being in possession of their room.

c. Family friends

These are less clear-cut. For example, if you are visiting a friend's house, does your friend have the legal right to grant you entry if the house is owned by her parents/guardians/relatives? Suppose they have told your friend that they strongly disapprove of your friendship and that she is not to meet you again? Or what if she is allowed to see friends at home but only for certain purposes, for example: not sex or drugs. Despite knowing this, you both intend to go to your friend's room to have sex?

There are no clear answers. Trespass can therefore be a rather technical issue which is problematic when applied to the criminal law which should be as clear as possible.

Exceeding permission with an unauthorised purpose

It may be possible to trespass by having permission to enter premises for one purpose but actually doing so with quite another unauthorised purpose. This has particular relevance where D enters a shop or supermarket in order to steal. Entry is only authorised for the purposes of browsing and buying goods. Is D's entry unauthorised and therefore a trespass? The following case suggests that this may be the case but it is somewhat controversial:

Jones & Smith [1976] 3 ALL ER 54 COURT OF APPEAL

Smith had general permission to enter his father's house. On one occasion at dead of night, he entered with Jones in order to steal two television sets. Their convictions for burglary under s9(1)(a) were upheld on the basis that entry with intent to steal exceeded the scope of permission to enter.

James LJ:

Counsel for the appellants argues that a person who had a general permission to enter premises of another person cannot be a trespasser. His submission is as short and as simple as that. Related to this case he says that a son to whom a father has given permission generally to enter the father's house cannot be a trespasser if he enters it even though he had decided in his mind before making the entry to commit a criminal offence of theft against the father once he had got into the house and had entered that house solely for the purpose of committing that theft . . . .

In our view the passage there referred to [of Edmund LJ in Collins] is consonant with the passage in the well-known case of *Hillen and Pettigrew v ICI (Alkali) Ltd* [[1936] AC 65 at 69] where, in the speech of Lord Atkin, these words appear:

'My Lords, in my opinion this duty to an invitee only extends so long as and so far as the invitee is making what can reasonably be contemplated as an ordinary and reasonable use of the premises by the invitee for the purposes for which he has been invited. He is not invited to use any part of the premises for purposes which he knows are wrongfully dangerous and constitute an improper use. As Scrutton LJ has pointedly said [*The Calgarth* [1927] . . .]: "When you invite a person into your house to use the staircase you do not invite him to slide down the banisters"'. . . .

Taking the law as expressed in *Hillen and Pettigrew v ICI (Alkali) Ltd* and *Collins*, it is our view that a person is a trespasser for the purpose of s9(1)(b) of the Theft Act 1968 if he enters premises of another knowing that he is entering in excess of the permission that has been given to him, or being reckless whether he is entering in excess of the permission that has been given to him to enter, providing the facts are known to the accused which enable him to realise that he is acting in excess of the permission given or that he is acting recklessly as to whether he exceeds that permission, then that is sufficient for the jury to decide that he is in fact a trespasser.

Clearly there are risks of over-criminalisation should this become a general principle. But there is a view that D's secret intention should determine the legality of entry. Therefore, a shopper who intends to steal commits not just theft but also burglary upon entry to a store. See on this point P.J. Pace, 'Burglarious Trespass' [1986] *Crim LR* 716 when discussing *Collins* and *Jones & Smith*:

In the case of shoplifting the scope of the purpose for which entry to shop premises is permitted to the general public poses a difficult problem. In general terms a shopkeeper's implied invitation to the public is to enter his premises for lawful purposes connected with buying. Does this include permission to enter in order to wait for a friend who is shopping or to take advantage of the shelter provided? . . . It need hardly be added that a person entering a shop with the sole intention of stealing could hardly be properly described as a 'prospective customer' . . . Another argument levelled against the common law approach as interpreted by *Jones and Smith* is that it renders the phrase 'as a trespasser' in section 9(1)(a) superfluous. This is so, the argument goes, because an intention to commit one of the specified ulterior offences, eg theft, exceeds any permission given to enter and therefore automatically produces a trespassory entry, provided always that the accused has the necessary mens rea as required by *Collins*.

Therefore, if the wider *Jones & Smith* interpretation is adopted, the word trespasser in s9(1) would be irrelevant and this cannot have been the intention behind the Act. As you can appreciate, trespass, along with several other Theft Act 1968 concepts such as dishonesty, remains a difficult term.

MR of trespass: intention or recklessness

In *Collins* it was held that no trespass could become a potential burglary unless it was either intentional or reckless at the point of entry. In other words, D must actually know he has no right to enter or know that he might not have such right. There was no equivalence in criminal law to the civil concept of trespass *ab initio*, that is: entering lawfully and then exceeding authority to become a trespasser or trespassing by mistake.

Therefore, in *Collins*, the issue was not only one of D's position on the window sill (inside or outside) when he received his invitation but also his *belief* as to the girl's authority to invite him in. Any intention to rape that might otherwise have satisfied the MR of burglary at that time was undermined by the possibility that he did not enter the room as a trespasser and that the girl consented to sexual intercourse, albeit under a mistake.

Edmund-Davies LJ approved the views of Professor J.C. Smith in *The Law of Theft* (1968):

> It is submitted that . . . D should be acquitted on the ground of lack of mens rea. Though, under the civil law, he entered as a trespasser, it is submitted that he cannot be convicted of the criminal offence unless he knew of the facts which caused him to be a trespasser or, at least, was reckless.

He also approved the following quote from *The Theft Act 1968* by Professor Griew:

> What if D wrongly believes that he is not trespassing? His belief may rest on facts which, if true, would mean that he was not trespassing: for instance, he may enter a building by mistake, thinking that it is the one he has been invited to enter. Or his belief may be based on a false view of the legal effect of the known facts: for instance, he may misunderstand the effect of a contract granting him a right of passage through a building. Neither kind of mistake will protect him from tort liability for trespass . . . . But for the purposes of criminal liability a man should be judged on the basis of the facts as he believed them to be, and this should include making allowances for a mistake as to rights under the civil law. This is another way of saying that a serious offence like burglary should be held to require mens rea in the fullest sense of the phrase: D should be liable for burglary only if he knowingly trespasses or is reckless as to whether he trespasses or not . . .

Intention or recklessness may be negated by D's honest mistake or an honest belief in a right of entry.

?! **THINKING POINT** 14.2

Is there a trespass in the following cases?

1. D is carried against her will into X's house and left there. She steals a necklace and escapes via an open window.

2. D mistakenly enters a neighbour's house through an open door one night after a furious row with his girlfriend. On turning to leave, he sees a huge box of chocolates by the front door. He takes it and leaves, intending to give it to his girlfriend the next time he sees her.

3. D gains entry into an 85-year-old person's home by fraudulently representing himself as a gas-meter reader. He then steals her purse and seriously assaults her.

4. An 18-year-old daughter living in her parents' home invites her boyfriend to her room for sex. On his way out, he steals her father's mobile phone.

'Any building or part'

Before the Theft Act 1968 burglary was confined to dwelling houses. The Act now refers to 'buildings or part' but no definition is provided. The word 'building' has been considered in various other statutory contexts and, in relation to burglary, is regarded as a matter of common sense. It would potentially include houses, blocks of flats, offices, barns, garages, shops and out-buildings. A temporary pre-fab building would be included but an articulated lorry trailer being used as a supermarket is not, even though steps and an electricity supply are attached (*Norfolk v Seekings & Gould* [1986] Crim LR 167). A tent would not be included, but might be if it was used as a dwelling for a long period.

Section 9(3) creates higher sentences for burglaries of buildings which are also dwellings. In fact, it now seems that burglaries of dwellings and non-dwellings are two separate offences (*Miller* [2010] EWCA Crim 809). This is explained by the fact we would feel a burglary of our home to be more of an invasion than a burglary of our work-places. Occupied residential ac-commodation, therefore, obviously constitutes a dwelling. Less obvious is the case of an empty residential house undergoing renovation. There appears to be little consistency in the cases. The Court of Appeal held in *Sticklen* [2013] EWCA Crim 615, for example, that this would be a non-domestic burglary since it was not a home, or dwelling, and no personal space had been violated. However, in *Flack (Perry)* [2013] EWCA Crim 115 the court held that similar facts should be left to the jury. The same problem arises in respect of buildings attached to 'dwellings', such as greenhouses and sheds. In *Miles* [2003] EWCA Crim 2893 burglary from a shed was held to constitute non-*domestic* burglary, whereas in *Alexander* [2008] EWCA Crim 2834 it was considered to be the opposite.

In *Hudson v Crown Prosecution Service* [2017] EWHC 841, the Queen's Bench Division of the High Court considered whether a property which was normally let out to tenants, but which was vacant two days before it was burgled, was a 'dwelling' for the purposes of s9 and not a commercial property. This was an appeal by way of case stated (an appeal on a point of law from the magistrates' court). The court said that there were many dwellings where frequent changes of occupancy took place and which would be vacant for short periods. See the case commentary by Harry O'Sullivan, 'When is a residential address a dwelling for the purposes of sentencing?'(2017) 2 *Sentencing News* 6–9 who argues for statutory clarification of the word 'dwelling':

> it is respectfully submitted that the court reached the wrong conclusion in this case. On the available facts, no reasonable tribunal of fact could have concluded that the property was a dwelling at the material time. No person was living in the property at the time, no person's personal and sentimental property was targeted and no person's personal domain or expectation of privacy and security were violated. Accordingly, this should not have amounted to a domestic burglary. There is a need for clear-er guidance on this point. . . . given the relative significance of the domestic distinction in burglary sentences, future Parliaments may wish to offer more precise legislative guidance on the definition the courts are required to employ.

Inhabited vehicle or vessel

Section 9(4) includes inhabited vehicles and vessels within the scope of burglary. This would include occupied caravans, trailers, dormobiles, motor-homes and houseboats. Difficult ques-tions can arise as to whether these vehicles are inhabited and in every case it would be a question of fact. It was held in *R v Coleman* [2013] EWCA Crim 544 that an inhabited narrow boat fell within the s9(4) definition of 'building', as would a caravan.

> **EXAMPLE** 14.1
>
> 1. You live in a motor-home but drive it around town for errands and leave it in a railway car park for a few days whilst you visit friends elsewhere. Is it inhabited?
> 2. Your motor-home is parked in a campsite for four months of each year and you only occupy it during the weekends. Same question.

Part of a building

D may have permission to be in part of a building but not other parts, for example: hotel/hostel dwellers have permission to enter the common parts and their own rooms, but not other people's rooms or offices. We all have permission to enter public premises such as shops, theatres, galleries, museums, libraries, sports facilities, etc but only those parts specifically designated for the public. An unauthorised entry to a part of a building from which we are excluded will therefore constitute trespass. If I invite an electrician into my house to fix a socket in the kitchen and I find him ten minutes later taking money from the bedroom, he will have trespassed to that room and committed burglary. Therefore, if you go uninvited behind a shop counter and steal from the till, this will be burglary (*Walkington* [1979] 2 All ER 716). Similarly, you can trespass by remaining on premises after being asked to leave within a reasonable time. If during that period, you trespass on to another part of the building and commit theft or grievous bodily harm, you commit burglary.

More difficult is the question of whether a block of flats/offices constitutes a building so that if you enter the flat above a shop intending to steal from the shop, have you committed burglary simply by entering the flat with the intention of stealing below? There is some support for the view that you have.

This can get even more complicated. Suppose you lawfully enter a building but hide until it closes, say in a cupboard or under the stairs, intending to steal when the building is closed and deserted. By entering the cupboard you will have trespassed into part of the building. But unless you intend to steal what is in there, you do not commit burglary in that part. When you re-emerge and enter into the general part, you trespass, even though you earlier entered lawfully, and if you steal you commit burglary.

On the other hand, if you hide in the general part of the shop until later, say behind a screen, and later emerge to steal, you do not technically trespass because you have not entered a building or part. Thus you cannot burgle. But clearly, you have no right to be in the building after closing time and so this might be considered a trespass on those grounds.

> **?!** **THINKING POINT** 14.3
>
> Has D entered any building or part?
>
> 1. D breaks into a derelict house and takes away a fireplace.
> 2. D goes to the local swimming pool and walks down a corridor passing a notice stating that access to the public is denied. He steals an employee's leather coat from a rack on the wall.
> 3. D enters a supermarket and hides behind a pallet of vegetables. When the supermarket closes, he emerges, steals £100 from a petty cash box and leaves through an open window.

14.1.3 Mens Rea

Entry as a trespasser must be intentional or reckless

This may be negated by an honest mistake or an honest belief in a right of entry as explained earlier.

Intention and the ulterior offences under s9(1)(a)

There must be proof of an intention to commit the ulterior offences at the time of entry as a trespasser: stealing, grievous bodily harm or criminal damage (NB: not fraud or the dishonest use of electricity under s13). The ulterior offences do not need to be committed provided there is proof of D's intention to do so. Note that electricity is not property under s4 Theft Act 1968 and therefore if D enters property as a trespasser and makes a telephone call, he does not commit burglary (*Low v Blease* [1975] Crim LR 513).

So far as grievous bodily harm is concerned, only grievous bodily harm with intent under s18 Offences Against the Person Act 1861 is envisaged for s9(1)(a) burglary. Either burglary or s18 could be charged. Therefore if D recklessly or intentionally commits assault, battery, actual bodily harm or grievous bodily harm under s20 Offences Against the Person Act 1861 this will be insufficient for s9(1)(a) burglary.

On the other hand, if D trespasses with intent to murder, this would probably satisfy the necessary ulterior intent.

MR for the offences under s9(1)(b) may consist of recklessness

This is not a crime of ulterior intent. There needs to be proof of MR for the offences of theft or grievous bodily harm or an attempt of either following entry. MR for the offences does not need to exist at entry. Section 20 grievous bodily harm, which can be committed either recklessly or intentionally, is envisaged by s9(1)(b).

In either case, a conditional intent will suffice.

?!   THINKING POINT 14.4

In which of the following does D have the MR for s9(1)(a) burglary?

D breaks into a dwelling house:

- to seek shelter for the night;
- to find food to eat;
- to rape any woman he finds there;
- with a view to stealing any credit card he might find and finds none;
- to make many long-distance telephone calls without paying;
- to spray paint the hallway;
- to take as much money as possible and to beat up the occupier if necessary.

14.1.4 Aggravated Burglary

Section 10 Theft Act 1968:

(1) A person is guilty of aggravated burglary if he commits any burglary and at the time has with him any firearm or imitation firearm, any weapon of offence, or any explosive; and for this purpose–

    (a) 'firearm' includes an airgun or air pistol and 'imitation firearm' means anything which has the appearance of being a firearm, whether capable of being discharged or not; and

    (b) 'weapon of offence' means any article made or adapted for use for causing injury to or incapacitating a person, or intended by the person having it with him for such use; and

    (c) 'explosive' means any article manufactured for the purpose of producing a practical effect by explosion, or intended by the person having it with him for that purpose.

This offence carries a maximum life sentence.

The requirement of firearms and explosives are relatively self-explanatory. Weapon of offence includes articles made or adapted for the purposes of injury or incapacitating a person. This could therefore include a broken bottle, handcuffs, tape, string, rope, a sack or any other item that could cause injury or incapacitation.

The weapon of offence must be present 'at the time' of the burglary, that is: under s9(1)(a) this means at the time of entry, and under s9(1)(b) at the time of the later offence. D must know he has a weapon with him. If he is unaware of that fact or has forgotten about it, this does not equate to knowledge.

SECTION SUMMARY

Burglary

Under s9(1) Theft Act 1968 burglary consists of two offences related to the entry of a building/part as a trespasser:

a. *where D has an intent to commit one of several ulterior offences: stealing, grievous bodily harm or criminal damage (here burglary is a crime of specific intent); OR*

b. *having entered as a trespasser, D goes on to steal or commit grievous bodily harm or attempts to do so.*

Actus reus: *The three AR elements are common to both offences:*

▪ *Entry*

▪ *As a trespasser*

▪ *Any building or part thereof.*

Mens rea:

▪ *Entry as a trespasser must be intentional or reckless.*

▪ *s9(1)(a): There must be proof of an intention to commit the ulterior offences at the time of entry as a trespasser.*

▪ *s9(1)(b): There needs to be proof of MR for the offences of theft or grievous bodily harm or an attempt of either following entry.*

▪ *The civil concept of trespass applies to burglary with the addition of MR.*

▪ *Any defence to the ulterior offences will act as a defence to burglary.*

Aggravated burglary consists of burglary accompanied by a firearm, weapon of offence or explosive.

14.2 Blackmail

14.2.1 Introduction

14.2.2 Actus Reus

14.2.3 Mens Rea

KEY CASES

Collister & Warhurst [1955] 39 Cr App R 100—demand with menaces can be implied;

Treacy [1971] AC 537—demand made when letter posted;

Harvey [1980] 72 Cr App R 139—whether demand is unwarranted is subjectively determined.

14.2.1 Introduction

A blackmail is an unwarranted demand with menaces, or threat, by D against V to gain something of value for himself or another or to cause loss to V. You may have read about blackmail in the newspapers whenever personalities in the public eye or public officials are reported to have been threatened with tabloid revelations about sexual indiscretions or corruption unless money is paid to the blackmailer.

In legal terms, the crime of blackmail raises questions about the boundary between a criminal threat amounting to 'menaces' and legitimate commercial bargaining. Blackmail is an offence of dishonesty, defined according to D's beliefs, and therefore, may admit somewhat variable standards from one case to another. Note that where the demand for property is accompanied by a coincident threat of violence, D will commit both robbery and blackmail.

The offence is defined by s21 Theft Act 1968.

> (1) A person is guilty of blackmail if, with a view to gain for himself or another or with intent to cause loss to another, he makes any unwarranted demand with menaces; and for this purpose a demand with menaces is unwarranted unless the person making it does so in the belief–
>
> (a) that he has reasonable grounds for making the demand; and
>
> (b) that the use of menaces is a proper means of reinforcing the demand.
>
> (2) The nature of the act or omission is immaterial, and it is also immaterial whether the menaces relate to action to be taken by the person making the demand.
>
> (3) A person guilty of blackmail shall on conviction on indictment be liable to imprisonment for a term not exceeding 14 years.

Neither 'demand' nor 'menaces' are defined. Under the previous law, the Larceny Act 1916, 'menaces' meant 'threat'.

Actus reus

- There must be a demand.
- The demand must be accompanied by menaces.
- The demand must be unwarranted.
- With a view to gain or intent to cause loss.

Mens rea

◾ Belief that the demand is unwarranted.

14.2.2 Actus Reus

Demand

The demand must be to make V do or stop doing something. It does not matter if V ignores it or is otherwise oblivious to it because it cannot be heard, read, seen or understood. The nature of the act or omission is immaterial. The demand can be express or implied.

Collister & Warhurst [1955] 39 CR APP R 100 COURT OF APPEAL

Two police officers implied to V that he would be prosecuted unless he met them the next day. At the meeting, they asked him if he had brought anything with him and he handed over £5. Both police officers were convicted of demanding money with menaces under s30 Larceny Act 1916, the judge commenting that a reasonable man would understand that a demand for money was being made and that it was accompanied by menaces.

Pilcher J to the jury:

> You need not be satisfied that there was an express demand for money in words. You need not be satisfied that any express threats were made, but if the evidence satisfies you that, although there was no such express demand or threat, the demeanour of the accused and the circumstances of the case were such that an ordinary reasonable man would understand that a demand for money was being made upon him and that that demand was accompanied by menaces—not perhaps direct, but veiled menaces—so that his ordinary balance of mind was upset, then you would be justified in coming to the conclusion that a demand with menaces had been made . . .

When is a demand made? Suppose the demand is by post, email, fax? This matters from the point of view of jurisdiction in cross-border cases.

Treacy v DPP [1971] AC 537 HOUSE OF LORDS

It was held that a demand was made when a letter was posted in England addressed to Germany.

Lord Diplock:

> So the question which has to be answered is: Would a man say in ordinary conversation: 'I have made a demand' when he had written a letter containing a demand and posted it to the person to whom the demand was addressed? Or would he not use those words until the letter had been received and read by the addressee?
>
> My answer to that question is that it would be natural for him to say 'I have made a demand' as soon as he had posted the letter, for he would have done all that was in his power to make the demand. He might add, if it were the fact: 'but it has not reached X yet', or: 'I made a demand but it got lost in the post.' What, at any rate, he would not say is: 'I shall make a demand when X receives my letter,' unless he contemplated making some further demand after the letter had been received . . . . 'Are the circumstances of this case such as would prompt a man in ordinary conversation to say: "I have made a demand"?'.

Appeal dismissed.

Note that two of the Law Lords thought that the demand was not made until received in Germany.

Menaces

Menaces can also be express or implied from the circumstances although the term is not defined in the Act. However, it had already developed a wide meaning under the former law.

In *Thorne v Motor Trade Association* [1937] AC 797 Lord Wright said that the word was to be liberally construed and not limited to threats of violence. It included threats of any action detrimental or unpleasant to V or warnings to that effect. It is now clear that the threat can be aimed at V, a third party or D himself. Furthermore, it is not necessary that D must be capable of carrying out the threat or capable of controlling whether the threat is executed. This was confirmed in *Lambert*:

R v Lambert [2009] EWCA CRIM 2860 COURT OF APPEAL

L was owed money by A. Posing as a victim and not an aggressor, L rang A's grandmother and said 'Nana, this is [A]. They've got me tied up. They want £5,000, Nana.' The grandmother believed it was A but did not have the money. L did the same thing again. On appeal against conviction of blackmail L argued that his demand was not unwarranted and that, in order to commit blackmail, D must propose to execute the menace attached to the demand (ie: against A), or have the power to do so. This was rejected because s21(2) states that 'it is immaterial whether the menaces relate to action to be taken by the person making the demand'.

Moses LJ:

> We think it makes absolutely no difference whether the person pretending that someone has been tied up and will be hurt if money is not handed over is pretending to be the victim, or pretending to be the aggressor or pretending that he has it within his power to see that harm comes to the fictitious victim. The essence of the offence which the prosecution must prove is, first of all, that there was an unwarranted demand. Mr Parish submits that there was no unwarranted demand in this case. But it is by now well established that the demand does not have to be made in terms of a demand or requirement or obligation. It can be couched in terms which are by no means aggressive or forceful. Indeed, the more suave and gentle the request, the more sinister in the circumstances it might be. If one needs authority for so obvious a proposition, one can find it in the decision of this court in R v Collister [1955] 39 Cr App R 100 and in particular in the approval by the court of the terms of Pilcher J's summing-up at page 102. In our view, there was clearly a demand in this case and it was unwarranted. No justification was offered for imposing pressure upon the grandmother to hand over money to her grandson so that this defendant could be paid what the grandson owed him. The next question is whether it was accompanied by menaces. Mr Parish again submits that it was not, since what was threatened by the caller was not that he would do something or allow others to do something but rather that he would suffer violence from others. That, as we have already indicated, is wholly irrelevant. What the caller was seeking to do was to impose upon the grandmother the pressure that were she not to hand over the money, her grandson would suffer violence. It is the essence of the offence that the offender intends and does impose what is described at paragraph 15 of this court's judgment in R v Jheeta [2007] EWCA Crim 1699 as 'menacing pressures'.

The Court of Appeal confirmed that the menaces may be directed against a third party and not the recipient victim of the threat. It is how the demand and menace affects the victim that matters.

Whether the demand will be sufficiently serious to constitute menaces is determined according to ordinary standards. Thus in *Clear* [1968] 1 QB 670 it was said that the threat must be such as to influence the mind of the ordinary person of normal stability and courage or make him apprehensive so as to unwillingly accede to the demand. It does not matter that V is not coerced or frightened by the demand. Blackmail is committed as soon as the demand is made.

THINKING POINT 14.5

1. Is the *Clear* test subjective or objective?
2. Do you consider that an ordinary person would be intimidated by the following demands for money:
   - Otherwise you will be killed?
   - Otherwise your daughter will be kidnapped?
   - Otherwise I shall slash your tyres?
   - Otherwise I shall tell your husband about your adulterous affair?
   - Otherwise I will go to the press about your criminal record?
3. D threatens V that if he does not pay him £1,000 by the end of the week he will beat V up. V is part of a criminal gang and is not concerned. Has D blackmailed V?

Unwarranted demand: an AR and MR element

A demand is not necessarily unwarranted if D has the legal right to make it, for example: demanding payment of an unpaid debt—'Repay me my £25 which you borrowed last week'. However, such a demand, if accompanied by menaces, will be unwarranted (see *Lambert*).

Whether or not a demand is unwarranted depends on D's belief.

THINKING POINT 14.6

Section 21(1)(a) states that a demand will not be unwarranted where D has a belief:

a. that he has reasonable grounds for making the demand; *and*

b. that the use of menaces is a proper means of reinforcing the demand.

Does s21(1) impose a subjective or objective test?

Therefore, D's state of mind and belief can provide a defence. What matters is the genuineness of D's belief not its reasonableness *and* his belief that the use of menaces is a proper means of enforcing the demand. See the following case:

R v Harvey [1980] 72 CR APP R 139 COURT OF APPEAL

D and others paid £20,000 to V for what was believed to be a consignment of cannabis. It was not. They kidnapped V's wife and small child and informed V they would kill his family unless he returned their money. They appealed against convictions of blackmail.

Bingham J:

> It matters not what the reasonable man, or any man other than the defendant, would believe save so far as that may throw light on what the defendant in fact believed. Thus the factual question of the defendant's belief should be left to the jury. To that extent the subsection is subjective in approach, as is generally desirable in a criminal statute.... In order to exonerate a defendant from

liability his belief must be that the use of the menaces is a 'proper' means of reinforcing the demand. 'Proper' is an unusual expression to find in a criminal statute. It is not defined in the Act, and no definition need be attempted here. It is, however, plainly a word of wide meaning, certainly wider than (for example) 'lawful.' But the greater includes the less and no act which was not believed to be lawful could be believed to be proper within the meaning of the subsection. Thus no assistance is given to any defendant, even a fanatic or a deranged idealist, who knows or suspects that his threat, or the act threatened, is criminal, but believes it to be justified by his end or his peculiar circumstances. The test is not what he regards as justified, but what he believes to be proper. And where, as here, the threats were to do acts which any sane man knows to be against the laws of every civilised country no jury would hesitate long before dismissing the contention that the defendant genuinely believed the threats to be a proper means of reinforcing even a legitimate demand.

Bingham J went on to say that D must hold both beliefs in s21(1)(a) and (b). Remember that D does not have to prove these beliefs. It is for the prosecution to prove that D had no such belief.

The test of whether the demand is unwarranted is subjective because it was felt by the Law Commission prior to enactment of the Theft Act 1968 that it would be wrong to convict when someone honestly believed their demand to be justified. Therefore, if D is owed money and V fails to pay, D may believe that he has justifiable cause for demanding it with menaces. Such a belief could exist where D is really hard up and V could easily pay. The question of whether the demand is unwarranted (it could be a threat of violence, revelation about sexual status or that V is a disreputable business associate) is determined according to D's belief. The difficulty here is to distinguish between different types of threat. Violence is clearly unwarranted and unlikely to be considered justified. In *Walker* [2010] EWCA Crim 2184, D demanded £150 for the return of V's missing dog on which he inflicted violence to induce V to pay. The dog died and D was convicted of blackmail. Revelation about a sexual past is not a crime but is it the right way to enforce a debt? In *Kewell* [2000] 2 Cr App R (S) 38 a threat to publish photographs of a former girlfriend to obtain a debt was held to constitute blackmail. Conversely, a threat to interfere with the debtor's business may not be dishonest.

?! THINKING POINT 14.7

D threatens V, a local councillor, that unless V repays a £5,000 debt D will go to a local newspaper with scandalous, but true, details of V's sexual past. In each case below, decide whether D is likely to be believed by a jury that:

a. he has a belief in reasonable grounds for making the demand; *and*

b. menaces are a proper means of reinforcing it.

1. D is a solicitor with a good reputation;
2. D is a banker;
3. D is unemployed and desperate for money;
4. D has a low IQ;
5. V was involved with D in his sexual past and feels abused.

You might wonder whether a demand that a debt be repaid amounts to an unwarranted threat. The case of *Parkes* says that it can. In each case, it will be a question of fact for the jury.

These examples draw attention to the difficulty of a subjective test. A demand might or might not be unwarranted depending on D's own view of it and this could vary according to D's social, moral or intellectual status. The reverse argument is, of course, that an objective standard would be unjust to those with genuine beliefs that what they had done was right.

With a view to gain or *an intent to cause loss*

Section 34(2) Theft Act 1968 provides assistance here:

For the purposes of this Act–

(a) 'gain' and 'loss' are to be construed as extending only to gain or loss in money or other property, but as extending to any such gain or loss whether temporary or permanent; and–

    (i) 'gain' includes a gain by keeping what one has, as well as a gain by getting what one has not; and

    (ii) 'loss' includes a loss by not getting what one might get, as well as a loss by parting with what one has.

Therefore, it is clear that the demand with menaces can extend to all sorts of gains and losses, financial or otherwise, temporary or permanent, immediate or future. In *Parkes* [1973] Crim LR 358 it was held by a Crown Court that the fact that D only sought repayment of a debt did not mean that it was not 'with a view to gain' and was thus capable of amounting to blackmail. In *Bevans* (1988) 87 Cr App R 64 D, an osteoarthritis sufferer was convicted of blackmail when he went to his doctor and threatened to shoot him unless he administered an injection of pain-killer!

?!   **THINKING POINT** 14.8

Consider whether the following examples are with a view to gain or intent to cause loss:

1. D, an employer, threatens V, an employee, that:
   a. she will lose her job unless she has sexual intercourse with him;
   b. she will lose her holiday pay unless she has sexual intercourse with him;
   c. she should have sexual intercourse with him.
2. D threatens V with harm unless he:
   a. repays £100 debt by the end of next week.
   b. returns his CD player in three days' time.

14.2.3 Mens Rea

The only MR relates to s21: that unless D believes that he has reasonable grounds for making the demand and that menaces are a proper means of reinforcing the demand, the demand will be unwarranted.

SECTION SUMMARY

Under s21 Theft Act 1968 blackmail consists of an unwarranted demand with menaces with a view to gain or causing loss to another.

Actus reus

■ *Demand*

■ *Menaces*

■ *Unwarranted demand*

■ *With a view to gain or intent to cause loss.*

Mens rea

■ *Lack of genuine belief that the demand is either reasonable or that the threat is a proper way of enforcing it.*

14.3 Criminal Damage

14.3.1 Introduction

14.3.2 Actus Reus

14.3.3 Mens Rea

14.3.4 Racially or Religiously Aggravated Criminal Damage

14.3.5 Criminal Damage with Intent or Recklessness as to Endangering Life

14.3.6 Arson

14.3.1 Introduction

Criminal damage represents 17 per cent of all recorded crime (http://webarchive.nationalarchives.gov.uk/20130128103514/http://www.homeoffice.gov.uk/science-research/research-statistics/) and has been decreasing since 2006/7. It is now at its lowest level since recording began in 1981. The majority of offences are against vehicles. Criminal damage encompasses five offences under the Criminal Damage Act 1971 (CDA 1971) of which only the first three will be dealt with in this chapter:

■ criminal damage (s1(1));

■ criminal damage with intent or recklessness as to endangering life (s1(2));

■ arson (criminal damage by fire) (s1(3));

■ threatening to damage (s2);

■ possessing anything with intent to damage (s3).

KEY CASES

Fiak [2005] EWCA Crim 2381—damage includes damage to usefulness;

Seray-Wurie v DPP [2012] EWHC 208—damage is not determined by D's opinion;

Denton [1981] 74 Cr App R 81—belief in consent must be as to a lawful purpose;

Hunt [1978] 66 Cr App R 105—belief in the need for protection of property must be reasonable;

Wenton [2010] EWCA 2361—damage was unrelated to risk of endangerment;

Unsworth v DPP [2010] EWHC 3037 (Admin)—the dual test of mistaken belief in the need to protect property.

Section 1(1) Criminal Damage Act 1971:

> A person who without lawful excuse destroys or damages any property belonging to another intending to destroy or damage any such property or being reckless as to whether any such property would be destroyed or damaged shall be guilty of an offence.

Maximum sentence: 10 years or life for arson under s1(3).

Actus reus of criminal damage

This consists of four elements:

- Destroys or damages
- Property
- Belonging to another
- Without lawful excuse.

Mens rea

- Intention or recklessness (*Cunningham* subjective recklessness. Recall that *Caldwell* recklessness was overruled and abolished by *R v G* [2003] UKHL 50).

14.3.2 Actus Reus

Destroys or damages

Destruction or damage is a question of fact. The former is a self-evident term and signifies finality and total uselessness. To be destroyed, a building or vehicle would need to be completely destroyed or smaller objects such as televisions/computers would need to be so broken that they could not be used. Damage, on the other hand, may take different forms. It is not always easy to discern how much and what type of damage is essential.

Damage to value

Damage signifies some sort of material change to either the *usefulness* or *value* of the property, whether permanent or temporary. Damage to the value of property may well be only superficial, such as a scratch to a car. It will nevertheless amount to damage for the purposes of the offence. A mark left on a valuable painting or sculpture, for example, will affect its value. A scratch on a scaffolding pole is not damage, however, because such a thing is incidental to scaffolding poles (*Morphitis v Salmon* [1990] Crim LR 48). Liquids which are upset or thrown on clothes or soft furnishings may damage their value.

Damage to usefulness

Damage to the usefulness of property will usually be obvious but can also include dismantling a machine without damage to the parts. If expense is involved in restoring the property, by removal of graffiti or paint, this will count as damage. It is a moot point as to whether all graffiti constitutes criminal damage, of course, because the addition of a 'Banksy' to a wall could considerably enhance its value. Damage to audio or video tapes/recorders is within s1(1). Damaging the plastic circuit card of a computerised saw to the value of £620 would be included (*Cox v Riley* [1986] 83 Cr App R 54). Altering data on discs in a computer network which impairs the value or usefulness of the disc to the owner constitutes damage (*R v Whiteley* (1991) 93 Cr App R 25). But damaging or erasing electronic computer data would now fall under the Computer Misuse Act 1990 (intentionally causing an unauthorised modification of the contents of any computer). Section 10(5) of the 1971 Act provides that modification of the contents of a computer shall not be regarded as damage unless its physical condition is impaired.

Spitting on a policeman's waterproof coat is not damage because the coat could be restored simply by wiping off the spittle (*A v R* [1978] Crim LR 689). In *Fiak* it was held that damage had been caused to a blanket and an impermeable floor of a police cell when D pushed a blanket into a toilet of the cell and repeatedly pulled the flush, flooding the floor.

Fiak [2005] EWCA CRIM 2381 COURT OF APPEAL

Judge LJ:

The issue in relation to criminal damage can be summarised very simply. Mr Belger argued that there was no evidence that either the blanket or the cells were damaged. He suggested that clean water had flooded onto a waterproof floor, and that in the process the blanket was made wet by clean water. The blanket would have been reusable when dry. Cleaning up a wet cell floor does not constitute damage to the cell itself. However widely interpreted 'damage' may be for the purposes of the Criminal Damage Act 1971, a wet blanket and a wet cell floor fall outside any sensible definition. The argument of course assumes the absence of any possible contamination or infection from the lavatory itself, and the confident expectation that there would be none.

In the 1971 Act, hardly surprisingly, the word 'damage' itself is not further defined. The Concise Oxford Dictionary explains damage as 'harm or injury impairing the value or usefulness of something . . . '. We need refer to only two authorities. The first is Morphitis v Salmon [1990] Crim LR 48, where the transcript of Auld J's judgment reads:

'The authorities show that the term 'damage' for the purpose of this provision, should be widely interpreted so as to conclude not only permanent or temporary physical harm, but also permanent or temporary impairment of value or usefulness.'

This analysis was approved in R v Whiteley [1991] 93 CAR 25 where, after a comprehensive examination of the authorities, Lord Lane CJ summarised their effect.

'Any alteration to the physical nature of the property concerned may amount to damage within the meaning of the section. Whether it does so or not will depend on the effect that the alteration has had upon the legitimate operator (who for convenience may be referred to as the owner) . . . where . . . the interference . . . amounts to an impairment of the value or usefulness of the [property] to the owner, then the necessary damage is established.'

Applying these principles to the present case, while it is true that the effect of the appellant's actions in relation to the blanket and the cell were both remediable, the simple reality is that the blanket could not be used as a blanket by any other prisoner until it had been dried out (and, we believe, also cleaned) and the flooded cells remained out of action until the water was cleared. In our judgment it is clear that both sustained damage for the purposes of the 1971 Act. There plainly was a case to answer.

Two different criticisms arise from the summing up. The judge directed the jury:

> 'What is required before you can be satisfied that this defendant is guilty of criminal damage? One, that he did damage the cell and the blanket. Now, in law, you damage a thing if you render it imperfect or inoperative and you know on the evidence, the uncontested evidence, that as a result of putting the blanket down the lavatory and flooding the cell, the blanket was not capable of being used, obviously, and the cell and the adjoining cells were not capable of being used for a period of time. That in law would amount to damage. So you have to consider the rest of it. Can you be satisfied that that is what this defendant intended to do?'

> Although this direction accurately described the constituents of criminal damage for the purposes of this case, Mr Belger nevertheless argued that the language amounted to a direction that on the basis of the uncontested facts the blanket and the cell did in fact sustain damage for the purpose of the statute. That is a fair reading of this passage. In the normal way we would expect an issue of this kind to be resolved by the jury. That said, assuming the jury addressed the uncontested facts in accordance with the appropriate legal principles, a conclusion that the blanket and the cell did not sustain damage for the purposes of the 1971 Act would have been incomprehensible. The argument to the contrary was not even superficially plausible. We cannot discern any basis for concluding that the safety of this particular conviction is undermined by the way in which the judge dealt with this issue.

D's opinion of whether what he did is damage is irrelevant if damage is actually caused: *Seray-Wurie v DPP* [2012] EWHC 208.

Mr Justice Lloyd Jones:

> The charge relates to the use of a black marker pen to write on two parking notices, placed by the management company in a private residential estate where Dr Seray-Wurie lives . . . 'Damage' is not defined by the Act. It has been interpreted broadly by the courts and includes permanent or temporary physical harm and also permanent or temporary impairment of value or usefulness (See . . . in particular *Rowe v Kingerlee* [1986] Crim LR 735 where eradicable graffiti was held to be capable of amounting to criminal damage). The Crown Court found that Dr Seray-Wurie intended to write on the signs. It must therefore have concluded that he intended that ink from the marker pen should be placed on the signs. However, it also concluded that it was not sure that Dr Seray-Wurie intended to cause damage . . . . I accept the submission of Mr Boyd . . . the prosecution must prove at least recklessness as to whether damage may be caused, but need not show recklessness as to whether what is intended to be caused constitutes damage in law. I consider therefore that the marker ink placed on the signs was damage. In the present case the Crown Court had found—indeed it was admitted—that the defendant intended to do that. Furthermore, it is clear that the Crown Court found as a fact that the writing constituted damage. In these circumstances I consider the Crown Court was wrong in law in concluding that Dr Seray-Wurie lacked the requisite intention.

The court was of the opinion that an earlier case of *Fancy* [1980] Crim LR 171 had been wrongly decided. There, D, a demonstrator, was found in possession of a bucket of paint and a roller. He admitted that he painted walls over National Front slogans. He was charged with possessing an article with intent to damage property, contrary to s3 of the Act. The judge upheld a submission of no case to answer on the basis that (1) D did not intend to cause damage as the only evidence available was of an intention to paint out slogans and (2) he was not satisfied that to apply white paint over 'mindless National Front graffiti' could constitute damage to a wall. This would now constitute damage.

?!   **THINKING POINT** 14.9

Has D damaged property belonging to another?

1. D sprayed graffiti over the wall of the local town hall which cost £1,000 to clean off.

2. In an argument, D threw a bucket of water on to the wooden floor of his neighbour's kitchen.

Property

Property is defined according to s10 CDA 1971:

In this Act 'property' means property of a tangible nature, whether real or personal, including money and:

(a) including wild creatures which have been tamed or are ordinarily kept in captivity, and any other wild creatures or their carcasses if, but only if, they have been reduced into possession which has not been lost or abandoned or are in the course of being reduced into possession; but

(b) not including mushrooms growing wild on any land or flowers, fruit or foliage of a plant growing wild on any land.

For the purpose of this subsection, 'mushroom' includes any fungus and 'plant' includes any shrub or tree.

The major difference between s10 and s4 Theft Act 1968 is that land is not excluded from criminal damage. Otherwise, they are quite similar.

?!   **THINKING POINT** 14.10

D drives to his friend's house to settle a dispute. He angrily swerves to a halt on the drive, colliding with his friend's pet dog. He runs over the dog, killing it. Has he damaged property belonging to another?

Belonging to another

This is defined in s10(2) CDA 1971:

(2) Property shall be treated for the purposes of this Act as belonging to any person:

(a) having the custody or control of it;

(b) having in it any proprietary right or interest (not being an equitable interest arising only from an agreement to transfer or grant an interest); or

(c) having a charge on it.

(3) Where property is subject to a trust, the persons to whom it belongs shall be so treated as including any person having a right to enforce the trust.

(4) Property of a corporation sole shall be so treated as belonging to the corporation notwithstanding a vacancy in the corporation.

Section 10(2) is quite similar to s5 Theft Act 1968 except for the reference to 'custody' or control in s10(2)(a) instead of 'possession' or control in s5.

THINKING POINT 14.11

D agrees to sell his car to a friend (V). He gives him the keys and allows him to take the car on condition that V pays the price in the next few weeks. One week later, D demands the money. V promises to pay next month and refuses to return the car. D sees the car outside V's house one night. He immobilises it by removing the battery leads. Has D committed criminal damage?

Without lawful excuse

D may have a very good reason for damaging property belonging to another such as self-defence, prevention of crime, arrest of offenders, necessity or duress. In addition, s5 provides two specific defences:

(2) A person charged with an offence to which this section applies shall, whether or not he would be treated for the purpose of this Act as having a lawful excuse apart from this subsection, be treated for those purposes as having a lawful excuse:

(a) if at the time of the act or acts alleged to constitute the offence he *believed* that the person or persons whom he believed to be entitled to consent to the destruction or damage to the property in question had so consented, or would have so consented to it if he or they had known of the destruction or damage and its circumstances; or

(b) if he destroyed or damaged or threatened to destroy or damage the property in question or, in the case of a charge of an offence under s3 above, intended to use or cause or permit the use of something to destroy or damage it, in order to protect property belonging to himself or another or a right or interest in property which was or which he believed to be vested in himself or another, and at the time of the act or acts alleged to constitute the offence he *believed*:

(i) that the property, right or interest was in immediate need of protection; and

(ii) that the means of protection adopted or proposed to be adopted were or would be reasonable having regard to all the circumstances.

(3) For the purpose of this section it is immaterial whether a belief is justified or not if it is honestly held.

(4) For the purpose of subsection (2) above a right or interest in property includes any right or privilege in or over land, whether created by grant, licence or otherwise.

(5) This section shall not be construed as casting doubt on any defence recognised by law as a defence to criminal damage.

[Question: Does s5(2) pose a subjective or an objective test of D's belief?]

NOTE 14.1

Section 5(2) confers two defences in addition to defences of incapacity or general defences:

■ s5(2)(a)—mistaken belief in consent; and

■ s5(2)(b)—mistaken belief in the immediate need for protection of the property in question.

Section 5(2)(a)

D's belief here need not be reasonable according to the standards of ordinary people provided it is honestly held. This is a subjective test which permits an honest and genuine mistake. D is judged on the facts as he believed them to be. Therefore, his *belief* may be mistaken, correct, reasonable or unreasonable. What matters is whether it is honest.

→ CROSS-REFERENCE
The facts of *Jaggard* are set out in Chapter 8, 8.3.8.

Therefore, unlike self-defence, even if D's mistaken belief is the result of intoxication, the defence will succeed provided D's drunken mistake is honest. The case of *Jaggard v Dickinson* [1980] 3 All ER 716 confirms this principle in relation to s5(2)(a).

Ms Jaggard's honest but drunken belief that her friend would consent to her breaking a window to gain access to her flat prevailed.

In addition, D's *purpose* may be dishonest but his belief can still be honest.

R v Denton [1981] 74 CR APP R 81 COURT OF APPEAL

D was charged with arson contrary to s1(1) and s1(3) CDA 1971 for having set fire to machinery in his employer's cotton mill. His defence was that his employer was in financial trouble and had asked him to start the fire with a view to making a fraudulent insurance claim. The defence was therefore belief in consent under s5(2)(a). The trial judge held that the words in the subsection 'entitled' to consent implied a lawful purpose and thus D was not entitled to the owner's consent for a fraudulent purpose. The judge's ruling was rejected by the Court of Appeal.

Lord Lane CJ:

> The fact that somebody may have had a dishonest intent which in the end he was going to carry out, namely to claim from the insurance company, cannot turn what was not originally a crime into a crime.
>
> There is no unlawfulness under the 1971 Act in burning a house. It does not become unlawful because there may be an inchoate attempt to commit fraud contained in it; that is to say it does not become a crime under the 1971 Act, whatever may be the situation outside of the Act.
>
> Consequently it is apparent to us that the judge, in his ruling in this respect, was wrong. Indeed it seems to us, if it is necessary to go as far as this, that it was probably unnecessary for the defendant to invoke s5 of the 1971 Act at all, because he probably had a lawful excuse without it, in that T (the employer) was lawfully entitled to burn the premises down. The defendant believed it. He believed that he was acting under the directions of T and that on its own, it seems to us, may well have provided him with a lawful excuse without having resort to s5.

The case is authority for the proposition that burning down your own property is no offence under the CDA 1971, because it does not belong to another (subject to the equitable interests of mortgagees and other registered parties) and that what is important is D's honest belief, not that the means are reasonable or that the purpose is necessarily lawful. Contrast s5(2)(b) next:

Section 5(2)(b)

The defence under s5(2)(b) of mistaken belief in the need for protection of property consists of two parts:

1. That the damage was in order to protect property and

2. s5(2)(b)(i): That D believed in the *immediate* need of protection and

   s5(2)(b)(ii): that he believed the means adopted were reasonable.

Whether the damage was in order to protect property under the first test (1) is determined objectively according to D's belief, very much like the test for mistaken belief in self-defence, where the force must be (*objectively*) reasonable according to the facts as D (*subjectively*) believed them to be.

R v Hunt [1978] 66 CR APP R 105 COURT OF APPEAL

D set fire to a guest room in an old people's home to draw attention to the defective fire alarm system. He was charged with arson contrary to s1(1) CDA 1971. He claimed a lawful excuse under s5(2) but was convicted. The court confirmed that what D had done was not in itself an act that protected or was capable of protecting property. It was an act which drew attention to the immediate need for protecting the building by repairing the alarm system. Section 5(2) did not apply. The appeal was dismissed.

Lord Roskill:

> The question whether or not a particular act of destruction or damage or threat of destruction or damage was done or made in order to protect property belonging to another must be, on the true construction of the statute, an objective test. Therefore we have to ask ourselves whether, whatever the state of this man's mind and assuming an honest belief, that which he admittedly did was done in order to protect this particular property, namely the old people's home in Hertfordshire? . . . . this was not done in order to protect property; it was done in order to draw attention to the defective state of the fire alarm. It was not an act which in itself did protect or was capable of protecting property.

The subjective/objective nature of the first part of s5(2)(b) was confirmed in the next case:

Unsworth v DPP [2010] EWHC 3037 (ADMIN), DIVISIONAL COURT

D lopped off her neighbour's trees which were blocking the light to her property and was charged with criminal damage. The right to light is called an easement. Section 5(2)(b) protects not only property but a right or interest in the property. Her defence failed but she successfully appealed against her conviction.

Munby LJ:

> . . . the objective element . . . could not in this case . . . be any difficulty in the way of Ms Unsworth establishing the defence. . . . Manifestly in the present case. . . . not merely were the steps which Ms Unsworth believed it proper to take steps which *could* ameliorate the problem; they were steps which of their very nature *would* ameliorate the problem and moreover do so immediately.

In other words, she was objectively justified in her belief that her actions were taken in order to protect her right to light.

The second test (2 under sub-heading 5(2)(b)) of D's beliefs in s5(2)(b)(i) and (ii) is entirely subjective. This means that D's honest belief is all important, even as to whether the means of protection would be reasonable. There is no objective element here and so this is wider than self-defence. However, the defence will fail unless the threat to the damaged property was really immediate:

R v Hill [1988] 89 CR APP R 74 COURT OF APPEAL

D was arrested outside a US naval base in Wales in possession of a hacksaw blade. She admitted intending to use the blade to cut the perimeter fence of the base. On appeal against conviction of having the blade with intent without lawful excuse to use it to damage property belonging to another contrary to s3 CDA 1971, she argued lawful excuse: an honest belief in the need for immediate protection of her nearby house because the presence of the base would at some future time attract a nuclear strike by Soviet missiles. Furthermore, she believed that her means were reasonable having regard to all the circumstances. On the authority of *Hunt*, the court dismissed the appeal.

Lord Lane CJ:

> He [the judge in the case] had to decide as a matter of law, which means objectively, whether it could be said that on those facts as believed by the applicant, snipping the strand of the wire, which she intended to do, could amount to something done to protect either the applicant's own home or the homes of her adjacent friends in Pembrokeshire.
>
> He decided, again quite rightly in our view, that that proposed act on her part was far too remote from the eventual aim at which she was targeting her actions to satisfy the test.
>
> It follows therefore, in our view, that the judges in the present two cases were absolutely right to come to the conclusion that they did so far as this aspect of the case is concerned, and to come to that conclusion as a matter of law, having decided the subjective test as the applicants wished them to be decided.
>
> The second half of the question was that of the immediacy of the danger . . . . Once again the judge had to determine whether, on the facts as stated by the applicant, there was any evidence on which it could be said that she believed there was an immediate need of protection from immediate damage. In our view that must mean evidence that she believed that immediate action had to be taken to do something which would otherwise be a crime in order to prevent the immediate risk of something worse happening . . . The evidence given by this woman . . . drives this Court to the conclusion . . . that there was no evidence on which it could be said that there was that belief . . .'

 NOTE 14.2

There was no immediate threat of a Soviet missile strike and therefore the threat was too remote.

The same principle applied in the next two cases:

Ashford & Smith [1988] CRIM LR 682 COURT OF APPEAL

This was an appeal against conviction under s3 CDA 1971 (possessing articles with intent to damage property). The Ds had been found in possession of wire-cutting equipment with which they had tried to cut a wire fence surrounding an RAF base as part of a demonstration against nuclear weapons. Their defence was one of protection of property abroad and in this country by reducing the risk of nuclear war. The court held that the test of lawful excuse was objective and that the need for protective action was not immediate.

Ayliffe v DPP [2005] EWHC 684, [2005] CRIM LR 959 COURT OF APPEAL

D's car was clamped after he parked on private land having seen notices that the cars of trespassers would be clamped and the clamp only removed on payment of £25. D refused to pay and cut the clamp with a disc cutter the following day. He was charged with criminal damage to the clamp.

Nolan LJ:

We are solely concerned with the question whether Mr Lloyd had a lawful excuse for damaging the property of South Coast Securities . . . . To my mind, it would be a truly absurd state of affairs if the appellant, having consented to the risk of clamping, was at liberty to withdraw his consent with immediate effect once clamping had occurred and to proceed at once to recover his car by force. I am satisfied that this is not the law. Even assuming in the appellant's favour that the refusal of South Coast Securities to let him remove his car save on payment of £25 was an unlawful restraint, it would by no means follow that there was a lawful excuse for his subsequent action. He had a choice. He could have paid the £25 under protest, removed his car and taken action against South Coast Securities in the county court. Instead he chose to re-enter the car park, once again quite plainly as a trespasser, and to retrieve his car by causing some £50-worth of damage to the property of South Coast Securities.

In my judgment, the suggestion that there was a lawful excuse for his action is wholly untenable. At the worst what he had suffered was a civil wrong. The remedy for such wrongs is available in the civil courts. That is what they are there for. Self-help involving the use of force can only be contemplated where there is no reasonable alternative . . . .

?! THINKING POINT 14.12

Does D have a defence of lawful excuse in the following?

1. D is visiting the home of a wealthy friend. A fire breaks out in the lounge caused by a cigarette. D rips some heavy and very expensive curtains from their rails and throws them on the fire so as to dampen it down and prevent it from spreading. The curtains are damaged.

2. D is having a drink one night in a pub. A drunken stranger approaches and threatens to punch him on the nose. D hits him over the head with his stool, breaking it.

3. D scrawls anti-war graffiti on the pavement outside the Houses of Parliament in the belief that this is necessary for the protection of innocent lives and property in Iraq.

14.3.3 Mens Rea

Two elements are required:

- Intention or recklessness as to damage/destruction of property;
- Knowledge or belief that the property belongs to another.

D must damage/destroy property intentionally or recklessly, knowing or believing that it belongs to another. If D is unaware the property belongs to another, he is not guilty of criminal damage. MR must therefore be proved in relation to both damage/destruction and belonging to another.

R v Smith [1974] 1 ALL ER 632 COURT OF APPEAL

D, the tenant of a flat, installed some wiring into the conservatory connected to his stereo. With the landlord's permission, he affixed roofing material, asbestos wall panels and floor boards to the premises. Two years later he wished to leave the tenancy and damaged the panels so as to remove the wiring. He was charged with criminal damage under s1(1) CDA 1971. His defence was that he honestly believed he had damaged his own property. As a matter of civil law, once the fixtures had been made, they became the property of the landlord. It was held that MR was required not only as to an intention to destroy or damage property but also in relation to whether the property belonged to another:

James LJ:

> Construing the language of s1(1) we have no doubt that the actus reus is 'destroying or damaging any property belonging to another'. Applying the ordinary principles of mens rea, the intention and recklessness and the absence of lawful excuse required to constitute the offence have reference to property belonging to another. It follows that in our judgment no offence is committed under this section if a person destroys or causes damage to property belonging to another if he does so in the honest though mistaken belief that the property is his own, and provided that the belief is honestly held it is irrelevant to consider whether or not it is a justifiable belief . . .

Appeal allowed.

→ CROSS-REFERENCE
For details of the facts and outcome in *Caldwell*, refer to Chapter 3.

Intention to destroy/damage property bears its ordinary meaning (direct: aim or purpose or oblique: foresight of a virtual certainty).

Recklessness is now subjective *Cunningham* recklessness following the abolition of *Caldwell* by *R v G* [2003] UKHL 50, [2004] AC 1034. In *R v G*, Lord Bingham applied the Draft Criminal Code definition of recklessness (cl 18) to criminal damage:

(c) A person acts recklessly within the meaning of section 1 of the Criminal Damage Act 1971 with respect to –

    (i)   a circumstance when he is aware of a risk that it exists or will exist;

    (ii)   a result when he is aware of a risk that it will occur;

and it is, in the circumstances known to him, unreasonable to take the risk.'

Therefore, recklessness is satisfied by:

    (i)   Awareness that property might belong to another (a circumstance);

    (ii)   Awareness that damage/destruction might occur to that property.

?!   **THINKING POINT** 14.13

Does D have the MR for criminal damage? Use this exercise to revise basic categories of MR.

D throws his wife's valued oriental vase across a room so it smashes against the wall. His state of mind is as follows:

a. He wanted to smash the vase to annoy his wife.

b. He did not want to destroy it but knew that it would certainly be damaged.

c. He thought it would probably be damaged.

d. He thought there was a small risk of damage.

e. He did not care whether it was damaged or not.

f. The risk of damage never entered his mind because he was drunk/too angry.

g. The risk of damage never entered his mind because he suffered from an episodic mental illness.

14.3.4 Racially or Religiously Aggravated Criminal Damage

This offence was created by s30 Crime and Disorder Act 1998. Higher penalties will apply on conviction in the same way as they do for racially or religiously motivated assaults.

➜ CROSS-REFERENCE
See Chapter 10 for a discussion of racially or religiously motivated assaults.

14.3.5 Criminal Damage with Intent or Recklessness as to Endangering Life

Section 1(2) CDA 1971 defines this aggravated form of criminal damage.

> A person who without lawful excuse destroys or damages any property, whether belonging to himself or another–
>
> (a) intending to destroy or damage any property or being *reckless* as to whether any property would be destroyed or damaged; and
>
> (b) intending by the destruction or damage to endanger the life of another or being reckless as to whether the life of another would be thereby endangered;
>
> shall be guilty of an offence.

The offence is punishable by a maximum of life imprisonment.

The aggravating element of this offence is the intent or recklessness to endanger the life of another and this makes ordinary criminal damage a far more serious offence, hence the potential life sentence. The AR elements are similar to ordinary criminal damage except for two differences:

Actus reus

▪ Damage/destruction

▪ Property

▪ Belonging to D or another

▪ Without lawful excuse (*s5(2) does not apply*).

Mens rea

▪ Intention or recklessness as to endangerment of life.

Actus reus

This is similar to ordinary criminal damage and therefore we need only examine the differences. Firstly, D may commit this offence by damaging his own property as well as that belonging to another.

EXAMPLE 14.2

D hits V over the head with his bottle of beer which gets broken in the assault.

Secondly, lawful excuse is not defined in accordance with s5(2). The defences of honest belief in consent or the need for immediate protection of property are excluded from the aggravated form of criminal damage. Lawful excuse is defined here under general principles and so the defences of self-defence, defence of another, duress or necessity could apply.

EXAMPLE 14.3

D hits V over the head with his bottle of beer which gets broken in the assault because:

a. V was about to stick a broken glass into D's face (self-defence) or

b. D had been threatened by X with serious violence unless he did so (duress).

Mens rea

■ Intention or recklessness as to *damage to property* + *endangerment of life by that damage* (NB: *Cunningham* subjective recklessness applies).

MR is as for ordinary criminal damage *plus* intention or recklessness as to endangerment of life *by that damage.* There are several points to make:

There must be an intention to endanger the life of another. Therefore, if D attempts suicide by setting fire to his car whilst inside, this offence is not committed (*Thakar* [2010] EWCA Crim 2136).

The damage which D intended or foresaw must be that by which he intends or is aware might endanger life. An example would be *Parker* [1993] Crim LR 856 where D started a fire in his own house and was convicted of s1(2) criminal damage for risking (being reckless as to) the lives of his neighbours even though they were absent. Therefore, if D only intends minor harm by the damage but it unexpectedly gets out of control and threatens life, D should not be guilty.

EXAMPLE 14.4

D1 and D2 light an unauthorised small fire in a wood for a picnic barbecue. An abnormally strong wind causes the fire to spread and a child playing nearby is burned. In the absence of foresight of personal endangerment, neither D will be guilty.

It follows that provided endangerment was intended or foreseen, the means by which it arises will not matter. In *Steer* the House of Lords held that D did not endanger the life of another simply by firing rifle shots at the windows of a house occupied by V. If D had taken aim specifically at V standing behind a window, then D's intention to endanger V's life would have been clear, but this was not the case.

R v Steer [1987] 2 ALL ER 833 HOUSE OF LORDS

D fired three shots from an automatic.22 rifle at the bedroom window and front door of his former business partner against whom he bore a grudge. It was in the early hours of the morning and he first rang the doorbell, waking up the man and his wife both of whom looked out of the bedroom window. None of the shots were aimed at either victim. D was convicted of damaging property with intent contrary to s1(2) and appealed.

Lord Bridge:

> It is to be observed that the offence created by sub-s(2), save that it may be committed by destroying or damaging one's own property, is simply an aggravated form of the offence created by sub-s(1), in which the prosecution must prove, in addition to the ingredients of the offence under sub-s(1), the further mental element specified by sub-s(2)(b) .... Of course, it is obvious that any danger to life in this case was caused by the shot from the rifle itself, not by any trifling damage done to the bedroom window or to any property in the bedroom .... the respondent, in firing at the bedroom window, had no intent to endanger life, but accepts that he was reckless whether life would be endangered.
>
> Under both limbs of s1 of the 1971 Act it is the essence of the offence which the section creates that the defendant has destroyed or damaged property .... To be guilty under sub-s(1) the defendant must have intended or been reckless as to the damage to property which he caused. To be guilty under sub-s(2) he must additionally have intended to endanger life or been reckless whether life would be endangered 'by the damage' to property which he caused. This is the context in which the words must be construed and it seems to me impossible to read the words 'by the damage' as meaning 'by the damage or by the act which caused the damage'.
>
> Counsel for the Crown did not shrink from arguing that s1(2) of the 1971 Act had created, in effect a general offence of endangering life with intent or recklessly, however the danger was caused, but had incidentally included as a necessary, albeit insignificant, ingredient of the offence that some damage to property should also be caused. In certain fields of legislation it is sometimes difficult to appreciate the rationale of particular provisions, but in a criminal statute it would need the clearest language to persuade me that the legislature had acted so irrationally, indeed perversely, as acceptance of this argument would imply.

It is necessary for the risk to life to arise from the damage D has caused, not from D's act. In other words, D had intentionally caused criminal damage to V's window. He was reckless as to endangering life but he did not foresee that risk arising from the broken glass, only from the bullet he had fired. Therefore, he was not guilty of s1(2).

Steer involved only one act: firing a rifle at a window. That act gave rise to both the damage and, potentially, the risk to life.

In the next case, there were two acts: throwing a brick through a window, which caused the damage, and throwing a petrol can and a burning piece of paper through the broken window, which gave rise to a risk to life. The Court of Appeal overturned D's conviction of aggravated criminal damage being reckless as to whether life was endangered, because the risk to life did not arise from the damage to the window. The prosecution argument that there had been a single, continuing act was rejected.

Luke Wenton [2010] EWCA CRIM 2361

Leveson LJ:

> The Crown relied on a course of conduct. The window is broken which made it possible for the petrol canister and lit paper immediately thereafter to be introduced. The two acts, it is submitted, cannot be divorced from each other but were inextricably intertwined as part of the execution by the appellant of a single course of conduct to insert the petrol into the premises. Mr Grant argues

that the principle in Steer was qualified in two other cases, although the fundamental principle had been correctly left untouched.

In Dudley [1989] Crim.L.R 57 the court made it clear that the destruction or damage referred back to the destruction or damage intended or as to which there was recklessness, rather than destruction or damage actually caused. In Asquith and others [1995] 1 Cr.App.R (S) 492 the court recognised as well established that an offence under section 1(2) of the 1971 Act required proof that the intention or recklessness related to life endangered by the damage or destruction of the property. In both cases, however, focus was placed upon the consequence of the damage caused which in Asquith was the damage caused to the roof of a railway carriage onto which stones had been projected which not surprisingly the court concluded could endanger the lives of passengers.

In Warwick (heard at the same time as Asquith) it was similarly held that from an intention to break a window a jury could infer an intention to shower the driver of a police car, which was bombarded with stones, with broken glass causing him to lose control of his vehicle and that a series of such incidents of damage could properly be charged as a single course of conduct. This case is far removed from that. The incident of damage was unrelated to the incident which gave rise to the risk of endangerment to life.

The Court of Appeal held that the correct offence with which D should have been charged was arson contrary to s1(3) CDA 1971.

Provided D intended or was reckless (ie: foresaw or was aware) as to the risk of endangerment, no-one's life need actually be put at risk. In *Sangha* [1988] 2 All ER 385 for example, D started a fire in his own flat. It could not spread because of the special construction of the block. No-one's life was actually threatened but as D was unaware of that fact, it was held that he had recklessly put the lives of others at risk. What is important is D's state of mind at the time of the damage/destruction.

?! **THINKING POINT** 14.14

Have the following committed criminal damage being intentional or reckless as to endangerment of life?

1. A gang of people throw a hail of bricks through the window of a man and his family intending to frighten the occupiers. The family are unhurt.

2. Two teenagers drop a concrete block over a railway bridge on to a train for a joke. It smashes a window but no-one is hurt.

3. D throws bricks from his car at passing police cars. One smashes the windscreen and covers the driver with broken glass.

14.3.6 Arson

Section 1(3):

An offence committed under this section by destroying or damaging property by fire shall be charged as arson.

Maximum life imprisonment.

[The maximum life sentence applies even if D is not intentional or reckless as to endangerment of life. Otherwise, the AR/MR elements are identical to s1(1) or s1(2) criminal damage, except that D must intend or be reckless as to damage by fire.]

SUMMARY

In this chapter we have looked at the following offences:

Burglary

Section 9(1) Theft Act 1968—intentional/reckless entry of a building/part as a trespasser:

a. with intent to commit an ulterior offence of stealing, grievous bodily harm or criminal damage *or*

b. having entered as a trespasser, D goes on to steal or commit grievous bodily harm or attempts to do so.

- s9(1)(a) requires an ulterior intent at the time of entry.
- s9(1)(b) requires proof of MR for and commission of the ulterior offences/attempt following entry.

Aggravated burglary

Burglary accompanied by a firearm, weapon of offence or explosive.

Blackmail

Section 21 Theft Act 1968—an unwarranted demand with menaces with a view to gain or causing loss to another. There must be a lack of genuine belief that the demand is either reasonable or that the threat is a proper way of enforcing it.

Criminal damage

Section 1(1) CDA 1971—intentional or reckless destruction/damage of property belonging to another without lawful excuse. Mistaken belief in consent and the need for protection of property can provide lawful excuse.

Criminal damage endangering life

Section 1(2) CDA 1971—intentional or reckless damage to property + endangerment of life (NB: *Cunningham* subjective recklessness applies to these offences).

Arson

Section 1(3) CDA 1971—Damage by fire.

PROBLEM SOLVING

D is asked by his neighbours (H and W) to look after their house whilst they are on an extended holiday. He agrees and they give him the keys. Each week D goes into the house to collect the mail. On one occasion he takes a bottle of brandy from the kitchen and several DVDs from the lounge. He drinks half the bottle of brandy and replaces it the following week along with the DVDs which he has copied for his own use. Whilst upstairs in the bedroom one day he discovers some letters written to H by a girlfriend from which it is apparent that H is having an illicit affair. D emails H at his hotel and demands £1,000 or else he will inform W. H refuses to pay.

D decides that he will therefore throw a concrete block into H and W's pond which is full of ornamental fish. The block damages the pond. It springs a leak and the fish die.

Discuss D's liability for burglary, blackmail and criminal damage.

Remember:

- **I: Identify** relevant issues
- **D: Define** offences/defences
- **E: Explain/evaluate** the law
- **A: Apply** law to facts.

See the online resources for further guidance on solving this problem: www.oup.com/uk/loveless6e/.

FURTHER READING

J. Child, 'Understanding Ulterior Mens Rea: Future Conduct Intention is Conditional Intention'
(2017) 76(2) *CLJ* **311–336**
Argues that conditional intention and future conduct intention is the same thing.

I. Edwards, 'Banksy's Graffiti: A Not So Simple Case of Criminal Damage' (2009) 73(4) *JCL* **345**
Discusses whether graffiti artists are liable for criminal damage—do they have the requisite mens rea?

K. Laird, 'Conceptualising the Interpretation of 'Dwelling' in Section 9 of the Theft Act 1968' [2013]
Crim LR **656**
Considers the concept of a dwelling under s9 Theft Act 1968 and whether it is a question of fact or law.

K. Laird, 'Hudson v Crown Prosecution Service' [2017] 9 *Crim LR* **703**
Examines the ruling in the above case and argues that the defendant should not have been convicted.

M. Maguire, 'The Impact of Burglary upon Victims' (1980) 20 *British Journal of Criminology* **261**
Assesses reactions of victims of crime and some of the ways in which the effects might be addressed. Considers this in the context of interviews of victims.

H. O'Sullivan, 'When is a Residential Address a Dwelling for the Purposes of Sentencing?' (2017) 2
Sentencing News **6–9**
Considers the sentencing implications of this definition.

Inchoate offences: attempt, conspiracy and assisting and encouraging under the Serious Crime Act 2007

15

Introduction

15.1 Attempt

15.2 Conspiracy

15.3 The Serious Crime Act 2007: Encouragement and Assistance

KEY POINTS

This chapter will help you to understand that:

■ inchoate offences impose liability for the early stages of suggesting, planning or embarking on the substantive offence;

■ they are crimes of specific intent;

■ the intended substantive offence does not need to be completed.

It will also help you to identify the differences between them:

■ Attempt: Steps which are more than merely preparatory to commission of the substantive offence;

■ Conspiracy: An agreement to commit a crime;

■ Assisting and encouraging an offence under the Serious Crime Act 2007.

By the end of this chapter you will be able to compare liability for each offence where it is impossible to commit the intended crime.

INTRODUCTION

This chapter examines the conditions of liability for offences which can be committed before any intended substantive crime actually occurs. 'Inchoate' means 'incomplete'. As we saw in Chapter 2 you cannot be punished by the criminal law for your guilty thoughts alone. There is no criminal liability for thoughts or planning until these are translated into the first stages of action. Inchoate offences are designed around the early stages and to catch offenders before final offences are committed.

The law on attempt prohibits acts which are more than merely preparatory to the completion of a crime. Therefore, D must have reached the stage where he is about to embark on the AR of the substantive offence intending to complete the crime.

Conspiracy, on the other hand, prohibits nothing more than an agreement between two or more people to commit an offence. No physical step towards completion of the crime need be undertaken. This of course looks very much like punishment for thoughts alone but the essence of the offence is a communicated agreement.

Three new offences under the Serious Crime Act 2007 replace the former common law crime of incitement. They will apply to one who 'facilitates' another's offence.

Rationale

The rationale for the law on attempt is that D's actions are thought to be sufficiently close to the completed offence as to warrant liability. So far as conspiracy and encouraging and assisting are concerned, the rationale for punishing such early stages of planning is that there is increased danger to society from two or more people intent on criminality. This bears similarity to the principles underlying joint ventures and secondary participation. In this area, as you have read, the rules on the mental element required have substantially changed.

→ CROSS-REFERENCE
Joint ventures and secondary participation are discussed in Chapter 5.

Inchoate offences: crimes of specific intent

An inchoate offence, therefore, consists of the initial steps towards the commission of an offence. All are crimes of specific intent. Recklessness is not enough. Remember that in relation to murder, intention takes two forms, direct (aim/purpose) and oblique (foresight of a virtual certainty). Whether oblique intention applies to inchoate offences is unclear.

15.1 Attempt

15.1.1 Definition

15.1.2 Actus Reus

15.1.3 Mens Rea

15.1.4 Impossibility

15.1.5 Reform

KEY CASES

Gullefer [1990] 3 All ER 882—proximity or 'more than merely preparatory': D must have embarked on the crime itself;

Jones [1990] 3 All ER 886—proximity does not mean 'the last act' test;

Geddes [1996] Crim LR 894—lying in wait is not an attempt;

White [1910] 2 KB 124—unsuccessful poisoning is an attempt;

Shivpuri [1987] AC 1—you can attempt the legally impossible;

Ferriter [2012] EWCA Crim 211—attempted rape consists of more than pulling down V's trousers;

Pace and Rogers [2014] EWCA Crim 186—intention as to circumstances.

15.1.1 Definition

All statutory references in this section are to the Criminal Attempts Act 1981 unless otherwise stated. The offence of attempt is defined in s1(1) Criminal Attempts Act 1981:

> If, with intent to commit an offence to which this section applies, a person does an act which is more than merely preparatory to the commission of the offence, he is guilty of attempting to commit the offence.

Actus reus

- An act (not an omission);
- Which is more than merely preparatory.

Mens rea

- Intention to commit the completed offence.

Certain offences (set out in s1(4)) cannot be attempted:

> This section applies to any offence which, if it were completed, would be triable in England and Wales as an indictable offence, other than–
>
> - *conspiracy* (at common law or under s1 of the Criminal Law Act 1977 or any other enactment);
> - *aiding, abetting, counselling, procuring or suborning* the commission of an offence;
> - offences under s4(1) (*assisting offenders*) or 5(1) (*accepting or agreeing to accept considera-tion for not disclosing information about an arrestable offence*) of the Criminal Law Act 1967.
>
> You can only attempt a certain classification of offence. What is it?

15.1.2 Actus Reus

D will have to commit an act which is more than merely preparatory to the commission of the offence, and this will be a question of fact for the jury in each case.

Whether an act is more than merely preparatory is not necessarily an easy matter to determine. First, the intended offence needs to be identified. Then the AR must be ascertained. Whether D's acts are more than merely preparatory involves taking a view of the past (ie: what counts as merely preparatory?) and looking forward to the future (ie: what more needs to be done in order to complete the offence?) Look at the following two scenarios:

1. D plans to rob a post office. He approaches wearing a crash helmet and gloves and carry-ing an imitation gun and a threatening note. He is stopped by police one metre from the post office doorway.

2. D plans to murder V by burning down his house in the middle of the night whilst V is asleep. He buys some paraffin and matches early that evening and sets off. He keeps watch until he sees all the upstairs lights of V's house go out. As he is about to pour paraffin through V's letter box he is arrested.

You might think that in (1) D's acts are more than preparatory because he is on the point of committing robbery but you would be wrong. These were the facts of *Campbell* [1991] Crim LR 268 where the Court of Appeal surprisingly held that a number of acts remained undone. If D had not even got to the place where he could carry out the offence, it is unlikely he could be said to have committed attempted robbery. One might wonder why it would be necessary to wait a couple more minutes and put lives at risk before he could be arrested for an attempt. Surely, the victim would have been robbed in a matter of minutes. As we shall see, the divide between being 'on the job' and acts which are merely preparatory is not entirely clear.

In (2), however, D is at the scene of the intended murder and is immediately about to embark on it. He would appear to have gone further than the preparatory stage (ie: buying the paraffin and matches and travelling to V's house) and must, therefore, have committed attempted murder.

The 1981 Act is unhelpful on the question of the distinction between preparation and attempt. It is for the jury to decide in each case. The following cases decide that D will not attempt a crime unless he can be said to have embarked on it and be 'on the job'. It is not necessary for D to be beyond the point of no return.

What does 'more than merely preparatory' mean?

'More than merely preparatory' is not explained in the 1981 Act. Under the common law, the test was one of proximity. This was a rather vague term and was sometimes explained as requiring D to have 'crossed the Rubicon' or to be beyond the point of no return. At other times, it was described as 'the last act' before embarking on the actual crime, or 'one of a series of acts which would lead to the crime'. A narrower interpretation was that the attempt had to be immediately connected to the commission of the offence (*Eagleton* (1855) 6 Cox CC 559). Under the new test of 'more than merely preparatory' it is not necessary to have crossed the Rubicon. This is more generous to prosecutors. The test was explained in a series of cases occurring shortly after the introduction of the 1981 Act.

More than merely preparatory ends when D embarks on the substantive crime

R v Gullefer [1990] 3 ALL ER 882 COURT OF APPEAL

D jumped on to a greyhound race track and waved his arms to distract the dogs during a race. He hoped to disrupt the race so as to be able to recover £18 he had placed on a poor bet. The case was an appeal against his conviction of attempted theft from the bookmaker.

Lord Lane CJ:

> Might it properly be said that when he jumped on to the track he was trying to steal £18 from the bookmaker?
>
> Our view is that it could not properly be said that at that stage he was in the process of committing theft. What he was doing was jumping onto the track in an effort to distract the dogs, which in its turn, he hoped, would have the effect of forcing the stewards to declare 'no race', which would in its turn give him the opportunity to go back to the bookmaker and demand the £18 he had staked. In our view there was insufficient evidence for it to be said that he had, when he jumped onto the track, gone beyond mere preparation . . . .
>
> *It seems to us that the words of the 1981 Act seek to steer a midway course. They do not provide, as they might have done, that the R v Eagleton test is to be followed, or that, as Lord Diplock suggested, the defendant must have reached a point from which it was impossible for him to retreat before the actus reus of an attempt is proved. On the other hand the words give perhaps as clear a guidance as is possible in the circumstances on the point at which Stephen's 'series of acts' begins. It begins when the merely preparatory acts come to an end and the defendant embarks on the crime proper. When that is will depend of course on the facts in any particular case.* [Emphasis added.]

Appeal allowed.

Gullefer was, in fact, still some way from embarking on the recovery of his money (theft) although the judgment does not examine how much more he had still to do. The court applied the 'series of acts' test which required considering how much more D still had to do to embark on the intended crime. This can produce somewhat arbitrary (or 'case sensitive') results. For example, the Divisional Court in *Mason v DPP* [2009] EWHC 2198 held that an attempted offence of driving whilst over the legal limit of alcohol under s5(1) Road Traffic Act 1988 is not committed until something is done to put the car in motion, such as turning the ignition key. Opening the car door is not enough. Yet in *Moore v DPP* [2010] EWHC 1822 (Admin) the court disagreed that the achievement of motion was critical to the distinction between attempt and driving. Here, after giving a positive breath test, D walked to his car and drove a short distance on a private road but was stopped by a police officer. This was held to be an attempt to drive on the public highway notwithstanding the fact that he was prevented from doing so. The question of the *number* of outstanding acts was considered in the next case:

Pointing a loaded gun at V, even with the safety catch on, is an attempt

R v Jones (Kenneth) [1990] 3 ALL ER 886 COURT OF APPEAL

D was a jilted lover who took revenge on the new partner of his former girlfriend. He jumped into the partner's car wearing a disguise (a crash helmet and visor) and pointed a sawn-off shot gun at him. The safety catch was on and it was unclear as to whether D's finger was ever on the trigger. A struggle ensued and the partner got hold of the gun. D tried to strangle him but he got free. D was convicted of attempted murder and appealed. On his behalf it was argued that there were three things D had still to do in order to commit murder and that he had not, therefore, performed acts which were more than merely preparatory: to remove the safety catch, to place his finger on the trigger and to pull it.

Taylor LJ:

> We do not accept counsel's contention that s1(1) of the 1981 Act in effect embodies the 'last act' test derived from *R v Eagleton*. Had Parliament intended to adopt that test, a quite different form of words could and would have been used.
>
> It is of interest to note that the 1981 Act followed a report from the Law Commission on *Attempt, and Impossibility in Relation to Attempt, Conspiracy and Incitement* (Law Com No 102). At para 2.47 the report states:
>
>> 'The definition of sufficient proximity must be wide enough to cover two varieties of cases; first, those in which a person has taken all the steps towards the commission of a crime which he believes to be necessary as far as he is concerned for that crime to result, such as firing a gun at another and missing. Normally such cases cause no difficulty. Secondly, however, the definition must cover those instances where a person has to take some further step to complete the crime, assuming that there is evidence of the necessary mental element on his part to commit it; for example, when the defendant has raised the gun to take aim at another but has not yet squeezed the trigger. We have reached the conclusion that, in regard to these cases, it is undesirable to recommend anything more complex than a rationalization of the present law.'
>
> ... the words 'an act which is more than merely preparatory to the commission of the offence' would be inapt if they were intended to mean 'the last act which lay in his power towards the commission of the offence.' ...
>
> *Clearly his [D's] actions in obtaining the gun, in shortening it, in loading it, in putting on his disguise and in going to the school could only be regarded as preparatory acts. But, in our judgment, once he had got into the car, taken out the loaded gun and pointed it at the victim with the intention of killing him there was sufficient evidence for the consideration of the jury on the charge of attempted murder. It was a matter for them to decide whether they were sure that those acts were more than merely preparatory. In our judgment, therefore, the judge was right to allow the case to go to the jury, and the appeal against conviction must be dismissed.* [Emphasis added.]

The crucial step would appear to have been the pointing of the gun.

Stevens v R [1985] LRC (CRIM)

But read the following by L. Blake, 'Court of Appeal—Stevens v R (St. Helena), *Attempt*,' (1986) 50 *JCL* 247:

> ... D (who had been menacing his estranged wife with a shotgun) shot a policeman ... He pulled his wife back into the room where the shooting had taken place, and told the 14 year old daughter of the family that she was going to see her mother die. He released the safety-catch on the (loaded) shotgun. At that point the policeman groaned, and the D allowed his wife to go and get medical help, but made her promise to return 'because the next shot in the gun was for her'. The law report does not make it clear whether the gun was ever pointed at the wife during this crucial time, but ... it was never fired at her ... The Court held, as a matter of law, that Stevens' conduct towards his wife fell short of the crime of attempt. Hurley, J.A ... stated that although the D had made threats, and had taken preparatory action to the extent of loading his gun and releasing the safety catch, he never made any attempt to shoot his wife ... [T]here cannot be, at common law, an attempted murder with a gun unless the D actually fires that gun, or (at least), attempts to do so.

The law of St. Helena was essentially identical to s1(1) Criminal Attempts Act 1981.

However, the current test sometimes fails to adhere to common sense. See the next case.

Lying in wait is not an attempt

R v Geddes [1996] CRIM LR 894 COURT OF APPEAL

D was found in the boys' toilet of a school. A policewoman saw him and shouted but he left. His rucksack was later found in some bushes containing a large kitchen knife, some lengths of rope and a roll of masking tape. These items suggested that he was preparing to kidnap a boy. He was convicted of attempted false imprisonment contrary to s1(1) 1981 Act and appealed on the grounds that his act was only preparatory and did not constitute an attempt. The Court of Appeal held that the demarcation between acts which were merely *preparatory* and acts which might amount to an *attempt* were not clear or easy to recognise. Had D done an act which showed that *he had actually tried to commit the offence* in question or had he *merely equipped* himself to commit it? The court held that since he had had no contact or communication with any boy, nor had he actually confronted a boy at the school, his actions were merely preparatory even though there was clear evidence of his intent.

 NOTE 15.1

It might be asked how the principle of this case provides adequate protection to the public from harm. If D plans to commit a property offence, and equips himself accordingly, he can be convicted of *going equipped* contrary to s25 Theft Act 1968. There is, however, no equivalent for offences against the person. An alternative now might be s63 Sexual Offences Act 2003 (trespass with intent to commit a sexual offence). As Professor J.C. Smith remarked in the commentary to this case ([1996] *Crim LR* at 896): 'Stealing a child is incomparably more serious than stealing a watch.' Compare *R v Robson* [2009] 1 WLR 713 in which D's text message to a prostitute asking for details of 12-year-olds for sex constituted an attempt to arrange a sexual offence with a child under s14 Sexual Offences Act 2003.

Attempted rape

To commit attempted rape, D must intend to rape, rather than commit another sexual offence, and it must be proved that his actions are more than merely preparatory to penile penetration:

R v Ferriter [2012] EWCA CRIM 2211

D, the last customer in a bar, walked behind the bar and struggled with V, the barmaid, both ending up on the floor. V escaped and D stole money and spirits from the till. V alleged D had tried to pull down her trousers more than once. He was convicted of theft, to which he pleaded guilty, and attempted rape.

Hughes LJ:

> To borrow the language of Lord Bingham in R v Geddes [1996] Crim LR 894, it is often helpful to invite the jury to consider whether the defendant has done an act which shows that he has actually tried to commit the offence in question, or whether he has only got ready or put himself into a position or equipped himself to do so in future.
>
> The defendant's case here . . . was that there was nothing sexual in his mind at all. His case was that what he wanted to do was to take the money out of the tills behind the bar . . . We are entirely satisfied that the jury had ample material on which to conclude that the intention was sexual molestation as distinct from robbery. If he had wanted the money, he would have said so and he did not. The attempt to remove her trousers, which the jury clearly accepted, is wholly inconsistent with robbery and only consistent with sexual intent . . . In those circumstances we are, we think, driven to the conclusion that the conviction for attempted rape is unsafe.

A conviction of sexual assault was substituted as permitted by s3 Criminal Appeal Act 1968.

Which offence is D attempting to commit?

There are thousands of offences in the criminal justice system. It is sometimes difficult to identify exactly which offence D is attempting to commit.

R v Nash [1999] CRIM LR 308 COURT OF APPEAL

D left two notes for paper boys in the street inviting them to meet him in order to perform indecent acts. A third note offered the recipient work with a company and requested a specimen of urine. He appealed against convictions of attempting to procure acts of gross indecency. His appeal failed in relation to the first two explicit notes but succeeded in relation to the third note. Note three did not contain an overtly sexual invitation as compared to the first two. It was not an unequivocal invitation and not sufficiently proximate to the act of procurement to amount to an attempt.

?! **THINKING POINT** 15.1

Has D attempted murder in the following scenarios?

1. D hands D2 poison and tells him to put it in V's tea the following day. D2 does so but V does not die.

2. D hands a child some poison and tells her to put it in V's tea the following day. The child does so but V does not die.

On whether these cases draw the line between an attempt and substantive crime too late for effective intervention or, conversely, too early so that people risk conviction on the basis of their guilty thoughts alone, read this extract from K.J.M. Smith, 'Proximity in Attempt: Lord Lane's Midway Course' [1991] *Crim LR* 576:

> The transition from a common law test to one based on statute has not lacked difficulty. This is largely attributable to the unrevealing quality of 'more than merely preparatory' combined with uncertainty over the state and subsequent status of pre-Act authorities. The predictable outcome has been a fair crop of conflicting and, sometimes, confusing judicial dicta . . . .
>
> Turning to the wording of the statutory test itself, in *Gullefer* Lord Lane tried to put a little meat on the bare bones of the Act's provisions by briefly identifying and comparing the 'two lines of authority' existing before the Act. The first of these, the 'last act' approach, was exemplified by *Eagleton*, as later endorsed by Lord Diplock in *D.P.P. v. Stonehouse*. The 'other line of authority' rested on the notion of an act 'forming part of a series of acts which would constitute . . . actual commission of [the crime] if it were not interrupted.' Neither test represents the current law. Rather, according to Lord Lane, the 'words of the Act seek to steer a midway course' between the two: an attempt 'begins when the merely preparatory acts come to an end and the defendant embarks upon the crime proper [or] the actual commission of the offence.'
>
> What can be extracted from these observations? Lord Lane's denial of the relevance of the 'last act' or Rubicon principle is clear enough. But when is a defendant to be regarded as having embarked upon the 'crime proper' or the 'actual commission' of the offence? Does this mean that the defendant must, then and there, have been actually engaged in trying to bring about some *actus reus* element of the substantive offence? Though not identical, in most situations this approach would be as restrictive as demanding the defendant's 'last act.' Certainly, on the showing of the facts in *Gullefer*, the scope for finding that acts earlier than the 'last act' were 'more than merely preparatory' appears to be exceedingly limited. If the appellant in *Gullefer* had succeeded in stopping the greyhound race his £18 stake would have been returnable under the governing wagering provisions –the 'bookmakers would have been obliged to repay.' The only further action required by the appellant was the collection of his refunded stake. Stopping the race would have qualified the appellant for a refund. His next move, requesting repayment of the £18, would have been his 'last act.' . . .
>
> Lord Lane's guiding comments were subsequently aired and applied by the Court of Appeal in *Jones*. Here the appellant had climbed into the victim's car and pointed a loaded sawn off shotgun at the victim. The appellant's conviction for attempted murder was challenged on the grounds that his conduct was insufficiently proximate in that at least three more actions were required to be carried out by him before the full offence could have occurred: removing the gun's safety catch, putting the appellant's finger on the trigger and pulling it. Expressly adopting Lord Lane's 'midway course' and 'looking at the plain natural meaning' of section 1(1), the court concluded that:
>
>> 'Clearly [the appellant's] actions in obtaining the gun, in shortening it, in loading it, in putting on his disguise, and in [lying in wait] could only be regarded as preparatory acts. But, in our judgment, once he had got into the car, taken out the loaded gun and pointed it at the victim with the intention of killing him, there was sufficient evidence for consideration of the jury on a charge of attempted murder.'
>
> Again, as in *Gullefer*, the Court of Appeal appeared to perceive the ambit of attempt in narrow terms. Only behaviour very close to the defendant's last possible act is recognised as capable of being 'More than merely preparatory.' Curiously the court in *Jones* felt able to fortify its tight construction of the 1981 Act by resort to extracts from Law Commission Report 102. The curiosity lies in the court confining its citation of elements of paragraph 2.48 of the Report to those indicating no more than a

desire to end the use of the 'last act' test. Yet the concluding portion of the same paragraph, and elsewhere in the Report, which implied the Commission's wish to see attempt construed to cover conduct no more proximate than that in *Robinson*, is ignored . . . .

. . . a matter of penal policy, so far as they can be determined at present, the boundaries of attempt have been too tightly drawn. Circumstances where the actor is physically or temporally close to, or on the verge of, his 'last act' appear to be the remotest point which the Court of Appeal is prepared to concede may be an attempt. Thus, cases where the defendant is caught aiming a loaded gun or poised, matches in hand, next to a haystack, will pass the proximity test. Examples where activities are more remote and which appear likely to be regarded as 'merely preparatory' include:

(i)   a gunman, or person with a remotely detonatable bomb, lying in wait for his victim to appear;

(ii)   the prospective burglar positioning his ladder prior to entering a building, and

(iii) the would-be insurance fraudster who, having faked the insured event, writes to his insurers indicating an intention to submit a claim in the near future.

Clearly, it is highly debatable just where the balance ought to be struck between an individual's freedom of action and the broader social need of facilitating timely pre-emptive intervention. But it is suggested here that the present state of the law is undesirably narrow and that examples similar to the hypothetical cases posed above should be brought within the ambit of attempt.

Q. Does the author think that the law on attempts is drawn widely or narrowly? Do you agree with the author's opinion in the final paragraph? Why?

The search for an adequate definition of the AR of attempt has proved elusive. Much seems to depend on distinctions of fine degree. There is no need to 'cross the Rubicon' or reach the point of no return but it appears that the stage of 'more than merely preparatory' is not reached until everything necessary has been done for the crime to result.

The Law Commission has recently confirmed that the test of 'more than merely preparatory' should remain, notwithstanding an earlier proposal to replace it by two new offences: 'attempt' and 'criminal preparation' ('Conspiracy and Attempts', Law Com No 138, December 2009). Read the following extract:

8.80 It is worth adding, in closing, that the flexibility inherent in the present definition of the offence of attempt means that the courts currently have the power to draw the line separating mere preparation (incurring no liability) from attempt differently depending on the nature of the harm intended.

8.81 Where the line separating attempt from non-criminal preparation is drawn under the current law may depend on how serious, damaging and anti-social the intended offence is. In other words, it may be that the line will be drawn further back from the commission of the intended offence in proportion to the seriousness and/or anti-social nature of that offence. We accept that, if this is the approach which the courts adopt, consciously or otherwise, there is no compelling need for guiding examples. The inherent flexibility of the present inchoate offence, whatever label it bears, means that, by and large, the right decision will be reached for the type of offence intended.

8.82 On this view, cases such as Geddes should be seen as aberrations or deviations from the proper approach, and dealt with, as we suggest, by the creation of new context-specific offences where necessary.

The approach of the courts to the question of how to distinguish an attempt from the substantive crime attempted is far from satisfactory. It concerns the balance between the rights of the individual and the need to protect society. The danger of the law intervening too soon is that people will be punished for their intentions on the basis of little action. The danger of leaving it too late is that there will be little to distinguish an attempt from the substantive offence. Withdrawal or police intervention will be impossible.

15.1.3 Mens Rea

All inchoate offences are crimes of specific intent. In order to attempt a crime D must intend to bring about the final result or consequence. This will be so even where recklessness may be sufficient for the completed substantive crime (ie: a crime of basic intent, such as criminal damage). However, the AR of most offences also refers to the circumstances in which the offence must be committed (see Example 15.1 in this chapter). A separate MR element is therefore required for this aspect of the attempted offence. The law on this has changed quite recently as we shall see.

Conditional intent

→ CROSS-REFERENCE
See *Easom* [1971] 2 QB 315 discussed in Chapter 12, 12.1.3.

A conditional intent is also sufficient. Usually, this is only relevant to property offences, that is: an intent to steal on condition that D finds something worth stealing. A conditional intent does not suffice for theft but does suffice for attempted theft. This will be so even though the object/s D is searching for may not exist in fact.

Whatever state of mind suffices for the substantive offence, the MR of attempt requires intention to commit the final result as illustrated in the following sections.

Attempted murder

The MR of murder is intention to kill or cause grievous bodily harm. For the purposes of the law of attempt, only an intention to kill will suffice. This principle derives from *Whybrow* (1951) 35 Cr App R 141 where D wired up a soap dish to the electricity supply to administer an electric shock to his wife in the bath. On appeal against conviction the Court of Appeal confirmed that the judge had been wrong to direct the jury that an intention to kill or cause grievous bodily harm would suffice for attempted murder.

There is no offence of attempting an offence by omission. The 1981 Act requires 'an act'. However, the Law Commission recommend that attempted murder be extended to murder by omission where D has an intent to kill and fails to discharge a legal duty to V where that omission, if completed, could have resulted in V's death (Recommendation 20, Law Com No 318).

Attempted criminal damage

In *O'Toole* [1987] Crim LR 759 and *Millard* [1987] Crim LR 393, both cases of attempted criminal damage/arson, it was held that the prosecution had to prove intention to damage/destroy property belonging to another without lawful excuse and not just recklessness.

However, in order to attempt the aggravated form of criminal damage under s1(2) Criminal Damage Act 1971 relating to endangerment of life, MR can be satisfied by recklessness as to the risk of endangerment provided D intended to cause the initial act of criminal damage. For the substantive offence, it does not matter that there is no risk to V's life in fact provided the ulterior offence of endangerment was intended or foreseen. Therefore, an attempt will consist of a failed intentional act of criminal damage plus foresight of the risk of endangerment.

> **EXAMPLE** 15.1
>
> D intends to throw a brick through V's bedroom window. He knows there is a risk that V will be harmed by both the brick and the broken glass because the room is very small, it is 2.00 am and he believes V is asleep in bed. In fact, the brick misses the window and hits a wall. D has attempted intentional criminal damage with foresight (subjective recklessness) as to endangerment of life under s1(2) CDA 1971: *Attorney-General's Reference (No 3 of 1992)* [1994] 1 WLR 409.

The justification for requiring intention as to the result is that the punishment of a failed attempt must demand the highest and clearest form of MR.

MR as to the circumstances

Until recently, it was thought that although D must intend to bring about the *result* of an attempted offence, he need only be reckless as to any *circumstance* required by the AR (ie: he must foresee the circumstance as a possible or probable risk). This is the case even where the offence is one of negligence or strict liability. The difference between a result and a circumstance can be explained as follows:

> **EXAMPLE** 15.2
>
> 1. Rape—s1 Sexual Offences Act 2003. For the completed crime there must be intentional penetration of the mouth, vagina or anus (result) and D must lack a reasonable belief in consent (negligence as to a circumstance). For an attempt, D must intend to penetrate, but need not actually do so provided his act is more than merely preparatory to penetration. In addition, D must foresee a lack of consent (although some have argued that D need only lack a reasonable belief in consent).
> 2. Criminal damage—s1(1) Criminal Damage Act 1971. For the completed crime D must be either intentional or reckless as to damage/destruction of property belonging to another (result) without lawful excuse (circumstance). For an attempt, D must intend to damage/destroy (and will fail to do so) but need only know of a risk that he may not have a lawful excuse (recklessness).

The requirement of recklessness as to a circumstance was the result of *Khan* [1990] 1 WLR 813, a case of attempted rape, where the victim was penetrated by three men whilst the four appellants tried but failed to do so. At that time, the MR for rape was defined as intentional penetration plus recklessness as to lack of consent. The MR for attempted rape was therefore the same. However, the Court of Appeal took a different view in *Pace and Rogers* [2014] EWCA Crim 186 where it was held that nothing less than intention as to both the result and the circumstances was required. The offence in question concerned attempting to convert 'criminal property' under s327(1) Proceeds of Crime Act 2002. The defendants had bought second-hand scrap metal which they suspected to be stolen. Had that been the case, they could have been convicted of the completed offence which required 'suspicion' as MR. However, the transaction was part of a police sting operation and the metal belonged to the police. The question was whether they were guilty of an attempted offence. Section 1 Criminal Attempts Act 1981 requires an intent to commit an offence. Since the defendants were only suspicious that the property was stolen, they did not intend or know that it was, and they were acquitted. Davis LJ:

> ... as a matter of ordinary language and in accordance with principle, an 'intent to commit an offence' connotes an intent to commit all the elements of the offence. ...
>
> A constituent element of the offence of converting criminal property is, as we have said, that the property in question *is* criminal property. That is an essential part of the offence. Accordingly, an intent to commit the offence involves ... an intent to convert criminal property: and that connotes an intent that the property should *be* criminal property.

The consequence of this decision is that convictions for attempted crimes, by requiring intention as to both results and circumstances, will become more difficult. Academic commentators are divided as to whether this decision was right or not. For example, M. Dyson in 'Scrapping *Khan*' [2014] 6 *Crim LR* 445 argues that:

> ... as a matter of policy, *Pace* cannot be right. For instance, it cannot be right that the defendant who, doing more than merely preparatory acts to rape a complainant, should only be liable for attempted rape if he intends that she does not consent, rather than if he has no reasonable belief that she does.

On the other hand, Professor P. Mirfield in 'Intention and Criminal Attempts' [2015] 2 *Crim LR* 142 considers that:

> Even if it would be better, in policy terms, for Khan ... to be guilty of attempted crime, it might be thought that there are two rather important policies or principles pointing the other way, not least because constitutional in nature. As Davis LJ clearly recognized, it is not for judges to overturn the clear words of a sovereign parliament even on the most convincing policy grounds. And he may also have had in mind the important idea, which is part of the rule of law, that, where there is uncertainty, criminal statutes should be interpreted in the way least favourable to the prosecution.

?! THINKING POINT 15.2

Has D committed an attempt?

D intends to have sexual intercourse with V not thinking about whether she will consent or not. She protests and D is physically unable to penetrate her.

As you will see, attempt is different from conspiracy which requires intention as to both consequences and circumstances.

15.1.4 Impossibility

Under the previous common law, D could not be liable for attempting an offence which was physically or legally impossible. Liability for attempting the impossible only existed in respect of ineptitude. We encountered one such example in Chapter 2, *White* [1910] 2 KB 124 Court of Appeal, where D put two grains of cyanide of potassium in his mother's drink, intending to kill her. She died, but from heart failure not the poison, which was insufficient to have killed her. His appeal against conviction of attempted murder failed, Bray J concluding that the jury must have found that the appellant intended to kill but was mistaken as to the necessary dose. This approach was confirmed by the House of Lords in *Haughton v Smith* [1975] AC 476 where D's conviction for attempting to handle stolen goods which were not, in fact, stolen, was overturned.

Under s1(2) Criminal Attempts Act 1981 you can attempt an offence which it is impossible to complete for various reasons:

- *physical impossibility* (eg: D intends to steal property which no longer exists or has been removed elsewhere); or
- *ineptitude* (eg: D intends to enter premises by breaking down the front door using a hammer but the hammer breaks); or
- *legal impossibility*. Here D commits a mistake of fact (eg: handling property believed to be stolen but which is not) or a mistake of law (eg: having sexual intercourse with a girl of 17 believing the age of consent to be 18 when it is 16).

Section 1(2) says that, regardless of the reason for impossibility, D may be convicted of an attempt:

> (2) A person may be guilty of attempting to commit an offence to which this section applies even though the facts are such that the commission of the offence is impossible.
>
> (3) In any case where–
>
> > (a) apart from this subsection a person's intention would not be regarded as having amounted to an intent to commit an offence: but
> >
> > (b) *if the facts of the case had been as he believed them to be*, his intention would be so regarded, then, for the purposes of subsection (1) above, he shall be regarded as having had an intent to commit that offence. [Emphasis added.]

This establishes that D may commit an attempt even though it is impossible for any reason. The basis of liability is D's belief which is subjectively assessed, that is: what did he actually believe?

Shortly after the Act, however, the House of Lords in *Anderton v Ryan* [1985] AC 560 refused to hold that s1(2) imposed liability for attempting the factually impossible and reverted to the common law test. Here D bought a video recorder believing it to be stolen when it was not. She was convicted and appealed. Lord Bridge held that the legislation led to absurd results. A man could be convicted under s1(3) of stealing an umbrella, believing it to be stolen, when it was his own. Liability would be imposed for his guilty thoughts but his actions would be innocent. The court thought that liability for attempting the impossible should exist for acts which were potentially harmful (such as rummaging around in someone's empty pocket) but not for those which were *objectively innocent* such as Mrs Ryan's. However, one year later, the House of Lords overruled *Anderton v Ryan*:

R v Shivpuri [1987] AC 1 HOUSE OF LORDS

D was found by customs officials in possession of a suitcase which he admitted he believed to contain prohibited drugs which consisted, in fact and unknown to him, of vegetable matter similar to snuff. He was convicted of attempting to commit the offence of being knowingly concerned in dealing with and harbouring prohibited drugs contrary to s170(1)(b) Customs and Excise Management Act 1979. He appealed on the basis that he had not done an act which was more than merely preparatory to the commission of the offence as required by s1(1) CAA 1981.

Lord Bridge:

. . . In each case the act was clearly more than preparatory to the commission of the intended offence; it was not and could not be more than merely preparatory to the commission of the actual offence, because the facts were such that the commission of the actual offence was impossible. Here then is the nub of the matter. Does the 'act which is more than merely preparatory to the commission of the offence' in s1(1) of the 1981 Act . . . require any more than an act which is more than merely preparatory to the commission of the offence which the defendant intended to commit? Section 1(2) must surely indicate a negative answer; if it were otherwise whenever the facts were such that the commission of the actual offence was impossible, it would be impossible to prove an act more than merely preparatory to the commission of that offence and sub-ss(1) and (2) would contradict each other.

This very simple, perhaps over-simple, analysis leads me to the provisional conclusion that the appellant was rightly convicted of the two offences of attempt with which he was charged. But can this conclusion stand with Anderton v Ryan? The appellant in that case was charged with an attempt to handle stolen goods. She bought a video recorder believing it to be stolen. On the facts as they were to be assumed it was not stolen. By a majority the House decided that she was entitled to be acquitted. I have re-examined the case with care . . . . Running through Lord Roskill's speech and my own in Anderton v Ryan is the concept of 'objectively innocent' acts which, in my speech certainly, are contrasted with 'guilty acts'. . . .

If we fell into error, it is clear that our concern was to avoid convictions in situations which most people, as a matter of common sense, would not regard as involving criminality. In this connection it is to be regretted that we did not take due note of para 2.97 of the Law Commission Report, Criminal Law: Attempt and Impossibility in relation to Attempt, Conspiracy and Incitement (1980) (Law Com no 102) which preceded the enactment of the 1981 Act, which reads:

> 'If it is right in principle that an attempt should be chargeable even though the crime which it is sought to commit could not possibly be committed, we do not think that we should be deterred by the consideration that such a change in our law could also cover some extreme and exceptional cases in which a prosecution would be theoretically possible. An example would be where a person is offered goods at such a low price that he believes that they are stolen, when in fact they are not; if he actually purchases them, upon the principles which we have discussed he would be liable for an attempt to handle stolen goods. Another case which has been much debated is that raised in argument by Bramwell B in Reg v Collins. If A takes his own umbrella, mistaking it for one belonging to B and intending to steal B's umbrella, is he guilty of attempted theft: Again, on the principles which we have discussed he would in theory be guilty, but in neither case would it be realistic to suppose that a complaint would be made or that a prosecution would ensue.'

I am satisfied on further consideration that the concept of 'objective innocence' is incapable of sensible application in relation to the law of criminal attempts. The reason for this is that any attempt to commit an offence which involves 'an act which is more than merely preparatory to the commission of the offence' but which for any reason fails, so that in the event no offence is committed, must ex hypothesi, from the point of view of the criminal law, be 'objectively innocent'. What turns what would otherwise, from the point of view of the criminal law, be an innocent act into a crime is the intent of the actor to commit an offence. [Emphasis added.]

Appeal dismissed.

 NOTE 15.2

1. Lord Hailsham LC would also have dismissed the appeal on the basis that the appellant was guilty on the clear wording of s1(1) and (2) of the 1981 Act without recourse to s1(3) because D's intention was to evade and cheat the customs authorities, an offence, and he had done an act which was more than merely preparatory to that offence.

2. Lord Bridge decided that the acts of retention and harbouring the packages and taking steps to meet a recipient were more than preparatory to the commission of the *intended* offence. This was sufficient under s1(3). Clearly, the acts could not be more than preparatory to an actual offence because it was physically impossible, but this was not relevant to s1(3).

?! **THINKING POINT** 15.3

Is D guilty of an attempt in the following scenarios?

1. D rummages through V's coat pocket hoping to steal something of value. The pocket is empty.
2. D buys what he believes to be cocaine from X. It is in fact baking powder.
3. D, aged 16, lives in London and believes he is fare-dodging by failing to pay for a bus ride. In fact, bus transport in London is free for children aged 16 and under.
4. D plunges a knife into his own pillow in his bed. D believes it to be his enemy V and intends to kill him.

15.1.5 Reform

Clause 49 Draft Criminal Code:

(1) A person who, intending to commit an indictable offence, does an act that is more than merely preparatory to the commission of the offence is guilty of attempt to commit the offence.

(2) For the purposes of subsection (1), an intention to commit an offence is an intention with respect to all the elements of the offence other than fault elements, except that recklessness with respect to a circumstance suffices where it suffices for the offence itself.

(3) 'Act' in this section includes an omission only where the offence intended is capable of being committed by an omission.

(4) . . . the question whether that act was more than merely preparatory is a question of fact.

This replicates the current law. Clause 50 would impose liability for attempting, inciting or conspiring to commit an offence even though it is impossible, if it would be possible on the facts which D hopes or believes will exist at the time of commission.

Attempt and conspiracy

The 'Conspiracy and Attempts: A Consultation Paper' (Law Com CP No 183, 2007) proposed the replacement of the current law on attempt with two new inchoate offences: 'criminal attempt' applying to the last act D needs to do before committing the intended offence and 'criminal preparation' covering much earlier acts. This proposal was abandoned in Law Com No 318 (2009) as indicated in the text.

SECTION SUMMARY

Attempt is defined by s1(1) Criminal Attempts Act 1981 and consists of:

Actus reus

■ *An act which is more than merely preparatory to commission of the substantive offence; and*

Mens rea

■ *Intention to bring about the result;*

■ *Intention can be direct/oblique/conditional;*

■ *Recklessness suffices as to a circumstance;*

■ *Recklessness suffices as to an ulterior offence.*

Impossibility: Under s1(2) and 1(3) you can attempt an offence which is impossible factually, legally or due to ineptitude.

15.2 Conspiracy

15.2.1 Introduction

15.2.2 Actus Reus

15.2.3 Impossibility

15.2.4 Conspiracy to Defraud

15.2.5 Conspiracy to Corrupt Public Morals and Conspiracy to Outrage Public Decency

15.2.6 Reform

KEY CASES

R v G, R v F [2012] EWCA Crim 1756—agreement to rape a child not proved by mere possession of indecent images;

R v Shillam [2013] EWCA Crim 160—no common design on the basis of separate but similar designs;

Saik [2006] UKHL 18—MR of conspiracy: intention as to consequences and knowledge/intention as to circumstances;

Siracusa [1990] Cr App R 340—conspiracy requires an intention that an offence should be committed;

Yip Chiu-Cheung [1994] 3 WLR 514—agents provocateurs have criminal intent;

Shaw [1961] 2 All ER 446—conspiracy to corrupt public morality: 'Ladies Directory';

Knuller [1972] 3 WLR 143—conspiracy to outrage public decency: 'IT Magazine'.

15.2.1 Introduction

The essence of conspiracy is 'an agreement' between two or more people to commit an offence. Here, the law intervenes at a much earlier stage than with an attempt for there need be no positive steps taken towards the commission of an offence beyond mere agreement. The rationale is based on the increased danger of group criminality. Conspiracy is a convenient offence for prosecutors where it is clear that one or several crimes have been committed by a diverse group of people but there is little direct evidence against them other than in relation to an original agreement. Therefore, no evidence of any criminal act beyond an agreement is required to obtain a conviction. Conspiracy is only triable on indictment even where the object of the agreement is to commit a summary offence. The sentence is now the maximum for the intended offence.

Conspiracy was a common law offence until the Criminal Law Act 1977 abolished all but two common law offences, conspiracy to defraud and conspiracy to corrupt public morals or outrage public decency, replacing them with statutory conspiracies.

At common law a conspiracy was an agreement between two or more people to do 'an unlawful act or to do a lawful act by unlawful means' (called the 'object' of the conspiracy). There was no necessity to prove an agreement to commit a *crime*. The unlawful act could be a tort, such as trespass, if there was also an intent to inflict damage, or economic injury. The sentence was unlimited. This extremely wide and infamous law led to several controversial convictions against squatters, demonstrators, strikers, picketers and individuals accused of terrorism. Conspiracies in respect of obscenity and indecency effectively controlled moral behaviour that was not otherwise criminal. Naturally, the law carried a great risk of injustice and conspiracy was largely reformed by the Criminal Law Act 1977 following 'Conspiracy and Criminal Law Reform' (Law Com No 76), which recommended that conspiracy be limited to agreements to commit crimes (statutory conspiracies). There are common elements to both statutory and the remaining common law conspiracies.

Many conspiracies have a transnational element: money laundering, drugs trafficking, people trafficking, arms trafficking and terrorism. Some will be domestic but with a transnational element, where the evidence is located abroad. Such conspiracies are difficult to prosecute, and rely on international mutual legal assistance agreements for investigation and detection of evidence.

Common law and statutory conspiracies

Actus reus

- Agreement between two or more people;
- Statutory conspiracies: s1(1) Criminal Law Act 1977.

Mens rea

- Intention to commit a criminal offence and intention that the result should occur;
- Knowledge or intention as to the circumstances of the offence;
- In the case of common law conspiracies to defraud and corrupt public morals or outrage public decency the intention may be to commit a result which may be wider than a crime.

15.2.2 Actus Reus

Definition of a statutory conspiracy (s1(1) Criminal Law Act 1977 as amended by s5 Criminal Attempts Act 1981):

(1) Subject to the following provisions of this Part of this Act, if a person agrees with any other person or persons that a course of conduct shall be pursued which, if the agreement is carried out in accordance with their intentions, either–

(a)   will necessarily amount to or involve the commission of any offence or offences by one or more parties to the agreement, or

(b)   would do so but for the existence of facts which render the commission of the offence or any offences impossible, he is guilty of conspiracy to commit the offence or offences in question.

(2)   Where liability for any offence may be incurred without knowledge on the part of the person committing it of any particular fact or circumstance necessary for the commission of the offence, a person shall nevertheless not be guilty of conspiracy to commit that offence by virtue of subsection (1) above unless he and at least one other party to the agreement intend or know that that fact or circumstance shall or will exist at the time when the conduct constituting the offence is to take place.

A new s1A concerns conspiracies to commit offences outside the UK. This provision was inserted by the Criminal Justice (Terrorism and Conspiracy) Act 1998 and amended by the Coroners and Justice Act 2009 s72.

Agreement between two or more people

The essence of conspiracy, whether common law or statutory, is an agreement between two or more people to commit a crime. It need not be followed by any act towards the commission of the crime. The offence is committed as soon as the agreement is made. To amount to an agreement, there must be a common purpose communicated to and shared by at least one other party to the conspiracy. Something more than just a mental process is required together with evidence of spoken or written words or some other form of act indicating agreement.

It was held in *R v G, R v F* [2012] EWCA Crim 1756, for example, that an agreement to rape a male child under 13 was not proved by mere possession of indecent images of children on both G and F's laptop and text messages between them. The evidence against them was equivocal and as consistent with fantasy as with an agreement to rape, especially since nothing further had happened.

The law requires a minimum of two people to the agreement. Provided there is evidence of agreement between D and at least one other person who must be of the age of criminal responsibility (10), D can be convicted of conspiracy even if the other parties cannot be identified, or they are acquitted (*R v Longman & Cribben* (1980) 72 Cr App R 121), or where one conspirator or both withdraw (*Austin* [2011] EWCA Crim 345).

Conspiracy is a continuing offence and thus parties can join an existing conspiracy after the initial agreement. It is not necessary for all conspirators to make an agreement with each other or even to make contact with each other provided each has agreed with one other person to commit a crime and, fundamentally, there is a common purpose. Where one person makes agreements with several others individually, it is known as a 'wheel conspiracy'. Where one person makes an agreement with another, who makes the same agreement with yet another and so on, it is known as a 'chain conspiracy'. It can sometimes be difficult to find the common purpose:

R v Shillam [2013] EWCA CRIM 160
. . . .

The appellant and X, neither of whom knew each other, separately purchased cocaine from Robb, a central supplier. Both the appellant and X supplied other people. They were charged, with Robb and others, of conspiracy to supply cocaine. The question was whether there was evidence of a conspiracy between all the parties:

Toulson LJ:

> Conspiracy requires a single joint design between the conspirators within the terms of the indict-ment. It is possible, as in *Mehta* [2012] EWCA Crim 2824, that the evidence may prove the existence of a conspiracy of narrower scope and involving fewer people than the prosecution originally al-leged, in which case it is not intrinsically wrong for the jury to return guilty verdicts accordingly, but it is always necessary that for two or more persons to be convicted of a single conspiracy each of them must be proved to have shared a common purpose or design.

The prosecution's argument that there was a 'wheel' or 'chain' conspiracy with Robb at its centre was rejected; but in such a case, although each conspirator need not necessarily know of the iden-tity or even the existence of all the other conspirators, there must be a shared criminal purpose or design in which all have joined, rather than merely similar or parallel ones. Neither was the court persuaded of an umbrella conspiracy, illustrated in *Mehta*:

> I employ an accountant to make out my tax return. He and his clerk are both present when I am asked to sign the return. I notice an item in my expenses of £100 and say: 'I don't remember incurring this expense.' The clerk says: 'Well, actually I put it in. You didn't incur it, but I didn't think you would object to a few pounds being saved.' The accountant indicates his agreement to this attitude. After some hesitation I agree to let it stand. On those bare facts I cannot be charged with 50 others in a conspiracy to defraud the Exchequer of £100,000 on the basis that this accountant and his clerk have persuaded 500 other clients to make false returns, some being false in one way, some in another, or even all in the same way. I have not knowingly attached myself to a general agreement to defraud.

The court concluded that you cannot prove a common design on the basis of separate but similar designs:

> Since Robb was put by the prosecution as the head of the alleged conspiracy, and the involvement of the appellant and Reid was with him, the jury should have been directed to consider first the case in relation to Robb. As to that, there was a strong case that he masterminded the acquisition and processing of the drugs for onward distribution, and that this must have involved the knowing participation of others, so rendering him guilty of the conspiracy charged. The jury should next have been told that if they were not sure of Robb's guilt, they should also acquit the other defend-ants; but that if they were sure of his guilt, they must then consider whether the prosecution had proved as against each of the other defendants that they shared a common purpose or design (as distinct from separate but similar designs) so as to be a party to the *same* conspiracy, i.e. a con-spiracy wider than the supply of cocaine to that particular defendant.

There is no liability if the only parties to the agreement are husband and wife but they can be liable if a third party joins the agreement. The Law Commission in Law Com No 318 (2009) would abol-ish this exemption. There is no liability if the agreement is with the intended victim. Alternatively, an agreement to commit a crime between an adult and a child below the age of 10 or between hus-band and wife may result in *secondary liability* if the crime is completed rather than conspiracy.

A person can be guilty of conspiracy even though he cannot commit the completed offence as a principal offender. Therefore, a woman can commit conspiracy to rape if she is party to an agreement with one or more people that X should rape V.

Statutory conspiracies

Section 1(1): 'course of conduct'

a. Intention as to consequences

The course of conduct must necessarily amount to or involve the commission of an offence. The mental element, apart from agreement, consists of an intention to pursue a course of conduct (ie: actions) leading to a crime which the conspirators intend to commit. Therefore, they must intend both the physical actions and the consequences or result of those actions.

R v Siracusa [1990] 90 CR APP R 340 COURT OF APPEAL

D was convicted of conspiracy to import heroin contrary to s170(1)(b) Customs and Excise Management Act 1979. He had agreed to smuggle cannabis into the country but it was in fact heroin. On appeal his conviction was overturned. The essence of conspiracy was agreement. One did not prove an agreement to import heroin by proving an agreement to import cannabis. However, he could be convicted of the substantive offence of importing heroin because the point had been previously established by case law that a person could be convicted of importing heroin where he believed he was importing cannabis.

This case demonstrates that although D may possess the mental element for a substantive offence he will not necessarily do so for conspiracy to commit it.

 EXAMPLE 15.3

Conspiracy to commit murder must involve an agreement and an intention to kill. If two people agree to shoot V in the leg they commit conspiracy to commit grievous bodily harm. If V dies, they have committed murder. But they have not committed conspiracy to murder. Intention to commit grievous bodily harm is insufficient. There must be an intention to kill.

b. Knowledge/intention of facts or circumstances

Under s1(2) a course of conduct includes any circumstances necessary for the commission of the substantive offence. Intention or knowledge as to the existence of certain circumstances is crucial even if recklessness or negligence would suffice for the substantive offence. Intention or knowledge must exist at the time of the agreement.

R v Saik [2006] UKHL 18 HOUSE OF LORDS

This was a case of conspiracy to launder money against D who operated a bureau de change in London. He had pleaded guilty at trial subject to the qualification that he only suspected but did not know the money was the proceeds of crime. The substantive offence of money laundering was satisfied by 'reasonable suspicion' and therefore D might have had the requisite mental element for that crime but the question was whether suspicion sufficed for conspiracy. The House held that in respect of a material fact or circumstance conspiracy has its own mental element. It is set as high as to 'intend or know'.

Lord Nicholls:

> Section 1(2) qualifies the scope of the offence created by section 1(1). This subsection is more difficult. Its essential purpose is to ensure that strict liability and recklessness have no place in the offence of conspiracy . . . .
>
> Under this subsection conspiracy involves a third mental element: intention or knowledge that a fact or circumstances necessary for the commission of the substantive offence will exist. Take the offence of handling stolen goods. One of its ingredients is that the goods must have been stolen. That is a fact necessary for the commission of the offence. Section 1(2) requires that the conspirator must intend or know that this fact will exist when the conduct constituting the offence takes place.

It follows from this requirement of intention or knowledge that proof of the mental element needed for the commission of a substantive offence will not always suffice on a charge of conspiracy to commit that offence. In respect of a material fact or circumstance conspiracy has its own mental element. In conspiracy this mental element is set as high as 'intend or know'. This subsumes any lesser mental element, such as suspicion, required by the substantive offence in respect of a material fact or circumstances. In this respect the mental element of conspiracy is distinct from and supersedes the mental element in the substantive offence. When this is so, the lesser mental element in the substantive offence becomes otiose on a charge of conspiracy.

Appeal allowed.

 NOTE 15.3

Suspicion, recklessness, negligence or strict liability as to circumstances do not apply in conspiracy. At the time of the agreement, each conspirator must intend or know the circumstances will exist when the crime is committed.

 EXAMPLE 15.4

D commits rape by intentionally penetrating the vagina, anus or mouth of another person with his penis non-consensually where D does not reasonably believe that the other consents (s1 Sexual Offences Act 2003). For conspiracy to rape, however, the conspirators would need to know or intend at the time of the agreement that the other person should not consent rather than suspect or fail to reasonably believe in consent, that is: 'whether he consents or not we will have sexual intercourse'. Once the agreement is made, the offence is committed.

Therefore, it would make no difference if the rape victim later consented to sexual intercourse at the time of the act. The intention of the conspirators *at the time of the agreement* is to have sexual intercourse even if the victim does not consent.

If one party to the agreement knows or intends that any circumstances necessary for the substantive offence should exist but the other does not, there can be no liability for conspiracy at all.

 EXAMPLE 15.5

D1 asks D2 to collect a consignment of goods which D1 knows to be stolen. D2 does not know the goods are stolen. There can be no liability for conspiracy to handle stolen goods at all. There was no agreement or meeting of minds on conduct which both D1 and D2 intended would lead to an offence.

The Law Commission in Law Com No 318 (2009) recommends that conspiracy should carry the same degree of fault as to circumstances as required by the relevant substantive offence (with the exception of offences of negligence when recklessness should be required). The current law is too generous to defendants.

c. 'If carried out'

The course of conduct agreed upon must necessarily amount to a crime if carried out in accordance with the conspirators' intentions. Again, this signifies the fundamental fact that there must be an agreement, or common purpose, to commit a crime not a civil or moral wrong. Whether or not the crime is subsequently committed is immaterial.

THINKING POINT 15.4

D1 agrees with D2 that D2 should steal V's watch as he walks down the street but only if it is a Rolex watch. D2 is nine years old.

Has D1 committed conspiracy to rob?

Conditional intent

The intention need only be conditional, that is: to steal only if the conspirators find anything of value. Therefore, in *Reed* [1982] Crim LR 819 the Court of Appeal explained that an agreement to rob a bank if it seemed safe to do so at the time of arrival sufficed. In *Jackson* [1985] Crim LR 444 an agreement to shoot a man in the leg to get him a reduced sentence if he received a conviction of burglary was sufficient. If the condition of the agreement occurred (ie: that he was actually convicted), the course of action would necessarily amount to the offence of perverting the course of justice.

d. 'In accordance with their intentions'

It would appear from the clear wording of s1(1) CLA 1977 that each party must intend that the agreed crime be committed. This was the position under the common law. However, surprisingly, the House of Lords decided otherwise:

R v Anderson [1986] AC 27 HOUSE OF LORDS

D, on remand in custody, agreed to supply diamond-cutting wire to cut through the bars of a prison cell in order to allow another prisoner to escape. He was charged with conspiracy to effect a prisoner's release. D claimed that he never expected the plan to be carried out and that his only intention was to supply the equipment and then leave the country. It was held that prosecutors should not be compelled to prove an intention by each conspirator that the offence would actually be carried out.

Lord Bridge:

> . . . an essential ingredient in the crime of conspiring to commit a specific offence or offences under section 1(1) of the Act of 1977 is that the accused should agree that a course of conduct be pursued which he knows must involve the commission by one or more of the parties to the agreement of that offence or those offences. But, beyond the mere fact of agreement, the necessary mens rea of the crime is, in my opinion, established if, and only if, it is shown that the accused, when he entered into the agreement, intended to play some part in the agreed course of conduct in furtherance of the criminal purpose which the agreed course of conduct was intended to achieve. Nothing less will suffice; nothing more is required. [Emphasis added.]

Appeal dismissed.

This decision led to the strange consequence that a person could be convicted of conspiring to commit a crime without actually intending that the crime be committed provided there was an agreement to *participate* in the crime. Yet, participation is not referred to in the definition of the offence. A conspiracy consists of an agreement that a crime will be committed and not an agreement that each conspirator will participate in the crime.

Lord Bridge's judgment can be explained by his acknowledgement that most conspiracies concern highly complex plans in which many people participate to a greater or lesser extent. It would be difficult to prove an intention on the part of each conspirator that the eventual crime be carried out. The requirement of participation was rejected in *Siracusa*.

R v Siracusa [1990] 90 CR APP R 340 COURT OF APPEAL

The case concerned prosecutions of conspiracy to import into the UK heroin from Thailand and cannabis from Kashmir. The intended destination was Canada and the acts concerned involved the organised smuggling of massive quantities of drugs.

O'Connor LJ:

> The appellants contend that where conspiracy to contravene section 170(2)(b) [Customs and Excise Management Act 1979] is charged, the position is . . . that [the prosecution] had to prove against each defendant that he knew that the Kashmir operation involved cannabis and that the Thailand operation involved heroin. If this submission is well-founded, then it is said that the learned judge's direction on conspiracy is flawed . . .
>
> We think it obvious that Lord Bridge [in Anderson] cannot have been intending that the organiser of a crime who recruited others to carry it out would not himself be guilty of conspiracy unless it could be proved that he intended to play some active part himself thereafter.

With reference to organised conspiracies:

> The present case is a classic example of such a conspiracy. It is the hallmark of such crimes that the organisers try to remain in the background and more often than not are not apprehended. Secondly, the origins of all conspiracies are concealed and it is usually quite impossible to establish when or where the initial agreement was made, or when or where other conspirators were recruited. The very existence of the agreement can only be inferred from overt acts. Participation in a conspiracy is infinitely variable: it can be active or passive. If the majority shareholder and director of a company consents to the company being used for drug smuggling carried out in the company's name by a fellow director and minority shareholder, he is guilty of conspiracy . . . .

Appeal dismissed.

The second point made by Lord Bridge in *Anderson*, regarding the innocence of agents provocateurs, was clarified in the next case:

Yip Chiu-Cheung v R [1994] 3 WLR 514 PRIVY COUNCIL

D was convicted of conspiracy to traffic heroin in Hong Kong. D had agreed with an American undercover agent (Needham) to meet in Hong Kong where D would supply the agent with five kilos of heroin which the agent would then take to Australia. The aim of the agent was to expose an international drug trafficking ring. The agent missed his flight to Australia and abandoned the plan. D was convicted and argued on appeal that as the agent lacked the MR for drug trafficking, D himself could not be guilty of conspiracy. It was held by the Privy Council that the agent's good motives were irrelevant. He still intended that the crime be committed. He was therefore a co-conspirator and it followed that D was guilty of conspiracy.

→ CROSS-REFERENCE
This aspect of the case is discussed further in Chapter 3, 3.1.7.

Lord Griffiths:

On the principal ground of appeal it was submitted that the trial judge and the Court of Appeal were wrong to hold that Needham, the undercover agent, could be a conspirator because he lacked the necessary mens rea or guilty mind required for the offence of conspiracy. It was urged upon their Lordships that no moral guilt attached to the undercover agent who was at all times acting courageously and with the best of motives in attempting to infiltrate and bring to justice a gang of criminal drug dealers. In these circumstances it was argued that it would be wrong to treat the agent as having any criminal intent, and reliance was placed upon a passage in the speech of Lord Bridge of Harwich in R v Anderson (William Ronald) [1986] AC 27, 38–39; but in that case Lord Bridge was dealing with a different situation from that which exists in the present case. There may be many cases in which undercover police officers or other law enforcement agents pretend to join a conspiracy in order to gain information about the plans of the criminals, with no intention of taking any part in the planned crime but rather with the intention of providing information that will frustrate it. It was to this situation that Lord Bridge was referring in *Reg v Anderson*. The crime of conspiracy requires an agreement between two or more persons to commit an unlawful act with the intention of carrying it out. It is the intention to carry out the crime that constitutes the necessary mens rea for the offence. As Lord Bridge pointed out, an undercover agent who has no intention of committing the crime lacks the necessary mens rea to be a conspirator.

The facts of the present case are quite different. Nobody can doubt that Needham was acting courageously and with the best of motives; he was trying to break a drug ring. But equally there can be no doubt that the method he chose and in which the police in Hong Kong acquiesced involved the commission of the criminal offence of trafficking in drugs by exporting heroin from Hong Kong without a licence. Needham intended to commit that offence by carrying the heroin through the customs and on to the aeroplane bound for Australia.

Appeal dismissed.

This Privy Council decision is persuasive. It cannot overrule *Anderson*. However, it is now accepted, following *Siracusa* and *Yip Chiu-Cheung*, that he who has an intention to commit a crime, without necessarily participating in it, commits conspiracy.

 THINKING POINT 15.5

On Monday, D1 and D2 agree to import amphetamines into the UK. D2 is an undercover police officer. On Friday, D1 withdraws from the agreement. In any case, he claims that his intention was not to import amphetamines but ephedrine (nose drops). D1 is charged with conspiracy to import amphetamines.

Has he committed conspiracy?

e. 'Necessarily amount to or involve the commission of any offence or offences by one or more parties to the agreement'

If the conduct agreed on does not amount to an offence by one or more parties to the agreement there is no liability, even though the participants believe it does.

 EXAMPLE 15.6

A and B agree to drink alcohol, without getting drunk, and sing in the street thinking that they are committing an offence. It may be anti-social behaviour but this is not a crime and they cannot therefore be convicted of conspiring to commit this act.

An agreement to aid and abet an offence is not sufficient (*R v Hollinshead* [1985] 1 All ER 850). That aiding and abetting is merely the process by which a secondary party can be convicted, rather than the offence which he has actually committed, was recently confirmed in relation to conspiracy to aid and abet *production* of cannabis (*R v Kenning* [2008] EWCA Crim 1534). The appellants had sold seeds and equipment to customers. They may have assisted the buyers to grow cannabis, but given that selling is not an offence, that neither defendant intended to grow the drug and that the buyers were not party to the agreement to sell, there was no liability. Put simply, none of the conspirators intended to be involved in *the production*. Therefore, there was no agreement to aid and abet. There was no question of conspiring to *aid and abet* in the similar case of *Dang* [2014] EWCA Crim 348 where the defendants were charged with conspiracy 'to be *concerned* in the production of a controlled drug, namely Cannabis, *by another* in contravention of s4(2)(b) of the Misuse of Drugs Act 1971'. They had sold equipment to Cannabis growers ('another'). Since this was preceded by an agreement that cannabis would be produced by another with the assistance of the equipment supplied, they were guilty of conspiracy to be *concerned* in the drug's production. An agreement to aid and abet an offence may now be an offence under s44 Serious Crime Act 2007.

➜ CROSS-REFERENCE

Section 44 is cited in 15.3.

15.2.3 Impossibility

Statutory conspiracies

Under s1(1)(b) 1977 Act, the actual existence of facts making the agreed crime impossible to carry out does not affect liability for statutory conspiracy. Impossibility due to circumstances, ineptitude or the absence of a quality will not affect liability. This is similar to impossibility concerning attempts and incitement.

Common law conspiracies

Under the common law, impossibility is a defence except for that arising due to ineptitude. This still applies to common law conspiracy to defraud and conspiracy to corrupt public morality. The authority for this is *DPP v Nock* [1978] AC 979 (HL) in which the defendants agreed to produce cocaine by pouring sulphuric acid on to powder which was, in fact, impossible to convert into cocaine. Neither was guilty of an attempt or conspiracy to commit the physically impossible.

?! THINKING POINT 15.6

Have D1 and D2 committed a statutory conspiracy?

1. They agree to rummage through V's coat pocket hoping to steal something of value. The pocket is empty.
2. They agree to buy what they believe to be cocaine from X. X secretly intends to supply baking powder.
3. Aged 16, they live in London and agree to fare-dodge by failing to pay for a bus ride. In fact, bus transport in London is free for children aged 16 and under.
4. They agree to kill V. V is already dead.
5. They agree to kill V in two weeks' time. V dies the following day.
6. They agree to break into a house by unscrewing the window. The screwdriver breaks.

15.2.4 Conspiracy to Defraud

This common law conspiracy was preserved by s5(2) of the 1977 Act:

(1) Subject to the following provisions of this section, the offence of conspiracy at common law is hereby abolished.

(2) Subsection (1) above shall not affect the offence of conspiracy at common law so far as relates to conspiracy to defraud . . . .

[This was amended by s12 Criminal Justice Act 1987:]

(1) If–

(a) a person agrees with any other person or persons that a course of conduct shall be pursued; and

(b) that course of conduct will necessarily amount to or involve the commission of any offence or offences by one or more of the parties to the agreement if the agreement is carried out in accordance with their intentions, the fact that it will do so shall not preclude a charge of conspiracy to defraud being brought against any of them in respect of the agreement.

(3) A person guilty of conspiracy to defraud is liable on conviction on indictment to imprisonment for a term not exceeding 10 years or a fine or both.

The offence was also excluded from the reform of deception offences under the Fraud Act 2006. The essence of the offence was described in *Wai Yu-Tsang v The Queen* [1992] 1 AC 269, 280:

that the conspirators have dishonestly agreed to bring about a state of affairs which they realise will or may deceive the victim into so acting, or failing to act, that he will suffer economic loss or his economic interests will be put at risk.

Actus reus

The AR consists of an agreement to pursue a course of conduct which, if carried out in accordance with the intentions of the conspirators, will necessarily amount to a fraud offence. These are now defined by s1 Fraud Act 2006. The definition of 'defraud' under the common law was tainted with uncertainty and was interpreted as meaning no more than 'dishonesty' (*Scott v Commissioner of Police* [1974] 3 WLR 741). This meant that it went wider than agreements to commit crimes and could include agreements to commit tortious and even lawful conduct. The offence is confined in practice to conspiracies to cause economic prejudice and to deceive a person into acting contrary to their public duty. It seems the offence must now involve unlawfulness, either in its object or in its means and it is a condition precedent that a proprietary right or interest of the victim is actually or potentially injured where the prosecution rely on 'economic prejudice': *R v Evans (Eric)* [2014] 1 WLR 2817.

→ CROSS-REFERENCE
The offence of fraud is discussed in Chapter 12.

Remember that the fraud offence in s1 Fraud Act 2006 is very wide and will therefore support agreements to defraud in a wide range of circumstances.

The Law Commission in 'Fraud' (Law Com No 276, 2002) acknowledged that conspiracy to defraud was an anomalous crime:

3.2 The concept of fraud, for the purposes of conspiracy to defraud, is wider than the range of conduct caught by any of the individual statutory offences involving dishonest behaviour. Thus it can be criminal for two people to agree to do something which it would not be unlawful for one person to do. . . .

3.4 The 1977 Act was the implementation of our Report on Conspiracy and Criminal Law Reform, which 'emphatically' concluded that the object of a conspiracy should be limited to the commission of a substantive offence and that there should be no place in a criminal code for a law of conspiracy extending beyond this ambit. An agreement should not be criminal where that which it was agreed should be done would not amount to a criminal offence by one person.

3.5 This Commission has repeated its adherence to this principle in subsequent reports and we believe it commands very wide support. Either conspiracy to defraud is too wide in its scope (in that it catches agreements to do things which are rightly not criminal) or the statutory offences are too narrow (in that they fail to catch certain conduct which should be criminal) – or, which is our view, the problem is a combination of the two. On any view, the present position is anomalous and has no place in a coherent criminal law.

The Commission was of the view that since a capitalist economy involves the pursuit of profit with consequent risk of loss to others, the wide definition of 'to defraud' involving a dishonest agreement to make a gain at another's expense may well encompass some aspects of legitimate commercial practice which are not dishonest. Dishonesty has no fixed meaning. It was defined according to the *Ghosh* test and will now be interpreted according to the new standard imposed by *Ivey v Genting Casinos*.

Ultimately, this is a question of fact for the jury according to ordinary standards which may be at variance with the standards of either the defendant or commercial practice. This contributes to the unacceptable width of the offence and is in potential violation of Article 7 ECHR (certainty). Conspiracy to defraud was not abolished by the Fraud Act 2006 for fear of creating unacceptable gaps in the law.

→ CROSS-REFERENCE
See Chapter 12 for further discussion on the *Ghosh* test and the changes made by this new standard.

Mens rea

MR consists of intention to defraud as defined in s2 Fraud Act 2006: false representation. Therefore, D must:

- make a false representation;
- knowing or intending that it was untrue or misleading;
- dishonestly.

Sentence

The maximum sentence is that which applies to the corresponding substantive offence.

 THINKING POINT 15.7

Two railway employees decide to make and sell their own sandwiches on a train and to keep the profits.
Have they committed conspiracy to defraud?

15.2.5 Conspiracy to Corrupt Public Morals and Conspiracy to Outrage Public Decency

In these offences we see how far morality is a matter for the criminal law. In practice, conspiracy to corrupt public morals has been used to control prostitution, sex shows and pornography. Many of the prosecutions stem from a time when public morality was more easily outraged by so-called obscene publications than is currently the case. Conspiracy to outrage public decency has been used to control public exhibitions.

These common law offences were preserved by s5 of the 1977 Act:

> (3)   Subsection (1) above shall not affect the offence of conspiracy at common law if and in so far as it may be committed by entering into an agreement to engage in conduct which–
>
> (a)   tends to corrupt public morals or outrages public decency, but
>
> (b)   would not amount to or involve the commission of an offence if carried out by a single person otherwise than in pursuance of an agreement.

Section 5(3) applies the common law rules to these two conspiracies so long as the object of the agreement does not amount to a crime. If it amounts to a crime, it will be charged as a statutory conspiracy under s1.

It was for many years unclear whether there were at common law substantive offences of corrupting public morality or outraging public decency and therefore whether the equivalent conspiracy offences involved an agreement to commit common law crimes as opposed to moral wrongs. The House of Lords in the next case held, by a 4:1 majority, that there was an offence of corrupting public morals and thus it was indictable as a conspiracy.

Shaw v DPP [1961] 2 ALL ER 446 HOUSE OF LORDS

The case arose out of the publication of a pamphlet called 'The Ladies' Directory' containing names, addresses, telephone numbers and details of perversions of prostitutes. The women paid for advertisements to be published. Shaw had, in fact, sought legal advice before publication and had left a copy of the magazine with Scotland Yard as a precaution. You should note that prostitution has never been prohibited by the criminal law.

The House stated in the broadest terms that the courts were the custodians of public morals and that this entitled them to 'superintend' offences prejudicial to the public welfare, particularly between the gaps created by piecemeal legislation.

'Corruption' was defined as 'to lead morally astray', and this was left to the jury, with the obvious risk of inconsistency between one jury and another. In the ten years between *Shaw* and the next case, there were 40 prosecutions for conspiracy to corrupt public morals only one of which was reported (*Anderson* [1972] 1 QB 304: the prosecution of the publishers of a student magazine called 'Oz' for showing a picture of Rupert the Bear with an erect penis. The prosecution failed but production of the magazine was halted). Although the 1970s ushered in a culture of relative moral permissiveness, the courts refused to abdicate their role of custodians of public morality.

Knuller v DPP [1972] 3 WLR 143 HOUSE OF LORDS

The case was concerned with an agreement by several defendants to insert into a column of an underground magazine (*International Times*) an advertisement for the purpose of arranging homosexual acts between consenting adult males in private. Homosexuality had been de-criminalised by the Sexual Offences Act 1967 and was therefore not a crime at the time of the agreement. However, the age of consent for homosexual males was 21 and the purpose of the prosecution was: (a) to deter young men under that age from responding to the advertisements; and (b) to protect public morality from 'lewd, disgusting and offensive' advertisements. Without deciding whether there was a substantive offence of outraging pubic decency, the House confirmed the corresponding conspiracy offence in relation to 'shocking, disgusting and revolting' public exhibitions. The conviction of conspiracy to corrupt public morality was, however, upheld.

Several subsequent decisions have found outraging public decency to be a substantive offence. For instance, *Gibson & Sylverie* [1990] 2 QB 619 where D exhibited earrings made from frozen human foetuses of three or four months' gestation. The necessary public element was held to be missing from *Rose v DPP* [2006] Crim LR 993, where the Court of Appeal overturned a conviction of outraging public decency in respect of a man who exposed his penis with a female performing an act of oral sex upon him at 00.54 am in the foyer of a bank containing ATM machines to which the public had access. The act was captured on CCTV but the only person who had witnessed the event was the manageress of the bank when she later viewed the recording. In *Hamilton* [2007] EWCA Crim 2062, where D secretly filmed up women's skirts in a shopping precinct, it was held that the substantive offence requires the presence of more than one person who is capable of being outraged. It remains the case, however, that the definitions of the substantive offence, and hence any conspiracy to commit it, are vague.

> **?! THINKING POINT** 15.8
>
> Which ECHR rights could be violated by the offences of conspiracy to corrupt public morality or to outrage public decency?

15.2.6 Reform

The Law Commission has recommended reform of conspiracy and attempts in the light of the expansion of organised and international crime (Law Com CP No 318, 2009). It is proposed that s1(1) Criminal Attempts Act 1981 should be abolished and replaced by two inchoate offences:

1. an offence of criminal attempt limited to D's last acts;

2. an offence of criminal preparation covering acts which are part of the execution of the plan.

Both would require an intention to commit the final offence. The existing boundaries of liability are not intended by these proposals to be extended. The two new offences would require a distinction between 'last acts' and 'preparatory acts'. It would not seem to avoid the current difficult distinction between 'more than merely preparatory' and 'merely preparatory' but does provide some guidance in the form of a list of examples of acts which should be more than merely preparatory.

SECTION SUMMARY

Common law and statutory conspiracies are defined by s1(1) Criminal Law Act 1977:
These are intentional crimes.

Actus reus

▨ *Agreement between two or more people to commit a crime.*

Mens rea

▨ *Intention to commit a criminal offence and that the result should occur.*

▨ *Knowledge or intention as to the circumstances of the offence.*

▨ *In the case of common law conspiracies to defraud and corrupt public morality or outrage public decency the intention may be to commit a result which may be wider than a crime.*

Impossibility

▨ *Statutory conspiracies—as for attempt—all types of impossibility are included (legal, factual and ineptitude).*

▨ *Common law conspiracies—only ineptitude.*

15.3 The Serious Crime Act 2007: Encouragement and Assistance

15.3.1 Introduction

15.3.2 Problems with the Old Law of Incitement

15.3.3 Section 44: Intending to Assist or Encourage

15.3.4 Section 45: Assisting or Encouraging Believing an Offence will be Committed

15.3.5 Section 46: Encouraging or Assisting Offences Believing One or More will be Committed

15.3.6 Defences

15.3.7 Conclusion

15.3.1 Introduction

Part 2 of the Serious Crime Act 2007 (SCA) came into force on 1 October 2008. It abolishes common law incitement and replaces it with three new offences covering 'assisting and encouraging' another (P) to commit an offence. These are inchoate offences. They overlap with secondary liability and are very broad. It has been said that the resulting offences are some of the most convoluted and complicated to have been enacted for decades (D. Ormerod & R. Furston 'Serious Crime Act 2007: The Part 2 Offences' [2009] *Crim LR* 389). Statutory offences of incitement such as soliciting murder are retained by the Act but these are beyond the scope of this book. Sentences for the new offences will be the maximum which is available for the completed crime.

KEY CASES

Blackshaw and Sutcliffe [2011] EWCA Crim 2312—s46 encouragement to riot;

Sadique [2013] EWCA Crim 1150—s46 requires one indictment for the various offences D believes might be committed.

15.3.2 Problems with the Old Law of Incitement

Incitement was an offence of suggesting, encouraging, persuading, influencing, threatening or pressurising another to commit an offence as opposed to a civil wrong.

The incitement occurred as soon as the suggestion was made. The suggested or incited crime did not have to be committed. Indeed, if it was, there would not have been an offence of incitement but of counselling or procuring a completed offence.

The old offence of incitement had been criticised as being uncertain. There was one, albeit rare, problem which provided practical difficulties: incitement provided no liability for 'facilitation', for example: if D supplied P with a weapon intending that P commit a crime with it but for some reason P did not do so, D would probably have escaped liability for incitement for lack of 'encouragement' which was essential to the offence. In the absence of any agreement between D and P neither could there be liability for conspiracy. Unless more than preparatory steps had been taken, there could be no liability for an attempt and there could be no liability for secondary participation unless the final offence had actually been committed. There was therefore a gap in the law in respect of one who 'facilitated' P's crime with the intention that it should be committed where it was not. This gap has already been plugged over the years in respect of serious crime and terrorism, where numerous specific offences of 'facilitation' have been created. And given that possession offences might also adequately deal with the example above, one has to question whether the new offences were really necessary. Every attempt has been made here to explain them briefly and intelligibly but whether the attempt succeeds is an open question.

15.3.3 Section 44: Intending to Assist or Encourage

In each of the three new offences, D's liability is not dependent on P and is complete as soon as D commits the act or omission in question.

> (1) A person commits an offence if–
>
>> (a) he does an act capable of encouraging or assisting the commission of an offence; and
>>
>> (b) he intends to encourage or assist its commission.
>
> (2) But he is not to be taken to have intended to encourage or assist the commission of an offence merely because such encouragement or assistance was a foreseeable consequence of his act.

This is an inchoate offence of 'facilitation' based on D's intention or purpose to do an act which is 'capable' of encouraging or assisting P to commit a crime. A s44 offence is committed even though P is not in fact encouraged and even though P does not commit the final offence. It will not matter that D is unaware that his act is an offence. This is what needs to be proved:

Actus reus

- There must be an act or course of conduct not an omission;
- It need only be 'capable' of encouraging or assisting P to commit a crime and need not actually do so;
- It can include a threat or coercion upon a third party to commit a crime;
- It can include arranging for another person to encourage or assist a further person to commit a crime (s65(1)).

Mens rea

- D must intend that conduct to encourage or assist P to commit a crime;
- s47(5)(a): where the offence being assisted or encouraged is one requiring MR, D must believe that the crime would be committed by another with that MR or he must be reckless as to that fact or, if D were to actually commit the offence in question, he would do it with that MR.

Therefore, D must either have belief or recklessness that P will commit the offence with MR (ie: conduct/circumstances and result elements) or he must himself have the MR for the final offence.

   EXAMPLE 15.7

D supplies P with a hammer to throw through a shop window. P never commits the offence. Section 44 will be proved by:

1. A deliberate act (supplying the hammer);

2. An intention to encourage or assist P to commit criminal damage;

3. An intention that P should commit the offence;

4. MR in relation to P's offence, that is:

   a. a belief that P will or awareness that P might intentionally or recklessly throw the hammer through the window (conduct);

   b. an intention, belief or awareness that the window does not or might not belong to P and that there is no lawful excuse for his actions (circumstances);

   c. an intention, belief or awareness that unlawful criminal damage will be caused by P's act (result); *or*

   d. D must himself possess the necessary intention or recklessness for criminal damage. This would apply where D has no belief or awareness that P has the MR for the offence.

5. Intention must be direct not oblique (s44(2)).

15.3.4 Section 45: Assisting or Encouraging Believing an Offence will be Committed

A person commits an offence if–

   (a) he does an act capable of encouraging or assisting the commission of an offence; and

   (b) he believes–

      (i)   that the offence will be committed; and

      (ii) that his act will encourage or assist its commission.

[D does not need to intend P to commit the final offence, merely to believe that P will do so. Again, P does not need to commit the offence.]

→ CROSS-REFERENCE
Section 44 is cited
in 15.3.3.

Actus reus

As for s44.

Mens rea

- D must believe: that P will (not might) commit an offence and that his act will (not might) encourage or assist P to commit it; and

- s47(5) applies in relation to s45 as it does in relation to s44.

'Belief' is not defined but under the common law it means more than suspicion and less than knowledge (*Moys* [1984] 79 Cr App R 72).

 EXAMPLE 15.8

D gives P a metal bar believing that P will use it in order to burgle a house. P never commits the offence. Section 45 will be proved by:

1. A deliberate act (supplying the metal bar);

2. A belief that P will commit burglary;

3. A belief that his act will encourage or assist P to burgle;

4. The MR of burglary in relation to P's offence, that is:

    a. A belief or awareness that P will commit burglary with MR as to entry (conduct);

    b. An intention, belief or awareness that he will do so as a trespasser (circumstances);

    c. An intention, belief or awareness that he will do so with intent to commit an ulterior offence (circumstances/result); *or*

    d. D must himself possess the necessary MR for burglary (ie intentional reckless entry as a trespasser with intent to commit an ulterior offence). This would apply where D has no belief or awareness that P has the MR for the offence.

A s45 offence is committed even though P is not in fact encouraged, P does not commit the final offence and D is unaware that burglary is an offence.

15.3.5 Section 46: Encouraging or Assisting Offences Believing One or More will be Committed

(1) A person commits an offence if–

    (a) he does an act capable of encouraging or assisting the commission of one or more of a number of offences; and

    (b) he believes–

        (i) that one or more of those offences will be committed (but has no belief as to which); and

        (ii) that his act will encourage or assist the commission of one or more of them.

(2) It is immaterial for the purposes of subsection (1)(b)(ii) whether the person has any belief as to which offence will be encouraged or assisted.

This section reflects the law on joint enterprise in secondary liability where D participates in conduct which he knows will lead to an offence but is unaware as to which final offence might be committed. A s46 offence is committed even though P is not in fact encouraged, P does not commit the final offence and D is unaware that any potential consequences amount to an offence.

Actus reus

As for s44.

→ CROSS-REFERENCE
Section 44 is cited
in 15.3.3.

Mens rea

- ▨ D must believe: that P will (not might) commit one or more offences and that his act will (not might) encourage or assist P to commit the offence/s; and

- ▨ s47(5) applies in relation to s46 as it does in relation to s44.

- ▨ s46(1)b(i): if D believes one offence in particular will be committed, the offence should be s45 not s46.

EXAMPLE 15.9

D drives P to a building aware of the fact that P will commit either burglary, criminal damage, GBH, murder or some or all of them, but he does not know which. P never commits the offence. Section 46 will be proved by:

1. A deliberate act (driving);

2. A belief that P will commit one or more of these offences;

3. A belief that his act will encourage or assist P to commit one or more of these offences;

4. a. A belief or awareness that P will have MR for any offence in relation to the conduct of any offence P commits;

    b. An intention, belief or awareness that P will have MR in relation to circumstances and result of any offence he commits; *or*

5. D must have the actual MR for any final offence as if he were going to commit it. This would apply where D has no belief or awareness that P has the MR for the offence.

'Encouraging' is not defined but should have the same meaning as for incitement, that is: 'to spur on by advice, encouragement or persuasion' (*Invicta Plastics Ltd v Clare* [1976] RTR 251 DC—a case of a company inciting readers of a magazine to commit an offence of avoiding police speed traps by buying their tailor-made devices). There have been only two reported appeals concerning s46:

Blackshaw and Sutcliffe [2011] EWCA CRIM 2312

Two defendants posted a message on Facebook for a 'Smash down in Northwick Town', encouraging people to meet behind McDonalds at 1.00 pm the next day to commit riot, burglary or criminal damage. There were convictions under s46 of (1) encouraging the commission of riot with intent to encourage that offence and (2) encouraging offences believing that one or more of them would be committed. Both were convicted and sentenced to four years' imprisonment.

The second Court of Appeal hearing in *Sadique* [2013] EWCA Crim 1150, seemed to justify the objections to s46: vagueness, width and complexity.

Sadique [2013] EWCA CRIM 1150

S and H were involved with a national distribution business supplying chemical cutting agents direct to drug dealers and to regional distributors of cutting agents. The supply was capable of assisting one or more offence/s of supplying Class A or Class B controlled drugs. Each is a separate offence but they were charged with a single count of assisting in the supply of Class A or Class B drugs. It was alleged that S and H believed that one or more of those offences would be committed and that their conduct would provide assistance. The Court of Appeal in a preparatory ruling (*Sadique (Omar)* [2011] EWCA Crim 2872) held that P must identify and charge a separate s46 count for each offence D's act was capable of encouraging and assisting. Professor Virgo in 'Encouraging or assisting more than one offence' [2012] *Archbold Review* 6 explained why this was wrong:

In the law of accessorial liability the leading case on the encouragement or assistance of more than one offence is Maxwell v DPP [1978] . . . In that case, the defendant had guided some members of a terrorist gang to an inn, knowing that they would commit a terrorist outrage there. He was not sure what form this outrage would take, but contemplated that it might involve an attack by bomb, incendiary device or bullet, either against people or property. It was held to be sufficient that the defendant had contemplated a range of possible crimes and that one of those offences was actually committed. Since this was a case of accessorial liability, requiring the commission of a substantive offence, it was sufficient that the defendant had foreseen the commission of a number of offences and that the offence which was actually committed was one of them. For the inchoate offence involving encouragement or assistance there is no need to establish that a substantive offence has been committed, and the appropriate mens rea is one of belief rather than recklessness as to whether a crime will be committed, but otherwise s46 is purporting to embody the same principle as Maxwell: a defendant should not be acquitted of assisting or encouraging a crime simply because his act might assist or encourage a number of offences, at least where the defendant has the appropriate mens rea in respect of those offences. . . . But there is a crucial difference between the application of the Maxwell principle where the substantive offence is committed and where no substantive offence is committed. . . . [S] 46 states that the defendant must believe that one or more of the offences which are capable of being encouraged or assisted by his act will be committed. . .

But does this mean that the defendant must believe that each identified offence will be committed, or is it sufficient that the defendant contemplates that each of the offences may be committed, as long as the defendant believes that one of those offences will be committed, although he is not sure which one?

The author concluded that since the Court of Appeal chose the first interpretation in its preliminary ruling, s46 was effectively redundant. Moreover, it rendered the conviction in *Blackshaw* suspect. On a further appeal against conviction, the Court of Appeal reversed its earlier ruling:

Judge LCJ:

As we have already explained, the 2007 Act created three distinct offences. It is not open to the court to set one or other of them aside and the legislation must be interpreted to give effect to the creation by statute of the three offences. It may well be that the common law offence of inciting someone else to commit an offence was less complex. It may equally be that the purpose of the legislation could have been achieved in less tortuous fashion. Nevertheless these three distinct offences were created by the 2007 Act, with none taking priority over the other two. S.46 creates the offence of encouraging or assisting the commission of one or more offences. Its specific ingredients and the subsequent legislative provisions underline that an indictment charging a s.46 offence of encouraging one or more offences is permissible. This has the advantage of reflecting practical reality. A defendant may very well believe that his conduct will assist in the commission of one or more of a variety of different offences by another individual without knowing or being able to identify the precise offence or offences which the person to whom he offers encouragement or assistance intends to commit, or will actually commit. As Professor Virgo explains in his most recent article, the purpose of the s.46 was 'to provide for the relatively common case where a defendant contemplates that one of a variety of offences might be committed as a result of his or her encouragement'. We entirely agree. . . .

 NOTE 15.4

The Court of Appeal's preliminary ruling had been wrong. It would have involved proving that D believed each such offence would actually be committed. This was surely a s45, not s46, offence. But if he believed only that the offence might occur, he would have to be acquitted of a s46 offence. This represented a narrowing of the offence and was contrary to the intention behind it.

The three offences are wider than incitement in these respects:

1. D need not actually communicate his encouragement to P. If he attempts to do so by email, text or letter but the message is never received, one of the new offences will be committed. Incitement had to be communicated.

2. P need not be aware of D's intention to encourage. An offence will be committed even where weapons/tools are received by P from D innocently.

3. Any of the offences may be committed where D anticipates that P will commit an inchoate offence or even one of the new offences. This makes them extremely wide and creates offences of double inchoate liability.

4. All three offences can be committed by D recklessly.

'Assisting' is very wide and includes acts designed to reduce the chance of criminal proceedings in respect of that offence or by failing to take reasonable steps to discharge a duty (s65). It seems quite likely that, despite the need for some sort of offence to fill the gap in the law, these offences will have to undergo future reform because they are too complicated.

15.3.6 Defences

General defences such as insanity will apply but there is no defence of withdrawal.

The Act provides certain statutory defences:

Section 50: Reasonableness

A person is not guilty of an offence if he *proves* knowledge or belief in certain circumstances and that it was reasonable for him to act in the circumstances as he believed them to be. Factors to be taken into account in determining reasonableness include:

→ CROSS-REFERENCE
For the criticisms of this type of provision see Chapter 1.

- the seriousness of the anticipated offence;
- D's purpose;
- any authority by which D claims to be acting.

This is a reverse-onus defence.

Section 51: Victimhood

If D is a victim or a member of a protected category, he cannot be guilty. This defence is aimed at children, the elderly and those trafficked for exploitation in relation to sexual offences.

15.3.7 Conclusion

The purpose behind these new offences was to plug a loophole in the law: to convict one who facilitates an offence which is not committed. They are, however, complex, technical and extremely wide. It remains to be seen to what extent their use will confirm their justification.

SUMMARY

- Inchoate offences impose liability for the early stages of suggesting, planning or embarking on the substantive offence.
- They are crimes of specific intent.
- The intended substantive offence does not need to be completed.
- Attempt: Steps which are more than merely preparatory to commission of the substantive offence.
- Conspiracy: An agreement to commit a crime.
- Assisting and Encouraging under the Serious Crime Act 2007.

PROBLEM SOLVING

X suggests to D1 that if D1 stole some designer handbags they could make a lot of money by selling them. D1 agrees with D2 to smash the window of a designer shop and grab several bags. D2 discusses the plan with D3 who agrees to sell the bags but only if they are made by a specific Italian fashion house. Two days later he withdraws from the plan when he hears from D2 that the type of bag cannot be guaranteed. D1 and D2 are husband and wife. D1 rides to the shop with a brick in his back-pack. He is standing on the pavement in front of the shop when he is arrested.

Discuss the liability of all parties, if any, for inchoate offences.

Remember:

- **I: Identify** relevant issues
- **D: Define** offences/defences
- **E: Explain/evaluate** the law
- **A: Apply** law to facts.

See the online resources for further guidance on solving this problem: www.oup.com/uk/loveless6e/.

FURTHER READING

Attempt

M. Bohlander, 'The Conflict Between the Serious Crime Act 2007 and s1(4)(b) of the Criminal Attempts Act 1981' [2010] *Crim LR* 483

Discusses the conflict between these provisions and argues that the SCA 2007 should implicitly repeal the CAA section in order to avoid confusion.

**Law Commission, 'Attempt, and Impossibility in relation to Attempt, Conspiracy and Incitement'
(Law Com No 102, 1980)**

The Law Commission's proposals on conspiracy and attempts. These were accepted but not implemented in new legislation.

P. Mirfield, 'Intention and Criminal Attempts' [2015] 2 *Crim LR* 142–148

Discusses changes in the courts' approach to mens rea in attempts.

J. Rogers, 'The Codification of Attempts and the Case for "Preparation"' [2008] *Crim LR* 937

Discusses the Law Commission's recommendation to replace the current offence of attempt with two separate offences—'attempts' or 'preparation'.

Conspiracy

P. Jarvis and M. Bisgrove, 'The Use and Abuse of Conspiracy' [2015] 4 *Crim LR* 261

Discusses the problems of charging a defendant with conspiracy when there are a number of substantive offences. Proposes that the charge should focus on a single agreement instead.

S. Lloyd Bostock, 'The Jubilee Line Jurors: Does their Experience Strengthen the Argument for Judge-only Trial in Long and Complex Fraud Cases?' [2007] *Crim LR* 255

Discusses the Jubilee Line fraud trial and asks whether there is a case for judge-only fraud trials in complex fraud cases.

Serious Crime Act

**The Act: www.legislation.gov.uk/ukpga/2007/27/contents
Explanatory notes: www.legislation.gov.uk/ukpga/2007/27/notes/contents**

Link to the legislation and its explanatory notes.

Child, J.J., 'Exploring the Mens Rea of the Serious Crime Act 2007 Assisting and Encouraging Offences' (2012) 76(3) *JCL* 220–231

Considers the mens rea elements of the crime—do they require intention or will recklessness suffice?

D. Ormerod and R. Furston, 'Serious Crime Act 2007: The Part 2 Offences' [2009] *Crim LR* 389

Asks whether it was necessary to abandon the offence of incitement in favour of a wider inchoate offence.

G. Virgo, 'Encouraging or Assisting More Than One Offence' [2012] 2 *Archbold Review* 6

Discusses whether s46 of the Serious Crime Act 2007 is compatible with the ECHR.

Index